Table 2
Future Value of an Annuity Factors

PERIOD	2.5%	3%	3.5%	4%	4.5%	5%	5.5%	6%	7%	8%	9%	10%	12%	15%
1	1.00000	1.00000	1.00000	1.00000	1.00000	1.00000	1.00000	1.00000	1.00000	1.00000	1.00000	1.00000	1.00000	1.00000
2	2.02500	2.03000	2.03500	2.04000	2.04500	2.05000	2.05500	2.06000	2.07000	2.08000	2.09000	2.10000	2.12000	2.15000
3	3.07562	3.09090	3.10622	3.12160	3.13702	3.15250	3.16802	3.18360	3.21490	3.24640	3.27810	3.31000	3.37440	3.47250
4	4.15252	4.18363	4.21494	4.24646	4.27819	4.31012	4.34227	4.37462	4.43994	4.50611	4.57313	4.64100	4.77933	4.99337
5	5.25633	5.30914	5.36247	5.41632	5.47071	5.52563	5.58109	5.63709	5.75074	5.86660	5.98471	6.10510	6.35285	6.74238
6	6.38774	6.46841	6.55015	6.63298	6.71689	6.80191	6.88805	6.97532	7.15329	7.33593	7.52333	7.71561	8.11519	8.75374
7	7.54743	7.66246	7.77941	7.89829	8.01915	8.14201	8.26689	8.39384	8.65402	8.92280	9.20043	9.48717	10.08901	11.06680
8	8.73612	8.89234	9.05169	9.21423	9.38001	9.54911	9.72157	9.89747	10.25980	10.63663	11.02847	11.43589	12.29969	13.72682
9	9.95452	10.15911	10.36850	10.58280	10.80211	11.02656	11.25626	11.49132	11.97799	12.48756	13.02104	13.57948	14.77566	16.78584
10	11.20338	11.46388	11.73139	12.00611	12.28821	12.57789	12.87535	13.18079	13.81645	14.48656	15.19293	15.93742	17.54874	20.30372
11	12.48347	12.80780	13.14199	13.48635	13.84118	14.20679	14.58350	14.97164	15.78360	16.64549	17.56029	18.53117	20.65458	24.34928
12	13.79555	14.19203	14.60196	15.02581	15.46403	15.91713	16.38559	16.86994	17.88845	18.97713	20.14072	21.38428	24.13313	29.00167
13	15.14044	15.61779	16.11303	16.62684	17.15991	17.71298	18.28680	18.88214	20.14064	21.49530	22.95338	24.52271	28.02911	34.35192
14	16.51895	17.08632	17.67699	18.29191	18.93211	19.59863	20.29257	21.01507	22.55049	24.21492	26.01919	27.97498	32.39260	40.50471
15	17.93193	18.59891	19.29568	20.02359	20.78405	21.57856	22.40866	23.27597	25.12902	27.15211	29.36092	31.77248	37.27971	47.58041
16	19.38022	20.15688	20.97103	21.82453	22.71934	23.65749	24.64114	25.67253	27.88805	30.32428	33.00340	35.94973	42.75328	55.71747
17	20.86473	21.76159	22.70502	23.69751	24.74171	25.84037	26.99640	28.21288	30.84022	33.75023	36.97370	40.54470	48.88367	65.07509
18	22.38635	23.41444	24.49969	25.64541	26.85508	28.13238	29.48120	30.90565	33.99903	37.45024	41.30134	45.59917	55.74971	75.83636
19	23.94601	25.11687	26.35718	27.67123	29.06356	30.53900	32.10267	33.75999	37.37896	41.44626	46.01846	51.15909	63.43968	88.21181
20	25.54466	26.87037	28.27968	29.77808	31.37142	33.06595	34.86832	36.78559	40.99549	45.76196	51.16012	57.27500	72.05244	102.44358
21	27.18327	28.67649	30.26947	31.96920	33.78314	35.71925	37.78608	39.99273	44.86518	50.42292	56.76453	64.00250	81.69874	118.81012
22	28.86286	30.53678	32.32890	34.24797	36.30338	38.50521	40.86431	43.39229	49.00574	55.45676	62.87334	71.40275	92.50258	137.63164
23	30.58443	32.45288	34.46041	36.61789	38.93703	41.43048	44.11185	46.99583	53.43614	60.89330	69.53194	79.54302	104.60289	159.27638
24	32.34904	34.42647	36.66653	39.08260	41.68920	44.50200	47.53800	50.81558	58.17667	66.76476	76.78981	88.49733	118.15524	184.16784
25	34.15776	36.45926	38.94986	41.64591	44.56521	47.72710	51.15259	54.86451	63.24904	73.10594	84.70090	98.34706	133.33387	212.793[illegible]
26	36.01171	38.55304	41.31310	44.31174	47.57064	51.11345	54.96596	59.15638	68.67647	79.95442	93.32398	109.18177	150.33393	245.71[illegible]
27	37.91200	40.70963	43.75906	47.08421	50.71132	54.66913	58.98911	63.70577	74.48382	87.35077	102.72313	121.09994	169.37401	283.56[illegible]
28	39.85980	42.93092	46.29063	49.96758	53.99333	58.40258	63.23351	68.52811	80.69769	95.33883	112.96822	134.20994	190.69889	327.10[illegible]
29	41.85630	45.21885	48.91080	52.96629	57.42303	62.32271	67.71135	73.63980	87.34653	103.96594	124.13536	148.63093	214.58275	377.16[illegible]
30	43.90270	47.57542	51.62268	56.08494	61.00707	66.43885	72.43548	79.05819	94.46079	113.28321	136.30754	164.49402	241.33268	434.74[illegible]
35	54.92821	60.46208	66.67401	73.65222	81.49661	90.32031	100.25136	111.43478	138.23688	172.31680	215.71076	271.02437	431.66350	881.17[illegible]
40	67.40255	75.40126	84.55027	95.02552	107.03032	120.79977	136.60561	154.76197	199.63511	259.05652	337.88245	442.59256	767.09142	1779.09[illegible]

FINANCIAL ACCOUNTING A FOCUS ON DECISION MAKING

2E

Michael C. Knapp
University of Oklahoma

SOUTH-WESTERN College Publishing
An International Thomson Publishing Company

Accounting Team Director: Richard K. Lindgren
Sponsoring Editor: Alex von Rosenberg
Developmental Editor: Sara E. Bates
Production Editor: Deanna Quinn
Production House: Litten Editing and Production
Composition and Art: GGS Information Services, Inc.
Cover and Internal Designer: Michael H. Stratton
Cover Illustrator: Dave Cutler/SIS
Photo Researcher: Jennifer Mayhall
Marketing Manager: Sharon Oblinger

Part and Chapter Opener Photo Credits: 1—© WEKA Publishing; 2—© Jon Riley/Tony Stone Images; 73—© Michael Newman/PhotoEdit; 152—© Lonnie Duka/Tony Stone Images; 231—© 1996 PhotoDisc, Inc.; 232—© 1996 PhotoDisc, Inc.; 285—© Greg Probst/Tony Stone Images; 339—© Ford Motor Company; 387—© 1996 PhotoDisc, Inc.; 388—© John Neubauer/PhotoEdit; 446—© Rosemary Weller/Tony Stone Images; 491—© WEKA Publishing; 493—Photography by Joe Higgins; 537—© Chromosohm/Sohm/Unicorn Stock Photos; 576—© Jeff Greenberg; 657—© 1996 PhotoDisc, Inc.; 658—© 1996 PhotoDisc, Inc.; 711—© 1996 PhotoDisc, Inc.

1 2 3 4 5 6 7 8 9 VH 5 4 3 2 1 0 9 8 7

Printed in the United States of America

Library of Congress Cataloging-in-Publication Data

Knapp, Michael Chris, 1954–
Financial accounting : a focus on decision making / Michael C. Knapp. —2nd ed.
p. cm.
Includes bibliographical references and index.
ISBN 0-538-87658-1 (hardcover : alk. paper)
1. Managerial accounting. 2. Decision-making. I. Title.
HF5657.4.K647 1998
658.15′11—dc21 97-20353
CIP

To my son
JOHN WILLIAM KNAPP

ABOUT THE AUTHOR

Michael Chris Knapp, Ph.D., CPA, CMA, has been a member of the faculty of the University of Oklahoma since 1988 and taught previously at the University of Southern California and Texas Christian University. Professor Knapp has published extensively in both academic research journals and practitioner-oriented journals. Included in his more than one dozen publications in refereed academic journals are papers appearing in *The Accounting Review, Auditing: A Journal of Practice & Theory,* the *Journal of Accounting, Auditing and Finance,* and *Behavioral Research in Accounting.* Among Professor Knapp's publications in practice journals are articles appearing in the *Journal of Accountancy,* the *CPA Journal,* and the *Internal Auditor.* Professor Knapp has also written numerous articles for major metropolitan newspapers on a wide range of business topics, including several articles appearing in the *Los Angeles Times.* Additionally, he has served on the editorial boards of several journals including *The Accounting Review, Auditing: A Journal of Practice & Theory, Advances in Accounting,* and *Research in Accounting Regulation.* Professor Knapp's popular auditing casebook, *Contemporary Auditing: Issues and Cases,* is now in its second edition.

Finally, Professor Knapp has received numerous teaching awards. Among these awards are the State Regents Award for Superior Teaching, Delta Sigma Pi Professor of the Year, Harrison Associates Master Teacher Award, and Mortar Board's Outstanding Faculty Member of the Year.

CONTENTS IN BRIEF

PART VI ANALYSIS OF ACCOUNTING DATA 657

CONTENTS

PART II THE ACCOUNTING MODEL 107

CHAPTER 4 THE MECHANICS OF DOUBLE-ENTRY ACCOUNTING 108

CHAPTER 5 THE ACCOUNTING CYCLE 152

PREFACE

FIVE POINTS MAKE A STAR

A Galaxy of Decisions

While business managers may use many different terms to describe their roles and responsibilities, the essence of operating a business is making decisions. Executives and managers must make fundamental decisions about their products, policies, people, and priorities. The purpose of these decisions is to enhance the economic value of the firm. Likewise, investors and financial analysts make decisions about the relative value of competing investment opportunities and strategies.

This decision-making process serves as a backdrop against which we must view accounting. Accounting information in a vacuum has no value to anyone. Only when such information is used to make economic decisions does accounting information accrue value. In fact, when the right information is collected and analyzed effectively, it may be a firm's or investor's most valuable asset.

Facilitating economic decision making is the purpose of accounting and, hence, the unifying theme of this text. The text is organized around key financial statement elements and decision makers' information needs regarding each of these elements. So, while accounting rules and procedures are integral to this text, they are consistently presented as a means of collecting information for decision making, rather than as ends in and of themselves. This decision focus not only mirrors the use of accounting information in the real world, but it also makes the text more readable and logical to students new to accounting.

What follows is a brief look at some of the features that make *Financial Accounting: A Focus on Decision Making, 2e* such a powerful tool for teaching and learning accounting in the context of making smart business decisions.

Integrative Module: Lighting the Way

"The decision-making focus comes through clearly, especially with...Module 1....The author's overview of where we've been and where we're going is helpful, giving the students a 'road map' approach."
—Lorraine Glasscock, University of North Alabama

The text begins with five chapters on accounting fundamentals and the accounting model. Next is a unique module: "An Integrative Framework for Understanding Accounting." This module pulls together the content of the first five chapters to convey to students a clear image of how accounting works in real business entities and sets the stage for the remainder of the text.

This module helps to clarify the nature, purpose, and structure of the accounting and financial reporting process. It defines the key elements of the integrated accounting model, provides a comprehensive overview of the key features of an accounting system, and defines the primary purpose of financial statement analysis. This module acts as a springboard to Parts III, IV, and V, which discuss accounting and control issues relevant to each major financial statement line item, and Part VI, which presents a comprehensive treatment of financial statement analysis.

Making a Star: The Five Points

"The five point organization scheme is very appropriate, particularly item 2 [information needs of decision makers]." —Larry Falcetto, Emporia State University

The five-point organizing framework utilized in *Financial Accounting: A Focus on Decision Making, 2e* gives the text its star quality. Each financial statement element is explored in relation to five key questions:

1. Why is the element important to financial decision makers?
2. What are the key information needs of decision makers regarding the element?
3. What accounting procedures are used to collect the needed information?
4. What control activities are necessary to ensure that the information collected is reliable?
5. How do decision makers interpret the information and use it to make sound decisions?

To illustrate this five-point framework, let's consider receivables, which are discussed in Chapter 6.

1. *Why are receivables an important financial statement element to financial decision makers?* Receivables are a primary source of cash flows for a firm. Collection problems can pose short-term liquidity challenges as well as hinder long-term growth opportunities.
2. *What are the information needs of decision makers with regard to a firm's receivables?* Most important, decision makers need to know whether a firm can collect its receivables and thus provide a steady source of cash flow.
3. *What accounting procedures are used to collect the needed information?* Businesses apply the allowance method to arrive at the estimated net realizable value of their receivables. Thus, they are estimating the cash flow to be realized from those receivables.
4. *What control policies and procedures are used to ensure that the collected information is reliable?* Here the role of an accounts receivable subsidiary ledger is discussed.
5. *How do decision makers interpret reported information regarding a firm's receivables?* At this point, the text discussion focuses on two important financial ratios involving receivables, the accounts receivable turnover ratio and the age of receivables.

As we see from this example, the information needs of decision makers with regard to a firm's receivables serve as the orienting focus of the text's discussion of accounting procedures, control activities, and analytical techniques applied to this important financial statement element. This systematic five-point presentation helps students see the rhyme and reason of otherwise mysterious accounting methods and procedures.

Decision making is further supported by each chapter's opening vignette, *Focus on Decision Making*. For instance, Chapter 6, Cash and Accounts Receivable, begins with a vignette entitled "Giving Credit to Whom Credit Is Due," which describes J.C. Penney's transition from a cash and carry policy to the use of credit. This vignette also examines the bigger picture, discussing the accounting and control issues faced by all firms that extend credit.

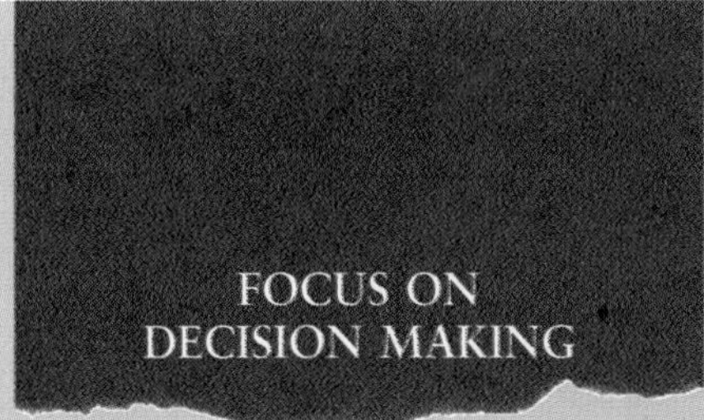

Corporate Accountants: "Toying" with Inventory

Accountants play a key role in monitoring inventory levels and helping management develop appropriate inventory policies. For a hot-selling item, accountants can assist management by preparing weekly or daily sales reports for each sales region. The limited inventory of such a product can then be diverted to those regions where the demand is highest and inventory is lowest.

Monitoring sales and inventory levels for slow-moving items is also an important responsibility of accountants. In the early 1970s, Mattel's accounting department was responsible for tracking weekly sales data for each of the company's toys. Based upon these data, the accountants were to write down the inventory values of those products that were selling poorly. However, Mattel's accountants failed to write down the company's inventory of Hot Wheels. Instead, those toys remained on the company's books at values well in excess of the prices for which they could be sold, a clear violation of generally accepted accounting principles. When this and other accounting oversights were disclosed, Mattel's management was sued by angry stockholders. Eventually, Mattel and its executives paid more than $30 million to settle the lawsuits stemming from the company's sloppy accounting practices.

Each chapter also includes a *Decision Case* where students explore complex issues with the goal of making the correct economic decision. The Decision Case at the end of Chapter 6 highlights cash flow problems experienced by Warnaco Group resulting from a buildup in the firm's receivables balance.

DECISION CASE

Renee Jenkins is the CEO of Marsh Industries, Inc., a manufacturing company that has two divisions. Each year, Ms. Jenkins evaluates the job performance of the two divisional managers. Following are financial data for the most recent fiscal year for Marsh Industries and its two divisions.

⋮

Required: Assume that you are a corporate accountant for Marsh Industries. Ms. Jenkins asks you to compute return on assets and the total asset turnover ratio for the Eastern and Western divisions and to provide a brief assessment of each divisional manager's job performance. She specifically asks that you indicate in your report which manager did a better job managing the assets assigned to his or her division.

Controls' Starring Role

"Great idea to focus on fraud cases to demonstrate the risk of poor internal controls." —Joseph O'Donnell, Canisius College

Internal controls are often discussed in only one chapter of a financial accounting textbook, but that approach is not sufficient. In *Financial Accounting, A Focus on Decision Making,* Chapter 3 introduces students to fundamental control concepts. Then, subsequent chapters that focus on major financial statement components address the control activities relevant to those specific components. Extensive coverage of control concepts and activities is particularly advantageous to nonaccounting majors who will likely have little exposure to these topics in other business courses.

Your Students: Future Stars of Business

In addition to decision making, four other essential themes help students recognize accounting's relevance to the ever-changing world of business and their future careers. Ethics, international issues, the mechanics of double-entry accounting as a tool for understanding, and flexibility of coverage add to the text's relevance and utility.

Ethical coverage is an important inclusion, not only relative to the AECC's directives but also because it enhances the text's connection to real world companies and situations. Each chapter includes at least one *Spotlight on Ethics* vignette that presents a real-world situation involving an ethical dilemma or issue related to the preparation, use, or interpretation of accounting data. Examples of these vignettes include: "Abusive Accounting and Abused Accountants" (Chapter 1), "Payroll Padding: A Case of Dodger Blue" (Chapter 9), and "Russians Say 'Nyet' to American Business Ethics" (Chapter 13).

Searching for Treasure on the High Seas Leads to Trouble with the SEC

In the early 1990s, Seahawk Deep Ocean Technology, Inc. (SDOT) was apparently the only public company whose principal line of business involved retrieving valuable artifacts from shipwrecks. SDOT searched the ocean floor off the southeastern United States to locate treasures carried more than three centuries earlier by Spanish galleons.

In 1994, the SEC filed a complaint against SDOT. This complaint alleged that the company overstated the value of items discovered in a shipwreck location off the Florida coast. The SEC eventually sanctioned SDOT and required the firm to record a large prior period adjustment to correct errors in earlier financial statements that resulted from the inflated values assigned to shipwreck artifacts.

In response to an economy that is becoming more global by the day, international issues are presented throughout the text, including in at least one *For Your Information* vignette in each chapter. These vignettes not only illuminate accounting methods used in other countries, but they also compare and contrast them to American accounting conventions. Examples include "Ru, Chu, and Yu: The Three Pillars of Chinese Bookkeeping" (Chapter 4), "Inventory Costing Methods in Europe" (Chapter 7), and "Tracking Cash Flows Around the World" (Chapter 14). In addition, the final section of Chapter 13 is devoted entirely to international accounting issues.

As for the ever-controversial debits and credits, they are a tool used in Part II, "The Accounting Model" to clarify how accounting information is generated and recorded. Clearly, accounting majors have a need to understand the mechanics of double-entry bookkeeping which forms the backbone of practically every modern organization's accounting system. But, just as important, nonaccounting majors who seek to be marketing experts, operations managers, and chief executive officers should be familiar with the mechanical features of an accounting system if they aspire to leadership roles in the business world. The organization of Part II makes that understanding possible without detracting emphasis from the essential focus of the text—making well-informed decisions.

Besides Module 1, which was described earlier, the text features two other supplemental modules, "The Time Value of Money" and "Partnerships and Proprietorships." These optional modules add flexibility to the financial accounting course, providing insight into important topics, while creating no continuity problems if they are omitted.

Stellar Real World Coverage

"I really enjoy the style that the author used in writing this text. Not only was it easy to read, but the real world examples made very good points. Students would be able to easily relate to the subject matter given the manner in which it is presented." —Ron Tunda, Birmingham Southern College

Throughout the text, real world examples are used extensively to introduce and clarify accounting, control, and financial reporting issues and practices. For quick access, names of companies, organizations, and governmental agencies are highlighted in the text's index. The text also cites financial data and other financial disclosures from a recent annual report of Outback Steakhouse, Inc., which is included as an appendix to the text.

In *Financial Accounting: A Focus on Decision Making,* students learn not only about accounting on the scale of the multinational corporation, but also at the human level. This text uses anecdotes and illustrations drawn from the lives of actual people to introduce important issues and concepts relevant to accounting. Among the individuals featured in this text are James Cash Penney, Milton Hershey, Mary Kay Ash, Ray Kroc, Arthur Andersen, Henry Ford, "Crazy Eddie" Antar, Betty the "sticky-fingered" cashier, Luca Pacioli, Walt Disney, Bill Gates, Barry Minkow, and many other unique personalities.

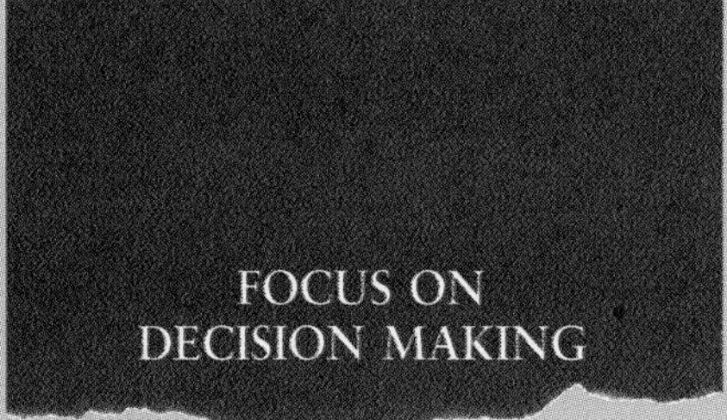

A Mickey Mouse Organization Built on Mickey Mouse Loans

In 1922, an artistic young man established Laugh-O-Gram Films, Inc., an animated film production company based in Kansas City. Only twenty-one years old at the time, the young man's artistic ability exceeded his business skills. Within one year, the company was bankrupt. After considerable pleading, the young entrepreneur convinced his creditors to allow him to keep one camera and one film he had produced. With fifty dollars in his pocket, his camera, and the film, Walt Disney boarded a train for California hoping that Hollywood would have a better appreciation for his animation skills than Kansas City.

In seven decades, the Walt Disney Company has gone from financing its operations with small loans from Walt Disney's friends and relatives to borrowing hundreds of millions of dollars on exotic debt instruments. Would the founder of the company be impressed? Probably not. Once, when asked about the financial empire he had built, Walt Disney modestly replied, "Always remember that this whole thing was started by a mouse."

End-of-Chapter Materials Shine Bright

This text provides a wide array of end-of-chapter assignment materials written by the author to support the decision making theme of the text, to reinforce the text's secondary themes, and to stimulate and challenge students. These materials are organized into Questions, Exercises, two parallel Problem Sets, Cases, and Projects. Each chapter's assignment materials contain an extensive number of items involving real world financial data. In Chapter 6, for example, you will find assignment materials that involve the following companies:

- Outback Steakhouse, a restaurant chain
- Macromedia, Inc., a computer software firm
- Campbell Soup Company, a food products firm
- KLM Royal Dutch Airlines, an international airline
- QLogic Corporation, a manufacturer of computer peripherals
- Melville Corporation, a general merchandiser
- Sotheby's Holdings, Inc., an international auction house
- Paychex, Inc., a provider of payroll processing services
- IFG, Inc., a conglomerate in the financial services industry

Many of the assignments with an ethics component are based on cases that appear in the author's widely used auditing casebook, *Contemporary Auditing: Issues and Cases,* including: The PTL Club; Suzette Washington, Accounting Major; The Trolley Dodgers; Crazy Eddie Inc.; ZZZZ Best Company; Howard Street Jewelers; and Cardillo Travel Systems, Inc.

The end-of-chapter items involving ethics and international accounting issues are identified with icons.

Included in the Cases and Projects for each chapter are at least one cooperative teamwork assignment and one assignment that requires students to access the Internet to obtain financial or other data. These items also are marked with icons.

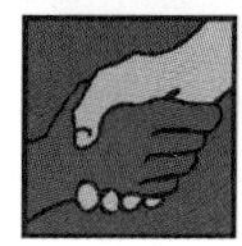

Examples of teamwork assignments include a project that requires students to study and document the cash processing controls of a small business and an assignment that requires students to analyze the ethical issues related to an actual case involving the illicit use of accounting data by corporate insiders. Several Internet projects require students to obtain financial statement data from the SEC's EDGAR Web site or other sites maintained by individual corporations.

65. SEC Disclosures for PP&E

Public companies registered with the Securities and Exchange Commission (SEC) must file an annual financial report or "10-K" statement with that agency. "Item 2" of a company's 10-K is entitled "Properties." This item provides a description of the major manufacturing, administrative, distribution, and other facilities owned by a company.

Required:

Using the Internet, access EDGAR, the SEC's electronic data gathering and retrieval system. Retrieve the most recent 10-K statements of two public companies that operate in the same industry and print "Item 2, Properties" from each of those statements. How do Item 2 disclosures supplement each firm's financial statements? Which company's Item 2 disclosures are most informative for financial decision makers? Defend your answer. Submit to your instructor the printed Item 2 disclosures for the two companies along with your answers to the previous questions.

Many of the Cases and Projects, as well as many Exercises and Problems, include a written or oral communication component to help students build these important skills.

All the Extras

FOR THE STUDENT:

Study Guide: Chapter overviews, outlines, and a self-test with answers are contained in this helpful study guide written by Lola Dudley, Eastern Illinois University. The solutions have been carefully verified to ensure quality. (0-538-87661-1)

PowerNotes: The author-created PowerPoint Presentation slides/transparencies have been duplicated along with note-taking space to assist students as the slides/transparencies are presented in class. (0-538-87663-8)

Student Solutions Manual: This student supplement, prepared from the instructor's solutions manual, contains complete solutions to alternate end-of-chapter exercises and problems. (0-538-87499-1)

Working Papers: Workpaper templates, prepared by Carol Knapp, University of Central Oklahoma, are provided for the problem assignments within each chapter. These templates include preprinted headings identifying the name of the company and/or the title of the financial statement or other item to be completed. (0-538-87662-X)

BusinessLink Video Workbook: Enrich student understanding of the BusinessLink video through questions and activities presented in this student workbook. (0-538-87336-1) Available 1998.

CONTACCT II, Version 3: Contained in this accounting cycle software package by Dasaratha Rama and K. Raghunandan, both of the University of Massachusetts at Dartmouth, are tutorials, practice assignments, graded homework assignments, and a student instruction booklet. This newly revised software works with the latest version of ToolBook. (A run-time version is provided in the package.) The presentation is livelier and, as in previous versions, allows students to use the package in a lab or at home. (0-538-87584-4)

QuickBooks for Windows (Trial Version): This commercial accounting software package gives students an opportunity to experience accounting processing through a computerized system. (0-538-87570-4)

FOR THE INSTRUCTOR:

Instructor's Manual: Prepared by the author, this supplement provides instructional materials for adopters that reinforce the key themes woven into his text. For each chapter, the manual contains a listing of the learning objectives, a glossary of terms, a lecture outline that closely correlates with the text material, and solutions to the Decision Case, questions, cases, and projects at the end of each chapter. Also included are a list of check figures for the exercises and problems included in the assignment materials and a complete set of PowerPoint Presentation slide transparency masters. Special feature: The *Turnkey Option*. This option allows instructors to use PowerPoint slides in conjunction with the lecture outlines included in the Instructor's Manual. Signposts in the lecture notes indicate when each slide is to be presented. When used together, the lecture outlines and PowerPoint slides provide adopters with a complete, classroom-ready set of instructional materials. Alternatively, instructors can selectively use hard copies of the PowerPoint slides as transparency masters. (0-538-87659-X)

Solutions Manual: Contained in the Solutions Manual are complete solutions to each problem and exercise in the text. The Solutions Manual was developed by Carol Knapp. Each solution was verified by Charles Pursifull, University of Central Oklahoma, and Michael Knapp. (0-538-87660-3)

Solution Transparencies: The solutions to the exercises and problems are available in transparency form. (0-538-87664-6)

PowerPoint Presentations: The author has created a set of more than 300 PowerPoint slides that provide instant organization to lectures and reduce class preparation time. Combined with the information in the Instructor's Manual, these slides are key elements in the *Turnkey Option*. (0-538-87667-0)

Test Bank: This test bank, written by Sue Cullers, Tarleton State University, consists of hundreds of multiple-choice items and problems. It has been carefully verified to ensure quality. (0-538-87665-4)

Westest: This electronic test bank is Windows-based. (0-538-87892-4)

Cooperative Learning Workshop Video: This workshop video presents Philip Cottell, Jr., Miami University, who explains a number of cooperative learning techniques for use in the teaching of accounting. (0-538-86498-2)

BusinessLink Video: Six video segments cover key financial accounting topics. Real companies are featured. (0-538-87335-3). Available 1998.

BusinessLink Video Instructor's Manual: This manual assists instructors in the use of the BusinessLink Video and student workbook. (0-538-87337-X) Available 1998.

CONTACCT II, Version 3, Manual: This manual provides solutions to the problems contained in the student software. (0-538-87586-0)

CONTACCT II, Version 3, Test Bank: This ASCII-format 3.5" disk contains problems for testing students using the student software. (0-538-87588-7)

Acknowledgments

Writing, revising, and publishing a textbook is much too large a project for any one person, so while my name appears on the cover, this text is the product of many people's input, energy, and effort. I am pleased to acknowledge the exceptional work of Carol Knapp, Charles Pursifull, Alice Sineath, and the South-Western College Accounting Team.

In addition, I wish to thank the reviewers below who submitted such comprehensive remarks about the manuscript and how it could be improved. These reviewers will see that their comments were taken to heart in the revision process.

S. Douglas Beets, Wake Forest University
Denise English, Boise State University
Larry Falcetto, Emporia State University
Lorraine Glasscock, University of North Alabama
Kenneth M. Hiltebeitel, Villanova University
Cynthia Jeffrey, Iowa State University
Ann Galligan Kelley, Providence College
Rebecca A. Kerr, Midlands Technical College
Jerry G. Kreuze, Western Michigan University
Ronald M. Mano, Weber State University
Gary J. Merz, Bellevue Community College
Paula Morris, Kennesaw State University
Marla Myers, University of Idaho
Joseph B. O'Donnell, Canisius College
Ron Tunda, Birmingham Southern College

ACCOUNTING FUNDAMENTALS

I

You begin your study of accounting in this textbook with Chapter 1, which acquaints you with the role of accounting in today's business world and provides you with an overview of the accounting profession. Before focusing on the accounting discipline, Chapter 1 introduces you to the major types of businesses, their legal forms, and their key internal functions.

Chapter 2 discusses the fundamental concepts, elements, and issues that are central to the accounting discipline. The chapter begins with an overview of the key objectives of accounting and financial reporting. Next, the four basic financial statements are discussed and illustrated. Chapter 2 also identifies the attributes that accounting information should possess and the conceptual principles that underlie accounting rules and procedures. This opening series of chapters concludes with Chapter 3, which presents an introduction to accounting information systems and internal control issues and concepts. By first studying accounting systems and internal control, you will find it much easier to grasp the procedural aspects of recording and reporting accounting information that are discussed in later chapters.

1 An Introduction to the Role of Accounting in the Business World

"Getting the facts is the key to good decision making. Every mistake that I made came because I didn't take the time. I didn't drive hard enough. I wasn't smart enough to get the facts."
Charles F. Knight, Chief Executive Officer, Emerson Electric Company

LEARNING OBJECTIVES

After studying this chapter, you should be able to do the following:

1. Identify the major types of business entities, their principal legal forms, and their key internal functions.
2. Identify the primary means accountants use to communicate financial information to decision makers.
3. Briefly describe how financial data are collected by an organization's accounting system.
4. Define the nature, structure, and major segments of the accounting profession and key changes presently taking place within the profession.

FOCUS ON
DECISION MAKING

Accounting and the Allocation of Scarce Economic Resources

To make rational economic decisions, a decision maker must have good information. In the business world, the quality of decisions made by corporate executives depends largely upon the relevance and reliability of the information supplied to them by their accountants. Take the case of Sears, Roebuck and Co., the giant merchandising firm. A few years ago, Sears executives faced an unpleasant realization. The company was losing market share to some of its more aggressive competitors, particularly Wal-Mart. Financial data supplied to Sears top management by the firm's accounting department zeroed in on the source of this problem.

The most common measure of productivity in merchandising operations is sales-per-square-foot of available selling space. In the early 1990s, Sears stores generated less than $300 of annual sales per square foot of selling space, considerably below the same measure for many of its competitors. To remedy this problem, Sears executives embarked on a $5 billion, five-year plan to remodel the company's retail outlets to better utilize their available selling space. As the remodeling plan neared completion, accounting data fed back to Sears executives by the company's accountants demonstrated that the plan was working. Sears' sales-per-square-foot of available selling space had leaped 20 percent to nearly $350 following the adoption of the new management strategy.

Business owners and managers must continually make decisions regarding how to utilize their organization's scarce economic resources. These decisions ultimately determine which companies are successful and which companies wind up in the corporate graveyard. The key scarce resource for Sears, Wal-Mart, and other retailers is the square footage available to display their merchandise. Portfolio managers of The China Fund, a large mutual fund traded on the New York Stock Exchange, must decide in which companies in the People's Republic of China they will invest the capital entrusted to them by thousands of investors. Executives of General Motors must determine how much of the company's large, but limited, manufacturing capacity should be devoted to the production of Camaros, Corvettes, and other GM models. Business executives make these important resource allocation decisions only after they have spent untold hours studying data supplied to them by their accountants. Even the most skilled and insightful managers will find profits elusive if they do not have access to relevant and reliable accounting data.

This chapter begins by introducing you to the business world, including the different types of businesses, their legal forms, and their key internal functions. Then, you examine more closely the accounting function of business organizations. You will become familiar with the means used by accountants to communicate financial data to decision makers and briefly review how accounting systems collect financial data for business organizations. This chapter concludes with an introduction to the accounting profession, including the important challenges it faces in coming years.

THE ORIGINS AND NATURE OF BUSINESS ORGANIZATIONS

LEARNING OBJECTIVE 1 ▶
Identify the major types of business entities, their principal legal forms, and their key internal functions.

You have certainly heard the expression "going into business." Richard Sears and his good friend, Alvah Roebuck, did just that in 1887. The two men hoped to earn a livelihood by selling watches by mail order to residents of small towns and rural areas in the Midwest. Since you have enrolled in an introductory accounting course, you are also apparently planning on "going into business," if not exactly in the same manner as Sears and Roebuck. Given your interest in business and given that accounting is one specialized business field, it seems reasonable to briefly explore the nature of the business world before we focus specifically on accounting.

Fred, Ray, and Mary Kay: Finding Success in the Business World

Like many college students, Fred Smith often waited until the last minute to complete a required class project. While a college junior during the 1960s, Fred faced a pressing deadline for a term paper assignment in an economics course. This assignment required Fred to develop an idea for a new business. Fred rushed through the paper and submitted it to his instructor. Unimpressed by Fred's effort, the instructor gave him a "C" for the paper. Not one to be easily discouraged, years later Fred pursued the business concept he had outlined in the term paper. By the late 1990s, the business that sprang from Fred's term paper, Federal Express Corporation, employed more than 100,000 people and had annual revenues exceeding $8 billion.

Many large corporations had modest beginnings. Take the case of Federal Express Corporation. The concept that led to the creation of the large company sprang from an economics term paper written by its founder when he was a college student.

You will become acquainted with many "Fred Smiths" as you pursue your study of business over the next few years. You may be introduced to Ray Kroc, who parlayed a small investment in a hamburger stand into McDonald's, the world's largest restaurant chain. Maybe you will analyze the business tactics of Mary Kay Ash, a door-to-door saleswoman who turned an initial investment of $5,000 in a small business, Mary Kay Cosmetics, into a multimillion dollar fortune. In fact, you may become familiar with the business strategies employed by Richard Sears and Alvah Roebuck.

If you study the case histories of individuals who have gone on to tremendous success in the business world, you will find that their stories typically share several common features. In most cases, these individuals were motivated by a simple economic need, namely, earning a "living." Industrious and independent by nature, these individuals chose to establish their own business rather than become, or remain, an employee of another firm. By hard work, ingenuity, or luck—or a combination of those factors, each of these individuals discovered a need for a product or service that was not being met or not being effectively met by an existing business. These individuals then had the courage to take a chance, to accept some risk of failure and disappointment, by creating their own business. Arguably, the most important trait common to these individuals was their ability to make wise economic decisions. Faced with limited economic resources—money, land, equipment, and so on—these individuals had a knack for knowing how to allocate these resources wisely to maximize the profitability of their new businesses.

Major Types of Business Entities

Those businesses that entrepreneurs like Fred Smith, Ray Kroc, and Mary Kay Ash establish are typically segregated into three broad groups: service companies, manufacturing companies, and merchandising companies. Exhibit 1.1 lists examples of each of these three groups of firms. That exhibit also reports the given firms' principal lines of business, their revenues for a recent year, and their total number of employees.

Businesses that provide professional, technical, or other types of services to their customers are referred to as service companies or organizations. Law firms, airlines, and advertising agencies are service businesses. One of the most widely known service companies in today's economy is Federal Express, the air courier company founded by the "mediocre" former college student, Fred Smith. Manufacturing firms such as Dow

Going Into Business . . . Going Out of Business

FOR YOUR INFORMATION

Starting a new business is a risky endeavor. In 1996, Dun & Bradstreet, an investment advisory firm, reported that approximately 200,000 new businesses were launched. Unfortunately, thousands of businesses go "belly up" each year, many of which have been in operation for only a few months. Dun & Bradstreet revealed that in 1996 approximately 71,200 businesses failed.

Sources: "Business Failures Decline, But Liabilities Increase," *The Wall Street Journal,* January 26, 1996, A8; "NFIB Reports High Number of Start-Ups," *The Wall Street Journal,* August 23, 1996, B2.

EXHIBIT 1.1 ▼
Three Major Types of Businesses

	Name	Principal Line of Business	Recent Annual Revenues	Number of Employees
Service Companies	Charles Schwab Corp.	Stock brokerage	$1.1 billion	6,500
	Federal Express Corp.	Air courier services	8.5 billion	110,000
	H&R Block, Inc.	Tax return preparation	1.4 billion	91,000
Manufacturing Companies	Chrysler Corp.	Automobile manufacturing	52.2 billion	123,000
	Dow Chemical Company	Chemical manufacturing	20.0 billion	62,000
	Xerox Corp.	Production of copiers	17.8 billion	87,600
Merchandising Companies	Eckerd Corp.	Drugstores	4.5 billion	43,000
	Egghead Inc.	Computer software stores	725 million	2,700
	Wal-Mart Stores, Inc.	Discount merchandising	82.5 billion	625,000

Chemical, Goodyear Tire & Rubber, and Bethlehem Steel convert raw materials of some type into finished products. These finished products are then sold, typically to wholesale merchandising companies. Wholesale merchandising companies are commonly referred to as wholesale distributors or, simply, wholesalers. An example of a wholesale distributor is United Stationers Inc., the largest wholesaler of office supply products in the United States. United Stationers purchases office supply products from more than 400 manufacturing companies. Then, the company resells these products to retail office supply stores from thirty regional distribution centers scattered across the United States.

Retail merchandising firms such as Sears, J.C. Penney, and Wal-Mart buy products principally from wholesalers and then resell these products to the public from retail outlets. Some retail merchandisers sell their goods by mail order, such as the apparel retailer Land's End. Other retailers sell their goods on a door-to-door basis, an example being Mary Kay Cosmetics, while a few futuristic companies market their goods via televised home shopping clubs and the Internet. In recent years, many large retailers have begun skipping the so-called middleman by purchasing their goods directly from manufacturers. Wal-Mart, in particular, has used this strategy to reduce the acquisition cost of the merchandise it sells.

Common Forms of Business Organizations

Business enterprises in the United States operate in several different legal forms, but the principal forms of business organization are sole proprietorships, partnerships, and corporations. As shown by Exhibit 1.2, the most common form of business organization in this country is the sole proprietorship. The *Statistical Abstract of the United States,* published annually by the U.S. Bureau of the Census, reported recently that there were approximately 15.5 million sole proprietorships in the United States. Although there are considerably fewer businesses operating as corporations, these firms account for the large majority of the total business revenues generated each year in the United States. According to the *Statistical Abstract of the United States,* corporations generated nearly $11 trillion in revenues by the mid-1990s and had more than $20 trillion in total assets.

EXHIBIT 1.2
Number of Business Organizations and Their Annual Revenues

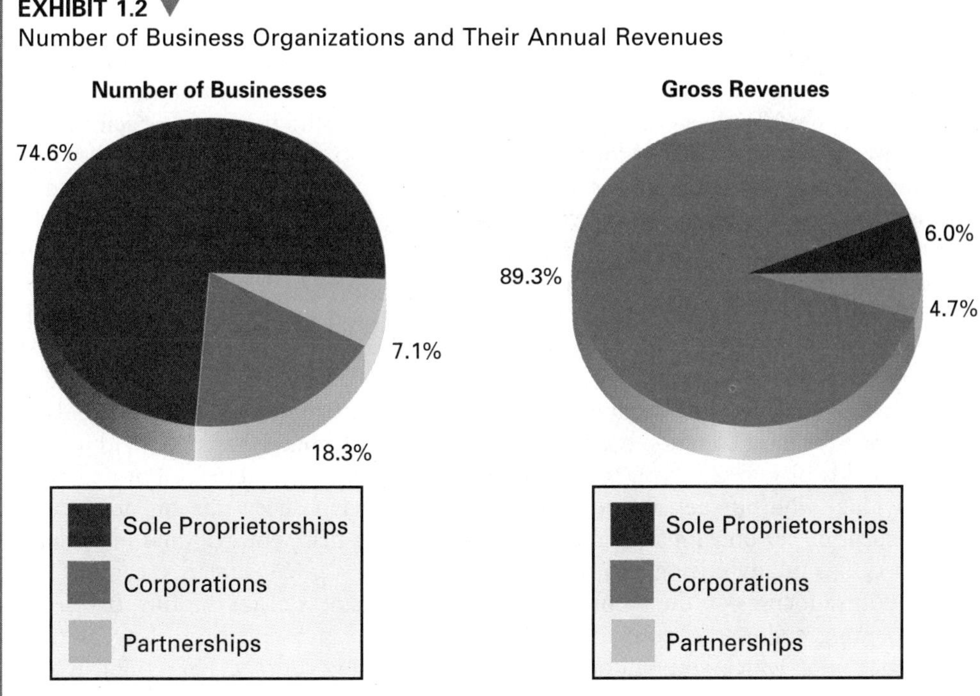

Source: U.S. Bureau of the Census, *Statistical Abstract of the United States, 1995.*

A **sole proprietorship**[1] is a business owned by one individual, the proverbial "Mom and Pop" operation. Granted, if both Mom and Pop are full partners in the business, then we have a **partnership.** More generally, a partnership is an unincorporated business with two or more owners. For instance, the Boston Celtics are owned by a partnership—one consisting of several thousand partners. Most of the largest companies in the United States operate as corporations, although many of these firms began operations decades earlier as either sole proprietorships or partnerships. *Random House Webster's College Dictionary* defines a **corporation** as "an association of individuals, created by law and having an existence apart from that of its members as well as distinct and inherent powers and liabilities." You will discover that there are several advantages of operating a business as a corporation. One of the most important of these advantages is that corporate stockholders, the owners of a corporation, have limited liability for the actions of their firm, which is not true of the owners of sole proprietorships and partnerships. In a lawsuit against a corporation, the plaintiffs cannot recover any settlement or judgment from the personal assets of the firm's individual stockholders. Instead, any settlement or judgment must be paid strictly from the corporation's assets.

sole proprietorship

partnership

corporation

In this text, we concentrate principally on corporations in studying the accounting function of business organizations. Fortunately, most of the accounting issues faced by large corporations are similar, if not identical, to the accounting issues faced by smaller, unincorporated businesses.

1. The first time that a substantive reference is made to a key term, that term is boldfaced in the text. At the end of each chapter is a glossary of key terms introduced in the chapter.

Internal Functions of Business Organizations

An individual, such as Fred Smith or Mary Kay Ash, who establishes a successful and growing business quickly learns that he or she needs the assistance of skilled employees. For example, most business owners are not accountants or do not have sufficient time to tend to the accounting tasks for their organizations. So, they must hire one or more accounting employees or retain the services of a "public" accountant to maintain their business's accounting records. Likewise, the owner of a growing business may have to hire marketing experts, personnel managers, production supervisors, and credit managers to perform important functions for the business.

Every large company has numerous internal functions carried out by individuals with specialized skills and training. Typically, individuals pursuing a degree in business concentrate on one of these specialized fields during their college programs. Management, marketing, finance, and accounting are among the most commonly recognized fields of business and the most common business majors available to college students. Within each of these fields of business, you will find an array of "sub-specialities." For example, an individual who pursues a career in management may concentrate on production management or personnel management. In the marketing field, you will find individuals who specialize in advertising and others who are experts in consumer research.

This course focuses on the accounting function of business organizations. If you are an accounting major, this course will provide you with a foundation of accounting knowledge upon which you will build in future accounting courses. This course is also important to those of you who intend to specialize in a field of business other than accounting. A primary goal of college business programs is to develop future business leaders. Even if you do not plan to pursue a career in accounting, you need a solid understanding of the accounting function of business organizations to enhance your chance of success in the business world. To be an effective sales manager, personnel specialist, or chief executive of a large corporation, you must understand the operations of your organization's accounting function and be able to interpret accounting data and recognize the limitations of those data.

▲ THE NATURE OF ACCOUNTING: A MEANS TO AN END

LEARNING OBJECTIVE 2 ▶ Identify the primary means accountants use to communicate financial information to decision makers.

To make wise decisions regarding the utilization of money, equipment, or people, business executives must have ready access to a wide array of financial information regarding their firms. Take the case of Fred Smith of Federal Express. In the mid-1970s, Federal Express was almost forced to file for bankruptcy. A sudden and significant increase in fuel prices resulting from a Middle Eastern oil crisis caused Federal Express to begin losing more than $1 million per month. Based on information supplied to him principally by his firm's accounting department, Fred Smith quickly implemented cost containment measures that saved Federal Express from financial ruin.

In today's business world, most of the information needed by business executives to make critical decisions regarding their firms is funneled to them by their accountants. In the so-called Information Age in which we presently live, accountants serve as information merchants for the business world. We take a closer look at the nature of the accounting function of business organizations in this section.

Defining the Societal Role of Accounting

In 1970, the Accounting Principles Board, a rule-making body within the accounting profession at the time, defined **accounting** as follows:

accounting

> Accounting is a service activity. Its function is to provide quantitative information, primarily financial in nature, about economic entities that is intended to be useful in making economic decisions—in making reasoned choices among alternative courses of action.[2]

Notice that first and foremost accounting is a service activity. Accounting is a means to an end, that end being to assist a wide variety of parties in making economic decisions. Accountants generally segregate these decision makers into two groups: external and internal decision makers. External decision makers are third parties who do not have ready access to an organization's financial records or accountants since they are not members of the organization. Internal decision makers, on the other hand, are executives or employees of a given entity.

Communicating Financial Information to External Decision Makers

Financial statements are the principal means accountants use to communicate financial information to external decision makers such as investors, suppliers, and bank loan officers. Most large companies prepare an annual financial report that they distribute to the public. A recent annual report of Outback Steakhouse, Inc., is included as an appendix to this text. Throughout the text, we will periodically refer to Outback's annual report to highlight key accounting and financial reporting issues. Among other items, an annual financial report contains four financial statements: a balance sheet, an income statement, a statement of stockholders' or owners' equity, and a statement of cash flows. Shown in Exhibit 1.3 is a condensed income statement for J.C. Penney Company, a large merchandising firm. This income statement reports that J.C. Penney

financial statements

EXHIBIT 1.3 ▼
Recent Income Statement (in thousands) for J.C. Penney Company

Retail sales	$ 20,380,000
Miscellaneous revenues	702,000
Cost of goods sold	(13,970,000)
Selling, general & administrative expenses	(4,783,000)
Miscellaneous expenses	(630,000)
Income tax expense	(642,000)
Net income	$ 1,057,000

2. *Statement of Accounting Principles Board No. 4,* "Basic Concepts and Accounting Principles Underlying Financial Statements of a Business Enterprise" (New York: American Institute of Certified Public Accountants, 1970), para. 40.

Abusive Accounting and Abused Accountants

Accountants who prepare and deliver financial statements documenting that a company is in poor financial health sometimes encounter a "kill the messenger" attitude. This was true during the 1980s when a financial crisis struck the savings and loan industry. Many accountants spoke out regarding improper accounting practices being used by hundreds of savings and loans at the time, accounting practices that obscured the failing health of these institutions. These warnings were largely ignored, and the accountants who voiced them were often chastised for being too conservative or pessimistic.

Consider the case of Phoenix-based Lincoln Savings and Loan, one of the nation's largest savings and loans in the 1980s. For several years, Lincoln's accounting firm was the large international firm of Arthur Young & Company, now known as Ernst & Young. In 1988, the Arthur Young accountant assigned to supervise the accounting services being provided to Lincoln vigorously contested aggressive accounting practices used by the savings and loan. Lincoln's chief executive, Charles Keating, did not appreciate this accountant's point of view and pressured top officials of Arthur Young to replace that accountant. To their credit, the executives of Arthur Young resigned from the Lincoln engagement rather than capitulate to Keating's demand. A few years later, Lincoln would be declared bankrupt, resulting in losses to investors, depositors, and taxpayers of more than $1 billion.

Source: M. C. Knapp, "Lincoln Savings and Loan Association," in *Contemporary Auditing: Issues and Cases*, 2d. ed. (Minneapolis/ St. Paul: West Publishing Co., 1996).

earned $1,057,000 during the year in question. That number sounds impressive enough, but notice that J.C. Penney's income statement, like the financial statements of many large companies, is presented in thousands. Consequently, J.C. Penney's actual net income was more than $1 billion!

External decision makers use financial statements as input to a wide range of decisions. These decisions include determining whether to invest in a given company, whether to extend a loan to a company, or, in the case of a regulatory authority, whether a company is complying with specific governmental regulations. In Chapter 2, we examine the four financial statements in more detail.

Information funneled to a company's executives by its accountants can often mean the difference between a firm surviving or becoming one of the tens of thousands of businesses that fail each year.

Communicating Financial Information to Internal Decision Makers

The form and content of financial statements prepared for external decision makers are specified by formal accounting rules and regulations. When accountants provide financial data to internal decision makers, such as production-line superintendents and advertising managers, most of these formal rules and regulations do not apply. To assist internal decision makers, accountants develop customized financial reports designed with the specific information needs of these parties in mind.

To illustrate how accountants are called upon to satisfy the information needs of internal decision makers, consider a recent series of events involving Holly Farms, Inc., a leading producer of poultry products. A few years ago, Holly Farms decided to market a product, roasted chicken, to retail grocery chains, the company's principal customers. The company invested $20 million in a production facility for this product and then spent several million dollars advertising the product when it went on the market. No doubt, after the roasted chicken had been on the market for a few months, company executives were more than a little interested in determining whether the venture was a financial success. To answer this question, the executives relied upon their accountants to collect, process, and analyze the appropriate financial data. These data included the total or "gross" sales generated by the product, sales returns made by customers, production and production-related expenses, advertising costs, and so on.

Determining whether a new product is profitable does not sound like a particularly challenging exercise. Simply add and subtract a few numbers, right? Wrong. Holly Farms' accountants had to address several contentious issues to determine whether the roasted chicken product was profitable. One of the toughest of these issues was the allocation of so-called "common" costs to the new product.

Since Holly Farms ships numerous products to market in its large fleet of trucks, the company's accountants must decide how to allocate delivery costs to these various products. Common costs can be allocated in several different ways. One method of allocating common delivery costs is based upon the proportionate weight of the products in each shipment. For example, assume that a delivery truck is carrying 10,000 pounds of product and the freight bill for this shipment is $1,000. In this case, the common cost of $1,000 could be allocated to the products at a rate of $.10 per pound ($1,000/10,000 pounds). Alternatively, the products' relative sales values could be used as the basis for allocating delivery costs or other common costs to the products. All common cost allocation methods are somewhat arbitrary, including the two just mentioned. If an allocation method is extremely arbitrary, the profitability of the products or product lines affected by that method may be significantly distorted. In turn, distorted accounting data may result in company executives making improper decisions.

So, was the roasted chicken product successful? No, at least not initially. The problem was not the quality of the product but Holly Farms' inability to get the product to market on a timely basis. By the time the roasted chicken reached retail grocery outlets, it had only a few days of shelf-life remaining, meaning that spoilage losses were high. To solve this problem, Holly Farms decided to develop a new distribution system for the roasted chicken product, a decision creating more data collection, processing, and analysis problems—or opportunities—for the company's accountants.

Capturing Accounting Data: From Pacioli to the FASB

LEARNING OBJECTIVE 3
Briefly describe how financial data are collected by an organization's accounting system.

So, accounting is a service activity that exists to provide needed information to decision makers both internal and external to business organizations. We also know that accountants communicate this information in different ways to these decision makers. But, exactly how is this information captured in the first place? At this early stage of your study of accounting, it will be helpful to become briefly acquainted with a few basic technical features of accounting.

Financial recordkeeping, in one form or another, has existed for thousands of years. However, the origins of modern accounting can be traced to a mathematics book

Luca Pacioli

double-entry bookkeeping

written in 1494 by **Luca Pacioli,** a Franciscan monk living in present-day Italy. Pacioli was a mathematics scholar and a close friend of Leonardo da Vinci. As a favor to local merchants, Pacioli included in his book a section on the mechanics of **double-entry bookkeeping,** a financial recordkeeping system that had been used for several decades in and around Venice.

Pacioli did not invent or claim to invent the "Method of Venice." However, his book did formalize and document this recordkeeping system. This system allowed merchants to maintain financial records that summarized the operating results and financial condition of their businesses in a logical and easily understood manner. More important, double-entry bookkeeping permitted merchants to make informed and timely decisions regarding their business affairs. Economic historians attribute the rapid spread of commerce across Europe during the sixteenth century in large part to the availability of this recordkeeping system. Five hundred years following the publication of Pacioli's book, double-entry bookkeeping serves as the backbone of accounting systems worldwide.

DOUBLE-ENTRY BOOKKEEPING AND THE LAWS OF PHYSICS The key premise underlying double-entry bookkeeping stems from a fundamental law of physics: For every action there is an equal and opposite reaction. You will discover that applying this natural law to bookkeeping is a bit of a stretch at times. Nevertheless, financial transactions are recorded as if they consist of two equal and opposite effects. A brief example may be helpful. Consider a purchase made by Chrysler Corporation from one of its suppliers. Assume that Chrysler purchases on credit $1,000 of supplies from Office Depot. From Chrysler's perspective, this transaction can be reduced to two parts: (1) the company obtains "assets" valued at $1,000, and (2) the company assumes a "liability" or debt in the same amount. Action . . . reaction. Another example? What about a personal transaction that each of us makes periodically? When you purchase a set of tires, that transaction can be reduced to two components: (1) you give up a certain amount of cash, and (2) you obtain a set of tires having a retail value equal to the cash you paid to acquire them.

Every transaction, regardless of how large or small, can be reduced by an accountant to two equal effects expressed in dollars. If a company properly records the dual nature of each of its transactions, the entity's financial records will be "in balance" at any given point in time. Failure to apply the basic premise of double-entry bookkeeping results in an "unbalanced" set of financial records. Many weary accountants have invested long and tedious overtime hours attempting to balance a set of accounting records. This frustrating exercise is very similar to reconciling your checkbook balance with your month-end bank statement balance when you have failed to record certain checks or deposits.

THE EVOLUTION OF ACCOUNTING SYSTEMS Double-entry bookkeeping provided businesses in the Middle Ages with a systematic method to record financial data. In addition to a financial recordkeeping system, these early businesses needed some place to record their financial transactions. At some point in the history of accounting, "journals" and "ledgers" were developed to meet this need. Journals and ledgers are financial diaries in which businesses and other organizations record their transactions. Later chapters discuss and illustrate journals and ledgers.

Before the Industrial Revolution of the eighteenth century, accounting systems were quite simple. Most business enterprises prior to the eighteenth century were small and engaged in only a few types of routine transactions. The Industrial Revolution resulted in much larger businesses and a wider array of business transactions, which led to a need for more elaborate accounting systems. In today's business world, huge companies such as Exxon, Microsoft, and General Electric spend millions of dollars each year to process and record their transactions. As you can imagine, these firms' enormous volume of transactions and the geographical dispersion of their operating units mandate that computers be an integral part of their accounting systems.

GENERALLY ACCEPTED ACCOUNTING PRINCIPLES: THE RULES OF THE GAME Double-entry bookkeeping provides the foundation upon which modern accounting is based. Since Pacioli's time, successive generations of accountants have developed a series of concepts, guidelines, and rules that are helpful in applying double-entry bookkeeping to the task of recording and reporting financial information. These concepts, guidelines, and rules are known collectively as **generally accepted accounting principles.** Accountants use the acronym GAAP to refer to these basic accounting principles. Notice the term "generally accepted." Most accounting principles have become established by general acceptance or usage over time.

generally accepted accounting principles

Accounting rules evolved over a period of several centuries on an industry-by-industry basis. For example, one set of accounting rules became generally accepted, or widely used, by merchants, while another set of accounting rules became generally accepted within the shipbuilding industry. Even today, there are significant differences in how similar transactions are recorded within different industries.

Eventually, accountants decided that allowing accounting rules to be validated strictly by general acceptance was not necessarily a good idea. As a result, during the latter part of this century the development of accounting rules or standards has been guided by several rule-making bodies. Presently, the **Financial Accounting Standards Board** (FASB) is the principal rule-making authority within the accounting profession in the United States. The FASB is an independent body that receives funding from several private sources, including substantial funds from major accounting firms. Before the creation of the FASB in 1973, the Accounting Principles Board and the Committee on Accounting Procedures served as the authoritative rule-making bodies in accounting for fourteen years and twenty years, respectively.

Financial Accounting Standards Board

AN OVERVIEW OF THE ACCOUNTING PROFESSION ▲

This final section of Chapter 1 introduces you to the accounting profession. Understanding the nature of the accounting profession will provide you with valuable insights on key accounting topics that you will encounter as you progress through this course.

LEARNING ◀ OBJECTIVE 4
Define the nature, structure, and major segments of the accounting profession and key changes presently taking place within the profession.

Accountant vs. CPA

To the proverbial man, or woman, on the street, accountant and **CPA—certified public accountant**—are essentially interchangeable terms. In fact, all CPAs are not practicing accountants, and many, many accountants are not CPAs. "Accountant" is a generic term that can be applied to anyone, including a CPA, who works in one of the fields of accounting. On the other hand, a CPA is an individual who has passed the rigorous CPA examination and met any other certification requirements established by his or her state. Most states, for example, require CPA candidates to complete an experience requirement ranging from six months to two years. (Like all professions, accounting is regulated primarily at the state level.) The CPA examination is administered twice

CPA—certified public accountant

American Institute of Certified Public Accountants (AICPA)

each year by the **American Institute of Certified Public Accountants (AICPA)**, a national professional organization of CPAs. By the late 1990s, there were approximately 350,000 CPAs in the United States.

Private vs. Public Accounting

Most businesspeople think of the accounting profession as consisting of two segments: private accounting and public accounting.[3] Accountants in private industry are employed by corporations and other business entities, not-for-profit organizations, and governmental agencies. Public accountants are employed by accounting firms or are sole proprietors or partners of their own firms.

Work Roles in Private Accounting

Individuals in private accounting have job titles such as controller, internal auditor, cost analyst, and tax accountant. A controller is the top accounting executive of an organization. A primary responsibility of a controller is to ensure that an entity's periodic financial statements are prepared on a timely and accurate basis. A controller usually reports to his or her organization's chief financial officer (CFO), who has the overall responsibility for supervising an organization's finance and accounting functions.

An internal auditor monitors the compliance of an organization's employees with its operating policies and procedures. Such monitoring is important if top management is to maintain effective control over an organization and keep its employees focused on the entity's short-term and long-term goals and objectives. Take the case of Hertz, the rental car company. Hertz has a large internal audit staff. These internal auditors regularly visit the hundreds of Hertz rental car agencies. An internal audit of a Hertz agency usually requires two weeks and involves a detailed review and study of the agency's financial records and day-to-day operations. Any significant deviations from Hertz's operating policies and procedures discovered during an internal audit are referred to a Hertz regional manager who then takes the proper corrective action.

An individual holding the job title of "cost analyst" may have any of a number of accounting-related responsibilities within an organization. These responsibilities may include maintaining production cost records for manufacturing processes, analyzing variances from budgeted expenditures, and preparing customized reports that forecast expected costs for a new operating unit. Finally, a tax accountant's principal duties involve the collection and processing of data needed to file an entity's periodic federal, state, and local tax returns.

certified management accountant (CMA)

Most organizations do not require their accountants to earn the CPA designation, although doing so nearly always furthers one's career in private accounting. A person interested strictly in a career in private accounting should consider the benefits of becoming a **certified management accountant (CMA)**. This professional designation is sponsored by the Institute of Management Accountants. CMAs specialize in assisting the management of business entities and other organizations in obtaining and making

3. The terms "private accounting" and "public accounting" refer to the two major employment sectors within the profession. College sophomores majoring in business tend to view the accounting domain as being segmented into "Financial Accounting" and "Management Accounting," the titles typically assigned to the two introductory level accounting courses in business programs. Financial accounting is generally concerned with the methods and procedures used to record financial data and to develop financial reports for decision makers external to organizations. Management or managerial accounting focuses on communicating financial data to decision makers within given enterprises.

optimal use of accounting information. To earn the CMA designation, an individual must have a college degree, pass the CMA examination, and work for two years in a field of private (management) accounting. Although the CMA designation has only existed since the early 1970s, it is now widely recognized as an important symbol of professional expertise in the field of private accounting.

Shown in Exhibit 1.4 are median 1996 salaries for several employment positions in private accounting. The consulting firm of Robert Half International, Inc., which compiled these data, disclosed that individuals possessing a CPA and/or CMA generally received a salary 10 to 20 percent higher than the figures reported in Exhibit 1.4.

Public Accounting: A Closer Look

Public accounting firms, like law firms, market their professional services to the general public. Among the services offered by public accounting firms to their clients are bookkeeping services, taxation services, auditing, and management consulting activities of various types. The preparation of tax returns is the professional service most closely identified with public accounting firms. Besides preparing tax returns for their clients,

EXHIBIT 1.4 ▼
Representative Salaries in Private Accounting

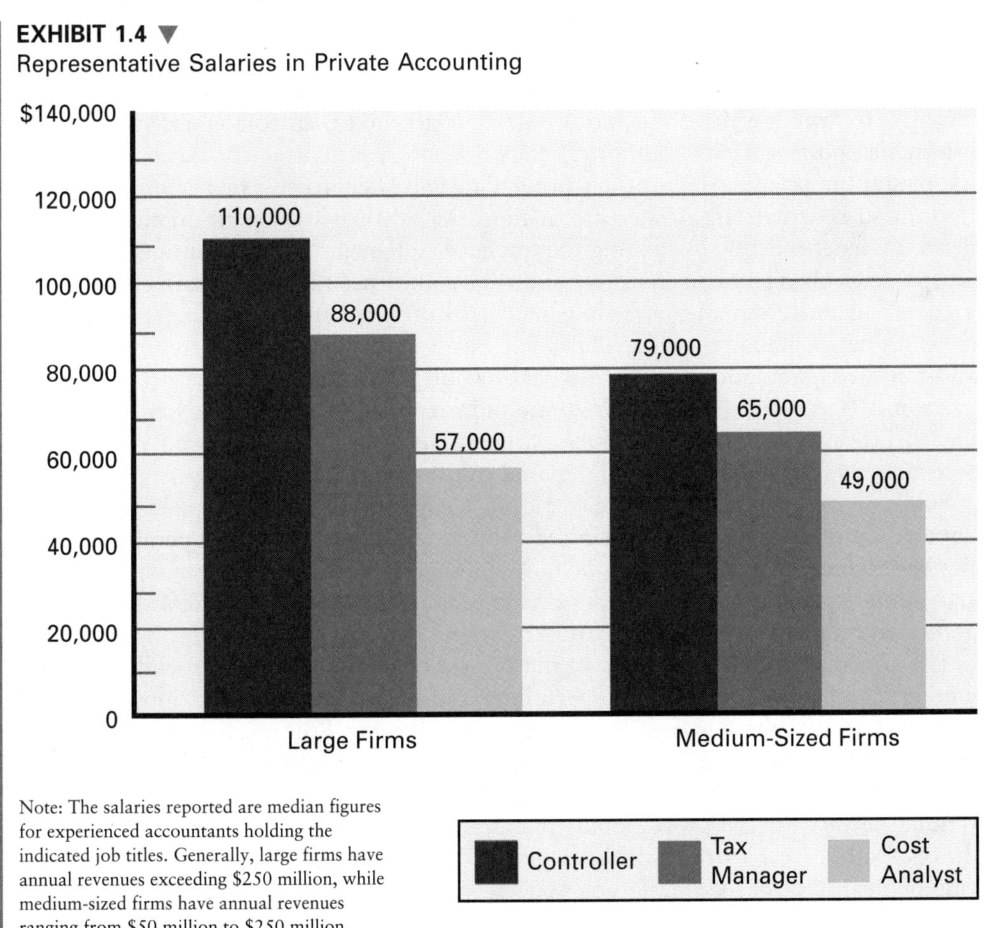

Note: The salaries reported are median figures for experienced accountants holding the indicated job titles. Generally, large firms have annual revenues exceeding $250 million, while medium-sized firms have annual revenues ranging from $50 million to $250 million.

Source: Robert Half/Accountemps, 1996 Salary Guide.

public accounting firms provide a wide range of other taxation services. Most important, these firms assist their clients in structuring personal and business transactions to minimize their taxes—legally.

Although not well understood by the public, independent auditing is arguably the most important professional service provided by public accounting firms. The independent audits performed by public accounting firms are much different from the services provided by internal auditors. One key difference is that an independent audit is just that, independent. A public accounting firm that has no financial interest in, or other important ties to, a business entity is retained to perform an independent audit of that entity's financial statements. On the other hand, internal auditors are not independent when they provide audit services to their employer. Why? Because the employer-employee relationship creates a strong financial bond or connection between the two parties.

The principal objective of an independent audit is to determine whether an entity's financial statements have been prepared in accordance with GAAP. That is, auditors examine an audit client's financial statements and accounting records to determine whether GAAP were used in recording the data summarized in those financial statements. If a company's financial statements have been prepared in accordance with GAAP, those statements are presumed to fairly reflect the financial affairs of the company.

In the absence of an independent audit, financial statement users would be much less likely to assume that a company's published financial statements are honest representations of its financial affairs. Why? Because business executives have an economic incentive to "window dress" financial statements to make their companies appear more profitable and financially stable than they actually are. If business executives report impressive financial results for their firms, they will likely receive higher salaries in the future and benefit from an increase in the value of their ownership interest in their firms. By independently examining the financial statements and accounting records of companies, public accounting firms bolster the confidence that third parties have in the accuracy of those statements. This higher level of confidence in financial statements increases the likelihood that individuals will invest in, or loan funds to, business entities and thus keep the national economy healthy and growing.

Exhibit 1.5 presents an example of an audit report on a company's financial statements. Ernst & Young, a large public accounting firm, issued this audit report on a recent set of financial statements prepared by Toys'R'Us, Inc.

Public accounting firms range in size from one-person proprietorships to huge international partnerships that have hundreds of partners and thousands of employees. The Big Six accounting firms, all of which are international in scope, dominate the public accounting profession in many respects. Exhibit 1.6 reports the worldwide revenues generated by the Big Six firms in a recent year.

The size and financial resources of the Big Six firms allow them to spend enormous amounts each year training their personnel and developing new and more effective means of serving the needs of their clients. The Big Six firm of Arthur Andersen & Co. operates the largest private educational center in the world. Located in St. Charles, Illinois, the Arthur Andersen & Co. Center for Professional Education is used as a training facility for the professionals that staff the several hundred Arthur Andersen offices scattered across the world. Exhibit 1.7 lists representative salaries for various employment positions within large public accounting firms. This latter group includes the Big Six firms and the handful of other accounting firms that have annual revenues exceeding $150 million. Recognize that the reported salaries shown in Exhibit 1.7 do

EXHIBIT 1.5 ▼
Audit Report Issued by Ernst & Young on Recent Financial Statements of Toys'R'Us, Inc.

Report of Independent Auditors
The Board of Directors and Stockholders
Toys'R'Us, Inc.

We have audited the accompanying consolidated balance sheets of Toys'R'Us, Inc. and subsidiaries as of February 3, 1996 and January 28, 1995, and the related consolidated statements of earnings, stockholders' equity and cash flows for each of the three years in the period ended February 3, 1996. These financial statements are the responsibility of the Company's management. Our responsibility is to express an opinion on these financial statements based on our audits.

We conducted our audits in accordance with generally accepted auditing standards. Those standards require that we plan and perform the audit to obtain reasonable assurance about whether the financial statements are free of material misstatement. An audit includes examining, on a test basis, evidence supporting the amounts and disclosures in the financial statements. An audit also includes assessing the accounting principles used and significant estimates made by management, as well as evaluating the overall financial statement presentation. We believe that our audits provide a reasonable basis for our opinion.

In our opinion, the financial statements referred to above present fairly, in all material respects, the financial position of Toys'R'Us, Inc. and subsidiaries at February 3, 1996 and January 28, 1995, and the consolidated results of their operations and their cash flows for each of the three years in the period ended February 3, 1996, in conformity with generally accepted accounting principles.

Ernst & Young LLP
New York, New York

March 13, 1996

EXHIBIT 1.6 ▼
Worldwide Revenues of Big Six Accounting Firms

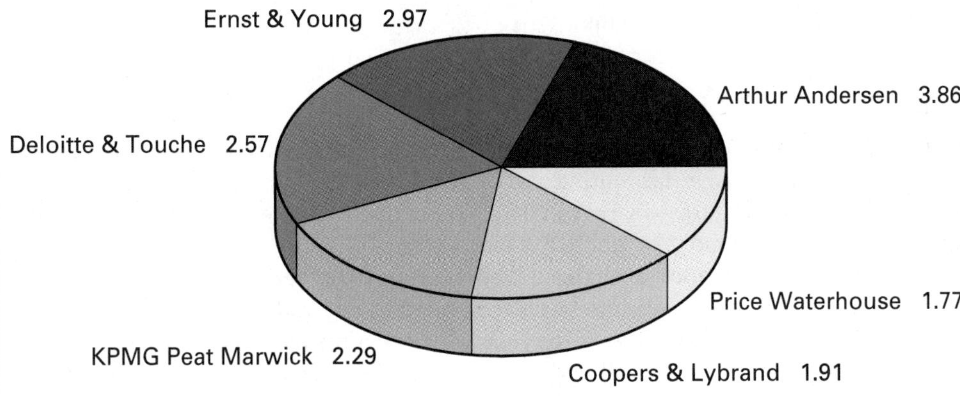

Source: Accounting Today, March 18–April 7, 1996.

EXHIBIT 1.7
Representative Salaries in Public Accounting: Large Firms

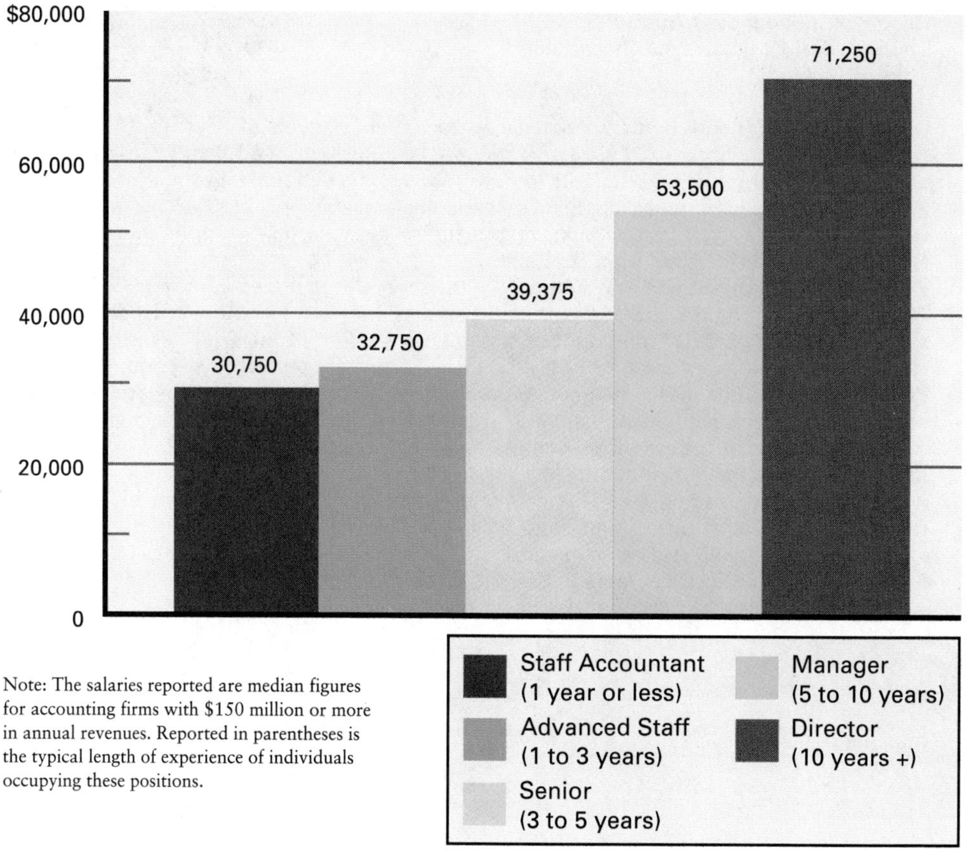

$80,000
60,000
40,000
20,000
0

30,750
32,750
39,375
53,500
71,250

Staff Accountant (1 year or less)
Advanced Staff (1 to 3 years)
Senior (3 to 5 years)
Manager (5 to 10 years)
Director (10 years +)

Note: The salaries reported are median figures for accounting firms with $150 million or more in annual revenues. Reported in parentheses is the typical length of experience of individuals occupying these positions.

Source: Robert Half/Accountemps, 1996 Salary Guide.

not include the profit distributions received by the partners, or owners, of these firms. Annual profit distributions range as high as several hundred thousand dollars for the partners of large accounting firms.

Regulation of the Accounting Profession

Securities and Exchange Commission (SEC)

In the early 1930s, Congress established the **Securities and Exchange Commission (SEC)** to deter the abusive accounting and financial reporting practices that contributed to the collapse of the stock market in 1929. The SEC regulates the sale of securities, such as stocks and bonds, by publicly owned companies and the subsequent trading of those securities on stock exchanges. (Companies that market their stocks, bonds, or other securities on an interstate basis are generally referred to as "publicly owned" companies.) The SEC also oversees the financial reporting and accounting practices of publicly owned companies. "Full and fair disclosure" is the SEC's motto. This federal agency does not assess the investment quality of the securities issued by the companies that it regulates, nor does it prohibit the sale of highly speculative securities. Instead, the SEC attempts to ensure that publicly owned companies provide third parties with sufficient information to make informed economic decisions regarding the securities these firms sell.

The SEC closely monitors the accounting profession's rule-making processes and has the authority to override any new rules issued by the FASB to the extent that those rules apply to publicly owned companies. However, the SEC has seldom interfered with rule-making bodies within the profession.

As indicated earlier, the accounting profession is regulated most directly at the state, rather than federal, level. Each state has established an agency to regulate the practice of accounting within its borders. Typically, this agency is known as the state board of accountancy or the state board of public accountancy. The primary responsibilities of this agency include issuing and renewing CPA licenses, monitoring compliance with continuing education requirements, and sanctioning CPAs who violate the agency's rules and regulations.

Accounting: A Profession in Transition

The past quarter of a century has brought extensive changes to the accounting profession and the business world. One of the most apparent changes in accounting over the past two decades has been a rapid growth in the use of computers by accountants. Much of the tedious clerical work previously performed by accountants can now be done in a matter of nanoseconds by modern computers. Take the case of independent auditing. With the aid of computers, auditors use statistical sampling techniques to audit efficiently and effectively populations of client transactions that can easily number in the tens of millions, if not more.

International Differences in Accounting Rules Spell Trouble for Decision Makers

FOR YOUR INFORMATION

To investigate the impact of differences in international accounting rules on companies' reported operating results, three researchers computed the profit of a hypothetical firm four times. Each time, these researchers based the profit computation on a different country's accounting rules. The results, reported in U.S. dollars, were as follows:

Country	Net Income
Australia	$240,000
United Kingdom	260,600
United States	34,600
West Germany	10,402

These data demonstrate that decision makers must be cautious when interpreting the financial statements of a foreign firm and suggest a strong need for uniform international accounting rules.

Source: D. E. Wygal, D. E. Stout, and J. Volpe, "Reporting Practices in Four Countries," *Management Accounting,* December 1987, pp. 37–42.

The growing trend toward multinational business enterprises and international trade promises to complicate the work roles of public and private accountants in the next several decades. Cultural differences in business practices, varying governmental regulations, and a lack of uniform international accounting rules create "global-sized" headaches for accountants of multinational companies.

One recent trend in the accounting profession is of special significance to prospective accountants. This trend involves requiring individuals sitting for the CPA examination to have completed a minimum of 150 hours of college credit. This requirement spread across the nation over the past decade. By the year 2000, most states are expected to have adopted this rule. A perceived need for future accountants to develop better communication, computer, and interpersonal skills motivated the profession to require a five-year educational program for its new members.

Business organizations and the accounting profession face several challenges as they prepare to enter the twenty-first century. Since the time of Pacioli and before, accountants have played an integral role in the economic success of business enterprises. Those businesses that thrive in the coming century will share several key attributes. One of these attributes will be a supporting staff of accountants who understand their organization, recognize the information needs of the organization's internal and external decision makers, and satisfy those needs on a timely basis with relevant and reliable accounting data.

SUMMARY

The three major types of business entities are service, manufacturing, and merchandising companies. The most common legal forms of business organizations are sole proprietorships, partnerships, and corporations. A large majority of businesses in the United States are sole proprietorships, although corporations account for nearly 90 percent of gross business revenues each year in this country. Large companies have several internal functions that are performed by individuals with specialized training and experience in a field of business. Management, marketing, finance, and accounting are the most commonly recognized specialized fields in business. This course focuses on the accounting function of business organizations. The principal role of the accounting function of business organizations is to provide financial information regarding those organizations to decision makers.

The manner in which accountants communicate financial data depends upon the identity of the decision maker who will utilize that data. Financial statements are the primary means accountants use to communicate financial information to investors, creditors, regulatory agencies, and other decision makers external to a given organization. Accountants communicate financial data oriented toward the needs of internal decision makers, such as production-line superintendents and advertising managers, in customized reports designed with the specific objectives of those decision makers in mind. A system of financial recordkeeping known as double-entry bookkeeping has been used for five centuries by businesses to capture financial data regarding their transactions and related events. The concepts, guidelines, and rules that accountants use in applying double-entry bookkeeping are known collectively as generally accepted accounting principles (GAAP).

Private accounting and public accounting are the two major segments of the accounting profession. Accountants in private industry are employed by businesses, not-for-profit organizations, and other entities in various accounting-related work roles. Public accountants are employees, partners, or proprietors of accounting firms. Public accounting firms provide an array of professional services to the public including bookkeeping, taxation services, auditing, and management consulting.

The business world and the accounting profession face several challenges as they prepare for the next century. Among the most important challenges facing the accounting profession are those posed by the increasing trend toward international trade and multinational business operations. This trend is important because the lack of uniform international accounting standards impairs the comparability of financial data prepared in different countries.

GLOSSARY

Accounting (p. 9) A service activity designed to provide quantitative information about economic entities that is intended to be useful in making economic decisions.
American Institute of Certified Public Accountants (AICPA) (p. 14) The national professional organization of CPAs that prepares and administers the CPA examination.
Certified management accountant (CMA) (p. 14) An individual who has passed the CMA examination and satisfied the other requirements to qualify for this professional designation; CMAs generally specialize in private (management) accounting.
Certified public accountant (CPA) (p. 13) An individual who has passed the CPA examination and satisfied any other requirements established by his or her state to qualify for this professional designation.
Corporation (p. 7) An association of individuals, created by law and having an existence apart from that of its members as well as distinct and inherent powers and liabilities.
Double-entry bookkeeping (p. 12) A method of maintaining financial records developed more than five hundred years ago that serves as the foundation of modern accounting systems worldwide.
Financial Accounting Standards Board (FASB) (p. 13) The rule-making body that has the primary authority for establishing accounting standards in the United States.
Financial statements (p. 9) The principal means accountants use to communicate financial information regarding business entities and other organizations to investors, creditors, and other decision makers external to those entities.
Generally accepted accounting principles (GAAP) (p. 13) The concepts, guidelines, and rules that accountants follow in recording and reporting financial information.
Luca Pacioli (p. 12) A Franciscan monk credited with formalizing and documenting double-entry bookkeeping in the late fifteenth century.
Partnership (p. 7) An unincorporated business with two or more owners.
Securities and Exchange Commission (SEC) (p. 18) A federal agency that regulates the sale and subsequent trading of securities by publicly owned companies; also oversees the financial reporting and accounting practices of these companies.
Sole proprietorship (p. 7) A business owned by one individual.

DECISION CASE

During the 1980s, Vincent Golden served as the chief financial officer of Regina Company, Inc., whose principal line of business was manufacturing and marketing vacuum cleaners. As Regina's chief financial officer, Golden was responsible for the company's accounting function. Golden's immediate superior was Donald

Sheelen, Regina's chief executive officer. Under Sheelen's leadership, Regina introduced several new products that were initially well received by the public. In the late 1980s, Regina began experiencing financial problems that stemmed primarily from poor quality controls over product development and manufacturing processes. Many of the new products developed by Sheelen and his subordinates were returned by customers because they suffered from a high rate of malfunctions.

In 1988, Sheelen became very concerned when he realized that Regina would not achieve target sales and earnings goals he had established for the company. Sheelen recognized that if Regina reported disappointing financial results, the company's stock price would decline. To prevent this from occurring, Sheelen instructed Golden to falsify Regina's accounting records. Among the steps taken by Golden to improve Regina's reported financial results were recording millions of dollars of nonexistent sales and ignoring $13 million of merchandise returned by customers.

As typically happens, Sheelen and Golden were unable to conceal Regina's financial problems indefinitely. When the fraud was revealed, both men were prosecuted and eventually pleaded guilty to federal mail fraud and securities fraud charges.

Required: Assume that in the future you are the chief financial officer of Boyd Enterprises. Near the end of a year, you realize that the company will not meet the target sales and earnings goals established at the beginning of that year by Boyd's new chief executive officer (CEO). Over the past year, you have realized that this individual has a very casual attitude toward financial reporting. When you inform the CEO that the company's financial goals will not be met, the CEO responds, "You can fix that by backdating the sales for the first two weeks of January as if they occurred in December. That will put us right on target." When a stunned look appears on your face, the CEO continues. "This is a one-time thing only. We're turning around this company. Next year's profit figures will be much better, and we won't have to get involved in any of these accounting shenanigans."

What would you do at this point? Before answering, identify the parties who will be affected by your decision. What responsibility, if any, do you have to each of these parties?

QUESTIONS

1. Identify the three general types of businesses and provide an example of each.
2. Identify the three common legal forms of business organizations. Which form of business organization is most common in the United States?
3. List the principal internal functions of businesses and briefly describe each.
4. What is the primary purpose of a business's accounting function?
5. Identify the four major financial statements. Why do businesses issue financial statements?
6. How does a business's accountant communicate financial information to internal decision makers?
7. To what fifteenth century scholar do we trace the origin of modern accounting?
8. What fundamental law of physics is reflected in double-entry accounting?
9. You just bought a new tennis racket for $125. Identify the two dimensions of this transaction and how these dimensions are equivalent in an economic sense.
10. Define "generally accepted accounting principles" (GAAP). What is the primary purpose of GAAP?

11. Identify the principal rule-making body within the accounting profession.
12. Is a CPA an accountant? Is an accountant a CPA? Distinguish between accountants and CPAs.
13. Distinguish between private and public accounting. Briefly describe several work roles in private accounting.
14. What services do public accounting firms typically offer to the public?
15. What is the principal objective of an independent audit?
16. What prompted the formation of the Securities and Exchange Commission (SEC), and what is its primary function?
17. List key factors or trends that have impacted the accounting profession in recent decades.

EXERCISES

18. True or False (LO 1–4)

Following are a series of statements regarding topics discussed in Chapter 1.

Required:

Indicate whether each statement is true (T) or false (F).

_____ a. Financial statements are the principal means accountants use to communicate financial information regarding business entities to external decision makers such as bank loan officers and investors.

_____ b. A key advantage of the corporate form of business organization is that the personal assets of a corporation's owners are not at risk if the business is sued.

_____ c. The Securities and Exchange Commission issues most new accounting rules in this country.

_____ d. Sole proprietorships are the most common form of business organization in the United States and account for the majority of business revenues generated in this country each year.

_____ e. A trait common to most successful businesspeople is an ability to make wise decisions regarding the allocation of their business's economic resources.

_____ f. Double-entry bookkeeping is a financial recordkeeping system used only in the United States and a few European countries.

_____ g. A key objective of independent auditors is to bolster the confidence of third parties in audited financial statements.

_____ h. Controller, internal auditor, and cost analyst are common job titles in private accounting.

_____ i. Because it is a "service" activity, accounting does not contribute significantly to the success of business organizations.

_____ j. The reported profits of multinational companies are not affected by their home country's accounting rules.

19. Analyzing Business Transactions (LO 3)

"Every transaction, regardless of how large or small, can be reduced by an accountant to two equal effects expressed in dollars." As you will discover in a subsequent chapter, all business transactions affect either assets (things owned), liabilities (amounts owed), owners' equity (the ownership interest in a business), or some combination of these items. Following is an analysis of the equal dollar effects of two transactions mentioned in this chapter.

	Assets	Liabilities	Owners' Equity
1. Purchased $1,000 of office supplies on credit	+ $1,000	+ $1,000	
2. Purchased a set of tires for $200 cash	+ $ 200 − $ 200		

Required:
Listed next are selected transactions of Fuente & Demond Realtors. Analyze the effect of each transaction on the firm's assets, liabilities, and owners' equity.

1. Purchased equipment for $12,500 cash.
2. Fuente & Demond's owners invested an additional $17,000 in the firm.
3. Paid $1,500 owed to an office supply store for a purchase made the previous month.
4. Purchased inventory for $4,000 on credit.

20. **Information Needs of External and Internal Decision Makers** (LO 2)
Consider the following items of information that may be obtained from a given company's accounting records.

a. Net income
b. Inventory cost per unit
c. Total liabilities (amounts owed)
d. Total sales by geographical area of business operations
e. Five-year trend in total sales
f. Employee salaries by department

Required:

1. Indicate a specific type of decision maker who would have a primary interest in each of these items of information. The decision maker may be an external party, such as an investor or bank loan officer, or an internal party, such as a departmental supervisor or president of a company.
2. Briefly explain why the decision makers identified in (1) would have a need for the given item of information.

21. **Analyzing the Financial Statements of Foreign Companies** (LO 2)
Joan Blake wants to invest in one or more firms in the automobile industry. Blake has obtained the most recent income statements of two foreign automobile manufacturers, Company A, which is based in Japan, and Company B, which is headquartered in Germany. She has translated each firm's net income into U.S. dollars. Company A's most recent net income expressed in U.S. dollars is $55 million, while Company B earned a net income equivalent to $702 million.

Required:

1. What additional information should Blake obtain before she can compare the translated profits of these two companies?
2. What challenges are posed for accountants by the growing trend toward multinational business operations?

22. **The Need for Financial Statements** (LO 2)
Jim Hardy opened a new business several months ago, which he named Jim's Bike Shop. Hardy sells and repairs bicycles. Since Hardy took several accounting courses in college, he has decided to maintain his business's accounting records. Although the bike shop has been in operation for more than three months, Hardy has not yet prepared any financial statements for the business. He has several friends who are business owners and is aware that they prepare monthly financial statements for their businesses. Nevertheless, Hardy has decided that it is too much of a "hassle" to prepare monthly financial statements for Jim's Bike Shop.

Required:
Write a memo to Hardy explaining why financial statements would help him operate his business more efficiently and effectively.

23. **Major Types of Businesses** (LO 1)
Businesses are often classified into three broad groups: service companies, manufacturing companies, and merchandising companies.

Required:

1. Identify each of the following well-known firms as either a service company (S), a manufacturing company (M), or a merchandising company (D).
   _____ a. General Motors
   _____ b. Kinko's
   _____ c. Merrill Lynch
   _____ d. Kmart
   _____ e. Levi Strauss
2. For the companies listed, identify a key business decision that each firm's management likely faces on a recurring basis. What type of data might each firm's management obtain from their accountants to help them make these decisions?

24. **Common Legal Forms of Business Organizations** (LO 1)
The text identified three common legal forms of business organizations: sole proprietorships, partnerships, and corporations.

Required:

1. Compare and contrast what you believe would be key advantages and disadvantages of operating a business as a sole proprietorship versus a corporation.
2. Compare and contrast what you believe would be key advantages and disadvantages of operating a business as a partnership versus a corporation.

PROBLEM SET A

25. **Use of Income Statement Information** (LO 2)
The following condensed income statement was taken from a recent financial report of CKE Restaurants, Inc. This company operates Carl's Jr. fast-food restaurants in the western United States and Mexico. Amounts are expressed in thousands.

Sales by company-operated restaurants	$ 381,733
Revenues from franchised and licensed restaurants	78,635
Other income	6,148
Operating expenses	(449,860)
Interest expense	(10,387)
Income tax expense	(1,836)
Other expenses	(768)
Net income	$ 3,665

Required:
Describe how the following three groups of decision makers might use CKE's income statement data: the company's stockholders (its owners), the company's executives, and the firm's bankers. Also identify additional information regarding this company's income statement data that each group of decision makers might request.

26. **Common Cost Allocation** (LO 2)
Little River Corporation manufactures ceramic ornaments. Two of the primary raw materials used by Little River are stone chips and cement colorants. These materials are often delivered to Little River's production plant in the same shipment, accompanied by a single freight bill.

Little River's management presently allocates common shipping costs for chips and colorants based on the total cost of each item in a shipment. For example, if a shipment contains $2,000 of chips and $1,000 of colorants, two-thirds of the common shipping costs would be allocated to chips and one-third to colorants. (Chips cost $.50 per pound, while colorants cost $.10 per pound.) Management is considering a second method of allocating common shipping costs. Under this method, shipping costs would be allocated based on the total weight of each inventory item in a shipment.

Required:

1. Little River recently received a shipment containing one ton of chips and four tons of colorants. The freight bill for this shipment was $600. Allocate this shipping cost between the two inventory items based on
   a. the total weight of each item in the shipment.
   b. the total cost of each item in the shipment.
2. Which allocation method would you recommend that Little River use? Why?
3. How, if at all, may the choice of a cost allocation method affect those parties who make decisions based on Little River's financial statements? Explain.

27. Effects of Industry Accounting Practices (LO 3)

During the 1980s, a special set of accounting rules was in effect for the savings and loan industry. These accounting rules allowed companies in that industry to recognize, or "write off," losses on sales of certain securities over a several-year period. For example, suppose that a savings and loan sold a security for $1 million that had originally cost $3 million. Rather than immediately reporting the loss on this sale, the company could have prorated the loss over several years.

Required:

1. In the example just given, how much loss would the savings and loan have reported in the year of sale had the special accounting rules not been in effect?
2. Assume now that the savings and loan prorated the loss on the sale of the security over a five-year period, recognizing an equal portion of that loss in each of those years. What portion of the loss did the savings and loan report in the year of sale?
3. How was this "special" accounting treatment for losses on the sale of certain securities misleading to financial statement users?

28. International Accounting Differences (LO 4)

In the United States, GAAP requires that long-term assets, such as buildings and equipment, be reported in financial statements at cost less accumulated depreciation. Accumulated depreciation represents the total "depreciation expense" recorded on an asset since its acquisition. For example, suppose an asset that cost $10,000 has an estimated useful life of 10 years and a zero estimated "salvage value" at the end of its useful life. This asset would be depreciated $1,000 per year for 10 years. So, after three years, the asset would be reported in a business's financial statements at $7,000—$10,000 cost less accumulated depreciation of $3,000. (Some of the finer points regarding the computation of depreciation are not discussed here but are instead deferred to a later chapter.)

Long-term assets should be "written off" more rapidly if they decline in value because of obsolescence or other factors. However, in the United States, these assets cannot be increased in value for accounting purposes even if their fair market values rise. This rule does not apply in many countries, such as Australia. In these countries, if the asset in the example just described had a fair market value of $14,000 after three years, that asset could be "written up" to $14,000. This new value would then be depreciated over the remaining seven years of the asset's useful life.

Required:

1. Consider the example presented. Assume the given asset was owned by a business operating in a country that allows long-term assets to be written up to their fair market values. If this asset had a fair market value of $14,000 after three years, how much depreciation expense would the business record each remaining year of the asset's life?
2. Compare the amount computed in (1) to the depreciation expense allowed for an identical asset owned by a U.S. business. All other relevant variables held constant,

which of the two businesses would report the higher net income for each of the next seven years?

3. "Financial decision makers must be very cautious when interpreting the financial statements of a foreign entity." Write a brief memo discussing the meaning of this statement given the example presented here and the related discussion in the text.

29. **Analyzing Financial Statement Data** (LO 2)
The following table lists the net income, or earnings, of three large companies over a recent three-year period. (In each case, Year 3 is the most recent year.)

	Year 1	Year 2	Year 3
The Reader's Digest Association	$207,300,000	$246,300,000	$264,000,000
Rio Hotel & Casino	10,649,000	15,966,000	18,745,000
Wendy's International	80,517,000	97,432,000	110,070,000

Required:

1. Which of these companies was most profitable over the given three-year period? Which company's profitability improved the most over this period?
2. What business trends, economic variables, or other factors likely influence the profitability of each of these firms? When responding to this question, consider the nature of each firm's principal line of business.

PROBLEM SET B

30. **Use of Income Statement Information** (LO 2)
The following information was taken from a recent annual financial report of Winnebago Industries, Inc. The company, headquartered in Forest City, Iowa, manufactures motor homes and recreational vehicles. Amounts are expressed in thousands.

Sales revenue	$ 432,406
Service revenue	19,710
Operating expenses	(435,322)
Interest expense	(661)
Other expenses	(19,108)
Net loss	$ (2,975)

Required:
Describe how the following three groups of decision makers might use Winnebago's income statement data: Winnebago's executives, potential lenders, and potential suppliers or vendors. Also identify additional information regarding this company's income statement data that each group of decision makers might request.

31. **Common Cost Allocation** (LO 2)
Kamoche Enterprises manufactures a number of unusual yard statuary items for sale to lawn and garden stores. Two of the primary raw materials used in these products are marble chips and polished stones. These materials are often delivered to Kamoche's facilities at the same time and in the same shipment, accompanied by a single freight bill covering both.

Kamoche's management is concerned about the appropriate way to allocate common shipping costs to the two raw material inventory items. Presently, the company allocates shipping costs based on weight. For example, if a shipment contains three tons of marble chips and one ton of polished stones, three-fourths of the shipping costs would be allocated to the chips and one-fourth to the stones. Another option being considered is to allocate shipping costs based upon the total cost of each item in a given order. Presently, marble chips cost $80 per ton, while polished stones cost $200 per ton.

Required:

1. Kamoche recently received a shipment containing five tons of marble chips and five tons of polished stones. The freight bill for this shipment was $400. Allocate this shipping cost between the two inventory items based on
   a. the total weight of each item in the shipment.
   b. the total cost of each item in the shipment.
2. Which allocation method would you recommend that Kamoche use? Why?
3. How may the cost allocation scheme used by Kamoche affect related decisions of the company's managers?

32. Effects of Industry Accounting Practices (LO 3)

Until recently in the savings and loan industry, losses on the sale of certain securities could be "written off" over several years rather than being recorded exclusively in the year of sale. Assume that the write-off period was four years under this special accounting rule and that a savings and loan sold a qualifying security for $1.6 million that had cost $4 million.

Required:

1. How much loss would the savings and loan have reported in the year of sale had the special accounting rule not been in effect?
2. How much loss did the savings and loan report in the year of sale under the special accounting rule? (Assume the firm prorated the loss equally over the four-year write-off period.)
3. How may this "special" accounting treatment have affected the economic decisions of parties relying on savings and loans' financial statements?

33. International Accounting Differences (LO 4)

Businesses in the United States must report their long-term assets, such as buildings and equipment, at cost less accumulated depreciation. Accumulated depreciation represents the total "depreciation expense" recorded on an asset since its acquisition. For example, suppose an asset that cost $40,000 has an estimated useful life of 10 years and a zero estimated "salvage value" at the end of its useful life. This asset would be depreciated $4,000 per year for 10 years. So, after four years, the asset would be reported in a business's financial statements at $24,000—$40,000 cost less accumulated depreciation of $16,000. (Some of the finer points regarding the computation of depreciation are not discussed here but are instead deferred to a later chapter.)

Accounting principles in the United States require long-term assets to be "written off" more rapidly if they decline in value because of obsolescence or other factors. However, these assets cannot be increased in value for accounting purposes even if their fair market values rise. This rule does not apply in many countries, such as Sweden. In these countries, if the asset in the example just described had a fair market value of $60,000 after four years, that asset could be "written up" to $60,000. This new value would then be depreciated over the remaining six years of the asset's useful life.

Required:

1. Consider the example presented. Assume the given asset was owned by a business operating in a country that allows long-term assets to be written up to their fair market values. If this asset had a fair market value of $60,000 after four years, how much depreciation expense would the business record each remaining year of the asset's life?

2. Compare the amount computed in (1) to the depreciation expense allowed for an identical asset owned by a United States business. All other relevant variables held constant, which of the two businesses would report the higher net income for each of the next six years?
3. Write a brief memo discussing why decision makers who rely on financial statements issued by companies from different countries must be knowledgeable of differences in international accounting rules.

34. **Analyzing Financial Statement Data** (LO 2)
Listed in the following table are the net income, or earnings, of three large companies over a recent three-year period. (In each case, Year 3 is the most recent year.)

	Year 1	Year 2	Year 3
Alberto Culver	$ 41,272,000	$ 44,068,000	$ 52,651,000
The Gap	258,424,000	320,240,000	354,039,000
Outback Steakhouse	43,376,000	61,318,000	71,613,000

Required:
1. Which of these companies was most profitable over the given three-year period? Which company's profitability improved the most over this period?
2. What business trends, economic variables, or other factors likely influence the profitability of each of these firms? When responding to this question, consider the nature of each firm's principal line of business.

CASES

35. **Improper Accounting Practices** (LO 2)

As the independent auditor of Makinson, Inc.'s financial statements for the year just ended, you are concerned that the company intentionally "window-dressed" those financial statements. In particular, you have uncovered evidence suggesting that the company "backdated" sales made in the first few days of the new year to make it appear that those sales occurred during the final week of the year just ended. You also suspect that the company overstated its assets in its recent financial statements. For example, you suspect that the company "double-counted" many inventory items on hand at the end of the year.

Required:
1. How would these improper accounting practices affect Makinson's financial statements for the year just ended?
2. How might these practices mislead investors, lenders, and other third parties who use Makinson's financial statements to make important decisions regarding that firm?
3. As Makinson's independent auditor, what should you do about this situation?

36. **Supplemental Financial Statement Information** (LO 2)
A company supplements its financial statements with a set of financial statement "footnotes," which are often referred to simply as financial statement "notes." These footnotes provide additional information regarding a company's accounting practices, unusual circumstances that it faces, and other issues that would be of interest to financial statement users.

Books-A-Million, Inc., is an Alabama-based company that operates a chain of retail bookstores. During a recent year, this company disclosed the following information in the footnotes to its financial statements.

a. The company revealed that a large portion of its annual inventory purchases was made from companies controlled by individuals having a substantial ownership interest in Books-A-Million.
b. A table included in Books-A-Million's financial statement footnotes reported the dollar amount the firm was required to pay each of the following five years under the terms of the long-term leases on its store locations.
c. One footnote discussed the details of an agreement that allowed company employees to purchase stock (ownership interests) in Books-A-Million at a 15 percent discount from the stock's market value.

Required:

For each item listed, discuss why external decision makers would have an interest in the information disclosed.

37. Analysis of the Audit Report (LO 4)

Review the audit report for Toys'R'Us included in this chapter and the related discussion in the text.

Required:

1. Based on your reading of this audit report, answer the following questions.
   a. What does an auditor audit?
   b. Who is ultimately responsible for a company's financial statements?
   c. What standards guide the conduct of an independent audit?
   d. What is the objective of an independent audit?
2. What role do independent auditors play in overseeing corporate financial reporting?
3. What role does the SEC play in overseeing corporate financial reporting?

PROJECTS

38. Origins of Major Corporations

Most large corporations had modest beginnings. This chapter briefly profiled the origins of several prominent corporations including Sears, Federal Express, and Mary Kay Cosmetics. In this project, you will research the origins of a major corporation.

Required:

Identify a company in which you have a particular interest. Using your school's library or other available resources, research this company with a particular focus on identifying how it was created, its founders, where it began operations, the company's initial products or services, and related information. If possible, identify the key factor primarily responsible for the ultimate financial success of the firm. Summarize your findings in a written report.

39. Proposed Accounting Rules and Criticism of the Accounting Profession

Corporate executives are often critical of proposed accounting rules that would negatively affect their firm's reported financial condition. In recent years, proposed accounting rules for stock options, postretirement employee benefits, certain investments in marketable securities, and permanent impairments in the value of long-term assets have resulted in criticism of the accounting profession.

In this project, which will be completed on a team basis, you will research one of the proposed accounting rules just mentioned, or another assigned by your instructor. Your project team will develop a written report summarizing the nature of the controversy involving the proposed rule. Among the items your report will cover are the following: (1) a brief summary of the proposed rule, (2) a brief overview of why the accounting profession believed the proposed rule was needed, (3) a summary of the reasons that certain parties opposed the rule, (4) a summary of the reasons that certain parties supported the rule, and (5) whether or not the rule was adopted.

Required:

1. Your instructor will assign you to a group or project team to complete this assignment. In your initial meeting, your group should allocate the responsibilities for completing this project. For example, one or more group members may have the primary responsibility to search on-line newspaper indices (*New York Times, The Wall Street Journal,* etc.) to identify articles relevant to the assigned topic. Another member may be assigned the responsibility of identifying and reviewing magazine articles related to this topic. Other tasks to be assigned individual group members include organizing and outlining the relevant materials collected, preparing the written report, critiquing the report, and presenting an in-class summary of the report.
2. Before the written report is submitted to your instructor and the in-class presentation is made, a final group meeting should be arranged. In this meeting, group members should review a draft of the written report and agree on its final content. The individual responsible for presenting the report in class should present the report to the group, which will then critique that presentation.

40. Accessing Financial Information Via the Internet

Exhibit 1.3 in this chapter presents a recent income statement for J.C. Penney Company. Financial statements of hundreds of large companies can be accessed via the Internet. Companies that have established a permanent site on the Internet typically make available a wide array of information from that site including recent financial statements. Financial statements for a large number of companies can also be accessed via the "EDGAR" Internet site maintained by the Securities and Exchange Commission (SEC). EDGAR is an acronym referring to the SEC's electronic data gathering and retrieval system. Corporate financial statements are included in "Form 10-K" statements at the EDGAR Internet site.

Required:

1. Select a large company and then access the company's financial statements on the Internet. Print this company's income statement. (The given company's income statement may have a slightly different title such as "Consolidated Statement of Income" or "Statement of Operations.')
2. Briefly summarize the nature of the business operations of the company you selected.
3. What was the company's net income or net loss for the most recent year for which data are reported? List the major "revenues" and 'expenses" of this company during that year.
4. Prepare a brief report summarizing your answers to (2) and (3). When submitting your report, include the copy of the printed income statement.

2 Accounting Concepts and Elements

> *"The beginning of wisdom is the definition of terms."*
> Socrates

LEARNING OBJECTIVES

After studying this chapter, you should be able to do the following:

1. Define the three financial reporting objectives of business entities.
2. Describe the nature, purpose, and content of each of the four financial statements.
3. Identify and define the key attributes or characteristics that accounting information should possess.
4. Identify and define the fundamental concepts that underlie accounting and financial reporting rules and practices.

FOCUS ON DECISION MAKING

Concept-Driven Businesses; Concept-Driven Accounting

Most successful businesses are founded on a few simple concepts. A key concept upon which Ray Kroc built McDonald's during the 1950s was consistency in the quality of food served to customers. Kroc rigorously controlled food preparation at McDonald's restaurants by establishing tight standards for each menu item. For example, the fat content of hamburger meat used by each McDonald's restaurant could not exceed 19 percent. French fries had to be sold in seven minutes or thrown away. Kroc even dictated the precise amount of onions used on each hamburger (one-quarter ounce). Such uniform standards allowed Kroc to assure McDonald's customers that the quality of menu items would not vary from one visit to the next, a pledge that most restaurants could not make at the time.

Michael Dell was a freshman at the University of Texas in Austin when he began selling computers from his dorm room in the early 1980s. Before launching his business, Dell had decided that price was the key selling feature of personal computers. By purchasing computer components at wholesale and assembling them himself, Dell believed he could undercut the prices charged for personal computers by retail stores. With the help of a 1-800 number and a modest amount of advertising in computer magazines, Dell's "concept" quickly succeeded. In 1984, Dell dropped out of school to devote full-time to his new business, Dell Computers. Within one year, his business was generating annual sales of more than $6 million.

During the early twentieth century, dozens of cereal companies were marketing flaked cereal products. In this very competitive environment, Will Kellogg established the Battle Creek Toasted Corn Flake Company in 1906. After deciding that name recognition was a critical success factor in the crowded cereal industry, Kellogg gambled and spent much of his small company's resources on an aggressive advertising campaign. Kellogg's gamble paid off. Within a few years, the renamed Kellogg Company was the dominant firm in the cereal industry.

Each of these individuals recognized the importance of one or more key "concepts" in their line of business. These individuals then made decisions based on these concepts, decisions that heavily contributed to the ultimate success of their organizations. This chapter introduces you to the key concepts that underlie accounting practices. To correctly record transactions and other events affecting organizations, accountants must understand the basic conceptual principles of accounting. Likewise, nonaccountants must have a solid understanding of these basic concepts to properly utilize accounting data in making financial decisions.

In Chapter 1 you learned that the primary objective of accounting and accountants is to provide useful information to financial decision makers. The principal focus of financial accounting is the information needs of decision makers who are external to an organization. You may enroll in a subsequent course entitled Management Accounting or Managerial Accounting. In that course, you will be concerned primarily with the information needs of internal decision makers.

In this textbook, we concern ourselves principally with accounting for business entities. The phrase "business entities" refers to organizations that have a profit motive, such as the Kellogg Company, a large corporation. Most of the examples in this textbook involve corporations rather than other types of business entities such as partnerships and sole proprietorships, which were discussed in Chapter 1. Many organizations do not have a profit motive. Municipal hospitals, charities such as the Salvation Army, and governmental agencies are examples of not-for-profit organizations. The accounting and financial reporting rules and methods used by not-for-profit organizations are often quite different from the corresponding rules and methods applied by businesses. If you continue your study of accounting, you may enroll in a course entitled Governmental Accounting or Fund Accounting that will focus on the accounting and financial reporting rules and methods used by not-for-profit organizations.

This chapter begins by identifying the financial reporting objectives of business entities. Next, you become acquainted with the four financial statements that are prepared and issued regularly by business enterprises to satisfy those objectives. The last two sections of this chapter discuss the qualitative attributes that the accounting information in financial statements should possess and describe the fundamental concepts that underlie accounting and financial reporting practices.

Most introductory financial accounting textbooks do not discuss accounting concepts in an early chapter. Instead, these textbooks quickly focus on the mechanics of accounting and delay a discussion of accounting concepts to a chapter much further along in the book. Here, we are going to take a different approach, a top-down approach. Beginning with a discussion of accounting concepts and the key elements of accounting can be intimidating to introductory accounting students. However, keep in mind that the purpose of this chapter is not to suddenly transform you into an accounting expert. Instead, the intent of this chapter is to allow you to "make sense" of the accounting rules and procedures discussed in later chapters. In fact, you may want to think of this chapter as a user's manual for the remainder of this textbook.

OBJECTIVES OF FINANCIAL REPORTING

LEARNING OBJECTIVE 1 ▶ Define the three financial reporting objectives of business entities.

***Statements of Financial Accounting Concepts* (SFACs)**

In the mid-1970s, the Financial Accounting Standards Board (FASB) decided that there was a need for a conceptual framework to guide the development of future accounting and financial reporting standards. From 1978 through 1985, the FASB issued six ***Statements of Financial Accounting Concepts*** **(SFACs)** to serve as this conceptual framework. These six statements are listed in Exhibit 2.1. Throughout Chapter 2, we will refer to these statements as we identify the basic concepts and elements of accounting.

According to *SFAC No. 1,* business enterprises have three financial reporting objectives. Exhibit 2.2 summarizes these objectives. Each of these objectives directly or indirectly concerns the need for the financial reports of business entities to assist third parties in making rational and informed economic decisions. A key responsibility of an organization's accountants is to collect, process, and summarize the data to be included in those financial reports.

If investors, creditors, and other external decision makers are to make sound economic decisions involving business enterprises, they need a wide array of financial information regarding those entities. To prove this point, consider the Strawberry House, a bed and breakfast inn located in Cripple Creek, Colorado. Cripple Creek was a prosperous

EXHIBIT 2.1 ▼
FASB's Conceptual Framework

- SFAC No. 1: Objectives of Financial Reporting by Business Enterprises
- SFAC No. 2: Qualitative Characteristics of Accounting Information
- SFAC No. 3: Elements of Financial Statements of Business Enterprises*
- SFAC No. 4: Objectives of Financial Reporting by Nonbusiness Organizations
- SFAC No. 5: Recognition and Measurement in Financial Statements of Business Enterprises
- SFAC No. 6: Elements of Financial Statements

*Superseded by *SFAC No. 6*

gold-mining town in the early 1900s, but now the principal industry in this small mountain village is tourism. The owners of the Strawberry House rent out its three bedrooms on a nightly basis and provide their guests with breakfast each morning. If the owners of this business decide to branch out and open bed and breakfast inns in other mountain resorts in Colorado, they may require funding (loans) from a bank. A banker approached by these individuals for a loan would insist on reviewing financial statements for the Strawberry House. The banker would use these financial statements to predict the net cash flows produced by the business after its expansion. Why? Because those cash flows would be the principal source of funds used to repay the loan and the interest on the loan. The financial reporting objective most pertinent to this context would be the second objective listed in Exhibit 2.2.

Now, let us turn the tables on the just described situation and consider the financial reporting objectives of a banking company. First Chicago Corporation has more than $50 billion in assets and owns and operates several banks, including the First National Bank of Chicago. Since the financial crisis of the 1980s in the banking and savings and loan industries, regulatory agencies have closely monitored the health of financial institutions. One item in a bank's financial statements monitored by regulatory authorities such as the Federal Reserve is the allowance for loan losses. This item represents a bank's best estimate of the dollar amount of its outstanding loans that will prove to

EXHIBIT 2.2 ▼
Financial Reporting Objectives of Business Enterprises

1. Financial reports should provide information that is useful in making investing, lending, and other economic decisions.
2. Financial reports should provide information allowing decision makers to predict the future cash flows of businesses and the future cash flows they will receive from those businesses.
3. Financial reports should provide information about the assets and liabilities of businesses and the transactions and other events that have resulted in changes in those assets and liabilities.

Source: Statement of Financial Accounting Concepts No. *1*, "Objectives of Financial Reporting by Business Enterprises" (Stamford, Conn.: FASB, 1980).

be uncollectible. A bank's financial health can be jeopardized if it begins experiencing problems collecting its outstanding loans. If these problems become severe, banking regulators may step in and force the bank to change its operating policies.

A check of recent financial statements issued by First Chicago Corporation reveals that the company's allowance for loan losses declined by nearly $100 million during the preceding twelve months. When banking regulators obtained these financial statements, you can be certain that they wanted to know exactly why First Chicago's allowance for loan losses had dropped sharply during the previous year. Here, the pertinent financial reporting objective is the third objective listed in Exhibit 2.2. First Chicago Corporation had a responsibility to provide banking regulators and other interested third parties with information explaining the large change in its allowance for loan losses. To the credit of First Chicago Corporation, the firm's financial statements included an extensive analysis of the large decrease in its allowance for loan losses.

▲ FINANCIAL STATEMENTS: NATURE, PURPOSE, AND DEFINITIONS OF KEY ELEMENTS

LEARNING OBJECTIVE 2 ▶
Describe the nature, purpose, and content of each of the four financial statements.

Accountants help satisfy the financial reporting objectives identified in the previous section by preparing periodic financial statements for business entities. These financial statements include a balance sheet, an income statement, a statement of stockholders' equity, and a statement of cash flows. In this section, we review the structure and content of each of these financial statements. Do not expect to become a financial statement guru from having studied this section. Here, the purpose is simply to introduce you to the four financial statements regularly prepared by businesses. Later chapters will provide you with an opportunity to obtain a more in-depth understanding of each major financial statement.

The Balance Sheet

balance sheet

Exhibit 2.3 presents a recent balance sheet for The Gap, an apparel retailer that operates more than 1,500 stores nationwide. Accountants sometimes refer to a **balance sheet** as a statement of financial condition or financial position. A more descriptive definition of a balance sheet is a financial statement that summarizes the assets, liabilities, and stockholders' or owners' equity of an entity at a specific point in time. When asked to define a balance sheet, accountants are prone to answer that it is a financial snapshot of a company at a specific point in time. For the balance sheet shown in Exhibit 2.3, the snapshot date was February 3, 1996.

The title "balance sheet" is appropriate because the sum of an entity's assets must equal the sum of its liabilities and stockholders' or owners' equity. Expressed in equation form for a corporation, this relationship appears as follows:

Assets = Liabilities + Stockholders' Equity

accounting equation

Accountants refer to this equation as the **accounting equation**, or the balance sheet equation. A generic version of this equation for all business entities is presented next.

Assets = Liabilities + Owners' Equity

EXHIBIT 2.3
The Gap, Inc., Balance Sheet as of February 3, 1996

THE GAP, INC.
BALANCE SHEET
FEBRUARY 3, 1996
(in thousands)

Assets		
Current assets:		
Cash and cash equivalents		$ 579,566
Short-term investments		89,506
Inventory		482,575
Prepaid expenses		128,398
Total current assets		$1,280,045
Property, plant & equipment	$1,562,582	
Less accumulated depreciation	604,830	
		957,752
Long-term investments		30,370
Intangible assets and other assets		74,901
Total assets		$2,343,068
Liabilities and Stockholders' Equity		
Current liabilities:		
Accounts payable		$ 262,505
Accrued liabilities		267,424
Notes payable		21,815
Total current liabilities		$ 551,744
Long-term liabilities		150,851
Total liabilities		$ 702,595
Stockholders' equity:		
Common stock		$ 15,799
Additional paid-in capital		335,193
Retained earnings		1,289,481
Total stockholders' equity		$1,640,473
Total liabilities and stockholders' equity		$2,343,068

Source: The Gap, Inc., Annual Report for the Year Ended February 3, 1996.

Notice the only difference in the two versions of the accounting equation is in the final term. Stockholders' equity represents the collective ownership interests in a corporation of its stockholders—which are a corporation's owners. Owners' equity is a general term that refers to the collective ownership interests of any business entity.

A balance sheet provides answers to many questions that investors, creditors, and other decision makers have regarding a business's financial status. Examples of these questions include: "How much cash does PepsiCo have on hand?" "Is that cash balance large enough to allow PepsiCo to pay off its debts that are coming due in the next few months?" "Is Kmart's inventory growing at a faster pace than Wal-Mart's?" "Does J.C. Penney have more long-term debt than Sears?" In later chapters, we consider a broad range of decision makers' information needs that a balance sheet satisfies. To acquaint you with the general structure and content of a balance sheet, let us "walk through" this financial statement and identify its key components.

assets

ASSETS *SFAC No. 6* defines **assets** as "probable future economic benefits obtained or controlled by a particular entity as a result of past transactions or events."[1] A nonaccountant might simplify this definition to "things that a company owns." The Gap prepares a classified balance sheet, like most companies. A classified balance sheet sorts assets, liabilities, and stockholders' equity into groups of similar items. Notice in Exhibit 2.3 that The Gap's assets are classified into four groups: current assets; property, plant & equipment; long-term investments; and intangible assets and other assets.

current assets

fiscal year

operating cycle

Current Assets Current assets typically are listed first in a balance sheet. Included in **current assets** are cash and other assets that will be converted into cash, sold, or consumed during the next fiscal year or the normal operating cycle of a business if its operating cycle is longer than a year. An entity's **fiscal year** is the twelve-month period covered by its annual income statement. Although not true of The Gap, the fiscal year of most companies coincides with the calendar year. A company's **operating cycle** is that

Like most merchandising companies, The Gap reports a large amount of inventory on its annual balance sheets. A recent balance sheet of the firm reported nearly $500 million of inventory.

1. *Statement of Financial Accounting Concepts No. 6*, "Elements of Financial Statements" (Stamford, Conn.: FASB, 1985), para. 25.

period of time elapsing from the use of cash in its normal operating, or profit-oriented, activities to the collection of cash from its customers. The operating cycle of a restaurant chain, such as Luby's Cafeterias, is usually just a few days. Luby's buys unprocessed raw materials—flour, fruit, vegetables, etc.—and converts those materials into ready-to-eat food items. It then sells these items to its customers for cash. The operating cycle of a manufacturing firm, such as the La-Z-Boy Chair Company, can be several months long, if not longer.

The most common current assets are cash, short-term investments, accounts receivable, inventory, and prepaid expenses. Current assets are typically listed in a balance sheet in order of "nearness to cash," which explains why cash is the first current asset reported in most balance sheets. Short-term investments generally include investments that a company expects to sell or otherwise convert into cash within the coming year. Common examples of such assets include certain investments in corporate stocks and bonds.

Companies that sell goods or provide services often extend credit to their customers, meaning that customers are not required to pay for the goods or services immediately. Amounts owed to a company by its customers are referred to as accounts receivable, or trade accounts receivable. Notice that The Gap's balance sheet in Exhibit 2.3 does not list any accounts receivable. Many retailers only allow customers to charge their purchases to national credit cards, such as VISA or MasterCard. These retailers typically collect such amounts on a daily basis, less a service fee, from the credit card companies.

Inventory consists of goods that an entity intends to sell directly to its customers or raw materials or in-process items that will be converted into saleable goods. Businesses often pay in advance relatively minor expense items such as rent, insurance, and advertising. These amounts are reported as "prepaid expenses" in the current assets section of a balance sheet.

Property, Plant & Equipment By definition, all assets other than current assets are long-term or noncurrent assets. Most companies have several categories of long-term assets, the largest typically being **property, plant & equipment**. This category of long-term assets includes buildings, machinery, furniture, and related assets used in the normal operating activities of a business. General Motors, the large automobile manufacturer, reported more than $73 billion of property, plant & equipment assets in a recent balance sheet.

property, plant & equipment

A Noncurrent Current Asset

FOR YOUR INFORMATION

Current assets are generally expected to be sold, consumed, or converted into cash within one year or less. However, if a company has an operating cycle longer than one year, current assets include those assets expected to be sold, consumed, or converted into cash within the next year or the company's operating cycle. Most companies have operating cycles shorter than twelve months. An example of a company with an operating cycle longer than one year is Philip Morris Companies Inc., a firm best known for its tobacco products. One of Philip Morris's current assets is its inventory of leaf tobacco. Leaf tobacco requires more than one year to age properly. Since this aging process is a component of the company's operating cycle, leaf tobacco is included as a current asset in Philip Morris's balance sheet, although it may be more than one year away from being converted into cash.

Those property, plant & equipment assets that have limited useful lives are referred to as depreciable assets. Accounting rules require that the cost of these assets be allocated or "written off" to expense over the time periods they benefit. The technical accounting term used to describe this cost allocation process is "depreciation." Chapter 8 discusses several approaches to computing depreciation. To briefly acquaint you with this subject, suppose that Westinghouse buys a piece of equipment on January 1, 1998, for use in a manufacturing process. The cost of the machinery is $120,000, and its expected useful life is four years, at the end of which it will have zero salvage, or scrap, value. If Westinghouse uses the straight-line depreciation method, it will depreciate the equipment $30,000 per year from 1998 through 2001 ($120,000/4 years).

"Accumulated depreciation" is the total amount of depreciation that has been recorded on a depreciable asset or group of depreciable assets since their acquisition. For balance sheet purposes, the accumulated depreciation for property, plant & equipment assets is subtracted from the collective dollar amount of these assets, as shown in Exhibit 2.3.

long-term investments

Long-Term Investments Investments in corporate stocks and bonds and other securities are considered short-term investments if they are expected to be converted into cash within the coming year. Similar investments that management intends to retain for more than one year are classified as **long-term investments**. Land and other noncurrent assets not used in the normal operating activities of a business are also classified as long-term investments for balance sheet purposes.

intangible assets

Intangible Assets **Intangible assets** are long-term assets that do not have a physical form or substance. An example of an intangible asset is a patent. A patent is an exclusive right granted by the United States Patent Office to manufacture a specific product or to use a specific process. Pfizer, Inc., a large pharmaceutical company, owns dozens of patents on pharmaceutical products. These patents prohibit other firms from producing or selling those products. Other examples of intangible assets include copyrights, trademarks, and goodwill. A catchall classification for miscellaneous long-term assets, other assets, is typically the last asset category appearing on a balance sheet. The total amount of these mystery assets is usually quite small compared to a business's total assets. Notice in The Gap's balance sheet shown in Exhibit 2.3 that other assets are combined with the company's intangible assets.

liabilities

LIABILITIES Liabilities generally are amounts owed by businesses to third parties. Following is the accounting profession's more technical, and long-winded, definition of **liabilities**: "probable future sacrifices of economic benefits arising from present obligations of a particular entity to transfer assets or provide services to other entities in the future as a result of past transactions or events."[2] The two major classifications of liabilities are current liabilities and noncurrent or long-term liabilities.

current liabilities

Current Liabilities **Current liabilities** are listed first in the liabilities section of a balance sheet. Included in this balance sheet classification are debts and other obligations that must be paid by a business during its next fiscal year or operating cycle, whichever is longer. Among the most common types of current liabilities are accounts payable, accrued liabilities, and notes payable.

---

2. *Statement of Financial Accounting Concepts No. 6*, para. 35.

© Liaison International/Wernher Krutein

The operating cycle of certain companies extends beyond one year. An example is lumber companies whose operating cycle includes the time to harvest, cure, and process timber.

Accounts payable represent amounts owed by a business to its suppliers. In a sense, accounts payable are the "flip side" of accounts receivable. For example, the amounts owed to Whirlpool Corporation by its customers would appear as accounts receivable in Whirlpool's balance sheet. Conversely, the amounts that Whirlpool owes to its suppliers would be reported in the company's balance sheet as accounts payable.

When a balance sheet is being prepared, a business's accountants must identify amounts the firm owes to third parties that previously have not been recorded as liabilities in its accounting records. These liabilities, referred to as accrued liabilities, typically relate to obligations incurred near the end of an accounting period. Quite often, accrued liabilities must be estimated, since their exact amount cannot be determined. For instance, at the end of an accounting period, a company will generally have to estimate the dollar amount of electricity it has consumed since the date of its last electric bill. This amount will then be recorded as a liability in its accounting records. Notice that The Gap's balance sheet in Exhibit 2.3 reported more than $267 million of accrued liabilities.

Companies frequently borrow money from their banks or other parties on a short-term basis and sign a promissory note, which is a legally binding commitment to repay borrowed funds. If due in one year or less, notes payable are listed as current liabilities on a company's balance sheet.

long-term liabilities

Long-Term Liabilities **Long-term liabilities** are the debts and obligations of a business other than those classified as current liabilities. Examples of long-term liabilities include long-term notes payable, mortgages payable, and long-term accrued liabilities. Quite often, a company reports the collective amount of several long-term liabilities on one balance sheet line item entitled "long-term debt" or simply "long-term liabilities."

STOCKHOLDERS' EQUITY As pointed out earlier, a balance sheet "balances" in the following sense: assets must equal the sum of liabilities and stockholders' or owners' equity. If you own a home, the difference between the value of your home and the unpaid balance of your mortgage is your ownership interest or equity in the home, often referred to as homeowner's equity by a bank. Applying this reasoning to a corporation, total assets less amounts owed to third parties (liabilities) equals **stockholders' equity**, or the stockholders' ownership interest in that corporation. Notice that The Gap's balance sheet in Exhibit 2.3 lists three components of stockholders' equity: common stock, additional paid-in capital, and retained earnings. Those are the three most common elements of stockholders' equity in a corporate balance sheet.

stockholders' equity

The composition of the assets, liabilities, and stockholders' equity of corporations varies widely from company to company. Exhibit 2.4 depicts the asset composition of four major corporations. Exhibit 2.5 reveals the composition of the liabilities and stockholders' equity of these same four corporations. Notice the sizable differences in the proportionate amounts of The Gap's liabilities and stockholders' equity versus those of Xerox. Xerox is a highly leveraged company; that is, it has borrowed heavily from third parties to obtain funds to finance its operations. The Gap, on the other hand, has relied principally on stockholders to finance its operations.

The Income Statement

Exhibit 2.6 presents a recent income statement for a small company, Lincoln Logs Ltd. Lincoln Logs markets prepackaged home building kits for do-it-yourselfers who want to construct their own homes. (No, the company does not market the toys that bear its name.) An **income statement** summarizes a business's "revenues" and "expenses" for a given accounting period. Just like a balance sheet, an income statement has a basic format. In this case, the format is revenues less expenses equals net income. Revenues result from the sale of merchandise, provision of services, and related

income statement

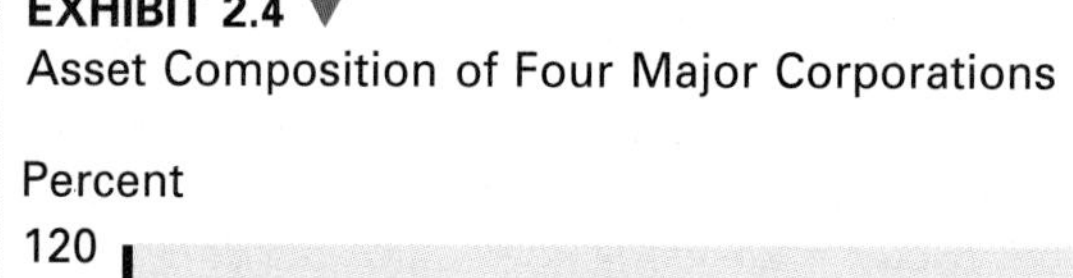

EXHIBIT 2.4 ▼
Asset Composition of Four Major Corporations

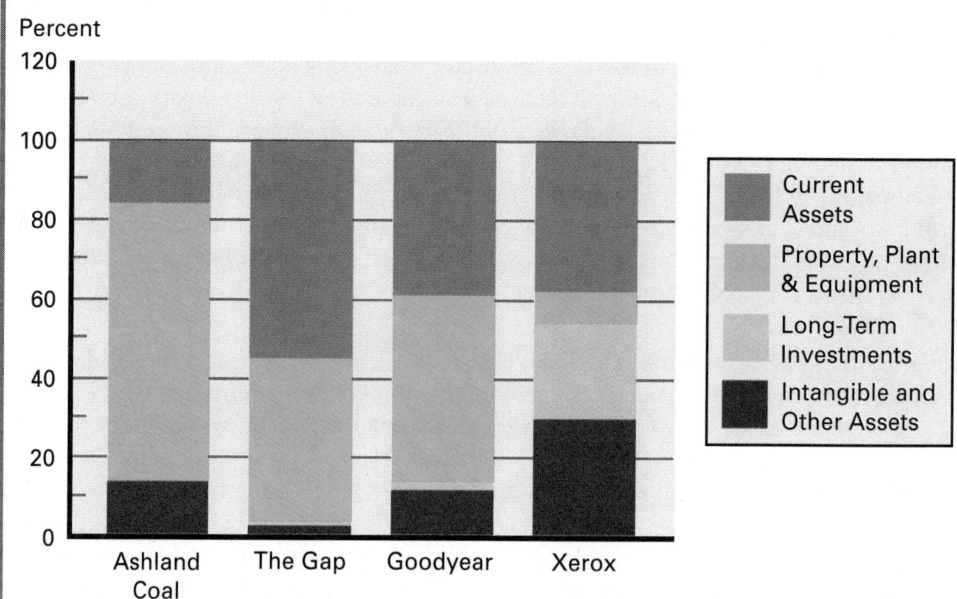

Source: Recent Annual Reports.

EXHIBIT 2.5 ▼
Composition of Liabilities and Stockholders' Equity of Four Major Corporations

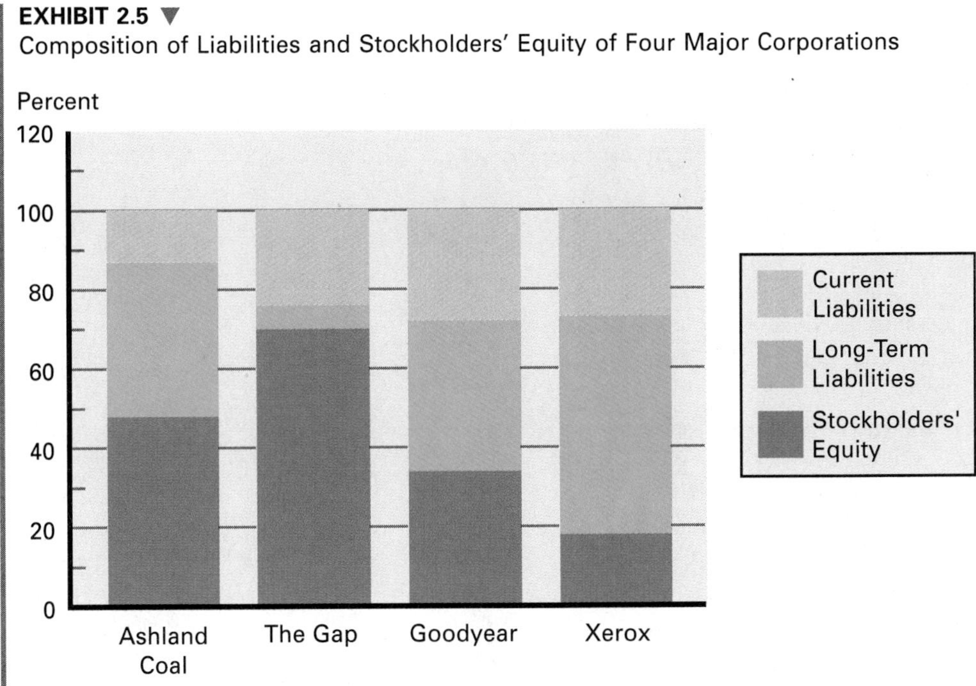

Source: Recent Annual Reports.

transactions. More formally, **revenues** are increases in assets and decreases in liabilities resulting from an entity's profit-oriented activities. **Expenses** are decreases in assets and increases in liabilities resulting from those same profit-oriented activities. Employee salaries are an example of an expense incurred by most businesses.

revenues

expenses

The Balance Sheet: A Malaysian Perspective

FOR YOUR INFORMATION

The general nature and purpose of accounting are much the same worldwide, although accounting methods and financial reporting practices vary considerably from country to country. Consider the financial statements of Sime Darby Berhad, a large Malaysian firm that owns and operates more than 300 businesses in 22 countries. Among the hundreds of products manufactured by Sime Darby are golf balls, batteries, handcrafts, and automobiles. A comparison of Sime Darby's financial statements to those of large U.S. firms reveals several distinctive differences. For example, Sime Darby uses an organizational scheme for its balance sheet that greatly differs from the scheme used by most large U.S. businesses. The first section of Sime Darby's balance sheet lists stockholders' equity instead of current assets. Next, the company's balance sheet reports long-term liabilities followed in order by current assets, current liabilities, and long-term assets. Not surprisingly, the amounts reported for each item in Sime Darby's balance sheet are denominated in Malaysian ringgits rather than U.S. dollars. To attract U.S. investors, many foreign firms issue financial statements denominated in both their home country's currency and U.S. dollars, an example being Honda Corporation, a Japanese firm.

EXHIBIT 2.6 ▼
Lincoln Logs Ltd., Income Statement

LINCOLN LOGS LTD. INCOME STATEMENT FOR THE YEAR ENDED JANUARY 31, 1996	
Net sales	$7,120,152
Cost of goods sold	4,821,560
Gross profit	$2,298,592
Operating expenses:	
Selling, general and administrative	2,171,317
Operating income	$ 127,275
Other revenues and expenses:	
Interest revenue	34,924
Interest expense	(195,383)
Miscellaneous revenue	78,862
Income before income taxes	$ 45,678
Income tax expense	1,600
Net income	$ 44,078
Earnings per share	$ .05

Source: Lincoln Logs Ltd., Annual Report for the Year Ended January 31, 1996.

Notice that not only is the basic format of an income statement different from that of a balance sheet, the two financial statements have different time frames as well. Recall that a balance sheet summarizes a business's assets, liabilities, and owners' equity at a specific point in time. An income statement, on the other hand, is prepared for a period of time, typically an entity's fiscal year. Lincoln Logs' fiscal year runs from February 1 of one year through January 31 of the following year.

You have probably heard someone in business, or another discipline, for that matter, refer to the "bottom line." In the business world, that phrase commonly refers to the net income figure reported on an income statement. Once we subtract a business's total expenses from its total revenues for a given period, the difference is the entity's profit or earnings or, best of all, **net income** for that period. ("Net loss" is the appropriate term for this difference if expenses exceed revenues.)

net income

Decision makers have certain questions in mind when they refer to a company's income statement, questions quite different from those answered by a firm's balance sheet. These questions typically concern that "bottom line" figure just mentioned: "Did IBM earn a profit during 1997?" "How does B.F. Goodrich's 'gross profit percentage' compare to that of Goodyear?" "What is Merrill Lynch's principal source of revenue" Now, let us briefly review the key items commonly appearing in an income statement.

gross profit

GROSS PROFIT Many companies, particularly those involved in merchandising and manufacturing, begin their income statements by computing gross profit. **Gross profit** is the difference between net sales—sales less any sales returns made by customers and certain other items—and the collective cost of the goods sold during a given period. Exhibit 2.6 shows that Lincoln Logs registered a gross profit of slightly less than $2.3 million for the year ended January 31, 1996. Gross profit is a very important and informative figure for financial statement users. Quite often, an early sign that a company's financial fortunes are on the decline is a decrease in its gross profit percentage, which is gross profit divided by net sales. In the early 1990s, intense price competition drove down the gross profit percentages of most companies in the personal computer industry. Apple Computer, in particular, was adversely affected by this cutthroat competition. When a company's gross profit percentage declines, it often has to compensate by slashing its operating expenses.

OPERATING EXPENSES Those expenses, other than cost of goods sold, that a company incurs in its principal business operations are known as **operating expenses.** Among the more common operating expenses are selling expenses, such as sales commissions and advertising costs, and administrative expenses, such as the salaries of top management. The difference between gross profit and a company's operating expenses is its **operating income,** or income from operations. Operating income is another important figure for financial statement users. The remaining revenues and expenses listed on an income statement are "nonoperating" items that do not result from an entity's principal business operations. Decision makers tend to pay less attention to nonoperating revenues and expenses, since a company's eventual success or failure hinges on the profitability of its principal line or lines of business.

operating expenses

operating income

OTHER REVENUES AND EXPENSES Most companies report miscellaneous revenues and expenses on their income statements. A heading frequently used for these items is "other revenues and expenses." The most common items included in this section of an income statement are interest revenue and interest expense.

EARNINGS PER SHARE Notice in Exhibit 2.6 that "income before income taxes" is determined by adding or subtracting the net amount of other revenues and expenses to, or from, operating income. After subtracting income tax expense from income before income taxes, we have finally arrived at net income. A corporation goes one step beyond net income to report an earnings per share figure for its common stock. The common stock of a corporation represents that firm's ownership interests. Since these ownership interests are sold in single units, or shares, corporations report earnings per share each period to assist stockholders in determining the profit that period attributable to their equity, or ownership interest, in the firm. Notice that Lincoln Logs reported earnings per share of $.05 for the year ended January 31, 1996. In Chapter 12, the computation of earnings per share is discussed and illustrated.

COMPREHENSIVE INCOME As this book was being written, the accounting profession was considering a proposal to require businesses to report both a net income and a "comprehensive income" in their financial statements. Many, if not most, businesses would continue to report only net income since they would not have any transactions or events requiring them to report comprehensive income. Under this proposal, a company that reports both net income and comprehensive income could prepare a single financial statement, "statement of income and comprehensive income," that discloses its net income and comprehensive income. Alternatively, such a company could choose to include both an income statement and a separate "statement of comprehensive income" in its annual financial report.

Statement of Stockholders' Equity

The third financial statement included in a corporation's annual financial report is a statement of stockholders' equity. (Statement of owners' equity is an alternate title used for this financial statement when prepared for unincorporated businesses.) Financial decision makers often disagree as to which of the four financial statements is the most important or informative. However, few decision makers would disagree with the assertion that the statement of stockholders' equity is the least important financial statement. Essentially, this statement is a supporting schedule to the balance sheet. A **statement of stockholders' equity** reconciles the dollar amounts of a corporation's stockholders' equity components at the beginning and end of an accounting period, typically the entity's fiscal year. The obvious question this statement addresses is "What events or transactions accounted for the changes in a company's stockholders' equity over the previous year?" Exhibit 2.7 presents a recent statement of stockholders' equity for NeoStar Retail Group, a company that sells computer software products.

statement of stockholders' equity

Statement of Cash Flows

The fourth and final financial statement is the statement of cash flows. Exhibit 2.8 presents a recent statement of cash flows for MacFrugal's Bargains and Close-Outs, a deep-discount retailer. As its title implies, a **statement of cash flows** reveals how a business generated and used cash during a given accounting period. Similar to an income statement and statement of stockholders' equity, the accounting period covered by a statement of cash flows is commonly a firm's fiscal year. The first three sections of a statement of cash flows summarize the cash inflows and outflows from three major types of activities engaged in by business entities: operating activities, investing activities, and financing activities. The final section of a statement of cash flows reconciles an entity's cash balance at the beginning of a period to its cash balance at the end of that period.

statement of cash flows

EXHIBIT 2.7 ▼
NeoStar Retail Group, Statement of Stockholders' Equity

NEOSTAR RETAIL GROUP
STATEMENT OF STOCKHOLDERS' EQUITY
FOR THE YEAR ENDED FEBRUARY 3, 1996
(in thousands)

	Common Stock	Additional Paid-In Capital	Retained Earnings
Balances, January 28, 1995	$147	$68,367	$13,153
Exercise of employee stock options	2	1,506	—
Income tax benefit from exercise of employee stock options	—	619	—
Net income	—	—	120
Balances, February 3, 1996	$149	$70,492	$13,273

Source: NeoStar Retail Group, Annual Report for the Year Ended February 3, 1996.

EXHIBIT 2.8
MacFrugal's Bargains and Close-Outs, Inc., Statement of Cash Flows

MACFRUGAL'S BARGAINS AND CLOSE-OUTS, INC.
STATEMENT OF CASH FLOWS
FOR THE YEAR ENDED JANUARY 28, 1996

Cash flows from operating activities:	
Cash received from customers	$704,934
Cash paid to suppliers and employees	(653,184)
Income taxes paid	(23,318)
Interest paid	(12,369)
Interest received	149
Net cash provided by operating activities	$ 16,212
Cash flows from investing activities:	
Capital expenditures	(26,117)
Proceeds from sale of property, plant & equipment	207
Net cash used in investing activities	$ (25,910)
Cash flows from financing activities:	
Net repayments under short-term borrowing arrangements	(80,500)
Repurchase of treasury stock	(1,573)
Net long-term borrowings	90,737
Proceeds from exercise of stock options	432
Other	1,213
Net cash provided by financing activities	$ 10,309
Net increase in cash and cash equivalents	611
Cash and cash equivalents, beginning of year	6,674
Cash and cash equivalents, end of year	$ 7,285

Source: MacFrugal's Bargains and Close-Outs, Inc., Annual Report for the Year Ended January 28, 1996.

When decision makers refer to a company's statement of cash flows, the question foremost in their minds is "How does the company's cash flows from its operating, or profit-oriented, activities compare to its net income?" Surprising to many nonaccountants is that the net cash flow generated each period by a business's operating activities is not closely correlated, necessarily, with its net income. Consider Exhibit 2.9, which compares Woolworth Corporation's net income and net cash flow from operating activities over a recent three-year period. Notice that during this period there were significant differences between this company's annual net income and net cash flow from operating activities.

Just because a company is earning large profits each year does not mean that the firm is generating sufficient cash flows to sustain its operations. A very profitable company may experience severe cash-flow problems, including falling behind on its debt payments

EXHIBIT 2.9 ▼
Woolworth Corporation: Net Income vs. Net Cash Flow from Operating Activities

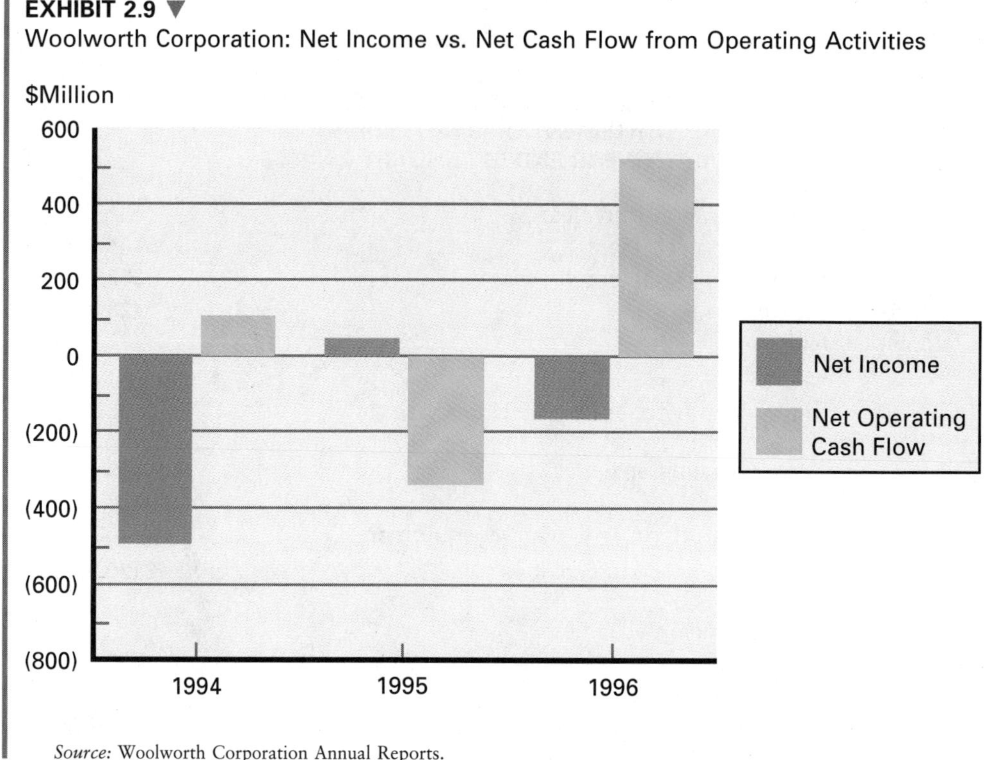

Source: Woolworth Corporation Annual Reports.

and being unable to replace inventory as it is sold. Several factors could account for a profitable company failing to generate sufficient cash flows from its principal profit-oriented activities. These factors include slow-paying customers and increasing prices for raw materials and other goods and services required in the firm's day-to-day operations.

So, there you have it. A brief—okay, not so brief—overview of the four financial statements regularly prepared by corporations and other businesses. Students new to accounting often fail to recognize that the four financial statements are closely linked despite their differing structures, contents, and objectives. For example, consider the close relationship between the balance sheet and income statement. Revenues and expenses are reported on a business's income statement, while assets and liabilities are reported on its balance sheet. However, most changes in a business's assets and liabilities during a given period are a direct result of the entity's revenues and expenses that period. In a later chapter, you will learn that the net income figure reported in a company's income statement directly affects stockholders' equity reported in the firm's balance sheet. As noted earlier, the statement of stockholders' equity is actually just a supporting schedule to the balance sheet. Finally, consider the statement of cash flows. This financial statement accounts for the change in the amount of cash reported in a company's balance sheet at the beginning and end of a given period.

Financial Statement Footnotes

Besides the four financial statements, the annual financial report (often shortened to "annual report") prepared by most businesses contains other important information as well. One particularly informative section of an annual report is the **financial statement footnotes**. These footnotes assist decision makers in interpreting and drawing the proper conclusions from a business's financial statements. Most important, the footnotes to a company's financial statements identify the specific accounting methods used by the company. If you refer to Outback Steakhouse's annual report in an appendix of this text, you will find that the company's first financial statement footnote is entitled "Summary of Significant Accounting Policies." Other information found in financial statement footnotes includes assumptions that underlie key financial statement amounts, financial data regarding a company's major business segments, and descriptions of any lawsuits pending against a company.

financial statement footnotes

KEY ATTRIBUTES OF ACCOUNTING INFORMATION

LEARNING OBJECTIVE 3
Identify and define the key attributes or characteristics that accounting information should possess.

You have now been introduced to each of the major financial statements. However, your introduction to these financial statements would be incomplete if we did not consider certain key attributes or traits that the data in these financial statements should contain. Because of the quantitative nature of accounting, decision makers often overlook important qualitative features of accounting information. The second of the FASB's six *Statements of Financial Accounting Concepts,* "Qualitative Characteristics of Accounting Information," defines and describes the qualitative attributes that accounting information should possess. If the accounting data included in financial statements do not exhibit these attributes, the information needs of decision makers are unlikely to be satisfied. That is, those statements are unlikely to be useful to decision makers. In fact, decision usefulness is the most important qualitative characteristic that accounting information should possess. To qualify as useful to decision makers, accounting information should be understandable, relevant, and reliable, as shown in Exhibit 2.10.

EXHIBIT 2.10 ▼
Key Attributes of Accounting Information

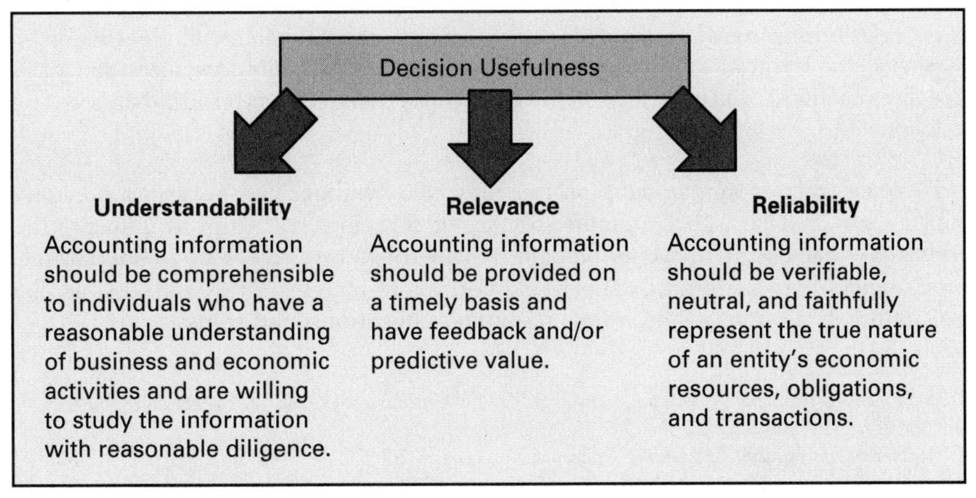

Understandability

For many years, the accounting profession debated the question of to whom accounting information should be understandable, or comprehensible. Many parties within the profession maintained that financial statements should be understandable by even naive, or unsophisticated, financial statement users. Other parties argued that financial statements should be oriented principally toward decision makers who have an in-depth understanding of financial reporting and accounting issues. *Statement of Financial Accounting Concepts No. 1* settled this debate. That pronouncement states that financial reports should be comprehensible to individuals who have a "reasonable understanding of business and economic activities" and are willing to "study the information with reasonable diligence."[3]

Relevance

For accounting information to be useful, it must possess a high degree of relevance. To qualify as relevant, accounting data must be timely and have feedback value and/or predictive value. By definition, if information is provided too late to influence financial statement users' decisions, then it is not relevant to those decisions. Feedback value is an important trait of accounting information because it enables decision makers to confirm or correct earlier expectations regarding, for instance, a business's operating results. If accounting data have feedback value, decision makers should become more proficient, over time, in using financial information to make economic decisions. Finally, predictive value is also an important trait of accounting information. For example, as suggested earlier, a banker considering a loan application from a company should be able to use the firm's financial statements to predict whether it can repay the loan if granted.

Reliability

Accounting information must also be reliable to be useful to decision makers. Generally, accounting information possesses reliability if it is characterized by the following traits: verifiability, neutrality, and representational faithfulness. Accounting data do not have to be subject to precise quantification to qualify as verifiable. In fact, most financial data are not subject to precise quantification.

> . . . despite the aura of precision that may seem to surround financial reporting in general and financial statements in particular, with few exceptions the measures are approximations, which may be based on rules and convention, rather than exact amounts.[4]

To be neutral, accounting data must be presented "without bias towards a predetermined result."[5] That is, accountants should not consciously attempt to influence the decisions of the users of accounting data. Finally, the term "representational faithfulness" implies that accounting data should portray, to the greatest extent possible, the true nature of a business's economic resources, obligations, and transactions.

---

3. *Statement of Financial Accounting Concepts No. 1,* "Objectives of Financial Reporting by Business Enterprises" (Stamford, Conn: FASB, 1978), para. 34.

4. *Statement of Financial Accounting Concepts No. 1,* para. 20.

5. *Statement of Financial Accounting Concepts No. 2,* "Qualitative Characteristics of Accounting Information" (Stamford, Conn.: FASB, 1980), para. 99.

Disappointing Financial Results? Blame the Weather

Certain corporate executives are inclined to 'pass the buck' when it comes to pinpointing responsibility for their firm's lackluster financial results. Claire Ansberry, a staff reporter for *The Wall Street Journal,* discovered several instances in recent annual reports in which corporate executives blamed the weather for their company's unimpressive bottom line. For example, a company in the recyclables industry complained that heavy snowfall during the winter of 1996 significantly reduced the volume of its business because recyclables are difficult to recover when they are buried under several feet of snow. Likewise, a home-building company's annual report noted that poor weather had stymied the pouring of foundations . . . and the stream of revenues pouring into the company. Finally, the vice president of investor relations for a large restaurant chain suggested that the snowy winter of 1996 had been particularly unkind to his line of business. "We don't mind if it [a snowstorm] falls on Monday or Tuesday, but we hate it if it falls on Saturday or Sunday. There seemed to be some seven-day cycle this year, and weekend timing of winter storms is detrimental to the restaurant business."

Source: C. Ansberry, "A Chill Wind Blows Through the Pages of Earning Reports," *The Wall Street Journal,* April 22, 1996, pp. A1 & A10.

Attributes of Accounting Information: A Few Other Issues

So, accounting information must first and foremost be useful to decision makers. To be useful, accounting information must be understandable, relevant, and reliable. Enough said? Not quite. There are a few other issues financial decision makers must grasp to fully appreciate the key qualitative attributes of accounting information. In certain situations, it is not necessary for accounting data to satisfy the understandability, relevance, and reliability criteria. For example, accountants do not have to ensure that accounting data are perfectly reliable if the imprecision in that data would not be sufficiently large to "matter" to decision makers. **Materiality** is the term that accountants use when referring to the relative importance of specific items of accounting information. An item is deemed material if it is large enough or significant enough to influence the decision of an investor, lender, or other financial statement user. The reverse is true for immaterial items.

materiality

Both preparers and users of accounting information should also recognize that the usefulness of accounting data is enhanced by comparability. **Comparability** refers to the degree to which a business entity's accounting information can be easily compared with similar information reported by the firm in prior accounting periods and with similar information reported by other business entities. One key threat to the comparability of accounting information is an entity's failure to use the same accounting rules from period to period. The financial statement data of a company will not be comparable from one period to the next if the firm does not consistently apply the

comparability

same set of accounting rules. Fortunately for decision makers, when a company changes an accounting principle, the effect of that change must be disclosed in its financial statements.

FUNDAMENTAL ACCOUNTING CONCEPTS

LEARNING OBJECTIVE 4 ▶

Identify and define the fundamental concepts that underlie accounting and financial reporting rules and practices.

Earlier sections of this chapter have acquainted you with financial reporting objectives, the nature and content of financial statements, and the key qualitative attributes that financial statement data should possess. Now, you are ready to tackle the basic conceptual issues that underlie accounting and financial reporting practices. The need for accountants to have a thorough understanding of these issues is underscored by the rapidly changing nature of the business world. Today's volatile business environment continually spawns new transactions and new variations of routine or familiar transactions. To record new or unusual transactions properly, accountants must have an in-depth knowledge of the fundamental conceptual principles of accounting.

Accounting concepts are not just for accountants. Financial decision makers can benefit greatly if they understand the basic concepts that dictate how accounting information is recorded and reported. Such an understanding allows decision makers to better grasp both the uses and limitations of accounting data. Exhibit 2.11 lists the key concepts that underlie the accounting and financial reporting rules, procedures, and practices discussed in the remainder of this textbook.

Entity Concept

entity concept

Business enterprises operate in several different legal forms, including sole proprietorships, partnerships, and corporations, as discussed in Chapter 1. Regardless of its legal form, for accounting purposes, a business enterprise is treated as a distinct and independent entity, meaning that its transactions should be accounted for separately from the personal transactions of its owners. This **entity concept** is particularly important for sole proprietorships. The owners of one-man and one-woman firms may see no need to separate the assets and liabilities of their businesses from their personal assets and liabilities. However, a sole proprietor will find it difficult to prepare financial statements that accurately depict the financial status of his or her company if personal and business assets and liabilities are commingled.

EXHIBIT 2.11 ▼

Fundamental Accounting Concepts

- Entity Concept
- Accounting Period Concept
- Going Concern Assumption
- Unit-of-Measurement Concept
- Historical Cost Principle
- Revenue and Expense Recognition Rules
- Full Disclosure Principle

Accounting Period Concept

Suppose that the Bobbsey twins operate a lemonade stand during the summer. At the end of August, the twins can easily determine how profitable their three-month business venture was by simply tallying up its receipts and expenditures. Unfortunately, determining the profitability of an ongoing business enterprise is not so easy. For instance, consider a large industrial concern such as Northrup Grumman Corporation, which is based in Los Angeles. Northrup signs multi-year contracts to build aircraft for several companies and the federal government. If we wanted to precisely determine the actual profitability of Northrup, we would have to wait until the company ceases operations.

Decision makers demand financial information on a regular basis regarding business entities, most of which continue operating indefinitely. The **accounting period concept** suggests that accountants can prepare meaningful financial reports for ongoing business enterprises by dividing their lives into reporting intervals of equal length. As a result, accountants "chop up" the life of a business entity into accounting periods. The accounting function of most businesses revolves around a monthly accounting period, or accounting cycle. However, for financial reporting purposes, businesses typically release financial statements to external decision makers on an annual basis at the end of each fiscal year. Publicly owned companies regulated by the Securities and Exchange Commission (SEC) must issue financial statements on a quarterly and annual basis.

accounting period concept

The need to prepare periodic financial statements for ongoing business enterprises poses several challenging problems for accountants. Assume that in the year 2000, Northrup Grumman signs a contract to deliver 25 aircraft to United Parcel Service (UPS) in 2005. During 2000 and 2001, Northrup will design the aircraft and develop the engineering specifications. In 2002, the company will begin constructing the aircraft. The final planes will be delivered to UPS in December 2005. Northrup expects to earn a large profit on this transaction, but the question is, when should Northrup report this profit in its periodic income statements? Should the profit be recorded only after all the aircraft have been delivered to UPS? Should the profit be recognized proportionately over the six years of the contract? In fact, practically all businesses face a similar problem in accounting for their operations. Somehow, accountants must allocate the economic impact of multi-period transactions to the accounting periods they affect. Much of the remainder of this textbook addresses the methods that accountants use to accomplish this objective.

Going Concern Assumption

Accountants assume that businesses are "going concerns" and thus will continue operating indefinitely unless there is evidence to the contrary. The **going concern assumption** has significant implications for the accounting and financial reporting decisions rendered for business enterprises. Consider a company that is thriving versus one that has such severe financial problems, slow-paying customers, declining sales, and so on, that there is substantial doubt it will continue to be a going concern. Now, assume that each of these companies applies for a loan from a local bank. The loan officer will need much more information from the company experiencing financial problems than from the financially healthy company. For instance, the loan officer will likely want to know what the troubled company's assets would be worth if they had to be sold hurriedly to pay off the firm's liabilities due to a bankruptcy filing. This information would not be necessary for the profitable company.

going concern assumption

When a company's status as a going concern is seriously in doubt, this fact should be disclosed in the firm's financial statements. Other supplemental disclosures may also be necessary for a financially troubled company. For example, as just suggested, the value of such a company's assets on an involuntary liquidation (bankruptcy) basis may need to be disclosed in the firm's financial statement footnotes.

Unit-of-Measurement Concept

unit-of-measurement concept

Long ago, in an empire far away, King Hammurabi proclaimed that silver would be the official measure of wealth and exchange in Babylon. A common denominator of economic value greatly facilitated commerce in the ancient world. Transacting business was made even easier by the first minting of coins, reportedly in the Kingdom of Lydia around 700 B.C. Today, thousands of years later, practically all business transactions in the United States are denominated in dollars. The **unit-of-measurement concept** mandates that businesses use a common unit of measurement in accounting for their transactions. The use of a common unit of measurement for accounting purposes allows financial data to be quantified, summarized, and reported in a uniform, timely, and consistent manner.

Historical Cost Principle

historical cost principle

In the United States, the **historical cost principle** dictates that the primary valuation basis for most assets is their original cost to a company. For instance, assume that a company acquires a tract of land at a cost of $500,000. Three years later, nearby urban development has caused the appraised value of the land to skyrocket to $2 million. At what dollar amount would the land most likely be reported in the company's balance sheet? No, not $2 million, but instead the original, or "historical," cost of $500,000.

The historical cost of an asset is often less informative or useful to third-party decision makers than the asset's current value. If you are considering buying a company, wouldn't you be more interested in the current value of that company's assets rather than their historical cost? Almost certainly. The principal justification for using historical costs instead of current values as the valuation basis for assets is the objectivity of historical costs. Historical costs are much more verifiable than current values. To determine the historical cost of the piece of land referred to in the previous paragraph, you would simply refer to the purchase contract. On the other hand, determining the current value of that property would be a much more subjective exercise. Generally, the current value of a piece of undeveloped land is established by obtaining one or more real estate appraisals. However, real estate appraising is not an exact science. Consequently, appraised values are subject to errors, sometimes very large errors.

conservatism principle

There are several exceptions to the general rule that assets are valued for accounting purposes at their historical cost. For example, many investments in corporate stocks and bonds are reported at their current value, rather than their historical cost, in financial statements. Likewise, when there is strong evidence that the value of an asset has permanently declined below its historical cost, that asset should be written down to its current value. This latter rule invokes the **conservatism principle** of accounting. More generally, when there are uncertainties regarding the valuation of assets or the magnitude of revenues, accountants are inclined to understate, rather than overstate, the recorded amounts for these items. Conversely, for liabilities and expenses the conservatism principle dictates that accountants resolve uncertainty in favor of higher recorded amounts for these items.

Revenue and Expense Recognition Rules

One of the most important accounting issues that businesses face is when to record revenues and expenses in their accounting records. Companies would generally prefer to record revenues as quickly as possible and to postpone the recording of expenses as long as possible to enhance (inflate?) their reported profits.[6] Allowing companies to record revenues and expenses whenever they wish is not in the best interests of financial statement users. Consequently, the accounting profession has established general rules to dictate the timing of revenue and expense recognition. These rules limit the ability of business executives to misrepresent their firms' operating results by selectively choosing the accounting periods in which to record revenues and expenses.

REVENUE RECOGNITION *SFAC No. 5* established a two-part **revenue recognition rule** for accountants to follow in deciding when to record revenues. Before revenue is recognized (recorded) in a business's accounting records, the revenue should be both realized and earned.

revenue recognition rule

> Revenues and gains are *realized* when products (goods or services), merchandise, or other assets are exchanged for cash or claims to cash. . . . revenues are considered to have been *earned* when the entity has substantially accomplished what it must do to be entitled to the benefits represented by the revenues.[7]

For merchandising companies, both requirements of the revenue recognition rule are usually satisfied at the point of sale.

EXPENSE RECOGNITION The **expense recognition rule** requires expenditures to be recognized as expenses in the accounting period they provide an economic benefit to a business. Typically, this rule means that an expenditure should be recorded as an expense in the accounting period when the related revenue is recorded. In other words, expenses should be "matched" with their corresponding revenues. This concept of matching revenues and expenses in the same accounting period is known as the **matching principle**. Consider sales commissions. Commissions paid to a company's sales staff should be recorded as expenses in the same accounting period that the related sales were recorded as revenues. When an expenditure, such as the purchase of production equipment, provides an economic benefit to several accounting periods, the dollar amount of the expenditure should be "capitalized." (Accountants use the term "capitalize" to refer to the process of recording the cost of an asset.) Then, the cost of the asset should be gradually written off to expense, that is, depreciated over its useful life.

expense recognition rule

matching principle

The expense recognition rule and related matching principle are often difficult to apply when there is no clear cause-and-effect relationship between an expenditure and the subsequent revenue that it generates. Consider the case of pharmaceutical companies, such as Abbott Laboratories and Upjohn, which engage in long-term, multimillion dollar research programs to develop new pharmaceutical products. Matching the cost of such programs with the subsequent revenues they generate is very difficult, since these companies seldom know which research efforts are likely to result in viable

6. For taxation purposes, businesses prefer just the opposite. By delaying the recording of revenues and accelerating the recording of expenses, businesses minimize the amount of income taxes payable to state and federal governments.

7. *Statement of Financial Accounting Concepts No. 5,* "Recognition and Measurement in Financial Statements of Business Enterprises," (Stamford, Conn.: FASB, 1984), para. 83.

products. When there is no clear cause-and-effect relationship between an expenditure and a business's subsequent revenues, the conservatism principle mandates that the expenditure be immediately recognized as an expense.

accrual basis of accounting

cash basis of accounting

ACCRUAL BASIS VS. CASH BASIS ACCOUNTING Companies that employ the revenue and expense recognition rules just discussed are said to use the accrual basis of accounting. Under the **accrual basis of accounting,** the economic impact of a transaction is recognized (recorded) whether or not the transaction involves cash. Many business entities, very small businesses for the most part, use the **cash basis of accounting** instead of the accrual basis. These businesses record revenues when they receive cash payments from their customers and record expenses when they disburse cash to their suppliers, employees, and other parties. When decision makers use cash-basis financial statements, they must be aware that the given business did not employ the appropriate revenue and expense recognition rules. As a result, the business's reported net income for a given period may not be a reliable indicator of its true profitability for that period.

Full Disclosure Principle

full disclosure principle

The **full disclosure principle** requires that all information needed to obtain a thorough understanding of a company's financial affairs be included in its financial statements or accompanying narrative disclosures. Certain information that external decision makers would find useful, if not essential, for their decision-making processes does not "fit" into any of the four financial statements discussed earlier. Examples of such information include the effect that inflation may have on a company's future operations, information regarding employee profit-sharing and pension plans, and the contractual details of any major transactions with related parties. Typically, such information is disclosed in the footnotes to a company's financial statements.

Consider one item of information often included in financial statement footnotes. Investors and lenders are interested in whether a company has engaged in major transactions with related parties, such as large stockholders of the firm. Why? Because a related party transaction may be structured to economically benefit one party to the transaction at the expense of the other. Disclosure of the key contractual details of related party transactions allows decision makers to assess the reliability of a given firm's reported financial results. A recent annual report issued by NeoStar Retail Group revealed that Barnes & Noble, the company that operates a chain of retail bookstores, was a major NeoStar stockholder. NeoStar's annual report went on to discuss several large transactions between the two companies and the key terms of those transactions.

▲ SUMMARY

During the mid-1970s, the FASB began developing a conceptual framework to guide the development of future accounting standards. This framework was completed in 1985 and consists of six *Statements of Financial Accounting Concepts* (SFACs). *SFAC No. 1* defines the three financial reporting objectives for business enterprises, each of which concerns the need to assist third parties in making rational and informed economic decisions. Business enterprises satisfy these reporting objectives by preparing four financial statements for distribution to interested third parties.

A balance sheet summarizes a business's assets, liabilities, and owners' equity at a specific point in time. An income statement reports on a business's profitability for a stated period of time, usually the entity's fiscal year. Net income, the difference between a business's revenues and expenses, is the key figure reported in an income statement. Similar to an income statement, a statement of stockholders' equity and a statement of cash flows present data for a specific period. Again, this period is most commonly an entity's fiscal year. A statement of stockholders' equity reconciles the balances of the individual components of a corporation's stockholders' equity at the beginning and end of an accounting period. A statement of cash flows reveals how a business generated cash and used cash during a given period.

The key attribute that the accounting information included in financial statements should possess is decision usefulness. For accounting information to be useful, it should be understandable, relevant, and reliable. The rapidly changing business environment continually yields new transactions and new variations of routine transactions. To account properly for new or unusual business transactions, accountants must have a thorough understanding of the conceptual principles that underlie accounting practices. Among these principles are the entity concept, the going concern assumption, the historical cost principle, and the full disclosure principle.

GLOSSARY

Accounting equation (p. 36) The mathematical expression indicating that the sum of an entity's assets must equal the collective sum of its liabilities and owners' equity.

Accounting period concept (p. 53) An accounting principle that suggests that accountants can prepare meaningful financial reports for ongoing business enterprises by dividing the lives of these entities into regular reporting intervals of equal length.

Accrual basis of accounting (p. 56) A method of accounting under which the economic impact of a transaction is recognized (recorded) whether or not the transaction involves cash.

Assets (p. 38) Probable future economic benefits obtained or controlled by a particular entity as a result of past transactions or events.

Balance sheet (p. 36) A financial statement that summarizes the assets, liabilities, and owners' equity of an entity at a specific point in time.

Cash basis of accounting (p. 56) A method of accounting under which revenues are recorded when cash is received and expenses are recorded when cash is disbursed.

Comparability (p. 51) The degree to which an entity's accounting information can be easily compared with similar information reported for the entity in prior accounting periods and with similar information reported by other entities.

Conservatism principle (p. 54) An accounting principle that dictates that uncertainty regarding the valuation of an asset or magnitude of a revenue should generally be resolved in favor of understating the asset or revenue; applies as well to liabilities and expenses, except that uncertainty should be resolved in favor of overstating these items.

Current assets (p. 38) Cash and other assets that will be converted into cash, sold, or consumed during the next fiscal year or the normal operating cycle of a business, whichever is longer.

Current liabilities (p. 40) Debts or other obligations of a business that must be paid during its next fiscal year or operating cycle, whichever is longer.

Entity concept (p. 52) An accounting principle dictating that a business enterprise be treated as a distinct entity independent of its owners.

Expense recognition rule (p. 55) An accounting rule that requires expenses to be recognized (recorded) in the accounting period in which they provide an economic benefit to an entity.

Expenses (p. 43) Decreases in assets and increases in liabilities resulting from an entity's profit-oriented activities.

Financial statement footnotes (p. 49) A section of an annual report intended to assist decision makers in interpreting and drawing the proper conclusions from an entity's financial statements.
Fiscal year (p. 38) The twelve-month period covered by an entity's annual income statement.
Full disclosure principle (p. 56) An accounting principle dictating that all information needed to obtain a thorough understanding of an entity's financial affairs be included in its financial statements or accompanying narrative disclosures.
Going concern assumption (p. 53) An accounting principle that dictates that entities should be treated as if they will continue to operate indefinitely, unless there is evidence to the contrary.
Gross profit (p. 44) The difference between an entity's net sales and cost of goods sold during an accounting period.
Historical cost principle (p. 54) An accounting principle dictating that the primary valuation basis for most assets is their historical or original cost.
Income statement (p. 42) A financial statement that summarizes a business's revenues and expenses for a given accounting period.
Intangible assets (p. 40) Long-term assets that do not have a physical form or substance.
Liabilities (p. 40) Probable future sacrifices of economic benefits; generally, amounts owed by an entity to third parties including such items as accounts payable, accrued liabilities, and notes payable.
Long-term investments (p. 40) Ownership interests in corporate stocks and bonds and other securities that an entity intends to retain for more than one year; also includes land and other long-term assets not used in an entity's normal operating activities.
Long-term liabilities (p. 41) The debts and obligations of an entity other than those classified as current liabilities.
Matching principle (p. 55) An accounting principle requiring that expenses be recorded in the same accounting period as the related revenues.
Materiality (p. 51) Refers to the relative importance of specific items of accounting information; an item is material if it is large enough or significant enough to influence the decision of a financial statement user.
Net income (p. 44) The difference between an entity's revenues and expenses during an accounting period.
Operating cycle (p. 38) The period of time elapsing from the use of cash in the normal operating activities of an entity to the collection of cash from the entity's customers.
Operating expenses (p. 45) Those expenses, other than cost of goods sold, that an entity incurs in its principal business operations.
Operating income (p. 45) An entity's gross profit less its operating expenses; represents the income generated by an entity's principal line or lines of business.
Property, plant & equipment (p. 39) Long-term assets such as buildings and machinery used in a business's operating activities.
Revenue recognition rule (p. 55) An accounting rule that requires revenues to be both realized and earned before they are recognized (recorded).
Revenues (p. 43) Increases in assets and decreases in liabilities resulting from an entity's profit-oriented activities.
Statement of cash flows (p. 46) A financial statement that reveals how an entity generated and expended cash during an accounting period.
Statement of stockholders' equity (p. 46) A financial statement that reconciles the dollar amounts of a corporation's stockholders' equity components at the beginning and end of an accounting period.
Statements of Financial Accounting Concepts (p. 34) Six technical pronouncements issued by the FASB from 1978 through 1985 to serve as the conceptual framework for the development of future accounting standards.
Stockholders' equity (p. 42) The total assets of a corporation less amounts owed to third parties; represents stockholders' collective ownership interest in a corporation.
Unit-of-measurement concept (p. 54) The accounting principle dictating that a common unit of measurement be used to record and report transactions and other financial statement items.

DECISION CASE

For several decades, Wilson Foods Corporation, based in Oklahoma City, was among the largest producers of processed pork products in the nation. One of the company's products was the Thomas E. Wilson Masterpiece Ham, which was named after the company's founder. Wilson ran a marketing promotion for this product each December for several years. Customers who purchased one of these hams could send a coupon and proof of purchase to Wilson and receive a rebate of a few dollars. The total rebates paid by Wilson each year amounted to several million dollars.

Wilson's fiscal year ended on December 31, the same date that the Masterpiece Ham promotional campaign ended. However, most of the coupons that were redeemed by customers were not received until January. Near the end of each year, Wilson retained the services of the A. C. Nielsen Company to estimate the number of Masterpiece Ham coupons that would be redeemed after December 31. Wilson's accounting staff multiplied this estimate by the rebate amount. The resulting dollar figure was then recorded as a marketing expense for the fiscal year ending December 31.

Required: Assume that you are the controller of a company that initiated a promotional campaign identical in all key respects to the one just described. On December 31, the date the month-long promotion ends, you estimate that $1.5 million of coupons will be redeemed after the end of the year. You then notify the sales manager of the product for which this promotional campaign was run that an additional $1.5 million of marketing expense must be recorded for that product as of December 31. The sales manager immediately becomes upset. "That's ridiculous. We haven't even paid those coupons yet. They won't be paid until the next fiscal year. In fact, most customers haven't even mailed in the coupons. How can you justify making my division absorb a phantom expense like that? If you force us to take that hit, my year-end bonus and the bonus of everyone in my division will be slashed by 30 percent!" A few minutes later, you receive a phone call from a senior vice-president in the marketing department. This individual also protests your decision. She insists that you write a memo justifying that decision.

Write the requested memo to the senior vice-president. In your memo, refer to one or more of the accounting concepts discussed in this chapter.

QUESTIONS

1. Serving whose information needs is the principal focus of financial accounting?
2. What is the common theme of the three financial reporting objectives of business entities?
3. List the four major financial statements.
4. What does a balance sheet contain? What is an alternative title for a balance sheet?
5. Write the accounting equation and explain its components.
6. What period of time does a company's fiscal year cover? What determines the length of a company's operating cycle?
7. In what order are current assets typically listed in a balance sheet?
8. What is the purpose of recording depreciation expense on long-term assets?
9. Define liabilities.
10. Identify the three common components of stockholders' equity.

11. Is the income statement a "point-in-time" statement or a "period-of-time" statement?
12. Briefly describe or define the following three items: revenues, gross profit, and net income.
13. List the three major types of business activities by which cash flows are classified in a statement of cash flows.
14. Identify types of information typically found in financial statement footnotes.
15. According to *SFAC No. 2,* what characteristics must accounting data possess to qualify as "useful"?
16. *SFAC No. 1* states that financial reports should be comprehensible to whom?
17. To qualify as "reliable," accounting information should have what three traits?
18. Materiality refers to the relative importance of specific items of accounting information. How is "relative importance" defined in this context?
19. To what does comparability refer?
20. What disclosures may be necessary in a company's financial statements if the going concern assumption is in doubt?
21. What is the principal justification for using historical costs instead of current values as the primary valuation basis for assets?
22. How may the conservatism principle affect the valuation of a company's assets and liabilities?
23. What two conditions must be met for a company to recognize revenue from a transaction or event in its accounting records?

EXERCISES

24. True or False (LO 1–4)
Following are a series of statements regarding topics discussed in Chapter 2.

Required:
Indicate whether each statement is true (T) or false (F).

_____ a. The revenue and expense recognition rules limit the ability of business executives to freely choose the accounting periods in which to record their firm's revenues and expenses.

_____ b. A key advantage of using historical costs for asset valuation purposes is that historical costs are more objective, or verifiable, than current values.

_____ c. Common current assets include cash, short-term investments, prepaid expenses, and intangible assets.

_____ d. The entity concept requires that all information needed to obtain a thorough understanding of a company's financial affairs be included in its financial statements or accompanying narrative disclosures.

_____ e. The conceptual framework of the Financial Accounting Standards Board consists of six *Statements of Financial Accounting Concepts.*

_____ f. A business's fiscal year is the twelve-month period covered by its balance sheet.

_____ g. The unit-of-measurement concept suggests that accountants can prepare meaningful financial reports for ongoing business enterprises by dividing their lives into reporting intervals of equal length.

_____ h. One purpose of a statement of cash flows is to reconcile a business's cash balance at the beginning of a period to its end-of-period cash balance.

_____ i. To qualify as "reliable," accounting information should be timely and have feedback value and/or predictive value.

_____ j. Examples of "operating expenses" include sales commissions, advertising costs, and the salaries of a firm's top executives.

25. Classification of Balance Sheet Items (LO 2)
Following are items you may find in a balance sheet:

Accounts payable
Inventory
Retained earnings
Notes payable (due in ten years)
Prepaid expenses
Common stock
Intangible assets
Cash
Accounts receivable
Notes payable (due in six months)
Additional paid-in capital
Property, plant & equipment

Required:
Determine the correct balance sheet classification for each item listed. Choices are current assets, long-term assets, current liabilities, long-term liabilities, and stockholders' equity.

26. **Operating Cycle** (LO 2)
Khalid, Inc., manufactures furniture for sale to department stores. On average, 90 days elapse between Khalid's payment for raw materials and the sale of furniture produced from those raw materials. On average, the firm's customers pay for the goods they purchase in 45 days. (All of Khalid's sales are on credit.)

Required:
1. What is the length of Khalid's operating cycle?
2. How does the length of a company's operating cycle affect the classification of items in its balance sheet?

27. **Current Asset Classification** (LO 2)
Following are current assets of Nunez Enterprises, Inc.:

Accounts receivable
Inventory
Cash
Prepaid expenses
Short-term investments

Required:
1. In what order would you usually find these accounts listed in the current assets section of a balance sheet?
2. Explain the significance of the ordering of these accounts.

28. **Liability Classification** (LO 2)
For the past several years, Farewell Distributors reported a long-term debt of $100,000 on its balance sheet. Next year, the company will begin paying off this debt in four annual installments of $25,000 each.

Required:
1. How should Farewell's $100,000 debt be reported in the company's balance sheet at the end of the current year?
2. Why is the proper balance sheet classification of a company's liabilities important to the firm's creditors and potential creditors?

29. **Accrued Liabilities** (LO 2)
BioTechnica International, an agricultural seed distribution company based in Peoria, Illinois, reported accrued liabilities of $2,847,000 at the end of a recent fiscal year.

Required:
Provide two examples of transactions or events that could result in a company recording accrued liabilities in its accounting records at the end of an accounting period.

30. **Balance Sheet Equation** (LO 2)
Rick Francis & Son, Inc., has assets equal to twice the amount of its liabilities.

Required:
1. Assuming Francis & Son's total stockholders' equity is $1,000,000, determine the company's total assets and total liabilities.
2. Assuming $750,000 of the company's stockholders' equity consists of common stock and additional paid-in capital, determine Francis & Son's retained earnings.

31. **Asset Valuation on the Balance Sheet** (LO 4)
Lightner & Associates acquired a parcel of land 10 years ago for $100,000. The company intended to build a factory on the land. Ten years later, the factory is still not built and the land has an appraised value of $1,200,000.

Required:
1. Under current accounting standards, at what amount must Lightner report the land on its balance sheet? What principle dictates this accounting treatment?
2. In your opinion, are Lightner's financial statements misleading? Defend your answer.

32. **Analyzing Balance Sheets of International Companies** (LO 2, 3)
This chapter's "For Your Information" vignette entitled "The Balance Sheet: A Malaysian Perspective" describes a recent balance sheet of Sime Darby Berhad, a Malaysian company. Reread that vignette if you do not recall its contents.

Required:
Suppose that you are considering investing in either Sime Darby Berhad or a similar company based in Italy. What problems would you likely encounter in comparing and contrasting the balance sheet data of the two firms?

33. **Preparing an Income Statement** (LO 2)
Following are the line items, presented in random order, that were included in a recent income statement of Malenski Corporation:

Selling, general and administrative expenses	$ 45,050
Operating income	?
Cost of goods sold	65,750
Net income	?
Income tax expense	1,500
Net sales	115,000
Income before income taxes	?
Gross profit	?
Interest revenue	5,000

Required:
1. Compute each missing amount.
2. Prepare an income statement for Malenski Corporation.

34. **Computing Depreciation Expense** (LO 4)
Assume that Tankersley Enterprises purchased a piece of machinery for $18,000 in early January 1998. The machinery's estimated useful life is five years, and it will have no salvage value at the end of its useful life.

Required:
1. Using the straight-line depreciation method discussed in this chapter, compute the annual depreciation expense on this asset.

2. What accounting principle or principles require companies to depreciate long-term assets over their useful lives instead of "expensing" their total cost in the year of purchase?

35. **Computing Gross Profit and Net Sales** (LO 2)
In 1997, Doolan Company sold 10,000 units of inventory at twice their purchase price of $27.50 each. In 1998, Doolan had a gross profit of $200,000 and cost of goods sold of $225,000.

Required:
1. What was Doolan's gross profit in 1997?
2. What was the company's net sales in 1998?

36. **Interpreting Gross Profit** (LO 2)
Company A and Company B operate in the same industry; both companies wholesale shoes in New Mexico. In 1998, Company A had a gross profit of $400,000, while Company B had a gross profit of $120,000. Both companies had approximately $1.2 million in sales.

Required:
1. Identify at least two factors that could account for the large difference in the two companies' gross profits.
2. If you were the president of Company B, what strategies might you implement to increase your firm's gross profit?

37. **Net Income and Net Cash Flow from Operating Activities** (LO 2)
Jack's Bakery earned a net income of $40,000 last year. However, the business's statement of cash flows for the year reflected a decrease in cash of $10,000.

Required:
Identify specific reasons why a business may have negative cash flow in a given year from its operating (profit-oriented) activities although the firm earned a profit that year.

38. **Qualitative Characteristics of Accounting Information** (LO 3)
The following narrative items refer to various qualitative characteristics of accounting information:
1. The relative importance of specific items of accounting information
2. Timeliness, predictive value, and/or feedback value
3. Verifiability, neutrality, and representational faithfulness

Required:
Match each narrative item with one of the following terms: understandability, relevance, reliability, materiality, comparability.

39. **Accounting Concepts and Principles** (LO 4)
The following narrative items refer to various accounting concepts and principles:
1. Accountants can prepare meaningful reports for ongoing businesses by dividing the lives of businesses into regular reporting intervals of equal length.
2. Businesses are expected to continue operating indefinitely unless there is evidence to the contrary.
3. All information needed to obtain a thorough understanding of a company's financial affairs should be included in its financial statements and accompanying footnotes.
4. A means of determining the expenses to be included in an income statement.
5. Business transactions must be accounted for separately from the personal transactions of a business's owner or owners.

Required:
Match each narrative item with the appropriate accounting concept or principle. Choices are entity, accounting period, unit-of-measurement, and going concern concepts; historical cost, revenue recognition, matching, and full disclosure principles.

40. **Violation of Accounting Concepts** (LO 4)
Mom and Pop's Diamond Boutique is located on Campus Corner between Toto's Pizza and the Quarterhorse Arcade. Among transactions entered recently in the business's accounting records are the following:

Purchase of jewelry
Payment of employee salaries
Payment of daughter's college tuition
Sale of jewelry
Payment of monthly rent on store
Payment of insurance on Mom and Pop's house
Payment of store utility bills

Required:
1. What accounting concept are Mom and Pop apparently violating? Why?
2. Identify each transaction that prompted your answer to (1).

41. **Statement of Stockholders' Equity** (LO 2)
Following is a recent statement of stockholders' equity for Tucson Company.

	Common Stock	Additional Paid-In Capital	Retained Earnings
Balances, January 1, 1998	$1,000,000	$200,000	$800,000
Sale of common stock	240,000	300,000	—
Exercise of employee stock options	10,000	15,000	—
Net income	—	—	125,000
Balances, December 31, 1998	$1,250,000	$515,000	$925,000

Required:
1. How does a company's statement of stockholders' equity articulate with, or relate to, the firm's balance sheet?
2. What transaction or event accounted for the largest increase in Tucson's stockholders' equity during 1998?

PROBLEM SET A

42. **Financial Reporting Objectives** (LO 1, 2)
Wagner Company operates a small chain of department stores. The owner of Wagner Company has decided to open two additional stores next year, but the company does not have sufficient cash to finance this expansion project. To raise the needed funds, Wagner's owner has asked several friends to consider investing in the firm. She has provided these individuals with audited financial statements for Wagner's most recent fiscal year.

Required:
1. Besides the audited financial statements, what additional information do you believe the potential investors would want to obtain regarding Wagner Company before deciding whether to invest in the firm? Be specific.
2. Which financial reporting objective or objectives will Wagner's audited financial statements help satisfy in this context?

3. Which of Wagner's financial statements do you believe the potential investors will find most useful? Defend your answer.

43. Analyzing Balance Sheet Data (LO 2, 4)

Following is the assets section of a recent balance sheet of First Union Real Estate Investments. This company owns and manages real estate properties throughout the United States. Amounts are expressed in thousands.

Investments in real estate:	
Land	$ 44,594
Buildings and improvements	391,800
	$436,394
Less accumulated depreciation	(111,972)
Total investments in real estate	$324,422
Mortgage loans receivable	35,761
Other assets:	
Cash	2,975
Accounts receivable and prepayments	4,594
Miscellaneous assets	8,437
Total assets	$376,189

Required:

1. First Union's balance sheet is unusual in that it begins with *Investments in Real Estate* instead of *Current Assets.* Why do you believe the company uses this format for the assets section of its balance sheet?
2. If most real estate companies use this format for the assets section of their balance sheets, what accounting principle would First Union violate by using a different format?

44. Analysis of Income Statement Data (LO 2, 3, 4)

Following is a recent income statement of Sizzler International, Inc., which operates a chain of family restaurants. Amounts are expressed in thousands.

Revenues:		
Restaurant sales	$471,290	
Franchise operations	16,214	
Investment income	1,212	
Total revenues		$ 488,716
Costs and expenses:		
Cost of goods sold	$170,480	
Labor and related expenses	143,413	
General and administrative expenses	171,789	
Depreciation and amortization	33,122	
Other operating expenses	99,287	
Interest expense	1,169	
Total costs and expenses		619,260
Income (Loss) before income taxes		$(130,544)
Income taxes		(35,651)
Net loss		$ (94,893)

Required:

1. Compare Sizzler's income statement to that of Lincoln Logs Ltd. shown in Exhibit 2.6. Identify differences in the formats of these two income statements.
2. In your opinion, which of the income statement formats is most informative for decision makers? Why?
3. Should all companies be required to use exactly the same format for their income statements? Defend your answer.
4. What accounting principle(s) or concept(s) requires businesses to prepare an annual income statement?

45. Interpreting Financial Statements (LO 2, 4)

PepsiCo, Inc., is a large diversified company. In a recent year, the firm's revenues exceeded $30 billion, while its net income topped $1.6 billion. PepsiCo ranks second only to Coca-Cola in annual sales of cola products. However, sales of beverage products account for just one-third of the firm's annual revenues. Sales of snack foods, such as Fritos and Cheetos, account for approximately 30 percent of PepsiCo's annual revenues. The company's principal source of revenues is fast-food sales. Taco Bell, Kentucky Fried Chicken (KFC), and Pizza Hut are each owned by PepsiCo.

Required:

1. What problems do investors, lenders, and other decision makers likely face when studying the financial statements of diversified companies such as PepsiCo?
2. How may a diversified company's financial statement footnotes help decision makers interpret its financial statement data?

46. Ethics and Financial Reporting (LO 1, 3)

Tim Michael, the chief executive officer of Kokomo Corporation, is very concerned about his company's profitability. In the next few weeks, Kokomo will apply for a large loan from a local bank. This loan is needed to replace several pieces of outdated equipment on the company's production line. Michael is worried that the loan will be rejected because Kokomo's profits have been declining over the past two years. Profits are declining because Kokomo's products cost more to produce than the comparable products of the company's primary competitor. In turn, these higher production costs are due to Kokomo's inefficient production equipment.

To ensure that Kokomo receives the loan, Michael decides to overstate the company's sales and net income for its most recent fiscal year. In his own mind, Michael believes this decision is justified. Why? Because if Kokomo obtains the loan and purchases the new equipment, he is almost certain that the company will generate sufficient profits and positive cash flows to repay the bank loan. "Besides," Michael reasons to himself, "if we don't get this loan, the company may go under, leaving more than one hundred people without jobs."

Required:

According to Tim Michael's way of thinking, the "end justifies the means." What would you do if you found yourself in Michael's shoes? If you were almost certain that your company would be able repay the loan if granted, could you justify being dishonest to protect the jobs of the company's employees? Do you believe that any other factors have entered into Michael's decision to misrepresent Kokomo's financial data? Explain.

47. Income Statement Data for an International Company (LO 3, 4)

Following is selected information included in a recent income statement of The Broken Hill Proprietary Company Limited (BHP), one of Australia's largest publicly owned companies. Amounts are expressed in millions of Australian dollars.

Sales	$17,739
Other revenue	748
Operating profit	4,583
Depreciation expense	1,651
Interest expense	407

Required:

1. Suppose that BHP's major competitor is a U.S. firm, J. Darcy & Co. Would the income statement data of BHP and J. Darcy & Co. be directly comparable? Why or why not?
2. Briefly explain the unit-of-measurement concept. Should BHP translate its financial statements that are distributed in the United States into U.S. dollars to avoid violating the unit-of-measurement concept?
3. Where in BHP's annual report would you likely find information regarding the accounting rules used by the company? How would this information be helpful to a U.S. citizen considering investing in this company?

48. Applying Accounting Concepts (LO 4)

The following situations involve the application of accounting concepts or principles. In some cases, more than one concept or principle may be involved.

a. Whitecotton Enterprises recently changed its method of computing depreciation for the third time in three years.

b. Hethcox Distributors sold two of its five divisions immediately after the close of its most recent fiscal year. Company executives included information regarding the sale of these two divisions in the footnotes to the company's financial statements.

c. Inventory is the largest asset of Still Gardening Company. Last year, Still's inventory was reported at its historical cost in the company's balance sheet. This year, the company intends to report its inventory at market value. Why? Because the inventory's market value is significantly below its historical cost.

d. A footnote to the recent financial statements issued by Mason, Inc., lists the cash payments that the company is required to make over the next several years under its long-term lease agreements.

Required:

1. Identify the accounting concepts or principles involved in each of these situations.
2. Indicate whether the given accounting concept or principle has been properly applied in each case. Explain your reasoning.

PROBLEM SET B

49. Financial Reporting Objectives (LO 1, 2)

The owner of Garrity's Greenhouse, Nina Garrity, wants to buy out a local competitor. The competing firm's owner has offered to sell his business to Nina for $400,000. Although Garrity's Greenhouse has total assets of $800,000, it has cash of only $12,000. Most of the business's assets are tied up in inventory and accounts receivable.

To finance the purchase of the competing business, Nina Garrity has decided to apply for a $400,000 loan from a local bank. Among other items of information, the bank has requested audited financial statements for Garrity's Greenhouse for the past five years.

Required:

1. What information will the bank obtain from this business's financial statements that will assist it in determining whether to grant the loan?
2. Which financial reporting objective listed in Exhibit 2.2 is most relevant in this context?

50. **Analyzing Balance Sheet Data** (LO 2, 4)
Following are selected assets included in a recent balance sheet of Kelly Services, Inc., a firm based in Troy, Michigan. Kelly provides "human resource solutions" (temporary workers) to remedy staffing problems faced by companies of all sizes. Amounts are expressed in thousands.

Land and buildings	$ 35,153
Cash	52,811
Accounts receivable	397,534
Short-term investments	74,737
Intangibles and other assets	75,697

Required:
1. How do businesses determine which of their assets are current assets and which are long-term assets?
2. Identify which of the listed assets of Kelly Services are current assets and which are long-term assets.
3. What valuation basis does Kelly Services use for its buildings? What accounting principle dictates that the company use this valuation basis?

51. **Analysis of Income Statement Data** (LO 2, 4)
Following is information included in a recent income statement of Barnes & Noble, Inc., which operates a chain of retail bookstores. Amounts are expressed in thousands.

Sales	$1,337,386
Depreciation expense	29,077
Selling and administrative expenses	262,861
Rental expenses	120,326
Cost of goods sold	874,038
Net income	7,753

Required:
1. What was Barnes and Noble's gross profit during the year in question? Suppose the previous year that Barnes & Noble had a gross profit percentage of 31.2 percent. Did the company's gross profit percentage improve or deteriorate during the year for which data are presented?
2. Assuming that "selling and administrative expenses" and "rental expenses" are Barnes & Noble's only operating expenses, determine the firm's operating income.
3. If Barnes & Noble fails to record depreciation expense in a given year on certain of its assets, what accounting principle or concept would this oversight violate?

52. **Interpreting Financial Statements** (LO 1, 2)
Masco Corporation manufactures kitchen and bathroom products, including Delta faucets, KraftMaid cabinets, and Thermador kitchen ranges. In a recent year, Masco reported sales of nearly $5 billion and a net loss of more than $440 million.

Required:
1. How would a potential investor use Masco's financial statements to identify the factors responsible for the company's sizable net loss?
2. Compare and contrast the insights regarding Masco's financial health that the company's balance sheet, income statement, and statement of cash flows would provide to potential investors.

53. **Ethics and Financial Reporting** (LO 1, 3)

Mei Wong is a loan officer employed by Capital City Bank. Recently, Mei was assigned the responsibility of processing a loan application for a local company, Kokomo Corporation. Mei is very familiar with this company; in fact, her younger brother and several of his friends work on Kokomo's production line.

After reviewing Kokomo's loan application, Mei is disturbed. Her brother recently told her that Kokomo's sales shipments have been declining due to an aggressive marketing effort by the firm's leading competitor. Mei is also aware that the company has been suffering an excessive amount of downtime on its production line. The company's outdated production equipment frequently malfunctions and must be repaired. Despite these problems, Kokomo's unaudited financial statements included in the loan application are "rosy." For Kokomo's most recent fiscal year, the company's financial statements report impressive increases in sales and net income. Mei suspects that the financial statements may have been tampered with by company executives to enhance the company's reported financial condition and operating results.

Required:

1. Does Mei have a right to question the integrity of the individuals who were responsible for the preparation of Kokomo's financial statements? Should she accept those financial statements at face value and make her loan recommendation accordingly? Explain.
2. What steps could Mei take to investigate the accuracy of Kokomo's financial statements?
3. Put yourself in Mei's position. Identify the parties who will be affected by Mei's decision regarding this loan application. What responsibility, if any, does she have to each of these parties?

54. **Income Statement Data for an International Company** (LO 2, 3, 4)

Following are selected items included in a recent income statement of Hitachi, Ltd., a Japanese electronics firm. Amounts are expressed in millions of Japanese yen.

Other revenue	104,972
Net sales	7,400,205
Selling, general and administrative expenses	1,874,824
Net income	65,279
Cost of goods sold	5,311,992

Required:

1. Determine Hitachi's gross profit and operating income for the year in question. Why are these two amounts important to financial statement users?
2. Suppose that you were considering investing in Hitachi's common stock, what additional information might you request to interpret this firm's income statement data? What information would you need to compare and contrast Hitachi's income statement data to that of a similar U.S. firm?

55. **Applying Accounting Concepts** (LO 4)

The following scenarios involve the application of accounting concepts or principles. In some cases, more than one concept or principle may be involved.

a. Gooch Corporation is being forced out of business due to large losses it has incurred in recent years. To pay off its creditors, the company has scheduled a going-out-of-business sale next month. The company's recently issued financial statements do not comment on this matter.

b. Wallestad Enterprises had sales of $45 million and net income of $7 million during its recently ended fiscal year. During the year, the company inadvertently failed to record depreciation expense of $1,100 on a piece of equipment.

c. Dunlap Distributors had several assets, principally buildings and equipment, increase in value during 1998. The company did not record these increases in asset value in its accounting records.

d. Mary Madison Dolls & Toys, Inc., had a poor year profit-wise in 1998. So, the company's owners decided to record a portion of the firm's January 1999 sales as if they had occurred in December 1998. These sales were not "double-counted," since they were only reflected in the company's accounting records in 1998.

Required:

1. Identify the accounting concepts or principles involved in each of these scenarios.
2. Indicate whether the accounting concepts and principles you identified in (1) were violated in the given scenarios.

CASES

56. **Information for Lending Decisions** (LO 1, 2)

Suppose that you are the president of a small bank in Winslow, Arizona. A group of local investors has approached you with a loan proposal. These individuals want to borrow $750,000 to build a new motel adjacent to Interstate 40 that bisects Winslow. Presently, there are several motels on the interstate access road on which the investors intend to build the new motel. However, the investors maintain that there is more than enough business to support a new motel.

Required:

1. What types of information would you require the investors to submit with their loan application? What do you hope to learn from this information?
2. Would it be appropriate for you to ask the investors to prepare projected financial statements for the first several years of the proposed motel's operations? Why or why not?
3. Suppose that the investors intend to operate their new business as a corporation. How, if at all, would this affect your decision of whether or not to grant the loan? Explain.

57. **Conflicting Accounting Principles and Concepts** (LO 4)

Quite often, accountants must consider multiple accounting concepts or principles when deciding how to record a transaction or event. It is not unusual for these concepts and principles to be in conflict with each other. That is, one concept may dictate that a business transaction or event be recorded in one way, while another concept suggests another accounting treatment for that same item.

Required:

1. Develop two scenarios in which there is a conflict between two or more accounting concepts or principles regarding how a given business event or transaction should be recorded.
2. For each of the scenarios you developed in (1), indicate which accounting concept or principle you believe should take precedence. Defend your answers.

58. **Manipulation of Accounting Data** (LO 3, 4)

As you will learn in a subsequent chapter, businesses can choose from among several methods of computing depreciation expense on assets such as buildings and equipment. Likewise, businesses often have several alternative methods to choose from in accounting for inventory, accounts receivable, and other key financial statement items.

Required:

1. Refer to the discussion of depreciation in this chapter. How might a company manipulate or distort its annual depreciation expense on a given asset? Be specific.
2. In general, what problems may result from allowing businesses to "pick and choose" from among different accounting methods for various financial statement items?
3. In your opinion, should businesses be allowed to choose the accounting methods they apply to their business transactions and related events? Or, should accounting methods for businesses be expressly dictated by law or by a regulatory body? Write a memo supporting your stance on this issue.

PROJECTS

59. "The Buck Stops Here" for Corporate Executives

Reread the Spotlight on Ethics vignette in this chapter entitled "Disappointing Financial Results? Blame the Weather." In this project, you will investigate whether corporate executives are prone to accepting responsibility for poor operating results reported by their firm.

Required:

1. Identify a public company that reported a net loss, as opposed to a net income, for its most recent fiscal year. Obtain this company's annual report from your school's library, directly from the company, or from another source.
2. Review this company's income statement for its most recent fiscal year and any related financial statement footnotes. What factor or factors were apparently responsible for the company's poor operating results?
3. Read the key narrative information included in the annual report by the company's executives. (Most companies include a "letter to stockholders," a "president's letter," or a comparable item in their annual reports.) Compare and contrast the financial data in the company's income statement, and any related disclosures in the company's financial statement footnotes, with the information included in management's narrative disclosures in the annual report. Did you discover any apparent attempt by the company's executives to "gloss over," to downplay, or to avoid responsibility for the firm's poor operating results? If so, briefly describe these efforts.
4. Write a brief report summarizing your findings.

60. Comparing and Contrasting Profits and Cash Flows

Meet with your assigned group or project team. For this project, your group should choose two large companies that are in the same industry.

Required:

1. One or more members of your group will prepare an exhibit similar to Exhibit 2.9. This exhibit should compare the net cash flow from operating activities for the two selected companies over a recent three-year period.
2. One or more other members of your group will prepare a second exhibit, similar in format to the first but focusing on different financial data. This exhibit should compare the gross profit, operating income, and net income of the two companies for the previously chosen three-year period.
3. As a group, discuss the two exhibits. In particular, focus on the following questions, defending your answers with appropriate data and/or reasoning in each case. Which company was more profitable over the three-year period? Is the overall trend in each firm's financial data positive or negative? Which company has a "brighter" future?

4. Your group should prepare a brief written report, accompanied by the two exhibits, that summarizes the group's findings. Be prepared to have one or more group members present this report to the class.

61. Full Disclosure Principle in Practice

Companies regularly disseminate information regarding their financial results, new products and services, changes in corporate executives, etc., to the public. In recent years, many large corporations have begun using the Internet for this purpose. Each of the following large companies maintains a "Web" (World Wide Web) site on the Internet. For example, Apple Computer, not included in this list, has the following Web site address: http://www.apple.com.

Aluminum Company of America (Alcoa)
American Standard Companies Inc.
Chevron Corporation
The Estee Lauder Companies Inc.
Levi Strauss Associates Inc.
Micron Technology, Inc.
Microsoft Corporation
The Procter & Gamble Company
Sprint Corporation
Union Pacific Corporation

Required:

1. Choose one of the companies listed and access its Web site on the Internet.
2. List the general types of information that the selected company makes available at its Web site.
3. What specific types of financial information does the company make available at its Web site?
4. Does any of the information available from the company's Web site reflect *unfavorably* on its products or services, personnel, recent financial results, etc.? If so, briefly describe such information.
5. Summarize your responses to (2)–(4) in a written report. Include in your report the location of the selected firm's headquarters, its principal products or services, and other key descriptive information regarding the firm. Also include in your report the selected company's Web site address.

Accounting Systems and Internal Control

3

"The system is the solution."
American Telephone & Telegraph, Inc.

LEARNING OBJECTIVES

After studying this chapter, you should be able to do the following:

1. Define an accounting system and identify its principal elements.
2. Briefly describe how an accounting system is used to record accounting data for a business each accounting period.
3. Define the internal control process for a business entity and identify its primary objectives.
4. Identify the key components of internal control.
5. Identify the principal differences between manual and computer-based processing of accounting data and the related internal control implications.
6. Discuss recent trends in computer processing and the related implications for organizations' accounting and control functions.
7. Identify internal control issues stemming from the growing trend toward multinational business operations.

FOCUS ON DECISION MAKING

In Controls We Trust

Dateline: New York City, September 1994. A social events coordinator with Salomon Brothers Inc. admits embezzling $1.1 million from the prestigious investment banking firm.

Dateline: Wilmington, Delaware, June 1995. The Roman Catholic Diocese of Wilmington discloses that a former employee stole more than $1 million of the diocese's funds. The employee attempted to conceal the theft by setting fire to the diocese's accounting records.

Dateline: Newark, New Jersey, August 1995. A former Continental Airlines customer service representative is arrested and charged with stealing nearly 1.5 million frequent-flier miles. The employee used a computer to transfer the frequent-flier miles to the accounts of friends and relatives.

Dateline: Tokyo, Japan, January 1996. The Bank of Tokyo reports that a former employee of a branch office stole 850 million yen ($8.1 million) over a five-year period by diverting funds into a bogus customer account.

Isolated instances? Hardly. Employee theft and fraud wreak havoc each year on the profits of businesses of all sizes. A recent study estimated that annual business losses due to employee theft approach $120 billion in the United States.[1] Restaurants, for example, are estimated to suffer more than $113 of theft losses per employee each year. Another study estimated that employee fraud and theft wipe out as much as 6 percent of an average company's annual revenues.[2]

The chairman of the Association of Certified Fraud Examiners suggests that small businesses are particularly vulnerable to employee fraud and theft. He notes that owners of small businesses tend to place a higher level of trust in their employees than do the owners and managers of larger firms.[3] That higher level of trust allows dishonest employees to take unfair advantage of small business owners. To protect themselves, their firms, and the parties that rely on their firms, business owners and managers must have a strategy to contend with employee fraud and theft. The most effective strategy for dealing with this problem is a network of rigorous internal controls. Such a network is costly for a business to establish and maintain. However, the alternative—placing complete trust in employees—may be even more costly in the long run.

This chapter introduces you to accounting systems and internal control concepts and issues. Before focusing on accounting procedures in later chapters, you will find it helpful to become acquainted with the general nature of accounting systems and internal control concepts. The introduction you receive to accounting systems in this

1. *The Wall Street Journal,* "A Special News Report About Life On the Job—and Trends Taking Shape There," 6 February 1996, p. A1.

2. J. R. Emshwiller, "Small Business Is the Biggest Victim of Theft by Employees, Survey Shows," *The Wall Street Journal,* 2 October 1995, p. B2.

3. Ibid.

chapter provides you with a basic framework for understanding how accounting data are systematically collected and processed. An organization's accounting system is one element, one key element, of a larger system used by business executives to maintain effective control over their organizations. To fully comprehend the purpose of specific accounting procedures, you must understand the objectives and nature of an organization's control system.

The opening section of this chapter presents a general overview of accounting systems, while the next section discusses fundamental internal control concepts as they relate to a business's accounting function. The final two sections of this chapter address the impact of two important trends on the accounting and control functions of businesses. These trends are the increasing use of computers to process accounting data and the growth in multinational business operations.

AN INTRODUCTION TO ACCOUNTING SYSTEMS ▲

How many times have you heard the now trite expression "You gotta have a system"? The systems mentality has invaded, if not conquered, the business world in recent decades. Without exception, the purpose of every system is to help individuals or groups of individuals "attack" some problem. If anyone needs a system to help solve a problem, it has to be accountants. Consider the task facing the accounting staffs of Wal-Mart, IBM, and McDonald's, corporations that engage in millions of transactions each year. To provide useful information to investors, creditors, and other decision makers regarding those companies, each firm's accountants must somehow convert a huge amount of transaction data into the four financial statements discussed in Chapter 2. Fortunately, each of those firms has in place a sophisticated system to help their accountants accomplish that task.

The Accounting Function as a System

LEARNING ◀ OBJECTIVE 1
Define an accounting system and identify its principal elements.

The unabridged version of the *Random House Dictionary* provides more than one dozen definitions for the term "system." Paraphrasing and merging several of those definitions, a **system** is a coordinated network of plans and procedures designed to achieve a stated goal in an orderly, effective, and efficient manner. Not surprisingly, this definition applies very well to the typical accounting system. For our purposes, let us define an **accounting system** as a systematic approach to collecting, processing, and communicating financial information to decision makers.

system

accounting system

Like most types of systems, accounting systems come in varying degrees of complexity and sophistication. Some small businesses still use manual accounting systems. A manual accounting system relies strictly on a "pen and paper" mode of processing financial data. Most businesses have integrated computer processing into their accounting systems. The accounting concepts and methods you encounter in this course apply equally well to manual and computer-based accounting systems.

Now, let us briefly walk through the principal elements of an accounting system. In the following two chapters, we examine accounting systems in much more detail. Here, the purpose is to provide you with an overview of accounting systems and how they convert raw financial data into financial statements useful to decision makers.

Accounts

accounts

Accounts are the basic storage units for financial data in an accounting system. Financial data related to the assets, liabilities, and other financial statement items of a business are recorded and stored in accounts either electronically or manually. Some primitive accounting systems used a very simple account format, a so-called T-account, that derived its name from its shape. T-accounts are not formally integrated into modern accounting systems. Nevertheless, accountants frequently use T-accounts for illustration or analytical purposes.

Exhibit 3.1 presents a cash T-account for the Strawberry House, the bed and breakfast inn mentioned in Chapter 2. This T-account summarizes the cash transactions of the Strawberry House during January 1998 and reveals the business's cash balance at the beginning and end of that month. Chapter 4 identifies the double-entry bookkeeping rules that dictate how financial data are recorded in individual accounts. Although we are "jumping the gun," let us briefly consider two of those rules so that you can better appreciate the nature and purpose of an account. When recording financial data in a T-account for an asset such as cash, the transactions and other events that increase the dollar amount of the asset are recorded on the left-hand or "debit" side of the account. Transactions and other events that decrease the dollar amount of the asset are recorded on the right-hand or "credit" side of the account. (If you are unfamiliar with the bookkeeping terms "debit" and "credit," do not be concerned. The next few chapters acquaint you with these terms.)

Notice that the Strawberry House began the month of January 1998 with a $525 debit balance in its Cash account. (The $525 is a "debit" balance because it appears on the left-hand or debit side of the Cash account.) By the end of January, the account had a debit balance of $815. This figure was determined by adding four bank deposits made during the month to the beginning-of-the-month cash balance and then subtracting from this total three checks written during the month. The four bank deposits, such as the $200 deposit on January 8, were entered on the left-hand side of the T-account. Why? Because bank deposits increase a business's cash and the relevant bookkeeping rule dictates that increases in asset accounts be entered on the left-hand (debit) side of a T-account. The three checks written during January 1998 by the Strawberry House were entered on the right-hand (credit) side of the Cash account shown in Exhibit 3.1. For example, on January 17 the Strawberry House issued a $120 check.

Your life will be much easier over the next several weeks or months if you recognize and accept the following fact: *bookkeeping rules are arbitrary.* We could just as easily

EXHIBIT 3.1 ▼
T-Account for Cash

Cash				
Balance	1/1/98	525		
	1/8/98	200	1/10/98	250
	1/15/98	430	1/17/98	120
	1/22/98	350	1/30/98	760
	1/29/98	440		
Balance	1/31/98	815		

record increases in assets on the right-hand side of an asset account and decreases in assets on the left-hand side of an asset account. But, someone in the Middle Ages decreed that increases in assets should be entered on the left-hand side of an asset account, while decreases in assets should be entered on the right-hand side of an asset account. Ever since, accountants have followed those arbitrary rules or conventions.

As noted previously, the T-account format is not used in modern accounting systems, even in those systems in which accounting data are processed manually. Instead, the four-column account format shown in Exhibit 3.2 is commonly used. The data included in the T-account shown in Exhibit 3.1 have been entered in the four-column account presented in Exhibit 3.2. A key advantage of the four-column account format is that it provides an updated account balance after each transaction has been entered. (In a later chapter, the purpose of the "post reference" column in the four-column account format is explained.)

Chart of Accounts

A **chart of accounts** is a numerical listing, by account number, of a business's accounts. Think of a chart of accounts as an address book. When recording a transaction, an accountant refers to the chart of accounts to identify the proper address for each account affected by the transaction. A chart of accounts speeds up the recording of transactions and minimizes the risk that transaction data will be recorded in the wrong accounts. Exhibit 3.3 contains a partial chart of accounts that a small business might use—assuming it is organized as a corporation rather than as a sole proprietorship or partnership.

chart of accounts

Notice that accounts appear in a chart of accounts in the same general order they appear in a balance sheet and income statement, respectively: assets, liabilities, stockholders' equity, revenues, and expenses. Most companies use a numbering system for a chart of accounts based on the fact that there are five types, or groups, of accounts. For instance, asset accounts are typically assigned an account number beginning with the numeral one.

EXHIBIT 3.2 ▼
Four-Column Account Format

Cash							**Account No. 101**
						Balance	
Date		**Explanation**	**Post Ref.**	**Debit**	**Credit**	**Debit**	**Credit**
1998							
Jan.	1	Balance Forward				525	
	8	Deposit		200		725	
	10	Check No. 112			250	475	
	15	Deposit		430		905	
	17	Check No. 113			120	785	
	22	Deposit		350		1,135	
	29	Deposit		440		1,575	
	30	Check No. 114			760	815	
	31	Balance				815	

EXHIBIT 3.3 ▼
Partial Chart of Accounts for a Small Business

101.	Cash	201.	Accounts Payable
102.	Accounts Receivable	250.	Notes Payable
103.	Supplies	300.	Common Stock
106.	Prepaid Insurance	310.	Additional Paid-In Capital
151.	Furniture and Fixtures	320.	Retained Earnings
152.	Furniture and Fixtures, Accumulated Depreciation	401.	Rental Revenue
157.	Equipment	404.	Interest Revenue
158.	Equipment, Accumulated Depreciation	503.	Repair Expense
		506.	Cleaning Expense
160.	Land	507.	Interest Expense

The General Journal and the General Ledger

When referring to the process of recording transactions, accountants often use the slang term "book," as in "Dennis, go ahead and book that sale to the Beresford Corporation." The principal accounting books, or records, for most business enterprises are journals and ledgers. At this point, we will become acquainted with the general journal and general ledger. Later chapters briefly introduce you to other journals and ledgers used in accounting systems.

journalizing

When Dennis, the accountant, was instructed to "book" the sale to the Beresford Corporation, he would have initially recorded this transaction in a journal. The technical term for "booking" a transaction in a journal is **journalizing.** More specifically, journalizing refers to the process of recording financial data in a journal for a transaction or other event affecting a business. Exhibit 3.4 presents a general journal format and a general journal "entry." This entry illustrates how our friend Dennis journalized the sale made by his employer to the Beresford Corporation.

Think of a journal as a financial diary in which accountants initially record the dollar amounts of transactions and other events that affect the financial status of a business. Some of these dollar amounts are recorded simultaneously. For instance, a small grocery

EXHIBIT 3.4 ▼
General Journal Format and Representative Journal Entry

GENERAL JOURNAL					**Page 12**
Date		**Description**	**Post Ref.**	**Debit**	**Credit**
1998					
Apr.	19	Cash		1,274	
		Sales			1,274
		To record sale made to Beresford Corporation			

store that uses a manual accounting system does not individually record each sale made to customers. Instead, the daily cash sales of such a business are typically recorded in one lump sum at the end of the day. Businesses that maintain only one journal initially record the dollar amounts for transactions and other financial events in a **general journal.** In the olden days, a general journal was known as the "book of original entry."

general journal

The **general ledger** is the accounting record that contains each of the individual accounts for a business's assets, liabilities, owners' or stockholders' equity, revenues, and expenses. A journal serves the purpose of establishing a historical record of the transactions and events affecting a business. As you might expect, accountants would have considerable difficulty preparing financial statements directly from the hundreds, thousands, or even millions of journal entries recorded for a business during a given accounting period. To expedite the preparation of financial statements at the end of an accounting period, accountants transcribe, or copy, accounting data from the general journal and other journals used by a business to the individual accounts in the general ledger.

general ledger

Posting is the term used by accountants when referring to the process of transferring accounting data from a journal to the appropriate general ledger accounts. Posting can be done daily, weekly, or monthly. In a computerized accounting system, the posting of transactions is often done simultaneously with the journalizing of transactions.

posting

At the end of an accounting period, accountants prepare a listing of the general ledger account balances of a business. The account balances in this listing, known as a trial balance or working trial balance, are eventually incorporated into the appropriate financial statements. For financial statement purposes, several account balances are often consolidated into one line item. For example, assume that a company has ten cash accounts. The balances in those accounts would be added and the resulting total listed on the balance sheet line item Cash.

The Accounting Cycle

LEARNING ◀ OBJECTIVE 2
Briefly describe how an accounting system is used to record accounting data for a business each accounting period.

Embedded in the preceding section is a condensed summary of the **accounting cycle,** which is the set of recurring accounting procedures that must be performed for a business each accounting period. First, financial data for transactions and other events affecting a business are journalized. Second, these data are posted to the appropriate general ledger accounts. Third, the period-ending general ledger account balances are organized into a trial balance. Finally, the account balances are consolidated and incorporated into the appropriate financial statements. Exhibit 3.5 summarizes these four general tasks and the related accounting procedures or activities required to accomplish them. In Chapter 5, you will become familiar with other tasks that must be completed in the accounting cycle.

accounting cycle

INTERNAL CONTROL FOR BUSINESS ORGANIZATIONS ▲

An accounting system is one element of a larger system that business executives use to maintain effective control over their organizations. For small companies, this control system is often quite informal. The principal method a sole proprietor may use to control his or her business is involvement in the day-to-day operations of the firm. Employees have less opportunity to take unfair advantage of their employer if he or she is working side by side with them. On the other hand, large corporations have extensive manuals documenting and defining the various aspects of their control systems. These manuals describe in tedious detail the specific responsibilities of each job position, the chain

EXHIBIT 3.5 ▼
Basic Steps in the Accounting Cycle

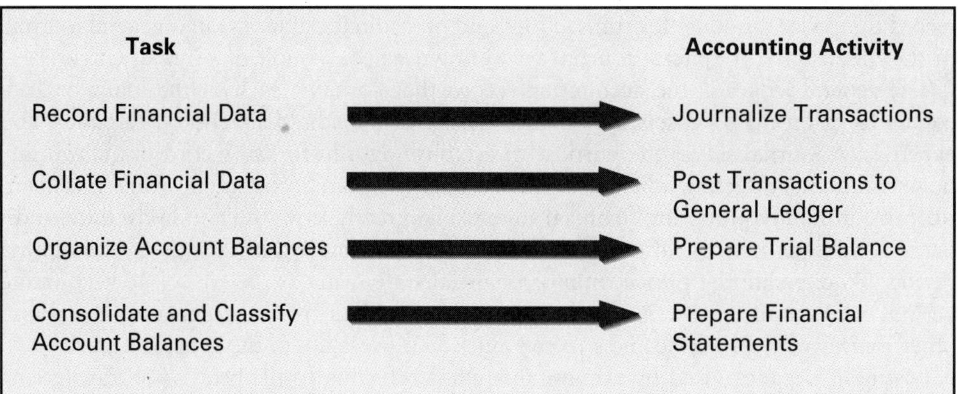

of command within each department, and so on. In this section, we focus on control concepts and issues, particularly as they relate to the accounting function of a business entity.

Internal Control as a Process

LEARNING OBJECTIVE 3 ▶
Define the internal control process for a business entity and identify its primary objectives.

internal control

The accounting profession views the organizational control function as an ongoing process. The phrase commonly used in referring to this process is "internal control." Following is a paraphrased version of the profession's formal definition of **internal control.**

> Internal control is a process—effected by an entity's board of directors, management, and other personnel—designed to provide reasonable assurance that key entity objectives will be accomplished.[4]

Two of the phrases in the previous definition are particularly important, "key entity objectives" and "reasonable assurance." Accountants tend to focus on a few specific entity objectives when helping to develop and maintain their organization's control function. Among these objectives are the maintenance of reliable financial records, compliance with applicable accounting and financial reporting rules and regulations, and the safeguarding of assets. Given their professional training, accountants are the individuals within an organization best equipped to develop and implement controls to provide for reliable financial records and to ensure compliance with accounting and financial reporting rules and regulations. Likewise, because of their thorough understanding of control concepts, accountants typically assume responsibility for developing specific procedures to minimize the risk that a business's assets will be stolen or misused.

The concept of reasonable assurance suggests that the costs of specific controls should not exceed the benefits they provide to an organization. For instance, elaborate security measures to prevent or minimize shoplifting losses in a retail store may be very effective.

4. *Statement on Auditing Standards No 78,* "Consideration of Internal Control in a Financial Statement Audit: An Amendment to SAS No. 55" (New York: American Institute of Certified Public Accountants, 1996), para. 6.

However, if the cost of such measures exceeds the shoplifting losses they prevent, these measures are not cost-effective and, as a general rule, should be discontinued.

Components of Internal Control

LEARNING OBJECTIVE 4
Identify the key components of internal control.

Each business's internal control process has several components. Three of these components are particularly relevant to an organization's accounting function. One internal control component involves the collection and communication of information needed by decision makers internal to an organization. An accounting system is the key element of this communication component of internal control. Two other components of an entity's internal control process that have important implications for accountants are the control environment and control activities.

control environment

CONTROL ENVIRONMENT Arguably the most important component of an organization's control function is its **control environment,** which refers to the degree of control consciousness within an organization. Executives of a company must impress upon their subordinates the importance of strong internal control. If top executives exhibit a lack of concern regarding internal control issues, their subordinates will likely follow suit. Even when an organization's executives exhibit a high degree of control consciousness, they may inadvertently undercut the effectiveness of their firm's internal control process. For instance, if executives impose too much pressure on their subordinates to attain targeted revenue and profit goals, the subordinates may bypass the organization's controls to ensure that those goals are reached. Similarly, incentive or bonus compensation plans that focus subordinates' attention on maximizing profits for their personal benefit can result in internal controls being undercut.

An example of a company that lacked a strong control environment was Crazy Eddie, Inc., a consumer electronics retailer based in New York City until the late

Safeguarding of assets is an important objective of a company's internal control process. For companies that retail jewelry and related products, providing adequate physical security for its merchandise inventory is a critical control issue.

Crazy Eddie: No controls . . . no company

In 1969, Eddie Antar opened a consumer electronics store near Coney Island in New York City. The store was tiny, 150 square feet of selling space, but Eddie, a 21-year-old high-school dropout, was a master salesman. Within a few months, Antar's aggressive and audacious sales tactics had earned him the nickname Crazy Eddie, which he soon loaned to his rapidly growing business. By the mid-1980s, Crazy Eddie, Inc., owned dozens of stores and was reporting several hundred million dollars of annual sales. During this period, Antar was among the best known celebrities in New York, thanks to his ear-piercing television commercials that proclaimed "Crazy Eddie—His prices are insane!!" commercials that were regularly parodied on *Saturday Night Live.*

Although a super salesman, Eddie Antar apparently lacked certain qualities needed to be a model chief executive. One such quality was an appreciation of the importance of internal control. Instead of hiring skilled professionals to staff key positions in his growing business, Eddie nearly always insisted on hiring a member of his family. At various times, Eddie's father, mother, wife, sister, two brothers, uncle, brother-in-law, and several cousins held key positions in his firm. Unfortunately, many of these individuals lacked the appropriate experience and training for their job roles. Eddie also thumbed his nose at technology. Instead of using a computer-based inventory control system developed for his business by an accounting firm, Eddie insisted on continuing to use a tedious and error-ridden manual inventory system.

Incompetence, greed, and weak or nonexistent controls eventually proved to be the undoing of Crazy Eddie, Inc. In 1987, the company was taken over by outside investors. A large inventory shortage discovered shortly after the takeover resulted in a bankruptcy filing for the firm in 1989 and in fraud charges being filed against Eddie Antar a few years later.

Source: M. C. Knapp, "Crazy Eddie, Inc.," *Contemporary Auditing: Issues and Cases,* 2d ed. (Minneapolis/St. Paul: West Publishing Company, 1996).

1980s. The Spotlight on Ethics vignette accompanying this section describes financial problems stemming from Crazy Eddie's inadequate control environment, problems that eventually led to the bankruptcy of the firm.

control activities

CONTROL ACTIVITIES **Control activities** are the policies and procedures established to help ensure that an entity's primary organizational objectives are accomplished. Exhibit 3.6 lists several examples of control activities relevant to an organization's accounting function. An important control activity is the segregation of key functional responsibilities or duties within an organization's accounting system. To minimize the potential for employee theft and undetected errors, the three types of duties shown in Exhibit 3.7—authorization, recordkeeping, and custodianship—should be segregated within each major segment of an accounting system. For instance, an

EXHIBIT 3.6
Examples of Control Activities

- Segregation of Key Functional Responsibilities
- Proper Authorization of Transactions
- Use of Prenumbered Accounting Documents
- Periodic Counts of Inventory
- Clerical Tests of the Mathematical Accuracy of Invoices and Other Accounting Documents
- Periodic Reconciliation of General Ledger Controlling Accounts with Balances of Subsidiary Ledgers

employee should not have custodial and recordkeeping responsibilities for cash. An individual with both of those responsibilities could steal cash and then conceal the theft by making the appropriate entries in the accounting records.

In the late 1970s, the Hermetite Corporation, a manufacturing firm, learned first-hand about the risks posed by assigning incompatible responsibilities to an employee.[5] Hermetite's office manager also served as the company's bookkeeper. This individual had access to the company's blank checks, its check-writing machine, the facsimile signature plate used to impress authorized signatures on checks, and the cash disbursements journal in which checks were recorded. The office manager also received the company's monthly bank statement and prepared the monthly bank reconciliation. Over a five-year period, the office manager stole more than $200,000 from Hermetite by writing and then cashing bogus checks made out to himself. To conceal the scheme, the office manager recorded the embezzled amounts as purchases of raw materials and then destroyed the canceled checks when they were returned by the company's bank.

Any of a number of control activities would have prevented or detected the office manager's embezzlement scheme. For instance, assume that another employee had been

EXHIBIT 3.7
Key Duties that Should Be Segregated in an Accounting System

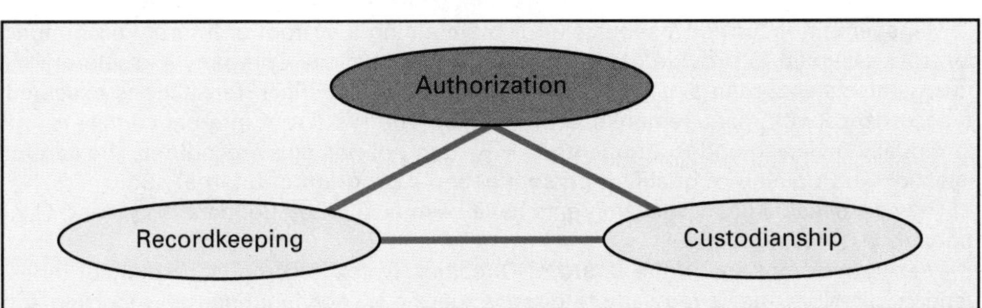

5. See Securities and Exchange Commission, *Accounting and Auditing Enforcement Release No. 2*, 18 August 1992.

responsible for receiving the company's monthly bank statement and preparing the monthly bank reconciliation. This individual would have discovered the suspicious checks that the office manager had written to himself.

Another common control activity involves clerical tests of the mathematical accuracy of invoices and other accounting documents, as indicated in Exhibit 3.6. Consider the embarrassment suffered by executives of the world's largest mutual fund, the Magellan Fund, when an accountant made a clerical error in a tax computation that went undetected. The error converted a $1.3 billion loss into a $1.3 billion gain. Magellan's shareholders were provided with a significantly overstated estimate of the fund's 1994 earnings because of the error. In January 1995, the mutual fund's executives had to relay the bad news to Magellan's shareholders, which, as you can imagine, was an unpleasant experience for both the executives and the shareholders.

Internal Control Reports

Okay, let's assume that you make it through college and land a great job. Because you are a forward-looking individual, you immediately begin planning for your retirement. You decide to make your initial nest egg investment in a company that manufactures semiconductor chips used in a wide array of computer products. Reportedly, the common stocks of such companies are "hot tickets" because of an increasing demand for semiconductor chips. Your broker has recommended the common stock of Zilog,

Report of Management, Tiffany & Co.

FOR YOUR INFORMATION

In 1961, Audrey Hepburn starred in the now classic movie Breakfast at Tiffany's. *Ms. Hepburn played the fictional role of Holly Golightly, but the setting that provided the name of the movie was not fictional. Tiffany & Co. markets jewelry, china, crystal, and related products in dozens of exclusive retail stores located throughout the world. Following is the Report of Management included in a recent annual report of Tiffany & Co.*

The Company's consolidated financial statements were prepared by management, who are responsible for their integrity and objectivity. The financial statements have been prepared in accordance with generally accepted accounting principles and, as such, include amounts based on management's best estimates and judgment.

Management is further responsible for maintaining a system of internal accounting controls designed to provide reasonable assurance that the Company's assets are adequately safeguarded and that the accounting records reflect transactions executed in accordance with management's authorization. The system of internal control is continually reviewed and is augmented by written policies and procedures, the careful selection and training of qualified personnel and a program of internal audit.

The consolidated financial statements have been audited by Coopers & Lybrand LLP, Independent Accountants.

The Audit Committee of the Board of Directors, which is composed solely of independent directors, meets regularly to discuss specific accounting, financial reporting and internal control matters. Both the independent accountants and the internal auditors have full and free access to the Audit Committee. Each year the Audit Committee selects the firm that is to perform audit services for the Company.

Source: Annual Report of Tiffany & Co. for the year ended January 31, 1996.

Inc., a small but growing semiconductor company. Now, the connection to internal control. Would you, as a prospective investor, be interested in information regarding Zilog's internal controls? Almost certainly. You have read about companies such as Crazy Eddie and Hermetite that were plagued by nonexistent or weak internal controls. As a result, one of your primary investment criteria is to buy stocks of companies that have rigorous internal controls. To your disappointment, you discover that Zilog's most recent annual report does not contain information regarding the company's internal controls.

Should companies regularly disclose information regarding their internal controls? That question has been widely debated in recent years. Presently, only certain financial institutions are required to include in their annual reports information concerning their internal controls. However, many companies voluntarily disclose such information in their annual reports.

Each year, the American Institute of Certified Public Accountants (AICPA) analyzes the accounting and financial reporting practices of 600 publicly owned companies. The results of this annual study are reported in a publication entitled ***Accounting Trends & Techniques.*** A recent edition of *Accounting Trends & Techniques* indicated that approximately 60 percent of public companies include a "Report of Management" in their annual report. This document nearly always contains at least brief disclosures regarding a company's internal controls. These voluntary disclosures are a step in the right direction. Hopefully, companies will become even more responsive in the future to decision makers' demand for internal control disclosures. A vignette accompanying this section presents a Report of Management included in a recent annual report of Tiffany & Co.

Accounting Trends & Techniques

INTERNAL CONTROL AND COMPUTER PROCESSING ▲

LEARNING OBJECTIVE 5
Identify the principal differences between manual and computer-based processing of accounting data and the related internal control implications.

Remember the scene from the hit movie *Jurassic Park* when the dinosaurs were about to crash into the control room and devour some human flesh? To the rescue came a teenage girl who navigated through a computer-based, three-dimensional representation of the electronic security system for the imaginary amusement park. Using a mouse to click her way through the various screens of the system, the teenager finally discovered what she was looking for and activated the locking mechanism for the door of the control room. Fantasy? Yes. At least the part about the dinosaurs. With the aid of computer visualization software, a company can construct a three-dimensional map of its corporate headquarters' security system, a map that would be considered a key internal control for the company.

Computers have dramatically influenced the methods used by business executives and their accountants to manage and control the day-to-day operations of business entities. In this section, we consider some key implications that computer processing has for an organization's accounting and control functions.

Integrating Computers into Accounting and Control Functions

Accountants increasingly rely on computer technology to develop more effective internal controls for businesses and to eliminate many tedious manual aspects of the monthly accounting cycle. No business is too small to benefit from the computerization of its accounting system. With a small investment in a personal computer and an accounting software package, such as the popular *QuickBooks* software marketed by Intuit, even a "Mom and Pop" business can have a computerized accounting system up and running in a matter of days. Once financial data are properly formatted and entered into such a system, the accounting software does most of the work for accountants. Among other tasks, accounting software packages can automatically post data from journals to the general ledger, print accounting documents, test the clerical accuracy of those documents, and generate a complete set of financial statements.

Sounds as if computer-based accounting systems may eventually eliminate the need for accountants, right? Wrong. Despite the widespread introduction of computers into accounting systems over the past few decades, the need for accounting professionals has continued to grow each year. Similarly, the computer has not diminished the importance of the 500-year-old double-entry bookkeeping system popularized by Pacioli. At the core of every multimillion-dollar, computerized accounting system are the centuries-old mechanics of double-entry bookkeeping.

The computer has changed the nature of accountants' work environment and the nature of their job responsibilities. The availability of powerful, low-cost computer resources provides accountants with the opportunity to allocate more of their time to challenging assignments. With the aid of a computer, accountants can easily develop financial forecasts based upon a variety of economic assumptions. In a matter of seconds, accountants can use a computer to analyze complex cost-behavior patterns both mathematically and graphically. Accountants can also use computers to develop and implement more effective and efficient internal controls for an organization. A three-dimensional representation of a company's security system is just one such example, an internal control that is particularly helpful when a company is attempting to thwart a dinosaur attack!

Computer vs. Manual Processing of Accounting Data: Internal Control Implications

When companies switch from manual to computer-based accounting systems, they should be aware of the important internal control implications this change has for their operations. Exhibit 3.8 lists six features that distinguish computer processing from manual processing of accounting data. Each of these features affects, to some degree, the ability of business executives to exercise effective control over their firm's operations.

UNIFORMITY IN THE PROCESSING OF TRANSACTIONS The use of computers in an accounting system increases the degree of uniformity with which similar transactions are processed and recorded. On the downside, computer processing of accounting data means that thousands (or millions) of similar transactions may be incorrectly processed if there is a "bug" in a computer program.

INITIATION AND EXECUTION OF TRANSACTIONS Computer processing can greatly expedite the initiation and execution of business transactions. For example, many retail stores use optical scanners to read bar-coded information from the price tags of merchandise. In a matter of moments, information scanned by a salesclerk is processed by a sales terminal, resulting in a quickly completed sale and thus a happy customer. The information scanned by the salesclerk is also fed into the store's accounting system via the sales terminal, resulting in the store's inventory records being updated immediately.

EXHIBIT 3.8 ▼
Computer Processing vs. Manual Processing of Accounting Data: Distinguishing Features

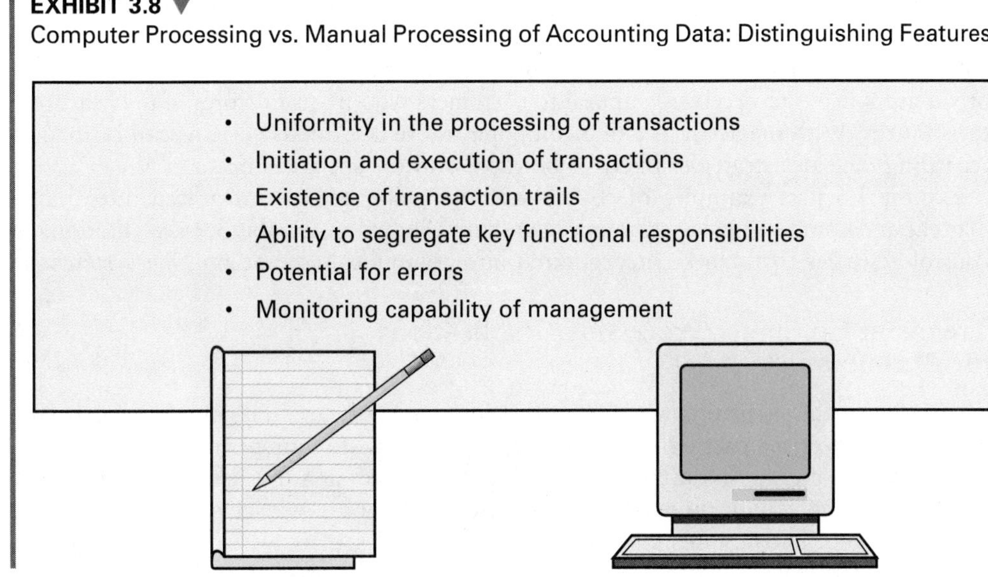

EXISTENCE OF TRANSACTION TRAILS As transactions are processed in a manual accounting system, they leave a trail of paper documentation such as sales invoices, purchase orders, and receiving reports. A visible transaction trail typically does not exist in a computer-based accounting system, making it more difficult to unravel errors when they occur.

ABILITY TO SEGREGATE KEY FUNCTIONAL RESPONSIBILITIES In a manual accounting system, organizations minimize the potential for employee theft and undetected errors by segregating authorization, recordkeeping, and custodianship responsibilities. Such segregation of responsibilities is much more difficult to accomplish in a computer-based accounting system without forfeiting many cost-saving benefits of computer processing.

POTENTIAL FOR ERRORS The potential for errors exists in both manual and computer-based accounting systems. Computer processing eliminates the occasional random errors that occur in a manual system due to human fatigue or oversight. Then again, if a computer operator becomes tired or distracted, the result may be thousands of "systematic" random errors. Computer processing is also perceived to be less subject than manual processing to errors resulting from unauthorized access to an entity's accounting records. However, when an unauthorized party obtains a valid password for a firm's computer system, the result may be devastating for the business.

MONITORING CAPABILITY OF MANAGEMENT Computer processing provides business executives and managers with a much greater ability to monitor the operating activities of their firms. Consider a retail store that has a fully computerized accounting system. At any point during a business day, the manager of the hardware department of this store can step up to a computer terminal and obtain a wide range of information regarding his or her department. For example, the manager can immediately determine how many electric sanders are in inventory, how many are on order, and whether the wholesale price of that item has changed recently. Business executives and managers can also utilize the speed and power of a computer to monitor buying trends at different stores in given sales districts or regions. Products that sell well in retail stores near urban areas may not necessarily appeal to customers who frequent stores in the heart of the suburbs. With the assistance of a computer, more informed decisions can be made regarding the sales strategies likely to be successful for specific stores.

Exhibit 3.6 lists examples of control activities that can be integrated into both manual and computer-based accounting systems. Shown in Exhibit 3.9 are additional control activities that can be incorporated into computer-based accounting systems.

Trends in Computer Processing: Implications for Accountants

LEARNING OBJECTIVE 6 ▶
Discuss recent trends in computer processing and the related implications for organizations' accounting and control functions.

The rate of technological change in both computer hardware and software has been phenomenal over the past two decades. If companies fail to monitor technological advances in the computer industry, they will find themselves at a distinct disadvantage to competitors who exploit those advancements. Given their knowledge of computers and their experience in using them, accountants are often designated the computer experts within an organization. As such, accountants assume the primary responsibility within many firms for monitoring new product offerings and technological changes in information processing and computer technology. This monitoring may include informal activities such as reading computer periodicals, for example, *PC Magazine* and *ComputerWorld*. More formal responsibilities may include attending computer trade shows and identifying vendors to make in-house presentations regarding their products.

Among the advancements in information processing and computer technology that businesses have utilized in recent years are on-line real-time processing, database management systems, local area networks (LANs), and microcomputer-based accounting packages. In subsequent business courses, you will be introduced to these technologies and recent refinements to them. Two trends in information processing and computer technology that have particularly important implications for the accounting and control functions of organizations are the outsourcing of information systems and the use of electronic data interchange (EDI).

OUTSOURCING OF INFORMATION PROCESSING In recent years, there has been a growing trend for businesses to outsource, or transfer, one or more components of their information system to consulting firms specializing in information processing services. This trend stems primarily from the rapid pace of technological change in

EXHIBIT 3.9 ▼
Examples of Control Activities for Computer-Based Accounting Systems

- Maintain back-up copies of key computer programs
- Periodically process test transactions to determine whether computer programs are properly functioning
- Establish controls to determine that data are not lost or modified when input into the computer
- Limit access to computer facilities to authorized personnel
- Establish procedures to identify parties accessing and operating each computer
- Limit access to key data files and computer programs by establishing a password access procedure

information processing. By choosing the outsourcing option, companies delegate the responsibility for monitoring changes in information processing technology and for updating their information processing functions to an external consulting firm. One such consulting firm is Electronic Data Systems Corporation (EDS), which was founded by Texas financier and politician Ross Perot. Other major outsourcing firms include Alltel Information Services, Inc., Fiserv, Inc., Computer Sciences Corporation, and Integrated Systems Solutions Corporation (ISSC), a subsidiary of IBM.

Among the largest outsourcing transactions to date involving information processing is a $3 billion deal between McDonnell Douglas, the large aerospace company, and ISSC. By outsourcing most of its information processing function to ISSC, McDonnell Douglas reduced its workforce by nearly 1,500 employees. Chase Manhattan, the large New York bank, recently announced the signing of a twelve-year outsourcing contract with Fiserv. Other major companies announcing large outsourcing arrangements in recent years involving their information systems include Bethlehem Steel, Deere and Co., Del Monte Foods, and General Dynamics.

The outsourcing of a company's information system, or major portions of that system, has important implications for its accounting and control functions. An information system includes many components of a company's internal control process. As a result, when a firm's information system is outsourced, its accountants must subsequently coordinate their control activities with an outside agency. The need for this coordination raises complex and often difficult to resolve issues. Duplication of effort and disputes over assigned areas of responsibilities, so-called "turf wars," are among the key problems that accountants face in these situations.

Will accounting systems be outsourced in the future by large public companies? Almost certainly. In fact, over the past two decades, many small businesses have outsourced segments of their accounting functions to data-processing firms or computer service bureaus. The payroll segment of an accounting system is the component of a small business's accounting function that is most frequently outsourced. The largest firm providing payroll accounting services is Automatic Data Processing, Inc. (ADP). ADP processes payroll checks for approximately 300,000 companies nationwide, companies with more than 16 million employees.

A very recent trend is for companies to outsource their internal audit function to a public accounting firm. In a few cases, a large corporation has outsourced its internal audit function to the accounting firm that performs its annual independent audit. This arrangement raises the critical question of whether an accounting firm can retain its independence if it provides both types of audit services to a client.

ELECTRONIC DATA INTERCHANGE Bill Gates, computer guru, is attempting to undo a tradition begun centuries ago by Cai Lun. Many historians credit Cai Lun, a Chinese court official, with inventing paper. Apparently, Cai Lun believed that important matters should be documented on paper rather than left floating somewhere in cyberspace. (Not that Mr. Lun had ever heard of cyberspace.) Gates, founder and chief executive officer of Microsoft Corporation, reportedly refuses to allow paper documents in any of his staff meetings. Despite the protestations of Bill Gates, each year U.S. businesses generate an enormous amount of paper documents. An estimated 360 billion business transactions take place annually in the United States.[6] The majority of these transactions, approximately 80 percent, involve the processing of one or more paper documents.

---

6. D. Akst, "In Cyberspace, Nobody Can Hear You Write a Check," *Los Angeles Times Magazine,* 4 February 1996, 20–32.

© Matthew McUay/SABA

Bill Gates, CEO of the computer software giant Microsoft Corporation, has long advocated that companies adopt a "paperless" mode of transacting business. Companies that take Gates' advice must rethink several important features of their accounting and control functions.

In total, an estimated four trillion business documents are produced annually in the United States, enough documents to wallpaper the Grand Canyon several hundred times, according to one trivia buff.[7] Corporations, alone, issue an estimated twelve billion checks annually. The cost of processing checks and other business documents is estimated to be as high as $100 billion per year. A large hidden expense related to transacting business on paper are the costs associated with lost documents. In 1994, the *Journal of Accountancy* reported that 7.5 percent of all business documents are lost and that $350 is spent on average recreating a lost document.[8]

The use of paper documents is not only costly to businesses but also adds significantly to the time required to complete business transactions. To remedy the shortcomings of paper-based transactions, many companies are adopting the philosophy of Bill Gates and switching to a "paperless" mode of transacting business. To date, the most successful of these approaches has been electronic data interchange (EDI), which involves the cooperative exchange of financial data via a computer network among companies that transact business with each other. One consulting firm estimated that by late 1997 the accounting departments of 30,000 businesses would be accepting payments funneled to them via EDI.[9]

EDI is particularly useful for merchandising companies that require large amounts of inventory. Companies such as Wal-Mart, J.C. Penney, and Sears allow suppliers to access their inventory records through an EDI network. For example, when the inventory of Levi's 501 Jeans in a retail store participating in an EDI network falls to a certain level, an electronic purchase order is automatically transmitted to Levi Strauss, which manufactures the jeans. For retailers, this arrangement significantly lowers the cost of processing purchase transactions and reduces lost sales due to inventory shortages.

---

7. G. Rifkin, "The Future of the Document," *Forbes ASAP,* 9 October 1995, 42–60.
8. M. J. Weiss, "The Paperless Office," *Journal of Accountancy,* November 1994, 73.
9. B. Orr, "EDI: Banker's Ticket to Electronic Commerce?" *ABA Banking Journal,* May 1996, 64–70.

Belly Basics: Say "Hello" to EDI and Outsourcing

FOR YOUR INFORMATION

In 1995, Jody Kozlow and Cherie Sorota faced a perplexing problem. The two women own and operate Belly Basics, a New York firm that markets maternity clothes. At the time, their largest customer, Federated Department Stores, had just announced that it was switching to an EDI order system. Belly Basics would be forced to interact electronically with Federated or immediately forfeit 25 percent of its annual sales. After considering their various options, Jody and Cherie decided that the most rational decision was to outsource their new electronic processing function to a consulting firm, Intercoastal Data. So, this story has a happy ending. Belly Basics kept the Federated account, while the firm's owners were introduced, if reluctantly, to two "cutting edge" phenomena in computer processing, namely, EDI and outsourcing.

Source: P. Hise, "How to Survive EDI," *Inc.*, December 1995, 131.

Many EDI systems involve dozens of firms, each of which can potentially access the accounting records of the other companies in the system. Companies involved in these computer networks must establish controls to minimize the likelihood of unauthorized access and use of their accounting records. The participants in an EDI network must also cooperate to develop standard methods of coding and transmitting financial data. If such methods are not developed and used consistently by all firms involved in an EDI network, numerous errors may be introduced into the accounting records of these companies.

INTERNAL CONTROL: AN INTERNATIONAL PERSPECTIVE

LEARNING OBJECTIVE 7
Identify internal control issues stemming from the growing trend toward multinational business operations.

Each year, more U.S. companies become involved in international trade. Entering international markets poses several challenges for a company's accountants, including designing effective internal controls for the firm's new operations. The procedures that are necessary to establish effective control over domestic business operations may not necessarily be effective or appropriate for business operations in other countries.

Cultural differences across the world translate into varying definitions of acceptable and ethical business practices. Bribes, kickbacks, and related payments made by companies to obtain unfair advantage over their competitors are certainly not unheard of in this country. Nevertheless, most large companies in this country have established controls to discourage executives and employees from making such payments and to detect such payments if they are made. A different attitude exists toward these types of inducements in many countries. For instance, although not encouraged by governmental authorities, bribes paid by businesses in France and Germany have long been tax-deductible expenses. In both Japan and Mexico, there is a long history of "under-the-table" payments to facilitate major business transactions. Over the past two decades in Japan, the disclosure of such payments to several high-ranking government officials abruptly ended those individuals' political careers. In Mexico, companies that refuse to pay *mordida* (a little bite) to government officials often have difficulty closing major transactions.

Banking on Internal Controls Around the World

FOR YOUR INFORMATION

For centuries, banks and other financial institutions have been perceived as conservative businesses managed by tight-fisted executives. Despite this perception, hundreds of financial institutions in the United States went "belly up" during the 1980s, thanks largely to aggressive and ill-advised investment and lending practices. In case after case, banking executives or their subordinates circumvented their institution's internal controls to invest in speculative securities or business ventures and to lend funds to clients that posed an excessive credit risk.

The 1990s proved that bank executives and employees in countries other than the United States can also give the proverbial "cold shoulder" to internal controls. In 1995, the Daiwa Bank, a Japanese firm, revealed that an employee had lost several hundred million dollars in speculative securities trades. For eleven years, the employee concealed the mounting losses by overriding key internal controls of the bank. In 1996, the Bank of Tokyo disclosed that an employee had embezzled more than $8 million over a five-year period. Press reports indicated that the bank's weak internal controls allowed the employee to easily conceal the theft. The most startling breach of an international bank's internal controls was revealed in 1995. Executives of the 233-year-old Barings Bank of the United Kingdom were stunned to learn that a 28-year-old securities trader in their Singapore branch had lost more than $1 billion in securities trades in a matter of months. During his wild investment binge, the employee repeatedly sidestepped internal controls established by the bank. In summarizing this embarrassing financial debacle, one banking official noted, "This represents a colossal failure of internal controls at Barings."[10]

So, what are U.S. companies to do when faced with transacting business in a foreign country that has a much different view of acceptable business practices than the prevailing view in this country? Should these companies ignore the controls they have established to discourage and detect questionable payments made by their personnel to third parties? Definitely not. The Foreign Corrupt Practices Act of 1977 expressly prohibits U.S. companies from paying bribes, kickbacks, or related inducements to officials of foreign countries to acquire business or maintain business relationships. This law also requires publicly owned companies, including those that do not have international operations, to establish internal controls that have a high likelihood of preventing and detecting bribes, kickbacks, and similar payments.

▲ SUMMARY

Systems technology is used extensively by businesses in the design of their accounting and control functions. An accounting system can be defined as a systematic approach to collecting, processing, and communicating financial information to decision makers. Financial data for a business are initially recorded in a journal. Then, these data are

10. W. B. Crawford, "Barings Fiasco a 'Colossal' Failure of Internal Controls," *Chicago Tribune*, 28 February 1996, Section 3, 1.

transferred or posted to the appropriate accounts in the general ledger. At the end of an accounting period, summary financial data drawn from the general ledger are used to prepare a business's financial statements.

The phrase "internal control" refers to an organization-wide process employed by a business to help ensure that its key objectives are achieved. A business's internal control process has several components, including a control environment and various control activities. "Control environment" refers principally to the degree of control consciousness within an organization. A primary responsibility of an organization's top executives is to ensure that their subordinates have an awareness and appreciation of the need for strong internal controls. Control activities are the specific policies and procedures established to ensure that an entity's primary objectives are accomplished. An example of an important control activity is the segregation of authorization, custodianship, and recordkeeping responsibilities within each major segment of an entity's accounting system.

The integration of computers into the accounting and control functions of a business significantly affects, both positively and negatively, the entity's ability to maintain effective control over its operations. Accountants must be aware of the key differences between manual and computer processing of accounting data and the related effects on an organization's accounting and control functions. Two fairly recent developments in information processing and computer technology have important implications for accountants. These developments are the outsourcing of information systems by businesses and electronic data interchange (EDI) among companies that transact business with each other.

U.S. companies that have international operations often encounter very different attitudes toward acceptable or ethical business practices in foreign countries. These differing attitudes affect the ability of these companies to exercise effective control over their foreign operations. Accountants must be aware of the requirements of the Foreign Corrupt Practices Act of 1977 when establishing internal controls for their companies. This law prohibits the payment of illegal inducements to officials of foreign countries to obtain overseas business. Additionally, this law requires all publicly owned companies to establish internal controls that have a high likelihood of preventing and detecting bribes, kickbacks, and similar payments.

GLOSSARY

Accounting cycle (p. 79) The set of recurring accounting procedures that must be performed for a business each accounting period.
Accounting system (p. 75) A systematic approach to collecting, processing, and communicating financial information to decision makers.
Accounting Trends & Techniques (p. 85) An annual publication of the AICPA that analyzes the accounting and financial reporting practices of 600 publicly owned companies.
Accounts (p. 76) The basic storage units for financial data in an accounting system.
Chart of accounts (p. 77) A numerical listing, by account number, of a business's accounts.
Control activities (p. 82) The policies and procedures established to help ensure that an entity's primary organizational objectives are accomplished.
Control environment (p. 81) A component of internal control that refers to the degree of control consciousness within an organization.
General journal (p. 79) The accounting record in which the dollar amounts for transactions and other financial events are initially recorded by businesses that maintain only one journal.

General ledger (p. 79) The accounting record that contains each of the individual accounts for a business's assets, liabilities, owners' or stockholders' equity, revenues, and expenses.
Internal control (p. 80) A process—effected by an entity's board of directors, management, and other personnel—designed to provide reasonable assurance that key entity objectives will be accomplished.
Journalizing (p. 78) The process of recording financial data in a journal for a transaction or other event affecting a business.
Posting (p. 79) The process of transferring accounting data from a journal to the appropriate general ledger accounts.
System (p. 75) A coordinated network of plans and procedures designed to achieve a stated goal in an orderly, effective, and efficient manner.

DECISION CASE

McGuire's Irish Pub and Brewery in Pensacola, Florida, has a particularly vexing internal control problem. Why? Because much of the business's cash is stapled to its walls or hanging from its rafters. A longstanding tradition of this establishment is for customers to write personal notes on dollar bills with a black magic marker. These bills are then displayed within the restaurant or adjacent bar. Although the customers provide the dollar bills, they become the property of McGuire's when they are stapled to a wall or a rafter or a wooden hand rail. "Hi Mom, stuck in Pensacola over spring break, send cash," "Seminoles Eat Gator Meat," "Roll Tide," and "Rock Chalk Jayhawk" are just a few samples of notes you will find scrawled on McGuire's monetary assets.

The internal control problem McGuire's management faces should be obvious: discouraging would-be bill snatchers. This is not a small problem since there is approximately $100,000 literally "hanging around" the business's interior.

Required: Assume that you accept a job with a restaurant that has a tradition identical to that of McGuire's Irish Pub and Brewery. On your first day of work, the owner of this business approaches you. He mentions that the restaurant has been suffering an increasing number of bill-snatching incidents over the past few months. The owner knows that you are enrolled in a financial accounting course at a nearby university and that internal control is a key topic in that course. So, he asks you to spend 10–20 hours developing a system of policies and procedures to safeguard the restaurant's "exposed" cash. Because the owner does not want to influence your report, he does not inform you of the controls that have been used in the past.

Develop a system to safeguard the restaurant's inventory of dollar bills. (You should first refer to the definition of a system included in this chapter.) Integrate at least four specific control activities into this system.

QUESTIONS

1. Why is it necessary for businesses to develop a comprehensive strategy for dealing with employee theft and fraud?
2. Define an "accounting system."
3. "Bookkeeping rules are arbitrary." Explain this statement.

4. What is a key advantage of the four-column account format over the T-account format?
5. What is the purpose of a chart of accounts? How are numbers typically assigned to accounts in a chart of accounts?
6. Identify the principal accounting books (or records) for business enterprises.
7. Why are accounting data posted to the general ledger from the general journal?
8. Identify the four key steps in the accounting cycle.
9. Define the phrase "internal control."
10. In reference to an organization's internal control process, define "control environment" and "control activities."
11. Where in a corporate annual report may you find information regarding a company's internal controls?
12. Identify common tasks performed by accounting software packages.
13. What do multimillion-dollar accounting systems have in common with the financial recordkeeping system popularized by Pacioli in the fifteenth century?
14. List two key advantages of computerized accounting systems over manual accounting systems. List two key disadvantages.
15. Explain what it means for a company to "outsource" its information system.
16. What segment of the accounting function is most frequently outsourced, especially by smaller companies?
17. Briefly describe the nature of "electronic data interchange" in a business environment.
18. What problems or challenges does a company's decision to join an EDI network pose for the organization's accountants?
19. How does a company's involvement in international trade affect the nature of its internal controls?
20. Identify the major internal control-related requirements of the Foreign Corrupt Practices Act of 1977.

EXERCISES

21. True or False (LO 1–7)

Following are a series of statements regarding topics discussed in Chapter 3.

Required:

Indicate whether each statement is true (T) or false (F).

_____ a. An accounting system is one element of a larger system that business executives use to maintain effective control over their organizations.

_____ b. A chart of accounts speeds up the recording of transactions and minimizes the risk that transaction data will be recorded in the wrong accounts.

_____ c. An important advantage of a computer-based accounting system is the existence of a trail of paper documentation for each transaction.

_____ d. Posting is the term used by accountants when referring to the process of recording in a journal financial data related to a business transaction.

_____ e. The costs of integrating computer processing into a small business's accounting system typically exceed the related benefits for such an entity.

_____ f. The Foreign Corrupt Practices Act of 1977 requires all publicly owned companies to establish internal controls that have a high likelihood of preventing and detecting bribes, kickbacks, and similar payments.

_____ g. Accounts are the basic storage units for financial data in an accounting system.

_____ h. The concept of reasonable assurance suggests that the cost of specific controls should not exceed the benefits the controls provide to an organization.

_____ i. The widespread integration of computers into accounting systems in recent decades has resulted in a decline in the need for accounting professionals.

_____ j. To enhance control over cash, an organization often assigns one employee both custodial and recordkeeping responsibilities for this asset.

_____ k. A large "hidden" expense related to transacting business on paper is the cost associated with lost documents.

_____ l. Income statement accounts are typically listed first in a business's chart of accounts.

22. **Purpose of an Accounting System** (LO 1, 2)
You have recently designed an accounting system for Amini's Art Gallery, a new business. The owner of this business, Alex Amini, intended to maintain its accounting records, a responsibility that he assumed would be simple given the small size of the business. However, after reviewing the accounting system you designed, Amini is having second thoughts. He does not understand why his small business must have a complete accounting system. Now, Amini is seriously considering "trashing" the accounting system you designed. Instead, Amini may simply maintain a checkbook as the only accounting record for his business.

Required:
Write a brief memo to Amini in which you describe the nature and purpose of an accounting system. Attempt to convince Amini that maintaining a checkbook as the only accounting record for his new business would not be a wise decision.

23. **Reasonable Assurance and Internal Controls** (LO 3)
Karen and Kelli Casteel own and operate Curly's Hamburger Shop on Campus Corner. The two partners have recently hired four college students to work part-time in the popular late-night hangout for college students. From 8 p.m. until closing at midnight, the hamburger shop will be staffed completely by college students. Because the two partners are concerned that they may be "ripped off" by their employees, they have decided to hire a security guard to watch over the restaurant in their absence.

Required:
1. Explain how the internal control concept of "reasonable assurance" may be relevant in this context.
2. Identify alternative control activities that the owners of this business could consider implementing to minimize the likelihood of being ripped off by their employees.

24. **Components of Internal Control** (LO 4)
Joseph Dredd owns a company that provides security and investigative services. Dredd employs ten security guards, three detectives, and four office workers. Dredd has never paid much attention to internal controls. He is much more interested in helping his detectives work on the latest "hot" case. Dredd's philosophy of internal control is simply to hire honest employees. Recently, Dredd has become more interested in internal control issues. Over the past few months, the cash inflows of his business have declined considerably. Apparently, one or more of Dredd's employees is stealing cash from the business.

Required:
1. Briefly describe the following three components of a business's internal control process: accounting system, control environment, and control activities.
2. How does Dredd's attitude toward internal controls affect the control environment within his firm?

25. **Analysis of a T-Account** (LO 1, 2)
Consider the following T-account for the machinery owned by the Von Rosenberg Construction Company:

Machinery

Balance	4/1/98	125,000		
	4/15/98	15,000		
			4/18/98	100,000
Balance	4/30/98	40,000		

Required:
Describe a transaction that might have resulted in the $15,000 amount posted to this account on April 15. What type of transaction might have resulted in the April 18 posting?

26. Creating a T-Account (1, 2)
Barb's Bike Shop engaged in the following transactions during the first week of May:
1. May 2: Sold a bike stand for $60 cash.
2. May 3: Bought three bikes from Trek for $600 on credit.
3. May 3: Sold a Cannondale bike for $500 on credit.
4. May 4: Paid an employee's wages, $50 cash.
5. May 5: Sold a bike bell for $20 cash.
6. May 6: Paid the electric bill of $70 by check.

Required:
Prepare a T-account for Barb's Bike Shop reflecting the transactions that affected the business's cash balance during the first week of May. The business's Cash account had a $720 balance on May 1.

27. Creating a Four-Column Account (LO 1, 2)

Required:
Prepare a four-column Cash account for Barb's Bike Shop using the information in Exercise 26.

28. Analysis of a Four-Column Account (LO 1, 2)
Consider the following four-column account of Von Sydow Enterprises:

Inventory						Account No. 103	
						Balance	
Date		Explanation	Post Ref.	Debit	Credit	Debit	Credit
1998							
March	1	Balance Forward				2,000	
	5			6,000		8,000	
	25				3,000	5,000	
	31	Balance				5,000	

Required:
Notice that the explanation column was left blank for the postings made to Von Sydow's Inventory account on March 5 and March 25. Describe a transaction that would have resulted in each of those postings.

29. Control Activities (LO 4)
Following are selected control activities established by the owner of Eddie's Ice Cream Shop:
1. Sales are made only on a cash basis.
2. Sales transactions must be recorded immediately in the cash register.
3. Ice cream inventory must be counted weekly.
4. Managers must approve all purchases of ice cream inventory.
5. Cash registers must be locked when not in use.

Required:
Briefly describe the purpose of each of these control activities.

30. **Internal Control Weaknesses** (LO 4)
Diane Hershey and Ray Assante are accountants for a small company, Leisure Time, that manufactures and sells hot tubs and spas. The owner of the business has assigned these two accountants the following responsibilities:

Diane: Maintains all inventory accounting records, authorizes inventory purchases, serves as the supervisor of the inventory warehouse.
Ray: Maintains accounts receivable accounting records, decides which customers will be granted credit, processes cash received from customers, prepares monthly bank reconciliation.

Required:
1. What benefit is realized by assigning one individual all key accounting and control responsibilities for a given asset such as inventory or accounts receivable?
2. Identify potential problems that Leisure Time may experience given the job responsibilities assigned to Diane and Ray.

31. **Internal Control for Multinational Businesses** (LO 7)
The owners of Zipf Productions, Inc., a manufacturing company, are developing a plan to build distribution facilities in several foreign countries. Each of these facilities would be staffed with as many as 50 to 100 employees hired from the local community, including an accounting staff of six to eight individuals.

Required:
1. What internal control issues and problems will Zipf face if its owners proceed with the expansion plan?
2. How will the Foreign Corrupt Practices Act of 1977 affect Zipf's foreign operations?

32. **Computer Processing and Control Activities** (LO 5)
Sue Thompson owns Thompson's Homebuilders, a local construction company. Because of a significant increase in the volume of her business in recent years, Sue has decided to computerize her company's accounting system. Sue is not sure how integrating a computer into the accounting system will affect the business's internal controls. She is particularly concerned about unauthorized access to the computerized accounting system.

Required:
Write a brief memo to Sue in which you describe key differences in manual and computer-based accounting systems that have important internal control implications for a business. In your memo, identify one or more specific control activities that Sue could adopt to minimize the risk of unauthorized access to her firm's computer-based accounting system.

33. **Computer Controls** (LO 3, 5)
Review Exhibit 3.9 from this chapter.

Required:
1. Of the six controls listed, which two do you believe would be the least costly for a business to implement? Explain.
2. Which two controls would likely be the most costly for a business to implement? Explain.
3. What role does cost play in a company's decision to implement (or not implement) a specific control?

34. **Reasonable Assurance and Internal Controls** (LO 3)
John Corso owns and operates a small business, Corso's Cakery, in a local mall. John estimates that his store loses the equivalent of one cake (retail value $12.50, cost $6.00) and one gallon of ice cream (retail value $10.00, cost $7.50) each day to employee theft. He is so disturbed by this problem that he is considering hiring a worker at $4.00/hour

for four hours per day just to "manage" (keep an eye on) the employees when he is out of the store. The worker would receive a $50 bonus for each employee caught stealing cake or ice cream.

Required:
Should John implement the new control activity? Explain.

35. **Computerizing an Accounting System** (LO 5)
Sheila Schwartz, the owner of Sheila's Auto Repair, is converting the business's manual accounting system to a computerized system. Sheila believes that a computer-based accounting system will be free of errors and that such a system will provide her with more timely access to the financial information she needs to make important decisions regarding her business.

Required:
Write a brief memo to Sheila summarizing the key strengths and weaknesses of a manual accounting system versus a computerized accounting system. In your memo, focus principally on the following issues:
1. Uniformity of processing transactions
2. Potential for errors
3. Monitoring capability of management

36. **Updating an Information System** (LO 6)
Rivera Corporation is a large publicly owned company that operates a chain of convenience stores in the eastern United States. Recently, Rivera's chief executive hired a consulting firm to perform an extensive review and critique of the company's information system including its accounting and control functions. The report prepared by this consulting firm suggests that Rivera consider outsourcing certain components of its accounting system, particularly the company's payroll function. The report also suggests that Rivera join an electronic data interchange (EDI) network. Several large convenience store chains and major suppliers in the industry are members of this network.

Required:
1. Briefly explain the key advantages a business realizes by (a) outsourcing components of its information system and (b) participating in an EDI network.
2. What new internal control issues or problems may Rivera encounter if it adopts the two recommendations made by the consulting firm?

PROBLEM SET A

37. **Using T-Accounts** (LO 1, 2)
Following are the transactions of Jane's Vines & Violets during the first week of June:

June 2: Sold $320 of plants on credit.
June 2: Sold $150 of plants for cash.
June 3: Collected $190 from a customer for a credit sale made in April.
June 5: Sold $810 of plants for cash.
June 6: Paid $750 for June rent.
June 6: Sold $240 of plants on credit.
June 7: Paid salaries of $380 to employees.

Required:
1. Prepare a T-account for cash as of June 7 for Jane's Vines & Violets. The balance of the business's Cash account was $7,000 on June 1.

2. Prepare a four-column account for cash as of June 7.
3. What is the principal function of accounts in an accounting system?

38. **Internal Controls for Small Businesses** (LO 3, 4)

Anderson Gardening is a retail lawn and garden supply store. The store has eight employees who are directly supervised by the business's owner. Five employees work as salesclerks. These employees also restock the store's departments when time permits. One of the three remaining employees operates the cash register; the owner operates a second cash register during peak business hours. Another employee serves as the business's accountant. The final employee is responsible for the purchasing function for the business. All purchases exceeding $100 must be personally approved by the owner. The owner also decides which customers will be granted credit; approximately 50 percent of the store's sales are made on a credit basis. Each month, the owner reconciles the store's bank statement balance with the amount of cash reported in the accounting records. Once per month, the inventory of each department is counted to determine whether the amount of inventory on hand agrees with the amount reported in the accounting records. The business also uses prenumbered accounting documents for all sales, purchases, and miscellaneous transactions such as merchandise returned by customers.

Johnson Gardening Supply is the principal competitor of Anderson Gardening. Johnson's owner is a local doctor who acquired the business two years ago. The owner has never been inside the store, although he has driven by it occasionally. Twice per month, the owner's business manager visits the store to make sure that everything is "okay." Day-to-day operations of the store are co-managed by its four full-time employees; the store also has four part-time employees. Each full-time employee has complete responsibility for one of the store's four departments including making all purchase decisions for that department, maintaining the department's inventory records, and operating the cash register located within his or her department. The store does not have a full-time accountant. Once per month, the owner's bookkeeper drops by the store to update the accounting records other than the inventory accounting records. The owner of Johnson Gardening Supply has a very simple internal control strategy: "Hire honest employees." The owner believes that if an employee intends to steal cash or inventory, he or she will find some way to subvert any existing controls. As a result, the owner does not require the use of prenumbered accounting documents, instructs the employees to count inventory only once per year for tax purposes, and does not require a monthly bank reconciliation to be prepared.

Required:

1. Define the "control environment" component of a business's internal control process. Which of the two businesses has a stronger control environment? Explain.
2. What is the purpose of control activities? Identify specific control activities within Anderson Gardening's internal control process.
3. Identify three examples of internal control weaknesses that exist at Johnson Gardening Supply. Identify one or more potential problems that the business may experience as a result of each internal control weakness.

39. **Control Activities: Benefits vs. Costs** (LO 3, 4)

Following is a list of control activities that the owner of Goodner's Grocery Store has implemented:

1. A timeclock is used to establish a record of the hours worked by each employee. Employees must "punch in" at the beginning of a work shift and "punch out" at the end of the shift.
2. Invoices received from suppliers are double-checked for mathematical accuracy before being paid.

3. Customers who want to purchase merchandise on credit are required to complete a credit application and provide three credit references. Approximately 25 percent of all credit applications are rejected.
4. A monthly statement is mailed to each customer who purchases merchandise on credit.
5. Out-of-state checks are not accepted for merchandise purchases.
6. Employees are allowed to purchase food from the store and eat it in the break room. However, if requested by a supervisor, an employee eating food must provide a sales register receipt for the merchandise.
7. The store is closed on the first Monday of every third month to allow employees to count the store's inventory. The owner reconciles the resulting dollar value of the inventory to the store's inventory accounting records.
8. Employees caught stealing merchandise are fired immediately.

Required:
Prepare a table with the following headings: "Key Benefit of Control Activity" and "Costs Associated with Control Activity." Complete this table for the eight control activities listed for Goodner's Grocery Store. When identifying the costs associated with a given control activity, describe not only the monetary costs stemming from that activity but also any hidden or 'opportunity" costs related to the activity. For example, a given control activity may result in fewer losses due to customer theft in a retail store, while at the same time discouraging customers from shopping in that store.

40. Integrating Computers into an Accounting System (LO 5)
Celeste's Arts & Crafts is a large retail store located in a rapidly growing suburb of Houston, Texas. By far, the largest asset of this business is inventory. Typically, the store has more than $250,000 of merchandise on hand in its ten departments. The store stocks more than 1,000 individual products, most of which have a retail sales value of less than $10. All sales are made on a cash basis. Recently, Celeste Ritchey, the owner of this business, has been considering the purchase of a computer-based accounting system for the store. She is particularly interested in the internal control implications that the acquisition of a computer-based accounting system would have for her store.

Required:
Write a memo to Celeste that analyzes the control-related advantages and disadvantages of a computer-based accounting system, compared with a manual accounting system. When writing this memo, keep in mind the nature of Celeste's business. In your memo, focus particular attention on how a computer-based accounting system would allow Celeste to improve control over her store's inventory.

41. An International Focus on Internal Controls (LO 7)

Gonzales Chili, Inc., a firm headquartered in El Paso, Texas, has recently begun selling frozen chili and other frozen food products in Central America. Company executives are aware that in many regions of Central America businesses are expected to pay bribes to local officials.

Required:
1. If Gonzales pays bribes to governmental officials in Central America, would this be considered an illegal activity in the United States?
2. Recommend specific control activities that Gonzales's management could implement to discourage the company's sales representatives from paying bribes to generate sales. Would these activities be cost-effective?
3. If the citizens of certain foreign countries believe that the payment of bribes is an acceptable business practice, do you believe that it is appropriate for U.S. companies to challenge that belief when doing business in those countries? Defend your answer.

PROBLEM SET B

42. Using T-Accounts (LO 1, 2)

Listed next are the transactions of Hilderbrandt Wholesalers for the first week of July. This company sells small tools to retail hardware stores.

July 2: Sold $400 of tools to Denco Retailers on credit.
July 3: Wrote check for $150 in payment of monthly electricity bill.
July 5: Collected $470 from a customer for a credit sale made in June.
July 5: Sold $280 of tools to Comanche Hardware for cash.
July 6: Sold $310 of tools to Symmes Tools on credit.
July 6: Sold $540 of tools to Eufaula Supply for cash.
July 7: Received tax rcfund of $600.

Required:

1. Prepare a T-account for cash as of July 7. The balance of Hilderbrandt's Cash account on July 1 was $4,300.
2. Prepare a four-column account for cash as of July 7.
3. Comment on the differing uses of the two types of accounts. Does a business typically use both types of accounts in its accounting system?

43. Internal Controls for a Small Business (LO 3, 4)

Tilt, Inc., is a video game arcade located in a suburban mall. Presently, Scott Tway is negotiating to purchase this business from a local attorney. Scott, who is also an attorney, has little time to devote to the business since he has a thriving law practice. However, Scott does not believe that the business requires much attention. Scott told a friend that owning the business would be comparable to owning his own mint. "Kids come in with five or ten bucks and don't leave until they have spent their very last quarter. And, there's very little overhead," he gleefully confided in the friend. "Sure, I'll have to pay rent for the floor space and the monthly electricity bill. But, the only other expense to speak of is the minimum wage salaries I'll pay to a few high-school students to run the place."

Tilt's operations are similar to those of most video game arcades. Customers either obtain quarters from a store employee in exchange for currency or obtain quarters directly from one of the store's two bill-changing machines. Coupons earned by playing the games can be exchanged for prizes at Tilt's redemption booth. The prizes range from rubber snakes (10 coupons) to small televisions (5,000 coupons). Tilt presently has five part-time employees, all of whom are high-school seniors. Unknown to Scott, the current owner is selling Tilt because of the constant headaches he has encountered attempting to prevent the employees from "stealing him blind." In addition to pilfering occasional $20 bills and handfuls of quarters when servicing the bill-changing machines, the employees habitually give away prizes to their friends.

Required:

1. Suppose that Scott purchases Tilt. The owner of a small business has the primary responsibility for establishing an effective control environment for that business. What type of control environment do you believe Scott would establish for Tilt? Explain.
2. What is the purpose of control activities?
3. Identify several control activities that could be implemented to minimize Tilt's employee theft problem. Would these control activities be cost-effective?

44. Control Activities: Benefits vs. Costs (LO 3, 4)

Following is a list of control activities that Claire Jameson has established for her business, Claire's Bookstore:

1. On a weekly basis, Claire compares the price lists of book distributors for newly issued books.
2. Customers are allowed to pay for their purchases with personal checks if they provide two forms of personal identification.
3. Claire approves all purchase orders that exceed $100.
4. A daily time log is maintained of the individuals operating the store's two cash registers.
5. Invoices received from suppliers are double-checked for mathematical accuracy before being paid.
6. Salesclerks are not allowed access to the store's inventory records.
7. Customers who want to purchase merchandise on credit are required to complete a credit application and provide three credit references. Approximately 20 percent of all credit applications are rejected.
8. When a customer returns a book, a prenumbered credit memo must be completed by a salesclerk. A refund is mailed to the customer only after Claire has reviewed the credit memo.

Required:
Prepare a table with the following headings: "Key Benefit of Control Activity" and "Costs Associated with Control Activity." Complete this table for the eight control activities listed for Claire's Bookstore. Identify both monetary costs and hidden or "opportunity" costs associated with each activity. For example, a given control activity may result in fewer losses due to customer theft in a retail store, while at the same time discouraging customers from shopping in that store.

45. Integrating Computers into an Accounting System (LO 5)
Regina's Fine Jewelry is a retail store located in LaClede's Landing, a suburb of St. Louis. The largest asset of this business is accounts receivable. At any point in time, the company typically has more than $3 million of outstanding receivables from as many as five hundred customers. Recently, Regina Break, the business's owner, has been considering the purchase of a computer-based accounting system for the store. Regina is particularly interested in the internal control implications that the acquisition of a computer-based accounting system would have for her business.

Required:
Write a memo to Regina that analyzes the control-related advantages and disadvantages of a computer-based accounting system, compared with a manual accounting system. When writing this memo, keep in mind the nature of Regina's business. In your memo, focus particular attention on how a computer-based accounting system would allow Regina to improve control over her receivables.

46. An International Focus on Internal Controls (LO 7)

Becker Brothers, Inc., is an international distributor of cosmetics. Company executives are aware that the payment of bribes to obtain business is a common practice in many countries, including certain countries in which the firm markets its products. Becker Brothers has a strict written policy prohibiting sales personnel from paying bribes to close sales transactions. The company compensates its sales personnel on a commission basis. Commission rates are 10 percent on domestic sales, and 15 percent on foreign sales. The higher commission rate for foreign sales stems from the company's strategy to expand its share of the international market for cosmetics which is growing much more rapidly than the domestic market.

Required:
1. Does Becker Brothers' commission rate structure conflict with the company's policy against the payment of bribes? Explain.

2. Other than the written policy against the payment of bribes, Becker Brothers does not have any control activities designed specifically to prevent or detect bribes paid by employees. What signal may the absence of such controls send to the company's sales personnel?
3. Identify specific control activities that Becker could implement to reinforce its written policy regarding the payment of bribes.

CASES

47. Ethics and Internal Control (LO 3)

Lee Venturi owns a propane and fuel oil supply business. Venturi supplies propane and fuel oil to hundreds of farmers and ranchers in west Texas. Besides approximately twenty truck drivers, Venturi employs ten individuals in his business office in Amarillo. Recently, Venturi has begun suspecting that one or more of his office employees is stealing cash from the business. Although the business's volume of deliveries is higher than ever before, monthly net cash flow has declined considerably in the past few months. To determine which of his employees is dishonest, Venturi has arranged to periodically have a third party offer bribes to individual employees. Venturi intends to dismiss any employee who fails to report a bribe offered to him or her.

Required:

Evaluate Venturi's plan for testing the honesty of his employees. In your opinion, is this plan ethical? Why or why not?

48. Recording Financial Data (LO 1, 2)

Mark's Raspberry Farms supplies raspberries and other fruits to restaurants and grocery stores in a large southwestern city. Mark, the business's owner, maintains his own financial records. Those records include two notebooks and a checkbook—Mark has a separate checking account for the business. In one notebook, Mark records credit sales made to his customers. For each credit sale, Mark records the date, amount, customer name, and a brief description of the product or products sold. In the second notebook, Mark enters similar information for each purchase that he makes on a credit basis. When Mark receives payment for a prior credit sale or pays for goods or services previously purchased on credit, he places a large check beside the original entry for that item in the appropriate notebook. Of course, Mark also records these cash receipts and cash payments in the business's checkbook. Cash sales and cash purchases are recorded only in the business's checkbook.

Required:

1. Does Mark have an "accounting system"? Why or why not?
2. A primary product of most accounting systems is a set of monthly or annual financial statements. Does Mark's "system" provide sufficient information to allow him to prepare periodic financial statements that document his business's assets, liabilities, and so on?
3. Other than providing the means to develop periodic financial statements, what other benefits do accounting systems typically provide to business owners or managers?

49. Financial Implications of Internal Control Weaknesses (LO 4)

In 1978, Harper & Row, a large publishing company, was negotiating to purchase a smaller competitor, J. B. Lippincott Company. Before finalizing the offer for Lippincott, Harper & Row's executives retained their independent audit firm to review Lippincott's accounting records. As a result of this review, numerous errors were discovered in Lippincott's accounting records. Most of these errors resulted from poor or absent internal controls. For example, Lippincott's accounts receivable were materially overstated by such simple errors as the duplicate recording of customer sales, failure to record credit memos issued to customers, and failure to test the clerical accuracy of the company's accounting records. Eventually, Harper & Row agreed to purchase Lippincott but at a price considerably below the original offer price.

Required:

1. Which individuals in an organization are ultimately responsible for the integrity of its internal control process? Explain.
2. Why should an organization's accountants have a significant role in the design and periodic review of its internal control process?

PROJECTS

50. Internal Control Reporting

The issue of whether companies should report on their internal controls has been widely debated in recent years. In this project, you will research this controversial topic.

Required:

1. Review recent editions of accounting periodicals such as the *Journal of Accountancy, Management Accounting, Internal Auditor,* and others recommended by your instructor and identify articles focusing on the subject of internal control reporting. Other sources of articles on this subject may include *The Wall Street Journal* and the business sections of major metropolitan newspapers.
2. Summarize in a written report the key arguments in support of companies reporting on their internal controls to the public and the major arguments opposed to such a requirement. In your report, indicate which arguments you believe are most persuasive and why.

51. Analyzing Internal Controls

For this assignment, your project group will study the accounting and control activities that an actual business applies to its cash transactions.

Choose any local business of interest to your group. One member of your group should contact the owner or manager of this business and obtain a signed permission to use information regarding the business to complete this project.

Required:

1. Your group will interview an owner or employee of the selected business who is familiar with its accounting function. One group member should lead the interview, but all group members should be present and participate. For example, each group member should be prepared to ask follow-up questions when appropriate. Among the items of information your group should obtain are the following:
   a. A brief history of the business.
   b. An overview of the nature of the business's operations, including the products it sells or services it provides.
   c. A summary of the key control issues and objectives related to the processing of cash transactions that the business has identified.
   d. A summary of the methods used by the business to process cash receipts and cash disbursements, including all relevant control activities.
2. Following the interview, the group should meet and discuss the information collected to ensure that there is consensus regarding the meaning or interpretation of that information.
3. Prepare a written report documenting the information collected in (1). One group member should be prepared to present a summary of this report to the class.

52. Accounting Software Packages

Visit one or more computer software stores and identify the accounting software packages that are available in that store or stores.

Required:

1. For each accounting software package you identified, obtain the following information:
   a. The name of the package
   b. The firm that developed the package
   c. The retail price of the package
   d. A summary of the software's key selling features which will be listed on the external packaging
2. What features seem to be the most important when it comes to successfully marketing an accounting software package?
3. Document your completion of (1) and (2) in a written report.

53. Searching for Internal Controls on the Internet

If you are familiar with the Internet, you realize that many businesses use the "net" to market their products and services. Among the thousands of products and services marketed on the Internet are a wide range of financial services. Many consulting firms, including CPA firms, market internal control-related services on the Internet. Among these services are forensic accounting, accounting systems design, internal control systems design, internal control audits, control risk assessment, and so on.

Required:

1. Using Yahoo, Excite, Lycos, or some other Internet cataloging service or search procedure, search the Internet for World Wide Web (Web) sites established by consulting firms that offer internal control-related services. Examples of phrases you might use during your search are "internal control," "financial controls," "fraud prevention," and "business fraud."
2. Choose the Web sites of two consulting firms that offer internal control-related services. For each firm, document in a written report the following items:
   a. The firm's name and location
   b. The firm's Web site address
   c. The specific types of internal-control related services offered by the firm and a brief description of each major service offered
   d. The professional qualifications of the firm and/or its members

II THE ACCOUNTING MODEL

The first three chapters introduced you to the business world and the accounting profession, the fundamental concepts and elements of accounting, and the nature of accounting systems and internal control. Chapters 4 and 5 acquaint you with the recordkeeping and data-processing aspects of accounting, including the basics of double-entry bookkeeping. Chapter 4 illustrates the procedures used to record financial data, with an emphasis on journalizing transactions and other events affecting businesses. Chapter 5 presents a sequential walk-through of the accounting cycle, the set of recurring accounting procedures that must be completed each accounting period for a business. In Chapter 5, you will learn how the transactions and other events affecting a business are summarized into a set of financial statements each accounting period. Part II concludes with Module 1, "An Integrative Framework for Understanding Accounting." The purpose of this module is to help you develop a comprehensive and integrative understanding of the accounting and financial reporting function of business entities.

4 The Mechanics of Double-Entry Accounting

"There is always a best way of doing everything, if it be to boil an egg."
Ralph Waldo Emerson

LEARNING OBJECTIVES

After studying this chapter, you should be able to do the following:

1. Analyze business transactions in reference to the accounting equation.
2. Determine whether increases and decreases in specific accounts are recorded as debits or credits.
3. Identify the normal balance, debit balance or credit balance, of the different types of accounts.
4. Prepare general journal entries.
5. Post general journal entries to a general ledger.
6. Prepare a trial balance of a general ledger.

FOCUS ON DECISION MAKING

From Clay Tokens to Computers: The History of Accounting

Accounting historians trace the beginning of the accounting profession to 1494 when Pacioli published a mathematics textbook that included a section on double-entry bookkeeping. In reality, the origins of accounting go back much further in time, before the beginning of recorded history.

Long before journals, ledgers, and accounting software packages, business owners had a need for a recordkeeping system to help them make informed economic judgments and to maintain control over their assets. From approximately 8,000 B.C. to 3,000 B.C., a method of financial recordkeeping that relied upon heat-baked clay tokens evolved in the Middle Eastern cradle of civilization located in present-day Iraq.[1] These tokens were of varying shapes and sizes. A cylinder-shaped token represented one sheep, while a triangular token represented a certain quantity of grain. Eventually, property owners, or their accountants, made the important realization that a one-to-one correspondence did not have to exist between individual assets and tokens. For example, a cylindrical token etched with five horizontal lines could be used to represent five sheep.

Cuneiform writing, a method of recording information on clay tablets, developed in Sumeria around 3,000 B.C. Initially, cuneiform writing was used exclusively to maintain financial records for wealthy merchants. For the next several thousand years, there would be few major advancements in the technology of financial recordkeeping. The earliest known example of financial records employing a form of double-entry bookkeeping has been traced to the mid-fourteenth century in Genoa, Italy. Of course, Pacioli in the late fifteenth century would set the stage for the widespread adoption of double-entry bookkeeping across Europe and eventually the world. Five centuries later, Pacioli's Method of Venice serves as the engine that drives the manual accounting systems of small corner gas stations and the multimillion-dollar computerized accounting systems of multinational petroleum companies.

Now that you have been introduced to the accounting profession, basic accounting concepts, and the nature of accounting and control systems, you are ready to tackle the mechanical aspects of accounting. In this chapter, you learn how to journalize transactions, post transactions to a general ledger, and prepare a trial balance from a general ledger. Once you acquire these skills, you will be prepared to "walk through" the entire accounting cycle for a business in Chapter 5.

Chapter 3 discussed the far-reaching impact computers have had on accounting systems and organizational control functions. In this chapter and the following chapter, we examine the mechanical features of accounting by focusing principally on manual accounting systems rather than computer-based accounting systems. Why? Because

1. For an excellent discussion of prehistoric accounting methods, see the following article: R. Mattesich, "Prehistoric Accounting and the Problem of Representation: On Recent Archeological Evidence of the Middle East From 8000 B.C. to 3000 B.C.," *The Accounting Historians Journal*, Fall 1987, 71–91.

manual accounting systems are more easily grasped by accounting novices, such as yourself, than computer-based accounting systems. You should recognize that the computer does not change the fundamental nature of how transaction data are processed. True, as pointed out in Chapter 3, a computer dramatically increases the speed with which transaction data are processed and generally enhances the reliability of accounting records. However, a manual accounting system and a computerized accounting system operate in fundamentally the same way: information regarding business transactions is collected, processed, and funneled into a set of financial statements. Throughout this chapter and Chapter 5, key differences between the processing of financial data in manual and computer-based accounting systems will be described at appropriate points.

THE ACCOUNTING EQUATION

LEARNING OBJECTIVE 1
Analyze business transactions in reference to the accounting equation.

In Chapter 2, you learned that a balance sheet balances in the sense that the assets of a business must equal the sum of its liabilities and owners' equity. This relationship, known as the accounting equation, is graphically illustrated in Exhibit 4.1 for a corporation. We all learned in grade school that the numerical amounts on each side of an equation must be equal. This basic mathematical rule applies to the accounting equation. *Every transaction of a business must be recorded in such a way that the accounting equation for that business remains in balance.* In this section, we consider a few transactions of a small business to become familiar with the accounting equation and how accountants analyze business transactions in reference to this equation.

Bitsy Black and Allison Bryant have been friends since grade school. After graduating from the University of Minnesota with political science degrees, Bitsy and Allison decided to try their hand at business. So, in April 1998, the two friends scraped together $20,000 to establish a pizza shop, B&B's Pizzeria, a few blocks from the university campus. Following are the first three transactions of this business venture.

1. April 5: Opened a checking account for B&B's Pizzeria at a local bank and deposited $20,000.
2. April 7: Purchased $12,000 of equipment, paying $5,000 in cash and signing a note payable for the balance.
3. April 8: Purchased $1,000 of baking supplies and $2,500 of cooking utensils for cash.

EXHIBIT 4.1
The Accounting Equation

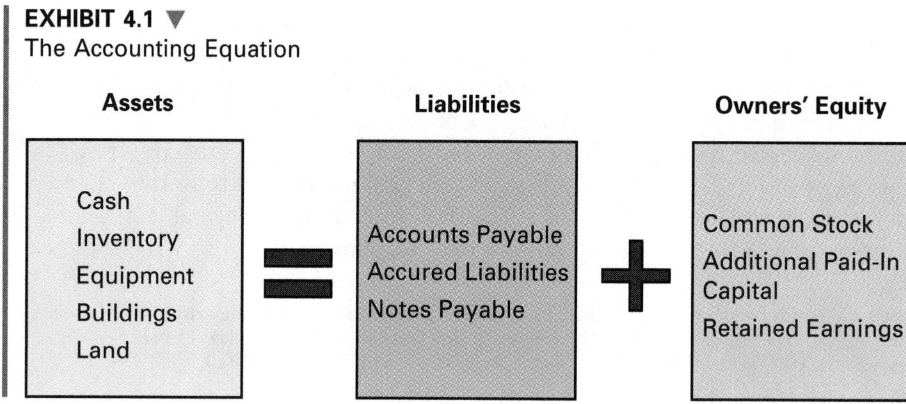

© Michael Newman/PhotoEdit

Businesses of all sizes and types, including neighborhood pizzerias, need a reliable accounting system to process their financial data and provide a means for preparing periodic financial statements.

We can use the accounting equation format shown next to record the first three transactions of this new business. This format contains a column for each financial statement item affected by these transactions. For the time being, think of these columns as simple accounts. Following each transaction, we will compute a new balance for the accounts affected by that transaction. Notice that the account for Bitsy and Allison's ownership interest in their business is entitled "B&B Equity." Separate equity accounts are typically established for each partner in a business venture, as discussed later in this textbook. Here, we will overlook that technicality and establish one equity account representing the joint ownership interest of the two co-owners of B&B's Pizzeria.

			Assets					Liabilities		Owners' Equity
Cash	+	Baking Supplies	+	Cooking Utensils	+	Equipment	=	Notes Payable	+	B&B Equity

When Bitsy and Allison launched their new business, they deposited $20,000 in a checking account entitled "B&B's Pizzeria" at a local bank. (Recall that the entity concept discussed in Chapter 2 requires business owners to segregate their personal assets from the assets of their business.) This initial transaction increased the business's assets from zero to $20,000 and established an equal amount of equity, or ownership interest, for Bitsy and Allison in the pizza shop. Following this transaction, the accounting equation for B&B's Pizzeria appeared as follows:

			Assets					Liabilities		Owners' Equity
Cash	+	Baking Supplies	+	Cooking Utensils	+	Equipment	=	Notes Payable	+	B&B Equity
$20,000							=			$20,000

When Bitsy and Allison purchased the equipment for their shop, they made a down payment of $5,000 and signed a note promising to pay the balance of the $12,000 purchase price by a specified date. This transaction affected three of the new business's accounts: (1) the balance of the Cash account decreased by $5,000, (2) the Equipment account increased from zero to $12,000, and (3) the Note Payable account increased from zero to $7,000. Notice that although two asset accounts and only one liability account were affected by this transaction, the net effect on each side of the accounting equation was $7,000: total assets and total liabilities both increased by that amount. So, our accounting equation for the pizza shop remains in balance.

Assets										**Liabilities**		**Owners' Equity**
Cash	+	Baking Supplies	+	Cooking Utensils	+	Equipment	=	Notes Payable	+	B&B Equity
$20,000							=			$20,000
– 5,000					+	12,000	=	+7,000		
$15,000					+	$12,000	=	$ 7,000	+	$20,000

Shortly after establishing their business, Bitsy and Allison purchased baking supplies at a cost of $1,000 and cooking utensils costing $2,500. The two owners paid cash for these items. This transaction only affected the assets component of the accounting equation, which is true of many business transactions. Two asset accounts, Baking Supplies and Cooking Utensils, increased from zero to $1,000 and $2,500, respectively, while another asset account, Cash, decreased from $15,000 to $11,500. Following this transaction, the total assets of B&B's Pizzeria remained at $27,000, which was also the sum of the business's liabilities and owners' equity.

Assets								**Liabilities**		**Owners' Equity**
Cash	+	Baking Supplies	+	Cooking Utensils	+	Equipment	=	Notes Payable	+	B&B Equity
$15,000	+					$12,000	=	$7,000	+	$20,000
– 3,500	+	1,000	+	2,500			=			
$11,500	+	$1,000	+	$2,500	+	$12,000	=	$7,000	+	$20,000

So, there you have it. After the first three transactions of B&B's Pizzeria, the business's accounting equation is in balance. The transactions illustrated for this business are simple ones. Additionally, each of these transactions affected only items appearing on the business's balance sheet. Later in this chapter we consider more complex, "real world" transactions, including transactions that affect revenues and expenses, that is, income statement items.

DOUBLE-ENTRY BOOKKEEPING RULES

Theoretically, we could use the accounting "system" illustrated in the previous section for an actual business. However, that simple system becomes cumbersome when the number of columns (accounts) becomes quite large. As you learned in Chapter 3, businesses

Accounting Software for Pizzerias . . . and Other Small Businesses

FOR YOUR INFORMATION

Chapter 3 mentioned that small business owners can establish their own accounting system with a small investment in a personal computer and an inexpensive accounting software package. Periodically, the *Journal of Accountancy* reviews accounting software packages available on the market. Following is a list of selected "low-end" accounting software programs profiled by that publication in May 1996. The retail price reported for each program is also listed.

BusinessWorks for Windows	$995.00
DacEasy Accounting & Payroll 95	149.95
Mind Your Own Business Accounting	209.95
One-Write Plus	69.00
Peachtree Accounting for Windows	169.00
Profit	299.00
QuickBooks for Windows	189.00
Simply Accounting	89.00

Source: W. Schulz, "Buyers' Guide to Low-End Accounting Software," *Journal of Accountancy,* May 1996, 49–60.

enter financial data in accounting records known as journals and ledgers. The rules of double-entry bookkeeping dictate how financial data are "booked" in those accounting records. This section presents the bookkeeping rules for each major type of account. Before these rules are presented, the bookkeeping terms "debit" and "credit" are discussed.

Debits and Credits?

LEARNING OBJECTIVE 2
Determine whether increases and decreases in specific accounts are recorded as debits or credits.

Accountants are often asked, "Exactly what is a debit and a credit?" An accountant steeped in the history of the profession might go into a long discourse regarding the original Latin terms from which "debit" and "credit" evolved. For our purposes, simply remember that **debit** refers to the left-hand side of a T-account, while **credit** refers to the right-hand side of a T-account. When an accountant refers to a "debit," he or she is typically referring to an amount entered on the left-hand side of an account. Shown next is a cash T-account for B&B's Pizzeria following the first three transactions of the new business. Notice that the account contains a $20,000 "debit," which stemmed from the owners' initial investment in the business. As a verb, "debit" means to enter a given amount on the left-hand side of an account. For example, following the initial transaction of B&B's Pizzeria, Allison may have said to her friend, business partner, and bookkeeper, "Bitsy, debit Cash $20,000."

debit

credit

Cash

	4/5/98	20,000	4/7/98	5,000
			4/8/98	3,500
Balance	4/9/98	11,500		

Alphonse Capone: Debit This

The bookkeeper for the infamous Chicago gangster, Al Capone, once bragged that he could steal much more with his bookkeeping tools—pen and paper, debits and credits—than Capone's henchmen could with their arsenal of guns. A common method that organized crime syndicates use to misappropriate funds from legitimate businesses they own is a so-called "skimming" operation. This scheme involves avoiding taxes by systematically understating or "skimming" the cash receipts taken in by a business.

Federal authorities uncovered and prosecuted a large-scale skimming operation in the early 1980s. This fraud involved several popular nightclubs in New York City including the Peppermint Lounge, the Mardi Gras, the Haymarket, and the Grapevine. Over a three-year period, federal prosecutors proved that the nightclubs' owners failed to report more than $2 million taken in by the Mardi Gras alone. A key figure in the skimming operation was an accountant who regularly made bookkeeping entries understating the cash receipts taken in by these Big Apple watering holes. Federal authorities indicted this individual on charges of preparing fraudulent financial statements and false tax returns for the nightclubs. Eventually, nine participants in the crime ring, including the accountant, were convicted of fraud.

In a four-column account format, the term "debit" refers to an amount entered in the debit column or to the process of entering an amount in the debit column. The phrase "debit balance" indicates that the net amount, or balance, of an account is a debit rather than a credit. (Notice that the Cash T-account of B&B's Pizzeria just shown had a debit balance of $11,500 on April 9, 1998.) Accountants use the term "credit" to refer to an amount entered on the right-hand side of a T-account or an amount entered in the credit column of a four-column account. Likewise, as a verb, "credit" refers to the process of entering an amount on the right-hand side of a T-account or in the credit column of a four-column account.

Accountants use debits and credits to define the bookkeeping rules and normal balance for each type of general ledger account. Exhibit 4.2 summarizes these bookkeeping rules and normal account balances. As shown in Exhibit 4.2, assets and expenses normally have debit balances, while liabilities, owners' equity items, and revenues are expected to have credit balances. Notice that Exhibit 4.2 identifies assets, liabilities, and owners' equity accounts as "permanent accounts," while revenues and expenses are identified as "temporary accounts." Shortly, the underlying meaning of each of these terms will be explained.

Recall a key point made regarding bookkeeping rules in Chapter 3, namely, that these rules are arbitrary. Many analogies to the arbitrary rules used by accountants can be drawn from the sports world—apologies to those of you who are non-sports types. For instance, in baseball why is first base to the right of the home plate umpire, while third base is to his (or her) left? Wouldn't it be just as reasonable for first base to be

EXHIBIT 4.2 ▼
Debit and Credit Rules

	Permanent Accounts			Temporary Accounts	
	Assets	Liabilities	Owners' Equity	Revenues	Expenses
To Increase	Debit	Credit	Credit	Credit	Debit
To Decrease	Credit	Debit	Debit	Debit	Credit
Normal Account Balance	Debit	Credit	Credit	Credit	Debit

third base, and vice versa? Likewise, why are horse races run in a counterclockwise direction in this country, while they are run in a clockwise direction in Great Britain? The answers to these and other probing questions will have to be examined later. For now, simply accept, and imprint into your long-term memory, the debit and credit rules summarized in Exhibit 4.2.

Recognize that the basic bookkeeping rules presented here are applied in both manual and electronic or computer-based accounting systems. In either type of accounting system, the key is to capture and record the dual nature of each transaction or event affecting a business. Accountants accomplish this objective by developing equivalent debits and credits for these transactions and events.

Asset Accounts

LEARNING ◀ OBJECTIVE 3
Identify the normal balance, debit balance or credit balance, of the different types of accounts.

Chapter 3 briefly introduced the bookkeeping rules for asset accounts. Allow Exhibit 4.2 to refresh your memory regarding those rules. Increases in assets are recorded as debits, while decreases in assets are recorded as credits. Also notice in Exhibit 4.2 that asset accounts normally have debit balances. Is it possible for asset accounts to have credit balances? Yes, but only under unusual circumstances. For example, suppose that a company overdraws its bank account by $250 and that its general ledger Cash account reflects a credit balance of that same amount. (You will learn in a subsequent chapter that the balance of a company's bank account and its corresponding Cash account in the general ledger are not necessarily equal.) Under these circumstances, the company owes its bank $250. If the company prepares a balance sheet at this point, it would not list the $250 as a negative cash item in that balance sheet. Instead, the $250 would be listed as an account payable in the current liabilities section of the balance sheet.

Liability Accounts

Liability accounts are, in a sense, mirror images of asset accounts. Accounts payable, notes payable, and other liability accounts normally have credit balances. Likewise, increases in liability accounts are recorded as credits, while decreases are recorded as debits, just the opposite of the bookkeeping rules for asset accounts. Like asset accounts, individual liability accounts may occasionally have an abnormal balance. As you would expect, a debit balance is considered abnormal for liability accounts.

Owners' Equity Accounts

Before considering the bookkeeping rules for owners' equity accounts, we should first define the terms "permanent accounts" and "temporary accounts." Balance sheet accounts are referred to as permanent accounts. The period-ending balances of **permanent accounts**, such as Cash and Equipment, are carried forward to the next accounting period. This is not true of income statement accounts, such as Interest Revenue and Advertising Expense. The dollar amounts associated with revenue and expense transactions are stored temporarily in revenue and expense accounts during an accounting period. At the end of each accounting period, after a business's net income has been determined, the balances of revenue and expense accounts are transferred or "closed" to an owners' equity account. As a result, revenue and expense accounts begin each new accounting period with a zero balance. For this reason, these accounts are referred to as **temporary accounts.**

permanent accounts

temporary accounts

The bookkeeping rules for owners' equity accounts are identical to the bookkeeping rules for liabilities. Increases in these accounts are recorded as credits, while decreases are recorded as debits. Likewise, these accounts normally have credit balances. **Retained Earnings** is a key stockholders' (owners') equity account of corporations. At any point in time, the balance of this account represents a company's net earnings (revenues minus expenses) since its inception less any dividends distributed to the firm's stockholders. As you may have guessed, Retained Earnings is the account to which the balances of revenues and expenses are "closed" each accounting period. Revenues closed to Retained Earnings increase the balance of that account, while expenses closed to Retained Earnings decrease the account's balance. More generally, revenues increase stockholders' (owners') equity, while expenses decrease stockholders' (owners') equity.

Retained Earnings

Temporary Accounts

Increases in revenue accounts are recorded as credits, while increases in expense accounts are recorded as debits. Seldom do either revenue or expense accounts have abnormal balances. Revenue accounts nearly always have credit balances, while expense accounts nearly always have debit balances.

Besides revenue and expense accounts, there is one additional temporary account not listed in Exhibit 4.2. For corporations, this account is typically entitled Dividends. Many corporations regularly distribute a portion of their earnings to stockholders. These distributions are referred to as dividends. For bookkeeping purposes, dividends are recorded similarly to expenses, that is, as debits. Likewise, a Dividends account normally has a debit balance and the period-ending balance of this account is transferred or closed to Retained Earnings. However, dividends paid by a corporation to its stockholders are not expenses and thus have no impact on the corporation's net income. These amounts are reported as a reduction in retained earnings in a company's statement of stockholders' equity.[2] In a subsequent chapter, we examine in more depth accounting issues related to the payment of dividends to stockholders.

Exhibit 4.2 summarizes bookkeeping rules in a tabular format. These same rules are integrated with the accounting equation and with the format of T-accounts in Exhibit 4.3. This latter exhibit also includes an expanded analysis of bookkeeping rules for

---

2. Companies often invest in the common stock of other firms. For example, on any given date, Exxon may own common stock of dozens of other companies. Dividends received by one company from another are typically recorded in a revenue account entitled Dividend Revenue and reported on the income statement under Other Revenues and Expenses.

EXHIBIT 4.3 ▼
Summary of Bookkeeping Rules Integrated with the Accounting Equation and the Format of T-Accounts

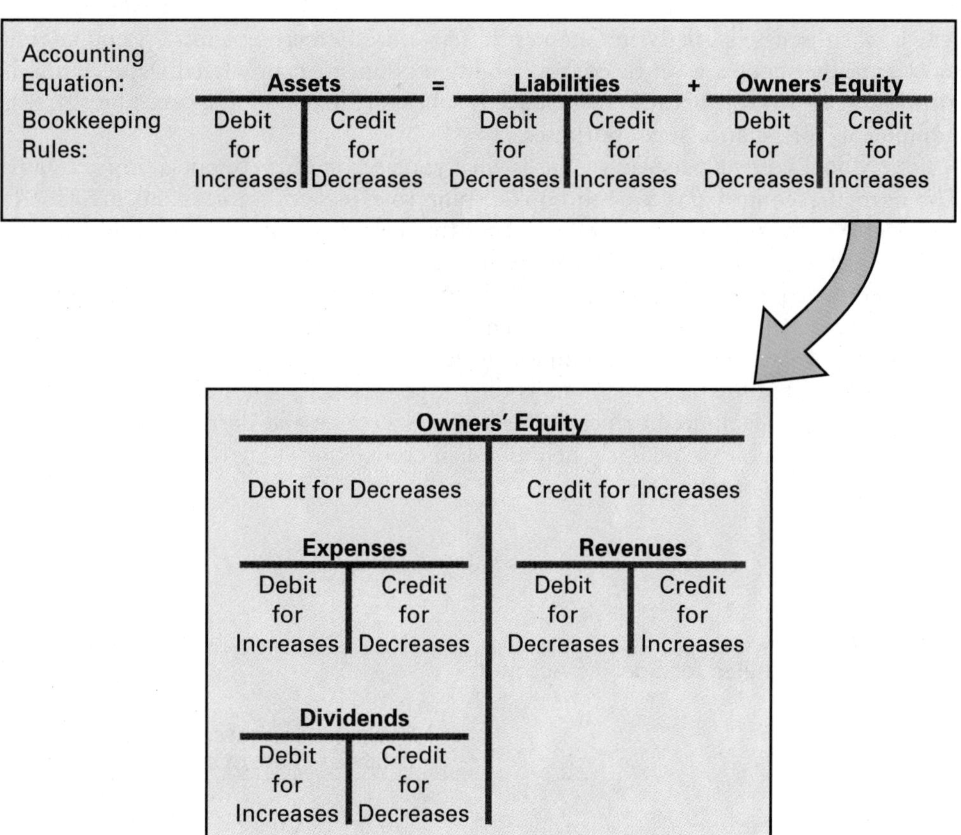

owners' equity accounts and the temporary accounts whose balances are eventually closed to an owners' equity account.

To help "cement" the debit/credit rules in your mind, you might correlate those rules with the accounting equation with the help of Exhibit 4.3. Assets appear on the left-hand side of the accounting equation. To increase an asset, you must debit the account or enter the given dollar amount on the left-hand side of the account. Liabilities and owners' equity appear on the right-hand side of the accounting equation. To record an increase in one of these accounts, you must credit the account, that is, enter the given dollar amount on the right-hand side of the account. If you can embed in your long-term memory the debit/credit rules for increases in given types of accounts, you can then remind yourself to use opposite debit/credit rules to record decreases in each type of account.

Contra Accounts

There is one final type of account that should be mentioned before we wrap up our overview of bookkeeping rules. **Contra accounts** are treated as offsets or reductions **contra accounts** to related accounts for financial statement purposes. These accounts are maintained independently during an accounting period, but then their balances are subtracted from related account balances in the appropriate financial statement at the end of the accounting period. An example of a contra account is Accumulated Depreciation, which was discussed briefly in Chapter 2. There are numerous contra accounts, but most are either contra asset or contra liability accounts. Accumulated Depreciation is a contra asset account because its balance is subtracted from an asset account, such as Equipment, for balance sheet purposes.

From a bookkeeping perspective, this is what you need to know about contra accounts: The normal account balances and bookkeeping rules for contra accounts are exactly the reverse of those shown in Exhibit 4.2 for the related type of account. For instance, contra asset accounts normally have credit balances and are increased by credits and decreased by debits. One more? Contra liability accounts normally have debit balances and are increased by debits and decreased by credits.

Exhibit 4.4 lists numerous examples of accounts that you will encounter in this course. Also listed for these accounts is their type (asset, liability, and so on), normal balance, and the debit/credit rules for recording increases and decreases in each. You may find this exhibit particularly helpful when completing homework assignments in this chapter and later chapters.

EXHIBIT 4.4 ▼
Debit and Credit Rules for Specific Accounts

Account	Type	Normal Balance	Increases Record as	Decreases Recorded as
Accounts Payable	Liability	Credit	Credit	Debit
Accounts Receivable	Asset	Debit	Debit	Credit
Accumulated Depreciation, Equipment	Contra Asset	Credit	Credit	Debit
Advertising Expense	Expense	Debit	Debit	Credit
Common Stock	Owners' Equity	Credit	Credit	Debit
Depreciation Expense	Expense	Debit	Debit	Credit
Equipment	Asset	Debit	Debit	Credit
Fee Revenue	Revenue	Credit	Credit	Debit
Income Taxes Expense	Expense	Debit	Debit	Credit
Interest Expense	Expense	Debit	Debit	Credit
Interest Revenue	Revenue	Credit	Credit	Debit
Inventory	Asset	Debit	Debit	Credit
Land	Asset	Debit	Debit	Credit
Notes Payable	Liability	Credit	Credit	Debit
Retained Earnings	Owners' Equity	Credit	Credit	Debit
Salaries Expense	Expense	Debit	Debit	Credit
Sales Revenue	Revenue	Credit	Credit	Debit
Service Revenues	Revenue	Credit	Credit	Debit
Short-Term Investments	Asset	Debit	Debit	Credit
Supplies	Asset	Debit	Debit	Credit

Arthur Edward Andersen: Credit This

An earlier vignette referred to the creative bookkeeping employed by the crime syndicate of Chicago gangster Al Capone. A contemporary of Alphonse Capone was Arthur Edward Andersen. The two men shared common backgrounds. Both men were born of immigrant parents of modest means during the late nineteenth century. Capone's parents immigrated to the United States from Italy, while Andersen's parents came from Norway. Both men were energetic, ambitious, and chose Chicago as their adopted hometown and the place where they would seek their fortune.

Unlike Capone, Andersen pursued a legitimate livelihood in Chicago. In 1908, the 23-year-old Andersen, then an employee of the prestigious accounting firm of Price Waterhouse, became the youngest CPA in Illinois. A few years later, Andersen formed an accounting firm of his own. Andersen, DeLany & Company soon became simply Arthur Andersen & Company when Arthur's partner left the firm. While Capone was overseeing his crime syndicate during the 1920s and 1930s, Andersen was expanding his accounting firm. Following his death in 1947, Andersen's fellow partners continued the legacy of his firm: hard work, uncompromising ethics, and a dedication to serving the public interest. By the late 1990s, Arthur Andersen & Company was the largest accounting firm worldwide with annual revenues of several billion dollars.

JOURNALIZING TRANSACTIONS

LEARNING OBJECTIVE 4
Prepare general journal entries.

This section acquaints you with the procedures to follow in journalizing transactions and other events affecting businesses. Preparing journal entries is the starting point of the accounting cycle that must be completed for a business each accounting period. If the journal entries prepared by an organization's accountants are incorrect or incomplete, these errors will be carried through the remainder of the accounting cycle. The eventual result will be inaccurate financial statements and potentially improper decisions by the parties relying on those statements.

Journalizing, Easy as 1, 2, 3 . . .

To illustrate the mechanical aspects of preparing a general journal entry, let us return to the initial transaction of B&B's Pizzeria. On April 5, 1998, our friends Bitsy Black and Allison Bryant deposited $20,000 in a bank account to establish their jointly owned business. At the top of the following page is the general journal entry reflecting this transaction.

Mechanically, the following steps are required to prepare a general journal entry that involves two accounts.

1. Enter the year, month, and date of the entry in the columns on the left-hand margin of the general journal as just shown. Typically, the year and month are recorded only at the top of each page of the general journal.

GENERAL JOURNAL					Page 1
Date		Description	Post Ref.	Debit	Credit
1998 Apr.	5	Cash		20,000	
		B&B Equity			20,000
		Initial investment in business			

2. Refer to the chart of accounts to identify the appropriate titles for the accounts affected by the transaction.
3. Enter the title of the account to be debited in the description column on the same line that the date was entered.
4. On the following line, indent two spaces and enter the title of the account to be credited.
5. Insert in the debit column—on the line on which the title of the account to be debited was entered—the amount of the transaction, and insert in the credit column—on the line on which the title of the account to be credited was entered —the same amount.
6. In the description column, two lines below the title of the account credited, write a brief explanation describing the nature of the transaction. This explanation may be omitted if the nature of the transaction is obvious.

compound journal entry

An entry that affects more than two accounts is known as a **compound journal entry.** The steps for recording a journal entry involving only two accounts must be modified, but only slightly, when recording a compound journal entry. To illustrate a compound journal entry, return to the second transaction of B&B's Pizzeria. On April 7, 1998, B&B's Pizzeria purchased $12,000 of equipment, paying $5,000 in cash and signing a note payable for the balance. Following is the general journal entry to record this transaction.

GENERAL JOURNAL					Page 1
Date		Description	Post Ref.	Debit	Credit
1998 Apr.	7	Equipment		12,000	
		Cash			5,000
		Notes Payable			7,000
		Purchased equipment; paid $5,000 down and signed note for balance			

Compound journal entries may have several debits and one credit, several credits and a single debit, or multiple debits and multiple credits. Like all journal entries, the dollar amount of debits and the dollar amount of credits in a compound journal entry must be equal.

Journalizing in Computer-Based Accounting Systems

Although the process of preparing a journal entry in a computer-based accounting system is very different than in a manual accounting system, the result is the same. In either case, the dual nature of the transaction is recorded in the given entity's accounting records. Likewise, as suggested earlier, journalizing in both types of systems relies on the double-entry bookkeeping rules summarized in Exhibit 4.2. In some computer-based accounting systems, data entry clerks "key" transaction data directly into a firm's accounting system. Typically, these clerks utilize electronic formats often referred to as templates to prepare electronic journal entries. These templates contain "blanks" for each major feature of a transaction, including the date, the accounts affected, the dollar amounts involved, and so on. The design of these templates allows data entry clerks who have little or no familiarity with the double-entry accounting rules discussed in this chapter to feed financial data into a company's accounting system.

In more sophisticated computer-based accounting systems, transaction data may be captured and fed into a company's accounting system electronically with little, or no, "human" assistance. For example, in department stores, data for sales transactions are often captured by electronic scanning devices at the point of sale. As discussed in Chapter 3, firms participating in an EDI (electronic data interchange) network have transactions "triggered" electronically. For example, a purchase transaction may be initiated when a company's inventory of a given item falls below a certain level. The electronic "purchase order" will be transmitted over the EDI network to the supplier's accounting system, which will then initiate a corresponding "sales order." Both companies' accounting records will be updated automatically—including all of the appropriate debits and credits—when the transaction is completed.

Even small businesses can integrate computer processing into their accounting systems to simplify and expedite tedious tasks such as journalizing transaction data. Among the most popular "low-end" accounting software packages used by small businesses is QuickBooks, which is produced and distributed by Intuit.

© Photography by Joe Higgins

Accounting Illustrated: A Sample of Real World Journal Entries

How do you learn to ride a bicycle, twirl a baton, or do the Cotton-Eyed Joe? Practice! Practice! Practice! The same is true for accounting, particularly when it comes to the basic bookkeeping rules that dictate how transactions should be journalized. To help you sharpen your journalizing skills, this section presents several business transactions for which journal entries are developed. These transactions were drawn from recent annual reports of large corporations.

For each transaction presented in this section, a transaction analysis is first performed. This analysis involves the following steps: identify the accounts affected by the transaction (since we do not have access to these companies' charts of accounts, an appropriate title is provided for each account); indicate whether these accounts are asset accounts, liability accounts, and so on; determine whether the transaction increased or decreased these accounts; and decide whether these increases or decreases should be recorded as debits or credits. After completing the transaction analysis, the effect of the transaction on the company's accounting equation is determined. Finally, a general journal entry is prepared for the transaction. Recognize that the journal entries illustrated in this section were not recorded by the given companies exactly as they are depicted here. For example, in most cases, numerous individual transactions have been consolidated into one "mega-transaction." Likewise, we will assume that each transaction involved the exchange of cash, which was not necessarily true.

The tasks just listed are completed for each of the real-world transactions presented; however, you may want to attempt these tasks yourself before reviewing the completed solutions. The format of the general journal entry developed for each transaction is a simplified version of the format illustrated earlier. This format contains only the titles of the accounts affected by the entry and the dollar amount of each debit and credit. For instance, the compound journal entry discussed earlier would be recorded as follows using this simplified format.

Equipment	12,000	
Cash		5,000
Notes Payable		7,000

Notice that in this format the accounts debited are listed first, followed by the accounts credited, which are indented two spaces. On the right-hand side of this format are two imaginary columns, one for debit amounts and one for credit amounts.

Noise Cancellation Technologies, Inc.

This company's name "gives away" its line of business. Noise Cancellation Technologies designs, develops, produces, and distributes electronic systems to reduce noise and vibration. To help finance its operations, Noise Cancellation Technologies borrows funds from various parties. During a recent year, the company paid $450,000 to retire a debt (note payable).

Transaction Analysis:

Account	Type	Increase/ Decrease	Debit or Credit	Amount
Notes Payable	Liability	Decrease	Debit	$450,000
Cash	Asset	Decrease	Credit	450,000

Effect on Accounting Equation:

Assets	=	Liabilities	+	Owners' Equity
−450,00		−450,000		

Journal Entry:

Notes Payable.	450,000	
Cash		450,000

Oriole Homes Corporation

Oriole Homes Corporation is a Florida-based homebuilding firm. During a recent year, Oriole Homes had income tax expense of $2,523,065, which was paid in cash.

Transaction Analysis:

Account	Type	Increase/ Decrease	Debit or Credit	Amount
Income Taxes Expense	Expense	Increase	Debit	$2,523,065
Cash	Asset	Decrease	Credit	2,523,065

Effect on Accounting Equation:

Assets	=	Liabilities	+	Owners' Equity
−2,523,065				−2,523,065

Journal Entry:

Income Taxes Expense	2,523,065	
Cash.		2,523,065

Excalibur Technologies Corporation

The core business of Excalibur Technologies is adaptive pattern recognition processing. This technology allows organizations to index and retrieve information electronically and to eliminate paper documentation. One important source of revenue for Excalibur is consulting services related to the installation and operation of its products. These service revenues totaled approximately $540,000 during a recent year.

Transaction Analysis:

Account	Type	Increase/ Decrease	Debit or Credit	Amount
Cash	Asset	Increase	Debit	$540,000
Service Revenues	Revenue	Increase	Credit	540,000

Effect on Accounting Equation:

Assets	=	Liabilities	+	Owners' Equity
+540,000				+540,000

Journal Entry:

Cash	540,000	
Service Revenues		540,000

Honda Motor Co., Ltd.

Like most large companies, Honda Motor Co. invests much of its excess cash in short-term certificates of deposit and other interest-yielding investments. A recent annual report of this company disclosed that it earned and received interest revenue of 34,382 million yen, which translated to $384,801,000. (The financial statements that Honda distributes in the United States express monetary amounts in both yen and U.S. dollars.)

Transaction Analysis:

Account	Type	Increase/ Decrease	Debit or Credit	Amount
Cash	Asset	Increase	Debit	$384,801,000
Interest Revenue	Revenue	Increase	Credit	384,801,000

Effect on Accounting Equation:

Assets	=	Liabilities	+	Stockholders' Equity
+384,801,000				+384,801,000

Journal Entry:

Cash	384,801,000	
Interest Revenue		384,801,000

Barnes & Noble, Inc.

During a recent fiscal year, Barnes & Noble, Inc., a retail bookstore chain, sold 321,724 copies of *The Rainmaker,* a novel written by accountant/attorney/author John Grisham. In the year in question, the company also paid $154,913,000 to acquire equipment and related assets.

Transaction Analysis:

Account	Type	Increase/ Decrease	Debit or Credit	Amount
Equipment	Asset	Increase	Debit	$154,913,000
Cash	Asset	Decrease	Credit	154,913,000

Effect on Accounting Equation:

Assets	=	Liabilities	+	Owners' Equity
+154,913,000				
−154,913,000				

Journal Entry:

Equipment	154,913,000	
Cash		154,913,000

Groundwater Technology, Inc.

Groundwater Technology provides environmental consulting and remediation services, principally to large oil firms. Remediation involves the restoration of soil and water contaminated by petroleum products. To motivate employees and executives to perform at a high level, this company has established a bonus incentive plan. During a recent year, Groundwater Technology paid out $283,000 under the terms of this plan.

Transaction Analysis:

Account	Type	Increase/ Decrease	Debit or Credit	Amount
Salaries Expense	Expense	Increase	Debit	$283,000
Cash	Asset	Decrease	Credit	283,000

Effect on Accounting Equation:

Assets	=	Liabilities	+	Owners' Equity
−283,000				−283,000

Journal Entry:

Salaries Expense.	283,000	
Cash		283,000

Entries, Entries, and More Entries

Most of the journal entries illustrated in this chapter have been for typical business transactions. Besides these normal, recurring journal entries, there are several "special" entries that accountants record either at regular intervals or whenever appropriate. These special entries include correcting entries, adjusting entries, and closing entries.

Correcting entries amend errors in previously recorded journal entries. For example, if a company paid cash of $3,500 for a piece of equipment but debited the Equipment account and credited the Cash account for $5,300, a correcting entry would be required. This entry would include a debit to the Cash account of $1,800 and an equal credit to the Equipment account. Correcting entries are typically made shortly following the discovery of bookkeeping errors. **correcting entries**

Adjusting entries and closing entries are made at the end of each accounting period. Accountants prepare **adjusting entries** to ensure that the revenue recognition and expense recognition rules discussed in Chapter 2 are properly applied each accounting period. **adjusting entries**

Ru, Chu, and Yu: The Three Pillars of Chinese Bookkeeping

FOR YOUR INFORMATION

Western accounting scholars credit Italian merchants of the Middle Ages with developing double-entry bookkeeping. However, elaborate financial records were maintained in ancient China well before the birth of Christ. Accountants for the dynasties that ruled ancient China developed sophisticated recordkeeping systems to document receipts and expenditures, to prepare budgets, and to issue periodic financial statements. Before the invention of paper around 100 A.D. by Chinese court official Cai Lun, Chinese financial statements were prepared on bamboo or silk scrolls.

Early Chinese accounting systems revolved around a single-entry, rather than double-entry, bookkeeping method. The monetary amount of each transaction was entered only once in early Chinese accounting records. The descriptive label, Ru (in), was used to identify each transaction involving a receipt, while Chu (out) was the label used to identify each disbursement transaction. At the end of an accounting period, the collective wealth or "equity" of a given entity was determined using the "three-pillars balancing equation": Ru (in) − Chu (out) = Yu (balance).

For example, adjusting entries are required to recognize expenses that a business has incurred at the end of an accounting period but not yet paid or recorded. As mentioned earlier, the balances of all temporary accounts including revenues, expenses, and dividends are transferred to an owners' equity account at the end of each accounting period. This task is accomplished by the preparation of **closing entries.**

closing entries

Journalizing: A Few Helpful Hints and Reminders

"Hints from Heloise" is a column that has appeared in international newspapers for decades. Heloise provides her readers, of all ages, with assorted helpful hints. These hints range from six ways to turn an empty milk carton into a Christmas gift for Grannie to advice for college students regarding everything from money management to doing their laundry. Exhibit 4.5 contains a few helpful hints and reminders for accountants-in-training who want to perfect their journalizing skills.

The most effective method of preventing or detecting journalizing errors is to review each journal entry carefully before turning your attention to another entry or accounting task. When reviewing a journal entry, one useful technique is to ask yourself whether the entry "makes sense" from the standpoint of the given business's normal operating activities. For example, a journal entry that includes a debit to Equipment and a credit to Salaries Expense is immediately suspect for any business and should be reviewed carefully.

Another helpful review technique is to analyze journal entries in reference to the accounting equation. Remember that the net dollar effect of a transaction on each side of the accounting equation must be equal. When all of the accounts affected by a transaction are on one side of the accounting equation, the net effect of the transaction on that side of the equation must be zero. For instance, a transaction that affects only assets must result in an increase in one or more asset accounts that is exactly equal to the decrease in one or more other asset accounts.

The most obvious hint when it comes to booking journal entries is that debits must equal credits. In entries involving only two accounts, violations of this fundamental rule are rare—but they still occur. Students are more prone to overlook this type of error when making compound journal entries, particularly compound journal entries that have several debits and several credits. Keep in mind that an entry may have an unequal number of debits and credits as long as the collective dollar amount of the debits is equal to the collective dollar amount of the credits. Also recognize that just because an entry has an equal dollar amount of debits and credits does not mean that

EXHIBIT 4.5 ▼
Journalizing: A Few Helpful Hints and Reminders

- Review the accounts affected by a journal entry to determine whether they "make sense" from the perspective of the business's normal operating activities.
- Determine that a journal entry is balanced in reference to the accounting equation and in terms of debits and credits.
- Review a journal entry for transposition errors and "slipped" decimals.
- Recognize that businesses use the terms "debit" and "credit" in reference to the impact that transactions have on their financial records instead of the impact those transactions have on the personal financial records of their customers.

it is free of error. For example, a "balanced" entry may contain a debit and/or credit to an improper account or an equal but incorrect dollar total for both debits and credits.

Among the more common journalizing errors are transposition errors and "slipped" decimals. Distracted or fatigued accountants often transpose two consecutive numerals in a journal entry. For instance, if an entry calls for a debit of $3,159 to Inventory and an equal credit to Cash, the journal entry may actually be recorded with a debit of $3,159 to Inventory and a $3,519 credit to Cash. An example of a slipped decimal would be recording a $42,300 decrease in Notes Payable as a decrease (debit) of $4,230. One important advantage of a computer-based accounting system is that controls can be written into accounting software to detect, and sometimes automatically correct, errors that occur during the journalizing process. For example, journal entries containing unequal debits or credits may be automatically included in an error listing that is periodically routed to an accountant's e-mail address.

Finally, you should be cautious when comparing the impact of debits and credits on the financial affairs of businesses with the implications those terms have for your own financial affairs. For a business, a debit to an asset account indicates that the given asset has increased, which is generally good news for the business. However, when you open your monthly bank statement and a "debit memo" falls out, that is not good news. A debit memo in your bank statement for a monthly service charge increases the bank's cash balance and decreases your cash balance. If you maintain a set of double-entry accounting records to keep track of your personal finances, you would credit, not debit, your cash account when you find a debit memo in your bank statement. Likewise, when you make a deposit and the bank clerk "credits" your savings account, your account balance will increase not decrease. Why does the bank clerk credit your account? Because your savings account is a liability from the bank's perspective and your deposit has increased that liability. The moral here is that when businesses use the terms "debit" and "credit," they use those terms in reference to the impact that transactions have on their financial records—not the financial records of their customers.

POSTING AND PREPARATION OF THE TRIAL BALANCE

LEARNING OBJECTIVE 5

Post general journal entries to a general ledger.

Besides journalizing, there are several other procedures that must be performed each accounting period in the accounting cycle. To set the stage for a discussion of the entire accounting cycle in Chapter 5, let us review two more of these procedures, the posting of data to the general ledger and the preparation of a trial balance.

Posting

Posting financial data from the general journal and other journals of a business to its general ledger serves the purpose of summarizing that data by specific type of account. These summarized data can then be used to prepare financial statements at the end of an accounting period for the business. In this section, we review the specific steps that should be followed in posting data from general journal entries to the appropriate general ledger accounts.

Following is the compound journal entry for B&B's Pizzeria that we developed to record the company's purchase of equipment. We will use this entry to illustrate the posting process. This entry affects three accounts. So, we will need to post data from this journal entry to three general ledger accounts.

GENERAL JOURNAL					Page 1
Date		Description	Post Ref.	Debit	Credit
1998 Apr.	7	Equipment Cash Notes Payable Purchased equipment; paid $5,000 down and signed note for balance		12,000	 5,000 7,000

After referring to the chart of accounts of B&B's Pizzeria, assume that we located the following general ledger accounts affected by the previous journal entry. Recognize that these accounts are presented before the posting of that journal entry. Notice that no prior amounts have been posted to two of the three accounts, Equipment and Notes Payable. The other account, Cash, has an existing balance of $20,000.

Cash							Account No. 101
						Balance	
Date		Explanation	Post Ref.	Debit	Credit	Debit	Credit
1998 Apr.	5	B&B investment	GJ1	20,000		20,000	

Equipment							Account No. 151
						Balance	
Date		Explanation	Post Ref.	Debit	Credit	Debit	Credit

Notes Payable							Account No. 241
						Balance	
Date		Explanation	Post Ref.	Debit	Credit	Debit	Credit

Listed next are the steps to follow in posting the data from the general journal entry for the purchase of equipment to the general ledger accounts affected by that transaction.

1. In the date column of each account, record the date of the transaction (April 7, 1998, in this case).
2. In each account's explanation column, enter a brief description of the transaction.
3. In the initial debit and credit columns for each account, enter the amount of the transaction affecting that account. If the amount affecting an account is a debit, the amount is entered in the debit column. Likewise, credit amounts are entered in the credit column.
4. Compute the new balance of each account and enter that amount in either the debit or credit balance column. (The new balance of the Cash account is a debit balance of $15,000, which is the original debit balance of $20,000 less the credit posted to that account of $5,000.)
5. In the post reference column of each account, indicate the journal from which the amount was posted and the page number of that journal. (In our example, "GJ1" is inserted in the post reference column to indicate that each amount was posted from page 1 of the general journal.)
6. For each account included in the journal entry, record in the post reference column of the general journal the number of that account to indicate that the given debit or credit amount was posted to the appropriate general ledger account.

Following are the general journal entry for the equipment purchase transaction and the general ledger accounts affected by this entry after the completion of the posting process.

GENERAL JOURNAL					Page 1
Date		Description	Post Ref.	Debit	Credit
1998					
Apr.	7	Equipment	151	12,000	
		Cash	101		5,000
		Notes Payable	241		7,000
		Purchased equipment; paid $5,000 down and signed note for balance			

Cash						Account No. 101	
						Balance	
Date		Explanation	Post Ref.	Debit	Credit	Debit	Credit
1998							
Apr.	5	B&B investment	GJ1	20,000		20,000	
	7	Equipment purchase	GJ1		5,000	15,000	

Equipment						Account No. 151	
			Post			Balance	
Date		Explanation	Ref.	Debit	Credit	Debit	Credit
1998 Apr.	7	Equipment purchase	GJ1	12,000		12,000	

Notes Payable						Account No. 241	
			Post			Balance	
Date		Explanation	Ref.	Debit	Credit	Debit	Credit
1998 Apr.	7	Equipment purchase	GJ1		7,000		7,000

Journal entry data may be posted only once per week, or even on a monthly basis, in a manual accounting system. In computer-based accounting systems, transaction data are typically posted to general ledger accounts simultaneously with the journalizing process. As the data for a transaction are keyed into a computerized accounting system by a data entry clerk or captured electronically by the system, a chronological record (journal entry) of the transaction is prepared. At the same time, the dollar amounts involved in the transaction are electronically routed (posted) to the computer files (accounts) of the financial statement items affected by the transaction. Of course, proper programming instructions "tell" the computer whether to add or subtract (debit or credit) these dollar amounts to the individual accounts to correctly update their balances.

Preparation of a Trial Balance

LEARNING OBJECTIVE 6 ▶
Prepare a trial balance of a general ledger.

trial balance

At the end of each accounting period, accountants "close the books" of a business. The primary purpose of the closing process is to prepare a set of financial statements for use by internal and external decision makers. The initial step in the closing process is the preparation of a trial balance. A **trial balance** is a two-column listing of general ledger account balances, one column for accounts with debit balances and one column for accounts with credit balances. The principal purpose of a trial balance is to help accountants determine whether the total debits and credits entered in a business's general ledger accounts during a given accounting period are equal. If a trial balance does not "balance," there are one or more errors in the accounting records. Those errors must be found and corrected before the closing process continues.

Unfortunately, even if a trial balance has equal debits and credits, there may be errors in the accounting records. For example, suppose that the debits and credits of a journal entry were posted to incorrect accounts. In such a case, the debit and credit columns of the trial balance would have equal totals although at least two of the accounts would have improper balances.

To prepare a trial balance in a manual accounting system, an accountant refers to a business's general ledger and lists each account in the order that they are listed in the chart of accounts. The balance of each account is entered either in the debit or credit column of the trial balance. Generally, accounts with zero balances are not included in a trial balance. In a computer-based accounting system, a trial balance can be prepared in a matter of minutes, or seconds, by activating the appropriate software instructions.

To illustrate the preparation of a trial balance, consider a small company, the Theta Travel Agency, that has ten general ledger accounts. Each of these accounts is listed next. To simplify matters, only the period-ending balances of these accounts—before the posting of adjusting and closing entries—are shown.

Cash						**Account No. 101**	
						Balance	
Date		**Explanation**	**Post Ref.**	**Debit**	**Credit**	**Debit**	**Credit**
1998 June	30	Balance				4,020	

Supplies						**Account No. 125**	
						Balance	
Date		**Explanation**	**Post Ref.**	**Debit**	**Credit**	**Debit**	**Credit**
1998 June	30	Balance				575	

Office Equipment						**Account No. 151**	
						Balance	
Date		**Explanation**	**Post Ref.**	**Debit**	**Credit**	**Debit**	**Credit**
1998 June	30	Balance				24,570	

Accumulated Depreciation, Office Equipment						**Account No. 152**	
						Balance	
Date		**Explanation**	**Post Ref.**	**Debit**	**Credit**	**Debit**	**Credit**
1998 June	30	Balance					6,200

Accounts Payable						Account No. 201	
Date		Explanation	Post Ref.	Debit	Credit	Balance	
						Debit	Credit
1998 June	30	Balance					1,200

Common Stock						Account No. 301	
Date		Explanation	Post Ref.	Debit	Credit	Balance	
						Debit	Credit
1998 June	30	Balance					2,000

Retained Earnings						Account No. 350	
Date		Explanation	Post Ref.	Debit	Credit	Balance	
						Debit	Credit
1998 June	30	Balance					18,850

Commission Revenue						Account No. 401	
Date		Explanation	Post Ref.	Debit	Credit	Balance	
						Debit	Credit
1998 June	30	Balance					3,200

Salaries Expense						Account No. 501	
Date		Explanation	Post Ref.	Debit	Credit	Balance	
						Debit	Credit
1998 June	30	Balance				1,960	

Miscellaneous Expense						Account No. 509	
						Balance	
Date		Explanation	Post Ref.	Debit	Credit	Debit	Credit
1998 June	30	Balance				325	

Following is the trial balance of the Theta Travel Agency's general ledger as of June 30, 1998. Fortunately for the company's accountants, the totals of the debit and credit columns are equal.

THETA TRAVEL AGENCY
TRIAL BALANCE
JUNE 30, 1998

	Debit	Credit
Cash	$ 4,020	
Supplies	575	
Office Equipment	24,570	
Accumulated Depreciation, Office Equipment		$ 6,200
Accounts Payable		1,200
Common Stock		2,000
Retained Earnings		18,850
Commission Revenue		3,200
Salaries Expense	1,960	
Miscellaneous Expenses	325	
	$31,450	$31,450

SUMMARY

The accounting equation expresses the mathematical relationship among the assets, liabilities, and owners' equity of a business. When journalizing transactions and other events affecting a business, accountants must ensure that each journal entry is balanced in reference to the accounting equation. Double-entry bookkeeping rules dictate how individual transactions and events are recorded. The key to understanding and applying these rules is the meaning and use of the terms "debit" and "credit." Debit refers to the left-hand side of a T-account, while credit refers to the right-hand side of a T-account. Likewise, to debit an account is to enter an amount on its left-hand side—or in the debit column of a four-column account. To credit an account is to enter an amount on its right-hand side—or in the credit column of a four-column account. Asset and expense accounts normally have debit balances and increases in these accounts are recorded as debits, while decreases are recorded as credits. Liability, owners' equity, and revenue accounts normally have credit balances. Increases in these accounts are recorded as credits, while decreases are recorded as debits.

When analyzing a transaction or event for the purpose of preparing a journal entry, a useful approach to follow is to first identify the type of each account (asset, liability, and so on) affected by the transaction. Next, decide whether the transaction increased or decreased these accounts. Then, after referring to the bookkeeping rules, determine whether these changes should be recorded as debits or credits. Finally, ensure that the transaction has an equal dollar effect on each side of the accounting equation.

The financial data recorded in the journals of a business should be transferred or posted periodically to the appropriate general ledger accounts. At the end of each accounting period, a trial balance of the general ledger accounts is prepared. A trial balance helps accountants determine whether the total debits and credits entered in a business's accounting records during a given accounting period are equal.

GLOSSARY

Adjusting entries (p. 125) Journal entries made at the end of an accounting period to ensure that the revenue recognition and expense recognition rules are properly applied that period.

Closing entries (p. 126) Journal entries made at the end of each accounting period to close out or transfer the balances of temporary accounts to the appropriate owners' equity account.

Compound journal entry (p. 120) A journal entry that affects more than two accounts.

Contra accounts (p. 117) Accounts that are treated as offsets or reductions to related accounts for financial statement purposes; an example is Accumulated Depreciation.

Correcting entries (p. 125) Journal entries made to correct errors in previously recorded journal entries.

Credit (p. 113) The right-hand side of a T-account or an entry made on the right-hand side of a T-account (or in the credit column of a four-column account); as a verb, to enter an amount on the right-hand side of a T-account or in the credit column of a four-column account.

Debit (p. 113) The left-hand side of a T-account or an entry made on the left-hand side of a T-account (or in the debit column of a four-column account); as a verb, to enter an amount on the left-hand side of a T-account or in the debit column of a four-column account.

Permanent accounts (p. 116) Accounts whose period-ending balances are carried forward to the next accounting period.

Retained Earnings (p. 116) An owners' equity account of corporations; the balance of this account represents the cumulative earnings of a company since its inception less any dividends distributed to the firm's stockholders.

Temporary accounts (p. 116) Accounts whose period-ending balances are transferred or closed to the appropriate owners' equity account.

Trial balance (p. 130) A two-column listing of a business's general ledger account balances, one column for debit balances and one column for credit balances.

DECISION CASE

If you are a bike rider, you are probably familiar with Cannondale Corporation, which manufactures bicycles and bicycle accessories. Included in Cannondale's product line are mountain, road, hybrid, and touring bikes. The company markets

its products in the United States, Europe, and Japan. The increasing popularity of biking has fueled rapid growth in Cannondale's revenues. Formed in the early 1970s, the company now has annual sales exceeding $100 million.

Cannondale provides a lifetime warranty on the frame of each bicycle it sells. The company also provides a one-year warranty on all bicycle components and accessories. Cannondale replaces a defective bicycle frame, or bicycle part still under warranty, at no cost to the purchaser.

Assume that in 1998 Cannondale sold 312,000 bicycles. The company estimated that .4% of these bicycles would have defective frames, each of which would eventually have to be replaced at a cost of $90. At the end of 1998, the company estimated that the following year $41,000 of replacement parts, not including bicycle frames, would be issued free of charge to the individuals who purchased Cannondale bikes or accessories during 1998.

Required: Suppose you are an accountant for Cannondale. At the end of 1998, how, if at all, would you recommend that the company account for the future warranty-related costs it will incur for bicycles and bicycle accessories sold in 1998? Justify your answer by referring to one or more of the accounting concepts discussed in Chapter 2.

QUESTIONS

1. List two examples of each of the following components of the accounting equation: assets, liabilities, and owners' equity.
2. Explain how it is possible for a transaction to affect only one side of the accounting equation. Provide an example of such a transaction.
3. What types of transactions affect the owner's equity of a business? Provide two examples.
4. List the debit and credit rules for assets. List the debit and credit rules for liabilities.
5. Define the terms "permanent accounts" and "temporary accounts." In which financial statement is each type of account found?
6. Revenue and expense accounts begin each new accounting period with what type of account balance?
7. Where is the Retained Earnings account presented in a set of financial statements and what does it represent?
8. What are "dividends" and where do they appear in a set of financial statements?
9. How are contra accounts treated in financial statements?
10. Who was Arthur Edward Andersen?
11. Briefly describe key differences in the journalizing process between manual and computer-based accounting systems.
12. Besides inaccurate financial statements, what is a potential result of incorrect journal entries?
13. What is a compound journal entry? What must be true with regard to the dollar amount of debits and credits in a compound journal entry?
14. Identify the steps involved in performing transaction analysis as described in this chapter.
15. Briefly describe the nature and purpose of correcting entries, adjusting entries, and closing entries.
16. Identify two common types of errors made during the journalizing process.
17. How does a "debit memo" that is included in your monthly bank statement affect the balance of your bank account? Explain.
18. What purpose is served by posting information from the general journal and other journals to the general ledger?

19. What is one key difference in how transaction data are posted in a manual and computer-based accounting system?
20. What is a trial balance and what is its purpose?

EXERCISES

21. **True or False** (LO 1–6)
Following are a series of statements regarding topics discussed in Chapter 4.

Required:
Indicate whether each statement is true (T) or false (F).

_____ a. If a journal entry affects one asset account and two liability accounts, that journal entry must be out of balance in reference to the accounting equation.
_____ b. If a business's trial balance is "in balance," then the entity's accounting records must be free of any errors.
_____ c. Contra accounts are typically treated as offsets or reductions to related accounts for financial statement purposes.
_____ d. Revenues, expenses, and dividends are all examples of temporary accounts.
_____ e. Correcting entries are made at the beginning of an accounting period to reverse, or cancel out, the effect of certain adjusting entries made at the end of the prior accounting period.
_____ f. Every transaction of a business must be recorded in such a way that the accounting equation for that business remains in balance.
_____ g. "Skimming" refers to a shortcut method used by accountants to transfer the balance of temporary accounts to the Retained Earnings account.
_____ h. Accountants use debits and credits to define the bookkeeping rules and normal balances for each type of general ledger account.
_____ i. Compound journal entries may contain several debits and one credit, several credits and one debit, or multiple debits and multiple credits.
_____ j. A company that has negative retained earnings will have a credit balance in its Retained Earnings account.

22. **Normal Account Balances** (LO 3)
Following are account titles taken from the financial statements of three large companies. Alcoa is the leading worldwide producer of aluminum, Honeywell produces a wide array of products including security systems, while Wendy's operates a chain of fast-food restaurants.

Alcoa and Subsidiaries:
_____ Short-term investments
_____ Accounts payable
_____ Retained earnings
_____ Operating expenses
_____ Sales revenue

Honeywell Inc.:
_____ Short-term debt
_____ Receivables
_____ Cash and cash equivalents
_____ Research and development expenses
_____ Property, plant & equipment

Wendy's International, Inc.
_____ Income taxes expense
_____ Inventories
_____ Income taxes payable
_____ General and administrative expenses
_____ Land

Required:
For each account listed, indicate its normal account balance: debit (D) or credit (C).

23. **Business Transactions and the Accounting Equation** (LO 1)
Lewis and Clare opened a tropical fish store, L&C's Fish Shop, on January 1. Following are the first four transactions engaged in by Lewis and Clare on behalf of their business:
1. Invested $25,000 in the business by depositing that amount in a checking account entitled "L&C's Fish Shop."
2. Borrowed $15,000 from a local bank on a five-year note payable.
3. Paid $10,000 for inventory (fish tanks and other merchandise) that was to be sold to customers.
4. Paid $8,000 for equipment to be used in the store.

Required:
1. Using the format illustrated in this chapter for B&B's Pizzeria, record the first four transactions of L&C's Fish Shop.
2. Determine the total assets, liabilities, and owners' equity of this business following its first four transactions.

24. **Using T-Accounts** (LO 2–5)
Refer to the information in Exercise 23.

Required:
1. Prepare T-accounts for L&C's Fish Shop and post the business's first four transactions to these T-accounts.
2. Determine the balance of each account.

25. **Analyzing General Journal Entries** (LO 2)
The following general journal entries (presented in a simplified format) were made recently by the bookkeeper of Chandlers' Hilltop Texaco:

	Debit	Credit
1. Supplies	400	
Cash		400
2. Interest Expense	270	
Cash		270
3. Equipment	4,000	
Notes Payable		4,000

Required:
1. Briefly describe the nature of the transactions that resulted in each of these journal entries.
2. Suppose that the bookkeeper inadvertently recorded the third entry by debiting Notes Payable and crediting Equipment, each for $4,000. How would this error have affected the assets and liabilities of Chandlers' Hilltop Texaco?

26. **The Accounting Equation** (LO 1)
Following are the balance sheet accounts of a small business.

Cash	$2,500
Accounts Payable	?
Equipment	5,200
Supplies	?
Land	8,200
Owners' Equity (total)	9,000
Notes Payable	5,400

Required:

1. Fill in the missing amounts assuming that the business has total assets of $18,000.
2. Fill in the missing amounts assuming that the business has total liabilities and owners' equity of $19,900.

27. **Transaction Analysis** (LO 1–4)
The Reader's Digest Association, Inc., is a publishing company best known for its namesake publication. During a recent year, this company purchased approximately $50 million of property, plant & equipment assets.

Required:
Assuming that Reader's Digest purchased the given assets in one transaction and paid cash, use the method presented in the text for developing "real-world" journal entries to complete the following tasks for this transaction:

1. Analyze the transaction.
2. Identify the effects on the company's accounting equation.
3. Prepare a journal entry using the simplified journal entry format shown in the text.

28. **Transaction Analysis** (LO 1–4)
Centex Corporation builds housing subdivisions and supplies homebuilders with building materials. During a recent year, this company paid $68,856,000 of interest expense on outstanding debt.

Required:
Assuming that Centex paid the interest in one transaction, use the method presented in the text for developing "real-world" journal entries to complete the following tasks for this transaction:

1. Analyze the transaction.
2. Identify the effects on the company's accounting equation.
3. Prepare a journal entry using the simplified journal entry format shown in the text.

29. **Correction of an Accounting Error** (LO 4)
Yeutter, Inc., recently acquired a piece of equipment for $2,190. Following is the entry—presented in the simplified format illustrated in the text—that was recorded in Yeutter's accounting records for this transaction:

Equipment	219	
Cash		219

Required:

1. What type of error was made in recording this transaction?
2. What effect does this error have on the two accounts involved and on Yeutter's total assets? Explain.
3. Prepare the journal entry needed to correct Yeutter's accounting records.

30. **Correction of an Accounting Error** (LO 4)
Earlier this year, Keller Corporation purchased a large tract of land for $2,450,000. Following is the entry—presented in the simplified format illustrated in the text—that was recorded for this transaction in Keller's accounting records:

Land	2,540,000	
Cash		2,540,000

Required:
1. What type of error was made in recording this transaction?
2. What effect does this error have on the two accounts involved and on Keller's total assets? Explain.
3. Prepare the journal entry needed to correct Keller's accounting records.

31. **Analyzing T-Accounts** (LO 2)
Consider the following T-accounts for cash and accounts payable:

Cash		Accounts Payable	
14,000	10,000	4,000	6,000
9,000	7,000	5,000	8,000
8,000	2,000	1,000	1,000

Required:
1. Compute the balance of each of these accounts.
2. How would each of these accounts be classified in a balance sheet?
3. Identify a transaction that would have resulted in the $8,000 posting to the Cash account.
4. Identify a transaction that would have resulted in the $5,000 posting to the Accounts Payable account.

32. **Analyzing T-Accounts** (LO 2)
Consider the following T-accounts for interest expense and interest revenue:

Interest Expense		Interest Revenue	
4,000			180
4,000			290
4,000			240
4,000			

Required:
1. Compute the balance of each of these accounts.
2. Where in a set of financial statements would each of these accounts appear?
3. Would you ever expect the Interest Expense account to have a credit balance? Why or why not?

33. **Trial Balance Errors** (LO 6)
The following year-end trial balance was hurriedly prepared by the accountant of Salter Company:

	Debit	Credit
Cash	$10,250	
Accounts Receivable	5,000	
Inventory	7,500	
Property, Plant & Equipment	13,000	
Accumulated Depreciation, Property, Plant & Equipment		$ 6,100
Accounts Payable		6,500
Common Stock	10,000	
Retained Earnings		4,050
Retained Earnings		4,050
Sales Revenue		20,000
Cost of Goods Sold		12,000
Other Revenue	500	
Depreciation Expense	1,200	
Totals	$47,450	$52,700

Required:

1. Prepare a corrected trial balance for Salter Company. The proper balance of the Inventory account is $5,700. (Hint: Each listed account has a "normal" balance.)
2. If a trial balance's total debits and credits are equal, can you assume that each account balance is correct? Explain.

34. **Posting General Journal Entries** (LO 5)
Following are several general journal entries of the Houseman Corporation during a recent month (the journal entry descriptions have been omitted):

GENERAL JOURNAL					Page 2
Date		Description	Post Ref.	Debit	Credit
1998 Jan.	2	Office Supplies		320	
		Cash			320
	5	Inventory		7,500	
		Accounts Payable			7,500
	12	Cash		5,750	
		Accounts Receivable			5,750
	17	Accounts Payable		4,300	
		Cash			4,300
	31	Utilities Expense		2,000	
		Cash			2,000

Following are the account number and the January 1 balance of each of the accounts affected by the listed journal entries:

	Account Number	January 1 Balance
Cash	101	$12,400
Accounts Receivable	111	9,300
Inventory	116	6,100
Office Supplies	121	840
Accounts Payable	201	14,200
Utilities Expense	505	0

Required:

1. What is the purpose of posting general journal entries to general ledger accounts?
2. Prepare a four-column account for each of the accounts affected by the general journal entries listed for the Houseman Corporation. Enter the January 1 balance in each of these accounts and then post the journal entries to the appropriate accounts.

35. **Trial Balance** (LO 6)
Moonlight Distributors has twelve general ledger accounts. Following are these accounts as of December 31, 1998. (Only the year-end balance is included in each account.)

Cash — Account No. 101

Date		Explanation	Post Ref.	Debit	Credit	Balance Debit	Balance Credit
Dec.	31	Balance				2,075	

Accounts Receivable — Account No. 111

Date		Explanation	Post Ref.	Debit	Credit	Balance Debit	Balance Credit
Dec.	31	Balance				1,750	

Inventory — Account No. 121

Date		Explanation	Post Ref.	Debit	Credit	Balance Debit	Balance Credit
Dec.	31	Balance				925	

Property, Plant & Equipment — Account No. 151

Date		Explanation	Post Ref.	Debit	Credit	Balance Debit	Balance Credit
Dec.	31	Balance				5,100	

Accumulated Depreciation, Property, Plant & Equipment						Account No. 152	
						Balance	
Date		Explanation	Post Ref.	Debit	Credit	Debit	Credit
Dec.	31	Balance					1,200

Accounts Payable						Account No. 201	
						Balance	
Date		Explanation	Post Ref.	Debit	Credit	Debit	Credit
Dec.	31	Balance					1,850

Common Stock						Account No. 301	
						Balance	
Date		Explanation	Post Ref.	Debit	Credit	Debit	Credit
Dec.	31	Balance					3,000

Retained Earnings						Account No. 321	
						Balance	
Date		Explanation	Post Ref.	Debit	Credit	Debit	Credit
Dec.	31	Balance					1,800

Sales Revenue						Account No. 401	
						Balance	
Date		Explanation	Post Ref.	Debit	Credit	Debit	Credit
Dec.	31	Balance					12,000

Cost of Goods Sold						Account No. 501	
						Balance	
Date		Explanation	Post Ref.	Debit	Credit	Debit	Credit
Dec.	31	Balance				7,000	

Salaries Expense						**Account No. 541**	
						Balance	
Date		**Explanation**	**Post Ref.**	**Debit**	**Credit**	**Debit**	**Credit**
Dec.	31	Balance				2,000	

Depreciation Expense						**Account No. 571**	
						Balance	
Date		**Explanation**	**Post Ref.**	**Debit**	**Credit**	**Debit**	**Credit**
Dec.	31	Balance				1,000	

Required:

1. What is the purpose of a year-end trial balance?
2. Prepare a December 31, 1998, trial balance for Moonlight Distributors.

PROBLEM SET A

36. Journalizing and Posting Transactions (LO 4, 5)

Orlando opened a hair salon recently. Orlando did not maintain a formal set of accounting records during the first week of his business's operations. Instead, he simply maintained a checkbook for the business. Following are the entries included in Orlando's checkbook for the period January 2–8.

January 2: Bank loan	$20,000
January 3: Rent to landlord	(500)
January 3: Hairstyling fees earned	650
January 4: Bought inventory	(7,000)
January 4: Bought inventory	(3,500)
January 8: Hairstyling fees earned	800

Required:

1. Prepare the necessary general journal entries for Orlando's Hair Salon for the period January 2–8.
2. Prepare T-accounts for Orlando's Hair Salon, and post the journal entries for the period January 2–8 to these accounts. Determine the account balances as of January 8.
3. In a short memo to Orlando, explain why his current method of recordkeeping does not provide him with the information he needs to monitor and evaluate the financial status of his business.

37. Journalizing Transactions (LO 4)

Jenonne's Gardening Supply had the following transactions involving cash during early August:

1. August 1: Purchased four lawnmowers for $300 each.
2. August 2: Purchased office supplies for $320.
3. August 4: Paid income taxes of $400.
4. August 4: Received $450 for lawn care services provided.

5. August 5: Paid salaries of $500.
6. August 7: Paid $1,000 of interest on a bank loan.

Required:

1. Prepare general journal entries for these transactions.
2. Suppose that you presented the journal entries prepared in (1) to the owner of Jenonne's Gardening Supply. After reviewing them, she is convinced that each transaction has been "double-counted." Write a short memo to the owner explaining why each entry requires at least one debit and one credit and why this procedure does not double-count the transactions.

38. **Correction of Accounting Errors** (LO 1, 2, 4)
Jabbar Company's inexperienced bookkeeper places a question mark next to a journal entry if he is uncertain the entry is correct. Question marks appear next to each of the following entries in Jabbar's accounting records.

1. Accounts Receivable	2,000	
Cash		2,000
To record collection of accounts receivable		
2. Property, Plant & Equipment	800	
Cash		800
To record purchase of office supplies for cash		
3. Cleaning Supplies	100	
Accounts Payable		100
To record purchase of cleaning supplies on credit		

Required:

1. Given each journal entry and its accompanying explanation, identify the nature of the error in the entry, if any, and how the entry should have appeared.
2. Given your responses to (1), prepare any necessary correcting entries.
3. Analyze each of the errors you identified in (1) in reference to the accounting equation. How would these errors have affected the accounting equation of Jabbar Company, if at all?

39. **Trial Balance** (LO 6)
Following are the general ledger account balances of Baggett Construction Company, Inc. (BCCI), as of September 30, 1998:

Cash	$ 25,000
Accounts Receivable	150,000
Inventory	150,000
Property, Plant & Equipment	425,000
Accumulated Depreciation, Property, Plant & Equipment	55,000
Accounts Payable	350,000
Income Taxes Payable	50,000
Common Stock	45,000
Retained Earnings	50,000
Sales Revenue	300,000
Operating Expenses	100,000

Required:

1. Prepare a trial balance for BCCI as of September 30, 1998. (Hint: Each account has a normal balance.)
2. As you read in the text, one or more general ledger accounts of a business may contain errors even if the firm's trial balance "balances." Provide a few examples of accounting errors that would *not* cause a business's trial balance to be unbalanced.
3. What steps could the management of BCCI take to help ensure that its accounts are error-free? Write a brief memo to the company's management listing your recommendations.

40. **Accounting, Canadian Style** (LO 2, 3)

Bombardier, Inc., is a Canadian company that designs, manufactures, and distributes transportation equipment. Following are selected accounts included in recent financial statements of this company.

	Classification	Normal Balance	Increase Recorded as
Term Deposits	______	______	______
Revenues from Subsidiary	______	______	______
Income Taxes Payable	______	______	______
Accounts Receivable	______	______	______
Fixed Assets	______	______	______
Short-Term Borrowings	______	______	______
Provision for Pension Costs	______	______	______
Property under Lease	______	______	______
Income Taxes	______	______	______

Required:

Using your "professional" judgment, classify each of the listed accounts as one of the following: asset, liability, owners' equity, revenue, or expense. Also identify the normal balance (debit or credit) of each account. Finally, indicate whether an increase in the balance of each account would be recorded with a debit or with a credit.

41. **Journalizing, Posting, and Preparing a Trial Balance** (LO 4–6)

Georgian Enterprises uses the following general ledger accounts in its accounting system. Listed for each account is its account number and balance as of January 1, 1999.

	Account No.	Balance
Cash	101	$ 60,000
Supplies	121	10,000
Office Equipment	151	170,000
Accumulated Depreciation, Office Equipment	152	45,000
Accounts Payable	201	70,000
Common Stock	301	90,000
Retained Earnings	350	35,000
Fee Revenue	401	0
Selling Expenses	501	0
Salaries Expense	511	0
Depreciation Expense	531	0

In early January 1999, Georgian Enterprises engaged in the following transactions:

January 2: Paid $30,000 on accounts payable.
January 3: Purchased $1,100 of supplies for cash.
January 4: Purchased office equipment for $2,700 cash.
January 6: Earned and received fees (revenues) from customers of $16,400.
January 7: Paid selling expenses of $7,100.
January 7: Paid employee salaries of $5,200.

Required:
1. Why do certain of Georgian's accounts have zero balances at the beginning of January?
2. Prepare a journal entry for each of the transactions listed.
3. Set up four-column accounts for Georgian Enterprises as of January 1, 1999. Post the journal entries from (2) to these accounts.
4. Prepare a trial balance for Georgian Enterprises as of the close of business on January 7, 1999.

PROBLEM SET B

42. Journalizing and Posting Transactions (LO 4, 5)
Priscilla recently opened a hair salon. Because she is unfamiliar with double-entry bookkeeping, Priscilla decided to maintain only a checkbook for her business. Following are the entries made in Priscilla's checkbook for the first week her business was open.

April 2:	Personal investment in business	$15,000
April 5:	Paid assistant's wages	(200)
April 6:	Hairstyling fees earned	900
April 6:	Purchased hairstyling supplies	(800)
April 8:	Purchased equipment for salon	(4,000)
April 8:	Hair styling fees earned	900

Required:
1. Prepare the necessary general journal entries for Priscilla's Hair Salon for the period April 2–8.
2. Prepare T-accounts for Priscilla's Hair Salon and post the journal entries prepared in (1) to these accounts. Determine the account balances as of April 8.
3. In a short memo to Priscilla, explain why her current method of recordkeeping does not provide her with the information she needs to determine how well her business is doing financially.

43. Journalizing Transactions (LO 4)
Paulette's Flower Shop had the following transactions involving cash during late November:
1. November 23: Paid $500 for newspaper ads.
2. November 24: Purchased equipment for $3,500.
3. November 27: Paid salaries of $500.
4. November 28: Borrowed $5,000 from a local bank (signed a two-year note payable).
5. November 29: Received $400 payment on account receivable.
6. November 29: Paid utility bill of $90.

Required:
1. Prepare general journal entries for the transactions listed.
2. After reviewing the journal entries prepared in (1), Paulette, the business's owner, is confused. She does not understand the meaning of the terms "debit" and "credit,"

nor how those items affect the recording of business transactions. Write a brief memo to Paulette explaining the meaning and use of the terms "debit" and "credit" from an accounting standpoint.

44. **Correction of Accounting Errors** (LO 1, 2, 4)
Cato's Towing Company recently hired a new and inexperienced bookkeeper. The bookkeeper places a question mark next to a journal entry if she is uncertain whether it is correct. A question mark appears next to each of the following entries in this business's accounting records.

1. Cash	300	
Interest Expense		300
To record interest paid on a bank loan		
2. Utilities Expense	100	
Cash		100
To record payment of monthly electricity bill		
3. Office Supplies	210	
Accounts Receivable		210
To record purchase of office supplies on credit		

Required:
1. Given each entry and its explanation, identify the nature of the error in the entry, if any, and how the entry should have appeared.
2. Given your responses to (1), prepare any necessary correcting entries.
3. Analyze each of the errors you identified in (1) in reference to the accounting equation. How would these errors have affected the accounting equation of Cato's Towing Company, if at all?

45. **Trial Balance** (LO 6)
Following are the general ledger account balances of Goldblum's Mercantile as of October 31, 1998:

Cash	$10,000
Accounts Receivable	700
Inventory	3,000
Equipment	2,000
Accumulated Depreciation, Equipment	400
Accounts Payable	800
Income Taxes Payable	200
Common Stock	1,000
Retained Earnings	3,600
Sales Revenue	20,000
Operating Expenses	10,300

Required:
1. Prepare a trial balance for Goldblum's Mercantile as of October 31, 1998. (Hint: Each account has a normal balance.)
2. What is the purpose of a trial balance?
3. Identify several examples of errors that would cause a trial balance not to balance.

46. Accounting, British Style (LO 2, 3)
British Airways plc is a London-based airline. Following is a list of selected general ledger accounts that appeared in recent financial statements of this company.

	Classification	Normal Balance	Increase Recorded as
Fleet	______	______	______
Trade Investments	______	______	______
Convertible Capital Bonds	______	______	______
Equipment	______	______	______
Administrative Expenses	______	______	______
Borrowings	______	______	______
Profit and Loss Account	______	______	______
Provisions for Liabilities and Charges	______	______	______

Required:
Relying on your accounting expertise, classify the listed accounts as one of the following: asset, liability, owners' equity, revenue, or expense. Also identify the normal balance (debit or credit) of each account. Finally, indicate whether an increase in the balance of each account would be recorded with a debit or with a credit.

47. Journalizing, Posting, and Preparing a Trial Balance (LO 4–6)
Mishell Realtors, Inc., uses the following general ledger accounts in its accounting system. Listed for each account is its account number and balance as of January 1, 1999.

	Account No.	Balance
Cash	101	$30,000
Supplies	131	4,000
Accounts Receivable	132	9,000
Office Equipment	152	46,000
Accumulated Depreciation, Office Equipment	153	35,000
Accounts Payable	201	9,000
Common Stock	301	10,000
Retained Earnings	350	35,000
Fee Revenue	401	0
Selling Expenses	501	0
Salaries Expense	511	0
Depreciation Expense	531	0

During the first week of January 1999, Mishell engaged in the following transactions:

January 3: Earned and received fees (real estate commissions) of $5,000.
January 4: Purchased $400 of supplies for cash.
January 5: Paid selling expenses of $1,100.
January 6: Paid $2,500 on accounts payable.
January 7: Paid employee salaries of $2,600.

Required:
1. Why do certain of this company's accounts have zero balances at the beginning of January?

2. Prepare journal entries to record Mishell's transactions during the first week of January 1999.
3. Set up four-column accounts for Mishell as of January 1, 1999, and then post the journal entries from (2) to the appropriate accounts.
4. Prepare a trial balance for Mishell as of the close of business on January 7, 1999.

CASES

48. Friends, Partners, and Accounting Records (LO 6)

Mary Jane's Shoes is co-owned by Mary Cellini and Jane Kleven. The two co-owners work at the store together Monday through Friday, while Mary works alone on Saturday. Mary also maintains the accounting records for the small business. Jane knows little about accounting and seldom reviews the business's accounting records.

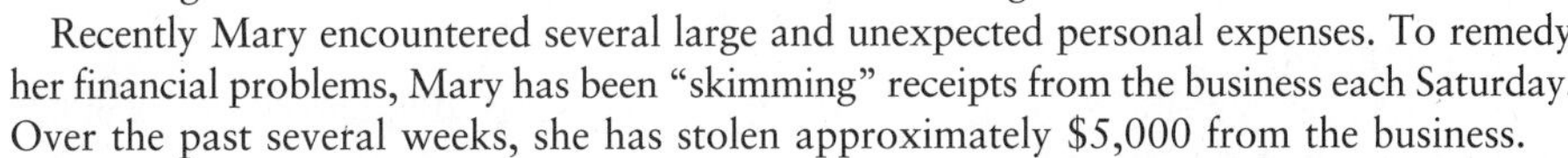

Recently Mary encountered several large and unexpected personal expenses. To remedy her financial problems, Mary has been "skimming" receipts from the business each Saturday. Over the past several weeks, she has stolen approximately $5,000 from the business.

Two days ago, Mary prepared the business's monthly trial balance. Jane stumbled across that trial balance today while she was searching for a lost document. Jane was shocked to discover that the company's cash balance was so low despite the increased customer traffic and booming sales of recent weeks. She realizes that either the accounting records must be wrong or someone, almost certainly Mary, has been stealing cash from the business. Jane is concerned by the latter possibility because she knows her friend and partner has been experiencing significant financial problems recently.

Required:
1. Assume the role of Jane Kleven. What would you do at this point? Would you ask your friend directly regarding your suspicions? Would you take the accounting records to a local accountant and ask him or her to review them? What factors would you consider in making this decision?
2. At a minimum, what should a co-owner of a small business know about accounting and internal control issues to minimize the possibility of becoming involved in a situation similar to that facing Jane Kleven? Be specific.

49. Chart of Accounts (LO 6)

Your best friend, Chris, recently dropped out of college to devote full-time to a new business that his father is bankrolling. Chris's business, Pizzas to Go, is located across the street from your college campus. Earlier this week, Chris asked you to help him set up an accounting system for his business. Chris enrolled in introductory financial accounting during his brief college career but dropped the course after "blowing" the first exam. So, his accounting expertise is limited. To this point, Chris has only created a chart of accounts for Pizzas to Go. Following is that chart of accounts.

Account No.	Account Title
1.	Accounts Payable
2.	Accounts Receivable
3.	Accumulated Depreciation, Equipment
4.	Cash
5.	Cleaning Supplies
6.	Delivery Fees
7.	Electricity
8.	Equipment
9.	Insurance
10.	Miscellaneous
11.	Taxes

Required:
Review the chart of accounts and write a short memo to Chris recommending how he should change it. (Note: You may find it helpful to review the discussion of the nature and purpose of a chart of accounts in Chapter 3 before completing this case.)

50. "Debit" This (LO 4)
A classmate of yours in introductory financial accounting received her monthly bank statement today. After opening the bank statement, she discovered a "debit memo" for $12. This debit memo was for services the bank provided to her during the previous month. Your classmate is confused. "I don't understand this," she said as the two of you sat in the student union sharing a hot fudge sundae. "Our accounting instructor insisted that increases in assets are *always* recorded with debits. Well, my checking account is an asset to me, but this debit memo in my bank statement caused my checking account balance to decrease *not* increase. What's going on here? Doesn't my bank know its debits from its credits?"

Required:
Write a brief memo to your classmate explaining the apparent inconsistency in her bank's use of the term "debit."

PROJECTS

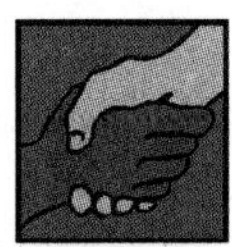

51. Accounting Terms Used by Foreign Companies
For this assignment, your project group will study the annual report of a foreign company. The purpose of this project is to acquaint you and your classmates with the differing account titles and other financial statement terms used by foreign firms compared with U.S. firms.

Required:
1. Obtain a recent annual report of a foreign company other than a Canadian firm. Each group member should review this annual report to become familiar with the company and its financial statements.
2. Meet as a group to discuss the annual report. The focus of your discussion should be the differing account titles and other financial statement terms used by the given company, compared with the corresponding terms you have been introduced to in this course and in other business courses. For example, "stocks" is a term found in many foreign annual reports that is usually synonymous with "inventory" in the annual reports of U.S. firms. Individual members of the group should be assigned responsibility for researching the meaning of unusual or unfamiliar terms identified in the selected company's annual report. Sources that may be particularly useful for interpreting such terms are the given firm's financial statement footnotes and international accounting textbooks.
3. One group member should compile the research completed by other members of the group into a written report that begins with a brief description of the company whose annual report was selected for this project. This description should indicate where the company is located, the types of products it sells or services it provides, and so on. The major section of your group's report should be a glossary of the unusual/unfamiliar financial statement terms identified by the group in the annual report and the group's interpretation of the meaning of each of those terms. One or more group members should be assigned responsibility for editing the group report before it is submitted to your instructor.
4. One group member should be prepared to present a summary of the group's written report to the remainder of the class.

52. History of Accounting

Relying on an accounting periodical, such as *The Accounting Historians Journal,* or another appropriate source, select and read an article dealing with the development and/or history of double-entry bookkeeping.

Required:

Identify and summarize in a written report the main points of the article you selected. Conclude your report by explaining how the article contributed to your understanding of the historical development of accounting.

53. Accounting for You

In this project, you will develop a chart of accounts that you could use to account for your personal financial affairs.

Required:

1. Identify the major categories of your personal assets. For example, your assets may include a car, a computer, a bike, and so on. You may "lump" similar assets into one category. For instance, you may define clothes as one of your asset categories. Similarly, identify your major types of liabilities, revenues, and expenses. Interest revenue, salaries or wages earned, college tuition, and utilities are examples of revenue and expense categories that you may define.
2. Develop a chart of accounts for your personal financial affairs using the information you developed in (1) and the organizational scheme discussed in Chapter 3 for a chart of accounts. You will need to include one "equity" account in your chart of accounts such as "Christina Duffield, Net Worth."
3. Identify five recent financial transactions in which you have engaged, such as, payment of college tuition, purchase of a new car, and so on. Using the chart of accounts you developed and your knowledge of double-entry bookkeeping rules, prepare journal entries to record these five transactions.

54. The Accounting Profession Joins the Internet

The American Institute of Certified Public Accountants (AICPA) is the national professional organization of CPAs. This organization was briefly discussed in Chapter 1. The AICPA supplies the public with information regarding the nature of the accounting profession and the services and products available from members of the profession. Another role of the AICPA is to disseminate important information to members of the accounting profession such as new accounting rules and pending legislation that may affect the profession.

Required:

1. Access the AICPA's World Wide Web (Web) site on the Internet.
2. Summarize the types of information that the AICPA provides to the public and members of the accounting profession from its Web site. Identify the titles of several AICPA publications that are listed at the organization's Web site.
3. Identify one other professional accounting organization's Web site on the Internet. Describe this organization and define its apparent role and purpose.
4. Summarize the information you collected in (2) and (3) in a written report. Include in that report the relevant Web site addresses.

5 The Accounting Cycle

"Begin at the beginning," the King said, gravely, "and go till you come to the end; then stop."
Lewis Carroll

LEARNING OBJECTIVES

After studying this chapter, you should be able to do the following:

1. Identify the major steps in the accounting cycle.
2. Develop period-ending adjustments to general ledger account balances.
3. Prepare an income statement, a statement of stockholders' equity, and a balance sheet.
4. Journalize and post closing entries.
5. Prepare a post-closing trial balance.

FOCUS ON DECISION MAKING

Beyond the Accounting Cycle

Much of the information that decision makers need regarding businesses does not "fit" into one of the four financial statements that you become familiar with in this course. Fortunately, thoughtful business owners and executives voluntarily disclose important nonaccounting information in their firms' annual reports.

A key issue that decision makers consider for any given company is how well the firm is utilizing its assets. Data reported in financial statements provide important, but limited, insight on this issue. For example, suppose that you intend to invest in the common stock of either British Airways or the Australian airline company, Qantas Airways. One question you would want to address is which firm is better utilizing its fleet of aircraft. Although not required to do so, both firms include asset utilization statistics in their annual reports. In a recent year, British Airways operated at 67.8 percent of its capacity (available seats and cargo area), while during the same year Qantas utilized 71.9 percent of its capacity.

An even more important issue for a business than asset utilization is future profit potential. Corporate executives are more than happy to disclose nonaccounting data indicating that their firm has a bright future. For example, take the case of Corrections Corporation of America (CCA), a company that builds and operates prisons. A recent CCA annual report noted matter-of-factly that there are 34 million crimes committed annually in the United States, while there are only 500,000 jail cells in this country—nearly every one of which is occupied. These two stark facts clearly communicate to readers of CCA's financial statements that the company operates in a "high-growth" industry. Applied Materials, a manufacturing firm, recently disclosed that its "backlog of orders" had doubled over each of the previous two years. Conclusion: the company's sales will be increasing dramatically in the future. Finally, Hershey Foods Corporation cheerily observed in a recent annual report that Americans consume more chocolate candy bars each successive year. The average American presently devours 22 pounds of chocolate candy bars per year, the highest level in history. Translation: more chocaholics means more profits for Hershey.

An organization's accountants typically assume responsibility for collecting, processing, and reporting both accounting and nonaccounting data. In fact, the distinction between "accounting" and "nonaccounting" data is becoming increasingly blurred. In the information age in which we live, financial decision makers insist on receiving the information they need to make rational economic judgments regardless of the labels attached to that data.

This chapter focuses exclusively on the accounting cycle, the set of recurring accounting procedures that must be completed for a business each accounting period. Even those of you who will not pursue a career in accounting need to understand how accounting data are collected, processed, and reported. Accounting data are central to most major decisions involving business organizations. Production supervisors, sales managers, loan officers, and other nonaccountants who understand the accounting cycle are better prepared to "hold their ground" when accounting data are the focus of important meetings with customers, bankers, and other parties.

THE ACCOUNTING CYCLE: AN OVERVIEW

LEARNING OBJECTIVE 1
Identify the major steps in the accounting cycle.

Chapter 3 presented an abbreviated version of the accounting cycle. Exhibit 5.1 presents the complete accounting cycle and lists the key documents or accounting records used or produced by accountants during each step of this cycle.

The accounting cycle begins with an analysis of a business's transactions. Recall from Chapter 4 that one purpose of this initial step of the accounting cycle is to identify the accounts affected by a transaction. Once these accounts have been identified, accountants must determine whether they were increased or decreased by the given transaction and whether these increases or decreases should be recorded with debits or credits. Accountants draw most of the information needed to analyze business transactions from **source documents.** Source documents identify the key features or parameters of business transactions and thus minimize the potential for misunderstanding between the parties to those transactions. Common types of source documents include invoices, legal contracts, checks, and purchase orders.

source documents

In the next section of this chapter, we "walk" through the accounting cycle for a small corporation, Snow Mountain Retreat, which operates a bed and breakfast inn. Exhibit 5.2 presents a source document for a transaction involving Snow Mountain Retreat. That exhibit contains an invoice issued by Snow Mountain Retreat to bill a customer for a three-day stay. In subsequent chapters, you will become familiar with additional source documents as we consider a wide range of business transactions.

Once a transaction has been analyzed, the information needed to prepare a journal entry is available. Posting of journal entries, the third step of the accounting cycle, involves transferring journal entry data to the appropriate general ledger accounts. In computerized accounting systems, the first three steps of the accounting cycle are typically performed on a daily basis. In fact, as suggested in Chapter 4, many sophisticated accounting systems automatically analyze, journalize, and post transaction data in a matter of nanoseconds.

EXHIBIT 5.1
The Accounting Cycle

Accounting Activity	Document or Accounting Record
1. Analyze Transactions	Source Documents
2. Journalize Transactions	General Journal
3. Post Journal Entires	General Ledger
4. Prepare Working Trial Balance	Working Trial Balance
5. Adjust the General Ledger Accounts	Adjusted Trial Balance
6. Prepare Financial Statements	Financial Statements
7. Journalize and Post Closing Entries	General Journal and General Ledger
8. Prepare Post-Closing Trial Balance	Post-Closing Trial Balance

EXHIBIT 5.2 ▼
Invoice Issued by Snow Mountain Retreat

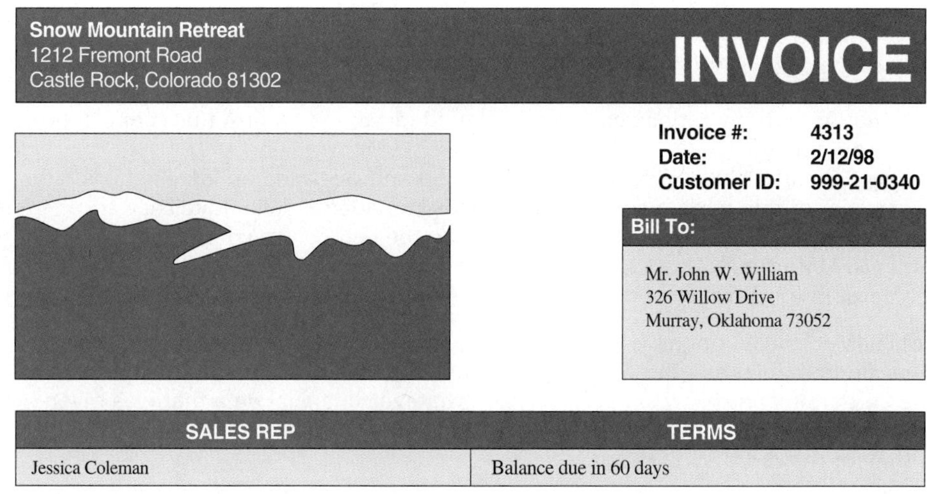

Snow Mountain Retreat
1212 Fremont Road
Castle Rock, Colorado 81302

INVOICE

Invoice #: 4313
Date: 2/12/98
Customer ID: 999-21-0340

Bill To:

Mr. John W. William
326 Willow Drive
Murray, Oklahoma 73052

SALES REP	TERMS
Jessica Coleman	Balance due in 60 days

ITEM	UNITS	DESCRIPTION	UNIT PR	TOTAL
Hope Room,	3 days	February 7–9, 1998	$125 per day	$ 375.00
double occupancy				

BAL DUE	$ 375.00

Quite often, accountants refer to "closing the books" at the end of the month. This monthly closing process involves the final five steps of the accounting cycle listed in Exhibit 5.1. The closing process begins with the preparation of a trial balance, sometimes referred to as a working trial balance. The final step of the closing process requires the preparation of another trial balance, a post-closing trial balance. Between the preparation of the working and post-closing trial balances, accountants adjust the general ledger accounts, prepare financial statements, and journalize and post closing entries.

As we progress through this chapter, keep in mind that the key purpose of the monthly accounting cycle is *to produce a set of financial statements that contain data*

A "Broken" Accounting Cycle for a Multinational Firm

FOR YOUR INFORMATION

Accountants integrate control activities into each step of a business's accounting cycle to enhance the reliability of the firm's periodic financial statements. This is a particularly challenging task for companies with foreign operations such as Fidelity Medical, Inc., a firm that manufactures medical equipment.

During the early 1990s, Fidelity Medical owned and operated an Israeli subsidiary. The controller of this foreign subsidiary regularly provided Fidelity Medical's corporate controller with financial data that were included in the company's consolidated financial statements. Unfortunately, these data contained numerous errors, errors not detected by the corporate controller but subsequently revealed by an SEC investigation.

> Fidelity Medical did not have internal controls in place to test the validity of foreign sales figures. In preparing Fidelity Medical's consolidated financial statements, [the corporate controller] simply included whatever financial data that was given her by the foreign controller and did not question or otherwise test the reliability of that information.

The SEC's investigation resulted in Fidelity Medical subsequently issuing corrected financial statements.

Source: The quotation and facts presented were drawn from Securities and Exchange Commission, *Accounting and Auditing Enforcement Release No. 558,* 5 May 1994.

needed by decision makers. Recall that publicly owned companies must submit annual and quarterly financial statements to the Securities and Exchange Commission (SEC). The SEC then makes these financial statements available to the public. Most privately owned companies prepare a formal set of financial statements for external users only once per year, at the end of their fiscal year. These financial statements are used in the preparation of income tax returns and are submitted to banks, other lenders, and investors. Both publicly and privately owned firms typically prepare financial statements each month for internal use.

THE ACCOUNTING CYCLE ILLUSTRATED

As noted earlier, Snow Mountain Retreat, a small corporation that operates a bed and breakfast inn, is used in this chapter to illustrate the accounting cycle. Exhibit 5.3 lists Snow Mountain Retreat's transactions for the first month of its existence, January 1998. If we are to record the transactions of this firm, we need a chart of accounts. Exhibit 5.4 contains Snow Mountain Retreat's chart of accounts.

Accounting Cycle, Step 1: Analyze Transactions

We begin our journey through Snow Mountain Retreat's accounting cycle by analyzing the company's January 1998 transactions. Accountants use their professional expertise to quickly dissect business transactions and determine how they should be recorded. Since

© Richard Elliot/Tony Stone Images

The accounting cycle for a business such as Snow Mountain Retreat begins with an analysis of individual transactions each accounting period and concludes with the preparation of a post-closing trial balance. The principal product of the accounting cycle is a set of financial statements.

EXHIBIT 5.3 ▼

Transactions of Snow Mountain Retreat during January 1998

1. January 1: Snow Mountain Retreat was incorporated by several investors. These individuals purchased 4,000 shares of Snow Mountain Retreat's common stock for $40,000.
2. January 1: Signed a one-year lease on a large, partially furnished house in Castle Rock, Colorado, to be operated as a bed and breakfast inn. Rent of $18,000 for one year was paid in cash.
3. January 1: Purchased furniture for $4,800, paying cash. The furniture is expected to have a useful life of two years and no salvage value at the end of its useful life.
4. January 3: Purchased $500 of supplies on credit.
5. January 8: Received $1,000 advance payment for two one-week rentals, January 22–28 and February 19–25.
6. January 19: Rented four rooms for the weekend, received cash of $1,500.
7. January 22: Paid part-time maintenance employee two-week salary of $400. Individual began working on January 8.
8. January 24: Rented two rooms for one week, received cash of $1,250.
9. January 26: Rented two rooms for weekend, received cash of $750.
10. January 30: Paid one-half of amount owed for supplies purchased on January 3.
11. January 31: Received $390 electricity bill for month of January.
12. January 31: Owners declared and paid themselves a dividend of $500.

EXHIBIT 5.4 ▼
Chart of Accounts for Snow Mountain Retreat

Balance Sheet Accounts	Income Statement Accounts
101 Cash	401 Rental Revenue
102 Interest Receivable	402 Interest Revenue
103 Supplies	501 Rent Expense
104 Prepaid Rent	502 Salaries Expense
105 Furniture	503 Utilities Expense
106 Accumulated Depreciation, Furniture	504 Supplies Expense
201 Accounts Payable	505 Depreciation Expense, Furniture
202 Unearned Rental Revenue	506 Income Taxes Expense
203 Salaries Payable	
204 Income Taxes Payable	
301 Common Stock	
302 Retained Earnings	
303 Dividends	
304 Income Summary	

you do not have such expertise at this point, let us use a condensed version of the format introduced in Chapter 4 to help us analyze Snow Mountain Retreat's transactions. Listed next are Snow Mountain Retreat's transactions for January 1998 and the accompanying analyses.

Transaction 1, January 1: Snow Mountain Retreat was incorporated by several investors. These individuals purchased 4,000 shares of Snow Mountain Retreat's common stock for $40,000. (At this point, we will credit the full amount of the proceeds from the sale of Snow Mountain Retreat's common stock to its Common Stock account. In a later chapter, we explore accounting for the issuance of common stock in more depth.)

Account	Type	Increase/ Decrease	Debit or Credit	Amount
Cash	Asset	Increase	Debit	$40,000
Common Stock	Owners' Equity	Increase	Credit	40,000

Transaction 2, January 1: Signed a one-year lease on a large, partially furnished house in Castle Rock, Colorado, to be operated as a bed and breakfast inn. Rent of $18,000 for one year was paid in cash.

Account	Type	Increase/ Decrease	Debit or Credit	Amount
Prepaid Rent	Asset	Increase	Debit	$18,000
Cash	Asset	Decrease	Credit	18,000

Transaction 3, January 1: Purchased furniture for $4,800, paying cash. The furniture is expected to have a useful life of two years and no salvage value at the end of its useful life.

Account	Type	Increase/ Decrease	Debit or Credit	Amount
Furniture	Asset	Increase	Debit	$4,800
Cash	Asset	Decrease	Credit	4,800

Transaction 4, January 3: Purchased $500 of supplies on credit.

Account	Type	Increase/ Decrease	Debit or Credit	Amount
Supplies	Asset	Increase	Debit	$500
Accounts Payable	Liability	Increase	Credit	500

Transaction 5, January 8: Received $1,000 advance payment for two one-week rentals, January 22–28 and February 19–25. This advance payment was refundable in full if the reservations were canceled. [Note: Revenue received before it is earned is recorded in a liability account. In this case, an appropriate title for such a liability account is Unearned Rental Revenue.]

Account	Type	Increase/ Decrease	Debit or Credit	Amount
Cash	Asset	Increase	Debit	$1,000
Unearned Rental Revenue	Liability	Increase	Credit	1,000

Transaction 6, January 19: Rented four rooms for the weekend, received cash of $1,500.

Account	Type	Increase/ Decrease	Debit or Credit	Amount
Cash	Asset	Increase	Debit	$1,500
Rental Revenue	Revenue	Increase	Credit	1,500

Transaction 7, January 22: Paid part-time maintenance employee two-week salary of $400. Individual began working on January 8.

Account	Type	Increase/ Decrease	Debit or Credit	Amount
Salaries Expense	Expense	Increase	Debit	$400
Cash	Asset	Decrease	Credit	400

Transaction 8, January 24: Rented two rooms for one week, received cash of $1,250.

Account	Type	Increase/ Decrease	Debit or Credit	Amount
Cash	Asset	Increase	Debit	$1,250
Rental Revenue	Revenue	Increase	Credit	1,250

Transaction 9, January 26: Rented two rooms for weekend, received cash of $750.

Account	Type	Increase/ Decrease	Debit or Credit	Amount
Cash	Asset	Increase	Debit	$750
Rental Revenue	Revenue	Increase	Credit	750

Transaction 10, January 30: Paid $250 of the $500 owed for the supplies purchased on January 3.

Account	Type	Increase/ Decrease	Debit or Credit	Amount
Accounts Payable	Liability	Decrease	Debit	$250
Cash	Asset	Decrease	Credit	250

Transaction 11, January 31: Received $390 electricity bill for month of January.

Account	Type	Increase/ Decrease	Debit or Credit	Amount
Utilities Expense	Expense	Increase	Debit	$390
Accounts Payable	Liability	Increase	Credit	390

Transaction 12, January 31: Owners declared and paid themselves a dividend of $500. (Note: Recall from Chapter 4 that the bookkeeping rules for Dividends are identical to those for expense accounts.)

Account	Type	Increase/ Decrease	Debit or Credit	Amount
Dividends	Contra Owners' Equity	Increase	Debit	$500
Cash	Asset	Decrease	Credit	500

Accounting Cycle, Steps 2 & 3: Journalize Transactions and Post Journal Entries

The second step of the accounting cycle is the journalizing of transactions, while the third step is the posting of journal entries to the general ledger. Chapter 4 listed the specific procedures to follow in preparing a journal entry and posting a journal entry to the general ledger. Applying these procedures to Snow Mountain Retreat's January 1998 transactions results in the journal entries shown in Exhibit 5.5 and the posted general ledger accounts shown in Exhibit 5.6. (Notice that in Exhibit 5.5 the appropriate account numbers are included in the post-reference column indicating that the journal entries at this point have been posted to the general ledger.)

Accounting Cycle, Step 4: Prepare a Working Trial Balance

To begin the process of closing the books at the end of an accounting period, accountants prepare a "working" trial balance of a business's general ledger accounts. Exhibit 5.7 presents a working trial balance for Snow Mountain Retreat as of January 31, 1998. The account balances listed in the trial balance in Exhibit 5.7 were taken from the general ledger accounts of Snow Mountain Retreat shown in Exhibit 5.6. Notice that only those general ledger accounts that have nonzero balances are included in a trial balance. If you refer to Exhibit 5.4, you will find that Snow Mountain Retreat had several accounts that had not been used during January 1998, at least to the point that the trial balance shown in Exhibit 5.7 was prepared. Since the total debits and credits in Snow Mountain Retreat's working trial balance in Exhibit 5.7 are equal, we can proceed to the next step of the accounting cycle, namely, adjusting the general ledger accounts.

EXHIBIT 5.5 ▼
General Journal Entries for Snow Mountain Retreat, January 1998

GENERAL JOURNAL					Page 1
Date		Description	Post Ref.	Debit	Credit
1998					
Jan.	1	Cash	101	40,000	
		Common Stock	301		40,000
		Sold 4,000 shares of common stock			
	1	Prepaid Rent	104	18,000	
		Cash	101		18,000
		Paid one year's rent in advance on rental property			
	1	Furniture	105	4,800	
		Cash	101		4,800
		Purchased furniture			
	3	Supplies	103	500	
		Accounts Payable	201		500
		Purchased supplies on credit			
	8	Cash	101	1,000	
		Unearned Rental Revenue	202		1,000
		Received advance payment for two one-week rentals			
	19	Cash	101	1,500	
		Rental Revenue	401		1,500
		Received payment for weekend rentals of four rooms			
	22	Salaries Expense	502	400	
		Cash	101		400
		Paid two-week salary of maintenance employee			
	24	Cash	101	1,250	
		Rental Revenue	401		1,250
		Received payment for two one-week rentals			

EXHIBIT 5.5 ▼
(Concluded)

GENERAL JOURNAL					Page 1
Date		**Description**	**Post Ref.**	**Debit**	**Credit**
1998					
Jan.	26	Cash	101	750	
		Rental Revenue	401		750
		Received payment for weekend rentals of two rooms			
	30	Accounts Payable	201	250	
		Cash	101		250
		Paid one-half of amount due for January 3 purchase of supplies			
	31	Utilities Expense	503	390	
		Accounts Payable	201		390
		Received January electricity bill			
	31	Dividends	303	500	
		Cash	101		500
		Declared and paid dividend			

EXHIBIT 5.6 ▼
General Ledger Accounts of Snow Mountain Retreat Following Posting of January 1998 Transactions

Cash							Account No. 101
						Balance	
Date		**Explanation**	**Post Ref.**	**Debit**	**Credit**	**Debit**	**Credit**
1998							
Jan.	1		GJ1	40,000		40,000	
	1		GJ1		18,000	22,000	
	1		GJ1		4,800	17,200	
	8		GJ1	1,000		18,200	
	19		GJ1	1,500		19,700	
	22		GJ1		400	19,300	
	24		GJ1	1,250		20,550	
	26		GJ1	750		21,300	
	30		GJ1		250	21,050	
	31		GJ1		500	20,550	

EXHIBIT 5.6
(Continued)

Supplies						Account No. 103	
Date		Explanation	Post Ref.	Debit	Credit	Balance Debit	Balance Credit
1998 Jan.	3		GJ1	500		500	

Prepaid Rent						Account No. 104	
Date		Explanation	Post Ref.	Debit	Credit	Balance Debit	Balance Credit
1998 Jan.	1		GJ1	18,000		18,000	

Furniture						Account No. 105	
Date		Explanation	Post Ref.	Debit	Credit	Balance Debit	Balance Credit
1998 Jan.	1		GJ1	4,800		4,800	

Accounts Payable						Account No. 201	
Date		Explanation	Post Ref.	Debit	Credit	Balance Debit	Balance Credit
1998 Jan.	3		GJ1		500		500
	30		GJ1	250			250
	31		GJ1		390		640

Unearned Rental Revenue						Account No. 202	
Date		Explanation	Post Ref.	Debit	Credit	Balance Debit	Balance Credit
1998 Jan.	8		GJ1		1,000		1,000

EXHIBIT 5.6
(Concluded)

Common Stock							Account No. 301
Date		Explanation	Post Ref.	Debit	Credit	Balance	
						Debit	Credit
1998 Jan.	1		GJ1		40,000		40,000

Dividends							Account No. 303
Date		Explanation	Post Ref.	Debit	Credit	Balance	
						Debit	Credit
1998 Jan.	31		GJ1	500		500	

Rental Revenue							Account No. 401
Date		Explanation	Post Ref.	Debit	Credit	Balance	
						Debit	Credit
1998 Jan.	19		GJ1		1,500		1,500
	24		GJ1		1,250		2,750
	26		GJ1		750		3,500

Salaries Expense							Account No. 502
Date		Explanation	Post Ref.	Debit	Credit	Balance	
						Debit	Credit
1998 Jan.	22		GJ1	400		400	

Utilities Expense							Account No. 503
Date		Explanation	Post Ref.	Debit	Credit	Balance	
						Debit	Credit
1998 Jan.	31		GJ1	390		390	

Tell Me No Secrets, and I'll Tell You No Lies

Suppose that you are the controller (chief accountant) for a company. Near the end of an accounting period, one of your subordinates informs you that there are large errors in a certain account. To prove his point, the employee hands you a sheet of paper listing the errors. What would you do at this point?

The controller of an Ohio-based company faced this very situation a few years ago. When the employee handed the sheet of paper to the controller, the controller refused to look at it. A subsequent investigation by the Securities and Exchange Commission (SEC) revealed that the controller did not inform other members of the company's accounting staff of the errors. Nor did the controller pass the information regarding the errors to the company's independent auditors. As a result, the SEC ruled that the controller had violated her responsibility to ensure that the company's financial statements were materially accurate.

Source: Securities and Exchange Commission, *Accounting and Auditing Enforcement Release No. 605*, 2 November 1994.

EXHIBIT 5.7 ▼
Working Trial Balance for Snow Mountain Retreat on January 31, 1998

SNOW MOUNTAIN RETREAT
TRIAL BALANCE
JANUARY 31, 1998

	Debit	Credit
Cash	$20,550	
Supplies	500	
Prepaid Rent	18,000	
Furniture	4,800	
Accounts Payable		$ 640
Unearned Rental Revenue		1,000
Common Stock		40,000
Dividends	500	
Rental Revenue		3,500
Salaries Expense	400	
Utilities Expense	390	
	$45,140	$45,140

Accounting Cycle, Step 5: Adjust the General Ledger Accounts

LEARNING OBJECTIVE 2 ▶
Develop period-ending adjustments to general ledger account balances.

Adjusting a business's general ledger accounts at the end of an accounting period is the most challenging step in the accounting cycle. To set the stage for our study of this step of the accounting cycle, let us first backtrack and examine why general ledger accounts must be "fine-tuned" at the end of an accounting period.

Chapter 2 discussed the two principal methods of accounting, accrual basis and cash basis. Under the cash basis of accounting, businesses generally record transactions *only* if they involve the payment or receipt of cash. Under the accrual basis of accounting, the economic impact of a transaction is recorded *whether or not* the transaction involves cash. With the primary exception of small businesses, most business entities use the accrual basis of accounting since it better represents the economic reality of their operations and financial condition. More to the point, accrual-basis accounting yields more useful information for internal and external users of financial statements.

At the end of each accounting period, a business that uses the accrual basis of accounting must adjust many of its general ledger account balances. These adjustments are required to ensure that the revenue and expense recognition rules (discussed in Chapter 2) have been properly applied each accounting period. For example, certain adjustments are required to ensure a proper matching of revenues and expenses each accounting period. That is, a business that applies the accrual basis of accounting must identify and record during each accounting period the expenses incurred to generate the revenues produced that period. Since some of these expenses have not been paid or recorded by the end of an accounting period, period-ending adjusting entries are necessary to "book" these expenses.

THE FOUR TYPES OF PERIOD-ENDING ADJUSTMENTS Accountants must identify the specific circumstances and events that require adjustments to a business's general ledger account balances at the end of each accounting period. Accountants identify such items by talking to management, scanning the accounting records, reviewing prior periods' adjusting entries, and, most important, using their intuition and accounting expertise. In sophisticated accounting systems, a computer may automatically "scan" the accounting records and produce a tentative list of adjusting journal entries. Nevertheless, one or more accountants will almost certainly review that list to ensure that it is complete.

Exhibit 5.8 presents the four general types of period-ending adjustments made by businesses that use the accrual basis of accounting. Notice that an example of each type of adjustment is included in Exhibit 5.8. Additionally, Exhibit 5.8 lists the basic form of each adjustment or adjusting journal entry. For example, notice that the first type of adjustment results in a debit to an expense account and a credit to an asset account. Finally, notice that embedded in Exhibit 5.8 are references to the following four terms: deferred expense, deferred revenue, accrued liability, and accrued revenue.

DEFERRALS AND ACCRUALS Before analyzing the period-ending adjustments for Snow Mountain Retreat, you will find it helpful to become familiar with deferrals and accruals. Accountants frequently use these terms when developing and referring to period-ending adjustments.

Assets such as prepaid rent and liabilities such as unearned rental revenue are often referred to as deferrals or, more specifically, as deferred expenses and deferred revenues, respectively. A **deferred expense** is an asset that represents a prepayment of an expense

deferred expense

EXHIBIT 5.8 ▼
Four Types of Period-Ending Adjustments

- Recognition of Expenses Related to Assets.
  Example: Adjusting entry to recognize expired portion of Prepaid Rent.
  Basic form: Debit Expense, Credit Asset
  Note: The asset credited in the above entry is a *deferred expense.*
- Recognition of Revenues Related to Liabilities.
  Example: Adjusting entry to recognize revenue for advance customer payments that have been earned by the end of an accounting period.
  Basic form: Debit Liability, Credit Revenue
  Note: The liability debted in the above entry is a *deferred revenue.*
- Recognition of Expenses Incurred but not yet Paid.
  Example: Adjusting entry to record wages owed to employees at the end of an accounting period.
  Basic form: Debit Expense, Credit Liability
  Note: The liability credited in the above entry is an *accrued liability.*
- Recognition of Revenues Earned but not yet Received.
  Example Adjusting entry to recognize interest revenue earned on a bank account during an accounting period.
  Basic form: Debit Asset, Credit Revenue
  Note: The asset debited in the above entry is an *accrued revenue.*

item. When a deferred expense is paid (prepaid), an asset account is debited and the Cash account credited. For example, assume that a company prepays the rent for a six-month equipment lease. The appropriate entry would be to debit Prepaid Rent, an asset account, and credit Cash. Over the term of the lease agreement, the economic benefit provided by the asset (prepayment) will be gradually consumed. As a result, by the end of the lease term, the full amount of the rent prepayment should be credited to Prepaid Rent and debited to Rent Expense, reflecting the fact that the asset has been consumed and "charged off" to an expense account. At the risk of being redundant, do not be misled by the phrase deferred *expense.* This term refers to an asset, *not* an expense. Granted, such assets are eventually recognized, or written off, as expenses. But, when they are initially recorded, these items are assets.

The terms "deferred expense" and "prepaid expense" are interchangeable. When deferred expenses are included in a balance sheet, they are most often referred to as prepaid expenses. Many companies consolidate several deferred expenses into a single balance sheet amount. For instance, Harry's Farmers Market, a Georgia-based retail chain specializing in perishable grocery products, reported $828,885 of "Prepaid Expenses" in a recent balance sheet.

deferred revenue

A **deferred revenue** is a liability resulting from an amount received by a business for a service or product that it will provide or deliver in the future. The Unearned Rental Revenue account of Snow Mountain Retreat is an example of a deferred revenue account. When the earnings process is completed for a deferred revenue, the appropriate deferred revenue account is debited with an offsetting credit to a revenue account. Why are deferred revenues treated as liabilities for balance sheet purposes? Because they are, in fact, liabilities: something is owed to the customer, either a product, or a service, or a refund. For example, although there are exceptions, amounts paid in advance on hotel, airline, and other reservations are generally refundable to customers if the reservations are canceled. A recent balance sheet of Southwest Airlines reported a $42

Airline passengers typically purchase their tickets several days or weeks in advance of taking a flight. Advance payments for airline tickets must be reported as current liabilities in the balance sheets of airline companies.

million deferred revenue liability. This amount represented payments received for tickets purchased in advance. Southwest Airlines included this liability in the current liabilities section of its balance sheet on a line item labeled "Air Traffic Liability."

Accountants use the term "accruals" to refer to asset and liability accounts that are entered in a business's accounting records via period-ending adjusting journal entries. "Accrued liabilities" and "accrued revenues" are the more specific terms commonly used when referring to these items. A liability stemming from an expense that has been incurred but not yet paid is referred to as an **accrued liability.** A common accrued liability is salaries payable. The end of a business's accounting period typically does not coincide with the end of a payroll period. So, at the end of most accounting periods, a business's employees have earned salaries or wages for which they have not been paid. These amounts are recognized via an adjusting entry by debiting an expense account, such as Salaries Expense, and crediting a liability account, such as Salaries Payable. A term used interchangeably with accrued liability is "accrued expense." Recognize that when an accountant uses the term accrued *expense,* he or she is referring to a liability, *not* an expense. Granted, when an accrued expense (accrued liability) is recorded, the offsetting debit is to an expense account.

accrued liability

An **accrued revenue** is a receivable resulting from revenue that has been earned but not yet received. At the end of a recent year, Morgan Stanley, a large investment banking company, reported Fees Receivable of more than $291 million on its balance sheet. This figure represented fees for services that Morgan Stanley had provided to customers but not collected by year-end. The offsetting credit for the $291 million debit to Fees Receivable was to a revenue account such as Fees Earned or Fee Revenue.

accrued revenue

ADJUSTING JOURNAL ENTRIES FOR SNOW MOUNTAIN RETREAT Now that we have become familiar with the purpose, types, and terminology associated with adjusting journal entries, we can go about the task of adjusting the general ledger accounts of Snow Mountain Retreat. Following are seven events or circumstances requiring adjustments to the company's general ledger account balances as of January 31,

1998. Since period-ending general ledger adjustments can be difficult for accountants-in-training to grasp, these items are analyzed by using the detailed format employed in Chapter 4 to acquaint you with the journalizing process.

Adjustment A: Expiration of Prepaid Rent

At the beginning of January 1998, the owners of Snow Mountain Retreat paid one year's rent, $18,000, in advance on the large house to be used in their business. By the end of January, one-twelfth, or $1,500, of this deferred or prepaid expense had been "used up" since one month of the twelve-month term of the lease had expired. The decrease in this asset should be recognized so that the company's assets are not overstated. Likewise, to satisfy the matching principle, an expense equal to the decline in the balance of the Prepaid Rent account should be recorded. This expense was one of many that the company's owners incurred to generate revenue during January 1998.

To decrease the balance of the Prepaid Rent account, an asset account, it must be credited. The offsetting debit is to Rent Expense, an expense account.

Analysis:

Account	**Type**	**Increase/ Decrease**	**Debit or Credit**	**Amount**
Rent Expense	Expense	Increase	Debit	$1,500
Prepaid Rent	Asset	Decrease	Credit	1,500

Effect on Accounting Equation:

Assets	=	Liabilities	+	Owners' Equity
− 1,500				− 1,500

Journal Entry:

Rent Expense.	1,500	
Prepaid Rent.		1,500

Adjustment B: Depreciation of Furniture

On January 1, 1998, the owners of Snow Mountain Retreat purchased furniture at a cost of $4,800 to place in their rental property. Recall from Chapter 2 that long-lived assets such as buildings, equipment, and furniture must be depreciated. Depreciation refers to the process of systematically allocating the cost of assets to the accounting periods that they provide an economic benefit to a business. A common depreciation method is the straight-line method, the method adopted by Snow Mountain Retreat. Under this method, the depreciable cost of an asset (total cost less estimated salvage value at the end of its useful life) is written off as "depreciation expense" in equal amounts over the accounting periods the asset is expected to be in service.

The depreciable cost of the furniture purchased by Snow Mountain Retreat is $4,800: purchase cost of $4,800 less a zero estimated salvage value. Since the furniture is expected to have a useful life of two years or twenty-four months, depreciation expense of $200 ($4,800/24) should be recognized (debited to Depreciation Expense) each month for this asset. The offsetting credit is not made to the account of the asset being depreciated. Instead, this credit is recorded in a contra asset account, Accumulated Depreciation, so that the historical cost of the asset is preserved in its general ledger account.

Analysis:

Account	Type	Increase/ Decrease	Debit or Credit	Amount
Depreciation Expense, Furniture	Expense	Increase	Debit	$200
Accumulated Depreciation, Furniture	Contra Asset	Increase	Credit	200

Effect on Accounting Equation:

Assets	=	Liabilities	+	Owners' Equity
− 200				− 200

Journal Entry:

Depreciation Expense, Furniture	200	
Accumulated Depreciation, Furniture		200

Adjustment C: Supplies Used

At the end of January 1998, the owners of Snow Mountain Retreat counted the business's supplies. The owners determined that $80 of the $500 of supplies purchased earlier in the month were used during January.

Analysis:

Account	Type	Increase/ Decrease	Debit or Credit	Amount
Supplies Expense	Expense	Increase	Debit	$80
Supplies	Asset	Decrease	Credit	80

Effect on Accounting Equation:

Assets	=	Liabilities	+	Owners' Equity
− 80				− 80

Journal Entry:

Supplies Expense	80	
Supplies		80

Adjustment D: Recognition of Revenue on Advance Rental Payment

On January 8, 1998, an individual paid $1,000 to Snow Mountain Retreat for two one-week room rentals, January 22–28 and February 19–25. When this amount was received, an entry debiting Cash for $1,000 and crediting the liability account Unearned Rental Revenue for the same amount was made. By the end of January, one-half of this $1,000 advance payment had been earned by Snow Mountain Retreat since the customer had used her reservation for the week of January 22–28. To recognize this revenue, the Rental Revenue account must be credited $500 with an offsetting debit in the same amount to Unearned Rental Revenue.

Analysis:

Account	Type	Increase/ Decrease	Debit or Credit	Amount
Unearned Rental Revenue	Liability	Decrease	Debit	$500
Rental Revenue	Revenue	Increase	Credit	500

Effect on Accounting Equation:

Assets	=	Liabilities	+	Owners' Equity
		− 500		+ 500

Journal Entry:

Unearned Rental Revenue	500	
Rental Revenue		500

Adjustment E: Recognition of Interest Revenue

During January 1998, Snow Mountain Retreat had cash on deposit in a bank account. By the end of the month, the company had earned interest revenue of $120 on this bank account, interest that had not been paid to Snow Mountain Retreat. To recognize this revenue, Interest Revenue is credited $120 with an equal debit to the asset account Interest Receivable.

Analysis:

Account	Type	Increase/ Decrease	Debit or Credit	Amount
Interest Receivable	Asset	Increase	Debit	$120
Interest Revenue	Revenue	Increase	Credit	120

Effect on Accounting Equation:

Assets	=	Liabilities	+	Owners' Equity
+ 120				+ 120

Journal Entry:

Interest Receivable	120	
Interest Revenue		120

Adjustment F: Recognition of Unpaid Salary Expense

On January 8, 1998, the owners of Snow Mountain Retreat hired a part-time maintenance employee. This individual is paid $400 every two weeks, which translates to $40 per day for Monday through Friday. (For the time being, we ignore payroll taxes and other deductions that affect the employee's take-home pay.) The employee received his first paycheck on January 22 and was scheduled to receive his second paycheck on February 5. As of January 31, the employee had worked eight days for which he had not been paid, meaning that Snow Mountain Retreat owed this individual $320 at the end of January. Likewise, the company had an unrecorded expense in the same amount.

Analysis:

Account	Type	Increase/ Decrease	Debit or Credit	Amount
Salaries Expense	Expense	Increase	Debit	$320
Salaries Payable	Liability	Increase	Credit	320

Effect on Accounting Equation:

Assets	=	Liabilities	+	Owners' Equity
		+ 320		− 320

Journal Entry:

Salaries Expense	320	
Salaries Payable		320

Adjustment G: Recognition of Estimated Income Tax Expense

At the end of each year, Snow Mountain Retreat will be required to pay a corporate income tax on any profit that it earns during that year. On January 31, 1998, the owners of Snow Mountain Retreat did not know how much their company would earn during 1998. Consequently, they could not determine exactly how much income tax, if any, the company would be required to pay at the end of the year. Nevertheless, a business must estimate its income tax expense each accounting period because of the expense recognition rule. The owners of Snow Mountain Retreat estimated that $200 of corporate income tax would eventually be paid on the profit earned by the company during January.

Analysis:

Account	Type	Increase/ Decrease	Debit or Credit	Amount
Income Taxes Expense	Expense	Increase	Debit	$200
Income Taxes Payable	Liability	Increase	Credit	200

Effect on Accounting Equation:

Assets	=	Liabilities	+	Owners' Equity
		+ 200		− 200

Journal Entry:

Income Taxes Expense	200	
Income Taxes Payable		200

Exhibit 5.9 contains Snow Mountain Retreat's adjusting journal entries for the accounting period ending January 31, 1998. After the period-ending adjustments have been journalized, they must be posted to the appropriate accounts in the general ledger. Exhibit 5.9 indicates that the posting has been completed since account numbers have been entered in the post-reference column of the general journal.

Accounting Cycle, Step 6: Prepare Financial Statements

LEARNING OBJECTIVE 3 ▶ Prepare an income statement, a statement of stockholders' equity, and a balance sheet.

Once a business's general ledger accounts have been adjusted at the end of an accounting period, the firm's accountants prepare an adjusted trial balance of those accounts. Exhibit 5.10 presents Snow Mountain Retreat's adjusted trial balance as of January 31, 1998. An adjusted trial balance contains the information needed to prepare a firm's income statement, statement of owners' or stockholders' equity, and balance sheet. (Recall that the preparation of a statement of cash flows is discussed in a later chapter.) A useful aid in sorting the account balances in an adjusted trial balance into the appropriate financial statements is a business's chart of accounts. Notice that Snow Mountain Retreat's chart of accounts in Exhibit 5.4 segregates the firm's accounts into balance sheet and income statement accounts. In the adjusted trial balance in Exhibit 5.10,

EXHIBIT 5.9 ▼
Adjusting Journal Entries for Snow Mountain Retreat, January 1998

GENERAL JOURNAL					Page 1
Date		**Description**	**Post Ref.**	**Debit**	**Credit**
1998					
Jan.	31	Rent Expense	501	1,500	
		Prepaid Rent	104		1,500
		To record rent expense for January			
	31	Depreciation Expense, Furniture	505	200	
		Accumulated Depreciation Furniture	106		200
		To record depreciation expense for January			
	31	Supplies Expense	504	80	
		Supplies	103		80
		To record supplies used in January			
	31	Unearned Rental Revenue	202	500	
		Rental Revenue	401		500
		To recognize the portion of an advance payment of revenue earned in January			
	31	Interest Receivable	102	120	
		Interest Revenue	402		120
		To recognize interest revenue earned in January			
	31	Salaries Expense	502	320	
		Salaries Payable	203		320
		To record salary owed to maintenance employee at the end of January			
	31	Income Taxes Expense	506	200	
		Income Taxes Payable	204		200
		To record estimated income tax expense for January			

Snow Mountain Retreat's accounts are presented in the same order they appear in the firm's chart of accounts. For example, the income statement accounts begin with Rental Revenue.

Exhibit 5.11 presents Snow Mountain Retreat's income statement for January 1998. Snow Mountain Retreat's revenues and expenses are listed in this income statement in the order they appear in the adjusted trial balance. In a later chapter, we review an income statement format that is more commonly used by corporations.

Exhibit 5.12 presents Snow Mountain Retreat's statement of stockholders' equity for January 1998. A statement of stockholders' equity reconciles the beginning-of-the-period and end-of-the-period balances of a corporation's stockholders' equity accounts. Notice in Exhibit 5.12 that three items must be considered when computing a company's period-ending retained earnings: the beginning-of-the-period retained earnings balance, net income for the period, and any dividends paid by the firm during the period.

If you refer to Exhibit 5.10, you will notice that Snow Mountain Retreat's Retained Earnings account was not included in the firm's adjusted trial balance prepared on

EXHIBIT 5.10 ▼
Adjusted Trial Balance for Snow Mountain Retreat

SNOW MOUNTAIN RETREAT
ADJUSTED TRIAL BALANCE
JANUARY 31, 1998

	Debit	Credit
Cash	$20,550	
Interest Receivable	120	
Supplies	420	
Prepaid Rent	16,500	
Furniture	4,800	
Accumulated Depreciation, Furniture		$ 200
Accounts Payable		640
Unearned Rental Revenue		500
Salaries Payable		320
Income Taxes Payable		200
Common Stock		40,000
Dividends	500	
Rental Revenue		4,000
Interest Revenue		120
Rent Expense	1,500	
Salaries Expense	720	
Utilities Expense	390	
Supplies Expense	80	
Depreciation Expense, Furniture	200	
Income Taxes Expense	200	
	$45,980	$45,980

EXHIBIT 5.11 ▼
Income Statement for Snow Mountain Retreat

SNOW MOUNTAIN RETREAT
INCOME STATEMENT
FOR THE MONTH ENDED JANUARY 31, 1998

Revenues		
Rental revenue	$4,000	
Interest revenue	120	
Total revenues		$4,120
Expenses		
Rent expense	$1,500	
Salaries expense	720	
Utilities expense	390	
Supplies expense	80	
Depreciation expense, furniture	200	
Income taxes expense	200	
Total expenses		3,090
Net Income		$1,030

January 31, 1998. Because Snow Mountain Retreat began operations on January 1, 1998, no dollar amounts had been posted to its Retained Earnings account at the point that the adjusted trial balance was prepared. But, all of the information needed to compute the firm's retained earnings as of January 31, 1998, is available in the adjusted trial balance. All we must do to compute Snow Mountain Retreat's January 31, 1998, retained earnings is to subtract the $500 of dividends paid during January from the firm's net income of $1,030 for the month. If the firm had been in existence prior to

EXHIBIT 5.12 ▼
Statement of Stockholders' Equity for Snow Mountain Retreat

SNOW MOUNTAIN RETREAT
STATEMENT OF STOCKHOLDERS' EQUITY
FOR THE MONTH ENDED JANUARY 31, 1998

	Common Stock	**Retained Earnings**
Balance, January 1, 1998	$ 0	$ 0
Sale of common stock	40,000	
Net income		1,030
Dividends		(500)
Balance, January 31, 1998	$40,000	$ 530

January 1, 1998, the beginning-of-the-period balance of Retained Earnings would have been included in the adjusted trial balance—and in the working trial balance, for that matter. Generally, a firm's period-ending retained earnings is computed by adding the beginning-of-the-period retained earnings to net income for the period and then subtracting dividends paid during the period. You will discover shortly that Snow Mountain Retreat's Retained Earnings account will have a balance of exactly $530 when we complete the closing process for the firm. Notice that amount is the retained earnings figure reported in Snow Mountain Retreat's statement of stockholders' equity shown in Exhibit 5.12.

Exhibit 5.13 presents Snow Mountain Retreat's balance sheet as of January 31, 1998. Notice that the company's balance sheet is "classified." That is, current assets and current liabilities are listed under separate headings—the company does not have any

EXHIBIT 5.13 ▼
Balance Sheet for Snow Mountain Retreat

SNOW MOUNTAIN RETREAT BALANCE SHEET JANUARY 31, 1998		
Assets		
Current assets:		
Cash		$20,550
Interest receivable		120
Supplies		420
Prepaid rent		16,500
Total current assets		$37,590
Furniture	$4,800	
Less: accumulated depreciation	(200)	4,600
Total assets		$42,190
Liabilities		
Current liabilities:		
Accounts payable		$ 640
Unearned rental revenue		500
Salaries payable		320
Income taxes payable		200
Total current liabilities		$ 1,660
Stockholders' Equity		
Common stock		$40,000
Retained earnings		530
Total stockholders' equity		$40,530
Total liabilities and stockholders' equity		$42,190

long-term liabilities. Classifying assets and liabilities into current and noncurrent items assists decision makers in analyzing a company's balance sheet data. Finally, notice that the retained earnings figure included in Snow Mountain Retreat's balance sheet is the amount previously computed for that account when the statement of stockholders' equity was prepared.

In most computerized accounting systems, financial statements are not prepared manually. In such systems, accountants can generate a set of financial statements electronically after adjusting the general ledger accounts. In fact, many large public companies not only prepare their financial statements electronically but also deliver them electronically to external users via the Internet. The EDGAR (electronic data gathering and retrieval system) Internet Web site maintained by the Securities and Exchange Commission provides investors and other interested parties timely access to hundreds of large companies' financial statements in an electronic format.

Accounting Cycle, Step 7: Journalize and Post Closing Entries

LEARNING OBJECTIVE 4
Journalize and post closing entries.

The temporary accounts of a business must begin each accounting period with a zero balance. The balances of temporary accounts are not simply erased at the end of an accounting period. Instead, they are transferred via closing entries to an owners' equity account. For a corporation, such as Snow Mountain Retreat, that account is Retained Earnings. Accountants typically establish an **Income Summary** account to help them close temporary accounts each accounting period. This account is used to "funnel" the balances of all temporary accounts into the Retained Earnings account via closing entries. Listed next are the four closing entries that businesses make at the end of an accounting period.

Income Summary

1. An entry to transfer credit balances of income statement accounts to the Income Summary account.
2. An entry to transfer debit balances of income statement accounts to the Income Summary account.
3. An entry to transfer the balance of the Income Summary account to the Retained Earnings account.
4. An entry to transfer the balance of the Dividends account to the Retained Earnings account.

Exhibit 5.14 contains the closing entries for Snow Mountain Retreat at the end of January 1998. The first entry in Exhibit 5.14 closes the two income statement accounts that have credit balances at the end of January 1998, namely, Rental Revenue and Interest Revenue. After this first closing entry is posted, the balances of those two accounts will be zero, while the Income Summary account will have a credit balance of $4,120.

The second entry shown in Exhibit 5.14 closes the income statement accounts of Snow Mountain Retreat that have debit balances at the end of January 1998. Following the posting of that entry, each of Snow Mountain Retreat's expense accounts will have a zero balance, while the Income Summary account will have a credit balance of $1,030. This latter amount equals Snow Mountain Retreat's net income for January 1998. By transferring the period-ending balances of all revenue and expense accounts to the Income Summary account, a business's accountants can confirm that the proper

EXHIBIT 5.14
Closing Entries for Snow Mountain Retreat

GENERAL JOURNAL					Page 1
Date		Description	Post Ref.	Debit	Credit
1998					
Jan.	31	Rental Revenue	401	4,000	
		Interest Revenue	402	120	
		Income Summary	304		4,120
		To close the revenue accounts			
	31	Income Summary	304	3,090	
		Rent Expense	501		1,500
		Salaries Expense	502		720
		Utilities Expense	503		390
		Supplies Expense	504		80
		Depreciation Expense, Furniture	505		200
		Income Taxes Expense	506		200
		To close the expense accounts			
	31	Income Summary	304	1,030	
		Retained Earnings	302		1,030
		To close the Income Summary account			
	31	Retained Earnings	302	500	
		Dividends	303		500
		To close the Dividends account			

net income amount was determined. Once this checking procedure has been completed, the next step is to close the Income Summary account by transferring its balance to the Retained Earnings account. The third closing entry shown in Exhibit 5.14 accomplishes this objective.

The final closing entry for Snow Mountain Retreat transfers the balance of the Dividends account to the Retained Earnings account. Since many companies do not pay dividends or pay dividends infrequently, this final closing entry is not always necessary.

The account numbers appearing in the post-reference column in Exhibit 5.14 indicate that Snow Mountain Retreat's closing entries have been posted to the appropriate general ledger accounts. Snow Mountain Retreat's general ledger accounts, after the posting of the adjusting and closing entries, are shown in Exhibit 5.15. Notice that, as promised earlier, Snow Mountain Retreat's Retained Earnings account has a balance of $530 following the completion of the closing process.

EXHIBIT 5.15

General Ledger Accounts of Snow Mountain Retreat Following the Posting of Adjusting and Closing Entries for January 1998

Cash — Account No. 101

Date		Explanation	Post Ref.	Debit	Credit	Balance Debit	Balance Credit
1998							
Jan.	1		GJ1	40,000		40,000	
	1		GJ1		18,000	22,000	
	1		GJ1		4,800	17,200	
	8		GJ1	1,000		18,200	
	19		GJ1	1,500		19,700	
	22		GJ1		400	19,300	
	24		GJ1	1,250		20,550	
	26		GJ1	750		21,300	
	30		GJ1		250	21,050	
	31		GJ1		500	20,550	

Interest Receivable — Account No. 102

Date		Explanation	Post Ref.	Debit	Credit	Balance Debit	Balance Credit
1998							
Jan.	31	Adjusting	GJ2	120		120	

Supplies — Account No. 103

Date		Explanation	Post Ref.	Debit	Credit	Balance Debit	Balance Credit
1998							
Jan.	3		GJ1	500		500	
	31	Adjusting	GJ2		80	420	

Prepaid Rent — Account No. 104

Date		Explanation	Post Ref.	Debit	Credit	Balance Debit	Balance Credit
1998							
Jan.	1		GJ1	18,000		18,000	
	31	Adjusting	GJ2		1,500	16,500	

EXHIBIT 5.15 ▼
(Continued)

Furniture							Account No. 105
						Balance	
Date		Explanation	Post Ref.	Debit	Credit	Debit	Credit
1998 Jan.	1		GJ1	4,800		4,800	

Accumulated Depreciation, Furniture							Account No. 106
						Balance	
Date		Explanation	Post Ref.	Debit	Credit	Debit	Credit
1998 Jan.	31	Adjusting	GJ2		200		200

Accounts Payable							Account No. 201
						Balance	
Date		Explanation	Post Ref.	Debit	Credit	Debit	Credit
1998 Jan.	3		GJ1		500		500
	30		GJ1	250			250
	31		GJ1		390		640

Unearned Rental Revenue							Account No. 202
						Balance	
Date		Explanation	Post Ref.	Debit	Credit	Debit	Credit
1998 Jan.	8		GJ1		1,000		1,000
	31	Adjusting	GJ2	500			500

Salaries Payable							Account No. 203
						Balance	
Date		Explanation	Post Ref.	Debit	Credit	Debit	Credit
1998 Jan.	31	Adjusting	GJ2		320		320

EXHIBIT 5.15 ▼
(Continued)

Income Taxes Payable						Account No. 204	
Date		Explanation	Post Ref.	Debit	Credit	Balance Debit	Balance Credit
1998 Jan.	31	Adjusting	GJ2		200		200

Common Stock						Account No. 301	
Date		Explanation	Post Ref.	Debit	Credit	Balance Debit	Balance Credit
1998 Jan.	1		GJ1		40,000		40,000

Retained Earnings						Account No. 302	
Date		Explanation	Post Ref.	Debit	Credit	Balance Debit	Balance Credit
1998 Jan.	31	Closing	GJ3		1,030		1,030
	31	Closing	GJ3	500			530

Dividends						Account No. 303	
Date		Explanation	Post Ref.	Debit	Credit	Balance Debit	Balance Credit
1998 Jan.	31		GJ1	500		500	
	31	Closing	GJ3		500	0	

Income Summary						Account No. 304	
Date		Explanation	Post Ref.	Debit	Credit	Balance Debit	Balance Credit
1998 Jan.	31	Closing	GJ3		4,120		4,120
	31	Closing	GJ3	3,090			1,030
	31	Closing	GJ3	1,030			0

EXHIBIT 5.15 ▼
(Continued)

Rental Revenue						**Account No. 401**	
						Balance	
Date		**Explanation**	**Post Ref.**	**Debit**	**Credit**	**Debit**	**Credit**
1998							
Jan.	19		GJ1		1,500		1,500
	24		GJ1		1,250		2,750
	26		GJ1		750		3,500
	31	Adjusting	GJ2		500		4,000
	31	Closing	GJ3	4,000			0

Interest Revenue						**Account No. 402**	
						Balance	
Date		**Explanation**	**Post Ref.**	**Debit**	**Credit**	**Debit**	**Credit**
1998							
Jan.	31	Adjusting	GJ2		120		120
	31	Closing	GJ3	120			0

Rent Expense						**Account No. 501**	
						Balance	
Date		**Explanation**	**Post Ref.**	**Debit**	**Credit**	**Debit**	**Credit**
1998							
Jan.	31	Adjusting	GJ2	1,500		1,500	
	31	Closing	GJ3		1,500	0	

Salaries Expense						**Account No. 502**	
						Balance	
Date		**Explanation**	**Post Ref.**	**Debit**	**Credit**	**Debit**	**Credit**
1998							
Jan.	22		GJ1	400		400	
	31	Adjusting	GJ2	320		720	
	31	Closing	GJ3		720	0	

Utilities Expense						**Account No. 503**	
						Balance	
Date		**Explanation**	**Post Ref.**	**Debit**	**Credit**	**Debit**	**Credit**
1998							
Jan.	31		GJ1	390		390	
	31	Closing	GJ3		390	0	

EXHIBIT 5.15 ▼
(Concluded)

Supplies Expense						**Account No. 504**	
			Post			**Balance**	
Date		**Explanation**	**Ref.**	**Debit**	**Credit**	**Debit**	**Credit**
1998							
Jan.	31	Adjusting	GJ2	80		80	
	31	Closing	GJ3		80	0	

Depreciation Expense, Furniture						**Account No. 505**	
			Post			**Balance**	
Date		**Explanation**	**Ref.**	**Debit**	**Credit**	**Debit**	**Credit**
1998							
Jan.	31	Adjusting	GJ2	200		200	
	31	Closing	GJ3		200	0	

Income Taxes Expense						**Account No. 506**	
			Post			**Balance**	
Date		**Explanation**	**Ref.**	**Debit**	**Credit**	**Debit**	**Credit**
1998							
Jan.	31	Adjusting	GJ2	200		200	
	31	Closing	GJ3		200	0	

Accounting Cycle, Step 8: Prepare Post-Closing Trial Balance

LEARNING ◄ OBJECTIVE 5
Prepare a post-closing trial balance.

The accounting cycle concludes with the preparation of a post-closing trial balance, which is a general ledger trial balance following the posting of adjusting and closing entries. Accountants prepare a post-closing trial balance to ensure that the general ledger is in balance at the end of the accounting cycle. If the totals of the debit and credit columns of this trial balance are equal, the adjusting and closing entries are assumed to have been entered correctly in the accounting records. Exhibit 5.16 presents the January 31, 1998, post-closing trial balance of Snow Mountain Retreat. Notice that only the company's permanent or balance sheet accounts are listed in this trial balance. At this point, each of the temporary accounts has been closed and thus has a zero balance.

You have been reminded on several occasions in this chapter and the previous chapter that most accounting tasks are generally much easier to complete in a computer-based accounting system compared with a manual accounting system. This observation also applies to closing a business's accounting records at the end of an accounting period. In

EXHIBIT 5.16 ▼
Post-Closing Trial Balance for Snow Mountain Retreat

SNOW MOUNTAIN RETREAT
POST-CLOSING TRIAL BALANCE
JANUARY 31, 1998

	Debit	Credit
Cash	$20,550	
Interest Receivable	120	
Supplies	420	
Prepaid Rent	16,500	
Furniture	4,800	
Accumulated Depreciation, Furniture		$ 200
Accounts Payable		640
Unearned Rental Revenue		500
Salaries Payable		320
Income Taxes Payable		200
Common Stock		40,000
Retained Earnings		530
	$42,390	$42,390

a fully computerized accounting system, accountants may close a company's accounting records and print a post-closing trial balance in a matter of seconds by activating the appropriate computer software instructions.

Turning the Tables on the IRS: Audit of Tax Agency Turns Up Messy Accounting Records

FOR YOUR INFORMATION

Just like the accountants for a private business, accountants for governmental agencies complete an accounting cycle each accounting period. During the late 1980s, Congress decided that the accounting practices of federal agencies should be reviewed periodically by federal auditors. In recent years, these reviews have uncovered significant lapses in accounting and control procedures at several federal agencies. Surprisingly, the federal agency that has been the target of the most criticism by federal auditors is staffed largely by accountants, namely, the Internal Revenue Service (IRS). For three consecutive years during the 1990s, the IRS's accounting records were in such disarray that federal auditors were unable to express an opinion on the reliability of the agency's financial statements.

Source: "Shoddy Bookkeeping by the IRS Draws Renewed Fire from the GAO," *The Wall Street Journal,* December 20, 1995, A1.

SUMMARY

Each accounting period, a set of accounting procedures referred to as the accounting cycle must be completed for a business. These procedures convert financial data resulting from a business's transactions during an accounting period into a set of financial statements. The accounting cycle begins with an analysis of these transactions. Key information regarding business transactions is obtained from source documents such as invoices, legal contracts, and purchase orders. After transactions have been analyzed, they are journalized and posted to the appropriate general ledger accounts.

At the end of each accounting period, accountants adjust a business's general ledger accounts and then prepare the firm's financial statements. Following the journalizing and posting of closing entries, a post-closing trial balance is prepared to determine whether the general ledger is in balance.

APPENDIX: USING A WORK SHEET IN THE CLOSING PROCESS

Accountants may use a "work sheet" to assist them in closing a business's accounting records at the end of each accounting period, particularly if the given firm has a manual accounting system. A work sheet is simply a schedule used by accountants to help them complete an accounting task. Work sheets come in various sizes and formats. The ten-column work sheet format shown in Exhibit 5.17 is designed specifically for use in the closing process at the end of an accounting period.

In this appendix, we briefly review the procedures used when a work sheet is integrated into the closing process. Tracking accounting data through the closing process via a work sheet will help you grasp the nature of this process and better understand the purpose of the various closing procedures. To illustrate the use of a work sheet, we will rely on Snow Mountain Retreat's accounting data for January 1998. The completed work sheet in Exhibit 5.17 could have been used during the closing of Snow Mountain Retreat's accounting records at the end of January 1998.

When a ten-column work sheet is used in the closing process, accountants enter their firm's working trial balance in the first two columns of the work sheet, as shown in Exhibit 5.17. Next, the period-ending adjustments are entered in the two Adjustments columns of the work sheet. If an account affected by an adjustment is not included in the working trial balance, the title of that account is entered below the accounts that were included in the trial balance. To minimize the likelihood of errors in preparing a work sheet, accountants code each adjustment. In Exhibit 5.17, notice that the adjustments are coded with the alphabetical references used when these adjustments were analyzed in this chapter. For example, adjustment "a" involves the $1,500 debit to the Rent Expense account and the equal credit to Prepaid Rent.

After entering all of the adjustments on the work sheet, the debit and credit Adjustments columns are "footed"—an accounting term that means to add a column of numbers—and the totals are entered at the bottom of those columns. If these two totals are unequal, an error has been made in developing the adjustments or entering them on the work sheet. Next, the appropriate additions and subtractions are made to determine the adjusted account balances. ("Crossfooting" is the term used by

EXHIBIT 5.17 ▼
Completed Work Sheet for Snow Mountain Retreat

SNOW MOUNTAIN RETREAT
WORK SHEET
FOR THE MONTH ENDED JANUARY 31, 1998

	Trial Balance		Adjustments		Adjusted Trial Balance		Income Statement		Balance Sheet	
Account Title	**Debit**	**Credit**	**Debit**	**Credit**	**Debit**	**Credit**	**Debit**	**Credit**	**Debit**	**Credit**
Cash	20,550				20,550				20,550	
Supplies	500			(c) 80	420				420	
Prepaid Rent	18,000			(a) 1,500	16,500				16,500	
Furniture	4,800				4,800				4,800	
Accounts Payable		640				640				640
Unearned Rental Revenue		1,000	(d) 500			500				500
Common Stock		40,000				40,000				40,000
Dividends	500				500				500	
Rental Revenue		3,500		(d) 500		4,000		4,000		
Salaries Expense	400		(f) 320		720		720			
Utilities Expense	390				390		390			
	45,140	45,140								
Rent Expense			(a) 1,500		1,500		1,500			
Depreciation Expense, Furniture			(b) 200		200		200			
Accumulated Depreciation, Furniture				(b) 200		200				200
Supplies Expense			(c) 80		80		80			
Interest Receivable			(e) 120		120				120	
Interest Revenue				(e) 120		120		120		
Salaries Payable				(f) 320		320				320
Income Taxes Expense			(g) 200		200		200			
Income Taxes Payable				(g) 200		200				200
			2,920	2,920	45,980	45,980	3,090	4,120	42,890	41,860
Net Income							1,030			1,030
							4,120	4,120	42,890	42,890

accountants when adding or subtracting amounts horizontally.) After each adjusted account balance has been entered in the appropriate Adjusted Trial Balance column of the work sheet, those two columns are footed. The resulting totals are entered at the bottom of each column. Again, these totals should be equal.

The next step in completing the work sheet is to transfer the adjusted account balances to the appropriate Income Statement and Balance Sheet columns. Notice in Exhibit 5.17 that the totals of the Income Statement debit and credit columns are not equal—at least not initially. The initial total of the debit column, $3,090, represents the total expenses of Snow Mountain Retreat for January 1998. Likewise, the total of the credit column, $4,120, represents the company's total revenues during that month. The company's net income for January 1998 is the difference between these two amounts, $1,030.

To balance the two Income Statement columns, we add the net income figure to the debit column. This amount is also added to the Balance Sheet credit column, as shown in Exhibit 5.17, to bring the debit and credit columns for that financial statement into balance. This apparent trickery causes the debit and credit columns for the two financial statements to have equal totals, but we are not "cheating" to bring these paired columns into agreement. The entry of $1,030 in the Income Statement debit column and the equivalent entry in the Balance Sheet credit column transfers Snow Mountain Retreat's net income to owners' equity for work sheet purposes.

When a work sheet is completed, a firm's accountants have the information needed to prepare the business's income statement, statement of stockholders' equity, and balance sheet. The information in the two Income Statement columns in Exhibit 5.17 would be organized into Snow Mountain Retreat's income statement that is presented in Exhibit 5.11. Next, the statement of stockholders' equity shown in Exhibit 5.12 and the balance sheet included in Exhibit 5.13 would be prepared.

Following the preparation of financial statements, the period-ending adjustments are journalized and then posted to the appropriate general ledger accounts. Journalizing adjustments is a simple task since the work sheet contains the information needed to prepare each adjusting journal entry. Once the adjusting journal entries are prepared and posted, the accounting cycle would be completed by preparing and posting the closing entries and, finally, by preparing a post-closing trial balance of the general ledger.

GLOSSARY

Accrued liability (p. 168) A liability stemming from an expense that has been incurred but not yet paid.

Accrued revenue (p. 168) A receivable resulting from a revenue that has been earned but not yet received.

Deferred expense (p. 166) An asset that represents a prepayment of an expense item.

Deferred revenue (p. 167) A liability resulting from an amount received by a business for a service or product that it will provide or deliver in the future.

Income Summary (p. 177) An account used only during the journalizing and posting of closing entries.

Source documents (p. 154) Documents that identify the key features or parameters of business transactions; examples include invoices, legal contracts, and purchase orders.

DECISION CASE

Assume that the owners of Snow Mountain Retreat have decided to expand their business by opening another bed and breakfast inn in a nearby town. Unfortunately, the owners do not have sufficient funds of their own to finance this expansion. So, they turn to a local bank. They provide the bank loan officer with Snow Mountain Retreat's financial statements that were prepared in this chapter. The owners hope that the profitable operations of Snow Mountain Retreat during January 1998 will convince this individual to loan them $20,000.

Patricia Rose (loan officer): *I see that you had a profitable month in January. Net income of $1,030, correct?*

Bud Hearst (part-owner): *Yes ma'am, Ms. Rose. We did very well, thank you.*

Ms. Rose: *You are keeping your accounting records on an accrual basis, correct?*

Mr. Hearst: *Well . . . I guess so. A local accountant who is a friend of mine is keeping the books for us.*

Ms. Rose: *I see.*

Mr. Hearst: *She's not a CPA or anything. But she sure knows her debits and credits.*

Ms. Rose: *Oh really. Okay. Let's see here. You and your two friends invested $40,000 in this business, correct?*

Mr. Hearst: *Yes ma'am, Ms. Rose. $40,000 hard-earned dollars.*

Ms. Rose: *And you ended the month with approximately $20,000?*

Mr. Hearst: *Uh . . . yes ma'am.*

Ms. Rose: *So, let me get this straight. You earned $1,030 in January, but your cash balance decreased by nearly $20,000 during the month, correct?*

Mr. Hearst: *Uh, well . . . yeah, uh . . . yes ma'am, that's correct.*

Ms. Rose: *And now, you want me to loan you another $20,000?*

Mr. Hearst: *Uh . . .*

Ms. Rose: *Appears to me that at the rate you're going through your cash, you will be back in a couple of months asking for another loan, correct?*

Mr. Hearst: *Well, I don't think so.*

Ms. Rose: *You "don't think so"?*

Mr. Hearst: *Uh . . .*

Ms. Rose: *Did you prepare a statement of cash flows for me to review?*

Mr. Hearst: *Statement of cash flows?*

Ms. Rose: *Mr. Hearst, do you understand the difference between cash flow and profit?*

Mr. Hearst: *Well, they're basically the same thing, aren't they?*

Required: Not surprisingly, the loan application of Snow Mountain Retreat was rejected. The firm's owners have decided to approach a second bank for this loan but realize they must be better prepared this time. Assume that they have retained you to negotiate this loan. To prepare for your meeting in the next few days with a bank loan officer, one of the co-owners hands you the following partially completed statement of cash flows that he has been working on for January 1998. This statement of cash flows has the same format as the one presented in Exhibit 2.8 of Chapter 2.

Cash flows from operating activities:	
Cash received from customers	$
Cash paid to employees	
Cash paid for rent and supplies	
Net cash used in operating activities	
Cash flows from investing activities:	
Purchase of furniture	(4,800)
Net cash used in investing activities	(4,800)
Cash flows from financing activities:	
Proceeds from sale of common stock	
Dividends paid	
Net cash provided by financing activities	39,500
Net Increase in Cash	$
Cash Balance, January 1, 1998	
Cash Balance, January 31, 1998	$20,550

By referring to the accounting data included in this chapter for Snow Mountain Retreat, complete the business's statement of cash flows for January 1998. Assuming the business's operations in February are similar to its operations in January, estimate the firm's cash balance at the end of February 1998. Make any assumptions you believe are necessary.

QUESTIONS

1. Identify several "source" documents from which accountants obtain information needed to journalize business transactions.
2. List the steps in the accounting cycle.
3. Which steps in the accounting cycle do accountants refer to as the "closing process"?
4. What is the key purpose of the accounting cycle?
5. If appropriate period-ending adjusting journal entries are not incorporated into a business's accounting records, what accounting rules will the business likely violate?
6. Where do accountants obtain the information needed to prepare adjusting journal entries?
7. Identify the four types of adjusting journal entries.
8. Define "deferred expense." Provide two examples of deferred expenses.
9. Why are adjusting entries generally required at the end of an accounting period for deferred expenses?
10. Why is a deferred revenue a liability? Provide two examples of deferred revenues.
11. Why is an accrued revenue an asset? Provide two examples of accrued revenues.
12. What is a term that accountants use interchangeably with "accrued liability"?
13. How does a company's net income for a given accounting period affect its period-ending balance sheet?

14. Why do accountants use an Income Summary account when closing revenue and expense accounts rather than simply transferring the proper amounts directly into the Retained Earnings account?
15. Describe the circumstances under which three, rather than four, closing entries are required at the end of a company's accounting period.
16. Explain the purpose of a post-closing trial balance.
17. Briefly describe several differences in the procedures performed in the accounting cycle of a firm that uses a manual accounting system compared with a firm that uses a computerized accounting system.
18. What is a "work sheet" and how do accountants generally use work sheets?
19. How may accountants integrate a work sheet into the period-ending "closing process" for a business?

EXERCISES

20. **True or False** (LO 1–5)
Following are a series of statements regarding topics discussed in Chapter 5.

Required:
Indicate whether each statement is true (T) or false (F).

_____ a. The terms "deferred expense" and "deferred revenue" refer to asset accounts.
_____ b. The initial step of the closing process is posting journal entry data to the appropriate general ledger accounts.
_____ c. An Income Summary account is an account that is used only during the preparation of period-ending adjusting journal entries.
_____ d. A primary purpose of period-ending adjusting journal entries is to avoid violations of the revenue recognition and expense recognition rules.
_____ e. Privately owned companies typically prepare a formal set of financial statements for external users only once per year.
_____ f. An "accrued revenue" account is included in a company's income statement.
_____ g. Salaries payable is an example of a deferred expense account.
_____ h. The temporary accounts of a business must begin each accounting period with a zero balance.
_____ i. Most of the information needed by accountants to analyze business transactions is drawn from source documents.
_____ j. A post-closing trial balance is prepared to determine whether a business's general ledger is in balance upon completion of the accounting cycle.

21. **General Journal Entries** (LO 1)
Listed next are two recent transactions of Grady Real Estate Company:
    1. Received $24,000 advance payment for one year's rent on an office building (the building is being leased to an accounting firm by Grady).
    2. Paid $6,000 in advance for six months of newspaper advertising.

Required:
    1. Prepare a general journal entry to record each of these transactions in Grady's accounting records.
    2. Prepare a general journal entry for each transaction from the point of view of the other party (company) to the transaction.
    3. Were Grady's total assets increased, decreased, or unchanged as a result of each of these transactions?

22. **Adjusting Journal Entries** (LO 2)
Fisher, Jones and Bottomley is a local law firm. Following are several transactions engaged in by this law firm during a recent month.

January 1: Purchased a laptop computer for $3,200.
January 1: Received a $4,000 advance payment from Smith Brothers, Inc., for legal services to be provided during January.
January 16: Paid $450 for a newspaper ad that ran for the three-day period January 12–14.
January 24: Prepaid February rent of $1,300 on leased office space.
January 31: Wrote a will for John Darden; Darden will be billed $300 for this service in February.

Required:

1. Prepare a general journal entry for each of these transactions in the law firm's accounting records.
2. Which of the items recorded in the journal entries in (1) will require an adjusting journal entry on January 31? Why?

23. **General Journal Entries** (LO 1)
Following are several recent transactions of the Saxe Detective Agency.

March 2: Purchased a van for $20,000 cash.
March 4: Paid the prior month's electricity bill of $400; an appropriate adjusting entry had been recorded for this item at the end of February.
March 15: Received payment of $1,300 for investigative services provided to a client for the period March 1–14.
March 19: Received advance payment of $4,000 for services to be provided in June to a client.
March 21: Purchased office supplies of $200 on credit.
March 24: Paid $2,000 premium on insurance policy for an office building; the term of the insurance policy covers April 1–October 1 of the current year.
March 31: Received $350 for interest that had been earned in February on a certificate of deposit; an appropriate adjusting entry had been recorded for this item at the end of February.

Required:

1. Prepare a general journal entry to record each of these transactions in the accounting records of Saxe Detective Agency.
2. Identify the accounts affected by the journal entries you prepared in (1) that qualify as: an accrued liability, an accrued revenue, a deferred expense, or a deferred revenue.

24. **Accrued Expenses vs. *Accrued Expenses*** (LO 2)
The following conversation took place between Erica Cain, an accountant for Seminole Freight Company, and Stuart Whitman, a senior vice president recently hired by the firm.

Stuart: *"Erica, why did you include $12,700 of expenses in our company's year-end balance sheet?"*
Erica: *"What are you talking about?"*
Stuart: *"I'm talking about this line item "Accrued Expenses, $12,700" in the current liabilities section of our year-end balance sheet."*
Erica: *"Those aren't* expenses.*"*
Stuart: *"What do you mean? You referred to them as expenses in the balance sheet."*
Erica: *"Stuart, accrued expenses aren't* expenses.*"*
Stuart: *"Huh?"*

Required:
Write a brief memo to Stuart explaining to him why the $12,700 of "accrued expenses" were included in Seminole Freight Company's balance sheet.

25. Adjusting Journal Entries for Balance Sheet Accounts (LO 2)
Following are several account balances of Brookhaven Square Inc., on December 31, prior to the preparation of year-end adjusting journal entries.

Property, Plant & Equipment	$1,530,200
Cash	120,600
Unearned Rental Revenue	72,000
Common Stock	30,000
Prepaid Rent	5,400
Land	340,500
Notes Payable	50,000
Retained Earnings	770,100

Required:
1. Identify the listed accounts that likely will require year-end adjusting journal entries.
2. Briefly describe the nature of the adjusting journal entries for the accounts you identified in (1).

26. Adjusting Journal Entries for Liability Accounts (LO 2)
Following is the liabilities section of a recent balance sheet of Thiokol Corporation. Among other products, Thiokol produces solid rocket motors for aerospace and defense applications. (Amounts are expressed in millions.)

Liabilities

Current liabilities:		
Short-term debt	$27.1	
Accounts payable	40.3	
Accrued compensation	46.4	
Other accrued expenses	28.9	
Income taxes payable	2.6	
Current portion of long-term debt	.1	
Total current liabilities		$145.4
Noncurrent liabilities:		
Long-term debt	$87.9	
Accrued retiree benefits		
Other than pensions	76.0	
Deferred income taxes	16.9	
Accrued interest and other	89.8	
Total noncurrent liabilities		270.6
Total liabilities		$416.0

Required:
1. Identify the current liabilities in Thiokol's balance sheet that may have been recorded in period-ending adjusting entries.
2. What type of adjusting entry related to Long-Term Debt may have been required in Thiokol's accounting records?
3. Assume that the Accrued Compensation liability was recorded in a period-ending adjusting entry. Prepare that entry.

27. Adjusting Journal Entries (LO 2)
Montana Designs, Inc., is an interior decorating firm. The company requires that customers pay 50 percent of their estimated bill before any work is performed. On November 20 of the current year, Montana Designs received and recorded a $5,000 partial payment from a customer on a new job that was scheduled to begin on December 1. The estimated bill for this job is $10,000. As of December 31, the job is 90 percent complete. No further payments have been received by December 31 from the customer, nor have any additional entries relating to this job been recorded in the accounting records of Montana Designs.

Required:
1. Prepare the entry to record the November 20 partial payment.
2. Prepare any necessary adjusting journal entry in Montana Designs' accounting records as of December 31.

28. Failure to Record Year-End Adjusting Journal Entry (LO 2)
Silverman & Sachs is a large investment banking firm. In December 1998, Silverman & Sachs earned fees of $4.1 million for investment banking services provided to three large clients. As of December 31, 1998, the firm had not been paid for these services.

Required:
1. Given the facts provided, prepare an appropriate adjusting journal entry as of December 31, 1998, in the accounting records of Silverman & Sachs.
2. Suppose that Silverman & Sachs' accountants fail to record the adjusting journal entry you prepared in (1). Which accounting principles or concepts would be violated by this oversight?

29. Failure to Record Year-End Adjusting Journal Entry (LO 2)
In December, Harsha's Cleaning Service, a new business, bought $6,500 of cleaning supplies. At the end of December, the business had $3,400 of supplies on hand.

Required:
1. Prepare an entry to record the purchase of the cleaning supplies and an adjusting entry to record the supplies used during December.
2. Suppose that neither of the entries in (1) were recorded in the business's accounting records. Indicate how the December 31 financial statements of Harsha's Cleaning Service would be affected. Consider only the firm's balance sheet and income statement.

30. Closing Entries (LO 4)
Listed next are selected account balances included in the December 31, 1998, adjusted trial balance of Hernandez Brothers Supply Company.

Cash	$ 2,000
Accounts Receivable	3,000
Unearned Rental Revenue	6,100
Utilities Expense	3,000
Income Taxes Expense	4,000
Accounts Payable	1,500
Sales Revenue	25,000
Selling Expenses	6,000
Prepaid Rent	4,500

Required:

1. Assuming that all of the company's temporary accounts are included in the listed accounts, prepare the appropriate December 31 closing entries for Hernandez Brothers.
2. How much net income did the company earn during the period in question?

31. **Need for Adjusting and Closing Entries** (LO 2, 4)
Theo's Tailors is a small business operated by Alex Theodorius. The accounting records for this business are maintained by Markey & Michaels, CPAs. Recently, Alex questioned the monthly accounting bill submitted to him by the CPA firm. Included in the bill were the following line items, among others:

Adjustment of year-end account balances:	5 hours × \$60 per hour	\$300
Year-end closing of revenue and expense accounts:	1 hour × \$60 per hour	60

Alex does not understand why his accounting records must be adjusted at year-end. In a recent telephone conversation, he complained to a partner of Markey & Michaels, "If you guys did my accounting records right the first time, you wouldn't have to adjust them at year-end." Alex went on to protest the \$60 charge for closing his business's revenue and expense acounts. "Why do you close those accounts every December 31? Don't you always use them again the next year? I think you're closing them just to run up my bill."

Required:
Write a memo to Alex Theodorius explaining the purpose of, and need for, period-ending adjusting and closing entries.

32. **Closing Entries** (LO 4)
Random Access, Inc., is a small business that leases computer equipment. Following are several account balances that were included in a year-end adjusted trial balance for the company.

Cash	\$100,000
Interest Revenue	5,000
Accounts Payable	40,000
Accumulated Depreciation, Equipment	36,000
Rental Revenue	152,000
Dividends	15,000
Salaries Expense	45,000
Depreciation Expense	12,000

Required:

1. Indicate which of the listed accounts are permanent accounts and which are temporary accounts.
2. Given the information provided, prepare all appropriate closing entries for Random Access.

33. **Preparation of an Income Statement** (LO 3)
Following is the adjusted trial balance of Blackburn Consultants, Inc., that was drawn from a work sheet prepared for the company for the year ended December 31, 1998.

	Debit	Credit
Cash	$ 24,000	
Accounts Receivable	71,000	
Interest Receivable	1,000	
Inventory	125,000	
Prepaid Insurance	6,000	
Equipment	242,000	
Accumulated Depreciation, Equipment		$ 31,000
Accounts Payable		17,000
Interest Payable		4,000
Income Taxes Payable		90,000
Notes Payable (Long-Term)		67,000
Common Stock		15,000
Retained Earnings		91,000
Consulting Fees Revenue		460,000
Interest Revenue		3,000
Salaries Expense	176,000	
Advertising Expense	22,000	
Utilities Expense	6,000	
Interest Expense	5,000	
Depreciation Expense, Equipment	10,000	
Income Taxes Expense	90,000	
	$778,000	$778,000

Required:
Prepare an income statement for Blackburn Consultants, Inc., for the year ended December 31, 1998.

34. **Preparation of Balance Sheet** (LO 3)
Refer to the information in Exercise 33.

Required:
Prepare a classified balance sheet for Blackburn Consultants, Inc., as of December 31, 1998.

PROBLEM SET A

35. **General Journal Entries** (LO 1)
Following are several recent transactions of Cerullo Electrical Contractors.

1. December 1: Purchased supplies for $300.
2. December 3: Paid $250 electricity bill for November that had been properly recorded with an adjusting entry on November 30.
3. December 9: Paid employee salaries for first week of December, $1,200.
4. December 16: Received $600 for interest that had been earned in November on a bank account; an appropriate adjusting journal entry had been recorded for this item on November 30.
5. December 22: Received $1,700 from customer in payment of account receivable.

6. December 26: Paid January rent on leased office space, $400.
7. December 30: Received $2,500 advance payment from a customer for work to be performed in January.
8. December 31: Purchased equipment on credit for $3,000.

Required:
1. Prepare general journal entries for these transactions.
2. Identify the accounts affected by the journal entries prepared in (1) that are a deferred expense, a deferred revenue, an accrued revenue, or an accrued liability.

36. "Window-dressing" Financial Statements (LO 2)

Suppose that you are an accountant for Kelberg, Inc., an advertising agency. You are preparing to close Kelberg's accounting records for the current year, since December 31 is only a few days away. The owner of this business is planning to apply for a loan from a local bank in early January. To "window dress" Kelberg's financial statements, the owner instructs you to credit a $31,000 advance payment received from a customer on December 27 to a revenue account. Kelberg will not provide the services paid for by this customer until March of next year. The owner also instructs you to not record a year-end adjusting entry for $7,500 of December rent owed to the real estate firm that leases office space to Kelberg.

Required:
1. If you comply with the owner's instructions, how will Kelberg's December 31 balance sheet for the current year be affected? How will the company's income statement for the current year be affected?
2. What accounting principles will be violated if you comply with the owner's instructions?
3. What will you do in this situation? Identify the parties likely affected by your decision to comply or not comply with the owner's requests. Indicate how each of these parties may be impacted by your decision.

37. Adjusting Journal Entries (LO 2)

The following information pertains to the operations of Story Investigating, a private detective agency, for the month of December.

1. Story's employees earn $420 of salary collectively each day. The employees work Monday through Friday and are paid each Friday. This year, December 31 falls on a Tuesday.
2. On December 31, Story's owner estimates that the business's electricity bill for December will be $240.
3. Story's owner also estimates that the firm will have income tax expense of $800 for the month of December. This amount will not be paid until March of the following year.
4. On December 1, Story received and recorded a $300 payment from a customer. This payment was for services to be rendered by Story during December, January, and February. By December 31, one-third of these services had been provided. (Note: Story's principal revenue account is Fee Revenue.)
5. Story received $680 from a new client on December 28. No services had been provided to this client as of December 31. This item was properly recorded by Story's bookkeeper on December 29.
6. Bonocher, Inc., owes Story $1,400 for services provided during December. No entry pertaining to these services has been recorded in Story's accounting records.

Required:
1. For each transaction or event identified, prepare any necessary adjusting journal entry as of December 31 in Story's accounting records.

2. Suppose that Story Investigating employs the cash basis of accounting instead of the accrual basis. That is, the company records revenues when it receives cash payments from customers and records expenses when it disburses cash to suppliers, customers, and other parties. Analyze the six items listed and determine how Story's revenues and expenses for December would be affected by using the cash basis instead of the accrual basis of accounting.
3. Write a brief memo indicating which method of accounting, cash basis or accrual basis, would provide a more appropriate measure of Story's net income each accounting period.

38. Adjusting Journal Entries and Financial Statement Errors (LO 2)
Providence, Inc., operates a chain of health food stores in New England. At the end of its most recent fiscal year, Providence reported total assets of $42,500,000 and total liabilities of $17,200,000. Unfortunately, those figures are unreliable since Providence's accountants made several errors when adjusting the company's general ledger accounts at year-end.

Required:
Listed next are the errors that Providence's accountants made when preparing year-end adjusting entries for the company. For each item, indicate whether the error resulted in an overstatement (O) or understatement (U) of the relevant component of Providence's accounting equation or whether the error had no effect (N) on the given component.

	Total Assets	Total Liabilities	Total Owners' Equity
1. Failed to record adjusting entry for depreciation expense on equipment.	______	______	______
2. Did not record an adjusting entry to recognize interest earned on certificate of deposit.	______	______	______
3. Recorded an adjusting entry for unpaid interest expense on a note payable by debiting Interest Expense and crediting Cash.	______	______	______
4. Recorded adjusting entry for supplies used during the last month of the year by debiting Supplies and crediting Supplies Expense.	______	______	______
5. Recorded year-end adjusting entry for unpaid income taxes by debiting Income Taxes Expense and crediting Accounts Payable.	______	______	______

39. (*Appendix*) Integrating a Work Sheet into the Accounting Cycle (LO 2–5)
Following is a trial balance for Resultan Corporation, as of January 31, 1998, prior to the closing of the company's books. Resultan rents various types of equipment to manufacturing companies. This firm began operations on January 1, 1998.

	Debit	Credit
Cash	$10,000	
Accounts Receivable	2,000	
Supplies	900	
Prepaid Insurance	1,200	
Equipment	48,000	
Accounts Payable		$ 200
Unearned Rental Revenue		700
Common Stock		12,000
Additional Paid-In Capital		46,000
Dividends	500	
Rental Revenue		8,000
Salaries Expense	3,200	
Utilities Expense	1,100	
	$66,900	$66,900

Listed next is additional financial information regarding Resultan Corporation.

a. On January 31, the company owed its employees $800 for salaries they had earned in the last few days of January.
b. Resultan earned $50 of interest on a bank account during January.
c. By January 31, the company had earned $500 of the $700 balance of the Unearned Rental Revenue account.
d. Resultan uses the straight-line depreciation method for its equipment. The equipment was purchased on January 1 for $48,000, has a four-year useful life, and is expected to have no salvage value at the end of its useful life.
e. On January 1, Resultan purchased and paid for a one-year insurance policy on its equipment. The cost of this policy was $1,200 and was debited to Prepaid Insurance.

Required:

1. Prepare four-column accounts or T-accounts for Resultan. Enter the January 31 balances in these accounts from the company's trial balance.
2. Enter Resultan's trial balance on a work sheet and complete the work sheet.
3. From the work sheet completed in (2), prepare the following financial statements for Resultan Corporation: an income statement and statement of stockholders' equity for the month of January 1998 and a classified balance sheet as of January 31, 1998.
4. Prepare all necessary adjusting journal entries for Resultan as of January 31, 1998. Post these adjusting entries to the appropriate accounts. When necessary, create new accounts.
5. Prepare closing entries as of January 31, 1998, for Resultan. Post the closing entries to the appropriate accounts.
6. Prepare a post-closing trial balance for Resultan as of January 31, 1998.

40. **Closing Entries** (LO 4)

Following is a list of certain account balances drawn from the adjusted trial balance of Sharon's Shoe Repair Shop as of December 31, 1998. This list includes all of the business's revenue and expense accounts as well as selected additional accounts.

Prepaid Rent	$ 4,500
Accounts Payable	8,200

Utilities Expense	$ 1,000
Cash	12,000
Accounts Receivable	3,000
Shoe Repair Revenue	35,000
Prepaid Insurance	5,500
Unearned Repair Revenue	700
Salaries Expense	12,000
Salaries Payable	900
Bonds Payable	1,500
Income Taxes Expense	8,000

Required:

1. Prepare all appropriate closing entries for Sharon's Shoe Repair Shop on December 31, 1998.
2. What was the company's net income (loss) for 1998?

41. Preparation of Financial Statements (LO 3)
Following is an adjusted trial balance for DGA & Associates for the year ended December 31, 1998.

	Debit	Credit
Cash	$112,500	
Accounts Receivable	95,000	
Supplies	12,000	
Prepaid Advertising	18,000	
Prepaid Rent	40,000	
Equipment	90,500	
Accumulated Depreciation, Equipment		$ 71,000
Accounts Payable		38,000
Salaries Payable		2,400
Unearned Fee Revenue		75,000
Common Stock		34,000
Retained Earnings		20,000
Fee Revenue		315,000
Interest Revenue		9,100
Rent Expense	69,500	
Income Taxes Expense	35,000	
Salaries Expense	75,000	
Depreciation Expense, Equipment	17,000	
Totals	$564,500	$564,500

Required:

1. Prepare an income statement for DGA & Associates for the year ended December 31, 1998.
2. Prepare a classified balance sheet for DGA & Associates as of December 31, 1998.
3. Identify three general classes of financial statement users who might make economic decisions based upon the financial statements of DGA & Associates. How might errors in these financial statements affect such decisions?

PROBLEM SET B

42. General Journal Entries (LO 1)
Following are several transactions engaged in by McDuffie Decorators, Inc., during a recent month.

1. December 1: Purchased supplies for $400.
2. December 3: Received $4,000 from customer for services to be provided in January.
3. December 6: Received $3,600 for interest that had been earned in November on a bank account; an appropriate adjusting journal entry had been recorded for this item on November 30.
4. December 11: Purchased equipment on credit for $2,500.
5. December 14: Received $2,500 from customer in payment of account receivable.
6. December 21: Paid employee salaries for third week of December, $3,900.
7. December 30: Paid December rent on leased office space, $800.
8. December 31: Paid January rent on leased office space, $800.

Required:

1. Prepare general journal entries for these transactions.
2. Identify the accounts affected by the journal entries prepared in (1) that are a deferred expense, a deferred revenue, an accrued revenue, or an accrued liability.

43. Intentional Manipulation of Financial Statement Data (LO 2)
Suppose that you are a local CPA and that once per month you update the accounting records of Pinpoint Printing Company. You also close this client's accounting records at the end of each year and prepare the firm's annual financial statements. Shortly after you arrive at Pinpoint's headquarters on December 31 of the current year, the business's owner asks to meet with you privately. The owner explains that she is attempting to sell Pinpoint to a much larger competitor. Because she wants to receive "top dollar" for the business, she asks you to ignore several of Pinpoint's unpaid expenses when you prepare year-end adjusting journal entries. These expenses include a $1,400 bill for newspaper ads run in December, a $2,100 electricity bill for December, and $3,700 of salaries earned by Pinpoint's employees during the last few days of the year. In an effort to convince you to overlook the period-ending adjustments for these items, the owner casually remarks to you, "Hey, we haven't even paid these items yet. So, why should we have to *pre-record* them as expenses?"

Required:

1. If you comply with the owner's request, how will Pinpoint's income statement for the current year be affected? How will the firm's December 31 balance sheet be affected?
2. Will you comply with the owner's request? Identify the parties who likely will be affected by your decision to comply or not comply with the owner's request. Indicate how each of these parties may be impacted by your decision.
3. Will the fact that you are a CPA influence your decision of whether or not to comply with the owner's request? Why or why not?

44. Adjusting Journal Entries (LO 2)
The following information pertains to the operations of Steeplechase Consultants, an architectural firm, for the month of December.

1. On December 31, Steeplechase's accountant estimates that the firm's water bill for December will be $2,100.
2. Steeplechase's accountant also estimates that the firm will have income taxes expense of $7,700 for the month of December. This amount will be paid in March of the following year.

3. Steeplechase received and recorded a $30,000 payment on December 2 from a customer. This payment was for services to be rendered by Steeplechase during December and January. By December 31, one-half of these services had been provided.
4. The employees of Steeplechase earn $12,000 of salary collectively each day. The employees work Monday through Friday and are paid each Friday. This year, December 31 falls on a Thursday.
5. Tarkanian, Inc., owes Steeplechase $13,400 for services provided during December. No entry pertaining to these services has been recorded in Steeplechase's accounting records.
6. Steeplechase received a $4,900 advance payment from a new client on December 29. No services have been provided to this client as of December 31. This item was properly recorded by Steeplechase's accountant on December 30.

Required:

1. For each transaction or event listed, prepare any necessary adjusting journal entry as of December 31 in Steeplechase's accounting records.
2. Suppose that Steeplechase employs the cash basis of accounting instead of the accrual basis. That is, the company records revenues when it receives cash payments from customers and records expenses when it disburses cash to suppliers, customers, and other parties. Analyze the six items listed and determine how Steeplechase's revenues and expenses for December would be affected by using the cash basis instead of the accrual basis of accounting.
3. Write a brief memo indicating which method of accounting, cash basis or accrual basis, would provide a more appropriate measure of Steeplechase's net income each accounting period.

45. Adjusting Journal Entries and Financial Statement Errors (LO 2)

Baldwin & Wallace Corporation wholesales sporting goods to retail outlets in the midwestern United States. At the end of its most recent fiscal year, Baldwin & Wallace reported total assets of $122,300,000 and total liabilities of $46,800,000. Unfortunately, those figures are unreliable since Baldwin & Wallace's accountants made several errors when adjusting the company's general ledger accounts at year-end.

Required:

Listed next are the errors that Baldwin & Wallace's accountants made when preparing year-end adjusting entries for the company. For each item, indicate whether the error resulted in an overstatement (O) or understatement (U) of the relevant component of Baldwin & Wallace's accounting equation or whether the error had no effect (N) on the given component.

	Total Assets	Total Liabilities	Total Owners' Equity
1. Recorded unpaid employee salaries at year-end by debiting Salaries Expense and crediting Income Taxes Payable.	_______	_______	_______
2. Recorded an adjusting entry for unpaid interest expense on a note payable by debiting Interest Receivable and crediting Cash.	_______	_______	_______

	Total Assets	Total Liabilities	Total Owners' Equity
3. Did not record adjusting entry for depreciation expense on an office building.	______	______	______
4. Recorded adjusting entry for supplies used during the last month of the year by debiting Interest Expense and crediting Supplies.	______	______	______
5. Failed to record an adjusting entry to recognize the portion of the Prepaid Insurance balance that had "expired" by the end of the year.	______	______	______

46. **(*Appendix*) Integrating a Work Sheet into the Accounting Cycle** (LO 2–5)
Following is a trial balance for Norman Enterprises as of January 31, 1998, prior to the closing of the company's books. Norman rents furniture, principally to college students. This company began operations on January 1, 1998.

	Debit	Credit
Cash	$ 17,000	
Accounts Receivable	4,500	
Supplies	1,800	
Furniture	90,000	
Accounts Payable		$ 1,600
Unearned Rental Revenue		2,200
Common Stock		104,000
Rental Revenue		12,800
Utilities Expense	1,500	
Salaries Expense	4,800	
Dividends	1,000	
	$120,600	$120,600

Listed next is additional financial information regarding Norman Enterprises.

a. By January 31, the company had earned $800 of the $2,200 balance of the Unearned Rental Revenue account.
b. On January 31, the company had $500 of supplies on hand; $1,800 of supplies were purchased during the month.
c. Norman earned $100 of interest on a bank account during January.
d. The company owed its employees $900 at the end of January for salaries the employees had earned but not yet been paid.
e. Norman uses the straight-line depreciation method for its furniture. The furniture was purchased on January 1 for $90,000, has a six-year useful life, and is expected to have no salvage value at the end of its useful life.

Required:
1. Prepare four-column accounts or T-accounts for Norman and enter the January 31 balances in these accounts from the company's trial balance.
2. Enter Norman's trial balance on a work sheet and complete the work sheet.
3. From the work sheet completed in (2), prepare the following financial statements for Norman Enterprises: an income statement and statement of stockholders' equity for the month ended January 31, 1998, and a classified balance sheet as of January 31, 1998.
4. Prepare all necessary adjusting journal entries for Norman as of January 31, 1998. Post these adjusting entries to the appropriate accounts. When necessary, create new accounts.
5. Prepare closing entries as of January 31, 1998. Post the closing entries to the appropriate accounts.
6. Prepare a post-closing trial balance as of January 31, 1998.

47. **Closing Entries** (LO 4)
Following is a list of account balances drawn from an adjusted trial balance for Beckwith Advertising Agency as of December 31, 1998. This list includes all of the business's revenue and expense accounts as well as selected additional accounts.

Salaries Expense	$ 5,500
Notes Payable	8,200
Utilities Expense	2,000
Cash	12,000
Accounts Receivable	3,000
Advertising Revenue	55,000
Prepaid Insurance	4,500
Unearned Advertising Revenue	6,100
Prepaid Rent	22,000
Salaries Payable	900
Accounts Payable	1,500
Income Taxes Expense	10,000

Required:
1. Prepare all appropriate closing entries for Beckwith on December 31, 1998.
2. What was Beckwith's net income (loss) for 1998?

48. **Preparation of Financial Statements** (LO 3)
On the following page is an adjusted trial balance for McCann Consulting, Inc., as of December 31, 1998.

Required:
1. Prepare an income statement for McCann's Consulting for the year ended December 31, 1998.
2. Prepare a classified balance sheet for McCann Consulting as of December 31, 1998.
3. Suppose this company is publicly owned and you are considering purchasing 100 shares of its common stock. Identify three questions pertaining to either McCann's balance sheet or income statement that you would want to ask of the company's chief executive officer before you decide whether to invest in the firm.

	Debit	Credit
Cash	$115,500	
Accounts Receivable	92,000	
Inventory	16,000	
Prepaid Insurance	20,000	
Prepaid Rent	40,000	
Machinery	85,500	
Accumulated Depreciation, Machinery		$ 20,000
Unearned Fee Revenue		46,100
Accounts Payable		3,400
Income Taxes Payable		19,000
Common Stock		9,000
Retained Earnings		45,000
Fee Revenue		425,000
Interest Revenue		8,000
Depreciation Expense, Machinery	14,500	
Rent Expense	50,000	
Income Taxes Expense	40,000	
Salaries Expense	80,000	
Utilities Expense	22,000	
Totals	$575,500	$575,500

CASES

49. **Analyzing Current Liabilities** (LO 3)
K.C. is a college student at Lehigh University. Thanks to his grandparents, K.C. has a large investment portfolio. One day, K.C. was browsing through the annual reports of several public companies in which he owns common stock. K.C. noticed the following information for Van Vleet Corporation.

	December 31, 1997	December 31, 1998
Accounts payable	$17,200,000	$ 8,300,000
Salaries payable	12,500,000	1,200,000
Income taxes payable	10,000,000	8,000,000
Interest payable	1,200,000	200,000
Total current liabilities	$40,900,000	$17,700,000

K.C., who enrolled in an introductory financial accounting course but dropped out after the first exam, turns to his roommate and observes, "What a crooked company! Look at this. Over $40 million in current liabilities one year and less than half that the next. You know this company has been playing around with its financial statements. I'm calling my broker and telling him to unload my stock in this company."

Required:
Write a brief memo to K.C. In this memo, identify legitimate reasons that may account for the large differences in Van Vleet Corporation's current liabilities at the end of 1997 and 1998.

50. **Year-End Expense Accruals** (LO 2)
Sawyer Brown is the bookkeeper for the Daniels Manufacturing Company. Recently, Daniels was audited for the first time by a public accounting firm. The auditors discovered that Brown never accrues expenses for such items as unpaid salaries and unpaid utilities at year-end. When asked, Brown explained that there is no need to accrue such expenses at year-end. "Every December 31 we have approximately the same amount of unpaid salaries, unpaid utility bills, etc., etc. So, why go to the trouble of recording such expenses since they net out each year?"

Required:
1. Explain Brown's reasoning. What does he mean when he maintains that the items in question "net out each year"?
2. What is wrong, if anything, with Brown's method of accounting (or not accounting) for unpaid expenses at year-end?

51. **Adjusting Entries and Accounting Concepts** (LO 2)
In 1970, a large warehouse of Mattel, Inc., the toy manufacturer, was destroyed by a fire. The contents of the warehouse were fully insured. In fact, Mattel's insurance policy contained a "business interruption" clause that compensated the company for up to $10 million of business profits lost as a result of a fire or other calamity. Near the end of 1970, Mattel recorded an adjusting entry debiting a receivable account for $10 million related to this clause of its insurance policy. The offsetting credit was to a revenue account. As it turned out, Mattel was overly optimistic in booking the receivable and revenue stemming from the insurance claim. Nearly seven years passed before Mattel collected on the insurance claim, and then it received only $4.4 million. The Securities and Exchange Commission (SEC) subsequently criticized Mattel for the accounting treatment it applied to the insurance claim. According to the SEC, Mattel was aware in 1970 that it would collect considerably less than $10 million from its insurance company.

Required:
What accounting concepts or principles did Mattel violate when it recorded the $10 million adjusting entry in 1970? Explain how these concepts or principles were violated. How were Mattel's subsequent financial statements affected by its improper accounting for the insurance claim.

PROJECTS

52. **"True and Fair" vs. "Present Fairly, in All Material Respects"**

Sophisticated decision makers recognize that financial statement data are always subject to some risk of being misleading even when prepared by business executives and accountants who are scrupulously honest. Such decision makers also recognize that the criteria or benchmarks against which the accuracy of financial statement data is measured often vary significantly from country to country. For example, in the United Kingdom, a public company is required to report financial statement data that provide a "true and fair view" of the firm's operating results, financial condition, and so on. In the United States, on the other hand, a public company has a responsibility to report financial statement data that "present fairly, in all material respects" the relevant dimensions of its financial health.

Required:
Research the meaning of "true and fair view" as that phrase is applied by the United Kingdom's accounting profession. Likewise, research the meaning of "present fairly, in all material respects," the comparable phrase applied by the accounting profession in this country. Summarize your research results in a written report.

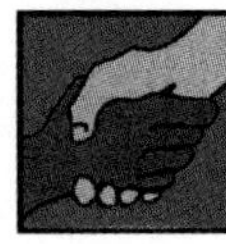

53. Prepaid Expenses and Accrued Liabilities in Corporate Balance Sheets

Meet with the project team to which you have been assigned by your instructor. Each member of your team should select a public company from a different industry that has the current asset "Prepaid Expenses" and the current liability "Accrued Liabilities" (or "Accrued Expenses") reported in its annual balance sheets. Each member should identify for his or her selected company the dollar amount of those two items each year for the most recent three years. For each company each year, the following percentages should be computed: Prepaid Expenses/Current Assets; Prepaid Expenses/Total Assets; Accrued Liabilities/Current Liabilities; Accrued Liabilities/Total Liabilities. (Note: Most companies report one lump sum amount in their balance sheet for prepaid expenses. On the other hand, companies typically report multiple accrued liabilities in their balance sheet. As a result, it may be necessary to compute total accrued liabilities for a given company by adding such items as "Salaries Payable," "Income Taxes Payable," and "Other Accrued Liabilities.")

Required:

Meet as a group and compare your findings. Discuss the factors that may account for any major differences in the computed percentages across the companies selected by individual group members. Prepare a written report summarizing these factors. Include in your report the financial data collected for each company and the corresponding percentages computed by group members.

54. Unearned Revenues in Corporate Balance Sheets

Identify three companies that report unearned revenues in their annual balance sheets. You may select these companies from annual report files available in your library or from other sources.

Required:

1. Prepare a brief written description of each of the three companies you selected. In this description, identify the location of the company's headquarters, describe the nature of the company's industry, and list the primary products or services that the company markets.
2. Determine whether the individual companies' financial statement footnotes describe the accounting method used for unearned revenues. If so, write a brief summary of each of these accounting methods.
3. Record the dollar amount of unearned revenues reported by each company in its balance sheet for each of the past three years. Is there a definite trend in these amounts for one or more of the companies? That is, have the unearned revenues reported by one or more of the companies steadily increased or decreased in recent years? Provide an explanation for any apparent trends in these data.
4. Why do some companies have large amounts of unearned revenues, while others have little or none?

55. Statement of Cash Flows

The Decision Case in Chapter 5 requires the preparation of a statement of cash flows for Snow Mountain Retreat, the hypothetical company used to illustrate the accounting cycle in this chapter. In this project, you will become more familiar with this important financial statement with the help of the Internet.

Required:

1. Access the Web sites of two large public companies that make their financial statements available on the Internet. Print the most recent statement of cash flows for each of these companies.

2. Prepare a written report that includes the information listed next. (Attach to your report the two statements of cash flows you printed.)
   a. Provide a brief description of each company selected in (1). In this description, identify the location of the company's headquarters, describe the nature of the company's industry, and list the primary products or services that the company markets. Also, list each company's Web site address.
   b. Using the statements of cash flows you printed, identify the net increase or decrease in each firm's cash balance for its most recent fiscal year.
   c. Identify each company's largest source of cash inflows and largest source of cash outflows during its most recent fiscal year.
   d. Relying exclusively on each company's statement of cash flows, which firm do you believe is in better financial condition? Defend your choice.

MODULE ONE

AN INTEGRATIVE FRAMEWORK FOR UNDERSTANDING ACCOUNTING

"Errors, like straws, upon the surface flow; He who would search for pearls must dive below."

—John Dryden

LEARNING OBJECTIVES

After studying this module, you should be able to do the following:

1. Define the key elements of the integrated accounting and financial reporting model for business entities.
2. Provide a comprehensive overview of the key features of an accounting system.
3. Define the primary purpose of financial statement analysis.
4. Compute the gross profit percentage and profit margin percentage ratios.

FOCUS ON DECISION MAKING

Milton Hershey's Recipe for Success: Regroup After Failure and Then Forge Ahead

Milton Hershey was born in 1857 in the small community of Derry Township, Pennsylvania. To help support his family, Hershey went to work for a local printer at the age of fourteen. Hershey showed little interest in the job and was soon fired. The young man then found work as an apprentice candymaker in nearby Lancaster. Immediately, Milton liked his new job. Four years later, after completing his apprenticeship, Hershey decided to strike out on his own. He chose Philadelphia as the site of his first business, The Spring Garden Steam Confectionery. For six years, Hershey sold candy from a horse-drawn wagon in the streets of Philadelphia, candy he had made the night before in his workshop. Hershey constantly tinkered with his recipes attempting to improve his candies. Unfortunately, his products didn't appeal to Philadelphians. By 1883, Hershey was broke and he was forced to close his business.

For the next several years, Milton Hershey drifted around the country working at various jobs. Eventually, he settled in New York City and established another small candy-making firm. Three years later, Hershey was bankrupt again.

In the late 1880s, Hershey returned home and founded the Lancaster Caramel Company, a business that quickly became profitable. The success of this new venture stemmed from a recipe that the persistent Hershey developed for a creamy caramel candy. Hershey used profits produced by the Lancaster Caramel Company to repay the remaining debts of his two failed business ventures. In 1901, Hershey sold the Lancaster Caramel Company for one million dollars and invested those funds in a new business venture, the Hershey Chocolate Company. For several years, Hershey had believed that there were large profits to be made in producing milk chocolate candy. And, he was right. Today, Hershey Foods Corporation is the largest candy company in the United States with annual sales approaching $4 billion.

What can we learn from the life and times of Milton Hershey? One obvious lesson is that going into business is a risky venture. Anyone going into business must assume a considerable risk of failing. Another important lesson is that a key factor in becoming successful in business is perseverance. Many individuals who went on to great success in business failed at more than one venture early in their careers. Milton Hershey eventually succeeded because he had confidence in himself and an ability to regroup and forge ahead after each trying episode in his life. So, if you experience failure in your business career, remind yourself of Milton Hershey. Take time out to regroup, to muster new energy and enthusiasm, and then forge ahead.

This module grants you a brief respite, a chance to take a page from the life of Milton Hershey and regroup before forging ahead. This interlude gives you an opportunity to digest the material you have covered so far and to prepare yourself for the topics presented in the chapters that follow. Most important, this module presents a model designed to help you develop a comprehensive and integrative understanding of the accounting and financial reporting function of business entities.

LOOKING BACK . . .

Accounting is considered a complex and challenging subject by the typical college student. When most of you sat through the first session of this course a few weeks ago, you had little or no prior experience or background in accounting. In recent weeks, you have been introduced to a wide range of accounting concepts, issues, and procedures. For many of you, this introduction may have seemed more like a barrage of terms, techniques, and topics hailing down upon you. Given your interest in business, you wanted to learn about accounting, but quite likely you wanted to obtain this knowledge at a more leisurely pace. Maybe you would equate your experience to date in this course with attempting to take a drink from a fully operational fire hose: you get what you want . . . and much, much more.

This module provides you with an integrative summary of what you have learned (should have learned?) to date and an overview of the subject matter that follows. A key factor in successfully completing a college course is obtaining, as quickly as possible, a "big picture understanding" (BPU) of the course's subject matter. A BPU does not include detailed knowledge of detailed subjects embedded in a course. Instead, a BPU implies that you grasp the fundamental nature of a given course's subject matter: you understand why the field of biochemistry exists; you can explain to a friend the origins of computer science and the key trends driving the future of that discipline; you can refute your uncle's assertion that accounting is just a "bean counting" activity.

A reasonable question at this point is, "Knapp, why didn't you give us a 'big picture' perspective on accounting earlier in the course?" Excusing your testy attitude, I respond by asserting that you were not ready for the big picture five chapters ago. Now that you have been introduced to the role of accounting in the business world, key accounting and control concepts, and the basic mechanical features of accounting, you are much better prepared to acquire a broad and integrated view of the nature of accounting and financial reporting for business entities. If you can obtain such a perspective on accounting and financial reporting for business entities, you will find the remainder of this course much more meaningful . . . and enjoyable.

AN INTEGRATIVE MODEL OF ACCOUNTING AND FINANCIAL REPORTING FOR BUSINESS ENTITIES

LEARNING OBJECTIVE 1
Define the key elements of the integrated accounting and financial reporting model for business entities.

James Carville was credited with developing a self-deprecating phrase that served as the motivating theme of President Clinton's 1992 campaign, which he managed. "It's the economy, stupid" continually reminded Carville that the key issue facing voters during the 1992 presidential campaign was the health of the national economy. Carville used that realization to continually focus his candidate's speeches and policy statements on the major concern of the voting public.

When writing this textbook, I used a modification of James Carville's phrase to repeatedly focus my attention on the key theme of this text, namely, "It's economic decisions, stupid." Throughout this text, discussions of key accounting issues, concepts, and procedures are linked, directly or indirectly, to economic decisions. This focus on decision making is evident in Exhibit M1.1, which presents a comprehensive accounting and financial reporting model for a business entity. In this section, we walk through this model to obtain a clearer understanding of the nature and purpose of accounting and financial reporting for business entities.

EXHIBIT M1.1
A Integrative Accounting and Financial Reporting Model for a Business Entity

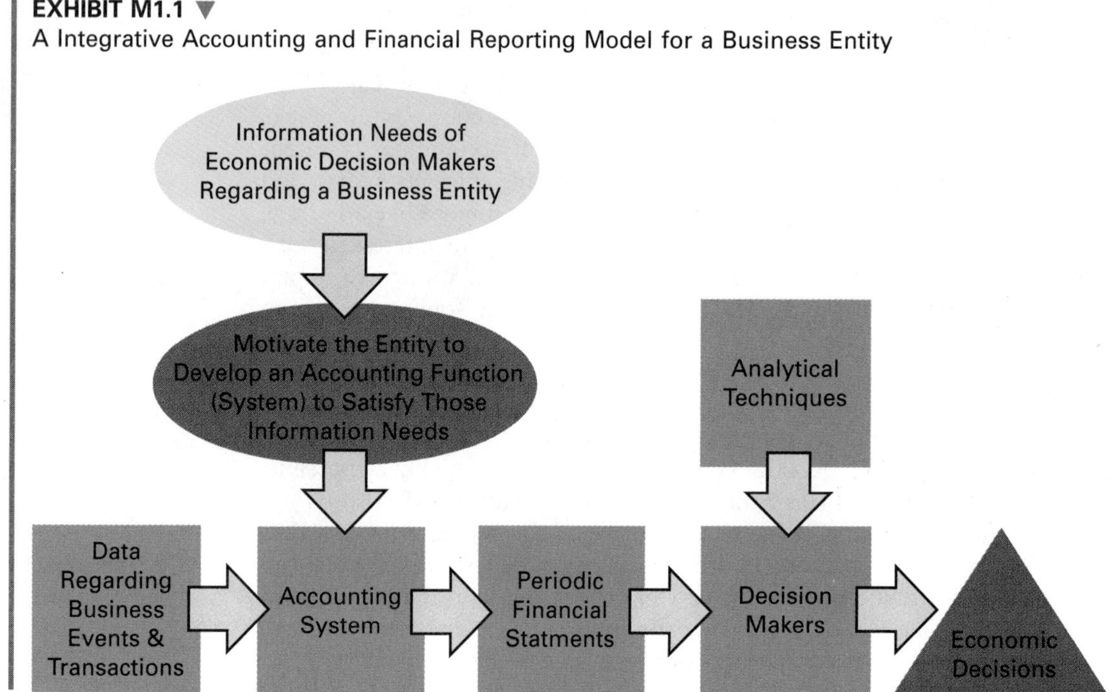

Information Needs of Decision Makers: *Raison d'etre* of Accounting

The *raison d'etre,* or key reason or justification, for accounting is to satisfy the information needs of financial decision makers. One important and expanding group of decision makers that rely heavily on accounting data to make economic judgments is mutual fund investors. Very likely, your parents, your grandparents, and/or yourself are among the millions of individuals who have cashed in certificates of deposit (CDs) and money market funds in recent years and invested the proceeds in mutual funds. Investment companies, such as Fidelity Investments and Vanguard, pool money contributed by individual investors and then purchase large blocks of securities, principally common stocks. *The Wall Street Journal* reported in 1997 that there are nearly 1,500 mutual funds, alone, that invest only in common stocks of U.S. companies.[1] Most mutual funds have a focused investment objective. For example, dozens of mutual funds purchase only the common stocks of high-technology companies, while others invest exclusively in healthcare firms. Mutual funds are particularly favored investments of small investors. Many mutual funds require a minimum initial investment of $1,000, or less, and allow additional investments of even smaller amounts.

Suppose that you are shopping for a mutual fund in which to invest $2,174.02 left to you by dear, departed Uncle Joe. How would you choose from among the hundreds of mutual funds that exist in today's economy? Clearly, you are facing an economic decision; clearly, you want to make a wise decision. To make an informed and rational choice, you would want to obtain financial data regarding the recent performance of

1. R. Lowenstein, "Time for Straight Talk From Mutual Funds," *The Wall Street Journal,* January 9, 1997, C1.

the various mutual funds that you are considering. The accounting systems of mutual funds regularly process such data for distribution to investors and potential investors. One fund you might consider is the world's largest mutual fund, the $50 billion Magellan Fund managed by Fidelity Investments. In early 1996, financial data released by the Magellan Fund indicated that the fund was profitable but not as profitable as many of its competitors. Result: in May 1996, alone, Magellan investors "cashed in" (sold) more than $1 billion of their holdings in that mutual fund and transferred the cash to other investments.

Mutual fund investors, "high rollers" on Wall Street, and bank loan officers working on Main Street, Smalltown USA, are just a few examples of decision makers who rely heavily, or exclusively, on accountants for needed financial information. In 1980, the accounting profession reaffirmed that its primary societal role is to satisfy the information needs of financial decision makers. In that year, the profession issued *Statement of Financial Accounting Concepts (SFAC) No. 1,* "Objectives of Financial Reporting by Business Enterprises." Recall from Chapter 2 that *SFAC No. 1* expressly states that the primary financial reporting objective of business entities is to provide *useful* information to decision makers. Also recall that to qualify as "useful," accounting information must be understandable, relevant, and reliable.

Developing an Accounting System

Businesses depend heavily on decision makers such as investors, lenders, and regulatory authorities. Many businesses rely on banks and other financial institutions to periodically extend them loans. Likewise, many large corporations are at the "beck and call" of governmental agencies, such as the Interstate Commerce Commission and the Federal Trade Commission. These agencies impose strict rules and regulations on corporations, which, if violated, may subject these firms to large penalties, or worse. Such dependence on external decision makers is a key factor that motivates businesses to develop and maintain an accounting system, as suggested by Exhibit M1.1.

When developing an accounting system, a business should consider several broad accounting concepts and principles. These concepts and principles were discussed in Chapter 2. For example, recall the *entity concept.* A business's accounting system must be designed to process only transactions directly related to its operations. Personal transactions of a business's owner or owners, such as the payment of Junior's college tuition, should not be recorded in the business's journals and ledgers. Another important accounting concept that influences the design of accounting systems is the *accounting period concept.* This concept dictates that a business prepare financial reports at regular intervals. As a result, an accounting system must be designed to capture and report financial data for discrete periods of time, known as accounting periods. As you know, the most common length of an accounting period is one month. Among other accounting concepts and principles that influence the design of an accounting system are the *unit-of-measurement concept,* the *historical cost principle,* and the *full disclosure principle.*

Dissecting an Accounting System

LEARNING OBJECTIVE 2

Provide a comprehensive overview of the key features of an accounting system.

Chapter 3 defined an accounting system as a systematic approach to collecting, processing, and communicating financial information to decision makers. To this point in the text, we have reviewed each major feature of accounting systems. Now, let us bring these features together to obtain a sharper and more comprehensive understanding of accounting systems.

Exhibit M1.2 presents an integrated view of the elements of an accounting system and the principal inputs and outputs of an accounting system. Chapter 3 discussed the key components of an accounting system including accounts, a chart of accounts, journals and ledgers, and the accounting cycle. Recall that accounts are the primary storage units for financial data in an accounting system and are maintained in a general ledger. A chart of accounts lists the "addresses"—identification numbers—assigned to general ledger accounts. Journals maintain a chronological record of a business's transactions and other events that affect its financial status. This record is established via the preparation of journal entries. Small businesses that maintain only one journal refer to that accounting record as the general journal. Accounting data originally recorded in journal entries are eventually posted to the appropriate general ledger accounts. In later chapters, we briefly consider other journals and ledgers maintained by businesses.

In one sense, an accounting system is a number-crunching machine. Accountants shovel into an accounting system raw data from hundreds, thousands, or even millions of transactions during an accounting period. The accounting system then "crunches," or compacts, that data into a neat and orderly set of four financial statements and accompanying footnotes. This number-crunching process is accomplished via an accounting cycle, the set of recurring accounting procedures that must be performed for a business each accounting period. Chapter 5 outlined the major steps in an accounting cycle, such as the analysis of transactions, preparation of a working trial balance, and journalizing and posting of adjusting and closing entries.

Notice that Exhibit M1.2 lists several operational facets or features of an accounting system. Returning to our analogy, these features include the guidelines, procedures, and rules to follow in operating an accounting (system) machine. Of course, we cannot

EXHIBIT M1.2 ▼
An Expanded View of an Accounting System

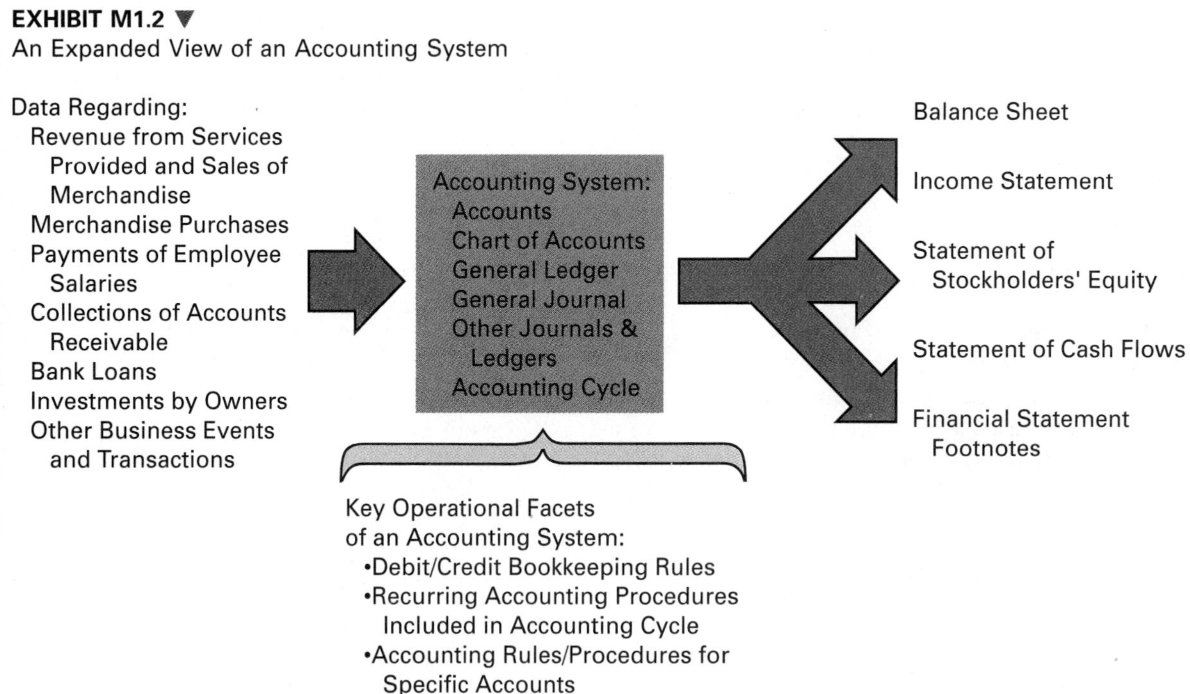

"book" transactions in journal entries without knowledge of the debit and credit rules made famous by our friend Luca Pacioli. Another operational feature of an accounting system is the set of recurring accounting procedures included in the accounting cycle. Chapter 5 illustrated an accounting cycle for a service business, Snow Mountain Retreat. Recall that there are three major types of business entities: service, merchandising, and manufacturing firms. Although there are minor differences, the structure of the accounting cycle for merchandising and manufacturing firms is very similar to the accounting cycle for service businesses.

Besides the procedures embedded in the accounting cycle, accountants must have a working knowledge of accounting rules and procedures for specific accounts. In future chapters, we tackle transactions and other business events that are more challenging to analyze for accounting purposes than those we have considered to date. For example, in Chapter 5 we applied the straight-line depreciation method for Snow Mountain Retreat. In a later chapter, we consider more "interesting" methods of computing periodic depreciation on property, plant & equipment assets.

Notice that control activities are listed as the final operational facet of an accounting system in Exhibit M1.2. Chapter 3 defined control activities as the policies and procedures established by an entity to ensure that its primary organizational objectives are accomplished. Included in these objectives are maintaining reliable financial records, ensuring compliance with applicable accounting and financial reporting rules and regulations, and safeguarding assets. A wide range of control activities is incorporated into an accounting system. In fact, if you think about it for a moment, accounting procedures qualify as control activities. Granted, when accountants use the phrase "control activities," they are typically referring to control-oriented procedures other than accounting procedures.

As noted in Chapter 5, an important control activity for a business is the segregation of key functional duties or responsibilities. In each major segment of an accounting system, three general types of responsibilities should be assigned to different employees: authorization, recordkeeping, and custodianship. For example, an employee who has direct access to a business's daily cash receipts should not maintain the accounting records for cash. Why? Because that individual might be tempted to steal cash and then conceal the theft by making improper entries in the accounting records. Segregation of key responsibilities in an accounting system helps ensure that each of the three organizational objectives referred to previously are satisfied. This control activity reduces the risk of inaccurate financial records, increases the likelihood of compliance with accounting and financial reporting rules, and enhances the physical security maintained over an entity's assets.

Again, the principal output of an accounting system is a set of financial statements and accompanying financial statement footnotes, as indicated in Exhibit M1.2. If an accounting system has been designed properly and operates as designed, the data in these financial statements will be understandable by decision makers, relevant to the decisions they face, and reliable. In other words, the financial statement data will be *useful* to decision makers.

Analyzing Financial Statement Data

LEARNING OBJECTIVE 3
Define the primary purpose of financial statement analysis.

Periodic financial statements provide the key input to the decision-making processes of investors, lenders, and other financial decision makers. To make the most effective use of a business's financial statements, decision makers apply various analytical techniques to financial statement data, as suggested by Exhibit M1.1. In a sense, decision makers

"Hacking Away" at Internal Controls: A Case of International Espionage

FOR YOUR INFORMATION

The accounting systems of major companies are heavily dependent on computer processing. As discussed in Chapter 3, integrating computers into accounting systems yields significant benefits, such as enhancing the speed and uniformity with which financial data are processed. But, there are also significant disadvantages of computer processing. Among these disadvantages is the threat posed by "computer hackers." In recent years, companies large and small have fallen victim to hackers who "invade" their computer systems and steal, destroy, or distort financial data and other important and confidential information.

Even the computer systems of the federal government are vulnerable to attacks by hackers. A key feature of the federal government's internal control process is the General Accounting Office (GAO), which implements and reviews control activities for federal agencies. The GAO reported in May 1996 that each year the Pentagon's computer system, alone, suffers an estimated 250,000 "break-ins" by hackers. One such incident involved a hacker known by the Internet handle "Datastream Cowboy." Military officials became alarmed when it appeared that Datastream Cowboy was attempting to hack into the computer system of a North Korean nuclear facility. This alarm stemmed from concern that North Korea would view the hacking incident as a hostile military action by the United States. Why? Because the cyberspace pirate had made the origin of the attempted break-in appear to be a U.S. military base. Fortunately, Datastream Cowboy's alias was "cracked" while this incident was unfolding, which led to his arrest.

Source: J. J. Fialka, "Pentagon Hacker Attacks Increase and Some Pose Threat, GAO Says," *The Wall Street Journal,* 23 May 1996, B2.

use these analytical techniques to force financial statements to "give up their secrets" regarding an entity's future prospects. What is the end result of prying such secrets from financial statements? Answer: more informed and rational economic decisions.

Exhibit M1.3 lists three types of analytical techniques applied by decision makers to financial statement data: trend analysis, the preparation of common-sized financial statements, and ratio analysis. In later chapters you will become familiar with each of these types of analytical techniques. To introduce you to financial statement analysis, let us briefly review the purpose and nature of ratio analysis, the most widely used approach to analyzing financial data.

financial ratios

Financial ratios express the relationship or interrelationships between, or among, two or more financial statement items. There are five general categories of financial ratios as shown in Exhibit M1.3. Each of these categories of ratios is used to investigate a different dimension of a company's financial health. Profitability ratios provide insight on how profitable a company is compared to its own historical standards and compared to competing firms. Liquidity ratios measure the ability of a company to pay off its short-term or current liabilities as they come due, while activity ratios reveal how effectively a company's executives are managing the firm's assets. A key question posed by decision makers is how a company has historically raised the funds needed to finance its operations. Leverage ratios reveal whether a company relies more heavily on borrowed funds or on "capital" invested by owners. Finally, market strength ratios reflect how a company's overall financial prospects are perceived by investors.

EXHIBIT M1.3 ▼
Techniques Used in Analyzing Financial Statement Data

- Trend Analysis
- Common-Sized Financial Statements
- Ratio Analysis:
  - *Profitability Ratios*
  - *Liquidity Ratios*
  - *Activity Ratios*
  - *Leverage Ratios*
  - *Market Strength Ratios*

LEARNING ◀ OBJECTIVE 4
Compute the gross profit percentage and profit margin percentage ratios.

To introduce you to analytical techniques applied to financial statement data, let us briefly review two important profitability ratios. Merchandising companies, such as Barnes & Noble, the retail bookstore chain, are in the business of buying goods at one price and selling them at a higher price. If a company buys a product for $60 and resells that same product for $100, it has earned a "gross profit" of $40. A company's **gross profit percentage** is computed by dividing its total gross profit for a given period by its net sales for that period.

gross profit percentage

Gross Profit Percentage = Gross Profit/Net Sales

For its fiscal year ending in 1995, Barnes & Noble realized a gross profit percentage of 35.3. The following year, this ratio showed a slight improvement, increasing to 35.8%.

Decision makers closely monitor the gross profit percentage of merchandising companies since this ratio is a key indicator of these firms' financial health. Operating problems facing a merchandising company are often quickly reflected in its gross profit percentage. For instance, if a merchandiser is forced to lower its selling prices to meet those of a competitor, the result will be a smaller gross profit percentage and usually a smaller net income for the company.

Another closely monitored financial ratio for merchandising companies is the **profit margin percentage,** which is computed as follows:

profit margin percentage

Profit Margin Percentage = Net Income/Net Sales

This ratio indicates the percentage of each sales dollar that contributes to a company's net income. A company's gross profit percentage and profit margin percentage tend to be highly correlated from one period to the next. When the relationship between these ratios diverge from their historical pattern for a given company, decision makers typically investigate the implications for the firm.

In Barnes & Noble's fiscal year ending in 1995, the company realized a profit margin percentage of 1.6, meaning that approximately one and one-half cents of each sales dollar contributed to net income. Stated another way, approximately 98.5 percent of each sales dollar was consumed by expenses. The following year, the firm's profit margin percentage plummeted to a *negative* 2.7 percent, despite the fact that its gross profit percentage rose slightly. Of course, a negative profit margin percentage means that a company experienced a net loss for the period in question.

The Sherlock Holmes of Accounting

Forcing accounting data to give up their secrets is not an easy task. However, an accounting professor does just that by applying a little known mathematical theory developed by a physicist several decades ago. Following is a condensed version of an article appearing in The Wall Street Journal *that explained how the professor has used this theory to become a financial detective.*

Some crime busters depend on fingerprints; others put their faith in DNA. Now one scholar in Nova Scotia has taken cooperation between law enforcement and science a step further. Mark Nigrini, an assistant professor of accounting at St. Mary's University in Halifax, is trapping tax cheats, check forgers, and embezzlers with an obscure theory known as Benford's Law. Formulated by Frank Benford in 1938, the law lays out the statistical frequency with which the numbers 1 through 9 appear in any set of random numbers.

Mr. Nigrini applies the law to the numbers on suspicious checks or tax returns. A series of legitimate check amounts or tax write-offs will be genuinely random, while those dreamed up by a human will not.

Benford's Law "gives Professor Nigrini a tool worthy of Sherlock Holmes," says Robert Burton, chief financial investigator for the district attorney's office in Brooklyn, N.Y. Mr. Burton spotted check fraud at seven companies using a Benford's Law computer program Dr. Nigrini sent him last year. Burton used that program to analyze 784 checks issued by those companies and found that check amounts didn't conform to random patterns. "Bingo, that means fraud," says Mr. Burton. The district attorney has since caught the culprits, which were bookkeepers and payroll clerks, and is charging them with theft from their companies.

Source: L. Berton, "He's Got Their Number: Scholar Uses Math to Foil Financial Fraud," *The Wall Street Journal,* 10 July 1995, B1. Reprinted by permission of *The Wall Street Journal,*

An investigation of Barnes & Noble's financial data for 1996 reveals that the company experienced some large and unusual expenses during that year, expenses responsible for the company's net loss and negative profit margin percentage. These expenses stemmed from management's decision to restructure the firm's operations, including closing many of its mall-based bookstores. Management believed that this restructuring would allow the firm to become more competitive in the future. So, in a sense, the restructuring expenditures were good news/bad news. The bad news was that they were necessary; the good news was that they would hopefully improve the firm's profits in the future.

LOOKING FORWARD . . .

Now that we have reviewed the highlights of the first five chapters, let us take a look ahead to the material covered in the remaining chapters of this text. The remainder of this text is organized into four segments. Parts III, IV, and V discuss accounting issues related to assets, liabilities, and stockholders' equity, respectively. A five-point organizational scheme is applied to each major financial statement item covered in these parts of the text. Exhibit M1.4 summarizes this organizational scheme.

The coverage of a major financial statement item, such as cash or inventory, begins with an introductory section. This section generally highlights the nature of the item, its relationship to other financial statement components, and key terms associated with the item. Next, important information needs of decision makers related to the given item are discussed. Remember, these needs are the primary reason that accounting exists. Obtaining a better understanding of decision makers' information needs for a financial statement item will allow you to better grasp the nature and purpose of the specific accounting procedures applied to that item, which are the third element of coverage.

The fourth element of coverage for each major financial statement item discussed in Parts III through V is control activities. As suggested earlier, control activities are important components of an accounting system. Included in these activities are measures to ensure that a business maintains reliable accounting records for financial statement items and procedures to safeguard a business's assets. The latter control activities are particularly critical for assets such as cash and inventory that are susceptible to theft. A company that fails to establish effective controls to safeguard these assets may soon be making an appointment with a bankruptcy judge.

Relevant financial ratios and other analytical techniques are the final element of coverage for each major financial statement item discussed in the following chapters. Whether you plan to be a public accountant or a bank loan officer or the chief executive of MegaCorp Consolidated, Inc., you will be responsible for making economic decisions or assisting others in making such decisions. Having available a toolbox of analytical techniques that you can use to crack open financial statements and discover their secrets will increase the likelihood that those economic decisions will be made wisely.

This textbook concludes with Part VI, which is entitled Analysis of Accounting Data. What? More financial statement analysis? Absolutely. Now, let me explain why.

Chapter 14, the first chapter in the final segment of this text, focuses exclusively on the statement of cash flows. A statement of cash flows provides important insights on the financial status of an entity that are not available from the other three major financial statements, which contain accrual-basis accounting data. Consider a company that has reported record profits for three successive years, although its cash resources have declined each of those years. You would find it difficult to locate the cause of this cash drain and its implications for the company if you only had access to the firm's

EXHIBIT M1.4 ▼

Organizational Scheme Applied to Key Financial Statement Items Discussed in Subsequent Chapters

- Introduction: Nature of Item, Relationship to Other Financial Statement Items, Key Terms
- Information Needs of Decision Makers
- Key Accounting Procedures
- Relevant Control Activities
- Relevant Financial Ratios and Other Analytical Techniques

accrual-basis financial statements. A review of the company's recent statements of cash flows would pinpoint why the firm is increasingly cash-poor. So, in one sense, a statement of cash flows is an analytical tool used by decision makers to interpret the accrual-basis data reported in a business's balance sheet, income statement, and statement of stockholders' equity.

The second and final chapter in Part VI, Chapter 15, highlights methods that decision makers can use to analyze and interpret accrual-basis financial statement data. Most of the techniques illustrated in Chapter 15 are introduced in earlier chapters. However, an integrated treatment of these techniques will reinforce your understanding of them, demonstrate how they complement each other, and illustrate how to comprehensively analyze a company's financial statements.

SUMMARY

This module provides you with an opportunity to take a brief look back at the key topics that have been covered to date and a brief look forward to the material covered in the remainder of this text. Most important, this module presents an integrative model of the accounting and financial reporting process used by business entities. Each element of this model has been discussed in the first two parts of this text. However, presenting these elements in an integrated model allows you to better understand the nature, purpose, and structure of the accounting and financial reporting process. This understanding will serve you well as you progress through the remaining four parts of this text. Parts III through V discuss accounting issues related to each major financial statement line item, while Part VI presents a comprehensive treatment of financial statement analysis.

GLOSSARY

Financial ratios (p. 216) Measures that express the relationship or interrelationships between, or among, two or more financial statement items.

Gross profit percentage (p. 217) Gross profit divided by net sales; a key ratio used to analyze a business's profitability.

Profit margin percentage (p. 217) Net income divided by net sales; indicates the percentage of each sales dollar that contributes to a company's net income.

DECISION CASE

The accounting systems of businesses produce a wide array of financial information, including the four major financial statements periodically made available to external decision makers. Certain financial information produced by the accounting systems of businesses is considered confidential and is not released to third parties. Businesses often face the perplexing problem of where to draw the line between the data to which external decision makers are entitled and the information that should be restricted to internal decision makers. A company that faced this dilemma several years ago was Burroughs Wellcome, a British pharmaceutical firm acquired in 1995 by Glaxo, another British firm.

In 1988, Burroughs Wellcome developed and patented AZT. Extensive clinical research had proven this drug effective in slowing the progression of AIDS-related symptoms in HIV-positive individuals. Initially, Burroughs Wellcome charged approximately $10,000 for a one-year supply of AZT, a price that reportedly yielded a large gross profit on the sales of this product. Critics claimed that Burroughs Wellcome was engaging in price-gouging by charging AIDS patients an exorbitant price for the drug. In testimony before Congress, Burroughs Wellcome's chief executive defended the high price of AZT by pointing out that his company had invested heavily in the development and marketing of the drug. He maintained that the pricing structure the company had established for AZT allowed Burroughs Wellcome to earn no more than a "reasonable" rate of return on this large investment. When pressed to disclose the accounting data regarding the costs associated with AZT, the chief executive refused. He maintained that those data were confidential and that releasing the data might be beneficial to competing companies.

In response to heavy criticism of its AZT pricing policy, Burroughs Wellcome gradually reduced the price of the drug. By the late 1990s, the average price of a one-year supply of AZT had declined to approximately $3,000.

Required: Assume that you are the chief executive of a biotechnology company that spent $10 million over the past three years developing a lifesaving drug for a rare disease. This disease is so rare that only 500 or so individuals are afflicted with it at any point in time in the United States. The total cost incurred by your firm to produce, package, and distribute a one-year supply of this drug is approximately $4,000. The New Product Committee of your firm, which includes two sales managers, a pharmacist, a cost accountant, and a research scientist, has recommended that the price for a one-year supply of this drug be established at $9,600.

When the price of this new drug is publicly announced, your company faces a storm of criticism. Similar to the Burroughs Wellcome case, critics demand that you release accounting data regarding the costs associated with this product. How would you respond to this demand? Does your firm have a responsibility to defend its pricing decision for this new drug by releasing the relevant accounting data? Finally, has your firm behaved unethically by establishing a price for this drug that will impose an economic sacrifice on those individuals who need it? Defend your answer.

QUESTIONS

1. According to *Statement of Financial Accounting Concepts No. 1,* what is the primary objective of financial reporting?
2. To qualify as "useful," what three traits must accounting information possess?
3. Identify three groups of decision makers who regularly use financial statement data.
4. Identify three accounting concepts or principles and briefly define each.
5. Define an "accounting system."
6. Identify three components of an accounting system.
7. Briefly describe the purpose and nature of the accounting cycle. List at least three steps in the accounting cycle.

8. Define "control activities."
9. What three types of responsibilities should be segregated or assigned to different employees in an accounting system?
10. Identify one key advantage of integrating computer processing into an accounting system. Identify one key disadvantage.
11. List three major types of analytical techniques that decision makers apply to financial statement data.
12. Define "financial ratios." Provide one example of a financial ratio.

EXERCISES

13. **True or False** (LO 1–4)
Following are a series of statements regarding topics discussed in Module 1.

Required:
Indicate whether each statement is true (T) or false (F).

_____ a. The unit-of-measurement concept dictates that a business entity prepare financial reports at regular intervals known as accounting periods.
_____ b. The principal output of an accounting system is a set of financial statements and accompanying footnotes.
_____ c. Activity ratios reveal how effectively a company's executives are managing the firm's assets.
_____ d. Accounts are the primary storage units for financial data in an accounting system.
_____ e. Among the activities that must be completed in the accounting cycle are the analysis of transactions and the preparation of a trial balance.
_____ f. An accounting system is that set of policies and procedures established by an entity to ensure that its primary organizational objectives are accomplished.
_____ g. Dependence on external decision makers is a key factor that motivates businesses to develop and maintain an accounting system.
_____ h. Profitability ratios measure the ability of a company to pay off its short-term or current liabilities as they come due.
_____ i. Among the primary objectives of an organization that are most relevant to its accounting and control functions are the maintenance of reliable financial records and the safeguarding of its assets.
_____ j. An important profitability ratio for merchandising companies is the gross profit percentage.
_____ k. A chart of accounts maintains a chronological record of the transactions and other events that affect a business's financial status.
_____ l. Accounting procedures qualify as control activities.

14. **Accounting as a Profession** (LO 1)
Chase Nordstrom is an accounting major at the University of Minnesota. Chase's friend from high school, Leah Olafson, also attends UM but has not yet chosen a major. Over lunch recently, Chase attempted to convince his friend to pursue an accounting degree.

Leah: *"I don't know, Chase. I had that high school accounting course, and I didn't much care for all of those debits and credits. Debit this, credit that . . . Ya know, that gets a little boring after a while."*

Chase: *"C'mon, Leah. That high school accounting course wasn't an* accounting *course. It was a bookkeeping course. Accounting is much more than debits and credits."*

Leah: *"Oh, so your accounting instructors never mention debits and credits?"*
Chase: *"Well, sure, we had to become familiar with debits and credits in the introductory financial accounting course. But, what accounting is really about is helping people."*
Leah: *"Now you've gone too far. If you really want to help people, Chase, you have to go into a professional field . . . like education, or social work, or medicine."*

Required:
Write a brief memo addressed to Leah. In that memo, help Chase convince his friend that accounting does have a "social mission" and that it qualifies as a profession.

15. Information Needs of Financial Decision Makers (LO 1)
Listed next are several individuals faced with an important financial decision.

Cindy Puccinelli: Cindy recently set up an IRA (individual retirement account) and made her first cash contribution of $2,000. Now, Cindy wants to invest that cash in the common stock of a "high-tech" company.
Johnny Branch: Johnny is a city council member in the small Kansas town of Augusta. Presently, Johnny and his fellow council members are attempting to decide how to finance the construction of a new municipal hospital.
Meisha Franklin: Meisha owns and manages a local building supply store. Recently, the owner of a homebuilding firm in a nearby city asked to set up a line of credit with Meisha's store.

Required:
1. For each individual listed, indicate the specific types of financial information that would be useful given the decision he or she faces.
2. How would these individuals likely obtain the financial information they need?

16. Design of an Accounting System (LO 2)
Rajendra Srivastava is opening a new business on campus corner, the Misal Restaurant. Since Raj has no accounting experience, he has come to you for advice on setting up an accounting system for his new business.

Required:
Following are a list of key elements of an accounting system. For the benefit of your friend Raj, briefly describe the nature of each element and the role it plays in an accounting system.
1. Accounts
2. Chart of accounts
3. Journals and ledgers
4. The accounting cycle
5. Double-entry bookkeeping rules
6. Control activities

17. Control Activities for Merchandising Businesses (LO 2)
Identify four merchandising businesses that you have visited in the past year. Make sure that each sells a different type of merchandise. Examples of businesses you might identify for purposes of this assignment include the following: grocery store, computer software store, campus bookstore, furniture store, large department store, and a pet shop.

Required:
1. List the four merchandising businesses you identified and briefly describe the nature of their operations.

2. Identify an internal control risk factor for each business. These factors may place the business's assets at some risk of being stolen or misused or have the potential to economically damage the business in some other way. As an example, a drugstore may be sued if it sells pharmaceutical products that are not labeled correctly.
3. Identify a control activity to minimize the potential problem or risk posed by each item you identified in (2).

18. **Gross Profit and Profit Margin Percentages** (LO 4)
Following are recent financial data for South Oval Enterprises, a plumbing supply business.

	Year 1	Year 2
Net sales	$520,000	$544,000
Gross profit	161,200	179,850
Net income	39,000	49,000

Required:
1. Compute South Oval's gross profit and profit margin percentages for each year.
2. Did these ratios improve or worsen in Year 2 compared with Year 1?
3. Suppose that plumbing supply businesses historically have a gross profit percentage of 30 percent and a profit margin percentage averaging 6 percent. Do the financial ratios you computed for South Oval compare favorably or unfavorably with those two benchmarks. If you were a potential investor in this business, would this additional information have a favorable or unfavorable influence on your investment decision?

19. **Gross Profit and Profit Margin Percentages** (LO 4)
Following are selected financial data for Conner Peripherals, Inc., for a recent three-year period. Conner markets computer disk drives and related products.

	December 31, Year 1	December 31, Year 2	December 31, Year 3
Net sales	$2,238,423	$2,151,672	$2,365,152
Gross profit	458,464	237,954	468,649
Net income (loss)	121,072	(445,314)	109,687

Required:
1. Compute Conner's gross profit percentage and profit margin percentage for each year listed.
2. Did these financial ratios improve or worsen between Year 1 and Year 3?

PROBLEM SET A

20. **Analyzing Financial Statement Data** (LO 1, 3, 4)
Honeywell, Inc., a large corporation headquartered in Minneapolis, sells a wide range of consumer and industrial products including home security systems. The following financial data (in thousands) were reported in a recent annual report of this company.

Quarter	Net Sales	Gross Profit	Net Income
1st, Year 1	$1,347.9	$430.6	$ 47.7
2nd, Year 1	1,463.8	462.0	56.9
3rd, Year 1	1,507.6	495.7	69.4
4th, Year 1	1,737.7	586.6	104.9
1st, Year 2	1,478.7	465.5	54.7
2nd, Year 2	1,655.6	517.8	68.9
3rd, Year 2	1,680.3	532.2	84.2
4th, Year 2	1,916.7	631.6	125.8

Required:

1. The Securities and Exchange Commission (SEC) requires public companies to prepare and distribute quarterly financial reports. These quarterly reports are in addition to annual financial reports that these companies must make available to the public. What factor(s) do you believe motivated the SEC to require companies to provide quarterly and annual financial data to the public?
2. Why do financial decision makers apply analytical techniques to financial statement data? Identify three major types of analytical techniques commonly used by financial decision makers.
3. Compute Honeywell's gross profit percentage and profit margin percentage for each quarter during Year 1 and Year 2.
4. Can you discern any definite trends from these data? If so, what are they and what factors may account for them?
5. Suppose that during the first few weeks of Year 3 you were considering a large investment in Honeywell's common stock. Identify three questions you would have wanted to ask the company's chief executive officer before deciding whether to invest in the firm's common stock.

21. **Control Activities in an Accounting System** (LO 2)

A large supermarket suffered several thousand dollars of losses over a period of a few years resulting from a scam perpetrated by the store's assistant managers. The assistant managers were responsible for periodically emptying and then counting each cash register till. One of the assistant managers pointed out to his colleagues that the cash count and the total of the cash register tape were nearly always different by some small amount. As a result, this individual persuaded two of the other assistant managers to take a quarter from each cash till that they counted each day—each assistant manager made as many as twenty to thirty till counts during each eight-hour workshift. "Who's going to miss a quarter here and a quarter there," was the argument of the master schemer.

Required:

1. Suppose that each of the three assistant store managers counted twenty cash tills daily and that each worked 250 days per year. Determine the supermarket's theft loss over a period of three years.
2. Control activities are an important feature of any accounting system. Identify specific control activities that might have prevented or detected the theft losses suffered by the supermarket.

22. **Impact of Financial Statement Errors on Decision Makers** (LO 3, 4)

Miranda LaBelle has just finished preparing the year-end financial statements for her employer, Rourke Merchandising. Rourke is a public company whose stock is traded on a national stock exchange. Following are several key amounts included in the company's financial statements.

Total assets	$2,530,000
Inventory	400,000
Retained earnings	310,000
Net sales	1,880,000
Gross profit	460,000
Net income	255,000

Miranda was putting her working papers away and preparing to lock up for the night when she found two items that had been placed in her "in box" late that afternoon. Both items affected the financial statements Miranda had just spent three days preparing. First, she found a memo from the warehouse accountant indicating that the year-end warehouse inventory was overstated by $24,000 due to a computer glitch. Second, she found an unpaid and unrecorded bill for an advertising expense of $12,000. These items caused Rourke's gross profit to be overstated by $24,000 and its net income to be overstated by $22,000. These items also caused Miranda to consider "pulling her hair." Why? Because the cut-off date for submitting such items had been one week earlier. Twice during the past week, Miranda had sent out a memo to each department asking if there were any additional transactions or events that should be incorporated in the company's year-end financial statements.

Required:

1. Suppose that Miranda does not make the appropriate corrections in the financial statements. Determine the impact on Rourke's gross profit percentage and profit margin percentage. Identify other errors that would remain in Rourke's financial statements if Miranda does not make the appropriate corrections in the company's accounting records.
2. What parties may rely on Rourke's financial statements to make economic decisions? How might those decisions be affected if Miranda does not correct the company's financial statements?
3. Does Miranda have a professional or ethical responsibility to correct Rourke's financial statements? Defend your answer.

PROBLEM SET B

23. Computing and Interpreting Profitability Ratios (LO 1, 3, 4)
Kellogg Company, headquartered in Battle Creek, Michigan, is the largest producer of cereal products worldwide. The following information (in millions) was included in a recent annual report issued by Kellogg.

Quarter	Net Sales	Gross Profit	Net Income
1st, Year 1	$1,518.4	$793.4	$179.2
2nd, Year 1	1,541.6	785.7	142.7
3rd, Year 1	1,669.2	897.3	209.3
4th, Year 1	1,566.2	830.0	149.5
1st, Year 2	1,611.2	879.2	183.9
2nd, Year 2	1,616.9	888.2	151.5
3rd, Year 2	1,741.9	985.7	216.7
4th, Year 2	1,592.0	858.2	153.3

Required:

1. What incentive would companies have to prepare and distribute periodic financial statements even in the absence of regulatory requirements to do so?

2. Why do financial decision makers apply analytical techniques to financial statement data? Identify three major types of analytical techniques commonly used by financial decision makers.
3. Compute Kellogg's gross profit percentage and profit margin percentage for each quarter during Year 1 and Year 2.
4. Are there any obvious trends in these data? If so, what are they and what factors may account for them?
5. Suppose that during the first few weeks of Year 3, you were considering a large purchase of Kellogg's common stock. Identify additional financial data you would have wanted to obtain regarding the company before deciding whether to invest in its common stock.

24. Control Activities for a Merchandising Business (LO 2)

Following are selected control activities that are integrated into the accounting system of Koh Imports, a retail store that sells household items such as rugs and lamps imported from South Korea.

a. Salesclerks are not allowed access to the store's accounting records.
b. The inventory of each of the store's five departments is counted once every three months.
c. The store owner must approve all purchases exceeding $100.
d. Before invoices are processed for payment, the store's accountant must test the mathematical accuracy of each invoice.
e. Salesclerks are not allowed to extend credit to customers; all credit-granting decisions are made by the store owner.

Required:

1. What general objectives does a business hope to accomplish by integrating control activities into its accounting system?
2. Identify the specific purpose of each control activity listed for Koh Imports. That is, comment on the potential problem or problems that each control is designed to avoid or minimize.

25. Impact of Financial Statement Errors on Decision Makers (LO 1, 3, 4)

Ray Burton is sitting on a couch in a small waiting room nervously counting the minutes down until he meets with Bonnie Tollison, the president of Muskogee National Bank. Burton owns a local office supply store. Three weeks ago, he submitted a loan application to Ms. Tollison requesting a $300,000 loan to expand his business. Burton intends to use the funds to build another office supply store on the other side of town. He hopes that his business's impressive financial data will convince Ms. Tollison to grant the loan. Presently, the average gross profit percentage and profit margin percentage in the office supply industry are 30 percent and 10 percent, respectively. Burton is well aware that his business's profitability ratios significantly exceed those industry averages.

Following is a list of several items that were included in the financial statements Burton attached as a supplement to his loan application. Those financial statements were for the recently ended fiscal year of Burton's business.

Net income	$ 93,000
Property, plant & equipment	290,000
Accounts receivable	75,000
Total assets	565,000
Total owners' equity	245,000
Net sales	405,000
Inventory	120,000
Gross profit	185,000

Burton's anxiety regarding his meeting with Ms. Tollison stems primarily from two sources. First, Burton is concerned that she may reject his loan application. Second, and more important, he is "sweating out" the possibility that Ms. Tollison may somehow realize that his business's financial statements contain large errors. To improve his chances of obtaining the loan, Burton overstated his store's year-end inventory by $20,000 and booked fictitious credit sales of $50,000. The net result of these two misrepresentations was to overstate the business's gross profit by $70,000 and its net income by $45,000.

Required:

1. Compute the actual gross profit percentage and profit margin percentage for Burton's office supply business.
2. Identify the listed financial statement items that are in error as a result of Burton's dishonesty—including the items already mentioned. Indicate how each of these items is misstated.
3. What parties, other than Bonnie Tollison, may be affected by the errors in the financial statements of Ray Burton's business?
4. Does a banker have a right to question the accuracy of a loan applicant's financial data? Does a banker have a professional or ethical responsibility to question the accuracy of that data? Explain.
5. What factor or factors may cause Ms. Tollison to question the accuracy of Burton's financial statements?

CASES

26. Responding to Management Scams (LO 1, 2)

In an earlier chapter, a brief anecdote described errors that executives of the now defunct Regina Company had intentionally incorporated into their firm's financial statements. Regina, which marketed vacuum cleaners and related products, was eventually forced into bankruptcy after the financial shenanigans were revealed. At one point, Regina's executives also concocted a marketing scam to increase the company's sales. In a commercial for one of the company's vacuum cleaners, a senior company executive spread crushed cereal on a carpet and then demonstrated how the Regina vacuum cleaner was much superior to the comparable product of Hoover, Regina's principal competitor. However, it was later discovered that the demonstration model used in the commercial had an industrial-strength suction that was not available on the model sold to the public.

Required:

The accountants of a business are responsible for ensuring that the financial statements and other financial data they prepare are free of material errors. However, what responsibility, if any, does an accountant of an organization have when he or she discovers unethical conduct in some other area of the organization? Suppose you were the controller (chief accountant) of Regina in the late 1980s and discovered the fraudulent nature of the commercial just described. What would you have done at that point? Why?

27. Analyzing Financial Statement Data of Foreign Firms (LO 1, 3)

The following information was taken from recent financial statement footnotes of KLM Royal Dutch Airlines. Because this company is based in The Netherlands, all amounts are expressed in millions of Dutch guilders.

Traffic Revenue:	
Passengers	5,934
Cargo and Mail	1,375
Total	7,309

Revenue by Traffic Routes:	
Europe	1,996
North America	1,731
Central and South America	809
Far East	1,350
Middle East	617
Africa	488
Total Scheduled Services	6,991
Charters	318
Total	7,309

Required:

1. What problems do U.S. citizens face when attempting to analyze financial statement data of foreign firms?
2. What specific questions might U.S. investors raise regarding KLM's revenue data? What additional information, if any, would these investors need to address these questions?
3. Develop "customized" financial ratios or other financial measures that decision makers, such as investors, might use to analyze an airline's operating results and financial condition. In developing these items, consider the nature of an airline's operations.

28. **Marketing, Accounting, and Goo Goo Clusters** (LO 1, 2)

Although accountants are not perceived as marketing types, they provide invaluable information to corporate executives responsible for developing a company's marketing strategy. This is particularly true for the pricing component of a company's marketing strategy. Take the case of the Standard Candy Company of Nashville, Tennessee, which sells Goo Goo Clusters, a very popular candy item in the South. In 1983, Standard Candy's executives decided to boost sales to their principal customers, retail stores, by discounting the wholesale prices of their candy products. Within a matter of weeks, the company's accounting department was feeding data to these executives regarding the financial implications of the new pricing strategy. These data revealed that the discounting tactic had been successful, in one respect, and a disappointing failure, in another. The new pricing strategy caused the sales of Goo Goo Clusters to increase dramatically. However, profits dropped even more dramatically because the company realized a much smaller "profit margin" on its sales due to the price discounts. After reviewing the relevant accounting data, management quickly reverted to its former pricing structure.

Required:

1. Develop a "before and after" numerical example to illustrate how Standard Candy Company's profits dropped following the implementation of the new pricing strategy despite an increase in the firm's revenues.
2. A business's accountants supply information to both internal and external decision makers. Identify specific types of financial data that the following internal decision makers might demand of Standard Candy Company's accountants:
   a. Production line supervisor
   b. Advertising executive
   c. Credit manager
   d. Property insurance clerk
   e. Manager of personnel department
3. Are the financial data items you identified in (2) typically reported in a business's financial statements? Explain.
4. In designing a business's accounting system, should the information needs of the firm's internal or external decision makers be given more consideration? Defend your answer.

PROJECTS

29. Analyzing Profitability of Competing Firms

Comparisons of profitability ratios across companies in the same industry can help investors determine which of those firms' common stocks are more attractive investments. In this project, you will compare the relative profitability of companies operating in several different merchandising lines of business.

Required:

1. In three of the following merchandising industries, identify two public companies (six in total): supermarkets, hardware supply, convenience stores, furniture retailers, bookstores, women's apparel, and men's apparel.
2. For each selected company, obtain the following data for the three most recent years for which data are available: net sales, gross profit, and net income. Compute each company's gross profit percentage and profit margin percentage for each year.
3. Given the data you collected and your "professional" insight, identify which company in each matched pair has been most profitable in recent years. Defend your choice in each case.
4. What factors likely contribute to the companies you identified in (3) being more successful than their competitors?

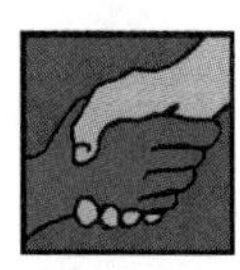

30. Investing in Mutual Funds

As discussed in this module, mutual funds have become an increasingly popular investment alternative in recent years. Presently, there are several thousand mutual funds from which investors can choose. The managers of many mutual funds use the Internet to distribute information regarding the funds they oversee. In this assignment, you and the fellow members of your project group will access the Internet to obtain information, including financial data, for a sample of mutual funds.

Required:

1. Each group member should search the Internet for mutual fund Web sites. After reviewing the information in several such Web sites, each group member should select a mutual fund that he or she believes would be a "good" investment. Each member should print key descriptive information, including financial data, for the selected mutual fund.
2. In a group meeting, each member of your project team will review the information obtained by the other members of the group for the mutual funds they selected. After reviewing this information, the group should discuss the factors that are relevant in determining whether a mutual fund is a "good" investment. At the conclusion of this discussion, one member of the group should develop a list of these factors.
3. Next, the group should determine, given the list of factors identified in (2), which of the individual mutual funds selected by group members is the best or most attractive investment.
4. One group member should prepare a written report that identifies the mutual funds selected by the members of the group, that lists the factors identified in (2), and that documents the selection made by the group in (3). A brief explanation should be included in the report to explain how the group arrived at its decision in (3). The Web site address of each mutual fund should also be included in the report. A group member should be prepared to present a brief summary of the written report in class.

ACCOUNTING FOR ASSETS AND RELATED TRANSACTIONS

III

Parts I and II of this text acquainted you with fundamental accounting concepts and with the basic accounting procedures that dictate how business transactions and events are recorded. Next, we consider key accounting issues related to specific financial statement items. The series of chapters in Part III focus on accounting for assets and related transactions. Chapter 6 examines accounting for cash and accounts receivable, Chapter 7 discusses accounting issues involving inventory, while Chapter 8 addresses accounting for long-term assets.

The key theme of this text is that an organization's accounting function should be responsive to the information needs of economic decision makers. You will find this theme interwoven throughout each of the three chapters in Part III. Among the issues relating to economic decision making that you will encounter in Chapters 6 through 8 are the following: What financial disclosures do investors and creditors demand regarding cash and accounts receivable? How can inventory accounting methods influence the reported profits of a business? What valuation methods for long-term assets provide bankers with the most insight as to their clients' true financial condition?

6 Cash and Accounts Receivable

"No man's credit is as good as his money."
Ed Howe

LEARNING OBJECTIVES

After studying this chapter, you should be able to do the following:

1. Define the key information needs of decision makers regarding cash and accounts receivable.
2. Account for the major types of transactions involving cash and accounts receivable.
3. Discuss key control activities for cash and accounts receivable.
4. Compute and interpret key financial ratios for cash and accounts receivable.
5. Use the aging method to estimate uncollectible accounts expense.
6. (Appendix) Prepare a bank reconciliation.

FOCUS ON DECISION MAKING

Giving Credit To Whom Credit Is Due

In 1902, James Cash Penney opened a dry goods store in the small mining town of Kemmerer, Wyoming. Penney was a hard-nosed businessman who believed that the secret to success in business was focusing on a few fundamental principles and implementing those principles more effectively than competitors. Keeping overhead as low as possible, offering merchandise at reasonable prices, and a cash-and-carry—no credit—sales policy were the principles around which Penney built his company. These principles worked well for Penney. By the mid-1920s, there were more than one thousand J.C. Penney stores scattered across the nation.

Penney was particularly adamant about the cash-and-carry sales policy. What else would you expect from a man whose middle name was Cash? Long after most retailers had begun extending credit to their customers, Penney refused to even consider selling merchandise on anything but a cash basis.

By the late 1950s, J.C. Penney's strict cash-basis sales policy was hurting the firm. Credit sales by competing retailers, Sears and Montgomery Ward in particular, were cutting into J.C. Penney's market share. Company executives realized they had to break with tradition and begin offering their customers credit or risk losing even more ground to their competitors. By 1962, all of J.C. Penney's stores were offering credit to their customers. Five years later, J.C. Penney had 12 million credit accounts and more than one-third of the company's annual sales were made on credit.

The decision to begin extending credit to customers significantly affects a business's operations. No longer do daily sales figures translate into equivalent bank deposits. Immediately, a credit department must be established. This new department must decide which customers will be extended credit, whether discounts for early payment will be offered, and the length of the discount period. Likewise, management must become concerned with collection activities. A collections department may be necessary to track down slow-paying customers. Alternatively, past-due accounts may be turned over to a collection agency that will take a hefty cut of the amounts it collects as the fee for its services.

The decision to extend credit to customers also imposes new responsibilities on an organization's accountants. Among these responsibilities are providing management with the data needed to monitor the collectibility of receivables. Revised cash forecasting techniques may be necessary to furnish management with reliable cash-flow projections. New control activities must be developed and implemented for the credit-granting function. Finally, the firm's accounting records and procedures may need to be redesigned to accommodate several types of new transactions.

No doubt, the grand old gentleman of merchandising would be more than a little annoyed with the extensive use of credit by modern merchandising companies. Imagine Jim Penney's chagrin if he picked up a copy of his namesake firm's financial statements in 1996 and discovered that the company was owed $5 billion by its customers! Then again, imagine the frustration that plastic-toting consumers would experience if merchandisers decided to return to the olden days and invoke the sales policy that worked so well for so many decades for James Cash Penney.

This chapter focuses on accounting issues for two important and closely related current assets, cash and accounts receivable. Accounts receivable are a major source of the cash required to keep many businesses "up and running." Declining cash inflows from accounts receivable collections can leave a business strapped for cash and searching for other ways to raise the funds needed to finance its day-to-day operations.

To illustrate basic accounting procedures in Chapters 4 and 5, service businesses were used. Double-entry bookkeeping rules and nearly all of the recurring procedures included in the accounting cycle are identical for service, merchandising, and manufacturing businesses. However, merchandisers and manufacturers engage in certain transactions that service businesses do not, an example being the sale of merchandise or other goods to customers. In this chapter and the following chapter, we consider many transactions unique to merchandising and manufacturing operations.

▲ CASH

This first section of Chapter 6 focuses on accounting issues related to cash. As pointed out in Module 1, the discussion of each major financial statement item in this chapter and the following several chapters begins with a brief overview of that item. Next, key information needs of decision makers regarding the given item are identified, followed by a discussion of accounting rules and procedures. The treatment of each financial statement item concludes with a review of relevant control activities and financial ratios.

Cash, Cash Equivalents, and Cash Flows

Most businesses list cash as the first line item on their balance sheet. The most common caption for cash in corporate balance sheets is "cash and cash equivalents." A recent edition of *Accounting Trends & Techniques* reported that nearly 80 percent of public companies use that balance sheet caption or its first cousin, "cash and equivalents."

cash equivalents

Cash equivalents include funds that companies have invested in short-term securities such as certificates of deposit (CDs), money market funds, and U.S. treasury bills. To qualify as cash equivalents, these investments must have 90 days or less to maturity when purchased.

Why has cash historically been the first line item on the balance sheet? Probably because cash has long been considered one of the most important assets of businesses. An old business axiom goes something like this, "Profit is an estimate, but cash is a fact." Although a company is posting large profits, it may find itself on shaky ground if those profits do not translate into positive cash flows. Recall from Chapter 2, specifically Exhibit 2.9, that a company's net income and net cash flow from profit-oriented activities may not be closely correlated. For example, suppose that the Choi Corporation is realizing impressive increases in sales each accounting period. This growth in sales volume is causing the company's cash outflows to increase due to larger payments to suppliers and higher operating expenses. Unfortunately, many of Choi's new customers are slow to pay their bills. As a result, the increase in the company's cash outflows is not being offset by a proportionate increase in cash inflows from customers. If this trend continues, the company may be forced to borrow funds so that it will not fall behind on payments to its suppliers and other creditors.

If you review the balance sheets of numerous public companies, you will find that their cash balances vary significantly, both in absolute terms and as a percentage of total assets. Consider Parametric Technology Corporation, a company that develops computer software, and Atmos Energy Corporation, a natural gas company. Recent balance sheets issued by these companies disclosed that each had approximately $450 million of total assets. However, Parametric Technology reported $146 million of cash, accounting for 32 percent of its total assets, while Atmos Energy reported $2.2 million of cash, which represented less than 1 percent of its total assets. Generally, the average cash balance of companies in most industries ranges from five to 10 percent of total assets.

One factor that significantly influences the cash needs of a company is the length of the firm's operating cycle. Recall from Chapter 2 that an operating cycle is the period of time elapsing between the use of cash in a business's normal operating activities and the collection of cash from customers. Exhibit 6.1 reports the average length of the operating cycle in six industries. As you would expect, grocery stores have short operating cycles since their inventory turns over quickly and most of their sales are on a cash basis. On the other hand, furniture stores, although they are merchandising operations like grocery stores, have a much longer operating cycle. Apparently, convincing Joan and John Q. Public to buy a La-Z-Boy recliner requires more time than selling the couple a jar of orange marmalade or a dozen farm fresh eggs.

EXHIBIT 6.1 ▼
Length of Operating Cycle for Selected Industries

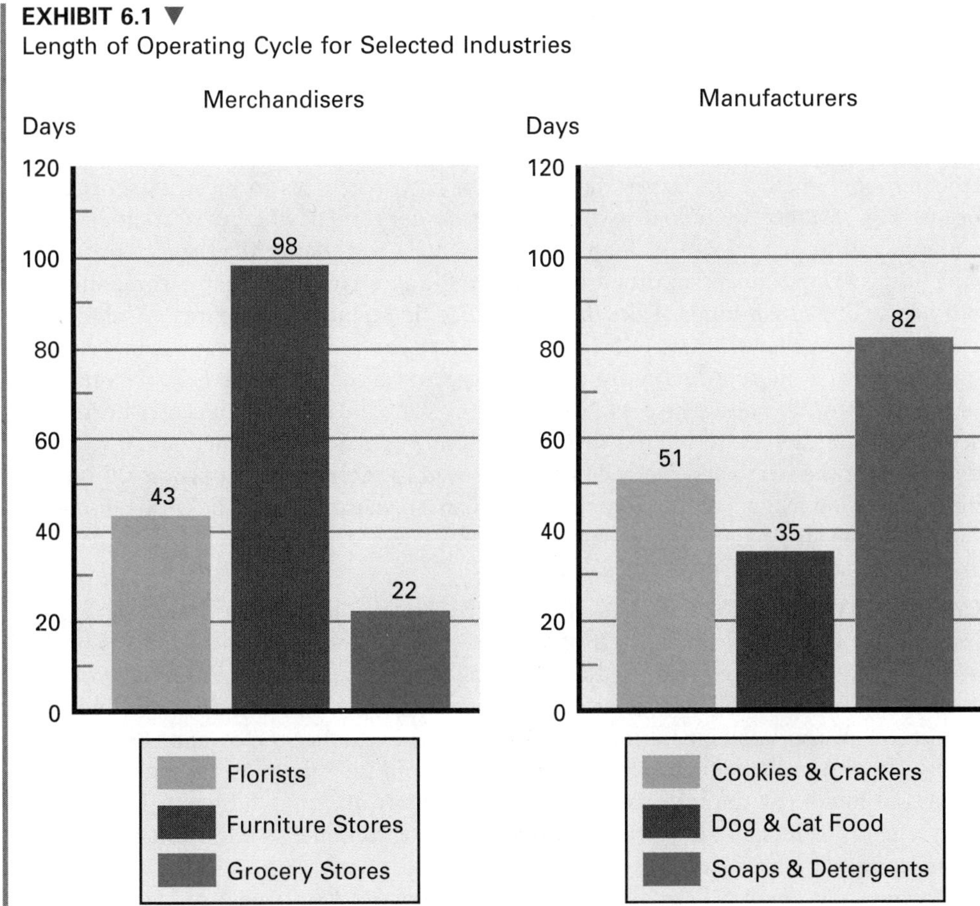

Cash Cache Causes Carmaker Concern

FOR YOUR INFORMATION

Can you ever have too much cash? Yes, just ask the executives of Chrysler Corporation, the large automobile manufacturer. During the mid-1990s, Chrysler accumulated a large war chest of cash to provide funds for various projects including the development of new products. By early 1996, Chrysler had nearly $7 billion of cash. The problem this large cash balance posed for Chrysler was that one of the firm's largest stockholders, Kirk Kerkorian, insisted that the funds be returned to stockholders as dividends. When Chrysler executives snubbed Kerkorian, the investment mogul attempted a hostile takeover of the company. Kerkorian's takeover attempt failed, but Chrysler's executives did agree to nearly double the firm's annual dividend.

Cash: Information Needs of Decision Makers

LEARNING OBJECTIVE 1 ▶ Define the key information needs of decision makers regarding cash and accounts receivable.

As pointed out repeatedly in this text, the key role of accounting and accountants is to provide information needed by decision makers. By continually focusing on the information needs of decision makers, accountants are better prepared to select the most appropriate accounting procedures for specific financial statement items. In this section, key information needs of decision makers regarding cash and cash equivalents are identified.

CASH BALANCES Decision makers should be informed of a business's total cash and cash equivalents as of each balance sheet date. Decision makers use this information to determine whether a business has sufficient cash resources to meet its short-term needs. For instance, potential investors may be concerned whether a company has enough cash to pay off a large loan that comes due shortly after the firm's fiscal year-end. Just as important is information regarding any restrictions that a company has on the use of its cash funds. Take the case of Pacific Scientific Company, a California-based firm that manufactures electrical and safety equipment. A recent balance sheet of Pacific Scientific reported more than $12 million of cash. However, over one-half of that amount was designated as "Restricted Cash." The company recently borrowed several million dollars to build a new manufacturing facility, and the loan agreement dictates that the borrowed funds can only be used for construction purposes. To fully inform decision makers of the restriction on its cash resources, Pacific Scientific discusses this matter in its financial statement footnotes.

CASH-FLOW INFORMATION Decision makers also demand information regarding the cash flows of businesses. Of prime interest to financial statement users is how a company both generated and used cash during a given period. For example, consider a company that realized a large increase in cash during a recent year. If this increase resulted from profitable operations, that is a positive signal of the company's financial health. However, if the increase in cash resulted from the sale of assets such as equipment and buildings, the implications for the company are quite different. If the company intends to remain an operating entity, it cannot continue to sell off its productive assets to raise cash.

Statement of Financial Accounting Standards No. 95, "Statement of Cash Flows," requires businesses to classify cash flows into three categories for financial statement purposes. These three categories are cash flows from operating activities, investing activities, and financing activities. Operating activities are those day-to-day, profit-oriented activities of a company, such as the sale of merchandise to customers. Investing activities involve such transactions as the acquisition and disposal of property, plant, and equipment assets. An example of a financing activity is the sale of common stock. Financial statement users tend to focus on cash flows related to operating activities. Why? Because over the long run, a business must generate positive cash flows from its profit-oriented activities to be economically viable.

FUTURE CASH FLOWS No doubt, what decision makers really want is information about a business's future cash flows. However, forecasts of cash flows, revenues, and earnings are rarely included in annual reports. Business executives are reluctant to include financial forecasts in their companies' annual reports because of the risk of being sued if their projections are not achieved. For example, Monsanto Chemical Corporation was sued several years ago when it released sales and profit projections and then saw its actual operating results fall short of the projected amounts. Thankfully for Monsanto, the suit against the company was unsuccessful. The judge hearing the case ruled that Monsanto was not liable because its forecasts had been based upon reasonable assumptions.

The Securities and Exchange Commission (SEC) encourages public companies to release financial forecasts. To promote the issuance of forecasted financial data, the SEC established a "safe harbor" rule. Under this rule, the SEC pledges to help protect a company from lawsuits if a financial forecast prepared by the firm in good faith proves to be a poor predictor of future operating results.

Accounting for Cash

LEARNING OBJECTIVE 2
Account for the major types of transactions involving cash and accounts receivable.

You may be surprised to learn, and happy as well, that there are not many "sticky" procedural accounting issues to discuss for cash. Cash sales to customers are among the most common cash-based business transactions. Another common transaction involving cash is the collection of "accounts receivable" from customers who purchase goods and services on credit. We consider credit sales, and the subsequent cash collections of accounts receivable, later in this chapter.

CASH SALES Revenue resulting from a sale of merchandise or other goods is recorded in a Sales account or Sales Revenue account. This is true whether a sale is made on a cash or credit basis. Suppose that a wholesaler of building supplies sells $900 of merchandise to an electrical contractor who pays cash for the goods. The following entry, in simplified general journal format, would be appropriate for this transaction in the wholesaler's accounting records.

Jan. 11	Cash	900	
	Sales		900
	Cash sale to Singh Contractors, invoice no. 2751		

In certain accounting systems, a second journal entry is necessary to record a sale of merchandise in the seller's accounting records. This second entry records the "cost of goods sold" related to a sales transaction. In Chapter 7, we consider accounting for cost of goods sold.

CASH OVER & SHORT Suppose that a retail store's cash register tape indicates $2,402.17 of cash sales for a given day of business. However, only $2,389.02 is found when the cash till is counted. How does the store's accountant deal with this cash shortage? Naturally, this situation raises control issues, particularly if such shortages are common, significant in size, or correlated with the presence of certain employees. Putting the control issues aside, the following entry would be appropriate, assuming the store's accountant records daily sales in one lump sum.

Mar. 17	Cash	2,389.02	
	Cash Over & Short	13.15	
	Sales		2,402.17
	To record daily cash sales		

If the cash count had exceeded the total sales reflected by the cash register tape, the difference would have been credited to Cash Over & Short. At the end of each accounting period, the balance of Cash Over & Short is treated as a miscellaneous revenue or expense for financial statement purposes. Since this account typically has a debit balance, it is most often classified as an expense account.

petty cash fund

PETTY CASH FUND Many businesses maintain a **petty cash fund** from which they pay minor expenses such as delivery fees and postage costs. Suppose that a company establishes a $100 petty cash fund on May 12 of a given year. On that date, the firm would debit Petty Cash Fund and credit Cash, each for $100.

For each disbursement made from a petty cash fund, the individual responsible for the physical security of the fund, the petty cash custodian, completes a petty cash voucher. Among the data items recorded on a petty cash voucher are the date and amount of the disbursement, the party to whom the disbursement was made, the goods or services acquired, and the account to which the disbursement amount will eventually be debited.

Periodically, a petty cash fund must be replenished. For example, suppose that the fund just referred to has only $15 remaining on June 17. At this point, the petty cash custodian might prepare a request for replenishment of the fund. In this request, the custodian would list the expenditures that account for the $85 of disbursements paid from the fund since it was established. Assume that the $85 of disbursements involved the following items: delivery expenses—$32, postage costs—$41, and purchases of supplies—$12. Following approval of the petty cash custodian's request, an $85 check would be written against a company bank account, cashed, and the proceeds turned over to the petty cash custodian. The following entry would be made to record the replenishment of the petty cash fund.

June 17	Delivery Expense	32	
	Postage Expense	41	
	Supplies Expense	12	
	Cash		85
	To reimburse petty cash fund for expenses paid		

Notice that this entry records the expenditures made from the petty cash fund in the appropriate expense accounts. Also notice that this entry credits Cash instead of the account Petty Cash Fund. Entries are made to the Petty Cash Fund account only when the fund is established, increased, decreased, or eliminated.

Key Control Activities for Cash

LEARNING OBJECTIVE 3
Discuss key control activities for cash and accounts receivable.

KPMG Peat Marwick, LLP, a large accounting firm, periodically surveys businesses to determine the most common types of frauds they encounter. Theft of cash and check forgery always rank high on Peat Marwick's "top ten" list of business frauds. Not surprisingly then, providing effective control over cash is an important priority of most businesses. In this section, we consider three general control activities for cash. These activities include physical security measures, cash-processing controls, and periodic independent checks and reconciliations of cash balances.

PHYSICAL SECURITY MEASURES Limiting the number of individuals who have access to cash and near-cash items is probably the most important physical security measure for these assets. A control activity that at first seems to contradict the general control concept just mentioned is the policy that banks have regarding access to a vault or other storage area containing cash or securities. Typically, a minimum of two people, each of whom has proper authorization and security clearance, must enter such areas. This policy minimizes the ability of one dishonest employee to "rip off" a bank.

Although businesses make every effort to hire honest individuals to work in cash-handling functions, they should also obtain fidelity bonds for these employees. Fidelity bonds are essentially insurance policies companies purchase to protect themselves from theft and other fraudulent activities by employees.

CASH-PROCESSING CONTROLS The use of standardized accounting procedures for cash transactions minimizes the likelihood that errors will occur in the processing of these transactions. Take the case of cash receipts. Exhibit 6.2 outlines a common approach to assigning responsibilities for processing customer remittances (checks) received in the mail.

Banks establish extensive internal control procedures to protect their cash resources. Nevertheless, two or more dishonest bank employees may collaborate to override a bank's control procedures.

EXHIBIT 6.2 ▼
Assignment of Key Accounting and Control Responsibilities for Processing Cash Receipts

Responsibility 1	On a daily basis, a mail clerk opens customer remittances and prepares a list of the checks for deposit. Three copies of this list are made, one of which is retained by the mail clerk. One copy of the list, along with the checks, is sent to the cashier, while the remaining copy is forwarded to the accounting department.
Responsibility 2	The cashier prepares a daily deposit slip listing the checks received from customers, makes the deposit, and then sends a duplicate copy of the deposit ticket to the accounting department.
Responsibility 3	An accounting clerk determines that the listing of receipts prepared by the mail clerk and the receipts reflected by the duplicate copy of the deposit ticket agree. Then, the clerk makes the appropriate entries to record the receipts.

The multiple copies of key accounting documents produced in the tasks outlined in Exhibit 6.2 increase the likelihood that errors made in processing cash receipts will be detected. Just as important, the division of responsibilities and system of checks allows a business to pinpoint when such errors occur and the party who most likely made them.

PERIODIC INDEPENDENT CHECKS AND RECONCILIATIONS OF CASH BALANCES To verify the accuracy of their cash accounting records and to detect losses of cash due to theft and other causes, businesses should periodically count their cash funds. The results of these cash counts should be reconciled with the corresponding cash balances reflected in a business's accounting records. Companies that maintain a petty cash fund typically require internal auditors to count that fund at irregular intervals. The sum of the cash in the fund and the total dollar amount of expenditures documented on completed petty cash vouchers should equal the fund's permanent balance. The appendix to this chapter discusses a related control activity completed each accounting period for cash maintained on deposit with banks and other financial institutions. Preparing a monthly "bank reconciliation" is a useful control procedure for businesses and individuals alike.

Analyzing Cash

LEARNING OBJECTIVE 4 ▶
Compute and interpret key financial ratios for cash and accounts receivable.

In Module 1, financial ratios were defined as measures that express the relationship or interrelationships between, or among, two or more financial statement items. A key financial ratio involving cash is the quick ratio, which is used to evaluate a business's liquidity. **Liquidity** refers to an entity's ability to finance its day-to-day operations and to pay its liabilities as they mature. Liquidity is heavily influenced by the amount of cash a business has on hand and the amount of cash it can quickly raise, such as by selling short-term investments. The **quick ratio** is computed by dividing the sum of a firm's "quick" assets by the sum of its current liabilities. Quick assets generally include cash and cash equivalents, short-term investments, and the net amount of current receivables.

liquidity

quick ratio

To introduce you to the quick ratio, let us review recent financial data for The Gymboree Corporation, a company that markets children's apparel. The following

Controlling Cash in "Lost Wages," Nevada

Imagine the control nightmare facing the executives and accountants of large Las Vegas casinos such as the Mirage, the Riviera, and the Tropicana. A few years ago, the movie *Casino,* which was filmed in the Riviera and starred Sharon Stone and Robert DeNiro, highlighted control problems faced by these businesses on a daily basis. Casinos must implement an extensive set of control policies and procedures to safeguard the steady stream of currency flowing into their cash vaults from customers' pockets. (Occasionally, very occasionally, the direction of this cash flow is reversed.) Recently, an accounting professor at the University of Nevada discussed the control activities that casinos use to maintain physical security over their cash resources. Listed next are a few of these controls.

1. Remote control cameras with zoom lenses are located throughout casinos, including "count" rooms where cash is tallied and corridors where cash and gambling chips are transported.
2. Cash collection and counting are performed on a regular schedule to ensure that these activities can be occasionally observed, on a surprise basis, by casino and government auditors.
3. Access to count rooms is strictly limited to authorized personnel.
4. When a table game is stocked or restocked with chips, four individuals are typically involved to decrease the likelihood that chips will be stolen by a dishonest employee.
5. Game dealers are generally not allowed to wear French cuffs to prevent them from easily concealing (and stealing) chips.

Source: J. R. Mills, "Controlling Cash in Casinos," *Management Accounting,* May 1996, 38–40. Reprinted from *Management Accounting.* Copyright by Institute of Management Accountants, Montvale, N.J. (May 1996).

schedule lists Gymboree's quick assets, current liabilities, and quick ratio for the firm's fiscal years ending in 1995 and 1996.

	Fiscal Year Ending In	
	1995	1996
	(in thousands)	
Cash and cash equivalents	$11,028	$ 8,755
Short-term investments	52,103	64,893
Accounts receivable (net)	2,141	2,868
Total quick assets	$65,272	$76,516
Current liabilities	$27,101	$26,637
Quick ratio	2.41	2.87

These data indicate that Gymboree's quick ratio improved during its fiscal year ending in 1996. Thus, Gymboree became more liquid during that fiscal year, meaning that it had a greater ability to pay its liabilities and finance its day-to-day operations.

Further insight on a company's liquidity can be gained by comparing the firm's quick ratios to key benchmarks. For example, Dun & Bradstreet, an investment advisory firm, suggests that businesses should generally maintain a quick ratio of at least 1.0. An even better yardstick for evaluating a company's quick ratio is the industry norm for that ratio. In 1996, the median quick ratio in Gymboree's industry was .6. Compared to either of these standards, Gymboree's 1995 quick ratio was very strong and its 1996 quick ratio stronger yet.

Okay, Gymboree was very liquid in the mid-1990s, but why? Many companies have a strong liquidity position because they have recently obtained long-term loans from banks or tapped the pocketbooks of investors. To determine the source of a company's liquidity, we must review the firm's recent cash-flow data.

In 1996, Gymboree's operating or profit-oriented activities produced positive cash flows of more than $32 million. During that year, the company did not borrow any funds, and stockholders invested only an additional $2.5 million in the firm. So, Gymboree's strong liquidity was apparently a direct result of profitable operations, which was excellent news for investors and potential investors. In fact, between 1994 and 1996, Gymboree's net income nearly doubled, increasing from $14.1 million to $26.4 million.

▲ ACCOUNTS RECEIVABLE

Now, let us examine accounting issues related to accounts receivable. This asset is particularly important for those firms that sell goods and services primarily on credit. Collections of accounts receivable are typically the largest source of cash inflows for such firms.

Credit Makes the (Business) World Go 'Round

When you graduate from college, expect your mail box to be deluged with credit applications. VISA, American Express, and, yes, even J.C. Penney, will somehow discover your new earnings potential. These firms and many others will invite you to join, assuming you have not already, the hoards of fully "ac-credited" American consumers. Increased sales and larger market shares await those companies that allow their customers to "charge" purchases of goods and services. As pointed out in the opening vignette for this chapter, there are drawbacks to a business's decision to extend credit to customers. The biggest problem stemming from this decision can be summarized in two words: bad debts. Unlike a cash sale, there are two key activities associated with a credit sale: making the sale and collecting the resulting receivable. Quite often, the latter task is the more challenging and frustrating of the two.

All 600 public companies surveyed in a recent year by *Accounting Trends & Techniques* listed receivables on their balance sheets under current assets. Approximately 88 percent of these companies used one of the following captions for those assets: "accounts receivable," "receivables," or "trade accounts receivable." For our purposes, we will define **accounts receivable** as amounts owed to businesses by their

accounts receivable

customers. These receivables arise from purchases of goods or services on credit by those customers.

The nature of a business's operations significantly influences the composition of its assets, including the proportion of its total assets "tied up" in accounts receivable. Refer to Exhibit 6.3. Notice that Churchill Downs, the company that operates the racetrack where the Kentucky Derby is run each year, has a relatively small amount of accounts receivables on its balance sheet. Churchill Downs' executives do not allow customers to charge their bets, clearly a wise policy. On the other hand, Bassett Furniture, a manufacturing firm, and Dillard's, a large department store chain, make extensive use of credit. Why? Principally because it has become common practice in these companies' industries to extend credit to customers. Companies in these industries that do not allow their customers to purchase merchandise on credit will find themselves at a significant competitive disadvantage.

EXHIBIT 6.3 ▼

Cash, Accounts Receivable, and Current Assets as a Percentage of Total Assets for Selected Companies

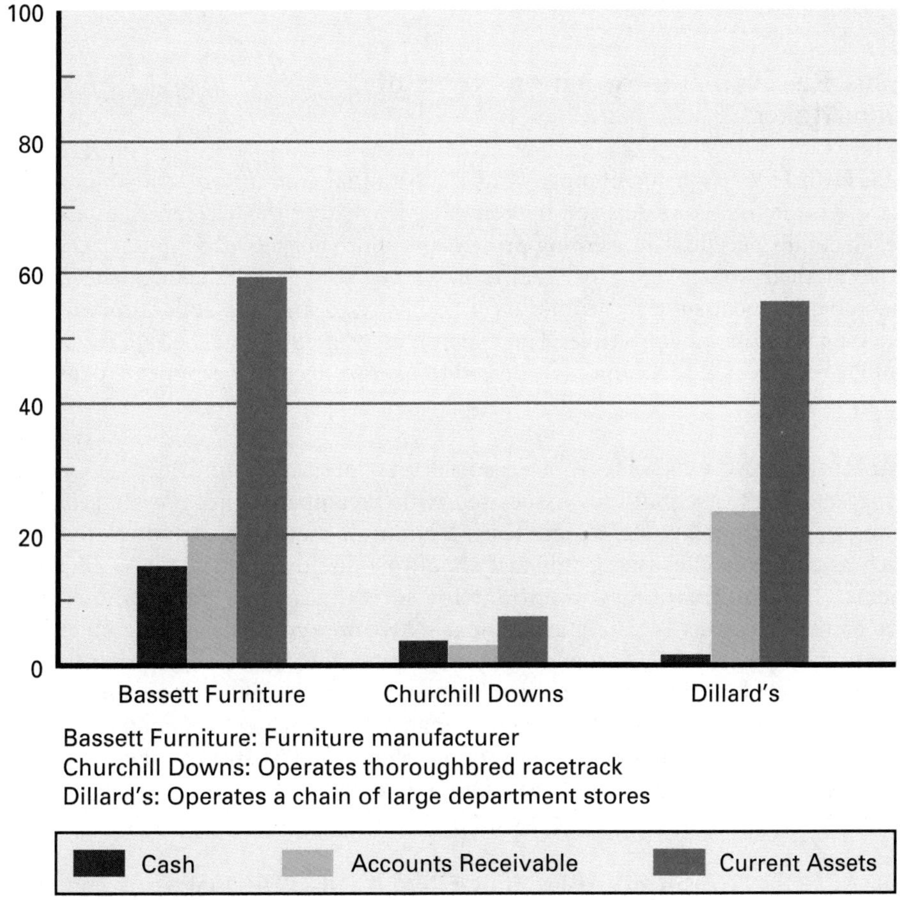

100
80
60
40
20
0

Bassett Furniture
Churchill Downs
Dillard's

Bassett Furniture: Furniture manufacturer
Churchill Downs: Operates thoroughbred racetrack
Dillard's: Operates a chain of large department stores

Cash
Accounts Receivable
Current Assets

Source: Recent Annual Reports.

The composition of a company's assets is heavily influenced by the nature of its operations. For example, you would not expect Churchill Downs, a company that owns and operates a thoroughbred racetrack, to have a significant amount of accounts receivable. Why? Just try "charging" a bet the next time you vist a racetrack.

© SuperStock

Accounts Receivable: Information Needs of Decision Makers

LEARNING OBJECTIVE 1 ▶
Define the key information needs of decision makers regarding cash and accounts receivable.

uncollectible accounts expense

COLLECTIBILITY When a company has a substantial amount of receivables on its balance sheet, the first issue decision makers raise is whether those receivables are collectible. Generally accepted accounting principles require businesses to report accounts receivable at their approximate net realizable value. That is, for balance sheet purposes, companies must subtract from their accounts receivable the dollar amount that will likely prove to be uncollectible. The expense associated with accounts receivable that cannot be collected is commonly referred to as **uncollectible accounts expense,** or bad debt expense.

UNUSUAL CHARACTERISTICS Decision makers need to be informed of any unusual characteristics or conditions associated with a company's accounts receivable. For example, if a company has a significant amount of receivables from related parties, such as company executives, this fact should be disclosed in the firm's financial statements. This information is important for several reasons. Probably the most obvious of these reasons is that management may not vigorously pursue collection efforts on such receivables. U.S. Pawn, Inc., a company that operates a chain of pawn stores, reported "Related Parties Receivables" on a separate line of a recent balance sheet. A footnote accompanying U.S. Pawn's financial statements explained that those receivables represented cash advances made to certain officers, stockholders, and employees. The footnote also reported the interest rate being charged these parties and the date they were responsible for repaying the amounts involved.

USE OF ACCOUNTS RECEIVABLE FOR FINANCING PURPOSES A company that becomes trapped in a liquidity crisis in which it is short of cash may be forced to sell its receivables to third parties. By definition, receivables that have been sold are no longer assets of a company and should not be included in the firm's periodic balance sheets. Accounts receivable can also be used as collateral for a loan. If a company defaults on such a loan, the lender can recover the amount it is owed from the subsequent cash collections on the "pledged" receivables. If a company has pledged its receivables as collateral, this fact should be disclosed in the firm's financial statement footnotes. Such disclosure alerts decision makers that the company has one less financing alternative available in the future.

Accounting Trends & Techniques recently reported that approximately 21 percent of public companies use their accounts receivable for financing purposes. One such company is Chock Full O'Nuts Corporation. Recent financial statements of this firm revealed that its accounts receivable, as well as certain other assets, were pledged as collateral for a large bank loan.

Accounting for Accounts Receivable

LEARNING OBJECTIVE 2
Account for the major types of transactions involving cash and accounts receivable.

Determining uncollectible accounts expense is typically the most important accounting task that must be completed for accounts receivable each accounting period. Before we consider that task, we should first review accounting procedures for credit sales, which are the source of accounts receivable.

CREDIT SALES Earlier in this chapter, we briefly examined accounting for cash sales. Recall that we "booked" an entry for a $900 cash sale made by a building supplies wholesaler. Suppose now that same sale was made on credit. The following journal entry would be appropriate to record that transaction under this new assumption.

Jan. 11	Accounts Receivable	900	
	Sales		900
	Credit sale to Singh Contractors, invoice no. 2751		

Notice that instead of debiting Cash for this transaction, we debit Accounts Receivable. Again, whether a sale is made on a cash or credit basis, the revenue account Sales is credited.

credit terms

The **credit terms** for a sales transaction express the agreement between the buyer and seller regarding the timing of payment and any discount available to the buyer for early payment. Egghead Software, a computer software retailer, offers its customers credit terms of n/30, which reads as "net 30." These credit terms require the buyer to pay the full invoice amount within thirty days of the invoice date—in other words, no discount is available to the buyer for early payment. This thirty-day period is known as the credit period and does not include the date of the invoice. For example, a customer that buys goods on May 1 with credit terms of n/30 would have until May 31 to pay for the goods.

sales discounts

To speed up the collection of cash on credit sales, many companies offer **sales discounts** to customers for early payment of their account balances.[1] Probably the most common credit terms that include a discount for early payment are 2/10, n/30. These credit terms allow buyers to subtract 2 percent from the invoice amount if payment

1. Besides these discounts for early payment, some companies offer "trade discounts" to certain of their customers. For instance, large volume customers may automatically receive a discount off selling prices quoted in a company's sales catalog. Typically, an invoice sales amount is recorded net of a trade discount. That is, a trade discount does not appear on the invoice, nor does the selling firm record a trade discount in its accounting records.

is made within ten days of the invoice date. This ten-day period is referred to as the discount period and begins the day following the invoice date. With credit terms of 2/10, n/30, if payment is not made within the ten-day discount period, the full or "net" amount of the invoice is due 30 days following the invoice date.[2]

To illustrate accounting for sales discounts, assume that a company sells $400 of merchandise on March 1 with credit terms of 2/10, n/30. At the time the sale is made, the company does not know whether the customer will take advantage of the discount. Consequently, the sales transaction is recorded at the amount reported on the sales invoice, $400.

Mar. 1	Accounts Receivable	400	
	Sales		400
	Credit sale to Hinton Brothers, invoice no. 189, credit terms 2/10, n/30		

If the customer does not take advantage of the sales discount and pays the invoice amount of $400 on March 31, the following entry would be required.

Mar. 31	Cash	400	
	Accounts Receivable		400
	Payment received for Mar. 1 sale, invoice no. 189		

Assuming the customer takes advantage of the available discount and makes payment on March 11, the last day of the discount period, the following entry would be appropriate.

Mar. 11	Cash	392	
	Sales Discounts	8	
	Accounts Receivable		400
	Payment received for Mar. 1 sale, invoice no. 189, 2% discount taken		

Most merchandising companies grant customers a full refund for damaged or defective merchandise they return. (This is true for sales made on either a cash or credit basis.) Customers may be granted an "allowance"—price reduction—to persuade them to keep damaged or defective merchandise. Collectively, these refunds and price reductions are referred to as **sales returns and allowances.**

sales returns and allowances

Suppose that a customer of the Shamrock Shoppe purchases a $120 dress only to discover a flaw in the dress a few days later. When the customer returns the dress to the store, the salesperson offers to "knock" $60 off the original selling price to encourage the customer to keep the dress. If the customer accepts this offer, a "credit memorandum," such as the one shown in Exhibit 6.4, would be prepared to document the price reduction. Preparation of credit memoranda is a control function that reduces the

2. The term "net" seems inappropriate since the customer is actually paying the full amount of the invoice. However, this term is widely used in this context because often a trade discount (see footnote 1) has been subtracted by the selling firm to arrive at the invoice sales amount.

risk of employees improperly granting price reductions or other concessions to customers. Typically, a manager must review and approve each credit memorandum prepared for his or her department or other area of responsibility. The credit memorandum shown in Exhibit 6.4 would serve as the source document for the sales allowance just described and would be the basis for the following journal entry.

Feb. 18	Sales Returns and Allowances	60	
	Accounts Receivable (or Cash)		60
	Sales allowance granted, credit memo no. 288		

EXHIBIT 6.4 ▼
Example of a Credit Memorandum

Shamrock Shoppe
1600 Clinton Avenue
Turlock, California 90544

CREDIT MEMO

Customer

Mary Nelle Jenkins
Rural Route 3
Modesto, CA 90044

No.: 288
Date: 2/18/98
Customer ID: 3481

ITEM	DESCRIPTION	TOTAL
32-5a	Dress returned by customer due to fabric flaw (size 7, Style 624, Crown Weavers). Customer kept dress but was granted an allowance of $60.	$ 60.00

REFUND DUE $ 60.00

Sales Returns and Allowances and Sales Discounts are contra revenue accounts. For financial statement purposes, the sum of these two accounts is subtracted from the balance of the Sales account to arrive at Net Sales, which is typically the first line item on a merchandising or manufacturing company's income statement.

NOTES RECEIVABLE When a customer cannot pay an account receivable by the due date, the company to whom the receivable is owed may ask the customer to sign a "promissory note." A promissory note is a legal document that formally recognizes a debt owed by one party to another. When such a note is signed, a customer's receivable balance is transferred from Accounts Receivable to Notes Receivable. Besides more formally documenting a customer's receivable, a promissory note typically requires the customer to begin paying interest on his or her unpaid receivable balance.

Except for banks and other financial institutions, few companies have notes receivable reported on their balance sheets. On the other hand, notes *payable,* which are liabilities, appear on the balance sheets of most companies. In Chapter 9, you will become familiar with notes payable and their accounting treatment. Much of what you will learn regarding notes payable applies as well to notes receivable.

DIRECT WRITE-OFF METHOD VS. THE MATCHING PRINCIPLE Companies that extend credit must establish some means for assessing the ability and intent of prospective customers to pay their debts. This task is the primary responsibility of a company's credit department. Despite the activities of a credit department, most companies do not collect all of their credit sales. A receivable should be "written off" by a business when it becomes apparent that the receivable will not be collected. Companies that use the **direct write-off method** debit Uncollectible Accounts Expense and credit Accounts Receivable when they determine that a receivable is unlikely to be collected. For example, assume that in November 1997 a small retail company sold $300 of merchandise on credit to a customer. In September 1998, after vigorous collection efforts had failed, the company decided to write off the $300 receivable. If this company uses the direct write-off method, the following entry would have been appropriate to write off the uncollectible receivable.

direct write-off method

Sep. 17	Uncollectible Accounts Expense	300	
	Accounts Receivable		300
	To write off receivable from D. R. Donaho		

Notice that the above entry was made in September 1998, while the credit sale resulting in the receivable was recorded in November 1997. Expressed another way, the revenue from the sale was recorded in 1997, while the related uncollectible accounts expense was recorded the following year. Something is amiss here. Recall the matching principle discussed in Chapter 2? The matching principle dictates that a company should attempt to "match" expenses with the corresponding revenues produced by those expenses. Companies expect to incur bad debts when they make sales on a credit basis. Consequently, companies should estimate the uncollectible accounts expense they will eventually realize from credit sales made during an accounting period and record that estimate as an expense *in that same period.*

Because the direct write-off method violates the matching principle, it is not considered a generally accepted accounting principle and thus should not be used for financial reporting purposes. Nevertheless, the direct write-off method must be used for federal taxation purposes by most businesses. You should recognize that federal taxation rules are intended to raise revenue for the federal government, not to provide for the most defensible method of accounting for business transactions.

LEARNING OBJECTIVE 5
Use the aging method to estimate uncollectible accounts expense.

ALLOWANCE METHOD OF ACCOUNTING FOR UNCOLLECTIBLE ACCOUNTS EXPENSE Because of the matching principle, most companies use the allowance method to estimate uncollectible accounts expense each accounting period. Under the **allowance method,** a business records uncollectible accounts expense at the end of each accounting period via an adjusting entry. This adjusting entry includes a debit to Uncollectible Accounts Expense and an equal credit to the contra asset account **Allowance for Doubtful Accounts.** For balance sheet purposes, the Allowance for Doubtful Accounts is subtracted from Accounts Receivable to reduce that asset to its approximate net realizable value.[3] The key to understanding the allowance method is to recognize that when uncollectible accounts expense is recorded at the end of an accounting period, *no specific customer receivables have been identified as uncollectible.* Like many expenses, uncollectible accounts expense must be estimated and booked in advance of the circumstances or events that confirm the existence of the expense.

allowance method

Allowance for Doubtful Accounts

Exhibit 6.5 presents five companies' allowance for doubtful accounts expressed as a percentage of their total accounts receivable. As you might expect, a company such as Caesar's World, which operates several large casinos, has a particularly difficult time collecting its receivables. Even compared to other companies in the casino industry, Caesar's has a poor track record of collecting its receivables. In a recent annual report, the company disclosed that approximately 61 percent of its receivables were from citizens of foreign countries. Apparently, once these individuals return to their home countries, they are not prone to render unto Caesar's what is Caesar's. Conversely, the rigorous credit policies of the fiscally conservative J.C. Penney Company result in a relatively low bad debt percentage for that firm.

When it comes to estimating uncollectible accounts, one of two approaches to applying the allowance method is commonly used. The net sales (allowance) method is an easy-to-use technique of estimating uncollectible accounts. Many businesses use this method each month until the final month of the year. At year-end, when it is necessary to prepare annual financial statements, the aging (allowance) method is commonly applied. The aging method is used to prepare a year-end adjusting entry that both establishes the proper balance of the Allowance for Doubtful Accounts and adjusts the uncollectible accounts expense for the year to a more appropriate figure. Here, only the aging method is illustrated.

Businesses realize that the likelihood of collecting accounts receivable is inversely related to the age of those receivables. The aging method of estimating uncollectible accounts expense is based upon this realization. Under the **aging method,** a business sorts its accounts receivable into several age categories. (In this context, "age" refers to the amount of time that has passed since a receivable was recorded.) Then, based upon historical experience and possibly other relevant factors, the dollar amount of the receivables in each age group that will not be collected is estimated.

aging method

Exhibit 6.6 presents an accounts receivable aging schedule for Woodruff Wholesale, Inc. In an aging schedule, a company typically classifies its receivables as either current or as past due by a given number of days. The number and width of past-due aging categories varies from firm to firm, but those shown in Exhibit 6.6 are fairly common.

---

3. Most accounting textbooks use the title "Allowance for Uncollectible Accounts" for this account. However, *Accounting Trends & Techniques* reports that "Allowance for Doubtful Accounts" is a more common title. Consequently, this latter title is used in this textbook.

EXHIBIT 6.5 ▼
Allowance for Doubtful Accounts as a Percentage of Accounts Receivable, Selected Companies

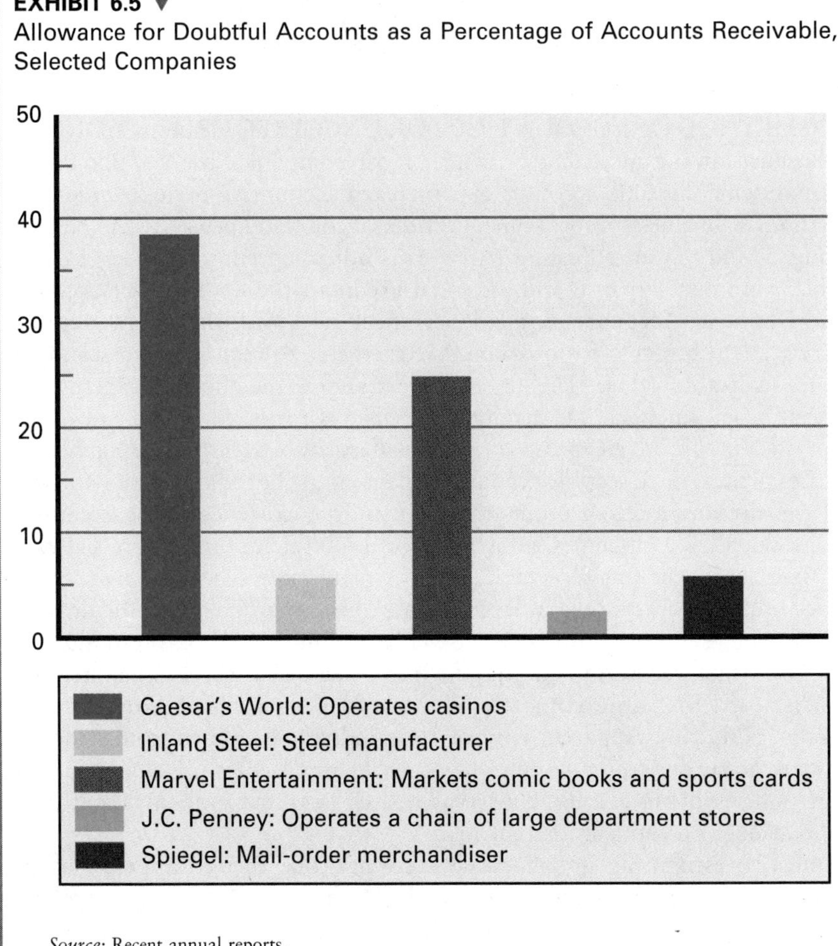

Source: Recent annual reports.

Notice at the bottom of Woodruff's aging schedule that historical bad debt percentages for each aging category are listed. To estimate this business's uncollectible accounts as of December 31, 1998, these percentages are multiplied by the total amount of receivables within each aging category. These computations are shown next.

Current receivables	$11,200 × .005 =	$ 56
Past-due receivables:		
1–30 days	2,120 × .025 =	53
31–60 days	1,560 × .075 =	117
61–90 days	720 × .200 =	144
91+ days	530 × .500 =	265
Total		$635

This analysis suggests that Woodruff's Allowance for Doubtful Accounts should have a balance of $635 on December 31, 1998. So, the appropriate adjusting entry on that date would be to debit Uncollectible Accounts Expense $635 and credit Allowance for Doubtful Accounts $635. Right? *Wrong.* An aging analysis reveals the proper year-end

EXHIBIT 6.6 ▼
Example of an Accounts Receivable Aging Schedule

WOODRUFF WHOLESALE, INC.
AGING SCHEDULE FOR ACCOUNTS RECEIVABLE
DECEMBER 31, 1998

			Days Past Due			
Customer	**Balance**	**Current**	**1–30**	**31–60**	**61–90**	**91+**
Madge Hale	$ 850	$ 220		$ 400		$230
Bud Kay	605	605				
Bess Penn	670	500			$170	
Dan Quinn	320		$ 320			
Gary Young	440	440				
Others	13,245	9,435	1,800	1,160	550	300
Totals	$16,130	$11,200	$2,120	$1,560	$720	$530
Historical bad debt percentages		.5	2.5	7.5	20.0	50.0

balance of the allowance account, *not* the required dollar amount of the year-end adjusting entry for uncollectible accounts expense.

Under the aging method, to determine the proper amount of the year-end adjusting entry to the Allowance for Doubtful Accounts, one must first refer to the preadjustment balance of that account. Following is the allowance account for Woodruff Wholesale on December 31, 1998, before the journalizing and posting of year-end adjusting entries.

Allowance for Doubtful Accounts						**Account No. 131**	
						Balance	
Date		**Explanation**	**Post Ref.**	**Debit**	**Credit**	**Debit**	**Credit**
1998 Dec.	31	Balance forward					140

Woodruff's allowance account has a credit balance of $140 prior to year-end adjusting entries. So, an adjusting (credit) entry to that account of $495 is necessary to establish the account's proper year-end balance of $635 that was determined by the aging analysis ($635 − $140 = $495). The offsetting debit in this adjusting entry is made to Uncollectible Accounts Expense. This adjusting entry is shown next followed by the allowance account after the posting of this entry.

Dec. 31	Uncollectible Accounts Expense	495	
	Allowance for Doubtful Accounts		495
	To record year-end adjusting entry for uncollectible accounts expense		

Allowance for Doubtful Accounts							Account No. 131
			Post			Balance	
Date		Explanation	Ref.	Debit	Credit	Debit	Credit
1998							
Dec.	31	Balance forward					140
	31	Adjusting	GJ5		495		635

WRITE-OFFS AND RECOVERIES OF DOUBTFUL ACCOUNTS Recall that under the direct write-off method, individual accounts receivable are written off when it is determined that they are unlikely to be collected. Write-off entries are also required under the allowance method. Under either variation of the allowance method, period-ending adjustments to record uncollectible accounts expense are based upon estimates. Again, when these estimates are made, no specific receivables have been identified as uncollectible. Later, when specific receivables are identified as uncollectible, they should be removed from a company's accounting records.

Suppose that a customer of Woodruff Wholesale filed for personal bankruptcy shortly after the close of the company's fiscal year on December 31, 1998. This customer, Dan Quinn, owed Woodruff $320, an amount the company did not expect to collect, given Quinn's financial problems. Under such circumstances, the following entry would have been appropriate to write off the receivable from Dan Quinn.

Jan. 20	Allowance for Doubtful Accounts	320	
	Accounts Receivable		320
	To write off receivable from D. Quinn		

Notice that the above entry does not include a debit to Uncollectible Accounts Expense. Why? Because the December 31, 1998, adjusting entry for uncollectible accounts expense took into consideration the likelihood that certain of the company's year-end receivables would not be collected. That adjusting entry properly allocated the bad debt expense associated with such receivables to Woodruff's 1998 fiscal year. When specific receivables existing at the end of 1998 later prove to be uncollectible, they must be charged off (debited) to the allowance account.

Now, assume that on March 21, 1999, Woodruff Wholesale unexpectedly received a check for $320 from Dan Quinn. Two entries would have been required in the firm's accounting records to record the receipt of this check. First, the receivable from Dan Quinn would have been reinstated in the accounting records. Second, the collection of this reinstated receivable would have been recorded.

Mar. 21	Accounts Receivable	320	
	Allowance for Doubtful Accounts		320
	To reinstate the receivable from D. Quinn written off on Jan. 20		
Mar. 21	Cash	320	
	Accounts Receivable		320
	To record payment by D. Quinn of reinstated receivable		

THE SPECIAL CASE OF CREDIT CARD RECEIVABLES Credit cards, such as VISA, MasterCard, and American Express, have become important fixtures in the national economy in recent decades. In 1996, more than $250 billion was charged by consumers on VISA credit cards, alone. Retailers realize several important benefits by having their customers make purchases with a credit card. One of these benefits is that credit card companies absorb bad debt losses resulting from credit card sales. In 1996, approximately 2 percent of the charges rung up on VISA credit cards were not collected. Credit card companies also relieve retail businesses of the need to do "credit checks" on prospective customers. Finally, credit card companies generally pay amounts owed to retailers on a more timely basis than do individual customers.

As you would expect, credit card companies charge for the services they provide. These companies typically deduct a 3 to 5 percent fee from the gross receipts they collect for retailers. So, for every $1,000 of credit card sales, a retailer may receive only $950 in payments from credit card companies.

To illustrate accounting for credit card receivables, suppose that Bonney's Dress Shop had $450 of credit card sales on May 5 of a given year, sales charged by Bonney's customers to their PlasticCard credit cards. The following entry would be made to book these sales, assuming the imaginary PlasticCard charges Bonney's a 4 percent fee for its services.

May 5	Accounts Receivable—PlasticCard	432	
	Credit Card Fees Expense	18	
	Sales		450
	To record credit card sales		

When Bonney's collects the receivable from PlasticCard, an accountant would debit Cash for $432 and credit Accounts Receivable—PlasticCard for the same amount.

Many companies that use the services of VISA or MasterCard have special bank accounts in which they deposit sales charged to these credit cards. Retailers typically deposit credit card receipts (sales slips) on a daily basis into these bank accounts. The

Accounting for Receivables on the Other Side of the World

FOR YOUR INFORMATION

Accounting practices in the Communist-ruled People's Republic of China differ significantly from accounting practices applied in capitalistic economies. In recent years, the Chinese government has begun making an effort to bring its country's accounting rules and procedures more in line with those used in other major countries. In 1985, the Chinese government issued *Accounting Law of the People's Republic of China,* the first nationwide law to dictate basic accounting policies and procedures. Since then, several additional laws and regulations affecting Chinese accounting practices have been issued.

Accounting laws and regulations issued by the Chinese government generally prohibit Chinese firms from using the allowance method to account for uncollectible accounts expense. Instead, the direct write-off method must be applied in most cases. However, a government regulation issued in 1992 allows a modified version of the allowance method to be used in certain limited situations.

amount of such a deposit, less the service fee, is treated as a cash deposit by the bank. As a result, the journal entry on a retailer's books to record daily VISA or MasterCard credit card sales may involve a debit to Cash instead of Accounts Receivable.

Key Control Activities for Accounts Receivable

LEARNING OBJECTIVE 3 ▶
Discuss key control activities for cash and accounts receivable.

special journal

subsidiary ledger

Many businesses integrate special journals and subsidiary ledgers into their accounting systems. A **special journal** is an accounting record in which a business journalizes a single type of transaction; a **subsidiary ledger** is an accounting record that contains the detailed support for an account balance in the general ledger. These accounting records enhance the degree of control over key financial statement items and provide for more efficient and uniform processing of financial data.

This section acquaints you with one example of a special journal, a sales journal, and one example of a subsidiary ledger, an accounts receivable ledger. These accounting records are specifically designed to help businesses establish and maintain effective control over accounts receivable and the transactions that are the source of accounts receivable, namely, credit sales transactions.

sales journal

SALES JOURNAL Many merchandising companies record all credit sales of merchandise in a **sales journal.** Exhibit 6.7 contains a one-day "window" of the sales journal of Bonney's Dress Shop. On May 1, 1998, three credit sales of merchandise were recorded in Bonney's sales journal. Since credit sales of merchandise require an equivalent debit and credit to Accounts Receivable and Sales, respectively, only one column for dollar amounts is necessary in a sales journal.

Periodically, the financial data recorded in special journals must be posted to the general ledger and, if necessary, to the appropriate subsidiary ledger. Assume that Bonney's Dress Shop posts journal data on a daily basis. The two three-digit numbers shown in parentheses at the bottom of the final column of Exhibit 6.7 indicate that the total credit sales for May 1, $1,082, have been posted to Accounts Receivable, account number 102 in Bonney's chart of accounts, and to Sales, account number 401. The check marks in the post reference column in Exhibit 6.7 indicate that the individual sales transactions have been posted to the accounts receivable ledger.

EXHIBIT 6.7 ▼
Entries in Sales Journal of Bonney's Dress Shop on May 1, 1998

SALES JOURNAL					Page 18
Date		Customer	Post Ref.	Invoice No.	Accounts Receivable Dr. Sales Cr.
1998					
May	1	Becky Orebel	✓	171	255
	1	Paula Hardy	✓	172	522
	1	Suzan Elliot	✓	173	305
					1,082
					(102) (401)

An **accounts receivable ledger** is a subsidiary ledger that maintains records (accounts) of the amounts owed to a company by its customers. Exhibit 6.8 contains the pages from Bonney's accounts receivable ledger for the three customers to whom credit sales were made on May 1, 1998. The credit sales made to these customers resulted in debits being posted to their accounts on May 1. The "S18" entry in the post reference column of each account indicates that these transactions were posted from page 18 of the sales journal. Notice that two of the three accounts had transactions posted to them earlier in 1998.

accounts receivable ledger

Keep in mind that Bonney's Dress Shop maintains both an accounts receivable ledger and a general ledger "controlling" account, Accounts Receivable. For control purposes, Bonney's accountant periodically reconciles the total of the customer account balances

EXHIBIT 6.8

Selected Customer Accounts Included in the Accounts Receivable Ledger of Bonney's Dress Shop

Name: Suzan Elliot
Address: 612 Persimmon Way, Alex Springs, OK 73151
Customer Account No.: 62 **Page 15**

Date		Explanation	Post Ref.	Debit	Credit	Balance
1998						
Feb.	2		S3	230		230
	26		CR11		230	0
May	1		S18	305		305

Name: Paula Hardy
Address: 515 Prairie Dog Drive, Penn Valley, OK 73048
Customer Account No.: 129 **Page 34**

Date		Explanation	Post Ref.	Debit	Credit	Balance
1998						
May	1		S18	522		522

Name: Becky Orebel
Address: 808 Cottonwood Lane, OK 73060
Customer Account No.: 155 **Page 39**

Date		Explanation	Post Ref.	Debit	Credit	Balance
1998						
Jan.	1	Balance Forward				600
	4		CR2		400	200
Feb.	3		CR9		200	0
Apr.	17		S15	120		120
May	1		S18	255		375

included in the accounts receivable ledger to the balance of the general ledger controlling account. Any difference between these two amounts is then investigated and eliminated. An accounts receivable ledger also provides the information needed to prepare periodic statements detailing the balances of individual customer accounts. To encourage prompt payment of outstanding receivables, companies typically mail a monthly statement to each of their customers.

In summary, maintaining a sales journal and accounts receivable ledger enhances an organization's control over credit sales and accounts receivable. A sales journal provides for uniform and efficient processing of credit sales transactions and collects the data needed to maintain an accounts receivable ledger. An accounts receivable ledger allows a business to periodically check the accuracy of the general ledger balance of Accounts Receivable and yields the data needed to prepare monthly statements to be mailed to customers.

Analyzing Accounts Receivable

LEARNING OBJECTIVE 4 ▶
Compute and interpret key financial ratios for cash and accounts receivable.

Ask a financial analyst what he or she first considers when evaluating a company's accounts receivable and that individual will likely reply "the 'quality' of those receivables." The quality of a company's receivables is largely a function of their collectibility. In turn, the collectibility of receivables is principally a function of their age. Determining the age of a company's receivables is a two-step process. First, the accounts receivable turnover ratio is computed.

accounts receivable turnover ratio

Accounts Receivable Turnover Ratio = Net Credit Sales/Average Accounts Receivable

Then, the accounts receivable turnover ratio is divided into 360 days, the number of days in a business year. (To simplify the computation of financial ratios and other financial measures, financial analysts typically define a "business year" as consisting of 360 days.)

age of receivables

Age of Receivables = 360 days/Accounts Receivable Turnover Ratio

To illustrate the computation of the age of receivables, consider the following data for Jensen Supply Co.

Accounts receivable, January 1, 1998	$ 82,000
Accounts receivable, December 31, 1998	74,500
Net credit sales, 1998	500,800

Listed next are the calculations to compute Jensen's age of receivables at the end of 1998.

Average Accounts Receivable = ($82,000 + $74,500)/2
= $78,250

Accounts Receivable Turnover Ratio = $500,800/$78,250
= 6.4

Age of Receivables = 360 days/6.4
= 56.25 days

Betty the Cashier: A Case of Misplaced Trust

For more than four decades, Lore and Julius Levi owned and operated Howard Street Jewelers. The business was very profitable until the late 1970s and early 1980s, when its financial condition began to deteriorate slowly. Mrs. Levi spent countless hours going over the store's accounting records trying to determine the cause of the downward trend in profits and net cash flow. Eventually, she developed a theory regarding the financial problems of Howard Street Jewelers. This theory focused on Betty the cashier, who had been a trusted and reliable employee for nearly twenty years.

Mrs. Levi concluded that Betty was stealing cash from the business. Besides occasionally working as a salesclerk, Betty handled all of the cash that came into the business and maintained the cash receipts, sales, and accounts receivable accounting records. Reluctantly, Mrs. Levi approached her husband about her theory. Mrs. Levi pointed out to Julius that Betty had unrestricted access to the cash receipts and accounting records of the business. Additionally, Lore noted that over the past few years Betty had developed a taste for more expensive clothes and had begun taking more frequent and costly vacations. Julius paid little attention to his wife's speculation regarding Betty. To him, it was preposterous to even consider the possibility that Betty might be stealing from the business.

Unfortunately, Julius's trust in Betty was misplaced. A few years later, the Levis stumbled across an embezzlement scheme that Betty had used for years to steal cash from the business. Included in this scheme was the theft of payments made by customers on their outstanding receivable balances, thefts that Betty easily concealed since she maintained the accounts receivable accounting records. Over the period she was employed by the Levis, Betty's thefts accumulated to an estimated $350,000.

Source: M. C. Knapp, "Howard Street Jewelers," *Contemporary Auditing: Issues and Cases,* Second Edition (Minneapolis/St. Paul: West Publishing Company, 1996).

The accounts receivable turnover ratio measures the number of times that a company collects or "turns over" its receivables each year. Companies want to convert their receivables into cash as quickly as possible. Consequently, the higher the accounts receivable turnover ratio, the better. The age of receivables indicates the average number of days that a company's receivables have been outstanding. Viewed another way, age of receivables indicates the average period required for a company to collect a receivable resulting from a credit sale.

Exhibit 6.9 reports the age of receivables for five companies. Many financial ratios, including age of receivables, vary significantly from company to company and industry to industry. Notice in Exhibit 6.9 that Starbucks' age of receivables is only six days, while Pfizer's receivables are more than ten times "older." Does this mean that Pfizer's receivables are of much lower quality than those of Starbucks? Not necessarily. Among other factors, differing credit terms offered by the two companies and varying economic conditions affecting each firm's industry may account for the large disparity in their age of receivables.

EXHIBIT 6.9 ▼
Age of Receivables, Selected Companies

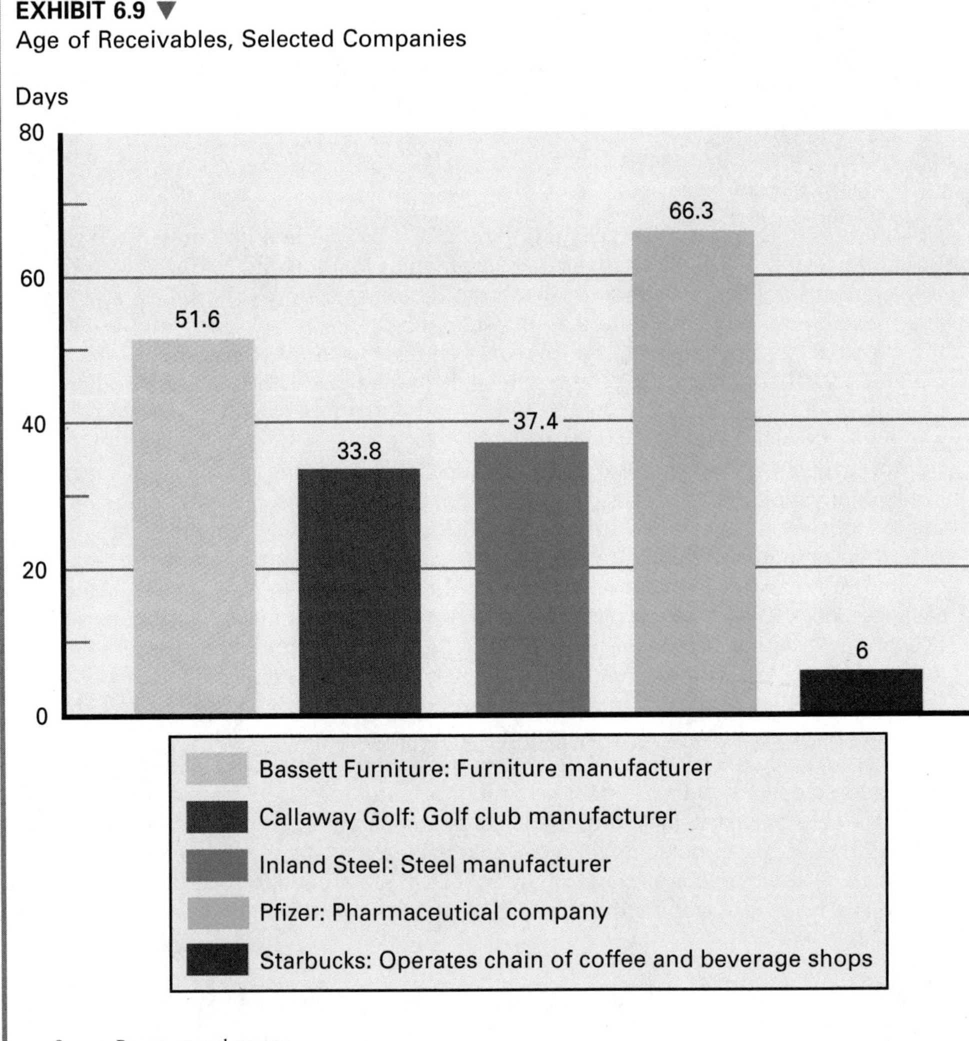

Source: Recent annual reports.

An important consideration in interpreting a specific financial measure for a company is the industry norm for that item. Regarding the age of receivables, the norm (median) for Starbucks' industry recently was nine days, while the corresponding norm for Pfizer's industry was 49 days. These industry data suggest that Starbucks collects its receivables more rapidly than the typical company in its industry, which should reduce Starbucks' bad debt losses relative to its competitors. Pfizer's receivables, on the other hand, are "elderly" compared to the industry norm, which suggests that the company faces a higher risk of bad debt losses than most firms in its industry.

▲ SUMMARY

Decision makers need and demand information regarding the major assets, liabilities, and other financial statement items of individual businesses. These information needs include any restrictions on the use of an entity's cash resources and information revealing a business's primary sources and uses of cash each accounting period. Collectibility is the key information need of decision makers regarding a business's accounts receivable. Decision makers realize that to provide a reliable source of cash for a business, accounts receivable must be collectible on a timely basis.

Cash typically does not pose complex accounting issues. For accounts receivable, the key accounting issue is arriving at a reliable estimate of uncollectible accounts expense. Businesses are generally required to use the allowance method to estimate uncollectible accounts expense for financial reporting purposes. A common approach to applying the allowance method is to prepare an aging schedule of accounts receivable at the end of an accounting period. Then, historical bad debt percentages for the various age groups of receivables are used to arrive at a collective estimate of uncollectible accounts.

The susceptibility of cash to being stolen or otherwise misused makes control issues for this asset an important concern for most organizations. Control activities must be established to provide for the physical security of cash funds and to ensure that cash transactions are processed correctly. Cash balances in accounting records should also be reconciled periodically to physical counts of those cash funds or to bank statement balances. To enhance control over accounts receivable and credit sales transactions, which are the source of accounts receivable, many businesses maintain an accounts receivable ledger and a sales journal.

Decision makers use financial ratios to assess the financial health of individual businesses. Liquidity is one aspect of a business's financial health that decision makers closely monitor. Liquidity refers to an entity's ability to finance its day-to-day operations and to pay its liabilities as they mature. A common measure of liquidity is the quick ratio. This ratio is computed by dividing total quick assets—cash and cash equivalents, short-term investments, and net current receivables—by total current liabilities. A financial ratio used to monitor the collectibility of accounts receivable is the age of receivables. As the average age of a company's accounts receivable increases, the percentage of those receivables that must be written off as uncollectible generally increases as well.

APPENDIX: PREPARING A BANK RECONCILIATION

LEARNING OBJECTIVE 6
(Appendix) Prepare a bank reconciliation.

Most cash resources of a business are maintained on deposit with banks and other financial institutions. Banks provide businesses with monthly statements that document the beginning-of-the-month and end-of-the-month balances of their bank accounts and the transactions affecting those accounts during the month. However, companies should not rely exclusively on the honesty and competence of their bank's personnel. Preparing a monthly **bank reconciliation** is a critical control activity for cash that a business has entrusted with a bank or other financial institution. A bank reconciliation is an accounting document that reconciles the cash balance reported in a bank statement to the corresponding cash balance reflected in a company's accounting records.

bank reconciliation

Exhibit 6.10 presents a bank statement for Hunt Brothers, Inc., for the month ended February 28, 1998. Although the formats of bank statements vary, the key elements or components of bank statements do not. The account summary in the Hunt Brothers bank statement lists the beginning and ending balances of the company's bank account for February 1998 and the total additions and deductions to the account during that month. Also included in this bank statement is a daily listing of the checks and other deductions made to the company's bank account, a similar listing for deposits and other additions to the account, and the daily account balances. Notice that a legend at the bottom of the bank statement provides brief descriptions for unusual or infrequent items appearing in the bank statement.

Sources of Differences Between Bank Statement and General Ledger Cash Balances

The cash balance reported on a company's bank statement nearly always differs from the corresponding cash balance in the company's general ledger. One source of such differences is the time required for cash transactions to be processed by the nation's

EXHIBIT 6.10 ▼
Bank Statement for Hunt Brothers, Inc., February 1998

LINCOLN NATIONAL BANK OF WALLVILLE

MEMBER FDIC
Wallville, OK 73000-3333

Hunt Brothers, Inc.
2122 Turner Avenue
Wallville, OK 73052-2122

Statement of Account
Account #441-230
From 2/1/98 To 2/29/98

Account Summary:

Opening Balance	5,254.19
Plus Deposits and Other Credits	13,518.55
Minus Checks and Other Debits	14,403.93
Ending Balance	4,368.81

CHECKS & OTHER DEBITS			DEPOSITS & OTHER CREDITS	DATE	DAILY BALANCE
1,106.77	212.59		2,429.66	02-01	6,364.49
345.78				02-03	6,018.71
55.43				02-06	5,963.28
101.44	352.21	49.03	3,021.18	02-08	8,481.78
22.13				02-09	8,459.65
2,986.42	707.53			02-10	4,765.70
112.09			2,783.91	02-15	7,437.52
984.25	101.78			02-16	6,351.49
565.02				02-17	5,786.47
3,476.82			2,141.17	02-22	4,450.82
202.88				02-23	4,247.94
1,190.31				02-24	3,057.63
789.52NSF	22.34		14.32INT	02-26	2,260.09
1,002.00	17.59SVC		3,128.31CM	02-28	4,368.81

CM—Credit Memo
DM—Debit Memo
INT—Interest Credited
NSF—Not Sufficient Funds
OD—Overdraft
SVC—Service Charge

banking system. Checks may take from a few days to more than one week to be processed. During the time that a check is "floating" through the banking system, it is referred to as an outstanding check. **Outstanding checks** have been deducted from a company's cash balance in its general ledger but were not subtracted from the company's cash balance in its most recent bank statement. Recognize that outstanding checks create only temporary differences between a general ledger cash balance and the corresponding bank statement balance. When outstanding checks clear the bank, these differences are eliminated.

outstanding checks

Deposits in transit also result in temporary differences between a general ledger cash balance and the corresponding bank statement balance. These amounts are deposits made near the end of an accounting period that have been added to an entity's general ledger cash balance but were not included in its most recent bank statement balance. Among other sources of differences between a general ledger cash balance and a bank statement balance are the following:

deposits in transit

- Bank service charges deducted from the bank statement balance but not from the general ledger balance.
- Amounts collected for a company by its bank that have been added to the bank statement balance but that have not yet been added to the general ledger balance. (For example, banks sometimes collect notes receivable for their customers.)
- Errors made in either a company's accounting records or its bank's accounting records.

Standard Format for a Bank Reconciliation

Exhibit 6.11 shows a format commonly used when reconciling a general ledger cash balance to a bank statement balance. Notice that when using this format, the objective is to arrive at the same adjusted balance in each column of the bank reconciliation. If a reconciliation does not result in the same adjusted balance at the bottom of each column, it is "back to the drawing board" to figure out why. As shown in Exhibit 6.11, there are four types of reconciling items in a bank reconciliation. These items include additions and deductions to the bank statement balance to arrive at the adjusted balance and additions and deductions to the general ledger balance to arrive at the adjusted balance. As a point of information, errors in a company's accounting records can appear as either additions or deductions to the general ledger balance in the bank reconciliation format shown in Exhibit 6.11. Similarly, errors in the accounting records of a company's bank can appear as either additions or deductions to the bank statement balance in a bank reconciliation.

Steps in Preparing a Bank Reconciliation

Listed next are the steps that are normally followed in preparing a monthly bank reconciliation. For control purposes, a bank reconciliation should be prepared by an individual who does not have access to cash or blank checks. Additionally, this individual should not maintain cash accounting records or have authorization responsibilities for cash transactions.

1. Compare deposits listed in the bank statement with the deposits included in the accounting records for the given month. Add any deposits in transit to the bank statement balance. Also review the deposits in transit included in the previous month's bank reconciliation to determine that those deposits appear in the most

EXHIBIT 6.11 ▼
Standard Bank Reconciliation Format

Balance per bank statement		$XX	Balance per general ledger		$XX
Add:	Deposits in transit and other items included in the general ledger balance but not yet included in the bank statement balance	XX	Add:	Amounts included in the bank statement balance, such as notes receivable collections, that have not yet been added to to the general ledger balance	XX
Less:	Outstanding checks and other reductions in the general ledger balance that have not yet been deducted from the bank statement balance	XX	Less:	Items deducted from the bank statement balance, such as service charges, that have not yet been deducted from the general ledger balance	XX
Adjusted balance		$XX	Adjusted balance		$XX

recent bank statement. If they do not, these are additional deposits in transit. The bank should be contacted immediately to determine why these deposits have not been processed.

2. List returned checks included in the bank statement in numerical order. Compare this listing with the checks recorded in the accounting records for the given month and with the list of outstanding checks included in the previous month's bank reconciliation. Identify outstanding checks and deduct them from the bank statement balance.
3. Review the bank statement and identify any additions to the bank statement balance that have not yet been added to the general ledger balance, such as the proceeds of a note receivable collected by the bank. Add these amounts to the general ledger balance.
4. Review the bank statement and identify any deductions to the bank statement balance, such as bank service charges, that have not yet been subtracted from the general ledger balance. Subtract these amounts from the general ledger balance.
5. While preparing the bank reconciliation, review the accounting records and the bank statement for any errors affecting either the general ledger balance or the bank statement balance. Make the appropriate additions to, or deductions from, the general ledger balance or the bank statement balance in the bank reconciliation.
6. Prepare any necessary journal entries for items included in the bank statement balance that have not yet been added to, or subtracted from, the general ledger balance.

Illustration of a Bank Reconciliation

To illustrate the preparation of a bank reconciliation, return to the bank account maintained by Hunt Brothers, Inc., at the Lincoln National Bank of Wallville, Oklahoma. (In the interest of full disclosure, there is no Lincoln National Bank in the great metropolis of Wallville, Oklahoma, which had a population of 52 at last count.) The bank statement for the Hunt Brothers account for the month ended February 28, 1998, reports a cash balance of $4,368.81, as shown in Exhibit 6.10. However, the general ledger cash balance was $1,213.14 on February 28, 1998. So, the objective here is to reconcile those two amounts. Assume that the following information was collected by a Hunt Brothers employee as that individual completed the first five steps of the six-step process for preparing a bank reconciliation.

Outstanding checks as of February 28:		
No. 667	$423.12	
No. 689	891.02	
No. 690	112.29	$1,426.43
Deposit made February 28 but not reflected in bank statement		606.28
Interest revenue earned in February but not recorded in accounting records as of February 28		14.32
Note collected by bank on February 28 but not recorded in accounting records as of that date		3,128.31
NSF (not-sufficient-funds) check charged against bank balance on February 26 but not recorded in accounting records as of February 28		789.52
Service charge for February, charged against bank balance on February 28 but not recorded in accounting records as of that date		17.59

Exhibit 6.12 contains the completed bank reconciliation for the Hunt Brothers bank account. Notice that the reconciliation was successful. After making the necessary adjustments to the bank statement balance and the general ledger balance, the two columns of the bank reconciliation "footed" to the same adjusted balance. One item included in the bank reconciliation may need some clarification. The NSF check is a "rubber" check that Hunt Brothers received from one its customers. This check was deposited by Hunt Brothers and added to the company's account balance at Lincoln National Bank. However, a few days later, the amount of this check was subtracted from that account. Why? Because Lincoln National Bank was informed by the bank of Hunt Brothers' customer that the individual did not have $789.52 in his or her account at that bank. So, the customer's bank refused to transfer that amount to Lincoln National Bank. Realize that Hunt Brothers had previously recorded this check by debiting Cash and crediting Accounts Receivable. The company was not aware that the check had "bounced" until it received the February 1998 bank statement. As a result, on February 28, 1998, the $789.52 was included in the general ledger cash balance.

Once a bank reconciliation has been completed, several journal entries are typically necessary to adjust the general ledger cash balance. For the bank reconciliation shown in Exhibit 6.12, the four entries listed next were needed. Entries were not required for the two reconciling items involving outstanding checks and the deposit in transit. When these items were processed by the bank the following month, the appropriate additions or deductions were made to the Hunt Brothers bank account. The reconciling items for which journal entries were necessary included only those items needed to

EXHIBIT 6.12 ▼
Bank Reconciliation for Hunt Brothers, Inc.

HUNT BROTHERS, INC.
BANK RECONCILIATION
FEBRUARY 28, 1998

Balance per bank, 2/28		$4,368.81	Balance per general ledger, 2/28		$1,213.14
Add:	Deposit in transit, 2/28	606.28	Add:	Note receivable collected on 2/28	3,128.31
				Interest revenue for February	14.32
Less:	Outstanding checks		Less:	NSF check	(789.52)
				Service charge for February	(17.59)
	No. 667 $423.12				
	No. 689 891.02				
	No. 690 112.29	(1,426.43)			
Adjusted balance, 2/28		$3,548.66	Adjusted balance, 2/28		$3,548.66

reconcile the general ledger balance to the adjusted balance. These were items that had not been entered in the accounting records at the point the bank reconciliation was prepared. Notice that an NSF check from a customer is recorded by debiting Accounts Receivable and crediting Cash. This entry is necessary to reestablish the customer's receivable balance on a company's books—obviously, an NSF check does not satisfy a customer's debt to a company. The debit amount of this entry will be posted to the general ledger controlling account, Accounts Receivable, and to the customer's account in the accounts receivable ledger.

Feb. 28	Cash	3,128.31	
	Notes Receivable		3,128.31
	To record collection by Lincoln National of note receivable from Ed Jones		
Feb. 28	Cash	14.32	
	Interest Revenue		14.32
	To record interest earned in February on bank account at Lincoln National		
Feb. 28	Accounts Receivable	789.52	
	Cash		789.52
	To record NSF check (from Lyn Wiggins) deducted from bank account at Lincoln National on 2/26		

Feb. 28	Miscellaneous Expense	17.59	
	Cash		17.59
	To record service charge for February on bank account at Lincoln National		

GLOSSARY

Accounts receivable (p. 242) Amounts owed to businesses by their customers.

Accounts receivable ledger (p. 255) A subsidiary ledger that maintains records (accounts) of the amounts owed to a company by its customers.

Accounts receivable turnover ratio (p. 256) Net credit sales divided by average accounts receivable; indicates how often a business collects or "turns over" its accounts receivable each year.

Age of receivables (p. 256) 360 days divided by the accounts receivable turnover ratio; a measure of the collectibility of accounts receivable.

Aging method (p. 249) One approach to applying the allowance method of estimating uncollectible accounts expense; under this method, an estimate of uncollectible accounts expense is determined by performing an aging analysis of accounts receivable.

Allowance for Doubtful Accounts (p. 249) A contra asset account subtracted from Accounts Receivable to reduce that asset to its approximate net realizable value.

Allowance method (p. 249) An accounting method used to estimate uncollectible accounts expense each accounting period.

Bank reconciliation (p. 259) An accounting document that reconciles the cash balance reported on a bank statement to the corresponding cash balance reflected in a company's accounting records.

Cash equivalents (p. 234) Investments in short-term securities, such as certificates of deposit (CDs), money market funds, and United States treasury bills, that have 90 days or less to maturity when purchased.

Credit terms (p. 245) The agreement between a buyer and seller regarding the timing of payment by the buyer and any discount available to the buyer for early payment.

Deposits in transit (p. 261) Deposits made near the end of an accounting period that have been added to the general ledger cash balance but that were not included in the most recent bank statement balance.

Direct write-off method (p. 248) An accounting method under which uncollectible accounts expense is recorded when it is determined that a specific account receivable is unlikely to be collected; this non-GAAP alternative to the allowance method is used for taxation purposes.

Liquidity (p. 240) Refers to a firm's ability to finance its day-to-day operations and to pay its liabilities as they mature.

Outstanding checks (p. 261) Checks that have been deducted from a company's cash balance in its general ledger but that were not subtracted from the company's cash balance in its most recent bank statement.

Petty cash fund (p. 238) A small cash fund from which a business pays minor expenses and other miscellaneous amounts.

Quick ratio (p. 240) Quick assets (cash and cash equivalents, short-term investments, and net current receivables) divided by current liabilities; measures a firm's liquidity.

Sales discounts (p. 245) Discounts offered to customers to entice them to pay their account balances on a timely basis.

Sales journal (p. 254) A special journal in which credit sales of merchandise are recorded.

Sales returns and allowances (p. 246) The sum of refunds paid to customers who return damaged or defective merchandise and price reductions granted to customers to persuade them to keep such merchandise.
Special journal (p. 254) An accounting record in which a business journalizes a single type of transaction.
Subsidiary ledger (p. 254) An accounting record that contains the detailed support for an account balance in the general ledger.
Uncollectible accounts expense (p. 244) The expense associated with accounts receivable that cannot be collected; sometimes referred to as bad debt expense.

DECISION CASE

Recently, Warnaco Group, a firm in the clothing industry, appeared to be a company on the move. Sales were increasing at a double-digit pace, and earnings were rising dramatically as well. The company was also expanding its product line to enter new markets. For years, a few high-profile and high-priced product lines generated the bulk of the company's sales. Christian Dior, Hathaway, and Ralph Lauren were a few of the prestigious brand names under which Warnaco's products had been marketed historically. Company executives believed that by selling selected products under less prestigious brand names, they could significantly increase Warnaco's market share in the clothing industry. Management intended to market these products to major discount chains, including Wal-Mart and Kmart.

Despite Warnaco's impressive income statement data and planned expansion strategy, financial analysts painted a less than rosy picture of the company's financial health in major business publications. For example, an article in *The Wall Street Journal* pointed out that although the company had annual sales exceeding $600 million, its cash balance was a measly $35,000. Apparently, the company's poor cash position stemmed principally from a buildup of accounts receivable. Sales were increasing, but receivables were increasing more rapidly. Over a two-year period, alone, the age of Warnaco's receivables had leaped nearly 40 percent, from 51 days to 70 days. Making matters worse for Warnaco's cash position were large interest and principal payments required on the company's $300 million of long-term debt. The company's weak cash position raised doubts regarding whether the firm could finance its new expansion strategy and ultimately caused its stock price to tumble.

Required: Assume that you are a stockholder of a company facing circumstances similar to those just described for Warnaco Group. The value of your investment has declined by 25 percent in recent weeks following the publication of articles in business publications that questioned the firm's future prospects. You will be attending the company's annual stockholders' meeting in a few weeks. You are aware that company officials representing its major departments, including accounting, will be present at the meeting and available to answer questions from stockholders. Additionally, representatives of the company's independent audit firm will be present.

Prepare a list of questions that you would address to officials of this company or representatives of its audit firm. Also, identify additional accounting data that you would request from company officials or obtain on your own to provide further insight on the company's financial health.

QUESTIONS

1. Identify three general types of control activities that businesses can implement to provide effective control over their cash resources.
2. Define "cash equivalents."
3. What is "restricted cash'?
4. Identify the three types of cash flows reported in a statement of cash flows.
5. Why are companies reluctant to provide information about future cash flows?
6. What types of decision makers would be particularly interested in information regarding a given business's future cash flows? Why?
7. Define the term "operating cycle." What determines the length of a company's operating cycle?
8. How does the length of a company's operating cycle affect its cash needs?
9. Define "liquidity."
10. What types of decision makers are most interested in a company's liquidity and why?
11. List the equation used to compute the quick ratio. How is a company's quick ratio used by decision makers?
12. Why would a company choose to sell on credit rather than strictly on a cash-and-carry basis?
13. Why do many companies grant their credit customers discounts for early payment?
14. What accounting concept requires businesses to estimate their uncollectible accounts expense each accounting period?
15. Explain why businesses integrate special journals and subsidiary ledgers into their accounting systems.
16. How are the accounts receivable turnover ratio and the age of receivables helpful in analyzing the collectibility of a company's accounts receivable?
17. Identify two factors that may cause age of receivables to vary significantly across different industries.
18. What is the purpose of a bank reconciliation?
19. Identify the four types of reconciling items included in a bank reconciliation and provide an example of each.
20. Which reconciling items in a bank reconciliation must be journalized?

EXERCISES

21. True or False (LO 1–6)

Following are a series of statements regarding topics discussed in Chapter 6.

Required:

Indicate whether each statement is true (T) or false (F).

_____ a. The Securities and Exchange Commission does not allow public companies to issue forecasted financial data because of the risk that the companies' projections may not be achieved.

_____ b. An important physical security measure for cash is limiting the number of individuals who have access to a business's cash and near-cash assets.

_____ c. Following the completion of the monthly bank reconciliation, deposits in transit must be recorded with a journal entry in the given business's accounting records.

_____ d. Sales Returns and Allowances is a contra revenue account.

_____ e. A statement of cash flows reports a business's cash flows from operating activities, investing activities, and budgeting activities.

_____ f. Collectibility is the key information need of decision makers regarding a business's accounts receivable.

_____ g. The direct write-off method results in an appropriate matching of sales revenues with bad debt expense.
_____ h. Inventory is an example of a quick asset.
_____ i. Cash equivalents are funds that companies have invested in short-term securities that mature six months or less from the date of purchase.
_____ j. For control purposes, the monthly bank reconciliation should be prepared by the person who makes the daily bank deposits for a business.
_____ k. The credit terms for a sales transaction express the agreement between the buyer and seller regarding the timing of payment and any discount available to the buyer for early payment.
_____ l. Despite rigorous and comprehensive physical security and cash-processing controls, there is always some risk that a business's cash will be stolen.

22. Analyzing Liquidity (LO 1, 4)
Refer to the annual report of Outback Steakhouse that is included as an appendix to this text.

Required:
1. Determine Outback's total quick assets at the end of 1995 and 1996. (Note: You will need to refer to Outback's financial statement footnote #2, "Other Current Assets," to identify one of the firm's quick assets.)
2. Compute Outback's quick ratio at the end of 1995 and 1996. Based strictly upon these ratios, did Outback's liquidity improve or worsen in 1996?
3. Besides the previous year's quick ratio, what benchmarks might decision makers use in evaluating a company's quick ratio in any given year?

23. Cash Flow Forecasts (LO 1)
The owner of Jim's Bike Shop has applied for a loan from a local bank to finance a planned expansion of his business. Before she would consider the loan application, the bank loan officer requested financial statements for Jim's Bike Shop for the past three years.

Required:
1. Describe how the loan officer might use recent financial statements of Jim's Bike Shop to predict whether the business will generate sufficient future cash flows to repay a loan if granted.
2. Why don't businesses include a cash-flow forecast in their annual financial reports for the benefit of external decision makers?

24. Cash Over and Short (LO 2, 3)
At the end of the day, the summary cash register tape for Pasquale's Deli indicated total sales of $1,342, but the cash and cash items in the register totaled only $1,325.

Required:
1. Prepare the journal entry to record this business's sales for the day in question.
2. Identify plausible explanations for the difference between the sales reflected by the summary cash register tape and the total cash in the register at day's end.

25. Petty Cash Fund (LO 2)
Stairwell's Home & Auto Insurance Agency periodically needs small amounts of cash on hand to pay minor expenses. As a result, the business's owner set up a $250 petty cash fund at the beginning of January. During January, the following amounts were paid from the fund. The expense account to which each item applies, such as Postage Expense, is indicated parenthetically.

Postage stamps (Postage)	$50.00
Flowers for a hospitalized employee (Miscellaneous)	15.00
Office supplies (Supplies)	80.00
Cost of taking customers to lunch (Selling)	60.00

Required:
Prepare the entry needed on January 31 to replenish Stairwell's cash fund.

26. **Computing the Quick Ratio** (LO 4)
Macromedia, Inc., designs and markets computer software products. Listed next are the year-end current assets and current liabilities of this San Francisco-based firm for two recent years.

	Year 1	Year 2
Accounts payable	$ 6,007	$11,364
Accounts receivable (net)	8,040	14,601
Accrued liabilities	3,492	8,956
Cash and cash equivalents	10,230	28,829
Inventory	1,601	1,568
Other current liabilities	347	331
Prepaid expenses	2,264	8,115
Short-term investments	23,751	87,833
Unearned revenue	2,767	1,235

Required:
1. Compute Macromedia's quick ratio for both Year 1 and Year 2. Did this ratio improve or weaken between the end of Year 1 and the end of Year 2?
2. Briefly discuss factors that may have accounted for the change in Macromedia's liquidity position between the end of Year 1 and the end of Year 2.

27. **Journal Entries for Accounts Receivable** (LO 2)
Following are recent transactions and other events involving Rodman's Rainbow, a company that markets hair-care products.

June 1: Customer purchased $400 of merchandise on credit with terms of n/60.
June 5: Wrote off an uncollectible account receivable of $350.
June 15: Customer purchased $1,200 of merchandise on credit with terms of 2/10, n/30.
June 17: Customer who purchased merchandise on June 1 returned $60 of that merchandise because it was defective.
June 25: Received amount due from customer who purchased merchandise on June 15.
June 29: Received payment in full from customer whose account balance was written off on June 5.
June 30: Received amount due from customer who purchased merchandise on June 1.

Required:
Prepare journal entries to record each of these transactions or events.

28. **Aging Method of Estimating Uncollectible Accounts Expense** (LO 5)
Payne Company has a $250,000 balance in Accounts Receivable at year-end. Payne uses the aging method to determine the proper year-end balance of its Allowance for Doubtful Accounts. Following is a year-end aging schedule for Payne's accounts receivable.

Aging Category	Amount	Percentage Estimated to Be Uncollectible
1–30 days (current)	$175,000	1
31–60 days	50,000	2
61–90 days	20,000	10
More than 90 days	5,000	25

Required:

1. Assume that Payne's Allowance for Doubtful Accounts had a credit balance of $1,500 at year-end before the posting of any adjusting entries. Prepare the appropriate year-end adjusting entry to record uncollectible accounts expense for this company.
2. Now assume that Payne's Allowance for Doubtful Accounts had a debit balance of $200 at year-end before the posting of adjusting entries. Prepare the appropriate year-end adjusting entry to record uncollectible accounts expense under this assumption.

29. **Subsequent Collection of Written-Off Accounts Receivable** (LO 2)

Gascho Enterprises had a $10,000 credit balance in Allowance for Doubtful Accounts at the beginning of the year. On September 10, Gascho wrote off $6,500 of accounts receivable. A customer whose $750 account balance was written off on September 10 unexpectedly paid his balance on December 2.

Required:

1. Prepare a journal entry to record the accounts receivable written off by Gascho.
2. Prepare the journal entries necessary to record the recovery of the previously written off account balance.
3. What was the balance of Allowance for Doubtful Accounts at year-end prior to the preparation and posting of any adjusting entries?
4. Gascho's chief executive officer (CEO) has questioned the company's controller regarding the allowance method of accounting for uncollectible accounts receivable. The CEO believes that it would be more efficient to simply write off individual receivables when it is determined that a customer will not pay. How should the controller respond to the CEO?

30. **Credit Card Sales** (LO 2)

The Magic Shoppe sells games, books, and party favors. Most of this business's customers charge their purchases to credit cards. Following is a summary of The Magic Shoppe's total credit card sales for July and the service fee of each credit card honored by the business.

	PlasticCard	BanCard	BigCard
July credit card sales	$10,500	$22,000	$37,250
Service fee	3%	3%	5%

Required:

1. Record these July credit card sales in The Magic Shoppe's accounting records and the subsequent collections from each credit card company.
2. Given the relatively high service fee charged by BigCard, why may The Magic Shoppe choose to honor that card? More generally, why do retail stores honor credit cards? Doesn't allowing customers to pay for their purchases with credit cards effectively reduce a business's profit?

31. **Analyzing Accounts Receivable** (LO 4)

Consider the following financial information for a recent year for two companies that are very similar in most respects:

	Altizer Corporation	Bechtel Corporation
Cash sales	$ 20,000	$ 40,000
Net credit sales	80,000	60,000
Total sales	$100,000	$100,000
Average accounts receivable during the year	$ 60,000	$ 30,000

Required:
1. Compute each company's accounts receivable turnover ratio and age of receivables.
2. Which of these companies is better managing its accounts receivable? Explain.

32. **Establishing a Credit Policy** (LO 3)
Recently, the owner of Erica's Electronics, Erica Lovell, decided to begin allowing her customers to purchase merchandise on credit. Customers who buy on credit will be given 60 days to pay for their purchases. No discounts will be granted for early payment. Erica believes this new policy will increase her store's sales because her principal competitor in town has a strict cash-and-carry sales policy.

Required:
Write a brief memo to Erica describing some of the problems her business may experience due to the new credit policy. Include in your memo internal control issues that Erica will confront following the implementation of this policy.

33. (*Appendix*) **Bank Reconciliation** (LO 6)
The following information is available for Lasher Company on June 30:

General ledger cash balance	$13,504.03
Deposit in transit	2,676.62
Outstanding checks	3,222.19

The following information was included in Lasher's monthly bank statement as of June 30:

Account balance	$14,012.10
Monthly service charge	55.50
Interest earned	18.00

Required:
1. Prepare a bank reconciliation for Lasher Company as of June 30.
2. Prepare any necessary journal entries in Lasher's accounting records related to this bank reconciliation.
3. Why should a business prepare a monthly bank reconciliation?

34. (*Appendix*) **Bank Reconciliation** (LO 6)
The following bank reconciliation for Dinero Enterprises is incomplete.

Balance per bank statement, October 31	$15,577.66
Add: Deposits in transit	?
Less: Outstanding checks	2,200.05
Adjusted balance, October 31	$?

Balance per general ledger, October 31	$ 9,769.36
Add: One-year note receivable collected for Dinero by bank on October 24	5,400.00
Less: Service charge for October	?
Adjusted balance, October 31	$15,128.11

Required:
1. Complete the bank reconciliation.
2. Prepare any necessary journal entries related to Dinero's bank reconciliation.

PROBLEM SET A

35. **Journal Entries for a Merchandising Company** (LO 2)
Following are selected transactions of Jenkins, Inc., which sells household appliances.

June 1: Cash sales for the day totaled $1,100.
June 4: Sold $2,000 of merchandise to another appliance retailer, JLK Company, with terms of 2/10, n/30.
June 6: Sold $300 of merchandise to Jae Lee, terms n/20.
June 8: Wrote off an uncollectible account receivable of $450.
June 12: JLK Company returned $500 of the merchandise purchased on June 4; the merchandise was defective.
June 14: JLK Company paid Jenkins the amount due for the June 4 transaction.
June 20: Sold $950 of merchandise to Larissa Rodriguez with terms of n/20.
June 26: Received payment from Jae Lee for merchandise sold to him on June 6.
June 28: Received a check for $450 from customer whose account balance had been written off on June 8.

Required:
Prepare general journal entries for these transactions.

36. **Credit Sales Policy and Internal Control** (LO 3)
Katie O'Reilly owns Mowers-n-More, a large store that sells lawn mowers, gardening equipment, and related products. Katie has recently tightened the business's credit policy. A written application and a credit check must be completed before a customer is extended credit. Katie has placed Matt Kilroy, her top salesman, in charge of the new credit department. Matt will continue working in sales since his new responsibilities will require no more than ten hours per week.

Like the other members of the sales staff, Matt is compensated principally on a commission basis. Given Matt's new responsibilities, Katie has restructured his compensation. Matt will receive the normal 15 percent commission on sales he makes plus an additional 3 percent commission on the sales of other members of the sales staff. This additional compensation is intended to make up for the commissions that Matt will lose as a result of the time he commits to his new responsibilities.

As Katie's accountant, you are glad to see that she has finally changed her credit policy. In the past, practically any customer who asked for credit was granted it "on the spot."

Required:
1. Comment on how the new credit policy adopted by Katie O'Reilly will likely affect her business, both positively and negatively.
2. How will the new policy affect the business's internal controls, both positively and negatively?

37. **Uncollectible Accounts Expense** (LO 1, 2, 5)
Following are the December 31 balances of Accounts Receivable and Allowance for Doubtful Accounts of Easton Hammer Corporation (EHC). These balances are prior to the preparation of any year-end adjusting entries.

Accounts Receivable	$3,200,000
Allowance for Doubtful Accounts (credit balance)	112,500

During the year, EHC wrote off several uncollectible accounts. Among these accounts and the dates they were written off were the following:

May 15	Jim Cantore, $1,425
July 6	Mike Bono, $930

Required:
1. On November 1, EHC unexpectedly received payment in full from Jim Cantore of his previously written off account balance. Prepare the journal entries that were made to record the write-offs of the Cantore and Bono accounts and the recovery of Cantore's account balance.
2. Suppose an accountant for EHC performs an aging analysis of the company's accounts receivable at year-end. Based upon this analysis, the accountant estimates that EHC has $363,000 of uncollectible accounts receivable. Prepare the appropriate adjusting journal entry to record uncollectible accounts expense at year-end.
3. Suppose that the accountant in (2) was too conservative in his estimate. Instead of uncollectible accounts receivable of $363,000, the company actually has uncollectible accounts of $278,000. How will the accountant's overstatement of year-end uncollectible accounts receivable affect EHC's income statement and balance sheet for the year in question? How may this overstatement affect the decisions of third parties, such as bankers and investors, who rely on those financial statements?
4. Will the assumed overstatement referred to in (3) affect EHC's financial statements for the following year? If so, explain how.
5. Is it ever permissible to intentionally overstate expenses in a company's financial statements? Defend your answer.
6. What accounting concepts or principles does the overstatement of expenses violate?

38. **Analyzing Liquidity** (LO 1, 4)
Shown next are recent balance sheet data of Campbell Soup Company. The amounts reported are in millions and represent year-end figures for the indicated years.

	Year 1	Year 2
Cash and cash equivalents	$ 94	$ 63
Short-term investments	2	7
Accounts receivable (net)	578	646
Inventories	786	804
Property, plant & equipment (net)	2,401	2,265
Current liabilities	1,665	1,851
Long-term liabilities	1,338	1,343

Required:
1. Explain the significance of the quick ratio. How is that ratio used by decision makers when interpreting a company's financial statements?

2. Compute Campbell's quick ratio for both years. Based strictly on these ratios, in which year was the company's liquidity position stronger?
3. If the average quick ratio in Campbell's industry is 1.2, how does the company's quick ratio compare with the industry norm?
4. Identify factors that could account for Campbell's quick ratio being significantly different from the industry norm.

39. Receivables: An International Perspective (LO 1)
Suppose that you are an investor and that you want to diversify your portfolio by investing in a foreign company. KLM Royal Dutch Airlines is one foreign company that a broker has recommended as a strong "buy." Being a conservative investor, you want to get a second opinion. You are in luck because one of your best friends is a Dutch exchange student who happens to be an accounting major. In flipping through a recent annual report of KLM, you notice that the company has accounts receivable of 2,540 million Dutch guilders.

Required:
1. Identify at least three questions that you would ask your friend regarding the Dutch accounting methods and financial disclosure rules for accounts receivable.
2. Suppose that another foreign company uses the direct write-off method of accounting for uncollectible accounts expense. How would this fact affect your comparison of that company's financial statements with those of a similar U.S. company? Explain.

40. Analyzing Accounts Receivable (LO 4)
QLogic Corporation designs and sells computer peripherals including an array of input/output products. Practically all of QLogic's sales are made on a credit basis. Following are selected financial data, expressed in thousands of dollars, for this California-based firm for a recent three-year period. (Note: QLogic had net sales of $52,257,000 in the year immediately preceding Year 1 and accounts receivable of $6,046,000 at the beginning of Year 1.)

	Year 1	Year 2	Year 3
Net sales	$44,902	$57,675	$53,779
Year-end accounts receivable	6,007	9,358	7,003

Required:
1. Compute QLogic's accounts receivable turnover ratio and age of receivables for Years 1 through 3.
2. Did these ratios improve or weaken over this three-year period? Explain.

41. (*Appendix*) Bank Reconciliation (LO 6)
Following is the daily transaction data included in the January bank statement of Farquay Imports.

Date	Transaction	Amount	Balance
1/1	Balance		$16,750.57
1/2	Deposit	$5,002.20	21,752.77
1/3	Check (#513)	(2,017.50)	19,735.27
	Check (#520)	(1,612.12)	18,123.15
1/6	Check (#521)	(506.73)	17,616.42
1/9	Check (#518)	(102.10)	17,514.32
	Check (#523)	(45.85)	17,468.47
	Deposit	7,310.19	24,778.66

Date	Transaction	Amount	Balance
1/11	Check (#522)	$(6,214.70)	$18,563.96
1/13	Deposit	4,440.13	23,004.09
	Check (#525)	(190.21)	22,813.88
1/16	Check (#524)	(12.00)	22,801.88
	Check (#526)	(63.17)	22,738.71
1/17	Check (#528)	(276.71)	22,462.00
1/18	Check (#519)	(712.93)	21,749.07
	Check Returned NSF	(1,500.00)	20,249.07
1/20	Deposit	2,612.52	22,861.59
	Note Collection	275.00	23,136.59
1/23	Check (#516)	(4,254.08)	18,882.51
	Check (#527)	(3,206.61)	15,675.90
1/25	Check (#517)	(408.04)	15,267.86
	Deposit	3,667.75	18,935.61
1/27	Check (#530)	(881.00)	18,054.61
	Check (#532)	(65.18)	17,989.43
1/31	Check (#533)	(1,129.33)	16,860.10
	Service Charge	(22.50)	16,837.60
	Interest Earned	72.15	16,909.75

Listed next is additional information regarding Farquay's cash transactions during January and its month-end general ledger cash balance.

a. Outstanding checks as of January 31:

#514	$ 754.27
#515	512.12
#529	400.00
#531	2,361.48
#534	1,052.14

b. Check #523 was recorded by Farquay as a credit to Cash for $48.45 rather than $45.85, the correct amount (as cleared by the bank).

c. On January 31, there was a deposit in transit of $7,500.00.

d. The January 31 balance of the general ledger Cash account was $20,502.49.

Note: Farquay does not become aware of any reductions to its bank account balance for such items as service charges or additions to its bank account balance for such items as note receivable collections until it receives its monthly bank statement.

Required:

1. Prepare Farquay's bank reconciliation for January.
2. Prepare any necessary journal entries in Farquay's accounting records as a result of the bank reconciliation.

42. (*Appendix*) **Bank Reconciliation** (LO 3, 6)

American Pillow Company is a firm struggling to develop a market for its principal product, duck feather pillows. The company is also struggling to maintain control over its cash accounting activities. Part of the problem is a new bookkeeper who cannot quite grasp how to prepare a monthly bank reconciliation. For the month of February, the bookkeeper documented the difference between the company's bank statement balance and general ledger cash balance in the following schedule:

Balance per bank statement on 2/28	$17,406.67
Balance per general ledger on 2/28	16,415.28
Difference	$ 991.39

Attached to this schedule is a sheet of paper with the heading "Bank Reconciliation Problems" that contains the following scribbled notes and dollar amounts:

1. Checks that we wrote and the bank seems to have lost:

#488	$ 623.14
#529	476.50
#530	1,100.00

2. I deposited $780.75 at the bank myself at 3:50 p.m. on February 28, but the deposit isn't listed in the bank statement.
3. There is a $27.50 service charge listed in the bank statement this month.
4. What is this $400 "NSF check" item in the bank statement?

Required:

1. Given the information provided, complete American Pillow's bank reconciliation for the month of February.
2. Prepare any journal entries needed as a result of this reconciliation.
3. Briefly describe the internal control objectives related to the preparation of a monthly bank reconciliation.

PROBLEM SET B

43. Journal Entries for a Merchandising Company (LO 2)
Following are selected transactions of Chautauqua, Inc., which sells construction supplies.

December 1:	Sold supplies of $700 to a local homebuilder, Gene Harrison, with terms of 1/10, n/30.
December 3:	Wrote off an uncollectible account receivable of $1,200.
December 8:	Sold merchandise of $1,600 to Kasulis Homes with terms of 2/10, n/30.
December 16:	Sold $1,800 of merchandise to another construction supply company, Alonso Supply, with terms of 2/10, n/30.
December 17:	Cash sales for the day totaled $550.
December 18:	Received payment from Kasulis Homes for December 8 transaction.
December 19:	Alonso Supply returned $200 of merchandise purchased on December 16 because it was defective.
December 26:	Received payment from Alonso Supply for December 16 transaction.
December 28:	Received payment in full from customer whose $1,200 account balance had been written off on December 3.
December 31:	Received payment from Gene Harrison for merchandise he purchased on December 1.

Required:
Prepare general journal entries for these transactions.

44. **Credit Sales Policy and Internal Control** (LO 3)
Mike Tarantino, the owner of Big Mike's Florist Shop, has recently begun allowing his customers to purchase merchandise on credit. Customers are not allowed to charge purchases on a credit card but are granted credit terms of n/30 by the florist shop. This policy has helped Mike increase his sales while at the same time avoiding the service fees charged by credit card companies.

Mike files each credit sales ticket by date sold. Once a week, he mails a bill to each customer who has an outstanding receivable. Once a month, Mike goes through the file of receivables and removes the sales tickets that have been paid. Already, Mike is encountering problems with his new credit policy and his method of keeping track of his receivables. He now has more than two hundred receivables in his file. In the past few weeks, several irate customers have called and complained that although they have paid for their credit purchase, they are still receiving a weekly bill in the mail. Additionally, Mike has several "deadbeat" customers who have not paid for credit purchases made more than two months ago.

Required:
Help Mike out. Write him a memo in which you suggest a few basic internal control activities to improve his credit-granting function and his accounting for unpaid credit sales (accounts receivable).

45. **Uncollectible Accounts Expense** (LO 2, 5)
Before the preparation of year-end adjusting entries, Chewels Company had a $70,500 debit balance in Accounts Receivable and a $4,250 credit balance in Allowance for Doubtful Accounts. Following is a year-end aging analysis of Chewels' accounts receivable.

Age of Receivables	Amount	Percentage Estimated to Be Uncollectible
1–30 days (current)	$40,500	4
31–60 days	20,000	6
61–90 days	10,000	12
Over 90 days	5,000	20

Required:
1. Prepare the year-end adjusting entry to record uncollectible accounts expense for Chewels.
2. Suppose that Chewels wrote off the following two accounts during the year in question: Jeanetta Jones, $1,250 (April 3); Vivian Brown, $3,100 (November 28). Prepare the entries made to write off these accounts. Also prepare the necessary entry, or entries, that were made to record the unexpected payment by Jeanetta Jones on December 7 of her previously written-off account balance.
3. What accounting concept or concepts dictate that Chewels use the allowance method of accounting for uncollectible accounts expense?
4. Why is the direct write-off method not considered a generally accepted accounting principle? Under what circumstances can businesses use the direct write-off method?

46. **Analyzing Liquidity** (LO 4)
Melville Corporation sells merchandise ranging from prescription drugs to toys to household furnishings. Presented next are selected balance sheet data (in thousands) for this company for two recent years.

	Year 1	Year 2
Cash and cash equivalents	$ 145,138	$ 80,971
Accounts receivable (net)	245,204	243,998
Inventories	1,806,550	1,858,772
Prepaid expenses	244,780	214,649
Total current assets	$2,441,672	$2,398,390
Total assets	$4,214,062	$4,272,400
Total current liabilities	$1,380,919	$1,328,097

Required:

1. Compute Melville's quick ratio for both Year 1 and Year 2. Did the company's liquidity improve or weaken between the end of Year 1 and the end of Year 2?
2. A common rule of thumb is that a company should maintain a quick ratio of 1.0. How do Melville's quick ratios in Year 1 and Year 2 compare with this benchmark? Instead of this general rule of thumb, identify a better measure to evaluate a company's quick ratio in any given year.
3. Notice that Melville's cash and cash equivalents declined by more than $64 million between the end of Year 1 and the end of Year 2. Which financial statement of Melville's would be particularly helpful in identifying the reasons for this large decrease in the company's cash resources over this twelve-month period?

47. **Receivables: An International Perspective** (LO 1)

In 1994, Sotheby's Holdings, Inc., celebrated its 250th anniversary. The London-based Sotheby's is the leading auction house worldwide. Each year, Sotheby's auctions millions of dollars of art, jewelry, rare books, and related items. The largest line item in Sotheby's periodic balance sheets is a current asset, Accounts and Notes Receivable. Each year, this line item accounts for approximately one-half of Sotheby's total assets. Sotheby's segregates its current receivables into three components in its financial statement footnotes: Auction Operations, Finance Operations, and Other.

Following are selected disclosures regarding current receivables that were included in a recent Sotheby's annual report. Sotheby's financial data in this report were denominated in U.S. dollars.

Auction receivables included $5.3 million . . . relating to the purchase of art objects at auction by employees, officers, directors and other related parties.

In certain situations, when the purchaser takes possession of the property [following a Sotheby's auction] before payment is made, the Company is liable to the seller for the net sale proceeds. . . . accounts and notes receivable included approximately $80.1 million of such sales.

The average interest rate charged on finance receivables was 6.8%.

Presently, credit losses on the client loan portfolio [included in finance receivables] are accounted for through the allowance for doubtful accounts, which is adequate to absorb losses inherent in this portfolio.

Required:

For each disclosure listed, indicate why external decision makers, such as investors and bankers, would need the information provided.

48. **Analyzing Accounts Receivable** (LO 4)

Paychex, Inc., provides payroll processing and payroll tax preparation services for more than 200,000 small and medium-sized businesses nationwide. Practically all of the company's services are provided on a credit basis. Following are selected financial data, expressed in thousands of dollars, for this New York-based firm for a recent three-year period. (Note: Paychex had net revenues of $190,032,000 in the year immediately preceding Year 1 and accounts receivable of $17,280,000 at the beginning of Year 1.)

	Year 1	Year 2	Year 3
Net revenues	$224,052	$267,176	$325,285
Year-end accounts receivable	21,965	30,772	37,527

Required:

1. Compute Paychex's accounts receivable turnover ratio and age of receivables for Years 1 through 3.
2. Did these ratios improve or weaken over this three-year period? Explain.

49. (*Appendix*) Bank Reconciliation (LO 6)

Following is the information needed to prepare a monthly bank reconciliation for Swank, Switzer & Hill, a law firm.

General ledger balance, October 31	$39,808.61
Bank statement balance, October 31	42,102.85
Outstanding checks, October 31	616.45
Deposits in transit, October 31	1,200.00
NSF check charged against bank balance on October 29	194.71
Bank service charge for October	37.50
Interest earned during October, added to bank account balance on October 31	110.00
Note receivable collected by bank for Swank, Switzer & Hill on October 30	3,000.00

Required:

1. Prepare a bank reconciliation for Swank, Switzer & Hill for the month of October.
2. Prepare any necessary journal entries in the law firm's accounting records as a result of this bank reconciliation.

50. (*Appendix*) Bank Reconciliation (LO 3, 6)

Linne Company has an inexperienced bookkeeper attempting to prepare the firm's December 31 bank reconciliation. Shown next is his effort to date.

Balance per books		$14,218.94
Add:	Bank service charge	47.12
Add:	Checks outstanding	2,491.29
Subtract:	Deposit in transit	(3,506.38)
Subtract:	Note receivable collected by the bank for Linne	(1,100.00)
NTB (needed to balance)		2,105.76
Balance per bank statement		$14,256.73

Required:

1. Prepare a proper bank reconciliation for Linne Company as of December 31.
2. Prepare any journal entries needed following the completion of the bank reconciliation.
3. Briefly describe the internal control objectives related to the preparation of a monthly bank reconciliation.

CASES

51. Cash Management (LO 1)

The owners of Adams & Hall Fine Furniture are planning their furniture store's grand opening for September 1. This fall, the owners plan to do extensive advertising of their store in the surrounding metropolitan area. They realize that a large percentage of new businesses fail in their first year, and they don't want to be "just another statistic." One problem, though. The owners are unsure whether they have sufficient cash to finance their large-scale advertising program. Following is a list of their planned expenditures for advertising this fall. These expenditures will be paid on the last day of each month.

September	$20,000
October	30,000
November	42,000
December	80,000

The owners hope that collections of accounts receivable (credit sales) in each month will be sufficient to pay for that month's advertising expenditures. Following are the store's expected credit sales for September through December. All of the store's sales will be on credit, and customers will be granted terms of n/45.

September	$ 70,000
October	40,000
November	50,000
December	100,000

The owners expect that each month's credit sales will be collected as follows: 30 percent in the month of sale and 65 percent in the following month. Uncollectible accounts are expected to average 5 percent.

Required:

1. Determine the store's cash collections from accounts receivable for each month, September through December.
2. Compare the projected cash collections with each month's planned advertising expenditures. In which months, if any, will cash collections from accounts receivable be less than the projected advertising expenditures?
3. Why is effective cash management important for businesses? How can accountants help business owners and executives properly manage a firm's cash resources?

52. Analyzing Receivables (LO 4)

Hee-Kyung Boutiques Inc. (HBI) began selling sportswear in the southwestern United States approximately five years ago. Although HBI has been growing rapidly, it has recently begun experiencing cash shortages. Mike Sung, HBI's president, asked his accounting department to collect the information shown in the following schedule to help him analyze the firm's cash-flow problems.

	Year 3	Year 4	Year 5
Net credit sales	$8,000,000	$9,000,000	$10,500,000
Year-end accounts receivable, net	3,000,000	4,000,000	6,000,000

(Note: HBI's net accounts receivable at the beginning of Year 3 was $2,000,000.)

Listed next is additional information that Mike Sung has collected to help him assess and respond to HBI's current financial crisis:

1. When HBI began operations five years ago, it chose not to accept credit cards of any kind, preferring to bill and collect its own receivables. Initially, the company granted credit terms of n/60 to its customers. Late in Year 3, the company switched to credit terms of n/120 to increase its sales.
2. HBI's uncollectible accounts expense was approximately 2 percent of credit sales during the first two years of its existence. However, uncollectible accounts expense as a percentage of credit sales increased to 4 percent in Year 3, to 5 percent in Year 4, and to 6 percent in Year 5.
3. If HBI begins allowing customers to charge their purchases to credit cards, service fees from the credit card companies will average 4 percent of total credit card sales.

Required:

1. Compute HBI's accounts receivable turnover ratio and its age of receivables for Years 3 through 5. Given these data, analyze the quality of HBI's receivables over this period. As suggested in the text, the quality of accounts receivable is primarily a function of their collectibility.
2. Write a memo to Mike Sung that comments on how the company's credit policy may have contributed to its cash-flow problems in Year 5. Include in your memo recommendations on how the company might resolve its cash-flow problems.

53. Doubtful Receivables (LO 3)

In the early 1980s, IFG Leasing was one of many subsidiaries of IFG, Inc., a Minneapolis-based corporation. IFG Leasing was engaged in the "small ticket" leasing industry. Small ticket leasing companies lease assets such as farm equipment, office furniture, and construction equipment to individuals and small businesses. Typically, the cost of the assets leased by small ticket leasing companies ranges from $2,000 to $10,000.

During the late 1970s and early 1980s, IFG Leasing experienced a huge increase in revenues. This period of time was characterized by steadily increasing interest rates that eventually "topped out" at more than 20 percent in the early 1980s. Since many individuals and businesses could not qualify for bank loans during this period, they turned to small ticket leasing companies to acquire assets they needed. As IFG Leasing's volume of business increased dramatically in the early 1980s, it began experiencing a high rate of default on its lease receivables. By early 1982, more than 20 percent of the company's receivables were past due. Since lease receivables accounted for more than 95 percent of the company's total assets, this situation posed a major problem for the firm.

To purchase new assets for their leasing business, IFG Leasing's executives regularly borrowed funds from local banks. Because the company's executives were worried that their loan applications might be rejected, they began understating the percentage of lease receivables that were past due in IFG Leasing's quarterly and annual financial statements. For example, in September 1982, IFG Leasing's accounting records indicated that the company had nearly $90 million of past-due lease receivables. However, the company's financial statement footnotes reported that past-due receivables totaled less than $34 million.

Allegedly, the chief executive of IFG Leasing threatened to fire any employee who reported the actual amount of the company's past-due receivables to anyone outside the company. Nevertheless, in late 1982, the chief accounting officer of IFG Leasing disclosed the actual dollar amount of the past-due receivables to an executive of IFG, Inc.

[Note: The facts of this case were drawn from the following source: Michael C. Knapp, "IFG Leasing," in *Contemporary Auditing: Issues and Cases,* 2d ed. (Minneapolis/St. Paul: West Publishing Co., 1996.)]

Required:

1. Refer to the definition of the internal control component "control environment" that was discussed in Chapter 3. Explain how IFG Leasing's control environment was flawed.

2. At one point, an executive of IFG Leasing maintained that a company's independent auditors have the primary responsibility for ensuring that the firm's past-due receivables are properly accounted for and disclosed in the company's financial statements. Is this true? If not, who has the final responsibility for ensuring that a company's financial statements are fairly presented? What is the role of independent auditors relative to an audit client's financial statements?
3. The chief accounting officer of IFG Leasing eventually ignored his superior's orders and disclosed the magnitude of the company's past-due receivables to a top executive of IFG, Inc. Identify the general circumstances under which an accountant, or other company employee, should intentionally ignore a superior's orders.

54. **Imprecise Accounting** (LO 2)
Many students are attracted to accounting by its apparent precision: debits and credits must be equal in each journal entry, the balance sheet balances, the financial statements must "tie" together, and so on. On the first day of an introductory financial accounting course, one student was startled to hear her instructor maintain that accounting is a very imprecise activity.

Required:
Write a short memo to this new accounting student. In this memo, comment on the imprecision in the allowance for doubtful accounts and the related financial statement item, uncollectible accounts expense. Then, provide other examples of imprecision in accounting that you have encountered to date in this course.

PROJECTS

55. **Controls Over Cash**
You are an accounting major at a local college and are currently working as an accounting intern at a large store in a shopping mall. One of your responsibilities involves the evaluation of internal controls. Two weeks ago, your department manager asked you to review the department's sales and cash receipts transactions and related accounting entries since the beginning of the year, a time period of approximately six months. For each sales transaction, a salesclerk enters the amount of the sale in a sales terminal, the type (cash, check, or credit card) and amount of payment made by the customer, and any change given to the customer. To date, you have reviewed computer printouts for each sales terminal in your department, related journal entries, and deposit slips for each day's sales over the past six months.

After reviewing several months of the department's cash and sales records, you began noticing a pattern for one particular sales terminal. You discovered that on weekday evenings, during the 5:00 p.m. to 9:00 p.m. shift, there is frequently a $5 to $10 difference between the total cash balance reported by the sales terminal and the total cash and cash items (checks and credit card sales slips) included in the sales terminal cash till at the end of the shift. Over the past six months, the collective cash shortage for this sales terminal is more than $500. Each of the other four sales terminals also has a collective cash shortage over the same time period, but the largest of these is less than $50. There is no indication that this particular sales terminal is malfunctioning. Each sales terminal is checked regularly with any needed maintenance performed immediately. You have discovered that the same employee is typically operating this terminal when the cash shortages occur. This employee was hired shortly after the beginning of the year. A check of last year's data for the sales terminal in question did not reveal a pattern similar to the one you have found for the past six months.

Required:
1. Meet with the other members of your project group to discuss this scenario.

2. Your group should develop a list of control activities that could be implemented to strengthen the degree of internal control over the given department's cash-processing activities.
3. As a group, develop a recommended course of action for the department manager regarding how he or she should deal with the frequent cash shortages in the one sales terminal.
4. One member of your group should be prepared to present a summary overview to the class of the group's discussion of this scenario. Included in this overview should be a list of the control activities developed in (2) and the recommendation developed in (3).

56. **Credit Policies**

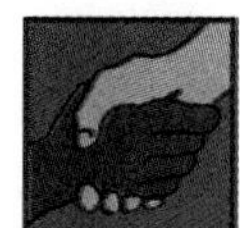

As a group, meet and identify three local businesses that extend credit to their customers. Make sure that the three businesses are quite different. If possible, include one service firm, one merchandiser, and one manufacturing firm in the businesses you select.

Each of the three businesses should be contacted by a member of the group—one member per business. These three group members should ask to visit with the credit manager of his or her assigned business or the individual, such as the business owner, responsible for making credit-related decisions for that firm. The three group members will obtain from the relevant individuals information documenting the objective and key features of each business's credit policy. For example, does the business accept credit cards? If so, which ones? Does the business manage its own credit function? If so, what credit terms are granted to customers, and what type of credit application, if any, must be completed? (Obtain a copy of this application, if possible.) Among other questions that may be posed to the appropriate individuals are the following: How often is the business's credit policy reevaluated? Has the credit policy been changed recently? If so, how and why? What percentage of the business's sales are on credit?

Required:

A written report should be prepared by your group. This report should begin with a brief overview of the nature of each business selected by your group. Document in your report the objectives and major features of the credit policies of the three selected businesses and the other information obtained during the interviews. The final section of the report should include a discussion of the factors that likely account for the key differences in the credit policies of the three businesses.

57. **Allowance for Doubtful Accounts**

Select two public companies that maintain a Web site on the Internet, make their annual financial statements available at their Web site, and regularly report a significant amount of accounts receivable in their annual balance sheets.

Required:

1. Access the Web site of each company you selected and print each firm's most recent balance sheet.
2. For each of the past five years, obtain the following data items for the selected companies.
   a. Total accounts receivable
   b. Allowance for doubtful accounts
   c. Total current assets
   d. Total assets
   e. Net sales
2. For each company, compute the following ratios for each of the past five years:
   a. Allowance for doubtful accounts/total accounts receivable
   b. Net accounts receivable/total current assets
   c. Net accounts receivable/total assets
   d. Net accounts receivable/net sales

3. Prepare a report containing the following information:
   a. A brief description of each company's principal line or lines of business.
   b. The data you computed in (2).
   c. Your analysis of any trends apparent in the data computed in (2). To interpret these trends, you may need to review narrative information included in the companies' annual reports.
   d. The Web site addresses from which you obtained the required data for each firm. (Attach to your report the balance sheet you printed for each firm.)

Inventory 7

"Every management mistake ends up in inventory [permanently]."
Mary Kay Ash, founder,
Mary Kay Cosmetics, Inc.

LEARNING OBJECTIVES

After studying this chapter, you should be able to do the following:

1. Define the key information needs of decision makers regarding inventory.
2. Account for common inventory transactions.
3. Apply the four major inventory costing methods.
4. Apply the lower-of-cost-or-market rule to inventory.
5. Identify key control activities for inventory.
6. Compute the inventory turnover ratio and the age of inventory.
7. (Appendix) Discuss key differences between the periodic and perpetual inventory systems.
8. (Appendix) Estimate inventory using the gross profit method.

FOCUS ON DECISION MAKING

Corporate Accountants: "Toying" with Inventory

In the early 1980s, first Mattel and then Fisher-Price were approached by an individual who wanted the toy manufacturers to market a line of "Little People" dolls he had developed. Both companies quickly rejected the proposal. Marketing experts within the two firms perceived the pudgy dolls as unattractive and unlikely to appeal to young children. The following year, Coleco Industries, another toy manufacturer, decided to take a chance on the dolls, which had been renamed by this time. During the fall of 1983, the dolls were placed on the market. Over the next several months, Cabbage Patch Kids took the country by storm.

The public's demand for the adoptable dolls surpassed Coleco's ability to produce them. The result was a nationwide shortage of the dolls in toy stores across the nation. Yelling and shoving matches between irate customers fighting over the scarce dolls were common, as were underground black markets for the dolls. To quell the nationwide furor, Coleco suspended its advertising campaign for Cabbage Patch Kids. Despite the shortage of the dolls, Coleco sold more than 2.5 million of them in the fall of 1983, generating total revenues of nearly $50 million.

In the early 1970s, Mattel faced a much different crisis for a toy that previously had been a best seller. Children's interest in Mattel's Hot Wheels plummeted unexpectedly in 1972, leaving the company with a large inventory of the toy. Mattel eventually sold nearly six million Hot Wheels en masse to a large oil company, which used them as a promotional item. In the process, Mattel was nailed with a whopping loss of $11 million.

Accountants play a key role in monitoring inventory levels and helping management develop appropriate inventory policies. For a hot-selling item, accountants can assist management by preparing weekly or daily sales reports for each sales region. The limited inventory of such a product can then be diverted to those regions where the demand is highest and inventory is lowest.

Monitoring sales and inventory levels for slow-moving items is also an important responsibility of accountants. In the early 1970s, Mattel's accounting department was responsible for tracking weekly sales data for each of the company's toys. Based upon these data, the accountants were to write down the inventory values of those products that were selling poorly. However, Mattel's accountants failed to write down the company's inventory of Hot Wheels. Instead, those toys remained on the company's books at values well in excess of the prices for which they could be sold, a clear violation of generally accepted accounting principles. When this and other accounting oversights were disclosed, Mattel's management was sued by angry stockholders. Eventually, Mattel and its executives paid more than $30 million to settle the lawsuits stemming from the company's sloppy accounting practices.

In Chapter 6, we focused on the assets that businesses acquire as a result of sales transactions, cash and accounts receivable. In this chapter, we focus on the asset that businesses exchange in sales transactions, inventory, and the related expense item, cost of goods sold.

INVENTORY: AN INTRODUCTION

In 1996, *The Wall Street Journal* reported that businesses in the United States owned \$982.6 billion of inventory.[1] Economists closely monitor changes in total business inventories to obtain clues regarding the health of the national economy. In turn, investors and other decision makers monitor individual businesses' inventory levels and related financial disclosures to evaluate their changing financial fortunes.

We begin our study of inventory by becoming familiar with terms commonly associated with this asset and by reviewing the two major approaches to accounting for inventory. This section also addresses the significant impact that errors in accounting for inventory can have on the reliability of a firm's financial statements.

Inventory Terms

inventory

Recall from Chapter 2 that **inventory** consists of goods businesses intend to sell to their customers or raw materials or in-process items that will be converted into salable goods. Inventory is classified as a current asset for balance sheet purposes. Like most accounting terms, "inventory" has several meanings. For example, accountants commonly refer to a company's inventory of equipment or its supplies inventory. In these contexts, the term "inventory" does not refer to salable goods but is being used in a more general way to refer to a group of assets. Accountants also frequently use the phrase "take inventory," as in, "We plan to take inventory on September 30." The phrase "take inventory" or "take a physical inventory" typically refers to an intention to count a company's salable goods on a specific date. A business can also "take inventory" of supplies, equipment, investments, or any other type of asset.

"Inventory cost flow" is another common expression used by accountants. Exhibit 7.1 depicts the inventory cost flow for a merchandising company. A merchandiser begins an accounting period with a certain amount of inventory. During the period, additional purchases of inventory are made. The sum of beginning inventory and merchandise purchases during an accounting period equals "cost of goods available for sale" for that period. The costs associated with merchandise that is sold during an accounting period flow out of cost of goods available for sale and into cost of goods sold. Cost of goods sold is the largest expense item of most merchandising companies. At the end of a period, the costs attached to unsold merchandise are designated as ending inventory and included as a current asset on a merchandiser's balance sheet. This cost flow cycle is repeated each accounting period.

Exhibit 7.2 presents an income statement for a recent fiscal year of Claire's Stores, Inc. This Florida-based merchandiser specializes in fashion accessories for young women. Although not shown in Claire's income statement, inventory is the key "player" in this financial statement. Why? Because the \$344.8 million revenue item "Net Sales" resulted from sales of inventory in the more than 1,500 Claire's stores scattered around the United States, the Caribbean, Japan, and the United Kingdom. Likewise, the largest expense item in Claire's income statement, "Cost of Goods Sold," is directly linked to inventory. In fact, we could just as easily refer to that item as "Cost of Inventory Sold." Notice that Claire's unsold inventory at the end of the year in question is not shown in the company's income statement. That figure, \$32,383,000, was reported in the current assets section of the company's balance sheet.

1. "Business Inventories," *The Wall Street Journal*, 22 March 1996, A1.

EXHIBIT 7.1 ▼
Inventory Cost Flow for a Merchandising Company

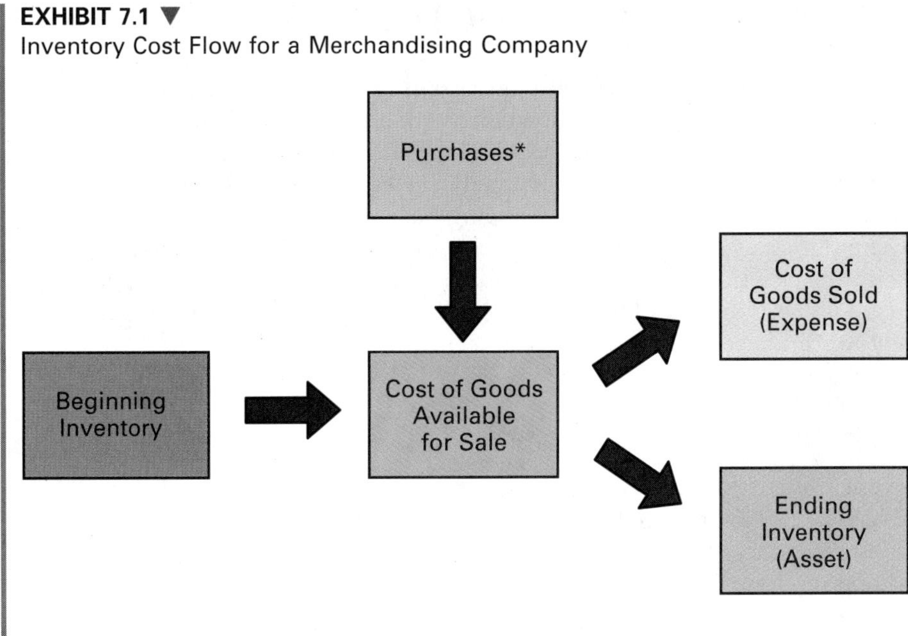

*Including delivery costs incurred to acquire merchandise

EXHIBIT 7.2 ▼
Recent Income Statement for Claire's Stores, Inc.

Net sales	$344,881,000
Cost of goods sold	157,857,000
Gross profit	$187,024,000
Operating expenses	139,430,000
Operating income	$ 47,594,000
Interest revenue	2,015,000
Income before income taxes	$ 49,609,000
Income taxes	18,694,000
Net income	$ 30,915,000

The flow of inventory costs through the accounting records of a manufacturing company is more complex than for a merchandising firm. One factor complicating a manufacturer's inventory cost flow is the existence of multiple types of inventory. Merchandisers typically have only one type of inventory, the goods they sell to their customers. Manufacturers generally have three types of inventory: raw materials, in-process or work-in-process inventory, and finished goods. For example, consider A.T. Cross, the company that manufactures Cross pens. On a recent balance sheet, A.T. Cross reported total inventories of $29.5 million, as shown in the following schedule.

Finished goods	$14,499,263
Work-in-process	7,837,532
Raw materials	7,128,544
Total inventories	$29,465,339

The examples in this chapter primarily involve accounting for the inventory of merchandising concerns. However, most of the accounting concepts, rules, and procedures we consider apply equally well to both merchandising and manufacturing firms. More advanced accounting topics unique to a manufacturing environment are deferred for coverage in subsequent accounting courses.

Periodic vs. Perpetual Inventory Systems

There are two general types of inventory accounting systems, perpetual and periodic inventory systems. In a **perpetual inventory system,** the revenue and cost of goods sold associated with sales transactions are recorded simultaneously when sales are made. Another key feature of a perpetual inventory system is the maintenance of a "perpetually" updated record of the quantity of individual inventory items and their per unit costs. In a **periodic inventory system,** the revenue from sales transactions is booked when sales are made but cost of goods sold is not. Additionally, a business that uses a periodic inventory system typically does not maintain records documenting the quantity and per unit costs of each inventory item. In a periodic inventory system, a business's inventory is counted at the end of each accounting period. Then, the quantity of each item is multiplied by the appropriate per unit cost to arrive at the dollar value of ending inventory. After that figure has been determined, the company's cost of goods sold for the period is computed.

perpetual inventory system

periodic inventory system

The key advantage of perpetual inventory systems, compared to periodic inventory systems, is the availability of a continually updated record of the quantity of each inventory item. Historically, the key disadvantage of perpetual inventory systems has been their cost. However, the declining cost of computer-based perpetual inventory systems and the increasing importance of their "information" advantage has convinced many businesses to switch from periodic to perpetual inventory systems. Since these systems are growing in popularity, this chapter focuses on perpetual inventory systems. The appendix to this chapter profiles the key differences between the two types of inventory systems.

Inventory Errors and the Bottom Line

You will find few accountants who downplay the importance of inventory and inventory accounting decisions. Accountants realize that improper inventory accounting decisions can significantly distort a company's balance sheet and income statement. Making matters worse, if a company's inventory is misstated at the end of one accounting period, the following period's beginning inventory will automatically be misstated. Why? Because inventory is a permanent account, meaning that its period-ending balance is carried over to the following period. Thus, an inventory error affects financial statement data for at least two consecutive accounting periods.

A misstatement of inventory typically results in a much larger error, on a percentage basis, in a company's net income. For example, suppose that a company reports $10

Cooking the Books at MiniScribe

Among the many business executives who have fallen victim to the temptation to overstate their firm's inventory were former officers of MiniScribe Corporation. MiniScribe, which no longer exists, was a Colorado-based company that manufactured computer disk drives. To inflate MiniScribe's profits during the late 1980s, company officials developed a computer program known internally as "Cook Book" to generate a large quantity of fictitious inventory. To conceal the overstatement of inventory from the company's independent audit firm, much of MiniScribe's fictitious inventory was "transferred" to a Far East subsidiary. Company personnel also broke into the auditors' workpaper files to determine which inventory items were being scrutinized. Additional overstatements were then made in the quantities of many inventory items that were not being tested by the auditors. A final fraudulent tactic used by MiniScribe was to stuff bricks and scrap materials into boxes and then label those boxes as containing computer disk drives.

million of inventory on its year-end balance sheet and net income of $1 million in its accompanying income statement. If this firm's ending inventory is overstated by 5 percent, or $500,000, then its gross profit (net sales less cost of goods sold) will be overstated by the same amount. Assume that after taxes, this $500,000 overstatement of gross profit translates to a $250,000 overstatement of net income. Given this scenario, the company's true net income is $750,000, instead of $1,000,000. So, the 5 percent overstatement of inventory resulted in a 33 percent overstatement of net income ($250,000/$750,000).

The latter analysis accounts for inventory often being the "weapon of choice" of corporate executives who want to misrepresent their company's bottom line. A Spotlight on Ethics vignette accompanying this section profiles a major accounting fraud involving inventory.

INVENTORY: INFORMATION NEEDS OF DECISION MAKERS

LEARNING OBJECTIVE 1 ▶
Define the key information needs of decision makers regarding inventory.

Earnings per share is no doubt the financial statement item most closely followed by decision makers. However, when it comes to the balance sheet, inventory likely garners more attention than any other asset, at least for merchandising and manufacturing companies. In this section, key information needs of decision makers regarding this important asset are identified.

Inventory Balances

"How much?" is the first question that decision makers pose regarding a company's inventory. Instead of focusing exclusively on the dollar amount of inventory for the most recent accounting period, decision makers also compare any significant change in inventory from one period to the next with changes in related financial statement items. An unusual or unanticipated change in inventory often provides definite clues regarding a company's future prospects.

Investors "downsized" the future prospects of Apple Computer in the mid-1990s when that firm's inventories began increasing much faster than its sales. In fiscal 1995, Apple's inventories increased by 63 percent, compared to a 20 percent increase in sales. Investors' concerns regarding Apple were confirmed the following year. In March 1996, the company reported that it would suffer a huge loss for the first three months of the year. Much of this loss stemmed from a nearly $400 million write-down in the value of the firm's slow-moving inventory.

Information Regarding Inventory Accounting Methods

Companies include in their financial statement footnotes a summary of the accounting methods applied to inventory and other major accounts. These disclosures are very important to financial statement users. The choice of an inventory accounting method can significantly affect the reported value of a firm's inventory and the periodic earnings reported by the firm. Inventory also impacts several key financial ratios. Consequently, decision makers should be aware of and understand the inventory accounting methods that a company applies.

Slow-moving inventory is often an early warning signal of financial problems for a company. In the mid-1990s, a large build-up of inventory preceded a huge loss reported by Apple Computer for the first quarter of 1996.

Photography by Photonics Graphics

Exhibit 7.3 presents excerpts from recent annual reports that describe the inventory accounting methods of several companies. These descriptions will be more meaningful to you after you have studied the accounting methods discussed later in this chapter.

"What If" Information

What may be most striking about the disclosures companies make regarding their inventories is the brief nature of those disclosures. Take the case of Duracell International Inc., a company that regularly has several hundred million dollars of inventory reported on its balance sheet. In a recent year, the key narrative information Duracell included in its annual report concerning inventory was the brief description shown in Exhibit 7.3. Unfortunately, most companies include very limited information in their annual reports regarding this important asset.

Decision makers would clearly benefit from additional financial statement disclosures for inventory. Particularly helpful would be "what if" disclosures revealing how companies' reported inventory values would have been affected had they used different accounting methods. An example of a company that makes such disclosures in its annual reports is FoxMeyer Corporation, the nation's third largest distributor of pharmaceutical products. FoxMeyer's principal inventory accounting method is LIFO (last-in, first-out), a method discussed later in this chapter. Although used by many companies, LIFO is not as popular as the FIFO (first-in, first-out) inventory accounting method. FoxMeyer discloses in its financial statement footnotes the dollar value that would have been assigned to its ending inventory under the FIFO method. With this information, decision makers can make more meaningful comparisons between FoxMeyer's financial data and that of competing companies that use the FIFO method. In a recent year, FoxMeyer reported that its ending inventory would have been $64 million larger if it had used the FIFO method.

EXHIBIT 7.3 ▼

Inventory Disclosures Made by Selected Companies in Recent Annual Reports

Inventories are stated at the lower of cost (first-in, first-out) or market. If the cost of inventories exceeds their market value, provisions are made currently for the difference between the cost and market value.

Apple Computer

Inventories are valued at the lower of cost or market using the first-in, first-out method.

Duracell

Inventories are valued at the lower of cost or market. Cost is determined on the last-in, first-out (LIFO) basis.

La-Z-Boy Chair Company

Inventories are valued at the lower of cost or market. Inventory cost is determined principally by the specific identification method. Market is replacement cost or net realizable value.

Trinity Industries

ACCOUNTING FOR INVENTORY

LEARNING OBJECTIVE 2
Account for common inventory transactions.

This section discusses and illustrates key accounting rules and procedures for inventory. We begin by examining the accounting treatment for several common transactions involving inventory. Next, four common inventory costing methods are illustrated. We also consider the appropriate accounting procedures for the occasional circumstances in which companies must value their inventories at other than cost. Recognize that the examples and scenarios we consider in this section assume that the given businesses use a perpetual inventory system. Again, the key differences between perpetual and periodic inventory systems are highlighted in the appendix accompanying this chapter.

Accounting for Common Inventory Transactions

To illustrate accounting for basic inventory-related transactions, let us consider several recent transactions of a small retail store, Marcia's Boutique. Exhibit 7.4 provides brief descriptions of these transactions.

INVENTORY PURCHASES Notice that the description of the August 1 purchase in Exhibit 7.4 reveals that this transaction has "credit terms" of 2/10, n/30, and "shipping terms" of "FOB shipping point." Recall that credit terms were discussed in Chapter 6. Credit terms of 2/10, n/30, indicate that Marcia's Boutique is entitled to a 2 percent discount if the invoice is paid within ten days of the invoice date. If payment is not made by August 11, Marcia's must pay the full amount of the invoice by August 31, the last day of the 30-day credit period. Suppliers offer **purchase discounts** to encourage prompt payment of credit purchases. The shipping terms for a transaction dictate which party, the seller or buyer, is responsible for paying the delivery cost of the goods. We will discuss this feature of merchandising transactions shortly. The initial entry for this purchase transaction would appear as follows in the accounting records of Marcia's Boutique.

purchase discounts

EXHIBIT 7.4 ▼
Recent Inventory-Related Transactions of Marcia's Boutique

1. **Inventory Purchase:** On August 1, Marcia's Boutique purchased twelve dresses from Kwon & Kwon Fashions at a cost of $50 each, $600 in total, with credit terms of 2/10, n/30, and shipping terms of FOB shipping point.
2. **Purchase Return:** On August 3, one of the dresses was discovered to have a fabric flaw and was returned to Kwon & Kwon.
3. **Inventory Sale:** Three of the dresses were sold on August 5 at a retail price of $110 each.
4. **Payment of Delivery Costs:** On August 7, Marcia's received and paid the $24 freight bill for the delivery of the dresses purchased from Kwon & Kwon.
5. **Sales Return:** On August 8, a customer returned the dress that she had purchased on August 5. The customer was given a full refund, and the dress was returned to inventory.
6. **Payment for Inventory:** Marcia's paid the amount due Kwon & Kwon on August 11.

Aug. 1	Inventory	600	
	Accounts Payable		600
	Purchase from Kwon & Kwon, invoice no. 361, credit terms 2/10, n/30, FOB shipping point		

purchase returns and allowances

PURCHASE RETURNS AND ALLOWANCES Just like their customers, merchandising companies are sometimes dissatisfied with the goods they purchase. Merchandise received is occasionally not the goods ordered, is defective, or was damaged when it was packaged. Reductions in amounts owed to suppliers resulting from returned goods or price concessions granted for defective or damaged goods are referred to as **purchase returns and allowances.** The source document for a purchase return or allowance is a "debit memorandum." (Recall that a "credit memorandum" was illustrated in Chapter 6.) The following entry records the purchase return made by Marcia's Boutique on August 3.

Aug. 3	Accounts Payable	50	
	Inventory		50
	Dress returned to Kwon & Kwon, debit memo no. 56		

You might have expected the $50 purchase return in the previous entry to be credited to an account entitled Purchase Returns and Allowances. Although such an account is used in a periodic inventory system, a Purchase Returns and Allowance account *typically* is not used in a perpetual inventory system. Instead, purchase returns and allowances are most often credited directly to the Inventory account in a perpetual inventory system.

Cost of Goods Sold

SALES OF INVENTORY Chapter 6 illustrated the accounting treatment of both cash and credit sales of merchandise. However, only the revenue "side" of such transactions was discussed in that chapter. In a perpetual inventory system, a sale of merchandise requires two journal entries. The first entry records the revenue resulting from the transaction, while the second entry records the related expense. A **Cost of Goods Sold** account accumulates the cost of inventory sold to customers during an accounting period when a perpetual inventory system is being used. Shown next are the two entries required to record the dresses sold by Marcia's Boutique on August 5.

Aug. 5	Accounts Receivable	330	
	Sales		330
	Credit sales		
Aug. 5	Cost of Goods Sold	150	
	Inventory		150
	To record cost of goods sold for credit sales		

PAYMENT OF DELIVERY COSTS When one business purchases goods from another, the two must agree on which will be responsible for paying the delivery costs for the goods. The point at which the legal title to goods transfers from the seller to the buyer dictates the party responsible for paying the delivery charges. In turn, the shipping terms for a transaction determine when legal title to goods transfers from the seller to the buyer.

The most common shipping terms are FOB shipping point and FOB destination. Under shipping terms of FOB shipping point, the seller delivers the goods free on board (FOB) to the shipping point, such as the seller's loading dock. There, a freight company usually takes possession of the goods and delivers them to the buyer. With these shipping terms, the buyer is responsible for paying the delivery charges since the title to the goods transfers to the buyer at the shipping point. When goods are shipped FOB destination, the seller retains legal title to the goods until they reach the destination point. As a result, the seller is responsible for paying the transportation charges.

The shipping terms for the dresses purchased by Marcia's Boutique on August 1 are FOB shipping point, as indicated in Exhibit 7.4. So, Marcia's is responsible for paying the delivery charges for those goods. When Marcia's receives and pays the $24 freight bill on August 7, the following entry would be appropriate in the business's accounting records.

Aug. 7	Inventory	24	
	Cash		24
	Freight charges on goods received from Kwon & Kwon on Aug. 1, invoice no. 216 of RTD Freight		

When businesses pay for the cost of delivering merchandise or other goods to their customers, such payments are *not* charged to the Inventory account. Instead, such expenses typically are debited to a Transportation Out account. For financial statement purposes, the balance of Transportation Out is treated as an operating expense, more specifically as a selling expense.

RETURN OF INVENTORY SOLD Recall from Chapter 6 that merchandisers typically establish a Sales Returns and Allowances account in which they record refunds and price concessions granted customers on previously sold merchandise. In a perpetual inventory system, a sales return or allowance requires two entries. The first entry records the return or allowance, while the second entry makes the necessary corrections to Inventory and Cost of Goods Sold. Following are the two entries required to record the dress returned to Marcia's Boutique on August 8.

Aug. 8	Sales Returns and Allowances	110	
	Accounts Receivable		110
	Sales return, credit memo no. 84		
8	Inventory	50	
	Cost of Goods Sold		50
	Sales return, credit memo no. 84		

PAYMENT FOR INVENTORY PURCHASES The credit terms for the purchase transaction described in Exhibit 7.4 are 2/10, n/30. As noted earlier, these credit terms allow Marcia's Boutique to deduct 2 percent from the gross amount owed Kwon & Kwon if payment is made by August 11, the final day of the 10-day discount period. Recognize that following the August 3 purchase return, the gross amount owed to Kwon & Kwon is $550 ($600 − $50). So, Marcia's is entitled to an $11 discount ($550 × 2%) if payment is made by August 11.

If Marcia's does not pay the $539 owed to Kwon & Kwon by August 11, the business has the use of that amount for an extra twenty days. Essentially, Marcia's will have borrowed $539 for a 20-day period at an interest charge of $11. The "effective" interest rate on this "loan" would be very high, more than 36% to be exact: ($11/$539) × (360 days/20 days) = 36.7%.

Let us assume that Marcia's Boutique realizes the heavy cost of not paying an invoice within the discount period established by a supplier. Given this assumption, Marcia's would pay Kwon & Kwon $539 by August 11. Shown next is the entry to record this payment. Notice that a purchase discount in a perpetual inventory system is credited to the Inventory account to reduce the cost of the goods acquired.

Aug. 11	Accounts Payable	550	
	Cash		539
	Inventory		11
	Paid for Aug. 1 purchase from Kwon & Kwon, invoice no. 361, less $50 purchase return, debit memo no. 56, and less 2% discount		

ALTERNATIVE ACCOUNTING PROCEDURES IN A PERPETUAL INVENTORY SYSTEM Thanks to Marcia's Boutique, we have now become well acquainted with the accounting treatment of basic inventory transactions in a perpetual inventory system. As noted on several occasions in this text, accounting is known for its diversity. You will find many different variations of perpetual inventory systems being used in practice. For example, some perpetual inventory systems make use of Purchase Returns and Allowances and Purchase Discounts accounts. You will also occasionally find in a perpetual inventory system a Transportation In account that accumulates the delivery cost of goods purchased. When these separate accounts are maintained in a perpetual inventory system, their balances are used at the end of each accounting period to arrive at the proper inventory and cost of goods sold figures for financial statement purposes.

As a point of information, you may have noticed that the August 5 entry to record cost of goods sold was for $150. That amount represented the original invoice cost of the three dresses sold that day: $50 cost per dress × 3. Of course, the actual cost of those dresses was affected by the $24 delivery charge paid on August 7 and the purchase discount that Marcia's Boutique took advantage of by paying for the dresses by August 11. When recording cost of goods sold in a perpetual inventory system similar to the one used by Marcia's Boutique, businesses must have some means for determining the impact that delivery charges and purchase discounts have on the per unit cost of items sold. Here, we ignore these matters for simplification reasons.

Inventory Costing Methods

LEARNING OBJECTIVE 3 ▶
Apply the four major inventory costing methods.

Like most assets, cost is the primary valuation basis for inventory. The most important accounting issue faced by many businesses, particularly merchandising and manufacturing firms, is how to determine the cost of ending inventory. On a moment's reflection, this may not seem to be a particularly challenging issue. From the previous section, you know that in a perpetual inventory system Cost of Goods Sold is debited and Inventory is credited for every sales transaction. Likewise, merchandise purchases and other transactions affecting inventory typically are recorded in the Inventory account. So, the period-ending cost of inventory should simply be the period-ending balance of the Inventory account. Right? Unfortunately, determining the cost of a business's period-ending inventory is not quite as simple as just described. Complicating inventory "costing" is the existence of several methods for choosing the inventory costs to charge off as cost of goods sold during an accounting period.

To explore the topic of inventory costing, we will use inventory data for a business with which you should be very familiar, namely, your local University Bookstore. Exhibit 7.5 lists inventory data for a recent year for one product sold by the University Bookstore, a principles of marketing textbook. Notice that the University Bookstore began the year with 100 copies of the marketing text, each of which cost $30. On January 8, the bookstore purchased an additional 400 copies at a per unit cost of $35, and on August 20 another 210 copies were purchased at a cost of $39 each. The Principles of Marketing course at our imaginary university is taught only during the fall and spring semesters, meaning that there are only two short "selling seasons" for this text. Prior to the spring semester, 360 copies of this book were sold by the bookstore during the week of January 13–17. For the week of August 25–29, shortly before the fall semester began, an additional 180 copies were sold, resulting in a year-end inventory of 170 copies of the marketing text, as indicated in Exhibit 7.5.

Notice that some key information is missing from Exhibit 7.5. For instance, the total cost of ending inventory is not listed. Likewise, the costs associated with the 540 books sold during the two one-week selling seasons are not reported in Exhibit 7.5. These missing data in Exhibit 7.5 raise the key inventory accounting issue facing companies that sell merchandise or other goods, namely: What per unit costs should be assigned to the goods sold during an accounting period and to those goods that remain unsold at the end of the period?

EXHIBIT 7.5 ▼

Inventory Data for Principles of Marketing Textbook for a Recent Fiscal Year

		Units		Cost per Unit		Total Cost
January 1	Beginning Inventory	100 books	@	$30 each	=	$ 3,000
January 8	Purchase	400 books	@	$35 each	=	14,000
Total		500 books	@	? each	=	$17,000
January 13–17	Sales	360 books	@	? each	=	(?)
Total		140 books	@	? each	=	$?
August 20	Purchase	210 books	@	$39 each	=	8,190
Total		350 books	@	? each	=	$?
August 25–29	Sales	180 books	@	? each	=	(?)
December 31	Ending Inventory	170 books	@	? each	=	$?
Cost of Goods Available for Sale:						
January 1	Beginning Inventory	100 books	@	$30 each	=	$ 3,000
January 8	Purchase	400 books	@	$35 each	=	14,000
August 20	Purchase	210 books	@	$39 each	=	8,190
Total		710 books				$25,190

Once we identify the total cost of goods available for sale during an accounting period and the cost of goods sold for that period, we can easily determine the cost of unsold items that comprise inventory at the end of the period. Why? Because we know from Exhibit 7.1 that the cost of goods available for sale during an accounting period less cost of goods sold must equal ending inventory.

Notice that the schedule near the bottom of Exhibit 7.5 summarizes the cost of goods available for sale, $25,190, for the present example. In this section, we consider four different inventory costing methods that can be used to "chop up" that cost of goods available for sale figure into cost of goods sold and ending inventory. To simplify matters, we ignore the fact that university bookstores typically sell both new and used textbooks. Here, we assume that the bookstore sells only new copies of the marketing text and that the selling price of this text was $50 throughout the year in question.

specific identification method

SPECIFIC IDENTIFICATION METHOD Generally accepted accounting principles (GAAP) allow a business to use any rational and systematic method to assign costs to the inventory sold during an accounting period. One costing method is the **specific identification method.** To use this method, a business must be able to identify the actual cost of each unit of inventory sold during an accounting period and the actual cost of each unsold unit at the end of an accounting period. Businesses that electronically code each inventory item and then scan these codes at the point of sale have ready access to the data needed to apply the specific identification method.

Let us assume that the University Bookstore uses an electronic scanning system to determine the specific units of each product sold during an accounting period and the corresponding cost of those units. In a perpetual inventory system, a business typically maintains a manual or electronic inventory ledger that contains an account or record for each inventory item. Exhibit 7.6 contains the inventory record for the principles of marketing text sold by the University Bookstore. As a point of information, the University Bookstore's inventory records are updated at the end of each week—a minor violation of the "perpetual" feature of a perpetual inventory system. For example, notice in Exhibit 7.6 that the perpetual inventory record for the principles of marketing text was updated at the end of each of the one-week selling seasons, January 17 and August 29, respectively. A truly perpetual inventory system updates inventory accounting records following each transaction affecting inventory.

The perpetual inventory record in Exhibit 7.6 reveals the cost of each textbook sold and purchased during the year and the cost of each book on hand at any point during the year. For example, 70 of the books sold during the week ending January 17 had a per unit cost of $30, while the remaining 290 books cost $35 each. Following the initial one-week selling season, the University Bookstore had 140 copies of the marketing text on hand at a total cost of $4,750. These 140 copies were distributed across two layers: 30 books having a per unit cost of $30 and 110 books having a per unit cost of $35.

The University Bookstore ended the year with 170 copies of the marketing text, which we already knew from Exhibit 7.5. Exhibit 7.6 indicates that the total cost of those 170 books was $6,120. Total cost of goods sold for the year was $19,070. That figure can be determined from Exhibit 7.6 by adding the four dollar amounts in the "Sold/Total" column ($2,100 + $10,150 + $1,750 + $5,070 = $19,070). Again, the sum of cost of goods sold and ending inventory for an accounting period must equal cost of goods available for sale for that period. For the present example, we can confirm the accuracy of the cost of goods sold and ending inventory figures by adding them together. The sum of those two figures is $25,190, which is the cost of goods available for sale figure reported in Exhibit 7.5.

EXHIBIT 7.6 ▼
Perpetual Inventory Record, Specific Identification Method

Item: Principles of Marketing

	Purchased			**Sold**			**Balance**		
Date	**#**	**Unit Cost**	**Total**	**#**	**Unit Cost**	**Total**	**#**	**Unit Cost**	**Balance**
Jan. 1							100	$30	$ 3,000
Jan. 8	400	$35	$14,000				100 400 500	30 35	3,000 14,000 17,000
Jan. 17				70 290	$30 35	$ 2,100 10,150	30 110 140	30 35	900 3,850 4,750
Aug. 20	210	39	8,190				30 110 210 350	30 35 39	900 3,850 8,190 12,940
Aug. 29				50 130	35 39	1,750 5,070	30 60 80 170	30 35 39	900 2,100 3,120 6,120

MOVING-AVERAGE METHOD Exhibit 7.7 presents the perpetual inventory record for the principles of marketing textbook assuming that the University Bookstore uses the **moving-average method** of inventory costing. Under this method, the average per unit cost for an inventory item is computed after each purchase. The cost basis of ending inventory for an item is determined by multiplying the number of unsold units of that item by its "moving-average" per unit cost at the end of the accounting period. Notice in Exhibit 7.7 that following the January 8 purchase of 400 books, the average per unit cost of the 500 books on hand was $34: [(100 × $30) + (400 × $35)/500]. So, the 360 books sold during the week ending January 17 were "costed out" at $34 per unit. Following the August 20 purchase, the new moving-average cost was $37 per unit: [(140 × $34) + (210 × $39)/350]. Thus, the total cost assigned to the 180 books sold during the week ending August 29 was $6,660 (180 × $37).

moving-average method

Under the moving-average method, the bookstore's ending inventory of marketing textbooks has a collective cost of $6,290, which is the year-end moving-average cost per unit of $37 multiplied by the 170 books on hand. Adding the two cost of goods

EXHIBIT 7.7

Perpetual Inventory Record, Moving-Average Method

Item: Principles of Marketing

	Purchased			Sold			Balance		
Date	**#**	**Unit Cost**	**Total**	**#**	**Unit Cost**	**Total**	**#**	**Unit Cost**	**Balance**
Jan. 1							100	$30	$ 3,000
Jan. 8	400	$35	$14,000				500	34	17,000
Jan. 17				360	$34	$12,240	140	34	4,760
Aug. 20	210	39	8,190				350	37	12,950
Aug. 29				180	37	6,660	170	37	6,290

sold amounts reported in Exhibit 7.7, we arrive at a total cost of goods sold for the year of $18,900 ($12,240 + $6,660). Alternatively, we can compute cost of goods sold by subtracting ending inventory, $6,290, from cost of goods available for sale, $25,190: $25,190 − $6,290 = $18,900.

FIFO (FIRST-IN, FIRST-OUT) METHOD When your local grocer restocks the dairy display, he or she moves the "old" milk forward and places the "new" milk near the back of the dairy display. The grocer's intention is to create a "first-in, first-out" inventory flow. A first-in, first-out inventory flow minimizes the risk of any given carton remaining on the shelves until its expiration date. Granted, customers often thwart the grocer's strategy by reaching to the back of the dairy display to find a carton of new milk.

FIFO (first-in, first-out) method

As you have probably surmised, the **FIFO (first-in, first-out) method** of inventory costing assumes that the oldest goods are sold first. In turn, the per unit costs of the most recently acquired goods are used to establish the collective cost of ending inventory under the FIFO method. Notice the word "assumes" in the first sentence of this paragraph. Both the FIFO and LIFO methods are often referred to as "inventory cost flow assumptions." A business is allowed to use an inventory cost flow assumption that is at variance with the actual physical flow of its goods. For example, although a company sells goods in a FIFO pattern, GAAP allow the firm to use the LIFO inventory costing method. A business whose inventory flows in a LIFO pattern may elect to use the FIFO inventory costing method. Similarly, a merchandiser that can identify the actual per unit costs of the items in ending inventory may still use the FIFO, LIFO, or the moving-average inventory costing method.

Exhibit 7.8 presents the perpetual inventory record for the principles of marketing text assuming that the University Bookstore applies the FIFO inventory costing method. On January 8, after the purchase of 400 books at a per unit cost of $35, notice that there were two layers of this inventory item: 100 books with a per unit cost of $30

EXHIBIT 7.8 ▼
Perpetual Inventory Record, FIFO Method

Item: Principles of Marketing									
	Purchased			Sold			Balance		
Date	#	Unit Cost	Total	#	Unit Cost	Total	#	Unit Cost	Balance
Jan. 1							100	$30	$ 3,000
Jan. 8	400	$35	$14,000						
							100	30	3,000
							400	35	14,000
							500		17,000
Jan. 17				100	$30	$3,000			
				260	35	9,100			
							140	35	4,900
Aug. 20	210	39	8,190						
							140	35	4,900
							210	39	8,190
							350		13,090
Aug. 29				140	35	4,900			
				40	39	1,560			
							170	39	6,630

and 400 books with a per unit cost of $35. During the week ending January 17, 360 books were sold. Applying the first-in, first-out concept, the bookstore assumed that all 100 of the oldest (first-in) books were sold. Naturally, the other 260 books sold were assumed to have been purchased on January 8 at a cost of $35 per unit.

Following the August 20 purchase, again there were two layers of inventory: 140 "old" books with a per unit cost of $35 and 210 "new" books with a per unit cost of $39. For the sales made during the week ending August 29, the 140 "old" books were assumed to have been sold first, as indicated in Exhibit 7.8. Additionally, 40 books from the "new" layer were also assumed to have been sold, leaving 170 of those books in ending inventory.

As shown in Exhibit 7.8, the total cost of ending inventory under the FIFO method was $6,630. Adding the cost of goods sold amounts in the "Sold/Total" column of Exhibit 7.8, we arrive at total cost of goods sold of $18,560. The sum of this figure and the ending inventory dollar amount of $6,630 equals $25,190, the cost of goods available for sale figure reported in Exhibit 7.5.

LIFO (last-in, first-out) method

LIFO (LAST-IN, FIRST-OUT) METHOD The **LIFO (last-in, first-out) method** of inventory costing assumes that the most recently acquired goods are sold first, while the oldest or earliest acquired goods remain in inventory. The perpetual inventory record for the principles of marketing text prepared under the LIFO cost flow assumption is shown in Exhibit 7.9.

EXHIBIT 7.9 ▼
Perpetual Inventory Record, LIFO Method

Item: Principles of Marketing									
	Purchased			Sold			Balance		
Date	#	Unit Cost	Total	#	Unit Cost	Total	#	Unit Cost	Balance
Jan. 1							100	$30	$ 3,000
Jan. 8	400	$35	$14,000						
							100	30	3,000
							400	35	14,000
							500		17,000
Jan. 17				360	$35	$12,600			
							100	30	3,000
							40	35	1,400
							140		4,400
Aug. 20	210	39	8,190						
							100	30	3,000
							40	35	1,400
							210	39	8,190
							350		12,590
Aug. 29				180	39	7,020			
							100	30	3,000
							40	35	1,400
							30	39	1,170
							170		5,570

Similar to the FIFO example just discussed, Exhibit 7.9 indicates that there were two layers of books following the January 8 purchase: 100 books that cost $30 per unit and 400 books that cost $35 per unit. Now, consider the sales made during the week ending January 17. Unlike the previous FIFO example, under the LIFO method the bookstore assumed that the 360 books sold during January were all "new" layer books costing $35 each. This assumption left intact the "old" layer of 100 books and reduced the new or "$35" layer to only 40 books.

Following the August 20 purchase, there were three layers of books: 100 books costing $30 each, 40 books costing $35 each, and the newest layer of 210 books costing $39 each. Applying the last-in, first-out concept, the layer of 210 books is reduced to only 30 books by the sale of 180 books during the week ending August 29. Notice that the other two layers existing prior to the August sales were left intact. Adding the costs associated with the three layers of books in ending inventory, we arrive at a collective LIFO cost for ending inventory of $5,570. Prove to yourself that cost of goods sold under the LIFO method is $19,620.

COMPARISON OF INCOME STATEMENT EFFECTS OF INVENTORY COSTING METHODS Exhibit 7.10 presents the gross profit for the principles of marketing text under each of the four inventory costing methods we have considered. Again, this schedule assumes that the bookstore sold the marketing text for $50 per unit throughout the year. These gross profit figures range from $7,380 for the LIFO method to $8,440 for the FIFO method, a difference of approximately 14 percent. In absolute terms, these differences are quite small. However, in a similar exercise for a large company, such as Sears or IBM, the differences in total gross profit would be much more impressive.

You may have noticed that the prices paid by the University Bookstore for the principles of marketing text increased during the year. The books in beginning inventory had a cost per unit of $30, while the subsequent purchases were made at $35 and $39 per unit, respectively. The U.S. economy has been characterized by steadily increasing prices over the past several decades. In an inflationary economic environment, the FIFO method yields a higher net income (or lower net loss) than the LIFO method when these methods are applied to the same financial data. The FIFO method yields a higher net income because more costly goods, those purchased later in the year, are assumed to be in ending inventory. This leaves the lower cost of "older" goods charged off to cost of goods sold. Just the reverse is true under the LIFO method. The goods assumed to be in ending inventory are the relatively low cost goods acquired early in the year or on hand at the beginning of the year. Alternatively, the cost of higher-priced goods purchased later in the year are assigned to cost of goods sold.

The moving-average method typically yields a net income between the net income figures produced by the FIFO and LIFO methods. Although not always true, the specific identification method usually results in a net income figure that approximates the net income produced by applying the moving-average method.

FIFO VS. LIFO: BALANCE SHEET VALUATION VS. INCOME DETERMINATION Exhibit 7.11 indicates that FIFO is the most popular inventory costing method among public companies. However, just because FIFO is the most widely used inventory costing method does not mean it is the method that yields the most useful information for decision makers. The question of whether FIFO or LIFO is the most informative (better) method for decision makers has been debated for years. The problem in resolving this debate is that there are two important but conflicting issues that must be considered.

EXHIBIT 7.10 ▼
Comparison of Income Statement Effects of Different Inventory Costing Methods

	Specific Identification	Moving Average	FIFO	LIFO
Sales*	$27,000	$27,000	$27,000	$27,000
Cost of goods sold	19,070	18,900	18,560	19,620
Gross profit	$ 7,930	$ 8,100	$ 8,440	$ 7,380

*540 books × $50 selling price

Which method results in the more appropriate balance sheet valuation for ending inventory is the first of these issues, while the second issue is which method does a better job of matching a business's expenses with its revenues.

For balance sheet purposes, FIFO assigns the per unit costs of the most recently acquired goods to ending inventory. LIFO, on the other hand, assigns "old" per unit costs to ending inventory. For this reason, accountants generally maintain that FIFO yields a more appropriate balance sheet valuation for ending inventory.

The next issue is which of the two most popular inventory costing methods accomplishes a better matching of a business's revenues and expenses. Here, LIFO is generally perceived to be superior to FIFO because LIFO produces a profit figure for accounting purposes that better reflects the economic reality facing a business enterprise.

Consider an extreme example. Suppose that the "FIFO" cost of an item is $10 per unit, the 'LIFO" cost is $50 per unit, and the item is presently being sold for $57 per unit. After selling one unit of inventory for $57, the business owner would likely spend $50 of that $57 to replace the unit. Why $50? Because that is the LIFO or recent purchase cost of the item. So, after selling and replacing one unit of inventory, the owner would "clear" $7 on the transaction—before considering other expenses such as income taxes. For accounting purposes, the owner would also "clear" $7, that is, earn a gross profit of $7, on the transaction if the LIFO method is used. However, if FIFO is used for accounting purposes, the gross profit entered in the accounting records would be $47 ($57 − $10).

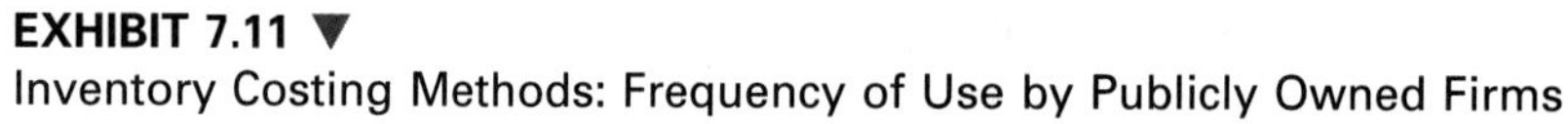

EXHIBIT 7.11 ▼
Inventory Costing Methods: Frequency of Use by Publicly Owned Firms

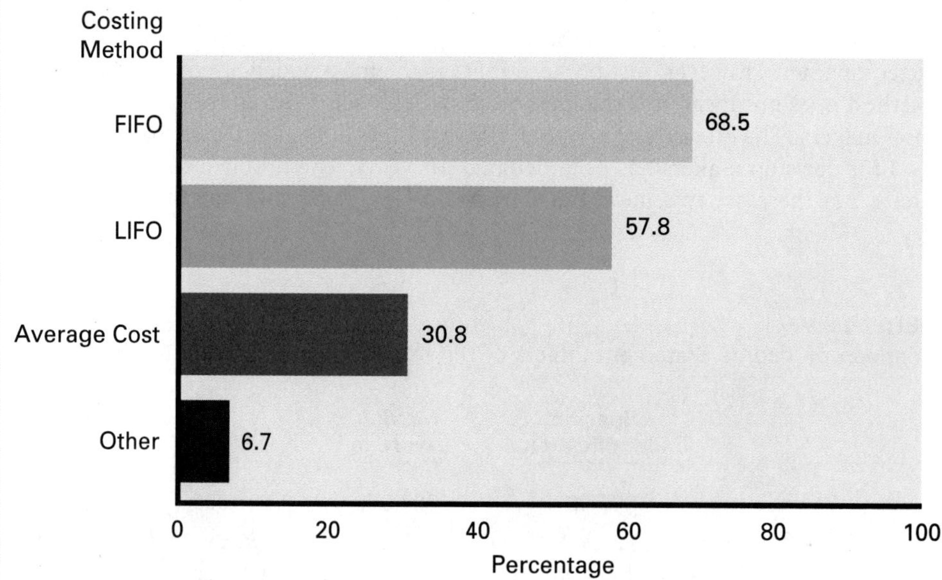

Note: Since some companies use different inventory costing methods for different classes of inventory, the percentages in the above table total more than 100 percent.

Source: *Accounting Trends & Techniques*, 1996.

In fact, business owners typically adopt a LIFO mindset when computing cost of goods sold, regardless of which inventory costing method is applied for accounting purposes. That is, business owners mentally compute the gross profit on a sales transaction by subtracting from the sales price the cost to replace the item sold, which generally approximates the cost of the most recently acquired inventory.

In summary, most accountants maintain that the LIFO costing method does a better job of matching revenues and expenses than the FIFO method. Consequently, when income determination is considered a more important issue than balance sheet valuation, the LIFO method is preferred to the FIFO method. Since most decision makers consider income determination a more critical issue than balance sheet valuation, they generally prefer businesses to use the LIFO method.

FIFO VS. LIFO: TAX CONSEQUENCES Tax consequences are an important consideration when choosing an inventory costing method. As pointed out earlier, LIFO yields lower profits than FIFO in a period of steadily rising prices, which translate into lower income tax payments. Thus, from a taxation standpoint, LIFO is generally preferred over FIFO by businesses in a period of rising prices. During the highly inflationary period of the late 1970s and early 1980s, hundreds of firms switched from FIFO to LIFO to reduce their income taxes.

There is a downside to using LIFO for taxation purposes. If a company uses the LIFO method for federal taxation purposes, it must also use LIFO for financial reporting purposes. Business executives would prefer to use the FIFO method for financial reporting purposes in a period of rising prices. Why? Because in such periods FIFO yields higher profits than LIFO, which, of course, reflect favorably on the performance of business executives. Again, notice in Exhibit 7.11 that the FIFO method is more widely used than the LIFO method. Apparently, many firms forfeit the considerable tax savings yielded by LIFO so that they can report more impressive profits on their annual income statements.

Valuing Inventory at Other Than Cost

LEARNING OBJECTIVE 4
Apply the lower-of-cost-or-market rule to inventory.

Cost is the primary valuation basis for inventory. However, businesses must occasionally depart from the cost basis of valuing inventory to prevent their financial statements

Inventory Costing Methods in Europe

FOR YOUR INFORMATION

Across Europe, the inventory costing methods commonly applied by businesses vary from country to country. In Great Britain, FIFO is used by most companies. The Republic of Ireland allows firms to use either the FIFO method or an average cost method but forbids the use of the LIFO method. Finland's "Bookkeeping Law" generally requires Finnish firms to use the FIFO method. Companies in France are allowed to use a variation of the FIFO method known as the "latest purchase price method." Under this method, the total quantity of an inventory item is costed out at the item's most recent purchase price. Finally, Greece and Poland allow businesses wide latitude in choosing inventory costing methods, meaning that FIFO, LIFO, and other reasonable costing methods are permissible.

lower-of-cost-or-market (LCM) rule

current replacement cost

from misleading decision makers. The **lower-of-cost-or-market (LCM) rule** requires businesses to value their ending inventories at the lower of cost, as determined by FIFO or some other costing method, and current market value. Market value for purposes of this rule is generally current replacement cost. **Current replacement cost** is the per unit amount that a business must pay to replace inventory items sold to customers. An inventory write-down resulting from application of the LCM rule is typically charged (debited) to Cost of Goods Sold.

Among the ways that the LCM rule can be applied are on an item-by-item basis and a total inventory basis. Here, we apply these two variations of the LCM rule to the inventory data reported in Exhibit 7.12 for Anthony's Department Store.

To apply the LCM rule on a total inventory basis, we simply compute the total cost and the total market value of a firm's inventory and select the lower figure. For Anthony's Department Store, the lower of total inventory cost and total inventory market value is $2,420, as reflected by Exhibit 7.12. In applying the LCM rule on an item-by-item basis, the lower of cost or market value is identified by each inventory item. Then, these amounts are added to determine the dollar amount of ending inventory for financial reporting purposes. Using the item-by-item version of the LCM rule, the year-end inventory of Anthony's Department Store would be valued at $2,120, as shown in the following table.

Item	Lower of Cost or Market
727 Jeans	$ 420
757 Jeans	340
Rockaway Shirts	800
Sparrow Shirts	560
Total	$2,120

EXHIBIT 7.12
Cost and Market Value Data for Year-End Inventory of Anthony's Department Store

Item	Quantity	Cost Per Unit	Market Value (Replacement Cost) Per Unit	Total Cost	Total Market
Jeans Department:					
727 Jeans	30	$14	$18	$ 420	$ 540
757 Jeans	20	24	17	480	340
Shirt Department:					
Rockaway Shirts	50	16	20	800	1,000
Sparrow Shirts	40	18	14	720	560
				$2,420	$2,440

Pacioli's Unique Approach to Inventory Valuation

FOR YOUR INFORMATION

Luca Pacioli, the fifteenth century Franciscan monk who is generally credited with being the father of modern-day accounting, was a mathematician, not an accountant. Recall that as a favor to local merchants Pacioli included a discussion of double-entry bookkeeping in a mathematics book he authored in 1494. Present-day scholars have uncovered several passages in Pacioli's text that question his familiarity with sound accounting practices. For example, in one passage Pacioli seemingly suggested that merchants should overstate the reported values of their period-ending inventories.

> And you will value them (inventories) according to your own judgment at their current value that should be rather high than low. For instance, if it seems to you that a thing is worth 20, value it 24, and you will thus obtain a greater profit.

Fortunately, subsequent generations of accountants identified and corrected Pacioli's sometimes unique interpretations of accounting rules and procedures.

Source: E. Hernandez-Esteve, "Comments on Some Obscure or Ambiguous Points of the *Treatise De Computis Et Scripturis* by Luca Pacioli," *The Accounting Historians Journal,* June 1994, 17–80.

KEY CONTROL ACTIVITIES FOR INVENTORY

Physical Security Controls

LEARNING OBJECTIVE 5
Identify key control activities for inventory.

In Chapter 6, the importance of physical security controls for cash was discussed. The cash resources of a business are nearly always kept under "lock and key." Inventory, on the other hand, is typically accessible to customers and employees and thus more susceptible to being stolen or otherwise misused. Additionally, inventory normally accounts for a much larger percentage of a business's total assets than cash. As a result, physical security controls are at least as important for inventory as they are for cash.

A recent survey of supermarkets, discount retailers, and other retail businesses revealed that retailers' losses due to customer and employee theft equal approximately 2 percent of annual sales.[2] Supermarkets are particularly susceptible to losses due to customer and employee theft. Recently, a large supermarket chain based in Texas, H.E. Butt Grocery Co., adopted a twenty-point plan to reduce theft losses and other sources of inventory "shrink."[3] Included in this plan is 24-hour electronic surveillance of all cash registers.

H.E. Butt's surveillance system allows store managers to recall for viewing sales transactions that meet any stated criteria. For example, if a store manager wants to review all "over-rings" of more than $3 on a given day or all "voids" made during a given shift by a specific checker, he or she can input those criteria into the system and retrieve the videotape of all such transactions. A company official estimated that reduction in inventory losses resulting from the surveillance system allowed the company to recoup the cost of that system in six to eight months.

2. D. Zimmerman, "Inventory Shrinkage Is Cut in Year," *Supermarket News,* 1 January 1996, 18.
3. C. O'Leary, "H-E-B Sets Broad Plan To Cut Loss From Shrink," *Supermarket News,* 15 December 1995, 19 & 21.

Manufacturing firms and wholesalers that maintain much of their inventory in large warehouses also face the potential for heavy inventory losses. In these settings, segregation of key functional responsibilities is a particularly important control activity. For example, a warehouse supervisor who has custodial responsibility for inventory should not maintain the warehouse's inventory accounting records or be allowed to authorize inventory transactions.

Periodic Inventory Counts

A business's perpetual inventory records typically are updated following each transaction affecting inventory. However, just because a company's perpetual inventory records indicate that there are 63 VCRs in the warehouse does not mean that are exactly 63 VCRs in the warehouse. A dishonest employee may have permanently "borrowed" one or two of those VCRs. To provide effective control over inventory, companies using a perpetual inventory system should periodically count their inventories and compare the results with their inventory records.

Companies employing a perpetual inventory system commonly take a physical inventory at the end of each fiscal year. Such companies then adjust their perpetual inventory records to bring them into agreement with the results of the physical inventory. Suppose that the perpetual inventory records of Stinson Distributors, Inc., indicate that the company's December 31 inventory balance is $425,000. However, the results of Stinson's year-end physical inventory reveal that the company's inventory totals only $404,000. The following adjusting entry would be necessary in the company's accounting records:

Dec. 31	Cost of Goods Sold	21,000	
	Inventory		21,000
	To bring perpetual inventory records into agreement with results of physical inventory		

Notice that the "missing" inventory is charged off to Cost of Goods Sold. When a physical inventory yields a lower inventory dollar value than the perpetual inventory records, which is commonly the case, the most plausible source of the difference is theft of inventory by customers, employees, or other parties. Nevertheless, companies typically charge off such inventory shrinkage to Cost of Goods Sold. When a physical inventory yields a higher inventory dollar value than the perpetual inventory records, the difference is recorded by debiting Inventory and crediting Cost of Goods Sold.

Inventory Management Systems

Many companies have developed computerized inventory management systems to enhance their control over inventory. PICOS is the acronym used by General Motors for its extensive inventory management system. (For you trivia buffs, PICOS is short for "purchased input concept optimization for supply.") A recent General Motors annual report disclosed that its PICOS system had reduced inventory levels by 47 percent. Floor space reserved for inventory had been reduced by 35 percent and time required to obtain inventory from suppliers by 52 percent. Another example of an inventory management system is the Smart Response system of American Greetings, which markets greeting cards. One important feature of the Smart Response system is its ability to capture "point-of-sale" data directly from the sales terminals of American Greetings' customers. Direct

Liz Claiborne: Fashion Conscious . . . Control Conscious

FOR YOUR INFORMATION

Elizabeth Claiborne always had an interest in clothes. As a teenager, she entered design contests sponsored by fashion magazines. At the age of twenty, she won such a contest and got the break that launched her career in the fashion industry. Over the next two decades, Liz worked as a fashion designer for several apparel firms. In the mid-1970s, Liz decided to start her own company so that she would have more freedom in designing clothes. Two decades later, Liz Claiborne, Inc., had annual sales exceeding $2 billion and was a leading firm in the very competitive women's apparel industry.

A key factor in the success of Liz Claiborne, Inc., has been the company's tight control over inventory. In the early 1990s, the company invested heavily in a state-of-the-art inventory management system known as LizRIM. The company provides this system to retail stores that are its major customers. The system allows these stores to identify the Liz Claiborne styles that are selling well and to quickly restock those styles while they are still in season. Liz Claiborne's rigorous inventory control policies allowed the company to decrease its investment in inventory by nearly $50 million during the mid-1990s. Lower inventory balances for the company translate into fewer write-downs and write-offs of slow-moving inventory.

access to these data has allowed American Greetings to reduce the time needed to restock customers' inventories. Additionally, American Greetings can now determine its future production needs much more accurately, thus reducing the risk of obsolete inventory.

ANALYZING INVENTORY

LEARNING OBJECTIVE 6
Compute the inventory turnover ratio and the age of inventory.

As noted in Chapter 6, decision makers closely monitor the age of a business's accounts receivable. Decision makers have a similar interest in inventory. As a company's inventory "ages," it becomes more subject to valuation concerns due to spoilage, obsolescence, and related problems.

Determining the age of inventory is a two-step process. First, the inventory turnover ratio must be computed.

inventory turnover ratio

Inventory Turnover Ratio = Cost of Goods Sold/Average Inventory

Then, the inventory turnover ratio is divided into 360 days, the number of days in a business year.

age of inventory

Age of Inventory = 360 days/Inventory Turnover Ratio

To illustrate the computation of the age of inventory, consider the following data for the Shapiro Mercantile Company.

Inventory, January 1, 1998	$ 232,200
Inventory, December 31, 1998	184,600
Cost of goods sold, 1998	1,563,000

Listed next are the calculations to compute Shapiro's age of inventory at the end of 1998.

$$\text{Average Inventory} = (\$232{,}200 + \$184{,}600)/2 = \$208{,}400$$

$$\text{Inventory Turnover Ratio} = \$1{,}563{,}000/\$208{,}400 = 7.5$$

$$\text{Age of Inventory} = 360 \text{ days}/7.5 = 48 \text{ days}$$

The inventory turnover ratio indicates the number of times that a company sells or "turns over" its inventory each year. As you would expect, businesses attempt to turn over their inventory as quickly as possible. A high rate of inventory turnover not only reduces the risk of inventory spoilage and obsolescence but also minimizes inventory carrying costs such as insurance and handling.

The age-of-inventory statistic indicates the average period required to sell an item of inventory. Unlike the inventory turnover ratio, lower is better when it comes to the age of inventory. Exhibit 7.13 reports the average age of inventory for six industries, including variety stores, the industry in which Woolworth Corporation operates. Shown in Exhibit 7.14 is Woolworth's age of inventory over a recent nine-year period. Notice that between 1988 and 1993, Woolworth's age of inventory gradually increased. To reverse this negative trend, company executives implemented an aggressive inventory management plan. This plan included establishing a system to monitor the age of individual inventory items and to expedite merchandise deliveries. Woolworth's inventory management plan was successful. Between 1993 and 1996, the age of Woolworth's inventory declined from 119 days to approximately 94 days. Woolworth's age of inventory in 1996 was particularly noteworthy since the industry norm for variety stores in the mid-1990s was nearly 120 days.

An aggressive plan implemented by the management of Woolworth Corporation in 1993 reversed a negative trend in the company's age of inventory. By 1996, Woolworth's age of inventory was significantly lower than the industry norm.

EXHIBIT 7.13 ▼
Age of Inventories, Selected Industries

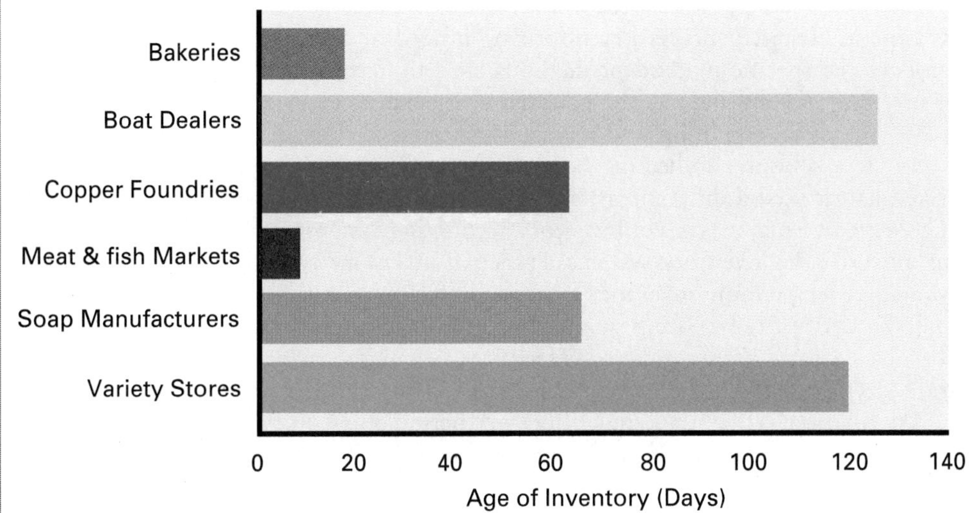

Source: Dun & Bradstreet's Industry Norms & Key Business Ratios, 1995–1996 (New York: Dun & Bradstreet, Inc., 1996).

EXHIBIT 7.14 ▼
Woolworth Corporation: Age of Inventory, 1988–1996

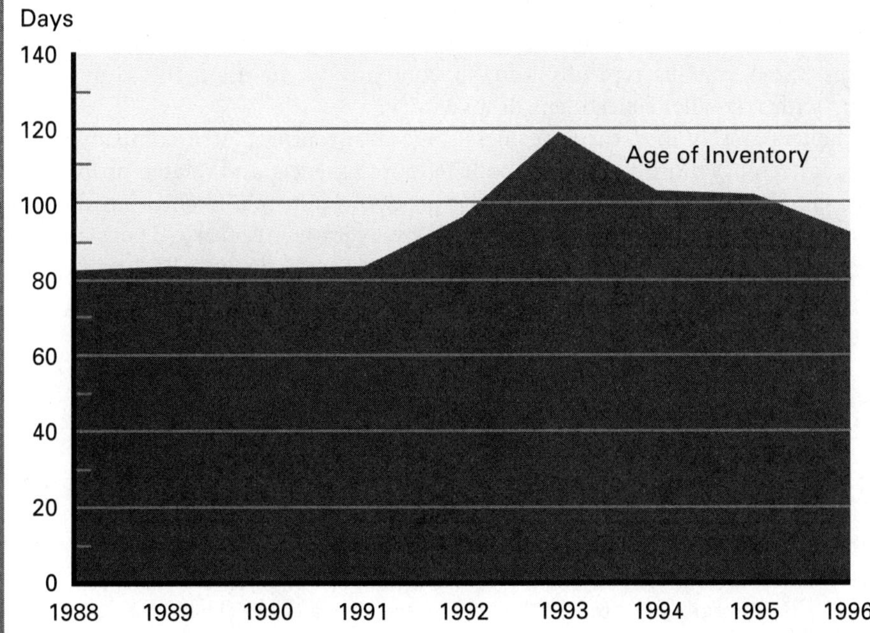

Source: Annual reports for fiscal years ending in years listed.

SUMMARY

Inventory is a focal point of attention for decision makers when they analyze a business's financial statements. A key information need of decision makers regarding inventory is the specific method or methods used to account for this important asset. The inventory accounting method adopted by a business can significantly influence its apparent financial condition and reported operating results. Also helpful to decision makers are disclosures indicating how a company's financial data would have been affected had it used a different inventory accounting method.

There are two major types of inventory accounting systems, perpetual inventory systems and periodic inventory systems. Perpetual inventory systems have an important advantage over periodic inventory systems, namely, the availability of a continually updated record of the existing quantity of each inventory item. In recent years, two factors have caused many firms to switch to perpetual inventory systems. These factors are the declining cost of perpetual inventory systems and the growing importance of the "information" advantage they offer over periodic inventory systems.

An important accounting task facing merchandising and manufacturing firms each accounting period is determining the cost of ending inventory. There are four major inventory costing methods businesses can apply in a perpetual inventory system: the specific identification method, the moving-average method, the FIFO (first-in, first-out) method, and the LIFO (last-in, first-out) method. Cost is the principal valuation basis used for inventory; however, businesses must occasionally value their inventories at other than cost. When the cost of inventory exceeds its market value, the lower-of-cost-or-market (LCM) rule requires the inventory to be written down to market value. Generally, current replacement cost is defined as market value for purposes of the LCM rule.

The susceptibility of inventory to theft makes physical security controls a critical consideration for this asset. A key control activity for businesses that use a perpetual inventory system is periodically counting inventory to confirm the accuracy of the perpetual inventory records. To gain more control over inventory, many companies in recent years have established comprehensive inventory management systems. Among other features, these systems typically allow a company to maintain the same level of operations with a smaller investment in inventory.

Decision makers closely monitor a business's age of inventory. As a company's inventory ages, it becomes more subject to spoilage, obsolescence, and related problems. Determining the age of inventory is a two-step process. First, the inventory turnover ratio is computed by dividing cost of goods sold by average inventory. Then, age of inventory is calculated by dividing the inventory turnover ratio into 360 days, the number of days in a business year.

APPENDIX: PERIODIC INVENTORY SYSTEMS

LEARNING OBJECTIVE 7 ▶
(Appendix) Discuss key differences between the periodic and perpetual inventory systems.

Recall that there are two key differences between perpetual and periodic inventory systems. A business that uses a periodic inventory system does not record cost of goods sold for each sales transaction and typically does not maintain records documenting the quantity of each inventory item. When a periodic inventory system is used, a business's inventory is generally counted at the end of each fiscal year. Then, the resulting quantities of each inventory item are multiplied by the appropriate per unit costs to arrive at the total dollar value of ending inventory. After that figure has been determined, the company's cost of goods sold for the year can be computed.

In this appendix, we take a closer look at periodic inventory systems. Among the topics we consider are determining inventory quantities in a periodic inventory system, key differences in the accounting treatment given basic inventory transactions in the two types of inventory systems, and the application of inventory costing methods in a periodic inventory system. We also review a common method for estimating the dollar value of inventory in a periodic inventory system.

Determining Inventory Quantities

In a periodic inventory system, the first step in determining a year-end dollar value for inventory is to count the quantity of each inventory item. When a company has a large amount of inventory, taking a physical inventory is not a simple or inexpensive task. To increase the likelihood of obtaining an accurate count of inventory, many businesses suspend their operations while the counting is being done.

When taking a physical inventory, a company must consider any goods in transit. Recall that the legal title to goods transfers between a buyer and seller at some specific point. Goods purchased with shipping terms of FOB shipping point are the buyer's property when the goods leave the seller's place of business. Goods purchased with shipping terms of FOB destination remain the property of the seller until they arrive at the buyer's place of business. So, a business must include in its year-end inventory in-transit goods purchased from suppliers with shipping terms of FOB shipping point. In-transit goods being shipped to customers with shipping terms of FOB destination must also be included in a business's year-end inventory.

Another issue that businesses must consider when taking a physical inventory is the need to exclude those items that they do not own. Sounds obvious, right? Nevertheless, many retail businesses have consigned inventory in their stores, that is, inventory owned by another party. For instance, supermarkets often have displays of hosiery products, greeting cards, and other goods that are owned by vendors. Albertson's, A&P, Safeway, and other supermarket chains receive a commission from the sale of these consigned goods. However, when taking a physical inventory, supermarkets must exclude such items. Including consigned goods in inventory would overstate a supermarket's ending inventory, understate its cost of goods sold, and overstate its net income.

Accounting for Common Inventory Transactions

To compare and contrast the accounting mechanics for perpetual and periodic inventory systems, it will be helpful to review journal entries within each system for several routine transactions. For this purpose, let us review the journal entries in a perpetual and periodic inventory system for the six transactions of Marcia's Boutique described in Exhibit 7.4. These journal entries are presented in Exhibit 7.15.

Notice in Exhibit 7.15 that none of the inventory-related transactions of Marcia's Boutique are recorded in an Inventory account when a periodic inventory system is being used. For example, consider the sale and sales return transactions in Exhibit 7.15, the third and fifth transactions, respectively. In a perpetual inventory system, two entries are required for each of these transactions. The initial entry records the revenue or contra revenue item and the corresponding impact on the appropriate asset account (Accounts Receivable). The second entry records the impact of the transaction on the Cost of Goods Sold and Inventory accounts. For a sale or sales return transaction, this second entry is not necessary in a periodic inventory system.

EXHIBIT 7.15 ▼
Comparative Journal Entries in Perpetual and Periodic Inventory Systems

	Perpetual Inventory System			Periodic Inventory System		
1.	Inventory	600		Purchases	600	
	Accounts Payable		600	Accounts Payable		600
2.	Accounts Payable	50		Accounts Payable	50	
	Inventory		50	Purchase Returns and Allowances		50
3.	Accounts Receivable	330		Accounts Receivable	330	
	Sales		330	Sales		330
	Cost of Goods Sold	150		No entry		
	Inventory		150			
4.	Inventory	24		Transportation In	24	
	Cash		24	Cash		24
5.	Sales Returns and Allowances	110		Sales Returns and Allowances	110	
	Accounts Receivable		110	Accounts Receivable		110
	Inventory	50		No entry		
	Cost of Goods Sold		50			
6.	Accounts Payable	550		Accounts Payable	550	
	Cash		539	Cash		539
	Inventory		11	Purchase Discounts		11

In a periodic inventory system, a Cost of Goods Sold account is not maintained and the Inventory account is not updated for each inventory-related transaction. Recall that in a periodic inventory system the dollar amount of ending inventory is determined by a physical count at the end of each accounting period. Cost of goods sold in a periodic inventory system is determined by combining several account balances in a cost of goods sold schedule. Shortly, we will review the steps in preparing a cost of goods sold schedule.

As indicated in Exhibit 7.15, purchases of inventory are debited to a Purchases account in a periodic inventory system. Similarly, purchase returns and allowances, transportation in (delivery costs paid for goods purchased), and purchase discounts are recorded in accounts bearing those names in a periodic inventory system. In a perpetual inventory system, these items are recorded directly in the Inventory account.

Exhibit 7.16 presents an example of a cost of goods sold schedule. A key figure in this schedule is cost of goods available for sale. Notice that this item is the sum of beginning inventory, "net" purchases, and transportation in. Net purchases is computed by subtracting from the total purchases for an accounting period the sum of purchase returns and allowances and purchase discounts. To determine cost of goods sold for an accounting period, ending inventory is subtracted from cost of goods available for sale, as shown in Exhibit 7.16.

EXHIBIT 7.16 ▼
Cost of Goods Sold Schedule in a Periodic Inventory System

Inventory, January 1, 1998			$23,980	
Purchases		$48,740		
Less: Purchase returns				
and allowances	$4,240			
Purchase discounts	1,200	5,440		
Net purchases			43,300	
Transportation in			3,320	
Cost of goods available for sale			$70,600	
Less: Inventory, December 31, 1998			26,230	
Cost of goods sold				$44,370

Recognize that Purchases, Purchase Returns and Allowances, Purchase Discounts, and Transportation In are temporary accounts in a periodic inventory system. At the end of each accounting period, these accounts are "zeroed out" in the closing process. Although not illustrated here, the closing entries in a periodic inventory system also establish the proper period-ending balance of the Inventory account. That account balance remains in the accounting records until the end of the following accounting period when the closing process results in the new period-ending inventory value being entered in (debited to) the Inventory account.

Inventory Costing Methods

The inventory costing methods discussed earlier can be integrated into either a perpetual or periodic inventory system. To illustrate the use of those methods in a periodic inventory system, let us return to the University Bookstore example and assume that business uses a periodic inventory system instead of a perpetual inventory system.

Under the current scenario, assume that the University Bookstore counts its inventory once per year, at the close of business on December 31. For the year in question, the University Bookstore determined that there were 170 copies of the marketing textbook on hand on December 31. (Of course, since we are working with the same set of facts, the ending inventory in the present scenario must agree with the ending inventory in the earlier scenario that illustrated the use of a perpetual inventory system.) After determining the ending inventory, the University Bookstore prepared the summary schedule of inventory data shown in Exhibit 7.17 for the marketing textbook.

Now that the data shown in Exhibit 7.17 have been compiled, the bookstore must go about the process of "costing out," or assigning a per unit cost to, each book in ending inventory. Once that process has been completed, the bookstore can compute its cost of goods sold for the year.

EXHIBIT 7.17 ▼
Inventory Data for Principles of Marketing Textbook for a Recent Fiscal Year

Cost of Goods Available for Sale:			
January 1	Beginning Inventory	100 books @ $30 each =	$ 3,000
January 8	Purchase	400 books @ $35 each =	14,000
August 20	Purchase	210 books @ $39 each =	8,190
Total		710 books	$25,190
Ending Inventory:		170 books @ ? each =	$?
Cost of Goods Sold:		540 books @ ? each =	$?

SPECIFIC IDENTIFICATION METHOD Whether a business uses a perpetual or periodic inventory system, the ending inventory and cost of goods sold for each accounting period will be exactly the same if the specific identification method is applied. So, if the University Bookstore uses a periodic inventory system and applies the specific identification method, the ending inventory for the principles of marketing text will be $6,120. That ending inventory figure was reported in Exhibit 7.6, which presents a perpetual inventory record prepared using the specific identification method.

weighted-average method

WEIGHTED-AVERAGE METHOD The "average" costing method in a periodic inventory system is referred to as the **weighted-average method.** Under this method, a weighted-average per unit cost is computed for each inventory item available for sale during an accounting period. Then, these per unit costs are multiplied by the quantity of each inventory item that remains unsold at the end of the period to arrive at the total cost of ending inventory.

For the year in question, the University Bookstore had 710 copies of the marketing text available for sale at a total cost of $25,190. Thus, the weighted-average cost of these books was approximately $35.48 ($25,190/710 books). This weighted-average cost yields an ending inventory value of $6,031.60 and cost of goods sold for the year of $19,158.40, as reflected by the following schedule.

Cost of goods available for sale	$25,190.00
Ending inventory: 170 books × $35.48	6,031.60
Cost of goods sold	$19,158.40

FIFO METHOD Similar to the specific identification method, the FIFO inventory costing method yields the same ending inventory and cost of goods sold figures each accounting period whether a business uses a perpetual or a periodic inventory system. To test this assertion, we can apply the FIFO method to the inventory data for the principles of marketing text, assuming this time that the University Bookstore uses a periodic inventory system.

Under the periodic FIFO method, the University Bookstore would automatically assume that the 170 unsold books in ending inventory were among the most recently acquired books during the year. The most recently acquired books for the year in question were the 210 books purchased on August 20. Thus, the University Bookstore would assign each of the 170 books in ending inventory a per unit cost of \$39, the purchase price of the books acquired on August 20. The resulting ending inventory value is \$6,630 (170 × \$39). The remaining cost of goods available for sale of \$18,560 (\$25,190 − \$6,630) would be allocated to cost of goods sold. If you refer to Exhibit 7.8, you will find that the ending inventory under perpetual FIFO was \$6,630, which meant that the cost of goods sold figure was \$18,560. So, there you have it. Perpetual FIFO and periodic FIFO yield identical ending inventory and cost of goods sold amounts when applied to the same inventory data.

LIFO METHOD Unlike perpetual FIFO and periodic FIFO, the two variations of the LIFO method typically result in different ending inventory and cost of goods sold amounts when applied to identical inventory data. These differences result from different timing in applying the last-in, first-out concept under periodic LIFO and perpetual LIFO. Under periodic LIFO, the last-in, first-out concept is applied only once per year, namely, at year-end. Under perpetual LIFO, the last-in, first-out concept is applied to each sales transaction or group of sales transactions.

When using periodic LIFO, the University Bookstore would assume that the marketing textbooks in ending inventory were among the "oldest" (first-in) books available for sale that year. The oldest books available for sale during the year were the 100 books in beginning inventory. So, the bookstore would assume that those 100 books remained unsold at the end of the year. Since there are 170 books in ending inventory, the bookstore would assume that 70 of the next oldest books, those purchased on January 8 at a per unit cost of \$35, were also unsold at year-end. Compiling these data in the following schedule yields an ending inventory of \$5,450 and cost of goods sold of \$19,740.

Cost of goods available for sale			\$25,190
Ending inventory (170 books):			
From beginning inventory:	100 books @ \$30 =	\$3,000	
From January 8 purchase:	70 books @ \$35 =	2,450	
Total ending inventory			5,450
Cost of goods sold			\$19,740

Referring to Exhibit 7.9, we find that the ending inventory when applying perpetual LIFO was \$5,570, while cost of goods sold was \$19,620.

Estimating Inventory

LEARNING OBJECTIVE 8 (Appendix) Estimate inventory using the gross profit method.

The absence of "perpetually" available inventory and cost of goods sold data sometimes presents a problem to businesses using a periodic inventory system. For example, what if such a business has a sudden need for financial statements in the middle of June to file with a loan application? Likewise, if such a business wants to prepare monthly financial statements, it must have some cost-effective means for determining cost of goods sold and ending inventory on a monthly basis. Taking a physical inventory each month is generally impractical because of the expense and time required.

When a company using the periodic inventory system needs to prepare financial statements at some point during a year but does not want to take a physical inventory, it can use the **gross profit method** to estimate its inventory and cost of goods sold. This method can also be used to estimate inventory losses due to fire or other causes. To use the gross profit method of estimating inventory, four items of information must be available. First, the beginning inventory must be known for the "interim" period. The interim period is the period of time that has elapsed since the taking of the previous physical inventory and also the period for which an income statement will be prepared. The other necessary items of information are the business's normal gross profit percentage and its sales and net purchases for the interim period.

gross profit method

Assume that the owner of Reba Jo's Fashions, a retail store, needs to prepare a set of financial statements for her business for the period January 1 to June 30. The owner intends to include these financial statements with a loan application for the business. Reba Jo's uses a periodic inventory system and has historically realized a gross profit of 40 percent on sales. On December 31 of the prior year, store personnel took a physical inventory that yielded an inventory value of $70,000. During the first six months of the current year, the store has had net purchases of $65,000 and net sales of $150,000. Exhibit 7.18 presents a schedule in which the June 30 inventory of Reba Jo's Fashions is estimated using the gross profit method.

The four steps in applying the gross profit method are listed next.

1. Determine cost of goods available for sale for the interim period by adding beginning inventory to net purchases and transportation in.
2. Estimate gross profit by multiplying the business's normal gross profit percentage by its sales during the interim period.
3. Estimate cost of goods sold by subtracting gross profit from sales.
4. Determine the estimated inventory dollar value by subtracting cost of goods sold from cost of goods available for sale.

EXHIBIT 7.18 ▼

Illustration of Gross Profit Method of Estimating Inventory

Inventory, January 1		$ 70,000
Net purchases, January 1–June 30		65,000*
Cost of goods available for sale		$135,000
Less: Estimated cost of goods sold		
Sales, January 1–June 30	$150,000	
Estimated gross profit (40%)	60,000	
Estimated cost of goods sold		90,000
Estimated inventory, June 30		$ 45,000

*Transportation in (delivery expenses for merchandise purchases) is included in this figure.

A company that uses the gross profit method to estimate inventory should apply this method cautiously if its gross profit percentage varies considerably from period to period. If a firm has a highly variable gross profit percentage, estimates of inventory yielded by the gross profit method may be unreliable.

GLOSSARY

Age of inventory (p. 309) 360 days divided by the inventory turnover ratio.

Cost of Goods Sold (p. 294) An account used in a perpetual inventory system to accumulate the cost of inventory sold to customers during an accounting period.

Current replacement cost (p. 306) The per unit cost that a business must pay to replace inventory items sold to customers.

FIFO (first-in, first-out) method (p. 300) An inventory costing method under which the per unit costs of the most recently acquired goods are used to establish the cost basis of ending inventory.

Gross profit method (p. 318) A method of estimating inventory in which the key factor is a business's normal gross profit percentage.

Inventory (p. 287) Goods that businesses intend to sell to their customers or raw materials or in-process items that will be converted into salable goods.

Inventory turnover ratio (p. 309) Cost of goods sold divided by average inventory; indicates how often a business sells or turns over its inventory each year.

LIFO (last-in, first-out) method (p. 301) An inventory costing method under which the per unit costs of the earliest acquired goods are used to establish the cost basis of ending inventory.

Lower-of-cost-or-market (LCM) rule (p. 306) An accounting rule that requires businesses to value their ending inventories at the lower of cost or market value, the latter typically being defined as current replacement cost.

Moving-average method (p. 299) An inventory costing method applied in a perpetual inventory system; under this method, the cost basis of ending inventory is determined by multiplying the number of unsold units of each inventory item by its moving-average per unit cost at the end of the accounting period.

Periodic inventory system (p. 289) An inventory accounting system in which the dollar value of ending inventory is determined by counting the goods on hand at the end of each accounting period and then multiplying the quantity of each item by the appropriate per unit cost.

Perpetual inventory system (p. 289) An inventory accounting system in which a perpetually updated record of the quantity of individual inventory items and their per unit costs is maintained.

Purchase discounts (p. 293) Discounts offered by suppliers to encourage prompt payment of credit purchases made by their customers.

Purchase returns and allowances (p. 294) Reductions in amounts owed to suppliers as a result of returned goods or price concessions granted for damaged or defective goods.

Specific identification method (p. 298) An inventory costing method under which actual per unit costs are used to establish the cost basis of ending inventory.

Weighted-average method (p. 316) An inventory costing method applied in a periodic inventory system; under this method, the cost basis of ending inventory is determined by multiplying the number of unsold units of each inventory item by its weighted-average cost during the accounting period.

DECISION CASE

Suppose that you were recently promoted to manager of a sales division of a large corporation. Your first responsibility was to analyze your division's operations and prepare a three-year forecast of its operating income. Following is the forecast you prepared.

	Year 1	Year 2	Year 3
Sales	$4,000,000	$4,400,000	$4,600,000
Cost of goods sold	2,000,000	2,100,000	2,200,000
Gross profit	$2,000,000	$2,300,000	$2,400,000
Operating expenses	800,000	850,000	900,000
Operating income	$1,200,000	$1,450,000	$1,500,000

After analyzing your division's operations, you realize that approximately one-third of the division's existing inventory is obsolete and unsalable at any price. This obsolete inventory has never been written down and has a book value of $100,000. You estimate that the insurance, handling, and other operating expenses associated with this obsolete inventory total $20,000 annually, expenses included in your forecasted data. These expenses affect you personally since you are entitled to a bonus each year equal to 10 percent of the amount that your division's operating income exceeds $1 million.

Your immediate superior is the vice-president of sales. This individual served several years as manager of the division that you now oversee. The two of you were promoted to your new positions at the same time. The vice-president is unhappy with your suggestion to write down your division's inventory by $100,000 since such a write-down would reflect poorly on his performance while he was divisional manager. Finally, he authorizes you to make the write-down if you insist. But he points out that the write-down will be included in cost of goods sold for Year 1, meaning that your bonus for that year will be reduced significantly. You immediately respond, "But that's not fair." The vice-president shrugs his shoulders indifferently and walks away.

Required: Compute your division's operating income and your bonus for the next three years under two assumptions: (1) the $100,000 write-down is taken for the obsolete inventory in Year 1 and (2) you retain the obsolete inventory without writing it down. Which of these two alternatives would be best for you? Which would be best for your company? (Ignore all tax and time value of money considerations and assume that the obsolete inventory can be disposed of at a nominal cost.) Do you believe the vice-president of sales has handled this matter properly? Explain. Would you discuss this matter with your company's chief executive? Why or why not?

QUESTIONS

1. Provide examples of how accountants can help their companies manage inventory.
2. Describe what is meant by the phrase "inventory cost flow."

3. Why is inventory always considered a current asset?
4. How is cost of goods available for sale determined for a merchandising company for a given accounting period?
5. For which type of companies, merchandisers or manufacturers, is inventory accounting more complex? Why?
6. Identify the key differences between a periodic and a perpetual inventory system.
7. Which type of inventory system, periodic or perpetual, has become increasingly popular in recent years? Why?
8. Define the shipping terms FOB shipping point and FOB destination for merchandising transactions. From the standpoint of the buyer, which terms are more advantageous? Why?
9. Identify the four most common inventory costing methods. Briefly describe each.
10. In a period of rising prices, which inventory costing method, FIFO or LIFO, generally yields the higher ending inventory value? Why?
11. Which inventory costing method, FIFO or LIFO, is generally considered the more appropriate method for balance sheet valuation purposes? Why?
12. Which inventory costing method, FIFO or LIFO, is generally considered the more appropriate method for income determination purposes? Why?
13. Briefly describe the lower-of-cost-or-market (LCM) rule.
14. Define "current replacement cost."
15. Describe three control activities commonly applied to inventory.
16. List the equations used to compute the inventory turnover ratio and the age of inventory.
17. How do decision makers use the inventory turnover ratio and the age of inventory when analyzing a company's financial data?
18. How do shipping terms determine whether a company includes in transit merchandise at year-end in ending inventory?
19. What is consigned inventory?
20. When a business uses the specific identification method of inventory costing, what information must it have available?
21. List the steps in applying the gross profit method of estimating inventory.
22. Why is the gross profit method of inventory estimation sometimes used to determine the dollar value of a business's inventory? Identify one key limitation of the gross profit method.

EXERCISES

Note: Unless indicated otherwise, Chapter 7 assignments assume that a perpetual inventory system is in use.

23. True or False (LO 1–8)

Following are a series of statements regarding topics discussed in Chapter 7.

Required:

Indicate whether each statement is true (T) or false (F).

_____ a. An error in a company's ending inventory balance automatically causes the following period's beginning inventory balance to be misstated.

_____ b. Companies may value inventory at current replacement cost if the historical cost of their inventory is lower than current replacement cost.

_____ c. The LIFO method of inventory costing assumes that the most recently acquired goods are sold first, while the oldest goods remain in inventory.

_____ d. Similar to perpetual FIFO and periodic FIFO, perpetual LIFO and periodic LIFO typically yield differing ending inventory and cost of goods sold amounts when applied to identical inventory data.

_____ e. When goods are shipped FOB destination, the seller is responsible for paying the transportation charges.

_____ f. Merchandising companies want to maintain as low an inventory turnover ratio as possible.

_____ g. Generally accepted accounting principles require a company to select the inventory cost flow assumption that most closely matches the physical flow of its goods.

_____ h. Consigned inventory items should be included in the physical inventory count at year-end.

_____ i. If a company uses the LIFO method of inventory costing for federal taxation purposes, it must also use LIFO for financial reporting purposes.

_____ j. Physical security controls are important control activities for inventory because of this asset's susceptibility to theft by customers and employees.

_____ k. Most companies provide only brief narrative disclosures in their annual reports regarding their inventories and their inventory accounting methods.

_____ l. In an inflationary economic environment, the FIFO inventory costing method typically yields a lower net income than the LIFO method when these methods are applied to the same financial data.

_____ m. If a firm has a highly variable gross profit percentage, estimates of inventory yielded by the gross profit method may be unreliable.

24. **Cost of Goods Available for Sale and Cost of Goods Sold** (LO 1, 2)
Ederington Enterprises is a merchandising company that uses a perpetual inventory system. At the end of each year, Ederington takes a physical inventory and adjusts its perpetual inventory records to agree with the results of the physical inventory. Following is selected financial information for 1998 for Ederington.

January 1, inventory	$150,000
Net merchandise purchases	625,000
December 31, inventory (perpetual inventory records)	125,000
December 31, inventory (physical inventory)	110,000

Required:

1. Prepare the appropriate year-end adjusting entry to bring Ederington's perpetual inventory records into agreement with the results of the physical inventory.
2. Compute Ederington's cost of goods available for sale and cost of goods sold for 1998.
3. How will the adjusting entry prepared in (1) affect Ederington's income statement for the year in question?
4. What factors may be responsible for the $15,000 difference between Ederington's perpetual inventory records and the dollar amount of inventory determined by the year-end physical count?

25. **Inventory Costing Methods** (LO 3)
Top of the World (TOW) is a retail store on Campus Corner that sells baseball caps. TOW had the following inventory purchases and sales during the year just ended:

	Units	Per Unit Cost	Per Unit Selling Price
Beginning inventory	1,000	$ 5	
Purchase, January 1	300	6	
Sales, first quarter	400		$12
Purchase, April 1	375	8	
Sales, second quarter	350		16
Purchase, July 1	400	9	
Sales, third quarter	500		17
Purchase, October 1	500	10	
Sales, fourth quarter	700		20

Required:
Determine TOW's ending inventory, cost of goods sold, and gross profit for the year in question assuming the company uses a perpetual inventory system and the following inventory costing methods:
1. FIFO
2. LIFO
3. Moving-average

26. **Lower-of-Cost-or-Market Rule** (LO 4)
Following is information regarding the year-end inventory of Madison County Steelworks.

Item	Quantity	Original Per Unit Cost	Replacement Cost Per Unit
Exgots	125	$17	$14
Ingots	100	12	13
Ongots	200	15	13
Ungots	50	20	19

Required:
1. Apply the lower-of-cost-or-market (LCM) rule to Madison County's ending inventory assuming that the company (a) uses the item-by-item version of that rule and (b) uses the total inventory version of that rule.
2. What accounting concept or concepts dictate that businesses apply the LCM rule?

27. **Analyzing Inventory** (LO 6)
Francesca Johnson owns and operates a sporting goods store. Listed next are selected financial data regarding Francesca's business over the past three years.

	Year 1	Year 2	Year 3
Sales	$280,000	$300,000	$330,000
Cost of goods sold	168,000	195,000	224,400
Net income	37,100	38,500	39,600
Ending inventory	80,000	110,000	130,000

Required:

1. Compute the inventory turnover ratio and age of inventory for Francesca's store for each year listed. (Note: On January 1, Year 1, the store's inventory was $60,000.)
2. Given the data provided and the ratios you computed in (1), evaluate Francesca's management of inventory over this three-year period.
3. Francesca is concerned by the slow growth in her business's net income in recent years. Given the data provided, identify factors that may be adversely affecting the business's profitability.

28. Perpetual vs. Periodic Inventory Systems (LO 2, 5, 7)

During July of the current year, Art's Auto Repair engaged in the following transactions involving car mirrors purchased from Prisms, Inc.:

July 1: Purchased ten car mirrors from Prisms, Inc., for $25 each, terms 2/10, n/30.
July 5: Sold six of the car mirrors on credit for $40 each, terms 1/10, n/30.
July 7: Two of the car mirrors sold on July 5 were returned by the customers because they were flawed.
July 9: Returned the two flawed car mirrors to Prisms, Inc.
July 11: Paid the amount due Prisms, Inc., for the car mirrors purchased on July 1.
July 15: Received full amount due from customer who purchased car mirrors on July 5.

Required:

1. Prepare the journal entries for each of the transactions listed, assuming that Art's Auto Repair uses a perpetual inventory system.
2. (Appendix) Prepare the journal entries for each of the transactions listed, assuming that Art's Auto Repair uses a periodic inventory system.
3. Suppose that Art's Auto Repair is a new business and has not yet selected an inventory accounting system. Write a brief memo to Art, the owner of the business, that identifies the factors he should consider in choosing between a periodic and perpetual inventory system. Include in your memo any relevant internal control issues that might influence Art's decision.

29. Income Statement Impact of Inventory Errors (LO 1, 2)

Robert Kincade owns and operates the Winterset Manufacturing Company. Following is the business's income statement for its most recent fiscal year.

Sales	$89,000
Cost of goods sold	31,000
Gross profit	$58,000
Operating expenses	10,000
Operating income	$48,000
Income taxes expense (30%)	14,400
Net income	$33,600

Shortly after the company's financial statements were distributed to external parties, Kincade's accountant discovered that the company's ending inventory had been inadvertently overstated by $12,000. This error stemmed from an oversight on the part of the accountant. The accountant forgot to record the year-end adjusting entry to bring the firm's perpetual inventory records into agreement with the results of the physical inventory. The perpetual inventory records reflected an inventory balance of $39,000, while the physical inventory yielded an ending inventory value of $27,000.

Required:

1. Prepare a corrected income statement for Winterset.
2. Suppose that Robert Kincade told his accountant to ignore the inventory error. "Why bother? The financial statements have already been issued, and besides, it was an honest error." Evaluate Kincade's decision. Has he behaved unethically? Why or why not? What parties may be affected by Kincade's decision? Explain.

30. **Analyzing Inventory** (LO 6)
Thiokol Corporation is a leading firm in the aerospace and defense industries. A recent annual report described one of the company's major products as "high-technology solid rockets for aerospace, defense, and commercial launch applications." Following are selected financial data (in millions) taken from that annual report.

	Year 1	Year 2	Year 3
Net sales	$1,311.7	$1,201.7	$1,043.9
Cost of goods sold	1,122.4	996.4	860.4
Net income	63.0	63.8	63.0
Ending inventory	164.0	118.4	121.9

Required:

1. Compute the inventory turnover ratio and age of inventory for Thiokol for each of the years listed. The company's inventory balance at the beginning of Year 1 was $153 million.
2. Did Thiokol's inventory ratios improve or deteriorate between Year 1 and Year 3? Explain.
3. In recent years, many companies in the aerospace and defense industries have been forced to "downsize." Is such downsizing evident in Thiokol's financial statements? Explain.

31. **Analyzing Inventory** (LO 6)
Listed next are Outback Steakhouse's total inventories at the end of three recent fiscal years.

December 31, 1994	$ 5,228,000
December 31, 1995	6,474,000
December 31, 1996	16,637,000

Required:

1. Refer to Outback's annual report that is included as an appendix to this text. Compute Outback's inventory turnover ratio for 1995 and 1996 and the firm's age of inventory at the end of each of those years. (Note: Outback's "Cost of revenues" is equivalent to cost of goods sold.)
2. Why would potential investors in Outback's common stock be interested in tracking the two inventory ratios you computed in (1)?
3. Did Outback's two inventory ratios improve or worsen during 1996? Explain.

32. ***(Appendix)*** **In-Transit Inventory** (LO 2, 7)
Victoria's Supply, a retail office supply company, both buys and sells goods on credit. At the end of each year, Victoria's typically has a significant amount of inventory in transit. Suppose that the merchandise Victoria's either bought or sold in the following transactions is in transit on December 31 of the current year.

a. Purchased goods on December 30, FOB shipping point.
b. Sold goods on December 29, FOB shipping point.
c. Sold goods on December 30, FOB destination.
d. Purchased goods on December 28, FOB destination.

Required:
Which in-transit items listed should be included in Victoria's December 31 inventory?

33. (*Appendix*) **Inventory Costing in a Periodic Inventory System** (LO 7)
Little Joe's T-Shirts is a retail store specializing in one-size-fits-all "Super T's." This business uses a periodic inventory system. Listed next is information regarding Little Joe's inventory during a recent year.

January 1	Beginning Inventory	100 T's @ $ 9 each	$ 900
March 15	Purchase	150 T's @ $10 each	1,500
July 20	Purchase	70 T's @ $ 9 each	630
December 10	Purchase	50 T's @ $11 each	550
Cost of Goods Available for Sale		370 T's	$3,580
Total Sales During the Year		260 T's @ $20	$5,200
Ending Inventory on December 31		110 T's @ $? each	$?

Required:
1. Compute Little Joe's ending inventory and cost of goods sold under each of the following assumptions:
   a. Little Joe's uses the specific identification method. Ending inventory consists of 60 T-shirts purchased on March 15 and 50 T-shirts purchased on December 10.
   b. Little Joe's uses the weighted-average inventory costing method.
2. The nature of a business often dictates the type of inventory costing method it uses. Identify two types of businesses that might use the specific identification costing method and two types of businesses that might use the weighted-average costing method.

34. (*Appendix*) **Inventory Costing in a Periodic Inventory System** (LO 7)
Refer to the information presented in Exercise 33.

Required:
1. Compute Little Joe's ending inventory and cost of goods sold assuming the business uses the:
   a. FIFO inventory costing method.
   b. LIFO inventory costing method.
2. Comment briefly on the advantages and disadvantages commonly associated with the FIFO and LIFO costing methods.

35. (*Appendix*) **Gross Profit Method of Estimating Inventory** (LO 8)
A fire destroyed Countess Company's inventory on October 1 of this year. For insurance purposes, Countess must estimate the dollar value of the inventory that was destroyed. Following is information obtained from Countess's accounting records.

Inventory, January 1	$100,000
Net purchases through October 1	350,000
Sales through October 1	600,000
Historical gross profit percentage	60%

Required:
Using the gross profit method, estimate the amount of inventory that Countess Company lost in the fire.

PROBLEM SET A

36. **Effects of Inventory Errors** (LO 1, 5)
Maxwell Machinery is a wholesale distributor of engine parts. This company is privately owned by two sisters, Laura Lambert and Jean Campeaux. Maxwell has a $300,000 loan outstanding from a local bank. The loan agreement requires the company to submit annual financial statements to the bank for its review. Following are Maxwell's income statements for 1997 and 1998.

	1997	1998
Sales	$620,000	$655,000
Cost of goods sold	299,000	391,000
Gross profit	$321,000	$264,000
Operating expenses	127,000	130,000
Operating income	$194,000	$134,000
Income taxes expense (40%)	77,600	53,600
Net income	$116,400	$ 80,400

In early 1998, shortly before Maxwell's 1997 financial statements were completed, Lambert and Campeaux discovered a large theft of inventory by a warehouse supervisor. This individual stole approximately $40,000 of goods and then sold them to an individual who allegedly smuggled the goods into Mexico. The theft occurred in June but went undetected until the results of the December 31, 1997, physical inventory had been tabulated. Maxwell's accountant failed to discover the theft because the warehouse supervisor also maintained the warehouse's perpetual inventory records.

Lambert and Campeaux did not prosecute the warehouse supervisor who had stolen the goods to obtain funds needed to support his drug habit. The owners agreed not to prosecute on the condition that the supervisor would check himself into a drug rehabilitation center. By settling the matter privately, the owners avoided publicly disclosing the incident. On the advice of their accountant, the owners also decided to report their business's year-end inventory for 1997 as $154,000, which was the amount reflected by the perpetual inventory records. The physical inventory had yielded a year-end dollar value of $114,000. "Don't worry about it," the accountant observed. "We will report the proper inventory balance at the end of 1998 and that will fix everything." (Recognize that the overstatement of the 1997 year-end inventory resulted in a $40,000 understatement of cost of goods sold for 1997 and a $40,000 overstatement of cost of goods sold for 1998.)

Required:

1. Prepare corrected income statements for Maxwell Machinery for 1997 and 1998. Compute the percentage misstatements in Maxwell's net income for 1997 and 1998 due to the failure to properly account for the $40,000 theft of inventory.
2. What effect did the overstatement of inventory have on Maxwell's total assets and owners' equity reported in its 1997 and 1998 balance sheets? How may these errors and the errors identified in (1) have impacted Maxwell's bank?
3. What internal control activities might have prevented or led to more timely disclosure of the inventory theft?
4. Did the owners behave ethically by failing to correct their company's accounting records at the end of 1997? Does the fact that their accountant advised them to ignore the error affect your answer? Why or why not?

37. Journalizing Transactions in a Perpetual Inventory System (LO 2)
House of Jeans is a retail store that specializes in denim jeans. This business uses a perpetual inventory system. Following are selected transactions of the House of Jeans for a recent month.

April 6:	Purchased thirty pairs of 404 Jeans with terms of 2/10, n/30; the per unit cost was $22.
April 9:	Returned ten pairs of the 404 Jeans purchased on April 6 due to fabric flaws.
April 13:	Sold two pairs of 303 Jeans for cash; the per unit cost of these jeans was $21. (House of Jeans has a "one price fits all" pricing strategy. All jeans are sold for $35 per pair.)
April 16:	Paid amount due supplier for jeans purchased on April 6.
April 17:	Purchased twelve pairs of 606 Jeans with terms of 2/10, n/30; the per unit cost was $18.
April 20:	Sold one pair of 909 Jeans on credit; the cost of this pair was $24.
April 21:	A customer returned a pair of 808 Jeans because they were the wrong size; the jeans, which cost $20, were returned to inventory.
April 27:	Sold two pairs of 101 Jeans on credit; the per unit cost of these jeans was $17.
April 27:	Paid amount due supplier for jeans purchased on April 17.

Required:
Prepare the journal entries necessary to record the listed transactions of House of Jeans.

38. Internal Control Activities for Inventory (LO 5)
Bob Goldstein owns and operates House of Jeans, the business referred to in Problem 37. Bob employs one full-time salesclerk, three part-time salesclerks who are high-school students, and a part-time accountant who is an accounting major at the local university. House of Jeans does not have a formal credit policy. Bob has given his salesclerks the following instructions when customers ask for credit: "If you know them, then give them credit." Bob's accountant, the accounting major, established a perpetual inventory system for the House of Jeans. Since the House of Jeans does not have a large volume of transactions, the accountant updates the business's accounting records when the in-basket on his desk is full of purchase invoices, return memos, and other source documents.

Besides the House of Jeans, Bob Goldstein also owns two other businesses in town, a convenience store and a hamburger stand located across the street from the high school. Typically, Bob spends ten to fifteen hours per week at each business, helping with sales, resolving employee problems, and so on.

On April 30 of the current year, House of Jeans took a physical inventory. Bob was shocked to find that his store's inventory was only $12,080. The store's perpetual inventory records indicated that $15,600 of inventory should have been on hand. Two years earlier, when the inventory was last counted, the dollar value reported by the business's perpetual inventory records had exceeded the dollar value determined by the physical inventory by less than $100.

Bob Goldstein is very concerned about the large difference between the dollar value of inventory as determined by the physical inventory and the corresponding amount reflected by the perpetual inventory records. He has retained you to develop a report identifying inventory-related internal control weaknesses existing at the House of Jeans. Bob has also asked you to include in your report specific control activities that he could adopt to tighten the business's control over inventory.

Required:
Write the report that Bob Goldstein has requested.

39. Lower-of-Cost-or-Market Rule (LO 1, 4)
Best Plumbing, Inc., sells plumbing fixtures. The company had the following inventory quantities, per unit costs, and per unit market values (current replacement costs) at the end of a recent fiscal year.

	Units	Per Unit Cost	Per Unit Market Value
Industrial Strength			
Item A	100	$160	$150
Item B	150	200	205
Medium Strength			
Item C	75	120	125
Item D	110	140	125
Low Strength			
Item E	80	80	80
Item F	130	75	70

Required:
1. Compute Best Plumbing's ending inventory by applying the item-by-item version of the lower-of-cost-or-market (LCM) rule.
2. Briefly describe how the application of the LCM rule will affect the financial statement data of Best Plumbing Supplies.
3. In your view, which of the following inventory valuation methods would provide the most relevant and reliable accounting data for external decision makers: valuing inventories strictly on a cost basis, valuing inventories strictly on a market basis, or valuing inventories on a lower-of-cost-or-market basis. Defend your choice.

40. Analyzing Inventory (LO 1, 6)
Cracker Barrel Old Country Store, Inc., is a Tennessee-based company that operates a large chain of restaurants. The following information was taken from a recent annual report of the firm.

	Year 1	Year 2	Year 3
Net sales	$400,577,451	$517,616,132	$640,898,529
Cost of goods sold	130,885,297	171,708,439	215,071,169
Net income	33,942,848	46,652,485	57,947,446
Ending inventory	23,192,110	28,426,408	41,989,546

Required:
1. Compute Cracker Barrel's inventory turnover ratio and age of inventory for Year 1 through Year 3. (The company's beginning inventory for Year 1 was $15,746,448.)
2. Comment on the ratios you computed in (1). Are there any definite trends in these ratios? If so, are these trends favorable or unfavorable? Explain.
3. Why do decision makers pay close attention to the age of inventory statistic for companies in the restaurant industry?

41. Inventory Costing Methods (LO 1, 3)
The following schedule summarizes the inventory purchases and sales of Brooks Street Enterprises during the year just ended:

	Units	Per Unit Cost	Per Unit Selling Price
Beginning inventory	400	$20	
Purchase, January 1	200	22	
Sales, first quarter	300		$40
Purchase, April 1	200	24	
Sales, second quarter	350		45
Purchase, July 1	200	25	
Sales, third quarter	150		45
Purchase, October 1	500	26	
Sales, fourth quarter	450		50

Required:

1. Determine Brooks Street's ending inventory, cost of goods sold, and gross profit for the year in question assuming the company uses a perpetual inventory system and the following inventory costing methods:
   a. FIFO
   b. LIFO
   c. Moving-average
2. Which of the three inventory costing methods yields the most impressive financial data for Brooks Street? Explain.
3. What factors should a company consider when choosing an inventory costing method? Should one of these factors be the inventory costing method preferred by the decision makers who will be using the company's financial statements?

42. (*Appendix*) **Inventory Costing Methods in a Periodic Inventory System** (LO 7)
Refer to the data presented in Problem 41 for Brooks Street Enterprises.

Required:

1. Determine Brooks Street's ending inventory, cost of goods sold, and gross profit assuming the company uses a periodic inventory system and the following inventory costing methods:
   a. FIFO
   b. LIFO
   c. Weighted-average
2. Identify the comparative advantages and disadvantages of periodic and perpetual inventory systems.

43. (*Appendix*) **Gross Profit Method of Estimating Inventory** (LO 8)
Louisa's Books is a large bookstore located in a local mall. The owner of this business, May Alcott, and her employees take an annual physical inventory on December 31. At the end of each quarter, other than year-end, Ms. Alcott uses the gross profit method to estimate the business's inventory since perpetual inventory records are not maintained. The following information is available for a recent quarter ending on September 30:

Beginning inventory, July 1	$ 72,000
Net purchases	123,000
Net sales	154,000
Normal gross profit percentage	40%

Required:

1. Estimate this business's cost of goods sold for the quarter ending September 30 and the inventory on that date applying the gross profit method.
2. May Alcott has determined that it costs her approximately $400 to take a physical inventory of her store at the end of each year. So, she is considering using the gross profit method to determine her year-end inventory. Is this a good idea? Why or why not?

PROBLEM SET B

44. Effects of Inventory Errors (LO 1)

Drexel & Clyde, Inc., operates a small chain of specialty stores that sell greeting cards, ceramic dolls, stuffed animals, and novelty gift items. Competition has been stiff in recent years for Drexel & Clyde, a company owned for four decades by two longtime friends. Over the past five years, a publicly owned company has begun building stores in Drexel & Clyde's market area. These new stores have caused Drexel & Clyde's annual sales to decline by nearly 40 percent.

During late 1997, the two owners began negotiations to sell Drexel & Clyde to their principal competitor. To improve their chances of obtaining a reasonable price for their company, the owners decided to "doctor" the firm's 1997 financial statements by overstating ending inventory for the year by $60,000 and understating cost of goods sold for the year by the same amount. They justified this decision to themselves by observing that if the competitor hadn't moved into their market area, their company's financial statements would have been much more impressive. "Besides," remarked one of the owners, "a large company like that is not going to be hurt by paying a little more than it should for our business."

In late 1998, the two owners were finalizing a buy-out agreement with their competitor. Before closing the deal, the other firm insisted on an audit of Drexel & Clyde's financial statements as of the end of 1998. Shown next are Drexel & Clyde's 1997 income statement and the audited 1998 income statement. (Recognize that the company's 1997 cost of goods sold is understated by $60,000, while the firm's 1998 cost of goods sold is overstated by $60,000. Both of these errors are due to the intentional overstatement of the year-end inventory for 1997.)

	1997	1998
Sales	$904,300	$862,000
Cost of goods sold	426,000	537,000
Gross profit	$478,300	$325,000
Operating expenses	241,000	221,000
Operating income	$237,300	$104,000
Income taxes expense (40%)	94,920	41,600
Net Income	$142,380	$ 62,400

Required:

1. Prepare corrected income statements for Drexel & Clyde for 1997 and 1998.
2. Compute the percentage decrease in Drexel & Clyde's reported net income in 1998 compared with the previous year. Compute the actual percentage decrease (or increase) in the company's 1998 net income compared with the previous year.

3. Do you believe the two owners' plan to increase the selling price of their business worked, or did it likely backfire on them? Explain.
4. Analyze the reasons used by the owners to rationalize their distortion of Drexel & Clyde's 1997 financial statements. Do you believe those reasons justified the owners' actions? Why or why not?

45. Journalizing Transactions in a Perpetual Inventory System (LO 2)

Roth, Inc., is a jewelry wholesaler specializing in diamond pendants, bracelets, and earrings. Roth uses a perpetual inventory system. Following are selected transactions of Roth during November.

November 2:	Sold three diamond pendants for $450 each to Loew's Jewelry with terms of 3/10, n/60; the pendants cost $200 each.
November 5:	Purchased ten diamond bracelets for $250 each from Horne Diamonds with terms of 2/10, n/30.
November 8:	Returned two of the diamond bracelets purchased on November 5 due to flaws.
November 9:	Sold five of the diamond bracelets purchased on November 5; selling price was $550 per unit with terms of n/30.
November 10:	Purchased thirty pairs of diamond earrings for $100 each from Gems Unlimited with terms of 3/10, n/60.
November 12:	Received payment in full from Loew's Jewelry for November 2 sales transaction.
November 14:	Sold ten diamond pendants for $500 each to Carr's Jewelry Stores with terms of 2/10, n/60; the pendants cost $200 each.
November 15:	Paid amount due Horne Diamonds for bracelets purchased on November 5.
November 19:	Carr's Jewelry Stores returned five of the pendants purchased on November 14 because they were not the style ordered.
November 20:	Paid amount due Gems Unlimited for earrings purchased on November 10.
November 24:	Received payment in full from Carr's Jewelry Stores for November 14 sales transaction.

Required:

Prepare the journal entries necessary to record the November transactions of Roth, Inc.

46. Internal Control Activities for Inventory (LO 5)

Christine Theroff owns Roth, Inc., the jewelry wholesaler referred to in Problem 45. Because of the nature of its inventory, Roth uses a perpetual inventory system. The company's inventory is maintained in a small warehouse located near its corporate headquarters. On November 30 of the current year, Roth's perpetual inventory records reflected a balance of $1,564,200. Following the taking of a physical inventory on that date, Roth's accountant determined that there was $1,511,900 of inventory on hand. Ms. Theroff is concerned by the large difference between the dollar value of inventory as determined by the physical inventory and the corresponding dollar value reflected by the perpetual inventory records. She has retained you to identify a list of control activities that could be implemented to safeguard the inventory maintained in the company's warehouse and to help ensure the accuracy of the perpetual inventory records.

Required:

Write a memo to Christine Theroff that includes the list of control activities she requested.

47. Lower-of-Cost-or-Market Rule (LO 1, 4)

Don Monroe owns and operates Opie's, Inc., a beverage distribution company. Opie's had the following inventory quantities, per unit costs, and per unit market values (current replacement costs) at the end of a recent fiscal year.

	Units	Per Unit Cost	Per Unit Market Value
Colas			
Item A	600	$180	$170
Item B	800	170	190
Non-colas			
Item C	450	120	130
Item D	500	140	150
Diet Drinks			
Item E	700	70	75
Item F	850	85	65

Required:

1. Compute Opie's ending inventory by applying the item-by-item version of the LCM rule.
2. Suppose that Opie's fails to apply the LCM rule to its inventory for the year in question. How will this oversight affect the business's financial statements? How may the decisions of those parties who rely on the business's financial statements be affected by this oversight?

48. Analyzing Inventory (LO 6)

Dress Barn, Inc., is a public company based in New York. A recent annual report described the nature of the firm's business as follows: "The Dress Barn, Inc., operates a chain of off-price women's apparel stores. Dress Barn emphasizes department store quality merchandise, primarily with nationally recognized brand names at substantial discounts from department store prices." The following financial information was taken from the company's annual report.

	Year 1	Year 2	Year 3
Net sales	$363,089,914	$419,585,581	$457,324,621
Cost of goods sold	231,829,749	266,867,616	291,937,984
Net income	16,194,118	19,039,260	16,153,216
Ending inventory	66,332,215	73,403,238	79,601,016

Required:

1. Compute Dress Barn's inventory turnover ratio and age of inventory for Year 1 through Year 3. (The company's beginning inventory for Year 1 was $48,427,296.)
2. Comment on the ratios you computed in (1). Are there any definite trends in these ratios? If so, are these trends favorable or unfavorable? Explain.
3. Consider the nature of the women's apparel industry. How may sudden changes in fashion trends be reflected in the inventory ratios of a company within this industry? Explain.

49. Inventory Costing Methods (LO 3)
J. Austin Enterprises (JAE) had the following inventory purchases and sales during the year just ended:

	Units	Per Unit Cost	Per Unit Selling Price
Beginning inventory	400	$20	
Purchase, January 1	200	24	
Sales, first quarter	300		$40
Purchase, April 1	200	22	
Sales, second quarter	350		45
Purchase, July 1	300	25	
Sales, third quarter	200		45
Purchase, October 1	400	23	
Sales, fourth quarter	450		50

Required:
1. Determine JAE's ending inventory, cost of goods sold, and gross profit for the year in question assuming the company uses a perpetual inventory system and the following inventory costing methods:
   a. FIFO
   b. LIFO
   c. Moving-average
2. Given your answers to (1), which of the three inventory costing methods yields the most impressive financial data for JAE? Explain.
3. If a company uses LIFO for federal taxation purposes, it must also use LIFO for financial reporting purposes. What is the purpose of this rule? Why isn't there a similar rule for FIFO?

50. (*Appendix*) Inventory Costing Methods in a Periodic Inventory System (LO 7)
Refer to the data presented in Problem 49 for J. Austin Enterprises (JAE).

Required:
1. Determine JAE's ending inventory, cost of goods sold, and gross profit assuming the company uses a periodic inventory system and the following inventory costing methods:
   a. FIFO
   b. LIFO
   c. Weighted-average
2. Briefly explain why periodic FIFO and perpetual FIFO yield the same ending inventory and cost of goods sold figures when applied to the same set of data. Likewise, explain why this is not true for periodic LIFO and perpetual LIFO.

51. (*Appendix*) Gross Profit Method of Estimating Inventory (LO 8)
Grass Point Lighthouse Supplies operates out of an old lighthouse on the coast of Maine. A once-in-a-century high tide has wiped out most of the business's inventory at midyear. Grass Point uses a periodic inventory system and keeps good accounting records, which fortunately were not lost in the flood. However, a physical count of inventory has not been taken since the beginning of the year.

Grass Point's insurance company has requested documentation for the amount of inventory lost in the flood. Following is information regarding Grass Point's inventory at the beginning of the year and inventory-related transactions from that point through the date of the loss:

Inventory, January 1	$ 75,000
Net purchases	238,300
Net sales	361,200

Note: Grass Point's gross profit percentages for the past three years are 42 percent, 48 percent, and 33 percent, respectively.

Required:

1. Estimate the inventory loss of Grass Point by applying the gross profit method. Use the business's average gross profit percentage for the past three years in making this computation.
2. Recompute the amount of inventory lost by Grass Point using its highest gross profit percentage (48 percent) for the past three years and its lowest gross profit percentage (33 percent) over that period.
3. Given your answers to (1) and (2), comment on the reliability of the inventory data yielded by the gross profit method.

CASES

52. Inventory Errors and Job Protection (LO 1)

Reread the Spotlight on Ethics vignette in this chapter entitled "Cooking the Books at MiniScribe."

Required:

1. Assume that some of MiniScribe's employees were being pressured by company executives to assist in overstating the firm's inventory. Place yourself in the position of one of these employees. What would you have done in that situation?
2. Again, place yourself in the position of the MiniScribe employees being pressured by company executives, but assume the following additional facts, considered independently:
   a. The officers believed that the company would eventually fail and the company's employees would lose their jobs unless ending inventory was overstated.
   b. The officers guaranteed you that the inventory overstatement would not be discovered or disclosed outside the company.
   c. The officers were convinced that the company would earn sufficient profits in the future to "wipe out" the illicit profits resulting from the intentional inventory overstatement.

Given these additional facts, would your answer to (1) change? Why or why not?

53. Inventory Errors and Materiality (LO 1)

Following are financial data (in thousands) for a recent fiscal year of Wm. Wrigley Jr. Company, the "chewing gum" company.

Net sales	$1,596,551
Cost of goods sold	697,442
Net income	230,533
Inventory	221,109

Listed next are comparable data (in thousands) drawn from a recent annual report of Whole Foods Market, a food retailer based in Austin, Texas.

Net sales	$401,684
Cost of goods sold	272,176
Net Income	8,638
Inventory	17,187

Note: For purposes of this case, assume that both companies have an effective income tax rate of 40 percent.

Required:

1. Suppose that the ending inventory of both Wrigley and Whole Foods was overstated by 5 percent. Refer to the concept of materiality discussed in Chapter 2. Did the (assumed) inventory error result in a material misrepresentation of either company's profitability for the year in question? Explain.
2. Suppose that the ending inventory of both Wrigley and Whole Foods was overstated by $7 million. Did the (assumed) inventory error result in a material misrepresentation of either company's profitability for the year in question? Explain.

54. **Meeting Profit Expectations** (LO 1)

Morehead Company did not meet its profit goal for Year 1, which ended today. At the previous stockholders' meeting, Morehead's chief executive officer (CEO) practically guaranteed that the firm would earn at least $1.2 million in Year 1. Preliminary financial data suggest that the company earned approximately $850,000 for the year. Since Year 1 has just ended, there is nothing Morehead can do to change the situation . . . or is there?

Morehead's annual physical inventory, which requires three days to complete, is in progress for Year 1. Morehead's independent auditors are busy going from warehouse to warehouse monitoring the counting of thousands of cartons and crates of merchandise. However, the auditors are unaware that each night several Morehead officers, including the CEO, are moving a large number of unmarked cartons and crates from warehouses that have been counted to warehouses that will be counted the following day.

Required:

1. How will the treachery of Morehead's officers affect the company's financial statements for Year 1?
2. Suppose the inventory scam goes undetected and Morehead reports a net income of slightly more than $1.2 million for Year 1 at the next stockholders' meeting. Also, assume that Morehead's CEO guarantees at the next stockholders' meeting that the company will earn $1.5 million during Year 2. How will the inventory scam perpetrated by Morehead's officers at the end of Year 1 affect the company's likelihood of legitimately reaching its profit objective for Year 2? Explain.
3. How might Morehead's independent auditors have prevented or detected the inventory scam?

55. **Applying the Lower-of-Cost-or-Market Rule** (LO 4)

Mega Computers produces a wide array of products used in the manufacture of personal computers. Recently, one of Mega's products became obsolete because a technologically advanced product was introduced by a competitor. Presently, Mega has 5,000 units of this product in inventory at a collective (FIFO) cost of $1,500,000. Mega plans to sell these units early next year for $110 each to a foreign firm that manufactures "clones" of U.S.-made personal computers. Mega will be required to pay freight charges of $14 per unit to deliver these items. Previously, this product was sold for $440 per unit by Mega with shipping terms of FOB shipping point.

Required:

At what value do you believe Mega should report the inventory of the obsolete product in its balance sheet? Defend your answer by referring to one or more accounting concepts or principles.

PROJECTS

56. International Inventory Accounting Practices

Refer to the For Your Information vignette entitled "Inventory Costing Methods in Europe." You and your project group will research the inventory accounting rules and practices of several foreign countries, using your college library as your principal source of information. These countries will be assigned to you by your instructor or selected by your group—do not choose countries mentioned in the vignette.

Required:

1. Each member of your group should identify a foreign country and research the inventory-related accounting rules and practices applied in that country. Examples of information that should be collected for each country include the acceptable inventory costing methods, the dominant inventory costing method, whether a version of the lower-of-cost-or-market rule is applied, mandatory financial statement disclosures for inventory, and so on.
2. Meet as a group and compare and contrast the information collected for each country. Which two countries of those researched by group members have the most similar accounting rules and practices for inventory? Which two countries have the most dissimilar inventory accounting rules and practices? As a group, identify factors that may account for the similarities and differences in inventory accounting rules and practices across the countries considered.
3. Your group should prepare a brief written report that summarizes the information collected in (1) and the results of the group discussion in (2). One group member should be prepared to present an oral summary of the report to the class.

57. Ethics, Inventory Controls, and College Students

Suzette Washington financed her college education by working as an inventory clerk for Bertolini's, a clothing store chain located in the southeastern United States. Bertolini's caters primarily to fashion-conscious young men and women. The Bertolini's store for which Suzette worked is located a few blocks from the campus of the large state university that she attended. Except for management personnel, most of Bertolini's employees are college students. Suzette's best friend and roommate, Paula Kaye, worked for Bertolini's as a salesclerk. Paula majored in marketing, while Suzette was an accounting major.

During Suzette's senior year in college, Bertolini's began experiencing abnormally high inventory shrinkage in the store's three departments that stocked men's apparel. Over lunch one day in the student union, Suzette casually mentioned the inventory problem to Paula. Paula quickly changed the subject by asking Suzette about her plans for the weekend.

"Paula, rewind for just a second. Do you know something that I don't?"

"Huh? What do you mean?"

"Missing inventory . . . shrinkage . . . theft?"

After a few awkward moments, Paula responded to her friend. "Suzette, I don't know if it's true, but I've heard a rumor that Alex and Matt are stealing a few things each week—polo shirts, silk ties, jeans. Every so often, they take something expensive, like a sports jacket."

"How are they doing it?"

"I've heard—and don't repeat any of this, now—I've heard that a couple of times per week, Alex stashes one or two items at the bottom of the trash container beneath the number two cash register. Then, Matt empties the trash in the dumpster in the back alley, pulls out the merchandise, and puts it in his car."

"Paula, we can't let them get away with this. We have to tell someone."

"No 'we' don't. Remember, this is just a rumor. I don't know that it's true. If you tell a manager, there will be questions. And more questions. Maybe even the police will be brought in. You know that eventually someone is going to find out who told."

"So, don't get involved? Just let those guys keep stealing?"

"Suze, you work in inventory. You know the markup they put on those clothes. They expect to lose a few things here and there to employees."

"Maybe the markup wouldn't be so high if theft wasn't a problem."

Now there was no doubt in Paula's mind that Suzette was going to tattle. "Two months, Suze. Two months till we graduate. Can you wait till then to spill the beans? Then we can move out of state before our cars are spray-painted."

One week following Suzette and Paula's conversation, a Bertolini's store manager received an anonymous typed message informing her of the two-person theft ring allegedly operating within the store. Bertolini's immediately hired a private detective. Over a four-week period, the detective documented the theft by Alex and Matt of merchandise with a retail value of approximately $500. After the police were notified, criminal charges were filed against the two young men.

Note: This vignette was adapted from an actual situation documented in the following source: M. C. Knapp, "Suzette Washington, Accounting Major," in *Contemporary Auditing: Issues and Cases,* 2d ed. (Minneapolis/St. Paul: West Publishing Co., 1996).

Required:

1. Meet with the members of your project group to discuss the following questions:
   a. What would you do if you found yourself in Suzette's position?
   b. Would it have been unethical for Suzette to report to a store manager what she had been told, considering that it was only a rumor? Would it have been unethical for Suzette not to report to a store manager what she had been told?
   c. Accounting majors are preparing to enter a profession recognized as having one of the strongest and most rigorously enforced ethical codes. Given this fact, do you believe that accounting majors have a greater responsibility than other business majors to behave ethically?
   d. What control activities might have prevented the theft losses suffered by Bertolini's?
2. One member of your group should be prepared to present to the class a brief oral summary of the group's discussion of this vignette and the questions included in (1).

58. Inventory Disclosures

Identify three companies in three different industries that make their financial statements available on the Internet. These financial statements may be available from the companies' Web sites or from the EDGAR (electronic data gathering and retrieval system) Web site maintained by the Securities and Exchange Commission. Access via the Internet the most recent financial statements and accompanying footnotes for each of these companies. Identify for each company the financial statement footnote disclosures regarding inventory.

Required:

Prepare a report containing the following items:

a. A summary of the inventory accounting policies of each company you selected.
b. A discussion of the factors that may account for the different inventory accounting policies used by these firms.
c. A discussion of how the different inventory accounting policies of the companies you selected may affect their reported profits.
d. The Web site addresses from which you obtained the required data for each firm.

Property, Plant & Equipment, and Intangible Assets

8

"It is said that one machine can do the work of fifty ordinary men. No machine, however, can do the work of one extraordinary man."
Tehyi Hsieh

LEARNING OBJECTIVES

After studying this chapter, you should be able to do the following:

1. Identify the key information needs of decision makers regarding property, plant & equipment.
2. Determine the acquisition cost of property, plant & equipment assets.
3. Compute depreciation expense using each of three major depreciation methods.
4. Distinguish between and account for revenue and capital expenditures.
5. Account for disposals of property, plant & equipment.
6. Discuss key control activities for property, plant & equipment.
7. Compute return on assets and the total asset turnover ratio.
8. Identify major types of intangible assets and the key accounting issues related to these assets.

FOCUS ON DECISION MAKING

Building Af*ford*able Cars

Suppose we used a popular game show format of recent years and asked 100 people to identify a corporate asset. "Machinery" would likely be the most popular response. The fastest growing sector of the U.S. economy is service industries. Nevertheless, the public still largely equates corporate America with towering smokestacks, long assembly lines, and noisy machinery.

Probably the person most responsible for creating the public's perception of corporate America is Henry Ford. Born on a farm near Detroit in 1863, Ford enjoyed tinkering with anything mechanical as a young boy. One of Ford's first jobs after he left home at age sixteen was repairing watches. In his early twenties, Ford landed a job with Edison Electric Lighting and Power Company. While working at that job, Ford met the company's founder, the famed inventor Thomas Edison. Ford discussed with Edison a project on which he had been working for several years, a gasoline-driven automobile. At the time, most leading engineers believed that to be commercially feasible an automobile would have to be powered by electricity. Surprisingly, Edison expressed interest in the project and encouraged Ford to pursue it.

In 1896, Ford took his first automobile for a spin on the streets of Detroit. A few years later, Ford quit his job with the Edison firm to establish an automobile company. That company soon failed, but Ford quickly organized another. Following a dispute with investors, Ford resigned from this second firm after only three months. This latter firm would eventually become the Cadillac Motor Car Company, which in turn would later become a prominent division of General Motors. Finally, at the age of forty, Henry Ford established a company he could call his own, and he did. The Ford Motor Company was founded in 1903 with two key assets: $28,000 in cash and the engineering genius of Henry Ford.

Ford decided that to be successful, his company would have to produce cars that the general public could afford. With this objective in mind, Ford perfected the concept of low-cost, mass production based on techniques and theories developed by numerous inventors, engineers, and economists. In 1914, a Ford plant in a Detroit suburb began operating the first large-scale, mechanized assembly line in the United States. This assembly line allowed the company's principal product, the Model T Ford, to be built in ninety minutes, a fraction of the time required under previous production methods. In 1908, Ford produced less than 10 percent of all automobiles sold in the United States. By 1914, following the introduction of the mechanized assembly line, Ford had captured one-half of the U.S. automobile market.

In this chapter, we focus on accounting issues for long-term assets such as those used on Henry Ford's assembly line. Business executives rely on accountants to provide them with a wide range of data regarding their firms' long-term assets. As you will learn in this chapter, external decision makers also rely on accountants to provide them with key information regarding the long-term assets of business enterprises.

In Chapter 2, assets were defined as probable future economic benefits obtained or controlled by a particular entity as a result of past transactions or events. Chapters 6 and 7 acquainted you with accounting issues for current assets including accounts receivable and inventory. Now, we turn our attention to long-term assets. The key difference between current and long-term assets is the timeframe over which these assets provide economic benefits to a business. Current assets provide economic benefits to a business over the coming twelve months, or the business's operating cycle, whichever is longer. Long-term assets typically provide economic benefits to a business for several years, if not several decades.

Those of you with an excellent long-term memory will recall that in Chapter 2 we identified four general types of long-term or noncurrent assets: property, plant & equipment; intangible assets; long-term investments; and other assets. This chapter principally concerns property, plant & equipment. The last section of this chapter provides a brief overview of accounting issues related to intangible assets. Long-term investments are discussed in Chapter 13. We do not consider "other assets," a catchall classification for miscellaneous and minor long-term assets.

PROPERTY, PLANT & EQUIPMENT: FORMERLY FIXED ASSETS ▲

Businesses typically classify the long-term assets used in their day-to-day operations as **property, plant & equipment** on their balance sheets. "Plant assets" and "operating assets" are among other balance sheet captions for this broad class of long-term assets. The cumbersome phrase "property, plant & equipment" is often shortened in this chapter to "PP&E," a term commonly used by accountants. A few decades ago, "fixed assets" was the most common balance sheet heading for these assets. However, the accounting profession in the United States decided that caption was too vague and encouraged businesses to replace it with a more descriptive term. Nevertheless, many accountants still refer to fixed assets in everyday conversation. Likewise, the annual reports of many foreign companies refer to fixed assets. Telecom Corporation of New Zealand recently reported "Fixed Assets" with a balance sheet value expressed in U.S. currency of nearly $2.3 billion.

property, plant & equipment

The following schedule presents an example of a PP&E section of a balance sheet. This example was drawn from a recent annual report of Community Psychiatric Centers (CPC), a California-based firm. The actual heading used for this section of CPC's balance sheet was "Property, Buildings and Equipment." Notice that accumulated depreciation was subtracted from the total cost of the company's PP&E assets to arrive at their net balance sheet value of approximately $354 million.

Land	$ 51,598,000
Buildings and improvements	300,388,000
Furniture, fixtures and equipment	92,933,000
Construction in progress	12,599,000
	$457,518,000
Less accumulated depreciation	(103,326,000)
Total property, buildings and equipment, at cost, less accumulated depreciation	$354,192,000

EXHIBIT 8.1 ▼
Property, Plant & Equipment as a Percentage of Total Assets, Selected Industries

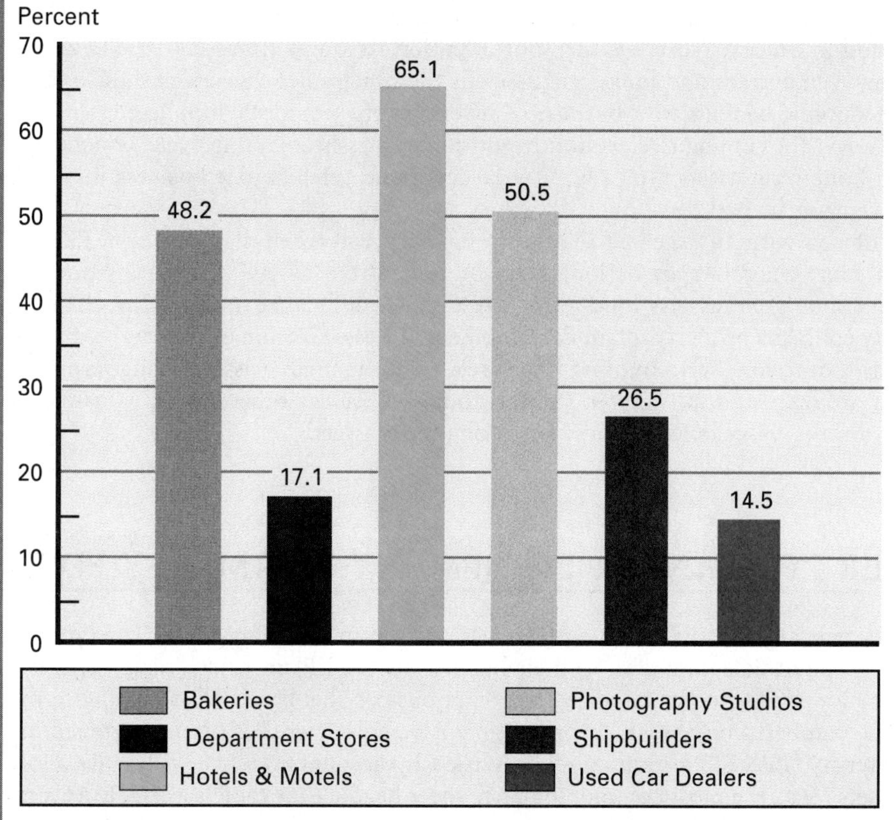

Source: Dun & Bradstreet's Industry Norms & Key Business Ratios, 1995–1996 (New York: Dun & Bradstreet, Inc., 1996).

The proportion of total assets invested in PP&E varies significantly across industries. Exhibit 8.1 reports PP&E as a percentage of total assets for six industries tracked by Dun & Bradstreet, the investment advisory firm.

PROPERTY, PLANT & EQUIPMENT: KEY INFORMATION NEEDS OF DECISION MAKERS

LEARNING OBJECTIVE 1 ▶
Identify the key information needs of decision makers regarding property, plant & equipment.

Take your average man or woman on the street who picks up an annual report of GetanGo Convenience Stores and discovers the balance sheet line item "Buildings . . . $20,994,038." This individual will probably interpret that item very literally. Uncle Jack, who has little or no formal training in the world of high finance, will likely assume that GetanGo's buildings could be sold for $20,994,038. When Jack discovers the line item "Accumulated Depreciation, Buildings," more confusion is likely. Even worse, assume that GetanGo uses the phrase "Allowance for Depreciation" instead of

"Accumulated Depreciation." At this point, Aunt Wilma may explain to her husband that GetanGo has obviously set aside a fund to provide for the replacement of its buildings or for future repairs to them. Finally, assume that Jack and Wilma turn to GetanGo's income statement and discover the line item "Depreciation Expense, Buildings . . . $1,050,264." Here, the logical, but incorrect, conclusion is that the value of GetanGo's buildings decreased by more than $1 million over the past year.

Of all the items appearing in financial statements, PP&E may be responsible for the most misconceptions in the minds of financial statement users. For this reason, it is very important that accountants include "user-friendly" information concerning PP&E and related accounting decisions in a business's annual report. This section identifies several general items of information that decision makers need regarding a business's PP&E.

Disclosures of Specific Types of Property, Plant & Equipment

Decision makers demand information regarding the composition of businesses' PP&E assets. Recall that Community Psychiatric Centers classified its total PP&E assets into five balance sheet line items, including accumulated depreciation. Disclosure of PP&E assets by major categories provides decision makers with insights as to a company's operating policies and strategies. This information also allows decision makers to draw more meaningful comparisons of different companies' financial data, particularly companies in the same industry.

Generally accepted accounting principles require businesses to disclose major classes of depreciable assets by nature or function in their financial statements. "Depreciable" assets include those long-term assets that must be depreciated for accounting purposes. The only major PP&E item that is not a depreciable asset, land, is also listed separately in the balance sheet. Among the most common types of depreciable assets reported on balance sheets are buildings, machinery or equipment, and land improvements. The latter category includes such assets as parking lots and driveways. Because land improvements are depreciable assets, they must be recorded separately from land. Construction in progress, furniture and fixtures, and automobiles are examples of other PP&E balance sheet classifications reported in recent editions of *Accounting Trends & Techniques.*

Valuation Issues

Nearly all businesses in the United States report their PP&E assets at historical cost less accumulated depreciation because of the historical cost principle. As noted in Chapter 2, a key advantage of historical costs is their objectivity. The historical cost of an asset is a "matter of record," while the current value of that same asset is a "matter of opinion."

Businesses occasionally must depart from the historical cost principle in valuing their long-term assets. For example, the conservatism principle requires businesses to write down long-term assets when their value has been permanently impaired. An accounting rule adopted recently, *Statement of Financial Accounting Standards No. 121,* "Accounting for the Impairment of Long-Lived Assets and for Long-Lived Assets to Be Disposed Of," provides guidelines for making such write-downs. If the book value (cost less accumulated depreciation) of a long-term asset is greater than the expected cash flows to be generated in the future by the asset, an impairment loss should be recorded. This loss is computed by subtracting the fair value of the asset from its book value. In this context, "fair value" is the amount at which an asset could be bought or sold in a transaction between "willing" parties.

To Depreciate or Not To Depreciate: A British Debate

FOR YOUR INFORMATION

Most businesses around the world record depreciation on PP&E assets. However, there are exceptions. For example, consider Great Britain. A British accounting rule requires businesses in that country to depreciate "fixed assets." Nevertheless, a recent survey of large British firms revealed that approximately 20 percent of those companies do not depreciate at least some of their PP&E assets. Why? Because in Great Britain, as well as numerous other countries, businesses are allowed to periodically "revalue" or write-up PP&E assets to their current values. Many British companies maintain that it is not reasonable to write up PP&E assets to their current values and then immediately record depreciation expense on those same assets.

Source: L. Hastie, "A Matter of Appreciating Depreciation," *Accountancy*, December 1995, 97.

Many companies have reported asset write-downs in recent years stemming from FASB *Statement No. 121*. Texaco, for example, recently reported a $640 million write-down of certain oil and gas properties related to this new accounting rule.

Depreciation Methods

depreciation

Generally accepted accounting principles require businesses to depreciate long-term assets. **Depreciation** is the process of allocating the cost of a long-term asset over its useful life in a rational and systematic manner. A long-term asset's useful life is that period of time it provides economic benefits to a business. Depreciating long-term assets is one method businesses use to match revenues recognized each accounting period with the expenses incurred to generate those revenues.

Later in this chapter, specific depreciation methods are discussed and illustrated. Similar to the choice of an inventory accounting method, the choice of a depreciation method can significantly influence a company's apparent financial condition and reported profits. Take the case of Sears, Roebuck & Co. In April 1996, Sears reported a net income of $1.8 billion for its most recent fiscal year. Sears' depreciation expense for that year applying the "straight-line" depreciation method was $631 million. If Sears had used a different depreciation method, its net income would likely have been materially different. To enhance the comparability of financial statement data, accounting standards require that businesses disclose in their financial statement footnotes the depreciation method or methods they use.

Restrictions on Use

Businesses should disclose in their financial statements any restrictions on the use of long-term assets. For example, many long-term assets are pledged as collateral for loans. In a recent year, Genzyme Corporation, one of the world's largest biotechnology firms, disclosed that certain of its land and buildings served as collateral for a $20 million loan. Genzyme cannot dispose of those assets without the prior approval of the lender.

ACCOUNTING FOR PROPERTY, PLANT & EQUIPMENT ▲

Property, plant & equipment assets pose four general accounting issues. First, accountants must determine the acquisition cost of these assets. Second, depreciation expense must be computed on these assets each accounting period. Third, expenditures related to PP&E assets following their acquisition must be analyzed and properly recorded. Finally, accountants must decide how to record the disposal of PP&E assets. In this section, we consider each of these issues.

Acquisition of Property, Plant & Equipment

LEARNING ◀ OBJECTIVE 2

Determine the acquisition cost of property, plant & equipment assets.

The acquisition cost of a PP&E asset includes all *reasonable* and *necessary* expenditures incurred to obtain the asset and to prepare it for use. Exhibit 8.2 lists examples of common acquisition costs for PP&E assets.

Suppose that Kinko's, the copy shop company, purchases a large copier. The suggested retail price of the copier is $40,000. However, the vendor grants a 10 percent discount to Kinko's to "close the deal," resulting in a net invoice cost of $36,000. Freight charges for the delivery of the copier are $550, and installation expenses total $320. During installation, a Kinko's employee accidentally damages the copier resulting in repair expenses of $410. The total acquisition cost of the copier is $36,870.

Net invoice cost	$36,000
Freight charges	550
Installation expenses	320
Total	$36,870

EXHIBIT 8.2 ▼

Common Acquisition Costs of Property, Plant & Equipment Assets

- Buildings (constructed): Cost of construction materials and labor, architectural fees, building permits, interest on loans obtained to finance construction,* insurance costs during construction.
- Buildings (purchased): Purchase price, real estate commissions, attorneys' fees, title fees, repair and remodeling expenses necessary to put into a usable condition.
- Equipment: Net invoice cost, transportation charges including in-transit insurance expense paid by purchaser, sales taxes, assembly and installation expenses, costs incurred to test once installed.
- Land: Purchase price, real estate commissions, attorneys' fees, title fees, surveying fees, accrued property taxes assumed by purchaser, cost to drain and otherwise prepare as a building site including the net cost of removing buildings or other structures.
- Land Improvements: All reasonable and necessary costs associated with the construction or installation of parking lots, driveways, fences, lighting systems, and irrigation systems.

*Only interest incurred on these loans during construction can be capitalized.

The major PP&E assets of Kinko's are copiers. Like other PP&E assets, the acquisition cost of a Kinko's copier includes all reasonable and necessary expenditures to obtain the copier and prepare it for use.

© Bonnie Kamin/PhotoEdit

Notice that the repair expenses are not considered a component of the copier's acquisition cost. Why? Because those expenses were not reasonable or necessary costs to obtain the copier or to ready it for use. The expenditures for the repairs would be recognized as an expense in the period incurred.

The following entry would be made to record the purchase of the copier. Included in the description for this entry is an asset number. For control purposes, an identification number is often assigned to each major PP&E asset of a business. More on this in a later section.

Apr. 19	Copier	36,870	
	Cash		36,870
	To record the acquisition of a copier (asset no. 231-7)		

Businesses often acquire several long-term assets in one transaction. For example, a company may purchase for one lump sum a production facility that includes land, land improvements, production equipment, and buildings. In such cases, the lump sum purchase price must be allocated to the specific assets acquired. This allocation is commonly based on the relative market values of the individual assets. Suppose that Hodnett Company purchases assets A, B, and C for $600,000 at a court-ordered auction of a bankrupt firm's assets. Individually, the assets have market values as follows: A—$160,000, B—$400,000, and C—$240,000. Given this information, the total cost of these assets would be allocated as follows based upon their relative market values.

Asset	Market Value	Percentage of Total Market Value	Allocation of Purchase Price		Cost Assigned to Each Asset
A	$160,000	20% ($160,000/$800,000)	20% × $600,000	=	$120,000
B	400,000	50% ($400,000/$800,000)	50% × 600,000	=	300,000
C	240,000	30% ($240,000/$800,000)	30% × 600,000	=	180,000
	$800,000	100%			$600,000

Depreciation of Property, Plant & Equipment

LEARNING OBJECTIVE 3
Compute depreciation expense using each of three major depreciation methods.

Again, depreciation is the process of systematically allocating the cost of an asset over its useful life. Three factors must be considered when computing depreciation expense: the given asset's cost, its estimated useful life, and its **salvage value,** or residual value. Salvage value is the estimated value of an asset at the end of its useful life. When computing depreciation, accountants often refer to the **depreciable cost,** or depreciation base, of an asset, which is the asset's acquisition cost less its salvage value. An asset's salvage value is *not* considered a part of its depreciable cost, since that portion of the asset's original value is not expected to be consumed or "used up" over its useful life.

salvage value

depreciable cost

Another phrase often used when referring to depreciable assets is "book value." The **book value,** or carrying value, of a depreciable asset is the difference between the asset's cost and the balance of its "accumulated depreciation" account. The balance of an asset's accumulated depreciation account reflects the total amount of the asset's original cost that has been depreciated or charged off as an expense since the asset was acquired. (Recall from an earlier chapter that accumulated depreciation is a "contra" asset account.)

book value

ILLUSTRATION OF DEPRECIATION METHODS Exhibit 8.3 documents the depreciation methods commonly used by public companies. The straight-line method is by far the most popular depreciation method. Besides the straight-line method, we consider here the units-of-production and declining-balance depreciation methods. To illustrate these three depreciation methods, let us use the following data for a depreciable asset acquired recently by the Riverside Construction Company.

Asset:	Drill press, asset no. 14-27B
Acquisition Date:	January 1, Year 1
Acquisition Cost:	$68,000
Useful Life:	4 years
Salvage Value:	$8,000
Depreciable Cost:	$60,000 ($68,000 − $8,000)

Straight-Line Method Under the **straight-line method,** a business allocates an equal amount of depreciation expense to each year of an asset's estimated useful life. The premise underlying this method is that an asset is equally productive each year that it is in service. Annual depreciation expense under the straight-line method can be computed by using either of the following two equations.

straight-line method

EXHIBIT 8.3
Depreciation Methods: Frequency of Use by Publicly Owned Companies

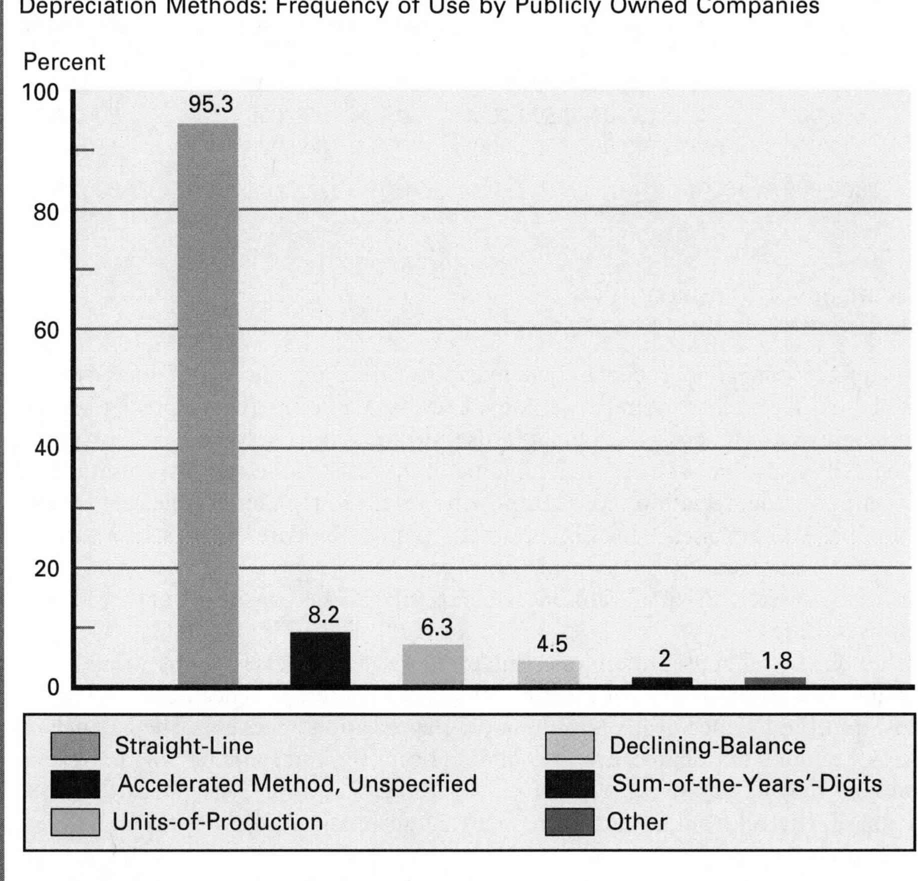

Source: Accounting Trends & Techniques, 1996.
Note: Some companies use different depreciation methods for different types of depreciable assets. As a result, the percentages in this graph accumulate to more than 100 percent.

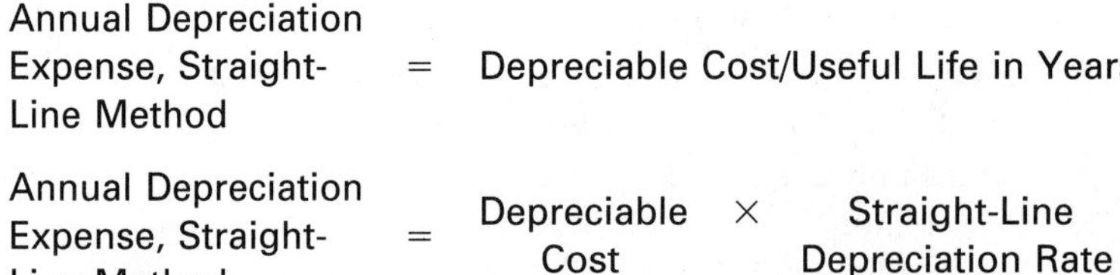

Applying the first equation to the drill press acquired by Riverside Construction Company yields an annual depreciation expense of $15,000 ($60,000/4). Alternatively, annual depreciation expense under the straight-line method can be computed by multiplying the depreciable cost of an asset by the appropriate depreciation rate. The depreciation rate represents the percentage of an asset's depreciable cost to be charged off to depreciation expense each year. For the drill press, the annual straight-line depreciation rate is 25 percent (100%/four years). Multiplying this percentage by the drill press's depreciable cost of $60,000 results, again, in an annual depreciation expense of $15,000. The following adjusting journal entry would be required to record depreciation expense at the end of the drill press's first year of service.

Dec. 31	Depreciation Expense, Drill Press	15,000	
	Accumulated Depreciation, Drill Press		15,000
	To record annual depreciation expense on drill press (asset no. 14-27B)		

Exhibit 8.4 presents a straight-line depreciation schedule for Riverside's drill press that documents the depreciation expense to be recorded each year of the asset's life. Also included in this depreciation schedule is the balance of the asset's accumulated depreciation account and the asset's book value at the end of each year. Notice in Exhibit 8.4 that the drill press will have a book value of $8,000 at the end of Year 4, an amount exactly equal to its salvage value. At this point, the depreciable cost of the asset will have been completely written off to depreciation expense. However, the machine will not necessarily be taken out of service. Unless the asset is unreliable or should be replaced for other reasons, it will be kept in service indefinitely. This is true even when a depreciable asset has a zero book value.

If the drill press was acquired in midyear, Riverside would likely compute depreciation expense for Year 1 by multiplying $15,000 by the fraction of the year the drill press was owned during Year 1. For example, if the drill press was purchased on March 1 of Year 1, the appropriate depreciation expense would be $12,500 ($15,000 × 10/12). Some businesses do not record depreciation expense for a partial year on newly acquired assets. Instead, these companies record a full year's depreciation expense for assets acquired in the first one-half of a year and no depreciation expense for assets acquired during the second one-half of a year.

Units-of-Production Method Under the **units-of-production method,** an asset's useful life is expressed in a number of units of production or use. The depreciation ex-

units-of-production method

EXHIBIT 8.4 ▼

Depreciation Schedule for Drill Press of Riverside Construction Company, Straight-Line Method

	Depreciation Computation					
Year	**Depreciation Rate**	**×**	**Depreciable Cost**	**Depreciation Expense**	**Year-End Balance of Accumulated Depreciation**	**Year-End Book Value***
1	25%	×	$60,000	$15,000	$15,000	$53,000
2	25%	×	60,000	15,000	30,000	38,000
3	25%	×	60,000	15,000	45,000	23,000
4	25%	×	60,000	15,000	60,000	8,000

*Computed as follows: Original cost of asset ($68,000) less year-end balance of accumulated depreciation account.

pense for any given period is a function of the asset's level of usage during that period. The units-of-production method is particularly well suited for a manufacturing environment. A piece of production equipment may have a useful life of ten years under normal conditions, which would typically involve one eight-hour work shift each day. However, if this equipment is used continually during three eight-hour work shifts each day, it is unlikely to be in service ten years from its purchase date.

Suppose now that Riverside applies the units-of-production method to its drill press. When the drill press is acquired, a production supervisor estimates that the asset will be used to produce 30,000 units of finished product over its useful life. Since the drill press's depreciable cost is $60,000, the per unit depreciation expense is $2: $60,000/30,000 units. For any given year, the asset's depreciation expense under the units-of-production method is determined by multiplying the per-unit depreciation cost by the number of units produced that year.

Annual Depreciation Expense, Units-of-Production Method	=	Per Unit Depreciation Cost	×	Total Units Produced During Year

The depreciation schedule shown in Exhibit 8.5 documents the expected depreciation expense for the drill press assuming the asset is used for four years and that the following number of units are produced each year.

Year 1	10,000 units
Year 2	8,000 units
Year 3	5,000 units
Year 4	7,000 units

Declining-Balance Method A few companies use "accelerated" methods to compute depreciation expense on PP&E assets. Under accelerated depreciation methods, larger amounts of depreciation are recorded in the early years of an asset's life compared to later years. The premise underlying these methods is that proportionately more of the economic benefit of depreciable assets is consumed during the early years of their useful lives. Machinery, for example, generally becomes less productive over time due to increasing breakdowns and more extensive maintenance requirements.

EXHIBIT 8.5 ▼

Depreciation Schedule for Drill Press of Riverside Construction Company, Units-of-Production Method

	Depreciation Computation					
Year	Depreciation Cost Per Unit	×	Expected Production	Depreciation Expense	Year-End Balance of Accumulated Depreciation	Year-End Book Value
1	$2	×	10,000 units	$20,000	$20,000	$48,000
2	$2	×	8,000 units	16,000	36,000	32,000
3	$2	×	5,000 units	10,000	46,000	22,000
4	$2	×	7,000 units	14,000	60,000	8,000

Under the **declining-balance method,** annual depreciation expense is computed by multiplying an asset's book value at the beginning of a year by an accelerated depreciation rate:

declining-balance method

Annual Depreciation Expense, Declining-Balance Method	=	Book Value (Beginning of the Year)	×	Accelerated Depreciation Rate

Accelerated depreciation rates under the declining-balance method are a multiple of the straight-line depreciation rate. If a company uses the **double declining-balance method,** the annual depreciation rate for an asset is twice the straight-line rate. The annual straight-line depreciation rate for an asset with a ten-year useful life is 10 percent (100%/10). Under the double declining-balance method, the annual depreciation rate for this asset would be 20 percent (2 × 10%).

double declining-balance method

For Riverside's drill press, the accelerated depreciation rate under the double declining-balance method is 50 percent, or twice the straight-line rate of 25 percent. At the beginning of Year 1, the asset's book value is equal to its cost of $68,000. So, Year 1 depreciation expense would be $34,000: $68,000 × 50%. The drill press's book value at the beginning of Year 2 would be $34,000 (cost of $68,000 less accumulated depreciation of $34,000). Depreciation expense for Year 2 would be $17,000: $34,000 × 50%.

A common mistake students make in applying the declining-balance method is multiplying the appropriate accelerated depreciation rate by the asset's depreciable cost instead of its book value. Another tricky aspect of the declining-balance method is that one must remember to stop depreciating an asset once its book value equals its salvage value. Recall that for both the straight-line and units-of-production methods an asset's salvage value is subtracted from its original cost to determine its depreciable cost. Then, a systematic method is used to allocate this latter amount over the asset's useful life. Under the declining-balance method, an asset's salvage value is ignored, at least initially, when computing periodic depreciation expense. However, once the asset's book value is equal to its salvage value, no further depreciation is recorded.

Exhibit 8.6 contains a depreciation schedule for Riverside's drill press based upon the double declining-balance method. Notice in the fourth year of the asset's life that

EXHIBIT 8.6 ▼

Depreciation Schedule for Drill Press of Riverside Construction Company, Double Declining-Balance Method

	Depreciation Computation					
Year	Depreciation Rate	×	Book Value	Depreciation Expense	Year-End Balance of Accumulated Depreciation	Year-End Book Value
1	50%	×	$68,000	$34,000	$34,000	$34,000
2	50%	×	34,000	17,000	51,000	17,000
3	50%	×	17,000	8,500	59,500	8,500
4	50%	×	8,500	500*	60,000	8,000

*Depreciation expense in Year 4 would be $4,250, applying the appropriate equation. However, since the asset's remaining depreciable cost is only $500 at the beginning of the year, depreciation expense for Year 4 is limited to that amount.

the depreciation computation yields a depreciation expense of $4,250 ($8,500 × 50%). However, since the book value of the asset at the beginning of Year 4 exceeds its salvage value by only $500 ($8,500 – $8,000), depreciation expense for that year is limited to $500.

COMPARISON OF DEPRECIATION METHODS Exhibit 8.7 summarizes the annual depreciation charges for Riverside's drill press under each of the three major depreciation methods. The straight-line and double declining-balance methods result in the general depreciation patterns shown in Exhibit 8.7 regardless of the length of an asset's useful life. Naturally, the depreciation pattern for the units-of-production method varies from case to case. Realize that whichever depreciation method Riverside uses for the drill press, the final result is the same: $60,000 of depreciation expense is recorded over the asset's useful life.

DEPRECIATION: OTHER ISSUES Besides the most common methods of computing depreciation expense, decision makers should be acquainted with certain other accounting issues related to the depreciation of PP&E assets. Among these issues are accounting for the depletion of natural resources and depreciation methods used for federal taxation purposes.

EXHIBIT 8.7 ▼
Annual Depreciation Expense for Drill Press of Riverside Construction Company Under Three Major Depreciation Methods

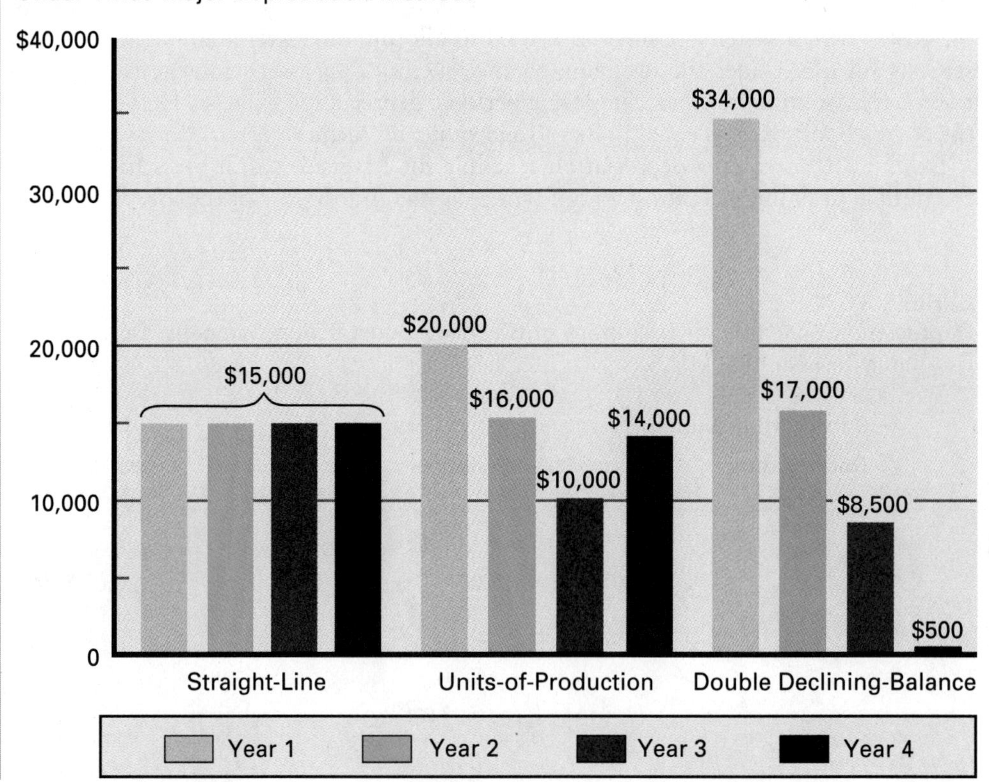

Depletion of Natural Resources The most important PP&E assets of mining firms, petroleum firms, and many other companies are natural resource properties. **Natural resources** include long-term assets such as coal deposits, oil and gas reservoirs, and tracts of standing timber that are extracted or harvested from the earth's surface or from beneath the earth's surface. Barrick Gold Corporation, based in Toronto, Canada, is the third largest producer of gold in the world and the largest gold production company in North America. A recent annual report issued by Barrick reported more than $2 billion of investments in natural resource properties, including a $44 million investment in the Bullfrog Mine of Beatty, Nevada. Union Texas Petroleum Holdings, Inc., a Houston-based oil and gas exploration company, recently reported assets of $1.8 billion, more than two-thirds of which were oil and gas properties.

natural resources

Natural resources are often referred to as wasting assets. The value of these properties gradually declines or "wastes away" as timber, gems, petroleum, and so on are extracted or harvested from them. Instead of depreciation, accountants use the term **depletion** to describe the allocation of the cost of natural resources to the periods in which they provide economic benefits to an entity. Barrick, Union Texas, and most other firms in the extractive industries apply the units-of-production concept to record depletion expense on natural resource properties. To compute annual depletion expense, the following adaptation of the units-of-production depreciation equation is used.

depletion

$$\text{Annual Depletion Expense, Units-of-Production Method} = \text{Per Unit Depletion Cost} \times \text{Total Units Recovered and Sold During Year}$$

Suppose Union Texas purchases an oil and gas property for $20 million that is estimated to have two million barrels of recoverable oil. The depletion expense per barrel of oil recovered and sold will be $10: $20,000,000/2,000,000 barrels. If the company recovers and sells 300,000 barrels from this property in a given year, the depletion expense for that year would be $3 million.

Certain industries are said to be "capital-intensive." Long-term assets, such as PP&E, typically account for a very high percentage of the total assets of firms in capital-intensive industries. An example of such an industry is oil and gas exploration.

© Courtesy of American Petroleum Institute

Annual Depletion Expense, Units-of-Production Method	=	Per Unit Depletion Cost	×	Total Units Recovered and Sold During Year
	=	\$10 × 300,000		
	=	\$3,000,000		

This depletion expense would be recorded with the following year-end adjusting entry.

Dec. 31	Depletion Expense	3,000,000	
	Accumulated Depletion		3,000,000
	To record depletion expense on reservoir B4-62 (300,000 barrels × \$10 per barrel)		

Suppose now that 100,000 barrels of the recovered oil were unsold at the end of the year. Under this assumption, the previous entry would include a \$2,000,000 debit to Depletion Expense, a \$1,000,000 debit to Inventory, and an offsetting credit of \$3,000,000 to Accumulated Depletion.

Depreciation for Federal Taxation Purposes The accounting methods businesses use for financial reporting purposes often differ from the accounting methods they apply for federal taxation purposes. Tax laws and regulations dictating the depreciation methods to be used for PP&E have been revised frequently in recent decades and at this point are quite complex. Here, the purpose is simply to provide you with a brief introduction to the acceptable depreciation methods for taxation purposes.

For PP&E assets acquired before 1981, businesses typically use one of the depreciation methods illustrated previously. In 1981, Congress enacted a law that created the Accelerated Cost Recovery System (ACRS). The ACRS introduced a new approach to computing depreciation for federal taxation purposes. This taxation system, which is used for assets acquired between 1981 and 1986, established six "cost recovery periods" over which different types of PP&E were to be depreciated. Generally, the cost recovery period assigned to a group of assets was much shorter than the useful lives of those assets.

Congress revised the ACRS when it established the Modified Accelerated Cost Recovery System (MACRS) in 1987. Businesses apply this depreciation system to assets acquired in 1987 and beyond. Under MACRS, most depreciable assets are assigned to one of seven classes, each of which has a different cost recovery period. For example, cars and general-purpose trucks are typically assigned a useful life of five years. The MACRS defines the depreciation methods that can be applied to each class of depreciable assets. The double declining-balance method is typically used for assets with short lives, while the straight-line method is mandated for certain long-lived assets.

The ACRS and MACRS generally allow companies to write off the cost of depreciable assets for tax purposes more rapidly than they had in the past. Congress hoped that allowing more liberal approaches to computing depreciation for tax purposes would motivate businesses to purchase new or additional PP&E assets and thus stimulate the economy. As a general rule, neither the ACRS nor the MACRS can be used for financial accounting or financial reporting purposes. Why? Because they violate certain of the accounting concepts discussed in Chapter 2. For example, these methods of computing depreciation typically violate the matching principle since they overstate the depreciation expense recorded during the early years of an asset's life.

Who Stole My Loblolly?

Imagine the control problems faced by paper, forestry, and other companies that own huge tracts of standing timber. Typically, these assets are located in remote areas far removed from "civilization," including a company's auditors. Companies with sizable investments in tracts of timber must establish some means for monitoring these sites before the trees are harvested. These companies must also implement rigorous controls over the harvesting process. A common fraud perpetrated in the timber industry is the theft of logs by contractors retained to harvest timber. A control activity designed to detect such theft is "stump cruising." Once a tract of timber has been harvested, a "stump cruiser" visits the site and selects random plots of a predetermined size. This individual counts and measures the tree stumps in the selected plots. With the help of mathematical equations, the stump cruiser can reliably estimate the amount of timber that should have been harvested from the site.

Source: T. J. Straka, "Auditing Timber Assets," *Management Accounting,* June 1995, 50–54.

Revenue Expenditures vs. Capital Expenditures

LEARNING OBJECTIVE 4
Distinguish between and account for revenue and capital expenditures.

Following the acquisition of PP&E assets, businesses incur a wide range of expenditures related to these assets. Accountants classify such expenditures as either revenue expenditures or capital expenditures. **Revenue expenditures** provide economic benefits to only one accounting period and thus are treated as expenses in the period incurred. Examples of revenue expenditures include maintenance expenses and minor repairs for PP&E assets. Expenditures to obtain, expand, or improve long-term assets or to extend their useful lives are known as **capital expenditures.** Unlike revenue expenditures, capital expenditures provide economic benefits to a business for more than one year. Because of the matching principle, capital expenditures are debited to an asset account and then written off as an expense over the appropriate number of accounting periods.

revenue expenditures

capital expenditures

Besides the acquisition cost of new PP&E assets, capital expenditures related to PP&E include additions, improvements, and extraordinary repairs. **Additions** are extensions or expansions of existing PP&E assets. For example, a new wing added to a production facility would qualify as an addition. **Improvements** are capital expenditures that enhance an existing asset's operating efficiency or reduce its operating costs. An example of an improvement is a new and more powerful engine installed on a piece of production machinery that increases the machinery's productive capacity by 20 percent. Generally, the cost of an improvement or addition is debited to the existing asset's general ledger account. (Recall that improvements made to land are recorded in Land Improvements instead of the Land account.)

additions

improvements

Additions and improvements increase the depreciable cost of PP&E and thus require revisions in the annual depreciation computations for these assets. Suppose that a company owns a building that cost $2.4 million to construct ten years ago. The building is expected to have a zero salvage value at the end of its forty-year useful life. Given the annual depreciation of $60,000 ($2,400,000/40 years) on the building, the balance of its accumulated depreciation account is presently $600,000 ($60,000 × 10 years). Now, assume that a new wing is added to the building at a cost of $1.2 million. This addition does not affect the asset's useful life or salvage value. The revised annual depreciation expense for the building would be $100,000, as shown by the following schedule.

Cost of addition		$1,200,000
Cost of existing building	$2,400,000	
Less accumulated depreciation	600,000	1,800,000
Total depreciable cost		$3,000,000
Useful life		÷ 30 years
Revised annual depreciation		$ 100,000

extraordinary repairs

A final type of capital expenditure is **extraordinary repairs.** Extraordinary repairs are major repair costs that extend the useful life of a PP&E asset but do not improve its operating efficiency or reduce its operating costs. Expenditures incurred during a major overhaul of a piece of production machinery typically qualify as extraordinary repairs. The cost of extraordinary repairs is debited to an asset's accumulated depreciation account. This accounting treatment serves to "erase" a part of the asset's accumulated depreciation, which is similar to the impact that extraordinary repairs have on an asset. That is, extraordinary repairs "turn back the clock" by extending an asset's useful life.

To illustrate accounting for extraordinary repairs, suppose that Knutson Engineering removes a piece of machinery from its production line shortly after the beginning of a new fiscal year. This machine is given a major overhaul at a cost of $3,000. The overhaul extends the machine's estimated useful life by two years. This $3,000 of expenditures would be recorded by debiting Accumulated Depreciation, Machinery, with an offsetting credit to Cash or an appropriate liability account.

Now, assume that this machine cost $44,000, was originally estimated to have a ten-year useful life and a $4,000 salvage value, and has been depreciated using the straight-line method at a rate of $4,000 per year (($44,000–$4,000)/10 years). The machine has been in service for seven years, resulting in accumulated depreciation of $28,000 before the overhaul ($4,000 annual depreciation × 7 years). Finally, assume that the overhaul did not affect the machine's salvage value. As illustrated in the following schedule, the machine would have a remaining depreciable cost of $15,000 after the extraordinary repairs are debited to its accumulated depreciation account.

Original cost		$44,000
Accumulated depreciation:		
Balance prior to overhaul	$28,000	
Cost of overhaul	(3,000)	
Revised balance		(25,000)
Salvage value		(4,000)
Remaining depreciable cost		$15,000

Since the remaining useful life of this machine has been extended from three years to five years by the overhaul, the revised annual depreciation expense would be $3,000 under the straight-line method ($15,000/5 years).

Disposal of Property, Plant & Equipment Assets

LEARNING OBJECTIVE 5
Account for disposals of property, plant & equipment.

Businesses dispose of PP&E assets in several ways. These assets may be removed from service and "junked," sold for cash, or exchanged for other assets. In this section, we consider the accounting procedures for disposals of PP&E assets. To illustrate these procedures, the now very familiar drill press of Riverside Construction Company is used. Recall that the drill press was purchased for $68,000, had an estimated useful life of four years, and an estimated salvage value of $8,000. The examples used here to illustrate disposals of PP&E assets assume that Riverside applied the straight-line depreciation method to this asset.

RETIREMENT OF PROPERTY, PLANT & EQUIPMENT ASSETS Suppose that Riverside's drill press suddenly becomes obsolete at the end of its third year of service because a new and more efficient model becomes available. The book value of the drill press at the end of Year 3 is $23,000 as indicated in Exhibit 8.4, the straight-line depreciation schedule we developed for the drill press. Unfortunately, the drill press has only a minimal salvage value given the new technology available. So, Riverside "cuts a deal" with the local junkyard. The junkyard hauls away the drill press for no charge in exchange for the scrap metal that can be recovered from the machine. Disposing of the drill press in this manner results in a loss equal to the asset's book value of $23,000. Following is the entry to record the retirement of the drill press under this assumption.

Jan. 4	Accumulated Depreciation, Drill Press	45,000	
	Loss on Retirement of Long-Term Assets	23,000	
	Drill Press		68,000
	To record the retirement of drill press (asset no. 14-27B)		

This entry removes from Riverside's accounting records both the cost of the drill press and its accumulated depreciation. Gains and losses on the disposal of long-term assets are generally classified as other revenues and expenses on an income statement.

CASH SALES OF PROPERTY, PLANT & EQUIPMENT ASSETS When a long-term asset is sold for less than its book value, a loss must be recorded equal to the difference between the asset's book value and selling price. To illustrate this scenario, assume that Riverside's drill press is sold for $10,000 on June 30 of Year 4. Here, we have an additional factor complicating the disposal of the drill press. If a depreciable asset is disposed of at midyear, an adjusting entry must be made to record depreciation expense on that asset before its disposal is recorded. This entry reflects the depreciation expense on the asset for the period that has elapsed since the most recent adjusting entry for depreciation expense was booked. Riverside records depreciation expense at the end of each year. On June 30 of Year 4 when the drill press is sold for $10,000, six months would have passed since the previous adjusting entry for depreciation. So, before recording the sale of the drill press, Riverside would record $7,500 of depreciation expense on June 30 of Year 4 to recognize the depreciation expense on the drill press for the first six months of the year.

Following the entry to record depreciation expense on the drill press for the first one-half of Year 4, the book value of the asset would be $15,500.

Original cost of drill press		$68,000
Less accumulated depreciation		
Accumulated depreciation, end of Year 3	$45,000	
Adjusting entry, June 30, Year 4	7,500	
Accumulated depreciation, June 30, Year 4		52,500
Book value, June 30, Year 4		$15,500

Given the assumed selling price of $10,000 and the book value of $15,500, Riverside would record a loss of $5,500 on the sale of the drill press, as reflected by the following entry.

June 30	Accumulated Depreciation, Drill Press	52,500	
	Cash	10,000	
	Loss on Sale of Long-Term Assets	5,500	
	Drill Press		68,000
	To record the sale of drill press (asset no. 14-27B)		

If Riverside sells the drill press for more than its book value, a gain equal to the difference between the asset's selling price and book value would be recorded. For example, suppose that the selling price of the drill press in the previous example was $25,000, rather than $10,000. In this case, Riverside would record a gain of $9,500. That gain represents the difference between the asset's $25,000 selling price and its book value of $15,500.

EXCHANGES OF PROPERTY, PLANT & EQUIPMENT ASSETS Businesses sometimes exchange existing PP&E assets for new models of those assets. Even when an asset is still functioning reliably, a business may decide to upgrade that asset for competitive reasons. A company that uses outdated equipment on its production line or in its distribution facilities likely will lag behind competitors in terms of operating efficiency and profits. Accounting for asset exchanges can be quite complex. Here, only two scenarios involving exchanges of *similar* assets are considered. A comprehensive discussion of accounting for asset exchanges, including the accounting rules for exchanges involving *dissimilar assets,* is deferred to advanced accounting courses.

Asset Exchanges Involving a Loss Assume that Riverside Construction Company decides to replace its drill press after using it for two years. The drill press has a $38,000 book value, $68,000 cost less $30,000 of accumulated depreciation, at this point, as shown in Exhibit 8.4. The replacement drill press is sold by a local equipment dealer at a cash price of $54,000. Besides trading in its original drill press on the new model, Riverside pays the equipment dealer $20,000. In other words, the dealer grants Riverside a $34,000 trade-in allowance on the old drill press, as shown by the following schedule.

Cash price of new drill press	$54,000
Cash paid in exchange by Riverside	20,000
Trade-in allowance for old drill press	$34,000

The $38,000 book value of the old drill press exceeds the trade-in allowance of $34,000. So, Riverside incurs a $4,000 loss on this asset exchange. As a general rule, when a loss is incurred on an exchange of similar assets, the loss is recognized and the newly acquired asset is recorded at its fair market value, which is typically its cash price. To record this asset exchange and the resulting loss, Riverside would make the following entry in its accounting records.

Jan. 1	Drill Press (new)	54,000	
	Accumulated Depreciation, Drill Press	30,000	
	Loss on Exchange of Assets	4,000	
	Drill Press (old)		68,000
	Cash		20,000
	To record exchange of drill press (asset no. 14-27B) for new drill press (asset no. 14-51A)		

Asset Exchanges Involving a Gain Assume the same facts as in the previous example with one difference: Riverside pays the dealer only $10,000 in the exchange of the drill presses. In this case, Riverside has received a trade-in allowance of $44,000 for the old drill press.

Cash price of new drill press	$54,000
Cash paid in exchange by Riverside	10,000
Trade-in allowance for old drill press	$44,000

Riverside's trade-in allowance for its old drill press exceeds that asset's book value by $6,000 ($44,000 − $38,000). However, generally accepted accounting principles do not allow gains on exchanges of similar assets to be recorded. Instead, the unrecognized gain of $6,000 is subtracted from the $54,000 cash price of the new asset in determining its acquisition cost. Alternatively, the acquisition cost of the new asset for accounting purposes, $48,000, can be determined by adding the book value of the old asset ($38,000) and the amount of cash paid ($10,000). In either case, the asset exchange is recorded as follows.

Jan. 1	Drill Press (new)	48,000	
	Accumulated Depreciation, Drill Press	30,000	
	Drill Press (old)		68,000
	Cash		10,000
	To record exchange of drill press (asset no. 14-27B) for new drill press (asset no. 14-51A)		

At this point, the obvious question is why accounting standards require losses on exchanges of similar assets to be recognized, while gains on such transactions are not. One reason stems from the conservatism principle. Recognizing a loss and not recognizing a gain both qualify as conservative accounting treatments. If you pursue further study of financial accounting, you will encounter additional rationale for the differing treatment of gains and losses on exchanges of similar assets.

You should recognize that the economic benefit of a gain on the exchange of similar assets is not totally disregarded for accounting purposes. Consider the example just discussed. In that case, the $6,000 unrealized gain on the exchange of the two drill presses is subtracted from the recorded cost of the new drill press. As a result, the depreciation expense recorded on the new drill press will be reduced by $6,000 over its useful life. So, instead of recognizing an "upfront" gain of $6,000 on this exchange, Riverside will recognize this gain gradually over the life of the new drill press in the form of lower depreciation expense.

KEY CONTROL ACTIVITIES FOR PROPERTY, PLANT & EQUIPMENT

LEARNING OBJECTIVE 6
Discuss key control activities for property, plant & equipment.

Property, plant & equipment assets pose different types of control issues compared with current assets such as cash and inventory. For example, for the latter two assets, physical security controls are especially important. However, the risk of someone walking off with a ten-story office building or a five-ton drill press is not very great. On the other hand, physical security controls are important for certain PP&E assets such as personal computers.

Insurance Coverage

An important control activity for PP&E is maintaining adequate insurance coverage for these assets. This is a particularly critical control for small businesses that would be devastated by a major fire or other calamity. Periodically, a firm's accountants should review the insurance coverage of all major PP&E assets. Significant changes in the current value of individual PP&E assets and capital expenditures, such as additions and improvements, may require that changes be made in the insurance coverage for these assets.

Authorization Controls

Businesses should have a strict policy that requires top executives to approve the acquisition and disposal of high-priced PP&E. Many companies require that major PP&E assets be purchased through a competitive bidding process. The intent of this control procedure is to ensure that these assets are acquired at the lowest possible cost. Following the acquisition or disposal of a major PP&E asset, the key terms of the transaction should be reviewed to ensure that those terms were the ones authorized by the appropriate company official.

Maintenance of a Property Ledger

property ledger

Businesses that have numerous PP&E assets usually maintain a property ledger. A **property ledger** is a subsidiary ledger in which key information is recorded for each major PP&E asset. Such information may include date of acquisition, acquisition cost, a depreciation record, location, intended use, insurance coverage, a maintenance record, and the employee primarily responsible for the asset.

A property ledger is often organized or indexed by asset identification numbers. When a company acquires a PP&E asset, the asset is assigned an identification number. This control number is stamped on the asset or permanently secured to it in some other manner. Businesses should periodically take a physical inventory of PP&E assets. This control activity ensures that each PP&E asset is in the appropriate department or operating unit, is being used in the intended manner, and is being properly maintained.

ANALYZING TOTAL ASSETS

LEARNING OBJECTIVE 7
Compute return on assets and the total asset turnover ratio.

Since PP&E is the last major asset category considered in Part III of this text, this section highlights two financial ratios related to the total assets of business entities. These ratios are return on assets and the total asset turnover ratio.

Return on Assets

A few years into the future when you are the chief executive officer (CEO) of a multibillion dollar firm, one of your major responsibilities will be performance appraisal. Granted, you will not be responsible for evaluating the work of production-line personnel. However, you will be responsible for regularly evaluating those individuals who manage your firm's major operating units. For example, if your company has three divisions, you will need some basis for measuring and comparing the job performance of the three divisional managers. A key measure used to assess the job performance of divisional managers, departmental supervisors, and CEOs, for that matter, is return on assets. **Return on assets** measures the rate of return earned on a business's total assets or on the total assets of a segment of a business. For an entire business, this ratio is computed by dividing the sum of the firm's net income and interest expense for an accounting period by its average total assets for that period.

return on assets

Return on Assets = (Net Income + Interest Expense)/Average Total Assets

Why is interest expense added to net income when computing return on assets? When return on assets is being used as a job performance measure, financing costs, such as interest expense, should generally be ignored. The issue in this context is how effectively an individual has managed the total assets in his or her area of responsibility regardless of how those assets were financed.

To illustrate the computation of return on assets, consider the following data for the Lehman Manufacturing Company. These data are for the company's fiscal year ending December 31, 1998.

Net sales	$7,200,000
Net income	320,000
Interest expense	24,000
Total assets, January 1	4,200,000
Total assets, December 31	4,400,000

Following is the computation of Lehman's return on assets for 1998.

Average Total Assets	=	($4,200,000 + $4,400,000)/2
	=	$4,300,000
Return on Assets	=	($320,000 + $24,000)/$4,300,000
	=	8%

Return on assets varies significantly across industries. Exhibit 8.1 of this chapter reported PP&E as a percentage of total assets in six industries. Exhibit 8.8 discloses the average return on assets for these same industries during a recent year.

Total Asset Turnover Ratio

total asset turnover ratio

Another measure of how effectively business executives utilize the total assets under their control is the **total asset turnover ratio.** This ratio is computed by dividing a company's net sales during an accounting period by its average total assets for that period.

Total Asset Turnover Ratio = Net Sales/Average Total Assets

EXHIBIT 8.8
Return on Assets, Selected Industries

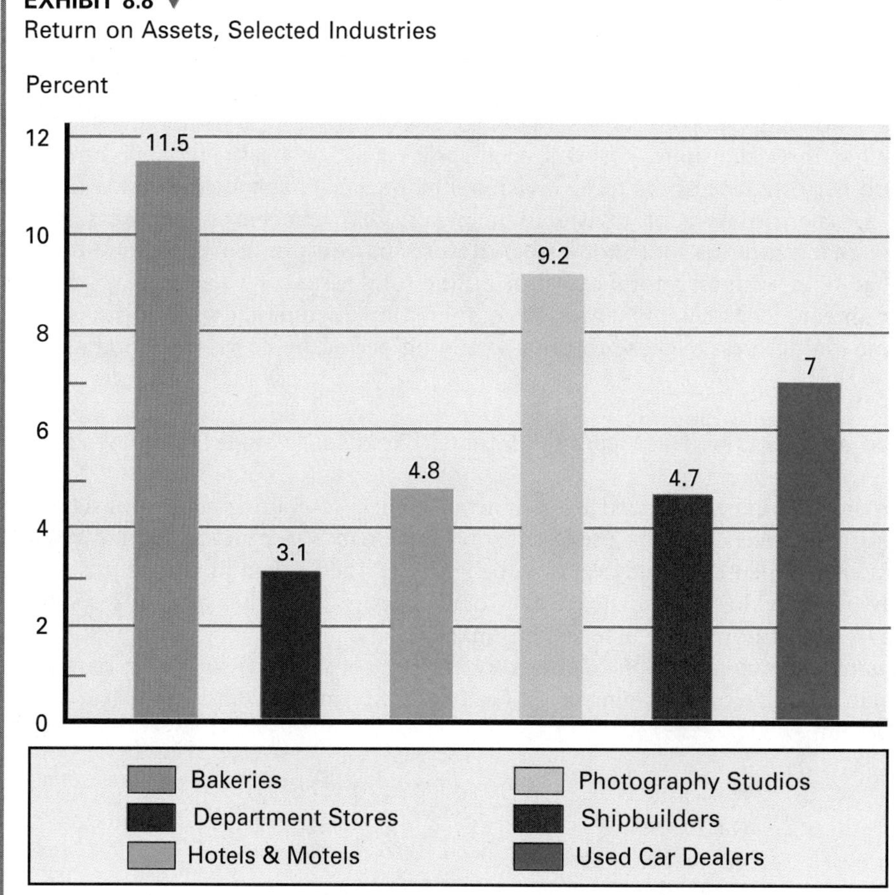

Source: Dun & Bradstreet's Industry Norms & Key Business Ratios, 1995–1996 (New York: Dun & Bradstreet, Inc., 1996).

In 1998, Lehman Manufacturing Company had net sales of $7.2 million and average total assets of $4.3 million, yielding a total asset turnover ratio of 1.67.

The total asset turnover ratio can be used to gauge executives' success in generating revenues relative to their organization's total asset base. Suppose that Faldo, Inc., and Singh Corporation, two companies in the same industry, each had total sales of $10 million during a recent year. However, Faldo had total assets of $9 million, while Singh had total assets of only $5 million. Focusing on this fact alone, Singh's executives appear to be better asset managers than Faldo's executives. In more concrete terms, Singh's executives generated $2 in revenues for every $1 investment in assets, while Faldo's executives produced only $1.11 in revenues for each dollar invested in assets.

INTANGIBLE ASSETS

LEARNING OBJECTIVE 8
Identify major types of intangible assets and the key accounting issues related to these assets.

intangible assets

Intangible assets are long-term assets that do not have a physical form or substance. Given their nature, the importance of these assets is sometimes discounted by decision makers. However, the financial success of many corporations stems largely from the intangible assets they have developed or purchased. Exhibit 8.9 lists examples of intangible assets reported recently by several publicly owned companies. *Accounting Trends & Techniques* suggests that goodwill, patents, copyrights, and trademarks are the most common types of intangible assets.

Accounting for Intangible Assets: An Overview

amortization

Intangible assets pose the same general types of accounting issues as their close cousins, long-term depreciable assets. For example, accountants must first determine the cost to assign to an intangible asset. Then, this cost must be systematically allocated to the accounting periods that the asset provides economic benefits to a business. For intangible assets, this allocation process is referred to as **amortization** instead of depreciation. Certain intangible assets, such as trademarks, have indefinite useful lives. Other intangible assets, such as patents, have a useful life that is limited by federal statute

EXHIBIT 8.9
Intangible Assets of Selected Companies

Company	Intangible Asset	Dollar Value
• Biogen, Inc.	Patents	$ 7,988,000
• Chrysler Corporation	Goodwill	767,000,000
• EZCORP/EZPAWN, Inc.	Noncompete Agreements	2,944,000
• Fingerhut Companies, Inc.	Customer Lists	11,201,000
• Fossil, Inc.	Trademarks	442,969
• Houghton Mifflin Company	Publishing Rights	18,523,000
• Westinghouse Electric Corporation	FCC Licenses	1,242,000,000

Source: Recent annual reports.

or by a contractual agreement. The general rule is that intangible assets should be amortized over their legal life, their useful life, or forty years, whichever is shorter.

To illustrate accounting for intangible assets, suppose that a record company purchases the copyright to a song for $100,000 on January 1 of a given year. This purchase would likely be recorded by debiting $100,000 to an account entitled "Copyrights" with an offsetting credit to Cash or an appropriate liability account. Under federal law, the legal life of a copyright extends over the life of the creator plus 50 years. However, assume that the record company believes its newly acquired copyright will have a useful life of only five years. Amortization of intangible assets is typically computed using the straight-line method. For the copyright, the annual amortization expense under the straight-line method would be $20,000 ($100,000/5 years). Shown next is the first year-end adjusting entry to record amortization expense on this asset.

Dec. 31	Amortization Expense	20,000	
	Copyrights		20,000
	To record annual amortization expense on copyright purchased on January 1		

Notice in the prior entry that the offsetting credit to Amortization Expense is made to the Copyrights account instead of to Accumulated Amortization, Copyrights. Some businesses use accumulated amortization accounts for intangible assets similar to the accumulated depreciation accounts used for depreciable assets. However, a more common practice is to credit amortization expense directly to the appropriate intangible asset account.

Disposals of intangible assets are accounted for much like the disposal of depreciable assets. If an intangible asset is sold, the gain or loss on the asset is computed by subtracting the unamortized cost of the asset from the selling price. Because of their nature, intangible assets are prone to losing their value rapidly. For instance, a patent held by a company may become worthless because a competitor develops a technologically advanced product. In such a case, the unamortized cost of the patent should be immediately written off as a loss.

Specific Types of Intangible Assets

There are dozens of different types of intangible assets that can be found on the balance sheets of businesses. In this section, the major types of intangible assets are discussed beginning with the most common, goodwill.

GOODWILL The 1996 edition of *Accounting Trends & Techniques* reported that approximately 67 percent of public companies listed goodwill as an asset on their balance sheets. What is goodwill? For John Q. Public, goodwill represents that "warm, fuzzy feeling" that makes him patronize Grandma Brinkley's Corner Grocery instead of Discount MegaMarkets USA. Superior service, excellent location, family ties to the community, and many other factors go into determining the goodwill associated with a business. However, just because Grandma Brinkley's Corner Grocery has accumulated a considerable amount of goodwill does not mean that goodwill can be "booked."

For accounting purposes, goodwill is generally recorded only when one business entity is acquired by another. In this context, **goodwill** is defined as the excess of the

goodwill

cost of a group of assets over their collective market value. Suppose that Exxon purchases for $25 million a company that operates a chain of service stations. If the collective market value of that company's assets is only $20 million, the remaining $5 million of the purchase price would be attributed to goodwill. Exxon must amortize this goodwill over a period not to exceed forty years. *Accounting Trends & Techniques* reveals that forty years is by far the most common amortization period for goodwill.

PATENTS The United States Patent Office grants patents on both new products and new processes. The holder of a **patent** has an exclusive right to manufacture a specific product or to use a specific process for 17 years.

patent

COPYRIGHTS AND TRADEMARKS The federal government grants the creators of songs, books, films, and other works of art the exclusive right to produce and sell those items. Such a grant is known as a **copyright.** Copyrights generally have a useful life of no more than a few years, although their legal lives extend fifty years beyond the life of the creator. The amortization period for a copyright cannot exceed forty years. Unlike patents and copyrights, trademarks have indefinite legal lives. A **trademark** is a distinctive word, symbol, or logo used to identify a specific business entity or one of its products. A trademark familiar to computer jockeys is the catchy two-word logo used by Intel Corporation. This logo is printed on adhesive labels applied to millions of personal computers to indicate that an Intel product is "inside." The next time you are sitting in front of a computer that displays Intel's logo, lean forward and you will discern a circled, capital letter R, which indicates the trademark is registered with the United States Patent Office. Although trademarks can be registered with the Patent Office, companies have the exclusive right to use the trademarks they have developed whether or not they are registered.

copyright

trademark

LEASEHOLDS AND LEASEHOLD IMPROVEMENTS Many businesses lease rather than purchase long-term assets. For example, a company that does not have sufficient funds to purchase a large production facility that it needs may choose instead to lease that facility for an extended period. The party that leases an asset, the lessee, acquires a **leasehold,** which is a legal right to use a leased asset for a specified period subject to any restrictions in the lease agreement. Technically, leaseholds are

leasehold

Hands Off My Trademarks!

FOR YOUR INFORMATION

Companies vigorously protect their patents, trademarks, and other important intangible assets from infringement by other firms. Estee Lauder, the skin-care and cosmetics distributor, recently filed a lawsuit against The Gap. The lawsuit alleges that The Gap chose a name for one of its products that was too similar to the name of an existing Estee Lauder product. A similar lawsuit involving The Quaker Oats Company was resolved in 1995. In earlier years, Quaker Oats had used the phrase "thirst aid" in advertising its popular product *Gatorade.* However, a competitor had a registered trademark for a product known as *Thirst-Aid.* Quaker Oats was ordered to pay approximately $30 million to compensate the competitor for alleged damages it suffered due to the infringement of its trademark.

intangible assets. As you will learn in Chapter 10, not all leaseholds are recorded as assets. Those leaseholds that are recorded are usually classified as PP&E assets for balance sheet purposes instead of being reported as intangible assets. Regardless of the balance sheet classification of a lease, its cost should be amortized over the term of the lease.

leasehold improvements

Companies that lease office buildings, retail stores, and production facilities often modify the leased properties to accommodate their operations. Expenditures for such modifications are referred to as **leasehold improvements.** Leasehold improvements revert to the owner of the property, the lessor, at the end of the lease term. Like leaseholds, leasehold improvements qualify as intangible assets. The cost of leasehold improvements should be amortized over their useful life or the term of the lease, whichever is shorter.

▲ SUMMARY

In the United States, the historical cost principle dictates that PP&E assets generally be reported at historical cost, less accumulated depreciation. Besides valuation issues related to a business's PP&E assets, decision makers should be informed of the specific types of these assets that a business owns, the depreciation methods applied to these assets, and any restrictions on their use.

The starting point in accounting for PP&E assets is determining their acquisition cost. Only those costs that are reasonable and necessary to acquire these assets and ready them for use should be capitalized, that is, debited to an asset account. Following their acquisition, the depreciable cost of PP&E assets should be allocated to the accounting periods that they will provide economic benefits to a business. Three major approaches to computing depreciation are the straight-line method, the units-of-production method, and the declining-balance method.

Accountants distinguish between two types of expenditures related to PP&E assets, revenue expenditures and capital expenditures. Revenue expenditures, such as maintenance costs, should be treated as expenses in the period incurred. Capital expenditures, such as additions and improvements, should be recorded in an asset account. A special type of capital expenditures, extraordinary repairs, involves major repairs that extend the useful life of an asset. These expenditures are debited to an asset's accumulated depreciation account.

PP&E assets can be disposed of in several ways, including retirements, cash sales, and exchanges for other assets. The disposal of a PP&E asset usually results in a gain or loss being recorded. However, when similar PP&E assets are exchanged, gains are not recorded. Instead, the unrecognized gain on such an exchange is subtracted from the cash price of the newly acquired asset to determine its acquisition cost for accounting purposes.

Given the nature of PP&E, the control activities for these assets are generally quite different from the comparable controls for other types of assets. Among control activities for PP&E are obtaining adequate insurance coverage and ensuring that the acquisition and disposal of these assets are properly authorized. Another control activity for PP&E is maintaining a property ledger that documents key data items for individual PP&E assets.

A major concern of external decision makers is how well a company's managers are utilizing the total assets at their disposal. Two financial ratios that can be used to address this issue are return on assets and the total asset turnover ratio.

Intangible assets are long-term assets that do not have a physical existence. Among the major types of intangible assets are goodwill, patents, copyrights and trademarks, leaseholds, and leasehold improvements. The cost of intangible assets must be systematically allocated to the accounting periods that they provide economic benefits to a business. Instead of depreciation, this cost allocation process for intangible assets is referred to as amortization.

GLOSSARY

Additions (p. 355) Capital expenditures that extend or expand existing property, plant & equipment assets.

Amortization (p. 363) The allocation of the cost of an intangible asset to the accounting periods that it provides economic benefits to an entity.

Book value (p. 347) For a depreciable asset, the difference between the asset's cost and the balance of its accumulated depreciation account; also referred to as carrying value.

Capital expenditures (p. 355) Expenditures to obtain, expand, or improve long-term assets or to extend their useful lives.

Copyright (p. 365) An exclusive right granted by the federal government to produce and sell a work of art such as songs, books, and films.

Declining-balance method (p. 351) A depreciation method under which annual depreciation expense is computed by multiplying an accelerated depreciation rate, which is a multiple of the straight-line rate, by an asset's book value at the beginning of the year.

Depletion (p. 353) The allocation of the cost of natural resources to the periods in which these assets provide economic benefits to an entity.

Depreciable cost (p. 347) The acquisition cost of a depreciable asset less its salvage value.

Depreciation (p. 344) The process of allocating the cost of a long-term asset over its useful life in a rational and systematic manner.

Double declining-balance method (p. 351) A variation of the declining-balance depreciation method under which the annual depreciation rate for an asset is twice the straight-line rate.

Extraordinary repairs (p. 356) Expenditures that extend the useful life of a property, plant & equipment asset.

Goodwill (p. 364) The excess of the cost of a group of assets over their collective market value.

Intangible assets (p. 363) Long-term assets that do not have a physical form or substance.

Improvements (p. 355) Capital expenditures that enhance an existing asset's operating efficiency or reduce its operating costs.

Leasehold (p. 365) A legal right to use a leased asset for a specified period subject to any restrictions in the lease agreement.

Leasehold improvements (p. 366) Improvements to a leased property made by a lessee that revert to the lessor at the end of the lease.

Natural resources (p. 353) Long-term assets, such as coal deposits, oil and gas reservoirs, and tracts of standing timber, that are extracted or harvested from the earth's surface or from beneath the earth's surface.

Patent (p. 365) An exclusive right granted by the United States Patent Office to manufacture a specific product or use a specific process.

Property ledger (p. 360) A subsidiary ledger in which key information is maintained for each major PP&E asset.

Property, plant & equipment (p. 341) The long-term assets used in the day-to-day operations of a business.
Return on assets (p. 361) The sum of net income and interest expense divided by average total assets for an accounting period.
Revenue expenditures (p. 355) Expenditures that provide economic benefits to only one accounting period and thus are expensed in the period incurred.
Salvage value (p. 347) The estimated value of an asset at the end of its useful life.
Straight-line method (p. 347) A depreciation method that allocates an equal amount of depreciation expense to each year of an asset's estimated useful life.
Total asset turnover ratio (p. 362) Net sales divided by average total assets for an accounting period; a measure of how effectively an entity's assets are being utilized.
Trademark (p. 365) A distinctive word, symbol, or logo used to identify a specific business entity or one of its products.
Units-of-production method (p. 349) A depreciation method under which an asset's useful life is expressed in a number of units of production or use; depreciation expense for any given period is a function of the level of usage of the asset during that period.

DECISION CASE

Renee Jenkins is the CEO of Marsh Industries, Inc., a manufacturing company that has two divisions. Each year, Ms. Jenkins evaluates the job performance of the two divisional managers. Following are financial data for the most recent fiscal year for Marsh Industries and its two divisions.

	Eastern Division	Western Division	Total
Sales	$6,000,000	$9,000,000	$15,000,000
Operating income	620,000	730,000	1,350,000
Corporate headquarters expenses	180,000	180,000	360,000
Interest expense	50,000	50,000	100,000
Income taxes expense	150,000	150,000	300,000
Net income	430,000	560,000	990,000
Average book value of total assets during year	4,200,000	8,300,000	12,500,000
Average market value of total assets during year	7,100,000	8,400,000	15,500,000

Notice in the schedule that Marsh Industries had interest expense of $100,000, income taxes expense of $300,000, and corporate headquarters expenses of $360,000. Historically, Ms. Jenkins has allocated these expenses equally to the two divisions. The interest expense is on a long-term loan obtained five years ago to construct a new factory in the Eastern Division. Also notice that the market value of the Eastern Division's assets is considerably above their book value. The division's new factory is located near the planned site for a major metropolitan airport that was announced within the past year. As a result, the value of the property on which the factory was built has increased dramatically in recent months.

Required: Assume that you are a corporate accountant for Marsh Industries. Ms. Jenkins asks you to compute return on assets and the total asset turnover ratio for the Eastern and Western divisions and to provide a brief assessment of each divisional manager's job performance. She specifically asks that you indicate in your report which manager did a better job managing the assets assigned to his or her division.

What additional information do you believe would be helpful in evaluating the performance of the two managers? What recommendations would you make to Ms. Jenkins regarding the use of return on assets and the total asset turnover ratio to evaluate the managers' job performance? Explain.

QUESTIONS

1. Identify the major types of long-term assets.
2. Define "property, plant & equipment" (PP&E) and provide several examples of assets that qualify as PP&E.
3. Identify key information needs of financial decision makers regarding a business's PP&E assets.
4. Identify advantages and disadvantages of using historical costs as the primary valuation basis for PP&E.
5. Under what circumstances can businesses depart from the historical cost principle for PP&E assets?
6. What alternative valuation basis is used for PP&E in certain countries?
7. Identify the four general issues that accountants must address in accounting for PP&E assets.
8. What types of expenditures are included in the acquisition cost of PP&E assets?
9. Describe the general method used to allocate the lump sum cost of a group of long-term assets to the individual assets acquired.
10. What is the objective of recording depreciation expense each accounting period on depreciable assets?
11. List the three factors that must be identified to compute depreciation expense on a depreciable asset.
12. Identify three common methods of computing depreciation expense. Briefly describe how each of these methods is applied.
13. Which depreciation method is most popular among publicly owned companies? What factor or factors may account for the popularity of this method?
14. How is the "book value" of a depreciable asset computed? How does a depreciable asset's book value change from one accounting period to the next?
15. Why are the depreciation methods applied for federal taxation purposes generally not permissible for financial accounting or financial reporting purposes?
16. Define the terms "revenue expenditures" and "capital expenditures" and provide examples of each.
17. Suppose that a company disposes of a depreciable asset by simply "junking" it. What is the amount of the loss, if any, that the company will record on this asset disposal?
18. Can a gain or loss be recorded when a business exchanges a depreciable asset for a similar asset? Explain.
19. Identify key control activities for PP&E assets.
20. How is return on assets computed? What does this ratio tell us about a business's operations?

21. How is the total asset turnover ratio computed? What does this ratio tell us about a business's operations?
22. Define "intangible assets."
23. Define the term "amortization" as it applies to intangible assets.
24. What is the difference between the legal life and the useful life of an intangible asset?

EXERCISES

25. **True or False** (LO 1–8)
Following are a series of statements regarding topics discussed in Chapter 8.

Required:
Indicate whether each statement is true (T) or false (F).

_____ a. Intangible assets should be amortized over their legal life, their useful life, or forty years, whichever is longer.

_____ b. Businesses are allowed to record gains realized on cash sales of PP&E assets.

_____ c. The "depreciable cost" and "acquisition cost" of a PP&E asset are interchangeable terms.

_____ d. Revenue expenditures provide economic benefits to a business for only one accounting period and, as a a result, are treated as expenses in the period incurred.

_____ e. A property ledger is a subsidiary ledger in which key information is recorded for each major PP&E asset.

_____ f. The salvage value of a PP&E asset is not relevant when a company applies the double declining-balance depreciation method.

_____ g. "Book value" and "carrying value" are interchangeable terms referring to the historical cost of an asset less the balance of its accumulated depreciation account.

_____ h. If a company can prove that the market value of a PP&E asset increased during a given accounting period, no depreciation expense must be recorded for the asset that period.

_____ i. "Land" generally qualifies as a long-term asset, a PP&E asset, and a depreciable asset.

_____ j. Leaseholds are typically classified for balance sheet purposes as PP&E assets although technically they are intangible assets.

_____ k. The method a company uses to finance the acquisition of long-term assets does not affect how the firm's "return on assets" is computed.

26. **Financial Statement Reporting of PP&E Assets** (LO 1)
Wiggins Corporation is a manufacturing firm that was established in 1992. Since that time, the company has acquired several long-term assets used in its operations at a collective cost of $3,600,000. Listed in the following schedule is the acquisition cost of each of these assets and the total depreciation expense recorded on them through the end of 1998.

Description	Acquisition Cost	Depreciation Expense through 1998
Office building	$1,400,000	$230,000
Production equipment	1,200,000	112,000
Office furniture	250,000	61,000
Land	350,000	0
Delivery trucks	400,000	125,000

Required:
1. Prepare the PP&E section of Wiggins Corporation's balance sheet at the end of 1998.
2. Why has no depreciation expense been recorded on the land owned by Wiggins?
3. Besides the information you developed in (1), what other information regarding Wiggins' PP&E assets is needed by decision makers who use the company's financial statements?

27. **Acquisition Cost of PP&E Assets** (LO 1, 2)
Fain Enterprises recently purchased new computer equipment for its company headquarters. Following is information regarding the various expenditures related to the acquisition of this equipment.
a. The original invoice price of the computer equipment was $400,000; however, Fain's owner negotiated a 15 percent price reduction.
b. The delivery cost for the equipment was $2,300 and was paid by Fain.
c. Three computer consultants were retained by Fain to install and test the new equipment at a cost of $1,500.
d. Supplies costing $200 were used in installing and testing the equipment.
e. The day following the installation of the equipment, Fain's owner decided to move the equipment to the floor on which her office was located. An additional $600 of costs were incurred in moving the equipment.

Required:
1. Determine the acquisition cost of the computer equipment for accounting purposes.
2. Prepare an appropriate journal entry to record the acquisition of the computer equipment. (Assume the expenditures listed were paid in cash.)
3. A computer purchased for several thousand dollars may have little resale value one year later because of technological changes in the computer industry. Given that the resale value of computers and computer equipment can decline rapidly, is historical cost the proper valuation basis to use for such assets? Defend your answer.

28. **Group Purchase of PP&E Assets** (LO 2)
Kelly's Garden Supply recently purchased a greenhouse for $360,000 from Wilmoth's Flowers, which was going out of business. Also included in the deal was a recently installed irrigation system, a forklift, and the land on which the greenhouse is located. Following are the individual market values of the assets acquired by Kelly's:

Asset	Market Value
Greenhouse	$250,000
Irrigation system	50,000
Forklift	50,000
Land	50,000

Required:
1. Allocate the $360,000 purchase price among the four assets acquired by Kelly's.
2. Why is it important to allocate the collective purchase price to the four individual assets instead of recording that amount in one aggregate asset account?

29. **Group Purchase of PP&E Assets** (LO 1, 2)

John Anderson, the owner of Anderson Landscaping, is considering buying out a competitor who is retiring. The principal assets of the competitor's business are several large pieces of equipment and the land on which the business is located. John knows that land is not depreciated. As a result, he plans to acquire the business for one lump sum and allocate all of the cost to the land. By not assigning any cost to the equipment, John will avoid recording depreciation expense on that equipment in the future, thus increasing his business's net income. John sees nothing wrong with this plan, since he views the recording of depreciation expense as an accounting "gimmick" anyway.

Required:
Write a memo to John Anderson explaining why his method of accounting for the assets he plans to purchase is inappropriate. Comment on how this method may be detrimental to third parties who will be relying on his business's financial statements.

30. **Computing Depreciation Expense** (LO 3)
Michelman Manufacturing purchased a piece of production equipment on January 1, 1997. The equipment cost $6,500 and was estimated to have a salvage value of $500 at the end of its six-year life.

Required:
1. Compute depreciation expense on the production equipment for both 1997 and 1998 and prepare the appropriate journal entries under the following two assumptions:
   a. Michelman uses the straight-line depreciation method.
   b. Michelman uses the double declining-balance depreciation method.
2. Suppose now that Michelman uses the units-of-production method. The new production equipment was expected to have a useful life of 12,000 hours. Compute the depreciation expense on the production equipment for 1997 and 1998 and prepare the appropriate journal entries, assuming the equipment was used 2,500 hours in 1997 and 1,900 hours in 1998.

31. **Choosing a Depreciation Method** (LO 3)
Albuquerque Stairs, which manufactures stairway railings, purchased a new lathe on January 1, Year 1. The lathe cost $15,000 and was estimated to have a salvage value of $1,000 at the end of its five-year useful life. Presently, the company's owner is trying to decide on a depreciation method to use for this new asset.

Required:
1. Compute depreciation expense on the new lathe for Year 1 and Year 2 assuming that Albuquerque Stairs uses:
   a. the straight-line method.
   b. the double declining-balance method.
2. Suppose that the company decides to apply the units-of-production depreciation method to the new lathe. The lathe will be used to produce approximately 3,500 units of finished product over its five-year useful life. Compute the depreciation expense on the lathe for Year 1 and Year 2 assuming that it is used to produce 550 units of finished product in Year 1 and 670 units of finished product in Year 2.
3. Which of the three major depreciation methods best satisfies the matching principle discussed in Chapter 2? Defend your choice.
4. Under which of the three depreciation methods will Albuquerque Stairs have the highest net income for Year 1? For Year 2?

32. **Depletion of Natural Resources** (LO 3)
On March 1, 1997, Smiley Corporation acquired a large oil reservoir that geologists estimated contained 3 million barrels of crude oil. Smiley paid $7.2 million for the reservoir, which is expected to have no salvage value after the oil has been extracted. During 1997, Smiley extracted and sold 1.2 million barrels of crude oil from the reservoir. During 1998, 1 million barrels of oil were extracted, of which 700,000 barrels were sold by year-end.

Required:

1. Compute the depletion cost per barrel of oil expected to be contained in the reservoir.
2. Prepare the appropriate journal entries in Smiley Corporation's accounting records for 1997 and 1998, given the information provided.
3. If the reservoir contains only 2.5 million barrels of oil, what will happen to the remaining book value of this asset after all the oil has been extracted?

33. **Identifying Revenue and Capital Expenditures** (LO 4)

On April 1, 1994, Dodson Enterprises acquired four bulldozers to be used in its construction and land development business. The bulldozers cost $246,000. Dodson chose to depreciate the bulldozers over useful lives of ten years. During the first several years the bulldozers were in use, Dodson incurred the following additional costs related to them:

a. Oil changes and lubrication of valves, $250 per month.
b. Replaced broken steering mechanism, $1,800.
c. Replaced the engine cooling system of each bulldozer at a total cost of $14,000 to significantly improve their operating efficiency.
d. Repaired a homeowner's fence that was accidentally destroyed by a bulldozer, $2,100.
e. State licensing fees on the bulldozers, $1,440 per year.
f. Paid $49,400 for a major overhaul of the bulldozers; these expenditures were estimated to extend the useful lives of the bulldozers by four years.

Required:

1. Identify those expenditures that were revenue expenditures and those that were capital expenditures. For those items that were capital expenditures, indicate the specific type of capital expenditure.
2. Why is it important for a business to properly distinguish between revenue and capital expenditures related to its long-term assets?

34. **Extraordinary Repairs** (LO 4)

In early January 1996, Talley & Hassee, a manufacturing firm, acquired a new hydraulic press. Talley & Hassee estimated that the machine would be in service for eight years. The machine cost $8,000 and was estimated to have a salvage value of $1,400 at the end of its useful life. The company uses the straight-line depreciation method.

On January 3, 1999, Talley & Hassee spent $2,000 overhauling the hydraulic press. This major overhaul was expected to extend the useful life of the asset by two years (to a total of ten years).

Required:

1. Prepare the appropriate journal entry to record the $2,000 spent to overhaul the hydraulic press in January 1999.
2. Compute the depreciation expense on the hydraulic press for 1999 and prepare the entry to record this depreciation.
3. Explain the reasoning that underlies the accounting treatment applied to extraordinary repairs.

35. **Sale of a PP&E Asset** (LO 3, 5)

On June 30, 1998, Newsom Company sold a computer for $1,250 that had been acquired on January 1, 1996. Newsom had originally estimated that the computer would have a five-year useful life and a $500 salvage value. The original cost of the computer was $2,500. Newsom uses the straight-line depreciation method. The company's fiscal year ends on December 31 and it records depreciation expense on its depreciable assets at the end of each fiscal year.

Required:

1. Determine the book value of the computer on June 30, 1998.
2. Prepare all entries needed to properly account for the disposal of the computer.

36. Disposals of PP&E Assets (LO 5)

Chandra Corporation traded in a 1995 Ford van on a new 1998 Chevy van in late December 1998. Chandra purchased the Ford van for $24,000 in early January 1995. Chandra recorded $4,000 of depreciation expense on the van each year from 1995 through 1998. The Chevy dealer had given Chandra the option of either paying $23,500 cash for the new Chevy van, or paying $17,500 plus trading in the Ford van.

Required:

1. Prepare the entry necessary to record this exchange transaction in Chandra's accounting records.
2. Suppose the cash price of the new Chevy van was $23,500 but that the deal negotiated by Chandra to acquire the new van involved a $14,500 cash payment plus the Ford van. Prepare the entry to record the exchange transaction under these circumstances.
3. What accounting principle or concept dictates the accounting treatment for gains and losses on exchanges of similar assets?

37. Accounting for Fully Depreciated Assets (LO 3)

Jim's Bike Shop purchased an air compressor four years ago at a cost of $2,400. The air compressor was estimated to have a four-year useful life when it was acquired. At the end of its useful life, it was projected to have no salvage value. This air compressor is now fully depreciated with a zero book value. Surprisingly to the business's owner, the air compressor "works like new" and he has no plans to replace it.

Required:

1. Should this business continue to record depreciation expense on the air compressor each year? Why or why not?
2. Should a business keep a fully depreciated asset on its books indefinitely as long as the asset is being used in the business?
3. Explain how the matching principle was violated by Jim's Bike Shop and how this violation affected the financial statements of the business. Was this violation intentional?

38. Disposals of PP&E Assets (LO 5)

On January 1, 1995, Landers Company purchased ten washing machines to be used in its coin-operated laundry. Each washer cost $400 and had an estimated salvage value of $40 at the end of its eight-year useful life. On September 30, 1998, Landers decided to purchase more efficient machines and sold the ten washers for $2,200. Landers Company uses the straight-line depreciation method for its depreciable assets and records depreciation expense at the end of each year.

Required:

1. Prepare the appropriate journal entry to record depreciation expense on the washers prior to their disposal. What is the book value of the washers following the posting of this journal entry?
2. Prepare the journal entry to record the sale of the washers.
3. Suppose that rather than being sold, the washers were simply hauled off to the junkyard. Prepare the journal entry to record the disposal of the washers under this assumption.
4. Suppose now that the old washers were exchanged for ten new washers that had a collective cash price of $5,100. In addition to trading in the old washers, Landers was required to pay cash of $3,300. Prepare the journal entry to record the disposal of the old washers under this assumption.

39. Analyzing Total Assets (LO 7)

The following information was taken from a recent annual report of TCBY Enterprises, Inc., which sells yogurt and other food items.

	Year 1	Year 2
Net sales	$107,633,301	$109,525,036
Interest expense	1,751,266	1,311,958
Net income	5,072,924	6,408,811
Average total assets	131,925,142	128,691,136

Required:

1. Compute TCBY's return on assets for Years 1 and 2. Given these measures, in which year did the company utilize its assets more effectively? Explain.
2. Compute TCBY's total asset turnover ratio for Years 1 and 2. Given these ratios, in which year did TCBY utilize its assets more effectively? Explain.
3. What other information would decision makers find useful in analyzing how effectively TCBY's management used the company's assets in Years 1 and 2?

40. **Intangible Assets** (LO 8)
Hulsey Company, a sporting goods manufacturer, began operations on January 1, 1998. On that date, the firm purchased two intangible assets from a competitor that was going out of business. The first patent involved a golf ball that corrects hooks and slices. Husley paid $300,000 for this patent, which had a remaining legal life of twelve years and a remaining estimated useful life of five years. The second intangible asset acquired by Hulsey was a trademark for a running shoe. Hulsey paid $100,000 for this trademark, which has an indefinite legal life and an estimated useful life of ten years.

Required:

1. Prepare the journal entries to record the acquisition of the patent and trademark by Hulsey. Prepare journal entries to record amortization expense on these two assets in 1998.
2. Why do decision makers sometimes overlook the importance of intangible assets?

41. **Internal Controls for PP&E Assets** (LO 6)
Eddie Garcia owns a small but rapidly growing plumbing business. Most of Garcia's assets are long-term assets including plumbing tools, several service vehicles, and office furniture and equipment. The collective book value of Garcia's long-term assets exceeds $300,000. Garcia has never developed a set of explicit internal controls for his long-term assets.

Required:

Write a brief memo to Eddie Garcia that emphasizes the importance of every business having reliable and cost-effective internal controls. Identify in your memo internal control risks related to Garcia's long-term assets. Conclude your memo with examples of control activities Garcia should consider implementing for his long-term assets.

42. **Financial Statement Disclosures for PP&E Assets** (LO 1)
Refer to the annual report of Outback Steakhouse that is included as an appendix to this text.

Required:

1. What balance sheet caption does Outback use in referring to its PP&E assets? List Outback's major classes of PP&E assets.
2. What depreciation method does Outback apply to its PP&E assets?
3. How much depreciation expense did Outback apparently record during 1996? How did you arrive at this figure?
4. What important narrative disclosures did you find in Outback's annual report regarding the firm's PP&E assets?

PROBLEM SET A

43. Acquisition of PP&E Assets (LO 2, 3, 4)

In 1998, Kare Corporation acquired several PP&E assets for its manufacturing operations. Following are descriptions of costs incurred by Kare during 1998 related to these assets. All amounts were paid in cash.

a. On January 1, Kare purchased a warehouse and the land on which it was located for $2,600,000. The land's appraised value was $700,000, while the warehouse had an appraised value of $2,100,000. The estimated useful life of the warehouse is twenty years, and its estimated salvage value is $200,000.
b. On January 3, Kare purchased production equipment for $1,000,000 that had an estimated useful life of five years and an estimated salvage value of $60,000. Delivery costs of $4,200 were paid by the seller of the equipment. Costs to repair the equipment after it was damaged during installation totaled $2,700.
c. On April 2, Kare purchased office furniture and fixtures for $400,000. These assets have an estimated useful life of ten years and an estimated salvage value of $30,000.
d. On July 1, Kare purchased four used delivery trucks at a cost of $12,000 each. Each truck had an estimated remaining useful life of four years and an estimated salvage value of $2,400. Expenses paid to deliver the trucks totaled $900, while insurance paid on the trucks while they were in transit amounted to $300. Kare immediately installed an alarm system on each truck at a cost of $600 per truck.

Required:

1. Prepare the journal entries to record the acquisitions of PP&E assets by Kare Corporation during 1998.
2. Kare records depreciation on its PP&E assets each December 31. Assuming that the company uses the straight-line method, prepare the December 31, 1998, adjusting entries for depreciation expense on the assets it acquired during 1998.

44. Alternative Depreciation Methods (LO 3)

Roslyn and Jimmy recently decided to open a restaurant specializing in Georgian cuisine. They purchased an existing restaurant on January 1, 1998, at a cost of $650,000. The two co-owners paid 10 percent of the purchase price in cash and financed the balance by obtaining a mortgage. The restaurant has an estimated useful life of twenty-five years and an estimated salvage value of $150,000. Also on January 1, 1998, Roslyn and Jimmy paid cash of $80,000 for used kitchen equipment. The equipment has an estimated useful life of four years and an estimated salvage value of $8,000.

Required:

1. Compute depreciation expense for 1998 and 1999 on the restaurant using the following methods:
   a. Straight-line
   b. Double declining-balance
2. Prepare year-end adjusting journal entries to record the depreciation expense amounts computed in (1).
3. Compute depreciation expense on the kitchen equipment for each year of its useful life, 1998 through 2001, assuming that the following depreciation methods are used:
   a. Straight-line
   b. Double declining-balance
4. Prepare year-end adjusting journal entries to record the depreciation expense amounts computed in (3).
5. Suppose that a business's owners believe that the double declining-balance method most accurately reflects the true depreciation pattern of their firm's depreciable assets. Would it be unethical for the owners to apply the straight-line depreciation method to these assets? Why or why not?

45. Alternative Depreciation Methods (LO 1, 3)

Midori Airlines is a small charter airline company that operates between San Francisco and Los Angeles. On January 1, 1998, Midori purchased a jet. The jet cost $1,600,000 and is estimated to have a salvage value of $100,000 at the end of its five-year useful life. Midori expects that the jet will be flown the following number of miles over the course of its useful life:

1998	100,000 miles
1999	120,000 miles
2000	130,000 miles
2001	90,000 miles
2002	60,000 miles

Required:

1. Prepare a depreciation schedule similar to the one shown in Exhibit 8.4, assuming that Midori uses the following depreciation methods:
   a. Straight-line
   b. Double declining-balance
   c. Units-of-production
2. In your opinion, which of these three depreciation methods is most consistent with the matching principle? Defend your answer.
3. Suppose that in early 1998 Midori had a large loan outstanding from a local bank. Which of the three depreciation methods might Midori's bank loan officer prefer the company use? Defend your answer.

46. Revenue and Capital Expenditures (LO 4)

On April 1, 1996, Krempler Enterprises purchased a new bookbinding machine for its manufacturing facility. The machine cost $241,000 plus sales taxes of 5 percent and a delivery charge of $2,200. Following are selected expenditures incurred by Krempler in the next few years related to this machine.

a. Valve adjustments on the machine were made in September 1996 at a cost of $600.
b. In September 1997, Krempler bought a special attachment for the machine to increase its operating efficiency. The attachment cost $8,000 plus $600 for installation. During installation, a Krempler employee damaged the attachment, resulting in repair costs of $240.
c. In December 1998, Krempler spent $24,000 overhauling the binding machine. This overhaul was estimated to extend the machine's useful life by two years.
d. Periodic maintenance expenses incurred in 1998 for the binding machine totaled $3,200.
e. In January 1999, the machine's cutting mechanism was replaced to accommodate special-order binding materials. This new mechanism, which cost $7,100, significantly reduced the costs to operate the machine.

Required:

1. For each expenditure related to the bookbinding machine, indicate whether the item was a revenue expenditure or a capital expenditure.
2. For the capital expenditures, indicate how each item should have been recorded in Krempler's accounting records.
3. Suppose that all of the listed expenditures were recorded as capital expenditures. What accounting principles or concepts were violated and why?

47. Depletion of Natural Resources (LO 3)

On February 12, 1997, Thayer Mining Corporation (TMC) acquired a large tract of land for $1,800,000. Geological reports indicate that this property contains 800,000 tons of ore. TMC estimates that the property can be sold for $360,000 following removal of the ore.

Required:

1. Assume that the following amounts of ore were recovered and sold during 1997 and 1998 from the TMC property:

	1997	1998
Tons of ore recovered	120,000	170,000
Tons of ore sold	110,000	180,000

   Determine the depletion expense recorded by TMC during 1997 and 1998.
2. Suppose that the property acquired by TMC actually has a negative salvage value of $280,000 because of large reclamation expenditures required to rehabilitate the property after the ore is extracted. Recompute the depletion expense for 1997 and 1998 given the data provided in (1).
3. What accounting principle dictates the accounting treatment given the reclamation expenditures referred to in (2)?

48. **Disposals of PP&E Assets** (LO 3, 5)

On January 1, 1995, Lein Phan Vending purchased five vending machines to place in a high school. Each vending machine cost $3,100 and was estimated to have a six-year useful life. The estimated salvage value of the vending machines was $400 each. Lein Phan uses the straight-line depreciation method. On April 1, 1998, the company decided to replace the vending machines and sold them collectively for $8,200.

Required:

1. Prepare the journal entry to record the depreciation expense on the vending machines for the first three months of 1998.
2. Determine the book value of the vending machines following the posting of the journal entry prepared in (1).
3. Prepare the journal entry to record the sale of the vending machines.
4. Prepare the journal entry to record the sale of the vending machines, assuming they were sold for $11,300.
5. Suppose now that rather than selling the vending machines, the company traded them in on six new machines that had a collective cash price of $25,300. In addition to trading in the old vending machines, Lein Phan was required to pay cash of $16,700. Prepare the appropriate journal entry to record this exchange transaction.

49. **Analyzing Total Assets** (LO 7)

Cardinal Health, Inc., and Herman Miller, Inc., are two companies in very different industries. Cardinal Health is a major distributor of pharmaceuticals, while Herman Miller markets office furnishings and related products. Following is selected financial information from recent years for each of these companies. (Amounts are presented in thousands of dollars.)

	Cardinal Health, Inc.		Herman Miller, Inc.	
	Year 1	Year 2	Year 1	Year 2
Net sales	$4,709,085	$5,790,411	$855,673	$953,200
Interest expense	26,174	18,140	2,089	1,828
Net income	39,298	33,931	22,054	40,373
Average total assets	1,048,752	1,273,013	477,805	509,044

Required:
1. Compute the return on assets and total asset turnover ratio for each company for both Year 1 and 2.
2. Based strictly on the data you computed in (1), which of these companies did a better job of managing its assets in Year 1 and 2? Defend your answer.
3. How may the nature of a company's industry affect the two ratios you computed in (1)? Explain by comparing the two industries represented by Cardinal Health and Herman Miller.

50. **Accounting for Intangible Assets** (LO 1, 8)
Coleman Pharmaceuticals is a leading manufacturer of pharmaceutical products. Following are transactions or events involving Coleman's intangible assets during a recent year.
a. January 4: Purchased a patent on the drug Zorcerin for $1,500,000.
b. February 9: Sold a patent with a book value of $753,000 to a competitor for $800,000.
c. June 30: A competitor introduced a new drug that made a patent held by Coleman obsolete; the book value of the patent was $607,000 at the time.
d. December 31: Recorded $300,000 of amortization expense on goodwill.
e. December 31: Recorded amortization expense on the Zorcerin patent, which had a legal life of twelve years when acquired on January 4 and an estimated useful life at the time of five years.

Required:
1. Prepare the appropriate journal entry for each transaction or event listed for Coleman Pharmaceuticals.
2. What accounting principles or concepts prevent a business from recording goodwill it has developed? In your opinion, would allowing businesses to record goodwill they have developed result in more useful financial statements for decision makers? Why or why not?

PROBLEM SET B

51. **Acquisition of PP&E Assets** (LO 2, 3, 4)
Beckwith Construction Corporation acquired several assets for its production operations during 1998. Following are descriptions of costs incurred by Beckwith related to these asset acquisitions. All amounts were paid in cash.
a. On January 4, Beckwith purchased a small factory, the land on which it was located, and the accompanying land improvements for $9,000,000. A real estate commission of $50,000 was also paid on this purchase. The factory had an appraised value of $8,000,000 versus an appraised value of $1,200,000 and $800,000 for the land and land improvements, respectively. The factory is expected to have a zero salvage value at the end of its estimated useful life of forty years. The land improvements are expected to have a salvage value of $20,000 at the end of their estimated useful life of ten years.
b. On July 1, Beckwith purchased a piece of used machinery at a cost of $320,000. At the end of its five-year useful life, the machinery is expected to have a salvage value of $40,000. Immediately after the machinery was acquired, Beckwith replaced its engine at a cost of $20,000.
c. On September 2, Beckwith purchased new furniture for its corporate headquarters. The furniture cost $9,600 and is expected to have a zero salvage value at the end of its three-year useful life.

d. On October 31, Beckwith purchased a flatbed truck at a cost of $26,000. The truck has an estimated useful life of four years and an estimated salvage value of $2,000. The company paid $1,400 to install a bed liner and sideboards on the truck immediately after it was purchased. An additional $450 was spent to repair damage to the truck's paint job during the installation of the sideboards. Beckwith's name and logo were painted on the doors of the truck at a cost of $200.

Required:

1. Prepare the journal entries to record the acquisitions of PP&E assets by Beckwith Construction Corporation during 1998.
2. Beckwith records depreciation on its PP&E assets each December 31. Assuming that the company uses the straight-line method, prepare the December 31, 1998, adjusting entries for depreciation expense on the assets it acquired during 1998.

52. **Alternative Depreciation Methods** (LO 3)
Wayne Garth opened a comedy club during the first few days of 1998. On January 2 of that year, Garth rented a building and then immediately furnished it at a cost of $100,000. The furniture has an expected useful life of five years and an estimated salvage value of $10,000. On January 6, 1998, Garth purchased $40,000 of sound equipment that has an estimated useful life of ten years. The salvage value of this equipment is estimated to be $4,000.

Required:

1. Compute the depreciation expense on the furniture for each year of its useful life, 1998 through 2002, assuming that the following depreciation methods are used:
   a. Straight-line
   b. Double declining-balance
2. Prepare year-end adjusting journal entries to record the depreciation expense amounts computed in (1).
3. Compute the depreciation expense for 1998 and 1999 on the sound equipment using the following methods:
   a. Straight-line
   b. Double declining-balance
4. Prepare year-end adjusting journal entries to record the depreciation expense amounts computed in (3).
5. Suppose that in early 1998, Wayne Garth asked your advice on which depreciation method, straight-line or double declining-balance, he should apply to his business's assets. What factors would you have suggested that he consider in making this decision?

53. **Alternative Depreciation Methods** (LO 1, 3)
On January 3, 1998, Faramarz Freight Lines purchased a new truck for local deliveries. The truck cost $62,000 and was estimated to have a $12,000 salvage value at the end of its five-year useful life. The owner of the company expected the truck to be driven the following number of miles over the course of its useful life:

1998	70,000 miles
1999	60,000 miles
2000	50,000 miles
2001	40,000 miles
2002	30,000 miles

Required:

1. Prepare a depreciation schedule similar to the one shown in Exhibit 8.4, assuming that Faramarz uses the following depreciation methods:
   a. Straight-line
   b. Double declining-balance
   c. Units-of-production
2. In your opinion, which of these three depreciation methods is most consistent with the matching principle? Defend your answer.
3. Suppose that in early 1998 Faramarz had a large loan outstanding from a local bank. Which of the three depreciation methods would Faramarz's bank loan officer have preferred the company use? Defend your answer.

54. **Revenue and Capital Expenditures** (LO 4)

On March 1, 1996, Audas & Ayres, a law firm, purchased a new computer system at a cost of $24,000, plus sales taxes of 8 percent. The computer system was estimated to have a five-year useful life and a salvage value of $3,000. Following are selected expenditures Audas & Ayres incurred in the next few years related to the computer system.

a. In September 1996, $200 was spent to replace a disk drive that had gone haywire.
b. In March 1997, a computer consultant was brought in to develop a local area network for the Audas & Ayres office. The law firm spent $3,200 for this project, which did not extend the life of the computer system but made it much more efficient.
c. In January 1998, a computer "checkup" was performed by a local computer technician. This checkup included vacuuming the inside of each computer to remove dust and testing for any malfunctioning parts. The cost of the checkup was $250.
d. In March 1998, an electrical malfunction damaged a computer monitor, resulting in a repair bill of $90.
e. In July 1998, several compact disk (CD) drives were added to the computer system at a cost of $3,800.
f. In December 1998, a computer consultant was brought in to reconfigure Audas & Ayres' computer system and its local area network at a cost of $8,200. Several additional components were added to the system, and several existing components were upgraded. Audas & Ayres estimated that the reconfiguration would extend the life of the computer system for two years beyond its original estimated useful life of five years.

Required:

1. For each expenditure related to the computer system, indicate whether the item is a revenue expenditure or a capital expenditure.
2. For the capital expenditures, indicate how each item should have been recorded in Audas & Ayres' accounting records.
3. Suppose that Audas & Ayres spend $65 on a new computer component that technically satisfies the definition of an "improvement" discussed in the text. Instead of capitalizing this expenditure, Audas & Ayres charge the $65 to an expense account. The firm's accountant justifies this treatment by maintaining that the expenditure is not "material." Explain the reasoning of the accountant.

55. **Depletion of Natural Resources** (LO 3)

On April 1, 1997, Gist Mining, Inc. (GMI), purchased a mining property that contains an estimated 30,000 ounces of the mineral lasordite. GMI paid $2,800,000 for the property and incurred another $800,000 digging a mine shaft. The property will have a salvage value of approximately $240,000 following the removal of the lasordite.

Required:

1. Assume that GMI recovered and sold the following amounts of minerals from the mine during 1997 and 1998:

	1997	1998
Ounces recovered	6,000	14,000
Ounces sold	4,500	12,000

   Determine the depletion expense recorded by GMI during 1997 and 1998.
2. Suppose that the property acquired by GMI actually has a negative salvage value of $150,000 because of reclamation expenditures required to rehabilitate the property after the lasordite is extracted. Recompute the depletion expense for 1997 and 1998, given the data provided in (1).
3. What accounting principle dictates the accounting treatment given the reclamation expenditures referred to in (2)?

56. **Disposals of PP&E Assets** (LO 3, 5)
On January 1, 1995, W & J Cabs purchased five new taxis. The taxis cost $20,000 each and were estimated to have a five-year useful life and a salvage value of $2,000 each. W & J uses the straight-line depreciation method. On September 30, 1998, W & J decided to replace the five taxis and sold them to an automobile wholesaler at a collective price of $24,200.

Required:

1. Prepare the journal entry to record the depreciation expense on the five taxis for the first nine months of 1998.
2. Determine the book value of the taxis following the posting of the journal entry prepared in (1).
3. Prepare the journal entry to record the sale of the taxis.
4. Prepare the journal entry to record the sale of the taxis, assuming they were sold for $39,400.
5. Suppose now that rather than selling the taxis, the company traded them in on five new taxis that had a collective cash price of $119,000. In addition to trading in the old taxis, W & J was required to pay cash of $47,300. Prepare the appropriate journal entry to record this exchange transaction.

57. **Analyzing Total Assets** (LO 7)
Presented in the following table are recent financial data for two companies that operate in very different industries. Clothestime, Inc., is a discount retailer of women's apparel, while Toll Brothers, Inc., is a homebuilder. (Amounts are presented in thousands of dollars.)

	Clothestime, Inc.		Toll Brothers, Inc.	
	Year 1	Year 2	Year 1	Year 2
Net sales	$315,164	$347,569	$392,560	$501,822
Interest expense	0	71	17,129	18,195
Net income	8,652	8,167	28,058	36,177
Average total assets	108,146	93,771	531,445	430,417

Required:

1. Compute the return on assets and total asset turnover ratio for each company for both Year 1 and Year 2.

2. Based strictly on the data you computed in (1), which of these companies did a better job of managing its assets in Year 1 and 2? Defend your answer.
3. How may the nature of a company's industry affect the two ratios you computed in (1)? Explain by comparing the two industries represented by Clothestime and Toll Brothers.

58. **Economic Benefits Associated with Intangible Assets** (LO 8)
Refer to Exhibit 8.9, which lists specific intangible assets of several companies. Recall the following definition of an asset: probable future economic benefits obtained or controlled by a particular entity as a result of past transactions or events.

Required:
For each intangible asset listed in Exhibit 8.9, briefly describe the "probable future economic benefit" it provides to the given company.

CASES

59. **Errors in Depreciation Computations** (LO 1, 3)

Jake Johannson is an accounting major at the local university and the accountant for Donnie's Delivery Service. The principal asset of this company is a fleet of ten identical delivery trucks purchased two years ago when the business was established. Jake has served as the accountant for Donnie's Delivery Service since its inception, having been hired by the business's owner, who is also the father of Jake's best friend.

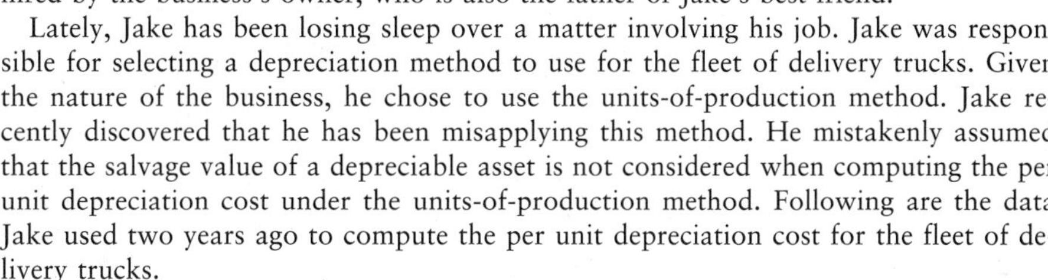

Lately, Jake has been losing sleep over a matter involving his job. Jake was responsible for selecting a depreciation method to use for the fleet of delivery trucks. Given the nature of the business, he chose to use the units-of-production method. Jake recently discovered that he has been misapplying this method. He mistakenly assumed that the salvage value of a depreciable asset is not considered when computing the per unit depreciation cost under the units-of-production method. Following are the data Jake used two years ago to compute the per unit depreciation cost for the fleet of delivery trucks.

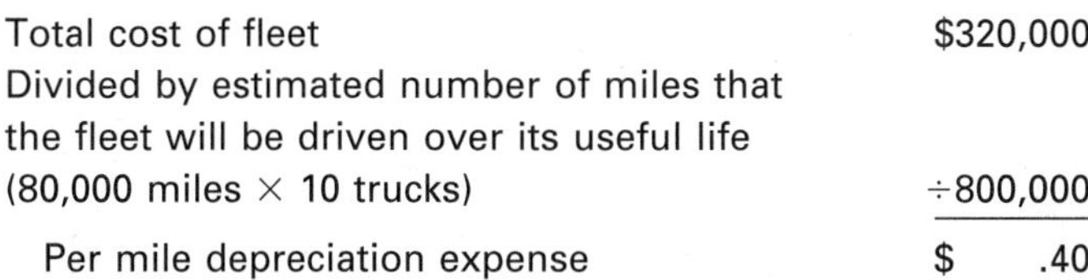

Total cost of fleet	$320,000
Divided by estimated number of miles that the fleet will be driven over its useful life (80,000 miles × 10 trucks)	÷800,000
Per mile depreciation expense	$ .40

As you can see, Jake ignored the fleet's estimated salvage value of $129,600 when he made this computation.

Jake is worried that if he tells Donnie about his oversight, he may lose his job. Additionally, he is concerned that Donnie may be in trouble for issuing incorrect financial statements the past two years to the bank that provided the financing for the fleet. (Note: The truck fleet was driven 200,000 miles in Year 1 and 250,000 miles in Year 2.)

Required:
1. Compute the depreciation expense that was included each of the past two years, Year 1 and Year 2, in the financial statements of Donnie's Delivery Service. Compute the depreciation expense that should have been included in the business's financial statements each of the past two years.
2. What information would you need to determine whether the financial statements of this business were "materially" misstated for the past two years? Explain.

3. Place yourself in Jake's shoes. One option is to say nothing; Jake will be graduating soon and moving out of state. Another option would be to go directly to the bank loan officer and admit the error and tell him that the misstated financial statements are his (Jake's) responsibility. Evaluate these and other options that Jake has. What would you do and why?

60. International Differences in Asset Valuation (LO 1)

Hanson Corporation is a Minnesota-based firm whose principal operating activities are carried on by three subsidiaries located in Ireland, France, and Sweden. You are the banker for Hanson Corporation. Recently, Hanson applied for a large loan. To supplement the company's loan application, you requested "consolidated" financial statements for Hanson and its three subsidiaries for the past three years. You are aware that certain countries allow businesses to periodically restate long-term assets to their current values. As you review Hanson's consolidated financial statements, you wonder whether revenues from such restatements are "buried" in the company's financial data.

Required:

1. Research the accounting standards for the three countries in which Hanson's subsidiaries are located. Do the accounting rules of these countries permit revaluations of long-term assets? If so, under what general conditions or circumstances are such revaluations permitted?
2. Explain how an asset revaluation affects a company's financial statements in the year of the revaluation and in subsequent years.

61. Human Resource Accounting (LO 1)

The most important long-term assets of most businesses are people. How long would a major manufacturing firm survive without a skilled sales staff, industrious production-line workers, product development specialists, and, yes, accountants to capture and record the firm's financial data? The same is true of those successful Mom-and-Pop businesses that survive and thrive primarily because Mom and Pop are dedicated and hardworking. Surprisingly, "human resource" assets very seldom appear on a balance sheet. In recent decades, there was a brief surge of interest in human resource accounting. However, the alleged difficulty of accounting for human resources discouraged most companies from seriously considering "booking" their people assets.

Required:

Refer to the discussion of fundamental accounting concepts in Chapter 2. Prepare a brief report identifying the conceptual principles that could be used to defend the inclusion of human resource assets on the balance sheets of business entities. Also identify in your report conceptual principles that could be used to argue against inclusion of human resource assets on balance sheets. Conclude your report by presenting a coherent argument either for or against the inclusion of human resources on the balance sheets of business entities.

PROJECTS

62. Valuation Adjustments for PP&E Assets

Last week, the chief accountant of LeBaron Enterprises, Jennifer Chavez, submitted a draft of the company's financial statements for its recently ended fiscal year to the firm's owner. Unfortunately, LeBaron, which wholesales foreign auto parts, did not have a good year. Sales declined by more than 15 percent in the past twelve months, and the company had a net loss for the first time in its history. The net loss of $37,000 is small compared with the company's sales, which exceeded $30,000,000. Nevertheless, it is still a loss, breaking a string of more than twenty-five straight years in which the company posted a profit.

Today, H. R. Holliday, LeBaron's owner and a prominent member of the local business community, approached Jennifer with a plan to improve his company's reported operating results. Five years ago, LeBaron purchased a large tract of land on the outskirts of the city. Property values have skyrocketed in the past few years in the area where that land is located, since several residential developments have been started nearby. Holliday has obtained three real estate appraisals indicating that the value of the property now exceeds $2 million—it was purchased for $350,000.

"Jennifer, you know, I have never asked you to do something like this before," Holliday said quietly after entering Jennifer's office and closing the door behind him. "But, I just can't stand to see our financial statements go out with a loss reported on them." Jennifer sat stoically behind her desk, realizing what was coming next. "I have three appraisals here in my hand proving that the Brookhaven property has increased in value by more than $1.5 million since we purchased it and by at least $600,000 in just the past year. Can't you find some way to squeeze a small part of this unreported gain into our income statement? Just enough to wipe out that loss? I know that we are going to get back on track this year. This will be a one-time thing only, I promise you."

"Mr. Holliday, accounting rules don't allow us to report unrealized gains like that in our income statement."

"Jennifer, I'm not asking you to report this as an unrealized gain on a real estate property. Just make up some vague type of miscellaneous revenue to hide this item in." Jennifer frowned and looked away. "Come on, Jenny. We're talking nickels and dimes here. Look, we have $30 million in revenues. Converting a small net loss into a small net income is not going to mislead anybody." Holliday opened Jennifer's door and then turned and added, "I want you to think about it overnight. Then, come into my office first thing tomorrow so that we can make our plans."

Required:

1. Break into your project groups to discuss this vignette. While discussing the vignette, develop a list of the factors that Jennifer should consider in deciding how to respond to Mr. Holliday's request. Also list the parties who may be affected by Jennifer's decision and briefly describe the potential impact on each of those parties. Finally, discuss and develop a list of the short-term and long-term implications that Jennifer's decision will have for her, both in terms of her employment situation and otherwise.
2. As a group, attempt to reach a consensus regarding (a) how Jennifer will likely respond to Mr. Holliday's request and (b) how Jennifer should respond to his request.
3. Identify other information that would be helpful in analyzing Jennifer's dilemma.
4. One member of the group should be prepared to present a summary overview to the class of the group's discussion of this vignette including the data items specifically required by (1) and (3).

63. Accounting for Research and Development Expenditures

One of the most debated accounting issues among accountants and business executives is the accounting treatment of so-called research and development expenditures. Many large companies spend millions of dollars each year researching and attempting to develop lifesaving drugs, faster and more efficient computers, fertilizers that are more effective and less hazardous to the environment, and so on. However, as a general rule, such expenditures must be written off in the period incurred instead of being capitalized.

Required:

1. Research the technical accounting rules for research and development expenditures. Also research accounting and business literature to identify articles and other publications focusing on the controversy regarding the accounting treatment of research and development expenditures.

2. Write a report that includes the following items:
   a. A brief summary of the key accounting rules related to research and development expenditures
   b. The arguments for capitalizing research and development expenditures
   c. The arguments against capitalizing research and development expenditures
   d. Your conclusion regarding whether the current accounting rules for research and development expenditures should be changed

64. Analyzing Total Assets

Identify three large companies with which you are familiar: one merchandising firm, one manufacturing firm, and one service firm. Obtain annual reports or other sources of financial data for these three companies for the past three years.

Required:

Compute the return on assets and total asset turnover ratio for the three companies that you selected for each of the years that you obtained data. Write a report addressing the following issues:

a. What factors likely account for the differences in these two financial measures across these three companies?
b. What trends are evident in these data for each company?
c. Are these trends favorable or unfavorable?
d. Given your familiarity with these companies, attempt to explain the reasons underlying these trends.

65. SEC Disclosures for PP&E

Public companies registered with the Securities and Exchange Commission (SEC) must file an annual financial report or "10-K" statement with that agency. "Item 2" of a company's 10-K is entitled "Properties." This item provides a description of the major manufacturing, administrative, distribution, and other facilities owned by a company.

Required:

Using the Internet, access EDGAR, the SEC's electronic data gathering and retrieval system. Retrieve the most recent 10-K statements of two public companies that operate in the same industry and print "Item 2, Properties" from each of those statements. How do Item 2 disclosures supplement each firm's financial statements? Which company's Item 2 disclosures are most informative for financial decision makers? Defend your answer. Submit to your instructor the printed Item 2 disclosures for the two companies along with your answers to the previous questions.

IV

ACCOUNTING FOR LIABILITIES AND RELATED TRANSACTIONS

Part IV of this text introduces you to accounting issues and rules related to liabilities. Chapter 9 focuses principally on current liabilities, such as short-term notes payable and accrued liabilities. Also included in Chapter 9 is an overview of contingent liabilities. Chapter 10 discusses accounting for long-term liabilities including bonds payable, capital lease obligations, and liabilities stemming from pension plans and other postretirement employee benefit plans. Sandwiched between Chapters 9 and 10 is Module 2, "The Time Value of Money." The time value of money concept is relevant to accounting decisions for several assets and liabilities, including bonds payable, the primary topic of Chapter 10.

The organizational scheme used in Chapters 6 through 8 is also applied in Chapters 9 and 10. Each major topical area focusing on a specific liability account or group of liability accounts has the following features:

1. An overview of that account (or accounts) including important terms and definitions.
2. Identification of decision makers' key information needs regarding the account.
3. A discussion of relevant accounting procedures.
4. A discussion of relevant control activities.
5. A description of financial ratios and other analytical measures that decision makers can use to interpret financial data related to the given account.

9 Current Liabilities and Contingent Liabilities

"Creditors are a superstitious sect, great observers of set days and times."
Ben Franklin

LEARNING OBJECTIVES

After studying this chapter, you should be able to do the following:

1. Define the key information needs of decision makers regarding current liabilities.
2. Account for the major types of transactions and events affecting current liabilities.
3. Discuss key control activities for current liabilities including the maintenance of a payroll register.
4. Compute and interpret the current ratio and working capital.
5. Define the key characteristics of, and account for, contingent liabilities.

FOCUS ON
DECISION MAKING

Pay Your Payables, or Pay the Piper

Accounts payable consume a large portion of the cash resources of most businesses and are the largest current liability of many firms. The following article focuses on a company whose executives realized—before it was too late—that gaining control over accounts payable is critical to sustaining good relationships with suppliers and to maintaining a firm's financial health.

It's easy to overlook the importance of a well-managed accounts payable system. Walter Pancewicz, vice-president of Aria Group Architects, an Oak Park, Illinois, architectural firm recalls, "Soon after we founded the company in 1989, we started falling dangerously behind on our payables."

The problem: Aria's early system had relied on all three owners' taking turns handling accounts payable. "It became clear to us that we needed one person to be fully responsible," Pancewicz notes. He assumed that job; later the firm hired an office manager.

As Aria has grown to nearly $2 million in sales, its accounts payable system has developed, too. Pancewicz explains, "We've tried to keep payments timely and accurate to protect ourselves against the risk of fraud." Here's the company's four-step system:

1. When a bill arrives, the office manager immediately logs it into the computer, recording the date of arrival, the amount, and the date it is due, and any relevant comments (such as order problems or discounts for early payment).
2. Pancewicz receives a weekly accounts payable report that details the key information for each payable and that highlights the bills due that week. The goal: to have all invoices paid within 30 days.
3. Once Pancewicz approves the weekly payment plan, checks are issued, which he then signs.
4. At the end of each month, Aria's outside accountant receives and reviews copies of the weekly accounts payable reports, copies of all signed checks, and a monthly report that summarizes all accounts payable activities for that period.

The precautions pay off, Pancewicz says. "Although we've never had a case of intentional fraud, our accountant did catch a $12,000 mistake. We had received the same bill twice and paid it without double-checking our records." He laughs. "That proved to us that it's worth having safeguards."

Source: "Accounts Payable: Creating a System of Safeguards," *Inc. Magazine,* February 1996, 104. Reprinted with permission.

This chapter addresses accounting issues for current liabilities and contingent liabilities. The major focus of this chapter is current liabilities, including notes payable, accrued liabilities, and related accounts. Contingent liabilities can be either current or long-term liabilities. Since these liabilities pose unique accounting issues, we consider them independently of other liabilities.

CURRENT LIABILITIES: AN INTRODUCTION

The Financial Accounting Standards Board defines liabilities as "probable future sacrifices of economic benefits arising from present obligations of a particular entity to transfer assets or provide services to other entities in the future as a result of past transactions or events."[1] Chapter 2 presented a more concise but less precise definition of liabilities: amounts owed to other parties. Those liabilities that must be paid by a business within one year or its operating cycle, whichever is longer, are classified as current liabilities.

We can identify two general types of current liabilities. The first type includes current liabilities whose dollar amounts are defined by a contractual or implied contractual agreement, such as accounts payable. Other current liabilities must be estimated, including many accrued liabilities that businesses record via adjusting entries at the end of each accounting period, for example, income taxes payable.

The individual line items included in the current liabilities section of a balance sheet vary from company to company. Exhibit 9.1 lists the current liabilities reported recently by two public companies. ShopKo Stores operates a chain of retail stores stretching from the company's home base in Wisconsin to the West Coast. Whole Foods

EXHIBIT 9.1 ▼
Current Liabilities on the Corporate Balance Sheet: Two Examples

SHOPKO STORES, INC.

Accounts payable—Trade	$149,293
Accrued compensation and related taxes	24,612
Accrued other liabilities	61,858
Accrued income and other taxes	29,955
Short-term debt	15,000
Current portion of long-term obligations	755
Total current liabilities	$281,473

WHOLE FOODS MARKET, INC.

Current installments of long-term debt and capital lease obligations	$ 1,815
Trade accounts payable	11,218
Accrued payroll, bonus and employee benefits	10,608
Other accrued expenses	12,200
Total current liabilities	$35,841

Note: Amounts reported are in thousands of dollars.
Source: Recent annual reports.

1. *Statement of Financial Accounting Concepts No. 6,* "Elements of Financial Statements" (Stamford, Conn.: FASB, 1985), para. 35.

Market, based in Austin, Texas, is the nation's leading retailer of organic foods. The largest current liabilities of ShopKo Stores and Whole Foods Market are accounts payable and various accrued liabilities, which is true of most corporations.

CURRENT LIABILITIES: KEY INFORMATION NEEDS OF DECISION MAKERS

Providing information useful to decision makers is the primary objective of an organization's accountants and the central theme of this textbook. In this section, we consider decision makers' key information needs regarding the current liabilities of business entities.

LEARNING OBJECTIVE 1
Define the key information needs of decision makers regarding current liabilities.

Completeness

In 1993, the Securities and Exchange Commission (SEC) reprimanded an accountant of U.S. Shoe Corporation for causing that firm's financial statements to contain material errors.[2] The accountant intentionally understated U.S. Shoe's accounts payable and failed to record certain accrued liabilities. Because of these and other errors, third-party decision makers may have made inappropriate decisions based upon the company's financial statements. When executives of U.S. Shoe learned of the accounting fraud, they informed the SEC and issued corrected financial statements.

The most important information need of decision makers when it comes to current liabilities is completeness. Decision makers must have confidence that a company's balance sheet reflects all of the firm's outstanding, or unpaid, current liabilities. Businesses implement a wide array of control activities to help ensure that their accounting systems "capture" all of their short-term liabilities.

Valuation Methods

Financial statement users need to be aware of the methods businesses use to assign dollar amounts to individual current liabilities. Sophisticated decision makers realize that the reported values of most current liabilities, such as accounts payable, are equal to the amount of hard, cold cash that must be paid when those liabilities come due. Occasionally, businesses extinguish their current liabilities by the delivery of goods or services. Included in a recent annual report of Harris Corporation, a manufacturing firm, was an $89 million current liability that represented advance payments received from its customers. Harris would eventually "wipe out" that liability by delivering completed goods to its customers.

A company should provide adequate disclosures in its financial statement footnotes to allow decision makers to decide whether the dollar amounts of estimated current liabilities have been properly determined. Apple Computer records an estimated current liability at the end of each year for product warranty expenditures that it will incur over the following twelve months. This product warranty liability totaled $181 million in a recent balance sheet issued by Apple. An accompanying financial state-

2. Securities and Exchange Commission, *Accounting and Auditing Enforcement Release No. 478,* 3 September 1993.

The Case of the Inflated Payables

Decision makers want to be assured that a business reports all of its liabilities in its periodic balance sheets. Seldom do financial statement users "lose sleep" over the possibility that a firm has intentionally overstated its liabilities. However, that was exactly what Comptronix Corporation did in the early 1990s.

Executives of Comptronix, an electronics manufacturer, entered fictitious sales in the company's accounting records to improve its reported profits. The executives realized that the phony sales would distort the relationships among certain key items in Comptronix's financial statements. To make the company's financial statements more realistic, the executives entered false merchandise purchases and corresponding accounts payable in Comptronix's accounting records. The executives went so far as to "pay" the fictitious liabilities with company-issued checks, which they eventually deposited in Comptronix bank accounts.

On the date the Comptronix fraud was revealed, the price of the company's common stock collapsed. After opening at $22 per share that day, the stock fell to less than $4 per share following disclosure of the fraud.

Source: Securities and Exchange Commission, *Accounting and Auditing Enforcement Release No. 543,* 29 March 1994.

ment footnote explained how Apple arrived at that figure and reinforced to financial statement users that the figure was a "best estimate." Following is a portion of that footnote.

> The Company's warranty and related accruals are based on the Company's best estimates of product failure rates and unit costs to repair. However, the Company is continually releasing new and ever-more complex and technologically advanced products. As a result, it is at least reasonably possible that product could be released with certain unknown quality and/or design problems. Such an occurrence could result in materially higher than expected warranty and related costs . . .

Unusual Circumstances

When unusual and material circumstances affect a major account balance or financial statement line item, those circumstances should be disclosed in a firm's financial statements. For current liabilities, an example of such a circumstance is an inability, or potential inability, to pay these liabilities as they come due.

Companies involved in bankruptcy proceedings face a significant risk of defaulting on their current liabilities. In late 1995, Clothestime, Inc., a women's apparel retailer, filed for protection from its creditors in federal bankruptcy court. The company's annual report issued in 1996 discussed the bankruptcy filing at length. Clothestime's balance sheet listed total liabilities of approximately $80 million, including $53.4 million

Balance Sheet Classification of Liabilities in Other Countries

FOR YOUR INFORMATION

Accounting and financial reporting rules for liabilities are very similar in developed countries across the world. Nevertheless, there are some unconventional rules and practices. For instance, Sweden's approach to distinguishing between current and long-term liabilities differs from that of the United States. In the United States, liabilities that must be paid within the following year or operating cycle of a business, whichever is longer, are classified as current liabilities. Sweden does not recognize the operating cycle concept when classifying liabilities. Instead, Swedish companies strictly classify liabilities as current or long-term depending upon their maturity date. Liabilities due within one year are considered current liabilities, while all other obligations are treated as long-term liabilities.

The Republic of Ireland and the Netherlands also classify liabilities differently than the United States. Both countries require businesses to classify certain obligations as "provisions" in their balance sheets. In the Netherlands, provisions generally include estimated liabilities. Polygram, the Dutch entertainment conglomerate, segregates its debts and other obligations into short-term provisions, long-term provisions, current liabilities, and long-term liabilities. Included in Polygram's provisions in a recent annual report were amounts the firm estimated it would eventually pay other entertainment companies under profit-sharing agreements for certain music albums.

of "Liabilities Subject to Compromise." The largest component of these liabilities was more than $20 million of accounts payable. Clothestime's annual report disclosed that negotiations with creditors and/or the bankruptcy court would determine the amount of these accounts payable the company would ultimately pay.

ACCOUNTING FOR CURRENT LIABILITIES

LEARNING OBJECTIVE 2
Account for the major types of transactions and events affecting current liabilities.

This section discusses accounting procedures for several current liabilities. Although there are dozens of different types of current liabilities, the accounting issues posed by most of them are very similar. Here, we consider accounting procedures for the most common current liabilities.

Accounts Payable

accounts payable

Earlier chapters introduced you to accounts payable. Let us formally define **accounts payable** as current liabilities that represent amounts owed by a business to its suppliers. To reacquaint yourself with the most frequently occurring transactions that involve accounts payable and the appropriate journal entries for those transactions, refer to Exhibit 7.15 in the appendix accompanying Chapter 7.

Notes Payable

notes payable

Notes payable are obligations documented by a legally binding written commitment known as a promissory note. These liabilities can be either current or long-term depending upon their maturity or payment date. For reporting purposes, some businesses combine short-term notes payable, short-term loans payable, commercial paper, and related current liabilities into one balance sheet classification entitled "short-term debt." These current liabilities are similar in that each is usually documented by a promissory note or similar legal instrument. Notice in Exhibit 9.1 that ShopKo Stores reported $15 million of "short-term debt" on a recent balance sheet. According to *Accounting Trends & Techniques,* approximately 71 percent of public companies report short-term debt in some form on their periodic balance sheets.

maker

payee

PROMISSORY NOTES: KEY TERMS No standard format exists for promissory notes. Occasionally, a promissory note is literally nothing more than a scribbled "note" on a piece of paper. Exhibit 9.2 presents an example of a promissory note. When he signs this note, Robert Brown, the **maker,** is promising to pay $2,000, plus interest, to Hunt Brothers, Inc., sixty days from the date of the signing. Hunt Brothers is the payee of the note. A **payee** is the party identified in a promissory note to whom payment will eventually be made. (Recognize that the promissory note shown in Exhibit 9.2 is a note receivable for Hunt Brothers, Inc., but a note payable for Robert Brown.)

principal

term of a note

maturity date

The amount initially owed by a maker of a note is the principal or **principal** amount. The **term of a note,** sometimes referred to as its duration, is the number of days from the date a note is signed, not counting the signing date, to the date the note matures. Suppose the note shown in Exhibit 9.2 is signed on July 15. The note's 60-day term would run from July 16 through September 13: 16 days in July, 31 days in August, and 13 days in September. Under this assumption, September 13 would be the **maturity**

EXHIBIT 9.2 ▼

PROMISSORY NOTE

$2,000 Lindsay, Oklahoma

I agree to pay the principal amount of $2,000 to Hunt Brothers, Inc., sixty days following the date of this note, plus interest accrued at an annual rate of 12%.

Robert Brown

Date

date, which is the date a note must be paid. Finally, the **maturity value** of a note is the total amount the maker must pay the payee on the maturity date. A note's maturity value equals the sum of its principal and any interest that accrues or accumulates on the note over its term.

maturity value

COMPUTING INTEREST ON A NOTE PAYABLE Shown next is the **interest equation** used to compute interest revenue or expense on a promissory note or, more generally, on any type of interest-bearing financial instrument.

interest equation

Interest = Principal × Rate × Time

The "rate" in this equation refers to the annual interest rate identified in a promissory note. The "time" component is expressed as a fraction with the term of the note as the numerator and 360 days as the denominator. (Financial analysts and other financial decision makers generally define a "business year" as 360 days.) Following is the computation of the interest that will accrue on the note shown in Exhibit 9.2.

Interest = Principal × Rate × Time

$40 = $2,000 × .12 × 60 days/360 days

Some promissory notes are noninterest-bearing. For example, if the note shown in Exhibit 9.2 simply stated that Robert Brown was responsible for paying Hunt Brothers $2,000 on the note's maturity date, the note would be noninterest-bearing. Discussion of the accounting treatment for noninterest-bearing notes is deferred to subsequent accounting courses.

ACCOUNTING FOR INTEREST-BEARING NOTES PAYABLE To illustrate accounting for interest-bearing notes payable, suppose that Bonney's Dress Shop borrows $5,000 from a local bank on October 2 of a given year. On that date, Bonney's chief executive signs a promissory note with a 120-day term obligating her firm to repay the $5,000 loan and interest on the loan at a 12 percent annual rate. The maturity date of this note is January 30 of the following year. (Remember that the term of a note includes the maturity date but not the date the note is signed.) Following is the entry to record the receipt of the $5,000 loan.

Oct. 2	Cash	5,000	
	Notes Payable		5,000
	To record note payable to First Bank of Rush Springs with terms of 120 days and 12 percent interest		

At year-end, Bonney's will record the interest expense on this note payable for the period October 2 through December 31. Since this note payable will have been outstanding for 90 days by December 31, $150 of interest will have accrued on the note by that date.

Interest = Principal × Rate × Time
Interest = $5,000 × 12% × 90/360
Interest = $150

The appropriate adjusting entry on December 31 to recognize this expense will include a debit of $150 to Interest Expense and an offsetting credit in the same amount to Interest Payable.

On January 30, the note's maturity date, Bonney's will repay the bank the $5,000 loan plus interest at a 12 percent annual rate for the note's 120-day term. The amount of interest due the bank will be $200 ($5,000 × 12% × 120/360). However, only $50 of interest expense will be recorded by Bonney's on the note's maturity date. This $50 is the interest expense on the note for the 30-day period January 1 through January 30. The remaining $150 of the interest paid to the bank will be debited to the current liability account Interest Payable, as shown in the following entry.

Jan. 30	Notes Payable	5,000	
	Interest Expense	50	
	Interest Payable	150	
	Cash		5,200
	To record payment of note payable and interest to First Bank of Rush Springs		

Current Portion of Long-Term Debt

current portion of long-term debt

For balance sheet purposes, businesses classify the portion of a long-term liability that must be paid within the coming twelve months as a current liability. **Current portion of long-term debt** is a common balance sheet caption for such a current liability. Notice in Exhibit 9.1 that "Current Portion of Long-Term Obligations" is included in ShopKo's current liabilities.

Deferred Revenues

Customers often pay businesses in advance for products and services. Since such amounts have not been earned when they are received, they are initially recorded as liabilities. Typically, accountants credit these amounts to a deferred revenue account such as Unearned Rental Revenue or Deferred Fee Revenue with an offsetting debit to Cash, as illustrated in Chapter 5. These advance payments are usually classified as current liabilities since the products or services that have been purchased will be delivered or provided to customers within twelve months. Jenny Craig, Inc., a company that operates weight-loss centers, reported $3.3 million of "Deferred Service Revenue" as a current liability in a recent balance sheet. That amount represented membership fees paid by the company's customers for the following year.

Accrued Liabilities

Each accounting period, businesses "match" the revenues earned that period with the expenses incurred to generate those revenues. Many expenses in a given accounting period will not have not been paid by the end of the period. Nevertheless, these items must be recognized as expenses via adjusting journal entries, otherwise the matching principle will be violated. When these unpaid expenses are recorded in adjusting entries, one or more expense accounts are debited and one or more accrued liability accounts are credited. Recall that in Chapter 5 an accrued liability was defined as a liability stemming from an expense that has been incurred but not yet paid.

Accountants often use the phrase "accrued expenses" interchangeably with "accrued liabilities." Notice in Exhibit 9.1 that Whole Foods Market applied the caption "Other Accrued Expenses" to its miscellaneous accrued liabilities. Recog-nize that when the phrase "accrued expenses" appears in a set of financial statements, it refers to a group of current liabilities *not* to a group of expenses. Granted, when accrued expenses are recorded, the offsetting debits are to expense accounts. But, these expenses are merged with similar expenses in an income statement instead of being listed separately on an income statement as "accrued expenses."

Several accrued liabilities have been discussed in earlier chapters, such as income taxes payable in Chapter 5. Interest payable, which was discussed earlier in this chapter, also qualifies as an accrued liability. In this section, we consider several additional accrued liabilities.

PRODUCT WARRANTY LIABILITY Many companies provide a guarantee or warranty for the goods or services they market, including Apple Computer, as noted earlier. A. T. Cross, the manufacturer of Cross pens, attaches a "forever guarantee" to its products. If a Cross pen malfunctions for any reason, the company promises to repair the pen or replace it free of charge. Clearly, there is a cost associated with product guarantees and warranties. A recent A. T. Cross annual report revealed that the firm had more than $750,000 of warranty expenses during the year in question.

Since A. T. Cross's warranty helps the firm sell its products, the company matches warranty costs with sales revenue each accounting period. More generally, businesses estimate the total warranty costs they will eventually absorb due to products sold during an accounting period and record that amount as an expense in that period. The offsetting credit to this expense is typically entered in a liability account entitled Product Warranty Liability.

Suppose that A. T. Cross repairs or replaces approximately 2 percent of the pens it sells and that the average repair or replacement cost is $15 per pen. If A. T. Cross sells 200,000 pens in a given month, the firm can expect to eventually repair or replace 4,000 (200,000 × 2%) of these pens at a cost of $60,000 (4,000 × $15). Given these facts, the adjusting entry to record warranty expense for the month in question would be as follows.

Jan. 31	Warranty Expense	60,000	
	Product Warranty Liability		60,000
	To record estimated warranty expense		

Assume that A. T. Cross records repairs and replacements of its pens on a weekly basis. Assume further that during a given one-week period the company incurs $15,100 of warranty costs. These costs would be recorded by debiting $15,100 to Product Warranty Liability with an offsetting credit to the appropriate account or accounts, such as Accounts Payable, Cash or Inventory.

For products with warranties that extend longer than one-year, such as Cross pens, the product warranty liability should be segregated into current and long-term components for balance sheet purposes. The current component represents the amount of warranty-related costs a company expects to incur in the coming twelve months, while the long-term component represents warranty costs expected to be incurred beyond one year.

© Liaison International/Wernher Krutein

Dell Computer Corporation was founded by Michael Dell when he was 19. Dell attaches a one-year warranty to the computers it sells. At the end of each year, Dell's accountants must estimate and record as an expense and current liability the future warranty-related expenditures the company will incur as a result of the computers sold that year.

VACATION PAY LIABILITY Besides earning their base salary or wages each payroll period, most employees also accumulate vacation pay each payroll period. Consider an employee who receives $400 of wages each week and is entitled to an annual two-week paid vacation. This individual earns $20,800 (52 × $400) each year, $800 of which qualifies as vacation pay. Expressed another way, this employee accumulates $16 of vacation pay ($800/50 weeks) for each week worked. Because of the matching principle, businesses recognize the cost of vacation pay earned by their employees each payroll period as a current liability. In a recent annual report, Pinkerton's Inc., the world's largest security services firm, reported a vacation pay liability of $6.8 million.

To illustrate accounting for vacation pay, assume that Jessica Linton & Co., Architects, provides each of its employees an annual two-week paid vacation. Each payroll period, the vacation pay accumulated by Linton & Co.'s employees equals 4 percent (2 weeks/50 weeks) of that week's payroll. If this company's payroll is $350,000 for its most recent two-week payroll period, the amount of vacation pay earned by its employees is $14,000 ($350,000 × 4%). A portion of the vacation pay accumulated by a company's workforce is usually forfeited because of employee turnover. Assume that in a typical year, 10 percent of all vacation pay accumulated by the employees of Linton & Co. is forfeited. Given this fact, the company would record only $12,600 ($14,000 × 90%) of vacation pay expense for its most recent payroll period. A company accountant would debit that amount to Vacation Pay Expense with an offsetting credit to Vacation Pay Liability.

When Linton & Co.'s employees take their vacations, Vacation Pay Liability will be debited for the cost of the vacation pay. Suppose that several employees take their vacations during a payroll period in April and receive vacation pay of $9,600. These payments would be recorded with a $9,600 debit to Vacation Pay Liability and an equal credit to Cash.

ACCRUED PAYROLL LIABILITIES Typically, the end of a business's fiscal year does not coincide with the end of a payroll period. Suppose that a company with a December 31 fiscal year-end pays its employees every two weeks. If December 23 is the last day of a two-week payroll period, by December 31 the employees will have worked several days for which they have not been paid. Like any other unpaid expense, unpaid payroll expenses must be recognized in an adjusting entry at the end of an accounting period.

As you are probably well aware, there is often a significant difference between a worker's gross pay and his or her net or take-home pay. The difference between gross pay and net pay is due to various payroll deductions. Among these deductions are an employee's portion of the Social Security tax, officially known as the Federal Insurance Contributions Act (FICA) tax,[3] federal and state income tax withholdings, union dues, and health insurance premiums. When accruing payroll expenses at the end of an accounting period, a business must also consider employee payroll deductions.

Suppose that as of December 31 of a given year, the employees of Cathy's Engineering Services have worked one week for which they have not been paid. The gross pay earned by Cathy's employees for this one-week period is $4,240, while their net pay for that period is $2,720, as shown by the following schedule.

Gross pay		$4,240
Less: Payroll deductions		
FICA taxes	$325	
Federal income taxes	810	
State income taxes	205	
Health insurance premiums	180	
Total payroll deductions		1,520
Net pay		$2,720

3. As of the writing of this book, the FICA tax rate is 7.65% on employee earnings. This tax is a composite of two elements: an old-age, survivors, and disability insurance (OASDI) component and a medicare component. For 1997, the OASDI tax rate was 6.2% of an employee's first $65,400 in annual earnings. The medicare tax rate for 1996 was 1.45% of the total annual earnings of an employee. Some companies account for these two components of FICA taxes separately. Here, they are combined into one item.

Given the previous data, Cathy's would make the following year-end adjusting entry to recognize unpaid salaries expense and the related employee payroll deductions.

Dec. 31	Salaries Expense	4,240	
	FICA Taxes Payable		325
	Employee Federal Income Taxes Payable		810
	Employee State Income Taxes Payable		205
	Employee Health Insurance Premiums Payable		180
	Salaries Payable		2,720
	To record unpaid salaries expense and related employee payroll deductions at year-end		

Businesses incur payroll-related expenses besides employee wages and salaries. For example, employers contribute to the Social Security program an amount equal to the FICA taxes paid by their employees. Likewise, employers must generally pay state and federal unemployment taxes on the earnings of their employees. A final component of payroll-related expenses is employee fringe benefits. Fringe benefits include such items as employer contributions to an employee pension fund and the portions of employees' health and other insurance premiums that an employer pays. At the end of each accounting period, businesses record these additional payroll-related expenses that they have incurred but not yet paid in adjusting journal entries.

KEY CONTROL ACTIVITIES FOR CURRENT LIABILITIES

LEARNING OBJECTIVE 3 ▶

Discuss key control activities for current liabilities including the maintenance of a payroll register.

Control activities that businesses implement for liabilities differ significantly from the control activities they establish for assets. These differences stem from the nature of assets and liabilities. A major control objective related to assets is minimizing the risk that they will be stolen or otherwise misused. A major control objective related to liabilities is minimizing the risk that suppliers, employees, and other parties will be paid more than they are due. Another important control objective for liabilities is ensuring that they are paid on a timely basis. Company owners and executives risk an unpleasant visit to the bankruptcy court if they do not pay outstanding debts when they are due.

As noted earlier in the chapter, accounts payable and accrued liabilities are typically the largest current liabilities reported in corporate balance sheets. The opening vignette for this chapter outlines a control strategy one firm implemented for its accounts payable. Here, we consider control activities specifically designed for a major class of accrued liabilities, namely, accrued payroll liabilities. Notice in Exhibit 9.1 that Whole Foods Market reported $10.6 million of accrued payroll liabilities on a recent balance sheet. That figure accounted for approximately 30 percent of the firm's current liabilities. A recent balance sheet issued by General Motors reported accrued payroll liabilities exceeding $2 billion.

The large amount of expenditures and period-ending accrued liabilities typically processed by a business's payroll function demand that rigorous control activities be established for this function. Maintaining a payroll register is among the most important of these activities. A **payroll register** is a subsidiary accounting record in which key payroll data, such as gross pay, payroll deductions, net pay, and payroll check number, are entered each payroll period for each employee. Exhibit 9.3 presents a simple example of a payroll register. As a point of information, notice that the payroll register in Exhibit 9.3 distinguishes between wages expense and office salaries expense. Businesses generally refer to compensation paid to hourly employees as wages expense and to compensation paid to salaried employees as salaries expense.

payroll register

A payroll register helps a business exercise effective control over its payroll function. For example, the use of a payroll register increases the likelihood that appropriate amounts are withheld each pay period from employees' paychecks. Companies face stiff fines and criminal penalties for failing to withhold the correct amounts from employees' paychecks for such items as federal and state income taxes and FICA taxes. A payroll register also helps ensure that only legitimate employees are receiving paychecks. Periodically, a firm's internal auditors should determine that the employees listed in the payroll register for each department are actually working in those departments. A dishonest supervisor who oversees a department of several hundred employees might attempt to maintain one or more former employees on the payroll and then obtain and cash their payroll checks.

The information needed to record periodic payroll disbursements is provided by a payroll register. For the data presented in Exhibit 9.3, the entry shown next would be made to record the weekly payroll.

Jan. 23	Wages Expense	2,328	
	Office Salaries Expense	1,150	
	FICA Taxes Payable		268
	Employee Federal Income Taxes Payable		461
	Employee Union Dues Payable		50
	Cash		2,699
	To record payroll for week ended January 23		

EXHIBIT 9.3 ▼
Weekly Payroll Register

Week Ended January 23, 1998

		Earnings			Deductions				Payment		Distribution	
Employee	Hours	Regular	Overtime	Gross	FICA Tax	Federal Income Tax	Union Dues	Total	Net Pay	Check No.	Wages Expense	Office Salaries Expense
Choo, L. T.	40	400		400	31	60	10	101	299	421	400	
Davis, Tom	40	400		400	31	44	10	85	315	422	400	
Earl, Will	41	480	12	492	38	60		98	394	423		492
Elliot, Jo	40	400		400	31	60	10	101	299	424	400	
Howe, Mimi	47	560	98	658	50	88		138	520	425		658
Martin, Sue	40	600		600	46	81	10	137	463	426	600	
Wills, M. W.	44	480	48	528	41	68	10	119	409	427	528	
Totals		3,320	158	3,478	268	461	50	779	2,699		2,328	1,150

Payroll Padding: A Case of Dodger Blue

Edward Campos accepted a position with the Los Angeles Dodgers in the late 1960s. By 1986, Campos had worked his way up the organization's employment hierarchy to become the operations payroll chief. After taking charge of the Dodgers' payroll department, Campos designed and implemented a new payroll system, a system that only he fully understood. Campos controlled the payroll system so completely that he personally filled out the weekly payroll cards for each of the Dodgers' more than four hundred employees. Even when he was on vacation, Campos returned to the Dodgers' accounting office once per week to complete the weekly payroll.

Unfortunately, the high level of trust that the organization's executives placed in Campos was not warranted. Over a period of a few years, Campos embezzled several hundred thousand dollars from the Dodgers. According to court records, Campos padded the Dodgers' payroll by adding fictitious employees to various departments. In addition, Campos inflated the number of hours worked by several employees and then split the resulting overpayments fifty-fifty with those individuals.

Campos' fraudulent scheme unraveled when he was unable to work for a short time due to illness and his responsibilities were assumed by the Dodgers' controller. While completing the payroll one week, the controller noticed that several employees, including ushers, security guards, and ticket salespeople, were being paid unusually large amounts. In some cases, employees earning $7 an hour were receiving weekly paychecks approaching $2,000.

After pleading guilty to embezzlement charges, Campos was sentenced to eight years in state prison and was required to make restitution to the Dodgers. Another of the conspirators also received a prison sentence, while the remaining individuals involved in the fraud made restitution and were placed on probation.

Source: M. C. Knapp, "The Trolley Dodgers," *Contemporary Auditing: Issues and Cases,* 2d ed. (Minneapolis/St. Paul: West Publishing Company, 1996).

A payroll register can also be designed to capture the data needed to record employer payroll taxes and fringe benefits expenses each payroll period. Finally, and most important in the present context, a payroll register can be used to collect the data needed to determine period-ending accrued payroll liabilities.

A wide range of electronic controls can be easily integrated into a computerized payroll accounting system. For example, a computer-based payroll system may automatically generate an "edit listing" that contains payroll data items each payroll period that are unusual in nature and/or in amount. Such an edit listing may include all employees who worked an unusually large number of hours during a payroll period. Possibly, these employees falsified the time cards on which they reported their hours worked. Alternatively, a data entry clerk may have inadvertently entered into the computer erroneous payroll data for one or more employees. For example, a distracted clerk may have entered 73 hours worked for a certain employee during a given week instead of the actual figure of 37 hours. Company executives typically delegate the responsibility for investigating such potential errors to their firm's internal auditors.

The Spotlight on Ethics vignette accompanying this section describes a payroll fraud perpetrated on the Los Angeles Dodgers professional baseball club. That fraud highlights the need for businesses to maintain effective control over their payroll functions. Among the control weaknesses evident in the Dodgers' payroll function was the vesting of too much authority in one individual. The Dodgers' operations payroll chief had such complete control over the organization's payroll system that he could steal almost at will from his employer.

ANALYZING CURRENT LIABILITIES

LEARNING OBJECTIVE 4
Compute and interpret the current ratio and working capital.

Liquidity refers to a business's ability to finance its day-to-day operations and to pay its liabilities as they come due. We considered one measure of liquidity, the quick ratio, in Chapter 6. Another widely used measure of liquidity is the current ratio. The current ratio expresses the relationship between a business's current assets and its current liabilities at a given point in time.

current ratio

$$\textbf{Current Ratio} = \frac{\text{Current Assets}}{\text{Current Liabilities}}$$

Another financial measure in which current liabilities figure prominently is working capital, which is the difference between an entity's current assets and current liabilities.

working capital

$$\textbf{Working Capital} = \text{Current Assets} - \text{Current Liabilities}$$

Besides tracking a firm's quick and current ratios, decision makers monitor the company's working capital from period to period to gauge its liquidity. A company that has a minimal amount of working capital, or, worse yet, a negative working capital, generally faces a higher than normal risk of defaulting on its current liabilities as they come due.

The Bombay Company, Inc., sells furniture and housewares from more than 400 retail stores in the United States and Canada. The following schedule lists this firm's working capital and current ratio for its fiscal years ending in 1994 through 1996.

	At Fiscal Year-End (in thousands)		
	1996	**1995**	**1994**
Current assets	$133,135	$127,482	$118,695
Current liabilities	31,669	50,050	29,305
Working capital	$101,466	$ 77,432	$ 89,390
Current ratio	4.20	2.55	4.05

Notice that Bombay's liquidity weakened during 1995. Both the company's working capital and current ratio declined during that year compared with the previous year. On the bright side, Bombay's liquidity bounced back strongly during 1996. A common rule of thumb across all industries is that a company should maintain a current ratio of at least 2.0. An even better benchmark for assessing a company's current ratio is the industry norm for that ratio. In 1996, the median current ratio for furniture retailers, such as the Bombay Company, was 2.8.[4] Compared to that industry norm, Bombay's 1996 current ratio was very impressive.

CONTINGENT LIABILITIES

LEARNING OBJECTIVE 5 ▶
Define the key characteristics of, and account for, contingent liabilities.

We all remember several years ago when Saddam Hussein's Iraqi troops invaded Kuwait. That invasion had financial implications for most firms engaged in the oil industry in the Middle East. One such firm was the Oklahoma-based Halliburton Company, an oil well servicing company. Shortly after Iraq invaded Kuwait, Halliburton recorded a $16.5 million expense—and a corresponding liability in the same amount—to recognize losses that it might realize due to the Iraqi occupation. Accountants refer to such potential losses as loss contingencies. Related to every loss contingency is a contingent liability. A **contingent liability** is a potential liability that may become an actual liability if one or more events occur or fail to occur.[5]

contingent liability

Lawsuits are the most common source of contingent liabilities. A company involved as a defendant in a lawsuit may eventually be forced to pay a legal judgment or settlement to a third party. Contingent liabilities can also result from potential impairments or losses of assets. The contingent liability recorded by Halliburton involved the possible destruction of oil field equipment.

Exhibit 9.4 summarizes the alternative accounting treatments for loss contingencies and the related contingent liabilities. The two factors to consider in determining the accounting treatment for a loss contingency are (1) the likelihood that an actual loss

EXHIBIT 9.4 ▼
Accounting Treatment of Contingent Losses and Related Contingent Liabilities

Likelihood of an Actual Loss	Potential Loss Subject to Reasonable Estimation	Accounting Treatment
Probable	Yes	Recorded by debiting an expense account and crediting a liability account
Probable	No	Disclosed in financial statement footnotes
Reasonably Possible	Yes/No	Disclosed in financial statement footnotes
Remote	Yes/No	Ignored

4. *Dun & Bradstreet's Industry Norms & Key Business Ratios,* 1995–1996 (New York: Dun & Bradstreet, 1996).

5. In some cases, a contingent liability is not a potential liability but rather an actual liability whose dollar amount is "contingent" on the outcome of some future occurrence.

will eventually result from the contingency, and (2) whether the amount of the potential loss can be reasonably estimated. Notice that a loss contingency is recorded only if it is *probable* that an actual loss will result from the contingency and the amount of the loss is subject to *reasonable estimation*. When a loss contingency is recorded, an appropriate expense or loss account is debited with an offsetting credit to a liability account.

Contingent liabilities can occasionally threaten the existence of companies. For several years, the survival of General Public Utilities (GPU), which owned and operated the ill-fated Three-Mile Island nuclear facility, was in doubt. Nevertheless, GPU survived and today is a financially healthy company.

As Exhibit 9.4 suggests, when certain conditions are met, a loss contingency is simply disclosed in the given firm's financial statement footnotes. Loss contingencies that have only a *remote* chance of resulting in actual losses should generally be ignored for accounting and financial reporting purposes. Large corporations regularly face nuisance lawsuits that pose no more than a minimal likelihood of resulting in actual losses. In 1996, PepsiCo, Inc., disclosed that it was a defendant in a lawsuit stemming from a large promotional campaign for Pepsi products. A fictitious prize in this program was a United States military jet featured in a Pepsi television commercial. An individual who had submitted the requisite number of proofs of purchase and a $700,000 check to PepsiCo to redeem the jet "prize" insisted that the company deliver the jet to him. In a legal brief filed with a New York federal court, PepsiCo asked the court to dismiss the individual's claim because it was "frivolous" and "without merit."[6]

Interpreting the meaning of the terms "probable," "reasonably possible," "remote," and "subject to reasonable estimation" is the key to accounting properly for loss contingencies. Accounting standards do not provide definitive guidelines regarding how those expressions should be interpreted. Consequently, accountants must rely on their own expertise and judgment when applying those terms.

Contingent liabilities can be current or long-term or have a component of each. General Public Utilities (GPU) operated the Three-Mile Island nuclear facility that was damaged in 1979 and leaked radioactive substances into the environment. The Three-Mile Island incident resulted in numerous contingent liabilities for GPU. Some of these contingent liabilities were current liabilities. An example was the large cost of an environmental remediation or cleanup program the company faced following the acci-

6. "Pepsi Moves to Thwart Suit Over Promotional Prize," *The Wall Street Journal*, 26 July 1996, A4.

Crying Over Spilled Oil

FOR YOUR INFORMATION

Companies in many industries face a risk of huge losses resulting from environmental calamities caused by their operations or by their employees. In 1989, the Exxon oil tanker Valdez ran aground in the Prince William Sound off the coast of Alaska and spilled 11 million gallons of oil. Exxon is still tallying the losses from the Valdez disaster. Besides cleanup costs and fines estimated at more than $3.5 billion, Exxon has been the target of numerous lawsuits stemming from that oil spill. In one such lawsuit, an Alaskan jury imposed $5 billion in punitive damages alone on Exxon.

dent. Other contingent liabilities arising from the accident were long-term in nature. GPU's annual report issued in early 1996 revealed that approximately 2,100 lawsuits resulting from the Three-Mile Island incident were still pending against the firm. Many of these lawsuits alleged personal injuries due to the radioactive emissions from the nuclear facility.

The 1996 edition of *Accounting Trends & Techniques* reported that most companies disclose contingent liabilities in their annual reports. There are two key sources of contingent liabilities. More than 70 percent of the public companies surveyed in 1996 by *Accounting Trends & Techniques* reported contingent liabilities due to pending litigation. Forty-nine percent of the companies surveyed disclosed contingent liabilities related to environmental issues or problems.

SUMMARY

Current liabilities involve obligations that must be paid or otherwise extinguished by a business within one year or its operating cycle, whichever is longer. Among the more common types of current liabilities are accounts payable, notes payable, the current portion of long-term debt, deferred revenues, and accrued liabilities.

The primary concern of decision makers regarding current liabilities is completeness. Decision makers need to be assured that a business has disclosed all of its current liabilities in its financial statements. A related information need of decision makers is the valuation of current liabilities, particularly estimated current liabilities. Decision makers should be provided with sufficient information to allow them to determine whether such liabilities have been reasonably estimated. Finally, decision makers need to be aware of any unusual and material circumstances related to a firm's current liabilities. For example, if there is substantial doubt that a company can pay its current liabilities as they come due, this fact should be disclosed in the company's financial statement footnotes.

Among key accounting procedures for current liabilities are accruing interest expense on notes payable at the end of an accounting period. The interest equation (Interest = Principal × Rate × Time) is used by accountants to accrue the proper amount of interest expense at the end of an accounting period on a note payable or other financial instrument. Other important accounting issues involving current liabilities include arriving at proper period-ending estimates of a firm's product warranty liability and vacation pay liability.

Control activities that businesses implement for liabilities differ significantly from the control activities they establish for assets. An example of an important control activity related to current liabilities is maintaining a payroll register. Companies maintain a payroll register to provide effective control over payroll-related expenses and period-ending accrued payroll liabilities.

Decision makers use the current ratio to evaluate a business's liquidity. This ratio is computed by dividing current assets by current liabilities. Although current ratios vary considerably from industry to industry, a common benchmark suggests that businesses should maintain a current ratio of at least 2.0.

A contingent liability is a potential liability that may become an actual liability if one or more events occur or fail to occur. Certain contingent liabilities must be recorded as if they are actual liabilities. Other contingent liabilities are simply disclosed in the footnotes of a firm's financial statements or ignored for financial statement purposes.

GLOSSARY

Accounts payable (p. 393) Current liabilities that represent amounts owed by a business to its suppliers.

Contingent liability (p. 404) A potential liability that may become an actual liability if one or more events occur or fail to occur.

Current portion of long-term debt (p. 396) The dollar amount of a long-term liability that must be paid in the coming twelve months.

Current ratio (p. 403) Current assets divided by current liabilities; a widely used measure of liquidity.

Interest equation (p. 395) The equation used to compute interest revenue or expense on a promissory note or other interest-bearing financial instrument: interest = principal × rate × time.

Maker (p. 394) The party who has signed a promissory note and is thus obligated to pay a certain amount to another party by a certain date.

Maturity date (p. 394) The date that the maker of a promissory note must pay its maturity value to the payee.

Maturity value (p. 395) The sum of the principal and interest due on a promissory note on its maturity date.

Notes payable (p. 393) Obligations that are documented by a legally binding written commitment known as a promissory note; can be either current or long-term liabilities depending upon their maturity date.

Payee (p. 394) The party to whom the maker of a promissory note must eventually pay the maturity value of that note.

Payroll register (p. 401) A subsidiary accounting record in which key payroll-related data, such as gross pay, payroll deductions, and net pay, are entered each payroll period for each employee.

Principal (p. 394) The amount initially owed by the maker of a promissory note.

Term of a note (p. 394) The number of days from the date a promissory note is signed, not counting the signing date, to the date the note matures.

Working capital (p. 403) The difference between an entity's current assets and current liabilities.

DECISION CASE

Manufacturers and wholesalers typically offer discounts for early payment to retailers who purchase merchandise from them on credit. Under credit terms of 2/10, n/30, retailers can deduct a 2 percent discount from the gross amount of an account payable if they make payment within ten days of the invoice date. As discussed in Chapter 7, retailers have a strong economic incentive to take advantage of such discounts. The effective interest rate for bypassing a purchase discount is more than 36 percent if the credit terms are 2/10, n/30.

A recent article in *Forbes* suggests that Wal-Mart routinely deducts purchase discounts from the gross amounts owed its suppliers, although the firm typically does not make payment within the suppliers' designated 10-day discount periods. According to the *Forbes* article, Wal-Mart generally waits until the final day of a 30-day credit period to pay an amount owed to a supplier. At that point, Wal-Mart is not entitled to a purchase discount since the 10-day discount period expired twenty days earlier. Nevertheless, Wal-Mart overlooks this "technicality" and sends the supplier a check equal to the invoice amount less the discount. Apparently, the size and "buying power" of Wal-Mart allows its executives to extract this concession from suppliers.

Required: Suppose that you own and operate a chain of retail stores in northern Louisiana. Your primary competitor is Wal-Mart. You recently discovered that Wal-Mart deducts purchase discounts from amounts owed suppliers although the company does not pay for those purchases within the 10-day discount period established by most of these suppliers. You purchase merchandise from these same suppliers and pay for your purchases within the allotted 10-day discount period. Thus, you are fully entitled to the purchase discounts that you deduct from the amounts remitted to suppliers.

How is your business affected, if at all, by the preferential treatment given Wal-Mart by suppliers? In your opinion, are suppliers behaving unethically by allowing Wal-Mart to take purchase discounts following the expiration of the discount period? What steps, if any, would you take to address this situation?

Source: M. Schifrin, "The Big Squeeze," *Forbes,* 11 March 1996, 45–46.

QUESTIONS

1. Define "liabilities."
2. Define "current liabilities." List several examples of common current liabilities.
3. Identify the two general types of current liabilities.
4. Describe the effects on a company's financial statements when one or more current liabilities are not recorded.
5. Identify key information needs of decision makers regarding current liabilities.
6. What is the difference between an account payable and a note payable?
7. Identify and describe the key terms related to a promissory note.
8. Explain how an interest-bearing note payable and a noninterest-bearing note payable differ.
9. Why are deferred revenues considered current liabilities?
10. Define "accrued liabilities." List several examples of accrued liabilities.

11. What is a product warranty liability?
12. Provide at least two examples of companies with which you are familiar that likely have a product warranty liability included in their balance sheets.
13. Briefly describe how a company's vacation pay liability is determined at the end of an accounting period.
14. Describe the items that employers commonly deduct from their employees' paychecks.
15. Besides salaries expense and wages expense, what payroll-related costs do companies typically incur?
16. Describe the information included in a payroll register. How does a payroll register help a business maintain control over its payroll function?
17. List the equation for computing the current ratio. How is the current ratio typically used by decision makers?
18. What constitutes a company's working capital? Explain briefly why decision makers closely monitor the amount of working capital maintained by a company.
19. Define "contingent liabilities."
20. Identify the issues that must be considered when determining how to account for a contingent liability.
21. What are the two most common types of contingent liabilities reported by public companies?

EXERCISES

22. **True or False** (LO 1–5)
Following are a series of statements regarding topics discussed in Chapter 9.

Required:
Indicate whether each statement is true (T) or false (F).

_____ a. For a loss contingency to be recorded in a company's accounting records, the amount of the loss must be subject to reasonable estimation.
_____ b. A note payable is an obligation documented by a legally binding written commitment known as a promissory note.
_____ c. Current liabilities are liabilities that must be paid by a business within one year or its operating cycle, whichever is shorter.
_____ d. Working capital is computed by subtracting current liabilities from quick assets.
_____ e. Financial decision makers generally do not consider the possibility that a company has intentionally overstated its current liabilities.
_____ f. Product warranty liability and vacation pay liability are examples of accrued liabilities.
_____ g. A "maker" is the party identified in a promissory note to whom payment will eventually be made.
_____ h. The maintenance of a payroll register increases the likelihood that the appropriate amounts are withheld each period from employees' paychecks.
_____ i. The current ratio is a common measure used by decision makers to evaluate a business's liquidity.
_____ j. A loss contingency that has a remote chance of resulting in an actual loss should be disclosed in a company's financial statement footnotes.

23. **Liability Classification** (LO 1, 2)
Hamilton's Bakery borrowed $50,000 on January 1, 1995. The repayment terms require Hamilton's to repay $5,000 of the principal amount of the loan on December 31 of each year, beginning December 31, 1995, plus 10 percent interest on the unpaid principal at the beginning of each year.

Required:

1. How will this debt be reported on Hamilton's December 31, 2000, balance sheet? How much interest expense related to this debt will be reported on Hamilton's income statement for the year ended December 31, 2000?
2. Suppose that Hamilton's fails to classify any portion of the outstanding bank loan as a current liability on its December 31, 2000, balance sheet. How will this error affect decision makers' analysis of the company's financial statements? Explain.

24. **Accounting for Interest-Bearing Note Payable** (LO 2)

Regier Homebuilders borrowed $10,000 from a local bank on October 2. On that date, Regier's chief executive signed a 10 percent, 180-day interest-bearing promissory note.

Required:

Prepare the appropriate journal entries in Regier's accounting records on the following dates:

1. October 2
2. December 31, the business's fiscal year-end
3. March 31, the date the note matures

25. **Accounting for Interest-Bearing Note Payable** (LO 2)

On December 1, 1998, Andersen Gardening bought a new computer for $4,000 from Computer Village. In exchange, Andersen signed a $4,000, 12 percent promissory note with a 180-day term. Andersen's fiscal year coincides with the calendar year.

Required:

1. Prepare the appropriate journal entries in Andersen's accounting records on the following dates: December 1, December 31, 1998, and the date the note matures.
2. On the date Andersen purchased the computer, the business had a cash balance of $8,000 on which it was earning interest at an annual rate of approximately 5 percent. What may have prompted Andersen to sign a 12 percent promissory note in payment for the computer instead of paying cash?

26. **Accounting for Current Liabilities** (LO 2)

FreeWheelers is a bike shop located near the campus of the University of Tennessee. FreeWheelers rents bikes on a nine-month basis. When a student rents a bike, he or she pays a security deposit equal to 50 percent of the bike's value. Typically, a bike is returned damaged in some way, causing some portion of the security deposit to be forfeited. When a security deposit is received, FreeWheelers' accountant debits Cash and credits Miscellaneous Revenue. If a bike is returned damaged, the accountant debits Repairs Expense and credits Cash or another appropriate account when the bike is repaired. Any portion of the deposit that is not required to repair the bike is returned to the student. Deposit amounts returned to students are recorded with a debit to Miscellaneous Expense and a credit to Cash.

Required:

Write a brief memo to FreeWheelers' accountant regarding the accounting treatment given security deposits on bike rentals. Explain why this accounting treatment is incorrect and how it may introduce errors into the business's financial statements. Also recommend a more appropriate method of accounting for security deposits.

27. **Recording Warranty Expense** (LO 2)

The bikes sold by Jim's Bike Shop carry a one-year warranty on parts and labor. Since Jim, the bike shop's owner, has experienced craftspeople assembling and fine-tuning the bikes, he expects very few warranty claims. Last year, Jim's Bike Shop sold two hundred bikes and made warranty repairs on three bikes at a total cost of approximately $500.

Required:

1. If Jim's Bike Shop fails to record a product warranty liability at the end of each fiscal year, how will the business's financial statements be affected? What accounting concepts or principles will be violated?

2. Under what condition or conditions could Jim reasonably argue that his business does not have to record a product warranty liability at year-end?

28. **Accounting for Vacation Pay Liability** (LO 2)
Hobbs Company grants its employees two weeks of paid vacation each year. As a general rule, 80 percent of the vacation pay earned by Hobbs' employees is eventually paid. Hobbs' payroll was $512,400 for the most recent two-week payroll period, which ended March 9.

Required:
1. Compute the amount of vacation pay earned by the employees of Hobbs Company for the payroll period ending on March 9.
2. Prepare the journal entry to record vacation pay expense for the payroll period ending on March 9.
3. Suppose that the actual vacation pay received by Hobbs' employees for the payroll period ending on August 8 totaled $82,300. Prepare the journal entry to record this vacation pay.

29. **Payroll Accounting** (LO 2)
Khalid Company pays its employees every two weeks. The firm just completed its fiscal year on September 30. Prior to year-end, the company last paid its employees on September 20. For the last ten days of the fiscal year, the employees of Khalid Company earned gross pay (salaries) of $8,200. Listed next are Khalid's employee payroll deductions for the period September 21–30.

	Employee Payroll Deductions
FICA taxes	$ 627
Federal income taxes	2,010
State income taxes	311
Health insurance premiums	225

Required:
1. Prepare the adjusting journal entry required on September 30 to record the unpaid salaries expense of Khalid on that date and the related employee payroll deductions.
2. What payroll-related expenses do businesses incur besides employee wages and salaries?

30. **Recognizing Warranty Expense** (LO 2)
Waurika Technologies, Inc., manufactures modems and disk drives. Waurika's revenues for the current year are nearly 20 percent below last year's level. As year-end approaches, the company president has instructed the accounting department not to record a December 31 adjusting entry for warranty expense on products sold during the year. "We can recognize that expense next year when we actually pay those costs. That makes more sense anyway. Why go to the trouble of estimating additional expenses at year-end? We have more than enough of the real thing."

Required:
Write a memo to Waurika's president explaining why it is necessary to recognize estimated warranty expense at the end of an accounting period. In your memo, point out how the company's financial statements will be misleading if this expense is not recorded.

31. **Working Capital and the Current Ratio** (LO 4)
Listed in the following schedule are the current assets and current liabilities of the Laoretti Cigar Company for the firm's fiscal years ending December 31, Year 1 and Year 2.

	December 31,	
	Year 1	Year 2
Cash and cash equivalents	$ 54,817	$ 48,902
Accounts receivable	63,295	59,748
Inventories	116,528	121,277
Other current assets	18,605	15,691
Total current assets	$253,245	$245,618
Accounts payable	$ 71,430	$ 73,819
Accrued payroll liabilities	26,608	28,456
Income taxes payable	12,089	11,572
Total current liabilities	$110,127	$113,847

Required:

1. Determine this company's working capital and current ratio as of December 31, Year 1 and Year 2.
2. Did the company's liquidity improve or weaken between the end of Year 1 and the end of Year 2? Explain.

32. **Working Capital and the Current Ratio** (LO 4)
Refer to the annual report of Outback Steakhouse that is included as an appendix to this text.

Required:

1. Compute Outback's working capital and current ratio at the end of 1995 and 1996.
2. Based upon the items computed in (1), did Outback's liquidity improve or worsen in 1996? What factors may have been responsible for the change in the company's liquidity between the end of 1995 and 1996?
3. What factors other than a company's working capital and current ratio are relevant in evaluating the firm's liquidity?

33. **Accounting for Contingent Liabilities** (LO 5)
Saddleback Sporting Goods, Inc., manufactures and sells a unique recreational footwear product, a convertible ice skate/roller blade. Periodically, the company is sued because someone using this product is injured. Saddleback is currently the defendant in one such lawsuit. The damages requested by the plaintiff in this lawsuit total $2,400,000. The company's net income for its fiscal year just ended was $460,000; the company's total assets at year-end were $1,232,000.

Required:

1. What factors should Saddleback consider in determining the accounting and financial statement treatment of this lawsuit?
2. In reference to the pending lawsuit against Saddleback, identify the conditions under which:
   a. Saddleback would record an expense and a liability in its accounting records.
   b. Saddleback would disclose the lawsuit in the footnotes to its financial statements.
   c. Saddleback would ignore the lawsuit for accounting and financial reporting purposes.

34. **Internal Controls for Payroll** (LO 3)
Reread the Spotlight on Ethics vignette in this chapter entitled "Payroll Padding: A Case of Dodger Blue."

Required:
Write a brief memo to the management of the Dodgers that identifies at least three specific control activities that might have prevented or detected the fraud perpetrated against the organization. You may find it helpful to review the internal control material in Chapter 3 before drafting this memo.

35. **Use of a Payroll Register** (LO 3)
Dick and Lucy Tracewski own a small trucking company that they established ten years ago. Initially, Dick and Lucy were not only the owners of the company but also represented its entire work force. Now the company has two office employees, ten drivers, and six dockworkers. Lucy has maintained the company's accounting records since the firm was established. Initially, Lucy's accounting system for the trucking company consisted only of a general journal and a general ledger. Over the years, she has gradually added other accounting records. One accounting record she does not maintain is a payroll register. In recent years, Lucy has experienced increasing difficulty keeping track of the data needed to prepare the weekly payroll for the company's employees.

Required:
Write a memo to Lucy explaining the nature of a payroll register and how one is usually formatted. Also include in your memo a discussion of how a payroll register can enhance a business's control over its payroll function. In this discussion, identify specific errors or problems that a payroll register can help prevent.

PROBLEM SET A

36. **Accounting for an Interest-Bearing Note Payable** (LO 2)
On April 1, a local bike club, Canadian River Racing Club (CRRC), approached Jim's Bike Shop with a proposal to buy on credit ten racing bikes with a cash price of $750 each. CRRC offered to pay for the bikes by making a $2,000 down payment and by signing a $5,500, 8 percent interest-bearing note. The interest and principal on this note would be due in one year.

Required:
1. Prepare the appropriate journal entries in the accounting records of CRRC on the following dates, assuming that Jim's Bike Shop agrees to the payment plan suggested by CRRC:
   a. April 1, the date the sales agreement is finalized
   b. December 31, the final day of CRRC's fiscal year
   c. April 1 of the following year when the note matures
2. Suppose that CRRC does not make an entry pertaining to this note payable in its accounting records on December 31. How will this oversight affect CRRC's financial statements for the year-ending December 31? For the following year?

37. **Current Ratio and Working Capital** (LO 1, 4)
Hormel Foods Corporation manufactures and distributes prepared foods. Bob Evans Farms, Inc., operates more than three hundred restaurants located in nineteen states. The following schedule lists the year-end current assets and current liabilities of these two firms for two recent years.

Hormel Food Corporation:

	Year 1	Year 2
	(in thousands)	
Cash and cash equivalents	$157,558	$248,599
Short-term marketable securities	14,862	11,360
Accounts receivable	218,487	228,369
Inventories	208,101	199,243
Deferred income taxes	12,393	14,213
Prepaid expenses	8,503	6,431
Total current assets	$619,904	$708,215
Accounts payable	$ 98,357	$112,851
Accrued liabilities	30,212	29,320
Accrued advertising	24,587	31,863
Employee compensation	40,195	41,989
Taxes, other than federal income taxes	14,011	17,606
Dividends payable	8,434	9,585
Federal income taxes	11,262	21,303
Current portion of long-term debt	0	400
Total current liabilities	$227,058	$264,917

Bob Evans Farms, Inc.:

	Year 1	Year 2
	(in thousands)	
Cash	$ 8,241	$ 6,699
Investments	1,947	1,399
Accounts receivable	12,545	15,445
Inventories	14,814	15,799
Deferred income taxes	4,249	4,585
Prepaid expenses	3,371	3,514
Total current assets	$45,167	$47,441
Line of credit	$ 0	$ 9,500
Accounts payable	9,530	12,200
Dividends payable	2,618	2,839
Federal and state income taxes	7,597	6,160
Accrued wages and related liabilities	10,163	10,830
Other accrued liabilities	17,185	18,023
Total current liabilities	$47,093	$59,552

Required:

1. Compute the following items for both companies for Year 1 and Year 2:
   a. Working capital
   b. Current ratio
   c. Quick ratio (discussed in Chapter 6)
2. Given the data computed in (1), which of these two companies had the stronger liquidity at the end of Year 1 and Year 2? Why?

3. In your opinion, which of the three measures that you computed in (1) is the best measure of liquidity? Explain.
4. Review the data presented for each company. Are there any unusual items or unusual relationships in either company's data that a decision maker might want to investigate further? If so, identify these items and the issues or questions that decision makers would likely raise.

38. **Current Ratio and Working Capital** (LO 4)
Presented in the table that follows are the total current assets and current liabilities of USA Truck, Inc., over a recent five-year period. USA Truck, based in Van Buren, Arkansas, describes itself as a "medium haul, common and contract carrier specializing in truckload quantities of general commodities." Amounts are expressed in millions of dollars.

	Year 1	**Year 2**	**Year 3**	**Year 4**	**Year 5**
Current Assets	$11.0	$8.9	$11.4	$12.5	$16.0
Current Liabilities	10.1	7.8	8.6	10.8	13.3

Required:
1. Compute USA Truck's current ratio and working capital for Year 1 through Year 5.
2. Did USA Truck's liquidity improve or deteriorate over this five-year period? Explain.
3. Suppose that the average current ratio in USA Truck's industry has historically been 1.8. Do the firm's current ratios compare favorably or unfavorably with that industry norm? Explain.

39. **Accounting for Contingent Liabilities** (LO 1, 5)
Consider the following three scenarios involving publicly owned companies in the United States.

Scenario A: One of the four wholly-owned subsidiaries of Option Plastics, Inc., is located in the South American country of San Turcia. Recent elections in the country have brought to power a political party that intends to nationalize all major businesses. The new president of San Turcia has indicated that the government will pay a "reasonable price" for these businesses. The manager of the San Turcia subsidiary estimates that Option Plastics will suffer a loss of between $4 million and $6 million when the government buys out the subsidiary sometime in the next two years.

Scenario B: Charles Ironworks has just been slapped with a $5.5 million fine by the Environmental Protection Agency (EPA). The company's legal counsel intends to contest the fine. When asked to evaluate the likelihood of overturning the EPA fine, the company's chief legal counsel responded, "I think there's a 50-50 chance that we can get the fine reduced. But I have no idea if we can reduce the fine by $2 or by $2 million."

Scenario C: Joy's Toys manufactures a wide range of toys designed for children one to four years of age. This past week, a competitor, Gaver Corporation, sued Joy's Toys for $17.2 million. The suit alleges that Joy's Toys infringed on a patent that Gaver holds on a popular toy. In a press release, the chief executive of Joy's Toys observed, "This suit is complete nonsense. Gaver knows that we haven't infringed on its patent. All this company is trying to do is harass us and damage our reputation."

Required:
1. Evaluate each of the three scenarios in reference to the accounting and financial reporting guidelines for contingent liabilities. How would you recommend that these items be accounted for and/or reported in each firm's financial statements? Support your recommendation for each scenario.
2. Do companies have an incentive to intentionally downplay the significance of contingent liabilities and thus exclude them from their financial statements? Explain. If this occurs, what is the impact on decision makers who rely on financial statement data?

40. **Accounting for a Product Warranty Liability** (LO 2)
Cool Air, Inc., wholesales air conditioners and related products to retail stores. Each product is sold with a one-year warranty covering parts and labor. The following table lists the company's three major product lines, the percentage of the products sold in each product line that are returned while under warranty, and the average warranty-related cost incurred on each returned item.

Product Line	Percentage of Products Sold That Are Returned While under Warranty	Warranty Cost Per Returned Item
Air conditioners	8%	$120
Air compressors	6%	50
Fans	3%	18

During the month of April, Cool Air had the following unit sales by product line:

Air conditioners	2,400
Air compressors	1,650
Fans	1,500

Required:
1. Compute the estimated product warranty expense that should be recorded by Cool Air at the end of April and prepare the appropriate adjusting entry to record this expense and the corresponding product warranty liability.
2. Suppose that during one week in May, the company pays warranty-related costs of $7,100. Prepare the entry to record these payments.

41. **Control Activities for Payroll** (LO 3)
Spencer Manufacturing produces fabricated steel products in six large factories located along the East Coast. Spencer has implemented the following control activities for its payroll function in each factory.
a. Initial hourly pay rates for production-line personnel are authorized by the assistant factory superintendent.
b. Hourly personnel "punch" a time clock at the beginning and end of each day and at the beginning and end of the daily lunch break.
c. Departmental supervisors review and approve the weekly time cards of all employees in their department before the weekly payroll is prepared.
d. Pay rates, hours worked, and all clerical computations are double-checked by payroll clerks before payroll checks are processed.

e. Departmental supervisors distribute employee paychecks. At least twice per year on a surprise basis, internal auditors distribute employee paychecks for each department.
f. Payroll checks are prenumbered. The numerical sequence of payroll checks used each week are accounted for by internal auditors.

Required:
Identify specific errors or problems that each of the control activities may help prevent or detect.

PROBLEM SET B

42. Accounting for an Interest-Bearing Note Payable (LO 2)

Jim Ed Brown, owner of B & B Farms, is negotiating with the local John Deere dealer to purchase a tractor. The dealer requires customers to make at least a 20 percent down payment when purchasing a tractor. The balance of the purchase price is placed on a 9 percent, one-year interest-bearing promissory note with both principal and interest due on the note's maturity date.

The tractor Jim Ed wants to purchase is a Model A that has a list price of $21,800. To close the deal, the dealer offers to sell the tractor to Jim at a "sacrifice" price of $19,000.

Required:
1. Prepare the appropriate journal entries in the accounting records of B & B Farms on the following dates, assuming that Jim Ed purchases the Model A and makes a 20 percent down payment.
   a. September 30, the date the sales agreement is finalized
   b. December 31, the final day of B & B Farms' fiscal year
   c. September 30 of the following year when the note matures
2. Suppose that B & B Farms does not make an entry pertaining to this note payable in its accounting records on December 31. How will this oversight affect B & B's financial statements for the year ending December 31? For the following year?

43. Current Ratio and Working Capital (LO 4)

The following table reports the year-end current assets and current liabilities of two companies over a recent five-year period. Kelly Services, Inc., provides temporary employees, principally office and clerical workers, to a wide range of businesses. Quantum Restaurant Group, Inc., operates two restaurant chains, Morton's of Chicago and Bertolini's Authentic Trattorias. Amounts are expressed in millions of dollars.

	Year 1	Year 2	Year 3	Year 4	Year 5
Kelly Services:					
Current assets	$411.4	$408.6	$447.1	$526.7	$558.6
Current liabilities	124.4	128.8	155.9	210.9	242.6
Quantum Restaurant Group:					
Current assets	4.5	6.7	13.0	15.4	35.4
Current liabilities	14.1	9.8	16.1	15.4	26.4

Required:
1. Compute each company's current ratio and working capital for Year 1 through Year 5.

2. Are there any apparent trends in the items you computed in (1)? If so, comment on them and how they reflect on the given company's liquidity.
3. Suppose that the average current ratio in each of these companies' industries is 1.6. Indicate whether each firm's current ratios compare favorably or unfavorably with the industry norm.

44. **Current Ratio and Working Capital** (LO 1, 4)
Following are the year-end current assets and current liabilities of Biogen, Inc., a leading biotechnology company, for a recent four-year period. Amounts presented are in thousands of dollars.

	Year 1	Year 2	Year 3	Year 4
Cash and cash equivalents	$ 56,647	$ 85,863	$ 74,546	$ 54,682
Short-term investments	129,343	142,025	195,805	213,120
Accounts receivable	18,389	33,415	31,695	18,502
Other	4,785	7,144	7,378	8,480
Total current assets	$209,164	$268,447	$309,424	$294,784
Accounts payable	$ 3,169	$ 3,896	$ 2,916	$ 9,991
Accrued liabilities	10,907	22,343	28,860	37,937
Total current liabilities	$ 14,076	$ 26,239	$ 31,776	$ 47,928

Required:
1. Compute the following items for Biogen for Year 1 through Year 4.
   a. Working capital
   b. Current ratio
   c. Quick ratio (discussed in Chapter 6)
2. Evaluate this company's liquidity over this four-year period. Was it strong or poor, improving or deteriorating? What other information would be helpful in evaluating Biogen's liquidity over this time period?
3. Suppose that early in Year 5, you were an investor considering a purchase of Biogen's common stock. What questions would you have wanted to pose to Biogen's executives, given the financial data presented and the financial measures you computed?

45. **Accounting for Contingent Liabilities** (LO 1, 5)
Consider the following three scenarios involving publicly owned companies.

Scenario A: Kasulis & Kenderine, a consulting firm, has recently been sued for $4.4 million by an employee. This individual alleges that the firm failed to provide a safe workplace for its employees. One month ago, the plaintiff slipped and fell on a banana peel near the front door of the firm. The chief executive of Kasulis & Kenderine maintains that her firm has no liability to the individual since three witnesses have testified that the alleged accident was "staged."

Scenario B: Jameson Exploration, Inc., an oil and gas exploration company, has been sued by a group of shrimp fishermen for an oil spill off the Louisiana coast. The suit is asking for damages of $3.3 million; however, Jameson's chief executive has publicly stated that his company will likely settle the suit for approximately $2 million.

Scenario C: Louis & Fred's Diners, Inc., has been named as the defendant in a class action lawsuit filed by representatives of an ethnic group who allegedly have been discriminated against by the firm. In responding to this lawsuit, the company's chief executive observed, "We are totally innocent of these charges. Nevertheless, our firm may have to spend several million dollars fighting this lawsuit in court."

Required:

1. Evaluate each of the three scenarios relative to the accounting and financial reporting guidelines for contingent liabilities. How would you recommend that these items be accounted for and/or reported in each firm's financial statements? Support your recommendation in each case.
2. Do companies have an incentive to intentionally downplay the significance of contingent liabilities and thus exclude them from their financial statements? Explain. If this occurs, what is the impact on decision makers who rely on financial statement data?

46. **Accounting for a Product Warranty Liability** (LO 2)
Standridge Farm Supply sells farm equipment through retail outlets in western Kansas. Several of the company's products are sold with a one-year warranty covering parts and labor. Listed in the following table are the products sold under warranty, the percentage of these products that are returned while under warranty, and the average warranty-related cost incurred on each returned item.

Product Line	Percentage of Products Sold That Are Returned While under Warranty	Warranty Cost Per Returned Item
Tractors	20%	$ 600
Plows	4%	130
Combines	25%	1,300
Irrigation equipment	10%	450

During March, Standridge had the following unit sales of products covered by a warranty:

Tractors	45
Plows	125
Combines	12
Irrigation equipment	70

Required:

1. Compute the estimated product warranty expense that should be recognized at the end of March. Also prepare the appropriate adjusting journal entry to record this expense and the corresponding product warranty liability.
2. Suppose that during one week in June, Standridge pays total warranty-related costs of $2,800. Prepare the entry to record these costs.

47. **Control Activities for Accounts Payable** (LO 3)
The opening vignette for this chapter identified control activities that an architectural firm, Aria Group Architects, has implemented for the processing and payment of accounts payable. These control activities are listed next.
    1. When a bill arrives, the office manager immediately logs it into the computer, recording the date of arrival, the amount, and the date it is due, and any relevant comments (such as order problems or discounts for early payment).

2. Pancewicz (the financial vice-president) receives a weekly accounts payable report that details the key information for each payable and that highlights the bills due that week. The goal is to have all invoices paid within 30 days.
3. Once Pancewicz approves the weekly payment plan, checks are issued, which he then signs.
4. At the end of each month, Aria's outside accountant receives and reviews copies of the weekly accounts payable reports, copies of all signed checks, and a monthly report that summarizes all accounts payable activities for that period.

Required:
Identify specific errors or problems that each of the control activities may help prevent or detect.

CASES

48. International Classification of Liabilities (LO 1, 4)

In the United States, current liabilities are debts and other obligations of a business that must be paid during the coming year or the business's operating cycle, whichever is longer. Under Swedish accounting rules, current liabilities are simply those liabilities that must be paid in the coming year. Swedish accounting rules ignore the operating cycle concept for the purpose of identifying current assets and current liabilities.

Assume that two shipbuilding companies have similar operations, except that one is located in the United States and one is located in Sweden. Each company complies with the accounting principles of its own country, and each company has an operating cycle of three years. These companies have approximately the same annual revenues each year and approximately the same amount of total assets. Following are selected financial data for these companies.

	Yankee Shipbuilders*	Viking Ships*	Viking Ships**
Current assets:			
Cash	$ 3,040,000	$ 5,276,000	$ 5,276,000
Short-term investments	9,222,000	8,322,000	6,703,000
Accounts receivable	68,609,000	72,555,000	33,808,000
Inventories	111,278,000	103,392,000	33,067,000
Prepaid expenses	8,231,000	16,449,000	4,611,000
Total	$200,380,000	$205,994,000	$ 83,465,000
Current liabilities:			
Accounts payable	$ 55,242,000	$ 51,002,000	$ 47,224,000
Accrued liabilities	32,139,000	38,864,000	34,375,000
Notes payable	107,878,000	91,053,000	62,630,000
Total	$195,259,000	$180,919,000	$144,229,000

*Compiled in accordance with GAAP.
**Compiled in accordance with Swedish accounting rules.

Required:
1. Analyze the liquidity of both companies by computing their current ratio, quick ratio, and working capital. Analyze the foreign company's liquidity using both the data based upon Swedish accounting rules and the GAAP-based data.

2. How do the different accounting rules in the United States and Sweden for classifying current assets and current liabilities affect the conclusions you draw about the liquidity of the foreign company?
3. Which accounting rule for classifying current assets and current liabilities do you believe is more appropriate? Defend your answer.

49. **Secret Payroll Account** (LO 1, 3)

Jim and Tammy Bakker founded the PTL Club, a religious broadcasting network, in 1974. A little more than one decade later, the PTL Club had 500,000 members and annual revenues of almost $130 million. Bakker and his close associates came under intense scrutiny in 1987 when it was disclosed that PTL funds had been used to pay a former church secretary to remain silent concerning a brief liaison involving herself and Bakker. In March 1987, Bakker was forced to resign as PTL's chairman. Two years later, he was convicted of fraud and conspiracy charges, fined $500,000, and sentenced to prison.

Prior to 1987, Bakker's critics had persistently called for greater disclosure of PTL's financial affairs. Bakker resisted these demands, repeatedly asserting that such disclosure was not necessary, since PTL had strong financial controls. Bakker also often reminded his critics that "[PTL] had excellent accountants and . . . external audits by reputable [CPA] firms." However, the results of numerous investigations of PTL during 1987 and 1988 by the FBI, IRS, and other agencies suggested that the organization's internal controls were extremely weak, and nonexistent in many cases. Investigators found that paychecks had been written to individuals who could not be identified, that large sums were paid to consultants who had not provided any services to PTL, and that there was no supporting documentation for millions of dollars of construction costs entered in PTL's accounting records.

The most troubling internal control problem that investigators uncovered in PTL's accounting system was the existence of a secret payroll bank account that was used to disburse funds to Bakker and his closest aides. This account was so secretive that the organization's chief financial officer was not informed of the nature of the expenses being paid through it. The members of PTL's board of directors were totally unaware of this payroll account. Surprisingly, the check register for the payroll account was maintained by a partner of Laventhol & Horwath, PTL's independent audit firm. In fact, that individual supervised the annual audits of PTL's financial statements. Bakker, or one of his aides, would telephone the Laventhol partner when a check was written on the account. The partner would also be called periodically to determine whether PTL needed to deposit additional funds into the account.

Note: This vignette was adapted from the following source: M. C. Knapp, "The PTL Club," in *Contemporary Auditing: Issues and Cases,* 2d ed. (Minneapolis/St. Paul: West Publishing Co., 1996).

Required:

1. Many large financial frauds have involved the illicit use of an organization's payroll function. List specific internal control weaknesses related to PTL's secret payroll bank account. Also identify control activities that would have prevented or detected the use of this account.
2. How do independent auditors enhance the credibility of an organization's periodic financial statements? Why should an audit firm be "independent" of its clients? Do you believe that Laventhol & Horwath was independent of PTL? Explain.

50. **Noninterest-Bearing Note Payable** (LO 2)

Howard Metzen recently purchased a used, twin-engine Cessna from a Cleveland-based plane dealer, Baum's & Whey. To finance the deal, Howard obtained a bank loan. Howard signed a $100,000, noninterest-bearing promissory note that comes due in one year. The "discount" rate applied to the note was 12 percent, meaning that Howard received only $88,000. A few days after signing the promissory note, Joel, a friend of Howard's, informed him that he had been "ripped off" by the bank. Why? Because according to Joel the true, or effective, interest rate on the bank loan is greater than 12 percent.

Required:

1. Explain Joel's reasoning, using a numerical example.
2. Was Howard "ripped off" by his bank? Defend your answer.

PROJECTS

51. Accounting for Contingent Liabilities

Consider the following three scenarios involving large public companies.

Scenario A: Augusta Appliances, Inc., manufactures a variety of household appliances. Augusta has recently been cited for dumping toxic waste in the South Canadian River. Estimated clean-up costs and fines amount to $4.3 million. Although the case is still being contested, Augusta's attorney believes there is an 80 percent chance that the firm will have to pay the clean-up costs and fines.

Scenario B: Edward Earl Inc. (EEI) has recorded a $1.2 million receivable from the IRS. This receivable stems from a refund claim that EEI filed with the IRS. EEI contends that the IRS inappropriately disqualified a large expense item the company deducted in a recent tax return. The IRS is contesting the claim in the federal courts. Privately, Will Charles, EEI's chief executive officer, believes there is only a 30 to 40 percent chance that the courts will rule in EEI's favor.

Scenario C: Washboard Abs, Inc., is the defendant in a patent infringement lawsuit filed against it by Ab Flexor Corporation. Washboard's attorney has informed the firm's chief executive that there is a 50 percent likelihood a judgment will be rendered in favor of Ab Flexor in this case. The attorney estimates that the amount of the judgment could range from $1 million to $14 million depending upon how the courts resolve several complex legal issues in the case.

Required:

1. Meet with the other members of your project group to discuss these scenarios. In each case, assume that the amounts involved are material to the relevant company.
2. Your group should evaluate each of the three scenarios in reference to the accounting and financial reporting guidelines for contingent liabilities. Develop a recommendation suggesting how each contingency should be accounted for by the relevant company and/or reported in its financial statements.
3. One member of your group should be prepared to present a summary overview to the class of the group's discussion of these scenarios. Included in this overview should be the recommendations developed in (2).

52. Litigation-Related Contingent Liabilities

Review the index of *The Wall Street Journal* or a major metropolitan newspaper such as *The New York Times* or *Los Angeles Times* for the past three years. Identify a major lawsuit filed against a public company by another firm, a group of investors, a governmental agency, or another party.

Required:

1. In a written report, summarize the nature of the lawsuit filed against the given company. Identify the plaintiff, the plaintiff's major allegations, the damages requested, and other key facts regarding the lawsuit.
2. Include in your report an assessment of the financial statement implications of this lawsuit. That is, evaluate whether or not the lawsuit should be ignored for account-

ing and financial reporting purposes by the company or should be included in some manner in the firm's financial statements. If the company has issued an annual report since the lawsuit was filed, determine whether the lawsuit was reflected in some way in the firm's financial statements or the accompanying footnotes.

53. **Interpreting Current Ratios**

Identify five different industries. Make sure that a variety of different types of industries are represented in your sample. For instance, your sample should include service, merchandising, and manufacturing industries.

Required:

1. Referring to recent data published by Dun & Bradstreet, Robert Morris Associates, or another investment advisory or financial services firm, identify the average or median current ratio for each industry included in your sample.
2. Analyze the nature of each industry in your sample and other relevant variables that may help explain the differences between and among the current ratio norms for these industries. Typically, such differences will be related to one or more key characteristics or facets of the given industries and/or to economic conditions that differentially affect individual industries.
3. Document in a written report the data collected in (1) and the results of your analysis in (2).

54. **Disclosure of Contingent Liabilities**

Identify several well-known public companies whose financial statements are available on the Internet. These financial statements may be available from the companies' Web sites or from the EDGAR (electronic data gathering and retrieval system) Web site maintained by the Securities and Exchange Commission. Browse through these companies' financial statements until you identify two firms that report a major contingent liability in their financial statements or the accompanying financial statement footnotes. (Note: Many companies include a financial statement footnote in their annual reports entitled "Contingencies" or "Commitments and Contingencies.')

Required:

Prepare a report containing the following items for each of the companies you identified:

a. The nature of the contingent liability.
b. The potential monetary effect on the company.
c. Management's evaluation of the likelihood that the contingent liability will eventually become an actual liability.
d. A brief discussion of whether you believe the contingency-related disclosures provide decision makers with a thorough understanding of the contingency and its potential economic impact on the company.
e. The Web site address from which you obtained the required data.

MODULE TWO

THE TIME VALUE OF MONEY

"Time is money."

—Benjamin Franklin

LEARNING OBJECTIVES

After studying this module, you should be able to do the following:

1. Distinguish between simple and compound interest.
2. Compute the future value of a single amount.
3. Compute the future value of an annuity.
4. Compute the present value of a single amount.
5. Compute the present value of an annuity.

FOCUS ON DECISION MAKING

Pay Me Now, or . . . Pay Me Later

You learned in Chapter 9 that most large companies disclose loss contingencies in their annual reports. The most common source of loss contingencies? Litigation. Accounting for litigation-related contingencies poses difficult accounting issues. Recall that companies must "book" a contingent loss and an offsetting contingent liability when it is both *probable* that an actual loss will result from the contingency and the amount of that loss is subject to *reasonable estimation.* Determining whether a pending lawsuit faced by a company satisfies these two conditions typically requires the exercise of considerable judgment, if not psychic insight. In fact, even when both conditions are clearly met, accounting for a loss contingency can be tricky.

Take the case of Shoney's, Inc., a company that operates a chain of restaurants. In the early 1990s, Shoney's tentatively agreed to pay more than $100 million over a five-year period to settle several lawsuits alleging that the company had discriminated against certain ethnic groups. While the final details of the settlement were being negotiated, Shoney's faced a contingent liability. This liability was both probable and the amount was subject to reasonable estimation. In fact, court documents identified the tentative amount of the settlement to be paid by Shoney's. So, Shoney's accountants "booked" the contingent loss and contingent liability. But, the accountants did not record the full amount of the proposed settlement figure as a loss (expense) and a liability in the firm's accounting records. Instead, the accountants "discounted" (reduced) the settlement to arrive at an appropriate debit and credit for accounting purposes. Why? Because the true economic value of a cash payment or receipt is a function of both the dollar amount involved *and* the timing of the receipt or payment.

You have probably heard the following good news/bad news joke. The good news: you just won $1 million. The bad news: your prize will be paid out $1 per year over the next one million years. Clearly, the economic value of $1 million to be received over an extended period of time is definitely less than the economic value of $1 million available today. The same reasoning applies to the legal settlement that Shoney's agreed to pay in the early 1990s.

For illustration purposes, suppose that on January 1 of Year 1 Shoney's tentatively agreed to pay $25 million annually to the plaintiffs in the lawsuit over a five-year period with the first payment due on December 31, Year 1. So, Shoney's agreed to pay $125 million in total. But, on January 1, Year 1, the economic cost associated with the settlement was an amount considerably less than $125 million given the payment plan agreed to by the two parties. If a "discount rate" of 10 percent is applied to the series of five $25 million payments, the true economic cost of the $125 million settlement on January 1, Year 1, was approximately $95 million. Consequently, on January 1, Year 1, Shoney's accountants were justified in booking a litigation loss and corresponding contingent liability of "only" $95 million.

This module focuses on the time value of money concept. This concept has accounting implications for many financial statement items. However, the time value of money is most often associated with long-term liabilities, such as bonds payable and capital lease obligations, both of which are discussed in Chapter 10.

TIME *IS* MONEY

In October 1994, four lucky individuals literally hit the jackpot when they won the New York state lottery.[1] These individuals split the $73 million Lotto jackpot that, at the time, was the largest in New York history. So, let's see, $73 million divided four ways means each of these winners walked away with approximately $18 million. Right? Wrong. Like most lottery prizes, this huge jackpot was not paid in a single amount. Instead, New York distributes the jackpot in a series of equal payments stretching over twenty-one years. Each of the four winners receives annual payments of approximately $863,000. Assuming an income tax rate of 50 percent for these individuals—they have to pay federal, state, and municipal income taxes on their winnings—each pockets less than $440,000 annually.

If we go one step further and apply the time value of money concept to the Lotto jackpot, we can determine the "present value" of each winner's $18 million share. The **time value of money concept** dictates that the economic value of a sum of cash to be received or paid is a function of both the amount and timing of that payment or receipt. In simple terms, the time value of money concept is based upon the premise that $1 in your pocket today is worth more to you than $1 you will receive sometime in the future. Applying the appropriate mathematical equation derived from the time value of money concept, the present value of each winner's share of the Lotto jackpot, again after taxes, is approximately $5 million. So, there you have it. Instead of winning $18 million each, these individuals were enriched to the tune of only $5 million, hardly enough to make an effort to collect. Right? Wrong.

time value of money concept

Scenarios involving the time value of money abound in the business world. For example, suppose that the owner of a hardware store is approaching retirement and wants to sell his business. The business's accounting records reveal that the hardware store generates a positive net cash flow of $80,000 per year. How much should someone be willing to pay for this indefinite stream of cash flows? A different type of time value of money scenario faces a small corporation with a long-range expansion plan that includes building a new factory in five years. The company intends to accumulate a $10 million building fund by making equal annual deposits in a savings account over the next five years. How large must these deposits be to allow the company to achieve its goal?

This module provides you with an introduction to the time value of money concept. Internal and external decision makers rely on this concept to help them make a wide array of economic decisions. Accountants apply this concept to analyze a variety of transactions and to assign dollar values to certain financial statement items. In the following chapter, we refer to the time value of money concept when reviewing the accounting treatment for bonds payable and capital lease obligations. If you take additional business courses in the future, you will find many other opportunities to apply your understanding of the time value of money.

1. "Four Hit the Lottery for $73 million Pot," *Los Angeles Times,* 3 October 1994, A15.

The next section of this module addresses the concept of interest, including the two methods of computing interest. The final four sections discuss and illustrate the four basic types of time value of money scenarios.

SIMPLE INTEREST VS. COMPOUND INTEREST

LEARNING OBJECTIVE 1 ▶ Distinguish between simple and compound interest.

interest

simple interest

compound interest

In Chapter 9, we used the interest equation (interest = principal × rate × time) to compute interest on notes payable. The key to understanding the time value of money is interest and the methods of computing interest. In an economic sense, **interest** is the expense of borrowing money for a specified period or, alternatively, the revenue earned from lending money for a specified period. If you borrow $1,000 from a bank for one year at an annual (simple) interest rate of 10 percent, the cost you will incur to use the bank's money is $100. That is, you will pay $100 of interest on the borrowed funds. Likewise, if you deposit money with a bank, that bank will pay you for its use of your money (but at an interest rate lower than the interest rate it charges on loans.)

Banks and other lenders have two choices when computing interest on a loan or other financial instrument, such as a certificate of deposit. They can calculate interest on a simple or a compound basis. **Simple interest** is computed only on the principal amount of a loan. **Compound interest** is computed on the principal amount of a loan plus any unpaid interest that has accumulated on the loan since its inception. Suppose that rather than borrowing $1,000 for one year at an annual interest rate of 10 percent, you borrow that amount for two years. If your bank charges you simple interest, at the end of two years you must pay the bank the $1,000 principal amount plus $200 of interest—$100 for each year that the loan was outstanding. Alternatively, assume that the bank charges you interest on a compound basis, which is more likely. In that case, $210 of interest will accrue, or accumulate, on your loan over its two-year term, as shown in the following schedule.

	Principal Amount of Loan Plus Unpaid Interest at Beginning of Year		Interest Rate		Interest
Year 1	$1,000	×	10%	=	$100
Year 2	1,100	×	10%	=	110
Total					$210

Unless stated otherwise, the examples and illustrations in this module assume that interest is computed on a compound basis.

FUTURE VALUE OF A SINGLE AMOUNT

LEARNING OBJECTIVE 2 ▶ Compute the future value of a single amount.

future value

In many situations, businesses need to know the future value of a single amount. In this context, **future value** refers to the sum of an invested amount plus any interest that will accumulate on that amount on a compound basis over a specified period of time. Suppose that a young woman has been given $25,000 by her grandmother, and she intends to invest this amount in a four-year certificate of deposit (CD) that pays 10 percent interest compounded annually. The young woman plans to use the accumulated balance of the CD at the end of four years to purchase a small business on Campus Corner. The question foremost in the young investor's mind is the "future value" of her CD, as suggested by the following graphic.

Present Value of CD: **\$25,000**		Future Value of CD: ?
	Four Years @ 10%	

Ignoring tax considerations, the CD's balance will be \$36,602.50 in four years, as demonstrated by the following schedule.

	CD Balance at Beginning of Year		**Interest Rate**		**Interest Revenue**	**CD Balance at End of Year**
Year 1	\$25,000	×	10%	=	\$2,500.00	\$27,500.00
Year 2	27,500	×	10%	=	2,750.00	30,250.00
Year 3	30,250	×	10%	=	3,025.00	33,275.00
Year 4	33,275	×	10%	=	3,327.50	36,602.50

Using the approach just shown to compute future values is tedious when a lengthy period is involved. For instance, if the young woman in our illustration plans to invest the \$25,000 gift for ten years, we would have to extend the previous schedule for six additional years.

Fortunately, there are two quick and easy approaches to computing future values. The first approach involves using the following equation.

$$\text{Future Value of a Single Amount} = \text{Present Value of the Amount} \times (1 + \text{Interest Rate})^t$$

where t represents the number of periods over which interest is to be compounded

More often than not, you will find the previous equation expressed as follows:

$$FV = PV \times (1 + R)^t$$

Shown next are the computations to determine the value of the \$25,000 gift both four years and ten years into the future.

$$\begin{aligned}
\text{Four Years: } FV &= PV \times (1 + R)^t \\
FV &= \$25{,}000 \times (1 + .1)^4 \\
FV &= \$25{,}000 \times (1.4641) \\
FV &= \$36{,}602.50 \\
\text{Ten Years: } FV &= PV \times (1 + R)^t \\
FV &= \$25{,}000 \times (1 + .1)^{10} \\
FV &= \$25{,}000 \times (2.59374) \\
FV &= \$64{,}843.50
\end{aligned}$$

The second approach to computing future values involves the use of a table, such as Exhibit M2.1. (The complete version of this table can be found on the inside front cover of this text.) Included in Exhibit M2.1 are numerical values that can be used to compute the future value of $1 amounts invested for a given number of periods at a specified compound rate of interest. These numerical values are referred to as future value factors. To find the future value factor (FVF) for the combination of four years and 10 percent, locate the 10 percent column in Exhibit M2.1 and then slide your finger down that column until it intersects with the 4 period row. At that intersection point, you will find the FVF of 1.4641, which is the figure we arrived at previously when we solved for the following term in the four-year scenario: $(1 + R)^t$. What does 1.4641 represent? Answer: the future value (approximately $1.46) of $1 invested at 10 percent for four years. At the intersection of the 10 percent column and 10 period row is the FVF of 2.59374. So, $1 invested at 10 percent for ten years will accumulate to the grand total of $2.59, approximately.

If you prefer to use Exhibit M2.1 to compute future values, you can use the following simplified future value equation. In this equation, FVF represents the appropriate future value factor drawn from Exhibit M2.1.

$$FV = PV \times FVF$$

For the four-year assumption in the present example, the future value is computed as follows.

$$FV = PV \times FVF$$
$$FV = \$25,000 \times 1.4641$$
$$FV = \$36,602.50$$

EXHIBIT M2.1 ▼
Future Value Factors for a Single Amount

Period	2.5%	3%	3.5%	4%	4.5%	5%	.....	8%	9%	10%
1	1.02500	1.03000	1.03500	1.04000	1.04500	1.05000	.....	1.08000	1.09000	1.10000
2	1.05063	1.06090	1.07123	1.08160	1.09203	1.10250	.....	1.16640	1.18810	1.21000
3	1.07689	1.09273	1.10872	1.12486	1.14117	1.15762	.....	1.25971	1.29503	1.33100
4	1.10381	1.12551	1.14752	1.16986	1.19252	1.21551	.....	1.36049	1.41158	**1.46410**
5	1.13141	1.15927	1.18769	1.21665	1.24618	1.27628	.....	1.46933	1.53862	1.61051
6	1.15969	1.19405	1.22926	1.26532	1.30226	1.34010	.....	1.58687	1.67710	1.77156
7	1.18869	1.22987	1.27228	1.31593	1.36086	1.40710	.....	1.71382	1.82804	1.94872
8	1.21840	1.26677	1.31681	1.36857	1.42210	**1.47746**	.....	1.85093	1.99256	2.14359
9	1.24886	1.30477	1.36290	1.42331	1.48610	1.55133	.....	1.99900	2.17189	2.35795
10	1.28008	1.34392	1.41060	1.48024	1.55297	1.62889	.....	2.15892	2.36736	**2.59374**
.	.	.	.	.	.	.	.	.	.	.
.	.	.	.	.	.	.	.	.	.	.
.	.	.	.	.	.	.	.	.	.	.
18	1.55966	1.70243	1.85749	2.02582	2.20848	2.40662	.....	3.99602	4.71712	5.55992
19	1.59865	1.75351	1.92250	2.10685	2.30786	2.52695	.....	4.31570	5.14166	6.11591
20	1.63862	1.80611	1.98979	2.19112	2.41171	**2.65330**	.....	4.66096	5.60441	6.72750

Note: The expanded table is located inside the front cover of this text.

Quite often, interest is compounded (added to the principal amount) on other than an annual basis. Fortunately, the "period" in Exhibit M2.1 can represent any length of time, such as one year, six months, or one quarter (three months). Returning to our hypothetical scenario, suppose the granddaughter invests the $25,000 for four years in a CD earning interest at a 10 percent annual rate but that the interest is compounded twice per year, or semiannually. In this case, there are eight six-month periods over which interest is computed at one-half the annual interest rate, or 5 percent. According to Exhibit M2.1, the appropriate FVF for eight periods and a 5 percent interest rate is 1.47746. The appropriate FVF for the ten-year assumption is 2.6533 if interest is compounded semiannually. Given these future value factors, the granddaughter would have the following amounts on deposit in her CD account under the four-year and ten-year assumptions.

$$\begin{aligned} \text{Four Years: } FV &= PV \times FVF \\ FV &= \$25{,}000 \times (1.47746) \\ FV &= \$36{,}936.50 \\ \text{Ten Years: } FV &= PV \times FVF \\ FV &= \$25{,}000 \times (2.6533) \\ FV &= \$66{,}332.50 \end{aligned}$$

Notice that for both the four-year and ten-year assumptions, the future value is greater when interest is compounded semiannually than when it is compounded annually. In fact, that is always the case. The more frequently interest is compounded, the greater the resulting future value.

FUTURE VALUE OF AN ANNUITY

LEARNING OBJECTIVE 3
Compute the future value of an annuity.

annuity

An **annuity** is a series of equal payments made, or received, at equal intervals on which interest is computed on a compound basis. In the business world, many financial transactions are structured as annuities. For example, suppose that a company must repay a $2 million loan that comes due in six years. The company could accumulate that amount by making equal annual deposits in a savings account that earns interest compounded annually. That series of equal annual deposits would qualify as an annuity.

In the previous section, we computed the future value of a single amount that was left on deposit with a bank. Now, let us tackle the slightly more challenging problem of computing the future value of an annuity. Suppose that on January 1 of Year 1, a sixteen-year-old young man sells his prized, and somewhat dilapidated, 1969 Chevy to his Uncle Buck. Since Uncle Buck is chronically short of funds, the two relatives agree that the $1,500 sales price for the car will be paid in three equal installments of $500 on December 31 of Year 1, Year 2, and Year 3. To guard against memory lapses, the teenager insists that Uncle Buck sign a sales contract documenting the payment terms. The teenager intends to deposit each of the three $500 payments in a bank account that earns 8 percent interest compounded annually. Now, suppose the young man wants to know exactly how much cash he will have in his account after the final payment is deposited on December 31 of Year 3. That is, he wants to determine the future value of a three-year, $500 annuity with interest compounded annually at 8 percent.

Exhibit M2.2 presents a diagram of this annuity. As indicated in that exhibit, the future value of the annuity is $1,623.20. In other words, by December 31, Year 3,

EXHIBIT M2.2 ▼
Diagram of the Future Value of a Three-Year, $500 Annuity with Interest Compounded Annually at 8 Percent

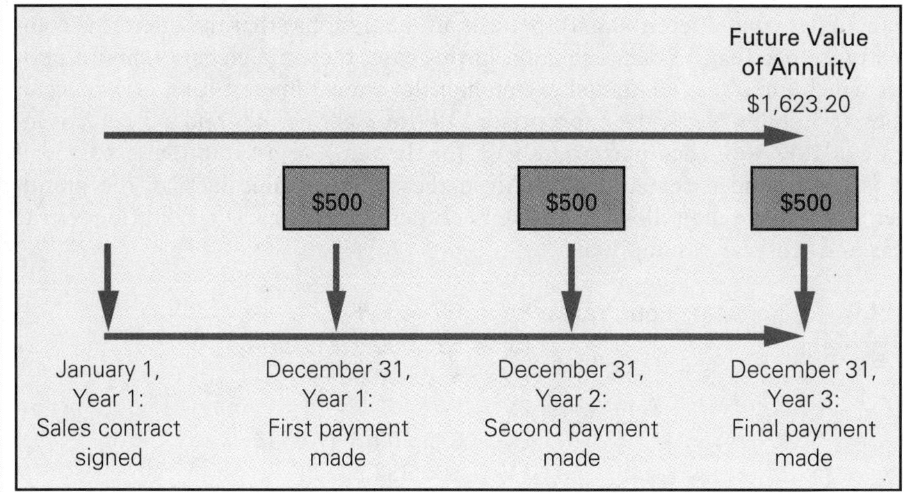

the former Chevy owner will have received the $1,500 in payments from his uncle and earned interest of $123.20 on those payments.

Refer to the following schedule for a year-by-year analysis of the activity in the teenager's bank account. This schedule indicates that no interest will be earned during Year 1. The initial deposit will not be made in the bank account until the final day of that year. During Year 2, $500 will be on deposit until the last day of the year, resulting in interest revenue of $40 ($500 × 8%). During Year 3, the balance of the bank account will be $1,040 until December 31, resulting in interest revenue of $83.20 ($1,040 × 8%). Final result: a $1,623.20 bank account balance on December 31 of Year 3.

	Balance of Bank Account at Beginning of Year	Interest Earned at 8%	December 31 Deposit	Balance of Bank Account at End of Year
Year 1	$ 0	$ 0.00	$500	$ 500.00
Year 2	500	40.00	500	1,040.00
Year 3	1,040	83.20	500	1,623.20

Again, the schedule approach to computing a future value (here, the future value of an annuity) is cumbersome. Shown next is the future value of an annuity (FVA) equation, which can be used instead.

$$FVA = A \times \{[(1 + R)^t - 1]/R\}$$

where: A = the dollar amount of the annuity
R = interest rate
t = the number of periods

If you have access to a future value of an annuity table, such as Exhibit M2.3, you can use a much simpler equation to determine the future value of an annuity. Exhibit

EXHIBIT M2.3 ▼
Future Value of an Annuity Factors

Period	2.5%	3%	3.5%	4%	4.5%	5%	5.5%	6%	7%	8%
1	1.00000	1.00000	1.00000	1.00000	1.00000	1.00000	1.00000	1.00000	1.00000	1.00000
2	2.02500	2.03000	2.03500	2.04000	2.04500	2.05000	2.05500	2.06000	2.07000	2.08000
3	3.07562	3.09090	3.10622	3.12160	3.13702	3.15250	3.16802	3.18360	3.21490	**3.24640**

Note: The expanded table is located inside the front cover of this text.

M2.3 contains future value of an annuity factors (FVAFs). These factors represent the following component of the future value of an annuity equation: $[(1 + R)^t - 1]/R$. The two parameters of the factors included in Exhibit M2.3 are an assumed interest rate and a given number of time periods. For the scenario just described, the appropriate FVAF, 3.2464, can be found at the intersection of the 8 percent column and the 3 period row. What does that figure represent? Answer: the amount of cash (approximately \$3.25) you will have in three years if you invest \$1 at the end of each of those years at an annual interest rate of 8 percent.

When a future value of an annuity table is available, the following simplified version of the future value of an annuity equation can be used:

$$FVA = A \times FVAF$$

For the annuity involving the sale of the 1969 Chevy, the future value is computed as follows.

$$FVA = A \times FVAF$$
$$FVA = \$500 \times 3.2464$$
$$FVA = \$1,623.20$$

Investing in Annuities

FOR YOUR INFORMATION

Many large firms in the financial services industries, including insurance companies and stock brokerage firms, sell annuities. Annuities are often used by individuals as a source of retirement income. For example, at age 55 an individual may purchase an annuity that will pay him $2,000 per month from age 65 until his death. If the individual is fortunate enough to live a long life, the investment in the annuity will have been a very wise (lucky?) decision. On the other hand, if the individual dies at age 66, the company that sold him the annuity will recognize a sizable profit on the transaction.

In fact, most annuities have a minimum guaranteed payout term. If an annuity investor does not live to see the end of that term, his or her heirs are entitled to collect the remaining guaranteed annuity payments. A common guaranteed payout term for annuities is ten years. For a description of factors to consider when purchasing an annuity and the key features of annuities, refer to the following source: J. B. Quinn, "A Check List: Should You Buy an Annuity?" *The Washington Post,* 3 March 1996, H2.

PRESENT VALUE OF A SINGLE AMOUNT

LEARNING OBJECTIVE 4 ▶
Compute the present value of a single amount.

present value

When we compute the future value of a single amount or of an annuity, we are looking forward in time. Another type of time value of money scenario requires us to do just the reverse. To compute a present value, we must "discount" a future value or a series of future values to their current dollar equivalent. A **present value** represents an amount that must be invested currently at a stated compound rate of interest to produce a given future value. Suppose that two members of a three-person partnership agree to buy out the third partner. The buy-out agreement includes a $100,000 payment to the withdrawing partner in three years. The two remaining partners want to know how much they must deposit currently in a CD earning 9 percent interest compounded annually to accumulate a fund of $100,000 in three years. Graphically, we can depict this scenario as follows:

We could use a year-by-year approach to finding the solution to this present value problem, as illustrated earlier. But, by now, you realize that there are more efficient approaches to solving time value of money problems. To compute the present value of a single amount to be received or paid in the future, we can utilize the following equation.

$$\text{Present Value of a Single Amount} = \text{Future Value of the Amount} \times \frac{1}{(1 + \text{Interest Rate})^t}$$

where t represents the number of periods over which the future value is to be discounted

Following is the shorthand version of this equation.

$$PV = FV \times [1/(1 + R)^t]$$

Applying this equation to the scenario described in the previous paragraph, we arrive at a present value of $77,218. That is, the two remaining partners must deposit $77,218 in the CD earning 9 percent interest compounded annually to accumulate the $100,000 needed in three years.

$$PV = \$100,000 \times [1/(1 + .09)^3]$$
$$PV = \$100,000 \times (1/1.29503)$$
$$PV = \$100,000 \times .77218$$
$$PV = \$77,218$$

The shortcut approach to computing present values involves using a present value factor (PVF) from Exhibit M2.4. Shown next is the present value equation to apply when using that exhibit.

$$PV = FV \times PVF$$

EXHIBIT M2.4 ▼
Present Value Factors for a Single Amount

Period	2.5%	3%	3.5%	4%	4.5%	5%	5.5%	6%	7%	8%	9%
1	0.97561	0.97087	0.96618	0.96154	0.95694	0.95238	0.94787	0.94340	0.93458	0.92593	0.91743
2	0.95181	0.94260	0.93351	0.92456	0.91573	0.90703	0.89845	0.89000	0.87344	0.85734	0.84168
3	0.92860	0.91514	0.90194	0.88900	0.87630	0.86384	0.85161	0.83962	0.81630	0.79383	**0.77218**

Note: The expanded table is located inside the back cover of this text.

For the partnership scenario, the appropriate PVF of .77218 can be found at the intersection of the 9 percent column and the 3 period row in Exhibit M2.4. This PVF indicates that the current value of $1 to be paid three years in the future is approximately $.77. Multiplying this PVF by $100,000, we again arrive at $77,218 as the amount that the two remaining partners must invest to accumulate the funds needed to pay off the retiring partner.

PRESENT VALUE OF AN ANNUITY ▲

LEARNING ◄ OBJECTIVE 5
Compute the present value of an annuity.

To illustrate computing the present value of an annuity, return to the scenario involving the teenager who is selling his 1969 Chevy to Uncle Buck. Previously, we determined that the future value of the series of three $500 payments is $1,623.20, as shown in Exhibit M2.2. Now, consider this scenario from the perspective of the teenager's uncle. Suppose that Uncle Buck wants to determine the cash equivalent price he is paying for the Chevy. Exhibit M2.5 presents another diagram of this three-year annuity. Here, the focus is on finding the present value, rather than the future value, of the annuity. Given an 8 percent interest rate, or discount rate, the present value of the payments to be made by Uncle Buck is $1,288.55, an amount that we will confirm not once, but twice.

The present value of an annuity (PVA) can be computed using the following equation:

$$\text{PVA} = \text{A} \times (\{1 - [1/(1 + \text{R})^t]\}/\text{R})$$

where: A = the dollar amount of the annuity
R = interest rate
t = the number of periods

We can apply this equation to our 1969 Chevy scenario as follows:

$$\text{PVA} = \$500 \times (\{1 - [1/(1 + .08)^3]\}/.08)$$
$$\text{PVA} = \$500 \times \{[1 - (1/1.259712)]/.08\}$$
$$\text{PVA} = \$500 \times 2.5771$$
$$\text{PVA} = \$1{,}288.55$$

EXHIBIT M2.5 ▼
Diagram of the Present Value of a Three-Year, $500 Annuity Applying a Discount Rate of 8 Percent

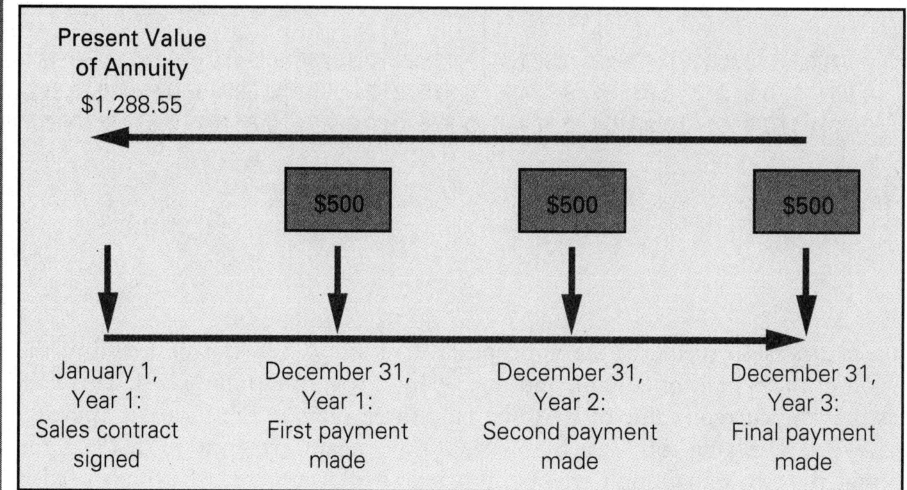

A simple version of the previous equation involves multiplying the annuity amount by the present value of an annuity factor (PVAF), as shown next.

$$PVA = A \times PVAF$$

Exhibit M2.6 lists present value of annuity factors. For the present example, the appropriate PVAF of 2.5771 can be found at the intersection of the 8 percent column and the 3 period row. Again, be sure you understand the literal meaning of that factor. That factor indicates that the present value of a series of $1 payments made at the end of each of the following three years and discounted at an 8 percent rate is equal to approximately $2.58. As you would expect, we arrive at the same present value for the three-year, $500 annuity using the complex and simple versions of the

EXHIBIT M2.6 ▼
Present Value of an Annuity Factors

Period	2.5%	3%	3.5%	4%	4.5%	5%	5.5%	6%	7%	8%
1	0.97561	0.97087	0.96618	0.96154	0.95694	0.95238	0.94787	0.94340	0.93458	0.92593
2	1.92742	1.91347	1.89969	1.88609	1.87267	1.85941	1.84632	1.83339	1.80802	1.78326
3	2.85602	2.82861	2.80164	2.77509	2.74896	2.72325	2.69793	2.67301	2.62432	**2.57710**

Note: The expanded table is located inside the back cover of this text.

present value of an annuity equation. Following is the computation of the present value of the annuity using the simple version of that equation.

$$\text{PVA} = \text{A} \times \text{PVAF}$$
$$\text{PVA} = \$500 \times 2.5771$$
$$\text{PVA} = \$1{,}288.55$$

SUMMARY

The time value of money concept dictates that the economic value of a sum of cash to be received or paid is a function of both the amount and timing of that payment or receipt. The key to understanding the time value of money is interest and the methods of computing interest. Interest is the expense of borrowing money for a specified period or, alternatively, the revenue earned from lending money for a specified period. Interest can be computed on a "simple" basis but is more often computed on a "compound" basis.

Accountants use the time value of money concept to analyze a variety of transactions and to assign appropriate dollar amounts to certain financial statement items. When applying this concept, accountants compute the present value or future value of a single dollar amount or an annuity. An annuity is a series of equal payments made, or received, at equal intervals on which interest is computed on a compound basis.

GLOSSARY

Annuity (p. 431) A series of equal payments made, or received, at equal intervals on which interest is computed on a compound basis.

Compound interest (p. 428) Interest computed on the principal amount of a loan (or other financial instrument) and any unpaid interest that has accumulated on the loan since its inception.

Future value (p. 428) The sum of an invested amount plus any interest that will accumulate on that amount on a compound basis over a specified period of time.

Interest (p. 428) The expense of borrowing money for a specified period, or, alternatively, the revenue earned by lending money for a specified period.

Present value (p. 434) An amount that must be invested currently at a stated compound rate of interest to produce a given future value.

Simple interest (p. 428) Interest computed only on the principal amount of a loan (or other financial instrument).

Time value of money concept (p. 427) Dictates that the economic value of a sum of cash to be received or paid is a function of both the amount and timing of that payment or receipt.

DECISION CASE

Suppose that you are the chief executive officer (CEO) of Threlkeld Corporation. Your company has recently been sued for $50 million by a competitor. The competitor alleges that your firm infringed on certain patents that it owns. Attorneys for your firm believe that there is a 50-50 chance that the courts would rule in favor of the competitor if the case goes to trial. The attorneys inform you that your firm will be required to pay either $20 million or $50 million in damages if the competitor wins the case. The amount of the settlement will depend on the court's interpretation of a legal technicality regarding how damages should be computed in such cases. The attorneys believe that the $20 million judgment is much more likely. If damages are awarded to the competitor, the attorneys estimate that there is an 80 percent chance the damages will total $20 million and a 20 percent chance that the damages will total $50 million. Given the probable length of the trial and subsequent appeals, such damages would not be paid for five years.

The CEO of your competitor has recently contacted you. She has offered to resolve this dispute by having your firm immediately pay her company $7 million. Alternatively, she has agreed to resolve the matter by having your firm pay her company $10 million in $2 million installments. These installments would be made at the end of each of the following five years.

Required: Ignoring taxes and other considerations, which of the following three alternatives is preferable from an economic standpoint for Threlkeld Corporation: taking the matter to court and assuming the risk of paying either $20 million or $50 million in damages five years from now; paying $7 million immediately to settle the dispute; or paying $10 million in $2 million installments over the next five years? (Use an 8 percent discount rate for any time value of money computations.) Defend your answer with the appropriate computations.

Besides taxes, what other issues should you consider in making this decision? Assuming that Threlkeld decides against settling the case, what type of accounting and financial statement treatment should be given this matter by the firm? Explain.

QUESTIONS

1. Define the "time value of money concept."
2. Provide three examples of business transactions in which the time value of money concept is relevant.
3. Define "interest." Distinguish between simple interest and compound interest.
4. What is a "future value"? A "present value"?
5. The factor 2.36736 can be found at the intersection of the 9% column and the 10 period row in Exhibit M2.1, "Future Value Factors for a Single Amount." Explain what that factor represents.
6. Explain the meaning of the following phrase: "The more frequently interest is compounded, the greater the resulting future value."
7. What is an annuity?
8. List two examples of financial transactions that are structured as annuities.

EXERCISES

Note: Unless indicated otherwise, assume that all time value of money applications involve interest compounded on an annual basis.

9. **True or False** (LO 1–5)
Following is a series of statements regarding topics discussed in Module 2.

Required:
Indicate whether each statement is true (T) or false (F).

_____ a. Interest compounded semiannually will result in a greater future value than interest compounded monthly.
_____ b. A present value represents an amount that must be invested currently at a stated compound rate of interest to produce a given future value.
_____ c. Individuals often purchase annuities from insurance companies to provide a source of retirement income.
_____ d. The time value of money concept is based on the premise that $1 to be received in the future is worth more than $1 available today.
_____ e. An annuity is a series of equal payments made, or received, at equal intervals on which interest is computed on a compound basis.
_____ f. A lender prefers that interest is computed on a simple basis, while a borrower prefers that interest is computed on a compound basis.

10. **Simple Interest vs. Compound Interest** (LO 1, 2)
Suppose that you have $5,000 to invest for five years. Because you are conservative by nature, you decide to invest your nest egg in an insured certificate of deposit (CD). You have identified the following five-year CDs being offered by local banks.

Jefferson Bank:	10 percent interest compounded annually
Lincoln Bank:	11 percent simple interest
Truman Bank:	9 percent interest compounded semiannually
Washington Bank:	10 percent interest compounded quarterly

Required:
In which CD will you invest? Why?

11. **Cashing in a Certificate of Deposit** (LO 2)
Today, you cashed in a certificate of deposit that you had acquired three years ago. You received $19,425.

Required:
Assume that your bank paid you 9 percent interest compounded annually on your certificate of deposit. How much did you deposit with your bank three years ago?

12. **Future Value of an Annuity** (LO 3)
Ben Campbell is the sole owner of Nighthorse Industries, a manufacturing firm. Campbell wants to double Nighthorse's production capacity by building another factory. His plan is to begin making annual deposits in a money market fund to accumulate the $4 million needed to finance the construction of the new factory. Suppose that Campbell needs to have the $4 million available at the end of seven years and that he can earn 7 percent interest compounded annually on deposits made in the money market fund.

Required:
1. Ignoring other considerations, how much must Campbell deposit in the money market fund each year for the next seven years to accumulate the $4 million needed to build the factory?
2. How would income taxes that Campbell must pay on interest revenue earned on the money market fund affect his plan to accumulate the $4 million within seven years? Explain.

13. Sell or Hold? (LO 2)
Real estate prices are escalating rapidly in your neighborhood. Presently, you believe that you can net $120,000 from the sale of your home. In five years, you believe that your net sales proceeds would be $200,000.

Required:
Suppose that you can earn an 8 percent annual compound rate of return on the $120,000 that you would receive from the sale of your home. Identify the factors you should consider in deciding whether to sell your home now or to wait and sell it in five years.

14. Annuities (LO 5)
Your cousin Larry sells annuities for the investment firm that he founded earlier this year. At a recent family reunion, Larry told you about two "super" annuity options that his firm is offering to individuals. The Cadillac Annuity pays $12,000 at the end of each of the following twenty years. The Infinity Annuity pays $8,000 at one-year intervals for the remainder of the purchaser's life.

Required:
Suppose that your mom is considering purchasing one of these two annuities. Write a brief memo to Mom in which you describe the time value of money concept, the nature of annuities, and the factors she should consider in choosing between the two annuity options.

15. Present Value of a Single Amount (LO 4)
Jim Gilliam is a major league baseball player. Under the terms of his new contract, Jim will receive an annual salary of $400,000 plus a one-time payment of $1 million on his fortieth birthday—Jim recently celebrated his twenty-eighth birthday.

Required:
Compute the present value of the lump sum payment to be made to Jim Gilliam on his fortieth birthday applying a discount rate of 10 percent.

16. Present Value of an Annuity (LO 5)
Wally Moon, the sole owner of Ebbets Enterprises, recently lost a lawsuit filed against him by a competitor, Cyndy Garvey. The presiding judge ruled that Wally must pay Cyndy $7,500 at the end of each of the following ten years.

Required:
Cyndy needs cash now, so she has offered Wally a deal. Rather than Wally paying her $75,000 over the next ten years, Cyndy has offered to accept a lump sum payment of $55,000. How can Wally determine whether this is a "good deal" for himself? Identify the specific circumstances under which this arrangement qualifies as a good deal for Wally.

17. Present Values (LO 5)
Leroy Chandler, owner of Goldseekers, Inc., has just struck gold, literally. Leroy discovered a vein of gold in a remote mine in the high Sierras. A geologist predicts that the mine will yield somewhere between 1,000 and 2,000 ounces of gold annually over the next decade. When pressed to be more precise, the geologist indicated that there was a 50 percent chance the mine will yield 1,200 ounces of gold per year and a 50 percent chance the mine will yield 1,800 ounces of gold annually. The geologist estimates that the gold can be recovered at a cost of $30 per ounce. Presently, economic forecasting models suggest that the price of gold will average $400 per ounce over the next decade. Since Leroy wants to enjoy the "good life," he plans to sell his gold mine as soon as possible.

Required:
1. Ignoring tax considerations, what present value would you assign to Leroy's gold mine? (Assume a discount rate of 8 percent.) Defend your answer.
2. Besides the figure you arrived at in (1), what other factors would you consider before deciding on the price you would be willing to pay for Leroy's gold mine?

PROBLEM SET A

18. **Time Value of Money Applications: Single Amounts** (LO 2, 4)
Following are two scenarios involving time value of money applications for single dollar amounts. In each scenario, interest is compounded annually. Ignore tax considerations.

Scenario A: Today, Roseboro Farms lost a lawsuit. The business has been ordered to pay the plaintiff \$200,000 two years from today's date and \$300,000 four years from today's date.

Scenario B: Wes Parker recently decided to sell the convenience store he owns. Parker believes that the business is worth \$90,000. Joe Pepitone wants to purchase Parker's convenience store. Pepitone has offered to sign a \$120,000 noninterest-bearing promissory note in payment for the store.

Required:
1. *Scenario A:* Roseboro Farms would prefer to resolve this matter immediately. How much should the plaintiff be willing to accept as a lump sum payment from Roseboro if the appropriate interest rate for this scenario is 7 percent?
2. *Scenario B:* If the appropriate interest rate in this scenario is 6 percent and Pepitone has suggested a five-year term for the promissory note, is this a "good deal" for Parker? Explain.

19. **Time Value of Money Applications: Annuities** (LO 3, 5)
Following are two time value of money scenarios involving annuities. In each scenario, interest is compounded annually. Ignore tax considerations.

Scenario A: Tommy Davis owns a local plumbing supply business. Tommy plans to build a second store on the other side of town but does not have sufficient cash to finance the project, and he doesn't want to borrow the required funds.

Scenario B: Lou Johnson is retiring after working forty years as a dentist in the small town of Maysville. Lou wants to sell his practice to another dentist and believes that a fair price is \$140,000.

Required:
1. *Scenario A:* If Tommy needs \$100,000 to build the store, how much must he deposit in his savings account at the end of each year over the next five years to accumulate the needed funds? Tommy's bank pays him 7 percent interest on his savings account.
2. *Scenario B:* Assume that another dentist agrees to purchase Lou's practice for \$140,000. However, the total amount received by Lou will exceed \$140,000, since the two parties agree on a ten-year payment plan. The other dentist will pay for Lou's practice in a series of equal annual installments over the next ten years. (The first payment is to be made one year from the date the sales agreement is finalized.) If the two parties agree that an 8 percent interest rate should be applied to this transaction, determine how much Lou will receive at the end of each of the following ten years.

20. **Time Value of Money Applications** (LO 2–5)
Following are two scenarios involving time value of money applications. In each scenario, interest is compounded annually. Ignore tax considerations.

Scenario A: Phyllis Regan replaces the delivery truck for her retail furniture store every five years. Phyllis estimates that the truck she will purchase in five years will cost approximately \$30,000.

Scenario B: Maurine Wills plans to purchase the local hardware store. She has offered to pay the store's present owner either $100,000 in cash, or $10,000 per year at the end of each of the next fifteen years.

Required:

1. *Scenario A:* How much must Phyllis deposit in an 8 percent certificate of deposit presently to accumulate the $30,000 she will need to purchase a new delivery truck in five years?
2. *Scenario B:* Suppose that the appropriate interest rate for this scenario is 5.5 percent. Should the owner of the hardware store accept the $100,000 lump sum payment, or the payment plan structured as an annuity? Will your answer change if the appropriate interest rate for this scenario is 7 percent?

PROBLEM SET B

21. **Time Value of Money Applications: Single Amounts** (LO 2, 4)

Following are two time value of money scenarios involving single dollar amounts. In each scenario, interest is compounded annually. Ignore tax considerations.

Scenario A: Richardson Real Estate leases the building in which its offices are located. The company wants to construct an office building of its own and believes that $164,000 will be required for this project. The company presently has $100,000 that it can invest in a savings account earning 7 percent interest.

Scenario B: Ford Electric Contractors is selling five used service vehicles. The company has received two bids for these vehicles. The first bid is a cash offer of $64,000 from Kubek Supply. Skowron Used Cars has offered to pay Ford $90,000 for the service vehicles in a series of three payments. The first payment would be $20,000 in two years, the second payment would be $30,000 in three years, and the final payment would be $40,000 in four years.

Required:

1. *Scenario A:* If Richardson deposits the $100,000 in the savings account, how many years must the company wait before the account has a balance of $164,000.
2. *Scenario B:* If the appropriate interest rate in this scenario is 9 percent, which bid should Ford accept? Besides time value of money considerations, what other factors should Ford consider in making this decision?

22. **Time Value of Money Applications: Annuities** (LO 3, 5)

Following are two time value of money scenarios involving annuities. In each scenario, interest is compounded annually. Ignore tax considerations.

Scenario A: Cleta Boyer owns the Bronx Carloading Company (BCC). Recently, Cleta decided to retire. She has received the following three bids for her company:

Bid A: $50,000 down payment plus 20 annual payments of $15,000
Bid B: $70,000 down payment plus 15 annual payments of $14,000
Bid C: $90,000 down payment plus 10 annual payments of $10,000

In each case, the down payment would be made on the date the sales agreement is finalized, while the first annual payment would be made one year following that date.

Scenario B: Elston Howard was seriously injured while working for his employer, Pinstripe Suit Manufacturers. He is presently negotiating to resolve this matter. The employer has offered to pay Elston $40,000 per year for the remainder of his life. Mortality tables used by the insurance industry indicate that Elston should live approximately twenty-five more years. Elston prefers to receive a lump sum payment.

Required:

1. *Scenario A:* Suppose that the appropriate interest rate for this scenario is 10 percent. Which offer should Cleta accept?
2. *Scenario B:* What lump sum payment would be equivalent to the present value of the annuity offered to Elston by his employer assuming that a 9 percent interest rate is appropriate for this scenario? What other factors should Elston consider in choosing between the annuity and a lump sum payment? Explain.

23. **Time Value of Money Applications** (LO 2–5)
Following are two scenarios involving time value of money applications. In each scenario, interest is compounded annually. Ignore tax considerations.

Scenario A: Tresh Lumberyard Company sold a used forklift to a local homebuilder. Because the customer was strapped for cash, Tresh agreed to accept a three-year, noninterest-bearing promissory note in payment for the forklift. (The cash price of the forklift was $15,000.)

Scenario B: Berra Bookstores has a "balloon payment" due on a loan that it obtained several years ago from a finance company. The $80,000 balloon payment is due in four years. Berra has created a savings account in which it will make annual deposits at the end of each of the following four years for the purpose of accumulating the required $80,000.

Required:

1. *Scenario A:* If Tresh charges its customers 8 percent interest on their unpaid balances, what should be the maturity value of the three-year, noninterest-bearing note that the customer signs in payment for the forklift?
2. *Scenario B:* If Berra earns 10 percent interest on its savings account, how much must it deposit in that account each year to accumulate the $80,000 needed for the balloon payment coming due in four years?

CASES

24. **Oil Wells and the Time Value of Money** (LO 2–5)
Bankhead Drilling Company, an oil and gas exploration firm, recently sold several oil wells to Hepburn Petroleum Corporation. The total payment to be received by Bankhead is dependent upon the amount of oil that Hepburn recovers from the oil wells. Initially, Hepburn will pay Bankhead $1,000,000 for the oil wells. At the end of each of the next five years, Hepburn will pay Bankhead an additional $100,000. At the end of ten years, if the oil wells have produced a specified number of barrels, Bankhead will receive an additional lump sum payment of $250,000. Bankhead's chief executive believes there is a 25 percent likelihood that her firm will be entitled to the $250,000 payment.

Required:

1. What amount do you believe Bankhead should record as the sales price of the oil wells? (Assume a discount rate of 10 percent.) Defend your answer.
2. Suppose that Bankhead's executives decide to deposit the cash received from the sale of these oil wells into a mutual fund that they believe will earn a 12 percent annual compound rate of return. Ignoring tax considerations, at the end of ten years, what will be the value of Bankhead's mutual fund investment assuming the company does not receive the $250,000 payment? What will be the value of the mutual fund investment after ten years if Bankhead receives the $250,000 payment?

25. **Real Estate and the Time Value of Money** (LO 2–5)
Wuerffel Distributors has just finalized a deal to sell a large tract of land to Busby Investors. The payment terms require Busby to pay Wuerffel $200,000 immediately in addition to $100,000 annually over a five-year period. The first of these annual payments will be made in three years. Wuerffel had acquired this land several years ago planning to use it as the site of a new warehouse. The land was purchased by Wuerffel for $185,000.

Required:

1. Compute the present value of the proceeds that Wuerffel will receive from the sale of the land. Assume that a discount rate of 8 percent is appropriate.
2. Prepare the journal entries to record this transaction in the accounting records of each company.

PROJECTS

26. **Time Value and Legal Judgments**
Today, Trent McIlhaney received some bad news. His firm, Heritage Hall Construction, Inc., will be required to pay $1.2 million in damages to several competing firms. A court ruled that Heritage Hall had engaged in "anticompetitive" business practices to gain an unfair advantage over four other local construction firms. Heritage Hall will pay the damages in six annual installments of $200,000 beginning one year from today.

Trent is discussing this matter with his firm's chief accountant, Susan Queary. Susan has informed Trent that the legal judgment must be recorded by debiting an expense account and crediting a liability account for the present value of the judgment.

Trent: "You mean we have to record the full $1.2 million as an expense and a liability immediately?"
Susan: "No. We have to record the *present value* of the judgment as both an expense and a liability."
Trent: "Okay. How do we do that?"
Susan: "By discounting the $1.2 million to an appropriate present value."
Trent: "So, what discount rate do we apply?"
Susan: "Well, I've thought about that already. I think we should use 9 percent, which is the approximate interest rate we would pay on a six-year, $1 million loan."
Trent: "Wait a minute. If we use a higher discount rate, won't we reduce the expense and liability that we book?"
Susan: "Sure."
Trent: "Okay. Use a 15 percent discount rate."
Susan: "Huh?"
Trent: "I said . . . use a 15 percent discount rate."
Susan: "Mr. McIlhaney, using a 15 percent discount rate would grossly understate the expense and liability that we record."

Trent: "That's exactly the idea. The judge made a mistake ruling against us in the first place. At the very least, we should be able to minimize the impact on our financial statements. Shouldn't we? Besides, the plaintiff and the judge couldn't care less how we account for the judgment. Right?"

Required:

Break into your project groups to address the following questions.

1. Ignoring tax considerations, what impact will using a 15 percent discount rate, rather than a 9 percent discount rate, have on Heritage Hall's financial statements over the next several years?
2. What factors should a firm consider when choosing a discount rate in a situation such as the one described? Was Susan's recommendation reasonable? Why or why not?
3. Evaluate Trent's decision to apply a 15 percent discount rate to the legal judgment. Has he behaved ethically? Why or why not? Is he likely correct that the plaintiff and the judge will have little interest in how Heritage Hall records the judgment? What other parties might have an interest in the accounting treatment Heritage Hall applies to this item?
4. Consider the circumstances facing Susan. Would it be unethical for her to record the legal judgment as suggested by Trent? If she does not agree with Trent's decision, how should she proceed?
5. One member of your group should be prepared to present to the class a brief oral summary of the group's discussion of this scenario and the accompanying questions.

27. Investing in Annuities

Reread the vignette in this module entitled "Investing in Annuities." In this project, you will become familiar with investment opportunities in annuities with the help of the Internet.

Required:

1. Search the Internet for Web sites that provide information regarding investment opportunities in annuities. Identify at these three such Web sites.
2. For each Web site you identified, select one annuity and summarize the key descriptive information available for that annuity. For example, identify the company that offers the annuity, the title of the annuity (if any), the descriptive label applied to the annuity such as "single premium, tax-deferred variable annuity," the minimum investment required, and so on.
3. Document the information you collected in (2) in a written report. Include in your report the addresses of the Web sites from which you obtained this information.

10 Long-Term Liabilities

"Banks will lend you money if you can prove you don't need it."
Mark Twain

LEARNING OBJECTIVES

After studying this chapter, you should be able to do the following:

1. Define the key information needs of decision makers regarding long-term liabilities.
2. Account for bonds payable and related interest expense.
3. Distinguish between operating leases and capital leases and describe the accounting treatment for each.
4. Discuss accounting issues for long-term liabilities stemming from pension and other postretirement employee benefit plans.
5. Identify key control activities for long-term liabilities.
6. Compute and interpret the long-term debt to equity and times interest earned ratios.
7. (Appendix) Amortize bond discount and premium using the effective-interest method.

FOCUS ON DECISION MAKING

A Mickey Mouse Organization Built on Mickey Mouse Loans

In 1922, an artistic young man established Laugh-O-Gram Films, Inc., an animated film production company based in Kansas City. Only twenty-one years old at the time, the young man's artistic ability exceeded his business skills. Within one year, the company was bankrupt. After considerable pleading, the young entrepreneur convinced his creditors to allow him to keep one camera and one film he had produced. With fifty dollars in his pocket, his camera, and the film, Walt Disney boarded a train for California hoping that Hollywood would have a better appreciation for his animation skills than Kansas City.

Walt and his brother Roy, who joined him in California, scraped together enough funds to rent a small studio in Los Angeles. The brothers borrowed most of these funds from friends and family members. An uncle loaned $500, Roy's fiancee $25, while a friend from Kansas City chipped in $275. The first few years were difficult ones financially for the new business. It was not until 1928 that Walt Disney got the break he had been looking for when he sketched an animation character, Mortimer the Mouse. Walt's wife, Lillian, liked the character but suggested what she thought was a more appealing name: Mickey. In less than twelve months, animated cartoons featuring Mickey Mouse were playing in movie theaters nationwide. The cartoons were so popular that they often received equal billing on theater marquees with feature films. With the profits produced by Mickey Mouse, Walt Disney was on his way to building a firm that would have nearly $20 billion of assets by 1997.

Friends and family members provide the initial financing for many small businesses. As businesses grow, they must turn to more substantial sources of financing. Not surprisingly, the Walt Disney Company often leads the way in developing creative approaches to borrowing funds. In 1993, Disney startled Wall Street by announcing plans to sell $300 million of bonds with a 100-year term. The normal term for corporate bonds is much shorter, 30 years being a common term. The following year, Disney announced that it was planning to sell an additional $400 million of bonds. These bonds are unique in that the interest rate is linked to the profitability of specific Disney films. In 1996, Disney again surprised the investment community by selling $2.6 billion of bonds, reportedly the largest "investment grade" bond issue in U.S. history.

In seven decades, the Walt Disney Company has gone from financing its operations with small loans from Walt Disney's friends and relatives to borrowing hundreds of millions of dollars on exotic debt instruments. Would the founder of the company be impressed? Probably not. Once, when asked about the financial empire he had built, Walt Disney modestly replied, "Always remember that this whole thing was started by a mouse."

In this chapter, we focus on accounting for long-term liabilities. The opening section of this chapter introduces you to the two basic types of long-term liabilities and provides examples of each. Next, we identify the key information needs of decision makers regarding long-term liabilities. Then, we consider specific accounting procedures for bonds payable, a common long- term liability of large public companies, and briefly review accounting issues for several other long-term liabilities. This chapter concludes by discussing control activities and financial ratios involving long-term liabilities.

LONG-TERM LIABILITIES: AN OVERVIEW

long-term liabilities

long-term debt

Long-term liabilities include the debts and obligations of a business other than those classified as current liabilities. Generally, long-term liabilities are of two types: amounts borrowed on a long-term basis and long-term accrued liabilities. Companies often report the total amount of their long-term borrowings on one balance sheet line item labeled **long-term debt.** Common long-term debt items include bonds payable, notes payable due more than one year from a firm's balance sheet date, and mortgages payable. Obligations arising from certain long-term leases are often classified as long-term debt although these obligations technically do not involve borrowed funds. Examples of long-term accrued liabilities include obligations stemming from pension and other postretirement benefit plans that many companies have established for their employees.

The types and dollar amounts of long-term liabilities reported by large corporations vary considerably from firm to firm. Consider two prominent companies, Microsoft Corporation and Campbell Soup Company. In 1996, Microsoft had total assets of approximately $10 billion, while Campbell Soup's assets totaled $6.5 billion. At the time, Microsoft had no long-term liabilities. Campbell Soup, on the other hand, reported long-term liabilities exceeding $1.6 billion, including notes payable, bonds payable, and long-term accrued liabilities. Most public companies have a significant amount of long-term liabilities. Microsoft is one of those fortunate companies that has not been forced to borrow on a long-term basis or to incur other long-term obligations to satisfy its financing needs. Instead, Microsoft generates sufficient funds through profitable operations to meet those needs.

Bill Gates, the founder of Microsoft Corporation, was declared the richest person in the United States in 1995. Gates' multibillion-dollar fortune stems largely from the stock he owns in Microsoft. In a recent balance sheet, Microsoft reported zero long-term liabilities, which is very unusual for a large public company.

LONG-TERM LIABILITIES: KEY INFORMATION NEEDS OF DECISION MAKERS

In Chapter 9, we identified decision makers' primary information needs for current liabilities. Decision makers have similar information needs for long-term liabilities. These needs include access to information concerning all of an entity's long-term obligations, information regarding valuation methods, and disclosure of any unusual and material circumstances involving long-term liabilities.

LEARNING OBJECTIVE 1
Define the key information needs of decision makers regarding long-term liabilities.

Completeness

Investors, creditors, and other decision makers rely on businesses to provide comprehensive disclosure of their long-term liabilities. Surprising to most nonaccountants is that businesses do not include certain long-term obligations in their periodic financial statements. These obligations result from "off-balance-sheet" financing techniques. **Off-balance sheet financing** involves the acquisition of assets or services by incurring long-term obligations that are not reported on an entity's balance sheet. For example, certain long-term leases qualify as off-balance sheet financing techniques. Fortunately for decision makers, the accounting profession has taken steps in recent years to reduce the number of off-balance sheet, long-term obligations.

off-balance sheet financing

Accounting and financial reporting rules require businesses to discuss in the footnotes to their financial statements any off-balance sheet financing methods they employ. Sears' annual report issued in 1996 contained a section entitled "Off-Balance Sheet Financial Instruments." That section revealed that Sears would pay more than $2 billion to retire off-balance sheet financial instruments coming due over the following five years. Those instruments included "interest swap agreements," "interest rate cap agreements," and "foreign currency hedge agreements." Advanced accounting courses explore in depth financial reporting issues for off-balance sheet financial instruments.

Valuation Methods

Proper valuation is a concern to decision makers for most financial statement items. Valuation issues are particularly important for long-term liabilities that must be estimated with the help of the time value of money concept discussed in Module 2. For example, companies with employee pension plans face complex computations each year to determine their long-term, pension-related obligations. These firms typically must project their employees' future salaries since pension benefits are usually linked to employee compensation in the final few years before retirement. A company that wants to minimize pension-related expenses and the present value of the related future obligations might intentionally underestimate future pay raises of its employees. To guard against this possibility, accounting standards require businesses to disclose key assumptions underlying their pension-related expense and liability computations. Comparable financial statement disclosures are required for other estimated long-term liabilities.

Unusual Circumstances

When a business borrows funds on a long-term basis, representatives of the borrower and lender sign a debt agreement. Such agreements often include restrictive debt covenants or conditions. Violations of these covenants typically cause the entire amount of the long-term debt to become immediately due and payable. Restrictive debt covenants that impose significant constraints on a company's future operations should be disclosed in its financial statement footnotes. Probably the most common restrictive debt covenant is a limitation on the payment of dividends. Following is a restrictive debt covenant disclosed in a recent annual report of Aaron Rents, Inc.

> The Company's credit agreement with the two banks restricts cash dividend payments and stock repurchases to 25% of net earnings since April 1, 1991, and places other restrictions on additional borrowings and requires the maintenance of certain financial ratios.

When a company violates a restrictive debt covenant, or faces a high risk of doing so, external decision makers should be informed. In January 1996, Chic by HIS, an apparel manufacturer, reported that poor operating results had caused it to violate certain restrictive covenants in its long-term debt agreements. These violations made the debt immediately due and payable. Chic revealed that it was contacting the lenders to ask them to waive (ignore) the violations of the debt covenants.[1]

▲ ACCOUNTING FOR BONDS PAYABLE

LEARNING OBJECTIVE 2 ▶ Account for bonds payable and related interest expense.

In this section and the following section we examine accounting issues for long-term liabilities. We begin by focusing on bonds payable for two reasons. First, bonds payable are among the most common long-term liabilities of many companies, particularly large public companies. Second, many accounting issues posed by bonds payable are relevant to other long-term liabilities. By focusing in depth on the accounting treatment for bonds payable, we can then touch only lightly on accounting decisions for similar long-term liabilities.

Corporate Bonds: An Introduction

Large corporations may borrow funds needed to finance the construction of new production facilities, the purchase of other companies, or the retirement of existing debt by selling bonds. For example, in July 1996, Texas Instruments announced plans to sell $400 million of bonds, in part to finance the acquisition of another company. The sale of bonds by corporations has been a particularly popular financing alternative in recent years when interest rates have been low by historical standards. The *Statistical Abstract of the United States* reveals that corporations were selling more than one-half trillion dollars of new bonds annually by the mid-1990s.[2] A wide range of investment objectives motivate external decision makers such as government agencies, charitable organizations, and individual investors to purchase these bonds.

bond

A **bond** is a long-term loan made by one party to another that is documented by a legal instrument known as a bond certificate. Exhibit 10.1 presents an example of a bond certificate. Let us define **bonds payable** as a long-term liability that represents the collective amount owed the parties who have purchased a company's bonds. Before discussing specific accounting issues for bonds payable, we should first become better

bonds payable

1. "Chic in Default on Bank Pacts," *WWD*, 9 January 1996, 2.
2. U.S. Bureau of the Census, *Statistical Abstract of the United States*, 1996.

SEC Says, "Tell It Like It Is!"

The early 1990s were unkind to America West Airlines, a publicly owned company based in Phoenix. High fuel prices following Iraq's occupation of Kuwait cut significantly into America West's profit margins. A nationwide "half-price sale" in 1991 also sliced into the company's profits. As America West's financial problems worsened, the company began experiencing cash flow problems. In June 1991, the company announced that it would not be making interest payments on its bonds payable. A few weeks later, America West filed for protection from its creditors in federal bankruptcy court.

In 1994, the Securities and Exchange Commission (SEC) chastised America West for not adequately warning creditors, investors, and other interested parties of its mounting financial problems during the early 1990s. Publicly owned companies must discuss their "liquidity and capital resources" in financial reports filed with the SEC. The SEC maintained that those disclosures by America West in the early 1990s were less than candid. An SEC "enforcement release" quoted several passages from America West's financial reports during that timeframe that downplayed the firm's financial problems. America West issued one of those reports just a few weeks before failing to make interest payments on its bonds payable. As always, the SEC's "full and fair disclosure" policy mandates that publicly owned companies "tell like it is" when it comes to their financial affairs.

Source: Securities and Exchange Commission, *Accounting and Auditing Enforcement Release No. 562*, 12 May 1994.

acquainted with these long-term liabilities. Here, we consider key terms related to corporate bonds, their various types, factors influencing their market prices, and how the selling price of newly issued bonds is determined.

KEY TERMS. Similar to other debt and equity securities, corporate bonds trade on major securities exchanges such as the New York Stock Exchange. Suppose you read in *The Wall Street Journal* that Exxon intends to sell a $700 million "bond issue." (A bond issue is simply a group of identical bonds sold at approximately the same point in time.) You could call up your broker and place an order to buy one or more of Exxon's bonds. Although you are buying these bonds, you are technically lending money to Exxon, which explains why the proceeds of a bond issue are recorded in a long-term liability account entitled Bonds Payable.

Corporations typically issue bonds in $1,000 denominations. That is, the face value or principal amount or maturity value, whichever term you prefer, of a corporate bond is usually $1,000. Most corporate bonds sell for slightly more or less than their face value. For instance, a $1,000 Exxon bond may sell for a discount of $20 from its face value, or $980. However, on the maturity date of that bond, the bondholder will be entitled to receive exactly $1,000 from Exxon.

EXHIBIT 10.1 ▼
Example of a Corporate Bond Certificate

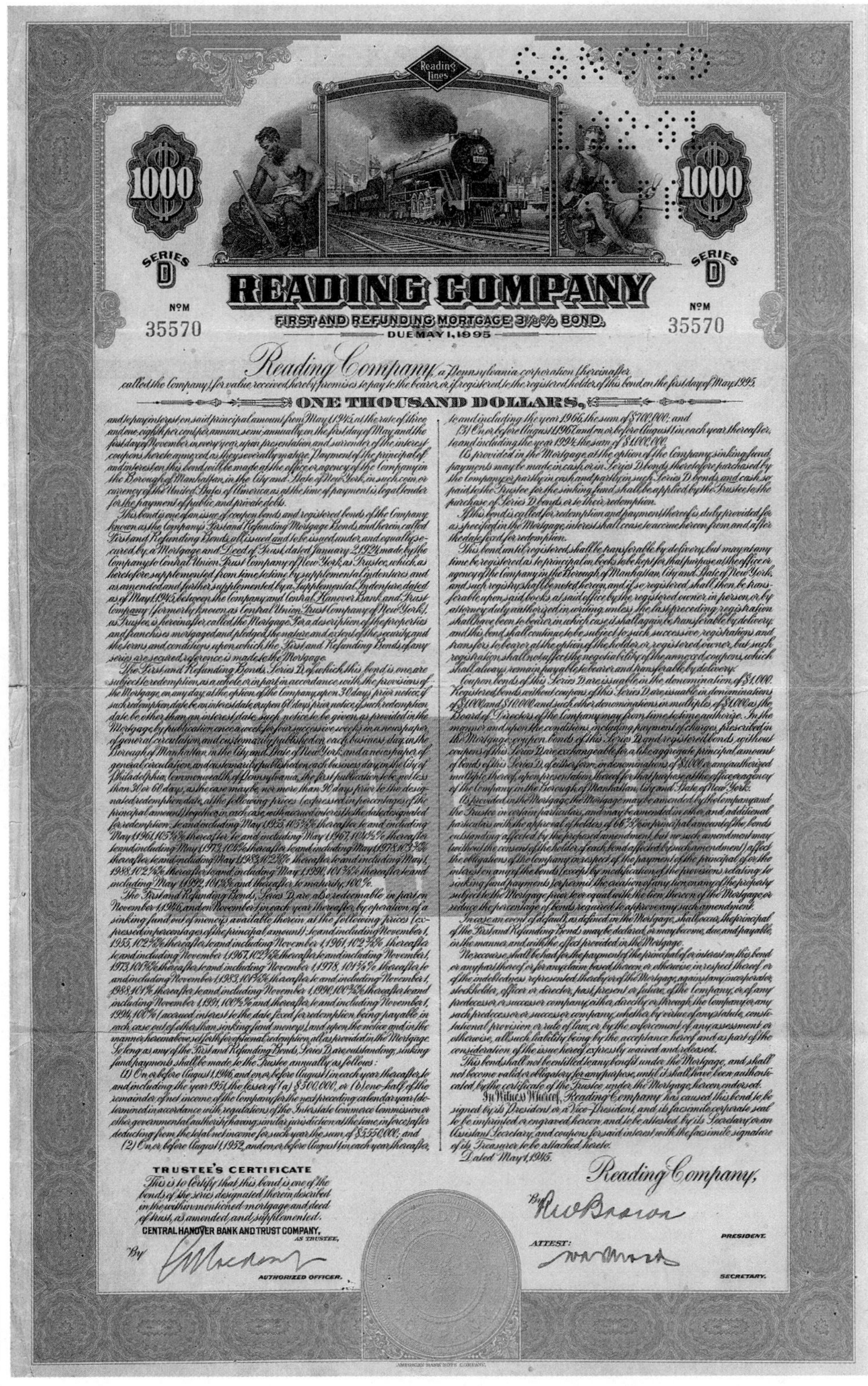

Prior to selling bonds, a company prepares a bond indenture. A **bond indenture** is the legal contract between a bond purchaser and the issuing company and identifies the rights and obligations of each party. For example, a bond indenture identifies the **stated interest rate** for a bond issue. The stated interest rate is the rate of interest paid to bondholders based upon the face value of the bonds. (Face interest rate and contract interest rate are terms interchangeable with stated interest rate.) An individual who purchases a $1,000 bond with a stated interest rate of 8 percent receives $80 of interest each year ($1,000 × 8%) from the company that issued the bond. Corporations typically pay interest on their bonds semiannually, that is, every six months, although some bond indentures specify quarterly or annual interest payments. A bond indenture also indicates the maturity date of a bond issue. On the maturity date, a company pays the face value of its bonds to the bondholders. The term of a bond issue is the period elapsing between the date bonds are first available for sale and the date they mature.

bond indenture

stated interest rate

TYPES OF BONDS. Bonds are often identified by one or more distinctive features or characteristics. **Secured bonds,** sometimes referred to as mortgage bonds, are collateralized by specific assets of the company issuing the bonds. **Unsecured bonds,** or debentures, are backed only by the legal commitment of the issuing firm to make all required principal and interest payments. Bond indentures typically include a call option and occasionally a convertible option. **Callable bonds** can be retired or redeemed by the issuing company when one or more conditions are met. The most common condition that activates a call option is simply the passage of time. For instance, a bond issue may be callable at the option of the issuing company at any point after the bonds have been outstanding for more than five years. If a bond issue is callable, the bond indenture usually requires the payment of a call premium to the bondholders. That is, the bondholders must be paid more than the face value of the bonds. Bondholders can exchange **convertible bonds** for stock in the issuing company. For example, a convertible option in a bond indenture may grant bondholders the right to exchange each $1,000 bond for 25 shares of the issuing company's common stock.

secured bonds

unsecured bonds

callable bonds

convertible bonds

BOND MARKET PRICES. Open *The Wall Street Journal* and turn to the section entitled "New York Exchange Bonds" and you will find price quotations for dozens of individual bond issues. Following is a recent price quotation line for a bond issue of Safeway, a supermarket chain.

	Cur Yld	Vol	Close	Net Chg
Safeway 10s01	9.2	20	108¼	−¾

The "10s01" indicates that Safeway's bonds have a 10 percent stated interest rate and that they mature in the year 2001—the "s" simply separates the interest rate on the bonds from their maturity date. According to the volume column, twenty of these bonds, each with a face value of $1,000, were sold on the day in question. The final or closing price for the Safeway bonds on this day was 108¼. No, these $1,000 bonds did not sell for $108.25. Bond prices are quoted as a percentage of their face value. So, a quoted selling price of 100 translates to an actual selling price of $1,000. Safeway's bonds closed the given day at a price of $1082.50 ($1,000 × 108.25%). The net change in the selling price of the Safeway bonds for the day was a decrease of ¾ or $7.50 per bond, meaning that the previous day these bonds closed at 109 ($1,090).

Finally, the closing price of the Safeway bonds on the day in question resulted in a current yield of 9.2 percent. Individuals who purchased a Safeway bond at a price of $1,082.50 on that date earn interest on their investments at an annual rate of approximately 9.2 percent. This current yield can be computed by dividing the interest earned on the bond each year, $100 ($1,000 × 10%), by the cost of the bond, $1,082.50.

Several factors influence the market price of Safeway's bonds at any point in time. These factors include Safeway's financial condition, the level of interest rates in the economy, the length of time to the bonds' maturity date, and investors' preferences. The market price of Safeway's bonds fluctuates as investors react to changes in these factors.

Several investment advisory firms, including Moody's Investors Service and Standard & Poor's Corporation, monitor hundreds of bond issues and assign each a risk assessment rating. Here, "risk" refers to the likelihood that a company will eventually default on its bonds, that is, fail to make required interest or principal payments. As the factors affecting the default risk associated with individual bond issues change, Moody's and Standard & Poor's update their risk assessment ratings. In late May 1996, Standard & Poor's upgraded certain bonds of Sears from a "BBB" rating to an "A-" rating. Standard & Poor's made this change because an extensive remodeling program for Sears' stores was having a positive impact on customer traffic, sales, and profits. At approximately the same time, Standard & Poor's downgraded certain Toys "R" Us bonds from "AA" to "A+." This move was made in reaction to growing competition among large toy retailers that was expected to have an unfavorable impact on the profits of Toys "R" Us.

Day-to-day changes in the market price of Safeway's bonds do not have accounting implications for that firm. Most of the accounting decisions for bonds payable are resolved on the date they are initially sold. To fully appreciate the accounting procedures for bonds payable, you need to understand how the selling price of newly issued bonds is determined.

DETERMINING THE SELLING PRICE OF NEWLY ISSUED BONDS. Suppose that Hardin Manufacturing Company plans to sell $100,000 of bonds. These bonds have a face value of $1,000 each and a five-year term that runs from April 1, Year 1, through April 1, Year 6. The stated interest rate on the bonds is 10 percent and interest is payable semiannually on April 1 and October 1. On each of those dates, Hardin will pay $5,000 ($100,000 × 5%) of interest to bondholders. The initial interest payment date is October 1, Year 1.

Now, assume that Hardin sells its bonds on April 1, Year 1, when the market interest rate is 11 percent. Here, "market interest rate" refers to the annual rate of return that investors can earn by purchasing any of a number of different corporate bonds that pose the same general level of default risk. The market interest rate represents the "yield to maturity" for a given bond. A bond's yield to maturity differs slightly from its "current yield, a term defined earlier in reference to the Safeway bonds." The current yield on a bond is simply the annual interest earned by a bondholder divided by the cost of the bond. A bond's yield to maturity takes into account both the interest earned on the bond each year *and* the impact of any bond discount or premium on the bond's rate of return over its term.

On April 1, Year 1, bonds that posed the same level of default risk as Hardin's bonds were selling at a price that provided investors an 11 percent rate of return through the bonds' maturity date. Because Hardin is paying only 10 percent interest on its bonds, the bonds will sell for less than their face value, that is, at a discount. This discount will be sufficiently large to allow the purchasers of Hardin's bonds to earn an 11 percent yield to maturity on their investments in these bonds.

Companies attempt to establish a stated interest rate on their bonds approximately equal to the market interest rate when the bonds are sold. However, since several weeks or longer may be required to process a bond issue, the stated interest rate must be "pegged" well in advance of the selling date of the bonds. Thus, the stated interest rate for a bond issue can be quite different from the market interest rate when the bonds are actually sold.

To determine the selling price of Hardin's bonds, we must apply the time value of money concept discussed in Module 2. The selling price of these bonds will be the present value of the cash outflows that Hardin will pay over the bonds' five-year term. These cash outflows consist of ten $5,000 semiannual interest payments and a $100,000 principal payment at the end of the bond term. Recall from Module 2 that the two key variables in a time value of money scenario are a given number of time periods and an interest or discount rate. In the present example there are ten time periods, the number of semiannual interest payment periods for Hardin's five-year bonds. The discount rate is 5.5 percent, one-half of the 11 percent market interest rate on the date the bonds are sold. *Key point to remember: The market interest rate on the date bonds are sold, not the stated interest rate, determines the present value of the future cash outflows related to a bond issue.*

Exhibit 10.2 contains a diagram of the present value of the cash outflows related to the Hardin bonds. On April 1, Year 1, the present value of the principal payment to be made on the bonds' maturity date (April 1, Year 6) is $58,543. This amount was determined by multiplying the bonds' $100,000 principal amount or face value

EXHIBIT 10.2 ▼

Determining the Selling Price of Five-Year Bonds With a 10 Percent Stated Interest Rate When the Market Interest Rate is 11 Percent

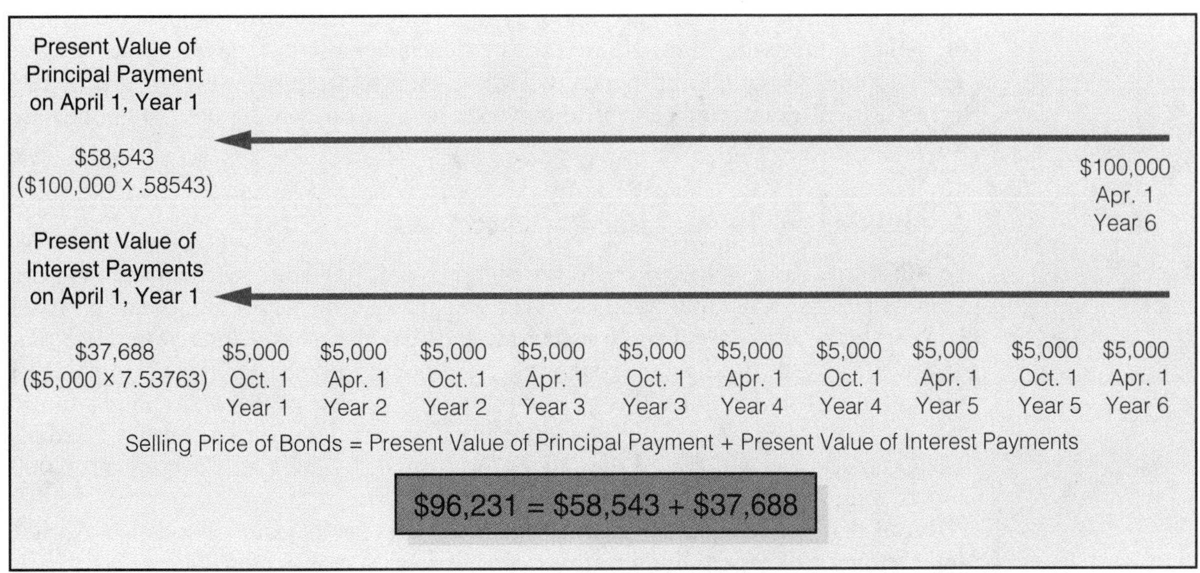

Zeroes, LYONS, TIGRS and . . . CATS?

FOR YOUR INFORMATION

Corporate financiers have become increasingly innovative in developing new methods of raising debt capital for large public companies. Complex borrowing arrangements create major headaches for corporate accountants who must record these transactions. One of the more popular new debt instruments is zero-coupon bonds or notes. In the early 1990s, Disney had more than $1 billion of "zeroes" outstanding.

If you purchase a $1,000 zero-coupon bond, you are entitled to one payment from the corporation issuing that bond. That one payment may be ten, twenty, or even thirty years following the bond's issue date. To compensate purchasers of these bonds for the lack of interest payments, zeroes sell at a large discount from their maturity value. For instance, a zero-coupon bond with a $1,000 maturity value may be purchased for $200, or even less, depending upon its maturity date.

Several prominent brokerage firms and investment bankers have created their own specialized long-term debt instruments. For example, Merrill Lynch markets LYONS (liquid yield option notes) and TIGRS (treasury investment growth receipts), while Salomon Brothers sells CATS (certificates of accrual on treasury securities). You may encounter these feline investment options in advanced finance courses.

by the appropriate present value factor for a single amount. That factor, .58543, is found at the intersection of the 5.5 percent column and the 10 period row in Table 3 (in the inside back cover of this text). To determine the present value of the series of interest payments, which is an annuity, we use the present value of an annuity table, Table 4. At the intersection of the 5.5 percent column and the 10 period row in Table 4 is the present value of an annuity factor 7.53763. When this factor is multiplied by $5,000, the result is $37,688, which is the present value of the ten semiannual interest payments on April 1, Year 1.

As shown in Exhibit 10.2, the Hardin bonds will sell for $96,231. Realize that although these bonds will sell for $96,231, Hardin will be required to pay the bondholders $100,000 on the bonds' maturity date. In essence, Hardin is being penalized for selling bonds with a stated interest rate that is less than the market interest rate. The discount on the Hardin bonds will allow their initial purchasers to earn a yield to maturity of exactly 11 percent, the market interest rate on the date the bonds are sold.

Accounting for Bonds Issued at Face Value

To illustrate basic accounting decisions for bonds payable, we can use Hardin Manufacturing's $100,000 bond issue. Assume that Hardin sells these bonds on April 1, Year 1, the first day of the bond term, and that the market interest rate on that date is 10 percent. Under this assumption, the bonds will sell for their face value of $100,000. You can confirm this by computing the present value of the bond's future cash outflows using a 5 percent semiannual discount rate. On April 1, Year 1, Hardin's accounting staff would record the sale of these bonds by debiting Cash for $100,000 and crediting Bonds Payable for the same amount.

Recall that the semiannual interest payment dates for Hardin's bonds are April 1 and October 1. The initial interest payment of $5,000 would be made on October 1,

Year 1, six months following the sale of the bonds. On that date, a Hardin accountant would debit Interest Expense and credit Cash for $5,000 each.

On December 31, an adjusting entry would be necessary to recognize interest expense on Hardin's bonds for the three-month period October 1 through December 31. Using the interest equation (interest = principal × rate × time), we can determine that the appropriate accrual for interest expense on that date is $2,500 ($100,000 × 10% × 3/12).

Dec. 31	Interest Expense	2,500	
	Interest Payable		2,500
	To recognize year-end interest expense on bonds payable		

Three months later, on April 1, Year 2, the second interest payment would be made and recorded.

Apr. 1	Interest Expense	2,500	
	Interest Payable	2,500	
	Cash		5,000
	To record interest payment on bonds payable		

Notice in the previous entry that two equal debits of $2,500 are required. The first debit records the interest expense on the bonds for the three-month period January 1 through March 31. The second debit reflects the payment of interest accrued as a liability on December 31 for the period October 1 through December 31.

On April 1, Year 6, Hardin would make the final semiannual interest payment and pay the principal amount of the bonds to the bondholders. The entry to record the payment of the principal amount of the bonds to the bondholders would consist of a $100,000 debit to Bonds Payable and an equal credit to Cash.

Accounting for Bonds Issued at a Discount

Now, let us assume that on April 1, Year 1, when Hardin sells its bonds the market interest rate is 11 percent. We have already determined that Hardin's bonds will sell for $96,231 under this assumption—see Exhibit 10.2. The difference between the $100,000 face value of the bonds and the bonds' selling price would be entered in a contra-liability account, Discount on Bonds Payable.

Apr. 1	Cash	96,231	
	Discount on Bonds Payable	3,769	
	Bonds Payable		100,000
	To record sale of five-year bonds with a stated interest rate of 10% and a maturity date of April 1, Year 6		

If Hardin prepares a balance sheet shortly after the sale of these bonds, the company would report the bonds payable at their carrying value, or book value, of $96,231. The carrying value of bonds that sell at a discount is the difference between their face value and the balance of the bond discount account.

When bonds are sold at a discount, the interest expense recorded each interest payment date is greater than the amount of the interest payment. In the present example, Hardin received $96,231 when it sold its bonds. However, the company will be required to pay the bondholders $100,000 when the bonds mature. The difference between these two amounts is additional interest expense on Hardin's bonds over their five-year term. Because of the matching principle, this additional interest expense must be prorated and recognized over the term of the bonds. One of two methods is used to amortize, or write off, bond discount, the straight-line method or the effective-interest method. Here, the straight-line method is illustrated. The appendix that accompanies this chapter illustrates the effective-interest method.

Under the straight-line method, an equal amount of bond discount is written off as interest expense each interest payment period. For the present example, the bond discount is $3,769 and there are ten semiannual interest payment periods. So, Hardin would amortize $377 ($3,769/10) of bond discount each interest payment period. (The small rounding error would be corrected during the final interest payment period.) Shown next is the October 1, Year 1, entry that would be made to record the first interest payment by Hardin under the present scenario.

Oct. 1	Interest Expense	5,377	
	Cash		5,000
	Discount on Bonds Payable		377
	To record interest payment on bonds payable		

On December 31, Year 1, an adjusting entry would be necessary to record the interest expense on Hardin's bonds for the period October 1 through December 31. The debit to Interest Expense in this adjusting entry would be $2,689. This amount equals the sum of the "normal" interest expense accrual of $2,500 for October 1 through December 31 and $189, which is approximately one-half of the $377 of bond discount amortized each six months. Since three months of the second six-month interest payment period would have elapsed by December 31, Year 1, one-half of $377 should be written off as interest expense on that date. On April 1, Year 2, the remaining one-half of the $377 would be charged off as interest expense. Following are the entries that would be necessary in Hardin's accounting records on December 31, Year 1, and April 1, Year 2.

Dec. 31	Interest Expense	2,689	
	Interest Payable		2,500
	Discount on Bonds Payable		189
	To recognize year-end interest expense on bonds payable		
Apr. 1	Interest Expense	2,688	
	Interest Payable	2,500	
	Cash		5,000
	Discount on Bonds Payable		188
	To record interest payment on bonds payable		

As the discount on bonds payable is amortized, the carrying value of the bonds gradually increases. In the present example, following the final interest payment on

April 1 of Year 6, Hardin's bond discount account would have a zero balance. The carrying value of Hardin's bonds payable at that point would be exactly $100,000. The journal entry to record the $100,000 payment of the principal amount of the bonds to the bondholders on April 1, Year 6, would include a debit of that amount to Bonds Payable with an offsetting credit in the same amount to Cash.

Accounting for Bonds Issued at a Premium

Now, let us consider a scenario in which Hardin's bonds sell for more than their face value. Hardin's bonds will sell for a premium if their stated interest rate is higher than the market interest rate on the date they are sold. Assume that on April 1, Year 1, when Hardin sells its bonds, the market interest rate is 9 percent. Here again, we can use what we learned in Module 2 regarding the time value of money to determine the selling price of the bonds. In this case, the appropriate semiannual discount rate is 4.5 percent, or one-half the market interest rate on the date the bonds are sold. Shown next are the computations to determine the bonds' selling price under this new assumption.

Present value of principal payment:	$100,000	×	.64393*	=	$ 64,393
Present value of interest payments:	$5,000	×	7.91272**	=	39,564
Selling price of bonds					$103,957

*Present value factor for 10 periods and 4.5% (see Table 3).

**Present value of an annuity factor for 10 periods and 4.5% (see Table 4).

Given a selling price of $103,957, the following entry would be made to record the sale of the bonds.

Apr. 1	Cash	103,957	
	Bonds Payable		100,000
	Premium on Bonds Payable		3,957
	To record sale of five-year bonds with a stated interest rate of 10% and a maturity date of April 1, Year 6		

Recognize that although Hardin sells its bonds for $103,957, the company will be required to pay its bondholders only $100,000 on the bonds' maturity date. One useful way to think of a bond premium is as a bonus payment made by bond purchasers to the company issuing the bonds. This bonus payment compensates the company for paying a higher interest rate on its bonds than the market interest rate when the bonds are sold. Bonds sold at a premium are reported on a company's balance sheet at their carrying value, which is the sum of their face value and the balance of Premium on Bonds Payable.

The matching principle requires a bond premium to be amortized over the term of a bond issue. The amortization of a bond premium reduces the interest expense recorded each accounting period and gradually reduces the bonds' carrying value. If Hardin uses the straight-line amortization method, each semiannual interest payment period $396 ($3,957/10) of the bond premium would be amortized. Following is the entry that would be made to record the first interest payment by Hardin on October 1, Year 1, assuming the bond premium is amortized on a straight-line basis.

Oct. 1	Interest Expense	4,604	
	Premium on Bonds Payable	396	
	Cash		5,000
	To record interest payment on bonds payable		

Early Retirement of Bonds Payable

If interest rates decline considerably after a company issues bonds, the firm's executives may decide to retire those bonds and issue new ones that have a lower stated interest rate. Such a decision is easier to implement if a call option is included in the bond indenture. If a company's bonds are not callable, the firm can purchase them on the open market and then retire them.

In 1996, TJX Cos., a Massachusetts-based firm that operates retail outlets including T.J. Maxx stores, "called in" $90 million of its outstanding bonds. As typically happens, TJX's bonds were not retired at their carrying value. A company records the difference between the carrying value of bonds retired and the amount paid to retire those bonds as an "extraordinary" gain or loss. TJX reported a $2.9 million extraordinary loss on the retirement of its bonds in 1996. Extraordinary gains and losses are unusual and infrequently occurring items that companies must report separately in their income statements. Chapter 12 discusses extraordinary gains and losses in more depth.

To illustrate accounting for an early bond retirement, suppose that the bonds retired by TJX had a face value of $90,000,000 and an unamortized bond discount of $1,600,000. So, these bonds had a preretirement carrying value of $88,400,000 ($90,000,000 − $1,600,000). If TJX paid $91,300,000 to purchase these bonds, the following entry would have been appropriate to record this bond retirement.

Apr. 3	Bonds Payable	90,000,000	
	Loss on Bond Retirement	2,900,000	
	Cash		91,300,000
	Discount on Bonds Payable		1,600,000
	To record retirement of bonds payable		

Russia and China "Bond" with the World

FOR YOUR INFORMATION

In 1996, both Russia and the People's Republic of China tested the international bond market on a large scale for the first time. Russia announced in March 1996 that it was selling $500 million of bonds to international investors. The instability of the Russian government and economy forced the Russian Finance Ministry to assign a steep 16.5 percent stated interest rate to these bonds. A few months later, an agency of the People's Republic of China reported that it would be selling $200 million of bonds with stated interest rates ranging from 9.125 to 11.5 percent. U.S. investment brokerage firms supervised both of these bond offerings. Merrill Lynch oversaw the Russian bond offering, while Morgan Stanley & Co. assisted China in selling its bonds.

Since these bonds were being retired, all account balances related to them had to be removed from TJX's accounting records. The previous entry eliminated the balance of the Bonds Payable account and the balance of Discount on Bonds Payable. Notice that the difference between the amount paid to retire the bonds, $91,300,000, and their carrying value, $88,400,000, was debited to the extraordinary loss account, Loss on Bond Retirement.

ACCOUNTING FOR LONG-TERM LIABILITIES OTHER THAN BONDS PAYABLE

Now that we have "nailed down" key accounting decisions for bonds payable, let us briefly address accounting issues related to other long-term liabilities. In this section, we review accounting for long-term notes payable, long-term lease obligations, pension liabilities, and other postretirement benefit liabilities.

Long-Term Notes Payable

The key accounting issues for long-term notes payable are very similar to the accounting issues posed by short-term notes payable, which we examined in Chapter 9. Let us briefly consider a special type of long-term notes payable, mortgage notes payable.

Many long-term notes payable are actually mortgage notes payable, or more commonly "mortgages payable." A company that borrows $10 million to purchase a new building may be required by the lender to sign a mortgage note. This note will likely pledge the building as security or collateral for the loan. If the company defaults on the mortgage note, the lender can obtain legal title to the building or force it to be sold to satisfy the unpaid balance of the mortgage. Mortgages payable usually require equal monthly payments consisting of both principal and interest. FHP International Corporation, a firm in the healthcare industry, reported $2.5 million of mortgages payable on a recent balance sheet. FHP listed the portion of this liability coming due in the following year as a current liability on its balance sheet.

Long-Term Lease Obligations

LEARNING OBJECTIVE 3
Distinguish between operating leases and capital leases and describe the accounting treatment for each.

As briefly noted in Chapter 8, a leasehold is a legal right to use a leased asset for a specified period subject to any restrictions in the lease agreement. The two parties to a lease agreement are the lessor, the owner of the asset being leased, and the lessee, the party leasing the asset. Leasing has become an increasingly popular method used by businesses to finance the acquisition of a wide range of assets including buildings, equipment, and automobile fleets. The growing popularity of leasing dictates that external decision makers become familiar with the impact of this financing technique on the financial statements of businesses. In this course, we consider accounting for leases strictly from the standpoint of lessees. Advanced accounting courses examine accounting and financial reporting issues for both lessees and lessors.

Leased assets and the long-term obligations stemming from lease agreements were largely ignored by lessees for accounting and financial reporting purposes until the mid-1970s. At that time, the accounting profession converted many leasing arrangements from off-balance sheet to "on-balance sheet" financing methods. When a business leases an asset under conditions that are comparable to purchasing that asset with borrowed funds, both the leased asset and the long-term lease obligation must be reported in the firm's balance sheet. Why? Because the economic substance of business transactions, instead of their legal form, should dictate how they are recorded. In substance, certain leases are equivalent to purchases of long-term assets that are financed by long-term loans. Consequently, these leases should result in both a long-term asset and a long-term liability being recorded in a lessee's accounting records.

Many companies now regularly report in their periodic balance sheets long-term liabilities related to lease agreements. Sonic Industries, based in Oklahoma City, operates the nation's largest chain of drive-in restaurants. The company's 1996 balance sheet reported $9 million of long-term lease obligations. That figure represented nearly 40 percent of the company's long-term liabilities and 25 percent of the firm's total liabilities.

operating lease

capital lease

OPERATING VS. CAPITAL LEASES. Accounting standards distinguish between operating leases and capital leases. An **operating lease** is usually cancelable by the lessee, has a relatively short term, and does not transfer ownership rights or risks to the lessee. A **capital lease** is generally noncancelable, long-term, and transfers at least some ownership rights or risks to the lessee. Leases that meet one or more of the following criteria qualify as capital leases, while all other leases are classified as operating leases.

1. The lease agreement transfers legal title to the leased asset to the lessee at the end of the lease term.
2. A "bargain purchase option" that can be exercised by the lessee is included in the lease agreement.
3. The term of the lease covers 75 percent or more of the economic life of the leased asset.
4. The present value of the lease payments is equal to 90 percent or more of the market value of the leased asset.

ACCOUNTING FOR OPERATING LEASES. Accounting for operating leases is straightforward. The lessee does not record the leasehold it obtains as an asset, nor does the lessee record a long-term liability related to the lease. When the lessee makes a lease payment, Rental Expense or Lease Expense is debited and Cash is credited.

ACCOUNTING FOR CAPITAL LEASES. Suppose that Holden Construction Company leases a bulldozer from Adams Equipment Supply at the beginning of a year and this lease qualifies as a capital lease. The lease agreement obligates Holden to make a $20,000 payment to Adams at the end of each year of the lease's five-year term. To record this lease, we must first determine the present value of the payments to be made over its term. The present value of the required payments under a capital lease is recorded as both an asset and a long-term liability in the lessee's accounting records.

For purposes of our example, assume that a discount rate of 10 percent is appropriate to compute the present value of the lease payments. Given this discount rate, the present value of the lease payments can be calculated by using the present value of an annuity equation.

$$\text{Present Value of an Annuity (PVA)} = \text{Annuity Amount (A)} \times \text{Present Value of an Annuity Factor (PVAF)}$$

Here, the appropriate present value of an annuity factor is 3.79079, which can be found in Table 4 at the intersection of the 10 percent column and the five-year row. We can now compute the present value of the lease payments as follows:

$$PVA = A \times PVAF$$
$$PVA = \$20{,}000 \times 3.79079$$
$$PVA = \$75{,}815.80$$

Shown next is the entry to record the present value of the lease payments in Holden's accounting records as both an asset and a long-term liability.

Jan. 1	Leased Equipment, Bulldozer	75,816	
	Capital Lease Obligation		75,816
	To record capital lease of bulldozer (asset no. 1-28)		

Over the term of a capital lease, a business depreciates the leased asset similar to depreciable assets that it owns. Besides adjusting entries to record depreciation, an entry is required each year to record the lease payment to the lessee. Examples of such entries are deferred to advanced accounting courses.

Like other long-term liabilities, a long-term lease obligation must be segregated into its current and long-term portions for balance sheet purposes. Additionally, for both operating and capital leases, lessees must disclose in their financial statements future minimum lease payments over the next five years. In its 1996 annual report, McKesson Corporation, a large pharmaceutical concern, disclosed the future minimum lease payments it would be required to make during the period 1997–2001.

Pension Liabilities

LEARNING OBJECTIVE 4
Discuss accounting issues for long-term liabilities stemming from pension and other postretirement employee benefit plans.

Most large companies and many smaller ones, as well, have established pension plans to provide a monthly retirement income for their employees. These pension plans come in two varieties: defined benefit plans and defined contribution plans. Under a defined contribution plan, employers make periodic contributions to a pension fund. These contributions are typically a percentage of each employee's gross earnings. Employers maintain an individual pension account for each employee in a subsidiary ledger. Following retirement, an employee receives a monthly, quarterly, or annual benefit based upon the size of his or her pension account. Accounting for a defined contribution plan is straightforward. When an employer determines the proper periodic contribution to the pension fund, Pension Expense is debited and Cash or a liability account is credited.

Unlike defined contribution plans, defined benefit plans pose contentious accounting issues. Under a defined benefit plan, employees are promised a monthly pension benefit. The size of this benefit depends on such factors as an employee's length of employment, age at retirement, and salary level over the last few years of employment. Until fairly recently, businesses accounted for the costs stemming from defined benefit pension plans on a cash basis. That is, the expense associated with a defined benefit plan was not recognized or accrued in a firm's accounting records as employees accumulated retirement benefits. Instead, when retirement benefits were paid to employees, an expense account was debited and a cash account credited. This "pay-as-you-go" approach to accounting for defined benefit pension plans violated the match-

Managing Pension Fund Assets

FOR YOUR INFORMATION

The pension plans of many large corporations have a huge amount of assets. In 1996, Eastman Kodak's pension plan assets exceeded $7 billion, while the pension plan assets of The Boeing Company topped $11.5 billion. An important issue facing such corporations is the investment strategy to use for pension plan assets. Numerous pension plans suffered large and embarrassing losses in recent years due to aggressive investment strategies. Many of these losses resulted from investments in so-called "financial derivatives." Financial derivatives are hybrid financial instruments that typically promise a potentially high rate of return and a correspondingly high degree of risk. Recently, The Common Fund, which manages pension plan assets for a wide range of companies and private institutions, reported a $128 million loss stemming from "index arbitrage trades."[3]

In 1995, Eastman Kodak announced that its pension plan managers would no longer invest in financial derivatives. For several years, Kodak posted impressive rates of return on its pension plan assets largely due to such investments. Company executives apparently decided that the key investment objective for the firm's pension plan should be safeguarding the plan's assets rather than seeking an abnormally high rate of return on those assets.

ing principle by not accruing a significant employment-related expense each accounting period. Additionally, this accounting treatment often resulted in a significant long-term liability going unreported on the balance sheets of companies having defined benefit pension plans.

Presently, businesses with defined benefit pension plans recognize pension expense on an accrual basis each accounting period. Businesses do not report pension plan assets on their balance sheets. However, if a company's pension fund assets are less than the present value of the pension benefits owed to employees, this difference must be reported as a liability on the company's balance sheet. Puritan-Bennett Corporation, a small manufacturing company, recently reported an $8 million long-term liability on its balance sheet stemming from its "underfunded" pension plan.

Other Postretirement Benefit Liabilities

LEARNING OBJECTIVE 4 ▶
Discuss accounting issues for long-term liabilities stemming from pension and other postretirement employee benefit plans.

Many businesses provide nonpension postretirement benefits to their employees, probably the most common being healthcare benefits. Similar to pension benefits, these "other postretirement benefits" (OPBs) were accounted for principally on a cash basis until recently. In the early 1990s, a new accounting standard issued by the Financial Accounting Standards Board mandated accrual-basis accounting for OPBs.

Many corporate executives apparently did not realize the economic implications that OPBs had for their firms before the adoption of accrual-basis accounting for these employee benefits. When IBM implemented this new accounting rule, the giant computer firm took a more than $2 billion "hit" on its income statement. That

3. S. Hemmerick, "Common Fund Loss Frightening," *Pensions & Investments,* 10 July 1995, 1 & 38.

expense item caused IBM to report its first ever quarterly loss. Likewise, consider the case of General Motors. General Motors revealed in the early 1990s that it was paying the healthcare costs of 386,000 employees, 358,000 retirees, and approximately one million dependents. In 1995, alone, General Motors reported $3.6 billion of healthcare expenses for these individuals. Even more staggering is the $41.6 billion long-term liability for OPBs that General Motors reported on a recent balance sheet.

KEY CONTROL ACTIVITIES FOR LONG-TERM LIABILITIES ▲

An important responsibility of an organization's accountants is to establish effective control activities for individual financial statement items, including long-term liabilities. Common control activities for long-term liabilities include proper authorization and documentation of these liabilities, controls over interest and principal payments, and monitoring compliance with restrictive debt covenants.

LEARNING ◄ OBJECTIVE 5
Identify key control activities for long-term liabilities.

Authorization and Documentation Controls

Achieving effective control over long-term liabilities begins with ensuring that long-term financing decisions are properly authorized. Decisions to sell corporate bonds, to borrow large sums on long-term promissory notes, or to create a pension plan must be approved by an organization's top executives. Once these transactions have been properly authorized, adequate documentation must be developed to meet all taxation, financial reporting, and other regulatory requirements for the resulting long-term liabilities. For example, federal regulations impose extensive recordkeeping requirements on employers for their employee pension plans. A company that fails to meet these requirements faces a risk of large fines and sanctions. Adequate documentation for bonds payable is also critical. Bond indentures must be written with extreme precision to protect the rights and privileges of both the company issuing bonds and the parties that subsequently purchase those bonds.

Payment Controls

Control activities should be implemented to ensure that interest and principal payments on long-term debt are made promptly, in the proper amounts, to the appropriate individuals, and are recorded correctly. Preparing an amortization schedule for long-term debt is one such control activity. An amortization schedule documents, among other items, the amounts to be included in the entries to record periodic interest payments on a long-term debt. The appendix to this chapter illustrates two amortization schedules.

Large public companies that have bonds payable outstanding often hire outside agencies to help them establish control over these liabilities. For example, a company that has bonds outstanding may retain a bank to serve as its transfer agent. A transfer agent maintains a current record of a company's bondholders and their addresses. This record serves as the basis for determining the individuals entitled to receive periodic bond interest payments.

Monitoring Compliance with Restrictive Covenants

Companies should closely monitor compliance with restrictive covenants included in a bond indenture or other long-term debt agreement. Such monitoring may result in early detection or prevention of debt covenant violations. As noted earlier, if a company violates one or more restrictive debt covenants, the entire long-term debt typically becomes immediately due and payable, which may force the firm into bankruptcy.

ANALYZING LONG-TERM LIABILITIES

LEARNING OBJECTIVE 6
Compute and interpret the long-term debt to equity and times interest earned ratios.

External decision makers monitor a firm's long-term liabilities and related financial data to gain insight on whether the firm can pay off those liabilities as they come due. Two financial ratios used to analyze long-term liabilities are the long-term debt to equity ratio and the times interest earned ratio. Exhibit 10.3 presents a five-year com-

EXHIBIT 10.3
Long-Term Debt to Equity and Times Interest Earned Ratios: American Greetings vs. Pioneer-Standard Electronics

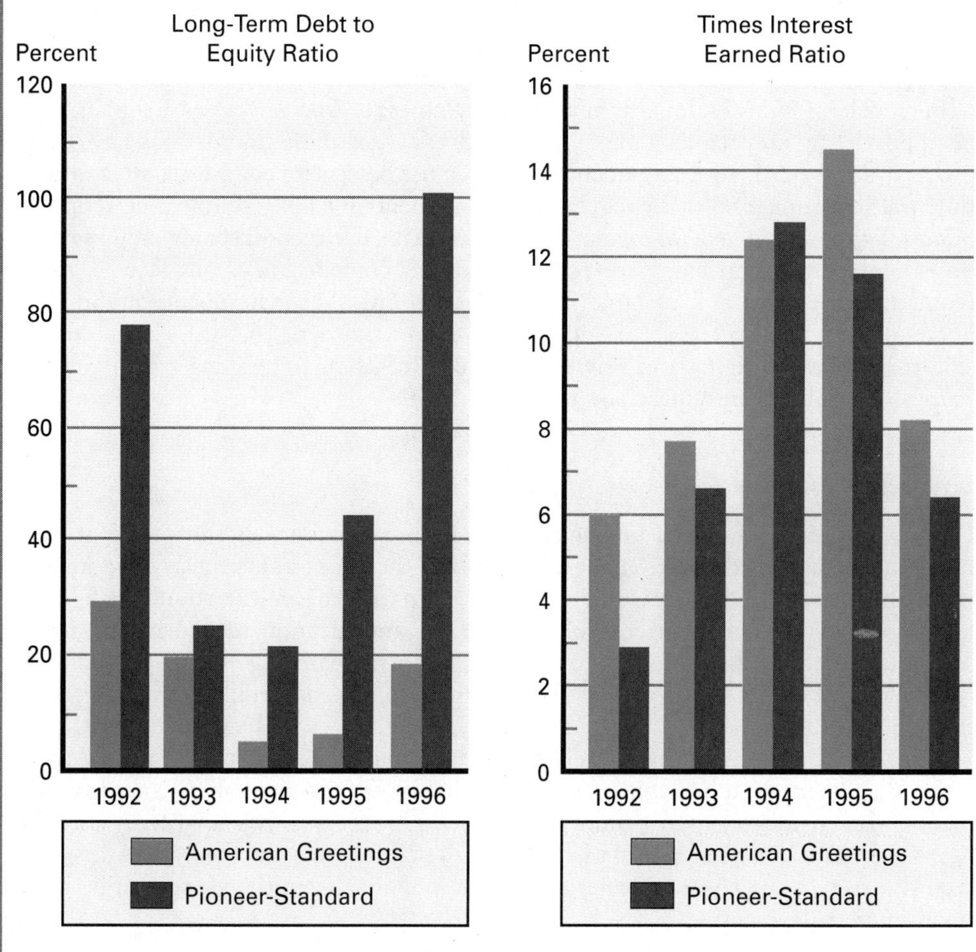

Source: Recent annual reports.

parison of these ratios for two public companies, American Greetings Corporation and Pioneer-Standard Electronics, Inc.

Long-Term Debt to Equity Ratio

A company that makes extensive use of long-term debt to meet its financing needs is said to be highly leveraged. Such companies generally face more risk of "going under" than firms that have little or no long-term debt on their balance sheets. Decision makers commonly use the **long-term debt to equity ratio** to measure financial leverage. This ratio is computed by dividing a company's total long-term debt by its total stockholders' equity. Notice in Exhibit 10.3 that Pioneer-Standard was more heavily leveraged than American Greetings throughout the period 1992–1996. By 1996, Pioneer-Standard's long-term debt exceeded its stockholders' equity. In that same year, American Greetings' long-term debt was less than 20 percent of its stockholders' equity. Notice also that each firm's long-term debt to equity ratio increased significantly during 1996. These increases resulted from long-term loans obtained by each firm to finance the acquisition of another company.

long-term debt to equity ratio

Exhibit 10.4 presents the average long-term debt to equity ratio for six industries in the mid-1990s. Included in these industries are electronic parts and equipment, Pioneer-Standard's industry, and greeting cards, the industry in which American Greetings operates. Notice that the norm for the long-term debt to equity ratio in both industries was slightly less than 20 percent. American Greetings' 1996 long-term debt to equity ratio paralleled the industry norm. Pioneer-Standard's corresponding ratio was significantly higher than the industry norm, indicating that the company had a much higher degree of financial leverage in 1996 than the typical firm in its industry.

Photography by Photonics Graphics

American Greetings produces and markets greeting cards for all occasions. Like most companies, American Greetings occasionally borrows funds on a long-term basis. In a recent year, this company's long-term debt was slightly less than 20 percent of its total stockholders' equity.

EXHIBIT 10.4 ▼
Long-Term Debt to Equity Ratio, Selected Industries

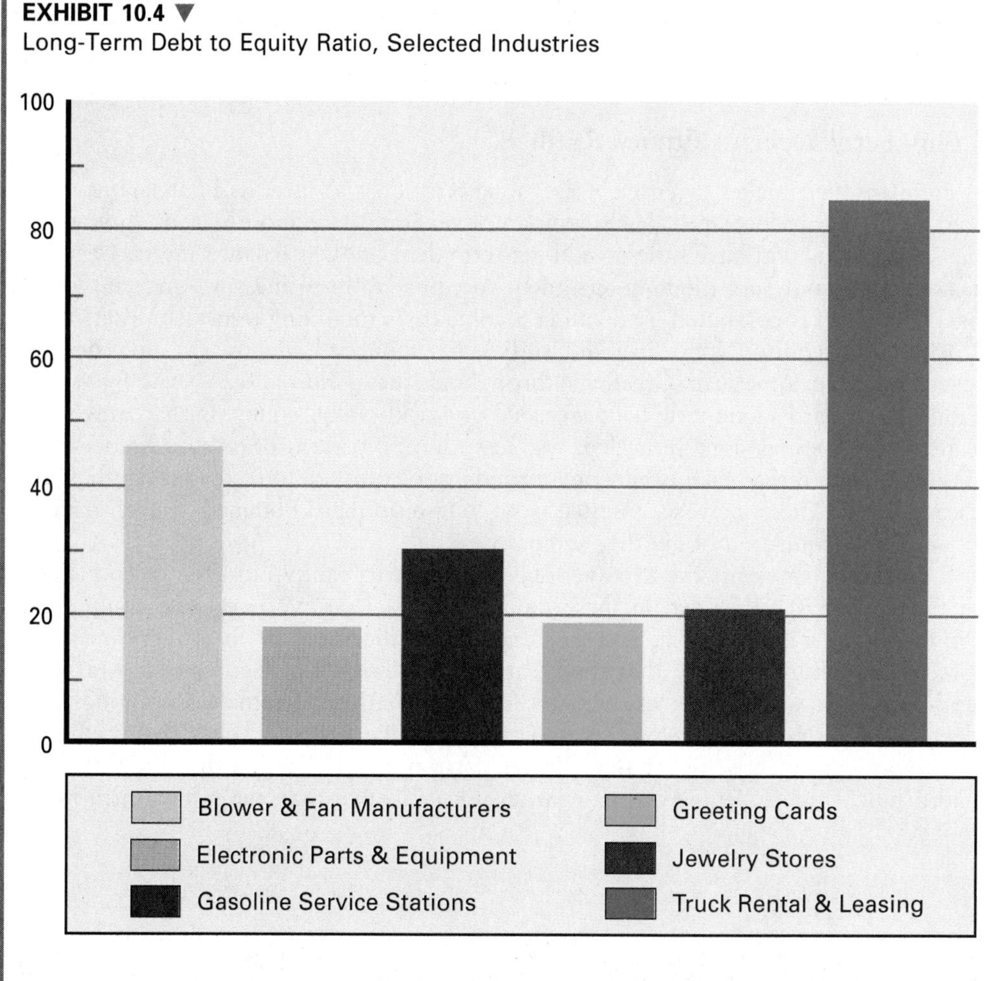

Source: *Industry Norms & Key Business Ratios, 1995–1996* (New York: Dun & Bradstreet, 1996).

Times Interest Earned Ratio

times interest earned ratio

A company that is highly leveraged is not necessarily at a high risk of defaulting on its long-term debt. The **times interest earned ratio** helps decision makers evaluate the ability of companies, particularly highly leveraged companies, to make interest payments on long-term debt as they come due. Following is the equation used to compute the times interest earned ratio.

$$\text{Times Interest Earned Ratio} = \frac{\text{Net Income} + \text{Interest Expense} + \text{Income Taxes Expense}}{\text{Interest Expense}}$$

The times interest earned ratio indicates the number of times that earnings before interest expense and income taxes expense "covers" a company's interest expense during a given period. The lower this ratio, the more risk a company generally faces of defaulting on interest payments on its long-term debt. As is true for most financial ratios, there is not complete agreement on what represents a reasonable level for the times interest earned ratio. Typically, this ratio is considered "comfortable" when it is 4.0 and higher. Exhibit 10.3 indicates that the times interest earned ratio of both American Greetings and Pioneer-Standard declined during 1996. Nevertheless, each company's 1996 ratio was easily within the "comfort zone."

SUMMARY

Long-term liabilities include the debts and obligations of a business other than those classified as current liabilities. Among the more common long-term liabilities are bonds payable, capital lease obligations, and long-term accrued liabilities stemming from employee benefit plans.

The information needs of external decision makers concerning long-term liabilities parallel those for current liabilities. Most important, decision makers need to be assured that all long-term liabilities are included in a firm's financial statements. Several recent accounting standards have reduced the number of "off-balance sheet" long-term liabilities, meaning that decision makers now obtain a more accurate picture of the financial condition of businesses. Decision makers also need to be informed of the methods used to assign dollar amounts to long-term liabilities, particularly those that must be estimated. Finally, businesses should disclose unusual and material circumstances related to long-term liabilities, such as potential violations of restrictive debt covenants.

The key accounting decisions for bonds payable are resolved on the date the bonds are initially sold. Newly issued bonds usually sell for more or less than their face value because their stated interest rate is either higher or lower than the market interest rate on the date they are sold. A bond discount or premium should be amortized over the term of a bond issue. The amortization of a bond discount increases the interest expense recognized on a bond issue, while the amortization of a bond premium reduces periodic interest expense on outstanding bonds.

When accounting for a long-term lease, the primary issue to consider is whether the lease qualifies as an operating lease or a capital lease. A lessee must record both an asset and a long-term liability in its accounting records for a capital lease. Accounting standards adopted recently require companies to record long-term liabilities resulting from commitments they have made to provide postretirement benefits to employees. These liabilities are often enormous and have dramatically affected the reported financial condition of many large companies.

Proper authorization of decisions to incur long-term liabilities is a key control activity for business entities. Businesses must also establish controls to ensure that interest and principal payments on long-term debt are made promptly, in the proper amounts, to the appropriate individuals, and are properly recorded. Finally, a company should closely monitor compliance with restrictive covenants included in long-term debt agreements to provide adequate warning of any potential violations of those covenants.

When decision makers analyze a company's long-term liabilities, they typically focus on the firm's degree of financial leverage and its ability to make periodic interest payments on long-term debt. A common measure of financial leverage is the long-term debt to equity ratio. A firm's ability to make periodic interest payments on long-term debt is commonly evaluated by referring to its times interest earned ratio.

APPENDIX: EFFECTIVE-INTEREST METHOD OF AMORTIZING BOND DISCOUNT AND PREMIUM

LEARNING OBJECTIVE 7 ▶ (Appendix) Amortize bond discount and premium using the effective-interest method.

Earlier in the chapter, we used the straight-line method to amortize a discount and a premium on bonds payable. The accounting profession considers the "effective-interest method" of amortizing bond discount and premium preferable to the straight-line method. Nevertheless, many companies employ the straight-line method, principally because it is easier to apply than the effective-interest method. The straight-line method is acceptable if the bond discount or premium amounts amortized each period are not materially different from the amounts that would be amortized applying the effective-interest method. Barnes & Noble, Inc., the retail bookstore chain, uses the straight-line method to amortize discount on certain long-term debt. The company's annual report issued in 1996 noted that the discount amortized each period under the straight-line method approximates the amount that would be amortized by applying the effective-interest method.

effective-interest method

effective interest rate

Under the **effective-interest method,** the interest expense recorded on bonds payable each interest payment period is a constant percentage of the bonds' carrying value. This constant percentage is the market interest rate on the date the bonds were initially sold, which is often referred to as the **effective interest rate.** The effective interest rate represents the true rate of interest incurred over the term of a bond issue by the company that issues the bonds.

Bonds Issued at a Discount

The first step in applying the effective-interest method is preparing an amortization schedule. Among other items, an amortization schedule documents the interest expense to be recognized each interest payment period on a long-term debt. Panel B of Exhibit 10.5 contains an amortization schedule for the bonds of Hardin Manufacturing Company that were discussed earlier in the chapter. Panel A of Exhibit 10.5 lists the key factual data for the Hardin bond issue, which are unchanged from the original example used to illustrate accounting for bonds sold at a discount. Recall that the market interest rate on the date the bonds were sold in this scenario was assumed to be 11 percent, which is higher than the bonds' stated interest rate of 10 percent.

The first column of the amortization schedule in Exhibit 10.5 lists the interest payment dates in chronological order. The second and third columns list the interest expense and interest payment amounts, respectively, for each interest payment period. Notice that interest expense for each six-month period is computed by multiplying the effective semiannual interest rate, 5.5 percent, by the bonds' carrying value at the end of the previous interest payment period. The interest payment, $5,000, does not vary over the bond term since it is contractually determined by the bond indenture. Included in the fourth column of the amortization schedule is the amount of bond discount amortized each interest payment period. These amounts equal the difference between the interest expense each period and the interest payment. The balance of the discount account at the end of an interest payment period is determined by subtracting the discount amortized that period from the account's previous balance. Finally, the carrying value of bonds payable at the end of an interest payment period is the difference between their face value and the period-ending balance of the bond discount account.

EXHIBIT 10.5 ▼
Effective-Interest Method of Amortizing Bond Discount

Panel A—Bond Data

Date Sold—April 1, Year 1
Face Value—$100,000
Stated Interest Rate—10%, paid semiannually
Market Interest Rate on Date Sold—11%
Selling Price—$96,231

Panel B—Amortization Schedule, Effective-Interest Method

Interest Payment Date	Interest Expense[1]	Interest Payment[2]	Discount Amortization[3]	Bond Discount Balance[4]	Bond Carrying Value[5]
Date Sold, Apr. 1, Year 1				$3,769	$ 96,231
Oct. 1, Year 1	$5,293	$5,000	$293	3,476	96,524
Apr. 1, Year 2	5,309	5,000	309	3,167	96,833
Oct. 1, Year 2	5,326	5,000	326	2,841	97,159
Apr. 1, Year 3	5,344	5,000	344	2,497	97,503
Oct. 1, Year 3	5,363	5,000	363	2,134	97,866
Apr. 1, Year 4	5,383	5,000	383	1,751	98,249
Oct. 1, Year 4	5,404	5,000	404	1,347	98,653
Apr. 1, Year 5	5,426	5,000	426	921	99,079
Oct. 1, Year 5	5,449	5,000	449	472	99,528
Apr. 1, Year 6	5,472*	5,000	472	0	100,000

[1]5.5% × Bond Carrying Value at the end of the prior interest payment period; for the initial interest payment date, interest expense is determined by multiplying 5.5% by the original carrying value (selling price) of the bonds.

[2]5% × Bond Face Value of $100,000; this is a cash payment.

[3]Interest Expense − Interest Payment.

[4]Prior Balance − current-period Discount Amortization.

[5]Bond Face Value of $100,000 − Bond Discount Balance.

*Difference due to rounding.

Once an amortization schedule has been prepared, recording periodic interest expense is a simple task. On October 1, Year 1, the following entry would be made to record the semiannual interest payment on Hardin's bonds, assuming the effective-interest method is used to amortize the bond discount.

		Debit	Credit
Oct. 1	Interest Expense	5,293	
	Cash		5,000
	Discount on Bonds Payable		293
	To record interest payment on bonds payable		

On December 31, Year 1, Hardin's accountants would prepare an adjusting entry to record interest expense on the bonds payable. At this point, one-half of the second semiannual interest payment period would have elapsed. So, one-half of the $309 discount amortization amount for that period reported in Exhibit 10.5 (approximately $155) would be recognized as interest expense. Shown next is the adjusting entry at the end of Year 1 to record interest expense on Hardin's bonds payable.

Dec. 31	Interest Expense	2,655	
	Interest Payable		2,500
	Discount on Bonds Payable		155
	To recognize interest expense on bonds payable		

EXHIBIT 10.6 ▼
Effective-Interest Method of Amortizing Bond Premium

Panel A—Bond Data

Date Sold—April 1, Year 1
Face Value—$100,000
Stated Interest Rate—10%, paid semiannually
Market Interest Rate on Date Sold—9%
Selling Price—$103,957

Panel B—Amortization Schedule, Effective-Interest Method

Interest Payment Date	Interest Expense[1]	Interest Payment[2]	Premium Amortization[3]	Bond Premium Balance[4]	Bond Carrying Value[5]
Date Sold, Apr. 1, Year 1				$3,957	$103,957
Oct. 1, Year 1	$4,678	$5,000	$322	3,635	103,635
Apr. 1, Year 2	4,664	5,000	336	3,299	103,299
Oct. 1, Year 2	4,648	5,000	352	2,947	102,947
Apr. 1, Year 3	4,633	5,000	367	2,580	102,580
Oct. 1, Year 3	4,616	5,000	384	2,196	102,196
Apr. 1, Year 4	4,599	5,000	401	1,795	101,795
Oct. 1, Year 4	4,581	5,000	419	1,376	101,376
Apr. 1, Year 5	4,562	5,000	438	938	100,938
Oct. 1, Year 5	4,542	5,000	458	480	100,480
Apr. 1, Year 6	4,520*	5,000	480	0	100,000

[1]4.5% × Bond Carrying Value at the end of the prior interest payment period; for the initial interest payment date, interest expense is determined by multiplying 4.5% by the original carrying value (selling price) of the bonds.

[2]5% × Bond Face Value of $100,000; this is a cash payment.

[3]Interest Payment − Interest Expense.

[4]Prior Balance − current-period Premium Amortization.

[5]Bond Face Value of $100,000 + Bond Premium Balance.

*Difference due to rounding.

Bonds Issued at a Premium

Panel B of Exhibit 10.6 contains a second amortization schedule for the Hardin bonds applying the effective-interest method. Here, we assume that the bonds are sold for a premium, as illustrated earlier in the chapter. Recall that under this assumption the market interest rate is 9 percent on the date the bonds are sold. An amortization schedule for bonds issued at a premium is nearly identical to an amortization schedule for bonds issued at a discount. Again, interest expense each six-month period is computed by multiplying the effective semiannual interest rate by the bonds' carrying value at the end of the previous period. Under the present scenario, the effective semiannual interest rate is 4.5 percent, or one-half of the market interest rate on the date the bonds were sold. Shown next is the entry to record the initial interest payment on Hardin's bonds, assuming the effective-interest method is used to amortize the bond premium.

Oct. 1	Interest Expense	4,678	
	Premium on Bonds Payable	322	
	Cash		5,000
	To record interest payment on bonds payable		

GLOSSARY

Bond (p. 450) A long-term loan made by one party to another that is legally documented by a bond certificate.

Bond indenture (p. 453) The legal contract between a bond purchaser and the issuing company; identifies the rights and obligations of each party.

Bonds payable (p. 450) A long-term liability that represents the collective amount owed the parties who have purchased a company's bonds.

Callable bonds (p. 453) Bonds that can be retired or redeemed by the issuing company when one or more conditions are met.

Capital lease (p. 462) A lease that is generally noncancelable, long-term, and transfers at least some ownership rights or risks to the lessee.

Convertible bonds (p. 453) Bonds that may be exchanged for stock in the issuing company at the option of the bondholders.

Effective-interest method (p. 470) A method of determining interest expense on bonds payable each interest payment period; under this method, interest expense is computed by multiplying the effective interest rate by the bonds' carrying value.

Effective interest rate (p. 470) The market interest rate on the date bonds are initially sold; represents the true rate of interest incurred over the term of a bond issue by the issuing company.

Long-term debt (p. 448) A business's liabilities resulting from amounts borrowed on a long-term basis.

Long-term debt to equity ratio (p. 467) A common measure of financial leverage; computed by dividing a company's long-term debt by its stockholders' equity.

Long-term liabilities (p. 448) The debts and obligations of a business other than those classified as current liabilities.

Off-balance sheet financing (p. 449) Involves the acquisition of assets or services by incurring long-term obligations that are not reported on an entity's balance sheet.

Operating lease (p. 462) A lease that is usually cancelable by the lessee, covers a short-term, and does not transfer ownership rights or risks to the lessee.

Secured bonds (p. 453) Bonds collateralized by specific assets of the issuing company; sometimes referred to as mortgage bonds.
Stated interest rate (p. 453) The rate of interest paid to bondholders based upon the face value of the bonds; also known as the face interest rate or contract interest rate.
Times interest earned ratio (p. 468) A financial ratio used to evaluate a firm's ability to make interest payments on its long-term debt; computed by dividing the sum of net income, interest expense, and income taxes expense by interest expense.
Unsecured bonds (p. 453) Bonds backed only by the legal commitment of the issuing firm to make all required principal and interest payments; often referred to as debentures.

DECISION CASE

You began your college career at Southwest Missouri State University as a marketing major and somehow wound up graduating with an accounting degree. You recently passed the CPA exam and are now a practicing public accountant in the small town of Hope, Arkansas. Like most small-town accountants, you generate the bulk of your revenue by preparing tax returns and performing bookkeeping services for local businesses. Occasionally, you serve as an informal financial advisor to your clients—no fees, just free, off-the-cuff advice.

Recently, Virgilene Crawford, former wife of your now deceased Uncle Rufus, asked you for advice on investing $100,000 she collected on her husband's life insurance policy. Aunt Virgie is a strong-willed woman. A friend of hers made a "killing" in the last couple of years in the corporate bond market. So, Aunt Virgie is dead set on investing her bundle of cash in corporate bonds. A cousin on the other side of the family suggested that she consider investing in the corporate bonds listed in the following table. The data in this table were taken from a recent edition of *The Wall Street Journal.*

Company	Stated Interest Rate	Current Yield	Market Price	Maturity Date
AMR	9.0%	9.8%	91 3/8	2016
IBM	6.375%	6.9%	92 1/4	2000
IBM	8.375%	8.6%	97	2019
U.S. Air	12.875%	14.3%	90	2000
Wendy's*	7.0%	5.3%	132	2006

*convertible bonds

Required: Aunt Virgie does not understand why there is such a disparity in the current yields on these bonds. In a brief memo, explain to her the key factors that may account for this disparity. When identifying these factors, refer to specific examples using the data provided in the table just shown. Also, identify additional information that she should obtain regarding these bonds before she makes her investment decision.

Applying the time value of money concept, demonstrate to Aunt Virgie how the market price of the AMR bonds can be confirmed mathematically. Assume that today's date is January 1, 1997, the bonds mature on December 31, 2016, the interest on the bonds is paid semiannually, and the market interest rate for comparable bonds is 10 percent. Finally, briefly explain to Aunt Virgie the difference between "current yield" and "yield to maturity."

QUESTIONS

1. Define "long-term liabilities." Provide several examples of long-term liabilities.
2. Identify the key information needs of external decision makers regarding the long-term liabilities of business entities.
3. Define "off-balance sheet financing." Provide one example of an off-balance sheet financing technique.
4. What are restrictive debt covenants? Provide an example.
5. What is a bond issue?
6. What is a bond indenture? Identify the key items of information included in a bond indenture.
7. Briefly describe callable and convertible bonds.
8. What factors influence the selling price of a corporate bond?
9. What is the actual selling price of a $1,000 bond that has a quoted market price of 97½?
10. Explain how the current yield on a bond is computed.
11. Why is a bond's stated interest rate usually different from the market interest rate on the date the bond is initially sold?
12. Will a bond with a stated interest rate of 10 percent that is issued when the market interest rate is 9 percent sell for more or less than its face value? Why?
13. How is the carrying value of bonds payable determined for balance sheet reporting purposes?
14. What is the advantage to a corporation of including a call option in a bond indenture?
15. What are mortgage notes payable?
16. Identify the two parties to a lease agreement.
17. Summarize the criteria used to determine whether a lease is a capital lease or an operating lease.
18. Identify the advantages and disadvantages of leasing assets as opposed to purchasing them.
19. How do defined benefit and defined contribution pension plans differ?
20. How did the pay-as-you-go, or cash-basis, method of accounting for defined benefit pension plans violate the matching principle?
21. Identify three control activities for long-term liabilities.
22. Define "financial leverage." Identify one method of measuring financial leverage.
23. How is the times interest earned ratio computed? How do decision makers use this ratio?
24. Compare and contrast the straight-line and effective-interest methods of amortizing bond discount and bond premium.
25. What is the purpose of an amortization schedule for bonds payable?

EXERCISES

26. True or False (LO 1–7)

Following are a series of statements regarding topics discussed in Chapter 10.

Required:

Indicate whether each statement is true (T) or false (F).

_____ a. Until fairly recently, businesses accounted for the costs stemming from defined benefit pension plans on a cash basis.

_____ b. Callable bonds may be exchanged for stock in the issuing company at the option of the bondholders.

_____ c. A key control activity for a long-term debt is the preparation of an amortization schedule.

_____ d. When bonds are sold at a discount, the interest expense recorded each interest payment date is less than the amount of the interest payment.

_____ e. The times interest earned ratio indicates the number of times that earnings before interest expense and income taxes expense covers a company's income taxes expense during a given period.

_____ f. Debentures are bonds backed only by the legal commitment of the issuing company to make all required principal and interest payments.

_____ g. The stated interest rate represents the true rate of interest incurred over the term of a bond issue.

_____ h. Secured bonds are collateralized by specific assets of the issuing company.

_____ i. Businesses must discuss in their periodic financial reports off-balance sheet financing methods that they employ.

_____ j. When a business leases an asset under conditions that are comparable to purchasing that asset with borrowed funds, both the leased asset and the long-term lease obligation must be reported on the firm's balance sheet.

_____ k. A common measure of financial leverage is the long-term debt to current liabilities ratio.

_____ l. A common restrictive debt covenant is a limitation on the payment of dividends.

_____ m. The market interest rate on the date bonds are sold determines the present value of the future cash outflows related to those bonds.

27. Bond Terminology (LO 2)

Following are definitions or descriptions of terms relating to corporate bonds.

_____ Bonds that may be exchanged for stock in the issuing company.

_____ Long-term loan made by one party to another.

_____ Legal instrument documenting a bond.

_____ $1,000 is the typical amount for corporate bonds.

_____ Bonds backed only by the legal commitment of the issuing company to make all required principal and interest payments.

_____ When bond principal is repaid.

_____ Bonds collateralized by specific assets of the company issuing the bonds.

_____ Legal contract between a bond purchaser and the company that issued the bond.

_____ Period elapsing between the date bonds are first available for sale and the date they mature.

_____ Rate of interest to be paid to bondholders based on the face value of the bonds.

Required:
Match each definition or description listed with the appropriate term from the following list.

1. Bond
2. Coupon bonds
3. Face value (or principal amount)
4. Maturity date
5. Bond indenture
6. Stated interest rate (or contract interest rate)
7. Term of the bonds
8. Serial bonds
9. Callable bonds
10. Registered bonds
11. Bond certificate
12. Term bonds
13. Secured bonds
14. Convertible bonds
15. Debentures

28. **Operating vs. Capital Leases** (LO 3)
Refer to the annual report of Outback Steakhouse that is included as an appendix to this text.

Required:
1. Review Outback's financial statements and accompanying footnotes. At the end of 1996, was Outback a "lessee" of any assets? If so, were the relevant leases operating leases or capital leases and what types of assets were involved in these leases?
2. Briefly describe the rationale for the accounting treatment applied to capital leases.

29. **Stated Interest Rate, Current Yield, and the Market Interest Rate** (LO 2)
Suppose you purchase a corporate bond with a face value of $1,000 that has a stated interest rate of 8 percent. Interest on the bond is paid semiannually.

Required:
1. How much interest will you receive on each interest payment date?
2. Suppose that you purchased this bond when the quoted market price was 98. How much did you pay for the bond? If you pay more or less than the face value of a bond, will the amount of interest you receive be affected? Why?
3. Suppose again that you purchase this bond at a quoted market price of 98. What is this bond's "current yield'? Why is the bond's current yield different from the bond's stated interest rate? Explain.
4. If you purchase this bond at a quoted market price of 98, is the market interest rate on the purchase date higher or lower than the bond's stated interest rate? Explain.

30. **Cash Flows Related to Bonds Payable** (LO 2)
Lomax Corporation issued $1,000,000 of six-year, 10 percent bonds on January 1 of Year 1. Interest on the bonds is payable semiannually on January 1 and July 1 of each year.

Required:
1. How much will Lomax pay its bondholders on each interest payment date? On the bonds' maturity date?
2. Determine the cash that Lomax will receive from the sale of these bonds on January 1, Year 1, if the market interest rate on that date is:
   a. 9 percent.
   b. 7 percent.

31. Journal Entries for Bonds Payable (LO 2)
On February 1, 1998, Ianello Company issued $10,000,000 of ten-year, 8 percent bonds at face value. Interest is payable semiannually on February 1 and August 1 of each year. Ianello's year-end is December 31.

Required:
Prepare the appropriate journal entries in Ianello's accounting records on the following dates for these bonds.
1. February 1, 1998
2. August 1, 1998
3. December 31, 1998

32. Straight-Line Method of Amortizing Bond Discount or Premium (LO 2)
Peterson Company issued $200,000 of five-year, 12 percent bonds on May 1, 1998, when the market rate of interest for similar bonds was 10 percent. The bonds pay interest semiannually on May 1 and November 1 of each year. Peterson's year-end is December 31.

Required:
Prepare the journal entries necessary on each of the following dates, assuming Peterson amortizes any bond discount or premium using the straight-line method.
1. May 1, 1998
2. November 1, 1998
3. December 31, 1998

33. (*Appendix*) Effective-Interest Method of Amortizing Bond Discount or Premium (LO 7)
Refer to the information in Exercise 32.

Required:
Prepare the journal entries necessary on each of the following dates, assuming Peterson amortizes any bond discount or premium using the effective-interest method.
1. May 1, 1998
2. November 1, 1998
3. December 31, 1998

34. Straight-Line Method of Amortizing Bond Discount or Premium (LO 2)
Sarkisian Company issued $700,000 of five-year, 8 percent bonds on March 1, 1998, when the market interest rate for similar bonds was 10 percent. The bonds pay interest semiannually on March 1 and September 1 of each year. Sarkisian's year-end is December 31.

Required:
Prepare the journal entries necessary on each of the following dates, assuming Sarkisian amortizes bond premium or discount using the straight-line method.
1. March 1, 1998
2. September 1, 1998
3. December 31, 1998

35. (*Appendix*) Effective-Interest Method of Amortizing Bond Discount or Premium (LO 7)
Refer to the information presented in Exercise 34.

Required:
Prepare the journal entries necessary on each of the following dates, assuming Sarkisian amortizes bond premium or discount using the effective-interest method.
1. March 1, 1998
2. September 1, 1998
3. December 31, 1999

36. **Key Bond Terms** (LO 2)
A. J. Coleman is a retired blacksmith who would like to invest some of his retirement funds in corporate bonds although he knows very little about the bond market. A. J. is particularly confused by the following terms associated with bonds: stated interest rate, current yield, face interest rate, and market interest rate.

Required:
Write a memo to A. J. explaining the meaning of the bond terms that have him confused. In your memo, indicate how these terms are related to each other.

37. **Retirement of Bonds Payable** (LO 2)
On December 31, 1998, Rockport Enterprises had a $10 million bond issue outstanding. The carrying value of this bond issue was $10,750,000. On that date, Rockport purchased these bonds on the open market and then immediately retired them. The bonds were purchased for $10,425,000.

Required:
1. Prepare the journal entry to record the purchase and retirement of Rockport's bonds.
2. Identify possible reasons that a company might choose to retire its outstanding bonds before their maturity date.
3. Is it ethical for a company to purchase its own bonds in the open market? Why or why not?

38. **Operating Leases and Capital Leases** (LO 3)
On January 11, 1998, Lonestar Gathering Hole leased a mechanical bull-riding machine for its entertainment room. The lease term is four years, and the lease contract calls for payments of $10,000 a year at the end of each year.

Required:
1. What is the primary difference between an operating lease and a capital lease?
2. Briefly describe the different accounting treatment given operating leases and capital leases by lessees.
3. Suppose that Lonestar's lease qualifies as a capital lease and that the appropriate discount rate to determine the present value of the payments to be made over the term of this lease is 7 percent. Prepare the journal entry in Lonestar's accounting records on January 11 to record the lease of the bull-riding machine.

39. **Buy vs. Lease Decision** (LO 3)
Aspereen Corporation needs a particular piece of equipment for its manufacturing operations. This equipment has an estimated useful life of six years and a zero salvage value. Johnson Equipment Supply will sell the equipment to Aspereen for $32,000 cash. Kelvin Equipment Supply will lease the equipment to Aspereen for six years with an annual lease payment of $7,000 due at the end of each year. The appropriate discount rate to determine the present value of the lease payments is 10 percent.

Required:
1. Based strictly on the information provided, which of the two alternative methods of acquiring the equipment appears to be more attractive to Aspereen? Why?
2. Identify factors other than acquisition cost that may influence a company's decision whether to buy or lease a long-term asset.

40. (*Appendix*) **Control Activities for Bonds Payable** (LO 5)
Scully Brothers is a manufacturing firm whose net income has ranged from $1.5 million to $2.1 million over the past five years. Two years ago, Scully sold $1 million of bonds that have a ten-year term, a stated interest rate of 8 percent, and pay interest semiannually. The sale of the bonds raised $950,000. Recently, Scully's accountant, Ross Porter, was having lunch with a friend who is also an accountant of a manufacturing firm. Porter

suggested to his friend that applying the effective-interest method to his company's bonds was a tedious task. "Every six months, I have to drag out all of this information regarding the bonds. Then I have to multiply this times that and subtract that from this. Man, it's a mess. It's impossible to make all of those computations without messing something up."

Required:

1. What control activity would simplify the accounting treatment applied to Scully's bonds? Identify other control activities relevant to bonds payable.
2. Suppose that the other accountant responded to Porter's complaint as follows: "Ross, why do you go to the trouble of using the effective-interest method? You can use the straight-line method, given the circumstances. That will solve most of your problems." Is Porter's friend correct? Under what condition is the straight-line method an acceptable alternative to the effective-interest method? Does that condition exist in this case?

41. Analyzing Long-Term Liabilities (LO 6)

Listed in the following schedule are selected financial data included in a recent annual report of Crown Cork & Seal Company. Based in Philadelphia, Crown Cork & Seal is the leading firm in the packaging industry. Amounts are expressed in millions of dollars.

	Year 1	Year 2
Total assets	$4,781.3	$5,051.7
Current assets	1,605.6	1,708.9
Current liabilities	1,483.0	1,279.0
Long-term debt	1,089.5	1,490.1
Stockholders' equity	1,365.2	1,461.2
Interest expense	98.8	148.6
Income taxes expense	55.6	24.9
Net income	131.0	74.9

Required:

1. Compute Crown Cork & Seal's long-term debt to equity and times interest earned ratios for Year 1 and Year 2.
2. How did the company's degree of financial leverage and interest coverage change over this two-year period?

42. Analyzing Long-Term Liabilities (LO 6)

Following is information drawn from a recent set of financial statements of Textronix, Inc., a publicly owned company based in Wilsonville, Oregon.

	Year 1	Year 2
Total assets	$1,218,302	$1,328,496
Current assets	666,135	753,580
Total stockholders' equity	604,215	675,322
Long-term debt	226,279	287,837
Net income	81,584	99,586
Interest expense	10,203	13,985
Income taxes expense	28,578	42,680

Required:

1. Suppose that Textronix has applied for a $50 million long-term loan from Lowell Bank, while Thomas Manufacturing is considering purchasing 10,000 shares of Textronix's common stock. Which of these two parties, Lowell Bank or Thomas Manufacturing, would likely be more interested in evaluating Textronix's financial leverage? Why?
2. Compute Textronix's long-term debt to equity ratio in Year 1 and Year 2. Did the company become more or less leveraged between the end of Year 1 and the end of Year 2?
3. Compute Textronix's times interest earned ratio in both Year 1 and Year 2. Did this ratio improve or deteriorate between the end of Year 1 and the end of Year 2? Explain.

PROBLEM SET A

43. Accounting for Bonds Payable, Straight-Line Method of Amortizing Bond Premium or Discount (LO 2)

The Doubleday Corporation issued $20,000,000 of five-year, 8 percent bonds on May 1, 1998. Interest payment dates are May 1 and November 1 of each year. Doubleday uses straight-line amortization for any bond premium or discount and has a December 31 fiscal year-end.

Required:

1. Determine the total proceeds Doubleday received from the sale of these bonds, assuming that the market interest rate for similar bonds on May 1, 1998, was:
   a. 6 percent.
   b. 10 percent.
2. Prepare the appropriate journal entries on the following dates for each assumption listed in Part 1:
   a. May 1, 1998
   b. November 1, 1998
   c. December 31, 1998
   d. May 1, 1999
3. For each assumption listed in (1), determine the carrying value of the bonds as of December 31, 1998.

44. Analyzing Long-Term Liabilities (LO 1, 6)

Station Casinos, Inc., is a Las Vegas-based firm that owns and operates casinos and other gaming operations. The following financial information was drawn from a recent set of financial statements for Station Casinos. Amounts are expressed in thousands.

	Year 1	Year 2
Total assets	$185,110	$301,486
Long-term debt	121,792	161,302
Stockholders' equity	37,153	95,791
Interest expense	8,949	9,179
Income taxes expense	4,806	6,100
Net income	9,417	11,840

In Station Casinos' annual report, the company's executives discussed aggressive expansion plans for the future. Following are specific comments addressing the issue of whether the company would be able to finance these plans.

The Company's plan for the development of new gaming opportunities, as well as further expansion of existing operations, may require substantial amounts of additional capital . . . There can be no assurance that any such financing would be available to the Company or, if available, that any such financing would be available on favorable terms.

Required:

1. Compute Station Casinos' long-term debt to equity and times interest earned ratios for Year 1 and Year 2. Did these ratios improve or weaken between the end of Year 1 and the end of Year 2?
2. Considering the financial data presented for the company, what factor was apparently most responsible for the significant change in the company's long-term debt to equity ratio between the end of Year 1 and the end of Year 2? Explain.
3. Suppose that the average long-term debt to equity ratio for the gaming industry is 50 percent and that the average times interest earned ratio is 4.5. Evaluate Station Casinos' ratios in reference to these industry norms.
4. What purpose is served by the narrative disclosures in Station Casinos' annual report regarding the company's potential need for additional capital?

45. Retirement of Bonds Payable (LO 2)

CookieTown Industries of CookieTown, Oklahoma, has a $10 million bond issue outstanding. These bonds were sold on February 1, 1995, have a ten-year term, and have a stated interest rate of 12 percent. Interest on the bonds is paid semiannually on February 1 and August 1. The bonds have a current carrying value of $9,877,000.

If CookieTown sold bonds in today's market, the company would be required to pay annual interest of only 9 percent. Consequently, the company's management wants to retire its outstanding bonds and sell new bonds. The current market price of CookieTown's bonds is 122¼.

Required:

1. At the present market price, how much will it cost CookieTown to purchase all of its outstanding bonds? What factor or factors may account for the difference between the collective market price and carrying value of CookieTown's bonds?
2. Suppose that CookieTown purchases and immediately retires the bonds. Prepare the appropriate journal entry to record this transaction.
3. What stipulation could have been included in the bond indenture that would have allowed the company to retire the bonds without being forced to purchase them in the open market?

46. Selected Long-Term Liabilities in Corporate Balance Sheets (LO 1, 4)

Suppose that a friend of yours is a social psychology major who is writing a term paper on the nature of large corporations. One feature she is studying is how corporations finance their operations. She has identified the following long-term liabilities, and related information, in recent corporate balance sheets.

a. *8 percent Convertible Debentures Due April 15, 2011—$19,975,000*
These debentures were included on a balance sheet of Quixote Corporation, a firm in the computer industry.

b. *Accrued Pension Costs—$12,265,000*
Hormel Foods Corporation, which reported this long-term liability, manufactures and markets prepared food products.

c. *Unearned Portion of Paid Subscriptions—$2,700,000,000*
This item was a long-term liability of Time Warner, which, among other lines of business, publishes *Time, People,* and *Sports Illustrated.*

d. *Mortgages on Property, Plant & Equipment—$4,952,000*
This item is a long-term liability of Tuesday Morning Corporation, a discount retailer.

Required:
Prepare a report for your friend. Begin your report with a brief overview of the nature of liabilities and the general types of long-term liabilities. Next, provide a brief description of the nature and source of each of the long-term liabilities identified by your friend. Include in these descriptions how each liability is related, or likely related if you are unsure, to the given company's profit-oriented activities.

47. **Liabilities in International Financial Statements** (LO 1, 6)

Many investors and other financial decision makers in this country are unaware that numerous, well-known companies are actually foreign corporations. Take the case of Nestlé, probably best known for its "crunchy" candy bar. Following are selected amounts included in Nestlé's recent annual report. Amounts are expressed in millions of Swiss francs.

	Year 1	Year 2
Short-term debts	18,166	17,297
Medium and long-term debts	10,424	10,156
Shareholders' funds	16,343	17,104
Net profit	2,887	3,250
Interest expense	1,284	1,118
Taxes	1,669	1,647

Required:
1. Compute Nestlé's long-term debt to equity ratio and its times interest earned ratio for Year 1 and Year 2.
2. Compare Nestlé's degree of financial leverage in Year 1 and Year 2 with the average degree of financial leverage for the U.S. industries listed in Exhibit 10.4. Is Nestlé generally more or less leveraged than the average company in each of those industries?
3. According to the text, a comfortable level for the times interest earned ratio is 4.0 and higher. Were Nestlé's times interest earned ratios in Year 1 and Year 2 "comfortable"?
4. Suppose that early in Year 3 you were considering buying several hundred shares of Nestlé's common stock. Identify three questions that you would have wanted to ask the company's controller regarding Nestlé's liabilities.

48. (*Appendix*) **Accounting for Bonds Payable, Effective-Interest Method of Amortizing Bond Premium or Discount** (LO 7)

The Naismith Corporation sold $4,000,000 of five-year, 7 percent bonds on June 1, 1998, when the market interest rate for similar bonds was 8 percent. Interest payment dates are June 1 and December 1 of each year. Naismith uses the effective-interest method to amortize bond discount or premium and has a December 31 fiscal year-end.

Required:
1. Prepare an amortization schedule for Naismith's bonds.
2. Prepare the appropriate journal entries in Naismith's accounting records on the following dates:
   a. June 1, 1998
   b. December 1, 1998
   c. December 31, 1998
3. Determine the carrying value of these bonds as of December 31, 1998.
4. Suppose now that on June 1, 1998, when these bonds were sold, the market interest rate for similar bonds was 6 percent. Prepare the appropriate journal entries in Naismith's accounting records on the following dates:
   a. June 1, 1998
   b. December 1, 1998
   c. December 31, 1998

PROBLEM SET B

49. Accounting for Bonds Payable, Straight-Line Method of Amortizing Bond Premium or Discount (LO 2)

The Hardaway Company issued $6,000,000 of four-year, 10 percent bonds on April 1, 1998. Interest payment dates are April 1 and October 1 of each year. Hardaway uses straight-line amortization for any bond premium or discount and has a December 31 fiscal year-end.

Required:

1. Determine the total proceeds Hardaway received from the sale of these bonds, assuming that the market interest rate for similar bonds on April 1, 1998, was:
   a. 8 percent.
   b. 12 percent.
2. Prepare the appropriate journal entries on the following dates for each assumption listed in (1):
   a. April 1, 1998
   b. October 1, 1998
   c. December 31, 1998
   d. April 1, 1999
3. For each assumption listed in (1), determine the carrying value of the bonds as of December 31, 1998.

50. Analyzing Long-Term Liabilities (LO 1, 6)

Pier 1 Imports, a Texas-based corporation, operates a chain of retail stores that sell furniture, decorative household items, gifts, and related items of merchandise. The following information was drawn from a recent set of Pier 1 financial statements. Amounts are expressed in thousands.

	Year 1	Year 2
Total assets	$460,497	$463,302
Long-term debt	167,073	169,798
Stockholders' equity	200,494	201,093
Interest expense	14,956	16,771
Income taxes expense	9,309	2,423
Net income	23,017	5,933

Required:

1. Compute Pier 1's long-term debt to equity and times interest earned ratios for Year 1 and Year 2. Did these ratios improve or weaken between the end of Year 1 and the end of Year 2?
2. Suppose that the average long-term debt to equity ratio for Pier 1's industry is 40 percent and that the average times interest earned ratio is 5.5. Evaluate the company's ratios in reference to these industry norms.
3. The following disclosure was included in a footnote entitled "Current and Long-Term Debt" that accompanied Pier 1's Year 2 financial statements.

   > The Company's loan agreements require that the Company maintain certain financial ratios and limit specific payments and equity distributions including cash dividends, loans to shareholders, and purchases of treasury stock. At year-end, the most restrictive of the agreements limits the aggregate of such payments to $10 million.

   What was the purpose of this disclosure?

51. Retirement of Bonds Payable (LO 2)

Follybeach Enterprises of Folly Beach, South Carolina, sold $5,000,000 of 8 percent bonds with a twenty-year term on May 15, 1992. Interest is paid semiannually on the bonds on May 15 and November 15. The bond indenture contains a call option that allows Follybeach to "call in" or retire the bonds on the ten-year anniversary date of their issue—May 15, 2002. This call provision requires Follybeach to pay the bondholders $1,050 for each bond.

Required:

1. Prepare the appropriate journal entry in Follybeach's accounting records if the company calls in the bonds on May 15, 2002. On that date, assume the carrying value of the bonds is $5,232,000.
2. Suppose that one of Follybeach's bondholders is very upset when he receives the notice that the bonds are being called in. He had purchased ten of the bonds six months earlier at a market price of 110. Is this person being "cheated" by Follybeach? Explain.

52. Selected Long-Term Liabilities in Corporate Balance Sheets (LO 1, 4)

Uncle Marcelle was until recently a retired truck driver who spent most of his free time either drinking coffee at the donut shop or playing bingo at the Moose hall. However, that changed recently when a large oil reservoir was discovered beneath three hundred acres of previously "dirt cheap" land he had inherited from his sister in west Texas. Now Marcelle is a "private investor." He has been studying recent financial statements of dozens of corporations and has uncovered the following long-term liabilities that he wants you to explain to him.

a. *Nonpension Postretirement Benefits—$486,800,000*
   This long-term liability was reported on a balance sheet of Kellogg, the cereal company.
b. *Convertible Debentures—$44,782,000*
   Dixie Yarns, Inc., a carpet and rug manufacturer, reported this long-term liability on a recent balance sheet.
c. *Long-Term Obligations under Capital Leases—$233,242*
   This item was included in a balance sheet of Jennifer Convertibles, Inc., a company that operates a line of specialty furniture stores.
d. *Deferred Service Contract Revenues—$29,058,000*
   Fretter, Inc., a consumer electronics retailer, recently reported this long-term liability.

Required:

Prepare a written report for Uncle Marcelle. Begin your report with a brief overview of the nature of liabilities and the general types of long-term liabilities. Next, provide a brief description of the nature and source of each of the long-term liabilities that Marcelle has identified. Include in your descriptions how each liability is related, or likely related if you are unsure, to the given company's profit-oriented activities.

53. Liabilities in International Financial Statements (LO 1, 6)

Rolls-Royce plc is an internationally known company headquartered in London. Following is selected information drawn from a recent annual report of Rolls-Royce. These amounts are expressed in millions of British pounds.

	Year 1	Year 2
Creditors—Amounts falling due within one year	1,263	1,173
Creditors—Amounts falling due after one year	543	514
Equity shareholders' funds	1,225	1,242
Interest payable (interest expense)	36	36
Taxation (income taxes expense)	18	20
Profit attributable to shareholders of Rolls-Royce plc (net income)	63	81

Required:

1. Compute Rolls-Royce's long-term debt to equity ratio and its times interest earned ratio for Year 1 and Year 2.
2. Compare Rolls-Royce's degree of financial leverage in Year 1 and Year 2 with the average degree of financial leverage for the U.S. industries listed in Exhibit 10.4. Was Rolls-Royce more or less leveraged in Year 1 and Year 2 than the average company in each of those industries?
3. According to the text, a comfortable level for the times interest earned ratio is 4.0 and higher. Were Rolls-Royce's times interest earned ratios in Year 1 and Year 2 "comfortable"?
4. Suppose that early in Year 3 you were considering investing in Rolls-Royce's common stock. Identify three questions that you would have wanted to ask of the company's controller regarding Rolls-Royce's long-term liabilities.

54. **(*Appendix*) Accounting for Bonds Payable, Effective-Interest Method of Amortizing Bond Premium or Discount** (LO 7)
The Anfernee Corporation sold $4,000,000 of four-year, 9 percent bonds on March 1, 1998, when the market interest rate for similar bonds was 8 percent. Interest payment dates are March 1 and September 1 of each year. Anfernee uses the effective-interest method to amortize bond discount or premium and has a December 31 fiscal year-end.

Required:

1. Prepare an amortization schedule for Anfernee's bonds.
2. Prepare the appropriate journal entries in Anfernee's accounting records on the following dates:
   a. March 1, 1998
   b. September 1, 1998
   c. December 31, 1998
3. Determine the carrying value of these bonds as of December 31, 1998.
4. Suppose now that on March 1, 1998, when these bonds were sold, the market interest rate for similar bonds was 10 percent. Prepare the appropriate journal entries in Anfernee's accounting records on the following dates:
   a. March 1, 1998
   b. September 1, 1998
   c. December 31, 1998

CASES

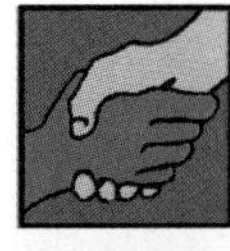

55. **Violation of Restrictive Debt Covenant** (LO 1)
Gharst Corporation is in danger of violating a restrictive debt covenant included in its bond indenture. The debt covenant requires Gharst to maintain no higher than a .5 long-term debt to equity ratio. If this ratio is higher than .5 at the end of any fiscal year, the bond issue becomes immediately due and payable. That is, the bondholders must immediately be paid the principal amount of the bonds they hold.

At the end of the third quarter of the current fiscal year, Gharst's long-term debt to equity ratio stood at .57. Gharst's management is now scrambling to find some way to reduce the ratio so that it is not above .5 at year-end. Several suggestions have been made by individual executives of the company.

a. One vice-president has suggested treating all new capital leases signed during the fourth quarter as operating leases. This will allow the company to avoid recording several hundred thousand dollars of capital lease obligations during the fourth quarter.

b. An assistant controller has suggested that the company sell a piece of land it has been holding to use as the site of a new production facility. The proceeds from the sale of this land could be used to pay down the balance of a large bank loan that Gharst has outstanding.
c. The chief financial officer believes the best solution is to sell additional Gharst common stock to outside investors. Selling additional common stock will increase total stockholders' equity and thus reduce the long-term debt to equity ratio.
d. A final solution recommended by another vice-president is to ask a finance company that Gharst owes nearly $1 million on a three-year note payable to change the note's maturity date. The finance company would be asked to temporarily change the note's maturity date so that it qualifies as a current liability at year-end.

Required:
1. Meet with the other members of your project group to discuss these suggestions. Why do lenders insist on including restrictive debt covenants in lending agreements?
2. Evaluate each of the proposed solutions to Gharst's problem. Are any of these solutions unethical? If so, why?
3. One member of your group should be prepared to present a summary overview to the class of the group's discussion of this case.

56. Times Interest Earned Ratio (LO 6)

A classmate of yours, Scott O'Grady, is having difficulty understanding the times interest earned ratio. Scott does not understand why interest expense and income taxes expense must be added to net income to determine the numerator of this ratio.

Required:
Write a concise but thoughtful memo to Scott explaining the "why" underlying the equation used to compute the times interest earned ratio. In your memo, use one or more examples to make your explanation crystal clear.

57. Financial Leverage (LO 2, 6)

Following are selected financial data for three companies of similar size that operate in the same industry. These amounts are in thousands of dollars and were taken from each firm's 1998 financial statements.

	Allen Company	Burns Company	Capote Company
Total assets	$100,600	$96,600	$105,400
Long-term debt	25,200	27,200	28,900
Stockholders' equity	41,200	37,300	44,600
Interest expense	4,900	3,000	3,500
Income taxes expense	1,600	2,500	2,700
Net income	2,500	3,800	4,100

Required:
1. Compute the long-term debt to equity and times interest earned ratios for each of these companies.
2. Suppose you discover that Allen Company is a foreign corporation. In Allen's home country, bond discount is not amortized over the term of bonds payable but instead is expensed in the year bonds are sold. In 1998, Allen wrote off as interest expense $2 million of bond discount on a new bond issue. Under GAAP, only $200,000 of this amount would have been charged off to interest expense.

Recompute Allen's interest expense, income taxes expense (assume an income tax rate of 40 percent), and net income for 1998 assuming the company used GAAP. Also, recompute the dollar amounts of Allen's year-end long-term debt and stockholders' equity. Finally, recompute Allen Company's long-term debt to equity and times interest earned ratios.

3. Are Allen's original financial data and financial ratios materially different from the company's financial data and financial ratios that result from applying the GAAP-based approach to accounting for bond discounts? Explain.

PROJECTS

58. Factors Affecting Bond Prices

In this group project, each group member should identify a corporate bond listed in the daily bond tables published in *The Wall Street Journal* and other major newspapers. The members of each group should select bonds of companies from different industries.

Required:

1. Each group member will plot the quoted market price of the bond he or she selected over the most recent one-year period. After you have selected a bond, identify the market price of the bond approximately one year ago. Then identify the bond's market price at monthly intervals up to the present date. These prices can be obtained from *The Wall Street Journal* or other major newspapers stored on microfilm or in some other form in your school's library. Once you have identified your bond's market price for each of the past twelve months, obtain a standard sheet of graph paper, prepare an appropriate scale, and then plot these market prices.
2. Meet as a group and compare and discuss the data individual group members collected in (1). Are the bond prices of the different companies closely correlated over the past twelve months? Is there a definite trend in these bond prices? If so, what factor or factors are likely responsible for this trend? If the market prices of one or more bonds are not consistent with an overall trend evident in bond prices over the past year, attempt to determine why by reviewing recent financial statements of the relevant firms and/or articles regarding those firms that have appeared recently in major business periodicals.
3. Each group should prepare a written report that summarizes the data collected by the individual group members in (1). The report should also summarize the issues addressed by the group in (2). One group member should be prepared to present a brief overview of the group's written report to the remainder of the class.

59. Classifying Liabilities

Companies in certain industries are not required to prepare classified balance sheets. Examples of such companies include stock brokerages, real estate firms, and life insurance companies. Generally, accounting standards allow companies to prepare unclassified balance sheets when the distinction between current and long-term assets and current and long-term liabilities is of little or no interest to financial statement users (*Statement of Financial Accounting Standards No. 6*, "Classification of Short-Term Obligations Expected to Be Refinanced").

Required:

1. Identify a company that does not prepare a classified balance sheet. List the liabilities included in this company's balance sheet and indicate those that you believe qualify as current liabilities and those that likely qualify as long-term liabilities. Next, compute the company's long-term debt to equity ratio. In your opinion, is this company highly leveraged? Explain.

2. Do you agree that assigning this company's assets and liabilities to current and long-term classifications would be irrelevant to financial statement users? Defend your answer.
3. Prepare a written report documenting your completion of (1) and (2).

60. Lease Disclosures

Identify several public companies whose financial statements are available on the Internet. These financial statements may be available from the companies' Web sites or from the EDGAR (electronic data gathering and retrieval system) Web site maintained by the Securities and Exchange Commission. Browse through these companies' financial statements until you identify two firms that have significant capital, or long-term, lease obligations reported on their balance sheets.

Required:

Prepare a report containing the following items for each of the companies you identified:

a. A summary of the key information included in the financial statement footnote that discusses the company's leasing transactions.
b. Each company's capital lease obligations as a percentage of (1) long-term liabilities, (2) total liabilities, and (3) property, plant & equipment.
c. Given the percentages just computed, your conclusion regarding whether or not leasing is a major method used by one or both companies to finance the acquisition of assets.
d. The Web site address from which you obtained the required data for each company.

V

ACCOUNTING FOR OWNERSHIP INTERESTS

Parts III and IV of this text addressed the principal accounting issues and rules related to assets and liabilities. This series of chapters focuses on the third of the three elements of the accounting equation, owners' equity. As you would expect given the major theme of this text, we will frequently consider the relevant information needs of decision makers as we discuss accounting for owners' equity. Because the corporation is the dominant form of business organization, our principal concern in these chapters is accounting for the stockholders' equity of corporations. Chapter 11 begins with an overview of the corporate form of business organization and then addresses the fundamental accounting issues and rules for stockholders' equity. Chapter 12 discusses financial reporting practices for corporations, including the structure and principal components of the corporate income statement and the statement of stockholders' equity.

Intercorporate investments and accounting for international operations are the topics of Chapter 13. Hostile takeovers, stock swaps, and other forms of intercorporate investments have become increasingly common in recent years. Another important business trend evident over the last few decades is the evolution of a global economy. To increase their revenues and profits, many U.S. businesses have established operating units in foreign countries or formed partnerships with foreign firms. The increasing frequency of intercorporate investments and international business operations complicate the efforts of accountants to provide useful financial data to decision makers.

This section concludes with Module 3, which discusses accounting for the ownership interests of sole proprietorships and partnerships. These business organizations account for approximately 11 percent of gross business revenues each year in the United States; corporations account for the remainder. Nevertheless, more than 80 percent of all businesses in this country are unincorporated. Approximately 75 percent of U.S. businesses are sole proprietorships, while approximately 7 percent are partnerships.

The Corporate Form of Business Organization: Accounting for Stockholders' Equity

11

"A corporation is an artificial being, invisible, intangible, and existing only in contemplation of law."
Chief Justice John Marshall

LEARNING OBJECTIVES

After studying this chapter, you should be able to do the following:

1. Describe the important characteristics, advantages, and disadvantages of the corporate form of business organization.
2. Identify the key characteristics of corporate stock and the rights and privileges of common and preferred stockholders.
3. Define the key information needs of decision makers regarding stockholders' equity.
4. Account for the issuance of corporate stock.
5. Account for treasury stock transactions, cash and stock dividends, and stock splits.
6. Discuss key control activities for stockholders' equity.
7. Compute and interpret return on equity.

FOCUS ON DECISION MAKING

Going Public: The Price Is Right . . . Hopefully

In 1992, Scott Beck, chief executive of Boston Chicken, Inc., realized his company needed cash, lots of cash. And fast. Boston Chicken (now known as Boston Market) was a small, privately owned corporation operating a chain of restaurants specializing in roasted chicken and healthy side dishes such as zucchini marinara. The company had grown rapidly since its founding in 1985. However, by the early 1990s, several larger and better financed competitors had recognized that Boston Chicken's menu items appealed to a wide cross section of health-conscious Americans. These companies were pouring millions of dollars into developing and advertising similar products. If Boston Chicken did not move quickly to expand, competitors would capture a significant portion of the company's potential market.

To raise the funds that his company needed, Scott Beck chose to do what hundreds of other executives of small but rapidly growing companies have done in recent years: sell stock to the public in an initial public offering or IPO. Each year during the mid-1990s more than 500 companies "went public." These firms raised more than $30 billion annually during that timeframe, principally from individual investors.

Accountants play an important role when a company goes public since an IPO involves complex accounting and financial reporting requirements. If these requirements are not met, an IPO can be delayed for weeks or months, leaving a company starving for cash. Accountants also help management collect and analyze the data needed to arrive at an initial selling price for a company's stock. Among the data used for this purpose are the company's projected future earnings and the relationship between similar firms' earnings and stock prices.

Establishing an initial selling price for a company's stock is a critical decision. If a company places an unrealistically high price on its stock, an IPO may fail because the stock sells poorly or not at all. Take the case of the 1993 IPO for Wilt Chamberlain's Restaurants. Despite the high or "tall" profile of the firm's principal owner, the company canceled the IPO after failing to generate sufficient interest in its stock. Apparently, investors perceived the "asking" price of the company's stock to be unreasonably high. On the other hand, if a company establishes an initial price for its stock that is too low, speculators will snap up the shares at that price and then resell them later at a higher price.

Scott Beck eventually settled on a $20 per share offering price for his company's stock. As it turned out, that price was too low, much too low. The perception that Boston Chicken was the next McDonald's of the restaurant industry sent the company's stock soaring. On the first day of trading, Boston Chicken's stock leaped from $20 to $51 per share. Boston Chicken raised approximately $38 million by selling 1.9 million shares in its IPO. However, if the company's stock had been initially priced at $51 per share, the company could have raised nearly $100 million. Over the next few years, the price of Boston Chicken's common stock gradually declined, falling by 1996 to near its original $20 offering price.

Photography by JoeHiggins

Corporations "go public" by selling their stock in an initial public offering or IPO. The company now known as Boston Market raised nearly $40 million of equity capital when it went public in 1992.

Business owners who need to raise a large amount of funds to build a factory, buy another company, or establish a foreign subsidiary have two principal financing alternatives. They can raise debt capital by borrowing funds, or they can raise equity capital by selling a portion of their ownership interests to outside parties. Corporations often raise equity capital by selling common stock, the approach taken by Boston Chicken in the early 1990s, as described in the opening vignette. This chapter focuses on the accounting issues and rules related to the stockholders' equity of corporations. The chapter begins with an overview of the corporate form of business organization. Next, the information needs of decision makers regarding stockholders' equity are identified, followed by a discussion of accounting procedures for major stockholders' equity transactions. The final two sections of this chapter focus on control activities and a key financial ratio related to stockholders' equity.

AN INTRODUCTION TO THE CORPORATE FORM OF BUSINESS ORGANIZATION

Although corporations have been used throughout this text to illustrate accounting issues and procedures, we have not yet examined in depth this form of business organization. This section better acquaints you with corporations by first defining a corporation and describing how one is created. Next, we identify the advantages and disadvantages of the corporate form of business organization. Finally, we consider the major types and characteristics of corporate stock, including the rights and privileges associated with each.

LEARNING OBJECTIVE 1
Describe the important characteristics, advantages, and disadvantages of the corporate form of business organization.

Corporations: Artificial and Invisible Beings

Chief Justice John Marshall provided a legalistic definition of a corporation in a famous legal case of the early nineteenth century. That definition serves as the opening

Dynatech Corporation's Statement of Corporate Citizenship

Corporations have often been criticized for being poor, or at least indifferent, citizens of the communities in which they maintain their major operating units. In recent years, many corporations have attempted to blunt such criticism by becoming more active in community affairs. One such firm is Dynatech Corporation, a company that markets voice, data, and video communication products. Following is Dynatech's Statement of Corporate Citizenship that appeared in a recent annual report of the company.

Statement of Corporate Citizenship, Dynatech Corporation As we produce growing profits for our employees and stockholders, we feel an obligation to reach out to the communities where we employ people. Our corporate contributions policy has therefore been changed to direct our contributions (money and volunteered employee time) primarily to the communities where we work. Charitable contributions are now focused on educational opportunities, medical care research, and children's issues. Our employees have the opportunities to select and concentrate efforts helping meet the needs of citizens in their own communities.

quote for this chapter. Recall that Chapter 1 presented the following definition of a corporation: an association of individuals, created by law and having an existence apart from that of its members as well as distinct and inherent powers and liabilities. When the owners of a business decide to incorporate, they file articles of incorporation with a state agency—corporations are established by individual states, not by the federal government. Among other items, articles of incorporation identify the business's purpose, its principal operating units, and the type and quantity of stock that it plans to issue. If all legal requirements are met, the state agency grants the business a corporate charter. A corporate charter is a contract between a corporation and the state in which it was created and identifies the corporation's principal rights and obligations.

When John Q. Public hears the term "corporation," names like Coca-Cola, General Motors, and United Airlines are likely to pop into his head. However, most corporations are small businesses and "closely-held." The stock of closely-held corporations is owned by a few individuals, often members of the same family, and is not publicly traded on a securities exchange. Approximately two million incorporated businesses, or roughly one-half of all corporations, qualify as "S corporations" under the Internal Revenue Code. One requirement to qualify as an S corporation is to have 35 or fewer stockholders. S corporations retain most of the advantages of the corporate form of organization, but they avoid a key disadvantage, namely, the double taxation of corporate profits, which is discussed shortly.

Key Advantages of the Corporate Form of Business Organization

Corporations have several advantages compared with the other primary types of business organizations, sole proprietorships and partnerships. There are also disadvantages of incorporating a business. Exhibit 11.1 summarizes the key advantages and disadvantages of the corporate form of business organization.

An important advantage of corporations over other forms of business organizations is the limited liability of corporate stockholders. In practically all cases, the maximum financial loss a stockholder faces is his or her original investment in a corporation. If a corporation files for bankruptcy, the unpaid debts of the firm cannot be recovered from the personal assets of its stockholders. If a partnership folds without paying all of its debts, each member of the firm is individually responsible for those debts. In the early 1990s, the accounting firm of Laventhol & Horwath, which was organized as a partnership, was declared bankrupt by a federal court. The former Laventhol & Horwath partners were required to contribute up to $400,000 each to pay off the firm's remaining liabilities.[1]

Unlike sole proprietorships and partnerships, the legal existence of a corporation is unaffected by the death or withdrawal of individual owners. Upon the death of a corporate stockholder, the individual's ownership interest in the firm passes directly to his or her estate or heirs. A partnership must be dissolved when one partner leaves the firm—although the remaining partners have the option of immediately forming a new partnership.

Corporations also benefit from the ease with which stockholders can transfer their ownership interests to other parties. A corporate stockholder can sell his or her ownership interest without the prior approval of the other owners, which is typically not true for the members of a partnership.

Generally, corporations can raise equity capital more readily and in larger amounts than unincorporated businesses. Even small corporations, as proven by Boston Chicken, can raise large amounts of capital very quickly by selling stock on a nationwide basis via an IPO.

EXHIBIT 11.1 ▼

Key Advantages and Disadvantages of the Corporate Form of Business Organization

Advantages	Disadvantages
• Limited liability of stockholders • Continuity of existence • Ease of transferring ownership interests • Access to equity capital • Professional management	• Double taxation of corporate profits • Extensive regulatory oversight • Potentially higher level of credit risk

1. L. Berton, "Laventhol Ex-Partners Face PTL Claims," *The Wall Street Journal,* 19 August 1992, B5.

An important advantage of large corporations is their ability to retain professional management teams. The resources of these firms allow them to employ skilled financial executives, marketing experts, professional accountants, and talented individuals in the other functional areas of business. Proprietorships, partnerships, and small corporations may also have talented individuals in their key positions. However, the limited financial resources of most small businesses makes it very difficult for them to compete with large corporations in hiring skilled professionals.

Key Disadvantages of the Corporate Form of Business Organization

The key disadvantage posed by the corporate form of business organization is the double taxation of corporate profits. Corporations are considered taxable entities, meaning that they must pay income taxes on their annual earnings. These profits are taxed again when corporations distribute earnings in the form of cash dividends since stockholders must report these dividends as income on their individual tax returns. The income of sole proprietorships and partnerships—and S corporations—is not taxed. Instead, the owners of such businesses report their firm's profits, or their proportionate share of their firm's profits in the case of partnerships, on their individual tax returns. (This is true whether or not the profits are distributed to the owners.)

All businesses are subject to some degree of regulatory oversight at the local, state, and federal levels. However, corporations are generally subject to more regulatory oversight than other businesses. For example, corporations that sell their stock to the public on an interstate basis must comply with the extensive accounting and financial reporting requirements of the Securities and Exchange Commission (SEC). If these firms list their stock on a securities exchange, such as the New York Stock Exchange, they are subject to the rules and regulations of that organization as well.

Occasionally, some of the items listed previously as advantages of the corporate form of business organization "backfire." For example, a small corporation may be rejected for a bank loan because of the limited liability feature of corporations. Bank loan officers realize that only corporate assets, not the personal assets of stockholders, can be seized to satisfy unpaid principal or interest payments if a corporation defaults on a loan. As a result, small corporations pose a higher level of credit risk than sole proprietorships and partnerships of comparable size. To gain approval of a loan application, one or more individual stockholders of a small corporation may agree to personally guarantee the loan.

Corporate Stock

LEARNING OBJECTIVE 2 ▶ Identify the key characteristics of corporate stock and the rights and privileges of common and preferred stockholders.

A corporation's charter grants it the right to issue a maximum number of shares of each designated class of stock. If a corporate charter identifies only one class of stock, that stock is automatically considered the corporation's **common stock.** Common stock represents the residual ownership interests in a corporation. If a corporation is liquidated (goes out of business), common stockholders are entitled to share proportionately in its remaining assets after all other obligations have been satisfied. These obligations include current and long-term liabilities and any amounts that must be paid to other classes of stockholders.

common stock

preferred stock

If a corporate charter identifies a second class of stock, it is usually a preferred stock. As you will discover, individuals who own a corporation's **preferred stock** have certain preferences or privileges compared with the company's common stockholders.

For each class of a corporation's stock, **authorized stock** refers to the maximum number of shares the firm is permitted to issue. **Issued stock** refers to the number of shares that have been sold or otherwise distributed, while **outstanding stock** is the number of shares owned by a company's stockholders. The corporate charter of The Home Depot, Inc., authorizes the company to issue up to one billion shares of common stock. A recent annual report of Home Depot disclosed that 477,106,000 shares of that stock were "issued and outstanding." Occasionally, companies reacquire some of their stock. **Treasury stock** is the term used when referring to such shares—these shares are typically maintained by a company's treasury department. When a company has reacquired some of its stock, the difference between the firm's issued stock and its treasury stock equals its outstanding stock.

authorized stock

issued stock

outstanding stock

treasury stock

COMMON STOCK: RIGHTS AND PRIVILEGES OF COMMON STOCKHOLDERS As just noted, common stockholders have the right to share proportionally in the residual assets of a corporation upon liquidation. Common stockholders also have the right to share proportionately in any distribution of earnings. For example, suppose that a company has 10,000 shares of outstanding common stock and decides to distribute a cash dividend of $50,000 to its common stockholders. Each common stockholder would be entitled to a $5 dividend ($50,000/10,000 shares) for each share he or she owns. The dividend could not be allocated exclusively to a few stockholders.

In most states, common stockholders have what is known as the **preemptive right,** or the right to retain their fractional ownership interest in a corporation. If a company issues additional common stock, each stockholder must be allowed to purchase a sufficient number of those shares to maintain his or her proportionate ownership interest in the firm.

preemptive right

Possibly the most important legal privilege of common stockholders is the right to vote on key matters facing a corporation, including the periodic election of a board of directors. A board of directors establishes a corporation's long-range objectives and operating policies. A corporation's officers, which are selected by its board of directors, have the responsibility for carrying out the board's policies. Typically, the top executives of a corporation, such as the chief executive officer and one or more senior vice presidents, serve on the firm's board of directors.

COMMON STOCK: PAR VALUE, NO-PAR, AND STATED VALUE Exhibit 11.2 presents an example of a common stock certificate. Most corporate charters designate par values for the different classes of stock that a company is permitted to issue. **Par value** represents a nominal dollar value assigned to each share of a given class of stock. In certain states, the collective par value of issued common stock establishes a firm's "legal capital." Corporations in these states are generally not permitted to allow their total stockholders' equity to fall below their legal capital. This requirement explains why par values are typically set at very low, or nominal, dollar amounts. For example, the par value of Home Depot's common stock is $.05, while the common stock of Dean Witter, Discover & Co. has a par value of $.01. Although a common stock's par value has limited, if any, economic significance, it does influence how the sale of the stock is recorded, as we shall see later.

par value

Some corporate charters do not designate a par value for a company's common stock. Such common stock is known as no-par stock. A company's board of directors may assign a **stated value** to a no-par common stock, which is a nominal dollar value essentially equivalent to a par value. Why go to the trouble of assigning a stated value

stated value

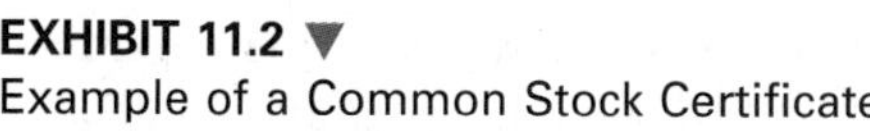

EXHIBIT 11.2 ▼
Example of a Common Stock Certificate

to no-par common stock? Answer: Because some states do not allow companies to issue common stock that does not have either a par value or a stated value.

PREFERRED STOCK: RIGHTS AND PRIVILEGES OF PREFERRED STOCKHOLDERS As noted previously, preferred stockholders have certain preferences relative to a corporation's common stockholders. The two most important of these preferences involve the payment of dividends, both normal cash dividends and liquidating dividends. Preferred stockholders are usually entitled to receive an annual cash dividend per share. For example, Alumax Inc., the nation's third largest producer of aluminum products, has preferred stock outstanding on which a $4.00 annual dividend is paid. Before Alumax's common stockholders can receive a dividend in a given year, the firm's preferred stockholders must be paid a $4.00 dividend. When a corporation is liquidated, preferred stockholders must be paid the par value, or other predetermined liquidation value, of their stock before common stockholders receive any distribution of cash or other assets.

Besides preferences to dividends, preferred stockholders have the same rights as those identified previously for common stockholders, unless stated otherwise in the corporate charter. One stockholder right that corporate charters typically withhold from preferred stockholders is the voting privilege.

cumulative preferred stock

PREFERRED STOCK: DISTINCTIVE FEATURES Preferred stocks typically have one or more distinctive features. For example, preferred stocks are usually cumulative. If a corporation fails to pay a dividend in a given year on a **cumulative preferred stock,** that dividend accumulates and must be paid in the future before common stockholders can receive a dividend. Most preferred stocks also have a call provision attached to them. **Callable preferred stock** can be reacquired, or "called in," at the option of the issuing corporation. When a company reacquires its preferred stock, a call premium must generally be paid. That is, the redemption price of a callable preferred stock usually exceeds its initial selling price. Similar to convertible bonds, **convertible preferred stock** may be exchanged at the option of preferred stockholders for the issuing corporation's common stock.

callable preferred stock

convertible preferred stock

STOCKHOLDERS' EQUITY: KEY INFORMATION NEEDS OF DECISION MAKERS

LEARNING OBJECTIVE 3
Define the key information needs of decision makers regarding stockholders' equity.

Corporate stockholders and potential stockholders represent a large and important class of financial decision makers. For these parties to make wise investment decisions regarding corporate equity securities, they need a wide range of financial information concerning the stockholders' equity of corporations. Here, we consider three such items of information.

Stockholder Rights and Privileges

Suppose your Uncle Bob has been given a "hot tip" by a domino-playing friend of his in the local old folks home. Because of this tip, Uncle Bob plans to invest much of his retirement nest egg in Woolworth Corporation's preferred stock. Before calling his broker, Bob asks for your advice on this matter. So, what do you do at this point? Probably first you would obtain a copy of Woolworth's most recent annual report. Being a sophisticated financial statement user, you realize that annual report will discuss the key features of the company's preferred stock. Exhibit 11.3 contains the paragraph describing Woolworth's preferred stock that was included in a recent annual report of the firm.

After reading the paragraph shown in Exhibit 11.3, you know much more about the preferred stock Uncle Bob plans to purchase. For example, you know the stock pays a \$2.20 annual dividend. After checking a recent edition of *The Wall Street Journal*, you determine that the stock is selling for \$120 per share. Now, you can compute the stock's "dividend yield," which is its annual dividend divided by its current

EXHIBIT 11.3 ▼
Disclosures in Recent Annual Report of Woolworth Corporation Regarding the Company's Preferred Stock

At January 27, 1996, the 97,326 outstanding shares of \$2.20 Series A Convertible Preferred Stock had a liquidation value of \$45.00 per share, or \$4.4 million. The stock is cumulative, voting and convertible at any time at the option of the holder, at the rate of 5.68 shares of common stock for each share of preferred stock, subject to anti-dilution provisions. A total of 552,812 shares of common stock has been reserved for the conversion. At the option of the company, the preferred stock is redeemable at liquidation value, subject to a holder's right to convert such shares into shares of common stock prior to the date fixed for redemption.

market price. The Woolworth preferred stock has a meager dividend yield of 1.8 percent ($2.20/$120). This surprises you since preferred stocks typically have a dividend yield comparable to the current yield on high-quality corporate bonds. Since such bonds currently yield 10 percent, the Woolworth preferred stock should be selling for about $22 per share, given its $2.20 annual dividend ($22 × 10% = $2.20).

Apparently, some factor other than dividend yield accounts for the current selling price of Woolworth's preferred stock. One such factor could be the stock's conversion feature. As indicated in Exhibit 11.3, each share of Woolworth's preferred stock can be converted into 5.68 shares of the company's common stock. You check the most recent price of Woolworth's common stock and discover that it is selling for $21 per share. So, the conversion feature of the preferred stock has a value of approximately $120 ($21 × 5.68) per share, which is also the current market price of that stock. In fact, the market price of a convertible preferred stock is often linked directly to the market price of the common stock to which it can be converted.

The disclosures included in Exhibit 11.3 provide you with other valuable information to pass along to Uncle Bob. For instance, the Woolworth preferred stock, like most preferred stocks, is cumulative. If Woolworth skips a dividend on the preferred stock, it must pay that dividend in the future before making any dividend payments to common stockholders. You will also want to explain to Uncle Bob that Woolworth can redeem the preferred stock for $45 per share. Before forcing preferred stockholders to cash in their shares at that price, Woolworth will permit them to convert those shares into common stock.

The moral to be learned from the Uncle Bob tale is that investors should identify the rights and privileges attached to the different classes of a corporation's stock. Identifying such information is particularly important for preferred stocks. Unlike common stocks, the rights and privileges assigned to preferred stocks typically vary across corporations.

Earnings Data

Current and prospective stockholders of a corporation need and demand information allowing them to assess the profitability of the firm. Of particular interest to these parties are earnings per share data for a company's common stock in recent years. (Chapter 12 illustrates the computation of earnings per share.) Investors often use a company's earnings trend to predict its future stock price. Unfortunately, the trend of a company's earnings is not necessarily a reliable predictor of the direction its stock price will take in the future. During the spring of 1996, both Baby Superstore, a retailer of children's products, and Compaq Computer reported significant increases in earnings.[2] Given this good news, one might reasonably expect that each company's stock price subsequently rose. But, that wasn't the case. Following the announcement of a 45 percent increase in earnings, the price of Baby Superstore's common stock plunged 12 percent. On the other hand, Compaq's stock leaped three dollars per share, more than 7 percent, shortly after the company announced an 8 percent increase in earnings.

There was a key difference between these two cases that explained the behavior of each company's stock price. At the same time that Baby Superstore reported an in-

2. D. A. Blackmon, "Baby Superstore Posts Rise in Net, But Stock Falls," *The Wall Street Journal,* 4 March 1996, A9; L. R. Rublin, "Compaq's Earnings Report Buoys the Market, But on Reflection, the Details Look Less Than Cheery," *Barron's,* 29 April 1996, MW3.

crease in earnings, financial analysts expressed concern regarding control weaknesses within the firm that had resulted in a significant error in the company's reported cash balance. This concern drove down the price of Baby Superstore's common stock despite the impressive increase in earnings. Investors bid up the price of Compaq's common stock following its reported increase in earnings. Investors' interest in the stock was fueled by anticipation that new Compaq products would send the firm's earnings even higher in the future. The moral here is that earnings per share data are important but must be used cautiously when the objective is to predict the future direction of a company's stock price. Besides earnings data, investors must obtain and analyze a wide array of other relevant information when forecasting the future price of a common stock.

Dividend Information

When it comes to any specific investment, the principal concern of most investors can be summarized in one brief question: "How much cash will this investment produce for me in the future?" To predict future cash flows from corporate investments, investors need information concerning the dividend policies of corporations and the factors that may affect those policies. Retirees, for example, often rely heavily on dividend income. The common stocks of "Baby Bells" are particularly favored investments of retirees since these stocks have historically paid high dividends. In 1996, PacTel (Pacific Telesis) slashed its dividend by more than 40 percent. Such dividend cuts force many retirees to suddenly rethink their cash budgets.

The SEC recognizes the importance of dividend information for decision makers. Companies subject to the SEC's regulations must disclose the cash dividends they have paid over their five most recent fiscal years. Additionally, these companies must disclose any significant restrictions on the payment of dividends, such as restrictive debt covenants included in a bond indenture. The SEC also encourages companies to discuss their dividend policies in their annual reports. Shown next is such a disclosure included in the annual report issued in 1996 by Mark Twain Bancshares, Inc., a St. Louis-based banking firm.

> Dividends paid during 1995 increased 12.5% to $1.08 per share from $0.96 per share in 1994. This represents a dividend payout ratio of 36.86%. The Company expects to maintain a payout ratio between 35% and 45%. [Note: A firm's dividend payout ratio is computed by dividing the firm's total dividend per share for a given year by its earnings per share for that year.]

Preferred stocks typically have a predetermined annual dividend rate. However, most corporate charters do not require preferred stock dividends to be paid in any given year. When a dividend is not paid on a cumulative preferred stock, a corporation must maintain a record of these **dividends in arrears.** As suggested earlier, before a company can pay a common stock dividend, dividends in arrears on cumulative preferred stock must be paid. Dividends in arrears should be disclosed in the footnotes to a company's financial statements. Talley Industries, Inc., a manufacturing firm, recently disclosed in its annual report approximately $10 million of dividends in arrears on its outstanding cumulative preferred stock. Investors find such disclosures informative since dividends in arrears affect the ability of a company to pay dividends in the future, particularly to common stockholders.

dividends in arrears

ACCOUNTING FOR STOCKHOLDERS' EQUITY

This section examines accounting decisions for the major types of stockholders' equity transactions. Among the stockholders' equity transactions we consider are the issuance of stock by a corporation, treasury stock transactions, dividends, and stock splits. Before considering procedural accounting issues for stockholders' equity, you will find it helpful to briefly review the stockholders' equity section of a corporate balance sheet.

Stockholders' Equity in the Corporate Balance Sheet

Exhibit 11.4 presents the stockholders' equity section of Dollar General Corporation's 1996 balance sheet. Dollar General operates a large chain of general merchandise stores located principally in the southeastern United States. Notice that instead of "stockholders' equity," Dollar General prefers the synonymous term "shareholders' equity." Also notice that there are five components of Dollar General's stockholders' equity: preferred stock, common stock, additional paid-in capital, retained earnings, and treasury stock. The stockholders' equity section of a balance sheet provides brief descriptive information regarding a company's equity securities. For example, Dollar General's balance sheet identifies the par value of its common and preferred stock and the number of authorized and issued shares of each.

book value per share

Many companies disclose in their annual report a book value per share for their common stock. **Book value per share** is computed by dividing total common stockholders' equity by the number of common shares outstanding. Dollar General's com-

EXHIBIT 11.4 ▼
Stockholders' Equity Section of Dollar General Corporation's 1996 Balance Sheet

	1995	1996
	(in thousands)	
Shareholders' equity:		
Preferred stock, stated value, $.50 per share:		
Shares authorized: 5,000,000		
Issued: 1995—1,716,000; 1996—1,716,000	$ 858	$ 858
Common stock, par value, $.50 per share:		
Shares authorized: 100,000,000		
Issued: 1995—67,942,000; 1996—85,524,000	33,971	42,762
Additional paid-in capital	283,323	303,609
Retained earnings	207,436	273,309
	$525,588	$620,538
Less treasury stock (common stock), at cost:		
Shares: 1995—11,472,000; 1996—13,404,000	201,832	200,527
Total shareholders' equity	$323,756	$420,011

mon stock had a book value per share of $5.72 and $5.81 at the end of 1995 and 1996, respectively. The book value per share at the end of 1996 was computed as follows:

$$\text{Book Value per Share} = \frac{\text{Common Stockholders' Equity}}{\text{Shares of Common Stock Outstanding}}$$

$$\text{Book Value per Share} = \frac{\$420{,}011{,}000 - \$858{,}000}{}$$

$$\text{Book Value per Share} = \$5.81$$

Notice that Dollar General's common stockholders' equity was determined by subtracting the company's preferred stockholders' equity from its total stockholders' equity. Additionally, the company's outstanding common stock was computed by subtracting its 13,404,000 shares of treasury stock from the total shares issued.

Issuance of Common Stock

Corporations issue stock in a wide array of different transactions. Here, we consider the accounting treatment for the most common of these transactions.

LEARNING OBJECTIVE 4
Account for the issuance of corporate stock.

SALE OF PAR VALUE COMMON STOCK According to *Accounting Trends & Techniques,* more than 90 percent of all common stocks have a par value. Suppose that Blue Onion Grill, Inc., a trendy restaurant chain, sells 30,000 shares of its $1 par value common stock for $12 per share. Following is the entry to record this transaction.

Mar. 9	Cash	360,000	
	Common Stock		30,000
	Additional Paid-In Capital, Common Stock		330,000
	To record sale of 30,000 shares of common stock at $12 per share		

Notice that the collective par value of the stock sold by Blue Onion Grill (30,000 shares × $1 = $30,000) is credited to Common Stock. The remaining proceeds from the sale ($360,000 − $30,000 = $330,000) are credited to Additional Paid-In Capital, Common Stock. *Key Point to Remember: Corporations are not allowed to recognize gains or losses on the sale of their own stock.* The sale of a corporation's own stock is a financing transaction. That is, the intent is to raise funds to meet the financing needs of the firm, not to generate a profit. Any amounts in excess of par value received from the sale of common stock must be recorded in a permanent stockholders' equity account.

EXCHANGE OF PAR VALUE COMMON STOCK FOR NONCASH ASSETS Occasionally, corporations exchange their common stock for equipment, buildings, or other assets. Either the fair market value of the stock issued or the asset acquired, whichever is more evident, should be used as the basis for recording such a transaction. Suppose that Blue Onion Grill agrees to exchange 9,000 shares of its $1 par value common stock for an office building. Blue Onion's stock is publicly traded and has a market value of $14 per share on the date this exchange takes place. Like most real estate, the fair market value of the building being acquired is not readily apparent. So, the total market value of the Blue Onion stock issued in exchange for the building, $126,000 (9,000 shares × $14), would be used to determine the building's acquisition cost. The following entry would be made to record this transaction.

Nov. 21	Buildings	126,000	
	Common Stock		9,000
	Additional Paid-In Capital, Common Stock		117,000
	To record exchange of 9,000 shares of common stock for office building (asset no. A-5)		

Suppose now that Blue Onion's common stock does not have a readily determinable market value because it is not publicly traded. In this case, company officials would use the appraised value of the building as the basis for recording the exchange transaction. Assume that a real estate appraiser assigns a fair market value of $133,000 to the building. The acquisition of the building would be recorded with a $133,000 debit to the Buildings account, a $9,000 credit to Common Stock, and a $124,000 credit to Additional Paid-In Capital, Common Stock.

SALE OF NO-PAR COMMON STOCK Baylee Almon, Inc., has no-par common stock to which a $5 stated value per share has been assigned. To record the sale of 5,000 shares of this stock for $17 per share, the entry shown next would be appropriate.

Apr. 19	Cash	85,000	
	Common Stock		25,000
	Additional Paid-In Capital, Common Stock		60,000
	To record sale of 5,000 shares of common stock at $17 per share		

Recognize that the entry just shown is no different from the entry that would be made if the stock had a par value of $5 instead of a stated value of $5. For companies whose common stock does not have a par value or a stated value, the total proceeds from the sale of common stock are credited to the Common Stock account. For example, if the no-par common stock of Baylee Almon did not have a stated value, the $85,000 proceeds from the sale of the 5,000 shares would be credited entirely to the Common Stock account.

Sale of Preferred Stock

Accounting Trends & Techniques reports that approximately 25 percent of publicly owned companies have one or more classes of preferred stock. Accounting for the issuance of preferred stock is very similar to accounting for the issuance of common stock. For example, suppose that Blue Onion Grill sells 6,000 shares of $100 par value preferred stock at a price of $102 per share. The total proceeds from the sale of this

Yahoo for *Yahoo!*

FOR YOUR INFORMATION

The opening vignette for this chapter focused on the 1992 IPO of Boston Chicken. Recall that Boston Chicken's stock soared from an original offering price of $20 per share to more than $50 per share on its first day of trading. The 1996 IPO of Yahoo! Inc. witnessed an even larger percentage increase in a new public company's stock price. Yahoo!, a company founded in the early 1990s by two college students, provides Internet search services. The company originally offered its common stock for sale in April 1996 at $13 per share. Midway through the first day the stock was publicly traded it was fetching a price of $43 per share. Once the mania surrounding a highly touted new stock subsides, the stock's price often plummets. By the late summer of 1996, Yahoo! stock was selling for $16 per share.

stock, $612,000, would be debited to Cash. The offsetting credits would be to Preferred Stock ($600,000) and Additional Paid-In Capital, Preferred Stock ($12,000).

Treasury Stock Transactions

LEARNING OBJECTIVE 5
Account for treasury stock transactions, cash and stock dividends, and stock splits.

In February 1997, Merck, & Co., one of the nation's largest pharmaceutical firms, announced plans to repurchase approximately four percent of its outstanding common stock.[3] Merck estimated that the stock buyback plan would cost $5 billion. Stock buyback plans are not unusual for large public corporations. If corporate executives believe their company's common stock is selling for less than its actual value, the firm may purchase large blocks of the stock. Corporations typically resell such shares at a later date when the stock's market price has risen.

To illustrate treasury stock transactions, we can use the data presented in Exhibit 11.4 for the treasury stock held by Dollar General Corporation. Like most companies, Dollar General records its treasury stock at cost. On a per share basis, the average cost of Dollar General's treasury stock at the end of 1996 was approximately $14.96 ($200,527,000/13,404,000). For illustration purposes, assume that Dollar General purchased the treasury stock in one transaction. The firm would have recorded this transaction by debiting Treasury Stock and crediting Cash for $200,527,000 each. Now, suppose that a few months later Dollar General resold 5,000 shares of this treasury stock at a price of $20 per share. The collective cost of these shares was $74,800 ($14.96 × 5,000), and Dollar General would have received $100,000 ($20 × 5,000) from their sale. Shown next is the entry to record this transaction.

May 15	Cash	100,000	
	Treasury Stock		74,800
	Additional Paid-In Capital,		
	Treasury Stock Transactions		25,200
	To record sale of 5,000 shares of treasury stock at $20 per share		

3. "Buyback Totaling $5 billion Is Unveiled by Drug Maker," *The Wall Street Journal*, 26 February 1997, B7.

When treasury stock is sold for more than cost, the difference between the proceeds and the stock's cost is credited to an additional paid-in capital account. Many novice accountants might be tempted to credit the $25,200 amount in the previous entry to an account such as "Gain on Sale of Treasury Stock." However, remember, a company cannot recognize gains or losses on the sale of its own stock, including treasury stock. If Dollar General subsequently sells 2,000 shares of its treasury stock for $12.00 per share, a loss would not be recorded on this transaction. Instead, the difference between the proceeds of the sale, $24,000 ($12 × 2,000), and the cost of the treasury stock, $29,920 ($14.96 × 2,000), would be debited to Additional Paid-In Capital, Treasury Stock Transactions as shown in the following entry.

June 12	Cash	24,000	
	Additional Paid-In Capital, Treasury Stock Transactions	5,920	
	Treasury Stock		29,920
	To record sale of 2,000 shares of treasury stock at $12.00 per share		

Dividends

LEARNING OBJECTIVE 5 ▶ Account for treasury stock transactions, cash and stock dividends, and stock splits.

Naive financial statement users often assume that the retained earnings figure reported in a corporate balance sheet represents a cash fund accumulated by a company over its existence. Not true. Retained earnings is simply a general ledger account in which entries are made each accounting period. Just because a company has a large amount of retained earnings does not mean it has the ability to pay dividends. Why? Because company executives may have reinvested those earnings in the company. A company's executives may have used the cash flows stemming from the firm's profits to purchase new equipment, develop new products, or acquire a jet aircraft to zip them to and from important meetings.

Here, our concern is not companies that choose to retain earnings indefinitely but instead those that "share the wealth" with their stockholders. Companies that have paid dividends regularly to their stockholders for an extended period typically broadcast this fact in their annual reports. Tootsie Roll Industries is one of the few companies that can boast of having paid quarterly cash dividends for more than fifty consecutive years.

cash dividend

CASH DIVIDENDS A **cash dividend** is a proportionate distribution of a company's prior earnings to its stockholders made in the form of cash. Companies that pay cash dividends typically do so on a regular basis. Although some companies pay semiannual or annual dividends, by far the most common approach is to pay quarterly cash dividends.

Before a company can distribute a cash dividend to its stockholders, three conditions must normally be met. First, a company must obviously have sufficient cash available. Second, a company must have sufficient "unrestricted" retained earnings. Suppose that a company has several million dollars of available cash and a $5 million balance in its Retained Earnings account. Although the firm has considerable cash and retained earnings, the company may be prohibited from paying dividends due to a restrictive covenant in a bond indenture. The final condition that must be met before a cash dividend can be paid is a formal dividend declaration, or authorization, by a company's board of directors.[4]

A corporation's accountants consider three dates when accounting for and maintaining control over cash dividend transactions. In chronological order, these three dates are the declaration date, the record date, and the payment date. On the dividend declaration date, a company's board of directors authorizes a cash dividend. On the record date, a list of the individuals who own the company's stock is prepared. This list becomes the official record of the stockholders entitled to receive the cash dividend. If an individual purchases a stock after the record date but before the dividend payment date, he or she is not entitled to receive the cash dividend.

Open any edition of *The Wall Street Journal* and you will typically find a large block of dividend announcements listed under "Corporate Dividend News." These announcements report the name of the company; whether the dividend is a quarterly, semiannual, or annual dividend payment; the dollar amount of the dividend; the dividend payment date; and, finally, the record date. On February 21, 1997, *The Wall Street Journal* reported 88 quarterly dividend announcements. Included in these announcements was a $.27 dividend declared by Sbarro, Inc., which operates a chain of Italian restaurants. This dividend was payable by Sbarro on April 2, 1997, to stockholders of record on March 18, 1997.

To illustrate the accounting entries for a cash dividend, assume that Charles & Edward, Inc., a stock brokerage firm, has two million shares of common stock outstanding. On January 16, the firm's board of directors declares a cash dividend of $.24 per share, $480,000 in total, to be paid February 16 to stockholders of record on February 2. When a dividend is declared, it becomes a liability of the company and should be recorded as such in its accounting records. The following entry would be made to record the cash dividend declared by Charles & Edward's board of directors.

Jan. 16	Dividends	480,000	
	Dividends Payable		480,000
	To record $.24 cash dividend declared on common stock		

Dividends is a temporary account closed to Retained Earnings at the end of each accounting period, while Dividends Payable is a current liability account.

No entry would be required in Charles & Edward's accounting records on the record date, February 2. On that date, a list of the individuals who own the company's stock would be prepared. On February 16, the firm's accounting staff would debit Dividends Payable and credit Cash, each for $480,000, to record the dividend payment.

STOCK DIVIDENDS Besides the impressive string of cash dividends paid by Tootsie Roll, that firm has also distributed an annual stock dividend for more than twenty-five consecutive years. A **stock dividend** is a proportionate distribution of a corporation's own stock to its stockholders. On February 26, 1997, Tootsie Roll declared a 3 percent stock dividend to be distributed on April 22, 1997, to stockholders of record on March 11, 1997. This stock dividend entitled a Tootsie Roll stockholder who

stock dividend

4. There are circumstances in which corporations can pay cash dividends even though the three conditions listed here are not satisfied. For example, certain states allow corporations to pay dividends that exceed the amount of their retained earnings if the "fair value" of the firms' assets are sufficiently greater than their book value.

A Yen for Dividends

FOR YOUR INFORMATION

In recent years, many U.S. citizens have diversified their investment portfolios by purchasing the stocks of foreign companies. Investing in foreign stocks can be tricky. At a minimum, investors considering such stocks should investigate the securities laws and other applicable regulations in the relevant countries. Take the case of Japan. Historically, Japanese companies have paid modest cash dividends. One factor affecting the dividend policies of Japanese firms is restrictions imposed by the Japanese Commercial Code. This code requires Japanese companies to establish a sizable legal reserve within their retained earnings, a reserve from which dividends cannot be paid.

owned 400 shares of the firm's common stock on March 11, 1997, to receive an additional 12 shares (400 × 3%) of that stock.

Accounting Impact of a Stock Dividend Generally accepted accounting principles classify stock dividends into two groups: small stock dividends and large stock dividends. There is not a clear line of demarcation between the two types of stock dividends. However, a small stock dividend generally involves a distribution of up to 20–25 percent additional stock to existing stockholders. All other stock dividends qualify as large stock dividends. Since most stock dividends are of the "small" variety, we will focus exclusively on accounting for small stock dividends and defer accounting treatment for large stock dividends to advanced accounting courses.

From an accounting standpoint, stockholders are essentially unaffected by the distribution of a stock dividend. To prove this point, refer to Exhibit 11.5. This exhibit

© Jeff Greenberg

When considering foreign stocks, U.S. investors must be wary. Many countries impose legal restrictions on the ability of companies to pay dividends. In Japan, for example, the Japanese Commercial Code limits the ability of companies to pay dividends to their stockholders.

presents the stockholders' equity of Erin Springs, Inc., both before and after the declaration and distribution of a 5 percent stock dividend. Exhibit 11.5 also analyzes the stock dividend's impact on the ownership interest of an Erin Springs stockholder, Chris Jennings. (For the time being, we ignore the technical aspects of accounting for a stock dividend.)

Notice in Exhibit 11.5 that the total stockholders' equity of Erin Springs was unchanged by the stock dividend. Now, consider Chris Jennings' ownership interest in the company before and after the stock dividend. Before the stock dividend, Jennings owned 100 shares of Erin Springs stock; following the stock dividend, he owned 105 shares. However, the collective book value of this individual's ownership interest in the company was $1,260 before and after the stock dividend. If we think of stockholders' equity as a pie that is cut into several slices, a stock dividend simply cuts that pie into a larger number of smaller slices.

Economic Impact of a Stock Dividend Despite the analysis shown in Exhibit 11.5, a company's stockholders may benefit from a stock dividend. Stockholders benefit from a stock dividend if the market price of the company's stock is unaffected by the dividend, which is often true for a small stock dividend. For example, assume Erin

EXHIBIT 11.5 ▼

Stockholders' Equity of Erin Springs, Inc., and Ownership Interest of an Individual Stockholder Before and After the Declaration and Distribution of a 5 Percent Stock Dividend

Erin Springs, Inc., Stockholders' Equity

	Before 5% Stock Dividend	**After 5% Stock Dividend**
Common stock, par value $1:		
Shares authorized—200,000;		
Shares issued and outstanding:		
100,000 before stock dividend	$ 100,000	
105,000 after stock dividend		$ 105,000
Additional paid-in capital	600,000	675,000
Retained earnings	560,000	480,000
Total stockholders' equity	$1,260,000	$1,260,000
Book value per share (common stockholders' equity/ number of shares outstanding)	$12.60	$12.00
Chris Jennings, Erin Springs stockholder:		
Shares owned	100	105
Percentage of outstanding shares owned	.1%	.1%
Total book value of shares owned	$1,260	$1,260

Springs common stock trades for $16 per share both before and after the declaration and distribution of the 5 percent stock dividend. Given this assumption, the market value of Chris Jennings' ownership interest in Erin Springs would increase from $1,600 ($16 × 100 shares) before the stock dividend to $1,680 ($16 × 105 shares) afterward.

Accounting for a Small Stock Dividend To illustrate accounting for small stock dividends, return to the data presented in Exhibit 11.5 for Erin Springs, Inc. Assume that the company's board of directors declares the 5 percent stock dividend on October 5 of the current year. The record date is October 25 and the distribution date is November 21. (A stock dividend is distributed rather than paid, so a stock dividend has a distribution date instead of a payment date). To account properly for a small stock dividend, we must know the market price of the stock on the dividend declaration date. Assume that the market price of Erin Springs common stock is $16 on the declaration date.

A small stock dividend is accounted for similarly to a cash dividend. Recall that on the date a cash dividend is declared, the Dividends account is debited for the amount of cash to be paid to the stockholders. That cash amount represents the economic benefit realized by the stockholders due to the dividend declaration. For a small stock dividend, the assumed economic benefit realized by stockholders is the total market value of the stock to be distributed. This amount is determined by multiplying the number of shares to be issued in the stock dividend by the stock's market price on the dividend declaration date.

On the declaration date of a stock dividend, the collective market value of the shares to be issued is debited to the Stock Dividends account. The offsetting credit in this entry consists of two amounts. First, the total par value of the shares to be issued is credited to Common Stock Dividend Distributable. Second, the difference between the market value of the stock to be distributed and its total par value is credited to Additional Paid-In Capital, Common Stock.

The Erin Springs stock dividend will result in an additional 5,000 shares (5% × 100,000) of common stock being issued by the company. Since the market price of the company's stock is $16 on the declaration date, the total market value on that date of the 5,000 shares to be issued is $80,000. Of this amount, $5,000, the collective par value of the new shares (5,000 shares × $1), is credited to Common Stock Dividend Distributable. The remaining $75,000 is credited to Additional Paid-in Capital, Common Stock, as shown in the following entry.

Oct. 5	Stock Dividends	80,000	
	Common Stock Dividend Distributable		5,000
	Additional Paid-In Capital, Common Stock		75,000
	To record declaration of 5 percent stock dividend		

On October 25, the record date for the Erin Springs stock dividend, a list of stockholders entitled to receive the dividend would be prepared. As with a cash dividend, no accounting entry is necessary on the record date for a stock dividend. On the stock distribution date of November 21, the firm's accounting staff would debit Common Stock Dividend Distributable and credit Common Stock, each for $5,000. On

Stock Dividends and the Supreme Court: A Taxing Matter

FOR YOUR INFORMATION

When Congress instituted a federal income tax in the early twentieth century, a long debate ensued regarding the "taxability" of stock dividends. This debate revolved around the issue of whether stock dividends provide economic income to stockholders. Congress insisted that stockholders benefit from stock dividends similar to cash dividends, meaning that stock dividends qualify as taxable income. Attorneys for corporate stockholders argued in case after case that stock dividends do not result in taxable income for stockholders. Instead, these attorneys contended that the effect of a stock dividend is simply to cut the stockholders' equity "pie" into a larger number of smaller pieces—an analogy you have heard before. After nearly a decade of legal wrangling, the Supreme Court resolved this controversy in 1920 by agreeing with the "pie" argument rather than the "income" argument.

December 31, the $80,000 balance of Erin Springs' Stock Dividends account would be closed to Retained Earnings—Stock Dividends is a temporary account similar to Dividends.

Accounting for Stock Splits

LEARNING ◀ OBJECTIVE 5
Account for treasury stock transactions, cash and stock dividends, and stock splits.

In February 1997, Boeing Company, the aircraft manufacturer, announced a 2-for-1 stock split.[5] A **stock split** is an increase in the number of shares of a company's stock accompanied by a proportionate reduction in the stock's par value. When the stock split was announced, Boeing's common stock was trading for $104 per share. Boeing's executives expected the stock's price to decline by approximately 50 percent following the 2-for-1 split, which would allow the company to sell the stock more readily to small investors.

stock split

When a company splits its stock, the firm issues new stock to stockholders and cancels the old shares. Assume that the board of directors of Erin Springs declares a 2-for-1 stock split on October 5 of the current year instead of declaring a 5 percent stock dividend. The par value of Erin Springs' common stock after the stock split would be $.50 per share instead of the original $1 per share. Additionally, the stock split would double the number of Erin Springs' authorized, issued, and outstanding shares and reduce the book value per share of the company's stock by one-half, from $12.60 to $6.30. Finally, consider the effect of the stock split on Chris Jennings, the Erin Springs stockholder. Following the stock split, Jennings would have 200 shares of the company's stock instead of the 100 shares he had before the stock split. But, the collective book value of Jennings' shares would be the same before (100 × $12.60 = $1,260) and after (200 × $6.30 = $1,260) the stock split. More important, the collective market value of his ownership interest in Erin Springs would likely be unaffected by the stock split. The market price of a company's stock typically drops proportionately following a stock split. For the present example, that would mean the

5. "Boeing Bids to Split Its Stock Two-for-One Effective This Spring," *The Wall Street Journal*, 27 February 1997, C20.

market price of Erin Springs stock would drop from \$16 to \$8 per share following the stock split. So, the market value of Jennings' ownership interest in Erin Springs would be \$1,600 before (\$16 × 100 = \$1,600) and after (\$8 × 200 = \$1,600) the stock split.

Because a stock split does not affect the balance of any account, a formal journal entry is not necessary to record the announcement of a stock split. However, some companies make a memorandum entry in their general journal to provide a historical record of a stock split. For example, Erin Springs might make the following memorandum entry in its general journal to record the 2-for-1 stock split.

Oct. 5 Board of directors announced a 2-for-1 stock split for company's common stock. The 200,000 shares of \$1 par value common stock will be canceled, and 400,000 shares of \$.50 par value common stock will be authorized. The new shares will be issued to stockholders on October 25.

KEY CONTROL ACTIVITIES FOR STOCKHOLDERS' EQUITY

LEARNING OBJECTIVE 6
Discuss key control activities for stockholders' equity.

Businesses typically focus their principal control activities on assets and liabilities. However, effective controls are also necessary for owner's equity. This is especially true for large corporations. Common control activities for stockholders' equity include proper authorization for the issuance of equity securities, controls to ensure compliance with state and federal securities laws and regulations, and the maintenance of reliable stockholder records.

Authorization Controls

The first step in achieving adequate control over stockholders' equity is to ensure that decisions to sell common or preferred stock are approved by a firm's board of directors. Such decisions are extremely important, particularly when common stock is involved. Individuals who become common stockholders vote on key matters facing a corporation and thus may influence the firm's long-range objectives and operating policies. Authorization controls for the issuance of stock should include determining that such transactions do not violate stipulations of a firm's corporate charter. Recall that these stipulations include restrictions on the classes and quantities of stock a firm can sell.

Monitoring Compliance with State and Federal Securities Laws and Regulations

A company that sells stock to the public must establish control activities to guard against violations of securities laws and other relevant regulations. Companies that sell stock on an interstate basis are subject to the extensive reporting and financial disclosure rules of the SEC. Many of these disclosure rules require publicly owned companies to include information in their financial reports that privately owned companies seldom release. For example, a company registered with the SEC must disclose the annual compensation of its five most highly paid executives. These disclosures must include "perks" and other employment benefits received by these executives in addition to their annual salaries. Violations of the SEC's disclosure rules may subject a firm and its executives to stiff sanctions and monetary fines.

Recordkeeping Controls

Following the issuance of common or preferred stock, a corporation should implement control activities to protect the rights and privileges of stockholders. One such control is maintaining complete and up-to-date name and address records for stockholders. Without such records, corporations would have difficulty notifying stockholders on a timely basis, as required by law, of stockholders' meetings. These records are also needed to determine the stockholders, past and present, who are entitled to receive dividend distributions. Most large corporations retain an outside firm, typically a bank, to maintain their stockholder records. Banks and other firms providing this service are specialists in this area and thus well equipped to keep track of a given corporation's several hundred, or several thousand, widely dispersed stockholders.

ANALYZING STOCKHOLDERS' EQUITY

LEARNING OBJECTIVE 7
Compute and interpret return on equity.

return on equity

As suggested earlier, investors continually monitor and assess the profitability of corporations whose stock they have purchased or are considering purchasing. A key financial measure used to evaluate the profitability of a corporation is return on equity. This financial ratio measures the rate of return earned on the capital invested in a firm by its residual owners, the common stockholders. **Return on equity** is computed by dividing a corporation's net income, less preferred stock dividends, by average common stockholders' equity for a given period.

$$\text{Return on Equity} = \frac{\text{Net Income} - \text{Preferred Stock Dividends}}{\text{Average Common Stockholders' Equity}}$$

Preferred stock dividends are subtracted from net income when computing return on equity because those dividends reduce a corporation's earnings available to common stockholders.

Following are the data needed to compute Nguyen Corporation's return on equity for a recent year.

Net income	$ 474,000
Preferred stock dividends	32,000
Common stockholders' equity, January 1	3,120,000
Common stockholders' equity, December 31	3,830,000

Given these data, Nguyen's return on equity for the given year was approximately 12.7 percent:

$$\text{Return on Equity} = \frac{\text{Net Income} - \text{Preferred Stock Dividends}}{\text{Average Common Stockholders' Equity}}$$

$$\text{Return on Equity} = \frac{\$474{,}000 - \$32{,}000}{(\$3{,}120{,}000 + \$3{,}830{,}000)/2}$$

$$\text{Return on Equity} = 12.7\%$$

The graphic in Exhibit 11.6 documents the annual return on equity over a recent seven-year period for two publicly owned corporations, Lowe's Companies, Inc., and Zero Corporation. Lowe's operates a chain of do-it-yourself home improvement centers. Zero designs and manufactures engineered cases used to protect electronic equipment, artwork, and other valuable items while they are in transit. Over the period covered by Exhibit 11.6, the average return on equity for these two companies was very comparable. However, Lowe's earnings were much more volatile over this period than Zero's. Why? One reason is that Lowe's historically relies more heavily on long-term debt to satisfy its financing needs than does Zero.

Generally, the more long-term debt a company has, the more volatile its earnings will be. The owners of a company benefit when the rate of return earned on assets financed by borrowed funds exceeds the interest rate paid on those loans. But, debt financing can also work to the detriment of companies. When a company's sales decline, most of its expenses decline as well, including cost of goods sold and major operating expenses. However, interest expense is unaffected by sales volume. When a company with a significant amount of long-term debt suffers a drop in revenues, its earnings are driven down even further by the large interest expense it continues to incur.

EXHIBIT 11.6 ▼

Return on Equity: Lowe's Companies vs. Zero Corporation

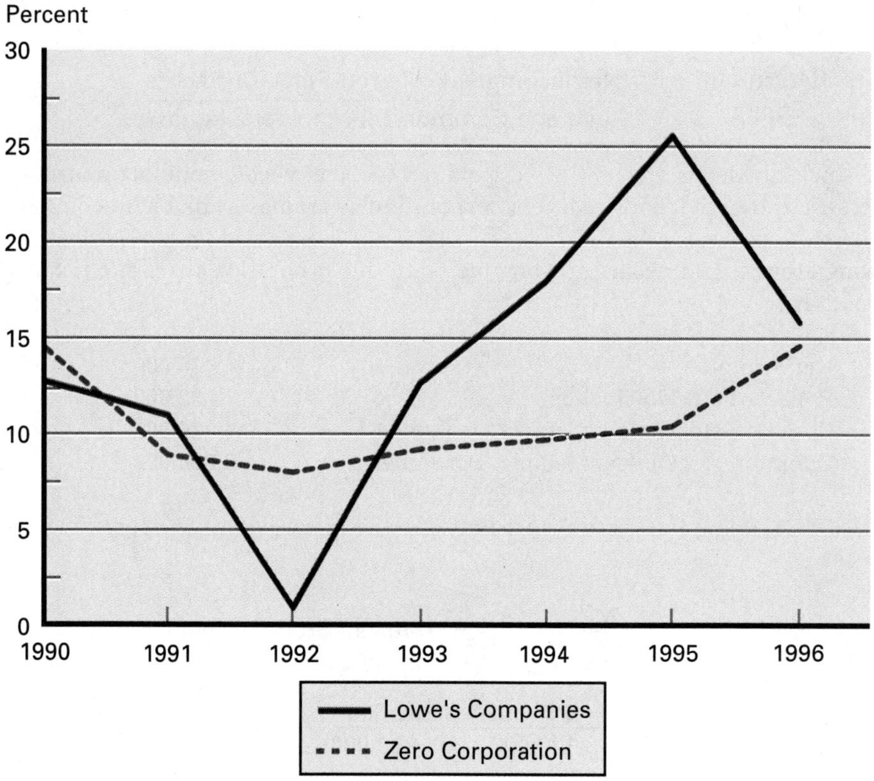

Source: Recent annual reports.

SUMMARY

Corporations have several advantages compared with the other primary types of business organizations, sole proprietorships and partnerships. Among the advantages of the corporate form of business organization are limited liability for corporate stockholders. Generally, the maximum financial loss a corporate stockholder faces is the amount he or she invested in the corporation's stock. The key disadvantage of the corporate form of business organization is the double taxation of corporate profits. Unlike the earnings of sole proprietorships and partnerships, corporate profits are taxed by the federal government and other governmental agencies. These profits are taxed again when they are distributed as cash dividends to stockholders.

When owners of a business decide to incorporate, they file articles of incorporation with an appropriate state agency. If all legal conditions for incorporation are met, the company is granted a corporate charter. A corporation's charter authorizes the firm to issue a maximum number of shares of one or more classes of stock. Common stock represents the residual ownership interests in a corporation. If a corporation is liquidated, its common stockholders are entitled to share proportionately in the firm's remaining assets after all other claims have been satisfied.

The owners of a corporation's preferred stock are granted certain preferences relative to the firm's common stockholders. For example, before common stockholders can be paid any dividends in a given year, preferred stockholders must receive the full amount of dividends to which they are entitled. Preferred stock often has one or more distinctive features. The most common preferred stock feature is a cumulative stipulation. If a dividend is not paid on a cumulative preferred stock in a given year, that dividend accumulates and must be paid in the future before common stockholders can receive a dividend.

Stockholders and potential stockholders represent a large and important class of financial decision makers. To make rational investment decisions regarding corporate stocks, investors must have access to key information regarding the stockholders' equity of individual corporations. Among these information needs are the specific rights and privileges of each class of a corporation's stock. Investors also need data allowing them to assess the profitability of corporations and information regarding corporate dividend policies.

Major types of stockholders' equity transactions include the issuance of common stock, the payment of cash dividends, the distribution of stock dividends, and stock splits. Among the most frequently occurring stockholders' equity transactions is the sale of common stock for more than its par value. Since the sale of a corporation's own stock qualifies as a financing activity, a firm cannot record a gain or loss on such a transaction. When common stock is sold for more than its par value, the difference between the proceeds and the common stock's collective par value should be credited to Additional Paid-In Capital, Common Stock. To account properly for a cash dividend, accountants must be aware of three relevant dates. These dates are the declaration, record, and payment dates for the dividend.

Proper authorization of corporate stock transactions is an important element of a firm's control over its stockholders' equity. A corporation must also establish control policies and procedures to ensure compliance with all state and federal securities laws and other applicable regulations. The maintenance of accurate name and address records for stockholders is an example of a control activity for stockholders' equity.

Current and prospective stockholders of a corporation closely monitor the firm's profitability. Return on equity is a key measure of a corporation's profitability. This financial ratio is computed by dividing net income, less any preferred stock dividends, by a corporation's average common stockholders' equity for a given period.

GLOSSARY

Authorized stock (p. 499) The maximum number of shares of a given class of stock a company is permitted to issue under the terms of its corporate charter.
Book value per share (p. 504) Common stockholders' equity per share for a corporation; computed by dividing total common stockholders' equity by the number of outstanding shares of common stock.
Callable preferred stock (p. 501) Preferred stock that can be reacquired at the option of the issuing corporation.
Cash dividend (p. 508) A proportionate distribution of a company's prior earnings to its stockholders made in the form of cash.
Common stock (p. 498) A class of stock that represents the residual ownership interests of a corporation.
Convertible preferred stock (p. 501) Preferred stock that can be exchanged at the option of preferred stockholders for common stock of the issuing corporation.
Cumulative preferred stock (p. 500) Preferred stock on which dividends that are not paid in a given year accumulate and must be paid in the future before common stockholders can receive a dividend.
Dividends in arrears (p. 503) Unpaid dividends on cumulative preferred stock; should be disclosed in a company's financial statement footnotes.
Issued stock (p. 499) The number of shares of a class of stock that has been sold or otherwise distributed by a corporation; these shares may be outstanding or held as treasury stock.
Outstanding stock (p. 499) The number of shares of a given class of stock owned by a company's stockholders.
Par value (p. 499) A nominal dollar value assigned to each share of a class of stock.
Preemptive right (p. 499) The right of stockholders to retain their fractional ownership interest in a corporation when additional stock is issued.
Preferred stock (p. 498) A class of stock that has certain preferences or advantages relative to a company's common stock.
Return on equity (p. 515) A key measure of a corporation's profitability; computed by dividing net income, less preferred stock dividends, by average common stockholders' equity for a given period.
Stated value (p. 499) A nominal value assigned to each share of a no-par common stock.
Stock dividend (p. 509) A proportionate distribution of a corporation's own stock to its stockholders.
Stock split (p. 513) An increase in the number of shares of a company's stock accompanied by a proportionate reduction in the stock's par value.
Treasury stock (p. 499) Common or preferred stock that has been issued by a corporation and then reacquired.

DECISION CASE

Suddenly, you find yourself at the advanced age of 40. For nearly two decades, you have worked for a large corporation but now want to go into business for yourself. You plan to start a real estate development company, Forest Pointe Enterprises (FPE). You believe that $4 million is needed to get this new company "off the ground," but you have only $1 million to invest. Presently, you are considering two alternative methods of raising the additional $3 million. The first alternative involves selling $2 million of common stock in your company to outside investors—you would purchase the remaining $1 million of the company's common stock. The other $1 million needed would be borrowed from a local bank on a long-term loan at a 10 percent interest rate. Under the second financing alternative, you would purchase all of FPE's common stock for $1 million and borrow $3 million at an interest rate of 10 percent.

To choose the optimal financing strategy, you must predict FPE's annual earnings. You have identified two possible earnings scenarios. Under the first scenario, FPE "scores" big and posts earnings before interest expense and income taxes of $700,000 annually. Under the second scenario, the company fails to realize its full potential and earns only $350,000 annually before interest and taxes. Following are projected financial data for FPE's first year for each earnings scenario and financing alternative.

	Scenario 1: Earnings Before Interest and Taxes of $700,000		**Scenario 2: Earnings Before Interest and Taxes of $350,000**	
	Financing Strategy 1*	**Financing Strategy 2†**	**Financing Strategy 1**	**Financing Strategy 2**
Capital structure:				
Owners' equity	$3,000,000	$1,000,000	$3,000,000	$1,000,000
Debt capital, 10% interest rate	1,000,000	3,000,000	1,000,000	3,000,000
Total capital	$4,000,000	$4,000,000	$4,000,000	$4,000,000
Earnings before interest and taxes	$ 700,000	$ 700,000	$ 350,000	$ 350,000
Interest expense	100,000	300,000	100,000	300,000
Pretax income	$ 600,000	$ 400,000	$ 250,000	$ 50,000
Income tax expense (40%)	240,000	160,000	100,000	20,000
Net income	$ 360,000	$ 240,000	$ 150,000	$ 30,000

*Invest $1 million in FPE's common stock, sell $2 million of common stock to external investors, and borrow $1 million on a long-term loan at a 10 percent interest rate.

†Invest $1 million in FPE's common stock and borrow $3 million on a long-term loan at a 10 percent interest rate.

Required: Compute the return on equity and times interest earned ratios for each of the four situations presented. (The times interest earned ratio was discussed in Chapter 10.) Which financing strategy poses the more risk for you personally? Why? Assuming Scenario 1 is realized, which financing strategy would be more advantageous for you? Support your answer with the appropriate data. Assuming Scenario 2 is realized, which financing strategy would be more advantageous to you? Again, defend your answer.

QUESTIONS

1. What is an "IPO"?
2. Identify two methods that business owners can use to raise a large amount of funds in a short period of time.
3. Define a "corporation." What is a "closely-held corporation"? an "S corporation"?
4. Identify the significance of each of the following items to a corporation.
    a. Articles of incorporation
    b. Corporate charter
5. Identify key advantages and disadvantages of the corporate form of business organization.
6. Explain how a corporation's income is taxed twice.
7. How do the common stock and preferred stock of a corporation differ?
8. Identify the primary rights and privileges of common stockholders and of preferred stockholders.
9. Briefly define the following terms:
    a. Authorized stock
    b. Issued stock
    c. Outstanding stock
    d. Treasury stock
10. What does the par value of a common stock represent?
11. Distinguish between and among cumulative preferred stock, callable preferred stock, and convertible preferred stock.
12. How is the book value per share of a corporation's common stock computed?
13. What are dividends in arrears? Of what significance to existing or potential common stockholders is information about a company's dividends in arrears?
14. When a corporation exchanges its common stock for an asset such as a building or a piece of equipment, how is the initial book value of the asset determined?
15. Why may a corporation decide to repurchase some of its outstanding common stock?
16. Does a corporation with a positive retained earnings balance have an equivalent amount of cash on hand? Explain.
17. Identify the three conditions that must be met before a corporation can distribute cash dividends to its stockholders.
18. What three dates are significant in accounting for a cash dividend? On which of these three dates is a cash dividend recognized as a liability by a corporation?
19. What is a stock dividend?
20. Does a stock dividend have a positive economic impact on a corporation's stockholders? Explain.
21. What is a stock split? Why are journal entries not necessary to record a stock split?
22. How does a stock split make a corporation's shares more affordable to potential investors? Provide a numerical example to support your answer.
23. Identify two control activities related to stockholders' equity.
24. How is the return on equity ratio computed?

EXERCISES

25. True or False (LO 1–7)

Following are a series of statements regarding topics discussed in Chapter 11.

Required:

Indicate whether each statement is true (T) or false (F).

_____ a. The first step in achieving adequate control over stockholders' equity is to ensure that decisions to sell common or preferred stock are approved by a firm's board of directors.

_____ b. Book value per share is computed by dividing retained earnings by the number of common shares outstanding.

_____ c. An important legal privilege of common stockholders is the right to vote on key matters facing a corporation.

_____ d. Among other items, articles of incorporation identify the given business's purpose, its principal operating units, and the type and quantity of stock that it plans to issue.

_____ e. Unlike sole proprietorships and partnerships, the legal existence of a corporation is unaffected by the death or withdrawal of individual owners.

_____ f. If a corporate charter identifies only one class of stock, that stock is automatically considered the corporation's preferred stock.

_____ g. Companies that pay cash dividends typically do so on a regular basis.

_____ h. "Authorized stock" refers to the number of shares of a corporate stock that have been sold or otherwise distributed.

_____ i. Callable preferred stock can be reacquired at the option of the issuing corporation.

_____ j. The stock of "closely-held" corporations is owned by a few individuals, often members of the same family, and is not publicly traded on a securities exchange.

_____ k. On the record date of a stock dividend, the collective market value of the shares to be issued is debited to the Stock Dividends account.

_____ l. Companies subject to the regulations of the Securities and Exchange Commission must disclose the cash dividends they have paid over their five most recent fiscal years.

_____ m. When corporations exchange their common stock for noncash assets, either the fair market value of the stock issued or the asset acquired, whichever is more evident, should be used as the basis for recording the transaction.

_____ n. Return on equity is computed by dividing a corporation's net income, less preferred stock dividends, by average common stockholders' equity for a given period.

26. Terms (LO 1, 2)

Following are definitions or descriptions of terms relating to corporations and corporate stockholders' equity.

_____ First-time sale of a corporation's stock to the general public.

_____ A minimal dollar value assigned to each share of a given class of stock.

_____ An association of individuals created by law and having an existence apart from that of its members as well as distinct and inherent powers and liabilities.

_____ The total number of shares of a given class of stock that a corporation is permitted to sell.

_____ Normally the only voting stock of a corporation.

_____ Items found in this document usually include the purpose of the organization and the type and quantity of stock it can issue.

_____ The number of shares of a class of stock that has been sold or otherwise distributed by a corporation.
_____ Permits a stockholder to maintain his or her existing ownership percentage in a company's stock when additional shares of that stock are issued.
_____ The number of shares of a given class of stock owned by a company's shareholders.
_____ Stock that has been issued and reacquired by a corporation.
_____ A contract between a corporation and the state in which it does business.

Required:
Match each definition or description with the appropriate term from the following list.

a. Corporation
b. Articles of incorporation
c. Corporate charter
d. Initial public offering
e. Stated value
f. Authorized stock
g. Issued stock
h. Outstanding stock
i. Treasury stock
j. Preferred stock
k. Common stock
l. Preemptive right
m. Par value

27. Common Stockholders' Rights (LO 2)
Suppose that you own 500 shares of the common stock of Cohen & Cohen Securities Brokers. The company has 50,000 shares of common stock outstanding. The par value of the stock is $40. Cohen & Cohen does not have any other classes of stock outstanding.

Required:
1. If Cohen & Cohen declares a cash dividend of $30,000, or $.60 per share, how much of this dividend can you expect to receive?
2. If Cohen & Cohen decides to sell an additional 14,000 shares of common stock, how many of these shares will you be entitled to purchase, if you so choose? Explain.
3. Presently, Cohen & Cohen has total stockholders' equity of $3,200,000 and the company's common stock is trading for $71 per share on a major stock exchange. What is the total "value" of the Cohen & Cohen shares that you own? Explain.

28. Preferred Stock Dividends (LO 3)
Biloxi Corporation has 10,000 shares of cumulative preferred stock outstanding. This stock has a $100 par value and an annual dividend rate of $5 per share. Biloxi has not paid any dividends to its preferred stockholders during the past three years.

Required:
1. What disclosure is Biloxi required to make in its annual report regarding the unpaid dividends on its preferred stock?
2. Where in Biloxi's financial statements will you find this disclosure?
3. Why is this information of interest to Biloxi's preferred and common stockholders?

29. Sale of Common Stock for Cash (LO 4)
On January 15, Shaller Legal Services, Inc., sold 20,000 shares of common stock for $14 per share.

Required:
Prepare the entry to record the sale of this stock, assuming that the stock has the following:
1. A $5 par value.
2. No par value but a stated value of $6 per share.
3. Neither a par value nor a stated value.

30. **Issuance of Common Stock for Noncash Assets** (LO 4)
Pincus Enterprises acquired a large tract of land from Mock Corporation. In exchange for the land, Pincus gave Mock 500 shares of its $2 par value common stock.

Required:
1. Prepare the appropriate journal entry to record this transaction in the accounting records of Pincus Enterprises, assuming that the company's stock is not publicly traded and that the land has an appraised value of $41,200.
2. Suppose now that Pincus common stock is actively traded on the New York Stock Exchange. Immediately before the tract of land was acquired from Mock Corporation, the Pincus stock was trading for $77 per share. Again, assume that the land has an appraised value of $41,200. Prepare the appropriate journal entry to record this exchange transaction in the accounting records of Pincus Enterprises.

31. **Accounting for Cash Dividends** (LO 3, 5)
Karlinsky Distributors has 1,000,000 shares of common stock outstanding. On January 11 of the current year, Karlinsky declared a cash dividend of $.20 per share, payable on March 9 to stockholders of record on February 12.

Required:
1. When did this dividend become a liability to Karlinsky?
2. Prepare any journal entries required in Karlinsky's accounting records relating to this cash dividend on the following dates in the current year:
   a. January 11
   b. February 12
   c. March 9
   d. December 31
3. What group of individuals within the Karlinsky firm authorized the payment of this dividend?
4. What general types of information must public companies regulated by the SEC disclose in their annual reports regarding their dividend policies? Why is this information important to potential investors?

32. **Accounting for Stock Dividends** (LO 5)
Savich, Inc., had 100,000 shares of $50 par value common stock outstanding on April 19 of the current year when the company declared a 10 percent stock dividend. The stock dividend was distributed on June 12 to stockholders of record on May 15. The market value of the stock on the declaration date was $61 per share; on the distribution date, the stock had a market value per share of $64.

Required:
1. Prepare any journal entries required in Savich's accounting records relating to this stock dividend on the following dates in the current year:
   a. April 19
   b. May 15
   c. June 12
   d. December 31
2. How does a stock dividend affect the total book value of a corporation's stock controlled by an individual stockholder? How does a stock dividend typically affect the collective market value of an individual stockholder's ownership interest in a corporation? Explain.

33. **Accounting for Preferred Stock Transactions** (LO 2, 4)
The corporate charter of Mosich Motors, Inc., authorizes the company to sell up to 20,000 shares of preferred stock. This preferred stock has a $20 par value and a $1 annual dividend rate. The stock is both cumulative and convertible. Each share of the preferred stock can be exchanged for two shares of Mosich's $3 par value common stock.

In 1998, Mosich had the following transactions involving its preferred stock.

March 25:	Sold 5,000 shares at a price of $24 per share.
May 24:	Sold 2,000 shares at a price of $25 per share.
August 8:	Declared a $1 preferred stock dividend payable September 13 to preferred stockholders of record on August 21.
September 13:	Paid dividend declared on August 8.

Required:

1. In what sense is preferred stock "preferred" compared with a corporation's common stock?
2. Mosich's preferred stock is both cumulative and convertible. Do these features make the stock more attractive to potential investors? Explain.
3. Prepare the appropriate journal entries for the 1998 transactions involving Mosich's preferred stock.

34. **Accounting for Treasury Stock Transactions** (LO 5)
Quick & Reilly is a large discount brokerage firm. At the end of a recent year, the stockholders' equity section of the company's balance sheet indicated that 69,400 shares of the company's common stock was being held as treasury stock. This treasury stock had been acquired at a total cost of $1,930,450, or approximately $27.82 per share. The company's common stock has a par value of $.10 per share.

Required:

1. Why do companies sometimes reacquire stock that they have previously issued?
2. Suppose that Quick & Reilly purchased all of the treasury stock on January 28, Year 1. Prepare the journal entry to record this transaction in the company's accounting records.
3. Assume that Quick & Reilly sold 2,000 shares of its treasury stock on April 3, Year 1, at a price of $35 per share. Prepare the journal entry to record this transaction in the company's accounting records.
4. Assume that on May 31, Year 1, Quick & Reilly sold another 3,000 shares of its treasury stock for $27 per share. Prepare the journal entry to record this transaction in the company's accounting records.

35. **Stockholders' Equity Section of a Corporate Balance Sheet** (LO 4, 5, 7)
Refer to the annual report of Outback Steakhouse, Inc., that is included as an appendix to this text.

Required:

1. Compute the book value per share of Outback's common stock at the end of 1995 and 1996.
2. Compute Outback's return on equity for 1995 and 1996. (Note: The company's common stockholders' equity at the beginning of 1995 was $186,697,000.)
3. Suppose that Outback sells 50,000 shares of its common stock for $14 per share on July 16 of a given year. Prepare the journal entry to record this transaction.
4. Suppose that in a given year Outback pays a $.12 per share cash dividend. During the year in question, assume that Outback has 50 million shares of com-

mon stock outstanding. Prepare any necessary journal entries related to this dividend in Outback's accounting records on the following dates:

a. April 5, declaration date
b. May 7, record date
c. June 1, payment date

36. **Accounting for Stock Splits** (LO 5)
Refer again to Outback Steakhouse's annual report that is included as an appendix to this text.

Required:

1. Suppose that on January 1, 1997, Outback announced a 2-for-1 stock split. Assume that the new stock was to be issued on January 31, 1997. Prepare a memorandum entry on January 1, 1997, in Outback's general journal to record the announcement of this stock split.
2. Following the stock split, determine the number of common shares that Outback would have had authorized, issued, and outstanding.

37. **Corporate Form of Business Organization** (LO 1)
Steven Anderson and Jason Martinkus own a small but rapidly growing business, Videos Unlimited. Anderson and Martinkus have been told by their attorney that they should consider incorporating their business, which they now operate as a partnership.

Required:
Suppose that you are the accountant for Videos Unlimited. Write a memo to Anderson and Martinkus that summarizes the key advantages and disadvantages of incorporating a business.

38. **Control Activities for Dividends** (LO 6)
Adequate controls over dividend transactions are very important for corporations. If a company's board of directors approves and pays a dividend that violates bond covenants, the directors and the company may be subject to prosecution by state and federal regulatory agencies and be held responsible for any resulting losses suffered by the bondholders. The company and its directors may also be held liable if dividends are not paid to stockholders who have a right to receive those dividends.

Required:

1. Develop a list of control activities that a company could adopt to ensure that bond covenants are not violated by dividend declarations.
2. What control activity would help ensure that a company pays dividends to the appropriate individuals and in the proper amounts?

39. **Book Value per Share and Return on Equity** (LO 3, 7)
Illinois Central Corporation operates the Illinois Central Railroad between Chicago and the Gulf Coast. Presented in the following table are key financial data for Illinois Central over a recent five-year period. Amounts are expressed in millions of dollars.

	Year 1	Year 2	Year 3	Year 4	Year 5
Revenues	$549.7	$547.4	$564.7	$593.9	$643.8
Net income	65.4	95.9	68.2	113.9	118.4
Common stockholders' equity (year-end)	260.3	338.8	377.4	454.1	470.1
Common shares outstanding (year-end)	59.7	63.9	64.0	64.1	62.9

Note: At the beginning of Year 1, Illinois Central had $128.4 million of common stockholders' equity.

Required:

1. Compute Illinois Central's book value per share at the end of each year listed. Also compute the company's return on equity for each year. Is there a definite trend apparent in either of these measures? If so, indicate whether a given trend is favorable or unfavorable.
2. Suppose that you are a potential investor in Illinois Central common stock. Identify three questions related to the company's financial data that you would want to ask of the company's top executives.

PROBLEM SET A

40. Accounting for Stockholders' Equity Transactions (LO 4, 5)
Arnold Manufacturing was granted a corporate charter on January 3, 1998, and began operations shortly thereafter. Arnold's corporate charter authorizes the firm to issue up to 100,000 shares of $3 par value common stock and 20,000 shares of $100 par value preferred stock. The preferred stock carries an annual dividend rate of $5, is cumulative, and can be converted into Arnold common stock through December 31, 2007. Each share of preferred stock can be converted into 2 shares of Arnold common stock. During 1998, the following events or transactions affected the stockholders' equity of Arnold:

January 10:	Sold 22,000 shares of common stock for $11 per share.
March 30:	Sold 5,000 shares of preferred stock for $101 per share.
June 12:	Exchanged 3,000 shares of common stock for a building with an appraised value of $37,000; on this date, Arnold's common stock was trading at $12 per share on a regional stock exchange.
October 3:	Sold 7,000 shares of common stock for $13 per share.
November 4:	Declared a cash dividend of $5 per share on outstanding preferred stock, payable on December 6, to stockholders of record on November 21.
December 6:	Paid dividend on preferred stock that was declared on November 4.
December 31:	Net income for 1998 was determined to be $89,000.

Required:

1. Prepare all appropriate journal entries for the events and transactions listed. Include in these journal entries the year-end closing entries for which you have the required data.
2. Prepare the stockholders' equity section of Arnold's balance sheet as of December 31, 1998.
3. Suppose now that Arnold's common stock has no par value. Prepare the appropriate journal entries to record the January 10, June 12, and October 3 transactions.
4. Suppose now that Arnold's common stock does not have a par value but has a $4 stated value. Prepare the appropriate journal entries to record the January 10, June 12, and October 3 transactions.
5. Refer to the transaction on June 12. Assume that Arnold's common stock is not publicly traded. Prepare the appropriate journal entry for this transaction given this assumption.

6. What accounting principle dictates that Arnold include information in its financial statement footnotes regarding the specific features or stipulations attached to its preferred stock?

41. **Analyzing Stockholders' Equity** (LO 3, 7)
King World Productions, Inc., produces and/or distributes several popular television shows. Included among these shows are *Jeopardy!*, *Wheel of Fortune*, and *The Oprah Winfrey Show*. Following is the stockholders' equity section of a recent King World balance sheet. Also listed for each year is King World's net income.

	Year 1 (in thousands)	Year 2
Stockholders' equity:		
Preferred stock, $.01 par value; 5,000,000 shares authorized, none issued	—	—
Common stock, $.01 par value; 75,000,000 shares authorized, 49,505,363 shares and 49,722,218 shares issued in Year 1 and Year 2, respectively	$ 495	$ 497
Additional paid-in capital	76,647	82,171
Retained earnings	577,039	665,339
Treasury stock, at cost; 12,207,794 shares and 12,960,894 shares in Year 1 and Year 2, respectively	(260,008)	(288,930)
Total stockholders' equity	$394,173	$459,077
Net income	$101,936	$ 88,300

Note: King World's common stockholders' equity at the beginning of Year 1 was $241,655,000.

Required:

1. Compute the book value per share of King World's common stock at the end of Year 1 and at the end of Year 2.
2. Compute King World's return on equity for Year 1 and Year 2. Did this ratio improve or deteriorate in Year 2 compared with the previous year?
3. Did King World declare any cash dividends during Year 2? any stock dividends? Explain.
4. Identify one reason that may explain why King World's common stock has such a low par value.

42. **Accounting for Treasury Stock Transactions** (LO 5)
Refer to the financial data presented in Problem 41 for King World Productions, Inc.

Required:

1. Compute the average cost of King World's treasury stock at the end of Year 2.
2. Suppose that King World purchased 5,000 shares of treasury stock on May 1, Year 2, at the average cost computed in (1). Prepare the appropriate journal entry to record this transaction.

3. Suppose now that 2,000 shares of the stock assumed purchased in (2) were sold for $27 per share on June 15, Year 3. Prepare the appropriate journal entry to record this transaction.
4. Finally, suppose that the remaining 3,000 shares of treasury stock assumed purchased in (2) were sold for $21 per share on July 29, Year 3. Prepare the appropriate journal entry to record this transaction.

43. Accounting for Stock Dividends and Stock Splits (LO 5)
Following is the stockholders' equity section of RocLee Corporation's December 31, 1997, balance sheet:

Common stock, $2 par value; 500,000 shares authorized, 120,000 shares issued	$240,000
Additional paid-in capital	90,000
Retained earnings	310,000
Total stockholders' equity	$640,000

Listed next are events and transactions involving RocLee's stockholders' equity during 1998.

a. On January 10, 1998, RocLee declared a 5 percent stock dividend. This stock dividend was distributed on March 1, 1998, to stockholders of record on January 31, 1998. RocLee's common stock opened the year at $3 per share and was trading for that same price on both January 10 and January 31. On March 2, the stock was trading for $3.75 per share.
b. On August 15, 1998, RocLee announced a 2-for-1 stock split. The new stock was issued on September 28. Immediately prior to the announcement of the stock split on August 14, the company's stock was trading for $3.50 per share. On October 1, 1998, the company's common stock was trading for $1.75 per share.
c. On December 31, 1998, RocLee's net income for the year was determined to be $64,000. The year-end market price of RocLee's common stock was $2.00.

Required:

1. Prepare all appropriate journal entries involving RocLee's stockholders' equity during 1998.
2. Prepare the stockholders' equity section of RocLee's balance sheet as of December 31, 1998.
3. Assume that you owned 100 shares of RocLee common stock on January 1, 1998. Determine the book value of your ownership interest in this company on the following dates (show your computations):
   a. January 1, 1998
   b. March 2, 1998
   c. August 14, 1998
   d. October 1, 1998
   e. December 31, 1998
4. Refer to (3). Determine the collective market value of your ownership interest in RocLee on each of the indicated dates. (Show your computations.)

44. Stockholders' Equity: Management Decisions (LO 3)
In early 1986, Cardillo Travel Systems, Inc., a publicly owned company, was experiencing severe financial problems. These problems worsened considerably when a large legal judgment was imposed on the firm following the settlement of a lawsuit. Public compa-

nies are required to disclose "material events," such as the loss of a major lawsuit, to the Securities and Exchange Commission (SEC). Such disclosures are then released to the public by the SEC. Instead of immediately disclosing the large legal judgment to the SEC, Cardillo's management delayed this disclosure for three weeks. In the meantime, Cardillo's chief executive sold 100,000 shares of the company's common stock in the open market. [Note: The facts in this problem were taken from the following source: M. C. Knapp, "Cardillo Travel Systems, Inc.," in *Contemporary Auditing: Issues and Cases,* 2d ed. (Minneapolis/St. Paul: West Publishing Co., 1996.)]

Required:

1. What is the purpose of the SEC rule requiring public companies to disclose "material events"?
2. Did the management of Cardillo behave ethically in the series of events described? Explain.
3. What parties were harmed as a result of the decisions made by Cardillo's management?

45. **Stockholders' Equity for an International Company** (LO 3)

Telefonaktiebolaget LM Ericsson (hereinafter "Ericsson"), one of the largest telecommunications firms in the world, is a Swedish company headquartered in Stockholm. Following is the stockholders' equity section included in a recent balance sheet of the company. Ericsson's financial data are presented in millions of Swedish kronor. Recently, one Swedish krona was equivalent to approximately $.13. Expressed another way, a U.S. dollar was roughly equivalent to 8 kronor.

	Year 1	Year 2
Stockholders' equity (note 19)		
Capital stock	2,172	2,172
Reserves not available for distribution	4,267	4,281
General reserve	100	100
Retained earnings	2,483	4,047
Reported net income	2,541	1,961
	11,563	12,561

Required:

1. Notice that one of the largest elements of Ericsson's stockholders' equity is "Reserves not available for distribution." This item represents the amount that Ericsson's long-term assets have been 'revalued" (written up) in excess of their cost. Would you find this item in the stockholders' equity section of a U.S. company? At the end of Year 2, the revaluation reserve was equal to approximately 11 percent of the company's total assets. In your opinion, does Ericsson's practice of periodically revaluing its long-term assets have a "material" effect on the firm's reported financial condition? Why or why not?
2. Sweden's federal securities laws prohibit Swedish companies from paying dividends from revaluation reserves included in their stockholders' equity. What is the likely purpose or intent of this rule?
3. Swedish companies are allowed to establish "general reserves" within their stockholders' equity. Notice that Ericsson had such a reserve in both Year 1 and Year 2. The company's financial statement footnotes did not explain the purpose of this reserve. What GAAP-based accounting concept or concepts would a U.S. firm violate by engaging in similar practices?

PROBLEM SET B

46. Accounting for Stockholders' Equity Transactions (LO 4, 5)

On February 4, 1998, Moore Industries received a corporate charter. A few days later, the new company began operations. The corporate charter of Moore Industries permits the firm to issue up to 400,000 shares of $1 par value common stock and up to 50,000 shares of $50 par value preferred stock. The preferred stock is cumulative and has a $3.50 annual dividend rate. Additionally, the preferred stock can be called in at the option of Moore within the first ten years of the corporation's existence. If the preferred stock is called in by Moore, the preferred stockholders must be paid $53 for each share they own. During 1998, the following events or transactions affected Moore's stockholders' equity:

February 16:	Sold 67,000 shares of common stock for $15 per share.
February 28:	Sold 3,000 shares of preferred stock for $52 per share.
May 15:	Exchanged 10,000 shares of common stock for a tract of land with an appraised value of $164,000; on this date, Moore's common stock was trading for $15 per share on a national stock exchange.
August 7:	Sold 7,000 shares of common stock for $17 per share.
October 22:	Declared a cash dividend of $3.50 per share on outstanding preferred stock, payable on November 21 to stockholders of record on November 5.
November 21:	Paid preferred dividend that was declared on October 22.
December 31:	Net income was determined to be $202,000.

Required:

1. Prepare all appropriate journal entries for the events and transactions listed. Include in these journal entries the year-end closing entries for which you have the required data.
2. Prepare the stockholders equity section of Moore's balance sheet as of December 31, 1998.
3. Suppose now that Moore's common stock has no par value. Prepare the appropriate journal entries to record the February 16, May 15, and August 7 transactions.
4. Suppose now that Moore's common stock does not have a par value but does have a $4 stated value. Prepare the appropriate journal entries to record the February 16, May 15, and August 7 transactions.
5. Refer to the transaction on May 15. Assume that Moore's common stock is not publicly traded. Prepare the appropriate journal entry for the May 15 transaction given this assumption.
6. Moore's executives considered not attaching a cumulative stipulation to the company's preferred stock. However, the company's investment banking firm informed Moore's executives that the preferred stock would likely sell for no more than $40 per share if it did not have a cumulative feature. Explain why this was the case. What other feature could Moore's management have assigned to the preferred stock to increase its initial selling price?

47. Analyzing Stockholders' Equity (LO 3, 7)

Circus Circus Enterprises, Inc., owns and operates several Las Vegas casinos including the Luxor and the Excalibur. Following is the stockholders' equity section that was included in a recent balance sheet issued by the company. Also listed is the company's net income for each year.

	Year 1	Year 2
	(in thousands)	
Stockholders' equity:		
Common stock, $.01 2/3 par value Authorized—450,000,000 shares Issued—95,914,143 and 96,168,179 shares in Year 1 and Year 2, respectively	$ 1,599	$ 1,603
Preferred stock, $.01 par value Authorized—75,000,000 shares	—	—
Additional paid-in capital	111,516	120,135
Retained earnings	502,257	618,446
Treasury stock, at cost; 8,663,214 shares and 10,062,814 shares in Year 1 and Year 2, respectively	(125,363)	(180,234)
Total stockholders' equity	$490,009	$559,950
Net income	$117,322	$116,189

Note: Circus Circus's common stockholders' equity at the beginning of Year 1 was $326,196,000.

Required:

1. Compute the book value per share of Circus Circus's common stock at the end of Year 1 and at the end of Year 2.
2. Compute Circus Circus's return on equity for Year 1 and Year 2. Did this ratio improve or deteriorate in Year 2 compared with the previous year?
3. Why do you believe Circus Circus listed its preferred stock in the stockholders' equity section of its balance sheet even though none of that stock was outstanding?
4. Did Circus Circus declare any cash dividends during Year 2? Any stock dividends? Explain.

48. **Accounting for Treasury Stock Transactions** (LO 5)
Refer to the financial data presented in Problem 47 for Circus Circus Enterprises, Inc.

Required:

1. Compute the average cost of Circus Circus's treasury stock at the end of Year 2.
2. Suppose that Circus Circus purchased 10,000 shares of treasury stock on May 1, Year 2, at the average cost computed in (1). Prepare the appropriate journal entry to record this transaction.
3. Suppose now that 4,000 shares of the stock assumed purchased in (2) were sold for $24 per share on June 15, Year 3. Prepare the appropriate journal entry to record this transaction.
4. Finally, suppose that the remaining 6,000 shares of treasury stock assumed purchased in (2) were sold for $17 per share on July 29, Year 3. Prepare the appropriate journal entry to record this transaction.
5. Why are corporations prohibited from recognizing gains or losses on treasury stock transactions? What accounting concept or concepts discussed in Chapter 2 would be violated if a company recorded a gain on the sale of its treasury stock?

49. **Accounting for Stock Dividends and Stock Splits** (LO 5)
Following is the stockholders' equity section of the December 31, 1997, balance sheet of Sampson & Schnell Associates (SSA), an investment advisory firm.

Common stock, $5 par value; 500,000 shares authorized, 80,000 shares issued	$400,000
Additional paid-in capital	80,000
Retained earnings	250,000
Total stockholders' equity	$730,000

Listed next are events and transactions involving SSA's stockholders' equity during 1998.

a. On January 25, 1998, SSA declared a 10 percent stock dividend. This stock dividend was distributed on March 4, 1998, to stockholders of record on February 16, 1998. SSA's common stock opened the year at $9 per share and was trading at that same price on January 25 and February 16. On March 5, the stock was trading for $8.50 per share.
b. On July 7, 1998, SSA announced a 2-for-1 stock split. The new stock was issued on August 8. Immediately prior to the announcement of the stock split on July 6, the company's stock was trading for $8.00 per share. On August 9, 1998, the company's common stock was trading for $4.25 per share.
c. On December 31, 1998, SSA's net income for the year was determined to be $112,000. The year-end market price of SSA's common stock was $4.75.

Required:

1. Prepare all appropriate journal entries involving SSA's stockholders' equity during 1998.
2. Prepare the stockholders' equity section of SSA's balance sheet as of December 31, 1998.
3. Assume that you owned 100 shares of SSA common stock on January 1, 1998. Determine the book value of your ownership interest in this company on the following dates (show your computations):
   a. January 1, 1998
   b. March 5, 1998
   c. July 6, 1998
   d. August 9, 1998
   e. December 31, 1998
4. Refer to (3). Determine the collective market value of your ownership interest in SSA on each of the indicated dates. (Show your computations.)

50. **Stockholders' Equity: Management Decisions** (LO 3, 6)

Four Seasons Nursing Centers of America was incorporated in 1967 in Oklahoma City. This company's principal line of business was the construction of nursing homes. During the first few years of its existence, the company recorded large profits, which caused the price of the firm's common stock to increase dramatically. In early 1968, Four Seasons' common stock was selling for $10 per share; eighteen months later the stock was trading for $100 per share. However, a large portion of the company's reported profits was bogus, the product of illicit accounting schemes by Four Seasons' executives. In the early 1970s, Four Seasons collapsed when the executives could no longer conceal the company's true financial condition and operating results. Nevertheless, before the company failed, several Four Seasons executives realized large gains on the sale of the company's common stock. One executive, alone, earned more than $10 million by selling stock he owned in the company after the stock's price had skyrocketed on the strength of the false earnings data.

Numerous lawsuits and criminal charges were filed against Four Seasons and its executives. An intercompany memo written by one Four Seasons executive to another was uncovered during the course of these lawsuits. This memo contained the following statement: "Let's get Walston's [one of the company's investment bankers] opinion as to when we could sell a sizable portion of our stock, while the stock is at a good price, to guard against having to sell after the public realizes that [our] nursing homes will not meet [profit] expectations." [Note: The facts in this problem were taken from the following source: M. C. Knapp, "Four Seasons Nursing Centers of America, Inc." in *Contemporary Auditing: Issues and Cases,* 2d ed. (Minneapolis/St. Paul: West Publishing Co., 1996.)]

Required:
1. What parties were harmed by the actions of Four Seasons' executives?
2. Refer to the concept of a "control environment" discussed in Chapter 3. What members of an organization are responsible for establishing an adequate control environment within the organization? Briefly analyze Four Seasons' control environment.
3. Can the establishment of a corporate code of conduct or mission statement, such as the one included in the Spotlight on Ethics vignette in this chapter, help to create a strong control environment in an organization? Why or why not?

51. **Stockholders' Equity for an International Company** (LO 3)

San Miguel Corporation is the largest publicly owned food products company in the Philippines. San Miguel accounts for approximately 4 percent of the country's gross national product and approximately 6 percent of the tax revenues collected by the Philippines federal government. A recent annual report issued by the company disclosed total stockholders' equity of approximately 21 billion Philippine pesos. (The U.S. equivalent of one Philippine peso was approximately $.04 when that annual report was issued.) A "Revaluation Increment" accounted for nearly 6 percent of San Miguel's stockholders' equity. This item resulted from San Miguel periodically revaluing or "writing up" the book values of property, plant & equipment assets to their approximate market values.

San Miguel's annual report indicated that the company was changing its method of accounting for its property, plant & equipment. This change was disclosed in the following financial statement footnote:

> Pursuant to the Company's internationalization thrust . . . the management decided to adjust the recorded appraised value of property, plant and equipment to conform with the historical cost method of valuation. The cost method is internationally the more widely accepted accounting principle for this account. This method, as well as the appraisal valuation method previously used, are both generally accepted accounting principles in the Philippines.

Required:
1. In your opinion, did San Miguel's practice of periodically revaluing its property, plant & equipment materially affect the firm's stockholders' equity? How would you assess "materiality" in this context?
2. What benefits may San Miguel realize as a result of adopting the historical cost principle for its property, plant & equipment? Explain.
3. Suppose that you want to compare the financial statements of a Philippines-based company that applies the "appraisal valuation" accounting method to the financial statements of a similar U.S. company. What specific information would you need to make valid comparisons between the two firms' financial data?

CASES

52. **Preferred Stock Features** (LO 2)

Larsen & O'Leary Publishing Company, a partnership, is preparing articles of incorporation to file with the state corporation commission. The present owners of the firm intend to purchase all 50,000 shares of the corporation's common stock, which will have a $10 par value. The owners also plan to sell 20,000 shares of $100 par value preferred stock to outside investors. This nonvoting preferred stock will have an annual dividend rate of $6 per share. The company's owners are attempting to decide what other features the preferred stock should have. Among the additional features they are considering are a call provision, a convertible option, and a cumulative stipulation. Following are brief descriptions of each of these features.

Call Provision: The preferred stock would be callable on the fifth anniversary date of its issuance. If Larsen & O'Leary exercises the call option, the preferred stockholders would receive $105 per share for the stock they own.

Convertible Option: After ten years, any preferred stock still outstanding could be converted at the option of the preferred stockholders into Larsen & O'Leary common stock. The exchange rate would be three shares of common stock for each share of preferred stock.

Cumulative Stipulation: Any annual dividend not paid on the preferred stock would accumulate as dividends in arrears. In subsequent years, before common stockholders would be entitled to receive any dividends, all dividends in arrears would have to be paid first. If the annual dividend is not paid on the preferred stock for three consecutive years, the preferred stockholders would be granted voting rights. Each share of preferred stock would be entitled to three votes. A one-share/one-vote rule will apply to the company's common stock.

Required:

1. What advantages will the owners of Larsen & O'Leary realize by retaining all of the common stock of the corporation and selling only preferred stock to outside investors?
2. Which of the three preferred stock features being considered would be advantageous to Larsen & O'Leary's common stockholders? Which would be advantageous to the company's preferred stockholders? Explain.
3. Why may the present owners of this firm, its future common stockholders, attach features to the company's preferred stock that would be disadvantageous to them?

53. **Corporate Stock Terminology** (LO 3)

Merle Hopkins is the only M.D. in the small town of Bitter Creek, Wyoming. Dr. Hopkins is beginning to develop a financial plan for his retirement years and has turned to you, a summer intern for a local bank, for some financial advice. Next fall, you will be returning to the University of Wyoming to complete your business degree. Dr. Hopkins realizes that you must have learned a great deal about corporate financial statements during your three years in Laramie. The first question Dr. Hopkins poses to you concerns the different values attached to corporate stocks.

Required:

Write a brief memo to Dr. Hopkins explaining the meaning of each of the following terms and how they are related: par value, stated value, book value per share, and market value (market price of common stock). Particularly perplexing to Dr. Hopkins is the wide disparity in these "values" for individual corporate stocks. In fact, he recently remarked to you, "Who would be fool enough to pay $89 per share for that big oil company's stock when its par value is only ten cents?!"

54. **Stock Split** (LO 3, 5)

The following footnote disclosure was included in a recent annual report of Circus Circus Enterprises, Inc.

In June, the board of directors declared a 3-for-2 stock split on the Company's common stock, which was distributed July 23 to stockholders of record on July 9. All share data have been adjusted retroactively in the accompanying financial statements for the 3-for-2 stock split.

Required:
Interpret this footnote. Why would per share data, such as earnings per share and book value per share amounts, be adjusted retroactively for a stock split—that is, restated from amounts reported in previously issued financial statements? Is this a dishonest practice? Or, are such restatements necessary to prevent the company's financial statements for two or more consecutive years from being misleading when the company's stock was split during the most recent of those years? Explain.

PROJECTS

55. Stockholders' Equity: Management Decisions

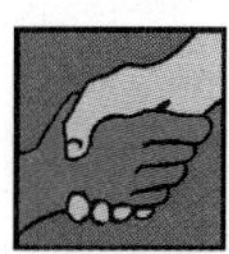

In early 1985, several key executives of a small biotechnology firm headquartered in Utah began negotiating a merger with the executives of another company. While this merger was being secretly negotiated, the executives of the Utah company purchased several hundred thousand shares of their firm's common stock on the open market. When the news of the merger was finally released, the market price of the Utah firm's common stock increased dramatically. At this point, the company's executives sold much of their stock at a large profit. (Note: The facts of this case were drawn from the following source: Securities and Exchange Commission, *Accounting and Auditing Enforcement Release No. 195,* 13 July 1988.)

Required:
Break into your project groups to discuss this case and the following questions.

1. Did the executives of the Utah company behave unethically? If so, who was disadvantaged by their actions?
2. In this case, corporate executives had access to "inside information" that induced them to purchase their company's common stock before that information became public. Often, just the reverse happens (see Problems 44 and 50). That is, corporate executives sell stock in their company before negative "inside information" regarding the company's financial condition or operations is released to the public. Should corporate executives be allowed to profit from inside information? If so, under what general conditions or circumstances? If not, how can corporate executives be prevented from benefitting from such information?
3. Consider this scenario. You are at lunch one day and hear two business executives quietly discussing an upcoming but unannounced merger of two publicly owned companies. You realize that the market price of each company's common stock will likely increase when the merger is announced. Would it be unethical for you to act on this information by purchasing stock in these companies? Keep in mind that you did not "steal" this information. Instead, you were simply in the right place at the right time.
4. Discuss the hypothetical scenario presented in (3). Individual members should defend the answer they gave to the question posed in (3). After this discussion, each group member should answer that question again.
5. One member of your group should be prepared to present a summary overview to the class of your group's discussion of this vignette.

56. Corporate Dividend Policies

Obtain a recent copy of *The Wall Street Journal* and turn to the section entitled "Corporate Dividend News." Choose any five companies for which a dividend announcement was reported on that date.

Required:
For each company selected, record the date the dividend was reported in *The Wall Street Journal,* the payment date, the record date, the amount of the dividend, and whether the dividend was a quarterly, semiannual, or annual dividend. For two of the companies selected, obtain and review their most recent annual reports. For each of these firms, identify information in the company's annual report regarding management's dividend policy or apparent dividend policy. This information may be included in a narrative disclosure within the annual report and/or disclosed in a tabular or graphical format. Prepare a brief written report that documents the information you obtained from *The Wall Street Journal* and the additional information you obtained regarding the dividend policies of two of the companies you selected.

57. Initial Public Offerings
In this project, you will search the Internet to identify three recent initial public offerings (IPOs) of common stock. Among the key phrases you may use in this search are "initial public offering" and related phrases such as "sale of common stock." After identifying these IPOs, you will document key information for each in a written report.

Required:
1. Summarize in a report the principal line of business of each company involved in the three IPOs you identified. Also, identify the principal reason that each company chose to raise funds by selling common stock. For example, was the purpose to provide funds needed to enlarge the company's production facilities, to expand overseas, or to purchase another company?
2. In your report, identify the initial selling price of the stock being sold in each IPO and the number of shares offered for sale. For each IPO that has already taken place, determine how many shares were sold, the stock's closing price on the first day it was traded, and its current market price. You will need to refer to the *The Wall Street Journal* or another source to obtain the latter data.
3. Document in your report the Web site addresses from which you obtained the key data for this project. Also, identify any other sources used for this project.

12 The Corporate Income Statement and Statement of Stockholders' Equity

"Prefer a loss to a dishonest gain: the one brings pain at the moment, the other for all time."
Chilon

LEARNING OBJECTIVES

After studying this chapter, you should be able to do the following:

1. Identify the key elements of the corporate income statement.
2. Compute earnings per share.
3. Account for corporate income taxes.
4. Describe the structure and purpose of a statement of stockholders' equity.
5. Account for prior period adjustments and appropriations of retained earnings.
6. Compute and interpret the price-earnings and market price to book value ratios.

FOCUS ON DECISION MAKING

Ben & Jerry and . . . Bob?

Probably the best known and most successful "corporation with a conscience" is Vermont-based Ben & Jerry's Homemade, Inc. Ben & Jerry's manufactures and markets super premium ice creams and related products. Founded in 1978 by two self-proclaimed hippies, Ben Cohen and Jerry Greenfield, the company quickly outgrew the former gas station that was its original home. Within a few years, the company was known nationwide for such tasty and memorable flavors as Cherry Garcia, Chunky Monkey, Wavy Gravy, and Chubby Hubby. The public's craving for Ben & Jerry's products translated into booming sales and profits for the company.

When it comes to social causes, Ben & Jerry's "puts its money where its mouth is." A longstanding company policy mandates that the firm donate 7.5 percent of pretax profits to a nonprofit corporation, Ben & Jerry's Foundation, Inc. Since the mid-1980s, this foundation has poured millions of dollars into a wide range of charitable organizations and social causes. Recipients of these grants include the Bay Area Nuclear Waste Coalition, the Brattleboro Area Aids Project, and the Vermont Clean Water Project.

Socially conscious firms such as Ben & Jerry's can become so preoccupied with their social causes that they neglect the fundamental business aspects of their operations. Even a "new age" corporation must establish strict collection procedures for receivables, implement inventory control measures, and closely monitor earnings and cash flows. In fact, rigorous financial controls are probably more important for these firms than most, since a sizable portion of their profits is siphoned off as charitable donations.

Economic realities caught up with Ben & Jerry's in the early 1990s. Aggressive competition from firms such as Haagen-Dazs loosened the company's stranglehold on the market for super premium ice creams. The company also had to cope with inventory control problems and disrupted production schedules stemming from the use of antiquated equipment. Collectively, these problems caused Ben & Jerry's growth rates in sales and profits to plummet, culminating in a large net loss for the firm in 1994. Worse yet, the company's stock price nose-dived from $33 to $10 per share. Recognizing that he was not the man to rescue Ben & Jerry's from its downward spiral, Ben Cohen resigned in 1994 as the company's chief executive officer and president.

The individual chosen to revive Ben & Jerry's was Robert Holland, a corporate turnaround specialist. Almost immediately, "President Bob" imposed more conventional operating policies and procedures on the free-spirited culture of Ben & Jerry's. In doing so, Holland often butted heads with Ben Cohen, who remained the firm's largest stockholder. For example, when Holland decided that the company should market its products in France, Ben Cohen disagreed. Cohen steadfastly maintained that the company's products should not be sold in France, in protest of that country's nuclear testing in the South Pacific.

By mid-1996, thanks largely to Holland's management style and executive decisions, Ben & Jerry's was again posting large profits. Outsiders expected the return to profitability to mend any hard feelings between President Bob and Ben Cohen. But, in late 1996, Holland abruptly resigned, forcing Cohen to search for another chief executive to take the reins of the company.

Chapter 11 focused on accounting for stockholders' equity. In this chapter, we again consider stockholders' equity but concentrate principally on financial reporting issues. First, we examine the structure and content of the corporate income statement and related taxation issues. Then, we review the statement of stockholders' equity. We wrap up this chapter by becoming familiar with two financial ratios, the price-earnings and market price to book value ratios. Investors frequently use these ratios when making investment decisions involving corporate common stocks.

THE CORPORATE INCOME STATEMENT

Corporate income statements have been presented in earlier chapters. For example, Chapter 1 presented a condensed income statement for J.C. Penney Company, while Chapter 2 contained a recent income statement of Lincoln Logs Ltd. This section examines in depth financial reporting issues related to the corporate income statement, which earlier chapters have not done. We begin by identifying information needs of decision makers that income statements address. Next, we review alternative titles and formats for corporate income statements and their key elements. This section concludes with an overview of corporate income taxes.

If we are going to analyze the corporate income statement, we need to have an example to which we can refer occasionally. Most corporate income statements do not contain all of the elements that we need to consider. So, for illustration purposes, we will use an income statement of an imaginary company, Happy Hollow Corporation. Exhibit 12.1 presents a recent income statement for this firm. The line items in Happy Hollow's income statement are numbered so that we can refer more easily to specific components of this financial statement. Notice also that certain key items in Happy Hollow's income statement are boldfaced.

Corporate Income Statements: Serving the Information Needs of Decision Makers

A wide range of decision makers rely on the information found in corporate income statements. As suggested in Chapter 11, investors need such information to make rational and informed investment decisions. Suppliers need to know whether their corporate customers are "moneymaking" operations so they can decide whether to continue extending credit to them. Prospective employees want to identify profitable corporations that promise a reliable source of employment income. Finally, consider executives of charitable organizations, a small subset of financial decision makers. These individuals study corporate income statements to identify profitable companies that can easily afford to donate "a few million here and there" to good causes.

Keep in mind as we study and dissect the corporate income statement that it is just one source of data regarding corporations. Decision makers must analyze each of a corporation's financial statements and the accompanying footnotes in addition to other relevant information to reliably evaluate the firm's financial status and future prospects.

EXHIBIT 12.1 ▼
Example of a Corporate Income Statement

HAPPY HOLLOW CORPORATION
INCOME STATEMENT
FOR THE YEAR ENDED DECEMBER 31, 1997

1	Net sales		$2,100,000
2	Cost of goods sold		1,240,000
3	Gross profit		$ 860,000
4	Operating expenses:		
5	Selling	$ 80,000	
6	General	47,000	
7	Administrative	130,000	257,000
8	Operating income		$ 603,000
9	Other gains or losses:		
10	Gain on sale of equipment		42,000
11	Income from continuing operations before income tax		$ 645,000
12	Income tax expense		258,000
13	**Income from continuing operations**		$ 387,000
14	**Discontinued operations:**		
15	Operating income, $24,000, less income tax of $9,600	$ 14,400	
16	Gain on disposal, $40,000, less income tax of $16,000	24,000	38,400
17	Income before extraordinary loss and cumulative effect of a change in accounting principle		$ 425,400
18	**Extraordinary loss due to tornado, $100,000, less income tax savings of $40,000**		(60,000)
19	**Cumulative effect of a change in accounting principle, $18,000, less income tax of $7,200**		10,800
20	Net income		$ 376,200
21	**Earnings per share of common stock:**		
22	Income from continuing operations		$3.87
23	Income from discontinued operations		.38
24	Income before extraordinary loss and cumulative effect of a change in accounting principle		$4.25
25	Extraordinary loss		(.60)
26	Cumulative effect of a change in accounting principle		.11
27	Net income		$3.76

Alternative Income Statement Titles and Formats

Corporations do not necessarily refer to the financial statement that reports their periodic revenues and expenses as an income statement. *Accounting Trends & Techniques* reveals that approximately 50 percent of all companies use a title other than "income statement." The two most common alternative titles are "statement of earnings" and "statement of operations." The latter caption is often used when

An Income Statement with a Northern Accent

FOR YOUR INFORMATION

Our friendly neighbors to the north, the Canadians, share most of our attitudes toward accounting and financial reporting. On certain matters of style, though, the Canadians often go their own way. Take the case of Hudson's Bay Company, Canada's largest department store chain and its oldest corporation, having been founded in 1670. Following is the company's statement of earnings for the year ended January 31, 1996. Contrast the format of Happy Hollow's income statement in Exhibit 12.1 with the income statement format used by Hudson's Bay. (As a point of information, The Bay and Zellers are the two major divisions of Hudson's Bay.)

HUDSON'S BAY COMPANY
CONSOLIDATED STATEMENT OF EARNINGS

	Notes	Year Ended January 31, 1996 $000's
Sales and revenue		
The Bay		2,348,571
Zellers		3,536,601
Other		99,346
		5,984,518
Operating profit		
The Bay		121,108
Zellers		106,730
Other		(13,378)
Earnings before interest and income taxes		214,460
Interest expense	3	(129,152)
Earnings before income taxes		85,308
Income taxes	4	(50,758)
Net earnings		34,550
Earnings per share	5	$0.59

a company has incurred a loss for one or more of the years for which financial data are being presented.

Corporations use one of two alternative formats for their income statements, the single-step format or the multiple-step format. In the single-step format, a company lists its revenues followed by its expenses and then computes net income as the difference between the totals of those two items. Many companies in service industries use the single-step format, for example, Quick & Reilly, the discount brokerage firm. Approximately two-thirds of all companies, according to *Accounting Trends & Techniques,* use the multiple-step format for their income statements. In a multiple-step income statement, certain revenues and expenses are netted to arrive at key subtotals, such as gross profit and operating income, before net income is presented. The accountants of Happy Hollow Corporation used the multiple-step format in preparing the income statement shown in Exhibit 12.1.

Key Elements of the Corporate Income Statement

LEARNING OBJECTIVE 1 ▶
Identify the key elements of the corporate income statement.

This section introduces you to the common elements or components of a corporate income statement. As we review Happy Hollow's 1997 income statement in Exhibit 12.1, recognize that corporations typically present income statement data on a comparative basis, that is, for multiple years. Corporations regulated by the Securities and Exchange Commission (SEC) generally present income statement data for their most recent fiscal year and the two preceding years.

INCOME FROM CONTINUING OPERATIONS In 1997, Happy Hollow had Income from Continuing Operations of $387,000, as shown on line 13 of Exhibit 12.1. That amount is net of income taxes of $258,000 reported on line 12. Later in this chapter, we examine several corporate taxation issues. For the time being, you should be aware of two "taxing" matters as they pertain to Happy Hollow's 1997 income statement. First, key items in a corporate income statement are presented "net of tax." This presentation method reveals to financial statement users the dollar effect of such items on an entity's net income. Second, corporations have different effective, or average, income tax rates. Happy Hollow's average income tax rate in 1997 was 40 percent. So, each income tax expense amount reported in Exhibit 12.1 is 40 percent of the related item. For instance, the income tax expense reported on line 12 of Exhibit 12.1 is 40 percent of Happy Hollow's Income from Continuing Operations Before Income Tax (line 11).

income from continuing operations

Income from continuing operations represents the earnings produced by a corporation's principal profit-oriented activities. Decision makers often use a firm's income from continuing operations as the starting point for developing profit forecasts for the firm. A company's expected growth rate in sales, competitive conditions in its industry, and the general health of the national economy are factors that decision makers can use to project the firm's future earnings given its current year's income from continuing operations as a base amount.

DISCONTINUED OPERATIONS Most large corporations have more than one line of business. For example, a corporation whose principal line of business is a chain of discount stores may also operate a trucking company and an equipment leasing firm.

discontinued operations

When a corporation decides to discontinue a line of business, a section entitled **discontinued operations** should be included in its income statement. This section of a corporate income statement normally contains two items: the operating income or loss for that business segment and the net gain or loss resulting from the disposal of the segment. Notice that line 15 of Happy Hollow's income statement reports operating income of $14,400, net of income tax, for a discontinued line of business. The following line reports a $24,000 after-tax gain on the disposal of that business segment. Listing these items in this manner clearly indicates that they are not components of continuing operations and thus should not be considered when making future profit projections.

When a company's income statement reports discontinued operations, an accompanying financial statement footnote typically describes the nature of those operations. That footnote provides additional details as well of the operating results and gains or losses attributable to the discontinued business segment. Halliburton Company, an oil well servicing firm, reported a loss from discontinued operations of $65.5 million in a recent annual report. A financial statement footnote entitled "Discontinued Operations" revealed that Halliburton had disposed of an insurance firm it had previously owned and operated. That footnote also presented a condensed income statement documenting the operating results of the discontinued business segment.

EXTRAORDINARY ITEMS Occasionally, companies incur material gains or losses—mostly losses—due to rare events such as a catastrophic fire. Because these "extraordinary items" are not normal components of a corporation's revenues and expenses, they should be shown separately in a corporate income statement. Accounting standards require that *both* of the following criteria be met before a gain or loss qualifies as an **extraordinary item:**

extraordinary item

1. *Unusual nature:* The underlying event or transaction should possess a high degree of abnormality and be of a type clearly unrelated to, or only incidentally related to, the ordinary and typical activities of the entity, taking into account the environment in which the entity operates.
2. *Infrequency of occurrence:* The underlying event or transaction should be of a type that would not reasonably be expected to recur in the foreseeable future, taking into account the environment in which the entity operates.[1]

According to *Accounting Trends & Techniques,* approximately 10 to 15 percent of publicly owned companies each year report extraordinary items in their income statements. Happy Hollow's income statement includes an extraordinary loss of $60,000 resulting from a tornado (line 18). The gross loss attributable to the tornado was $100,000; however, the loss reduced the company's income tax expense by $40,000. As recommended by accounting standards, Happy Hollow reported this extraordinary item following the discontinued operations section of its income statement.

Businesses often incur gains or losses that meet one of the two criteria for extraordinary items but not both. For example, a company that grows agricultural products in a flood-prone area may suffer material losses every five to ten years because of a flood. Since the floods occur periodically, the resulting losses do not meet the "infrequency of occurrence" requirement for extraordinary items. On the other hand, these losses may qualify as unusual in nature. Typically, gains or losses that meet only one of the two criteria for extraordinary items are reported as separate components of an entity's income from continuing operations. Apparently, Happy Hollow Corporation considers the disposal of equipment an unusual or infrequently occurring transaction. Notice in Exhibit 12.1 (line 10) that the $42,000 "Gain on Sale of Equipment" is re-

1. "Reporting the Results of Operations" *Accounting Principles Board Opinion No. 30* (New York: AICPA, 1973), para. 20.

ported as a separate component of Happy Hollow's income from continuing operations. Unlike an extraordinary item, an unusual or infrequently occurring gain or loss is *not* presented net of taxes.

Cabletron Systems, Inc., markets products used in local area computer networks. Cabletron reported a net income of $164.4 million in its 1996 annual report. The continuing operations section of the company's income statement separately listed $85.7 million of "nonrecurring expenses." A footnote to Cabletron's financial statements described the nature of those expenses.

CUMULATIVE EFFECT OF A CHANGE IN ACCOUNTING PRINCIPLE Cascade Corporation designs and manufactures materials handling equipment. In 1994, Cascade reported a $2 million expense item due to a change in the method it used to account for postretirement benefits other than pensions (OPBs). As noted in Chapter 10, a new accounting standard adopted in the early 1990s mandated that companies begin accounting for OPBs on an accrual basis. Like most companies, Cascade had previously accounted for OPBs on a cash basis.

cumulative effect of a change in accounting principle

A company that changes from one accounting principle to another must report a **cumulative effect of a change in accounting principle** in its income statement for the year in which the accounting change is made. For our purposes, let us define such an item as the change in an entity's collective net income for prior years assuming a newly adopted accounting principle had been used during those years. If Cascade had used the accrual basis of accounting for OPBs since its inception, the company's cumulative, after-tax earnings before 1994 would have been nearly $2 million less. So, in 1994, when Cascade switched to the accrual basis of accounting for OPBs, the firm had to record a "catch-up" expense of $2 million.

As shown in Exhibit 12.1 (line 19), Happy Hollow Corporation reported a $10,800 cumulative effect of a change in accounting principle in its 1997 income statement. A cumulative effect item is inserted in an income statement following any extraordinary items and immediately before net income. Recognize that the impact of a newly adopted accounting principle on an entity's *current* year revenues or expenses is included in income from continuing operations. The $10,800 cumulative effect item shown in Exhibit 12.1 relates to Happy Hollow's pre-1997 fiscal years. The impact of the new accounting principle on Happy Hollow's 1997 operations is included in the firm's income from continuing operations for that year.

The annual surveys that are the basis for each edition of *Accounting Trends & Techniques* reveal that most changes in accounting principles, or "accounting changes," result from companies implementing new accounting standards adopted by the FASB. Examples of other accounting changes include switching from one inventory accounting method to another, changing depreciation methods, and capitalizing costs formerly expensed. One final point. When a company changes an accounting principle, it must justify the change in the footnotes to its financial statements. That justification should explain why the new accounting principle is preferable to the principle that was formerly used.

LEARNING OBJECTIVE 2 ▶ Compute earnings per share.

EARNINGS PER SHARE No doubt, earnings per share is the most closely monitored and eagerly awaited financial disclosure each year for publicly owned companies. A lower than expected earnings per share typically causes a company's stock price to decline, while a positive earnings surprise generally triggers an increase in a company's stock price. Notice in Exhibit 12.1 that Happy Hollow reported an overall earnings per share of $3.76 for 1997. The company also reported separate per share amounts for income from continuing operations, among other items. Segmenting earnings per share into its various components allows decision makers to interpret earnings data more quickly and accurately.

Earnings per share is generally computed by dividing a company's net income by the weighted-average number of shares of common stock outstanding during the year. Happy Hollow had 100,000 shares of common stock outstanding throughout all of 1997. Dividing that number of shares into Happy Hollow's net income of $376,200 for 1997 yields the earnings per share of $3.76 shown on line 27 of Exhibit 12.1. Suppose now that Happy Hollow had 80,000 shares of common stock outstanding for the first six months of 1997. Then, on July 1, the company issued an additional 20,000 shares, resulting in 100,000 shares being outstanding over the final six months of the year. The weighted-average number of shares outstanding for 1997 under this scenario would have been 90,000: (80,000 × 6/12) + (100,000 × 6/12). Thus, Happy Hollow's overall earnings per share would have been $4.18 ($376,200/90,000).

earnings per share

The term "earnings per share" is used only in reference to common stock. There is no such "animal" as earnings per share of preferred stock. However, if a company has preferred stock outstanding, its earnings per share computation is affected. Such a company first subtracts dividends on preferred stock from net income when computing earnings per share. Assume that in 1997 Happy Hollow had 10,000 shares of preferred stock outstanding on which a $3 per share dividend was paid. If the firm had 100,000 shares of common stock outstanding throughout the year, the company's earnings per share would have been $3.46.

$$\text{Earnings per Share} = \frac{\text{Net Income} - \text{Preferred Stock Dividends}}{\text{Weighted-Average Number of Shares of Common Stock Outstanding}}$$

$$\text{Earnings per Share} = \frac{\$376{,}200 - \$30{,}000}{100{,}000}$$

$$\text{Earnings per Share} = \$3.46$$

Polishing the Corporate Brass

Compensation of top executives is a major expense for most large corporations, such as Ben & Jerry's Homemade, Inc., the firm profiled in the opening vignette of this chapter. Until the mid-1990s, Ben & Jerry's linked the pay of its top executives to the wages earned by the company's unskilled workers. Annual salaries of company executives could not exceed seven times the annual wages of the janitor, mail clerk, or delivery person who happened to be the lowest paid employee of Ben & Jerry's. The firm voided that policy in 1994 during its search for a chief executive officer to replace Ben Cohen.

Escalating salaries for corporate executives in recent years have caused many stockholders' rights activists to demand that corporations adopt compensation policies similar to the one scrapped by Ben & Jerry's in 1994. So, just how much do corporate executives earn? In 1996, the CEO of U.S. Robotics earned a cool $34 million, while H.J. Heinz's CEO pocketed more than $64 million. Those figures are impressive by most standards yet relatively modest compared to the $102 million of compensation earned in 1996 by the CEO of Green Tree Financial Corporation, a firm based in St. Paul, Minnesota.

Corporate Income Taxes

LEARNING OBJECTIVE 3 ▶
Account for corporate income taxes.

Before dissecting Happy Hollow's income statement, we briefly touched on the subject of corporate income taxes. Given the magnitude of income tax expense for most corporations and the resulting implications for decision makers, this section examines corporate income taxes in more depth. To simplify matters, we consider only the federal income taxes that corporations pay. Recognize that most corporations pay other income taxes as well.

CORPORATE INCOME TAX RATES Congress historically has imposed a graduated, or progressive, tax rate structure on corporations. As corporations earn more taxable income, the percentage of that income that must be paid to the federal government generally increases. Notice the term "taxable income." Corporations pay taxes based upon their taxable income, not their pretax accounting income, which is commonly referred to as income before income taxes. Exhibit 12.2 lists the tax rates that corporations were subject to when this book was being written.

Suppose that a corporation has $150,000 of taxable income. Given the tax rates shown in Exhibit 12.2, this corporation would owe federal income taxes of $41,750:

Federal Income Tax Payable = $22,250 + .39($150,000 − $100,000)
Federal Income Tax Payable = $22,250 + $19,500
Federal Income Tax Payable = $41,750

temporary differences

TEMPORARY DIFFERENCES Accountants use the phrase **temporary differences** when referring to certain differences between an entity's taxable income and its pre-

The Internal Revenue Service (IRS) oversees the collection of federal income taxes from individuals and corporations. Income taxes are typically a significant expense item for most corporations. For example, in recent years, the income tax expense of Sears, Roebuck & Co. has approached one-half billion dollars.

EXHIBIT 12.2 ▼
Federal Income Tax Rates for Corporations

If taxable income is: Over—	But not over—	Tax is—	Of the amount over—
$ 0	$ 50,000	15%	$ 0
50,000	75,000	$ 7,500+25%	50,000
75,000	100,000	13,750+34%	75,000
100,000	335,000	22,250+39%	100,000
335,000	10,000,000	113,900+34%	335,000
10,000,000	15,000,000	3,400,000+35%	10,000,000
15,000,000	18,333,333	5,150,000+38%	15,000,000
18,333,333	—	35%	0

Note: The 39% and 38% rates are imposed to phase out the benefits of the lower brackets for high-income corporations.

Source: 1997 U.S. Master Tax Guide (Chicago: Commerce Clearing House, 1996).

tax accounting income. These items arise from applying different accounting methods for taxation and financial accounting purposes. For example, recall that companies must use the direct write-off method to account for bad debt expense for taxation purposes, while they typically apply the allowance method for financial accounting purposes. In a given year, a company may have bad debt expense of $14,000 for taxation purposes and $25,000 for financial accounting purposes. The $11,000 difference between these amounts is a temporary difference. "Temporary" is an appropriate adjective for such items because eventually these differences disappear. For instance, in the example just given, the firm's total bad debt expense over its entire existence will be the same for taxation and financial accounting purposes.

Exhibit 12.3 lists sources of temporary differences identified in a recent annual report of Pinkerton's, Inc., the security services firm. For each financial statement item listed in Exhibit 12.3, Pinkerton's applies a different accounting method for taxation and financial accounting purposes.

Temporary differences generally work to the benefit of corporations. Corporations tend to use accounting methods for taxation purposes that postpone the recognition

EXHIBIT 12.3 ▼
Sources of Temporary Differences for Pinkerton's, Inc.

- Allowance for Doubtful Accounts
- Self-Insurance Reserves
- Depreciation
- Retirement Benefits
- Investment Losses
- Vacation Pay
- Amortization of Intangibles

of revenues or accelerate the recognition of expenses. This strategy allows corporations to defer taxes owed to Uncle Sam. Recall the famous adage used for years in a series of television commercials, "You can pay me now, or you can pay me later." In the case of taxes, the latter alternative is clearly preferred.

ACCOUNTING FOR CORPORATE INCOME TAXES Temporary differences, changes in tax rates, and the huge volume of tax laws and regulations complicate accounting for income taxes. Because of the complex nature of this subject, only a brief overview is provided here.

As noted earlier, corporations pay taxes to the federal government based upon their taxable incomes. However, a corporation's income tax expense is based upon its pretax accounting income. Consider the following entry to record a corporation's income tax expense at year-end.

Dec. 31	Income Tax Expense	143,000	
	Income Taxes Payable		106,000
	Deferred Income Taxes		37,000
	To record federal income tax expense		

Notice in this example that the corporation's income tax expense exceeds the firm's income taxes currently payable by $37,000. This latter amount represents income tax payments that the firm has postponed or deferred. Appropriately, such amounts are recorded in an account entitled **Deferred Income Taxes.**

Deferred Income Taxes

Deferred Income Taxes can be either a current or long-term liability but is more often a long-term liability. Thanks to their knowledgeable tax accountants, many large corporations report huge deferred tax liabilities in their balance sheets. A recent balance sheet of Procter & Gamble included a $347 million long-term liability for deferred taxes, while Computer Associates recently reported a comparable long-term liability of $460 million. Occasionally, Deferred Income Taxes has a debit balance, in which case it is classified as either a current or long-term asset for balance sheet purposes.

▲ STATEMENT OF STOCKHOLDERS' EQUITY

LEARNING OBJECTIVE 4 ▶
Describe the structure and purpose of a statement of stockholders' equity.

The SEC does not require companies that it regulates to prepare a statement of stockholders' equity. What the SEC does require is a reconciliation of the beginning-of-the-year and end-of-the-year balance of each stockholders' equity account. A company can include a schedule of these reconciliations in its financial statement footnotes. More commonly, the SEC's requirement is met by preparing a statement of stockholders' equity. According to *Accounting Trends & Techniques,* more than 80 percent of all public companies include a statement of stockholders' equity in their annual reports. One of these firms is Outback Steakhouse, Inc., the company whose 1996 annual report is included as an appendix to this text.

Statement of Stockholders' Equity Illustrated

Exhibit 12.4 presents a recent statement of stockholders' equity for ShopKo Stores, Inc. As advertised, this statement reconciles the beginning-of-the-year and end-of-the-

EXHIBIT 12.4 ▼
Statement of Stockholders' Equity for ShopKo Stores, Inc., for the Year Ended February 24, 1996 (in thousands)

	Common Stock		Additional Paid-In Capital	Retained Earnings
	Shares	Amount		
Balances at February 25, 1995	32,005	$320	$242,843	$154,112
Net income				38,439
Cash dividends declared on common stock—$.44 per share				(14,083)
Balances at February 24, 1996	32,005	$320	$242,843	$178,468

year balances of ShopKo's stockholders' equity accounts. Companies with capital structures that include preferred stock, treasury stock, and other stockholders' equity items have more elaborate statements of stockholders' equity. However, those statements have the same general format as ShopKo's statement of stockholders' equity.

Notice that only two items affected ShopKo's stockholders' equity during its fiscal year ended February 24, 1996. Net income of $38.4 million and cash dividends of slightly more than $14 million were closed to the company's Retained Earnings account. If you refer to Outback Steakhouse's annual report in an appendix to this text, you will find that only two items affected that firm's stockholders' equity during its fiscal year ended December 31, 1996. Those two items were net income of nearly $72 million and the issuance of additional common stock.

Prior Period Adjustments

LEARNING ◀ OBJECTIVE 5
Account for prior period adjustments and appropriations of retained earnings.

A **prior period adjustment** is a correction of a material error occurring in a previous accounting period that involved a revenue or expense. This correction is made directly to a firm's Retained Earnings account in the accounting period when the error is discovered. Because prior period adjustments are recorded in the Retained Earnings account instead of a revenue or expense account, they appear in a firm's statement of stockholders' equity rather than its income statement. Errors that may result in prior period adjustments include fraud, mathematical mistakes, misapplication of accounting principles, and misinterpretation of facts. Suppose that in May 1998 a company discovers that its prior year's depreciation expense was accidentally understated. This error resulted in a $24,000 overstatement of the company's 1997 net income, net of the related tax effect. This $24,000 would be reported as a prior period adjustment in the firm's 1998 statement of stockholders' equity.

prior period adjustment

Prior period adjustments are rare, so rare, in fact, that the financial statements of the 600 companies surveyed annually by *Accounting Trends & Techniques* seldom yield one example of a prior period adjustment. The Spotlight on Ethics vignette accompanying this section describes the circumstances surrounding a prior period adjustment reported in the early 1990s by a public company.

Searching for Treasure on the High Seas Leads to Trouble with the SEC

In the early 1990s, Seahawk Deep Ocean Technology, Inc. (SDOT) was apparently the only public company whose principal line of business involved retrieving valuable artifacts from shipwrecks. SDOT searched the ocean floor off the southeastern United States to locate treasures carried more than three centuries earlier by Spanish galleons.

In 1994, the SEC filed a complaint against SDOT. This complaint alleged that the company overstated the value of items discovered in a shipwreck location off the Florida coast. The SEC eventually sanctioned SDOT and required the firm to record a large prior period adjustment to correct errors in earlier financial statements that resulted from the inflated values assigned to shipwreck artifacts.

Appropriations of Retained Earnings

LEARNING OBJECTIVE 5 ▶ Account for prior period adjustments and appropriations of retained earnings.

appropriation of retained earnings

Occasionally, a statement of stockholders' equity includes one or more appropriations of retained earnings. An **appropriation of retained earnings** is a part of retained earnings that has been "earmarked," or restricted, for a special purpose. (Recognize that a company does not necessarily have cash funds equal to the amount of appropriated retained earnings or "unappropriated" retained earnings, for that matter, as suggested in Chapter 11.)

To illustrate an appropriation of retained earnings, assume that on December 31, 1998, the Red Horse Freight Company has $7.5 million of retained earnings. On that date, the company borrows $5 million from a bank on a five-year promissory note. One stipulation of the loan agreement makes $4 million of Red Horse's retained earnings unavailable for the declaration of dividends over the note's term. This restrictive debt covenant protects the economic interests of the lender. By limiting Red Horse's ability to pay dividends, the restrictive debt covenant increases the likelihood that the firm will be able to make the required principal and interest payments on the note. Although not required to do so by GAAP, Red Horse may recognize this restriction on retained earnings in its accounting records with the following entry.

Dec. 31	Retained Earnings	4,000,000	
	Retained Earnings, Appropriated due to Restrictive Debt Covenant		4,000,000
	To record appropriation of retained earnings due to restrictive debt covenant in loan agreement with Altamesa National Bank		

Red Horse's statement of stockholders' equity for the year ended December 31, 1998, may include a column for both unrestricted retained earnings and appropriated, or restricted, retained earnings. Additionally, in its December 31, 1998, balance sheet, Red Horse would report its total retained earnings of $7.5 million as follows:

Retained earnings:		
Appropriated under terms of long-term debt agreement	$4,000,000	
Unrestricted	3,500,000	
Total retained earnings		$7,500,000

This balance sheet treatment effectively communicates to decision makers that the ability of the company to pay dividends is limited. When Red Horse pays off the note payable, the appropriated retained earnings will be returned to unrestricted retained earnings by reversing the original appropriation entry.

ANALYZING CORPORATE COMMON STOCKS AS POTENTIAL INVESTMENTS

LEARNING OBJECTIVE 6
Compute and interpret the price-earnings and market price to book value ratios.

Investors are a large and important class of financial decision makers. A free market economy relies on investors to allocate their resources (investment funds) to productive business ventures. Society benefits if individuals invest in companies that provide a stable source of income for employees, sizable tax revenues for governmental agencies, and a reasonable rate of return for stockholders. To make optimal investment decisions, investors need relevant, reliable, and understandable accounting information. Such information helps investors identify companies with strong liquidity, good earnings potential, and solid cash flow prospects.

Investors cannot rely exclusively on accounting information when analyzing common stocks for investment purposes. A company that has impressive financial statements may be a poor investment. Why? Because the market price of its stock is too high. Here we consider two financial ratios that investors use to analyze the reasonableness of a company's stock price at any point in time. These ratios are the price-earnings and market price to book value ratios.

Price-Earnings Ratio

price-earnings (P/E) ratio

The **price-earnings (P/E) ratio** is computed by dividing the current market price of a company's common stock by its earnings per share for the most recent twelve-month period, as indicated by the following equation.

$$\text{Price-Earnings Ratio} = \frac{\text{Current Market Price of Common Stock}}{\text{Earnings per Share for Most Recent 12-Month Period}}$$

If a corporation's common stock has a much higher P/E ratio than its historical norm, sophisticated investors will likely conclude that the stock is overpriced. If a common stock is selling for an abnormally low P/E ratio by historical standards, investors will likely view the stock as a bargain.

If you read *The Wall Street Journal* regularly, you will often find references to bulls and bears. On Wall Street, a bull is someone who believes that stock prices are on the rise, while a bear is someone who believes that stock prices will be trending downward in the future.

© Bill Losh/FPG International

Like most financial statistics, there are limitations of the P/E ratio that can make it unreliable when used independently of other available information. For example, changes in a company's industry, the retirement of key executives, and many other factors may cause a company's normal P/E ratio to change over time. Likewise, a company's P/E ratio can be significantly distorted in any one year by extraordinary losses and other "special" income statement items discussed earlier in this chapter.

P/E ratios are particularly insightful when analyzed on a comparative basis. Exhibit 12.5 presents the P/E ratios of several well-known corporations in August 1996. Notice the large range of P/E ratios across these firms. The most striking contrast is the difference between the P/E ratio of Coca-Cola (40) and that of Philip Morris (13). Think of it this way. In August 1996, investors were willing to pay $13 for every $1 of Philip Morris's earnings but were willing to pay a whopping $40 for each $1 of Coca-Cola's earnings. By comparison, the average P/E ratio for large corporations at the time was approximately 19.[2]

Financial analysts track the prices of common stocks and periodically make recommendations regarding which are good investments. In September 1996, a prominent financial analyst with Goldman Sachs, a Wall Street investment banking firm, recommended that investors not purchase Coca-Cola stock at the time.[3] Although the analyst

2. "Investment Figures of the Week," *Business Week,* 26 August 1996, 79. As a point of information, each week *Business Week* reports the average P/E ratio of the five hundred large firms that make up the Standard & Poor's 500.

3. L. Washington, "Always Coca-Cola? Not If You're Marc Cohen," *Smart Money,* September 1996, 30, 32.

EXHIBIT 12.5 ▼
Price-Earnings Ratios, Selected Companies

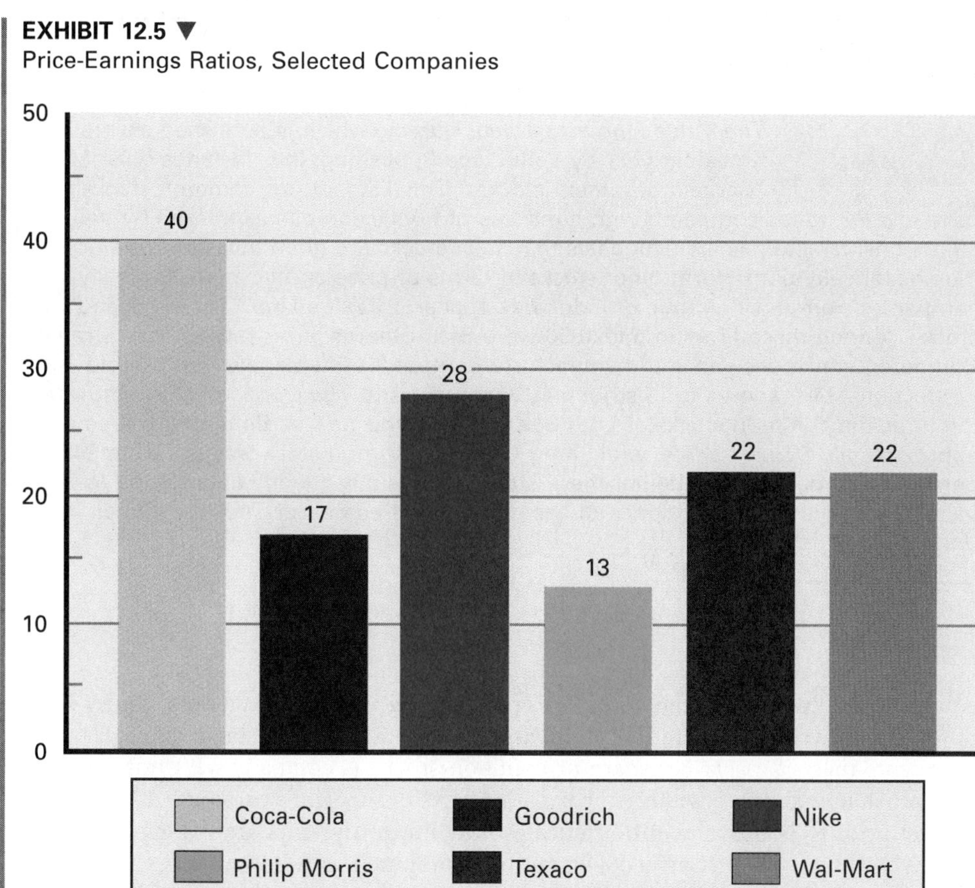

Source: The Wall Street Journal, August 27, 1996.

believed that Coca-Cola was a financially strong company, he maintained there was only a minimal likelihood the firm's stock price would increase in the near future given the stock's high P/E ratio. The same analyst was "bullish" on Philip Morris common stock. The analyst pointed out that negative publicity stemming from numerous large lawsuits filed in the mid-1990s against tobacco companies, including Philip Morris, had driven these firms' stock prices down to modest levels by historical standards.

Well, you have the final word in this matter. How did the stock prices of Coca-Cola and Philip Morris fare during the late 1990s? In late August 1996, Coca-Cola traded for $51 per share, while Philip Morris was selling at $90 per share. Pick up a recent edition of *The Wall Street Journal* and check out the price of each stock and its corresponding P/E ratio.

Market Price to Book Value Ratio

Many companies regularly report a book value per share for their common stock although not required to do so by accounting standards or the SEC. Recall from Chapter 11 that book value per share is computed by dividing total common stockholders'

Bargain Basement Stocks

FOR YOUR INFORMATION

The Value Line Investment Survey, which is published several times per year by Value Line Publishing, Inc., includes a list of "bargain basement stocks." This list features common stocks that have low P/E ratios compared with hundreds of public companies tracked by Value Line. Considerable research suggests that such stocks are good investments since they historically outperform other stocks in terms of price appreciation. Typically, companies from a wide range of industries appear on Value Line's list of "cheap" stocks. Among these firms in mid-1996 were Bear Stearns, a brokerage firm; Stratus Computer, which designs and manufactures computer systems; and King World Productions, best known for distributing *Jeopardy!* and *The Oprah Winfrey Show.* At the time, the common stocks of both Bear Stearns and Stratus Computer traded at approximately $23 per share, while King World's common stock was priced at $43 per share. To determine whether these stocks have subsequently appreciated in value, check out the current price of each in a recent edition of *The Wall Street Journal.*

equity by the number of common shares outstanding. Since stockholders' equity is the difference between a corporation's total assets and total liabilities, book value per share represents the net assets per share of common stock. A company's P/E ratio reveals how much investors are willing to pay for each $1 of the firm's earnings. A company's **market price to book value ratio** indicates how much investors are willing to pay for each $1 of the firm's net assets. This ratio is computed as follows:

market price to book value ratio

$$\text{Market Price to Book Value Ratio} = \frac{\text{Current Market Price of Common Stock}}{\text{Book Value per Share}}$$

A naive investor might assume that the market price to book value ratio for most common stocks is 1.0, or thereabouts. That is, if a company's common stock has a book value per share of $24, the stock's current market price should be approximately $24. In fact, the market price of a common stock often differs considerably from its book value per share. Why? Because the accounting-based book value, or net asset value per share, does not necessarily reflect the "true" economic value of a corporation's common stock. Recall that for accounting purposes, historical cost, rather than market value or true economic value, is the primary valuation basis used for most assets.

Exhibit 12.6 lists market price to book value ratios for the common stocks of six companies in 1996. At the time, the average market price to book value ratio for large firms was approximately 3.5.[4] However, notice that investors were willing to pay nearly $6 for every $1 of Cabletron Systems' net assets, while the "going price" for $1 of The Good Guys' net assets was only $.64. A review of these firms' operations and future prospects in 1996 provides insight as to why there was such a large disparity in their market price to book value ratios.

4. R. D. Hylton, "Is the Stock Market Too Pricey?" *Fortune,* 1 April 1996, 151–152.

EXHIBIT 12.6 ▼
Market Price to Book Value Ratios, Selected Companies

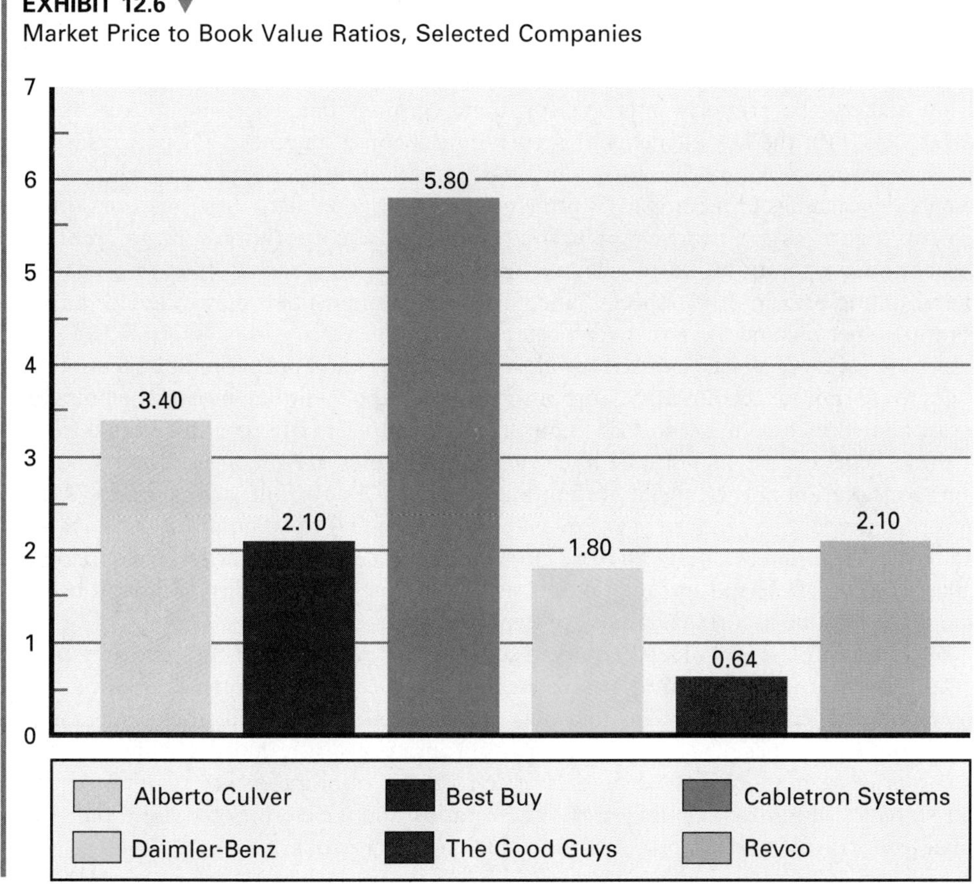

Cabletron markets products used in local area computer networks. A growing demand for such products in the late 1990s caused investors to perceive that Cabletron had tremendous profit potential in the years to come. That perception, in turn, caused investors to bid up the price of Cabletron's stock to a level several times greater than its book value per share. On the other hand, the future prospects of The Good Guys were much dimmer at the time. The Good Guys retails consumer electronic products from more than seventy outlets in the western United States, principally California. In 1996, the company was facing stiff competition from several larger competitors. For example, Best Buy's new "superstores" in California were cutting sharply into The Good Guys' sales in its primary market area. Financial analysts projected that The Good Guys would continue to face difficult competitive conditions in the late 1990s, meaning that the firm's profit potential was modest, at best.

Recognize that neither P/E ratios nor market price to book value ratios reveal which stocks' market prices will definitely increase or decrease in the future. Nevertheless, these ratios provide strong clues regarding the stock market's perception of the investment potential of common stocks. If an investor can identify stocks for which this perception is wrong or will change in the near future, that individual can make a "bundle" in the stock market.

SUMMARY

Corporate income statements are an important source of information for financial decision makers. To properly interpret corporate earnings data, decision makers must be familiar with the key elements of a corporate income statement. Of particular interest to investors is a corporation's income from continuing operations, which represents the earnings of a company's principal profit-oriented activities. Investors often use this figure as the starting point for predicting a corporation's future profits. Discontinued operations, extraordinary items, and the cumulative effect of a change in accounting principle are "special" income statement items that may influence a corporation's net income for any given year.

Income taxes are a large expense for most corporations and pose complex accounting issues for corporate accountants. Corporations must report key income statement items net of related income taxes so that financial statement users can determine the impact of these items on net income. Different accounting rules are often used by corporations for taxation and financial accounting purposes. As a result, a corporation's income tax expense for a given year typically does not equal the amount of tax payable that year. The difference between these two amounts is recorded in the Deferred Income Taxes account. Deferred income taxes is usually a long-term liability, although occasionally it may be a current liability or even an asset.

A statement of stockholders' equity reconciles the beginning-of-the-year and end-of-the-year balances of a corporation's stockholders' equity accounts. Besides net income and dividends, other items that may appear in a statement of stockholders' equity include prior period adjustments and appropriations of retained earnings.

The price-earnings (P/E) and market price to book value ratios are two key financial statistics monitored by investors. These ratios allow investors to assess the reasonableness of the market prices of individual common stocks.

GLOSSARY

Appropriation of retained earnings (p. 550) A part of a corporation's retained earnings that has been restricted for a special purpose; limits the ability of a corporation to pay cash dividends.

Cumulative effect of a change in accounting principle (p. 544) The change in an entity's collective net income for prior years assuming a newly adopted accounting principle had been used during those years.

Deferred Income Taxes (p. 548) An account in which a corporation records the difference between its income tax expense and income tax payable each year; typically a long-term liability account.

Discontinued operations (p. 542) A section of a corporate income statement devoted to a business segment that is being discontinued.

Earnings per share (p. 545) Generally, net income divided by the weighted-average number of shares of common stock outstanding during a given year.

Extraordinary item (p. 543) A material gain or loss that is both unusual in nature and infrequent in occurrence.

Income from continuing operations (p. 542) Represents the earnings produced by a corporation's principal profit-oriented activities.

Market price to book value ratio (p. 554) Computed by dividing the current market price of a company's common stock by its book value per share.

Price-earnings (P/E) ratio (p. 551) Computed by dividing the current market price of a company's common stock by its earnings per share for the most recent twelve-month period.

Prior period adjustment (p. 549) A correction of a material error occurring in a previous accounting period that involved a revenue or expense; the correction is made directly to the Retained Earnings account in the accounting period when the error is discovered.

Temporary differences (p. 546) Differences between an entity's taxable income and pretax accounting income that arise from applying different accounting methods for taxation and financial accounting purposes.

DECISION CASE

In the early 1990s, public interest groups sharply criticized Ben & Jerry's Homemade Inc., the company highlighted in the opening vignette of this chapter. Much of this criticism stemmed from the high-fat content of Ben & Jerry's most popular products. In 1993, the Center for Science in the Public Interest placed Ben & Jerry's super premium ice creams on the top ten list of foods that you should never eat. Tobacco firms, fast-food restaurant chains, and companies producing alcoholic beverages are among other corporations that have been lambasted recently by public interest groups.

Suppose that you are the chief executive officer (CEO) of Carol Ann's Homemade Cookies, Inc. Revenues and earnings skyrocketed over the past few years after your company introduced a new line of cookies, Donut-Dough Delites. The public simply cannot get enough of these high-fat, cholesterol-laden cookies. Although your competitors have tried, they have been unable to develop a product that mimics the taste of Donut-Dough Delites. Nevertheless, trouble is on the horizon. Several public interest groups have banded together and organized a nationwide boycott of your products. These groups insist that your company is profiting at the expense of the public's health. Your accountants have been monitoring the impact of the boycott on monthly sales and profit figures. So far, the boycott's impact is minimal. But, you are concerned that the boycott may eventually cut significantly into your sales.

Required: As the CEO of this company, identify the parties to whom you have a responsibility and briefly describe the nature of each of those responsibilities. Do any of these responsibilities conflict with each other? If so, explain how these conflicts should be resolved.

What accounting and/or financial reporting implications, if any, does the boycott have for your firm? Explain. Finally, evaluate the feasibility and acceptability of the following responses to the boycott:

1. Stop producing the cookies, in which case your company's annual sales and profits will decline by approximately 35 percent.
2. Donate 10 percent of the profits from the cookies to a nonprofit group that researches heart disease.
3. Put a highly visible disclaimer on the cookies' packaging that discloses their high fat and cholesterol content.
4. Threaten to sue the public interest groups if they continue the boycott.

QUESTIONS

1. Identify several classes of financial decision makers that rely on corporate income statements. Indicate the types of decisions these parties make based in part on the data they obtain from corporate income statements.
2. List alternative titles that some corporations use for their annual income statements.
3. Briefly describe the single-step and multiple-step income statement formats.
4. Companies regulated by the SEC generally include how many years of income statement data in their annual financial reports?
5. How do decision makers often use a firm's income from continuing operations?
6. Why are financial data for a discontinued line of business reported separately in a corporate income statement?
7. What two criteria must be met for a gain or loss to qualify as an "extraordinary item" for income statement purposes?
8. If a gain or loss meets only one of the two criteria for being classified as an extraordinary item, how may it be reported in a corporate income statement?
9. Define a "cumulative effect of a change in accounting principle."
10. In general, how is earnings per share computed?
11. What is meant by a graduated, or progressive, income tax rate structure?
12. Distinguish between "taxable income" and "income before income taxes."
13. Why do companies often use different accounting methods for taxation and financial accounting purposes?
14. Define what is meant by the term "temporary difference" in reference to corporate income taxes.
15. When does a corporation use a Deferred Income Taxes account? Is this account typically a liability or an asset account? Current or long-term?
16. What is the purpose of a statement of stockholders' equity?
17. Define "prior period adjustment." Are prior period adjustments frequently found in financial statements?
18. What is an "appropriation of retained earnings"?
19. Identify the equation used in computing the price-earnings (P/E) ratio. How is this ratio used by investors?
20. Why is the market price of a corporation's common stock often considerably different from the common stock's book value per share?

EXERCISES

21. True or False (LO 1–6)

Following are a series of statements regarding topics discussed in Chapter 12.

Required:

Indicate whether each statement is true (T) or false (F).

_____ a. An appropriation of retained earnings is a part of retained earnings that has been earmarked, or designated, for a special purpose.

_____ b. Corporations pay taxes based upon their taxable income, not their pretax accounting income.

_____ c. The Securities and Exchange Commission requires companies that it regulates to include a statement of stockholders' equity in their annual financial reports.

_____ d. A company that changes from one accounting principle to another must report a "catch-up" effect in its income statement in the year following the change.

_____ e. A prior period adjustment is a revenue or expense item reported in an income statement that involves a correction of a material error that occurred in a previous accounting period.

_____ f. Income from continuing operations represents the earnings produced by a corporation's principal profit-oriented activities.

_____ g. The market price to book value ratio indicates how much investors are willing to pay for each $1 of a company's net assets.

_____ h. Earnings per share is generally computed by dividing net income by the number of common shares outstanding at year-end.

_____ i. Because extraordinary items are not normal components of a corporation's revenues and expenses, they should be shown separately in a corporate income statement.

_____ j. Accountants use the term "temporary differences" to refer to certain differences between an entity's net income and its taxable income.

_____ k. If a corporation's common stock has a much higher P/E ratio than its historical norm, sophisticated investors will typically view that stock as "bargain" priced.

22. **Elements of a Corporate Income Statement** (LO 1)
Listed next are items often reported in corporate income statements.

- Operating Income
- Cumulative Effect of a Change in Accounting Principle
- Gross Profit
- Discontinued Operations
- Net Income
- Extraordinary Loss
- Income from Continuing Operations

Required:
1. List these items in their proper order in a corporate income statement.
2. Why is there a distinction in a corporate income statement between transactions and events involving "continuing operations" and transactions and events involving "discontinued operations"?
3. Why are extraordinary items included as separate components of a corporate income statement?

23. **Terms** (LO 1)
Following are definitions or descriptions of terms relating to corporate income statements or income measurement.

_____ The change in an entity's collective net income for prior years assuming a newly adopted accounting principle had been used during those years.

_____ Differences between an entity's taxable income and pretax accounting income that arise from applying different accounting methods for taxation and financial reporting purposes.

_____ An account in which a corporation records the difference between its income tax expense and income tax payable each year; typically a long-term liability account.

_____ Generally, net income divided by the weighted-average number of shares of common stock outstanding during a given year.

_____ A part of a corporation's retained earnings that has been restricted for a special purpose; limits the ability of a corporation to pay cash dividends.

_____ A material gain or loss that is both unusual in nature and infrequent in occurrence.

_____ Represents the earnings produced by a corporation's principal profit-oriented activities.

____ A correction of a material error occurring in a previous accounting period that involves a revenue or expense; the correction is made directly to the Retained Earnings account in the accounting period when the error is discovered.

____ A section of a corporate income statement devoted to a business segment that is being discontinued.

Required:
Match each definition or description with the appropriate term from the following list.

a. Discontinued operations
b. Temporary differences
c. Earnings per share
d. Income from continuing operations
e. Deferred income taxes
f. Appropriation of retained earnings
g. Prior period adjustment
h. Cumulative effect of a change in accounting principle
i. Extraordinary item

24. **Preparing a Corporate Income Statement** (LO 1)
Derinda Bentz is a business major at Southwest Missouri State University. Presently, Derinda is struggling with an accounting homework assignment. Derinda's task is to prepare an income statement for an imaginary firm, Harsha Corporation. Derinda has decided that the following items should be included in this income statement.

Cost of goods sold
Income taxes payable
Accounts receivable
Income tax expense
Loss from discontinued operations
Net sales
Appropriation of retained earnings
Accounts payable
Dividends (paid to stockholders)
Gain on sale of equipment
Salaries payable
Administrative expenses

Required:
Help Derinda complete her homework assignment. Which of the items listed should be included in Harsha Corporation's income statement?

25. **Multiple-Step Income Statement** (LO 1)
Following is information taken from the accounting records of Tarrasco Company at the end of 1998.

- Net sales, $220,000
- Operating income (discontinued operations), $12,000
- Cost of goods sold, $120,000
- Gain on sale of assets (discontinued operations), $20,000
- Operating expenses, $60,000
- Flood loss, $25,000 (an extraordinary item)
- Cumulative effect of a change in depreciation methods, $12,000 (credit balance)

Tarrasco had 10,000 shares of common stock issued and outstanding throughout the year. Tarrasco's effective tax rate is 40 percent.

Required:

1. Prepare a multiple-step income statement for Tarrasco for 1998.
2. Is the single-step or multiple-step income statement format more informative for financial decision makers? Defend your answer.

26. **Computation of Earnings Per Share** (LO 2)

Jericho Corporation had 100,000 shares of common stock outstanding for the first three months of the year. The company issued an additional 20,000 shares on April 1, and another 30,000 shares on September 1. Jericho reported net income of $371,250 for the year ended December 31.

Required:

1. Compute the weighted-average number of shares of common stock Jericho had outstanding during the year.
2. Compute Jericho's earnings per share for the year.
3. Why is the weighted-average number of shares of common stock outstanding during a year used in an earnings per share computation instead of the number of shares outstanding at the end of the year?

27. **Computation of Income Taxes Payable** (LO 3)

Refer to Exhibit 12.2, which lists the federal income tax rates for corporations.

Required:

1. Following is a list of taxable incomes for several corporations. Compute the amount of federal income taxes owed in each case.
   a. $117,000
   b. $37,500
   c. $12,000,000
   d. $62,000
   e. $25,000,000
2. Define a graduated, or progressive, income tax rate structure.
3. What is the reasoning underlying a graduated income tax rate structure?

28. **Deferred Income Taxes** (LO 3)

Suppose that for the current year, College Station Corporation (CSC) has a $10,000 difference between its pretax accounting income and its taxable income, as indicated in the following schedule.

	Pretax Accounting Income	Taxable Income
Income before depreciation expense	$100,000	$100,000
Depreciation expense	(20,000)	(30,000)
	$ 80,000	$ 70,000

Required:

1. Define "temporary difference" as it applies to the pretax accounting income and taxable income of a corporation. What is the dollar amount of the temporary difference in this scenario?
2. Prepare CSC's year-end adjusting entry to record income tax expense for the current year. Assume that CSC's effective income tax rate is 40 percent for both financial accounting and taxation purposes.
3. Suppose that CSC pays the amount of tax due for the current year on January 15 of the following year. Record this payment.
4. How much less income tax did CSC pay in the entry recorded in (3) due to the temporary difference related to depreciation expense?

5. Will CSC eventually pay the dollar amount you computed in (4)? If so, what advantage does CSC realize as a result of the depreciation-related temporary difference?

29. **Temporary Differences** (LO 3)
Following are the 1998 pretax accounting income and taxable income of two corporations. Each firm began operating in 1998 and each has an effective income tax rate of 40 percent for financial accounting and taxation purposes.

	Pretax Accounting Income	Taxable Income
Hartman Corporation	$35,000	$30,000
Reckers Corporation	34,000	38,000

Required:
1. The difference between each company's taxable income and pretax accounting income is due to a "temporary difference." Identify one possible source of each of these temporary differences.
2. Indicate whether the year-end balance of each company's deferred tax account will be reported as an asset or a liability in its December 31, 1998, balance sheet.

30. **Statement of Stockholders' Equity** (LO 4)
Following is an incomplete statement of stockholders' equity for Mufasa Corporation:

	Common Stock		Additional Paid-In Capital	Retained Earnings
	Shares	Amount		
Balances, January 1		$500,000	$150,000	$250,000
Net income				
Sale of common stock	10,000			
Cash dividends declared				
Balances, December 31		$	$	$

Additional Information:
a. Mufasa's common stock has a $10 par value.
b. Net income for the year was $40,000.
c. The common stock issued during the year was sold for $22 per share on July 1.
d. Two $1.50 cash dividends per share were declared and paid during the year. The first dividend was declared on March 1 and paid on April 11 to stockholders of record March 21. The second dividend was declared on August 6 and paid on September 4 to stockholders of record August 21.

Required:
Complete Mufasa's statement of stockholders' equity.

31. **Prior Period Adjustment** (LO 5)
Al-Sherazi Enterprises had no changes in stockholders' equity in 1998 other than in retained earnings. The following schedule analyzes the changes in the company's Retained Earnings account during that year.

Retained earnings, January 1, 1998	$200,000
Net income	40,000
Dividends declared	(10,000)
Retained earnings, December 31, 1998	$230,000

On March 2, 1999, Al-Sherazi discovered that depreciation expense on a piece of equipment had been understated by $10,000 during 1998. Al-Sherazi's effective income tax rate is 40 percent for both financial accounting and taxation purposes.

Required:

1. How much was Al-Sherazi's net income understated or overstated in 1998?
2. Describe the accounting treatment that Al-Sherazi will apply to this item.

32. **Overlooking Prior Period Adjustments** (LO 5)

Jane Byrd, the owner of Jane's Greenhouse, hired an accountant, Mary, a few weeks ago to maintain the business's accounting records. In the past, Jane kept the books herself, although she is not an accountant. This past week, Mary discovered three errors that Jane had made in the accounting records during the previous year. These errors caused the business's net income for last year to be overstated by a material amount. Net income was reported as $83,200, when it was actually $46,300. The only external party who received a copy of the business's financial statements was the president of a local bank. Jane's Greenhouse has an outstanding loan of $50,000 from that bank.

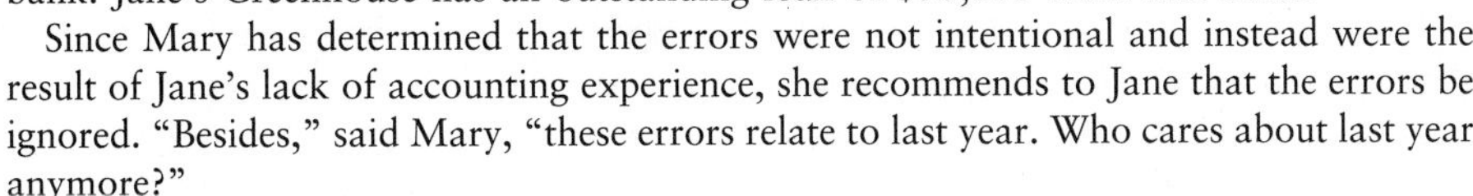

Since Mary has determined that the errors were not intentional and instead were the result of Jane's lack of accounting experience, she recommends to Jane that the errors be ignored. "Besides," said Mary, "these errors relate to last year. Who cares about last year anymore?"

Required:

Was Mary's advice to Jane appropriate? Does Jane have a responsibility to inform the local banker of the errors in the previous year's financial statements even if those financial statements are not corrected and reissued? Write a brief memo to Jane regarding these issues. Include in this memo your recommendation regarding how she should resolve this matter.

33. **Appropriation of Retained Earnings** (LO 5)

Falcetto Corporation must record an appropriation of retained earnings at the end of the current year because of a restrictive debt covenant in a new bond indenture. The amount of the appropriation is $100,000. Assume that the company will have total retained earnings of $500,000 at year-end.

Required:

1. Prepare the year-end entry to record the appropriation of retained earnings in Falcetto's accounting records.
2. Indicate how Falcetto's retained earnings will appear in the company's year-end balance sheet.
3. What "signal" does an appropriation of retained earnings send to users of a company's financial statements?

34. **Price-Earnings Ratio** (LO 6)

The following table lists recent financial data for five large corporations.

Company	Market Price of Common Stock	P/E Ratio
Caterpillar	$ 76.50	12
IBM	151.62	16
Marriott International	53.25	25
PepsiCo	26.87	36
Union Carbide	41.50	9

Required:

1. For each company listed, determine the twelve-month earnings per share figure used in computing the firm's reported P/E ratio.
2. What factors may account for large publicly owned companies having very different P/E ratios?

35. **Market Price to Book Value Ratio** (LO 6)

The ratio of a stock's market price to its book value per share reveals how much investors are willing to pay for each $1 of a company's net assets per share. The following information is available for Companies A, B, and C.

	Company A	Company B	Company C
Total assets	$1,000,000	$750,000	$2,000,000
Total liabilities	$250,000	$400,000	$1,500,000
Number of shares of common stock outstanding*	100,000	200,000	125,000
Year-end stock price	$8.00	$7.00	$24.00

*Note: None of the companies have preferred stock outstanding.

Required:

1. For each of the companies listed, compute the book value per share and the market price to book value ratio.
2. How is it possible for a company's market price to book value ratio to differ significantly from 1.0?

36. **Market Price vs. Book Value per Share** (LO 6)

Logan LaChance was born on a ranch in the Big Bend region of southwest Texas. For forty years, Logan punched cows, rode fences, and made annual deposits in his IRA (individual retirement account). Now retired, Logan spends most of his days sitting on the porch of his small house in Wink, Texas, chewing tobacco and reading Zane Grey and Louis L'Amour novels.

Logan has a large cash balance in his IRA that he wants to invest in one or more common stocks. He has narrowed down his investment alternatives to five stocks. Listed next are the companies whose common stocks he is considering along with selected financial data for each.

	Current Market Price	P/E Ratio	Book Value per Share
Coahuila Oil & Gas Exploration	$ 83	28	$29.42
Portales Manufacturing	$14\frac{1}{8}$	10	15.75
San Jacinto Silver Mines, Inc.	7	5	9.90
Texas Computer Peripherals	$102\frac{5}{8}$	33	17.48
Watters Electric Utility	$25\frac{3}{4}$	11	17.89

Nathan Lockett, Logan's nephew who doubles as his financial advisor, has suggested that his uncle invest all of his available cash in the common stock of San Jacinto Silver Mines. "Uncle Logan, you can't go wrong here," Nathan observed. "You'd be paying only five bucks for every $1 of earnings being reported by San Jacinto. Plus, for every seven bucks you invest in the company, you'd be gettin' nearly $10 of net assets."

Required:

Has Nathan given his uncle good investment advice? Explain. Identify other factors or issues that Logan should consider before choosing to invest in the common stock of San Jacinto Silver Mines.

PROBLEM SET A

37. Preparing a Corporate Income Statement (LO 1, 2)
Following are income statement data for Shaw Corporation for the year ended December 31, 1998. These items are presented in random order.

Cost of goods sold	$360,000
General expenses	18,000
Gain on sale of machinery	22,000
Income tax expense (related to income from continuing operations before income tax)	?
Operating income from discontinued line of business, $10,000, less income tax of $4,000	6,000
Selling expenses	20,000
Extraordinary loss due to fire, $20,000, less income tax savings of $8,000	12,000
Net sales	520,000
Loss on disposal of discontinued line of business, $20,000, less income tax savings of $8,000	12,000
Administrative expenses	19,000
Cumulative effect of a change in accounting principle, $5,000, less income tax of $2,000	3,000

Shaw's average income tax rate is 40 percent. Throughout 1998, Shaw had 50,000 shares of common stock outstanding.

Required:
Prepare a multiple-step income statement for Shaw Corporation, including an earnings per share section.

38. Earnings Per Share Computations (LO 2)
Following are income statement data for Ellis & Reddings Corporation for the company's most recent fiscal year:

Income from continuing operations before income tax		$800,000
Income tax expense		320,000
Income from continuing operations		$480,000
Discontinued operations:		
Operating income, $40,000, less income tax of $16,000	$24,000	
Loss on disposal, $50,000, less income tax savings of $20,000	(30,000)	
		(6,000)
Income before extraordinary item		$474,000
Extraordinary loss due to plane crash, $100,000, less income tax savings of $40,000		(60,000)
Net income		$414,000

At the beginning of the year, Ellis & Reddings had 100,000 shares of common stock outstanding. On October 1, Ellis & Reddings sold an additional 80,000 shares of common stock.

Required:

1. Compute the weighted-average number of shares of common stock that Ellis & Reddings had outstanding during the year.
2. Compute and clearly label the earnings per share figures you would expect to see in Ellis & Reddings' income statement.

39. **Statement of Stockholders' Equity** (LO 4, 5)
Hatlan Company had the following balances in its stockholders' equity accounts on January 1, 1998:

Common Stock	$ 32,000
Additional Paid-In Capital	310,500
Retained Earnings	2,664,200

On May 15, 1998, Hatlan sold an additional 11,000 shares of common stock for $24 per share. Hatlan's common stock has a $2 par value. On September 13, Hatlan declared a $2 per share cash dividend. The dividend was payable on October 25 to stockholders of record on October 3. Hatlan's net income for 1998 was $229,300.

Required:

1. Prepare a statement of stockholders' equity for Hatlan Company for the year ended December 31, 1998.
2. Suppose that on January 25, 1999, Hatlan issues bonds payable. One stipulation of the bond indenture requires Hatlan to make $1.5 million of its existing retained earnings unavailable for the declaration of dividends over the term of the bonds. Prepare the journal entry to record this appropriation of retained earnings.

40. **Analyzing Stockholders' Equity** (LO 6)
Listed next is selected financial information for Thiokol Corporation, an aerospace firm, for a recent three-year period.

	Year 1	Year 2	Year 3
Total revenues*	$ 1.32	$ 1.21	$ 1.06
Net income**	63.00	63.80	60.30
Earnings per share	3.12	3.13	(.18)
Book value per share of common stock	19.44	21.94	20.52
Year-end market price of common stock	16.00	21.88	24.13
Cash dividends per share	.36	.47	.68

*In billions
**In millions

Required:

1. How do investors use the P/E and market price to book value ratios to analyze a company's common stock as a potential investment?
2. Compute Thiokol's year-end P/E ratio and market price to book value ratio for Year 1 through Year 3.

3. Analyze the financial information presented for Thiokol and the ratios you computed in (2). Are there any unusual or unexpected relationships in these data? If so, what factor or factors may be responsible for these relationships?
4. In Year 3, Thiokol's earnings per share was reduced by a $3.20 after-tax charge related to a cumulative effect of an accounting change. Recompute Thiokol's year-end P/E ratio based upon the company's earnings per share before the cumulative effect of the accounting change. Is there any evidence which suggests that investors ignored the impact of the cumulative effect item on Thiokol's Year 3 earnings? Explain.
5. Suppose that you were considering an investment in Thiokol common stock early in Year 4. Identify three questions that you would have wanted to ask the company's chief executive officer before deciding whether to invest in the company.

41. Temporary Differences for Tax Purposes (LO 3)

Over a recent three-year period, Timber Country Enterprises (TCE) had the following pretax accounting incomes and taxable incomes.

	Pretax Accounting Income	Taxable Income
Year 1	$440,000	$380,000
Year 2	470,000	410,000
Year 3	370,000	490,000

For each year, the difference between TCE's pretax accounting income and its taxable income was due to the different depreciation methods the company uses for financial accounting and taxation purposes. Recently, a local attorney, who is a new member of TCE's board of directors, reviewed the company's financial records. At the next board meeting, this individual suggested that the use of different accounting methods for financial accounting and taxation purposes was, in her opinion, unethical.

Required:

1. Is it unethical to use different accounting methods for financial accounting and taxation purposes? Why or why not?
2. TCE's effective tax rate in recent years has been 40 percent for both financial accounting and taxation purposes. Compute the company's income tax expense and income tax payable for Year 1.
3. Prepare an appropriate journal entry to record TCE's income tax expense for Year 1.

42. Ethics and the Corporate Income Statement (LO 1, 3)

In 1984, executives of Berkshire Hathaway, Inc., a large investment company, became involved in a dispute with representatives of their independent audit firm. The focus of this dispute was a large payment received by Berkshire Hathaway during 1984 from another company. Berkshire's executives maintained that this payment should be treated as a dividend for financial accounting purposes, the treatment prescribed for taxation purposes. The company's independent auditors insisted on another accounting treatment for this transaction for financial accounting purposes. This alternative treatment was not preferred by Berkshire's executives because it would reduce the company's 1984 net income by approximately 8 percent. If Berkshire's executives failed to adopt the accounting treatment for this transaction suggested by the independent auditors, the auditors would issue an unfavorable audit opinion on Berkshire's 1984 financial statements.

Eventually, Berkshire's executives agreed to the accounting treatment suggested by their independent auditors. However, the following year, company management retained another accounting firm to audit the company's financial statements. [Note: The facts of this problem were drawn from the following source: M. C. Knapp, "Berkshire Hathaway, Inc.," in *Contemporary Auditing: Issues and Cases,* 2d ed. (Minneapolis/St. Paul: West Publishing Co., 1996).]

Required:

1. Who has the final responsibility for determining the accounting methods that a company should use, its management or its independent auditors?
2. What responsibility do independent auditors have regarding the annual financial statements of their audit clients?
3. In your opinion, should the prescribed treatment for a transaction for taxation purposes be used as the basis for determining its treatment for financial accounting purposes? Explain.

PROBLEM SET B

43. Preparing a Corporate Income Statement (LO 1, 2)

Following are income statement data for Shank Corporation for the year ended December 31, 1998. These items are presented in random order.

Administrative expenses	$ 9,000
Selling expenses	29,000
Income tax expense (related to income from continuing operations before income tax)	?
Cumulative effect of a change in accounting principle, $10,000, less income tax of $4,000	6,000
Gain on sale of equipment	16,000
Loss on disposal of discontinued line of business, $30,000, less income tax savings of $12,000	18,000
Extraordinary loss due to flood, $25,000, less income tax savings of $10,000	15,000
Cost of goods sold	440,000
Operating income from discontinued line of business, $15,000, less income tax of $6,000	9,000
General expenses	33,000
Net sales	810,000

Shank's average income tax rate is 40 percent. Throughout 1998, Shank had 100,000 shares of common stock outstanding.

Required:

Prepare a multiple-step income statement for Shank Corporation, including an earnings per share section.

44. Earnings per Share Computations (LO 2)

Following are income statement data for the most recent fiscal year of Andrew & DuPraine Corporation:

Income from continuing operations before income tax		$725,000
Income tax expense		290,000
Income from continuing operations		$435,000
Discontinued operations:		
Operating income, $30,000, less income tax of $12,000	$18,000	
Gain on disposal, $25,000, less income tax of $10,000	15,000	33,000
Income before cumulative effect of a change in accounting principle		$468,000
Cumulative effect of a change in accounting principle, $35,000, less income tax of $14,000		21,000
Net income		$489,000

At the beginning of the year, Andrew & DuPraine had 90,000 shares of common stock outstanding. On September 1, Andrew & DuPraine sold an additional 30,000 shares of common stock.

Required:

1. Compute the weighted-average number of shares of common stock that Andrew & DuPraine had outstanding during the year.
2. Compute and clearly label the earnings per share figures you would expect to see in Andrew & DuPraine's income statement.

45. **Statement of Stockholders' Equity** (LO 4, 5)
Brooks Corporation had the following balances in its stockholders' equity accounts on January 1, 1998:

Common Stock	$ 66,000
Additional Paid-In Capital	230,800
Retained Earnings	1,243,800

On January 1, 1998, Brooks had 22,000 shares of common stock outstanding. The company sold an additional 5,000 shares of its $3 par value common stock for $17 per share on October 15, 1998. On June 12, 1998, Brooks declared a $1.50 per share cash dividend. The dividend was payable on August 8 to stockholders of record on July 16. Brooks' net income for 1998 was $101,700.

Required:

1. Prepare a statement of stockholders' equity for Brooks Corporation for the year ended December 31, 1998.
2. Assume that on January 15, 1999, Brooks obtains a large loan from a local bank. One stipulation of the loan agreement is that Brooks make $1 million of its existing retained earnings unavailable for the declaration of dividends over the term of the loan. Prepare the journal entry to record this appropriation of retained earnings.

46. **Analyzing Stockholders' Equity** (LO 6)
Listed next is selected financial information for Hudson's Bay Company, the large Canadian retailer, for a recent three-year period. Amounts are expressed in Canadian dollars.

	Year 1	Year 2	Year 3
Total revenues*	$ 5.15	$ 5.44	$ 5.83
Net earnings (net income)**	117.00	147.70	151.30
Earnings per share	2.32	2.72	2.66
Book value per share of common stock	25.92	28.56	30.76
Year-end market price of common stock	24.00	32.00	29.25
Cash dividends per share	.80	.80	.92

*In billions
**In millions

Required:

1. How do investors use the P/E and market price to book value ratios to analyze a company's common stock as a potential investment?
2. Compute the year-end P/E ratio and market price to book value ratio for Hudson's Bay for Year 1 through Year 3.
3. Analyze the financial information presented for Hudson's Bay and the ratios you computed in (2). Are there any unusual or unexpected relationships in these data? If so, what factor or factors may be responsible for these relationships?
4. What factors may cause the market price of a company's common stock to be different from the stock's book value per share?
5. Suppose that you were considering an investment in the common stock of Hudson's Bay early in Year 4. Identify three questions that you would have wanted to ask the company's chief executive officer before deciding whether to invest in the company.

47. **Temporary Differences for Tax Purposes** (LO 3)
Thunder Gulch Developers (TGD) uses the direct write-off method to account for bad debt expense for taxation purposes and the allowance method to account for bad debt expense for financial accounting purposes. Shown in the following table is TGD's annual bad debt expense under each of these accounting methods for a recent three-year period.

	Direct Write-Off Method	Allowance Method
Year 1	$40,000	$60,000
Year 2	50,000	50,000
Year 3	80,000	60,000

A major stockholder of TGD was surprised when she reviewed these data. She immediately telephoned and then chastised TGD's controller. "You're the chief accountant of this organization. How can you allow TGD to keep two sets of accounting records? That's got to be illegal!"

Required:

1. Is it permissible for a company to maintain different accounting records for financial accounting and taxation purposes? Explain.
2. Is it ethical for a company to choose accounting methods for taxation purposes that minimize and/or delay the income taxes paid to governmental agencies? Why or why not?

3. Assume that in Year 1 TGD had a pretax accounting income of $200,000 and a taxable income of $220,000. Also assume that the company's effective tax rate for both financial accounting and taxation purposes was 40 percent. Prepare an appropriate journal entry to record TGD's income tax expense for Year 1.

48. Ethics and the Corporate Income Statement (LO 1)

Kim Caraway is the controller of Cotton Industries, a large manufacturing firm. During the current year, Cotton suffered a $4.2 million loss, after taxes, as a result of being forced to write off a large piece of machinery that became outdated after the firm's production process was redesigned. In the preliminary financial statements that Kim has drafted for the current year, she reports this loss as "Other gains or losses," a component of income from continuing operations, on Cotton's income statement. After reviewing the preliminary financial statements, Cotton's chief executive officer (CEO) insists that the loss be reported as an extraordinary item.

Required:

1. Why would it be advantageous for Cotton Industries to have this loss reported as an extraordinary item rather than as a component of income from continuing operations? Explain.
2. In your opinion, does this item qualify as an extraordinary item? Why or why not?
3. Suppose that after studying this matter, Kim decides that the relevant accounting rules do not expressly prohibit reporting this type of loss as an extraordinary item. Nevertheless, Kim believes the item is most appropriately classified as a component of income from continuing operations. Given this additional information, do you believe that it would be unethical for Kim to treat the item as an extraordinary loss? Why or why not?

CASES

49. Statement of Added Value (LO 1)

Electrolux Group is a large Swedish company based in Stockholm. Electrolux's operations are segregated into four lines of business: household appliances, commercial appliances, outdoor products, and industrial products. In the United States, Electrolux is probably best known for its vacuum cleaners.

Each Electrolux annual report contains a "Statement of Added Value." The firm defines "added value" as follows:

> Added value represents the contribution made by a company's production, i.e., the increase in value arising from manufacturing, handling, etc. within the company. It is defined as sales revenues less the cost of purchased goods and services.

On the following page is a recent statement of added value issued by Electrolux. The amounts in this statement are expressed in millions of Swedish kronor. Recently, one Swedish krona was equivalent to approximately $.13.

Required:

1. Review Electrolux's statement of added value. What do you believe is the principal purpose of this statement?
2. What information does a statement of added value provide that is not contained in an income statement of a U.S. corporation?
3. How would the information you identified in (2) be used by financial decision makers? Is this information particularly useful to certain types of decision makers? If so, identify these decision makers.
4. Do you believe that U.S. corporations should be required to include a statement of added value in their annual reports? Defend your answer.

Calculation of Added Value:

		%
Total Sales	108,004	100
Cost of Purchased Goods and Services	(70,610)	(65)
Added Value	**37,394**	**35**

Distribution of Added Value:

To Employees:		
Wages and Salaries	19,431	52
Employer Contributions	5,939	16
	25,370	*68*
To Central and Local Governments:		
Taxes	1,444	4
To Credit Institutions:		
Interest, etc.	1,439	4
To Shareholders:		
Dividend Payments	915	2
	3,798	*10*
Retained in the Group:		
For Wear on Fixed Assets (Depreciation)	4,214	11
Other	4,012	11
	8,226	*22*
Added Value	**37,394**	**100**

50. **1920 Income Statement** (LO 1)
Following is an income statement of the Frederick Kahl Iron Foundry for the company's fiscal year ended May 31, 1920. This income statement is formatted as originally issued by the company's accountants.

INCOME	MAY 31–1920
Net Sales	$284,158.85
Cost of Sales	199,866.63
MANUFACTURING PROFIT	$ 84,292.22
EXPENSES	
Administrative, General and Selling	39,545.55
OPERATING PROFIT OR LOSS	$ 44,746.67
Other Deductions or Other Income—Net	5,836.15
PROFIT OR LOSS (Before Federal Taxes)	$ 38,910.52
Provision for Federal Taxes—Estimated	10,500.00
NET PROFIT OR LOSS	$ 28,410.52

Required:

1. Identify the differences and similarities between this 1920 income statement and the income statements presently prepared by U.S. corporations.
2. What factors likely account for the evolution of the content and format of financial statements over a period of several decades?

51. **Elements of Corporate Income Statements** (LO 1)
Norton Warden has worked for many years as a state employee of Maine. With less than ten years to retirement, Norton realizes that he must begin planning for his retirement. Lately, Norton has begun reading *The Wall Street Journal* and studying the financial statements of dozens of publicly owned companies. When Norton identifies an item that he does not understand, he writes it down. Following is a list of mysterious items Norton has stumbled across in recent corporate income statements.

• Orbital Sciences Corporation:	
Cumulative effect of change in accounting for income taxes	$200,000
• First Union Real Estate Investments:	
Extraordinary loss from early extinguishment of debt	$1,200,000
• National Pizza Company:	
Loss on disposition of underperforming assets	$4,000,000
• Occidental Petroleum Corporation:	
Loss from discontinued operations	$622,000,000

Required:
Write a memo to Norton Warden explaining the nature of each item in his list. While writing this memo, keep in mind that Norton knows very little about accounting and financial reporting rules.

PROJECTS

52. **Tracking P/E Ratios over Time**
Select three industries of particular interest to you and then identify two major companies within each of these industries.

Required:
1. Using *The Wall Street Journal* or other sources, find the P/E ratio of each of the companies you selected at the end of each quarter for the past three years. (The specific dates for which you should obtain P/E ratios for these companies are March 31, June 30, September 30, and December 31.) Plot these twelve P/E ratios for each firm on a piece of graph paper with an appropriate numerical scale.
2. Study the data collected and plotted in (1). Among the issues you should address are the following: Are the P/E ratios of the paired companies within each industry fairly consistent over the three-year period? Are the P/E ratios of the paired companies in each industry more consistent than the P/E ratios of companies not in the same industry? Are there any apparent trends for the P/E ratios within specific industries? If so, attempt to identify factors that may account for these trends.
3. Write a brief report containing the data you collected in (1) and your analysis of that data in (2).

53. **Analyzing Statements of Stockholders' Equity**
To obtain the data required to complete this project, you will need to select ten companies that include a statement of stockholders' equity in their annual reports.

Required:
Prepare a written report to be submitted to your instructor that includes the following:
1. A list of the specific activities that affected the stockholders' equity of the companies you selected during the most recent year for which financial statement data are available.

2. An indication of how many of the ten companies report each of the activities identified in (1).

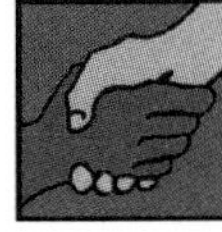

54. Income Statements of a Failing Business

For this project, your project group will identify a company that went into bankruptcy within the past three years. There are several readily available sources that can be used to identify such companies. One such source is the entries listed under the "bankruptcies" heading in the hard copy or on-line indices of *The Wall Street Journal.*

Required:

1. For the company your group selected, obtain a copy of the firm's annual income statement for each of the five years immediately preceding the bankruptcy filing. Each group member should be provided copies of these income statements. Meet as a group and discuss these income statements after each group member has had an opportunity to study them. The key issue you should address as a group is whether the series of income statements contains any "red flags" or warning signals regarding the company's financial problems. Specific tasks that should be completed by individual group members include the following:
   a. Compute and interpret key financial ratios for this company.
   b. Document and study any trends apparent in the company's income statements.
   c. Investigate unusual or "special" items included in the company's income statements.
   d. Compare and contrast the company's income statement data and related ratios and trends with comparable data of similar companies and the company's industry as a whole.
2. A written report summarizing the group's analysis of the selected company's income statements should be prepared. This report should identify any "red flags" that suggested the company might eventually fail. Your report should also contain recommendations that decision makers might use to identify companies that are in the process of failing.
3. One group member should be prepared to present a brief overview of the group's written report to the class.

55. Analyzing Corporate Profitability

Following are several large corporations that maintain Web sites on the Internet.

Ace Hardware Corporation
Baxter International Inc.
Centex Corporation
Dole Food Company, Inc.
Gateway 2000, Inc.
Lear Corporation
Merck & Co., Inc.
Pennzoil Company
Pittston Company
Shaw Industries, Inc.
The Times Mirror Company
Trans World Airlines, Inc.

Required:

1. Choose two of these companies and access their Web sites on the Internet. Document these Web site addresses, the headquarters location of each firm, and briefly describe the principal line or lines of business of each company.

2. Prepare a schedule of each company's net income or net loss over the most recent five-year period for which financial statement data are available. Also compute each firm's return on equity for each of these five years. (Return on equity was discussed in Chapter 11.)
3. Which of the two companies you selected has been the most profitable over the past five years? Explain. After reviewing the narrative and financial information available for each firm at its Web site, which firm do you believe has the most "profit potential" in the future? Defend your choice.

13 Intercorporate Investments and Accounting for International Operations

"It is not the return on *my investment that I am concerned about; it is the return* of *my investment."*
Will Rogers

LEARNING OBJECTIVES

After studying this chapter, you should be able to do the following:

1. Discuss the principal motives for intercorporate investments.
2. Define the key information needs of decision makers regarding intercorporate investments.
3. Account for each of the five types of intercorporate investments.
4. Identify important control issues related to intercorporate investments.
5. Discuss how intercorporate investments affect decision makers' analysis of financial statement data.
6. Discuss the challenges that multinational business operations pose for the accounting profession.
7. Account for realized and unrealized foreign currency transaction gains and losses.

FOCUS ON DECISION MAKING

LBOs & CPAs

As documented in the hit film *Wall Street,* Corporate America viewed "bigger as better" during the 1980s. One result of the so-called "decade of greed" was a record pace of corporate takeovers and other intercorporate investments. The Wall Street underwriting firms that typically coordinate corporate takeovers structured many of the mega-deals of the 1980s as leveraged buyouts or LBOs. In an LBO, the bulk of the funds required to finance the acquisition of one company by another is supplied by bank loans. The acquiring company or syndicate of investors generally provides 10 percent, or even less, of the funds needed to finance an LBO.

A company acquired via an LBO typically faces a heavy burden of debt following the change in its ownership. As a result, a temporary downturn in sales or an unexpected series of expenses can jeopardize such a company's ability to make principal and interest payments on its debt. Many companies involved in LBOs during the 1980s did fail, resulting in huge losses for the large metropolitan banks that financed these deals. To persuade these banks to continue participating in LBOs, underwriters began obtaining "solvency letters" from the Big Six accounting firms. In a solvency letter, an accounting firm offered an opinion on the likelihood that a company emerging from an LBO would survive for at least two to five years. A solvency letter typically indicated that the post-LBO company would be financially viable over that period. Given this assurance, banks were much more likely to participate in an LBO.

Consider the 1987 leveraged buyout of Southland Corporation, the owner of the nationwide chain of 7-Eleven convenience stores. The prospective purchaser of Southland requested a $2 billion loan from five large banks to finance the acquisition. The underwriters negotiating the LBO asked the accounting firm of Touche Ross, now known as Deloitte & Touche, to provide the five banks a solvency letter. Touche Ross supplied the solvency letter without which the banking syndicate reportedly would not have financed the takeover of Southland.

Solvency letters not only helped sustain the corporate takeover frenzy of the 1980s but also provided large accounting firms with a significant source of revenue. Accounting firms received as much as one million dollars per solvency letter. In 1986 and 1987, alone, the Big Six accounting firms earned nearly $100 million for the solvency letters they issued.

The solvency letter bonanza was short-lived for the major accounting firms. Critics of solvency letters maintained that accounting firms were not qualified to make the financial assertions contained in these letters. Rule-making authorities within the accounting profession sided with these critics and in February 1988 prohibited accounting firms from issuing solvency letters.

Following the late 1980s, the annual dollar volume of LBOs plummeted. Data reported in the *Statistical Abstract of the United States* indicate that the dollar volume of LBOs in 1993 was only 20 percent of the corresponding figure for 1988.

Chapters 6 through 8 focused on accounting for assets. Two classes of assets not considered in those chapters were short-term and long-term investments. Among the most common short-term and long-term investments of corporations are investments in debt and equity securities of other corporations. In this chapter, we examine accounting issues for intercorporate investments. We begin by considering the motives for these investments. Next, the key information needs of decision makers regarding these assets are discussed, followed by an overview of accounting decisions for the five major types of intercorporate investments. Finally, we highlight the major control issues for intercorporate investments and describe how these investments affect decision makers' analysis of corporate financial data.

The second section of this chapter focuses on accounting for international business operations. Each year, more U.S. companies expand their operations across international borders. Many firms expand abroad by investing in foreign companies, while other firms establish foreign subsidiaries. Regardless of the approach taken to enter foreign markets, multinational firms pose challenging accounting and financial reporting issues.

INTERCORPORATE INVESTMENTS

LEARNING OBJECTIVE 1 ▶
Discuss the principal motives for intercorporate investments.

Corporations invest in other firms' stocks and bonds for various reasons. As you will discover, the motives for these investments often dictate the accounting methods used for them. Many companies invest in corporate stocks and bonds to make effective use of excess cash. Generally, the rates of return yielded by corporate stocks and bonds are more attractive than the interest rates available on certificates of deposit and savings accounts. Stock and bond investments also provide an opportunity for corporations to earn "trading" profits by taking advantage of short-term fluctuations in securities prices. Many corporations have a long-term perspective when they purchase the stocks and bonds of other companies. Corporate executives make such investments with the hope of realizing a reasonable rate of return over an extended period. The principal components of this rate of return are dividends, interest revenue, and capital appreciation—that is, an increase in the market value of the given securities.

Another common motivation for intercorporate investments is to control, or at least influence, another firm's operations. Consider a company that retails large home appliances such as microwave ovens, washers, and dryers. To ensure that it has a reliable supply of such appliances, this retailer may "vertically integrate" by purchasing an appliance manufacturing company. Then again, instead of purchasing this company outright, the appliance retailer may choose to buy a controlling interest in the manufacturer's common stock. By purchasing slightly more than 50 percent of the manufacturer's outstanding common stock, the retailer can dictate the operating policies of that firm.

Intercorporate Investments: Key Information Needs of Decision Makers

LEARNING OBJECTIVE 2 ▶
Define the key information needs of decision makers regarding intercorporate investments.

Decision makers demand several items of information regarding a company's intercorporate investments. Most important, decision makers want to be aware of the nature and purpose of those investments. Decision makers also demand information regarding the market values of intercorporate investments and disclosures of the revenues and expenses related to these assets.

NATURE OF INTERCORPORATE INVESTMENTS Intercorporate investments often signal a shift in the objectives and operating policies of a firm. Consequently, financial statement disclosures concerning the nature and purpose of a company's intercorporate investments are of considerable interest to investors, lenders, and other external decision makers. As always, the need for external decision makers to be well informed must be balanced against a company's need to protect its economic interests. For example, suppose that Union Pacific Corporation, a company in the railroad industry, begins accumulating stock in a competitor. Union Pacific's eventual objective is a "hostile takeover" of that firm. Clearly, Union Pacific would not want to immediately disclose its intention. Doing so would drive up the price of the competitor's stock and provide its executives with a head start in foiling the takeover.

Financial statement footnotes typically contain important information regarding the nature of a company's intercorporate investments. Exhibit 13.1 presents an example of a footnote disclosure for an intercorporate investment. This disclosure was included in a recent annual report of BancTec, Inc. BancTec describes itself as a leading worldwide provider of electronic and document-based processing systems for financial transactions. The footnote in Exhibit 13.1 does not explicitly indicate the nature of BancTec's investment. Nevertheless, the information provided suggests that BancTec is expanding its operations into South America.

MARKET VALUE INFORMATION "What's it worth?" is a common question posed by decision makers regarding most assets of business entities. As you know, this question often goes unanswered. Two major classes of intercorporate investments are reported at their fair values, or current market values, on corporate balance sheets including "trading securities," which are discussed shortly. Investments in "held-to-maturity securities," also discussed later in this chapter, are not reported at their fair values on a balance sheet. However, companies must disclose the fair values of held-to-maturity securities in their financial statement footnotes.

The fair values of certain intercorporate investments are not reported on either an entity's balance sheet or in its financial statement footnotes. Among these investments are ownership interests in common stocks accounted for using the equity method, such as the BancTec investment in Servibanca described in Exhibit 13.1. Because a company intends to retain such investments indefinitely, the accounting profession maintains that fair value disclosures for these assets are not relevant to decision makers.

EXHIBIT 13.1 ▼

Footnote Included in Recent Financial Statements of BancTec, Inc., Describing Investment in a South American Company

... BancTec contributed approximately $500,000 in cash and certain other considerations in exchange for a 33% equity interest in Servibanca, S.A., a Chilean company. Servibanca is a check processing service bureau as well as a distributor of BancTec image processing systems, document processing systems, and stand alone reader/sorters to banks, service bureaus, and other financial processors in Chile and other South American countries. BancTec's investment in and share of Servibanca's earnings ... are recorded using the equity method of accounting.

Millions of investors rely on *The Wall Street Journal* for price quotations for corporate securities, investment advice, and general news stories involving U.S. and international businesses.

REVENUES AND EXPENSES RELATED TO INTERCORPORATE INVESTMENTS Companies typically report the net amount of revenues and expenses related to their intercorporate investments as a separate item on their income statements. Reporting this item separately allows decision makers to gauge whether it is a "material" source of income for a company. Tommy Hilfiger Corporation designs and markets sportswear. The company's 1996 income statement reported $5,712,000 of "investment income." A footnote to the company's financial statements revealed that all of this income resulted from interest revenue earned on investments.

Companies do not separately report the income associated with certain intercorporate investments. As discussed later in the chapter, if one company owns a "controlling" interest in another, the two companies are treated as one economic entity for financial reporting purposes. Such companies prepare a consolidated income statement in which they merge their sales, cost of goods sold, and other revenues and expenses.

Accounting for Intercorporate Investments

LEARNING OBJECTIVE 3 ▶ Account for each of the five types of intercorporate investments.

In this section, we consider accounting and financial reporting rules for the five major types of intercorporate investments identified by accounting standards. Exhibit 13.2 lists these investments along with a brief description of each.

The five types of intercorporate investments pose similar accounting issues. However, the specific accounting rules applied to each are often considerably different. Discussing all of the "ins and outs" of accounting for intercorporate investments is beyond the scope of this text. Here, the objective is to acquaint you with the major accounting issues for these investments.

TRADING SECURITIES As indicated in Exhibit 13.2, trading securities are short-term investments in debt and equity securities that may be sold to generate cash or to realize trading profits due to fluctuations in market prices. Since a company's man-

Red Herrings and White Knights

FOR YOUR INFORMATION

The rapid pace of intercorporate investments during the 1980s spawned a colorful Wall Street dialect to describe these investments and related management strategies. Following are definitions for a sample of Wall Street slang terms related to intercorporate investments that appeared in an Educational Edition of The Wall Street Journal. *A complimentary copy of this annual edition of* The Wall Street Journal *is available upon request from the publisher, Dow Jones & Company, Inc.*

Golden Parachute: When a company anticipates a future takeover, its executives may approve a lucrative termination package for themselves. If a takeover occurs, the executives can "parachute" to safety if their positions are eliminated by the new owners.

Red Herring: A preliminary prospectus or sales document describing the details of a planned offering of securities. The term is derived from a disclaimer printed in red ink along the border of the document that warns readers that key features of the securities offering may be changed.

Scorched Earth Tactic: A corporate defense tactic whereby a company sells off its most attractive assets to discourage an unwelcome takeover attempt by another firm.

Toehold Purchase: Term used to describe a purchase of less than 5 percent of a company's common stock. Once the purchaser owns 5 percent or more of the company's stock, a public disclosure of the purchaser's identity and the percentage of stock that it owns must be made to the SEC.

White Knight: An individual or corporate investor that rescues a corporation from an unfriendly takeover by purchasing the company on terms more agreeable to its owners.

EXHIBIT 13.2 ▼

Five Major Types of Intercorporate Investments for Accounting and Financial Reporting Purposes

Trading Securities: Investments in debt and equity securities that may be sold in the near term to generate cash or to realize trading profits due to fluctuations in market prices. Classified as current assets for balance sheet purposes.

Available-for-Sale Securities: Investments in debt and equity securities that do not qualify as one of the other types of intercorporate investments. Classified as either current or long-term assets depending upon the length of time that management intends to hold the securities.

Held-to-Maturity Securities: Investments in debt securities acquired with the positive intent and ability to hold them to maturity. Classified as long-term assets unless they mature in the coming year, in which case they are classified as current assets.

Influential but Noncontrolling Investments: Investments in equity securities in which the "investor" corporation generally owns at least 20 percent but not more than 50 percent of the "investee" corporation's common stock. Classified as long-term assets for balance sheet purposes.

Controlling Investments: Investments in equity securities in which the "parent company" owns more than 50 percent of the common stock of the "subsidiary." Consolidated financial statements are prepared for a parent company and its subsidiaries.

agement does not intend to hold these investments for an extended period, trading securities are classified as current assets. Accounting standards require trading securities to be reported on a balance sheet at their fair value. The **fair value** of a debt or equity security is generally the security's closing price on a given date on a securities exchange.

fair value

Purchase of Trading Securities To illustrate accounting for trading securities, suppose that on April 1, Year 1, Exxon purchases 200 shares of IBM common stock and five corporate bonds of Apple Computer. The Apple bonds have a \$1,000 face value, a 10 percent stated interest rate, and semiannual interest payment dates of April 1 and October 1. Assuming Exxon pays \$50 per share for the IBM common stock and \$1,000 for each Apple bond, the cost of these securities is \$10,000 and \$5,000, respectively. (Illustrations of purchases and sales of securities in this chapter ignore brokerage commissions and other transaction costs.) Listed next is the entry to record the purchase of these securities in Exxon's accounting records.

Apr. 1	Investment in Trading Securities	15,000	
	Cash		15,000
	To record stock and bond investments classified as trading securities		

Recording Interest and Dividend Revenue on Trading Securities Companies that have investments in trading securities periodically earn interest and dividend revenue on these investments. For example, on October 1, Year 1, Exxon will receive a \$250 interest payment from Apple Computer. Shown next is the computation of this amount given the information previously provided for the Apple bonds purchased by Exxon.

$$\text{Interest} = \text{Principal} \times \text{Rate} \times \text{Time}$$
$$\$250 = \$5{,}000 \times 10\% \times 6/12$$

The interest received from Apple Computer will be recorded in Exxon's accounting records with a \$250 debit to Cash and an equal credit to Interest Revenue. If Exxon receives a dividend from IBM, Exxon's accounting staff would debit the amount of the dividend to Cash with an offsetting credit to Dividend Revenue.

Year-End Adjusting Entries for Trading Securities At the end of an accounting period, adjusting entries typically are required for investments in trading securities held by a company. Returning to our example, Exxon's accountants will record an adjusting entry at the end of Year 1 to recognize \$125 (\$5,000 × 10% × 3/12) of interest earned on the Apple bonds but not yet received. This entry will include a \$125 debit to Interest Receivable and an equal credit to Interest Revenue.

A year-end adjusting entry will also be required in Exxon's accounting records to restate the recorded values of its trading securities to their year-end fair values. For illustration purposes, suppose that IBM common stock has a closing price on the New York Stock Exchange of \$56 per share on December 31, Year 1. Assume that the Apple bonds end the year at a quoted price of 97, which translates to an actual selling price per bond of \$970 (\$1,000 × 97%). Given these market prices, Exxon's investment in IBM stock will have a year-end fair value of \$11,200 (200 × \$56), while the fair value of the investment in Apple bonds will be \$4,850 (5 × \$970). The difference between the year-end fair value of trading securities and their book value is an "unrealized" gain or loss. These gains or losses are unrealized because the securities have not yet been sold. "Paper" gains or losses are terms that investors commonly use when referring to such amounts. The following table illustrates the computation of the net unrealized gain on Exxon's trading securities at year-end.

	Book Value	Year-End Fair Value	Unrealized Gain or (Loss)
IBM common stock	$10,000	$11,200	$1,200
Apple Computer bonds	5,000	4,850	(150)
	$15,000	$16,050	$1,050

To recognize the net unrealized gain on Exxon's trading securities, the following entry would be made on December 31, Year 1.

Dec. 31	Market Adjustment—Trading Securities	1,050	
	Unrealized Gain on Trading Securities		1,050
	To adjust investments in trading securities to their year-end fair values		

Market Adjustment—Trading Securities is a "valuation" account comparable to the Allowance for Doubtful Accounts discussed in Chapter 6. For financial reporting purposes, the balance of Market Adjustment—Trading Securities is added to (or subtracted from) the balance of Investment in Trading Securities. The resulting amount is then typically merged with the year-end values of other short-term investments and reported as "Short-term investments" or "Temporary investments" on a company's balance sheet.

Although the net gain of $1,050 on the trading securities owned by Exxon is unrealized at the end of Year 1, that gain will be reported in the company's income statement. Mark Twain Bancshares, Inc., reported approximately $64 million of trading securities on a recent balance sheet. Included in the company's "Other income" on its income statement was a $2.3 million unrealized gain on its portfolio of trading securities.

When a company sells trading securities, it records a "realized" gain or loss. Advanced accounting texts illustrate the accounting treatment for sales of trading securities.

AVAILABLE-FOR-SALE SECURITIES Investments in debt and equity securities that do not qualify as one of the other four types of investments listed in Exhibit 13.2 are classified as available-for-sale securities. A common account title for these assets is Investment in Available-for-Sale Securities. These investments can be classified as either current or long-term assets. If management intends to sell these securities within one year, they should be included in the current assets section of the balance sheet. Otherwise, these investments should be considered long-term assets.

The accounting and financial reporting rules for available-for-sale securities are similar to those applied to trading securities. Most important, both types of investments are reported on a balance sheet at their fair values. There is one major difference between the accounting methods used for trading and available-for-sale securities. This difference involves the classification of unrealized gains and losses on these securities for financial statement purposes.

Return to the previous example used to illustrate accounting for trading securities. Recall that at year-end Exxon recorded a net unrealized gain of $1,050 on the investment in Apple Computer bonds and IBM common stock. Now, assume that Exxon's investments in IBM common stock and Apple bonds qualify as available-for-sale securities rather than trading securities. Under this assumption, the following year-end adjusting entry would be appropriate to record the unrealized gain on these securities.

Dec. 31	Market Adjustment—Available-for-Sale Securities	1,050	
	Unrealized Gain on Available-for-Sale Securities		1,050
	To adjust available-for-sale securities to their year-end fair values		

Market Adjustment—Available-for-Sale Securities is a valuation account that is merged with Investment in Available-for-Sale Securities for balance sheet purposes. Merging the balances of these two accounts yields the collective fair value of a company's available-for-sale securities. Now, turn your attention to the account credited in the previous entry. Unrealized Gain on Available-for-Sale Securities is an *equity* account. (Recall that Unrealized Gain on Trading Securities is a *revenue* account.) An unrealized gain or loss on available-for-sale securities is included as a separate line item in the stockholders' equity section of a corporate balance sheet. An unrealized gain on available-for-sale securities increases a firm's stockholders' equity, while an unrealized loss on such an investment reduces a firm's stockholders' equity.

Shown next is the stockholders' equity section of a recent balance sheet for Gymboree Corporation. Included in this section of Gymboree's balance sheet is a $402,000 unrealized gain on available-for-sale securities. A schedule included in Gymboree's accompanying financial statement footnotes listed the cost and fair value of each available-for-sale security held by the firm.

Stockholders' Equity: (in thousands)	
Common stock, including excess paid-in capital, $.001 par value: 100,000,000 shares authorized; 24,992,276 shares issued	$ 56,687
Restricted stock deferred compensation	(1,139)
Unrealized investment gain	402
Retained earnings	67,984
Total stockholders' equity	$123,934

The obvious question here is why unrealized gains and losses on available-for-sale securities and trading securities are classified differently for financial reporting purposes. To answer this question, we must consider the nature of each of these investments. Recall that a key objective of investing in trading securities is to generate short-term profits due to fluctuations in stock prices. Given this motive for these investments, it seems reasonable that short-term changes in the market values of trading securities should be recognized for income statement purposes whether they are realized or not. Generating short-term trading profits is not an objective related to investments in available-for-sale securities. Consequently, the accounting profession has decided that it is inappropriate to report unrealized gains and losses on these investments as a component of a firm's periodic income. On the other hand, similar to trading securities, *realized* gains and losses on the *sale* of available-for-sale securities are reported on a company's income statement.

HELD-TO-MATURITY SECURITIES Trading and available-for-sale securities can be either debt or equity securities. However, only debt securities can be classified as held-to-maturity securities. (Equity securities, such as common stock, do not have a maturity date and thus cannot be "held to maturity.") Among the more common types of held-to-maturity securities are corporate bonds. Accounting standards require that an investor firm must have both the "positive intent" and "ability" to hold debt securities until their maturity date for these investments to qualify as held-to-maturity securities. If both criteria are not met, investments in debt securities are usually classified as available-for-sale securities.

Unlike trading and available-for-sale securities, held-to-maturity securities are not accounted for on a fair value basis. Since a company's management intends to hold these securities until their maturity date, fluctuations in their market values are generally ignored for accounting purposes. Nevertheless, as indicated earlier, the fair value of held-to-maturity securities must be disclosed in a firm's financial statement footnotes.

Accountants apply the "amortized cost method" in accounting for held-to-maturity securities. To illustrate key features of this accounting method, we will focus on investments in corporate bonds. The amortized cost method of accounting for bond investments is similar to the accounting treatment applied to bonds payable. Recall from Chapter 10 that a premium or discount on bonds payable is amortized over the term of the bonds using either the straight-line or effective-interest method. Under the **amortized cost method,** a company amortizes a "purchase" premium or discount on held-to-maturity securities over their remaining term. For balance sheet purposes, a company reports held-to-maturity securities at their original cost adjusted for any amortized premium or discount.

amortized cost method

The following table lists key facts for an investment in corporate bonds that qualify as held-to-maturity securities. These bonds were issued by Drexel Corporation and recently purchased by Manhattan Company.

Purchase date:	April 1, Year 1
Cost:	$14,400
Face value:	$15,000
Stated interest rate:	10%
Interest payment dates:	April 1 and October 1
Maturity date:	April 1, Year 4

On April 1, Year 1, Manhattan's accountants recorded the purchase of the Drexel bonds by debiting Investment in Held-to-Maturity Securities $14,400 and crediting Cash an equal amount. Recognize that Manhattan purchased the Drexel bonds at a $600 discount ($15,000 – $14,400) from their face value. When corporate bonds are purchased as an investment, a purchase premium or discount is generally not recorded in a separate account. Instead, the total cost of the bonds is simply debited to the investment account.

Assume that Manhattan amortizes the $600 discount on the investment in Drexel bonds on a straight-line basis. Given this assumption, Manhattan will amortize $100 of the discount in each of the six remaining semiannual interest payment periods in the bonds' term. On October 1, Year 1, Manhattan will make the following entry to record the $750 ($15,000 × 10% × 6/12) of interest received from Drexel and to amortize $100 of the discount on the bond investment.

Oct. 1	Cash	750	
	Investment in Held-to-Maturity Securities	100	
	Interest Revenue		850
	To record interest revenue on bond investment		

The amortization of a discount on a bond investment increases the interest revenue recognized each interest payment period on the investment and increases the investment's book value. Conversely, the amortization of a premium on a bond investment decreases the interest revenue recognized each interest payment period and reduces the investment's book value. By the end of the bond term, the balance of the bond investment account in the present example will be $15,000, which is the face value of the Drexel bonds purchased by Manhattan. If a company sells held-to-maturity securities before their maturity date, the firm records a realized gain or loss equal to the difference between the bonds' selling price and book value.

An example of a company reporting held-to-maturity securities in its financial statements is Cabletron Systems, Inc. On its 1996 balance sheet, Cabletron listed its investments in these securities under "Long-Term Investments." The company also included the following financial statement footnote in its annual report to describe these investments.

> Held-to-maturity securities are those investments in which the Company has the ability and intent to hold the security until maturity. Held-to-maturity securities are recorded at cost, adjusted for the amortization of premiums and discounts which approximates market value . . . Due to the nature of the Company's investments and the resulting low volatility, the difference between fair value and amortized cost is not material.

INFLUENTIAL BUT NONCONTROLLING INVESTMENTS Accountants apply the "equity method" of accounting to "influential but noncontrolling" intercorporate investments. These investments generally involve ownership by an "investor" corporation of 20 to 50 percent of an "investee" corporation's common stock. Accounting standards assume that an ownership interest in that range allows an investor firm to exercise significant influence over the investee's operations. An ownership interest of more than 50 percent of another firm's common stock represents a "controlling investment." Accounting for controlling investments is discussed shortly.

equity method

Under the **equity method** of accounting, the investor corporation records its investment in the common stock of the investee corporation at cost. Subsequently, the investor records its proportionate interest in the investee's periodic earnings (losses) as an addition (reduction) to the investment's book value. Any dividends received from the investee reduce the book value of the investment. This accounting treatment is appropriate because of the assumption that the investor can influence the timing and size of the investee's dividend distributions. Suppose for the moment that investor corporations recorded dividends received from investee corporations as revenue. Clearly, an investor's management might be tempted to pressure an investee to increase its dividend distributions in those years when the investor's profits were unimpressive or nonexistent.

To illustrate the key features of the equity method, suppose that on January 1 of a given year, BancTec purchased 40 percent of CheckTec Company's common stock for $300,000. During this year, CheckTec reported net income of $50,000 and distributed a cash dividend of $25,000, $10,000 of which ($25,000 × 40%) was paid to BancTec. Exhibit 13.3 presents the three journal entries required in BancTec's accounting records during the year in question for its investment in CheckTec.

Notice in Exhibit 13.3 that BancTec debited Investment in CheckTec Common Stock for 40 percent of the investee's reported earnings and credited the investment account for the cash dividend received. The year-end balance of the investment account was $310,000 ($300,000 + $20,000 − $10,000). That figure was the amount reported on BancTec's balance sheet for this asset. Again, because influential but noncontrolling investments are held indefinitely, unrealized gains and losses on these investments are not included in an investor's financial statements or disclosed in its financial statement footnotes. If these investments are sold, the realized gain or loss is the difference between the investment's book value and the cash received from the sale.

CONTROLLING INVESTMENTS A controlling investment exists when one company owns more than 50 percent of another company's common stock. Here, the investor corporation is known as the **parent company**, while the investee company is the **subsidiary.** Large corporations typically have many subsidiaries, most of which are 100 percent or "wholly-owned." When a parent company owns between 50 and 100 percent of a subsidiary's common stock, the subsidiary is referred to as "majority-

parent company

subsidiary

EXHIBIT 13.3 ▼

Common Journal Entries for Influential but Noncontrolling Investments

Jan. 1	Investment in CheckTec Common Stock	300,000	
	Cash		300,000
	To record purchase of 40 percent of CheckTec's common stock		
Dec. 31	Investment in CheckTec Common Stock	20,000	
	Investment Revenue		20,000
	To record proportionate interest in CheckTec's earnings ($50,000 × 40%)		
Dec. 31	Cash	10,000	
	Investment in CheckTec Common Stock		10,000
	To record cash dividend received from CheckTec		

owned." Since a parent company's executives can dictate the operating policies of a subsidiary, the accounting profession views a parent company and its subsidiaries as one economic entity although the firms may maintain separate accounting records.

consolidated financial statements

For financial reporting purposes, a parent company and its subsidiaries must combine their financial data into a set of **consolidated financial statements.** To illustrate the nature and preparation of consolidated financial statements, let us focus on the balance sheet. Procedures similar to those discussed here are used to prepare other consolidated financial statements such as a consolidated income statement.

Preparing Consolidated Financial Statements Suppose that on December 30, 1998, Pecos Corporation purchased all of Sunset Corporation's common stock at a cost of $66,000, which was exactly equal to the book value of Sunset's stockholders' equity. The entry to record this transaction in Pecos' accounting records included a debit of $66,000 to Investment in Sunset Corporation and an equal credit to Cash.[1] This transaction did not require an entry in Sunset's accounting records since it only involved a change in that company's stockholders.

intercompany transactions

Transactions between a parent company and a subsidiary, between two or more subsidiaries, or between other operating units of a company are known as **intercompany transactions.** For example, assume that Pecos loaned Sunset $50,000 immediately following the acquisition of that firm. To record this transaction, an entry was necessary in the accounting records of both Pecos and Sunset. The entry in Pecos' accounting records included a $50,000 debit to Note Receivable from Sunset Corporation and an offsetting credit to Cash. The corresponding entry in Sunset's accounting records consisted of a $50,000 debit to Cash and an equal credit to Note Payable to Pecos Corporation.

Exhibit 13.4 presents separate balance sheets as of December 31, 1998, for Pecos Corporation and Sunset Corporation. If Pecos intended to distribute financial statements to external decision makers as of December 31, 1998, the company was required to consolidate its financial statements with those of Sunset. Why? Because, again, for financial reporting purposes the two companies are considered one economic entity.

One approach to preparing a consolidated balance sheet for Pecos and Sunset would be to simply add the assets, liabilities, and stockholders' equity amounts shown in Exhibit 13.4. However, that method of combining the two companies' balance sheets would result in certain financial statement items being counted twice. For example, consider the $50,000 loan from Pecos to Sunset. If we treat Pecos and Sunset as one entity, that loan is comparable to an individual lending himself $20 by transferring that amount from one pocket to another. When consolidated financial statements are prepared, intercompany transactions and related account balances must be eliminated to avoid "double-counting" those items.

The balance of the Investment in Sunset Corporation account on Pecos' books and Sunset's stockholders' equity must also be eliminated when a consolidated balance sheet is prepared for the two companies. The $66,000 balance of the investment account on December 31, 1998, represents Pecos' ownership of Sunset's net assets of $66,000 ($136,000 of assets less $70,000 of liabilities). If the balance of Pecos' in-

1. Two methods can be used to account for "business combinations," the purchase method and the pooling-of-interests method. The purchase method is by far the most commonly applied of the two methods and is assumed to have been used by Pecos Corporation. Advanced accounting texts discuss both approaches to accounting for business combinations.

EXHIBIT 13.4 ▼

Balance Sheets for Pecos Corporation and Sunset Corporation as of December 31, 1998

Assets	Pecos Corporation	Sunset Corporation
Cash	$ 10,000	$ 55,000
Accounts receivable	72,000	16,000
Note receivable from Sunset Corporation	50,000	—
Inventory	46,000	26,000
Property, plant & equipment (net)	224,000	39,000
Investment in Sunset Corporation	66,000	—
Total assets	$468,000	$136,000
Liabilities and Stockholders' Equity		
Accounts payable	$ 18,000	$ 20,000
Note payable to Pecos Corporation	—	50,000
Bonds payable	100,000	—
Common stock	10,000	6,000
Retained earnings	340,000	60,000
Total liabilities and stockholders' equity	$468,000	$136,000

vestment account in Sunset is included in a consolidated balance sheet along with Sunset's individual assets, those assets would be counted twice. Similarly, Sunset's $66,000 of stockholders' equity on December 31, 1998, must be eliminated in a consolidated balance sheet. Why? Because the ownership interest of Pecos' stockholders in Sunset on that date is already reflected in the common stockholders' equity of Pecos.

Accountants use a consolidation work sheet, such as the one shown in Exhibit 13.5, to minimize the risk of "double-counting" items when they prepare consolidated financial statements. A consolidation work sheet allows accountants to merge the accounting data of two or more entities *without making actual entries in the entities' accounting records.*

Notice in Exhibit 13.5 that only two elimination entries are needed to consolidate the financial data of Pecos and Sunset. The first elimination entry cancels the note receivable on Pecos' books and the note payable on Sunset's books that resulted from the $50,000 intercompany loan. The second elimination entry wipes out the investment account on Pecos' books and Sunset's stockholders' equity. After these two entries are recorded on the consolidation work sheet, the work sheet is crossfooted to arrive at the consolidated amounts shown in the final column. The amounts in this column can then be organized into a balance sheet for the consolidated Pecos-Sunset entity as shown in Exhibit 13.6. Again, recognize that elimination entries are not

EXHIBIT 13.5 ▼
Consolidation Work Sheet for Pecos Corporation and Sunset Corporation as of December 31, 1998

Assets	Pecos Corporation	Sunset Corporation	Eliminations Debit	Eliminations Credit	Consolidated Amounts
Cash	$ 10,000	$ 55,000			$ 65,000
Accounts receivable	72,000	16,000			88,000
Note receivable from Sunset Corporation	50,000	—		(a) 50,000	—
Inventory	46,000	26,000			72,000
Property, plant & equipment (net)	224,000	39,000			263,000
Investment in Sunset Corporation	66,000	—		(b) 66,000	—
Total assets	$468,000	$136,000			$488,000
Liabilities and Stockholders' Equity					
Accounts payable	$ 18,000	$ 20,000			$ 38,000
Note payable to Pecos Corporation	—	50,000	(a) 50,000		—
Bonds payable	100,000	—			100,000
Common stock	10,000	6,000	(b) 6,000		10,000
Retained earnings	340,000	60,000	(b) 60,000		340,000
Total liabilities and stockholders' equity	$468,000	$136,000	$116,000	$116,000	$488,000

EXHIBIT 13.6 ▼
Consolidated Balance Sheet for Pecos Corporation and Sunset Corporation as of December 31, 1998

Cash	$ 65,000
Accounts receivable	88,000
Inventory	72,000
Property, plant & equipment (net)	263,000
Total assets	$488,000
Accounts payable	$ 38,000
Bonds payable	100,000
Common stock	10,000
Retained earnings	340,000
Total liabilities and Stockholders' equity	$488,000

recorded in either the accounting records of a parent company or a subsidiary. Elimination entries appear only on a consolidated work sheet.

Consolidated Financial Statements: Other Issues Suppose that Pecos Corporation acquired 80 percent, instead of 100 percent, of Sunset Corporation's common stock. In this case, Sunset would be a majority-owned subsidiary of Pecos. Stockholders other than Pecos Corporation would control the remaining 20 percent of Sunset's stockholders' equity. **Minority interest** is the term used when referring to the stockholders' equity of a subsidiary that is not controlled by the parent company. Typically, minority stockholders have little, if any, influence on key matters facing a corporation. Why? Because the majority stockholder or stockholders, by definition, control enough stock to determine the outcome of any issue brought to a vote of the stockholders.

minority interest

On a consolidated balance sheet, minority interest is listed between long-term liabilities and stockholders' equity. Battle Mountain Gold Company is a Houston-based firm that owns a 50.5 percent stake in Niguini Mining Limited, an Australian gold mining company. A recent balance sheet of Battle Mountain reported a minority interest of $112 million. Included in that amount was the ownership interest of the minority stockholders of Niguini Mining.

Corporations sometimes pay more for a controlling interest in another company than appears justified by the fair value of that company's net assets (assets less liabilities). This purchase premium may be to due any of several factors. Probably most often, such a purchase premium is due to a higher than normal earning power of the company being acquired. In turn, this abnormally high earning power may stem from an expert management team, a superior business location, or simply from providing a higher quality product or service than competing firms.

Suppose in the original Pecos-Sunset illustration, that the fair value of Sunset's net assets on December 30, 1998, was $66,000, an amount exactly equal to the company's stockholders' equity. Also assume that Pecos paid $75,000, instead of $66,000,

A Pig in a Poke

FOR YOUR INFORMATION

Corporations, like individual investors, sometimes make "bum" investments. Take the case of Texas-based Pier 1 Imports, the nation's largest retailer of home furnishings and accessories. In 1995, Pier 1 swallowed a $14 million loss resulting from the sale of its 50 percent interest in Sunbelt Nursery Group. Much worse was the loss suffered the following year by Novell, Inc., a computer software distributor, when that firm sold its WordPerfect division. Novell paid $855 million for WordPerfect in 1994. Two years later, the company sold WordPerfect for less than $200 million to another software company, Corel Corporation.

Finally, consider the quandary faced recently by Morgan Stanley, the prominent Wall Street investment banking firm. During the early 1990s, Morgan Stanley invested nearly $200 million in a joint venture to finance a large pig farming operation. The futuristic pig farm included genetic breeding techniques intended to develop more tasty pork for American consumers. Unfortunately, by 1996, *The Wall Street Journal* reported that the pig farm was "wallowing" in huge losses. No doubt, Morgan Stanley will avoid joint ventures in the future that involve "a pig in a poke."

to acquire all of Sunset's common stock. This $9,000 difference is referred to as "goodwill" for accounting purposes and would be reported as an intangible asset on the consolidated balance sheet of the two companies. When resulting from the purchase of a wholly-owned subsidiary, goodwill represents the amount by which the purchase price exceeds the fair value of the subsidiary's net assets. Recall from an earlier chapter that goodwill is more generally defined as the amount by which the cost of a group of assets exceeded the sum of their individual market values when they were acquired. *Accounting Trends & Techniques* reveals that approximately 67 percent of public companies report goodwill in their consolidated balance sheets.

Intercorporate Investments, Other Issues

Exhibit 13.7 presents summary information for the five major types of intercorporate investments. Notice that the last column of Exhibit 13.7 identifies a key accounting procedure for each type of investment. Before closing the books on intercorporate investments, let us consider two final and important issues related to these assets. First, corporations that invest in other companies must adopt policies and procedures to maintain effective control over these investments. Second, intercorporate

EXHIBIT 13.7 ▼

Summary of Accounting Methods for Intercorporate Investments

Type of Investment	Type of Securities	Accounting Method	Key Accounting Rule
Trading Securities	Debt and Equity	Fair Value	Unrealized gains and losses reported on income statement
Available-for-Sale Securities	Debt and Equity	Fair Value	Unrealized gains and losses reported as component of stockholders' equity
Held-to-Maturity Securities	Debt	Amortized Cost	Interest revenue equals interest payments received plus or minus the periodic amortization of discount or premium
Influential but Noncontrolling Investments	Equity	Equity Method	Book value of investment increased (decreased) for investor's proportionate interest in investee's earnings (losses) and decreased by dividends received from investee
Controlling Investments	Equity	Consolidated Financial Statements	All intercompany items eliminated in consolidated financial statements

investments complicate the efforts of decision makers to analyze a company's financial statement data.

CONTROL ACTIVITIES FOR INTERCORPORATE INVESTMENTS The extent and nature of controls exercised over intercorporate investments vary depending upon the size and type of these investments. For example, control issues related to intercorporate investments are of much more concern when a company purchases a controlling interest in a firm than when it purchases one hundred shares of another company's common stock. When a controlling interest in another firm is acquired, the investor corporation should perform a comprehensive review of the subsidiary's controls. This review should include such issues as whether key accounting and control responsibilities are properly segregated and whether access to assets is limited to authorized personnel. Based upon this review, the parent company can make any necessary changes in the subsidiary's controls. A recurring control activity for controlling investments is periodic compliance audits of a subsidiary by the parent company's internal auditors. These audits ensure that the subsidiary's personnel are not violating control policies and procedures or other administrative rules and guidelines.

LEARNING ◀ OBJECTIVE 4
Identify important control issues related to intercorporate investments.

Providing adequate physical security for bond and stock certificates is an important control activity for all intercorporate investments. Most large corporations retain an external firm to serve as the custodian for bond and stock certificates. If a company's own personnel maintain physical custody of investment certificates, those individuals should be bonded to protect the company from losses due to theft. These certificates should also be counted periodically by internal auditors. Companies that have numerous intercorporate investments establish an investment ledger comparable to an accounts receivable ledger to enhance their control over these assets.

FINANCIAL STATEMENT ANALYSIS AND INTERCORPORATE INVESTMENTS Although there are exceptions, intercorporate investments other than controlling investments typically do not represent a large percentage of the total assets of investor corporations. As a result, such investments are generally not a critical consideration when analyzing the financial status of corporations. On the other hand, controlling investments tend to be much larger, and thus decision makers should carefully consider them when performing financial statement analysis.

LEARNING ◀ OBJECTIVE 5
Discuss how intercorporate investments affect decision makers' analysis of financial statement data.

The rapid pace of business combinations in recent years has created hundreds of large companies that have multiple lines of business. The financial statements of such companies, often referred to as conglomerates, are more difficult to analyze than the financial statements of companies that operate only one line of business. For example, suppose a furniture manufacturer acquires a chain of retail toy stores. When evaluating this company's financial condition, decision makers must analyze the financial data of the two business segments independently since the two lines of business are unrelated.

Companies with multiple lines of business must generally disclose in their financial statement footnotes key financial data for each major business segment. These data allow decision makers to analyze the financial status of a company's major segments and thus reach a more reliable conclusion about the firm's overall financial condition and future prospects. An example of a company with multiple business segments is Stewart & Stevenson Services, Inc. Exhibit 13.8 presents the descriptions of the company's three business segments that were included in a recent annual report of the firm. For each of these segments, Stewart & Stevenson disclosed sales, total assets, and other key financial data in a financial statement footnote.

EXHIBIT 13.8 ▼
Description of Business Segments of Stewart & Stevenson Services, Inc.

Engineered Power Systems Segment: Includes the designing, packaging, and manufacturing and marketing of diesel and gas turbine engine-driven equipment.

Distribution Segment: Includes the marketing of diesel engines, automatic transmissions, material handling equipment, transport refrigeration units and construction equipment and the provision of related parts and service.

Tactical Vehicle Systems: Includes the designing, manufacturing and marketing of tactical vehicles, primarily $2\frac{1}{2}$-ton and 5-ton trucks under contract with the United States Army.

ACCOUNTING FOR INTERNATIONAL OPERATIONS

Every year, hundreds of U.S. companies increase their revenues and profits by selling goods and services in previously untapped foreign markets. Many of this nation's largest companies already sell more goods and services abroad than they do in the United States as demonstrated by Exhibit 13.9, which lists the ten largest U.S. multinational firms. A recent edition of the *Statistical Abstract of the United States* reported that foreign affiliates of U.S. firms had total assets approaching $2 trillion and nearly 7 million employees. The trend toward multinational business operations cuts both ways. BASF, Daimler-Benz, Honda, Michelin, and Sony are just a few examples of foreign corporations that have strong and growing annual sales in this country.

The recent growth in multinational business operations poses several challenges for the accounting profession. In the following section, we examine these challenges. Then, we focus on technical accounting issues for multinational business operations and review disclosure requirements for multinational firms.

EXHIBIT 13.9 ▼
Ten Largest U.S. Multinational Firms

	Foreign Sales*	As % of Total Sales
Exxon	$83.9	77.8%
General Motors	49.0	29.0
IBM	45.2	62.8
Mobil	44.3	66.4
Ford Motor	41.8	30.5
Texaco	27.0	56.1
Citicorp	18.8	59.3
Philip Morris	18.2	34.2
Chevron	18.0	45.6
General Electric	17.8	25.5

*In billions

Source: Forbes, July 15, 1996.

Challenges Posed for the Accounting Profession by Multinational Business Operations

LEARNING OBJECTIVE 6
Discuss the challenges that multinational business operations pose for the accounting profession.

The trend toward multinational business operations in recent decades has focused increasing attention on the need for uniform international accounting standards. Investors, creditors, and even skilled accountants often have difficulty interpreting accounting data from other countries given the variation in accounting methods applied across the world. Take the case of Germany. In the early 1990s, a frustrated partner of the British affiliate of Deloitte & Touche, a large international accounting firm, observed that a German financial statement is equivalent to a "crossword puzzle where you're not given all the clues."[2] Even countries with similar economic and political systems, such as the United States and the United Kingdom, often account for identical transactions quite differently. A perfect example is inventory accounting. In the United States, the LIFO inventory costing method is widely used; in the United Kingdom, LIFO is seldom used, with most companies opting instead for the FIFO method.

The organization leading the way in creating a uniform set of international accounting concepts and procedures is the International Accounting Standards Committee (IASC), which was founded in the early 1970s in London. By the late 1990s, the IASC had issued more than thirty accounting standards on such topics as income taxes, leases, depreciation, and business combinations. However, the IASC does not have the authority to require companies across the world to apply its accounting standards. As a result, the IASC's technical pronouncements have not been widely adopted. In the United States, the IASC's standards are not considered generally accepted accounting principles, nor does the SEC accept financial statements prepared according to the IASC's rules.

© Phil Borden/ PhotoEdit

Microsoft Corporation is one of the most profitable and well known companies in the world, thanks largely to the efforts of Bill Gates, the firm's industrious chief executive. In the early 1990s, Gates visited China for several weeks to introduce the Chinese people to Windows, Microsoft's computer operating system.

2. B. Hagerty, "Differing Accounting Rules Snarl Europe," *The Wall Street Journal,* 4 September 1992, A4A.

Bill Gates: On the Road to China

FOR YOUR INFORMATION

U.S. companies often face significant barriers to entering foreign markets. The most formidable of these barriers can be cultural differences that influence the nature of business practices in the United States and foreign countries. Take the case of Microsoft Corporation, the California-based software firm. In the early 1990s, the company's chief executive, Bill Gates, was frustrated by Microsoft's inability to "crack" the Chinese market. So, Gates decided to apply a modified version of an old and familiar American axiom: "If you can't beat them, visit them." In 1994, Gates took a long vacation in China during which he spent considerable time meeting with key "movers" and "shakers" in the Chinese government. Gates also invested considerable time and effort becoming better acquainted with Chinese history, culture, and business practices. Reportedly, Chinese officials greatly appreciated the executive's effort to acquaint himself with their country.

To date, the Chinese vacation taken by Gates has paid large dividends. In 1995, the Chinese government officially endorsed Microsoft's Windows operating system. Obtaining that endorsement was a large hurdle Microsoft faced in accomplishing its objective of making Windows the dominant operating system in China.

On a technical level, accountants of multinational firms must wrestle with such problems as having business transactions denominated in more than one currency. Consider the dilemma faced by the accountants of a U.S. company that has several subsidiaries scattered around the globe. This company must file consolidated financial statements with the SEC that are denominated in U.S. dollars. The company's accountants may be required to translate financial statement amounts expressed in South African rands, Brazilian reals, Malaysian ringgits, and Pakistani rupees into U.S. dollar equivalents.

Realized Gains and Losses on Currency Exchange

LEARNING OBJECTIVE 7 ▶
Account for realized and unrealized foreign currency transaction gains and losses.

exchange rate

A U.S. company that transacts business in a foreign currency must convert those transactions into U.S. dollar equivalents for accounting purposes. For example, suppose that on June 1 of a given year a U.S. company sells goods on credit to a French firm for Fr 20,000 (Fr = francs). The payment date for these goods is June 30. To convert this transaction into a U.S. dollar equivalent, we must know the "exchange rate" for U.S. dollars and French francs on the transaction date. An **exchange rate** is the value of one currency expressed in terms of another. Assume that on June 1 the exchange rate for converting francs into dollars is $.25 per franc. That is, a franc brought into the U.S. by a French tourist on that date could be exchanged for $.25. Alternatively, a U.S. dollar could be exchanged for four francs on that date. Given this exchange rate, the U.S. dollar equivalent for the sales transaction just described is $5,000 (Fr 20,000 × $.25). This transaction would be recorded as follows in the U.S. firm's accounting records.[3]

---

3. If this company uses a perpetual inventory system, a second entry would be required to record cost of goods sold for this transaction. Since the accounting treatment for cost of goods sold would not be affected by the multinational nature of this transaction, we will ignore cost of goods sold in this example.

June 1	Accounts Receivable	5,000	
	Sales		5,000
	To record sale of goods to D'Boughre Farms (Fr 20,000 × $.25)		

When the U.S. company receives payment on June 30, the Fr 20,000 received will be converted into U.S. dollars *at the exchange rate existing on that date.* Suppose that by June 30 the exchange rate has dropped from $.25 per franc to $.20 per franc. As a result, the Fr 20,000 received from the French customer can be exchanged for only $4,000 (Fr 20,000 × $.20). The U.S. firm has suffered a foreign currency transaction loss of $1,000 because of the change in the dollar-franc exchange rate. A **foreign currency transaction gain or loss** results from a change in the exchange rate for a credit transaction denominated in a foreign currency before the transaction is completed by the payment or receipt of cash. Shown next is the entry in the U.S. company's books to record the payment received from the French customer and the related foreign currency transaction loss.

foreign currency transaction gain or loss

June 30	Cash	4,000	
	Foreign Currency Transaction Loss	1,000	
	Accounts Receivable		5,000
	To record payment received from D'Boughre Farms ($.20 × Fr 20,000)		

Recognize that the change in the exchange rate would have no impact on the recording of this transaction by the French firm that purchased the goods. On June 1, an accountant of that firm would debit Inventory and credit Accounts Payable, each for Fr 20,000. On June 30, Accounts Payable would be debited and Cash credited for Fr 20,000.

U.S. firms can also realize foreign currency transaction gains and losses on purchase transactions. For example, assume that on June 16 the U.S. company in the previous illustration purchases goods on credit from a British firm. The quoted purchase price in British pounds is £3,000, and the exchange rate on the date of purchase is $1.60 per British pound. Given this exchange rate, the U.S. dollar equivalent for the transaction is $4,800 ($1.60 × £3,000). This purchase transaction would be recorded on June 16 by debiting Inventory $4,800 and crediting Accounts Payable an equal amount.

Suppose the payment date for this transaction is July 16 and that the exchange rate for the U.S. dollar and British pound has dropped to $1.50 per pound by that date. To pay the debt owed to the British supplier, the U.S. firm must first purchase the required £3,000. Given the change in the exchange rate, only $4,500 ($1.50 × £3,000) will be required to purchase the £3,000 on July 16. As a result, the U.S. firm will realize a $300 foreign currency transaction gain on the payment of this debt. The appropriate entry on July 16 to record the payment to the British supplier will include a $4,800 debit to Accounts Payable, a $4,500 credit to Cash, and a $300 credit to Foreign Currency Transaction Gain.

Unrealized Gains and Losses on Currency Exchange

The foreign currency transaction gain and loss in the previous examples were realized when cash exchanged hands between the U.S. company and its foreign customer or supplier. U.S. companies that engage in international commerce also have "unrealized" foreign currency transaction gains and losses. These unrealized gains and losses result from credit transactions denominated in foreign currencies that have not been completed by the end of an accounting period. That is, at the end of an accounting period cash has not changed hands between the parties to the transactions. Unrealized gains and losses are recorded via adjusting entries. For financial reporting purposes, a multinational company "nets" its realized and unrealized foreign currency transaction gains and losses into one amount. Consequently, all foreign currency transaction gains and losses can be recorded in the same account. The net foreign currency transaction gain or loss for an accounting period is typically reported in an income statement under a caption such as "Other revenues and expenses."

To illustrate an unrealized foreign currency gain, assume that a U.S. company purchases goods from a Japanese supplier, Katsura Corporation, on December 11 of a given year. The selling price of these goods expressed in Japanese yen is ¥132,000. Since the exchange rate for the U.S. dollar and Japanese yen on this date is $.011 per yen, the U.S. dollar equivalent of this purchase transaction is $1,452 ($.011 × ¥132,000). The U.S. company would record this purchase as shown in the following entry.

Dec. 11	Inventory	1,452	
	Accounts Payable		1,452
	To record purchase of inventory from Katsura Corporation ($.011 × ¥132,000)		

Now, assume that on December 31, the U.S. company's fiscal year-end, the dollar-yen exchange rate is $.01 per yen. Given this exchange rate, the liability to Katsura Corporation, expressed in U.S. dollars, is only $1,320 ($.01 × ¥132,000). The U.S. firm will record the following year-end adjusting entry to recognize the unrealized gain of $132 ($1,452 − $1,320) on this account payable and to reduce the book value of the payable to $1,320.

Dec. 31	Accounts Payable	132	
	Foreign Currency Transaction Gain		132
	To record unrealized foreign currency transaction gain on account payable to Katsura Corporation		

Consolidation of Foreign Subsidiaries

The executives of many U.S. companies believe that the best strategy for quickly establishing a strong economic presence in a foreign country is to set up a subsidiary in that country. This strategy provides greater access to a foreign country's economic markets and often results in considerable tax advantages as well. A foreign subsidiary's financial statements in most cases must be consolidated with those of its U.S. parent company. Since the subsidiary's financial data will be denominated in another currency, the parent must translate that data into U.S. dollars before preparing consolidated financial statements. Advanced accounting texts illustrate the conversion of a foreign subsidiary's financial statements into U.S. dollars.

Russians Say "Nyet" to American Business Ethics

The collapse of the U.S.S.R. in the early 1990s encouraged many U.S. companies to begin marketing their goods and services in the newly formed Russian republic. These companies soon recognized that Russians' attitudes about what constitutes acceptable business practices differed greatly from the attitudes of U.S. citizens. No doubt, firmly entrenched cultural norms in the two countries account for these differing attitudes. A recent study profiled opposing views that Russians and Americans have when it comes to business ethics. The following table lists several of these differences.

	Russia	United States
Large salary differences between business executives and employees	Unethical	Ethical
Price fixing	Ethical	Unethical
"Whistleblowing"	Unethical	Ethical
"Grease" payments to facilitate business deals	Ethical	Unethical
Employee layoffs when economic conditions deteriorate	Unethical	Ethical
Ignoring business regulations that seem to serve little, if any, purpose	Ethical	Unethical

Source: S.M. Puffer and D.J. McCarthy, "Finding the Common Ground in Russian and American Business Ethics," *California Management Review,* Winter 1995, 29–46.

Financial Disclosures for International Operations

Accounting standards require many U.S.-based multinational companies to disclose financial data regarding their foreign operations. These disclosures provide decision makers with a better understanding of the nature and scope of a multinational company's operations and the business risks it faces. U.S. multinational companies must disclose in their financial statement footnotes key data regarding their foreign operations if at least one of two conditions is met:

1. The revenue generated by their foreign operations account for at least 10 percent of their consolidated revenues; or,
2. The "identifiable" assets of their foreign operations account for at least 10 percent of the assets reported on their consolidated balance sheet.

An example of a U.S. company that has significant foreign operations is Integrated Device Technology, Inc. (IDT). IDT designs, manufactures, and markets several hundred computer-related products including a wide array of microprocessors. In a footnote to a recent set of financial statements, IDT disclosed key financial data for each geographic region in which it operates. For example, IDT provided the following breakdown of its total sales by geographic region (000s omitted).

United States	$404,994
Japan	72,530
Europe	144,154
Asia-Pacific	57,819
Total	$679,497

SUMMARY

Corporations purchase debt and equity securities of other companies for a variety of reasons. Among these reasons are generating trading profits on short-term fluctuations in securities prices and obtaining a sufficiently large ownership interest in another company to control its operations. Disclosures regarding the nature and purpose of a company's intercorporate investments often provide external decision makers with important insight on the company's future plans. Other information needs of external decision makers regarding a firm's intercorporate investments include market value disclosures and revenues and expenses related to these investments.

There are five major types of intercorporate investments: trading securities, available-for-sale securities, held-to-maturity securities, influential but noncontrolling investments, and controlling investments. Trading securities and available-for-sale securities can be either debt or equity securities. For balance sheet purposes, these two classes of intercorporate investments are reported at their fair values. Unrealized gains and losses on trading securities are reported on the income statement. In contrast, unrealized gains and losses on available-for-sale securities are a component of stockholders' equity on the balance sheet. The amortized cost method is used to account for held-to-maturity securities, which include only investments in debt securities. Under the amortized cost method, debt securities are reported on a balance sheet at their original cost adjusted for any amortized premium or discount.

The equity method must be used to account for influential but noncontrolling investments in equity securities. An influential but noncontrolling investment generally exists when a corporation owns 20 to 50 percent of another firm's common stock. Under the equity method, an investor firm reports an intercorporate investment on its balance sheet at adjusted historical cost. The original cost of the investment is increased (decreased) by the investor's proportionate interest in the investee's earnings (losses). Dividends paid to the investor by the investee reduce the investment's book value. When one company owns more than 50 percent of the common stock of another, the firms must prepare consolidated financial statements each reporting period. Accountants use a consolidation work sheet to merge the accounting data of a parent company and its subsidiaries.

Recent decades have witnessed a significant trend toward international business operations. A major problem faced by multinational companies is the absence of uniform accounting standards across the world. Accountants for multinational companies must also cope with transactions denominated in different currencies and constantly changing foreign currency exchange rates. A U.S. multinational company includes in its income statement realized and unrealized gains and losses due to the conversion, or anticipated conversion, of funds from one currency to another. U.S. multinational companies must also prepare consolidated financial statements with foreign subsidiaries. Finally, U.S. companies that have significant foreign operations must include in their financial statement footnotes key financial data for each major geographical area in which they operate.

GLOSSARY

Amortized cost method (p. 585) A method of accounting for investments in held-to-maturity securities under which any premium or discount on the purchase of these securities is amortized over their remaining term.

Available-for-sale securities (p. 581) Investments in debt or equity securities that do not qualify as one of the other types of intercorporate investments.

Consolidated financial statements (p. 588) The combined financial statements of a parent company and its subsidiaries.

Controlling investments (p. 581) Investments in equity securities in which the parent company owns more than 50 percent of the common stock of the subsidiary.

Equity method (p. 586) The accounting method used for influential but noncontrolling investments; the investor's proportionate interest in the investee's periodic earnings (losses) is treated as an addition (reduction) to the book value of the investment, while dividends received from the investee reduce the book value of the investment.

Exchange rate (p. 596) The value of one currency expressed in terms of another.

Fair value (p. 582) Generally, the closing price of a debt or equity security on a given date on a securities exchange.

Foreign currency transaction gain or loss (p. 597) A gain or loss resulting from a change in the exchange rate for a credit transaction denominated in a foreign currency before the transaction is completed by the payment or receipt of cash.

Held-to-maturity securities (p. 581) Investments in debt securities acquired with the positive intent and ability to hold them to maturity.

Influential but noncontrolling investments (p. 581) Investments in equity securities in which the investor corporation generally owns at least 20 percent but not more than 50 percent of the investee corporation's common stock.

Intercompany transactions (p. 588) Transactions between a parent company and a subsidiary, between two or more subsidiaries, or between other operating units of a company.

Minority interest (p. 591) The stockholders' equity of a subsidiary that is not controlled by the parent company.

Parent company (p. 587) A company that owns more than 50 percent of another company's common stock.

Subsidiary (p. 587) A company that has more than 50 percent of its common stock owned by another company.

Trading securities (p. 581) Investments in debt and equity securities that may be sold in the near term to generate cash or to realize trading profits due to fluctuations in market prices.

DECISION CASE

Isis Pharmaceuticals, Inc., is a California-based company that develops and markets pharmaceuticals. Ciba-Geigy, a large Swiss pharmaceutical company, owns 6 percent of Isis' common stock. Recently, Boehringer Ingelheim International (BII), a German pharmaceutical firm, announced plans to purchase approximately 10 percent of Isis' common stock and disclosed that it might purchase additional Isis stock in the future. BII also revealed that it had extended a $40 million line of credit to Isis and would be working with the company to develop a new line of anti-inflammatory drugs.

Suppose that you are the chief executive officer of Vitale, Inc., a pharmaceutical company that finds itself in the same circumstances as Isis. Two foreign competitors are Vitale's largest stockholders. Together, these competitors own approximately 20 percent of Vitale's outstanding common stock and have been gradually increasing their ownership interests. Each firm has also provided your company with substantial loans. In recent months, you have become concerned because the two firms have been working together to exert increasing influence on your company's operations. For example, executives of the firms have suggested that two of Vitale's laboratories should be moved overseas. The executives maintain that such a move would both reduce labor costs and minimize the "interference" of the FDA (Food and Drug Administration) in Vitale's operations.

In a recent conference call, the chief executives of these firms voiced displeasure with several financial reporting requirements of the SEC. They pointed out that their countries' comparable regulatory agencies do not require the extensive financial disclosures mandated by the SEC. One of the executives suggested that certain disclosures required by the SEC would be useful to competitors and thus should not be made. The executive then explained that he was familiar with the SEC's rules and believed that the disclosures could be avoided because of "loopholes" in those rules.

Required: Analyze your present situation as the chief executive officer of Vitale. How may the future operations of your firm be influenced by its two largest stockholders? What actions on your part, if any, do you believe are appropriate at this point and why?

The one executive is correct that the SEC has more extensive disclosure requirements than comparable regulatory agencies in other countries. Would it be appropriate for you to accept the executive's suggestion and avoid making certain financial disclosures because of "loopholes" in the SEC's rules? What factors should you consider in making this decision? Ignoring existing rules and regulations, do you believe public companies should disclose in their financial statements the identities of stockholders that control large blocks of their common stock? Explain.

QUESTIONS

1. The initials "LBO" refer to what kind of business acquisition? Briefly describe the nature of an LBO.
2. Identify common reasons that corporations invest in the stocks and bonds of other corporations.

3. When a company anticipates a future takeover, its executives may approve a lucrative termination package for themselves. What is such a package called?
4. What are the five major types of intercorporate investments? Identify one key characteristic of each.
5. In what sense are available-for-sale securities a "catchall" category for intercorporate investments?
6. How is the fair value of an investment in a debt or equity security usually determined for balance sheet purposes?
7. Where is an unrealized gain or loss on trading securities reported in a set of financial statements?
8. Where is an unrealized gain or loss on available-for-sale securities reported in a set of financial statements?
9. What is the logic underlying the different financial statement treatment applied to unrealized gains and losses on trading securities and available-for-sale securities?
10. Why can only investments in debt securities be classified as held-to-maturity securities?
11. When a company purchases corporate bonds at a price different from the bonds' face value, how does the company determine the periodic interest revenue to be recognized on this investment assuming it qualifies as a held-to-maturity security?
12. When should the equity method be used by a company to account for an investment in the common stock of another company?
13. When should two or more companies prepare consolidated financial statements? What is the justification for preparing consolidated financial statements for two or more legally separate entities?
14. Define "minority interest." Where on a consolidated balance sheet is minority interest typically reported?
15. Distinguish between a wholly-owned and a majority-owned subsidiary.
16. Define the term "goodwill" as it relates to business combinations.
17. Why is a company concerned with the internal controls of its subsidiaries?
18. Why do controlling investments make financial statement analysis more complicated?
19. What is the IASC and what is its objective?
20. What is a foreign currency exchange rate? How are exchange rates used in accounting for multinational business transactions?
21. How do foreign currency transaction gains and losses arise? When are these gains and losses realized? When are they unrealized?
22. U.S. multinational companies must disclose information about their foreign operations if either of two conditions are met. What are these conditions?

EXERCISES

23. True or False (LO 1–7)

Following is a series of statements regarding topics discussed in Chapter 13.

Required:

Indicate whether each statement is true (T) or false (F).

_____ a. The fair value of a debt or equity security is generally the security's closing price on a given date on a securities exchange.

_____ b. Market Adjustment—Trading Securities is a "valuation" account comparable to the Allowance for Doubtful Accounts.

_____ c. External decision makers want to be informed of the general purpose and nature of a company's intercorporate investments.

_____ d. For the benefit of decision makers, companies must generally disclose in their financial statement footnotes key financial data for each of their major business segments.

_____ e. Investments in debt and equity securities that do not qualify as one of the other four types of intercorporate investments are classified as trading securities.

_____ f. Accounting standards require trading securities to be reported on a balance sheet at their historical cost.

_____ g. Since a parent company's executives can dictate the operating policies of a subsidiary, the accounting profession views a parent company and its subsidiaries as one economic entity.

_____ h. Providing adequate physical security for bond and stock certificates is an important control activity for intercorporate investments.

_____ i. The amortized cost method is applied to held-to-maturity securities.

_____ j. One common motivation for intercorporate investments is to control, or at least influence, another firm's operations.

_____ k. Under the equity method of accounting for investments, an investor corporation records its proportionate interest in the investee's periodic earnings (losses) as an addition (reduction) to the investment's book value.

_____ l. A consolidation work sheet allows accountants to merge the accounting data of two or more companies without making actual entries in their accounting records.

_____ m. The accounting rules issued by the International Accounting Standards Committee (IASC) are considered generally accepted accounting principles in the United States.

_____ n. Realized foreign currency transaction gains and losses result from credit transactions denominated in foreign currencies that have not been completed by the end of an accounting period.

24. Short-Term Investments (LO 1, 2, 3)

Ellen and Jason McDougal own a retail business, Shoes 'n' Boots, Inc. The corporation presently has excess cash of $25,000. The McDougals would like to invest this cash. However, they do not want to "tie up" the cash for an extended period, since they plan to open another retail store within the next twelve months.

Required:

1. List several investment alternatives available to the McDougals. Identify an advantage and disadvantage of each of these alternatives.
2. Suppose that the McDougals invest the $25,000 in 500 shares of a corporate common stock. How would this intercorporate investment be classified for accounting purposes? Why?
3. How will dividends received on this investment be reported in Shoes 'n' Boots' financial statements?
4. Suppose that by the next balance sheet date, the market value of the 500 shares of stock is $3,500 less than the amount paid for the stock. Will this "paper loss" be reported in Shoes 'n' Boots' financial statements? If so, how?

25. Accounting for Stock and Bond Investments (LO 3)

Suppose that on April 1, 1998, Alpha Company acquires 1,000 shares of Omicron Company common stock for $15 a share and 25 corporate bonds of Epsilon Company for their face value of $1,000 each. The bonds have a 6 percent stated interest rate; the interest is paid semiannually on April 1 and October 1 of each year. Omicron Company pays a dividend of $1 per share on October 31 each year. Alpha's fiscal year ends on December 31.

Required:

1. How will Alpha likely classify these investments on its year-end balance sheet if it intends to hold the stock and bonds:
   a. indefinitely?
   b. until their market prices increase significantly (which management expects to be a period of no more than six months)?

2. Prepare the journal entries to record Alpha's two investments under both assumptions "a" and "b" in (1).
3. Assuming Alpha's two investments are considered trading securities, prepare the journal entries to record the dividends and interest revenue received by Alpha during 1998.
4. Suppose that Omicron's common stock is trading for $14 per share on December 31, 1998, and the Epsilon bonds have a quoted market price of 97 on that date. Prepare any necessary adjusting journal entries in Alpha's accounting records on December 31, 1998, again assuming that both investments qualify as trading securities.

26. **Accounting for Available-for-Sale Securities** (LO 3)
On October 14, 1997, Zeile Company purchased for $14.25 per share 1,000 shares of The China Fund, a mutual fund listed on the New York Stock Exchange. Zeile received a cash dividend of $.64 per share from this mutual fund on November 28. On December 31, 1997, The China Fund was trading for $11.50 per share. Zeile accounts for the investment in The China Fund as an available-for-sale security.

Required:
1. Under what conditions do intercorporate investments qualify as available-for-sale securities?
2. Prepare all necessary journal entries in Zeile Company's accounting records during 1997 related to its investment in The China Fund.

27. **Balance Sheet Treatment of Investments** (LO 2, 3)
Following is the stockholders' equity section included in a recent balance sheet of Orbital Sciences Corporation (OSC).

Common stock	$ 202
Additional paid-in capital	201,328
Unrealized losses on marketable securities	(462)
Retained earnings	978
Total stockholders' equity	$202,046

Required:
1. What type of intercorporate investments resulted in the unrealized losses reported in the stockholders' equity section of OSC's balance sheet?
2. The marketable securities referred to in the stockholders' equity section of OSC's balance sheet were reported as current assets in that same balance sheet. Does this change your answer to (1)? Why or why not?
3. What is the rationale for reporting unrealized gains and losses of this type in the stockholders' equity section of a company's balance sheet? Is this approach to reporting such gains and losses beneficial to external decision makers? Explain.

28. **Accounting for Trading Securities** (LO 3)
During 1998, Ashley Fay Fashions had the following transactions involving intercorporate investments.

March 11:	Purchased 500 shares of Maxim Co. common stock for $21 per share
May 3:	Purchased 1,200 shares of El Cortez Co. common stock for $7 per share
June 1:	Received a $.44 per share cash dividend from Maxim Co.
November 1:	Purchased 600 shares of Binion Co. common stock for $8 per share

Following are the December 31, 1998, stock prices of the companies in which Ashley Fay Fashions had an ownership interest at the end of 1998:

Maxim Co.	$17.25
El Cortez Co.	9.50
Binion Co.	6.75

Required:

1. Under what circumstances should intercorporate investments be classified as trading securities?
2. Suppose that each of the investments made by Ashley Fay Fashions during 1998 qualifies as a trading security. Prepare the appropriate journal entries to record the investment transactions of the company during 1998.
3. Prepare any necessary year-end adjusting entry related to the company's trading securities.

29. **Accounting for Held-to-Maturity Securities** (LO 1, 2, 3)
On March 1, 1998, Emerson, Inc., purchased 60 Branson Corporation bonds. The bonds have a 10 percent stated interest rate, pay interest semiannually on March 1 and September 1, and mature on March 1, 2008. Emerson paid $65,000 for these bonds, $5,000 more than their collective face value, and plans to hold the bonds until they mature.

Required:

1. Prepare the journal entry in Emerson's accounting records to record the acquisition of these bonds.
2. Prepare the journal entry to record Emerson's receipt of interest from Branson Corporation on September 1, 1998. Emerson uses the straight-line method to amortize any discount or premium on bond investments.
3. What is the rationale for applying the amortized cost method to held-to-maturity securities rather than accounting for these investments on a fair value basis? Are external decision makers provided with fair value disclosures for these investments?

30. **Classification of Investments** (LO 3)
On January 1, 1998, McQuig Corporation purchased 30 percent of the outstanding common stock of B. C. Clark, Inc., for $500,000. B. C. Clark reported net income of $100,000 for its fiscal year ending December 31, 1998. On November 1, 1998, B. C. Clark paid a $60,000 cash dividend to its common stockholders.

Required:

1. What accounting method did McQuig likely use to account for its investment in B. C. Clark?
2. Given the accounting method identified in (1), prepare the appropriate journal entries in McQuig's accounting records during 1998 for the company's investment in B. C. Clark common stock.

31. **Equity Method of Accounting for Intercorporate Investments** (LO 1, 3)
Barkley Enterprises purchased 40 percent of the common stock of Majerle Company on January 1, 1995, paying $370,000. Barkley uses the equity method to account for this investment. Following is Majerle's net income (net loss) for each year 1995 through 1998 and the total cash dividends paid by the company during each of those years.

	Net Income	Cash Dividends
1995	$ 25,000	$20,000
1996	(90,000)	10,000
1997	100,000	50,000
1998	35,000	45,000

Required:

1. When the equity method of accounting is appropriate for an intercorporate investment, what does the accounting profession assume was the principal motivation for that investment? Explain.
2. Determine the balance of the Investment in Majerle Common Stock account in Barkley Enterprises' accounting records at the end of each year 1995 through 1998.

32. **Accounting for Intercorporate Investments** (LO 1, 3)
Review the annual report of Outback Steakhouse that is included as an appendix to this text to identify information regarding the firm's intercorporate investments.

Required:

1. Has Outback Steakhouse made any intercorporate investments in recent years? If so, provide brief descriptions of some of these investments and the stated or apparent motive for each.
2. What accounting methods does Outback Steakhouse apply to its intercorporate investments? Where did you find this information?

33. **Consolidated Financial Statements** (LO 2, 3, 5)
Following are the trial balances of Parent Company and Subsidiary Company following Parent's purchase of 100 percent of Subsidiary's common stock. Parent Company loaned $5,000 to Subsidiary Company immediately after the stock purchase was completed.

	Parent	Subsidiary
Assets		
Cash	$ 15,000	$ 10,000
Accounts receivable (net)	25,000	22,500
Note receivable from Subsidiary Co.	5,000	—
Inventory	17,500	12,750
Property, plant & equipment (net)	72,650	55,275
Investment in subsidiary	66,075	—
Total assets	$201,225	$100,525
Liabilities and Stockholders' Equity		
Accounts payable	$ 17,400	$ 9,450
Note payable to Parent Co.	—	5,000
Bank loan payable	50,000	20,000
Common stock	110,000	60,000
Retained earnings	23,825	6,075
Total liabilities and stockholders' equity	$201,225	$100,525

Required:

1. How much did Parent Company pay for the common stock of Subsidiary Company?
2. Will there be any "minority interest" included in the consolidated financial statements of Parent and Subsidiary? Why or why not?
3. Assume that the fair value of Subsidiary's assets is approximately equal to their book value. Will any "goodwill" be included in the consolidated financial statements of Parent and Subsidiary? Why or why not?
4. Using the work sheet format shown in Exhibit 13.5, prepare any eliminating entries needed to consolidate the two companies' balance sheets.
5. Prepare the consolidated balance sheet for Parent and Subsidiary.

6. How does the acquisition of a controlling investment by one company in another affect decision makers' ability to analyze the combined entity's financial statement data? Explain.

34. Accounting for Goodwill and Minority Interest (LO 2, 3, 4)

El Palacio Restaurants purchased 80 percent of the common stock of a competing firm, Casa del Sol Restaurants, on May 5. El Palacio paid $3,357,000 for that common stock. Casa del Sol had net assets (total assets less total liabilities) of $4,030,000 immediately prior to El Palacio's takeover of the firm. The book value of these assets was approximately equal to their fair market value.

Required:

1. If a consolidated balance sheet is prepared for these two companies immediately following this stock purchase, how much minority interest will be reported on that balance sheet?
2. Will the consolidated balance sheet for the two firms include any goodwill? If so, how much?
3. What types of control activities related to the investment in Casa del Sol should El Palacio consider implementing?
4. Briefly explain why the preparation of consolidated financial statements for a parent company and its subsidiaries is beneficial to external decision makers.

35. Accounting for Foreign Currency Transactions (LO 7)

On April 1, Le Plume Fragrances, a company based in Paris, sold 100,000 pounds of perfume to a U.S. firm, Ou Pew Corporation. Ou Pew agreed to pay six francs for each pound of perfume. The credit terms for the transaction are n/30. The dollar-franc exchange rates on the relevant dates for this transaction are as follows:

April 1: $.20 per franc
May 1: $.22 per franc

Required:

1. Prepare the journal entry in Ou Pew's accounting records for the purchase of merchandise from Le Plume on April 1.
2. Prepare the journal entry in Ou Pew's accounting records for the payment made to Le Plume on May 1.
3. Prepare the appropriate journal entries in Le Plume's accounting records on April 1 and May 1. Record these entries in francs, not dollars.

36. Accounting for Foreign Currency Transactions (LO 7)

Takaguchi Company, a Japanese firm, sold 42,000 pounds of a metal alloy to Wolverine Metals, a U.S. company, on December 4. The price per pound was 21 yen, and the credit terms were n/60. Following are the dollar-yen exchange rates on the relevant dates for this transaction.

December 4: $.11
December 31: $.10
February 2: $.12

Required:

1. Prepare the journal entry in Wolverine's accounting records for the purchase of the metal alloy from Takaguchi on December 4.
2. Wolverine's fiscal year ends on December 31. Prepare any necessary adjusting journal entry in Wolverine's accounting records related to the December 4 purchase transaction.
3. Prepare the journal entry in Wolverine's accounting records on February 2 to record the payment made to Takaguchi.

37. **International Ethics** (LO 6)
Refer to the Spotlight on Ethics vignette in this chapter entitled "Russians Say 'Nyet' to American Business Ethics."

Required:
For each of the business practices listed in that vignette, indicate whether you believe the practice is ethical or unethical. Defend your answer in each case.

PROBLEM SET A

38. **Accounting and Financial Reporting Decisions for Intercorporate Investments** (LO 1, 2, 3)
In January 1998, Tervino Corporation purchased 41 percent of the outstanding common stock of Azle Landers, Inc., at a cost of $7.2 million. The chief executive officer (CEO) of Tervino believed the large block of Azle Landers common stock was a bargain at that price. In the previous five years, Azle Landers' net income had averaged $2.6 million, and the firm had paid out approximately $1.4 million in cash dividends each year. Tervino's CEO was so impressed with Azle Landers that she would have purchased all of its outstanding common stock. However, the remaining 59 percent of the company's common stock is owned by a foreign corporation, Resolut, Ltd, which intends to retain its ownership interest in Azle Landers indefinitely.

Unfortunately, 1998 was not a good year for Azle Landers. A strike by production personnel and problems with new machinery contributed to a 20 percent decline in Azle Landers' revenues compared with 1997 and resulted in a $400,000 loss for the year, the first in the company's twenty-five-year history. Because of Azle Landers' financial problems, the company's board of directors, which is controlled by Resolut, voted not to pay any cash dividends during 1998.

Tervino's controller prepared a draft of his company's 1998 financial statements in early January 1999. When Tervino's CEO reviewed the draft of the 1998 income statement, she "hit the roof" after discovering the $164,000 "investment loss" related to the company's ownership interest in Azle Landers. The CEO immediately stormed into the controller's office. "Are you telling me that not only did we receive zero dividends from Azle Landers, but we also have to report a portion of its loss in our financial statements? This can't be right. Who came up with this rule?"

Required:
Write a memo to Tervino's CEO in which you explain the logic underlying the equity method of accounting for influential but noncontrolling investments. In this memo, discuss whether there may be any rationale for not applying the equity method to Tervino's investment in Azle Landers.

39. **Classification of Intercorporate Investments** (LO 1, 3)
Thanos Corporation acquired the following corporate securities on the indicated dates during the current year:

January 12: Purchased 55,000 shares of Elektra, Inc., common stock at a cost of $12 per share. Elektra has 250,000 shares of common stock outstanding.

January 17: Purchased 500 shares of Namor Enterprises preferred stock at a cost of $17 per share. Thanos intends to hold these shares indefinitely.

March 9: Purchased 15 bonds of Sunfire Company at a quoted market price of 104. These bonds have a stated interest rate of 10 percent, pay interest semiannually on May 1 and November 1, and mature on May 1, 2009.

June 29: Acquired 75 percent of the outstanding common stock of Kraven Company at a cost of $3.2 million.

August 3: Acquired 2,000 of the 5,000 outstanding bonds of Mephisto Enterprises. These bonds were purchased at a quoted market price of 96, have a stated interest rate of 12 percent, and pay interest semiannually on June 1 and December 1. Thanos executives believe that these bonds will provide a high rate of return and pose a low level of default risk. Consequently, the executives intend to retain these bonds until their maturity date which is June 1, 2007.

Required:
Classify each of the intercorporate investments acquired by Thanos Corporation into one of the five categories identified in this chapter. If there is not sufficient information to classify one of these investments, indicate the classes to which the investment could potentially be assigned and the conditions under which it would be assigned to each of those classes.

40. Accounting for Intercorporate Investments (LO 1, 2, 3)
Pembroke Enterprises held the following investments in corporate securities on December 31, 1998, the company's fiscal year-end.

	Cost	Fair Value
Locus Corporation common stock	$ 65,000	$ 62,500
Excelsior Enterprises bonds	200,000	208,000

The Locus common stock was purchased on April 4, 1998, while the Excelsior bonds were acquired a few months later on October 1. Excelsior's bonds pay interest semiannually on March 31 and September 30 of each year. The stated interest rate on the bonds is 8 percent. Pembroke purchased the Excelsior bonds at a quoted market price of 100.

Required:
1. Prepare all necessary journal entries related to Pembroke's investments during 1998, assuming that they are considered trading securities. Include the year-end adjusting entry to record any unrealized gain or loss on these investments.
2. Prepare all necessary journal entries related to Pembroke's investments during 1998, assuming that they are considered available-for-sale securities. Include the year-end adjusting entry to record any unrealized gain or loss on these investments.
3. Indicate how any unrealized gain or loss on Pembroke's intercorporate investments would be reported in the company's December 31, 1998, financial statements, assuming these investments are classified as:
   a. trading securities.
   b. available-for-sale securities.
4. Briefly discuss the rationale underlying the different accounting and financial reporting treatment applied to trading and available-for-sale securities.

41. Accounting for Intercorporate Investments (LO 1, 2, 3)
On January 1, 1998, Eggling Corporation invested in the bonds of Rinker Company. Eggling purchased 100 of Rinker's $1,000 bonds at a quoted market price of 105. Rinker's bonds have a 10 percent stated interest rate, semiannual interest payment dates of January 1 and July 1, and a maturity date of January 1, 2003. On December 31, 1998, Eggling's fiscal year-end, Rinker's bonds have a quoted market price of 107.

Required:
1. Under what condition or conditions would Eggling Corporation account for the investment in Rinker Company's bonds as a held-to-maturity security?
2. Assuming that the investment in Rinker bonds is treated as a held-to-maturity security by Eggling, prepare the appropriate journal entries in Eggling's accounting records on January 1 and July 1, 1998. (Eggling uses the straight-line method to amortize any premium or discount on a bond investment.)

3. Assume that the book value of the investment in Rinker bonds is $104,000 on December 31, 1998. At what dollar amount will this investment be reported in Eggling's year-end balance sheet?
4. What other financial statement disclosures, if any, will Eggling include in its 1998 financial statements related to this investment?

42. Accounting for Intercorporate Investments (LO 1, 3)
On January 1, 1996, Grabbe Company acquired 35 percent of the outstanding common stock of Soledad Corporation for $4,000,000 and 45 percent of the outstanding common stock of MultiMax Corporation for $2,000,000. The following schedule presents the annual net income (net loss) of Soledad and MultiMax for the period 1996 through 1998 and the total dividends paid by each firm over that period.

	Net Income or (Loss)			Total Dividends Paid		
	1996	**1997**	**1998**	**1996**	**1997**	**1998**
Soledad	$1,000,000	$800,000	$1,500,000	$500,000	$500,000	$800,000
MultiMax	300,000	(200,000)	500,000	50,000	50,000	100,000

Required:
1. How should Grabbe account for its investments in Soledad and MultiMax? Briefly explain the logic underlying this accounting method.
2. Prepare any entries needed in Grabbe's accounting records for 1996 through 1998 to account for its investments in Soledad and MultiMax.

43. Consolidation Work Sheet for a Wholly-Owned Subsidiary (LO 3, 4, 5)
On December 31, 1998, Phoenix Trucking purchased all of the outstanding common stock of Sabretooth Resorts for $250,000. Immediately following the acquisition of Sabretooth, Phoenix extended a loan of $100,000 to its new subsidiary. Following are the separate balance sheets of the two companies at the close of business on December 31, 1998.

	Phoenix	**Sabretooth**
Assets		
Cash	$ 24,000	$112,000
Supplies	5,000	4,200
Prepaid expenses	11,200	3,100
Note receivable from Sabretooth	100,000	—
Buildings and land (net)	596,000	275,000
Investment in Sabretooth	250,000	—
Total assets	$986,200	$394,300
Liabilities and Stockholders' Equity		
Accounts payable	$ 74,100	$ 44,300
Note payable to Phoenix	—	100,000
Bonds payable	250,000	—
Common stock	120,000	55,000
Additional paid-in capital	303,100	—
Retained earnings	239,000	195,000
Total liabilities and stockholders' equity	$986,200	$394,300

Required:

1. Assume that the fair value of Sabretooth's assets is approximately equal to their book value. Should any "goodwill" be included in the consolidated balance sheet of these two companies? Explain.
2. Prepare any journal entries required on December 31, 1998, in either the accounting records of Phoenix Trucking or Sabretooth Resorts. Indicate in which company's accounting records each journal entry belongs.
3. Complete a postacquisition consolidation work sheet for Phoenix and Sabretooth.
4. Prepare a consolidated balance sheet for Phoenix and Sabretooth as of December 31, 1998.
5. Many large companies have one or more subsidiaries. What control activities should a company implement when it acquires a controlling interest in another firm?
6. How do controlling investments complicate decision makers' analysis of financial statement data?

44. Accounting for Foreign Currency Transactions (LO 6, 7)

Vermont Creations, Inc., a U.S. firm, wholesales stuffed toys to retail companies in several countries. For the convenience of its customers and suppliers, the company transacts business in the currency of each customer's or supplier's home country. Following are selected transactions engaged in by Vermont Creations during 1998. The company's 1998 fiscal year ended on June 30.

March 26:	Sold a shipment of stuffed toys to Colebridge Corporation, a London-based firm. The sales price was 8,000 pounds, and the credit terms were n/60.
April 1:	Purchased 500 cubic yards of raw materials from Chevalier Corporation, a French firm, for 15,000 francs. The credit terms were n/20.
April 21:	Paid Chevalier Corporation the amount due for the April 1 purchase.
May 15:	Sold a shipment of stuffed toys to Bee Choo Corporation, a Malaysian firm. The sales price was 22,000 ringgits, and the credit terms were n/60.
May 25:	Received payment from Colebridge Corporation for March 26 sale.
July 14:	Received payment from Bee Choo Corporation for May 15 sale.

Following are the assumed foreign exchange rates that are relevant to the listed transactions of Vermont Creations.

March 26:	$1.60 per pound
April 1:	$ .20 per franc
April 21:	$ .22 per franc
May 15:	$ .40 per ringgit
May 25:	$1.55 per pound
June 30:	$ .42 per ringgit
July 14:	$ .41 per ringgit

Required:

1. Identify the key accounting and control issues that multinational business operations pose for U.S. companies.
2. Prepare appropriate journal entries for the listed transactions in the accounting records of Vermont Creations. Include the required journal entry to record any unrealized foreign currency transaction gain or loss as of June 30, 1998. (Notes: Round all amounts to the nearest dollar. For sales transactions, you are not required to record the cost of goods sold.)
3. Considering only the transactions presented, compute the net foreign currency transaction gain or loss for Vermont Creations during 1998.

PROBLEM SET B

45. Accounting and Financial Reporting Decisions for Intercorporate Investments (LO 1, 2, 3)
You are the controller of Psylocke Company, a conglomerate that has two major subsidiaries, Silver Surfer Corporation and Sauron Company. The CEO of Psylocke is presently negotiating to obtain a large bank loan desperately needed by the company. He asks you to provide him with both consolidated financial statements for Psylocke and its subsidiaries and separate financial statements for Psylocke Company alone. The CEO is planning to review these two sets of financial statements and include the set that he believes is most impressive with the application for the bank loan.

Required:
Write a memo to the CEO of Psylocke explaining the purpose of consolidated financial statements. In this memo, comment on whether you believe it is appropriate for the CEO to choose the most "impressive" of the two sets of financial statements to file with the loan application.

46. Classification of Intercorporate Investments (LO 1, 3)
Recently, Gambit, Inc., acquired the following corporate securities:

January 29: Purchased 200 shares of Rhino, Inc., common stock at a cost of $3 per share. Gambit's executives believe the price of these shares will likely increase significantly in a few months, at which point they will be sold.

March 6: Purchased 20 bonds of Morbius Company. These bonds have a stated interest rate of 9 percent, pay interest annually on July 1, and mature on July 1, 2004. The bonds were purchased at a quoted market price of $92\frac{1}{2}$.

May 11: Purchased 100 shares of Jubilee, Inc., common stock at a cost of $29 per share. Gambit plans to hold these shares indefinitely.

June 2: Acquired 1,200 of the 4,000 outstanding bonds of Mystique Corporation. These bonds were purchased at a quoted market price of 101, have a stated interest rate of 12 percent, and pay interest semiannually on April 1 and October 1. Because these bonds have a high yield to maturity, Gambit's management intends to retain them until their maturity date, which is April 1, 2004.

June 12: Acquired 61 percent of the outstanding common stock of Xavier Company at a cost of $10 per share, or $5,200,000 in total.

Required:
Classify each of the intercorporate investments acquired by Gambit, Inc., into one of the five categories identified in this chapter. If there is not sufficient information to classify one of these investments, indicate the classes to which the investment could potentially be assigned and the conditions under which it would be assigned to each of those classes.

47. Accounting for Intercorporate Investments (LO 1, 2, 3)
Carner Enterprises held the following investments in corporate securities on December 31, 1998, the company's fiscal year-end.

	Cost	Fair Value
Steinhauer Corporation preferred stock	$ 77,100	$ 78,400
Sheehan Corporation bonds	240,000	231,000

Carner purchased the Steinhauer preferred stock on May 22, 1998, while the Sheehan bonds were purchased on September 1, 1998. Carner received a $2,200 dividend from Steinhauer on December 1, 1998. Sheehan's bonds have a stated interest rate of 9 percent. The bonds' interest payment dates are February 28 and August 31. Carner purchased the Sheehan bonds at a quoted market price of 100.

Required:

1. Assume that both of Carner's investments qualify as trading securities. Prepare all necessary journal entries for 1998 in Carner's accounting records for these investments, including any appropriate year-end adjusting entries.
2. Assume that both of Carner's investments qualify as available-for-sale securities. Prepare all necessary journal entries for 1998 in Carner's accounting records for these investments, including any appropriate year-end adjusting entries.
3. Indicate how any unrealized gain or loss on Carner's intercorporate investments would be reported in the company's December 31, 1998, financial statements, assuming these investments are classified as:
   a. trading securities.
   b. available-for-sale securities.
4. Briefly discuss the rationale underlying the different accounting and financial reporting treatment applied to trading and available-for-sale securities.

48. Accounting for Intercorporate Investments (LO 1, 2, 3)

On April 1, 1998, Lopez Enterprises purchased 200 of Mocchrie Company's $1,000 corporate bonds. Lopez purchased these bonds at a quoted market price of 98. Mocchrie's bonds have an 8 percent stated interest rate and interest payment dates of March 31 and September 30. The bonds mature on March 31, 2002. On December 31, 1998, Lopez's fiscal year-end, Mocchrie's bonds have a quoted market price of 96.

Required:

1. Under what condition or conditions would Lopez Enterprises account for the investment in Mocchrie Company's bonds as a held-to-maturity security?
2. Assuming that the investment in Mocchrie bonds is treated as a held-to-maturity security by Lopez, prepare the appropriate journal entries in Lopez's accounting records on April 1 and September 30 1998. (Lopez uses the straight-line method to amortize any premium or discount on a bond investment.)
3. Assume that the book value of the investment in Mocchrie bonds is $196,750 on December 31, 1998. At what dollar amount would this investment be reported in Lopez's year-end balance sheet?
4. What other financial statement disclosures, if any, will Lopez include in its 1998 financial statements related to this investment?

49. Accounting for Intercorporate Investments (LO 3)

On January 18, 1996, Greystoke, Inc., purchased 30 percent of the outstanding common stock of Weiss Corporation for $4,500,000 and 40 percent of the outstanding common stock of Muller Corporation for $1,500,000. The following schedule presents the annual net income (net loss) of each firm for the period 1996 through 1998 and the total dividends paid by each firm over that period.

	Net Income (Loss)			Total Dividends Paid		
	1996	1997	1998	1996	1997	1998
Weiss	$1,500,000	$(800,000)	$1,000,000	$500,000	$600,000	$800,000
Muller	500,000	200,000	400,000	50,000	100,000	150,000

Required:

1. What accounting method should Greystoke use to account for its investments in Weiss and Muller? Briefly explain the logic underlying this accounting method.
2. Prepare any entries needed in Greystoke's accounting records for 1996 through 1998 to account for its investments in Weiss and Muller.

50. **Consolidation Work Sheet for a Wholly-Owned Subsidiary** (LO 3, 4, 5)
On December 31, 1998, Puppet Masters, Inc., a toy company, purchased all of the outstanding common stock of Stryfe Company, a financial consulting firm. Puppet Masters paid $200,000 for this stock and immediately loaned Stryfe $40,000. Following are the separate balance sheets of the two companies after the close of business on December 31, 1998.

	Puppet Masters	Stryfe
Assets		
Cash	$ 12,000	$ 43,000
Accounts receivable (net)	121,000	78,500
Note receivable from Stryfe	40,000	—
Inventory	77,000	35,500
Property, plant & equipment (net)	242,000	98,000
Investment in Stryfe	200,000	—
Total assets	$692,000	$255,000
Liabilities and Stockholders' Equity		
Accounts payable	$154,500	$ 15,000
Note payable to Puppet Masters	—	40,000
Bonds payable	250,000	—
Common stock	50,000	20,000
Additional paid-in capital	120,000	40,000
Retained earnings	117,500	140,000
Total liabilities and stockholders' equity	$692,000	$255,000

Required:

1. Assume that the fair value of Stryfe's assets is approximately equal to their book value. Should any "goodwill" be included in the consolidated balance sheet of these two companies? Explain.
2. Prepare the journal entries required on December 31, 1998, in the accounting records of both Puppet Masters and Stryfe. Indicate in which company's accounting records each journal entry belongs.
3. Complete a postacquisition consolidation work sheet for Puppet Masters and Stryfe.
4. Prepare a consolidated balance sheet for Puppet Masters and Stryfe as of December 31, 1998.
5. Many large companies have one or more subsidiaries. What control activities should a company implement when it acquires a controlling interest in another firm?
6. How do controlling investments complicate decision makers' analysis of financial statement data?

51. Accounting for Foreign Currency Transactions (LO 6, 7)
Wisconsin Cheeses, Inc. (WCI), is a U.S. firm that has four large warehouses located in foreign countries. WCI wholesales cheese to retailers in more than forty countries. For the convenience of its customers and suppliers, WCI transacts business in the currency of each customer's or supplier's home country. Following are selected transactions engaged in by WCI during 1998. The company's 1998 fiscal year ended on December 31.

August 28:	Sold a shipment of 5,000 pounds of cheese to O'Shaughnessey & Sons, an Irish firm. The sales price was 4,300 punts, and the credit terms were n/90.
September 13:	Sold 6,000 pounds of cheese to Hansmeier Corporation, an Austrian firm. The sales price was 70,000 schillings, and the credit terms were n/30.
October 13:	Received payment from Hansmeier Corporation for September 13 sale.
November 14:	Purchased 3,000 pounds of packing supplies from Troberg of Stockholm, a Swedish firm. The purchase price was 6,000 kronor, and the credit terms were n/60.
November 26:	Received payment from O'Shaughnessey & Sons for August 28 sale.
January 13:	Paid amount due Troberg of Stockholm for November 14 purchase.

Following are the assumed foreign exchange rates that are relevant to the listed transactions of WCI.

August 28:	$1.65 per punt
September 13:	$ .11 per schilling
October 13:	$ .10 per schilling
November 14:	$ .14 per krona (singular of kronor)
November 26:	$1.70 per punt
December 31:	$ .13 per krona
January 13:	$ .12 per krona

Required:
1. What unique accounting and control issues do multinational business operations pose for U.S. companies?
2. Prepare appropriate journal entries for the listed transactions in the accounting records of WCI. Include the required journal entry to record any unrealized foreign currency transaction gain or loss as of December 31, 1998. (Notes: Round all amounts to the nearest dollar. For sales transactions, you are not required to record the cost of goods sold.)
3. Considering only the transactions presented, compute the net foreign currency transaction gain or loss for WCI during 1998.

CASES

52. Preventing Hostile Takeovers (LO 1)
Kowalsky Clothiers, Inc., has been a very successful company over the past two decades. The owners of this retail business began operations with one small store in Stow, Ohio. Now, Kowalsky stores are located in twenty-two states, and the company's common stock is listed on the New York Stock Exchange. The two founders of this company own 25 percent of Kowalsky's outstanding common stock. The remaining shares are widely

held by individual and institutional investors. Recently, there have been rumors that a large company is planning a hostile takeover of Kowalsky.

Required:
The two founders and principal stockholders of Kowalsky are very concerned by the rumors of the hostile takeover. Write a brief memo to these individuals identifying strategies they can use to reduce the risk of a hostile takeover of their company.

53. Classification of Intercorporate Investments (LO 1, 2, 3)

Piazza Engineering, Inc., recently purchased 6 percent of the outstanding common stock of Yeager Tools for $450,000. Piazza's controller has determined that this investment should be classified as an available-for-sale security and reported as a long-term asset on the company's periodic balance sheets. A key factor in reaching this decision was the stated intention of Piazza's chief executive officer (CEO) to hold this stock indefinitely. As the fiscal year-end approaches, the market value of this investment has increased to nearly $1 million. Because the company's net income for the year will be unimpressive, Piazza's CEO has suggested that the Yeager investment be classified as a trading security. When Piazza's controller asked the CEO whether he intended to sell the Yeager stock in the near term, the CEO responded, "Oh, sure," as he winked at the controller and slapped him heartily on the back.

Required:
1. Explain how the classification of the investment in Yeager common stock will affect Piazza's financial statements for the year in question.
2. Should a company allow the financial statement impact of alternative accounting methods to dictate which accounting method it selects? Why or why not?
3. Identify the parties that may be affected by Piazza's classification of the Yeager investment. How may these parties be affected by this decision?
4. Should Piazza's controller classify the Yeager investment as a trading security given the circumstances? Defend your answer.

54. Foreign Companies and U.S. Accounting Standards (LO 6)

Hitachi, Ltd., is a large Japanese company that manufactures a wide range of products including semiconductors, televisions, and large computer systems. Hitachi's common stock is traded on the New York Stock Exchange. The following footnote concerning Hitachi's accounting for investments in debt and equity securities was included in a recent annual report issued by the company. (Note: *SFAS #115* is the accounting standard that dictates the accounting treatment for trading, available-for-sale, and held-to-maturity securities.)

> SFAS No. 115, *"Accounting for Certain Investments in Debt and Equity Securities," which is effective for fiscal years beginning after December 15, 1993, was issued in May 1993. Regarding the method of implementation of* SFAS No. 115, *the Company requested the United States Securities and Exchange Commission (SEC) for special treatment, which allows the Company to provide the required* SFAS No. 115 *disclosure in a footnote to its financial statements, instead of implementing it in the body of its consolidated financial statements.*
>
> *This request is based upon the following reasons:*
>
> *Most marketable equity securities in Hitachi's portfolio are semi-permanent investments for maintaining business relationships with investee companies and management generally has no current plans to sell such securities.*
>
> *The Company files its consolidated financial statements with both the SEC and the Ministry of Finance in Japan utilizing accounting principles generally accepted in the United States. If* SFAS No. 115 *is implemented, the comparability among Japanese companies' financial statements would be considerably reduced. Many Japanese companies prepare their consolidated financial statements utilizing accounting practices generally accepted in Japan which generally reflect historical cost accounting.*

The SEC Division of Corporate Finance approved the Company's request. Consequently, the Company has decided to disclose the effect of its departure from SFAS No. 115 *in an audited footnote to its consolidated financial statements and not to implement* SFAS No. 115 *in the body of its consolidated financial statements.*

Required:

1. Do you agree with the SEC's decision in this case? Defend your answer.
2. If foreign companies are allowed to issue financial statements in this country that do not fully comply with GAAP, what problems may this pose for investors and other decision makers who use these companies' financial statements?

PROJECTS

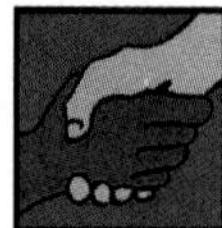

55. Business Combinations

Each project group will either be assigned a major business combination that occurred in the past five to ten years or choose such a business combination. The indices of business periodicals and metropolitan newspapers are a good source for locating information regarding major business combinations.

Required:

1. Each project group should obtain the following information for the business combination it has been assigned or has selected. Each group member should participate in obtaining and documenting this information.
   a. A description of the two companies involved in the business combination, including their headquarters location and principal lines of business.
   b. Key financial information for each company immediately prior to the business combination (total assets, most recent annual sales, most recent net income, and so on).
   c. The nature of the business combination. (For instance, was the combination a mutually agreed-upon merger, a "hostile takeover," or some other type of business combination?)
   d. The key terms of the business combination. (For example, were the stockholders of one firm "bought out" with cash payments or did they receive shares of stock in the surviving firm or the newly created firm, were the key executives of both firms given positions in the newly created or surviving firm, were certain segments of one or both firms eliminated following the combination, and so on?)
   e. The stated objective or purpose of the business combination. (For example, was the stated purpose of the combination to achieve economies of scale and thus reduce operating costs, to achieve stated profit or revenue goals, or to create the dominant firm in a given industry?)
2. For the five- to ten-year period following the business combination, your group should research the financial condition and operating results of the newly created firm or the surviving firm. Document the key financial trends evident in the given firm's financial data over this period.
3. After completing (1) and (2), meet as a group and review and discuss the information collected. The key issue you should address is whether the business combination has apparently been a success to date. The group's decision should be supported with the appropriate financial data and other relevant information.
4. The research and conclusions of the group should be documented in a written report. One group member should be prepared to present an in-class summary of this report.

56. Foreign Currency Exchange Rates

A key factor influencing the operating results of multinational companies is foreign currency exchange rates. These rates affect how much multinational firms must pay for goods and services they purchase in foreign countries and how much they receive for goods and services sold in foreign countries. To complete this project, you should select three foreign countries in which you have a particular interest.

Required:

1. For the three countries you selected, identify their present currency exchange rate relative to the U.S. dollar. Then identify each country's currency exchange rate relative to the U.S. dollar one, three, five, and ten years ago. This information can be obtained from *The Wall Street Journal* and several other business publications.
2. Plot the currency exchange rates for each country on a piece of graph paper with an appropriate numerical scale.
3. Interpret the data you collected. What factor or factors likely account for the variations apparent in these exchange rates over the past ten years? (Research relevant articles in business periodicals if necessary to address this issue.) What implications do the changes in the exchange rates you plotted have for U.S. firms transacting business in each of these countries?
4. Document your completion of (1)–(3) in a written report.

57. Consolidated Financial Statements

Browse the Internet and identify a publicly owned company that maintains a Web site on the Internet and issues consolidated financial statements.

Required:

1. Identify the company you selected, its headquarters location, its principal line of business, and its Web site address.
2. Identify the names and principal line of business of each subsidiary of the company you selected. If this information is not available at the parent company's Web site, obtain the information from the firm's most recent 10-K statement at the SEC's EDGAR (electronic data gathering and retrieval system) Web site or from a hard copy of the firm's 10-K.
3. Determine whether the consolidated balance sheet of the parent company and its subsidiaries contains minority interest and/or goodwill. If so, list the dollar amounts of these items and indicate how they are reported on the consolidated balance sheet.
4. After reviewing the financial and narrative information you accessed, briefly summarize why you believe the parent company acquired a controlling investment in each subsidiary you identified in (2). For example, did the parent company acquire the subsidiary to "vertically integrate" or possibly to achieve "economies of scale" by expanding its operations?
5. Document your responses to (1) through (4) in a written report.

MODULE THREE

PARTNERSHIPS AND PROPRIETORSHIPS

"I will have no one work for me who has not the capacity to become a partner."

—J.C. Penney

LEARNING OBJECTIVES

After studying this module, you should be able to do the following:

1. Identify the key advantages and disadvantages of the partnership and proprietorship forms of business organization.
2. Account for initial investments in partnerships.
3. Apply several methods of allocating partnership profits and losses to individual partners.
4. Prepare a statement of partners' capital.
5. Account for the dissolution of a partnership.
6. Account for the liquidation of a partnership.
7. Account for the ownership interest of a proprietorship.

FOCUS ON DECISION MAKING

Sinking Partner-Ships

Until the late nineteenth century, most large businesses in the United States operated as partnerships. Corporations were rare, principally because the incorporation of a business in most states required the approval of the state legislature. Gradually, states began passing laws that made it easier for businesses to incorporate. These laws spurred many partnerships to reorganize as corporations to take advantage of key benefits offered by the corporate form of organization. By the mid-1990s, there were more than twice as many corporations as partnerships in the United States—3.8 million corporations versus 1.5 million partnerships.[1]

The factor most responsible for the popularity of the corporate form of business organization is the limited liability feature of corporations. Individual stockholders face the risk of losing their total investment in a corporation if the firm goes "belly up." However, the creditors of a bankrupt corporation cannot collect their unpaid bills by filing legal claims against the personal assets of individual stockholders. On the other hand, if a partnership folds while it still has unpaid debts, the former partners are liable individually for the partnership's debts.

To find examples of the financial risk faced by the members of a partnership, one has to look no further than the accounting profession. Many of the large partnerships that dominated the profession throughout the twentieth century suffered huge financial losses in recent years due to class-action lawsuits filed by unhappy investors and creditors. Consider the case of Laventhol & Horwath, which in the late 1980s was one of the ten largest accounting firms in the United States. In 1990, Laventhol was forced out of business following several legal judgments imposed on the firm. When it disbanded, the firm owed creditors nearly $50 million. Former Laventhol partners contributed up to $400,000 each to pay off the partnership's remaining debts.

The Big Six accounting firms have been the hardest hit by litigation losses. In 1992, Ernst & Young settled several lawsuits filed against it by the federal government. These lawsuits charged Ernst & Young with negligently auditing savings & loans that eventually failed, resulting in significant losses for depositors, investors, and other parties. The price tag of the Ernst & Young settlement? $400,000,000. During the next few years, Deloitte & Touche and KPMG Peat Marwick paid $312 million and $186 million, respectively, to the federal government to settle similar legal claims.

This module focuses principally on accounting for the ownership interests of unincorporated businesses, namely, partnerships and sole proprietorships. However, first we become better acquainted with these two forms of business organization including key issues that external decision makers should consider when dealing with such businesses.

1. U.S. Bureau of the Census, *Statistical Abstract of the United States, 1995* (Washington, D.C.: U.S. Government Printing Office, 1995), 543.

UNINCORPORATED BUSINESSES: AN INTRODUCTION ▲

To this point, we have focused principally on corporations in addressing accounting and financial reporting issues. In terms of revenue production, the corporation is clearly the dominant form of business organization in this country. Each year, corporations account for nearly 90 percent of the nation's gross business revenues. Nevertheless, unincorporated businesses play an important role in our national economy. Millions of investors, lenders, suppliers, and other parties rely on the financial data of partnerships and proprietorships to make important economic decisions.

Partnerships and Proprietorships Defined

In Chapter 1, we defined a partnership as an unincorporated business with two or more owners. The Uniform Partnership Act, a law that has been adopted by most states, provides a more formal definition of a partnership. According to this statute, a partnership is "an association of two or more persons to carry on as co-owners a business for profit." Some partnerships are based on a "handshake" agreement between, or among, the partners. However, to avoid misunderstandings, the formation of a partnership should be documented with a written contract. A **partnership agreement** identifies the contractual rights and responsibilities of each member of a partnership. Among other issues, a partnership agreement specifies how profits and losses are allocated to individual partners and the procedures followed when partners withdraw or new partners are admitted.

partnership agreement

A sole proprietorship is a business owned by one individual. By far, proprietorships are the most common type of business entity. In the early 1990s, the U.S. Bureau of the Census reported that there were approximately 15.5 million nonfarm businesses operating as proprietorships, nearly three times the number of partnerships and corporations combined.[2]

Size vs. Legal Form of Business Entities

The term "corporation" typically brings to mind a business that has thousands of employees, millions if not billions of dollars of assets, and sprawling headquarters that cover several city blocks. Nevertheless, most of the 3.8 million corporations in the United States are "S corporations," which are typically small, family-owned businesses. On the other hand, some unincorporated businesses are huge. For example, many large oil exploration firms are organized as partnerships. Thus, the size and legal form of business entities are not necessarily correlated.

In the following sections, we focus on the legal form of unincorporated businesses to identify their key advantages and disadvantages compared with corporations. However, recognize that both the size and legal form of individual businesses significantly impact their operations. In fact, in many important respects, large unincorporated businesses are more similar to large corporations than to small unincorporated businesses. Likewise, small unincorporated businesses tend to be more similar to small corporations in several key respects than to large unincorporated businesses. For example, small businesses, regardless of their legal form, generally encounter more difficulty borrowing funds than large corporations and large unincorporated businesses.

2. Ibid.

Key Advantages and Disadvantages of Partnerships

LEARNING OBJECTIVE 1 ▶
Identify the key advantages and disadvantages of the partnership and proprietorship forms of business organization.

Unlike corporations, partnerships are not taxable entities. Recall that corporations—with the exception of S corporations, pay income taxes on their annual profits. When these profits are distributed in the form of cash dividends, corporate stockholders must pay personal income taxes on these distributions. The income of a partnership "flows through" to the tax returns of its individual partners. Clearly, avoiding "double taxation" of business profits is an important advantage of the partnership form of business organization and its close cousin, the S corporation.

Generally, partnerships are subject to less regulatory and governmental oversight than corporations. For example, most large corporations sell their stock on an interstate basis and thus must comply with the extensive financial reporting rules and regulations of the Securities and Exchange Commission. At the state level, partnerships also avoid some of the regulatory scrutiny imposed on corporations. By definition, partnerships are exempt from the regulatory purview of the state agency that charters and oversees corporations in a given state. A related advantage of partnerships, compared with corporations, is that they are typically less expensive to establish and operate since they are subject to less regulatory supervision.

The most important disadvantage of the partnership form of business organization is the unlimited liability of partners for their firm's debts. If a failed partnership's assets are depleted before all of its debts are paid, creditors can file legal claims against the individual partners, as documented in the opening vignette of this module. In fact, one "deep-pocketed" partner may find herself or himself totally responsible for the remaining liabilities of a bankrupt partnership.

To reduce the financial risk faced by individual partners, many large partnerships are organized as limited partnerships. Limited partnerships typically have at least one "general" partner and dozens, or even thousands, of "limited" partners. The unlimited liability feature of partnerships applies only to the general partners of a limited partnership. Limited partners may lose their investment in a partnership, but their personal assets are not at risk if the firm fails.

One defining characteristic of partnerships is *mutual agency,* which is the authority of individual partners to enter into contracts binding on the entire partnership. For example, individual partners can sign lease agreements and employment contracts on behalf of their firm. Many partners in business ventures have been "burned" because of poor decisions made by fellow partners. The moral here is to make sure you trust the judgment of your prospective partners before you sign the dotted line at the bottom of a partnership agreement.

Recall that an important advantage of corporations is "continuity of existence." A corporation's legal existence is unaffected when the firm's ownership interests change hands. This feature of corporations does not apply to partnerships. As a general rule, when at least one partner withdraws or one new partner is admitted, a partnership agreement becomes void and the partnership terminates.

LEARNING OBJECTIVE 1 ▶
Identify the key advantages and disadvantages of the partnership and proprietorship forms of business organization.

Key Advantages and Disadvantages of Sole Proprietorships

The sole proprietorship form of business organization shares many of the advantages and disadvantages of the partnership form of business organization. Like partnerships, the profits of proprietorships are taxed only once, when they are reported on proprietors' individual tax returns. Proprietorships are also generally subject to less regulatory oversight than corporations. Similar to the members of a partnership, sole proprietors face unlimited liability for the debts of their businesses. If a sole proprietorship fails, the firm's creditors can attempt to recoup amounts owed to them by filing claims against the owner's personal assets. Sole owners of businesses do not face the problems posed by the mutual agency feature of partnerships. Then again, the members of a partnership benefit from the individual and collective insight and experience of their fellow partners, a resource unavailable to sole proprietors.

External Decision Makers and Unincorporated Businesses

Investors, lenders, suppliers, and other external decision makers must be aware of the legal form of a business that they plan to loan funds, invest in, or interact with in some other way. Why? Because the distinguishing traits of the three major types of business entities impact the financial risks faced by such decision makers. For example, if you intend to invest in a large firm, your ownership rights and privileges will vary depending upon whether the firm is organized as a corporation or a partnership. Similarly, if you plan to extend a loan to a business, your ability to recover that loan may be impacted by the legal form of the business.

Fortunately, the information needs of external decision makers regarding the assets and liabilities of unincorporated businesses parallel those of corporations. Likewise, external decision makers apply the same analytical tools to the financial data of unincorporated and incorporated businesses. Finally, unincorporated businesses pose the same general internal control concerns faced by corporations. So, in this module we do not need to address those three topics when comparing and contrasting accounting and financial reporting issues for unincorporated businesses and corporations. Instead, we focus exclusively in the following two sections on the unique accounting and financial reporting treatments applied to the ownership interests of partnerships and sole proprietorships.

PARTNERSHIPS

LEARNING OBJECTIVE 2
Account for initial investments in partnerships.

In this section, we examine several events or transactions involving the owners' equity of partnerships and the related accounting decisions. We begin by considering initial investments in a new partnership.

Initial Investments of Partners

Suppose that Chris Austen and Jane Everett decide to form a partnership to operate a sporting goods store. If each individual contributes $20,000 to this new venture, the following entry would be made in the partnership's accounting records.

Apr. 19	Cash	40,000	
	C. Austen, Capital		20,000
	J. Everett, Capital		20,000
	To record partners' initial investments		

Owning a (Small) Piece of the Boston Celtics

FOR YOUR INFORMATION

Among the most well known partnerships in the United States is the limited partnership that operates the Boston Celtics. Equity interests in the Boston Celtics Limited Partnership, which are known as "units" instead of "shares," are traded on the New York Stock Exchange. For approximately $22 in March 1997, you could brag to your friends that you owned part of an NBA franchise. Of course, you probably would not mention that your ownership interest represented .0000167 percent of the total owners' equity of the Boston Celtics.

Notice that the investments of the partners are credited to their individual "capital" accounts. The maintenance of separate capital accounts allows a partnership to easily determine the ownership interest of each partner at any point in time.

Partners sometimes contribute assets other than cash to a new partnership. Noncash assets contributed to a partnership should be recorded at their fair market value. In this context, "fair market value" generally means a value mutually agreed upon by the partners.

Division of Partnership Profits and Losses

LEARNING OBJECTIVE 3 ▶ Apply several methods of allocating partnership profits and losses to individual partners.

When two or more individuals decide to form a partnership, they must tackle the difficult issue of how to divide the partnership's profits and losses between, or among, themselves. Several factors may be considered in reaching this decision. Among these factors are the original investments of each partner, the relevant skills of the individual partners, and the amount of time each partner commits to the firm's daily operations. If the partnership agreement does not indicate how profits and losses are to be divided, partnership profits and losses must be split equally among all partners.

PROFIT SHARING BASED UPON INITIAL CAPITAL INVESTMENTS Tim Johnson, Sadi Karim, and Larissa Lopez formed Hair Care Distributors, a partnership, on January 1, 1997, to distribute hair care products to salons. Johnson, Karim, and Lopez agreed that their initial investments would be $30,000, $60,000, and $90,000, respectively. The partners also agreed that the profits and losses of the firm would be allocated in the same proportions as their initial investments. Suppose that during 1997 Hair Care Distributors earned a net income of $135,000. This profit would have been allocated as follows to the three partners.

Johnson:	($30,000/$180,000) × $135,000 =	$ 22,500
Karim:	($60,000/$180,000) × $135,000 =	45,000
Lopez:	($90,000/$180,000) × $135,000 =	67,500
Total		$135,000

Like corporations and other business entities, partnerships close their books at the end of each accounting period. At the end of 1997, the Income Summary account of Hair Care Distributors would have had a credit balance of $135,000 after the firm's revenue and expense accounts were closed. Instead of transferring the balance of the Income Summary account to retained earnings, partnerships close this account balance directly to the partners' capital accounts. The following entry would have been necessary to close the Income Summary account of Hair Care Distributors at the end of 1997.

Dec. 31	Income Summary	135,000	
	T. Johnson, Capital		22,500
	S. Karim, Capital		45,000
	L. Lopez, Capital		67,500
	To allocate net income to the partners' capital accounts		

Recognize that the previous entry served only to allocate the annual profit of this partnership to the partners' capital accounts. At this point, none of the profit had actually been distributed to the partners. Nevertheless, each partner was required to report the appropriate portion of the $135,000 profit in his or her 1997 income tax return.

PROFIT SHARING INCLUDES SALARY ALLOWANCES Suppose now that the three partners of Hair Care Distributors agreed to a profit-sharing plan that took into consideration the time each devotes to the partnership's daily operations. Tim Johnson works full-time in the business, while Sadi Karim and Larissa Lopez spend approximately 50 percent and 25 percent, respectively, of each work week involved with the business. The three partners decided that Johnson would receive an annual salary allowance of $40,000 to compensate him for the time he devotes to the partnership. Karim and Lopez receive salary allowances of $20,000 and $10,000, respectively. The partners also agreed that any profit or loss remaining after the allocation of the salary allowances would be divided equally. Recognize that "salary allowances" are *not* considered expenses of a partnership for accounting purposes. That is, a partnership's net income is unaffected by salary allowances. The intent of such allowances is simply to help allocate a partnership's profits to the individual partners in a fair manner.

If Hair Care Distributors earned a net income of $124,000 during 1997, the three partners would have received their salary allowances totaling $70,000 and then shared equally in the remaining profit of $54,000 ($124,000 – $70,000). The following schedule indicates the amount of profit allocated to each partner under this scenario.

	Salary Allowance	Equal Share of Remaining Profit	Profit Allocated to Each Partner
Johnson	$40,000	$18,000	$ 58,000
Karim	20,000	18,000	38,000
Lopez	10,000	18,000	28,000
Net income			$124,000

Instead of a $124,000 net income, assume that Hair Care Distributors earned only $62,500 during 1997. In this case, the partners' total salary allowances would have exceeded the company's net income by $7,500 ($70,000 – 62,500). This amount, known as an "income deficiency," would have been allocated to the partners as shown in the following schedule.

	Salary Allowance	Equal Share of Remaining Profit (Income Deficiency)	Profit Allocated to Each Partner
Johnson	$40,000	$(2,500)	$37,500
Karim	20,000	(2,500)	17,500
Lopez	10,000	(2,500)	7,500
Net income			$62,500

PROFIT SHARING INCLUDES SALARY ALLOWANCES AND INTEREST ALLOWANCES ON INITIAL INVESTMENTS The final profit-sharing plan we consider for Hair Care Distributors involves each partner receiving a salary allowance and an interest allowance based upon his or her initial investment. Let us again assume that the annual salary allowances for Johnson, Karim, and Lopez are $40,000, $20,000, and $10,000, respectively. The annual interest allowance granted to each partner is 10 percent of his or her original capital investment. Given the initial investments of $30,000, $60,000, and $90,000, by Johnson, Karim, and Lopez, respectively, the partners would receive the following annual interest allowances under this profit-sharing agreement.

Johnson	$30,000 × 10% =	$ 3,000
Karim	60,000 × 10% =	6,000
Lopez	90,000 × 10% =	9,000
Total		$18,000

Any profit or income deficiency remaining after the distribution of salary and interest allowances is split equally among the partners of Hair Care Distributors. For example, assume that the partnership earned a profit of $130,000 during 1997. After the salary allowances ($70,000) and interest allowances ($18,000) were allocated, $42,000 ($130,000 − $88,000) remained to be allocated among the partners. The following schedule indicates the profit allocations to each partner under this scenario.

	Salary Allowance	Interest Allowance	Equal Share of Remaining Profit	Profit Allocated to Each Partner
Johnson	$40,000	$3,000	$14,000	$ 57,000
Karim	20,000	6,000	14,000	40,000
Lopez	10,000	9,000	14,000	33,000
Net income				$130,000

If the sum of the salary and interest allowances had exceeded the partnership's net income, the income deficiency would have been allocated equally to the three partners. Like salary allowances, interest allowances are *not* considered expenses of a partnership for accounting or financial reporting purposes.

A Partnership Gone Sour: The Sad Story of Claude & Harry

In 1978, two businessmen formed a partnership to operate a real estate development company. Claude contributed an undivided piece of land to the partnership that had an appraised value of $640,000, while Harry contributed an equal amount of cash. Partnerships, like other relationships, have their ups and downs. And so it was with Claude and Harry. After a few years, Harry accused Claude of squandering most of the business's cash. To settle the dispute, Claude allowed Harry to retain an accounting firm to examine the partnership's accounting records.

The young and inexperienced accountant assigned to review the partnership's accounting records discovered that the legal title to the partnership's principal asset, the land contributed to the firm by Claude, was still in Claude's name. Immediately, the accountant accused Claude of attempting to defraud his partner. The accountant charged that Claude intended at some point to claim that the land and the considerable improvements made to it were his personal property, leaving Harry out in the proverbial cold. When Harry learned of this matter, he insisted that Claude buy his share of the partnership at an inflated price. In fact, Claude had never intended to defraud his partner. Nevertheless, after being convinced that his actions could be construed as fraudulent, he agreed to a buyout deal structured by the accounting firm. Within a matter of days, Claude arranged to borrow $900,000 to purchase Harry's share of the partnership.

After the partnership with Harry collapsed, Claude lost interest in the real estate venture and eventually sold it at a large loss. Several months later, Claude discovered that he had not been required to transfer the legal title of the land to the partnership. According to the applicable state law, the stated intentions of partners are the controlling factor in determining whether a partner's personal assets have been contributed to a partnership. Claude immediately filed a large civil suit against the accounting firm that had accused him of defrauding his partner. Unfortunately, Claude's health had deteriorated rapidly following the termination of the partnership and he died of a heart attack before the lawsuit was resolved. Claude was later vindicated completely when the accounting firm settled the lawsuit by making a sizable payment to his estate. The accounting firm also apologized to Claude's family for the unfortunate incident.

Source: Adapted from the following: M. C. Knapp, "Laurel Valley Estates," in *Contemporary Auditing, Issues and Cases*, 2d ed. (Minneapolis/St. Paul: West Publishing Company, 1996).

Partnership Drawing Accounts

When a partnership's profits are allocated at year-end to the individual partners, cash or other assets are typically not distributed to the partners. However, a partnership agreement usually allows partners to withdraw assets from their firm. Withdrawals made by partners are recorded in "drawing" accounts, which are temporary equity accounts similar to the Dividends account for a corporation.

To illustrate the use of drawing accounts, suppose that during 1997 the three partners of Hair Care Distributors withdrew the following amounts: Johnson, $5,000; Karim, $3,000; and Lopez, $12,000. To simplify matters, assume that these withdrawals were all made on December 1, 1997. Following is the compound journal entry to record these withdrawals.

Dec. 1	T. Johnson, Drawing	5,000	
	S. Karim, Drawing	3,000	
	L. Lopez, Drawing	12,000	
	Cash		20,000
	To record partner withdrawals		

At the end of an accounting period, the balances of drawing accounts are closed to the capital accounts of the individual partners. The balances of the drawing accounts for Hair Care Distributors would have been closed at the end of 1997 with the following entry.

Dec. 31	T. Johnson, Capital	5,000	
	S. Karim, Capital	3,000	
	L. Lopez, Capital	12,000	
	T. Johnson, Drawing		5,000
	S. Karim, Drawing		3,000
	L. Lopez, Drawing		12,000
	To close partners' drawing accounts		

Statement of Partners' Capital

LEARNING OBJECTIVE 4 ▶ Prepare a statement of partners' capital.

statement of partners' capital

Partnership financial statements are very similar to corporate financial statements. In fact, the only major differences in the financial statements of the two types of business organizations involve owners' equity. Partnerships do not maintain a Retained Earnings account. Capital accounts are maintained for each individual investor (partner) in a partnership, which is not true for corporations. Finally, instead of a statement of stockholders' equity, partnerships typically prepare a **statement of partners' capital** to document the changes in partners' capital account balances during a given period.

To illustrate a statement of partners' capital, return to the earlier scenario presented for Hair Care Distributors in which the firm earns $130,000 and both salary and interest allowances are provided to each partner. The profit allocations to Johnson, Karim, and Lopez for this scenario are $57,000, $40,000, and $33,000, respectively. Also assume that the three partners made the December 1, 1997, withdrawals discussed previously: Johnson, $5,000; Karim, $3,000; Lopez, $12,000. Exhibit M3.1 presents a Statement of Partners' Capital for Hair Care Distributors for the year ended December 31, 1997, based upon these assumptions.

LEARNING OBJECTIVE 5 ▶ Account for the dissolution of a partnership.

Dissolution of a Partnership

dissolution

As a general rule, when there is a change in the composition of a partnership, the partnership must be terminated. **Dissolution** is the term commonly used to refer to the termination of a partnership. When a partnership is dissolved, the firm can continue op-

EXHIBIT M3.1 ▼
Statement of Partners' Capital for Hair Care Distributors

HAIR CARE DISTRIBUTORS
STATEMENT OF PARTNERS' CAPITAL
FOR THE YEAR ENDED DECEMBER 31, 1997

	Johnson	Karim	Lopez	Total
Balances, January 1, 1997	$ 0	$ 0	$ 0	$ 0
Add: Investments during 1997	30,000	60,000	90,000	180,000
Profit allocations	57,000	40,000	33,000	130,000
Total	$87,000	$100,000	$123,000	$310,000
Less: Withdrawals	5,000	3,000	12,000	20,000
Balances, December 31, 1997	$82,000	$ 97,000	$111,000	$290,000

erating while a new partnership agreement is being reached. If the new set of partners cannot reach a mutually acceptable agreement, the partnership will discontinue operations and be "liquidated." **Liquidation** involves the process of converting a discontinued partnership's assets into cash, paying its liabilities, and then distributing any remaining cash to the partners.

liquidation

Here, we consider several scenarios involving the dissolution of a partnership and the related accounting decisions. As a point of information, before a new partner is admitted or an existing partner withdraws, a partnership's assets are restated to their current values. Such restatements ensure that partners only participate in increases and decreases in the value of partnership assets that occur while they are a member of the firm. Any gain or loss resulting from a restatement of partnership assets to their current values is allocated to the existing partners according to their profit-sharing agreement.

ADMISSION OF A PARTNER A new partner can be admitted to a partnership by either purchasing the ownership interest of an existing partner or by investing assets in the partnership. To illustrate the first of these possibilities, assume that Bill Hardy wants to purchase an ownership interest in Newby Enterprises. The firm has total owner's equity of $372,000, as reflected by the following schedule.

Chad Keith	$121,000
Earl Stacy	106,000
Paula Tate	145,000
Total partnership capital	$372,000

Because he is anxious to join the partnership, Hardy offers Chad Keith $140,000 for his interest in the firm, or $19,000 more than the balance of Keith's capital account. After obtaining approval from the other two partners, Keith accepts Hardy's offer. (Generally, a new partner cannot be admitted to a partnership without the prior approval of existing partners.) The exchange of the $140,000 between these two individuals is a personal transaction that does not affect the partnership's assets or liabilities. The only entry required in the partnership's books would be to transfer the balance of Chad Keith's capital account to the new capital account of Bill Hardy. This entry would include a debit of $121,000 to C. Keith, Capital, and an equal credit to B. Hardy, Capital.

Instead of purchasing an existing partner's ownership interest in Newby Enterprises for $140,000, suppose now that Bill Hardy invests that amount of cash directly into the partnership. For his cash contribution of $140,000, the three existing partners agree to assign a one-fourth ownership interest in their firm to Bill Hardy. Following the admission of Hardy, the total partnership capital of Newby Enterprises will increase to $512,000, as documented by the following schedule.

Existing partnership capital	$372,000
Additional capital to be invested by Hardy	140,000
Total partnership capital following Hardy's admission	$512,000

Since Hardy is acquiring a one-fourth interest in Newby Enterprises, the balance of his capital account immediately following his admission should equal $128,000, or one-fourth of the partnership's total capital ($512,000/4). This raises a question. Since Hardy is investing $140,000 to obtain $128,000 of equity, what happens to the other $12,000 that he contributes to the partnership?

The "extra" $12,000 that Hardy contributes to the partnership is treated as a "bonus" paid to the existing partners. This bonus is allocated to existing partners according to their profit-sharing agreement. Assume that the three partners of Newby Enterprises shared profits and losses equally before Hardy's admission. Following is the entry to record Hardy's admission to the partnership and the allocation of the $12,000 bonus to his new partners.

May 15	Cash	140,000	
	B. Hardy, Capital		128,000
	C. Keith, Capital		4,000
	E. Stacy, Capital		4,000
	P. Tate, Capital		4,000
	To record admission of Bill Hardy to partnership		

Now, consider a situation in which the existing partners of Newby Enterprises are very eager to convince Hardy to join their firm because he possesses skills particularly needed by the partnership. To persuade Hardy to "join up," the existing partners offer him a one-fourth ownership interest in the firm for $100,000. Following Hardy's investment of $100,000, the partnership will have total capital of $472,000. Because of the deal he struck, Hardy's capital account upon his admission should have an initial balance of $118,000, or one-fourth of the partnership's total capital ($472,000/4). The $18,000 bonus credited to Hardy's capital account must be charged (debited) to the capital accounts of the existing partners. Under this scenario, the entry to record Hardy's admission to the partnership would include a $100,000 debit to Cash, equal debits of $6,000 to each existing partner's capital account, and a credit of $118,000 to B. Hardy, Capital.

WITHDRAWAL OF A PARTNER A partner may withdraw from a partnership by selling his or her ownership interest to an outside party as illustrated in the previous section. Alternatively, a partner can withdraw by "selling out" to another partner or to the partnership as a whole. In this section, we consider the latter alternative.

Partnership agreements typically dictate the payments partners are entitled to receive when they withdraw from a partnership. The most common arrangement is for a withdrawing partner to receive an amount equal to the balance of his or her capital account. Suppose that Carla Vecchia decides to withdraw from a partnership that operates a small business, Landscape By Design. Following the restatement of the partnership's assets to their current values, the balances of the partners' capital accounts are as follows.

Kelli Jennings	$21,000
Lesley Kovich	17,000
Carla Vecchia	13,000
Total partners' capital	$51,000

If Vecchia is paid cash for her ownership interest in the firm when she withdraws, the entry to record her withdrawal would include a $13,000 debit to C. Vecchia, Capital, and an equal credit to Cash.

Occasionally, a partner receives more or less than the balance of his or her capital account upon withdrawing from a partnership. The difference between the amount paid to a withdrawing partner and the balance of his or her capital account is treated as a bonus to the withdrawing partner or as a bonus to the remaining partners.

Partnership Liquidation

LEARNING ◀ OBJECTIVE 6 Account for the liquidation of a partnership.

When a partnership discontinues operations, the firm's accountants first close the books as if it were the end of a normal accounting period. Then, a three-step liquidation process is generally followed. First, the partnership disposes of its noncash assets. Second, the partnership pays its liabilities. Finally, any remaining cash is distributed to the partners.

To illustrate a partnership liquidation, consider the untimely demise of Newcastle Communications, a mail-order business operated by three partners. Like many small businesses, Newcastle Communications encountered cash-flow problems stemming principally from slow-paying customers. So, the partners decided to shut down their business as of April 1, 1998. Exhibit M3.2 contains a post-closing trial balance as of that date for Newcastle.

When a business is liquidated, the owners often suffer losses resulting from the sale of its assets. Why? Because the owners typically have to sell the business's assets at unfavorable prices to quickly raise cash needed to pay off nervous creditors. In the present example, assume that Newcastle Communications sold its accounts receivable to a finance company for $28,000, resulting in a loss of the same amount. The equipment that had a net book value of $33,000 was sold for $21,000. In total, then, the partnership suffered a loss of $40,000 on the sale of these assets. Newcastle's partners shared profits and losses in the following proportions: Hale, 20%; McGill, 30%; and Polumbra, 50%. Consequently, the loss on the disposal of Newcastle's noncash assets was allocated as follows to the partners.

Hale	$40,000 × 20% =	$ 8,000
McGill	40,000 × 30% =	12,000
Polumbra	40,000 × 50% =	20,000

EXHIBIT M3.2 ▼
Newcastle Communications, Post-Closing Trial Balance as of April 1, 1998

	Debit	Credit
Cash	$10,000	
Accounts Receivable (net)	56,000	
Equipment (net)	33,000	
Accounts Payable		$27,000
M. Hale, Capital		19,000
L. McGill, Capital		41,000
J. Polumbra, Capital		12,000
Total	$99,000	$99,000

Listed next are the entries to record the sale of Newcastle's accounts receivable and equipment and to allocate the resulting loss to the partners' capital accounts. When a partnership is being liquidated, losses on the disposal of assets are closed directly to the partners' capital accounts instead of being funneled through the Income Summary account.

Apr. 21	Cash	49,000	
	Loss on Disposal of Assets	40,000	
	Accounts Receivable		33,000
	Equipment		56,000
	To record loss on disposal of accounts receivable and equipment		
Apr. 21	M. Hale, Capital	8,000	
	L. McGill, Capital	12,000	
	J. Polumbra, Capital	20,000	
	Loss on Disposal of Assets		40,000
	To allocate loss on disposal of accounts receivable and equipment		

The liquidation of a partnership may require several weeks, several months, or even longer to complete. To keep partners informed of the status of a liquidation as it progresses, a statement of partnership liquidation may be prepared periodically. A **statement of partnership liquidation** is a financial report of a partnership's account balances at various stages of its liquidation. Exhibit M3.3 presents a statement of partnership liquidation for Newcastle Communications. Notice that this statement was prepared as of April 21, 1998, following the sale of the firm's noncash assets. At that point, one partner, Polumbra, had already seen his ownership interest in the partnership totally "wiped out." In fact, Polumbra owed the partnership $8,000 following the disposal of the firm's noncash assets.

statement of partnership liquidation

The next step in the liquidation of Newcastle Communications was to pay off its debts, which consisted of $27,000 of accounts payable. The entry to record the pay-

EXHIBIT M3.3 ▼
Preliminary Version of Statement of Partnership Liquidation for Newcastle Communications

NEWCASTLE COMMUNICATIONS
STATEMENT OF PARTNERSHIP LIQUIDATION
AS OF APRIL 21, 1998

	Cash	Noncash Assets	Liabilities	Hale, Capital	McGill, Capital	Polumbra, Capital
Beginning balances	$10,000	$89,000	$27,000	$19,000	$41,000	$12,000
Sale of noncash assets and allocation of loss	49,000	(89,000)		(8,000)	(12,000)	(20,000)
Updated balances	$59,000	$ 0	$27,000	$11,000	$29,000	$ (8,000)

ment of these liabilities included a $27,000 debit to Accounts Payable and an equal credit to Cash.

After the liabilities of Newcastle Communications were paid, the three partners had to resolve the matter of Polumbra's "capital deficiency." There were two possibilities at this point. Either Polumbra was solvent and would pay the $8,000 to the partnership, or he was insolvent and the $8,000 would be treated as a loss by the other two Newcastle partners. Fortunately for the other partners, Polumbra paid the $8,000 to the partnership. This payment was recorded by debiting Cash $8,000 and crediting J. Polumbra, Capital, an equal amount.

The final step in the liquidation process was to distribute Newscastle's remaining cash to its partners. After updating the partnership's account balances for the two previous entries, the partnership had three nonzero account balances: Cash, $40,000; M. Hale, Capital, $11,000; and L. McGill, Capital, $29,000. The following entry recorded the distribution of the firm's cash to Hale and McGill. Exhibit M3.4 con-

Using Offshore Partnerships to Avoid Taxes

FOR YOUR INFORMATION

Corporate tax accountants invest considerable time and effort devising legal "schemes" to lower their firms' income taxes. One such method used by many public corporations is to divert large chunks of their revenue to offshore partnerships in which they have a controlling ownership interest. Corporations establish such partnerships in "tax havens" that levy no, or only minimal, income taxes on businesses. Among the most popular tax havens for U.S. firms is the Cayman Islands. Increasing criticism of this innovative method of avoiding corporate income taxes has recently forced Congress to consider closing this loophole in the federal taxation laws.

Source: R. Vartabedian, "Loral Used Offshore Partnership for Tax Haven," *Los Angeles Times,* 20 April 1996, D1, D7.

EXHIBIT M3.4 ▼
Final Version of Statement of Partnership Liquidation for Newcastle Communications

NEWCASTLE COMMUNICATIONS
FINAL STATEMENT OF PARTNERSHIP LIQUIDATION
APRIL 1, 1998–JUNE 30, 1998

	Cash	Noncash Assets	Liabilities	Hale, Capital	McGill, Capital	Polumbra, Capital
Beginning balances	$10,000	$89,000	$27,000	$19,000	$41,000	$12,000
Sale of noncash assets and allocation of loss	49,000	(89,000)		(8,000)	(12,000)	(20,000)
Updated balances	$59,000	$ 0	$27,000	$11,000	$29,000	$ (8,000)
Payment of liabilities	(27,000)		(27,000)			
Updated balances	$32,000	$ 0	$ 0	$11,000	$29,000	$ (8,000)
Receipt of deficiency	8,000					8,000
Updated balances	$40,000	$ 0	$ 0	$11,000	$29,000	$ 0
Distribution of cash to partners	(40,000)			(11,000)	(29,000)	
Final balances	$ 0	$ 0	$ 0	$ 0	$ 0	$ 0

tains the final version of the statement of partnership liquidation for Newcastle Communications.

June 30	M. Hale, Capital	11,000	
	L. McGill, Capital	29,000	
	Cash		40,000
	To record distribution of remaining cash to partners		

PROPRIETORSHIPS

In this section, we focus on accounting issues unique to sole proprietorships. Again, as was true for partnerships, the unique accounting issues for sole proprietorships involve the ownership interests of these firms.

Proprietorships: Accounting on a "No Frills" Budget

The defining characteristic of most proprietorships is their size. Referring again to statistics published by the U.S. Bureau of the Census, proprietorships had average annual revenues in the mid-1990s of approximately $49,000. The comparable figures for partnerships and corporations were $348,000 and $2.9 million, respectively.[3] The small size of most proprietorships has a pervasive influence on their accounting and control functions. For example, a small business owner typically cannot justify investing considerable resources in an accounting system. In fact, many small businesses still use "pen and paper" accounting systems. Nevertheless, the steadily declining cost of personal computers and computer software convinces more small business owners each year to buy computer-based accounting systems "off the shelf." By the late 1990s, a comprehensive set of accounting software programs for a small business could be purchased for less than $100.

Although a small business may have its own high-tech, if low cost, accounting system, the reliability of that system largely depends upon the accounting expertise of the individual entering the debits and credits. Possibly the most common error made by small business owners who double as "do-it-yourself" accountants is the commingling of their personal assets and liabilities with those of their business. Unlike a corporation, a proprietorship is not a legal entity distinct from its owner. Nevertheless, proprietorship accounting records should reflect only the business's assets and liabilities, not the personal assets and liabilities of the owner.

Quite often, a small business owner who doubles as the company bookkeeper has a sudden change of heart. When a banker rejects a loan application because accounts payable are listed under owner's equity on the firm's balance sheet or an IRS agent points out that a depreciation schedule does not balance, the owner will likely reach for the telephone and dial C-P-A.

Accounting for the Ownership Interest of a Proprietorship

LEARNING OBJECTIVE 7
Account for the ownership interest of a proprietorship.

Accounting for the owner's equity of a proprietorship is fairly simple since, by definition, there is only one owner. There is no need to compute earnings per share for a proprietorship or to allocate earnings at year-end among several partners' capital accounts. To illustrate accounting for the owner's equity of a proprietorship, consider a bakery owned and operated by Buffy Gibson. Buffy established this business recently by transferring $25,000 from her personal savings account to a checking account entitled Buffy's Bakery. This initial transaction was recorded by debiting Cash $25,000 and crediting Buffy Gibson, Capital, an equal amount.

In the next few weeks, Buffy leased a small shop, purchased various supplies and equipment, and placed an advertisement in the local paper to announce her grand opening. Accounting for rental expense, purchases of supplies, and other common business transactions is no different for a proprietorship than for a corporation or partnership. So, there is no need for us to examine Buffy's accounting entries for such transactions.

Similar to the owners of a partnership, a sole proprietor may "pay" herself or himself a salary allowance. Again, such payments are not considered expenses for accounting purposes. If such payments qualified as expenses, a sole proprietor could easily manipulate a firm's profit for a given accounting period by varying the amount of salary he or she received. Salary allowances and other assets withdrawn by a proprietor from a business are recorded in a drawing account. For example, assume that Buffy Gibson withdraws $2,200 from her business for personal use. This withdrawal would be recorded by debiting Buffy Gibson, Drawing, and crediting Cash, each for $2,200.

3. Ibid.

At the end of each accounting period, Buffy's accountant will close the business's books. First, the accountant will close the revenue and expense accounts to the Income Summary account. Next, he will transfer the balance of the Income Summary account to Buffy's capital account. Finally, he will close the balance of Buffy's drawing account to her capital account. Assume that the following schedule summarizes the revenues, expenses, and withdrawals of Buffy's Bakery during a future accounting period.

Sales	$3,800
Baking supplies used	900
Utilities	200
Advertising	100
Withdrawals	1,100

The following entries would be necessary to close Buffy's books at the end of this accounting period.

Date	Account	Debit	Credit
Nov. 30	Sales	3,800	
	Income Summary		3,800
	To close the Sales account		
Nov. 30	Income Summary	1,200	
	Baking Supplies Expense		900
	Utilities Expense		200
	Advertising Expense		100
	To close expense accounts		
Nov. 30	Income Summary	2,600	
	Buffy Gibson, Capital		2,600
	To close Income Summary account		
Nov. 30	Buffy Gibson, Capital	1,100	
	Buffy Gibson, Drawing		1,100
	To close drawing account		

SUMMARY

A partnership is an unincorporated business with two or more owners. The key features of the contractual arrangement between, or among, the partners of a firm are documented in a partnership agreement. An important advantage of the partnership form of business organization, compared with the corporate form of business organization, is the absence of "double taxation" of partnership profits. A key disadvantage of partnerships compared with corporations is the unlimited liability of individual partners for a partnership's debts.

For accounting purposes, a separate capital or equity account is maintained for each member of a partnership. The fair market value of the assets initially contributed by partners to a partnership is credited to their capital accounts. Several methods can be used to allocate a partnership's profits and losses to the capital accounts of individual partners. For example, profits and losses may be allocated in proportion to the partners' initial investments. Partners often withdraw assets, typically cash, from a partnership. These withdrawals are recorded in a drawing account, which is a temporary equity account. A statement of partners' capital documents the changes in partners' capital accounts during a given period.

A partnership is usually dissolved, or terminated, whenever a new partner is admitted or an existing partner withdraws. Although a partnership is formally dissolved, the firm's business operations can continue while a new partnership agreement is being reached between, or among, the new set of partners. A new partner can be admitted by either purchasing the ownership interest of an existing partner or by contributing assets to the partnership. When a partner is admitted, a "bonus" may be credited to the new partner's capital account or to the capital accounts of the existing partners. A partner withdrawing from a partnership typically receives a distribution of partnership assets equal to the balance of his or her capital account.

When a partnership discontinues its business operations, a three-step liquidation process is followed. First, the partnership disposes of its noncash assets, which may require the allocation of gains or losses to the partners' capital accounts. Second, the partnership pays its liabilities. Third, the remaining cash of the partnership is distributed to the partners. As a partnership is being liquidated, a statement of partnership liquidation may be prepared periodically to keep partners informed of the status of the liquidation.

A sole proprietorship is a business owned by one individual. The small size of most proprietorships has important implications for their accounting and control functions. For example, proprietorships typically cannot justify investing considerable resources in an accounting system. Accounting for the owner's equity of a proprietorship is similar to accounting for a partnership's ownership interests. A capital account and drawing account are established for the owner of a proprietorship. At the end of each accounting period, the net income of a proprietorship and the balance of the drawing account are closed to the proprietor's capital account.

GLOSSARY

Dissolution (p. 630) The termination of a partnership.

Liquidation (p. 631) The process of converting a discontinued partnership's assets into cash, paying its liabilities, and distributing any remaining cash to the partners.

Partnership agreement (p. 623) A contract between, or among, the members of a partnership that defines the contractual rights and responsibilities of each partner.

Statement of partners' capital (p. 630) A partnership financial statement that documents the changes in partners' capital accounts during a given period; equivalent to a corporation's statement of stockholders' equity.

Statement of partnership liquidation (p. 634) A financial report of a partnership's account balances at various stages of its liquidation.

DECISION CASE

Suppose that you have recently been contacted by a friend from your hometown. This individual and her two partners own 3D Mining, a small mining company that operates in the Powder Basin of Wyoming. 3D Mining has a five-year lease on a mining site. When that lease expires, the partnership will be liquidated. Your friend has invited you to join the partnership by investing $100,000. The company needs the additional funds to purchase new mining equipment.

The existing partners have given you a choice between two profit-sharing arrangements if you join the partnership. Under Option A, each of the other three partners would receive an annual salary allowance of $20,000. They each work in the business, while you would be a "passive" partner. Any profit remaining after the salary allowances would be allocated 50 percent to the existing partners and 50 percent to you. Any income deficiency would be allocated in the same manner. Under Option B, the three existing partners would each receive an annual salary allowance of $20,000, while you would receive a 5 percent interest allowance on your initial investment. Any profit or income deficiency remaining after the distribution of the salary and interest allowances would be divided equally among you and the other three partners. That is, you would be allocated 25 percent of that profit or income deficiency.

The existing partners also offer you Option C, which is to borrow $100,000 from you at an annual interest rate of 10 percent. A final option available to you is to invest your $100,000 nest egg in a five-year CD (certificate of deposit) that pays interest at an annual rate of 7 percent.

Required: Suppose that you have analyzed the financial statements of 3D Mining and thoroughly investigated the company's business operations. You believe that over the next five years there is a 25 percent likelihood the company will earn $60,000 annually before any salary and interest allowances paid to partners. Likewise, the probability that the company will earn the following amounts, before salary and interest allowances, is 25 percent each: $80,000, $100,000, and $120,000.

Given the information provided, decide which of the following investment alternatives is optimal for you: Option A, Option B, Option C, or Option D (investing the $100,000 in a 7 percent CD). Which investment alternative has the highest potential return for you? Which alternative has the lowest potential return for you? Suppose the company actually earns $80,000 over its remaining five years. Under this assumption, which investment alternative would be optimal for you? Finally, what factors, other than those specifically mentioned, should you consider in making this decision?

QUESTIONS

1. Identify several advantages and disadvantages of operating a business as a partnership rather than a corporation.
2. What advantages and disadvantages are commonly associated with the sole proprietorship form of business organization?
3. What is a partnership agreement and why is it important to the proper functioning of a partnership?

4. Define the terms "dissolution" and "liquidation" as they apply to partnerships.
5. Are partnerships taxable entities? Explain.
6. What is one key difference in the method used to account for the stockholders' equity of a corporation versus the owners' equity of a partnership?
7. How should noncash assets contributed to a partnership by a new partner be valued when initially recorded in the partnership's accounting records?
8. Identify factors that partners may consider in deciding how to allocate a partnership's profits among themselves.
9. How are partnership profits and losses divided if the partnership agreement is silent on this point?
10. Why are salary and interest allowances granted to partners not considered expenses for purposes of a partnership's accounting records?
11. What is the purpose of partnership drawing accounts?
12. Drawing accounts are equivalent to what account of a corporation?
13. Briefly describe the differences in the period-ending closing procedures for a corporation versus a partnership.
14. A statement of partners' capital is equivalent to what financial statement of a corporation?
15. What are the two ways that an individual can be admitted to an existing partnership?
16. Describe the meaning of the term "bonus" as it relates to the admission of a new partner to a partnership.
17. When a partner withdraws from a partnership, how much cash or other assets is he or she generally entitled to receive?
18. Identify the three steps typically followed in liquidating a partnership.
19. What is the purpose of a statement of partnership liquidation?
20. Which business entities collectively generate more annual revenues in the United States: partnerships or proprietorships?
21. What is the defining characteristic of most proprietorships? How does this characteristic affect the accounting function of proprietorships?
22. Compare and contrast the accounting methods used for the owner's equity of a proprietorship versus the owners' equity of a partnership.

EXERCISES

23. **True or False** (LO 1–7)
Following are a series of statements regarding topics discussed in Module 3.

Required:
Indicate whether each statement is true (T) or false (F).

_____ a. A statement of partnership liquidation is a financial report of a partnership's account balances at various stages of its liquidation.

_____ b. Similar to a corporation's stockholders, the owners of a partnership cannot be held individually responsible for the liabilities of their firm.

_____ c. A statement of partners' capital is similar to a corporation's statement of stockholders' equity.

_____ d. As a general rule, an existing partnership agreement is voided if one partner withdraws.

_____ e. If a partnership agreement does not indicate how profits and losses are to be divided, partnership profits and losses are allocated in proportion to the partners' initial investments.

_____ f. The final step in the liquidation of a partnership is disposing of its noncash assets.

_____ g. The balance of a partnership's Income Summary account is closed to its Retained Earnings account during period-ending closing procedures.

_____ h. A new partner can be admitted to a partnership only by purchasing the ownership interest of an existing partner.

_____ i. A partnership agreement identifies the contractual rights and responsibilities of each member of a partnership.

_____ j. Salary allowances received by a sole proprietor are considered an expense of his or her firm for accounting purposes.

24. Partnership Characteristics (LO 1)

Following are definitions or descriptions of terms relating to partnerships.

_________ The account in which individual partners' withdrawals are recorded each period.

_________ A financial report prepared at various stages of a partnership's liquidation.

_________ The account in which a partner's initial investment and subsequent allocations of his or her share of partnership profits are recorded.

_________ The termination of a partnership.

_________ A contract between, or among, the members of a partnership that defines the key contractual rights and responsibilities of each partner.

_________ The process of converting a discontinued partnership's assets into cash, paying its liabilities, and then distributing any remaining cash to the partners.

_________ The authority of individual partners to enter into contracts binding on the entire partnership.

_________ A partnership financial statement that documents the changes in partners' capital accounts during a given period.

Required:

Match each definition or description listed with the appropriate term from the following list.

a. Partnership agreement
b. Statement of partnership liquidation
c. Mutual agency
d. Capital account
e. Dissolution
f. Liquidation
g. Statement of partners' capital
h. Drawing account

25. Advantages and Disadvantages of Partnerships (LO 1)

Charles Xavier is planning to form a partnership along with several of his close friends. Xavier is unfamiliar with the specific features of partnerships and other forms of business organizations.

Required:

Write a memo to Xavier explaining how a partnership differs from a corporation and a proprietorship. In your memo, be sure to comment on the key features of partnerships and whether these features are generally advantages or disadvantages of the partnership form of business organization.

26. Partnership Formation (LO 2)

John Burr and Alex Hale have decided to form a partnership. Following are the book values and fair market values of the assets contributed to this new partnership by each of these individuals who previously operated their own businesses as sole proprietors.

	Burr		Hale	
	Book Value	Fair Market Value	Book Value	Fair Market Value
Cash	$22,000	$22,000	$ 0	$ 0
Inventory	20,000	28,000	0	0
Building	0	0	150,000	160,000
Land	0	0	25,000	40,000

Required:
1. Prepare an entry to record the initial investments of the partners in the partnership.
2. Suppose that because Hale was eager to have Burr as a partner, he granted Burr a 50 percent ownership interest in the new partnership. Prepare the entry to record the formation of the partnership under this assumption.

27. **Allocation of Partnership Profits and Losses** (LO 3)
Mathis Furniture is a retail furniture store owned by Jonetta, Kiana, and Laura, three sisters. The partners' initial capital contributions to the partnership were $50,000, $30,000, and $20,000, respectively. The partnership agreement states that partnership profits and losses are to be allocated in the same proportions as the partners' initial capital investments.

Required:
1. Assume that during 1998, Mathis Furniture earned a profit of $240,000. Allocate this profit to the business's three partners.
2. Allocate the $240,000 profit to the three partners assuming that the partnership agreement is silent on how profits and losses are to be allocated.

28. **Allocation of Partnership Profits and Losses** (LO 3)
Three individuals own and operate St. Croix Enterprises, a real estate development company. Following are the names of these individuals, their initial capital investments, their annual salary allowances, and the balances of their capital accounts on January 1, 1998.

Partner	Initial Capital Investment	Annual Salary Allowance	Balance of Capital Account, January 1, 1998
R. Hearst	$ 50,000	$40,000	$105,000
C. Kane	70,000	30,000	84,000
O. Welles	100,000	20,000	110,000

Besides an annual salary allowance, each partner is granted an annual interest allowance equal to 10 percent of his or her initial capital investment. Any profit or income deficiency remaining after the allocation of the salary and interest allowances is divided equally among the partners.

Required:
Allocate the 1998 profit of St. Croix Enterprises to its three partners assuming that profit is:
1. $142,000.
2. $103,000.

29. **Allocation of Partnership Profits and Losses** (LO 3)
Four Star Partnership operates an oil exploration business in the Permian Basis of west Texas. Following is a partially completed profit allocation schedule for the firm's most recent year.

Partner	Salary Allowance	Interest Allowance	Remainder	Total
Star 1	$12,000	$?	$(4,000)	$?
Star 2	16,000	?	?	?
Star 3	0	5,000	?	?
Star 4	?	?	?	?
Totals	$50,000	$?	$?	$?

Three of the partners of this firm receive salary allowances, Star 3 being the exception. Each partner receives an annual interest allowance equal to 10 percent of the balance of his or her capital account at the beginning of the year. The balances of the partners' capital accounts at the beginning of the year were as follows:

Star 1	$40,000
Star 2	20,000
Star 3	50,000
Star 4	60,000

After the allocation of salary and interest allowances, the remaining profit or income deficiency is allocated in the following proportions to the partners' capital accounts:

Star 1	1/5
Star 2	1/5
Star 3	1/5
Star 4	2/5

Required:
Complete the 1998 profit allocation schedule for Four Star Partnership.

30. **Partnership Drawing Accounts** (LO 4)
In accordance with their partnership agreement, the three partners of Oak Tree Developers are allowed to withdraw cash from the partnership for their personal use. The only restriction in the partnership agreement is that a partner may not withdraw more than $5,000 per month. The following schedule lists the withdrawals made by the Oak Tree partners during December 1998 and the total withdrawals for the year:

	December Withdrawals	Total Withdrawals During Year
M. Donahue	$4,500	$52,500
S. Jude	3,500	47,000
D. Thomas	5,000	60,000

Required:
1. Prepare the journal entry to record the withdrawals made by the partners during December 1998.
2. Prepare the entry to close the partners' drawing accounts at the end of 1998.

31. **Admission of a New Partner** (LO 5)
Nancy Belmont wants to purchase an interest in Seal Beach Imports, a partnership with total capital of $720,000. Following are the capital account balances of the firm's existing partners:

Jack Alamitos, Capital	$120,000
Katie Bolsa, Capital	350,000
Tom Chica, Capital	250,000
Total	$720,000

The existing partners of Seal Beach Imports have approved admitting Nancy to the partnership under either of two options she negotiated. The first option involves Nancy purchasing Tom Chica's ownership interest for $300,000, while the second option involves Nancy contributing $280,000 to the partnership for a one-fourth ownership interest in the firm.

Required:
1. Why is it important that all existing partners of a firm approve the admission of a new partner?
2. Prepare the journal entry necessary to record the admission of Nancy if she purchases Tom Chica's ownership interest.
3. Prepare the journal entry necessary to record the admission of Nancy if she contributes $280,000 to obtain a one-fourth ownership interest in the firm.

32. **Withdrawal of a Partner** (LO 5)
Sharon Regard has decided to withdraw from Penisula Exports, a four-person partnership. The partners in the firm share profits and losses equally. Presently, the balances of the partnership's capital accounts are as follows:

T. Beau, Capital	$100,000
O. Corne, Capital	150,000
S. Regard, Capital	110,000
J. Wallis, Capital	135,000
Total	$495,000

Required:
Prepare the appropriate journal entry to record the withdrawal of Sharon Regard from this partnership under each of the following assumptions:
1. She receives cash equal to the balance of her capital account.
2. She receives $120,000.
3. She receives $80,000.

33. **Partnership Liquidation** (LO 6)
On June 30, 1998, the partners of Brown, McGrew & Associates decided to liquidate

their law firm. The firm's three partners share profits and losses equally. Following is the post-closing trial balance of Brown, McGrew & Associates on June 30, 1998.

	Debit	Credit
Cash	$ 50,000	
Accounts Receivable (Net)	60,000	
Furniture and Equipment (Net)	80,000	
Accounts Payable		$ 25,000
Brown, Capital		70,000
Herrick, Capital		70,000
McGrew, Capital		25,000
	$190,000	$190,000

On July 15, the accounts receivable were sold to a local collection agency for $48,000. Two weeks later, the furniture and equipment were sold for $44,000. On August 5, the firm's outstanding liabilities were paid. Finally, on August 14, the firm's remaining cash was distributed to the partners.

Required:
1. Prepare all journal entries necessary to record the liquidation of this partnership.
2. Prepare a final statement of partnership liquidation.
3. Notice that in each case the assets of this company were sold for a loss. Why do businesses that are being liquidated typically incur losses when they dispose of their assets?

34. **Accounting for a Proprietorship** (LO 7)
Luther McCord went into business for himself on January 1, 1998, by opening Luther's Music Store. Following is the working or pre-closing trial balance of this business on January 31, 1998.

	Debit	Credit
Cash	$ 6,450	
Inventory	9,000	
Note Payable		$ 5,000
L. McCord, Capital		10,000
L. McCord, Drawing	1,000	
Sales		17,500
Cost of Goods Sold	12,450	
Rent Expense	2,350	
Utilities Expense	1,200	
Interest Expense	50	
Total	$32,500	$32,500

Required:
Prepare the journal entries needed to close the accounting records of Luther's Music Store on January 31, 1998.

PROBLEM SET A

35. **Partnership Formation and Allocation of Partnership Profits and Losses** (LO 1–4)
Alexis Pavin and her two brothers, Boba and Corey, set up a partnership to operate a business entitled Family Counseling Services. The firm began operations on January 1, 1998. The individual partners' initial investments in the partnership are listed in the following schedule.

	A. Pavin	B. Pavin	C. Pavin
Cash	$10,000	$ 15,000	$60,000
Supplies	1,000	—	—
Equipment	9,000	30,000	—
Furniture	—	30,000	—
Building	—	105,000	—
Note Payable	—	(90,000)	—
	$20,000	$ 90,000	$60,000

Alexis will be the head counselor and general manager of Family Counseling Services. Boba will devote approximately 50 percent of his time to the business performing maintenance and janitorial services, while Corey will work full-time as an associate counselor in the business. Given the division of work responsibilities, each partner will be granted the following annual salary allowances: Alexis, $50,000; Boba, $15,000; and Corey, $40,000. Each partner will also be entitled to an annual interest allowance equal to 10 percent of the balance of his or her capital account at the beginning of the year. Any profit or income deficiency remaining after the allocation of salary and interest allowances will be divided equally among the partners.

Required:

1. Prepare the journal entry necessary on January 1, 1998, to record the partners' initial investments in Family Counseling Services.
2. Suppose that during 1998 the partnership earned a profit of $140,000. Allocate this profit to the partners and prepare the entry to close the balance of the Income Summary account to the partners' capital accounts at year-end.
3. Suppose that during 1998 the partnership earned a profit of $90,000 and the three partners withdrew the following amounts of cash from the business during the year: Alexis, $7,200; Boba, $14,300; and Corey, $9,000.
   a. Allocate the partnership's profit to the three partners.
   b. Prepare the entries to close the balance of the Income Summary account and the drawing accounts to the partners' capital accounts at year-end.
   c. Prepare a statement of partners' capital for 1998 for Family Counseling Services.
4. Suppose that Family Counseling Services applies for a bank loan of $50,000 in early 1999. Other than the firm's financial statements, what other financial information might a bank loan officer request from the individual partners that would not be requested from the executives of a large corporation applying for a similar loan? Explain.

36. **Allocation of Partnership Profits and Losses** (LO 3)
The Sutter brothers, Brent, Daryl, and Rich, have recently established Ice Rinks of America, a company that operates ice skating rinks in large malls. The brothers are presently at-

tempting to agree on a method for allocating the firm's profits among themselves—the firm is organized as a partnership. The following options are being considered.

- **Option A:** Salary allowance to Brent and Daryl equal to 25 percent of any partnership profit if the partnership earns a profit of at least $100,000. If the partnership suffers a loss during a given year or does not earn a profit of at least $100,000, no salary allowances will be granted. Each partner will also receive an annual interest allowance equal to 10 percent of his capital account balance at the beginning of the year. Any remaining profit or income deficiency after the allocation of salary and interest allowances will be divided equally among the partners.
- **Option B:** Partnership profits and losses divided equally among the three partners.

The initial investments of the three brothers in the partnership are as follows: Brent, $0; Daryl, $50,000; and Rich, $500,000.

Required:

1. Determine how much profit or loss will be allocated to each Sutter brother under each profit allocation scheme assuming the following profits for the business's first year of operations:
   a. $243,000
   b. $91,000
   c. $108,000
2. Suppose that Rich maintains the accounting records for the partnership. What ethical or "conflict of interest" issue may this raise if Option A is adopted? Explain. How could the partnership eliminate this conflict of interest or minimize its potential impact on the firm?

37. Admission of a Partner (LO 5)

Barry, Dewey, and LeRoy Watts own and operate the Eufaula Ironworks. Recently, a cousin, J. C. Gibbs, inquired about joining the firm. The Watts brothers have agreed to admit Gibbs to the firm, which is organized as a partnership. Presently, the capital account balances of the three partners are as follows:

B. Watts	$117,000
D. Watts	161,000
L. Watts	163,000

The three Watts brothers share profits and losses equally.

Required:

Prepare the journal entry to admit J. C. Gibbs to the Eufaula Ironworks partnership under each of the following assumptions:

1. Gibbs purchases the ownership interest of Barry Watts for $132,000.
2. Gibbs invests $159,000 in the firm in exchange for a one-fourth ownership interest.
3. Gibbs invests $119,000 in the firm in exchange for a one-fourth ownership interest.

38. Withdrawal of a Partner (LO 5)

Foxx & Pryor, Attorneys at Law, is a law partnership. Recently, one of the partners of this firm, Ellen Boosler, has indicated that she would like to withdraw from the partnership to establish her own law firm. Listed next are the updated balances of the firm's capital accounts following Boosler's announcement:

E. Boosler	$500,000
R. Foxx	874,000
R. O'Donnell	604,000
R. Pryor	522,000

The partnership agreement dictates that 50 percent of the firm's annual profit or loss be allocated to the firm's senior partner, R. Courtney Foxx. The remaining profit or loss is shared equally by the other partners.

Required:

1. Prepare the journal entry to record the withdrawal of Boosler from the law partnership under the following independent assumptions:
   a. Boosler is paid $470,000 for her ownership interest in the firm.
   b. Boosler receives $550,000 for her ownership interest in the firm.
2. Suppose that immediately following Boosler's withdrawal from the partnership, six clients of Foxx & Pryor inform R. Courtney Foxx that they will be using the services of Boosler's new law firm in the future. How could Foxx & Pryor have prevented Boosler from "taking" several clients with her when she left the firm?

39. **Partnership Liquidation** (LO 6)
Green Valley Hardware is a retail store located in Green Valley, Nevada. The four partners who own and operate Green Valley Hardware decided to liquidate the business beginning July 1, 1998. Following is the partnership's post-closing trial balance as of June 30, 1998:

	Debit	Credit
Cash	$ 12,500	
Accounts Receivable (Net)	25,000	
Inventory	40,000	
Equipment & Fixtures (Net)	70,000	
Accounts Payable		$ 30,250
J. Berwanger, Capital		30,000
J. Capiletti, Capital		40,000
T. Detmer, Capital		31,250
A. Griffin, Capital		16,000
Total	$147,500	$147,500

The partners share profits and losses as follows:

J. Berwanger	30%
J. Capiletti	15%
T. Detmer	20%
A. Griffin	35%

Following is a list of the transactions required to liquidate Green Valley Hardware:

July 7: Sold accounts receivable to a finance company for $15,000.
July 15: Sold inventory and equipment & fixtures to another hardware store for $80,000.
July 22: Paid accounts payable.
July 31: Disbursed remaining cash to partners.

Required:

1. Prepare the necessary journal entries to record the liquidation of this business.
2. Prepare a final statement of partnership liquidation.

40. Accounting for Owner's Equity of a Proprietorship (LO 7)
In January 1998, Merlie O'Shea established a plumbing supply business. Following is the adjusted trial balance on December 31, 1998, of Merlie's Plumbing Supply:

	Debit	Credit
Cash	$ 25,000	
Inventory	52,000	
Supplies	4,350	
Equipment	70,000	
Accumulated Depreciation, Equipment		$ 5,000
Accounts Payable		1,750
Note Payable		80,000
M. O'Shea, Capital		50,000
Sales		148,250
Cost of Goods Sold	75,700	
Salaries Expense	32,500	
Interest Expense	6,100	
Depreciation Expense	5,000	
Rent Expense	10,500	
Utilities Expense	3,100	
Advertising Expense	750	
	$285,000	$285,000

Merlie is the sole proprietor of her store and its only employee. The salaries expense shown in the business's adjusted trial balance represents cash amounts paid by Merlie to herself.

Required:

1. Explain the nature of any errors that Merlie made in accounting for her business. Prepare any entry or entries necessary to correct the accounting records of Merlie's Plumbing Supply as of December 31, 1998. Would this entry or entries be necessary if Merlie prepares financial statements only for her benefit and not for any external parties such as a local bank? Explain.
2. Prepare the closing entries for Merlie's Plumbing Supply on December 31, 1998.
3. What is Merlie O'Shea's total ownership interest in her business at the end of 1998?

PROBLEM SET B

41. Partnership Formation and Allocation of Partnership Profits and Losses (LO 1–4)
Josie Alou and her two brothers, Felipe and Mattie, operate an architectural firm, Alou Architects & Associates. The firm, which is organized as a partnership, began operations on January 1, 1998. Josie's initial investment in the partnership was a building valued at $120,000. Felipe and Mattie contributed cash of $60,000 and $100,000, respectively, as their initial investments in the partnership.

The three Alous, all licensed architects, receive an annual salary allowance based on the number of "chargeable" hours they work for the firm each year. In 1998, each partner received $100 per chargeable hour. Each partner is also entitled to an annual interest allowance equal to 10 percent of the balance of his or her capital account at the beginning of the year. Any profit or income deficiency remaining after the allocation of salary and interest allowances is divided equally among the partners.

Required:

1. Prepare the journal entry necessary on January 1, 1998, to record the partners' initial investments in Alou Architects & Associates.
2. Suppose that during 1998, the partnership earned a profit of $424,000 and the three partners had the following number of chargeable hours: Felipe, 1,200; Josie, 1,500; and Mattie, 1,100. Allocate the firm's profit to the partners and prepare the entry to close the balance of the Income Summary account to the partners' capital accounts at year-end.
3. Suppose that during 1998, the partnership earned a profit of $265,000 and the partners had the following number of chargeable hours: Felipe, 1,000; Josie, 1,600; and Mattie, 1,300. Additionally, the partners withdrew the following amounts of cash from the business during the year: Felipe, $60,000; Josie, $55,000; and Mattie, $68,000.
   a. Allocate the partnership's profit to the three partners.
   b. Prepare the entries to close the balance of the Income Summary account and each drawing account to the partners' capital accounts at year-end.
   c. Prepare a statement of partners' capital for 1998 for Alou Architects & Associates.
4. Suppose that this firm applies for a bank loan of $200,000 in early 1999. Other than the firm's financial statements, what other financial information might a bank loan officer request from the individual partners that would not be requested from the executives of a large corporation applying for a similar loan? Explain.

42. Allocation of Partnership Profits and Losses (LO 3)

The three Fitzgerald sisters, Eunice, Jean, and Rose, have recently established Honey Fitz Enterprises, a movie production company. The sisters are presently considering two methods of allocating the annual profits and losses of this business, which will be operated as a partnership, to their capital accounts. These two profit allocation schemes are as follows:

- **Option A:** Salary allowance of $100,000 each to Eunice and Jean if the business earns a profit of $500,000 or more during a given year. Rose will be a passive partner and thus not entitled to a salary allowance. Each partner will also receive an annual interest allowance equal to 8 percent of her capital account balance at the beginning of the year. Any remaining profit or income deficiency after the allocation of salary and interest allowances will be divided equally among the partners.
- **Option B:** Partnership profits and losses divided equally among the three partners.

The initial investments of the three sisters in the partnership are as follows: Eunice, $200,000; Jean, $100,000; and Rose, $1,000,000.

Required:

1. Determine how much profit or loss will be allocated to each Fitzgerald sister under each profit allocation scheme assuming the following profits for the business's first year of operations:
   a. $490,000
   b. $510,000
   c. $840,000
2. If the company's annual profit is expected to average slightly less than $500,000 each year, which profit allocation scheme do you believe Rose will prefer? Why?
3. Suppose that Rose maintains the accounting records for the partnership. What ethical or "conflict of interest" issue may this raise if Option A is adopted?

Explain. How could the partnership eliminate this conflict of interest or minimize its potential impact on the firm?

43. **Admission of a Partner** (LO 5)
Billy, Gomer, and Steve Vessels own and operate the Uptown Athletic Club. Recently, Bud Sims inquired about joining the firm. The Vessels brothers have agreed to admit Sims to the firm, which is organized as a partnership. Presently, the capital account balances of the three partners are as follows:

B. Vessels	$252,000
G. Vessels	188,000
S. Vessels	196,000

Profits and losses are divided as follows among the three partners: Billy, 40 percent; Gomer, 30 percent; and Steve, 30 percent.

Required:
Prepare the journal entry to admit Bud Sims to the Uptown Athletic Club partnership under each of the following assumptions:
1. Sims purchases the ownership interest of Steve Vessels for $183,000.
2. Sims invests $164,000 in the firm in exchange for a one-fourth ownership interest.
3. Sims invests $244,000 in the firm in exchange for a one-fourth ownership interest.

44. **Withdrawal of a Partner** (LO 5)
Jeni Leatherworks is a firm that makes and repairs leather products, including shoes, cowboy boots, and purses. The four partners of Jeni Leatherworks share equally in the annual profits and losses of the firm. Patricia Poundstone recently announced that she will be withdrawing from the partnership. Listed next are the balances of the firm's capital accounts immediately following Poundstone's announcement:

R. Jeni	$84,000
A. Lubell	42,000
M. Smith	36,000
P. Poundstone	60,000

Required:
1. Prepare the journal entry to record the withdrawal of Poundstone from the partnership under the following independent assumptions:
   a. Poundstone is paid $66,000 for her ownership interest in the firm.
   b. Poundstone is paid $55,500 for her ownership interest in the firm.
2. Suppose that immediately following Poundstone's withdrawal from the partnership, she establishes her own firm, Poundstone Leatherworks, directly across the street from Jeni Leatherworks. How could Jeni Leatherworks have prevented Poundstone from establishing a competing business following her withdrawal from the partnership?

45. **Partnership Liquidation** (LO 6)
For several decades, the Five & Dime Store of Holbrook, Arizona, was a small but prosperous business. During the mid-1990s, two large retail chains opened competing stores in Holbrook. These competitors caused steady declines in the revenues and profits of the Five & Dime Store. The three partners who operated the Five & Dime Store decided to liquidate the business beginning October 1, 1998. Following is the post-closing trial balance for this business as of September 30, 1998:

	Debit	Credit
Cash	$ 23,750	
Accounts Receivable (Net)	30,000	
Inventory	52,250	
Property, Plant & Equipment (Net)	70,250	
Accounts Payable		$ 45,750
Note Payable		25,000
M. Bogues, Capital		10,500
S. Bradley, Capital		30,000
B. Reeves, Capital		65,000
	$176,250	$176,250

The partners shared profits and losses as follows:

M. Bogues	40%
S. Bradley	20%
B. Reeves	40%

Following is a summary of the transactions required to liquidate the business:

October 1:	Sold accounts receivable to a finance company for $24,000.
October 9:	Sold inventory and property, plant & equipment at a public auction for $82,500.
October 16:	Paid liabilities in full.
October 31:	Remaining cash disbursed to partners.

Note: Any deficiency in partners' capital accounts was paid in full by the partner(s) on October 30.

Required:

1. Prepare the necessary journal entries to record the liquidation of this business.
2. Prepare a final statement of partnership liquidation.

46. Accounting for Owner's Equity of a Proprietorship (LO 7)

Tillman Rollins experienced a very interesting 1998. Besides learning how to operate a business, Tillman also became a self-taught accountant during 1998. On February 2, 1998, Tillman opened a small country store, the Wallville General Store. To cut down on overhead, Tillman "hired" himself as the business's bookkeeper. On the following page is the adjusted trial balance of the Wallville General Store's accounting records as of December 31, 1998.

Tillman was disappointed by his store's operating results for 1998. According to his computations, the store had a net loss during the year. But, that loss was more than offset by the $24,000 Tillman earned working as the business's sole employee. Plus, he received $4,800 of interest revenue on the $40,000 he invested in the business during the year.

Required:

1. Prepare any necessary correcting entries to the accounts of the Wallville General Store as of December 31, 1998. Why are these correcting entries necessary?
2. Prepare the closing entries for the Wallville General Store on December 31, 1998.
3. What was Tillman's total ownership interest in his business at the end of 1998?

	Debit	Credit
Cash	$ 2,500	
Inventory	15,000	
Accounts Receivable	10,000	
Building	18,000	
Accumulated Depreciation, Building		$ 1,800
Accounts Payable		4,100
T. Rollins, Capital		40,000
Sales		65,200
Cost of Goods Sold	31,600	
Salaries Expense	24,000	
Interest Expense	4,800	
Depreciation Expense	1,800	
Utilities Expense	2,400	
Advertising Expense	1,000	
	$111,100	$111,100

CASES

47. **Withdrawal of a Partner** (LO 5)
Joyce Whitmore and James Somerset have owned and operated the Dublin Brewery in south Boston for twenty-five years, sharing profits and losses equally. Somerset informed Whitmore during July that he wanted to retire from the business at year-end. After the partnership's accounting records were closed at the end of the year, the partners had the following balances in their capital accounts:

J. Whitmore	$490,000
J. Somerset	550,000

Two independent appraisals of the Dublin Brewery obtained in late December established an appraised value of $1,200,000, net of liabilities, for the business. On January 2, Somerset offered to accept $600,000 as payment for his share of the business. Whitmore immediately accepted that offer. Because approximately two weeks would be required to draw up the legal documents for the buy-out agreement, the two partners decided to formally "close the deal" on January 16. On January 10, Whitmore was approached by a much larger brewery. This brewery offered Whitmore $1.4 million for the Dublin Brewery.

Required:
Whitmore has decided not to inform Somerset of the buy-out offer from the larger brewery. Since Somerset had already decided to retire from the business before this buy-out offer was received, Whitmore believes that Somerset is not entitled to profit from that offer. Do you agree with Whitmore's reasoning? Why or why not? Is this an example of a situation or issue that should be dealt with in a partnership agreement?

48. **Limited Liability Partnerships** (LO 1)
The Big Six accounting firms that dominate the public accounting profession faced a serious problem in the early 1990s. As indicated in the opening vignette for this chapter, three of these large partnerships were forced to pay hundreds of millions of dollars to settle legal claims filed against them. Faced with such large legal settlements, the Big Six firms were forced to either "close their doors" or find some way to limit their litigation losses.

In July 1994, Ernst & Young, a Big Six firm, announced that it was reorganizing as a "limited liability partnership" (LLP) to reduce its partners' exposure to litigation losses. An LLP's total capital can be wiped out by litigation judgments. However, the personal assets of an LLP's individual partners are not at risk—with one key exception. Partners who were directly involved in a "bum" audit or other professional services engagement that was negligently performed are not protected by the limited liability feature of an LLP. These partners can lose their investment in an LLP and have their personal assets seized to satisfy any remaining portion of a legal judgment imposed on the firm. Shortly after Ernst & Young announced its decision to reorganize as an LLP, several other Big Six accounting firms quickly followed suit.

Required:

1. Why do partnerships have the unlimited liability feature discussed in this chapter? If necessary, review a business law text or other relevant materials in your school's library to address this issue. What benefit does this feature of partnerships provide to society? What disadvantage does this feature impose on the members of partnerships?
2. Do you agree that large accounting firms should be allowed to reorganize as limited liability partnerships? Defend your answer. Should all partnerships be allowed to reorganize as limited liability partnerships? Why or why not?

PROJECTS

49. Success and Failure Factors for Small Businesses

Most small businesses in the United States are either sole proprietorships or partnerships. Today's business environment poses a wide range of problems and opportunities for small businesses. In this group project, you will study these problems and opportunities.

Required:

1. Each member of your project group should research major business publications to identify small business "success" and "failure" stories. Among the publications that individual group members may research are *Business Week, Inc., Success,* and *The Wall Street Journal.*
2. The articles collected by individual group members should be shared with other group members. After each group member has had an opportunity to read or review the articles collected by all group members, meet as a group and discuss these articles. Your discussion should focus on identifying key success and failure factors for small businesses.
3. A written report should be prepared by each group. This report should begin with a list of the articles identified in (1). The major focus of the report should be an overview and brief explanation of each factor identified by the group in (2).
4. One group member should be prepared to present a summary of the written report in class.

50. Small Businesses: Going Global

To expand the markets for their products and services, each year more U.S. businesses look to international markets. "Going global" is generally more difficult for small businesses. However, the payoffs in increased revenues and profits for small businesses can be substantial. In this project, you will identify methods that small businesses have used to become involved in international commerce.

Required:

1. Review on-line and/or hard copy indices of business publications available in your library and identify articles focusing on how small businesses have become involved in international commerce. Identify at least three examples of such businesses.

2. Prepare a written report summarizing the following items, if available, for each small business you identified in (1):
   a. The name of the business, its location, its approximate size in terms of total assets and annual revenues, and its principal line or lines of business.
   b. The method used by the business to become involved in international commerce.
   c. How the business's operations have been favorably and/or unfavorably affected by the involvement in international commerce.
   d. Whether the business intends to expand its international operations in the future and, if so, how the business intends to accomplish this objective.

51. FLIPs: Family Limited Partnerships

Family limited partnerships, often referred to as FLIPs, have become a popular form of business organization in recent years. In this project you will become familiar with FLIPs with the help of the Internet.

Required:

1. Search the Internet for Web sites that provide information regarding family limited partnerships (FLIPs).
2. In a written report, describe the key features of FLIPs. For example, comment briefly on how FLIPs are formed, limitations imposed on them by law, relevant taxation issues, and so on. Also include in your report at least two examples of FLIPs that you identified on the Internet. Provide a brief overview of the nature of these FLIPs. Finally, document in your report the Web site addresses from which you obtained the information for this project.

ANALYSIS OF ACCOUNTING DATA

VI

The final two chapters of this textbook focus principally on methods used by financial decision makers to analyze and interpret accounting data. Chapter 14 acquaints you with the statement of cash flows and methods used to analyze cash-flow data. Chapter 15 presents a comprehensive discussion of financial ratios and other analytical techniques that can be applied to accrual-basis accounting data.

In the late 1980s, the accounting profession responded to a longstanding demand for cash-flow data by financial decision makers. Since 1987, businesses have been required to include a statement of cash flows in their annual financial reports. Cash-flow data provide decision makers with important insights regarding the financial health of businesses that are not available from accrual-basis financial data. In Chapter 14, we first become familiar with the purpose, content, and preparation of a statement of cash flows. Then, we discuss approaches to use in analyzing cash-flow data.

Earlier chapters introduced numerous financial ratios and other financial measures that can be used to analyze and interpret accrual-basis data reported in an income statement and balance sheet. Chapter 15 presents a comprehensive discussion of financial statement analysis. Included in this discussion are the financial ratios and measures highlighted in earlier chapters as well as several additional analytical techniques.

14 Statement of Cash Flows

"Though my bottom line is black, I am flat upon my back, My cash flows out and customers pay slow. The growth of my receivables is almost unbelievable; The result is certain—unremitting woe! And I hear the banker utter an ominous low mutter, 'Watch cash flow.' "

Herbert S. Bailey,
Publishers' Weekly
January 13, 1975

LEARNING OBJECTIVES

After studying this chapter, you should be able to do the following:

1. Identify the principal uses of the statement of cash flows for financial decision makers.
2. Identify and distinguish among operating, investing, and financing activities.
3. Prepare a statement of cash flows using the indirect method.
4. Interpret cash-flow data by comparatively analyzing the three components of an entity's cash flows.
5. Compute and interpret cash flow per share.
6. (*Appendix*) Prepare a statement of cash flows using the direct method.

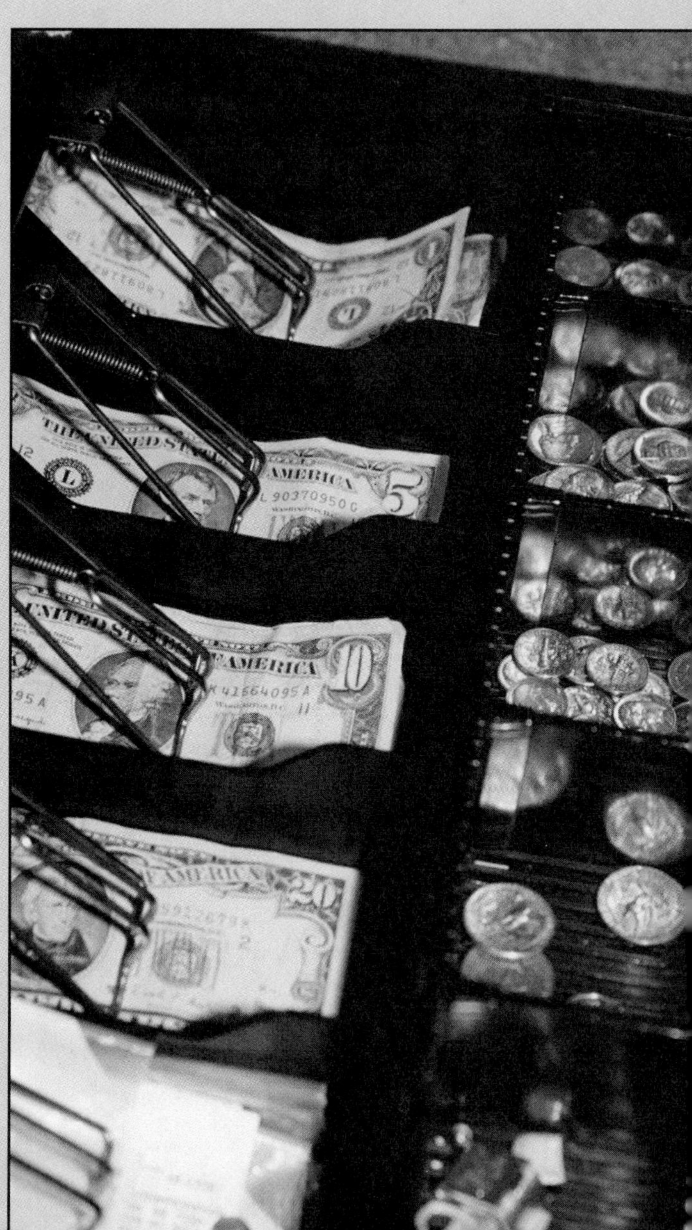

FOCUS ON
DECISION MAKING

Paging for Cash Flow

Under the accrual basis of accounting, companies recognize revenue from credit sales when the goods go out the front door. However, a company that cannot collect its receivables will soon find itself closing that front door—permanently. The following article, which appeared in Inc., *profiles a small business owner who uses an innovative and high-tech method to closely monitor his firm's cash collections on receivables and other cash flows.*

Joseph Popper's pager doesn't just reach out and touch him—it also sends him vital figures for company sales, accounts receivable, and cash flows on a daily basis. "We've been paranoid about cash from day one," says Popper, CEO of a small but rapidly growing computer firm based in Palm Desert, California. Popper's banker frequently reminds him that small businesses experiencing strong sales growth can encounter serious cash-flow problems even when their receivables are current. That's why "I monitor cash-flow numbers daily," Popper observes.

With his AirNote alphanumeric pager, Popper can get those cash-flow numbers wherever his frequent travels take him. The pager is lighter than a laptop and outdistances cellular-phone networks. When Popper purchased the AirNote, it was one of the few pagers offering electronic-mail capabilities; messages sent to an Internet or online-service address are routed to the pager, which displays 240 characters and saves 20 messages to its memory.

Popper wrote a software program that automatically extracts sales, receivables, and cash-flow data from his Excel spreadsheet back home and e-mails those figures to his pager each day when he is on the road. Those figures help him better manage the daily deposits that go into his two bank accounts, as well as track sales and receivables on a daily basis.

"If you grow too fast, you run out of cash," Popper says, "and we've been undercapitalized from the start." Downloading key financial numbers from his business's accounting system on a daily basis has allowed Popper to avoid serious cash-flow crises for his fast-track business.

Source: P. Hise, "Paging for Cash Flow," *Inc.*, December 1995, 131. Reprinted with permission.

The opening section of this chapter introduces you to the statement of cash flows. Two methods for preparing a statement of cash flows, the indirect and direct methods, are discussed in the next section. The following section illustrates how the more popular of these two methods, the indirect method, is applied. An appendix accompanying this chapter discusses the direct method of preparing a statement of cash flows. This chapter concludes with an overview of two approaches that can be used to analyze and interpret cash-flow data.

FINANCIAL DECISION MAKING AND CASH-FLOW DATA

As the opening vignette for this chapter suggests, business executives must be concerned not only with generating revenues but also with managing their firms' cash resources. Many companies with a long history of reporting profits eventually fail because their owners or managers did not pay sufficient attention to cash flows. The classic example of such a firm is W. T. Grant Company, one of the nation's largest retail chains until the mid-1970s.

No Cash, No Company: The Case of W. T. Grant Company

W. T. Grant Company experienced dramatic growth rates in revenues and profits between 1962 and 1972. Over that decade, Grant's annual earnings increased by 340 percent, topping out at almost $40 million in 1972 on sales of nearly $2 billion. These impressive financial figures caused Grant's common stock to be among the "hottest" investments on Wall Street. However, appearances can be deceiving. Less than three years later, Grant filed for protection from its creditors in bankruptcy court. The following year, a federal judge ordered the company to be liquidated.

Apparently, Grant's executives believed that if they could generate sufficient revenues and profits, the company's cash flows would follow suit. That was clearly not the case. Although the company was very profitable during the early 1970s, its net cash flows during that period were negative. The chief culprit was an aggressive expansion program that consumed large amounts of cash. In 1973, alone, Grant had a negative cash flow of more than $100 million from its principal business operations. Suddenly, there was no cash to pay the bills. Result: bankruptcy court. The liquidation of Grant led to the closing of more than 1,000 retail stores, the loss of 80,000 jobs, and huge write-offs by the company's creditors.

Statement No. 95 to the Rescue

The W. T. Grant debacle and several similar cases resulted in increasing demands by financial decision makers for businesses to report cash-flow data. In 1987, the Financial Accounting Standards Board (FASB) responded by adopting *Statement on Financial Accounting Standards No. 95,* "Statement of Cash Flows." This accounting standard requires businesses to include a statement of cash flows in their annual financial reports.

statement of cash flows

A **statement of cash flows** accounts for the net change in a business's cash balance during a given period by summarizing the business's cash receipts and disbursements by three major types of activities: operating, investing, and financing activities. The statement of cash flows is not intended to replace either the balance sheet or income statement. Decision makers jointly use these three major financial statements to analyze the financial condition, operating results, and future prospects of business entities.

LEARNING OBJECTIVE 1 ▶
Identify the principal uses of the statement of cash flows for financial decision makers.

Principal Uses of the Statement of Cash Flows

Exhibit 14.1 lists the principal uses of a statement of cash flows according to *FASB Statement No. 95*. Most important, a statement of cash flows helps decision makers

EXHIBIT 14.1 ▼
Principal Uses of the Statement of Cash Flows by Decision Makers

- Evaluate a business's ability to generate positive net cash flows in the future.
- Determine whether a business will be able to generate sufficient cash flows to pay its liabilities as they mature, pay dividends to stockholders, and satisfy its other obligations.
- Identify the sources of any major differences between a business's net income and its related cash receipts and payments.
- Analyze the effects on a business's financial position of both its cash and noncash investing and financing transactions during a given period.

Source: Statement of Financial Accounting Standards No. 95, "Statement of Cash Flows."

evaluate a business's ability to generate positive net cash flows in the future. Economists define the true value of an asset—or entire business—as the present value of the cash flows it will produce in the future. Although a statement of cash flows reports historical cash-flow data, a strong correlation usually exists between a company's future cash flows and its historical cash flows.

The second use of cash-flow data noted in Exhibit 14.1 refers principally to the information needs of specific types of financial statement users. As you would expect, individual decision makers are most concerned with how a given business's cash flows will benefit them directly. For example, suppliers want to be reassured that their customers can generate sufficient cash to pay their bills when they come due. A supplier

When a Cash Crisis Strikes

FOR YOUR INFORMATION

Many businesses encounter a cash crisis at some point during their existence that threatens their survival. Business executives should be prepared to cope effectively with such situations well before they occur. A recent article in Inc. *provides business executives with a four-prong plan for surviving a cash crisis.*

1. **Develop a credible plan for overcoming a cash crisis.** Such a plan should be action-oriented. Aim for a realistic assessment of your cash-flow problems, and then focus specifically on measures that will resolve those problems.
2. **Telephone each creditor to suggest meeting with them and their lawyers.** Be sure to schedule these meetings before payments are due. To show good faith, attempt to make at least a small payment to each creditor.
3. **Behave appropriately during these meetings.** Be poised and respectful in discussions with creditors. If creditors perceive that you are prepared to address your business's problems, they will be more likely to support you.
4. **Beware of creditor panic.** You must be honest with your creditors, but make every effort to avoid panicking them. If they panic, creditors will almost certainly refuse to provide any further goods and services to your business.

Source: J. A. Fraser, "When a Cash Crisis Strikes," *Inc.*, February 1996, 104. Reprinted with permission.

is not concerned with a customer's ability to generate sufficient excess cash each accounting period to pay dividends. Stockholders, on the other hand, are often preoccupied with the latter issue.

A statement of cash flows also allows decision makers to reconcile a business's net income to the cash receipts and disbursements produced by its principal operating activities. Profitable companies do not necessarily generate sufficient cash to finance their day-to-day operations. If a company's net income significantly exceeds the cash generated by its principal business operations, decision makers will want to investigate this difference. Consider a company that reports a large increase in net income but a negative cash flow from its operating activities in a given year. Further investigation may reveal that the firm increased its net income by adopting a more liberal credit policy that resulted in increased sales to high-risk customers. If many of these new customers are unable to pay their bills, this company essentially inflated its reported profit over the short-term by giving away inventory.

Finally, a statement of cash flows can help decision makers assess the impact of investing and financing transactions on a business's financial position. For example, a company may be financing the cost of its operations—inventory purchases, payroll costs, etc.—by selling off its property, plant & equipment assets. Clearly, that source of financing is very short-lived. To be economically viable over the long term, a company must eventually generate positive net cash flows from its principal operating activities.

In summary, a statement of cash flows has a variety of important uses. Listed next are examples of specific questions that decision makers can address with the data found in a statement of cash flows.

- Will a company generate sufficient cash to retire a large long-term debt that comes due in the next few years?
- Since a company has reported record profits over the past two years, why is the firm being forced to obtain short-term loans to finance its day-to-day operations?
- Will a company's board of directors suspend dividend payments in the near future because the firm's net cash flows have recently plummeted?
- Is a company producing sufficient cash flows from its principal operations to finance an aggressive expansion program, or will additional debt or equity capital be required to finance this program?
- How does the composition of a company's cash flows compare to that of its principal competitors?
- How does a company's cash flows this year compare to previous years? Are any important trends evident in these data?

THE STATEMENT OF CASH FLOWS: A CLOSER LOOK

Now that you are better acquainted with how decision makers use cash-flow data, we can focus on the technical features of the statement of cash flows. This section begins by reviewing two examples of statements of cash flows drawn from recent annual reports of large corporations. Then, the three types of cash flows produced by businesses are discussed. This section concludes with an overview of the two methods that can be used to prepare a statement of cash flows.

The Statement of Cash Flows: Two Examples

Exhibits 14.2 and 14.3 present recent statements of cash flows for two public companies. Exhibit 14.2 contains a statement of cash flows for Hughes Supply, Inc., while Exhibit 14.3 presents a statement of cash flows for Cabletron Systems, Inc. *FASB Statement No. 95* specifies two acceptable methods of preparing a statement of cash flows, the direct method and the indirect method. Hughes Supply uses the direct method, while Cabletron Systems applies the indirect method.

EXHIBIT 14.2 ▼

Statement of Cash Flows—Direct Method, Hughes Supply, Inc.

HUGHES SUPPLY, INC.
STATEMENT OF CASH FLOWS
FOR THE YEAR ENDED JANUARY 26, 1996 (in thousands)

Cash flows from operating activities:	
Cash received from customers	$ 1,073,951
Cash paid to suppliers and employees	(1,034,589)
Interest received	3,454
Interest paid	(7,273)
Income taxes paid	(15,230)
Net cash provided by operating activities	**$ 20,313**
Cash flows from investing activities:	
Proceeds from sale of property and equipment	$ 1,228
Capital expenditures	(11,853)
Business acquisitions, net of cash	(10,009)
Net cash used in investing activities	**$ (20,634)**
Cash flows from financing activities:	
Net borrowings under short-term debt arrangements	$ 6,245
Principal payments on:	
Long-term notes	(4,150)
Capital lease obligations	(844)
Proceeds from issuance of common shares under stock option plans	1,273
Purchase of common shares	(520)
Dividends paid	(1,736)
Net cash provided by financing activities	**$ 268**
Net decrease in cash and cash equivalents	(53)
Cash and cash equivalents, beginning of year	3,485
Cash and cash equivalents, end of year	$ 3,432

EXHIBIT 14.3 ▼
Statement of Cash Flows—Indirect Method, Cabletron Systems, Inc.

CABLETRON SYSTEMS, INC.
STATEMENT OF CASH FLOWS
FOR THE YEAR ENDED FEBRUARY 29, 1996 (in thousands)

Cash flows from operating activities:	
Net income	$ 164,418
Adjustments to reconcile net income to net cash provided by operating activities:	
Depreciation and amortization	32,061
Provision for losses on accounts receivable	356
Losses on disposals of property, plant & equipment	93
Deferred taxes	(38,766)
Changes in current assets and liabilities:	
Accounts receivable	(55,101)
Inventories	(50,483)
Prepaid expenses and other assets	(18,844)
Accounts payable and accrued liabilities	62,908
Income taxes payable	3,705
Net cash provided by operating activities	**$ 100,347**
Cash flows from investing activities:	
Capital expenditures	$ (65,035)
Purchase of available-for-sale securities	(79,427)
Purchase of held-to-maturity securities	(205,852)
Maturities of marketable securities	208,922
Net cash used in investing activities	**$ (141,392)**
Cash flows from financing activities:	
Repayments of notes receivable from stockholders	$ 174
Repurchase of common stock	(1,173)
Tax benefit of options exercised	7,215
Common stock issued to employee stock purchase plan	3,323
Proceeds from stock option exercise	16,021
Net cash provided by financing activities	**$ 25,560**
Effect of exchange rate changes on cash	**$ 166**
Net decrease in cash and cash equivalents	$ (15,319)
Cash and cash equivalents, beginning of year	114,032
Cash and cash equivalents, end of year	$ 98,713

From a technical standpoint, a statement of cash flows has one primary objective: account for the change in a business's cash balance during a given accounting period. If a company's balance sheet indicates that its cash increased by $8,421,000 during 1998, the firm's statement of cash flows for the year will account for that increase down to the last dollar. To document the change in a business's cash resources during a given period, accountants must identify all transactions that affected the firm's cash during that period. For purposes of the statement of cash flows, "cash" includes both cash and cash equivalents. Recall from Chapter 6 that cash equivalents are generally investments in short-term securities that have 90 days or less to maturity when purchased.

A statement of cash flows consists of four sections. The first three sections summarize the cash inflows (receipts) and cash outflows (disbursements) from a business's operating, investing, and financing activities. The final section reconciles a business's cash balance at the beginning and end of an accounting period. This reconciliation involves adding the net cash provided or used by operating, investing, and financing activities to the beginning cash balance to arrive at the period-ending cash balance.

When preparing the statement of cash flows shown in Exhibit 14.2, the objective of Hughes Supply's accountants was to explain the $53,000 decline in the company's cash balance during the fiscal year ending January 26, 1996. This change in Hughes Supply's cash balance was attributable to the following net cash flows that are boldfaced in Exhibit 14.2.

Net cash provided by operating activities	$ 20,313,000
Net cash used in investing activities	(20,634,000)
Net cash provided by financing activities	268,000
Net decrease in cash and cash equivalents	$ (53,000)

In Exhibit 14.3, a fourth item, "Effect of exchange rate changes on cash," was necessary to account for the change in Cabletron's cash balance during its fiscal year ending in 1996. The annual change in the cash balance of companies with international operations is partially explained by changes in foreign currency exchange rates. Since the impact of this factor on a business's cash balance is typically very small, we do not consider it further in this chapter.

Three Major Types of Business Activities and Related Cash Flows

LEARNING OBJECTIVE 2
Identify and distinguish among operating, investing, and financing activities.

We have referred several times to the three types of business activities by which cash flows are classified in a statement of cash flows. Now, let us define exactly what each of those activities involve, beginning with operating activities. Technically, the FASB defines operating activities as the transactions and events affecting a business other than investing and financing activities. That definition is not very helpful at this point since we have not yet defined investing and financing activities. **Operating activities** are generally those transactions and events related to the production and delivery of goods and services by businesses. In other words, operating activities are the day-to-day profit-oriented activities of a business.

operating activities

The principal cash inflows from operating activities are cash receipts from customers, both cash sales and collections of accounts receivable. Notice in Exhibit 14.2 that Hughes Supply reported more than $1 billion of cash receipts from its customers. Other

Cabletron Systems is a "high-tech" company that in recent years has generated large positive cash flows from its operating activities. Much of this cash flow has been reinvested by company executives into PP&E assets.

Courtesy Cabletron Systems Corp.

cash inflows from operating activities include cash dividends received, receipts of interest revenue, and cash provided by the sale of investments in trading securities. Major sources of cash outflows from operating activities include payments to suppliers, payroll expenditures, interest payments, and payments of taxes. Note that each operating activity impacts one or more revenues or expenses reported on the income statement.

investing activities

Investing activities include the making and collecting of loans, the acquisition and disposal of property, plant & equipment, and the purchase and sale of debt and equity securities other than trading securities and cash equivalents. Notice in Exhibit 14.2 that Hughes Supply's primary investing activities for the given year were approximately $12 million of capital expenditures to acquire property, plant & equipment. Exhibit 14.3 indicates that Cabletron had cash outlays of slightly more than $65 million for capital expenditures in its comparable fiscal year.

financing activities

Financing activities involve obtaining cash from lenders and repaying those amounts as well as obtaining cash from investors and providing them with a return of and a return on their investments. Hughes Supply's financing activities for its fiscal year ending January 26, 1996, included approximately $6 million of cash raised via short-term loans. Cabletron realized cash receipts of more than $3 million during its fiscal year ending February 29, 1996, by selling stock to employees via its employee stock purchase plan.

Exhibit 14.4 lists the principal cash inflows and outflows from operating, investing, and financing activities. Notice that the classification of cash flows from the sale or purchase of investments in debt and equity securities depends upon the type of investment. Cash receipts and disbursements from the sale or purchase of trading securities qualify as cash flows from operating activities. Cash receipts and disbursements from the sale or purchase of investments in debt and equity securities other than trading securities and cash equivalents are reported as cash flows from investing activities.

Direct Method vs. Indirect Method of Preparing a Statement of Cash Flows

The only major difference between the two methods of preparing a statement of cash flows concerns how net cash flow from operating activities is determined and reported. Notice in Exhibit 14.2 that the initial section of Hughes Supply's statement of cash flows lists specific cash inflows and outflows from operating activities. This approach

direct method

to preparing a statement of cash flows is known as the **direct method.** Now, refer to Exhibit 14.3, which presents a statement of cash flows for Cabletron Systems. In this

EXHIBIT 14.4 ▼
Examples of Common Cash Inflows and Cash Outflows from Operating, Investing, and Financing Activities

Operating Activities

Cash Inflows	Cash Outflows
Receipts from customers	Payments to suppliers
Receipts of interest and dividends	Payments to employees
Receipts from the sale of investments in debt and equity securities classified as trading securities	Payments of interest
Miscellaneous receipts related to operating activities	Payments of taxes
	Purchases of debt and equity securities classified as trading securities
	Miscellaneous payments related to operating activities

Investing Activities

Cash Inflows	Cash Outflows
Receipts from the sale of property, plant & equipment	Payments to acquire property, plant & equipment
Receipts from the sale of investments in debt and equity securities other than trading securities and cash equivalents	Payments to acquire investments in debt and equity securities other than trading securities and cash equivalents
Receipts from the repayment of long-term loans	Loans made to other firms

Financing Activities

Cash Inflows	Cash Outflows
Receipts from the issuance of common stock and preferred stock	Dividend payments
Receipts from the issuance of bonds	Payments to acquire treasury stock
Amounts borrowed from banks and other parties	Payments to retire principal amounts of bonds payable and to repay bank loans

case, specific cash flows from operating activities, such as cash received from customers, are not listed in the initial section of the statement of cash flows. When the **indirect method** is used to prepare a statement of cash flows, the net cash flow from operating activities is determined indirectly by making certain adjustments to net in-

indirect method

come. The indirect method yields the net cash flow from operating activities without revealing the individual cash inflows and outflows from those activities. Cash flows from investing and financing activities are determined and reported in the same manner under both the direct and indirect methods.

Companies that apply the direct method of preparing a statement of cash flows must include in their annual reports a schedule reconciling net cash flow from operating activities to net income. That is, these companies must essentially prepare the initial section of the statement of cash flows twice. This "double-trouble" feature of the direct method apparently causes it to be less popular than the indirect method. *Accounting Trends & Techniques* reports that more than 97 percent of public companies use the indirect method to prepare a statement of cash flows. Ironically, the FASB expressly stated a preference for the direct method in *Statement No. 95*. Because the direct method discloses specific types of operating cash flows, the FASB believes this method is more informative for financial statement users than the indirect method. Here, we focus primarily on the indirect method given its widespread use.

INDIRECT METHOD OF PREPARING A STATEMENT OF CASH FLOWS

LEARNING OBJECTIVE 3 ▶
Prepare a statement of cash flows using the indirect method.

In this section, we first review the steps in preparing a statement of cash flows using the indirect method. Then, we apply what we have learned by preparing a statement of cash flows for a small business, Cherokee Station, Inc. The appendix accompanying this chapter illustrates the direct method of preparing a statement of cash flows for Cherokee Station.

Source of Data for a Statement of Cash Flows

When preparing a statement of cash flows, the initial issues to address are where to obtain and how to organize the data to be incorporated in this financial statement. Recall from Chapter 5 that the information needed to prepare a balance sheet and income statement are general ledger account balances. Unlike the balance sheet and income statement, few of the items in a statement of cash flows are general ledger account balances. Cash flow amounts must be "filtered" from a business's accounting records. Intermediate accounting textbooks illustrate a work sheet approach to collecting and collating the data needed to prepare a statement of cash flows. However, the work sheet approach to preparing a statement of cash flows is cumbersome. Here, the objective is to introduce you to the statement of cash flows, while avoiding becoming "bogged down" in procedural details. So, we will use a streamlined approach to collecting and organizing the data for a statement of cash flows.

The data we need to prepare a statement of cash flows for Cherokee Station for the year ended December 31, 1998, are included in Exhibits 14.5, 14.6, and 14.7. Exhibit 14.5 presents Cherokee Station's 1998 income statement, while Exhibit 14.6 contains balance sheets for the firm as of December 31, 1998 and 1997. The accounting entries listed in Exhibit 14.7 summarize the company's transactions during 1998. For example, the first entry combines the journal entries made to record Cherokee Station's credit sales during 1998—all of the company's sales are on a credit basis. Notice that

EXHIBIT 14.5 ▼
Cherokee Station, Inc., Income Statement

CHEROKEE STATION, INC. INCOME STATEMENT FOR THE YEAR ENDED DECEMBER 31, 1998		
Sales		$44,900
Cost of goods sold		26,200
Gross profit		$18,700
Operating expenses:		
Selling & general expenses	$10,600	
Depreciation expense	4,200	14,800
Operating income		$ 3,900
Gain on sale of land		700
Income before income tax		$ 4,600
Income tax expense		1,000
Net income		$ 3,600

the final column of Exhibit 14.7 indicates the type of activity—operating, investing, or financing—to which each summary journal entry relates. (Note: When you are attempting to classify a specific event or transaction as either an operating, investing, or financing activity, refer to Exhibit 14.4.)

Determining Cash Flows from Operating Activities: The Indirect Method

The starting point for "indirectly" determining net cash flow from operating activities is a business's net income. The schedule shown in Exhibit 14.8 lists the general types of adjustments necessary to convert net income to net cash flow from operating activities. Recall that operating activities are the profit-oriented activities of a business. A company's net income for a given period seldom equals the net cash flow generated by its operating activities during that period for two reasons. First, certain "nonoperating" items, such as gain and losses on the sale of property, plant & equipment assets, are considered in computing net income. Second, net income is determined on an accrual basis, while cash flows from operating activities are, of course, cash-basis amounts. For example, suppose that during a given year a company earned $2,000 of interest revenue on an investment. However, the company had received none of that interest by the end of its fiscal year. If this company had no other revenues or expenses during the year in question, its net income was $2,000, while its net cash flow from operating activities was $0.

DEPRECIATION AND AMORTIZATION EXPENSES Depreciation and amortization are noncash expenses. That is, neither of these expenses results in cash outflows. However, these expenses decrease net income. So, to reconcile net income to

EXHIBIT 14.6 ▼
Cherokee Station, Inc., Balance Sheets

CHEROKEE STATION, INC.
BALANCE SHEETS
DECEMBER 31, 1998, AND 1997

		1998		1997
Assets				
Cash		$15,000		$ 6,100
Accounts receivable		5,500		3,300
Inventory		10,800		12,000
Prepaid expenses		2,500		1,400
Total current assets		$33,800		$22,800
Equipment	$35,000		$24,000	
Less: Accumulated depreciation	10,100	24,900	5,900	18,100
Land		—		1,900
Total assets		$58,700		$42,800
Liabilities				
Accounts payable		$ 5,900		$ 5,600
Accrued liabilities		4,600		5,800
Total current liabilities		$10,500		$11,400
Stockholders' Equity				
Common stock		$ 3,600		$ 3,600
Preferred stock		18,000		3,000
Additional paid-in capital		12,500		12,500
Retained earnings		14,100		12,300
Total stockholders' equity		$48,200		$31,400
Total liabilities and stockholders' equity		$58,700		$42,800

net cash flow from operating activities depreciation and amortization expenses must be added to net income.

GAINS AND LOSSES Several examples of gains and losses have been discussed in earlier chapters, including gains and losses on the disposal of property, plant & equipment. As shown in Exhibit 14.8, losses must be added to net income when computing net cash flow from operating activities, while gains must be subtracted from net income. To illustrate the rationale for this treatment of gains and losses, consider a gain realized on the sale of land. Assume that Zimbelman, Inc., sells for $33,000 a piece of land classified as a property, plant & equipment asset. This land had a book value of $24,000, meaning that Zimbelman realized a gain of $9,000 on its disposal.

EXHIBIT 14.7 ▼

Cherokee Station, Inc., Summary Journal Entries for the Year Ended December 31, 1998

	Debit	Credit	Type of Activity
1. Credit Sales:			Operating
Accounts Receivable	44,900		
Sales		44,900	
2. Collections of Accounts Receivable:			Operating
Cash	42,700		
Accounts Receivable		42,700	
3. Cost of Goods Sold:			Operating
Cost of Goods Sold	26,200		
Inventory		26,200	
4. Credit Purchases of Merchandise:			Operating
Inventory	25,000		
Accounts Payable		25,000	
5. Payments of Accrued Operating Liabilities:			Operating
Accrued Liabilities	5,800		
Cash		5,800	
6. Payments of Operating Expenses:			Operating
Selling & General Expenses	3,600		
Cash		3,600	
7. Prepayments of Operating Expenses:			Operating
Prepaid Expenses	3,500		
Cash		3,500	
8. Expiration of Prepaid Expenses:			Operating
Selling & General Expenses	2,400		
Prepaid Expenses		2,400	
9. Payments to Suppliers:			Operating
Accounts Payable	24,700		
Cash		24,700	
10. Purchase of Equipment:			Investing
Equipment	11,000		
Cash		11,000	
11. Sale of Land:			Investing
Cash	2,600		
Land		1,900	
Gain on Sale of Land		700	
12. Sale of Preferred Stock:			Financing
Cash	15,000		
Preferred Stock		15,000	
13. Declaration and Payment of Dividends:			Financing
Dividends	1,800		
Cash		1,800	

(*continued*)

EXHIBIT 14.7 ▼
(Concluded)

	Debit	Credit	Type of Activity
14. Payments of Income Taxes:			Operating
Income Tax Expense	1,000		
Cash		1,000	
15. Accrual of Unpaid Operating Expenses at Year-End:			Operating
Selling & General Expenses	4,600		
Accrued Liabilities		4,600	
16. Adjusting Entry to Record Depreciation Expense:			Investing
Depreciation Expense, Equipment	4,200		
Accumulated Depreciation, Equipment		4,200	
17. Entry to Close Net Income to Retained Earnings:			N/A
Income Summary	3,600		
Retained Earnings		3,600	
18. Entry to Close Dividends to Retained Earnings:			N/A
Retained Earnings	1,800		
Dividends		1,800	

For purposes of the statement of cash flows, transactions involving the purchase or sale of property, plant & equipment qualify as investing activities, as indicated in Exhibit 14.4. So, the $33,000 cash inflow from Zimbelman's sale of the piece of land should be reported as a component of "net cash provided by investing activities" in the firm's statement of cash flows. This presents a problem since the $9,000 gain on this transaction will also be included in the firm's net income, which, again, is the starting point for determining net cash flow from operating activities under

EXHIBIT 14.8 ▼
Standard Format for Determining Net Cash Flow from Operating Activities under the Indirect Method

Net income	$ x,xxx
Plus: Depreciation and amortization expenses	xxx
Losses	xxx
Decreases in current assets (other than cash)	xxx
Increases in current liabilities	xxx
Less: Gains	xxx
Increases in current assets (other than cash)	xxx
Decreases in current liabilities	xxx
Net cash flow from operating activities	$ x,xxx

the indirect method. Without an appropriate adjustment in the statement of cash flows, the total cash flow from this transaction will be reported as $42,000 in Zimbelman's statement of cash flows: $9,000 included in cash flows from operating activities via net income and $33,000 included in cash flows from investing activities. To remedy this problem, the $9,000 gain must be subtracted from net income in Zimbelman's statement of cash flows to determine net cash flow from operating activities. If the land had been sold for $21,000, the $3,000 loss would have been added to net income when computing Zimbelman's net cash flow from operating activities.

CHANGES IN CURRENT ASSET AND CURRENT LIABILITY ACCOUNTS

Most of the adjustments to net income required to determine net cash flow from operating activities under the indirect method involve noncash current asset and current liability accounts. As indicated in Exhibit 14.8, changes in these accounts must be added to, or subtracted from, a business's net income when computing net cash flow from operating activities.

Current Assets To illustrate the logic underlying the adjustments to net income shown in Exhibit 14.8 for changes in current assets, let us focus on accounts receivable. Assume that a company began operations on January 1 of a recent year. At the end of the year, the company's general ledger reflected total sales of $60,000 and accounts receivable of $5,000. As a result, the company's sales for that year produced cash flows from operating activities of only $55,000 ($60,000 − $5,000). So, when computing the firm's net cash flow from operating activities, $5,000 must be deducted from its net income. (To simplify matters, in the examples illustrated in this chapter we assume that there are no uncollectible accounts receivable and thus no allowance for doubtful accounts.)

More generally, when accounts receivable increase during a year, this increase must be deducted from net income when computing net cash flow from operating activities. This adjustment gives recognition to the fact that the cash inflows from customers were less than the sales recorded during the year. Conversely, when accounts receivable decrease during a year, this decrease must be added to net income when computing net cash flow from operating activities. This adjustment gives recognition to the fact that the cash inflows from customers exceeded the sales recorded during the year. Similar reasoning can be applied to other noncash current assets. In summary, *increases in noncash current assets are deducted from net income and decreases in these assets are added to net income when computing net cash flow from operating activities under the indirect method.*

Current Liabilities Now, consider income taxes payable to illustrate the rationale for the treatment of current liabilities shown in Exhibit 14.8. (Notice in Exhibit 14.4 that the payment of income taxes qualifies as an operating activity.) Assume that during 1998, a company paid $14,000 of income taxes on its previous year's taxable income. This entry was booked as follows:

Mar. 15	Income Taxes Payable	14,000	
	Cash		14,000
	To pay 1997 income taxes		

At the end of 1998, the company recorded the following adjusting entry to recognize its income tax expense for 1998.

Dec. 31	Income Tax Expense	12,000	
	Income Taxes Payable		12,000
	To record income tax expense for 1998		

Given the previous entries, we can easily determine that the company's income tax payments during 1998 exceeded its income tax expense for that year by $2,000. To reconcile net income to net cash flow from operating activities, this $2,000 difference must be subtracted from net income.

A shortcut method of arriving at this $2,000 adjustment is to analyze the change in the Income Taxes Payable account during 1998. Generally, there are only two types of entries that affect Income Taxes Payable. Accruals of income tax expense result in credits to this account, while income tax payments result in debits to the account. The balance of Income Taxes Payable in the present example decreased by $2,000 in 1998, meaning that debits to the account exceeded credits to the account by $2,000. So, we can conclude that the company's 1998 income tax payments exceeded its income tax expense for that year by $2,000. Again, this $2,000 item is deducted from net income to arrive at net cash flow from operating activities. Other current liabilities can be analyzed in the same manner using such "bookkeeping logic." As a general rule, then, *increases in current liabilities are added to net income and decreases in current liabilities are deducted from net income when computing net cash flow from operating activities under the indirect method.*

Determining Cash Flows from Investing and Financing Activities: The Indirect Method

Most businesses have only a few transactions or events each year that qualify as investing or financing activities. An accountant of a small company may simply scan the company's journals and ledgers to identify transactions involving cash flows from investing and financing activities. Accountants of larger companies often use the work sheet method alluded to previously to identify these items.

Companies occasionally engage in significant noncash investing or financing activities. For example, a company might acquire a building by issuing a long-term promissory note to the seller. Although these types of transactions do not involve cash, *FASB Statement No. 95* requires that they be disclosed in a firm's financial statements. Such disclosure is required whether the indirect or direct method of preparing a statement of cash flows is used. Typically, noncash investing and financing activities are included in a schedule added to the statement of cash flows.

Cherokee Station, Inc.: The Indirect Method of Preparing a Statement of Cash Flows

Our task now is to prepare a statement of cash flows for Cherokee Station, Inc., using the indirect method. Referring to Exhibit 14.6, we find that the company's cash balance increased from $6,100 at the beginning of 1998 (end of 1997) to $15,000 on December 31, 1998. So, our objective is to account for the $8,900 increase in Cherokee Station's cash balance during 1998.

CASH FLOWS FROM OPERATING ACTIVITIES The first step in preparing Cherokee Station's 1998 statement of cash flows is to derive the company's net cash flow from operating activities from its net income using the format shown in Exhibit 14.8. Since Cherokee Station's transactions for 1998 have been summarized in Exhibit 14.7, we can refer to that exhibit to identify the adjustments to net income necessary to determine the company's net cash flow from operating activities. One such item is the $700 gain on the sale of land (see journal entry #11 in Exhibit 14.7). As explained earlier, such a gain must be subtracted from net income to determine a firm's net cash flow from operating activities. A second adjustment item is the $4,200 depreciation expense recorded during 1998 (see journal entry #16 in Exhibit 14.7). This item is a noncash expense that must be added to net income to compute net cash flow from operating activities.

Next, we must analyze the changes in Cherokee Station's noncash current asset and current liability accounts during 1998 to determine their impact on the company's cash flows from operating activities. This is easily done by referring to Exhibit 14.6 and subtracting the December 31, 1997, balance of each of these accounts from the corresponding December 31, 1998, balance. Following are the resulting amounts and the type of adjustment that must be made for each item when computing net cash flow from operating activities.

		Type of Adjustment to Net Income to Determine Net Cash Flow from Operating Activities
Increase in accounts receivable	$2,200	Deduction
Decrease in inventory	1,200	Addition
Increase in prepaid expenses	1,100	Deduction
Increase in accounts payable	300	Addition
Decrease in accrued liabilities	1,200	Deduction

We now have the information needed to compute Cherokee Station's net cash flow from operating activities. Shown next is this information organized as it would appear in the company's statement of cash flows for 1998.

Cash flows from operating activities:	
Net income	$ 3,600
Adjustments to reconcile net income to net cash provided by operating activities:	
Depreciation expense	4,200
Gain on sale of land	(700)
Changes in current assets and liabilities:	
Increase in accounts receivable	(2,200)
Decrease in inventory	1,200
Increase in prepaid expenses	(1,100)
Increase in accounts payable	300
Decrease in accrued liabilities	(1,200)
Net cash provided by operating activities	$ 4,100

CASH FLOWS FROM INVESTING AND FINANCING ACTIVITIES After the net cash flow from operating activities has been determined, the next step in preparing a statement of cash flows is to identify the cash flows from investing and financing activities. Scanning the data in Exhibit 14.7, we find that Cherokee Station engaged in three investing activities during 1998. One of these investing activities, the recording of depreciation expense, did not produce a cash inflow or outflow.[1] So, we ignore that item. (Recall that depreciation expense is added to net income when computing net cash flow from operating activities.) The other two investing activities were the sale of land and the $11,000 purchase of equipment. Given these two transactions, we can prepare the following schedule of Cherokee Station's cash flows from investing activities during 1998.

Cash flows from investing activities:	
Sale of land	$ 2,600
Purchase of equipment	(11,000)
Net cash used in investing activities	$ (8,400)

During 1998, Cherokee Station also engaged in two financing activities. The company received $15,000 from the sale of preferred stock and paid dividends of $1,800. The following schedule summarizes these cash flows from financing activities.

Cash flows from financing activities:	
Sale of preferred stock	$15,000
Dividend payments	(1,800)
Net cash provided by financing activities	$13,200

COMPLETING THE STATEMENT OF CASH FLOWS Recall that our objective in preparing a statement of cash flows for Cherokee Station is to account for the $8,900 increase in the company's cash balance during 1998. To ensure that we have accomplished this objective, we can add the net cash flows from Cherokee Station's operating, investing, and financing activities as shown in the following schedule.

Net cash provided by operating activities	$ 4,100
Net cash used in investing activities	(8,400)
Net cash provided by financing activities	13,200
Net increase in cash	$ 8,900

Exhibit 14.9 presents Cherokee Station's completed statement of cash flows applying the indirect method. Notice that the final section of this statement reconciles

1. *FASB Statement No. 95,* paragraph 28, indicates that depreciation and amortization expenses are investing activities for purposes of the statement of cash flows. However, for income statement purposes, these items are considered operating expenses. As a result, in Cherokee Station's income statement shown in Exhibit 14.5, depreciation expense is listed under operating expenses.

EXHIBIT 14.9 ▼
Cherokee Station, Inc., Statement of Cash Flows—Indirect Method

CHEROKEE STATION, INC.
STATEMENT OF CASH FLOWS
FOR THE YEAR ENDED DECEMBER 31, 1998

Cash flows from operating activities:	
Net income	$ 3,600
Adjustments to reconcile net income to net cash provided by operating activities:	
Depreciation expense	4,200
Gain on sale of land	(700)
Changes in current assets and liabilities:	
Increase in accounts receivable	(2,200)
Decrease in inventories	1,200
Increase in prepaid expenses	(1,100)
Increase in accounts payable	300
Decrease in accrued liabilities	(1,200)
Net cash provided by operating activities	$ 4,100
Cash flows from investing activities:	
Sale of land	$ 2,600
Purchase of equipment	(11,000)
Net cash used in investing activities	$ (8,400)
Cash flows from financing activities:	
Sale of preferred stock	$15,000
Dividend payments	(1,800)
Net cash provided by financing activities	$13,200
Net increase in cash	$ 8,900
Cash balance, December 31, 1997	6,100
Cash balance, December 31, 1998	$15,000

the company's beginning and ending cash balances with the net cash flow generated during the year. As a point of information, if a company uses the indirect method to prepare its statement of cash flows, *FASB Statement No. 95* requires that two specific operating cash outflows be disclosed in the firm's financial statements. These two cash outflows are interest payments and income tax payments. Companies typically disclose these two items in a note or schedule attached to the statement of cash flows.

Tracking Cash Flows Around the World

FOR YOUR INFORMATION

Unlike the balance sheet and income statement, the statement of cash flows is not universally recognized across the world as a major financial statement. In fact, most countries do not require businesses to include a statement of cash flows in their annual financial reports. Instead of requiring a statement of cash flows, accounting and financial reporting standards in some countries, Sweden, for example, require businesses to prepare a funds statement. A funds statement analyzes the changes in a business's working capital accounts—current assets and current liabilities—during an accounting period. Several developed countries do not require businesses to prepare a statement of cash flows or a funds statement. Among these countries are Denmark, Italy, the Netherlands, and Switzerland. Even in the absence of requirements to do so, many multinational companies voluntarily include a statement of cash flows in their annual reports because of the demand for that statement by financial decision makers.

INTERPRETING CASH-FLOW DATA

The ability to prepare a statement of cash flows is an important skill, particularly for accountants. However, a more important skill for financial decision makers is the ability to interpret cash-flow data. In this section, we consider two approaches to analyzing cash-flow data. The first approach involves a comparative analysis of an entity's cash flows from its operating, investing, and financing activities. The second approach focuses specifically on operating cash flows and involves computing and interpreting cash flow per share.

Comparative Analysis of an Entity's Cash Flows

LEARNING OBJECTIVE 4 ▶
Interpret cash-flow data by comparatively analyzing the three components of an entity's cash flows.

Much can be learned about a company's financial status and future prospects by analyzing the three components of its cash flows. For example, refer to Exhibit 14.10, which presents cash-flow data over a three-year period for Zero Corporation, a manufacturing firm. Notice that in each year from 1994 through 1996, Zero Corporation's operating activities produced a positive net cash flow. As noted earlier in the chapter, for a company to be financially viable over the long run its operating activities must generate positive net cash flows. There is a limit to the amount of cash a company can raise by selling stocks or bonds or by taking out long-term loans—examples of financing activities. Likewise, a company cannot survive for long if it must sell equipment or other productive assets—an investing activity—to generate needed cash.

Zero's 1994–1996 statements of cash flows reveal that a large proportion of the company's investing cash outflows stemmed from the purchase of property, plant & equipment. Here again is a positive indication of the company's future prospects. The company is investing cash produced by its operating activities into additional productive assets to expand the scope of those activities. Finally, dividend payments accounted for a significant portion of Zero's financing cash outflows for the period

EXHIBIT 14.10 ▼
Zero Corporation: Cash Flows, 1994–1996

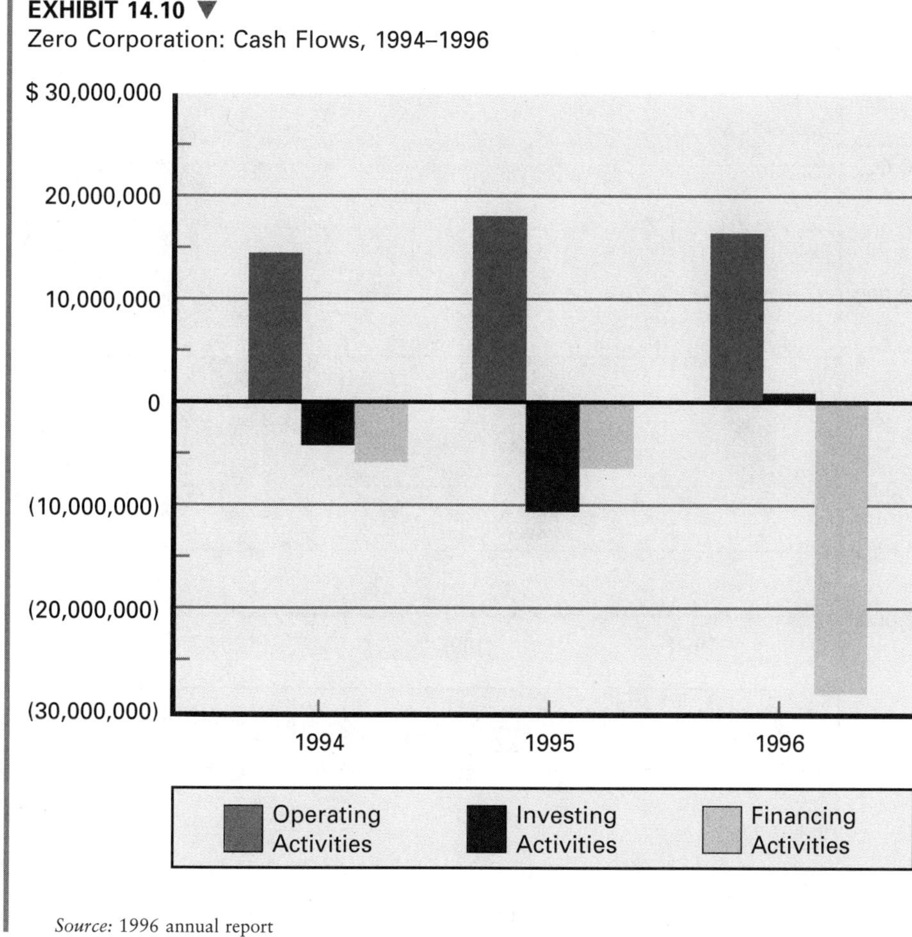

Source: 1996 annual report

1994–1996. Few stockholders or potential stockholders will complain regarding that use of a company's cash resources.

Now, consider the cash-flow data presented in Exhibit 14.11 for Allou Health & Beauty Care, Inc. Allou distributes health and beauty aids, fragrances, and cosmetics to thousands of retailers nationwide. Unlike Zero Corporation, Allou's operating activities did not produce positive net cash flows over the three-year period 1994–1996. This was true despite the company earning a net income ranging from $3.7 to $4.7 million in each of those years. Instead of relying upon its operating activities to generate positive net cash flows, this company relied heavily upon bank loans to satisfy its cash needs during 1994–1996.

Allou's 1996 annual report reveals that a buildup of inventory was largely responsible for the company's negative net cash flow from operating activities during the mid-1990s. In 1996, alone, the company saw its inventory increase by more than $14 million. Further investigation reveals that the company's inventory increased by 25 percent during fiscal 1996 compared with a 15 percent increase in sales. When a company's inventory increases more rapidly than sales for an extended period, the firm may eventually be forced to write down or write off excess inventory it has accumulated.

EXHIBIT 14.11 ▼
Allou Health & Beauty Care: Cash Flows, 1994–1996

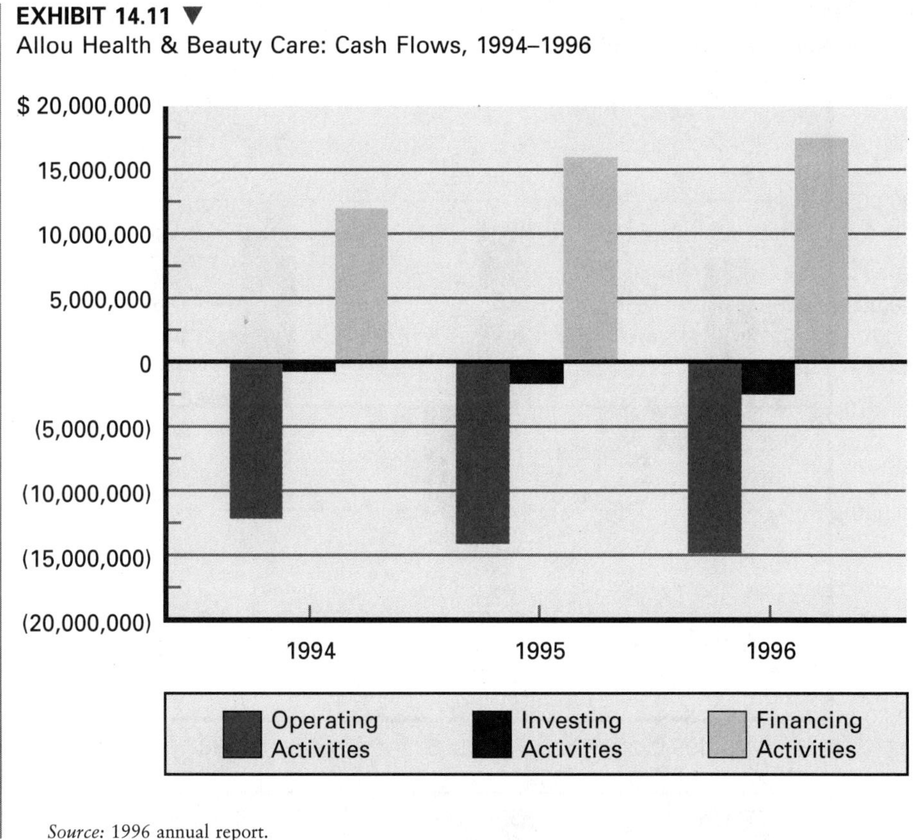

Source: 1996 annual report.

Computing and Interpreting Cash Flow per Share

LEARNING OBJECTIVE 5 ▶ Compute and interpret cash flow per share.

Cash flow per share is another financial measure tracked by decision makers. Ironically, in *Statement No. 95* the FASB prohibits businesses from reporting cash flow per share. Why? Principally because the FASB believes that reporting both earnings per share and cash flow per share would confuse financial statement users. A related concern is that decision makers would rely too heavily on cash flow per share as a measure of financial performance. Despite the important uses of cash-flow data, the accounting profession firmly believes that accrual-basis earnings data yield more reliable measures of the financial performance of business entities.

Since companies are not allowed to disclose cash flow per share in their annual reports, this "service" is provided by investment advisory firms. A problem arising from the absence of formal rules for cash flow per share disclosures is a lack of consistency in how this financial measure is computed. The following equation provides one of the more widely accepted approaches to computing **cash flow per share** for an accounting period:

cash flow per share

$$\text{Cash Flow per Share} = \frac{\text{Net Cash Flow from Operating Activities} - \text{Preferred Stock Dividends}}{\text{Weighted-Average Number of Shares of Common Stock Outstanding}}$$

Exhibit 14.12 presents a ten-year comparison of Compaq Computer's earnings per share and cash flow per share. As you might expect, these two measures tend to be closely correlated. Over the period covered by Exhibit 14.12, Compaq's earnings increased significantly. A comparable increase in net cash flow from operating activities accompanied this increase in profits. Notice that each year Compaq's cash flows per share exceeded its earnings per share, which is true for most companies. The gap between these two amounts is largely due to noncash expenses, principally depreciation expense.

When a company's earnings per share and cash flow per share diverge in a given year, decision makers want to know why. Quite often, a company's operating cash flows begin declining in advance of a decrease in earnings. For example, during the early stages of an economic recession, a company's sales may remain stable. However, the collection period on those sales may lengthen if the recession continues, causing cash flows from operating activities to decline. If economic conditions fail to improve, a company's earnings will likely begin declining as well. This drop in earnings may result from falling sales, increases in bad debt expense, and write-offs or write-downs of slow-moving inventory.

EXHIBIT 14.12 ▼
Compaq Computer: Earnings per Share vs. Cash Flow per Share

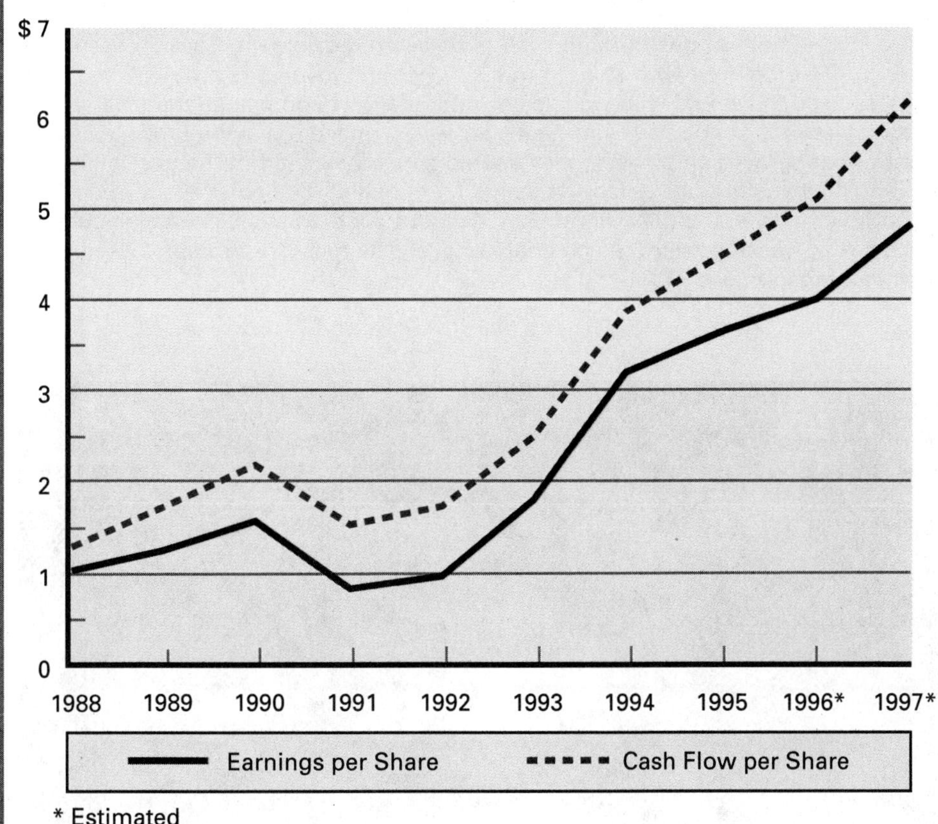

Source: Value Line investment advisory service.

Too Much Trust Can Lead to Too Little Cash

Cash-flow problems are a common bugaboo of businesses of all sizes. Slow-paying customers, economic downturns, and periods of "tight" credit are among the leading causes of depleted bank accounts. Another major source of cash-flow problems is employee theft.

Earlier chapters highlighted several incidents involving employees stealing cash from their employers. Two prominent business organizations that suffered embarrassing embezzlement losses in recent years are Salomon Brothers (Chapter 3) and the Los Angeles Dodgers (Chapter 9). A key administrative employee ripped off Salomon Brothers, the investment banking firm, for more than one million dollars. Recall that the Dodgers incurred several hundred thousand dollars of losses due to the scheming of a dishonest payroll chief. Then, there was the case of Howard Street Jewelers discussed in Chapter 6. Betty, the trusted but sticky-fingered cashier, stole $350,000 from her employer. Even accounting firms fall victim to dishonest employees. In 1995, Arthur Andersen & Co., a Big Six accounting firm, revealed that a former long-time employee had embezzled more than $2 million from the firm (M. O'Connor, "Accounting Firm Victim of Embezzling," *Chicago Tribune,* 23 June 1995, Section 2, p. 3).

A common thread runs through each of these embezzlement cases. In each instance, the employee who stole from his or her employer was a well-liked and respected individual who was perceived to be very competent and loyal to the organization. Although business owners and managers may be predisposed toward trusting their employees, they should never lose sight of the possibility that an employee may be quietly "stealing them blind." The most effective deterrent to employee theft is a rigorous network of control activities that includes occasionally "looking over the shoulder" of even the most trusted employees within an organization.

To properly interpret a statement of cash flows prepared for Compaq Computer, or any other business, a financial decision maker must first understand the nature of the business.

Another approach to tracking cash flow per share and earnings per share is to express one of these financial measures as a percentage of the other. This technique allows decision makers to more readily compare and contrast the relationship between the net operating cash flows and earnings of two or more companies. Exhibit 14.13 presents a ten-year summary of the relationship between earnings per share and cash flow per share for Compaq Computer and Ohio Edison, a large electric utility. Notice that during each year of this period, Ohio Edison's earnings per share as a percentage of cash flow per share was much lower than the comparable measure for Compaq Computer. Why? Principally because electric utilities have relatively high depreciation expenses each year that cause their earnings to be significantly lower than their net cash flow from operating activities.

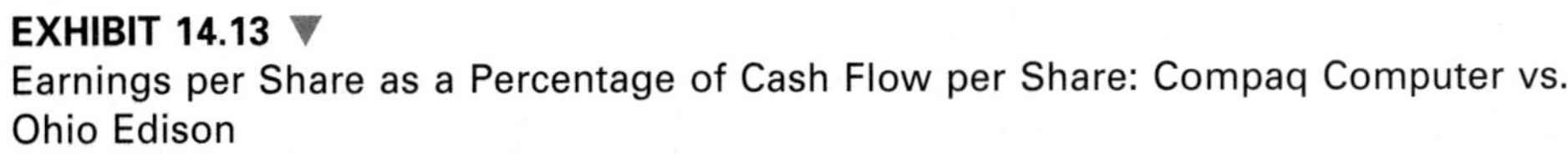

EXHIBIT 14.13 ▼
Earnings per Share as a Percentage of Cash Flow per Share: Compaq Computer vs. Ohio Edison

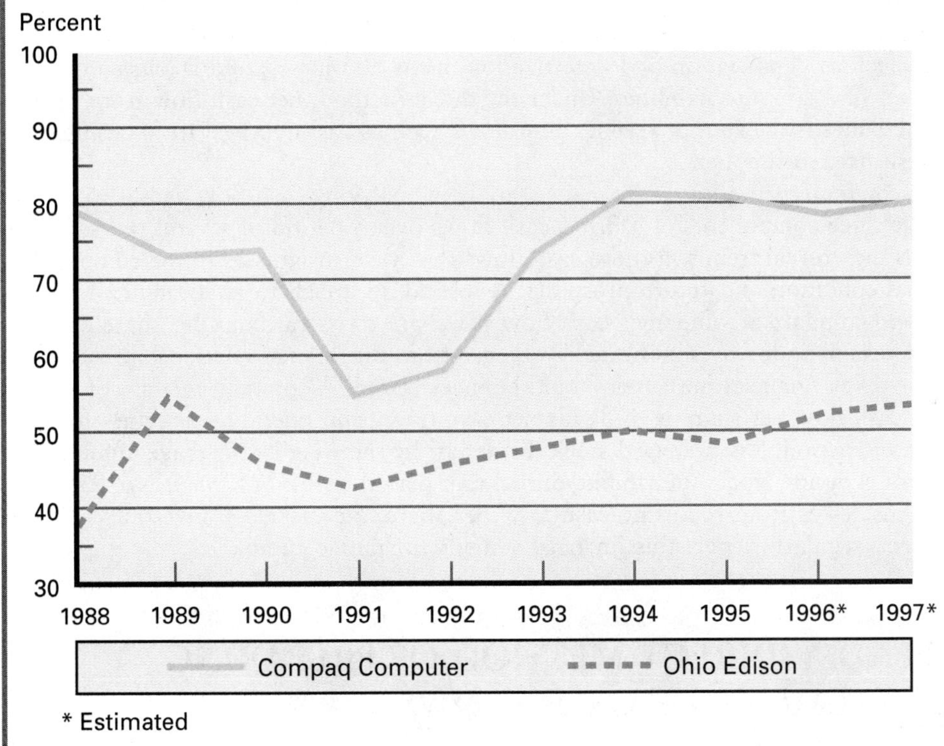

* Estimated

Source: Value Line investment advisory service.

SUMMARY

In 1987, the FASB issued *Statement of Financial Accounting Standards No. 95*, "Statement of Cash Flows." This accounting standard requires businesses to include a statement of cash flows in their annual financial reports. Among other uses, a statement of cash flows allows decision makers to evaluate a business's ability to generate positive net cash flows in the future.

Businesses engage in three principal activities that result in cash inflows and outflows: operating, investing, and financing activities. Operating activities involve transactions and events related to the production and delivery of goods and services. Receipts from customers are the primary cash inflows from operating activities for most businesses, while payments to suppliers are typically among the largest operating cash outflows. The acquisition and disposal of property, plant & equipment and the purchase and sale of investments in debt and equity securities, other than trading securities and cash equivalents, are important sources of cash flows from investing activities. Finally, examples of cash flows from financing activities include proceeds from the sale of a firm's common stock, payments of dividends, and principal payments on long-term loans.

FASB Statement No. 95 permits businesses to use either the direct or indirect methods of preparing a statement of cash flows. The only major difference between these two methods concerns the computation of net cash flow from operating activities. Under the indirect method, net cash flow from operating activities is computed by making certain adjustments to net income. These adjustments involve noncash expenses such as depreciation and amortization, gains and losses, and changes in noncash current assets and liabilities. Under the direct method, net cash flow from operating activities is the sum of specific cash flows such as cash received from customers and cash paid to suppliers.

One common method decision makers apply in analyzing cash-flow data is to compare the three components of a firm's cash flows over a period of several years. Such analysis may reveal trends in those cash flows that yield insights as to the company's financial condition and future prospects. A second approach to analyzing cash-flow data is to compare a company's cash flow per share to its earnings per share over a several-year period. Any significant divergence from the normal relationship between these two key financial measures should be investigated. A common method of computing cash flow per share is to divide net cash flow from operating activities for an accounting period, less preferred stock dividends, by the weighted-average number of shares of common stock outstanding during that period. *FASB Statement No. 95* prohibits businesses from reporting cash flow per share. Nevertheless, investment advisory firms regularly report this financial statistic for public companies.

▲ *APPENDIX:* DIRECT METHOD OF PREPARING A STATEMENT OF CASH FLOWS

LEARNING OBJECTIVE 6 ▶
(*Appendix*) Prepare a statement of cash flows using the direct method.

As mentioned previously, the only major difference between the indirect and direct methods of preparing a statement of cash flows involves the computation of net cash flow from operating activities. Under the indirect method, net cash flow from operating activities is derived from net income through a series of adjustments. Under the direct method, the specific cash inflows and outflows from operating activities must be identified and reported in the statement of cash flows. Exhibit 14.2 presents a statement of cash flows for Hughes Supply, Inc., prepared using the direct method. Shown next is the initial section of that financial statement, which lists Hughes Supply's cash flows from its operating activities.

Cash flows from operating activities:	
Cash received from customers	$ 1,073,951
Cash paid to suppliers and employees	(1,034,589)
Interest received	3,454
Interest paid	(7,273)
Income taxes paid	(15,230)
Net cash provided by operating activities	$ 20,313

Determining Cash Flows from Operating Activities: The Direct Method

The summary journal entries listed in Exhibit 14.7 provide the data we need to determine Cherokee Station's net cash flow from operating activities applying the direct method. If such data are not available, a business's cash flows from operating activities can be determined by using an account-analysis technique. This technique involves identifying the accounts in which cash flows from operating activities are recorded and then analyzing the activity in these accounts to filter out the cash-flow data.

Suppose that we want to determine a business's cash inflows from customer receipts using the account-analysis technique. The accounts that must be considered for this purpose are Sales and Accounts Receivable. Assume that Crimson Corporation had total sales of $424,000 during 1998. On January 1, 1998, the company had accounts receivable of $34,200, while at the end of the year the firm had accounts receivable of $29,500. Given these balances, we know that cash receipts from customers exceeded sales recorded during 1998 by $4,700.[2] So, Crimson's operating activities during 1998 produced cash receipts from customers of $428,700 ($424,000 + $4,700). This process of converting accrual-basis sales to cash receipts from customers is captured by the following equation.

$$\text{Sales}\left\{\begin{array}{c}+\text{ decrease in accounts receivable}\\ \text{or}\\ -\text{ increase in accounts receivable}\end{array}\right\} = \begin{array}{c}\text{Cash}\\ \text{Received from}\\ \text{Customers}\end{array}$$

2. We can prove this by using the following equation:

$$\begin{array}{c}\text{Year-End}\\ \text{Receivables Balance}\end{array} = \begin{array}{c}\text{Beginning}\\ \text{Receivables Balance}\end{array} + \begin{array}{c}\text{Credit}\\ \text{Sales}\end{array} - \begin{array}{c}\text{Collections}\\ \text{of Receivables}\\ \text{during Year}\end{array}$$

$$\begin{array}{c}\text{Year-End}\\ \text{Receivables Balance}\end{array} - \begin{array}{c}\text{Beginning}\\ \text{Receivables Balance}\end{array} = \begin{array}{c}\text{Credit}\\ \text{Sales}\end{array} - \begin{array}{c}\text{Collections}\\ \text{of Receivables}\\ \text{during Year}\end{array}$$

$$\$29{,}500 - \$34{,}200 = \begin{array}{c}\text{Credit}\\ \text{Sales}\end{array} - \begin{array}{c}\text{Collections}\\ \text{of Receivables}\\ \text{during Year}\end{array}$$

$$(\$4{,}700) = \begin{array}{c}\text{Credit}\\ \text{Sales}\end{array} - \begin{array}{c}\text{Collections}\\ \text{of Receivables}\\ \text{during Year}\end{array}$$

By definition, cash sales cannot result in any difference between a business's recorded sales during an accounting period and its cash receipts from customers that period. Consequently, the above analysis ignores cash sales. Also, recall that in this chapter we assume that all receivables are collectible. Thus, the above analysis is not affected by the write-off of uncollectible receivables.

Plugging in the numbers for the example just given to the previous equation, we again arrive at cash receipts from customers of \$428,700.

$$\$424{,}000 + \$4{,}700 = \$428{,}700$$

One more example? Suppose that Crimson Corporation had salaries expense of \$356,400 during 1998. The balance of the firm's Salaries Payable account was \$4,600 on January 1, 1998, and \$2,800 on December 31, 1998. Using the following equation, we determine that the company paid salaries to employees during 1998 of \$358,200.

$$\text{Salaries Expense} \left\{ \begin{array}{c} +\text{ decrease in salaries payable} \\ \text{or} \\ -\text{ increase in salaries payable} \end{array} \right\} = \text{Salaries Paid to Employees}$$

$$\$356{,}400 + \$1{,}800 = \$358{,}200$$

Determining Cash Flows from Investing and Financing Activities: The Direct Method

Cash flows from investing and financing activities are determined and reported in the same manner under the indirect and direct methods. Again, when summary journal entry data are available, such as the data shown in Exhibit 14.7, those data can be scanned to identify the cash flows from investing and financing activities.

Cherokee Station, Inc.: The Direct Method of Preparing a Statement of Cash Flows

CASH FLOWS FROM OPERATING ACTIVITIES To determine Cherokee Station's net cash flow from operating activities under the direct method, we identify those summary journal entries in Exhibit 14.7 that involve both operating activities and cash flows. For example, consider the initial two entries in Exhibit 14.7. The first entry summarizes the company's credit sales transactions during 1998. Although credit sales are an important operating activity, they do not directly yield cash flows. Instead, cash flows result from the collection of accounts receivable. The second entry in Exhibit 14.7 indicates that Cherokee Station's collections of accounts receivable totaled \$42,700 during 1998. Listed next are the summary transactions for Cherokee Station during 1998 that involved both operating activities and cash inflows or outflows.

Summary Journal Entry (SJE)	Cash Effect	
Collections of Accounts Receivable (SJE #2)	Increase	\$42,700
Payments of Accrued Operating Liabilities (SJE #5)	Decrease	5,800
Payments of Operating Expenses (SJE #6)	Decrease	3,600
Prepayments of Operating Expenses (SJE #7)	Decrease	3,500
Payments to Suppliers (SJE #9)	Decrease	24,700
Payments of Income Taxes (SJE #14)	Decrease	1,000

Given the previous data, we can now determine Cherokee Station's net cash flow from operating activities under the direct method, as shown in the following schedule.

Cash flows from operating activities:	
Cash received from customers	$ 42,700
Cash paid for operating expenses	(12,900)
Cash paid to suppliers	(24,700)
Income taxes paid	(1,000)
Net cash provided by operating activities	$ 4,100

Notice that the payments of accrued operating liabilities ($5,800), payments of operating expenses ($3,600), and prepayments of operating expenses ($3,500) were consolidated into one amount ($12,900). Finally, notice that the net cash provided by operating activities is the same amount determined previously under the indirect method.

CASH FLOWS FROM INVESTING AND FINANCING ACTIVITIES Again, the net cash flows from investing and financing activities are determined in the same manner under the indirect and direct methods. Since these items were discussed earlier when the indirect method was illustrated for Cherokee Station, here we simply list the schedules of these cash flows.

Cash flows from investing activities:	
Sale of land	$ 2,600
Purchase of equipment	(11,000)
Net cash used in investing activities	$ (8,400)

Cash flows from financing activities:	
Sale of preferred stock	$ 15,000
Dividend payments	(1,800)
Net cash provided by financing activities	$ 13,200

COMPLETING THE STATEMENT OF CASH FLOWS Exhibit 14.14 presents Cherokee Station's statement of cash flows for the year ended December 31, 1998, applying the direct method. Recall that *FASB Statement No. 95* requires companies that use the direct method to include in their financial statements a supporting schedule reconciling net income to net cash flow from operating activities. The reconciliation of Cherokee Station's net income to its net cash provided by operating activities is included as a supporting schedule to the statement of cash flows. Notice in Exhibit 14.2 that Hughes Supply did not include this reconciliation as a supporting schedule to its statement of cash flows. Instead, Hughes Supply, like many companies applying the direct method, included this reconciliation in a financial statement footnote.

EXHIBIT 14.14 ▼
Cherokee Station, Inc., Statement of Cash Flows—Direct Method

CHEROKEE STATION, INC.
STATEMENT OF CASH FLOWS
FOR THE YEAR ENDED DECEMBER 31, 1998

Cash flows from operating activities:	
Cash received from customers	$ 42,700
Cash paid for operating expenses	(12,900)
Cash paid to suppliers	(24,700)
Income taxes paid	(1,000)
Net cash provided by operating activities	$ 4,100
Cash flows from investing activities:	
Sale of land	$ 2,600
Purchase of equipment	(11,000)
Net cash used in investing activities	$ (8,400)
Cash flows from financing activities:	
Sale of preferred stock	$ 15,000
Dividend payments	(1,800)
Net cash provided by financing activities	$ 13,200
Net increase in cash	$ 8,900
Cash balance, December 31, 1997	6,100
Cash balance, December 31, 1998	$ 15,000
Reconciliation of net income to net cash flow from operating activities:	
Net income	$ 3,600
Adjustments to reconcile net income to net cash provided by operating activities:	
Depreciation expense	4,200
Gain on sale of land	(700)
Changes in current assets and liabilities:	
Increase in accounts receivable	(2,200)
Decrease in inventories	1,200
Increase in prepaid expenses	(1,100)
Increase in accounts payable	300
Decrease in accrued liabilities	(1,200)
Net cash provided by operating activities	$ 4,100

GLOSSARY

Cash flow per share (p. 680) Net cash flow from operating activities for an accounting period, less preferred stock dividends, divided by the weighted-average number of shares of common stock outstanding during that period.

Direct method (p. 666) An approach to preparing the statement of cash flows in which specific cash inflows and outflows from a business's operating activities are identified and listed in the initial section of this financial statement.

Financing activities (p. 666) Those activities of businesses that involve obtaining cash from lenders and repaying those amounts as well as obtaining cash from investors and providing them with a return of and a return on their investments.

Indirect method (p. 667) An approach to preparing the statement of cash flows in which net cash flow from operating activities is determined by making certain adjustments to a business's net income.

Investing activities (p. 666) Those activities of businesses that include the making and collecting of loans, the acquisition and disposal of property, plant & equipment, and the purchase and sale of debt and equity securities other than trading securities and cash equivalents.

Operating activities (p. 665) Those transactions and events related to the production and delivery of goods and services by businesses.

Statement of cash flows (p. 660) A financial statement that accounts for the net change in a business's cash balance during a given period; this statement summarizes the cash receipts and disbursements from a business's operating, investing, and financing activities.

DECISION CASE

Suppose that you have decided to enter the business world by becoming the sole proprietor of Acme Roadrunning Enterprise (ARE), a company that manufactures wear-resistant soles for running shoes. The major asset required by this business is a piece of production machinery. Presently, there are two models of this machinery available. Model A costs $300,000 and produces a higher-quality sole than Model B, which costs $180,000. Each machine has a three-year useful life and a zero estimated salvage value. You have sufficient resources available to purchase either Model A or Model B for cash. In either case, you will invest an additional $60,000 in your business by transferring that amount from your personal bank account to ARE's bank account.

The following table presents forecasted operating data, in condensed form, for the first three years of ARE's existence. Data are presented under the assumption that Model A is acquired and then under the assumption that Model B is acquired. In either case, the straight-line depreciation method will be used for the production machinery. The table does not include information regarding two transactions of ARE in Year 1—namely, the purchase of either Model A or Model B and your investment of an additional $60,000 in the business. You estimate that the replacement cost of Model A in three years will be $410,000, while the replacement cost of Model B at that point will be $200,000. Your decision to purchase either Model A or Model B is an important one. The products (soles) produced by the two models would be sold to different customers and require different business plans and strategies. As a result, it would not be economically feasible to switch from Model A to Model B, or vice versa, in the future.

	Year 1	Year 2	Year 3
Model A:			
Net income	$ 40,000	$ 50,000	$ 85,000
Depreciation expense	100,000	100,000	100,000
Year-end inventory	25,000	65,000	125,000
Year-end receivables	20,000	50,000	120,000
Year-end payables and accrued liabilities	10,000	25,000	50,000
Model B:			
Net income	$ 30,000	$ 35,000	$ 40,000
Depreciation expense	60,000	60,000	60,000
Year-end inventory	10,000	20,000	40,000
Year-end receivables	10,000	20,000	35,000
Year-end payables and accrued liabilities	5,000	10,000	20,000

Required: Prepare statements of cash flows for ARE for Years 1–3 assuming that Model A is purchased. Then prepare comparable statements of cash flows assuming Model B is acquired. Which model will produce the largest positive (net) cash flow over this period? Given the available data, which model should be purchased and why? What other factors should you consider in making this decision?

QUESTIONS

1. What is the principal use of a statement of cash flows from the perspective of financial decision makers?
2. Why do profitable companies not necessarily generate sufficient cash to finance their day-to-day operations?
3. From a technical standpoint, what is the primary objective of a statement of cash flows?
4. Identify the four sections of a statement of cash flows.
5. Define and provide an example of each of the following: operating activities, investing activities, and financing activities.
6. What are the principal cash inflows from operating activities for most businesses?
7. List several examples of cash outflows from operating activities.
8. What is the only major difference between the direct and indirect methods of preparing a statement of cash flows?
9. What factor or factors likely account for the popularity of the indirect method of preparing a statement of cash flows?
10. Why does the FASB prefer the direct method of preparing a statement of cash flows?

11. What is the starting point for determining a business's net cash flow from its operating activities under the indirect method?
12. List two reasons why a company's net income for a given period seldom equals the net cash flow generated by its operating activities during that period.
13. Under the indirect method of preparing a statement of cash flows, why is depreciation expense added to net income when determining net cash flow from operating activities?
14. How are gains and losses on the sale of property, plant & equipment dealt with in a statement of cash flows when the indirect method is being used? Why?
15. How do increases in current assets affect the determination of net cash flow from operating activities under the indirect method? What about decreases in current liabilities?
16. How are "noncash" investing and financing activities typically reported in a set of financial statements?
17. Identify the two specific cash outflows from operating activities that a company using the indirect method of preparing a statement of cash flows must disclose in its financial statements.
18. "For a company to be financially viable over the long run its operating activities must generate positive net cash flows." Explain the reasoning underlying this statement.
19. Why does the FASB prohibit businesses from reporting cash flow per share?
20. How is cash flow per share typically computed?
21. Which amount is typically larger each year for a business, cash flow per share or earnings per share? Why?
22. What is a common mistake business owners and executives make relative to their internal controls over cash and cash processing functions?
23. What is a business's most effective deterrent to employee theft?
24. Briefly describe how the account-analysis technique can be used to determine cash flows from operating activities under the direct method of preparing a statement of cash flows.

EXERCISES

25. True or False (LO 1–6)

Following are a series of statements regarding topics discussed in Chapter 14.

Required:

Indicate whether each statement is true (T) or false (F).

_____ a. Increases in noncash current assets are added to net income when computing net cash flow from operating activities under the indirect method.

_____ b. Profitable companies do not necessarily generate sufficient cash to finance their day-to-day operations.

_____ c. Financing activities are generally those transactions and events related to the production and delivery of goods and services by businesses.

_____ d. The Financial Accounting Standards Board permits businesses to report cash flow per share in their financial statement footnotes.

_____ e. Decision makers use a statement of cash flows to evaluate a business's ability to generate positive net cash flows in the future.

_____ f. The only major difference between the two methods of preparing a statement of cash flows concerns how net cash flow from operating activities is determined.

_____ g. Decision makers prefer companies to generate most of their cash inflows from investing and financing activities.

_____ h. The acquisition and disposal of property, plant & equipment are examples of operating activities.

_____ i. When the indirect method is used to prepare a statement of cash flows, the net cash flow from operating activities is determined by making certain adjustments to net income.

_____ j. The Financial Accounting Standard Boards expressly stated a preference for the indirect method of preparing a statement of cash flows.

_____ k. Similar to the balance sheet and income statement, the statement of cash flows is recognized around the world as a major financial statement.

_____ l. Cash flows from investing and financing activities are reported in the same manner under the indirect and direct methods.

26. Classification of Cash Flows (LO 2)

Following are examples of cash inflows and outflows that appear in statements of cash flows.

_________ Payments to employees
_________ Loans made to other firms
_________ Payments to acquire trading securities
_________ Receipts from customers
_________ Receipts from the sale of property, plant & equipment
_________ Payments of interest
_________ Payments made to acquire controlling interests in other firms
_________ Receipts of interest and dividends
_________ Payments to retire outstanding bonds
_________ Payments to suppliers

Required:

Classify each of the listed cash flows as one of the following:

a. Cash inflow from operating activities
b. Cash outflow from operating activities
c. Cash inflow from investing activities
d. Cash outflow from investing activities
e. Cash inflow from financing activities
f. Cash outflow from financing activities

27. Classification of Cash Flows (LO 2)

Following are examples of cash inflows and outflows that appear in statements of cash flows.

_________ Receipts from the sale of investments in trading securities
_________ Receipts from the issuance of common stock
_________ Dividend payments
_________ Payments to acquire property, plant & equipment
_________ Receipts from the sale of controlling investments
_________ Receipts from the issuance of bonds
_________ Amounts borrowed from banks
_________ Payments of taxes
_________ Payments to acquire treasury stock

Required:

Classify each of the listed cash flows as one of the following:

a. Cash inflow from operating activities
b. Cash outflow from operating activities

c. Cash inflow from investing activities
d. Cash outflow from investing activities
e. Cash inflow from financing activities
f. Cash outflow from financing activities

28. **Corporate Statement of Cash Flows** (LO 3)
Individual companies often use unique methods to prepare and present financial data. Take the case of Microsoft Corporation. Presented next are the exact line items, in random order, that appeared in the initial section of a recent statement of cash flows prepared by Microsoft. (Amounts are expressed in millions of dollars.)

Accounts receivable	$(146)
Inventories	23
Current liabilities	360
Net income	1,146
Other current assets	(27)
Depreciation and amortization	237
Net cash from operations	1,593

Required:
Prepare the initial section of Microsoft's statement of cash flows using the format shown in Exhibit 14.3.

29. **Net Income vs. Net Cash Flow from Operating Activities** (LO 1)
Conner Peripherals, Inc., manufactures computer disk drives and related computer products. Connor Peripherals suffered a loss of nearly $450 million in a recent year. However, the company's statement of cash flows for that year reported a net cash flow from operating activities of approximately $20 million.

Required:
How could Conner incur a large loss in a given year but still have a positive cash flow from operating activities for that year?

30. **Completing a Statement of Cash Flows** (LO 3)
Following is a partially completed statement of cash flows for Brigham Company. (Amounts are expressed in thousands of dollars.)

Cash flows from operating activities:	
Net income	$ 1,433
Adjustments to reconcile net income to net cash provided by operating activities:	
Depreciation expense	?
Gain on sale of land	(115)
Changes in current assets and liabilities:	
Increase in accounts receivable	(863)
Decrease in inventories	350
Decrease in prepaid expenses	667
Decrease in short-term notes payable	(400)
Decrease in accrued liabilities	(1,004)
Net cash provided by operating activities	$?

(continued)

Cash flows from investing activities:	
Sale of land	$?
Purchase of property, plant & equipment	(7,639)
Net cash used by investing activities	$ (1,113)
Cash flows from financing activities:	
Sale of common stock	$ 6,329
Dividend payments	?
Net cash provided by financing activities	$ 4,072
Net increase in cash	$ 4,115
Cash balance, December 31, 1997	?
Cash balance, December 31, 1998	$11,332

Required:

1. What method does Brigham Company use to prepare its statement of cash flows?
2. Complete Brigham's statement of cash flows.
3. What was Brigham's largest source of cash during the year in question?

31. **Classification of Cash Flows from Sales of Debt and Equity Securities** (LO 2)
Lodi Corporation had the following sales of debt and equity securities during its fiscal year just ended:

January 12:	300 shares of Exxon common stock classified as available-for-sale securities.
March 19:	42,500 shares of a controlling investment in MacDonald Manufacturing, Inc.
June 4:	300 short-term government securities classified as cash equivalents.
July 16:	500 shares of IBM common stock classified as trading securities.
October 3:	11,400 shares of Othello Restaurants, Inc., classified as an influential but noncontrolling investment.

Required:
Indicate how the cash receipts from each sale would be reported in Lodi's statement of cash flows.

32. **Corporate Statement of Cash Flows** (LO 2)
Refer to Outback Steakhouse's statements of cash flows included in the annual report in the appendix of this text.

Required:

1. What method does Outback use to prepare its statement of cash flows?
2. Does Outback have a "normal" relationship between net income and net cash flow from operating activities? Explain.
3. What was Outback's largest cash outflow from investing activities in 1996? What was Outback's largest cash inflow from financing activities in 1996?
4. What supplemental disclosures does Outback include in its statement of cash flows?

33. **Interpreting Cash-Flow Data** (LO 1)
Over a recent three-year period, Kellogg Company's statements of cash flows revealed cumulative increases in the company's accounts receivable of $145 million.

Required:

1. How does an increase in accounts receivable affect a company's net cash flow from operating activities?
2. If a company's accounts receivable balance is continually increasing from one year to the next, does that indicate, necessarily, that the firm is doing a poor job of "managing" or collecting its accounts receivable? Explain.

34. **Analyzing Cash-Flow Effects** (LO 3)
Motta Storage Company had the following balances in its Equipment and Accumulated Depreciation, Equipment accounts at the beginning and end of 1998.

	January 1, 1998	December 31, 1998
Equipment	$100,000	$120,000
Accumulated Depreciation, Equipment	25,000	18,000

During 1998, Motta engaged in the following transactions involving equipment:

March 9: Purchased new equipment for $40,000.
July 16: Sold for $16,500 equipment that originally cost $20,000 and had accumulated depreciation of $12,000.

Required:

1. How much depreciation expense did Motta Storage Company record on its equipment during 1998?
2. Indicate how Motta's depreciation expense and its transactions involving equipment would appear in the company's 1998 statement of cash flows, assuming the company uses the indirect method of preparing a statement of cash flows.

35. **Comparative Analysis of Cash Flows** (LO 4)
The following data were included in a recent annual report of Whole Foods Market, Inc., a firm headquartered in Austin, Texas.

	Year 1	Year 2	Year 3
Net income	$ 3,716,084	$ 3,818,190	$ 8,638,658
Net cash flow from operating activities	7,460,501	12,556,072	15,390,336
Net cash flow from investing activities	(7,792,408)	(41,527,077)	(32,850,636)
Net cash flow from financing activities	15,113,487	17,478,816	14,982,854

Required:

1. Why is a company's net income typically less than its net cash flow from operating activities?
2. Why do most companies, including Whole Foods, typically have negative cash flows from investing activities?
3. Over the three-year period for which data are reported, what type of activities was the largest source of funds for Whole Foods? Do business executives want these activities to be their firm's principal source of funds? Explain.

36. Cash Flow per Share (LO 5)
The following data were included in the a recent annual report of the large discount retailer, Dollar General Corporation.

	Year 1	Year 2	Year 3
Net income	$35,574,000	$48,557,000	$73,634,000
Net cash flow from operating activities	42,713,000	36,196,000	43,257,000
Weighted-average number of shares of common stock outstanding	66,306,000	67,281,000	69,009,000
Preferred stock dividends paid	—	—	772,000

Required:
1. Compute Dollar General's earnings per share and cash flow per share for each year listed.
2. For each year, express Dollar General's earnings per share as a percentage of its cash flow per share.
3. What factors possibly accounted for Dollar General's net cash flow from operating activities being less than the firm's net income in Year 2 and Year 3? Why would a potential investor in this firm want to identify these factors? Explain.

37. (*Appendix*) Account-Analysis Technique of Determining Cash Flows (LO 6)
Micah Manufacturing, Inc., had total sales of $4,232,000 during 1998, 50 percent of which were made on credit. On January 1, 1998, Micah had accounts receivable of $237,100, while on December 31, 1998, the company had accounts receivable of $303,900.

Required:
1. Assuming that Micah collects all of its credit sales, use the account-analysis technique to determine the cash collected from its customers during 1998.
2. For which method of preparing a statement of cash flows, the direct or indirect method, is the account-analysis technique useful?

38. (*Appendix*) Account-Analysis Technique of Determining Cash Flows (LO 6)
On January 1, 1998, Nahum Corporation had salaries payable of $22,340. The year-end balance of this account was $17,890. Nahum's salaries expense during 1998 was $957,316.

Required:
Using the account-analysis technique, determine the amount of salaries paid by Nahum during 1998.

PROBLEM SET A

39. Classification of Cash Flows (LO 2)
Following are line items included in recent statements of cash flows prepared by Tuesday Morning Corporation, a discount retailer, and America Online, Inc., a leading provider of on-line information and entertainment services.

_________ Repurchase of common stock
_________ Interest received
_________ Income taxes refunded
_________ Principal payments on long-term notes payable
_________ Cash paid to suppliers and employees
_________ Purchase of property and equipment
_________ Proceeds from (long-term) note payable
_________ Principal payments under capital lease obligations
_________ Payment of dividends on convertible redeemable preferred stock
_________ Principal payments on mortgages
_________ Proceeds from common stock offering
_________ Loans to officers
_________ Proceeds from the sale of property, plant & equipment
_________ Cash received from customers

Required:
Classify each of the line items listed as one of the following:
a. Cash inflow from operating activities
b. Cash outflow from operating activities
c. Cash inflow from investing activities
d. Cash outflow from investing activities
e. Cash inflow from financing activities
f. Cash outflow from financing activities

40. **Corporate Statement of Cash Flows** (LO 3)
Following are the line items included in a recent statement of cash flows prepared by Goody's Family Clothing, Inc. (Amounts are expressed in thousands of dollars.)

Proceeds from sale of long-term investments	$ 8,077
Depreciation and amortization	5,285
Increase in miscellaneous current assets	(1,396)
Increase in accounts payable	12,590
Purchase of long-term investments	(34,959)
Net income	16,214
Increase in accrued liabilities	4,072
Proceeds from sale of property and equipment	192
Increase in inventories	(11,320)
Long-term loans	500
Reductions of long-term debt	(172)
Gain on disposal of long-term assets	(135)
Issuance of common stock	126
Cash and cash equivalents, beginning of the year	31,350
Increase in income taxes payable	2,108
Acquisitions of property and equipment	(11,043)
Net increase (decrease) in cash and cash equivalents	?
Cash and cash equivalents, end of year	?

Required:
Prepare Goody's statement of cash flows using the indirect method.

41. **Determining Net Cash Flow from Operating Activities, Indirect Method** (LO 1, 3)
Following is an income statement for Cline Pacific Corporation for the year ended December 31, 1998, and a schedule listing the company's current assets and current liabilities at the end of 1997 and 1998.

CLINE PACIFIC CORPORATION
INCOME STATEMENT
FOR THE YEAR ENDED DECEMBER 31, 1998

Sales		$77,600
Cost of goods sold		44,400
Gross profit		$33,200
Operating expenses:		
Selling & general expenses	$ 8,800	
Depreciation expense	1,900	10,700
Operating income		$22,500
Gain on sale of land		5,500
Income before income tax		$28,000
Income tax expense		11,200
Net income		$16,800

	1997	1998
Cash	$11,700	$ 4,100
Accounts receivable	4,500	9,800
Inventory	6,700	11,300
Prepaid expenses	3,500	800
Accounts payable	2,900	5,600
Accrued liabilities	1,600	2,800

Required:
1. Prepare a schedule documenting Cline Pacific Corporation's net cash flow from operating activities for the year ended December 31, 1998, using the indirect method.
2. Briefly evaluate the schedule you prepared in (1). Does this schedule provide any clues regarding the financial health of Cline Pacific? Explain.

42. **(*Appendix*) Determining Net Cash Flow from Operating Activities, Direct Method** (LO 6)

Problem 41 presents an income statement for Cline Pacific Corporation for the year ended December 31, 1998, and the company's current assets and current liabilities at the end of 1997 and 1998. Following is additional information obtained from Cline Pacific's 1998 accounting records.

a.	Collections of accounts receivable	$72,300*
b.	Merchandise purchases	49,000*
c.	Payments to suppliers (of merchandise)	46,300
d.	Payments of accrued (operating) liabilities	1,600
e.	Payments of operating expenses	2,500
f.	Prepayments of operating expenses	800
g.	Expiration of prepaid (operating) expenses	3,500
h.	Payment of 1998 income tax expense	11,200
i.	Accrual of unpaid operating expenses at year-end	2,800
j.	Year-end adjusting entry to record depreciation expense	1,900

*All of Cline Pacific's sales and merchandise purchases are made on a credit basis.

Required:

1. Using the account-analysis technique illustrated in the text, confirm that Cline Pacific Corporation collected cash of $72,300 from its customers during 1998.
2. Prepare a schedule documenting Cline Pacific Corporation's net cash flow from operating activities for the year ended December 31, 1998, using the direct method.

43. **Preparing a Statement of Cash Flows, Indirect Method** (LO 3)
Following is an income statement for Knob Hill, Inc., for the year ended December 31, 1998, and the company's balance sheets as of December 31, 1997 and 1998.

KNOB HILL, INC.
INCOME STATEMENT
FOR THE YEAR ENDED DECEMBER 31, 1998

Sales		$92,900
Cost of goods sold		36,800
Gross profit		$56,100
Operating expenses:		
Selling & general expenses	$14,600	
Depreciation expense	5,700	20,300
Operating income		$35,800
Loss on sale of land		2,500
Income before income tax		$33,300
Income tax expense		13,300
Net income		$20,000

KNOB HILL, INC.
BALANCE SHEETS
DECEMBER 31, 1997 AND 1998

		1997		1998
Assets				
Cash		$12,100		$36,500
Accounts receivable		10,600		12,700
Inventory		14,700		13,000
Prepaid expenses		1,300		700
Total current assets		$38,700		$62,900
Equipment	$52,000		$52,000	
Less accumulated depreciation	16,300	35,700	22,000	30,000
Investment in land		5,100		—
Total assets		$79,500		$92,900

(*continued*)

	1997	1998
Liabilities		
Accounts payable	$ 7,100	$ 5,200
Accrued liabilities	3,300	3,700
Total current liabilities	$10,400	$ 8,900
Stockholders' Equity		
Common stock	$ 4,500	$ 4,800
Additional paid-in capital	18,200	20,300
Retained earnings	46,400	58,900
Total stockholders' equity	$69,100	$84,000
Total liabilities and stockholders' equity	$79,500	$92,900

The prepaid expenses and accrued liabilities included in Knob Hill's balance sheets involve selling or general (operating) expenses. All of Knob Hill's sales and merchandise purchases are made on a credit basis. Following is additional financial information that was obtained from Knob Hill's accounting records for 1998:

a.	Collections of accounts receivable	$90,800
b.	Purchases of merchandise	35,100
c.	Payments of accrued (operating) liabilities	3,300
d.	Payments of operating expenses	9,600
e.	Prepayments of operating expenses	700
f.	Expiration of prepaid (operating) expenses	1,300
g.	Payments to suppliers	37,000
h.	Proceeds from sale of land	2,600
i.	Sale of 300 shares of $1 par value common stock for $8 per share	2,400
j.	Declaration and payment of cash dividends on common stock	7,500
k.	Payment of 1998 income taxes	13,300
l.	Accrual of unpaid operating expenses at year-end	3,700
m.	Year-end adjusting entry to record depreciation expense on equipment	5,700

Required:
Prepare a statement of cash flows for Knob Hill for the year ended December 31, 1998, using the indirect method.

44. **(*Appendix*) Preparing a Statement of Cash Flows, Direct Method** (LO 6)
Refer to the information presented in Problem 43 for Knob Hill, Inc.

Required:
Prepare a statement of cash flows for Knob Hill for the year ended December 31, 1998, using the direct method.

45. **Comparative Analysis of Cash Flows** (LO 4)
Following are data obtained from recent financial statements of Biogen, Inc., one of the nation's leading biotechnology firms. (Amounts are expressed in thousands of dollars.)

	Year 1	Year 2	Year 3	Year 4	Year 5
Net income	$ 7,720	$ 7,186	$38,311	$32,417	$ (4,987)
Net cash flow from operating activities	10,721	5,884	43,052	47,570	34,886
Net cash flow from investing activities	(29,551)	(48,334)	(23,869)	(66,695)	(70,295)
Net cash flow from financing activities	(1,797)	86,253	10,033	7,808	15,545

Required:

1. In Year 5, Biogen's operating activities produced almost $35 million in positive cash flow although the firm had a loss of approximately $5 million for the year. How is this possible?
2. Explain how a company's net income can exceed its net cash flow from operating activities, which was the case for Biogen in Year 2.
3. Biogen's total assets increased by more than 50 percent between Year 1 and Year 5. What activities were the largest source of the funds used to finance this growth?
4. What factor or factors likely account for the large negative net cash flows from investing activities experienced by Biogen between Year 1 and Year 5?

46. Cash Flow per Share (LO 5)

Following are selected financial data for Claire's Stores, Inc., a women's apparel retailer, and Pioneer Standard Electronics, Inc., a distributor of industrial electronic supplies and components.

	Year 1	Year 2	Year 3
Claire's Stores:			
Net income	$14,551,000	$23,634,000	$23,855,000
Net cash flow from operating activities	$34,430,000	$34,750,000	$37,030,000
Weighted-average number of shares of common stock outstanding (in millions)	21.8	22.0	22.2
Pioneer Standard Electronics:			
Net income	$5,327,000	$12,913,000	$19,676,000
Net cash flow from operating activities	$2,450,000	$16,104,000	$9,531,000
Weighted-average number of shares of common stock outstanding (in millions)	8.2	9.2	10.1

Neither Claire's Stores nor Pioneer Standard Electronics has preferred stock outstanding.

Required:

1. Compute earnings per share and cash flow per share for Claire's Stores and Pioneer Standard Electronics for Year 1 through Year 3.
2. For each year, express each company's earnings per share as a percentage of its cash flow per share.

3. Which of these two companies had a more "normal" relationship between earnings per share and cash flow per share for the period Year 1 through Year 3? Explain.
4. Why does the FASB prohibit companies from disclosing cash flow per share in their annual financial statements?

PROBLEM SET B

47. Classification of Cash Flows (LO 2)

Following are line items included in recent statements of cash flows prepared by United States Surgical Corporation, a medical supply company, and Pacific Scientific Corporation, a company that manufactures electrical equipment.

________ Dividends paid
________ Acquisition of common stock for treasury
________ Long-term borrowings under credit agreements
________ Cash received from customers
________ Proceeds from disposition of property
________ Cash paid to vendors, suppliers, and employees
________ Issuance of common stock
________ Income tax paid
________ Payments for business acquisitions
________ Additions to property, plant & equipment
________ Interest payments

Required:
Classify each of the line items listed as one of the following:
a. Cash inflow from operating activities
b. Cash outflow from operating activities
c. Cash inflow from investing activities
d. Cash outflow from investing activities
e. Cash inflow from financing activities
f. Cash outflow from financing activities

48. Corporate Statement of Cash Flows (LO 3)

Following are the line items included in a recent statement of cash flows prepared by Hormel Foods Corporation. (Amounts are expressed in thousands of dollars.)

Amortization of intangibles	$ 2,956
Loss on sale of long-term investments	4,368
Increase in accounts receivable	(9,882)
Cash and cash equivalents, beginning of the year	157,558
Decrease in income taxes payable	(5,859)
Sale of long-term investments	3,309
Acquisitions of businesses	(9,750)
Purchase of property & equipment	(65,441)
Sale of property & equipment	1,575
Depreciation	33,655
Acquisition of miscellaneous long-term assets	(3,973)

Decrease in inventories and prepaid expenses	$ 10,930
Purchase of long-term investments	(357)
Increase in accounts payable and accrued liabilities	40,686
Proceeds from long-term borrowings	5,000
Net income	117,975
Dividends paid on common stock	(38,463)
Loss on sale of idle facility	4,312
Net increase (decrease) in cash and cash equivalents	?
Cash and cash equivalents, end of the year	?

Required:
Prepare Hormel's statement of cash flows using the indirect method.

49. **Determining Net Cash Flow from Operating Activities, Indirect Method** (LO 1, 3) Following is an income statement for Yates & Callahan, Inc., for the year ended December 31, 1998, and a schedule listing the company's current assets and current liabilities at the end of 1997 and 1998.

YATES & CALLAHAN, INC.
INCOME STATEMENT
FOR THE YEAR ENDED DECEMBER 31, 1998

Sales		$88,200
Cost of goods sold		39,800
Gross profit		$48,400
Operating expenses:		
Selling & general	$ 6,200	
Depreciation expense	2,700	8,900
Operating income		$39,500
Loss on sale of equipment		1,400
Income before income tax		$38,100
Income tax expense		15,200
Net income		$22,900

	1997	1998
Cash	$ 5,700	$ 6,100
Accounts receivable	7,500	6,800
Inventory	7,700	5,300
Prepaid expenses	1,200	1,800
Accounts payable	2,500	2,600
Accrued liabilities	1,100	900

Required:
1. Prepare a schedule documenting Yates & Callahan's net cash flow from operating activities for the year ended December 31, 1998, using the indirect method.
2. Briefly evaluate the schedule you prepared in (1). Does this schedule of cash flows from operating activities provide any clues regarding the financial health of Yates & Callahan? Explain.

50. (*Appendix*) Determining Net Cash Flow from Operating Activities, Direct Method (LO 6)

Problem 49 presents an income statement for Yates & Callahan, Inc., for the year ended December 31, 1998, and the company's current assets and current liabilities at the end of 1997 and 1998. Following is additional information obtained from Yates & Callahan's 1998 accounting records.

a.	Collections of accounts receivable	$88,900*
b.	Merchandise purchases	37,400*
c.	Payments to suppliers (of merchandise)	37,300
d.	Payments of accrued (operating) liabilities	1,100
e.	Payments of operating expenses	4,100
f.	Prepayments of operating expenses	1,800
g.	Expiration of prepaid (operating) expenses	1,200
h.	Payment of 1998 income tax expense	15,200
i.	Accrual of unpaid operating expenses at year-end	900
j.	Year-end adjusting entry to record depreciation expense	2,700

*All of Yates & Callahan's sales and merchandise purchases are made on a credit basis.

Required:

1. Using the account-analysis technique illustrated in the text, confirm that Yates & Callahan collected cash of $88,900 from its customers during 1998.
2. Prepare a schedule documenting Yates & Callahan's net cash flow from operating activities for the year ended December 31, 1998, using the direct method.

51. Preparing a Statement of Cash Flows, Indirect Method (LO 3)

Following is an income statement for Back Bay Corporation, for the year ended December 31, 1998, and the company's balance sheets as of December 31, 1997 and 1998.

BACK BAY CORPORATION
INCOME STATEMENT
FOR THE YEAR ENDED DECEMBER 31, 1998

Sales		$82,300
Cost of goods sold		41,800
Gross profit		$40,500
Operating expenses:		
Selling & general expenses	$12,600	
Depreciation expense	2,400	15,000
Operating income		$25,500
Gain on sale of equipment		1,500
Income before income tax		$27,000
Income tax expense		10,800
Net income		$16,200

BACK BAY CORPORATION
BALANCE SHEETS
DECEMBER 31, 1997 AND 1998

		1997		1998
Assets				
Cash		$ 9,200		$18,700
Accounts receivable		8,300		14,400
Inventory		12,500		14,700
Prepaid expenses		800		300
Total current assets		$30,800		$48,100
Equipment	$39,200		$29,200	
Less accumulated depreciation	8,000	31,200	1,400	27,800
Total assets		$62,000		$75,900
Liabilities				
Accounts payable		$ 7,100		$ 2,700
Accrued liabilities		3,300		3,600
Total current liabilities		$10,400		$ 6,300
Long-term note payable		—		$10,000
Stockholders' Equity				
Common stock		$12,000		$12,000
Additional paid-in capital		24,000		24,000
Retained earnings		15,600		23,600
Total stockholders' equity		$51,600		$59,600
Total liabilities and stockholders' equity		$62,000		$75,900

The prepaid expenses and accrued liabilities included in Back Bay's balance sheets involve selling or general (operating) expenses. All of Back Bay's sales and merchandise purchases are made on a credit basis. Following is additional financial information obtained from Back Bay's accounting records for 1998:

a.	Collections of accounts receivable			$76,200
b.	Purchases of merchandise			44,000
c.	Payments of accrued (operating) liabilities			3,300
d.	Payments of operating expenses			8,200
e.	Prepayments of operating expenses			300
f.	Expiration of prepaid (operating) expenses			800
g.	Payments to suppliers			48,400
h.	Sale of piece of equipment:			
	Selling price		$2,500	
	Original cost	$10,000		
	Less accumulated depreciation	(9,000)		
	Book value		1,000	
	Gain			1,500

i.	Bank loan obtained at year-end	$10,000
j.	Declaration and payment of cash dividends on common stock	8,200
k.	Payment of 1998 income taxes	10,800
l.	Accrual of unpaid operating expenses at year-end	3,600
m.	Year-end adjusting entry to record depreciation expense on equipment	2,400

Required:
Prepare a statement of cash flows for Back Bay for the year ended December 31, 1998, using the indirect method.

52. **(*Appendix*) Preparing a Statement of Cash Flows, Direct Method** (LO 6)
Refer to the information presented in Problem 51 for Back Bay Corporation.

Required:
Prepare a statement of cash flows for Back Bay for the year ended December 31, 1998, using the direct method.

53. **Comparative Analysis of Cash Flows** (LO 4)
The Dress Barn, Inc., operates a chain of women's apparel stores, while Tommy Hilfiger Corporation markets sportswear through department stores and specialty stores. The following schedule presents cash-flow data for these two companies for a recent three-year period.

	Year 1	Year 2	Year 3
Dress Barn:			
Net cash flow from operating activities	$24,391,633	$29,046,893	$23,704,087
Net cash flow from investing activities	(21,704,345)	(25,032,079)	(27,678,458)
Net cash flow from financing activities	354,795	1,408,732	578,585
Tommy Hilfiger:			
Net cash flow from operating activities	$(8,589,000)	$ 4,335,000	$ 4,326,000
Net cash flow from investing activities	(3,451,000)	(12,186,000)	(50,776,000)
Net cash flow from financing activities	14,300,000	24,116,000	65,924,000

Over the three-year period for which data are presented, Dress Barn purchased $36 million of property and equipment, compared with $33 million of such purchases by Tommy Hilfiger. Dress Barn raised approximately $2 million by issuing common stock during this time frame, compared with $112 million raised in this manner by Tommy Hilfiger.

Required:
1. What activities (operating, investing, or financing) were the principal source of funds for Dress Barn and Tommy Hilfiger during the period for which data are presented?
2. For each year over this period, Dress Barn's net income was considerably less than its net cash flow from operating activities. Is this the "normal" relationship between net income and net operating cash flow? Explain.

3. In Year 3, Tommy Hilfiger reported a net income of $25.3 million, which was considerably more than its $4.3 million net cash flow from operating activities for that year. What factor or factors may have accounted for the large disparity between these two amounts?
4. To remain financially viable over the long run, a company's principal source of funds must be its operating activities. Do you agree with that statement? Explain.

54. **Cash Flow Per Share** (LO 5)
Following is selected financial information for two companies, Airgas, Inc., a supplier of medical and specialty gases and related equipment, and Toll Brothers, Inc., a home builder.

	Year 1	Year 2	Year 3
Airgas:			
Net income	$ 7,292,000	$ 12,469,000	$ 20,290,000
Net cash flow from operating activities	$ 51,682,000	$ 58,321,000	$ 64,798,000
Weighted-average number of shares of common stock outstanding (in millions)	28.0	30.9	32.4
Toll Brothers:			
Net income	$ 16,538,000	$ 28,058,000	$ 36,177,000
Net cash flow from operating activities	$(25,898,000)	$(54,196,000)	$(29,514,000)
Weighted-average number of shares of common stock outstanding (in millions)	33.2	33.5	33.6

Neither Airgas nor Toll Brothers has preferred stock outstanding.

Required:
1. Compute earnings per share and cash flow per share for Airgas and Toll Brothers for Year 1 through Year 3.
2. For each year, express each company's earnings per share as a percentage of its cash flow per share.
3. What factor or factors may have accounted for the large difference between Airgas's net income and its net cash flow from operating activities over the given three-year period?
4. During the period Year 1–Year 3, Toll Brothers' inventory increased by more than $280 million. What effect did this factor have on the company's net cash flow from operating activities over this time frame? Explain.
5. Over the long run, what relationship would you expect to observe between a company's net income and its net cash flow from operating activities? Why?

CASES

55. **Classification of Cash Flows by Foreign Companies** (LO 2)
As noted in this chapter, the statement of cash flows is not a mandatory financial statement in most countries. However, large multinational corporations often include a statement of cash flows in their annual reports whether or not they are required to do so by their home country's accounting standards.

Following are line items included in recent statements of cash flows issued by the following foreign-based corporations: Telecom Corporation of New Zealand, Lloyd's of London (Great Britain), Ito-Yokado Co., Ltd. (Japan), Barclay's plc (Great Britain), Thyssen AG (Germany), and San Miguel Corporation (Philippines).

_________ Disposals of fixed assets
_________ Increase in gross financial indebtedness
_________ Preference dividends paid
_________ Proceeds from issuance of long-term debt
_________ Purchase of investments
_________ Investment income
_________ Issue of ordinary shares
_________ Purchase of associated undertakings
_________ Cash received from customers
_________ Dividends paid to minority interests
_________ Redemption of (short-term) notes receivable
_________ Interest paid on debt
_________ Proceeds from sales of distribution and food center assets
_________ Payments under revolving credit facilities
_________ Redemption of preference shares
_________ Prior year cash dividend

Required:
Indicate how you believe each of the listed items would appear in a statement of cash flows prepared by a U.S. firm. Use the following key:

a. Cash inflow from operating activities
b. Cash outflow from operating activities
c. Cash inflow from investing activities
d. Cash outflow from investing activities
e. Cash inflow from financing activities
f. Cash outflow from financing activities

If you are unsure of the nature of a given item, list an assumption regarding your interpretation of that item and then classify it accordingly.

56. Safeguarding Cash in a Small Business (LO 1)
Speedy Papers is a small business that provides word processing services to students of a large state university. The owner of the business supervises six typists (word processors) who work from a leased office in the university's student union. Approximately 50 percent of the company's services are provided on a credit basis with terms of n/30. The accounting records of Speedy Papers are maintained by a part-time bookkeeper. The bookkeeper also processes cash collections and cash disbursements. These responsibilities include making daily cash deposits and reconciling the monthly bank statement.

Recently, the owner of Speedy Papers has become concerned by a negative trend in the business's cash flows. After reviewing the business's bank statements for the past six months and those for the comparable period in the two previous years, the owner determined that the average monthly net cash inflow is down approximately 10 percent for the current year compared with the two previous years. This downward trend in cash flows has occurred despite the owner's impression that Speedy Papers has been busier than ever in recent months.

After work one night, the owner reviewed the cash receipts records of the business. She compared the daily cash receipts entered in the accounting records for two recent months with the daily bank deposit slips, finding no differences. While flipping through the other accounting records, something did catch her eye. The business's write-offs of uncollectible accounts receivable had increased considerably in the past six months. "Aha!" the owner thought to herself. "Here's the problem. Maybe I'll have to rethink my credit policy."

Required:
Is the owner's analysis of Speedy Papers' negative cash-flow trend necessarily correct? Explain. Write a memo to the owner that identifies further steps she could take to investigate the source of her business's cash-flow problem. Also identify in the memo control activities she could implement to enhance the degree of control over the business's cash and cash processing functions.

57. **Manipulation of Cash-Flow Data** (LO 1)

Suppose that you are the CEO of a major corporation. Your company's fiscal year will be ending in three weeks. This year has not been a memorable one. Your company will barely eke out a profit for the year. You realize that financial analysts pay considerable attention to both earnings per share and cash flow per share. There is not much you can do at this late date to improve your company's earnings per share for the year without violating GAAP. However, you have the ability to significantly improve your firm's reported cash flow per share for the year without violating GAAP. For example, you can instruct your collections department to make every effort to collect outstanding receivables even to the point of offering customers small price concessions on purchases they will make in coming months. You can also delay the payment of many expenses until next year.

Required:
1. Is it unethical for business executives to intentionally "manage" or manipulate their firms' reported cash-flow data although there are no explicit rules prohibiting them from doing so? Defend your answer.
2. In your opinion, should rule-making bodies in the accounting profession prohibit businesses from manipulating reported cash-flow data? Again, support your answer.

PROJECTS

58. **The FASB and Cash Flows**

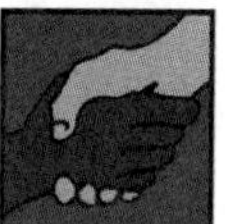

The FASB has stated that it prefers the direct method of preparing a statement of cash flows. Why? Because the direct method provides more useful information to financial decision makers than the indirect method. Nevertheless, more than 97 percent of all large corporations use the indirect method of preparing their annual statements of cash flows. Regarding a related financial reporting issue, the FASB prohibits businesses from reporting cash flow per share. However, investors and a wide range of other decision makers demand and obtain cash flow per share data from financial analysts and apparently use that data when making important financial decisions.

Required:
1. Break into your project groups for a discussion of the FASB's accounting rules for cash flows. Specifically address the following issues:
    a. Should the FASB continue to allow businesses to use either the direct or indirect method of preparing a statement of cash flows? Develop an argument defending the FASB's present stance on this issue and a counterargument suggesting that the FASB should require the direct method to be used exclusively. When appropriate, refer to the key attributes of accounting information discussed in Chapter 2 and other relevant accounting concepts.
    b. Should the FASB allow businesses to report cash flow per share data in their periodic financial statements? Develop an argument defending the FASB's present stance on this issue and a counterargument suggesting that the FASB should allow cash flow per share data to be reported by businesses. Again, when appropriate, refer to the key attributes of accounting information discussed in Chapter 2 and other relevant accounting concepts.

2. One group member should be prepared to provide a brief oral report to the class of the group's discussion and analysis of the issues raised in (1).

59. Cash Management Practices

In recent years, "cash management" has become a hot topic among the executives of large corporations that may have hundreds of millions, if not billions, of dollars of cash at any point in time.

Required:

1. Research the topic of cash management in your school's library, focusing particular attention on recent articles in business periodicals addressing this topic.
2. Write a brief report summarizing three cash management practices that have been used successfully in recent years by businesses of any size.

60. Comparing Cash Flows across Industries

Select three large public companies that make their financial statements available via the Internet either at their own Web site or the EDGAR (electronic data gathering and retrieval) Web site maintained by the Securities and Exchange Commission. One of these companies should be involved in merchandising, another in manufacturing, while the final company should be a service firm.

Required:

1. Access the most recent annual report or 10-K statement of each of the firms you selected. These annual reports or 10-Ks will contain statements of cash flows for each firm for the past three years. Compare and contrast the cash-flow data of these firms. Prepare appropriate graphs or exhibits to highlight the similarities and differences in these data.
2. Discuss in a written report the major differences and similarities apparent in the cash-flow data of the three firms you selected. Also, attempt to identify the source or sources of the major differences in these firms' cash-flow data. Attach to your report the graphs or exhibits you prepared in (1). Document in your report the Web site addresses from which you collected the data for this project.

Financial Statement Analysis 15

"I keep six honest serving-men
(They taught me all I knew);
Their names are What and Why and When
And How and Where and Who."
Rudyard Kipling

LEARNING OBJECTIVES

After studying this chapter, you should be able to do the following:

1. Discuss the objectives of financial statement analysis for different types of decision makers.
2. Identify the key sources of information for financial statement analysis.
3. Prepare trend analyses of financial statement data.
4. Prepare common-sized financial statements.
5. Compute key financial ratios including liquidity, leverage, activity, profitability, and market strength ratios.
6. Assess earnings quality.

FOCUS ON DECISION MAKING

Too-Good-to-Be-True Financial Statements Are Usually Too Good to Be True

On May 19, 1987, *The Wall Street Journal* reported that ZZZZ Best Company, Inc., had signed a contract for a $13.8 million building restoration project. This project was just the most recent of a series of such jobs obtained by ZZZZ Best (pronounced "zee best"), a leading firm in the building restoration industry. Located in the San Fernando Valley of southern California, ZZZZ Best had begun operations in the fall of 1982 as a small, door-to-door carpet-cleaning operation. Under the direction of Barry Minkow, the 16-year-old who founded the company and initially operated it from his parents' garage, ZZZZ Best experienced explosive growth during the first few years of its existence. In the three-year period from 1984 to 1987, the company's reported net income surged from less than $200,000 to more than $5 million on revenues of $50 million.

When ZZZZ Best went public in 1986, Minkow became a multimillionaire overnight. By early 1987, Minkow's stock in the company had a market value exceeding $100 million. Minkow's charm and entrepreneurial genius made him a sought-after commodity on the television talk show circuit. On *The Oprah Winfrey Show* in April 1987, Minkow exhorted his peers to "Think big, be big" and encouraged them to adopt his personal motto, "The sky is the limit."

Less than two years after appearing on *The Oprah Winfrey Show,* Barry Minkow began serving a 25-year prison sentence. Tried and convicted on 57 counts of securities fraud, Minkow had been exposed as a fast-talking con artist who bilked the public out of millions of dollars. Federal prosecutors estimate that Minkow cost investors and creditors $100 million. The company that Minkow founded was an elaborate scam. The reported profits of the firm were nonexistent and the huge restoration contracts, imaginary. In July 1987, just three months after the company's stock reached a market value of $220 million, an auction of its few actual assets netted only $62,000. After serving nearly six years of his sentence, Barry Minkow was released from federal prison in December 1994. Shortly thereafter, Minkow documented his rags-to-riches-to-rags story in his autobiography entitled *Clean Sweep.*

Minkow succeeded in duping investors for several years because they failed to rigorously analyze his company's financial statements. For example, investors failed to notice that ZZZZ Best's reported revenues exceeded the total annual revenues of the small building restoration industry. Likewise, the number of multimillion-dollar restoration jobs allegedly obtained by ZZZZ Best surpassed the total number of such jobs available during the mid-1980s according to industry statistics. Finally, ZZZZ Best's gross profit percentage was much higher than the normal gross profit percentage within the building restoration industry.

The lesson to be learned from ZZZZ Best and similar financial frauds is for investors to do their homework before making a decision to invest their hard-earned savings. A careful, painstaking analysis of financial statements should reveal when a company's profits are too good to be true.

Source: M. C. Knapp, "ZZZZ Best Company, Inc.," *Contemporary Auditing, Issues and Cases,* 2d ed. (Minneapolis/St. Paul: West Publishing Company, 1996).

In earlier chapters, we considered a wide array of financial ratios and other financial measures that can be used to analyze specific financial statement components. In this chapter, we take a "big picture" approach to financial statement analysis. Here, we consider several approaches to comprehensively analyzing the financial performance and financial condition of businesses as reflected by their income statements and balance sheets, respectively. Since Chapter 14 discussed approaches to analyzing and interpreting cash-flow data, the statement of cash flows is not a major focus of this chapter.

The initial section of this chapter identifies the key objectives of financial statement analysis and the principal sources of information used when analyzing financial statement data. Specific analytical techniques are discussed in the following section. The final section of this chapter identifies factors that influence "earnings quality" and discusses measures decision makers can use to analyze this important characteristic of earnings data.

FINANCIAL STATEMENT ANALYSIS: MAKING INFORMED ECONOMIC DECISIONS ▲

Recall from Chapter 1 that accounting is principally a service activity whose primary function is to provide information useful to financial decision makers. As proven by the ZZZZ Best fraud discussed in this chapter's opening vignette and other recent financial frauds, decision makers need more than just access to financial data. Decision makers must have the skills to analyze financial data if they are to make informed economic decisions. In this section, we focus on the objectives of financial statement analysis and identify the information sources used by decision makers to obtain and analyze financial statement data.

Objectives of Financial Statement Analysis

LEARNING ◄ OBJECTIVE 1
Discuss the objectives of financial statement analysis for different types of decision makers.

The objectives of financial statement analysis vary across different types of decision makers. Suppliers are very concerned with a given firm's liquidity. A company that has a poor liquidity position may be unable to pay its accounts payable as they come due in the following weeks and months. Bank loan officers, bondholders, and other long-term creditors are more concerned with a firm's ability to generate sufficient profits and cash flows to pay its debts over an extended number of years. The main concern of customers when it comes to financial statement analysis is which businesses will provide a reliable source of products or services. Prospective employees may analyze financial statements to identify companies that offer secure, long-term employment opportunities.

Investors are the decision makers who by necessity must take the most comprehensive approach to financial statement analysis. If you are considering becoming a part owner of Texaco or Tex's Corner Gas Station, you should be concerned with every aspect of those businesses' financial status. For example, you should be concerned with their liquidity. If a company in which you invest encounters short-term, cash-flow problems and cannot pay its suppliers, your investment will likely go down the proverbial drain. Investors also want to be reassured that a firm can retire its long-term debt as it matures. Bondholders and other long-term creditors can seize a company's assets and force the firm out of business if they are not paid on a timely basis. A business's profitability is of obvious concern to investors. Potential investors want to be assured that a company will generate sufficient profits to provide a reasonable rate of return on owners' equity.

This chapter illustrates a comprehensive approach to financial statement analysis that would be suitable to prospective investors. However, the techniques discussed in this chapter can also be used by other decision makers to focus on one or more specific aspects of a business's financial performance or financial condition.

Information Sources for Financial Statement Analysis

LEARNING OBJECTIVE 2 ▶ Identify the key sources of information for financial statement analysis.

A recent television commercial highlights the dilemma of a professional couple who suddenly realize that they should begin creating a portfolio of investments in preparation for their not-too-distant retirement years. Eventually, the couple turns to a local stockbroker to help them select common stocks and other investments for their retirement portfolio. Here, we identify sources of information that can be used by couples planning for retirement, stockbrokers, and a wide range of other parties, including yourself, to obtain financial data regarding individual companies.

ANNUAL REPORTS By now, you are probably very familiar with the annual report of Outback Steakhouse that is included as an appendix to this text. The annual reports of publicly owned companies not only contain financial statements for these firms but are also the principal source of information needed to analyze those financial statements. Many privately owned companies also prepare annual reports for their bankers, customers, employees, and other parties. Typically, a public company's annual report is a condensed version of its 10-K registration statement that it must file each year with the Securities and Exchange Commission (SEC). Investors can request a "hard copy" 10-K for a public company directly from the firm or, for many large companies, access their most recent 10-K at the EDGAR (electronic data gathering and retrieval) Web site maintained by the SEC on the Internet (Web address: *http://www.sec.gov/edgarhp.htm*).

The organizational scheme and content of annual reports vary from company to company. However, most annual reports contain several items of particular interest to investors and other decision makers. These items include financial statements and accompanying footnotes, a financial highlights table, management's discussion and analysis (MD&A) of a firm's financial condition and operating results, and an independent auditor's report.

Most companies include a financial highlights table in their annual report that tracks important financial items over a several-year period. Notice that Outback Steakhouse's annual report contains a three-year financial highlights table that emphasizes the significant growth the company realized in key financial statement items over the period 1994–1996. The MD&A section of an annual report contains a summary discussion of the factors that have recently affected a company's financial status. This section also typically includes a general overview of management's key plans for the future.

A company's independent auditor's report should be read carefully by decision makers. Included in this report are a discussion of such items as departures from generally accepted accounting principles (GAAP) and inconsistent application of those principles. Auditors must also disclose in their reports any conditions that may threaten

Financial Fraud in Cyberspace

As investors have become more sophisticated so, too, have the con artists and flim-flam men—and women—who prey on them. In recent years, growing numbers of investors have begun tapping the Internet for information regarding potential investments. Many such investors have been trapped by "cyberfraud" schemes involving electronic bulletin boards accessed via the Internet. One such scam works something like this. A group of subscribers to an on-line computer service will purchase stock of a small but little known company. Then, one of these subscribers will post a hot tip in an electronic bulletin board regarding this stock. The other participants in the scheme will hype that stock by posting messages confirming that it is a "can't miss" investment. If the scheme is successful, the stock's price will increase rapidly in a period of a few days. The schemers will then sell their stock at the inflated price.

the survival of a firm. Notice in Outback Steakhouse's annual report (page 15) that Deloitte & Touche, a "Big Six" accounting firm, gave the company a "clean bill of health" in an independent auditor's report issued on February 21, 1997.

INVESTMENT ADVISORY SERVICES If you browse through the business section of your college library, you will find an assortment of reference materials published by investment advisory firms. Value Line, Standard & Poor's, Moody's, Dun & Bradstreet, and Robert Morris Associates are among the best known of these firms. The *Value Line Investment Survey,* for example, provides a detailed analysis of key financial statistics and the future prospects of approximately 1,600 public companies. Included in this analysis is Value Line's best estimate of each company's stock price several years into the future. In April 1997, Value Line predicted that Delta Air Lines' common stock would have a price range of $115–$160 per share between 2000 and 2002. At the time, Delta's stock traded for $86 per share.

Decision makers often evaluate a company's financial data by comparing that data to the company's historical norms and to industry norms. For example, suppose that a company has a quick ratio of 1.2 at the end of a given year. Decision makers can better interpret that ratio if they have access to the company's quick ratio in prior years and to the current industry norm. Historical data for companies that do not include a comprehensive financial highlights table in their annual report can be found in financial databases published by investment advisory firms. Disclosure, Inc., distributes a popular computerized financial database that contains information on several thousand companies. Industry norms for a wide range of financial ratios and other financial measures are also available. Two popular sources of such information are *Industry Norms & Key Business Ratios* published by Dun & Bradstreet and *RMA Annual Statement Studies* published by Robert Morris Associates.

OTHER SOURCES Financial and nonfinancial information for individual companies can also be obtained from business periodicals such as *Barron's, Business Week, Forbes,* and *The Wall Street Journal.* A recent trend is for investors and other decision makers to access financial data through a personal computer by logging on to the Internet. Web sites maintained by large public companies nearly always contain extensive information regarding their financial condition, past operating results, and future plans. As mentioned earlier, the EDGAR Web site maintained by the SEC provides recent financial statement data for many large public companies. Do-it-yourself investors can obtain a free directory of on-line financial services and related computer software from the American Association of Individual Investors in Chicago.

ANALYTICAL TECHNIQUES

This section discusses and illustrates three general approaches to financial statement analysis. These approaches are trend analysis, the preparation of common-sized financial statements, and ratio analysis. The methods we consider in this section provide decision makers with powerful tools for analyzing and interpreting financial statements. Nevertheless, these methods also have certain limitations, which we will review briefly.

Decision makers analyze a company's financial statements to identify unusual or unexpected relationships in the firm's financial data. Further investigation, though, is usually required to determine whether these "red flags" are a signal that a company's financial health is changing—for the better or worse. Analytical techniques can also be used to make predictions regarding a given business's future financial performance and financial condition based upon its past financial data. However, changes in a company's operations, its industry, and the overall economic environment can cause historical data to be less than a reliable indicator of the firm's future prospects. Finally, data drawn primarily from companies that have one line of business are used to illustrate analytical techniques in this chapter. You should recognize that financial statement analysis is more difficult for companies that have two or more major lines of business. For such a company, analytical techniques are most useful if they are applied independently to the financial data of each major business segment of the firm.

Trend Analysis

LEARNING OBJECTIVE 3 ▶ Prepare trend analyses of financial statement data.

trend analysis

Much can be learned about a company's financial condition and financial performance by simply studying changes in key financial statement items over a period of time. For example, an investor might plot a company's net income for ten successive years to monitor the company's profitability. To track the proportionate changes in individual financial statement items from period to period, the dollar amounts of these items can be converted into percentages. Investors often use the trend of such percentages to predict future dollar amounts for given financial statement items. The study of percentage changes in financial statement items over a period of time is known as **trend analysis.**

To illustrate trend analysis, suppose that we have an interest in monitoring the net cash flow from operating activities of American Greetings, the large greeting card company. Shown next are the net cash flows from operating activities reported by this company for the period 1994–1996.

1994—$ 75,613,000
1995— 106,998,000
1996— 32,822,000

To apply trend analysis to these data, we must first select a base year and then express each amount as a percentage of the base-year figure. Typically, the first or earliest year for which data are available is selected as the base year. Applying this rule, 1994 becomes the base year for the present example. By dividing each of the dollar amounts in the previous schedule by the base-year figure of $75,613,000, we arrive at the following percentages.

1994—100%
1995—142%
1996— 43%

As suggested earlier, trend analysis provides a simple method of predicting a future financial statement amount. Suppose that we want to predict the net cash flow from operating activities that American Greetings realized in 1997. Unfortunately, the trend percentages just computed are not very useful for this purpose. That is, we cannot be very confident in making an extrapolation to 1997 based upon these trend percentages since they are so volatile. Cash-flow data tend to be more variable and thus more difficult to predict than accrual-basis data.

Let us try another application of trend analysis, this time using accrual-basis data. The following schedule lists the 1992–1995 annual sales of Darden Restaurants, Inc., a company best known for its Red Lobster and Olive Garden restaurants.

1992—$2,542,018,000
1993— 2,737,044,000
1994— 2,962,980,000
1995— 3,163,289,000

Trend analysis can help potential investors identify patterns in a company's financial data and predict sales before making an investment decision. The 1996 downturn of the sales trend of Darden Restaurants, Inc., owner of the Olive Garden and Red Lobster restaurant chains, would have been revealed through trend analysis.

EXHIBIT 15.1 ▼
Darden Restaurants, Inc., Sales Trend: 1992–1996

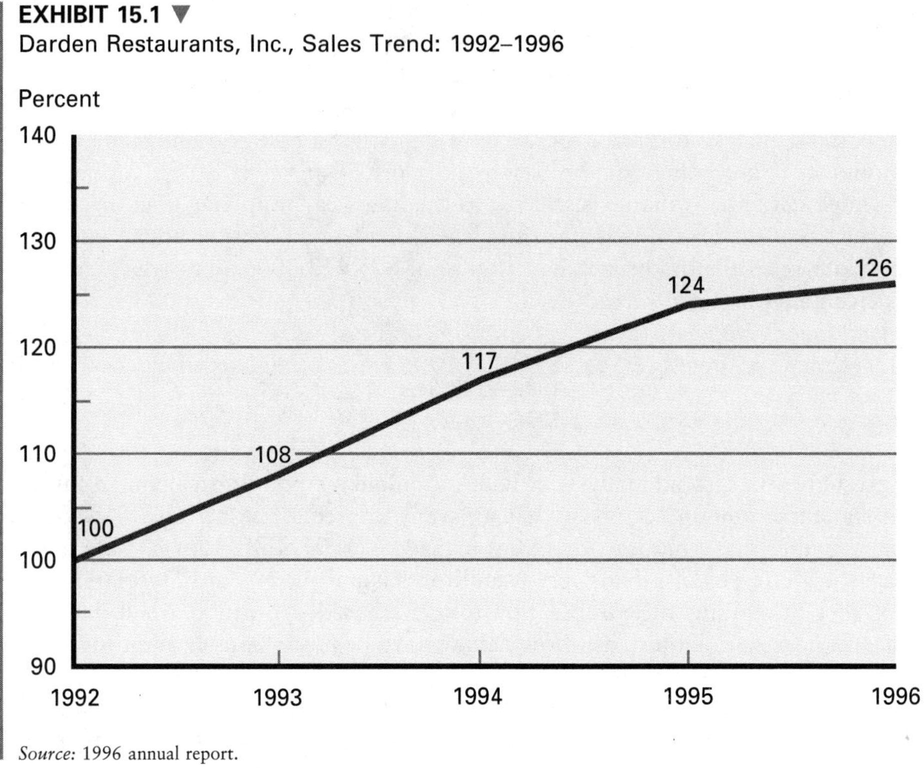

Source: 1996 annual report.

Applying trend analysis, we convert these data to percentages using 1992 as the base year.

1992—100%
1993—108%
1994—117%
1995—124%

Unlike the previous example, the latter percentages reveal a definite pattern in Darden's annual sales. By "eyeballing" this trend, we would predict the company's 1996 sales to be roughly 132 percent of its 1992 sales. Multiplying 132 percent by Darden's 1992 sales, we arrive at predicted sales for 1996 of $3,355,464,000. In fact, Darden's 1996 sales totaled $3,191,779,000. So, our prediction was off by "just" $164 million, or so. The moral of this story is that trend analysis can help decision makers identify patterns in financial data. However, trend analysis is a very crude financial forecasting technique. Although beyond the scope of this text, there are several sophisticated and more reliable techniques decision makers can use to forecast future financial data. You will be introduced to one such technique, regression analysis, a distant cousin of trend analysis, in subsequent business courses.

Trend analysis, and other analytical techniques for that matter, can be enhanced by using computer-based graphics. Computer software packages such as *PowerPoint, Freelance Graphics,* and *Harvard Graphics* allow decision makers to more easily analyze and interpret financial data. Exhibit 15.1 presents the sales trend of Darden's Restaurants for 1992–1996. That exhibit visually documents that Darden's sales trend changed abruptly in 1996. An investor considering a purchase of Darden's common stock in early 1997 would almost certainly have sought an explanation for this downturn in the company's sales trend. The weakening of Darden's sales may have been a temporary "blip" in the financial performance of the company. On the other hand, it may have been an early warning signal of financial problems for the firm.

Common-Sized Financial Statements

LEARNING OBJECTIVE 4
Prepare common-sized financial statements.

common-sized financial statements

Decision makers use common-sized financial statements to obtain a better understanding of the relationships among the items in a financial statement or series of financial statements. In **common-sized financial statements** each line item is expressed as a percentage of a major financial statement component. For example, in a common-sized balance sheet each line item is expressed as a percentage of total assets. In a common-sized income statement each line item is expressed as a percentage of net sales.

To illustrate common-sized financial statements, consider a hypothetical company, Lindsay Hardware Stores, Inc. Exhibit 15.2 contains income statements and common-sized income statements for Lindsay Hardware Stores for the three-year period 1996–1998. Exhibit 15.3 presents year-end balance sheets and common-sized balance sheets for this company for the same period. Lindsay's common-sized income statements were developed by dividing each line item in the company's 1996–1998 income statements by the net sales for the given year. For example, the percentages in Lindsay's 1998 common-sized income statement were determined by dividing each income statement amount for that year by $920,000, Lindsay's net sales for the year. Lindsay's 1998 common-sized balance sheet was derived by dividing each balance sheet amount for that year by $424,000, the company's total assets at the end of 1998.

Common-sized financial statements can be used to identify structural changes in a company's operating results and financial condition over a period of time. For example, Exhibit 15.2 demonstrates that Lindsay's cost of goods sold as a percentage of net sales steadily decreased between 1996 and 1998. On the other hand, the company's selling expenses increased significantly during this time period relative to net sales. Among other changes, the common-sized balance sheets in Exhibit 15.3 indicate that Lindsay's accounts receivable and inventory increased as a percentage of total assets between 1996 and 1998. Any unexpected changes or unusual relationships in a company's common-sized financial statements should be investigated. Such investigation should reveal whether these items point to developing financial problems for the firm. In the next section, we apply ratio analysis to Lindsay's financial data to gain further insight as to potential issues and questions raised by the company's common-sized financial statements.

Common-sized financial statements also allow decision makers to more easily compare and contrast the financial data of two or more companies. Suppose that Company A and Company B are the two leading firms in an industry. However, Company A is much larger than Company B. This size difference makes it difficult to compare the companies' financial data. To minimize this problem, we can prepare common-sized financial statements for the two firms. These financial statements may reveal key clues regarding the firms' comparative financial health. For example, common-sized income statement data will indicate the proportion of each company's sales that is absorbed by cost of goods sold and by operating expenses. Although Company A may have a much larger net income than its smaller competitor, inefficiencies in that firm's operations may cause it to have disproportionately high operating expenses. Over the long run, these inefficiencies may spell serious problems for Company A—and a window of opportunity for Company B.

EXHIBIT 15.2 ▼
Lindsay Hardware Stores, Inc., Income Statements and Common-Sized Income Statements for the Years Ended December 31, 1996–1998

	1998	1997	1996
Net sales	$920,000	$864,000	$704,000
Cost of goods sold	506,000	493,000	408,000
Gross profit	$414,000	$371,000	$296,000
Operating expenses:			
Selling	144,000	95,000	74,000
General	77,000	72,000	60,000
Administrative	72,000	71,000	63,000
Operating income	$121,000	$133,000	$ 99,000
Interest revenue	3,000	2,000	2,000
Interest expense	12,000	11,000	8,000
Income before income taxes	$112,000	$124,000	$ 93,000
Income tax expense	45,000	50,000	37,000
Net income	$ 67,000	$ 74,000	$ 56,000

	1998	1997	1996
Net sales	100.0%	100.0%	100.0%
Cost of goods sold	55.0	57.1	58.0
Gross profit	45.0	42.9	42.0
Operating expenses:			
Selling	15.7	11.0	10.5
General	8.4	8.3	8.5
Administrative	7.8	8.2	8.9
Operating income	13.1	15.4	14.1
Interest revenue	.3	.2	.3
Interest expense	1.3	1.3	1.1
Income before income taxes	12.1	14.3	13.3
Income tax expense	4.9	5.8	5.3
Net income	7.3%	8.5%	8.0%

Decision makers can also use common-sized financial statements to more easily compare a company's financial data to industry norms. Dun & Bradstreet's annual publication *Industry Norms and Key Business Ratios* provides a common-sized balance sheet for each of several hundred industries. The percentages reflected in these common-sized balance sheets are averages for each industry. One industry tracked by Dun & Bradstreet is "hardware stores." Following are selected items from a recent common-sized balance sheet for that industry. The corresponding percentages from the 1998 common-sized balance sheet of Lindsay Hardware Stores are presented for comparison purposes.

	Lindsay Hardware Stores	Industry Norm
Cash	2.1%	8.0%
Accounts receivable	17.0%	13.0%
Inventory	57.4%	51.6%
Property, plant & equipment	17.1%	14.2%
Accounts payable	12.3%	13.0%

EXHIBIT 15.3 ▼
Lindsay Hardware Stores, Inc., Balance Sheets and Common-Sized Balance Sheets as of December 31, 1996, 1997, and 1998

	1998	1997	1996
Assets			
Cash	$ 8,700	$ 2,200	$ 4,300
Accounts receivable	72,000	46,300	37,500
Inventory	243,700	188,000	151,900
Prepaid expenses	11,200	9,700	8,300
Total current assets	$335,600	$246,200	$202,000
Property, plant & equipment (net)	72,500	76,000	74,200
Other assets	15,900	20,300	19,800
Total assets	$424,000	$342,500	$296,000
Liabilities			
Accounts payable	$ 52,000	$ 39,600	$ 26,100
Accrued liabilities	25,400	23,400	14,200
Notes payable	20,000	18,000	17,000
Total current liabilities	$ 97,400	$ 81,000	$ 57,300
Long-term debt	110,000	110,000	110,000
Total liabilities	$207,400	$191,000	$167,300
Stockholders' Equity			
Common stock	$ 5,000	$ 5,000	$ 5,000
Additional paid-in capital	85,000	85,000	85,000
Retained earnings	126,600	61,500	38,700
Total stockholders' equity	$216,600	$151,500	$128,700
Total liabilities and stockholders' equity	$424,000	$342,500	$296,000

(continued)

EXHIBIT 15.3
(Concluded)

	1998	1997	1996
Assets			
Cash	2.1%	.6%	1.5%
Accounts receivable	17.0	13.5	12.7
Inventory	57.4	54.9	51.3
Prepaid expenses	2.6	2.9	2.8
Total current assets	79.1	71.9	68.3
Property, plant & equipment (net)	17.1	22.2	25.0
Other assets	3.8	5.9	6.7
Total assets	100.0%	100.0%	100.0%
Liabilities			
Accounts payable	12.3%	11.6%	8.8%
Accrued liabilities	6.0	6.8	4.8
Notes payable	4.7	5.3	5.7
Total current liabilities	23.0	23.7	19.3
Long-term debt	25.9	32.1	37.2
Total liabilities	48.9	55.8	56.5
Stockholders' Equity			
Common stock	1.2	1.4	1.7
Additional paid-in capital	20.0	24.8	28.7
Retained earnings	29.9	18.0	13.1
Total stockholders' equity	51.1	44.2	43.5
Total liabilities and stockholders' equity	100.0%	100.0%	100.0%

The previous data indicate that Lindsay had much less cash, on a proportionate basis, than the average hardware store company. Lindsay also had more of its assets invested in inventory than the typical company in its industry. An investor considering Lindsay's common stock might investigate these differences and assess their implications for the company's future prospects before pulling out her checkbook.

Common-sized financial statements can be presented graphically. Exhibit 15.4 presents common-sized financial data for Lindsay Hardware Stores in a bar graph. In this graph, you can see that the composition of Lindsay's assets changed from 1996 to 1998. In 1998, versus 1996, the company obviously had a smaller proportion of its total assets invested in property, plant & equipment and more of its assets invested in inventory and accounts receivable.

EXHIBIT 15.4
Lindsay Hardware Stores: Common-Sized Financial Statement Data for Assets

1996
1997
1998
0 20 40 60 80 100
Percent

Cash
Accounts Receivable
Inventory
Prepaid Expenses
PP&E
Other Assets

From Guilders to GAAP

FOR YOUR INFORMATION

Foreign companies that want to market their securities in the United States must first register those securities with the SEC. The SEC requires these firms to reconcile in their annual reports the net income reported under their home country's accounting rules to the net income that would have been reported under GAAP. These companies must also reconcile their stockholders' equity as determined by their home country's accounting rules to a GAAP-based stockholders' equity figure. The starting point for decision makers who wish to compare and contrast these companies' financial data to that of similar U.S. firms are these two reconciliations. These reconciliations often reveal large differences between foreign companies' reported net income and stockholders' equity and the comparable GAAP-based amounts.

In a recent annual report released in the United States, PolyGram, the Dutch entertainment conglomerate, reported net income determined under "Dutch legal requirements" of 741 million Netherlands guilders. If the company had used GAAP, its net income would have been 649 million guilders—the equivalent of $463 million. Under Dutch accounting rules, the company reported total stockholders' equity of 2.7 billion guilders. Under GAAP, this figure would have been more than 20 percent higher.

Ratio Analysis

LEARNING OBJECTIVE 5 ▶
Compute key financial ratios including liquidity, leverage, activity, profitability, and market strength ratios.

ratio analysis

cross-sectional ratio analysis

longitudinal ratio analysis

The most widely used method to analyze financial data is ratio analysis. **Ratio analysis** typically involves studying the relationship between two financial statement items. For example, the current ratio measures a business's liquidity at a specific point in time by comparing its current assets and current liabilities. Decision makers use financial ratios on both a cross-sectional and longitudinal basis. **Cross-sectional ratio analysis** involves comparing a company's financial ratios with those of competing companies and/or with industry norms. **Longitudinal ratio analysis** focuses on changes in a firm's financial ratios over a period of time, typically a time span measured in several years.

Financial ratios discussed in earlier chapters are presented in Exhibit 15.5 along with the equations used to compute them and a brief explanation of their purpose. Notice that Exhibit 15.5 classifies these ratios into five categories. These categories represent key features of the financial status of businesses that decision makers monitor. In the following sections, we review these five categories of financial ratios. Since the ratios shown in Exhibit 15.5 have been discussed previously, we do not dwell on their computational aspects. Instead, we focus on applying these ratios to financial data and interpreting the results.

LIQUIDITY RATIOS Liquidity refers to a firm's ability to finance its day-to-day operations and to pay its liabilities as they mature. Decision makers commonly use the current ratio and the quick ratio to assess the liquidity of businesses. The data from Exhibit 15.3 were used to compute the current and quick ratios for Lindsay Hardware Stores listed in the following table. Also included in this table are the approximate industry norms for these ratios in recent years.

	Lindsay Hardware Stores			Industry
	1998	1997	1996	Norm
Current ratio	3.45	3.04	3.53	3.2
Quick ratio	.83	.60	.73	.7

Notice that Lindsay's liquidity ratios between 1996 and 1998 closely paralleled the industry norms. Given these data, it appears that Lindsay Hardware Stores did not have any significant liquidity problems during the late 1990s. This conclusion is tempered by one minor caution. Recall that data reported previously indicated that companies in this industry, on average, had 8 percent of their assets invested in cash during the relevant time period. From 1996 through 1998, cash accounted for a much smaller percentage of Lindsay Hardware Stores' total assets, as shown by the common-sized balance sheets in Exhibit 15.3. The company's relatively small cash balances during this time span could have presented a problem if a sudden and unexpected need for a significant amount of cash had arisen.

LEVERAGE RATIOS Financial leverage refers to the degree that a business relies on debt, or borrowed, capital instead of equity, or invested, capital to finance its operations. A company's stockholders, or other owners, benefit if the rate of return earned on borrowed funds exceeds the interest rate paid on those funds. Financial leverage works to the disadvantage of a business's owners when the interest rate paid on borrowed funds exceeds the rate of return earned on those funds. The long-term debt to equity ratio is a key measure of financial leverage. As shown in Exhibit 15.5, this ratio relates a corporation's total long-term debt to its total stockholders' equity.

The second leverage ratio shown in Exhibit 15.5 does not directly measure financial leverage. Instead, the times interest earned ratio provides a margin of safety measure that is particularly useful when analyzing highly-leveraged companies. This ratio indicates how many times a company's interest expense was "covered" by earnings

EXHIBIT 15.5 ▼
Summary of Key Financial Ratios

Ratio	Equation	Purpose
Liquidity Ratios		
Current ratio	$\frac{\text{Current assets}}{\text{Current liabilities}}$	Measures a firm's ability to pay its current liabilities from its current assets
Quick ratio	$\frac{\text{Cash + cash equivalents + net current receivables + short-term investments}}{\text{Current liabilities}}$	Measures a firm's ability to pay its current liabilities without relying on the sale of its its inventory
Leverage Ratios		
Long-term debt to equity ratio	$\frac{\text{Long-term debt}}{\text{Stockholders' equity}}$	Measures a firm's degree of financial leverage
Times interest earned ratio	$\frac{\text{Net income + interest expense + income taxes expense}}{\text{Interest expense}}$	Indicates the number of times that a firm's interest expense is covered by earnings
Activity Ratios		
Accounts receivable turnover ratio	$\frac{\text{Net credit sales}}{\text{Average accounts receivable}}$	Indicates the number of times that a firm collects or turns over its accounts receivable each year
Age of receivables	$\frac{\text{360 days}}{\text{Accounts receivable turnover ratio}}$	Indicates the length of time normally required to collect a receivable resulting from a credit sale
Inventory turnover ratio	$\frac{\text{Cost of goods sold}}{\text{Average inventory}}$	Indicates the number of times that a firm sells or turns over its inventory each year
Age of inventory	$\frac{\text{360 days}}{\text{Inventory turnover ratio}}$	Indicates the length of time normally required to sell an inventory item
Total asset turnover ratio	$\frac{\text{Net sales}}{\text{Average total assets}}$	Measures a firm's ability to generate sales relative to its investment in assets

(continued)

EXHIBIT 15.5 ▼
(Concluded)

Ratio	Equation	Purpose
Profitability Ratios		
Profit margin percentage	Net income / Net sales	Indicates the percentage of each sales dollar that contributes to net income
Gross profit percentage	Gross profit / Net sales	Indicates the percentage of each sales dollar not absorbed by cost of goods sold
Return on assets	(Net income + interest expense) / Average total assets	Measures the rate of return a firm realizes on its investment in assets
Return on equity	(Net income − preferred stock dividends) / Average common stockholders' equity	Measures the rate of return on a firm's common stockholders' equity
Market Strength Ratios		
Price-earnings ratio	Current market price of common stock / Earnings per share for most recent 12-month period	Indicates the amount that investors are willing to pay for each dollar of a firm's earnings
Market price to book value ratio	Current market price of common stock / Book value per share	Indicates the amount that investors are willing to pay for each dollar of a firm's net assets

before income taxes and interest charges for a given period. For example, if this ratio is 2.0, a company covered its interest charges twice with its earnings during the period in question. The lower this ratio, the more risk a company faces of defaulting on its periodic interest payments.

Listed next are Lindsay Hardware Stores' long-term debt to equity and times interest earned ratios for 1996–1998 and the corresponding industry norms.

	Lindsay Hardware Stores			Industry
	1998	1997	1996	Norm
Long-term debt to equity ratio	.5	.7	.9	.3
Times interest earned ratio	10.3	12.3	12.6	2.4

The data just shown indicate that Lindsay became less leveraged between 1996 and 1998. If you refer to Exhibit 15.3, you will notice that Lindsay's long-term debt was unchanged during this period. However, due to profitable operations, the company's total stockholders' equity increased significantly between 1996 and 1998, causing the company's long-term debt to equity ratio to decline.

The average long-term debt to equity ratio for companies operating hardware stores was approximately .30 in the late 1990s. Although Lindsay's long-term debt to equity ratio steadily decreased from 1996 to 1998, the company was still more highly leveraged in 1998 than the typical firm in its industry. Again, financial leverage can be good or bad. If Lindsay continually earns a higher rate of return on its borrowed funds than the interest rate it pays on those funds, stockholders will benefit. However, unlike most expenses, interest expense does not decline if a company's revenues fall. As a result, when a company with a heavy debt burden experiences a drop in sales, its earnings are dragged down even further by the large interest expense it continues to incur.

Lindsay's times interest earned ratio decreased from 1996 through 1998, indicating that the company's coverage of its interest payments was declining. However, this ratio was well above the industry norm during each of these years, suggesting that the company faced a minimal risk of defaulting on its interest payments.

ACTIVITY RATIOS Activity ratios measure how well a company is managing its assets. For example, these ratios reveal how quickly a company is converting receivables into cash and how quickly it is selling or "turning over" inventory. Exhibit 15.5 lists five common activity ratios. Shown in the following schedule are these activity ratios for Lindsay Hardware Stores for 1997 and 1998 along with the corresponding industry norms.

	Lindsay Hardware Stores		Industry
	1998	1997	Norm
Accounts receivable turnover ratio	15.6	20.6	18.9
Age of receivables	23.1 days	17.5 days	19 days
Inventory turnover ratio	2.3	2.9	2.8
Age of inventory	157 days	124 days	129 days
Total asset turnover ratio	2.4	2.7	2.1

Before we discuss Lindsay's activity ratios, a few explanatory comments are necessary. First, all of Lindsay's sales are on a credit basis. As shown in Exhibit 15.5, the numerator of the accounts receivable turnover ratio is net credit sales. Second, the denominator of three of the five activity ratios is an average asset amount. These averages were computed by adding the appropriate beginning-of-the-year and end-of-the-year amounts and then dividing by two. For example, Lindsay's average accounts receivable for 1998 was determined by dividing by two the sum of its December 31, 1997, receivables and its December 31, 1998, receivables. Finally, Lindsay's activity ratios are not presented for 1996. To compute those ratios we would need asset balances as of December 31, 1995.

Lindsay's accounts receivable and inventory turnover ratios declined from 1997 to 1998, meaning that the company was not collecting its receivables as quickly nor selling its inventory as rapidly in 1998 compared with 1997. In 1997, Lindsay collected a receivable, on average, in a little more than 17 days, while the company required 23 days to collect a credit sale made during 1998. The average collection period for receivables in the hardware stores industry in the late 1990s was approximately 19 days. Consequently, in 1997, Lindsay outperformed its typical competitor in terms of how quickly receivables were converted into cash. The reverse was true in 1998. In

1997, Lindsay sold its inventory more rapidly than the average hardware retailer, while in 1998 the firm lagged behind its average competitor in this regard. Industry statistics during the late 1990s revealed that approximately 129 days were required to sell a typical inventory item in a hardware store. Notice that Lindsay's average time to sell an inventory item leaped from 124 days in 1997 to 157 days in 1998.

Recall that Lindsay's common-sized balance sheets indicated that both its receivables and inventory increased as a percentage of total assets during the period 1996–1998. Earlier, the meaning of these increases relative to the company's overall financial health was unclear. The company's activity ratios provide further insight on these changes. These ratios suggest that the company did not manage receivables and inventory as effectively in 1998 as it did in 1997. Receivables become more susceptible to bad debt losses the longer they go uncollected. Similarly, the longer the time required to sell inventory, the higher the risk that inventory items will become obsolete, damaged, or stolen.

Finally, Lindsay's total asset turnover ratio decreased (worsened) from 2.7 in 1997 to 2.4 in 1998. This change indicates that the company did a poorer job of generating sales relative to its total assets in 1998 compared with 1997. However, the industry average for the total asset turnover ratio in the late 1990s was approximately 2.1. So, in both 1997 and 1998, Lindsay bettered the industry, as a whole, in producing sales relative to its asset base.

PROFITABILITY RATIOS Profitability ratios measure a business's earnings performance. The most common benchmarks against which to evaluate a firm's profitability are its sales, assets, and owners' equity. Exhibit 15.5 lists four common profitability ratios. These profitability ratios for Lindsay Hardware Stores for 1997 and 1998 and the related industry norms are listed in the following schedule. Again, since we do not have the data necessary to compute certain of these ratios for 1996, none of the ratios for that year are presented.

	Lindsay Hardware Stores		Industry
	1998	1997	Norm
Profit margin percentage	7.2%	8.5%	2.6%
Gross profit percentage	45.0%	42.9%	35.0%
Return on assets	20.6	26.6	5.1
Return on equity	36.4	52.8	9.6

Notice that in both 1997 and 1998, Lindsay outperformed the typical hardware retailer across the board in terms of the four profitability ratios listed in Exhibit 15.5. In the late 1990s, Dun & Bradstreet reported that only 25 percent of all hardware retailers had a return on assets exceeding 11 percent. Additionally, only 25 percent of these companies had a return on equity exceeding 22 percent. These additional industry statistics reveal that Lindsay's return on assets and return on equity ratios were not only impressive, they were exceptional. But, are these ratios reasonable? At a minimum, when a company has very impressive financial ratios, decision makers should consider the possibility that errors, intentional or unintentional, artificially inflated those ratios.

If errors in Lindsay's financial data overstated its profitability ratios, the most likely culprit was the company's cost of goods sold. Companies frequently make mistakes in counting and pricing year-end inventory, errors that result in their reported cost of goods sold being incorrect. Firms that wish to distort their earnings data may intentionally misrepresent their year-end inventory to understate their cost of goods sold. In either case, the result is that a company's gross profit percentage and its other profitability ratios are misstated.

For illustration purposes, suppose that Lindsay's year-end inventory for 1998 was overstated by \$50,000, or approximately 20 percent. We know from an earlier chapter that an overstatement of year-end inventory causes a firm's cost of goods sold for that year to be understated by the same amount. The following schedule shows a side-by-side comparison of Lindsay's reported income statement data for 1998 and that same data corrected for the assumed \$50,000 overstatement of year-end inventory. (Note: Lindsay's average income tax rate is approximately 40%.)

	Reported 1998 Income Statement Data	Corrected 1998 Income Statement Data
Net sales	\$920,000	\$920,000
Cost of goods sold	506,000	556,000
Gross profit	\$414,000	\$364,000
Operating expenses	293,000	293,000
Operating income	\$121,000	\$ 71,000
Other revenues and expenses (net)	(9,000)	(9,000)
Income before income taxes	\$112,000	\$ 62,000
Income taxes	45,000	25,000
Net income	\$ 67,000	\$ 37,000
Gross profit percentage	45.0%	39.6%
Profit margin percentage	7.2%	4.0%

Notice the impact of the assumed inventory error on the company's gross profit and profit margin percentages. Also notice that an assumed 20 percent overstatement of inventory resulted in an 81 percent overstatement of Lindsay's net income (\$67,000/\$37,000 = 181%). As you can see, inventory errors typically have a greatly magnified effect, on a percentage basis, on a business's net income.

Now, let us take an intuitive, or common sense, approach to assessing Lindsay's profitability ratios. Suppose that all hardware retailers purchase a certain type of hammer from Hammers 'n Nails, Inc., at a wholesale cost of \$20. Lindsay would have to sell this item at a retail price of \$36.36 to realize a 45 percent gross profit—its 1998 gross profit percentage.[1] Conversely, a competitor that realizes the average gross profit percentage of 35 percent for hardware retailers would sell this hammer at a price of \$30.76. Question: Would Joe or Josephine "Home Improvement" pay \$36.36 for this hammer at Lindsay Hardware Stores instead of driving a mile or so to a competitor to purchase the same item at less than \$31? Answer: No. In other words, it is quite unlikely that Lindsay Hardware Stores could realize a gross profit percentage on its sales of 45 percent when the industry norm is 35 percent.

1. A selling price of \$36.36 would yield a gross profit of \$16.36. When this gross profit is divided by the selling price, the result is a 45 percent gross profit: \$16.36/\$36.36 = 45%.

When interpreting financial statements, a decision maker must be well versed in how to compute financial ratios but must also exercise common sense in interpreting those ratios. In the final section of this chapter, we expand upon this intuitive approach to financial statement analysis when we discuss the concept of earnings quality.

MARKET STRENGTH RATIOS The first four categories of financial ratios we have considered focus on a company's financial condition or operating results. Market strength ratios, on the other hand, provide insight on how the capital markets, as a whole, perceive a company's common stock. Despite impressive operating results and a strong financial condition, a company's common stock may fare poorly in the capital markets. In the 1990s, the stock prices of many electric utilities plummeted when regulatory authorities took steps to introduce more competition into the electric utility industry. Investors discounted the strong financial condition and operating results of these companies because they believed the firms' future prospects were uncertain.

Chapter 12 introduced you to two market strength ratios, the price-earnings (P/E) ratio and the market price to book value ratio. Recall that the P/E ratio indicates how much investors are willing to pay for each $1 of earnings reported by a company over the previous twelve months. The market price to book value ratio indicates how much investors are willing to pay for each $1 of a company's net assets.

Market strength ratios tend to be more volatile than other financial ratios because they are influenced by investors' perceptions and expectations, both of which can change rapidly. The following schedule documents the 1991–1996 year-end market price to book value ratios of Telxon Corporation, a company in the computer industry. Notice that this ratio ranged from approximately 1.2 to 3.0 over this period. If we considered intra-year measures of this ratio, we would discover that it fluctuated over an even larger range between 1991 and 1996.

	1996	1995	1994	1993	1992	1991
Market price to book value ratio, Telxon Corporation	2.12	1.68	1.55	1.19	2.71	3.00

Exhibit 15.6 presents two charts. The first chart depicts a graphical format used by security analysts to plot stock market prices. This chart presents four data points each fiscal year from 1991 through 1996 for Telxon's common stock: the opening price for the year, the highest price of the year, the lowest price of the year, and the stock's closing price for the year. At the beginning of fiscal 1996, Telxon's common stock had a market price of approximately $15 per share; the stock closed the year at a price of $21.25. During the year, the stock topped out at nearly $26 per share and bottomed out at $14.50 per share. The second chart in Exhibit 15.6 documents Telxon's beginning-of-the-year book value for each year from 1991 through 1996. Notice that unlike Telxon's stock market price, the company's book value per share was very stable over this period.

What accounts for the significantly different behavior patterns of Telxon's stock price and book value per share shown in Exhibit 15.6? Again, stock prices are driven by investors' perceptions and expectations. Security analysts suggest that investors often overreact to quarterly earnings data, changes in management, and news reports regarding a company's future prospects or those of its industry. The result is volatile stock prices. On the other hand, book value per share is based strictly upon financial data methodically captured by a firm's accounting system.

EXHIBIT 15.6 ▼
Market Price vs. Book Value: Telxon Corporation

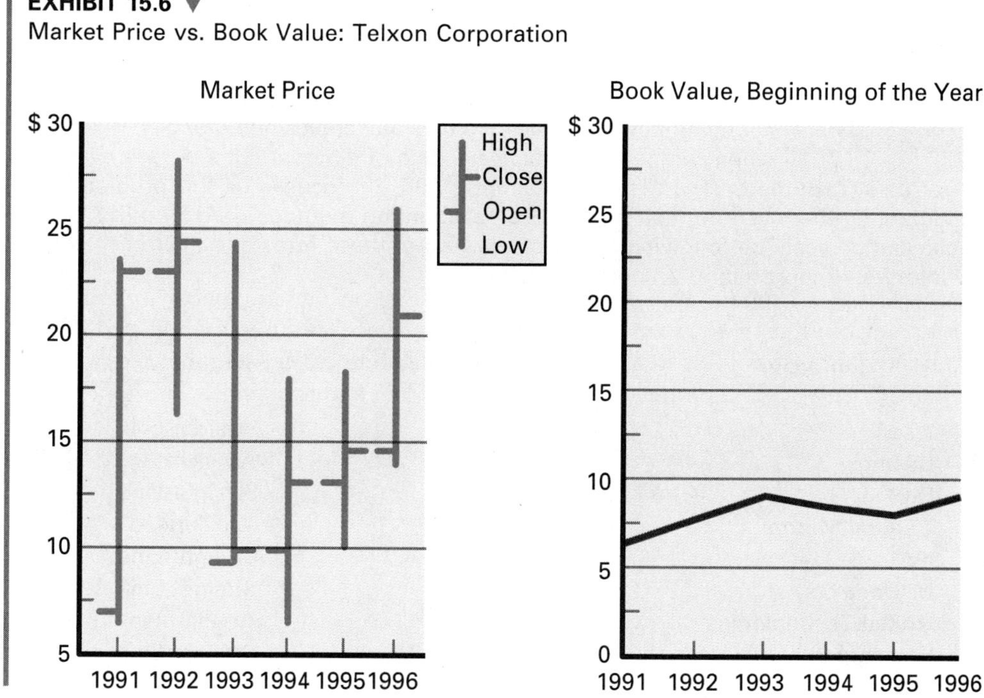

ASSESSING EARNINGS QUALITY

LEARNING ◀ OBJECTIVE 6
Assess earnings quality.

earnings quality

In recent years, the concept of earnings quality has become increasingly important to financial statement users. Although not rigidly defined, **earnings quality** generally refers to the degree of correlation between a firm's economic income and its reported earnings determined by GAAP. So, what is "economic income"? Economists define economic income as the change in the total value, or "well-offness," of a business from one point in time to another.[2] The analytical techniques illustrated in the previous section, including the profitability ratios, do not allow decision makers to comprehensively assess the quality of a firm's reported earnings. In this section, we consider the principal factors that influence earnings quality. Then, we identify specific measures that can be used to assess earnings quality.

Factors Influencing Earnings Quality

The opening vignette for this chapter described a large-scale financial fraud involving ZZZZ Best Company. Financial fraud obviously diminishes the correlation between a company's economic income and its reported accounting earnings. However, business executives, or their accountants, can manipulate a firm's reported earnings without engaging in financial fraud. As you know, there are often several alternative methods that can be used to account for a specific type of transaction or event. Depreciation

2. S. Cottle, R. F. Murray, and F. S. Block, *Graham and Dodd's Security Analysis* (New York: McGraw-Hill, 1988), 138.

Comparing Apples and Oranges

FOR YOUR INFORMATION

Because companies pick and choose from among alternative accounting methods, investors face an "apples and oranges" problem when comparing the financial data of different firms. A recent article in *Barron's* (T. Burnett, "Twin Towers," 15 July 1996, 20) focused on this problem by documenting the inventory and depreciation accounting methods used by thirty large public companies. The following table lists several of these firms and their primary inventory and depreciation accounting methods.

Company	Inventory Accounting Method	Depreciation Accounting Method
AT&T	FIFO	Straight-Line
Boeing	Average Cost	Accelerated
DuPont	LIFO	Straight-Line
General Motors	LIFO	Accelerated
IBM	Average Cost	Straight-Line
McDonald's	FIFO	Straight-Line
United Technologies	LIFO	Accelerated
Westinghouse	Average Cost	Straight-Line

expense, cost of goods sold, and uncollectible accounts expense are examples of income statement items that may be materially affected by a firm's choice of accounting methods. (For a related discussion, refer to the For Your Information vignette accompanying this section.) Business executives can also influence their firms' reported earnings by modifying operating decisions. For example, if a company is having a poor year profit-wise, management may purposefully delay discretionary expenses such as advertising and maintenance. Delaying these expenditures may improve a company's reported accounting earnings for a given year, while actually diminishing the overall economic value of the business.

A company's reported profits may not be closely correlated with its economic income even if there have been no explicit efforts to distort those profits. Many financial statement items are estimates, such as warranty expense and expected losses from pending lawsuits. These estimates may be materially in error although they are made honestly and objectively. Additionally, GAAP do not capture, or quantify, all events that affect the change in the economic value of a business during a given period. In fact, GAAP are not intended to capture all of these variables. For example, as you know, the change in the current value, or market value, of most assets is not considered a revenue item by GAAP.

Measures to Use in Assessing Earnings Quality

Analyzing the quality of a company's reported accounting earnings requires the exercise of considerable judgment on the part of financial decision makers. An understanding of the economic factors that influence given companies' operations, knowledge of accounting rules and concepts, and simple intuition—common sense—are the principal tools used in analyzing earnings quality. Exhibit 15.7 lists several measures decision makers can use to assess the quality of a firm's reported earnings.

EXHIBIT 15.7 ▼
Examples of Measures to Use in Assessing the Quality of a Firm's Reported Earnings

- Compare accounting principles employed by a firm to those used by competitors. Does the set of accounting principles used by the firm tend to inflate its reported earnings?
- Analyze any recent changes in accounting principles or accounting estimates to determine whether they inflated reported earnings.
- Read the footnotes to the financial statements to identify any unusual events that may have affected reported earnings.
- Read the footnotes to the financial statements to determine whether any major loss contingencies exist that could negatively affect future earnings.
- Review extraordinary losses included in the income statement to determine that they are actually nonoperating items.
- Attempt to determine whether there are any significant expenses not reflected in the income statement, such as warranty expense on products sold.
- Attempt to determine whether discretionary expenditures, such as advertising and maintenance expenses, have been delayed.

The starting point for analyzing the quality of a company's earnings is the accounting methods it uses. The initial financial statement footnote in a company's annual report summarizes its principal accounting methods. A review of this footnote should reveal whether a company uses income-inflating accounting methods. For example, as explained in Chapter 7, the FIFO inventory method generally results in a higher net income than the LIFO method during a period of steadily rising prices. Financial statement footnotes also disclose whether a company has changed accounting methods recently and the impact of such changes on its reported earnings.

Another reason to review a company's financial statement footnotes is to identify unusual items that affected the firm's past earnings or have the potential to affect its future earnings. An example of an unusual transaction that may artificially inflate a company's reported earnings is a "LIFO liquidation," which is the subject of the Decision Case at the end of this chapter. Most large companies are involved in litigation. Quite often, pending litigation has the potential to significantly influence the future earnings of a business. A company's financial statement footnotes will provide a summary of the major litigation cases in which it is involved. These footnotes typically assess the likely financial statement impact of these cases as well. Decision makers should review these disclosures and determine whether they agree with management's assessment of how pending legal matters may affect a company's financial status.

When analyzing a firm's reported earnings, decision makers generally focus on the income generated by its continuing operations. Extraordinary gains and losses are discounted since those items involve nonrecurring and unusual events or transactions that are unlikely to affect a company's future earnings. One method that business executives can use to inflate income from continuing operations is to classify operating expenses and losses as extraordinary losses. When assessing the quality of a company's reported earnings, decision makers should review any extraordinary losses in the firm's income statement. Footnote disclosures for extraordinary items often signal whether such items have been properly classified for income statement purposes.

Decision makers should also question whether a company's income statement includes all of the firm's expenses. To address this issue, decision makers must be familiar with the nature of a company's operations and its industry. A review of

Is choosing profitable stock investments a skill, an art, or simply "dumb luck"? In an ongoing experiment, *The Wall Street Journal* suggests that financial analysts, on average, can do a better job of choosing profitable stock investments than a random technique such as throwing darts at a stock market table.

competitors' financial statements is one useful technique for identifying expenses that a company may have omitted from its income statement. Finally, a comparison of a company's financial statements over several years may reveal that discretionary expenses, such as advertising and maintenance, have been postponed in the most recent year. Again, the postponement of such expenses may increase a company's reported accounting earnings while damaging the company economically. For example, the postponement of maintenance expenses may result in a higher rate of equipment breakdowns, higher repair bills in the future, and a decline in production efficiency.

SUMMARY

To make informed economic decisions, financial statement users must be able to analyze financial data and draw proper conclusions from such analysis. The objectives of financial statement analysis vary across different types of decision makers. This chapter focuses on financial statement analysis from the standpoint of investors since those decision makers must take the most comprehensive approach to analyzing and interpreting financial data.

Annual reports are the principal source of information used in analyzing financial statement data. The following sections of an annual report are particularly useful for this purpose: the financial statement footnotes, the financial highlights table, management's discussion and analysis of financial condition and operating results, and the independent auditor's report. Another important source of information for decision makers when analyzing financial statements is various publications of investment advisory firms such as Dun & Bradstreet and Robert Morris Associates. Among other data, these firms regularly publish key financial ratios for a wide range of industries.

Common approaches to analyzing financial statements include trend analysis, the preparation of common-sized financial statements, and ratio analysis. Trend analysis is the study of percentage changes in financial statement items over a period of time and is often used to predict the future value of a financial statement item. Decision makers can use common-sized financial statements to better grasp the relationships among the items in a financial statement or series of financial statements and how these relationships have changed over time. Ratio analysis involves a comparison of the relationship between two financial statement items. A company's financial ratios are often compared to its historical norms for those ratios and to industry norms. There are five general types of financial ratios: liquidity, leverage, activity, profitability, and market strength.

In recent years, financial statement users have focused increasing attention on assessing "earnings quality." Earnings quality generally refers to the degree of correlation between a business's economic income and its reported accounting earnings. Among factors influencing earnings quality are the efforts of business executives to manipulate, or distort, their firm's financial data. The need to estimate many financial statement amounts can also negatively affect earnings quality. Specific measures that can be used to assess earnings quality include comparing a firm's accounting methods to those used by its competitors. The earnings of companies that use income-inflating accounting methods are generally of lower quality than the earnings of competitors that use more conservative accounting methods.

GLOSSARY

Common-sized financial statements (p. 719) Financial statements in which each line item is expressed as a percentage of a major financial statement component.

Cross-sectional ratio analysis (p. 724) Comparison of a company's financial ratios with those of competing companies and/or with the industry norms for those ratios.

Earnings quality (p. 731) The degree of correlation between a firm's economic income and its reported earnings determined by GAAP.

Longitudinal ratio analysis (p. 724) A variation of ratio analysis that focuses on the changes in a business's ratios over a period of time.

Ratio analysis (p. 724) An analytical technique that typically involves studying the relationship between two financial statement items.

Trend analysis (p. 716) The study of percentage changes in financial statement items over a period of time.

DECISION CASE

Suppose that you are the controller of DeQuasie Corporation. This company is a wholesale distributor of lasonics, an electronic component used by computer manufacturers. Presently, in late November, sales forecasts indicate that DeQuasie will sell 10,000 lasonics at an average selling price of $50 per unit during the last month of the year. DeQuasie uses the LIFO costing method to account for its inventory of lasonics and by the end of November will have approximately 12,000 lasonics in inventory at a per unit LIFO cost of $20. The per unit cost of the lasonics in inventory at the beginning of the year was $20, and that per unit cost was paid by DeQuasie to purchase additional units through the first eleven months of the year. However, a recent strike has driven the replacement cost of lasonics up to $35 per unit. Unfortunately, DeQuasie cannot pass this price increase along to its customers given competitive conditions in the computer industry.

DeQuasie typically stocks up on inventory during the first few days of December to prepare for January and February, which are historically its busiest sales months. As a matter of company policy, the year-end inventory of lasonics is expected to be no less than 20,000 units. Given this policy, the company should purchase 18,000 units of inventory during the first few days of December, as determined by the following equation:

Required Inventory Purchases in early December	=	Desired Inventory, December 31	+	Expected Sales during December	−	December 1 Inventory
	=	20,000 + 10,000 − 12,000				
	=	18,000				

The current year has been a poor one for DeQuasie. Operating expenses are up and sales are down. Latest projections indicate that the company's net income for the year will be a meager $200,000, down from nearly $600,000 the previous year. At a recent management meeting, your immediate superior, the chief financial officer (CFO), suggested delaying additional inventory purchases until after January 1. The CFO pointed out that by delaying inventory purchases, the company could record a significantly higher gross profit in the last month of the year.

Required: Assume that your firm accepts the CFO's recommendation and delays all inventory purchases until after year-end. Explain how this decision will affect DeQuasie's earnings and determine the impact on the company's gross profit and net income for the year. (DeQuasie has an effective income tax rate of 40 percent.) Is your company's decision appropriate? Is it ethical? Why or why not? Identify the parties potentially affected by this decision and how they may be affected. What action, if any, should you take regarding this matter, given your position with the firm?

QUESTIONS

1. What is the primary purpose of the accounting function within a business organization?
2. Briefly explain why the objectives of financial statement analysis vary across different types of financial decision makers.
3. Why must investors take a comprehensive approach to financial statement analysis?
4. List several items included in an annual report that are of particular interest to investors and other financial decision makers.
5. What is the purpose of a financial highlights table in a company's annual report?

6. What type of information is generally included in the "MD&A" section of an annual report?
7. Identify several prominent investment advisory firms that publish financial data, statistical measures, and other information regarding business entities.
8. Identify two annual publications that report industry norms for financial ratios and other financial measures.
9. What type of information can be obtained from the EDGAR Web site maintained on the Internet by the SEC?
10. Describe the nature and purpose of trend analysis.
11. What are common-sized financial statements and how are they used by decision makers?
12. What is ratio analysis? Identify two approaches to applying ratio analysis.
13. Identify five general categories of financial ratios.
14. Define liquidity and identify two ratios commonly used to analyze a business's liquidity.
15. When do a company's stockholders benefit from the use of financial leverage? When are they disadvantaged by the use of financial leverage?
16. What does the times interest earned ratio measure?
17. What aspect of a company's financial performance do activity ratios measure?
18. What problems may a business face if its inventory turnover declines?
19. The benchmarks used in evaluating a company's profitability generally involve what major financial statement items?
20. How might a company manipulate its ending inventory to intentionally distort its earnings data?
21. What do market strength ratios measure?
22. Why are market strength ratios generally more volatile than other financial ratios?
23. Define earnings quality.
24. Identify several factors that influence the quality of a company's reported earnings.
25. Identify several measures that decision makers can use to evaluate the quality of a company's earnings.

EXERCISES

26. True or False (LO 1–6)

Following are a series of statements regarding topics discussed in Chapter 15.

Required:

Indicate whether each statement is true (T) or false (F).

_____ a. A price-earnings ratio reveals how much investors are willing to pay for each $1 of earnings reported by a company over the previous twelve months.

_____ b. Public companies are required to file a 10-K registration statement with the Securities and Exchange Commission each year.

_____ c. Decision makers commonly use activity ratios to evaluate a given business's liquidity.

_____ d. Accrual-basis data tend to be more variable and thus more difficult to predict than cash-basis data.

_____ e. The starting point for analyzing the quality of a company's earnings is the accounting methods it uses.

_____ f. Common-sized financial statements can be used to identify important structural changes in a company's operating results and financial condition over a period of time.

_____ g. Cross-sectional ratio analysis focuses on changes in a firm's financial ratios over a period of time, typically a time span measured in several years.

_____ h. Departures from generally accepted accounting principles are an example of key disclosures that may be found in the independent auditor's report accompanying a firm's financial statements.

_____ i. Financial leverage works to the advantage of a business's owners when the interest rate paid on borrowed funds exceeds the rate of return earned on those funds.

_____ j. The study of percentage changes in financial statement items over a period of time is known as trend analysis.

_____ k. Earnings quality generally refers to the degree of correlation between a firm's economic income and its reported earnings determined by generally accepted accounting principles.

_____ l. In a common-sized balance sheet each line item is expressed as a percentage of net sales.

27. **Terminology** (LO 5)
Following are definitions or descriptions of terms relating to ratio analysis.

_________ Involves studying the relationship between two or more financial statement items.
_________ Indicates the amount that investors are willing to pay for each dollar of a company's earnings over the past twelve months.
_________ Involves a comparison of a company's financial ratios with those of competing companies or industry norms.
_________ Measures a firm's ability to generate sales relative to its investment in assets.
_________ Focuses on changes in a firm's ratios over a period of time.
_________ Ratios that indicate how the capital markets as a whole perceive a company's common stock.
_________ Indicates the percentage of each sales dollar that contributes to net income.
_________ Measures a firm's ability to pay its current liabilities without relying on the sale of its inventory.
_________ Ratios used to evaluate how well a company is managing its assets.
_________ Indicates the number of times that a firm sells or turns over its inventory each year.
_________ Measures a firm's ability to pay its current liabilities from its current assets.

Required:
Match each definition or description listed with an appropriate term from the following list:

a. Ratio analysis
b. Inventory turnover ratio
c. Cross-sectional ratio analysis
d. Current ratio
e. Total asset turnover ratio
f. Longitudinal ratio analysis
g. Liquidity ratios
h. Gross profit percentage
i. Leverage ratios
j. Activity ratios
k. Market strength ratios
l. Age of inventory
m. Quick ratio
n. Price-earnings ratio
o. Accounts receivable turnover ratio
p. Profit margin percentage

28. Objectives of Financial Statement Analysis (LO 1)
Red Roof Inns, Inc., is the third largest operator of "economy" hotels in the United States. The company has nearly 300 inns, most of which are located west of the Mississippi River. For a recent year, the company reported net income of approximately $18 million on revenues of nearly $300 million.

Required:
1. Indicate what objective or objectives the following decision makers would likely have in mind when reviewing the financial statements of Red Roof Inns:
   a. potential investors in the company's common stock
   b. an individual applying for a management position with the company
   c. a banker reviewing a loan application submitted by the firm
   d. businesses that supply goods or services to the company
2. Identify information sources that the parties listed in (1) could use to analyze the financial statement data of Red Roof Inns.

29. Trend Analysis (LO 3)
Logicon, Inc., headquartered in Torrance, California, provides advanced technology systems and services to support national security, civil, and industrial needs. Presented in the following schedule are selected financial data reported recently by Logicon. Amounts are expressed in millions of dollars except for dividends per share.

Year	Total Revenues	Dividends Per Share	Total Assets
1	$258.5	$.180	$102.8
2	260.0	.180	98.4
3	299.1	.195	113.8
4	325.1	.240	119.8

Required:
1. Prepare a trend analysis for each of the three financial statement items listed for Logicon using Year 1 as the base year.
2. Predict the Year 5 figure for each financial statement item. In which of these predicted amounts do you have the most confidence? Why?
3. During Year 5, Logicon actually had total revenues of $320.2 million, paid dividends of $.28 per share, and had total assets at year-end of $129.3 million. Compute the percentage error between each of these actual amounts and the corresponding prediction you made in (2). Comment on any additional insight these results provide you regarding trend analysis.

30. Common-Sized Financial Statements (LO 4)
On the following page are balance sheets for Gabe's Shoe Repair Shop as of December 31, 1997 and 1998.

Required:
1. How are common-sized financial statements used by decision makers?
2. Prepare common-sized balance sheets for Gabe's Shoe Repair Shop as of December 31, 1997 and 1998.
3. What major structural changes occurred in this business's balance sheet during 1998? What factors may have accounted for these changes?

GABE'S SHOE REPAIR SHOP
BALANCE SHEETS
DECEMBER 31, 1997 AND 1998

	1997	1998
Assets		
Cash	$ 9,200	$18,700
Accounts receivable (net)	8,300	14,400
Inventory	12,500	14,700
Prepaid expenses	800	300
Total current assets	$30,800	$48,100
Equipment (net)	31,200	27,800
Total assets	$62,000	$75,900
Liabilities		
Accounts payable	$ 7,100	$ 2,700
Accrued liabilities	3,300	3,600
Total current liabilities	$10,400	$ 6,300
Long-term bank loan	10,000	10,000
Total liabilities	$20,400	$16,300
Stockholders' Equity		
Common stock	$12,000	$12,000
Additional paid-in capital	24,000	24,000
Retained earnings	5,600	23,600
Total stockholders' equity	$41,600	$59,600
Total liabilities and stockholders' equity	$62,000	$75,900

31. **Common-Sized Financial Statements** (LO 4)
Following is a recent income statement for Cable Company (amounts are expressed in thousands of dollars). Also presented is the average common-sized income statement for Cable Company's industry.

	Cable Company	Industry
Sales	$44,900	100.0%
Cost of goods sold	21,700	47.3
Gross profit	$23,200	52.7
Operating expenses	16,100	30.3
Operating income	$ 7,100	22.4
Other revenue (expense)	(1,300)	(2.9)
Income before income tax	$ 5,800	19.5
Income tax expense	2,300	8.2
Net income	$ 3,500	11.3

Required:
1. Prepare a common-sized income statement for Cable Company.
2. What major differences exist between the common-sized income statement of Cable Company and that of its industry?

32. **Liquidity and Leverage Ratios** (LO 5)
P. R. Williamson Company operates two small clothing stores in southeastern Idaho. Following are this company's income statements for the years ended December 31, 1996 through 1998, and the company's year-end balance sheets for 1996 through 1998.

P. R. WILLIAMSON COMPANY
INCOME STATEMENTS
FOR THE YEARS ENDED DECEMBER 31, 1996–1998

	1996	1997	1998
Sales*	$641,900	$652,000	$654,500
Cost of goods sold	304,500	323,700	339,200
Gross profit	$337,400	$328,300	$315,300
Operating expenses	154,200	155,800	161,900
Operating income	$183,200	$172,500	$153,400
Other revenue (expense)**	13,400	(6,400)	(1,200)
Income before income tax	$196,600	$166,100	$152,200
Income tax expense	78,600	66,400	60,900
Net income	$118,000	$ 99,700	$ 91,300

*All of the company's sales are on a credit basis.
**Includes interest expense of the following amounts: 1996—$9,900, 1997—$7,400, and 1998—$7,100.

P. R. WILLIAMSON COMPANY
BALANCE SHEETS
DECEMBER 31, 1996–1998

	1996	1997	1998
Assets			
Cash	$ 22,000	$ 9,100	$ 3,700
Accounts receivable (net)	72,500	103,300	116,900
Inventory	109,800	102,000	89,000
Prepaid expenses	2,500	1,400	1,700
Total current assets	$206,800	$215,800	$211,300
Property & equipment (net)	212,000	201,500	189,400
Other assets	3,200	2,600	1,500
Total assets	$422,000	$419,900	$402,200

(continued)

	1996	1997	1998
Liabilities			
Accounts payable	$ 51,900	$ 57,200	$ 64,900
Notes payable	25,000	15,000	12,000
Accrued liabilities	41,100	35,800	7,400
Total current liabilities	$118,000	$108,000	$ 84,300
Bonds payable	100,000	80,000	80,000
Total liabilities	$218,000	$188,000	$164,300
Stockholders' Equity			
Common stock	$ 50,000	$ 50,000	$ 50,000
Additional paid-in capital	130,000	130,000	130,000
Retained earnings	24,000	51,900	57,900
Total stockholders' equity	$204,000	$231,900	$237,900
Total liabilities and stockholders' equity	$422,000	$419,900	$402,200

Required:
1. Compute the liquidity and leverage ratios discussed in this chapter for P. R. Williamson Company for 1996 through 1998.
2. Overall, did the company's liquidity improve or deteriorate between 1996 and 1998? Explain.
3. Did this company become more or less leveraged between 1996 and 1998?

33. **Activity Ratios** (LO 5)
Refer to the data presented in Exercise 32 for P. R. Williamson Company.

Required:
1. Compute the activity ratios discussed in this chapter for P.R. Williamson Company for 1997 and 1998.
2. Indicate which of these ratios improved and which deteriorated during 1998.
3. Overall, did the company do a better job of managing its accounts receivable, inventory, and total assets in 1998 compared with 1997? Explain.

34. **Profitability and Market Strength Ratios** (LO 5)
Refer to the information presented in Exercise 32 for P. R. Williamson Company. This company had 50,000 shares of common stock outstanding throughout the period 1996–1998. Following are the market prices of P. R. Williamson's common stock at the end of each year 1996 through 1998: 1996, $8.50; 1997, $7.75; and 1998, $6.50.

Required:
1. Compute the profitability and market strength ratios discussed in this chapter for P. R. Williamson Company for 1996 through 1998. (Note: The company had total assets on January 1, 1996, of $425,000, while the company's total stockholders' equity on that date was $186,000.)
2. Evaluate the company's profitability ratios for the period 1996–1998. Did the company become more or less profitable over this time period? Explain.
3. Evaluate the company's market strength ratios for the period 1996–1998. What do the changes in these ratios over this period indicate?

35. Ethics and Investment Advice (LO 1, 2)

Suppose that you are considering an investment in the common stock of Merck & Company, a large pharmaceutical firm. You recently read a very favorable analysis of this company's future prospects. The investment advisor who prepared this analysis indicated that, in her opinion, Merck common stock was a "strong buy."

Required:

1. Would the degree of reliance that you place on this investment advisor's analysis of Merck common stock be affected by whether or not the advisor owns Merck stock? Why or why not?
2. Should investment advisors be required to disclose whether or not they own stock in the companies they analyze and discuss in published articles and reports? Defend your answer.
3. What information sources could you use to perform your own analysis of Merck's recent financial statement data?

36. Accounting Errors and the Impact on Financial Ratios (LO 5)

Moses & Stanley, Inc., is a retail company that has a large amount of obsolete inventory. This inventory is carried in the company's accounting records at its original cost although the true value of the inventory is essentially zero.

Required:

1. Refer to Exhibit 15.5. Identify the financial ratios that would be affected by the failure of a company to write off obsolete inventory.
2. Is it unethical for a company to refuse to write off or write down inventory that has little or no value?
3. What accounting principle or principles are violated by a company's failure to write off or write down obsolete inventory?

37. Accounting Errors and the Impact on Financial Statement Data (LO 5)

Following is a condensed version of the 1998 income statement of Linton Supply Company.

Sales	$725,400
Cost of goods sold	404,300
Gross profit	$321,100
Operating expenses	111,300
Operating income	$209,800
Other revenues (expenses)	10,200
Income before income tax	$220,000
Income tax expense	88,000
Net income	$132,000

Linton's accountant overlooked a $3,200 utility bill at the end of 1998. This bill should have been recorded with a debit to Utilities Expense and a credit to Accrued Liabilities. The company's year-end inventory account balance was also incorrect. Because of errors made during the counting of inventory, Linton's year-end inventory was listed as $174,300 in its accounting records instead of the correct figure of $151,200. This overstatement of year-end inventory caused Linton's cost of goods sold for the year to be understated by an equal amount.

Following is other information regarding Linton Supply:

Average total assets during 1998	$820,500*
Interest expense for 1998 (included in Other revenues and expenses)	34,000
Average common stockholders' equity	380,000*
Average income tax rate	40%

*This average was computed by adding the beginning-of-the-year and end-of-the-year amounts and dividing by two.

Required:

1. Ignoring the two errors discovered in Linton's accounting records, compute the company's profitability ratios for 1998.
2. Compute Linton's profitability ratios for 1998 after adjusting the company's financial data for the two errors.
3. Did the two errors have a material effect on Linton's profitability ratios? Defend your answer.

38. Market Price to Book Value Ratio (LO 5)

Ryder System, Inc., is a publicly owned company based in Miami, Florida. The company's principal line of business is truck leasing. Presented in the following schedule are selected financial data for Ryder's common stock over a recent five-year period.

	Year 1	Year 2	Year 3	Year 4	Year 5
Earnings per share	$ .05	$ 1.51	$ (.84)	$ 1.95	$ 1.86
Dividends per share	.60	.60	.60	.60	.60
Book value per share	17.50	18.26	12.81	14.33	15.64
Market price per share	21.63	28.87	26.63	28.00	26.13

Required:

1. Compute Ryder's market price to book value ratio for Year 1 through Year 5.
2. What factors may have contributed to the decline in Ryder's book value per share in Year 3?

39. Price-Earnings Ratio (LO 5)

Listed next are recent P/E ratios of several prominent companies:

	P/E Ratio
Abbott Laboratories	23
The Home Depot, Inc.	29
Maytag Corporation	17
Merrill Lynch & Co., Inc.	11
Texas Instruments Incorporated	33
Union Carbide Corporation	9

Required:

1. What factors may account for the large variance in the P/E ratios of the companies listed?
2. Explain the difference between a company's P/E ratio and its market price to book value ratio. Which of these two ratios do you believe is more relevant to potential investors? Defend your answer.

40. Earnings Quality (LO 6)

Charlie Turner wants to begin investing in the stock market but knows very little about accounting and financial reporting practices. Recently, he stumbled across a brief article in *The Wall Street Journal* that focused on the subject of "earnings quality." After reading this article, Charlie was baffled. "How can there be a difference in the quality of earnings across companies?" he asked a friend after reading the article. "Corporate earnings are cold, hard facts, right? Accountants just add numbers here and subtract numbers there to arrive at a company's net income, right? Any way you cut it, two plus two equals four . . . right?"

Required:

Write a memo to Charlie that explains the concept of earnings quality. Comment in this memo on several factors that influence earnings quality. Since Charlie is unfamiliar with accounting and financial reporting practices, include numerical examples in the memo to clarify how these factors influence earnings quality. Conclude your memo with a few suggestions to Charlie regarding how he can evaluate the quality of reported earnings data.

41. Earnings Quality (LO 6)

An appendix to this text presents a recent annual report of Outback Steakhouse, Inc., a Florida-based firm that operates in the restaurant industry. Refer to that annual report when completing this exercise.

Required:

1. Define earnings quality and briefly explain why potential investors in Outback's common stock would want to assess the quality of the firm's earnings.
2. Identify information available in Outback's annual report that would help you evaluate the quality of the company's reported earnings in recent years.
3. Other than Outback's annual report, what other sources of information would you rely on to evaluate the quality of the company's reported earnings?

PROBLEM SET A

42. Trend Analysis (LO 1, 3)

Following are selected financial data for a recent five-year period for Whole Foods Market, Inc., a company headquartered in Austin, Texas. (Amounts are expressed in thousands of dollars, except for per share data.)

	Year 1	Year 2	Year 3	Year 4	Year 5
Sales	$144,267	$173,164	$205,348	$322,308	$401,685
Operating income	3,546	5,023	5,842	8,343	14,666
Earnings per share	.26	.31	.37	.29	.61
Book value per share	.99	1.16	4.02	5.77	6.87

Required:

1. Prepare a trend analysis for each listed financial item of Whole Foods Market using Year 1 as the base year.
2. Why aren't the trend percentages you computed in (1) consistent across each financial statement item?
3. How is trend analysis used by financial decision makers? What are the limitations of trend analysis?

43. Common-Sized Financial Statements (LO 4)
The News Corporation Limited is a large Australian company that publishes newspapers and magazines and operates television stations. Following are income statements for The News Corporation over a recent three-year period. (Amounts are expressed in millions of Australian dollars.)

THE NEWS CORPORATION
INCOME STATEMENTS
FOR THE YEARS ENDED JUNE 30, YEAR 1–YEAR 3

	Year 1	Year 2	Year 3
Revenues	$10,189	$10,686	$11,621
Costs and expenses	8,373	8,753	9,788
Earnings before interest, taxes depreciation and amortization	$ 1,816	$ 1,933	$ 1,833
Depreciation and amortization	225	231	236
Operating income	$ 1,591	$ 1,702	$ 1,597
Other income (expense):			
Equity income (losses) of associated companies	(57)	177	394
Net interest expense	(932)	(737)	(667)
Other	20	19	40
Income before income taxes, outside equity interests, and abnormal items	$ 622	$ 1,161	$ 1,364
Income tax expense	25	110	132
Outside equity interests	67	72	20
Income before abnormal items	$ 530	$ 979	$ 1,212
Abnormal items:			
Parent entity and controlled entities	(18)	(7)	105
Associated items	(11)	(108)	18
Net income	$ 501	$ 864	$ 1,335

Required:

1. Prepare common-sized income statements for The News Corporation for Year 1 through Year 3.
2. What major structural changes occurred over this three-year period in The News Corporation's income statement data? Are these changes apparently favorable or unfavorable? Explain.

44. Comparative Analysis of Financial Data (LO 2, 5)
The schedule on the following page provides key financial ratios for three companies in the same industry and the industry norm for each of these ratios.

Required:

1. Evaluate the overall financial health of these three firms. Given the information provided, which firm do you believe is in the strongest financial condition? Explain.
2. Again, based only upon the data provided, which firm's common stock do you believe would be the most attractive investment alternative? Why?
3. List three other items of financial or nonfinancial information that you would want to review before making an investment decision regarding the common stocks of these companies.

	Industry Norm	Alonso Company	Buckley, Inc.	Cosgrove Corp.
Current ratio	2.4	1.6	2.3	2.5
Quick ratio	1.0	.4	1.3	1.2
Long-term debt to equity ratio	.5	.6	.4	.2
Times interest Earned ratio	4.5	2.4	5.6	14.9
Age of receivables	89 days	101 days	77 days	80 days
Age of inventory	97 days	99 days	92 days	76 days
Profit margin percentage	3.4%	2.3%	3.6%	4.7%
Return on assets	4.9%	3.4%	5.6%	6.0%
Return on equity	7.1%	4.9%	7.1%	8.9%
Price-earnings ratio	10.2	7.5	7.7	12.7
Market price to book value ratio	1.8	1.3	1.2	3.2

45. Impact of Accounting Errors on Financial Ratios (LO 5)
Following are examples of errors that can be made in processing accounting data. Listed next to each error is a financial ratio.

Accounting Error	Financial Ratio	Impact of Error on Financial Ratio: *Increase*	*Decrease*	*No Effect*
a. Recording a sales transaction twice	Gross profit percentage	______	______	______
b. Overstatement of ending inventory	Quick	______	______	______
c. Debiting a payment of a long-term note payable to a short-term payable account	Return on assets	______	______	______
d. Understating the estimated useful life of a depreciable asset	Return on equity	______	______	______
e. Failing to prepare a year-end adjusting entry to record interest revenue	Price-earnings	______	______	______
f. Failing to record the declaration of a cash dividend shortly before year-end	Profit margin percentage	______	______	______
g. Recording a purchase of a long-term asset in a current asset account	Market price to book value ratio	______	______	______

Required:
Indicate whether each error increases (overstates), decreases (understates), or has no impact on the financial ratio with which it is coupled.

46. **Comprehensive Financial Statement Analysis** (LO 2, 5)
Shown next are the income statements for the three most recent fiscal years of Wichita Enterprises. Following those income statements are the company's balance sheets at the end of those fiscal years.

WICHITA ENTERPRISES
INCOME STATEMENTS
FOR THE YEARS ENDED DECEMBER 31, YEAR 1–YEAR 3

	Year 1	Year 2	Year 3
Sales*	$685,300	$702,000	$730,900
Cost of goods sold	384,800	378,400	373,800
Gross profit	$300,500	$323,600	$357,100
Operating expenses	124,300	158,100	179,300
Operating income	$176,200	$165,500	$177,800
Other revenue (expense)**	2,000	400	1,300
Income before income tax	$178,200	$165,900	$179,100
Income tax expense	71,200	66,400	71,600
Net income	$107,000	$ 99,500	$107,500

*All of the company's sales are on a credit basis.
**Includes interest expense of the following amounts: Year 1, $17,940; Year 2, $17,940; and Year 3, $14,820.

WICHITA ENTERPRISES
BALANCE SHEETS
DECEMBER 31, YEAR 1–YEAR 3

	Year 1	Year 2	Year 3
Assets			
Cash	$ 6,200	$ 1,500	$ 2,300
Accounts receivable (net)	51,000	47,300	38,600
Inventory	132,500	188,000	251,500
Supplies	1,100	2,400	1,700
Prepaid expenses	10,200	8,600	8,900
Total current assets	$201,000	$247,800	$303,000
Property, plant & equipment (net)	512,500	511,400	520,300
Other assets	5,700	7,300	3,600
Total assets	$719,200	$766,500	$826,900

(continued)

	Year 1	Year 2	Year 3
Liabilities			
Accounts payable	$ 81,000	$ 99,600	$ 98,100
Accrued liabilities	55,600	43,400	32,200
Total current liabilities	$136,600	$143,000	$130,300
Bonds payable	230,000	230,000	190,000
Total liabilities	$366,600	$373,000	$320,300
Stockholders' Equity			
Common stock	$ 12,000	$ 12,000	$ 16,000
Additional paid-in capital	122,000	122,000	142,000
Retained earnings	218,600	259,500	348,600
Total stockholders' equity	$352,600	$393,500	$506,600
Total liabilities and stockholders' equity	$719,200	$766,500	$826,900

During Year 1 and Year 2, Wichita Enterprises had 80,000 shares of common stock outstanding. The company had 90,000 shares of common stock outstanding throughout Year 3. Following are the market prices of Wichita's common stock at the end of Year 1 through Year 3: Year 1, $12.50; Year 2, $11.75; and Year 3, $10.50.

Listed next are key financial norms in Wichita Enterprises' industry during the period Year 1–Year 3.

Liquidity Ratios:	
Current	2.1
Quick	.8
Leverage Ratios:	
Long-term debt to equity	.4
Times interest earned	7.0
Activity Ratios:	
Accounts receivable turnover	10.0
Age of receivables	36 days
Inventory turnover	4.5
Age of inventory	80 days
Total asset turnover	1.2
Profitability Ratios:	
Profit margin percentage	12.5
Gross profit percentage	42.1
Return on assets	11.4
Return on equity	16.1
Market Strength Ratios:	
Price-earnings	12
Market price to book value	6.2

Required:

1. Compute Wichita Enterprises' financial ratios for Year 1 through Year 3. (Compute all of the ratios for which an industry norm is listed. Given the data provided, you can compute certain ratios for only Year 2 and Year 3.)
2. Analyze the financial ratios of Wichita Enterprises on a longitudinal basis. What positive and negative trends are apparent in the company's financial data?
3. Analyze the ratios of Wichita Enterprises by comparing each with the corresponding industry norm. Comment on which of the company's ratios are significantly different from the industry norm and whether these differences are favorable or unfavorable.
4. Identify unusual or unexpected relationships in Wichita Enterprises' financial data that you believe decision makers relying on this company's financial statements would want to investigate.
5. Comment on the overall financial status of Wichita Enterprises as of December 31, Year 3. In your opinion, did the company's financial status improve or deteriorate during the period Year 1 through Year 3? Explain.
6. List additional financial and nonfinancial information you would want to obtain before reaching a final conclusion concerning this company's future prospects.

47. **Earnings Quality** (LO 6)
Pickard Corporation and Jenkins Company are two firms in the same industry. These two firms have approximately the same annual revenues and total assets. Following is the most recent income statement of each firm.

	Pickard Corporation	Jenkins Company
Sales	$1,324,900	$1,337,300
Cost of goods sold	690,200	640,900
Gross profit	$ 634,700	$ 696,400
Operating expenses:		
Selling	90,000	86,400
General & administrative	72,000	87,000
Depreciation	102,000	71,000
Operating income	$ 370,700	$ 452,000
Other revenue (expense)	5,200	3,700
Income before income tax	$ 375,900	$ 455,700
Income tax expense	150,400	182,300
Net income	$ 225,500	$ 273,400

Pickard Corporation uses the LIFO inventory costing method and an accelerated depreciation method, while Jenkins Company uses FIFO inventory costing and the straight-line depreciation method.

Required:

1. Define earnings quality.
2. Why is earnings quality an important consideration for financial decision makers when evaluating financial statement data?
3. Suppose that a friend of yours is considering investing in the common stock of either Pickard Corporation or Jenkins Company. Write a memo to your friend explaining the concept of earnings quality and comment on how the quality of these firms' reported earnings may be affected by their use of different accounting methods.

PROBLEM SET B

48. Trend Analysis (LO 1, 3)

Following are recent financial data for King World Productions, Inc., which distributes *The Oprah Winfrey Show* and *Jeopardy!* (Amounts are expressed in thousands of dollars except for per share data.)

	Year 1	Year 2	Year 3	Year 4	Year 5
Total revenues	$453,749	$475,909	$503,174	$474,312	$480,659
Operating income	142,828	154,084	152,481	150,950	127,578
Total assets	406,950	500,834	498,240	535,546	569,562
Earnings per share	2.15	2.31	2.43	2.65	2.33

Required:

1. Prepare a trend analysis for each listed financial item of King World Productions using Year 1 as the base year.
2. How is trend analysis used by decision makers? What are the limitations of trend analysis?
3. Why aren't the trend percentages you computed in (1) consistent across each financial statement item?

49. Common-Sized Financial Statements (LO 4)

The News Corporation Limited is a large Australian company that publishes newspapers and magazines and operates television stations. Following are balance sheets for The News Corporation at the end of two recent fiscal years. (Amounts are expressed in millions of Australian dollars.)

THE NEWS CORPORATION
BALANCE SHEETS
JUNE 30, YEAR 1 AND YEAR 2

	Year 1	Year 2
Assets		
Current assets:		
Cash	$ 659	$ 433
Receivables	1,984	2,127
Inventories	972	984
Other	180	199
Total current assets	$ 3,795	$ 3,743
Noncurrent assets:		
Investments	$ 3,268	$ 3,396
Property, plant & equipment (net)	3,691	3,545
Goodwill	527	457
Publishing rights, titles and television licenses	13,317	13,162
Long-term receivables	364	480
Inventories	1,751	1,635
Other	559	528
Total noncurrent assets	$23,477	$23,203
Total assets	$27,272	$26,946

(continued)

	Year 1	Year 2
Liabilities and Shareholders' Equity		
Current liabilities:		
Current maturities of long-term debt	$ 18	$ 112
Accounts payable and other	3,245	3,539
Total current liabilities	$ 3,263	$ 3,651
Noncurrent liabilities:		
Long-term debt	$10,162	$ 7,793
Accounts payable and other	1,073	1,039
Total noncurrent liabilities	$11,235	$ 8,832
Redeemable preference shares	$ 228	$ 11
Outside equity interests	448	476
Shareholders' equity	12,098	13,976
Total liabilities and shareholders' equity	$27,272	$26,946

Required:

1. Prepare common-sized balance sheets for The News Corporation for Year 1 and Year 2.
2. What major structural changes occurred during Year 2 in this company's balance sheet data? Are these changes apparently favorable or unfavorable? Explain.

50. **Comparative Analysis of Financial Data** (LO 2, 5)
The following schedule provides key financial ratios for three companies in the same industry and the industry norm for each of these financial ratios.

	Industry Norm	Razook, Inc.	Schumacher Enterprises	Tersine Corporation
Current ratio	2.2	2.0	1.8	1.3
Quick ratio	.8	.8	.9	.5
Long-term debt to equity ratio	.3	.2	.4	.9
Times interest earned ratio	6.5	11.4	12.1	3.9
Age of receivables	72 days	73 days	76 days	80 days
Age of inventory	83 days	75 days	79 days	97 days
Profit margin percentage	4.4%	5.3%	4.6%	3.1%
Return on assets	5.7%	7.4%	6.2%	3.7%
Return on equity	8.1%	9.2%	7.7%	4.9%
Price-earnings ratio	12.5	16.5	9.7	13.4
Market price to book value ratio	2.2	3.5	1.3	2.7

Required:

1. Evaluate the overall financial health of these three firms. Given the information provided, which firm do you believe is in the strongest financial condition? Explain.

2. Again, based only upon the data provided, which firm's common stock do you believe is the most attractive investment alternative? Why?
3. List three other items of financial or nonfinancial information that you would want to review before making an investment decision regarding the common stocks of these companies.

51. Impact of Accounting Errors on Financial Ratios (LO 5)
Following are examples of errors that can be made in processing accounting data. Listed next to each error is a financial ratio.

Accounting Error	Financial Ratio	Impact of Error on Financial Ratio		
		Increase	*Decrease*	*No Effect*
a. Failing to record a year-end adjusting entry for amortization of discount on bonds payable	Return on equity	______	______	______
b. Understating the estimated salvage value of a depreciable asset	Gross profit percentage	______	______	______
c. Failing to prepare a year-end adjusting entry to record interest revenue	Return on assets	______	______	______
d. Overstatement of prepaid expenses	Quick	______	______	______
e. Debiting the prepayment of an insurance premium near year-end to an expense account	Times interest earned	______	______	______
f. Understating the year-end estimate of uncollectible accounts receivable	Current	______	______	______
g. Recording a sales transaction twice	Price-earnings ratio	______	______	______

Required:
Indicate whether each error increases (overstates), decreases (understates), or has no impact on the financial ratio with which it is coupled.

52. Comprehensive Financial Statement Analysis (LO 2, 5)
Shown next are the income statements for the three most recent fiscal years of Tulsa Corporation. Following those income statements are the company's balance sheets at the end of those fiscal years.

TULSA CORPORATION
INCOME STATEMENTS
FOR THE YEARS ENDED DECEMBER 31, YEAR 1–YEAR 3

	Year 1	Year 2	Year 3
Sales*	$484,200	$523,000	$576,600
Cost of goods sold	234,300	259,200	291,000
Gross profit	$249,900	$263,800	$285,600
Operating expenses	104,100	104,600	106,200
Operating income	$145,800	$159,200	$179,400
Other revenue (expense)**	12,000	5,400	11,300
Income before income tax	$157,800	$164,600	$190,700
Income tax expense	63,100	65,800	76,200
Net income	$ 94,700	$ 98,800	$114,500

*All of the company's sales are on a credit basis.
**Includes interest expense of the following amounts: Year 1, $14,280; Year 2, $11,220; and Year 3, $9,180.

TULSA CORPORATION
BALANCE SHEETS
DECEMBER 31, YEAR 1–YEAR 3

	Year 1	Year 2	Year 3
Assets			
Cash	$ 16,700	$ 21,500	$ 52,300
Accounts receivable (net)	81,000	94,300	139,800
Inventory	52,500	56,000	58,200
Prepaid expenses	6,200	4,600	5,600
Total current assets	$156,400	$176,400	$255,900
Property, plant & equipment (net)	$488,900	$539,300	$529,200
Total assets	$645,300	$715,700	$785,100
Liabilities			
Accounts payable	$ 71,400	$ 79,100	$ 81,200
Accrued liabilities	35,600	41,700	12,200
Total current liabilities	$107,000	$120,800	$ 93,400
Bonds payable	140,000	110,000	95,000
Total liabilities	$247,000	$230,800	$188,400
Stockholders' Equity			
Common stock	$ 5,000	$ 5,000	$ 6,000
Additional paid-in capital	62,000	62,000	99,000
Retained earnings	331,300	417,900	491,700
Total stockholders' equity	$398,300	$484,900	$596,700
Total liabilities and stockholders' equity	$645,300	$715,700	$785,100

During all of Year 1 and Year 2, Tulsa Corporation had 100,000 shares of common stock outstanding. Throughout Year 3, the company had 120,000 shares of common stock outstanding. Following are the year-end market prices of Tulsa's common stock for Year 1 through Year 3: Year 1, $17.75; Year 2, $20.25; and Year 3, $26.50.

Listed next are key financial norms in Tulsa Corporation's industry during the period Year 1–Year 3.

Liquidity Ratios:	
Current	1.5
Quick	.5
Leverage Ratios:	
Long-term debt to equity	.6
Times interest earned	4.5
Activity Ratios:	
Accounts receivable turnover	7.5
Age of receivables	48 days
Inventory turnover	4.0
Age of inventory	90 days
Total asset turnover	1.3
Profitability Ratios:	
Profit margin percentage	13.6
Gross profit percentage	52.8
Return on assets	12.4
Return on equity	16.9
Market Strength Ratios:	
Price-earnings	14
Market price to book value	3.1

Required:

1. Compute Tulsa Corporation's financial ratios for Year 1 through Year 3. (Compute all of the ratios for which an industry norm is listed. Given the data provided, you can compute certain ratios for only Year 2 and Year 3.)
2. Analyze the financial ratios of Tulsa Corporation on a longitudinal basis. What positive and negative trends are apparent in the company's financial data?
3. Analyze the ratios of Tulsa Corporation by comparing each with the corresponding industry norm. Comment on which of the company's ratios are significantly different from the industry norm and whether these differences are favorable or unfavorable.
4. Identify unusual or unexpected relationships in Tulsa Corporation's financial data that you believe decision makers relying on this company's financial statements would want to investigate.
5. Comment on the overall financial status of Tulsa Corporation as of December 31, Year 3. In your opinion, did the company's financial status improve or deteriorate during the period Year 1 through Year 3?
6. List additional financial and nonfinancial information you would want to obtain before reaching a final conclusion concerning Tulsa Corporation's future prospects.

53. **Earnings Quality** (LO 6)
Monnett Enterprises and Page Company are two firms in the same industry. These two firms have approximately the same annual revenues and total assets. Following is the most recent income statement of each firm.

	Monnett Enterprises	Page Company
Sales	$6,727,800	$6,638,900
Cost of goods sold	3,190,200	3,385,100
Gross profit	$3,537,600	$3,253,800
Operating expenses:		
Selling & general	424,600	456,700
Depreciation	305,000	394,000
Operating income	$2,808,000	$2,403,100
Other revenue (expense)	(34,200)	53,700
Income before income tax	$2,773,800	$2,456,800
Income tax expense	1,109,500	982,700
Net income	$1,664,300	$1,474,100
Earnings per share	$ 1.66	$ 1.47
Recent market price of common stock	$18.50	$16.75

Page Company uses the LIFO inventory costing method and an accelerated depreciation method, while Monnett Enterprises uses FIFO inventory costing and the straight-line depreciation method. If Page had used the FIFO method during the year in question, the company's cost of goods sold would have been reduced by $240,000. If Page had used the straight-line depreciation method, its depreciation expense for the year would have been reduced by $70,000. Both firms have an effective income tax rate of approximately 40 percent.

Required:
1. Define earnings quality.
2. Prepare a revised income statement for Page Company for the year in question, assuming it had used FIFO inventory costing and the straight-line depreciation method. Compute Page's profit margin percentage and gross profit percentage for both sets of income statement data. Also, compute Monnett Enterprises' profit margin percentage and gross profit percentage.
3. Which of these two companies was more profitable during the year in question? Explain.
4. If Page Company had issued the revised income statement you prepared, do you believe that the market price of its common stock would have been affected? Explain.

CASES

54. **Managing Earnings** (LO 1)
In 1985, the Securities and Exchange Commission (SEC) charged that Oak Industries, Inc., a California-based firm, was "managing" its earnings (Securities and Exchange

Commission, *Accounting and Auditing Enforcement Release No. 63,* 25 June 1985). In both 1980 and 1981, Oak Industries reported record earnings. However, the company's earnings for those years would have been higher if company officials had not intentionally overstated certain expenses.

Required:

1. Why might a company's executives intentionally overstate the firm's expenses during a given accounting period?
2. Is it ethical for business executives to intentionally overstate their firm's expenses or understate its revenues? Defend your answer.
3. Does the conservatism principle permit businesses to intentionally overstate expenses and understate revenues? Explain.

55. Analyzing International Financial Statements (LO 6)

Problems 43 and 49 present recent income statements and balance sheets, respectively, for The News Corporation, a large Australian conglomerate. Accounting and financial reporting rules and practices vary considerably from country to country. This is true even of countries that have similar political and social systems, such as Australia and the United States.

Required:

1. Review the financial statements of The News Corporation that are presented in Problems 43 and 49. Prepare a list of unusual or unfamiliar features of these financial statements that you have not observed in the financial statements of U.S. companies.
2. Research the accounting and financial reporting rules applied by Australian companies. Identify the key differences between those rules and the comparable rules applied by U.S. firms.
3. Write a brief memo to an individual who is considering investing in an Australian company. Inform this individual of key differences in the accounting and financial reporting practices of Australian and U.S. firms. Indicate in the memo how these differences may cause the financial statement data of Australian firms to differ from the financial statement data of similar U.S. firms.

56. Stock Market Prices and Financial Data (LO 1)

Sears, Roebuck and Co. is one of the most recognizable corporate names in the United States. This company's common stock is listed on stock exchanges around the world, including exchanges in Great Britain, Switzerland, Japan, and Germany. In the mid-1990s, the company had approximately 400 million shares of common stock outstanding which were owned by nearly 300,000 stockholders. Sears' financial data and key developments affecting its operations are monitored by thousands of sophisticated investors, including financial analysts of large brokerage firms. Given how closely this firm is followed by the investment community, you might expect there to be little variability in the market price of its common stock, at least over the short term. However, in a span of less than four years in the early 1990s, Sears' common stock traded in a range of $22 per share to more than $60 per share. One year, alone, the stock traded in a range from $22 to $42 per share.

Required:

1. Why do the market prices of common stocks of even the largest corporations fluctuate significantly over a short period of time?
2. Is it possible to identify the "true" economic value of large corporations and their common stocks at any given point in time? Explain.
3. How do investors use accounting data to gain insight on the economic value of a corporation and its common stock?

PROJECTS

57. The Big Bath Theory

In recent years, the "big bath theory" has been discussed in the business press. According to this theory, when companies are experiencing a poor year profit-wise, they may overstate their expenses and losses for that year—that is, they may take a "big bath." By doing so, such a company increases its chances of returning to a profitable status the following year.

Required:

1. Research business periodicals and identify articles that directly or indirectly address the big bath theory.
2. Identify at least one example of a company that apparently, or at least allegedly, took a "big bath" in recent years.
3. Prepare a written report that summarizes the key issues raised in the articles you identified in (1). Also include in your report the circumstances surrounding the "big bath" case you identified in (2). Identify the company, its location and principal line of business, and the apparent or alleged activities it engaged in that were consistent with the big bath theory.

58. Financial Statement Analysis for Investors

Each member of your project group should select a publicly owned company whose common stock he or she believes is an attractive investment. Each member should select his or her company independently of the other group members.

Required:

1. Each group member will obtain a recent set of financial statements for the company he or she selected and then analyze the company's financial data by applying the techniques discussed in this chapter. These analytical techniques include trend analysis, the preparation of common-sized financial statements, and ratio analysis.
2. Each group member should also prepare a brief summary of key nonfinancial information relevant to the company he or she selected. An impending merger, the release of new products, a planned expansion into international markets, and the hiring of new executives are a few examples of key nonfinancial information that should be obtained and documented for each selected company. This information may be obtained from the given firm's annual reports, from articles in recent business periodicals, from investment advisory services, or other relevant sources.
3. After each group member has obtained the information identified in (1) and (2) for his or her firm, the group should meet and discuss this information for each selected firm. The purpose of the group's discussion will be to choose the firm, among the several identified by group members, whose common stock is the most attractive investment.
4. A written report should be prepared by the group. This report should document the individual companies selected by group members and provide a brief summary of the key financial and nonfinancial information collected for each of these companies. The final section of the report should explain how and why the group selected one of these companies' common stock as the most attractive investment alternative.
5. One group member should be prepared to present a brief overview of the group's written report to the remainder of the class.

59. Analyzing Investment Advice

Contact a stockbroker and ask him or her to identify two common stocks that are presently recommended by his or her firm.

Required:

1. Obtain the most recent financial statements available for the two companies identified by the stockbroker that you contacted.
2. Analyze the financial statements of these firms using the techniques discussed in this chapter. Also, identify key nonfinancial information that provides insight on the future prospects of each firm. This information may be obtained from the firms' annual reports, from articles in recent business periodicals, from investment advisory services, or other relevant sources.
3. Write a report summarizing your research. Identify in this report the firms you researched, their locations, and their principal lines of business. Include in your report your analyses of the firms' financial data and the key nonfinancial information you collected regarding these firms. Conclude your report by indicating whether you agree that these firms' common stocks are attractive investments.

60. On-Line Financial Statement Analysis

The Internet is an important source of financial information for many investors. In this project, you will search the Internet to identify Web sites that individual investors can use to make more informed investment decisions.

Required:

1. Browse the Internet and identify ten Web sites that could be used as key information sources for individuals who want to invest in common stocks. The specific Web sites you select may be broad-based or industry-specific. That is, a selected Web site may contain relevant information for a wide range of companies or focus specifically on companies in a particular industry. The Web sites you select may contain financial databases, nonfinancial information, analyses of the investment potential of specific stocks, "how to" guides on investing, or any other type of information useful to investors.
2. Document in a report the ten Web sites you identified in (1). List the address of each Web site and provide a brief explanation of its contents.

APPENDIX

OUTBACK STEAKHOUSE ANNUAL REPORT

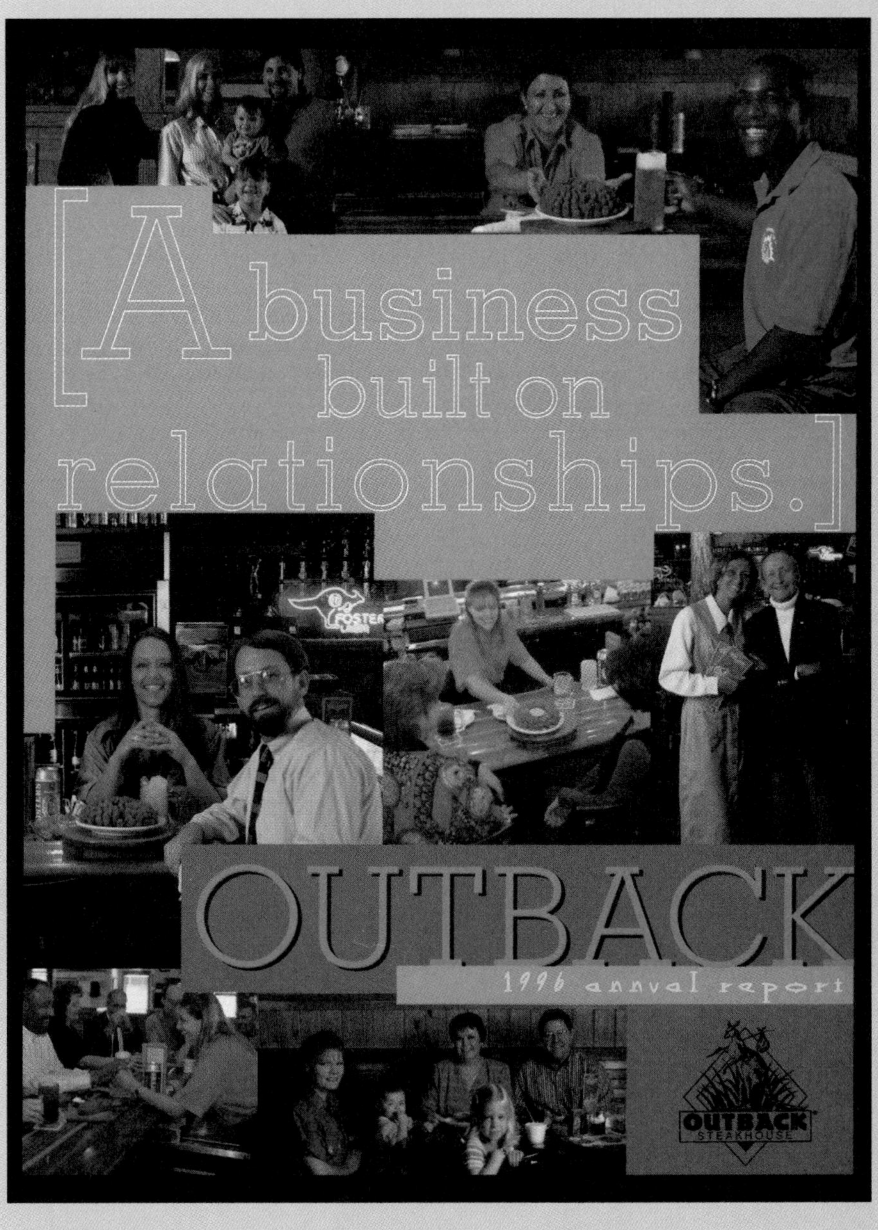

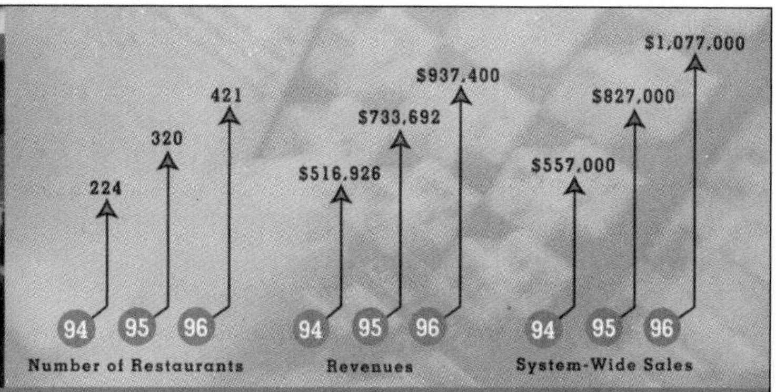

Number of Restaurants: 94 — 224; 95 — 320; 96 — 421

Revenues: 94 — $516,926; 95 — $733,692; 96 — $937,400

System-Wide Sales: 94 — $557,000; 95 — $827,000; 96 — $1,077,000

financial highlights

	Year Ended December 31,		
	1996	1995	1994
Statements of Income Data:	(in thousands, except per share data)		
Revenue	$ 937,400	$ 733,692	$516,926
Income from Operations	130,917	107,041	77,210
Net Income	71,613	57,911	41,196
Earnings Per Share	$ 1.45	$ 1.19	$ 0.86
Operating Data:			
System-wide Restaurant Sales			
Outback Steakhouses			
Company-owned restaurants	$ 892,000	$ 716,000	$516,000
Franchised and joint venture restaurants	125,000	82,000	33,000
	$1,017,000	$798,000	$549,000
Carrabba's Italian Grills			
Company-owned restaurants	$ 39,000	$ 14,000	
Joint venture restaurants	21,000	15,000	$ 8,000
	$ 60,000	$ 29,000	$ 8,000
System-wide total	$1,077,000	$827,000	$557,000
Number of restaurants (at end of period):			
Outback Steakhouses			
Company-owned restaurants	318	258	193
Franchised and joint venture restaurants	55	39	21
	373	297	214
Carrabba's Italian Grills			
Company-owned restaurants	36	13	
Joint venture restaurants	12	10	10
	48	23	10
System-wide total	421	320	224

Counting on our friends.

We are proud to report that despite soft casual dining industry sales patterns and fierce competition, we achieved another year of revenue and earnings growth in excess of 20%. We also opened 76 new Outback Steakhouses and 25 new Carrabba's Italian Grills.

For the year ended December 31, 1996, Company revenues increased by 28% to $937,400,000, and system-wide sales rose by 30%, to $1,077,000,000. Net income grew by 24%, to $71,613,000 and earnings per share by 22%, to $1.45. Return on average equity for 1996 was 24%.

But 1996 was a year that brought us face to face with several significant challenges. The echo baby boom now going on is having a significant effect on casual dining sales as many people with small children find it difficult to visit restaurants as frequently as they have in the past. We have seen a significant increase in the number of childrens meals we serve in our restaurants - now almost 8% of entrees sold. Food for take out, a less profitable sale for us because beverages are not usually purchased along with the meal, has also increased materially.

In addition to changing demographics, the number of casual dining restaurants in operation continues to grow at a pace that exceeds the small increase in industry sales, resulting in declining average sales per store. The industry experienced this kind of hyper-competition in the 1980's, but as capital dried up and marginal concepts failed, supply and demand changes came back into balance and the industry recovered and flourished.

Another challenge for the industry is the tight labor market resulting from the relatively low number of people in their early 20's, an important part of our labor pool. This has resulted in increased hourly wages in our restaurants which in turn put some pressure on our margins in 1996. While the pressure is not expected to go away in 1997, the demographic charts predict that things should improve going forward.

Someone once said that, "At times like this, you find out who your friends are". In 1996, we confirmed that we can count on the friends that we have made to help us prosper and grow. From the beginning, this Company was built upon relationships, from the bond between partners to our "one meal, one person at a time" philosophy. Our investment in the people who work with us and dine with us and our commitment to give back to the communities in which we operate and live, has allowed us to build a business far beyond our expectations.

In 1996, the first international Outback Steakhouse was opened in Toronto, Canada. Although there are many hurdles ahead for international expansion, we are pursuing relationships and exploring opportunities worldwide.

In 1997, we expect to open another 75 Outback Steakhouses and 25 Carrabba's Italian Grills in the United States. International expansion of Outback will continue with 7-10 new restaurants from Canada to the Far East. For the first time in our history, we expect that all of the capital needed for expansion will be generated internally.

Many of the challenges ahead can be viewed as opportunities. We have increased the value of our childrens meals to entice parents to continue to dine with us. We are testing enhanced service systems for food to ensure that customers who cannot dine in our restaurants still receive service that will exceed their expectations. We will continue to address competition by focusing on the execution of one meal, one person at a time and by continuing and expanding upon the relationships among partners, customers and staff. You will see a sampling of these relationships in the following pages.

Thank you.

Chris T. Sullivan
Chairman of the Board and Chief Executive Officer

Robert D. Basham
President and Chief Operating Officer

Just right, right from the start.

THE LEVINE FAMILY
Friday Night Regulars

"From the minute we walk in the door and see Beth smiling, we know everything is going to be just right," says Outback regular, Shelly Levine. "The kids see Beth and just light up." Her young family's visits to their favorite Outback Steakhouse have been a regular Friday night ritual for over five years. Hostess Beth Horton is part of what makes Outback a special place for the Levines, a place where their relationship with the staff makes for more than a great meal.

Beth considers the friendship she and her fellow Outbackers have with the Levines one of the perks of the job. "I really look forward to seeing them. They've been coming in since Samantha was an infant. Now little Sydney is one of our latest 'Outback babies.'"

"I kind of grew up here myself," observes Beth, who started while a 20-year old student. A seasoned veteran at 27, Beth is proud of "the consistent ability to deliver on the total guest experience" she feels is key to Outback's success. "This area has tons of young families," observes Beth. "We know how important that big night out is, and we go out of our way to accommodate them."

Shelly notes that, "Friday night at Outback is our reward to ourselves. Beth does all the little extras to get it off on the right foot."

"But it's not just us," adds Phil, "you can see Beth and the staff treating everyone the exact same way. It's just a very special restaurant and it's fun to feel like a part of it." It's employees like Beth Horton doing their part that keeps families like the Levines coming back to Outbacks across the country.

Team spirit, Outback style.

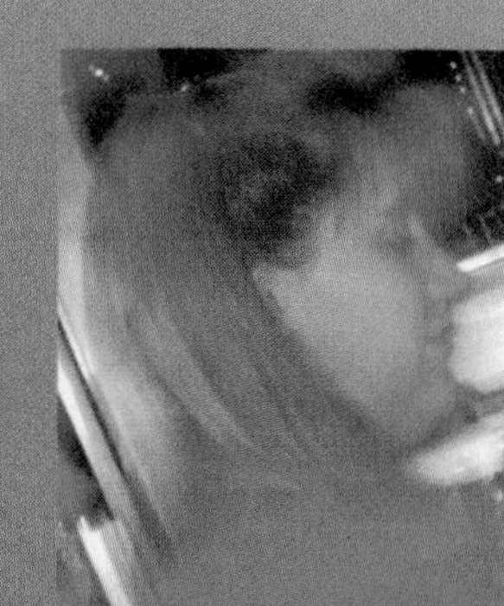

ARNOLD GWINN
Counting On Outback

When he moved from big city Pittsburgh, PA to small town Port Richey, Florida "there weren't many places to go around here," recalls gymnastics coach Arnold Gwinn. "But the minute that Outback opened, it was the place to be." Arnold and Outback bartender, Tina Swezey, have known each other "ever since he was one of my single-guy regulars through his stint as one of Port Richey's most eligible bachelors to happily married man."

Through it all, there's been Tina and the gang at Outback.

Arnold's gymnastics center has several students with a shot at making the nationals, but travelling around the country to competitions can get expensive for young families and their Olympic hopefuls. That's where Outback comes in. "Tina and the Outback gang have been with us all the way," says Arnold, "helping with fundraisers, donating gift certificates. You name it, Outback really supports us. They're part of the team."

"Arnold's like family," says Tina, proud to be able to do her part. Arnold feels the same way about Outback. "Tina and everybody go out of their way, do the little extras to make you feel special, ask how business is, how the team is doing. You feel good bringing your business to a place that gives back to the community."

For the past five years, Arnold's bride, Cindy, has been joining him at his favorite restaurant. "The food is always fantastic, but the people make the difference," insists Arnold. "That's why, even with all the competition around now, we'd just rather be at Outback."

A family tradition.

THE REXRODE FAMILY
Spreading the Word

"We're an Outback family," declares David Rexrode, whose wife Sally and two adoptive daughters, Sarah and Caroline, have made Outback Steakhouse their restaurant of choice for nine years. "It's our family clubhouse," says Sally, "where everyone knows your name."

Outback server, Annette Lampert, confirms the Rexrode's longstanding loyalty. "They've been regulars from day one. Just David and Sally at first. Sarah's been coming since she was 18 days old!"

"We know how difficult a family with young kids can be to wait on," says Sally. "But no matter how demanding we are, with all our special little requests, we know Annette will do anything it takes."

"Whenever they come in, they ask for my section," says Annette, whose relationship with the Rexrodes is just one more example of what makes Outback customers among the industry's most loyal. "They are the sweetest people," she smiles. "I always look forward to seeing them. It's not about the job, it's about spending time with them and their kids every week."

"We're Outback ambassadors," beams David. "This is where we entertain clients, bring friends. We're here for birthdays, anniversaries...and we love to give the gift certificates as gifts, because people love getting them!"

"The food and service are so consistently outstanding. You can count on it. That's what makes Outback the perfect place to bring people," adds Sally. "Our daughters are both adopted and we feel like Annette and Outback adopted us." Asked what makes Outback Steakhouse her favorite restaurant, five-year old Sarah sums it up this way: "Yum, yum!"

At Carrabba's, our secret is out in the open.

JIM McCUE
A Home Away From Home

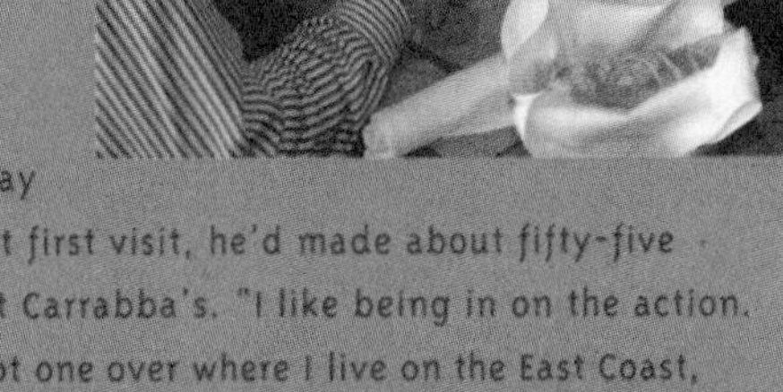

If there's a secret to the success of Carrabba's Italian Grill, it's an open one – the open grill and pasta bar where our quality is always on display and guests can always see what's cookin.' Salesman Jim McCue's business brings him to Tampa, often for weeks at a time. Any night he's in town, you'll find him up at the counter at Carrabba's, watching the cooks prepare his favorite Italian food.

That's were he got to know line cook, Celso Mascimento, Carrabba's 1996 Employee of the Year. "Just like this place, he impressed me right from the start," says Jim. "Friendly, and one hard worker."

Carrabba's is a place where even the cooks take time to get to know their guests. "Dining alone can be lonely," says Jim, "but from the moment I walked in the door, everyone went out of their way to make me feel welcome. Like Celso," says Jim, "by the end of that first visit, he'd made about fifty-five dinners and I'd made a new friend." Jim enjoys his ringside seat at Carrabba's. "I like being in on the action. And besides, it's the best Italian food I've ever found. Now we've got one over where I live on the East Coast, I take people all the time, and they love it."

Cooking in an open kitchen is extra pressure, but Celso enjoys the friendly competition among the line

cooks. "It keeps us on our toes, but we trust in our quality. We don't want our dishes coming back with anything but compliments to the chef."

As Jim puts it, "I got to know Carrabba's in Tampa, but now I look for them wherever I go. It's my home away from home."

Management's Discussion and Analysis of Financial Condition and Results of Operations

Introduction

At December 31, 1996, Outback Steakhouse, Inc. and Affiliates (the "Company") had 318 Outback Steakhouse restaurants in which it had a direct ownership interest ("Company-owned"), and 55 Outback Steakhouse restaurants operated by unaffiliated franchisees. The system also included 36 Company-owned Carrabba's Italian Grills and twelve Carrabba's Italian Grills operated by joint ventures in which the Company had a 45% interest ("Development Joint Ventures").

All of the Company-owned restaurants are organized as partnerships in which the Company is a general partner. The Company's ownership interests range from 71% to 90%, and the minority interests are owned by the restaurant managers and area operating partners. The results of operations of Company-owned restaurants are included in the consolidated operating results of the Company. The portion of the income attributable to the minority interests of restaurant managers and area operating partners is eliminated in the line item in the Company's Consolidated Statements of Income entitled "Elimination of minority partners' interest."

The Development Joint Venture restaurants are organized as general partnerships in which the Company owns 50% of the partnership and its joint venture partner owns 50%. The restaurant manager of each restaurant owned by a Development Joint Venture purchases a 10% interest in the restaurant he or she manages. The Company is responsible for 50% of the costs of new restaurants operated as Development Joint Ventures and the Company's joint venture partner is responsible for the other 50%. The income derived from restaurants operated as Development Joint Ventures is presented in the line item"Loss (income) from operations of unconsolidated affiliates" in the Company's Consolidated Statements of Income.

The Company derives no direct income from the operations of franchised restaurants other than franchise fees and royalties, which are included in the Company's revenues.

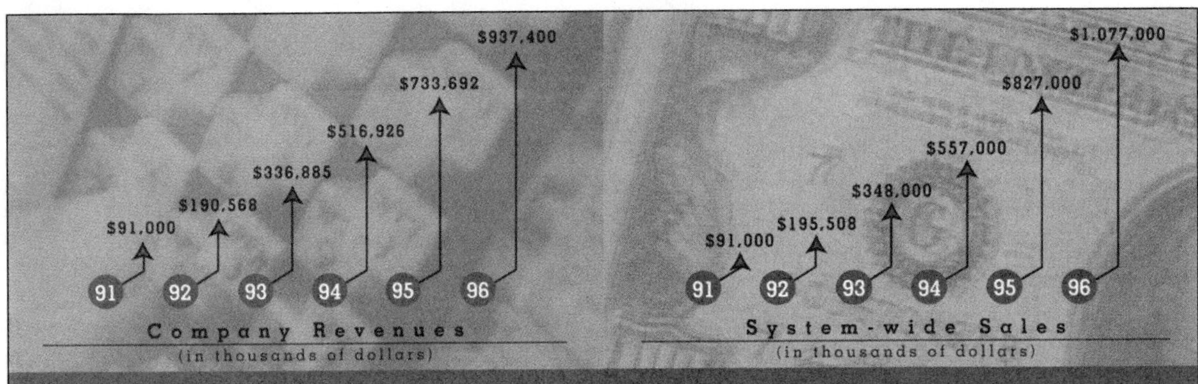

Results of Operations

The following table sets forth, for the periods indicated, (i) the percentages which the items in the Company's Consolidated Statements of Income bear to total revenues or restaurant sales, as indicated, and (ii) selected operating data:

	Years Ended December 31,		
Statements of Income Data:	1996	1995	1994
Revenues:			
Restaurant sales	99.3%	99.5%	99.7%
Franchise fees	0.7	0.5	0.3
	100.0	100.0	100.0
Costs and expenses:			
Cost of sales (1)	39.0	39.3	39.2
Labor and other related (1)	23.0	22.4	21.5
Other restaurant operating (1)	21.0	20.6	21.1
General and administrative	3.6	3.6	3.7
Loss (income) from operations of unconsolidated affiliates		(0.1)	(0.3)
Income from operations	13.9	14.6	15.0
Interest income (expense), net	(0.1)	(0.2)	(0.1)
Income before elimination of minority partners' interest and provision for income taxes	13.8	14.4	14.9
Elimination of minority partners' interest	1.9	2.1	2.3
Income before income taxes	11.9	12.3	12.6
Provision for income taxes (2)	4.3	4.4	4.6
Net income (2)	7.6%	7.9%	8.0%
System-wide sales (millions of dollars):			
Outback Steakhouses			
Company-owned restaurants	$ 892	$716	$516
Franchised and joint venture restaurants	125	82	33
	$ 1,017	$798	$549
Carrabba's Italian Grills			
Company-owned restaurants	$ 39	$ 14	
Joint venture restaurants	21	15	$ 8
	$ 60	$ 29	$ 8
System-wide total	$1,077	$827	$557
Number of restaurants (at end of period):			
Outback Steakhouses			
Company-owned restaurants	318	258	193
Franchised and joint venture restaurants	55	39	21
	373	297	214
Carrabba's Italian Grills			
Company-owned restaurants	36	13	
Joint venture restaurants	12	10	10
	48	23	10
System-wide total	421	320	224

(1) As a percentage of restaurant sales. (2) Amounts are pro forma for 1995 and 1994. See Note 11 of Notes to Consolidated Financial Statements.

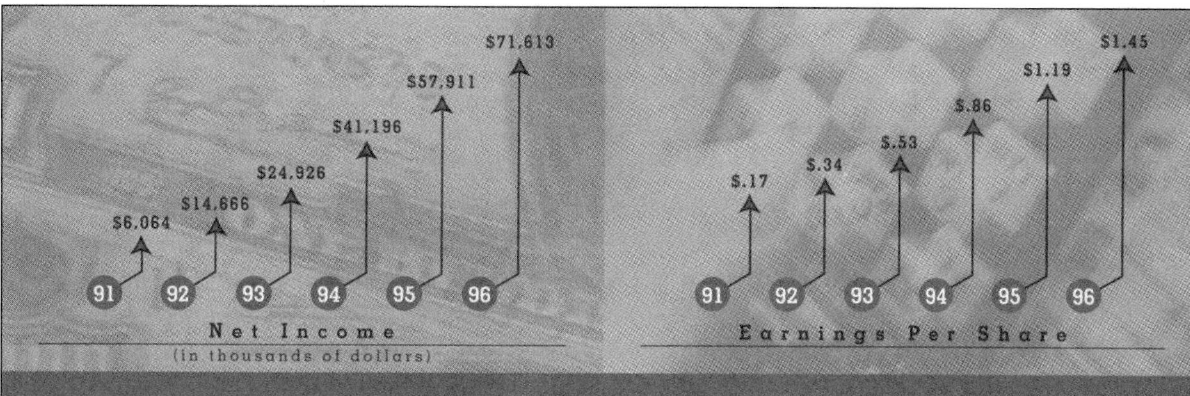

Fiscal years 1996, 1995 and 1994

Revenues. Total revenues increased by 27.8% between 1995 and 1996, and by 41.9% between 1994 and 1995. The increase in revenues in 1996 was attributable to the opening of new restaurants partially offset by a 1.1% decrease in comparable store sales. The decrease in comparable store sales resulted from lower customer check averages in the second quarter of 1996, the impact of the Olympics in July and August, and reduced customer counts resulting from increased competition in the last quarter of 1996. The increase in revenues in 1995 as compared with 1994 was attributable to the opening of new restaurants and a 1.1% increase in comparable store sales. The increase in comparable store sales reflected an increase in customer counts and a 1.2% menu price increase in September 1995.

Costs and expenses. Costs of sales, consisting of food and beverage costs, decreased by 0.3% of restaurant sales to 39.0% in 1996 as compared with 39.3% in 1995. Of the decrease, 0.1% resulted from an increase in the proportion of Carrabba's Italian Grills ("Carrabba's") in operation which have lower average food costs than Outback Steakhouses. The remainder of the decrease resulted from commodity cost decreases for shrimp and produce, partially countered by price increases in meat and dairy. Cost of sales increased as a percentage of restaurant sales to 39.3% in 1995 as compared with 39.2% in 1994. Commodity cost increases in shrimp, produce and baby back ribs in 1995 were partially offset by favorable meat prices and menu price changes in September 1995.

Labor and other related expenses include all direct and indirect labor costs incurred in operations. Labor expenses as a percentage of restaurant sales increased by 0.6% to 23.0% in 1996 as compared with 22.4% in 1995. Of the increase, 0.4% was attributable to an increase in the proportion of Carrabba's in operation which have higher average labor costs than Outback Steakhouses. The remainder of the increase resulted from higher labor costs in new markets, an increase in wage rates in certain markets, and an overall increase in back of the house wage rates due to a competitive labor market. Labor expenses as a percentage of restaurant sales increased to 22.4% in 1995 from 21.5% in 1994. This increase was attributable to the cost of the Company's health insurance plan implemented in February 1995, higher labor costs in new markets, and increased wage rates in certain other markets.

Restaurant operating expenses include all other unit-level operating costs, the major components of which are operating supplies, rent, repairs and maintenance, advertising expenses, utilities, depreciation and amortization and other occupancy costs. A substantial portion of these expenses are fixed or indirectly variable. These costs as a percentage of restaurant sales increased by 0.4%, to 21.0%, during 1996 as compared with 20.6% in 1995. This increase was attributable to an increase in the proportion of Carrabba's in operation which have higher operating expenses as a percentage of restaurant sales than Outback Steakhouses due to lower average unit volumes. In 1995 as compared with 1994, restaurant operating expenses decreased by 0.5% to 20.6% of restaurant sales. This decrease was attributable to improved operating efficiencies achieved by mature restaurants combined with lower occupancy expenses as the proportion of owned versus leased restaurants increased in 1995.

General and administrative expenses as a percentage of revenues was 3.6% in both 1996 and 1995 and 3.7% in 1994. The decrease from 1994 to 1995 was due to the opening of new restaurants.

Loss (income) from operations of unconsolidated affiliates. Loss (income) from operations of unconsolidated affiliates represents the Company's portion of net income or loss from Carrabba's Italian Grills and Outback Steakhouses operated as Development Joint Ventures. The loss from Development Joint Ventures was $102,000 in 1996 compared with income of $442,000 in 1995 and $1,269,000 in 1994. These decreases were attributable to

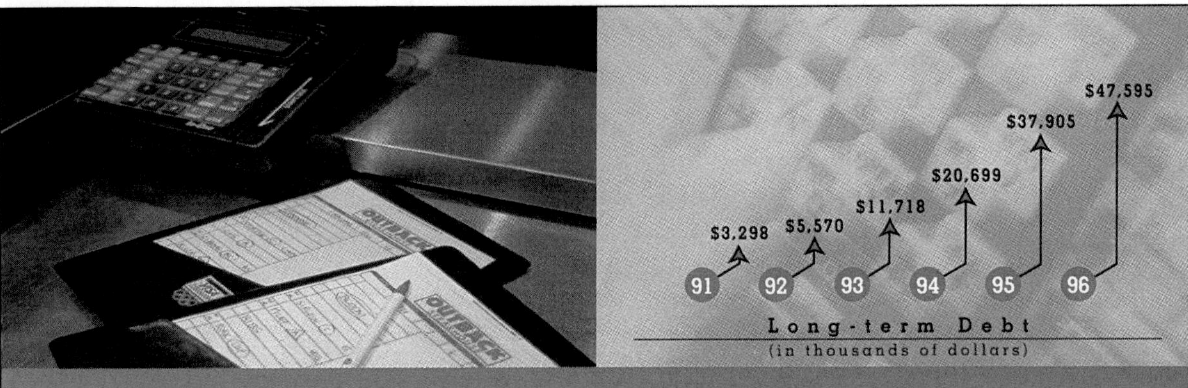

losses from Carrabba's Texas operations, and to fewer Outback Steakhouses operating as Development Joint Ventures as a result of the restructuring of the Company's Nevada operations in April 1996.

Income from operations. As a result of the increase in revenues, the changes in the relationship between revenues and expenses discussed above and the opening of new restaurants, income from operations increased by $23,876,000 to $130,917,000 in 1996 as compared with $107,041,000 in 1995, and by $29,831,000 to $107,041,000 in 1995 as compared with $77,210,000 in 1994.

Interest income (expense), net. Net interest expense was $1,096,000 in 1996 as compared with $1,375,000 in 1995 and $302,000 in 1994. The year to year changes in interest expense reflected changes in available cash and cash equivalents and investment securities earning interest, fluctuations in interest rates on the Company's line of credit, and changes in borrowing needs as funds have been expended to finance new restaurants. See Note 5 of Notes to Consolidated Financial Statements.

Elimination of minority partners' interest. This line item represents the portion of income from operations included in consolidated operating results attributable to the ownership interests of restaurant managers and area operating partners in Company-owned restaurants. As a percentage of revenues these costs were 1.9%, 2.1% and 2.3% in 1996, 1995 and 1994, respectively. The decrease in this ratio from year to year reflected changes in overall restaurant operating margins combined with changes in minority partners' ownership interests as a result of the restructuring of the Company's Dallas and Houston joint ventures in 1995.

Pro forma provision for income taxes. The provision for income taxes, in all three years presented reflected expected income taxes at the federal statutory rate and state income tax rates, net of the federal benefit. The effective income tax rate for pro forma income taxes was 36% in both 1996 and 1995 and 36.6% in 1994. The decrease in the effective tax rate from 1994 was attributable to changes in the federal income tax statutes in 1995.

Net income and earnings per common share. Net income for 1996 was $71,613,000, an increase of 23.7% over pro forma net income of $57,911,000 in 1995. Pro forma net income for 1994 was $41,196,000. Earnings per common share increased to $1.45 for 1996 from pro forma earnings per common share of $1.19 in 1995, an increase of 21.9%. Pro forma earnings per common share increased to $1.19 for 1995 as compared with $0.86 in 1994, an increase of 38.4%.

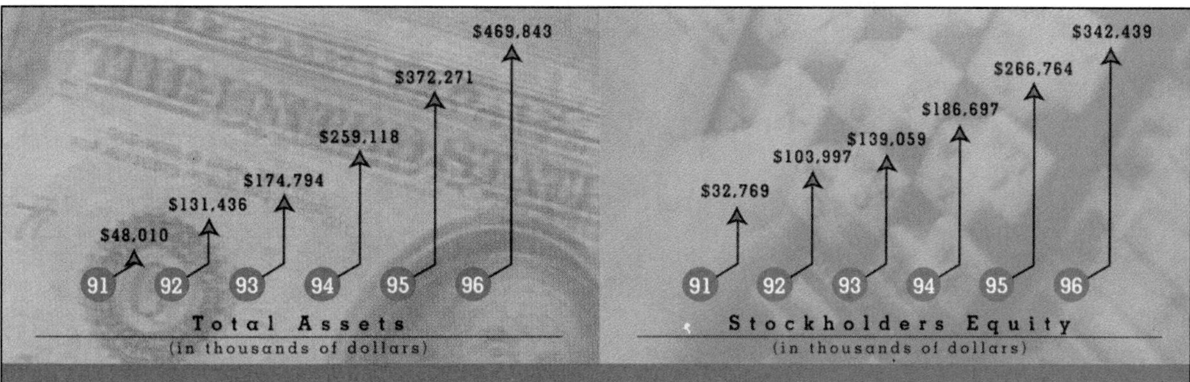

Liquidity and Capital Resources

The following table presents a summary of the Company's cash flows for the last three fiscal years:

	(in thousands)		
	1996	1995	1994
Net cash provided by operating activities	$122,799	$100,758	$75,976
Net cash used in investing activities	(126,631)	(119,104)	(86,845)
Net cash (used in) provided by financing activities	(7,596)	24,063	5,858
Net (decrease) increase in cash and cash equivalents	$ (11,428)	$ 5,717	$ (5,011)

The Company requires capital principally for the development of Company-owned and Development Joint Venture restaurants. Capital expenditures totalled approximately $130,987,000, $121,552,000 and $84,320,000 in 1996, 1995 and 1994, respectively. The Company either leases its restaurants under operating leases for initial periods ranging from five to 15 years or purchases free standing restaurants where it is cost effective. As of December 31, 1996, there were approximately 192 restaurants developed on properties which were owned by the Company. See Note 9 of Notes to Consolidated Financial Statements.

At December 31, 1996 the Company has two unsecured lines of credit totalling $82,500,000. Approximately $3,300,000 is committed for the issuance of letters of credit, some of which are to secure loans made by the bank to certain franchisees, and $45,320,000 has been drawn by the Company to finance capital expenditures. See Note 5 of Notes to Consolidated Financial Statements.

The Company's goal is to add new restaurants to the Outback system in each of 1997 and 1998, primarily through the development of 50 to 55 Company-owned Outback Steakhouses and 15 to 20 franchised Outback Steakhouses each year. The Company also intends to add 20 to 25 Carrabba's Italian Grills, the majority of which will be Company-owned restaurants in each of 1997 and 1998. The Company estimates that its capital expenditures for the development of new restaurants will be approximately $128 million in each of 1997 and 1998 and intends to finance this development with income from operations and the unused portion of the revolving line of credit referred to above. The Company anticipates that 80% to 90% of the Company-owned restaurants to be opened in 1997 will be free-standing units.

The Company notes that a variety of factors could cause the actual results and experience to differ from the anticipated results referred to in the previous paragraph. The Company's forward looking statements regarding its development schedule for new restaurant openings are subject to a number of risk factors including:

(i) Ability to secure appropriate real estate sites at acceptable prices;
(ii) Ability to obtain all required governmental permits including zoning approvals and liquor licenses on a timely basis;
(iii) Impact of government moratoriums or approval processes which could result in significant delays;
(iv) Ability to secure all necessary contractors and sub-contractors;
(v) Union activities such as picketing and hand billing which could delay construction;
(vi) Weather and acts of God beyond the Company's control resulting in construction delays.

Impact of Inflation

The Company has not operated in a highly inflationary period and does not believe that inflation has had a material effect on sales or expenses during the last three years. To the extent permitted by competition, the Company expects to mitigate increased costs by increasing menu prices.

Independent Auditors' Report

To the Board of Directors and
Stockholders of Outback Steakhouse, Inc.
Tampa, Florida

We have audited the accompanying consolidated balance sheets of Outback Steakhouse, Inc. and Affiliates (the "Company") as of December 31, 1996 and 1995, and the related consolidated statements of income, stockholders' equity, and cash flows for each of the three years in the period ended December 31, 1996. These financial statements are the responsibility of the Company's management. Our responsibility is to express an opinion on these financial statements based on our audits.

We conducted our audits in accordance with generally accepted auditing standards. Those standards require that we plan and perform the audit to obtain reasonable assurance about whether the financial statements are free of material misstatement. An audit includes examining, on a test basis, evidence supporting the amounts and disclosures in the financial statements. An audit also includes assessing the accounting principles used and significant estimates made by management, as well as evaluating the overall financial statement presentation. We believe that our audits provide a reasonable basis for our opinion.

In our opinion, such consolidated financial statements present fairly, in all material respects, the financial position of Outback Steakhouse, Inc. and Affiliates as of December 31, 1996 and 1995, and the results of their operations and their cash flows for each of the three years in the period ended December 31, 1996 in conformity with generally accepted accounting principles.

Deloitte & Touche LLP

Deloitte & Touche LLP
Tampa, Florida
February 21, 1997

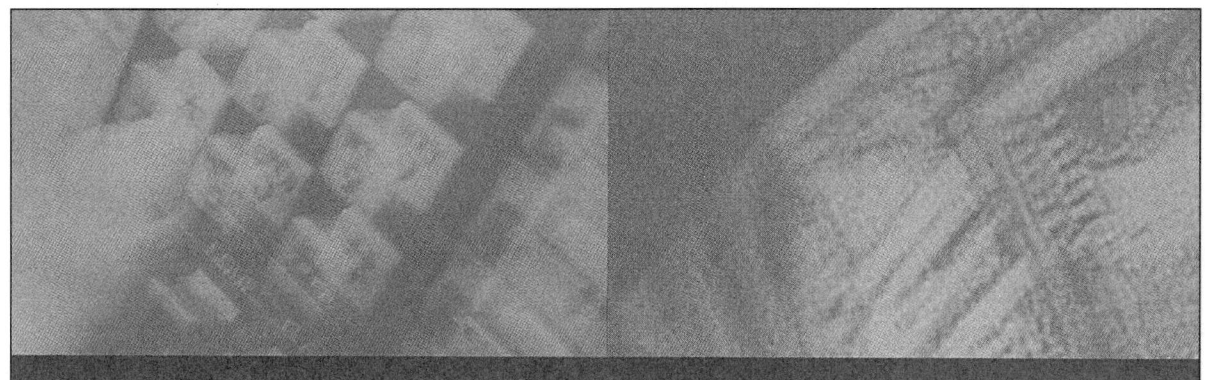

Outback Steakhouse, Inc.

Consolidated Balance Sheets (in thousands)

	December 31, 1996	December 31, 1995
Assets		
Current Assets		
Cash and cash equivalents	$ 15,661	$ 27,089
Short-term investment securities		1,176
Inventories	16,637	6,474
Other current assets	8,810	12,984
Total current assets	41,108	47,723
PROPERTY, FIXTURES AND EQUIPMENT, NET	397,759	290,630
INVESTMENTS IN AND ADVANCES TO UNCONSOLIDATED AFFILIATES	13,968	17,250
OTHER ASSETS	17,008	16,668
	$469,843	$372,271
Liabilities and Stockholders' Equity		
Current liabilities		
Accounts payable	$ 27,824	$ 20,285
Sales taxes payable	6,027	4,358
Accrued expenses	19,208	13,331
Unearned revenue	20,334	17,632
Current portion of long-term debt	706	3,000
Total current liabilities	74,099	58,606
DEFERRED INCOME TAXES	1,141	1,298
LONG-TERM DEBT	47,595	37,905
INTEREST OF MINORITY PARTNERS IN CONSOLIDATED PARTNERSHIPS	1,569	2,698
OTHER LONG-TERM LIABILITIES	3,000	5,000
Total liabilities	127,404	105,507
COMMITMENTS AND CONTINGENCIES (Notes 5 and 9)		
STOCKHOLDERS' EQUITY		
Common stock, $0.01 par value, 100,000 shares authorized; 48,009 and 47,503 shares issued and outstanding as of December 31, 1996 and 1995, respectively	480	475
Additional paid-in capital	111,941	107,884
Retained earnings	230,018	158,405
Total stockholders' equity	342,439	266,764
	$469,843	$372,271

See Notes to Consolidated Financial Statements.

Outback Steakhouse, Inc.

Consolidated Statements of Income (in thousands, except per share data)

	Years Ended December 31,		
	1996	1995	1994
REVENUES	$937,400	$733,692	$516,926
COSTS AND EXPENSES			
Cost of revenues	363,285	286,762	202,250
Labor and other related	214,038	163,747	110,787
Other restaurant operating	195,229	150,409	108,952
General and administrative	33,829	26,175	18,996
Loss (income) from operations of unconsolidated affiliates	102	(442)	(1,269)
	806,483	626,651	439,716
INCOME FROM OPERATIONS	130,917	107,041	77,210
NON-OPERATING INCOME (EXPENSE)	(1,096)	(1,375)	(302)
INCOME BEFORE ELIMINATION OF MINORITY PARTNERS' INTEREST AND PROVISION FOR INCOME TAXES	129,821	105,666	76,908
ELIMINATION OF MINORITY PARTNERS' INTEREST	17,925	15,181	11,930
INCOME BEFORE PROVISION FOR INCOME TAXES	111,896	90,485	64,978
PROVISION FOR INCOME TAXES	40,283	29,167	21,602
NET INCOME	$ 71,613	$ 61,318	$ 43,376
EARNINGS PER COMMON SHARE	$ 1.45	$ 1.25	$ 0.91
WEIGHTED AVERAGE NUMBER OF COMMON SHARES OUTSTANDING	49,289	48,877	47,674
PRO FORMA:			
PROVISION FOR INCOME TAXES		32,574	23,782
NET INCOME		$ 57,911	$ 41,196
EARNINGS PER COMMON SHARE		$ 1.19	$ 0.86

See Notes to Consolidated Financial Statements.

Outback Steakhouse, Inc.
Consolidated Statements of Stockholders' Equity (in thousands)

	Common Stock Shares	Common Stock Amount	Additional Paid-In Capital	Retained Earnings	Total
Balance, December 31, 1993	46,111	$ 461	$ 83,139	$ 55,459	$ 139,059
Issuance of Common Stock	488	4	6,006		6,010
Distributions				(1,748)	(1,748)
Net income				43,376	43,376
Balance, December 31, 1994	46,599	465	89,145	97,087	186,697
Issuance of Common Stock	904	10	18,739		18,749
Net income				61,318	61,318
Balance, December 31, 1995	47,503	475	107,884	158,405	266,764
Issuance of Common Stock	506	5	4,057		4,062
Net income				71,613	71,613
Balance, December 31, 1996	48,009	$480	$111,941	$230,018	$342,439

See Notes to Consolidated Financial Statements.

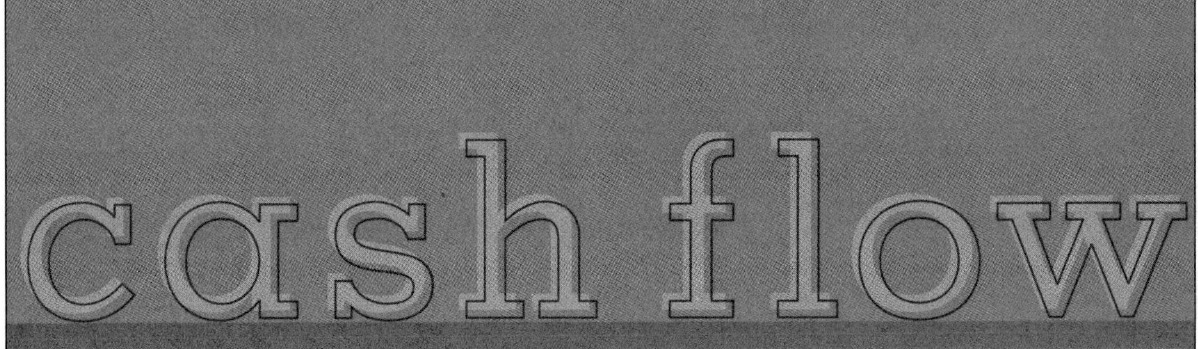

Outback Steakhouse, Inc.

Consolidated Statements of Cash Flow (in thousands)

	Years Ended December 31,		
Cash flows from operating activities:	1996	1995	1994
Net income	$71,613	$61,318	$43,376
Adjustments to reconcile net income to net cash provided by operating activities:			
Depreciation	23,858	15,699	11,362
Amortization	11,670	10,151	6,604
(Gain) loss from sale of investment securities		(133)	29
Minority partners' interest in consolidated partnerships' income	17,925	15,181	11,930
Loss (income) from operations of unconsolidated affiliates	102	(442)	(1,269)
Change in assets and liabilities:			
Increase in inventories	(10,163)	(1,246)	(859)
Increase in other current assets	4,174	1,636	(9,212)
Increase in other assets	(12,010)	(13,997)	(9,146)
Increase in accounts payable, sales taxes payable and accrued expenses	15,085	7,916	16,760
Increase in unearned revenue	2,702	4,426	6,525
Decrease in other long-term liabilities	(2,000)		
(Decrease) increase in deferred income taxes	(157)	249	(124)
Net cash provided by operating activities	122,799	100,758	75,976
Cash flows used in investing activities:			
Purchases of investment securities			$ (163)
Sales of investment securities	$ 1,176	$ 5,012	9,613
Capital expenditures	(130,987)	(121,552)	(84,320)
Payments from unconsolidated affiliates		732	1,472
Distribution to unconsolidated affiliates	(312)	(344)	(539)
Change in investments in and advances to unconsolidated affiliates	3,492	(2,952)	(12,908)
Net cash used in investing activities	(126,631)	(119,104)	(86,845)
Cash flows (used in) provided by financing activities:			
Adjustments from stock transactions	$ 4,062	$18,749	$ 6,010
Proceeds from issuance of long-term debt	48,037	35,198	24,580
Proceeds from minority partners' contributions	2,100	2,150	1,775
Distributions to minority partners' and shareholders	(21,154)	(17,042)	(10,907)
Repayments of long-term debt	(40,641)	(14,992)	(15,600)
Net cash (used in) provided by financing activities	(7,596)	24,063	5,858
Net (decrease) increase in cash and cash equivalents	(11,428)	5,717	(5,011)
Cash and cash equivalents at the beginning of the period	27,089	21,372	26,383
Cash and cash equivalents at the end of the period	$15,661	27,089	21,372
Supplemental disclosures of cash flow information:			
Cash paid for interest	$ 2,419	$ 1,586	$ 1,332
Cash paid for income taxes	53,261	29,100	24,625

See Notes to Consolidated Financial Statements.

Outback Steakhouse, Inc.
Notes to Consolidated Financial Statements

1. Summary of Significant Accounting Policies

Basis of Presentation – Outback Steakhouse, Inc. and Affiliates (the "Company") was formed for the purpose of developing casual dining restaurants. The Company's restaurants are generally organized as partnerships, with the Company as the general partner.

Profits and losses of each partnership are shared based on respective partnership interest percentages, as are cash distributions and capital contributions with certain defined exceptions.

Additional Outback Steakhouse restaurants in which the Company has no direct investment are operated under franchise agreements.

Principles of Consolidation – The consolidated financial statements include the accounts and operations of the Company and affiliated partnerships in which the Company is a general partner and owns more than a 50% interest. All material balances and transactions between the consolidated entities have been eliminated.

Unconsolidated affiliates are accounted for using the equity method.

Cash and Cash Equivalents – Cash equivalents consist of investments which are readily convertible to cash with maturities of three months or less.

Investment Securities – Investment securities are classified as "available for sale" and reported at amortized cost which approximates market value.

Inventories – Inventories consist of food and beverages, and are stated at the lower of cost (first-in, first-out) or market. The Company will periodically make advance purchases of various inventory items to ensure adequate supply or obtain favorable pricing. At December 31, 1996, inventories included approximately $7,300,000 in advance purchases.

Preopening costs – Preopening costs, consisting of marketing and training costs, are amortized primarily over twelve months.

Unearned Revenues – Unearned revenues represent gift certificates sold but not yet redeemed. Sales are recognized upon redemption of the gift certificates.

Property, Fixtures and Equipment – Property, fixtures and equipment are stated at cost. Depreciation and amortization are provided on a straight line basis over the estimated useful service lives of the related assets which range from 3 to 39.5 years.

Periodically, the Company evaluates the recoverability of the net carrying value of its property, fixtures and equipment by estimating its fair value. The fair value is compared to the carrying amount in the consolidated financial statements. A deficiency in fair value relative to carrying amount is an indication of the need for a writedown due to impairment. If the total of future undiscounted cash flows were less than the carrying amount of the property, fixtures and equipment, such carrying amount would be written down to the fair value, and a loss on impairment recognized by a charge to earnings. The Company's accounting policy complies with Statement of Financial Accounting Standards No. 121.

Construction in Progress – The Company capitalizes all direct costs incurred in the construction of its restaurants. Upon opening, these costs are depreciated or amortized and charged to expense based upon their property classification. The amount of interest capitalized was $1,084,000 in 1996, $400,000 in 1995, and insignificant in 1994.

Income Taxes – The Company uses the asset and liability method which recognizes the amount of current and deferred taxes payable or refundable at the date of financial statements as a result of all events that have been recognized in the financial statements as measured by the provisions of enacted tax laws.

The minority partners' interest in affiliated partnerships includes no provision or liability for income taxes as any tax liability related thereto is the responsibility of the individual minority partners.

Outback Steakhouse, Inc.

Notes to Consolidated Financial Statements

1. Summary of Significant Accounting Policies (continued)

Earnings Per Common Share – Earnings per common share is computed by dividing net income by the weighted average number of shares of common stock and dilutive options outstanding during the year.

Reclassification – Certain amounts shown in the 1994 and 1995 financial statements have been reclassified to conform with the 1996 presentation.

Certain Significant Risks and Uncertainties – The preparation of financial statements in conformity with generally accepted accounting principles requires management to make estimates and assumptions that affect the reported amounts of assets and liabilities and disclosure of contingent assets and liabilities at the date of the financial statements and the reported amounts of revenues and expenses during the reporting period. Actual results could differ from those estimated.

2. Other Current Assets

Other current assets consisted of the following (in thousands):

	December 31, 1996	December 31, 1995
Deposits (including income tax deposits)	$ 755	$ 6,310
Accounts receivable	1,898	1,667
Prepaid expenses	4,961	3,100
Other current assets	1,196	1,907
	$8,810	$12,984

3. Property, Fixtures and Equipment

Property, fixtures and equipment consisted of the following (in thousands):

	December 31, 1996	December 31, 1995
Land	$ 85,255	$ 64,923
Buildings and building improvements	153,212	96,676
Furniture and fixtures	36,794	22,592
Equipment	92,800	67,345
Leasehold improvements	74,858	67,232
Construction in progress	18,084	11,248
Accumulated depreciation	(63,244)	(39,386)
	$397,759	$290,630

Outback Steakhouse, Inc.

Notes to Consolidated Financial Statements

4. Other Assets

Other assets consisted of the following (in thousands):

	December 31, 1996	1995
Preopening costs, net	$ 8,818	$ 8,134
Intangible assets (including liquor licenses)	4,485	3,009
Other assets	3,705	5,525
	$17,008	$16,668

5. Long-Term Debt

Long-term debt consisted of the following (in thousands):

	December 31, 1996	1995
Notes payable to banks, collateralized by various items including stock, investment securities, property, fixtures and equipment, interest at rates ranging from 8.825% to 9.9% at December 31, 1996	$ 1,336	$ 14,794
Notes payable to leasing companies, collateralized by equipment, interest rates ranging from 8% to 13.2%	127	409
Note payable to corporation, collateralized by real estate, interest at 9.0%	455	553
Other notes payable, unsecured, interest ranging from 5.36% to 7.99%	1,063	749
Revolving line of credit, interest ranging from 6.19% to 6.37% at December 31, 1996 (see below)	45,320	24,400
	48,301	40,905
Less current portion	706	3,000
Long-term debt	$47,595	$37,905

Approximately $1,336,000 and $14,794,000 of the notes payable outstanding at December 31, 1996 and 1995, respectively, were assumed by the Company in connection with the mergers discussed in Note 10. The majority of the notes payable outstanding at December 31, 1995 were paid down with the Company's revolving line of credit during 1996.

The Company has an unsecured revolving line of credit which permits borrowing up to a maximum of $75,000,000 at a rate of 75 basis points over the 30, 60, 90 or 180 day London Interbank Offered Rate (LIBOR) (5.5% to 5.6% at December 31, 1996). At December 31, 1996, the unused portion of the revolving line of credit was $29,680,000. The line matures in June 1999.

The Company has a $7,500,000 unsecured line of credit bearing interest at the rate of 75 basis points over LIBOR. Approximately $3,300,000 of the line of credit is committed for the issuance of letters of credit, $703,000 of which is to secure loans made by the bank to certain franchisees.

The aggregate payments of long-term debt outstanding at December 31, 1996, for the next five years, are summarized as follows: 1997 - $706,000; 1998 - $610,000; 1999 - $45,958,000; 2000 - $295,000; 2001 - $52,000.

The carrying amount of long-term debt at December 31, 1996 approximates fair value.

accrued expenses

Outback Steakhouse, Inc.
Notes to Consolidated Financial Statements

6. Accrued Expenses

Accrued expenses consisted of the following (in thousands):

	December 31, 1996	1995
Accrued payroll	$ 4,624	$ 3,423
Accrued advertising	2,876	1,517
Accrued rent	1,148	1,490
Accrued insurance	4,490	2,090
Accrued ESOP contribution	1,150	1,375
Other	4,920	3,436
	$19,208	$13,331

7. Stockholders' Equity

On February 18, 1994, a three-for-two split of the Company's Common Stock was effected through distribution of one additional share for every two shares already issued. All applicable share and per share data has been restated to give retroactive effect to the stock split.

8. Income Taxes

Income tax expense consisted of the following (in thousands):

	Years Ended December 31, 1996	1995	1994
Federal:			
Current	$29,838	$ 23,296	$ 18,193
Deferred	3,765	995	(293)
	33,603	24,291	17,900
State:			
Current	6,268	4,623	3,738
Deferred	412	253	(36)
	6,680	4,876	3,702
	$40,283	$29,167	$ 21,602

Outback Steakhouse, Inc.

Notes to Consolidated Financial Statements

8. Income Taxes (continued)

The Company's effective tax rate differs from the federal statutory rate for the following reasons:

	Years Ended December 31,		
	1996	1995	1994
Income taxes at federal statutory rate	35.0%	35.0%	35.0%
State taxes, net of federal benefit	3.8	3.9	4.0
Earnings not subject to corporate income taxes		(3.8)	(3.3)
Other, net	(2.8)	(2.9)	(2.4)
Total	36.0%	32.2%	33.3%

As discussed in Note 10, in certain periods presented, the Company's net income included earnings attributable to Aussie Enterprises, Inc. ("Aussie Enterprises"), Connerty, Inc. ("Connerty"), the Hal Smith Restaurant Group (the "Hal Smith Group"), Garob, Inc. ("Garob"), FBS Enterprises, Inc. ("FBS"), the Fore Management Group ("Fore Management"), and the Brenica Restaurant Group ("Brenica"). These companies had elected under Subchapter S of the Internal Revenue Code to have their shareholders pay any federal income tax due on their earnings. Although income prior to the mergers attributable to the merging companies is included in the Company's consolidated financial statements, the Company is not required to pay income taxes on the income since they are the responsibility of the shareholders of the merging companies.

The income tax effects of temporary differences that give rise to significant portions of deferred tax assets and liabilities are as follows:

Deferred income tax assets (in thousands):	December 31,	
	1996	1995
Insurance reserves	$ 3,147	$ 2,725
Amortization		200
Advertising expense reserves	854	
Intangibles	9,760	2,813
	$13,761	$5,738

Deferred income tax liabilities (in thousands):	December 31,	
	1996	1995
Depreciation	$10,683	$3,847
Marketing and training costs	4,219	2,995
	$14,902	$6,842

Outback Steakhouse, Inc.
Notes to Consolidated Financial Statements

9. Commitments and Contingencies

Operating Leases – The Company leases restaurant and office facilities and certain equipment under operating leases having terms expiring between 1997 and 2012. The restaurant facility leases primarily have renewal clauses of five to 20 years exercisable at the option of the Company. Certain of these leases require the payment of contingent rentals based on a percentage of gross revenues, as defined. Total rental expense for the years ended December 31, 1996, 1995 and 1994 was approximately $18,353,000, $16,054,000 and $13,035,000, respectively, and included contingent rent of approximately $2,369,000, $2,048,000 and $1,570,000, respectively.

Future minimum lease payments on operating leases (including leases for restaurants scheduled to open in 1997), are as follows (in thousands):

1997	$ 13,825
1998	13,356
1999	12,430
2000	11,781
2001	9,906
Thereafter	29,570
Total minimum lease payments	$90,868

The Company has a line of credit of which approximately $703,000 is committed to secure loans made by banks to certain franchisees. See Note 5.

The Company is subject to legal proceedings claims and liabilities which arise in the ordinary course of business. In the opinion of management, the amount of the ultimate liability with respect to those actions will not materially affect the Company's financial position or results of operations.

10. Business Combinations

In April 1994, the Company issued 831,000 shares of Common Stock to the shareholders of Aussie Enterprises, the Company's franchisee in Louisiana in connection with the merger of Aussie Enterprises into the Company.

In May 1994, the Company issued 1,700,000 shares of Common Stock to Connerty, Inc. the Company's franchisee in Georgia and Jacksonville, Florida, in connection with the merger of Connerty's interest in Outback restaurants into the Company.

In December 1995, the Company issued 1,329,000 shares of Common Stock to the Hal Smith Group, the Company's franchisee in Oklahoma, Nebraska, Arkansas, and Kansas, in connection with the merger of the Hal Smith Group into the Company.

In 1996, the Company issued approximately 2,348,000 shares of Common Stock to the shareholders of four of its franchisees in exchange for all of their outstanding interests in 28 Outback Steakhouses in Ohio, Kentucky, Virginia, Illinois, Missouri, and Tennessee. The franchise groups include Garob, FBS, Fore Management and Brenica.

The mergers discussed above have been accounted for by the pooling of interest method using historical amounts and the financial statements presented herein have been restated to give retroactive effect to the mergers for the applicable periods presented.

Outback Steakhouse, Inc.
Notes to Consolidated Financial Statements

11. Pro Forma Earnings and Earnings Per Share

As discussed in Note 8, no income tax expense has been provided in the Company's historical consolidated financial statements on income attributable to the merging companies discussed in Note 10. Pro forma net income includes an adjustment to increase the provision for income taxes to reflect the anticipated tax as if the merging companies had not elected to be taxed under Subchapter S of the Internal Revenue Code.

12. Stock Option Plan

The Company's amended and Restated Stock Option Plan (the "Stock Option Plan") was approved by the shareholders of the Company in April 1992, and has subsequently been amended as deemed appropriate by the Company's Board of Directors or shareholders. There are currently 10,000,000 shares of the Company's Common Stock which may be issued and sold upon exercise of stock options ("Options"). The maximum term of Options granted is ten years, and optionees generally vest in the Options over a five year period.

The purpose of the Stock Option Plan is to attract competent personnel, to provide long-term incentives to Directors and key employees, and to discourage employees from competing with the Company.

Options under the Stock Option Plan may be Options which qualify under Section 422 of the Internal Revenue Code ("Incentive Stock Options") or Options which do not qualify under Section 422 ("Nonqualified Options"). The term of Options granted are generally 5 years and the price cannot be less than the fair market value of the shares covered by the Option.

At December 31, 1996, Options to purchase 5,901,346 shares of the Company's Common Stock had been granted to employees of the Company at prices ranging from $0.28 to $38.33 per share which was the estimated fair market value at the time of each grant. As of December 31, 1996, Options for 1,886,381 shares were exercisable.

Options to purchase 686,756, 1,429,000 and 827,000 of the Company's Common Stock were issued to employees during 1996, 1995 and 1994 with exercise prices ranging from $25.34 to $38.33, $23.38 to $32.15 and $23.75 to $30.88 for each respective period.

Activity in the Company's Stock Option Plan was:

	Shares	Weighted average Exercise Price
Outstanding at December 31, 1994	3,815,979	$11.30
Granted	1,429,000	25.78
Exercised	(628,029)	16.74
Forfeited	(28,200)	23.28
Outstanding at December 31, 1995	4,588,750	15.90
Granted	686,756	27.87
Exercised	(349,033)	17.44
Forfeited	(15,699)	28.09
Outstanding at December 31, 1996	4,910,774	21.13

Outback Steakhouse, Inc.

Notes to Consolidated Financial Statements

12. Stock Option Plan (continued)

Had the compensation cost for the Company's Stock Option Plan been determined based on the fair value at the grant dates for awards under the plan consistent with the method of FASB Statement 123, the Company's net income and earnings per share on a pro forma basis would have been (in thousands, except per share data):

	December 31, 1996	1995	1994
Net income	$68,154	$50,923	$37,159
Earnings per common share	$1.38	$1.04	$0.78

The preceding pro forma results were calculated with the use of the Black Scholes option-pricing model. The following assumptions were used for the years ended December 31, 1996, 1995 and 1994, respectively: (1) risk-free interest rates of 6.05%, 5.83%, and 5.45%; (2) dividend yield of 0.0%, 0.0%, and 0.0%; (3) expected lives of 3.5, 3.5, and 3.5 years; and (4) volatility of 25%, 25%, and 30%. Results may vary depending on the assumptions applied within the model.

13. Selected Quarterly Financial Data (unaudited)

The following table presents selected quarterly financial data for the periods indicated (in thousands, except per share data):

1996	March 31	June 30	September 30	December 31
Revenues	$216,102	$236,481	$236,730	$248,087
Income from operations	31,732	33,748	31,351	34,086
Income before provision for income taxes	26,546	28,719	27,242	29,389
Net income	16,857	18,236	17,712	18,808
Earnings per share	0.34	0.37	0.36	0.38
1995	**March 31**	**June 30**	**September 30**	**December 31**
Revenues	$162,623	$182,723	$191,259	$197,087
Income from operations	23,957	27,349	25,535	30,200
Income before provision for income taxes	20,080	22,845	21,856	25,704
Net income	13,283	15,290	14,716	18,029
Earnings per share	0.28	0.31	0.30	0.36
Pro forma net income	12,670	14,396	14,133	16,712
Pro forma earnings per share	0.26	0.30	0.29	0.34
1994	**March 31**	**June 30**	**September 30**	**December 31**
Revenues	$114,544	$127,414	$132,664	$142,304
Income from operations	16,773	20,201	19,755	20,481
Income before provision for income taxes	13,952	16,883	16,682	17,461
Net income	9,065	11,107	11,027	12,177
Earnings per share	0.19	0.23	0.23	0.26
Pro forma net income	8,766	10,586	10,488	11,356
Pro forma earnings per share	0.19	0.22	0.22	0.23

outback steakhouse, inc.

The Common Stock of the Company is traded in the over-the-counter market and is quoted on the NASDAQ National Market System under the symbol OSSI. The following table sets forth, for the fiscal years ended December 31, 1994, 1995, and 1996, the high and low per share prices of the Company's Common Stock as reported by NASDAQ, after giving effect to the 1994 stock split. See Note 7 of Notes to the Consolidated Financial Statements.

	High	Low
1994		
First Quarter	29.50	23.33
Second Quarter	28.75	22.75
Third Quarter	30.88	23.75
Fourth Quarter	32.00	22.63
1995		
First Quarter	29.25	22.88
Second Quarter	30.13	23.38
Third Quarter	35.50	28.50
Fourth Quarter	37.80	29.25
1996		
First Quarter	40.63	29.75
Second Quarter	40.75	34.00
Third Quarter	35.00	23.00
Fourth Quarter	29.63	21.50

The Company has never paid a cash dividend on its Common Stock. As of January 24, 1997 there were approximately 2,742 registered shareholders of record of the Company's Common Stock.

Reports On Form 10-K

A copy of the Company's annual report to the Securities and Exchange Commission on Form 10-K will be furnished to any shareholder without charge upon written request. Address to Investor Relations Department at the address below:

Outback Steakhouse, Inc.,
550 N. Reo Street, Suite 200, Tampa, FL 33609

Stock Transfer Agent and Registrar, Bank of New York, 101 Barclay Street, 12 West, New York, NY 10286

Independent Accountants, Deloitte & Touche LLP, Tampa, Florida

Company News

The Company's news releases, including quarterly earnings announcements, are available at no charge through Company News-On-Call. To receive a faxed copy of recent news releases, call 1-800-758-5804. Enter the Outback six digit code of 673313 and the requested release will be faxed within minutes of inquiry. This service is available 24 hours a day, 7 days a week.

Additional information, including a business description, annual report and restaurant locations, can be accessed through Company News-On-Call Plus on the PR Newswire Web site at http://www.prnewswire.com.

Annual Meeting

The annual meeting of shareholders will be held on Wednesday, April 23, 1997 at 10:00 a.m. local time at the Tampa Convention Center, 333 South Franklin Street, Tampa, Florida.

Officers

OUTBACK STEAKHOUSE, INC. and AFFILIATES

Chris T. Sullivan
Chairman of the Board and
Chief Executive Officer

Robert D. Basham
President and Chief Operating Officer

J. Timothy Gannon
Sr. Vice President

Robert S. Merritt
Sr. Vice President,
Chief Financial Officer and Treasurer

Paul E. Avery
Sr. Vice President, Operations

Trudy I. Cooper
Vice President,
Training and Development

Nancy Schneid
Vice President, Marketing

Steven C. Stanley
Vice President, Construction

Joseph J. Kadow
Vice President,
General Counsel and Secretary

Lauren C. Cooper
Vice President and Controller

Carl W. Sahlsten
President - Carrabba's Italian Grill

Steven T. Shlemon
Vice President and Director of Operations
Carrabba's Italian Grill

Address for all officers:
550 North Reo Street, Suite 200,
Tampa, Florida 33609

Top row (left-right): Lauren Cooper, Chris Sullivan, Tim Gannon, Paul Avery, Bob Basham
Bottom row: Joe Kadow, Trudy Cooper, Bob Merritt, Nancy Schneid, Steve Stanley, Lindon Richardson (Chief Designer), Denny Rouse (Director of Real Estate)

Board of Directors OUTBACK STEAKHOUSE, INC.

Chris T. Sullivan
Chairman of the Board and
Chief Executive Officer

Robert D. Basham
President and Chief Operating Officer

J. Timothy Gannon
Sr. Vice President

Robert S. Merritt
Sr. Vice President,
Chief Financial Officer and Treasurer

John A. Brabson, Jr.
Chairman of the Board, Lykes Bros. Inc.
Chairman, Chief Executive Officer and
President, Peoples Gas Systems, Inc.

Charles H. Bridges
Former Chairman and Chief Executive
Officer, Francois L. Schwartz, Inc.

W.R. "Max" Carey, Jr.
President
Corporate Resource Development

Debbi Fields
Founder and Former Chairperson
Mrs. Fields Cookies

Edward L. Flom
Former Chairman
and Chief Executive Officer
Florida Steel Corporation

Nancy Schneid
Vice President, Marketing
Outback Steakhouse, Inc.

Lee Roy Selmon
Associate Athletic Director
University of South Florida

OUTBACK
STEAKHOUSE
550 North Reo Street, Suite 200, Tampa, Florida 33609 813-282-1225

GLOSSARY

Accounting A service activity designed to provide quantitative information about economic entities that is intended to be useful in making economic decisions.

Accounting cycle The set of recurring accounting procedures that must be performed for a business each accounting period.

Accounting equation The mathematical expression indicating that the sum of an entity's assets must equal the collective sum of its liabilities and owners' equity.

Accounting period concept An accounting principle that suggests that accountants can prepare meaningful financial reports for ongoing business enterprises by dividing the lives of these entities into regular reporting intervals of equal length.

Accounting system A systematic approach to collecting, processing, and communicating financial information to decision makers.

Accounting Trends & Techniques An annual publication of the AICPA that analyzes the accounting and financial reporting practices of 600 publicly owned companies.

Accounts The basic storage units for financial data in an accounting system.

Accounts payable Current liabilities that represent amounts owed by a business to its suppliers.

Accounts receivable Amounts owed to businesses by their customers.

Accounts receivable ledger A subsidiary ledger that maintains records (accounts) of the amounts owed to a company by its customers.

Accounts receivable turnover ratio Net credit sales divided by average accounts receivable; indicates how often a business collects or 'turns over' its accounts receivable each year.

Accrual basis of accounting A method of accounting under which the economic impact of a transaction is recognized (recorded) whether or not the transaction involves cash.

Accrued liability A liability stemming from an expense that has been incurred but not yet paid.

Accrued revenue A receivable resulting from a revenue that has been earned but not yet received.

Additions Capital expenditures that extend or expand existing property, plant & equipment assets.

Adjusting entries Journal entries made at the end of an accounting period to ensure that the revenue recognition and expense recognition rules are properly applied that period.

Age of inventory 360 days divided by the inventory turnover ratio.

Age of receivables 360 days divided by the accounts receivable turnover ratio; a measure of the collectibility of accounts receivable.

Aging method One approach to applying the allowance method of estimating uncollectible accounts expense; under this method, an estimate of uncollectible accounts expense is determined by performing an aging analysis of accounts receivable.

Allowance for Doubtful Accounts A contra asset account subtracted from Accounts Receivable to reduce that asset to its approximate net realizable value.
Allowance method An accounting method used to estimate uncollectible accounts expense each accounting period.
American Institute of Certified Public Accountants (AICPA) The national professional organization of CPAs that prepares and administers the CPA examination.
Amortization The allocation of the cost of an intangible asset to the accounting periods that it provides economic benefits to an entity.
Amortized cost method A method of accounting for investments in held-to-maturity securities under which any premium or discount on the purchase of these securities is amortized over their remaining term.
Annuity A series of equal payments made, or received, at equal intervals on which interest is computed on a compound basis.
Appropriation of retained earnings A part of a corporation's retained earnings that has been restricted for a special purpose; limits the ability of a corporation to pay cash dividends.
Assets Probable future economic benefits obtained or controlled by a particular entity as a result of past transactions or events.
Authorized stock The maximum number of shares of a given class of stock a company is permitted to issue under the terms of its corporate charter.
Available-for-sale securities Investments in debt or equity securities that do not qualify as one of the other types of intercorporate investments.

Balance sheet A financial statement that summarizes the assets, liabilities, and owners' equity of an entity at a specific point in time.
Bank reconciliation An accounting document that reconciles the cash balance reported on a bank statement to the corresponding cash balance reflected in a company's accounting records.
Bond A long-term loan made by one party to another that is legally documented by a bond certificate.
Bond indenture The legal contract between a bond purchaser and the issuing company; identifies the rights and obligations of each party.
Bonds payable A long-term liability that represents the collective amount owed the parties who have purchased a company's bonds.
Book value For a depreciable asset, the difference between the asset's cost and the balance of its accumulated depreciation account; also referred to as carrying value.
Book value per share Common stockholders' equity per share for a corporation; computed by dividing total common stockholders' equity by the number of outstanding shares of common stock.

Callable bonds Bonds that can be retired or redeemed by the issuing company when one or more conditions are met.
Callable preferred stock Preferred stock that can be reacquired at the option of the issuing corporation.
Capital expenditures Expenditures to obtain, expand, or improve long-term assets or to extend their useful lives.
Capital lease A lease that is generally noncancelable, long-term, and transfers at least some ownership rights or risks to the lessee.
Cash basis of accounting A method of accounting under which revenues are recorded when cash is received and expenses are recorded when cash is disbursed.
Cash dividend A proportionate distribution of a company's prior earnings to its stockholders made in the form of cash.
Cash equivalents Investments in short-term securities, such as certificates of deposit (CDs), money market funds, and U.S. treasury bills, that have 90 days or less to maturity when purchased.

Cash flow per share Net cash flow from operating activities for an accounting period, less preferred stock dividends, divided by the weighted-average number of shares of common stock outstanding during that period.
Certified management accountant (CMA) An individual who has passed the CMA examination and satisfied the other requirements to qualify for this professional designation; CMAs generally specialize in private (management) accounting.
Certified public accountant (CPA) An individual who has passed the CPA examination and satisfied any other requirements established by his or her state to qualify for this professional designation.
Chart of accounts A numerical listing, by account number, of a business's accounts.
Closing entries Journal entries made at the end of each accounting period to close out or transfer the balances of temporary accounts to the appropriate owners' equity account.
Common-sized financial statements Financial statements in which each line item is expressed as a percentage of a major financial statement component.
Common stock A class of stock that represents the residual ownership interests of a corporation.
Comparability The degree to which an entity's accounting information can be easily compared with similar information reported for the entity in prior accounting periods and with similar information reported by other entities.
Compound interest Interest computed on the principal amount of a loan (or other financial instrument) and any unpaid interest that has accumulated on the loan since its inception.
Compound journal entry A journal entry that affects more than two accounts.
Conservatism principle An accounting principle that dictates that uncertainty regarding the valuation of an asset or magnitude of a revenue should generally be resolved in favor of understating the asset or revenue; applies as well to liabilities and expenses, except that uncertainty should be resolved in favor of overstating these items.
Consolidated financial statements The combined financial statements of a parent company and its subsidiaries.
Contingent liability A potential liability that may become an actual liability if one or more events occur or fail to occur.
Contra accounts Accounts that are treated as offsets or reductions to related accounts for financial statement purposes; an example is Accumulated Depreciation.
Control activities The policies and procedures established to help ensure that an entity's primary organizational objectives are accomplished.
Control environment A component of internal control that refers to the degree of control consciousness within an organization.
Controlling investments Investments in equity securities in which the parent company owns more than 50 percent of the common stock of the subsidiary.
Convertible bonds Bonds that may be exchanged for stock in the issuing company at the option of the bondholders.
Convertible preferred stock Preferred stock that can be exchanged at the option of preferred stockholders for common stock of the issuing corporation.
Copyright An exclusive right granted by the federal government to produce and sell a work of art such as songs, books, and films.
Corporation An association of individuals, created by law and having an existence apart from that of its members as well as distinct and inherent powers and liabilities.
Correcting entries Journal entries made to correct errors in previously recorded journal entries.
Cost of Goods Sold An account used in a perpetual inventory system to accumulate the cost of inventory sold to customers during an accounting period.
Credit The right-hand side of a T-account or an entry made on the right-hand side of a T-account (or in the credit column of a four-column account); as a verb, to enter an amount on the right-hand side of a T-account or in the credit column of a four-column account.

Credit terms The agreement between a buyer and seller regarding the timing of payment by the buyer and any discount available to the buyer for early payment.

Cross-sectional ratio analysis Comparison of a company's financial ratios with those of competing companies and/or with the industry norms for those ratios.

Cumulative effect of a change in accounting principle The change in an entity's collective net income for prior years assuming a newly adopted accounting principle had been used during those years.

Cumulative preferred stock Preferred stock on which dividends that are not paid in a given year accumulate and must be paid in the future before common stockholders can receive a dividend.

Current assets Cash and other assets that will be converted into cash, sold, or consumed during the next fiscal year or the normal operating cycle of a business, whichever is longer.

Current liabilities Debts or other obligations of a business that must be paid during its next fiscal year or operating cycle, whichever is longer.

Current portion of long-term debt The dollar amount of a long-term liability that must be paid in the coming twelve months.

Current ratio Current assets divided by current liabilities; a widely used measure of liquidity.

Current replacement cost The per unit cost that a business must pay to replace inventory items sold to customers.

Debit The left-hand side of a T-account or an entry made on the left-hand side of a T-account (or in the debit column of a four-column account); as a verb, to enter an amount on the left-hand side of a T-account or in the debit column of a four-column account.

Declining-balance method A depreciation method under which annual depreciation expense is computed by multiplying an accelerated depreciation rate, which is a multiple of the straight-line rate, by an asset's book value at the beginning of the year.

Deferred expense An asset that represents a prepayment of an expense item.

Deferred Income Taxes An account in which a corporation records the difference between its income tax expense and income tax payable each year; typically a long-term liability account.

Deferred revenue A liability resulting from an amount received by a business for a service or product that it will provide or deliver in the future.

Depletion The allocation of the cost of natural resources to the periods in which these assets provide economic benefits to an entity.

Deposits in transit Deposits made near the end of an accounting period that have been added to the general ledger cash balance but that were not included in the most recent bank statement balance.

Depreciable cost The acquisition cost of a depreciable asset less its salvage value.

Depreciation The process of allocating the cost of a long-term asset over its useful life in a rational and systematic manner.

Direct method An approach to preparing the statement of cash flows in which specific cash inflows and outflows from a business's operating activities are identified and listed in the initial section of this financial statement.

Direct write-off method An accounting method under which uncollectible accounts expense is recorded when it is determined that a specific account receivable is unlikely to be collected; this non-GAAP alternative to the allowance method is used for taxation purposes.

Discontinued operations A section of a corporate income statement devoted to a business segment that is being discontinued.

Dissolution The termination of a partnership.

Dividends in arrears Unpaid dividends on cumulative preferred stock; should be disclosed in a company's financial statement footnotes.

Double declining-balance method A variation of the declining-balance depreciation method under which the annual depreciation rate for an asset is twice the straight-line rate.

Double-entry bookkeeping A method of maintaining financial records developed more than five hundred years ago that serves as the foundation of modern accounting systems worldwide.

Earnings per share Generally, net income divided by the weighted-average number of shares of common stock outstanding during a given year.

Earnings quality The degree of correlation between a firm's economic income and its reported earnings determined by GAAP.

Effective-interest method A method of determining interest expense on bonds payable each interest payment period; under this method, interest expense is computed by multiplying the effective interest rate by the bonds' carrying value.

Effective interest rate The market interest rate on the date bonds are initially sold; represents the true rate of interest incurred over the term of a bond issue by the issuing company.

Entity concept An accounting principle dictating that a business enterprise be treated as a distinct entity independent of its owners.

Equity method The accounting method used for influential but noncontrolling investments; the investor's proportionate interest in the investee's periodic earnings (losses) is treated as an addition (reduction) to the book value of the investment, while dividends received from the investee reduce the book value of the investment.

Exchange rate The value of one currency expressed in terms of another.

Expense recognition rule An accounting rule that requires expenses to be recognized (recorded) in the accounting period in which they provide an economic benefit to an entity.

Expenses Decreases in assets and increases in liabilities resulting from an entity's profit-oriented activities.

Extraordinary item A material gain or loss that is both unusual in nature and infrequent in occurrence.

Extraordinary repairs Expenditures that extend the useful life of a property, plant & equipment asset.

Fair value Generally, the closing price of a debt or equity security on a given date on a securities exchange.

FIFO (first-in, first-out) method An inventory costing method under which the per unit costs of the most recently acquired goods are used to establish the cost basis of ending inventory.

Financial Accounting Standards Board (FASB) The rule-making body that has the primary authority for establishing accounting standards in the United States.

Financial ratios Measures that express the relationship or interrelationships between, or among, two or more financial statement items.

Financial statement footnotes A section of an annual report intended to assist decision makers in interpreting and drawing the proper conclusions from an entity's financial statements.

Financial statements The principal means accountants use to communicate financial information regarding business entities and other organizations to investors, creditors, and other decision makers external to those entities.

Financing activities Those activities of businesses that involve obtaining cash from lenders and repaying those amounts as well as obtaining cash from investors and providing them with a return of and a return on their investments.

Fiscal year The twelve-month period covered by an entity's annual income statement.

Foreign currency transaction gain or loss A gain or loss resulting from a change in the exchange rate for a credit transaction denominated in a foreign currency before the transaction is completed by the payment or receipt of cash.

Full disclosure principle An accounting principle dictating that all information needed to obtain a thorough understanding of an entity's financial affairs be included in its financial statements or accompanying narrative disclosures.

Future value The sum of an invested amount plus any interest that will accumulate on that amount on a compound basis over a specified period of time.

General journal The accounting record in which the dollar amounts for transactions and other financial events are initially recorded by businesses that maintain only one journal.

General ledger The accounting record that contains each of the individual accounts for a business's assets, liabilities, owners' or stockholders' equity, revenues, and expenses.

Generally accepted accounting principles (GAAP) The concepts, guidelines, and rules that accountants follow in recording and reporting financial information.

Going concern assumption An accounting principle that dictates that entities should be treated as if they will continue to operate indefinitely, unless there is evidence to the contrary.

Goodwill The excess of the cost of a group of assets over their collective market value.

Gross profit The difference between an entity's net sales and cost of goods sold during an accounting period.

Gross profit method A method of estimating inventory in which the key factor is a business's normal gross profit percentage.

Gross profit percentage Gross profit divided by net sales; a key ratio used to analyze a business's profitability.

Held-to-maturity securities Investments in debt securities acquired with the positive intent and ability to hold them to maturity.

Historical cost principle An accounting principle dictating that the primary valuation basis for most assets is their historical or original cost.

Improvements Capital expenditures that enhance an existing asset's operating efficiency or reduce its operating costs.

Income from continuing operations Represents the earnings produced by a corporation's principal profit-oriented activities.

Income statement A financial statement that summarizes a business's revenues and expenses for a given accounting period.

Income Summary A temporary account used only during the journalizing and posting of closing entries.

Indirect method An approach to preparing the statement of cash flows in which net cash flow from operating activities is determined by making certain adjustments to a business's net income.

Influential but noncontrolling investments Investments in equity securities in which the investor corporation generally owns at least 20 percent but not more than 50 percent of the investee corporation's common stock.

Intangible assets Long-term assets that do not have a physical form or substance.

Intercompany transactions Transactions between a parent company and a subsidiary, between two or more subsidiaries, or between other operating units of a company.

Interest The expense of borrowing money for a specified period, or, alternatively, the revenue earned by lending money for a specified period.

Interest equation The equation used to compute interest revenue or expense on a promissory note or other interest-bearing financial instrument: interest = principal × rate × time.

Internal control A process—effected by an entity's board of directors, management, and other personnel—designed to provide reasonable assurance that key entity objectives will be accomplished.

Inventory Goods that businesses intend to sell to their customers or raw materials or in-process items that will be converted into salable goods.

Inventory turnover ratio Cost of goods sold divided by average inventory; indicates how often a business sells or turns over its inventory each year.

Investing activities Those activities of businesses that include the making and collecting of loans, the acquisition and disposal of property, plant & equipment, and the purchase and sale of debt and equity securities other than trading securities and cash equivalents.
Issued stock The number of shares of a class of stock that has been sold or otherwise distributed by a corporation; these shares may be outstanding or held as treasury stock.

Journalizing The process of recording financial data in a journal for a transaction or other event affecting a business.

Leasehold A legal right to use a leased asset for a specified period subject to any restrictions in the lease agreement.
Leasehold improvements Improvements to a leased property made by a lessee that revert to the lessor at the end of the lease.
Liabilities Probable future sacrifices of economic benefits; generally, amounts owed by an entity to third parties including such items as accounts payable, accrued liabilities, and notes payable.
LIFO (last-in, first-out) method An inventory costing method under which the per unit costs of the earliest acquired goods are used to establish the cost basis of ending inventory.
Liquidation The process of converting a discontinued partnership's assets into cash, paying its liabilities, and distributing any remaining cash to the partners.
Liquidity Refers to a firm's ability to finance its day-to-day operations and to pay its liabilities as they mature.
Long-term debt A business's liabilities resulting from amounts borrowed on a long-term basis.
Long-term debt to equity ratio A common measure of financial leverage; computed by dividing a company's long-term debt by its stockholders' equity.
Long-term investments Ownership interests in corporate stocks and bonds and other securities that an entity intends to retain for more than one year; also includes land and other long-term assets not used in an entity's normal operating activities.
Long-term liabilities The debts and obligations of a business other than those classified as current liabilities.
Longitudinal ratio analysis A variation of ratio analysis that focuses on the changes in a business's ratios over a period of time.
Lower-of-cost-or-market (LCM) rule An accounting rule that requires businesses to value their ending inventories at the lower of cost or market value, the latter typically being defined as current replacement cost.
Luca Pacioli A Franciscan monk credited with formalizing and documenting double-entry bookkeeping in the late fifteenth century.

Maker The party who has signed a promissory note and is thus obligated to pay a certain amount to another party by a certain date.
Market price to book value ratio Computed by dividing the current market price of a company's common stock by its book value per share.
Matching principle An accounting principle requiring that expenses be recorded in the same accounting period as the related revenues.
Materiality Refers to the relative importance of specific items of accounting information; an item is material if it is large enough or significant enough to influence the decision of a financial statement user.
Maturity date The date that the maker of a promissory note must pay its maturity value to the payee.
Maturity value The sum of the principal and interest due on a promissory note on its maturity date.
Minority interest The stockholders' equity of a subsidiary that is not controlled by the parent company.

Moving-average method An inventory costing method applied in a perpetual inventory system; under this method, the cost basis of ending inventory is determined by multiplying the number of unsold units of each inventory item by its moving-average per unit cost at the end of the accounting period.

Natural resources Long-term assets, such as coal deposits, oil and gas reservoirs, and tracts of standing timber, that are extracted or harvested from the earth's surface or from beneath the earth's surface.

Net income The difference between an entity's revenues and expenses during an accounting period.

Notes payable Obligations that are documented by a legally binding written commitment known as a promissory note; can be either current or long-term liabilities depending upon their maturity date.

Off-balance sheet financing Involves the acquisition of assets or services by incurring long-term obligations that are not reported on an entity's balance sheet.

Operating activities Those transactions and events related to the production and delivery of goods and services by businesses.

Operating cycle The period of time elapsing from the use of cash in the normal operating activities of an entity to the collection of cash from the entity's customers.

Operating expenses Those expenses, other than cost of goods sold, that an entity incurs in its principal business operations.

Operating income An entity's gross profit less its operating expenses; represents the income generated by an entity's principal line or lines of business.

Operating lease A lease that is usually cancelable by the lessee, covers a short term, and does not transfer ownership rights or risks to the lessee.

Outstanding checks Checks that have been deducted from a company's cash balance in its general ledger but that were not subtracted from the company's cash balance in its most recent bank statement.

Outstanding stock The number of shares of a given class of stock owned by a company's stockholders.

Par value A nominal dollar value assigned to each share of a class of stock.

Parent company A company that owns more than 50 percent of another company's common stock.

Partnership An unincorporated business with two or more owners.

Partnership agreement A contract between, or among, the members of a partnership that defines the contractual rights and responsibilities of each partner.

Patent An exclusive right granted by the U.S. Patent Office to manufacture a specific product or use a specific process.

Payee The party to whom the maker of a promissory note must eventually pay the maturity value of that note.

Payroll register A subsidiary accounting record in which key payroll-related data, such as gross pay, payroll deductions, and net pay, are entered each payroll period for each employee.

Periodic inventory system An inventory accounting system in which the dollar value of ending inventory is determined by counting the goods on hand at the end of each accounting period and then multiplying the quantity of each item by the appropriate per unit cost.

Permanent accounts Accounts whose period-ending balances are carried forward to the next accounting period.

Perpetual inventory system An inventory accounting system in which a perpetually updated record of the quantity of individual inventory items and their per unit costs is maintained.

Petty cash fund A small cash fund from which a business pays minor expenses and other miscellaneous amounts.
Posting The process of transferring accounting data from a journal to the appropriate general ledger accounts.
Preemptive right The right of stockholders to retain their fractional ownership interest in a corporation when additional stock is issued.
Preferred stock A class of stock that has certain preferences or advantages relative to a company's common stock.
Present value An amount that must be invested currently at a stated compound rate of interest to produce a given future value.
Price-earnings (P/E) ratio Computed by dividing the current market price of a company's common stock by its earnings per share for the most recent twelve-month period.
Principal The amount initially owed by the maker of a promissory note.
Prior period adjustment A correction of a material error occurring in a previous accounting period that involved a revenue or expense; the correction is made directly to the Retained Earnings account in the accounting period when the error is discovered.
Profit margin percentage Net income divided by net sales; indicates the percentage of each sales dollar that contributes to a company's net income.
Property ledger A subsidiary ledger in which key information is maintained for each major PP&E asset.
Property, plant & equipment Long-term assets such as buildings and machinery used in the day-to-day operations of a business.
Purchase discounts Discounts offered by suppliers to encourage prompt payment of credit purchases made by their customers.
Purchase returns and allowances Reductions in amounts owed to suppliers as a result of returned goods or price concessions granted for damaged or defective goods.

Quick ratio Quick assets (cash and cash equivalents, short-term investments, and net current receivables) divided by current liabilities; measures a firm's liquidity.

Ratio analysis An analytical technique that typically involves studying the relationship between two financial statement items.
Retained Earnings An owners' equity account of corporations; the balance of this account represents the cumulative earnings of a company since its inception less any dividends distributed to the firm's stockholders.
Return on assets The sum of net income and interest expense divided by average total assets for an accounting period.
Return on equity A key measure of a corporation's profitability; computed by dividing net income, less preferred stock dividends, by average common stockholders' equity for a given period.
Revenue expenditures Expenditures that provide economic benefits to only one accounting period and thus are expensed in the period incurred.
Revenue recognition rule An accounting rule that requires revenues to be both realized and earned before they are recognized (recorded).
Revenues Increases in assets and decreases in liabilities resulting from an entity's profit-oriented activities.

Sales discounts Discounts offered to customers to entice them to pay their account balances on a timely basis.
Sales journal A special journal in which credit sales of merchandise are recorded.
Sales returns and allowances The sum of refunds paid to customers who return damaged or defective merchandise and price reductions granted to customers to persuade them to keep such merchandise.
Salvage value The estimated value of an asset at the end of its useful life.

Secured bonds Bonds collateralized by specific assets of the issuing company; sometimes referred to as mortgage bonds.
Securities and Exchange Commission (SEC) A federal agency that regulates the sale and subsequent trading of securities by publicly owned companies; also oversees the financial reporting and accounting practices of these companies.
Simple interest Interest computed only on the principal amount of a loan (or other financial instrument).
Sole proprietorship A business owned by one individual.
Source documents Documents that identify the key features or parameters of business transactions; examples include invoices, legal contracts, and purchase orders.
Special journal An accounting record in which a business journalizes a single type of transaction.
Specific identification method An inventory costing method under which actual per unit costs are used to establish the cost basis of ending inventory.
Stated interest rate The rate of interest paid to bondholders based upon the face value of the bonds; also known as the face interest rate or contract interest rate.
Stated value A nominal value assigned to each share of a no-par common stock.
Statement of cash flows A financial statement that accounts for the net change in a business's cash balance during a given period; this statement summarizes the cash receipts and disbursements from a business's operating, investing, and financing activities.
Statement of partners' capital A partnership financial statement that documents the changes in partners' capital accounts during a given period; equivalent to a corporation's statement of stockholders' equity.
Statement of partnership liquidation A financial report of a partnership's account balances at various stages of its liquidation.
Statement of stockholders' equity A financial statement that reconciles the dollar amounts of a corporation's stockholders' equity components at the beginning and end of an accounting period.
Statements of Financial Accounting Concepts Six technical pronouncements issued by the FASB from 1978 through 1985 to serve as the conceptual framework for the development of future accounting standards.
Stock dividend A proportionate distribution of a corporation's own stock to its stockholders.
Stock split An increase in the number of shares of a company's stock accompanied by a proportionate reduction in the stock's par value.
Stockholders' equity The total assets of a corporation less amounts owed to third parties; represents stockholders' collective ownership interest in a corporation.
Straight-line method A depreciation method that allocates an equal amount of depreciation expense to each year of an asset's estimated useful life.
Subsidiary A company that has more than 50 percent of its common stock owned by another company.
Subsidiary ledger An accounting record that contains the detailed support for an account balance in the general ledger.
System A coordinated network of plans and procedures designed to achieve a stated goal in an orderly, effective, and efficient manner.

Temporary accounts Accounts whose period-ending balances are transferred or closed to the appropriate owners' equity account.
Temporary differences Differences between an entity's taxable income and pretax accounting income that arise from applying different accounting methods for taxation and financial accounting purposes.
Term of a note The number of days from the date a promissory note is signed, not counting the signing date, to the date the note matures.

Time value of money concept Dictates that the economic value of a sum of cash to be received or paid is a function of both the amount and timing of that payment or receipt.

Times interest earned ratio A financial ratio used to evaluate a firm's ability to make interest payments on its long-term debt; computed by dividing the sum of net income, interest expense, and income taxes expense by interest expense.

Total asset turnover ratio Net sales divided by average total assets for an accounting period; a measure of how effectively an entity's assets are being utilized.

Trademark A distinctive word, symbol, or logo used to identify a specific business entity or one of its products.

Trading securities Investments in debt and equity securities that may be sold in the near term to generate cash or to realize trading profits due to fluctuations in market prices.

Treasury stock Common or preferred stock that has been issued by a corporation and then reacquired.

Trend analysis The study of percentage changes in financial statement items over a period of time.

Trial balance A two-column listing of a business's general ledger account balances, one column for debit balances and one column for credit balances.

Uncollectible accounts expense The expense associated with accounts receivable that cannot be collected; sometimes referred to as bad debt expense.

Unit-of-measurement concept The accounting principle dictating that a common unit of measurement be used to record and report transactions and other financial statement items.

Units-of-production method A depreciation method under which an asset's useful life is expressed in a number of units of production or use; depreciation expense for any given period is a function of the level of usage of the asset during that period.

Unsecured bonds Bonds backed only by the legal commitment of the issuing firm to make all required principal and interest payments; often referred to as debentures.

Weighted-average method An inventory costing method applied in a periodic inventory system; under this method, the cost basis of ending inventory is determined by multiplying the number of unsold units of each inventory item by its weighted-average cost during the accounting period.

Working capital The difference between an entity's current assets and current liabilities.

INDEX

Entries in italics indicate exhibits or illustrations.
Entries in bold indicate definitions.
Entries in color indicate companies, organizations, and governmental agencies.

A

B

C

J

K

L

M

N

O

P

Q

R

S

T

U

DATE DUE

OCT 11 2004			
MAR 01 2005			
OCT 20 2011			

Table 3
Present Value Factors for a Single Amount

Period	2.5%	3%	3.5%	4%	4.5%	5%	5.5%	6%	7%	8%	9%	10%	12%	15%
1	0.97561	0.97087	0.96618	0.96154	0.95694	0.95238	0.94787	0.94340	0.93458	0.92593	0.91743	0.90909	0.89286	0.86957
2	0.95181	0.94260	0.93351	0.92456	0.91573	0.90703	0.89845	0.89000	0.87344	0.85734	0.84168	0.82645	0.79719	0.75614
3	0.92860	0.91514	0.90194	0.88900	0.87630	0.86384	0.85161	0.83962	0.81630	0.79383	0.77218	0.75131	0.71178	0.65752
4	0.90595	0.88849	0.87144	0.85480	0.83856	0.82270	0.80722	0.79209	0.76290	0.73503	0.70843	0.68301	0.63553	0.57175
5	0.88385	0.86261	0.84197	0.82193	0.80245	0.78353	0.76513	0.74726	0.71299	0.68058	0.64993	0.62092	0.56743	0.49718
6	0.86230	0.83748	0.81350	0.79031	0.76790	0.74622	0.72525	0.70496	0.66634	0.63017	0.59627	0.56447	0.50663	0.43233
7	0.84127	0.81309	0.78599	0.75992	0.73483	0.71068	0.68744	0.66506	0.62275	0.58349	0.54703	0.51316	0.45235	0.37594
8	0.82075	0.78941	0.75941	0.73069	0.70319	0.67684	0.65160	0.62741	0.58201	0.54027	0.50187	0.46651	0.40388	0.32690
9	0.80073	0.76642	0.73373	0.70259	0.67290	0.64461	0.61763	0.59190	0.54393	0.50025	0.46043	0.42410	0.36061	0.28426
10	0.78120	0.74409	0.70892	0.67556	0.64393	0.61391	0.58543	0.55839	0.50835	0.46319	0.42241	0.38554	0.32197	0.24718
11	0.76214	0.72242	0.68495	0.64958	0.61620	0.58468	0.55491	0.52679	0.47509	0.42888	0.38753	0.35049	0.28748	0.21494
12	0.74356	0.70138	0.66178	0.62460	0.58966	0.55684	0.52598	0.49697	0.44401	0.39711	0.35553	0.31863	0.25668	0.18691
13	0.72542	0.68095	0.63940	0.60057	0.56427	0.53032	0.49856	0.46884	0.41496	0.36770	0.32618	0.28966	0.22917	0.16253
14	0.70773	0.66112	0.61778	0.57748	0.53997	0.50507	0.47257	0.44230	0.38782	0.34046	0.29925	0.26333	0.20462	0.14133
15	0.69047	0.64186	0.59689	0.55526	0.51672	0.48102	0.44793	0.41727	0.36245	0.31524	0.27454	0.23939	0.18270	0.12289
16	0.67362	0.62317	0.57671	0.53391	0.49447	0.45811	0.42458	0.39365	0.33873	0.29189	0.25187	0.21763	0.16312	0.10686
17	0.65720	0.60502	0.55720	0.51337	0.47318	0.43630	0.40245	0.37136	0.31657	0.27027	0.23107	0.19784	0.14564	0.09293
18	0.64117	0.58739	0.53836	0.49363	0.45280	0.41552	0.38147	0.35034	0.29586	0.25025	0.21199	0.17986	0.13004	0.08081
19	0.62553	0.57029	0.52016	0.47464	0.43330	0.39573	0.36158	0.33051	0.27651	0.23171	0.19449	0.16351	0.11611	0.07027
20	0.61027	0.55368	0.50257	0.45639	0.41464	0.37689	0.34273	0.31180	0.25842	0.21455	0.17843	0.14864	0.10367	0.06110
21	0.59539	0.53755	0.48557	0.43883	0.39679	0.35894	0.32486	0.29416	0.24151	0.19866	0.16370	0.13513	0.09256	0.05313
22	0.58086	0.52189	0.46915	0.42196	0.37970	0.34185	0.30793	0.27751	0.22571	0.18394	0.15018	0.12285	0.08264	0.04620
23	0.56670	0.50669	0.45329	0.40573	0.36335	0.32557	0.29187	0.26180	0.21095	0.17032	0.13778	0.11168	0.07379	0.04017
24	0.55288	0.49193	0.43796	0.39012	0.34770	0.31007	0.27666	0.24698	0.19715	0.15770	0.12640	0.10153	0.06588	0.03493
25	0.53939	0.47761	0.42315	0.37512	0.33273	0.29530	0.26223	0.23300	0.18425	0.14602	0.11597	0.09230	0.05882	0.03038
26	0.52623	0.46369	0.40884	0.36069	0.31840	0.28124	0.24856	0.21981	0.17220	0.13520	0.10639	0.08391	0.05252	0.02642
27	0.51340	0.45019	0.39501	0.34682	0.30469	0.26785	0.23560	0.20737	0.16093	0.12519	0.09761	0.07628	0.04689	0.02297
28	0.50088	0.43708	0.38165	0.33348	0.29157	0.25509	0.22332	0.19563	0.15040	0.11591	0.08955	0.06934	0.04187	0.01997
29	0.48866	0.42435	0.36875	0.32065	0.27902	0.24295	0.21168	0.18456	0.14056	0.10733	0.08215	0.06304	0.03738	0.01737
30	0.47674	0.41199	0.35628	0.30832	0.26700	0.23138	0.20064	0.17411	0.13137	0.09938	0.07537	0.05731	0.03338	0.01510
35	0.42137	0.35538	0.29998	0.25342	0.21425	0.18129	0.15352	0.13011	0.09368	0.06763	0.04899	0.03558	0.01894	0.00751
40	0.37243	0.30656	0.25257	0.20829	0.17193	0.14205	0.11746	0.09722	0.06678	0.04603	0.03184	0.02209	0.01075	0.00373